HOW TO PRACTICE
MAYAN
ASTROLOGY

HOW TO PRACTICE
MAYAN
ASTROLOGY

The Tzolkin Calendar and Your Life Path

BRUCE SCOFIELD

and

BARRY C. ORR

Bear & Company
Rochester, Vermont

Bear & Company
One Park Street
Rochester, Vermont 05767
www.BearandCompanyBooks.com

Bear & Company is a division of Inner Traditions International

LIBRARY OF CONGRESS CATALOGING-IN-PUBLICATION DATA

Scofield, Bruce.
    How to practice Mayan astrology : the Tzolkin calendar and your life path /
Bruce Scofield and Barry C. Orr.
        p. cm.
    Includes bibliographical references.
    ISBN-13: 978-1-59143-064-3
    ISBN-10: 1-59143-064-X
    1. Maya astrology. I. Orr, Barry C. II. Title.
    F1435.3.A8S36 2007
    529'.32978427—dc22

                                                            2006031596

Printed and bound in the United States by Lake Book Manufacturing

10   9   8   7   6   5   4   3   2   1

Text design and layout by Virginia Scott Bowman
This book was typeset in Sabon with Frutiger, Avenir, and Agenda as the display
typefaces

Part-title illustration: Cosmogram from the Maya Codex Madrid, from *Myths and
Symbols of Aboriginal Religions in America* by Stephen J. Peet

To send correspondence to the authors of this book, mail a first-class letter to the
authors c/o Inner Traditions • Bear & Company, One Park Street, Rochester, VT
05767, and we will forward the communication.

CONTENTS

List of Figures

•••

INTRODUCTION

MAYAN ASTROLOGY FOR MODERN TIMES

This book presents a simple approach for learning and practicing the intricate system of astrology invented by the Maya in ancient Meso-america. People today have much to learn from the profound intellectual and spiritual heritage of the Native American peoples who lived for millennia in today's Mexico and Central America and still live there today. Their knowledge and understanding of the influences of the cosmic environment on human life was encoded into a system that has survived the book-burnings of religious fanatics.

Mayan astrology offers a perspective on human existence not found elsewhere. The authors have devised a unique and practical way of interpreting the components of this lost system, since no one really knows how they were originally used. Our reconstruction of the astrological symbols and techniques is a work in progress that it is based on many sources of information: indigenous sources, including ancient manuscripts, inscriptions, and the oral traditions; academic studies by archaeoastronomers, ethnoastronomers, and anthropologists; and real-life observations—anecdotal evidence gathered in the course of over twenty-five years of correlating the characteristics of individuals with their Mayan birth data.

The major difference between Western and Mayan astrology is that Western astrology interprets sky-events (i.e., astronomical cycles, eclipses, planetary alignments, etc.) spatially while Mayan astrology interprets them in blocks of time. Western astrology focuses on zodiac signs, houses, and aspects that measure space. In ancient Mexico, the same sky-events were interpreted in terms of their significant influence on the period of time in which they occurred.

THE MAYAN CALENDAR

At the center of the Mayan astrological system are several calendar-like groupings of days. The most important of these is the 260-day sacred astrological calendar, known as the tzolkin. This mathematic and scientific marvel organizes intricate correlations between time, number, and astronomy and exists separately from the 365-day civil calendar that was used to govern mundane matters of day-to-day life. The 260-day tzolkin was strictly a Mesoamerican intellectual creation; nothing like it has been found in any other part of the world. As a calendar it serves many purposes, including divination and the timing of rituals and events. But perhaps its most important use, and one that is still valid today, was as a matrix of personality types.

The features of the calendar that are most significant in our approach to practicing Mayan astrology are as follows:

- **The Day-Sign.** The Mayan calendar divides its year into periods of twenty days. Each of the twenty days has its own sign. Like the signs of the Western zodiac, these day-signs reveal important components of personality and destiny.
- **The Trecena.** The 260-day astrological calendar is divided into twenty blocks of thirteen days that also function like signs. Trecenas are a kind of subset of the day-signs, and they seem to describe qualities of the personality that are similar to those described by the moon in Western astrology.
- **The Lord of the Night.** A repeating sequence of nine days is named for important gods of the underworld. It may be that these "Lords of the Night" symbolize one's deep unconscious, hidden motivations, and even one's dark side.
- **The Year.** In the Mayan calendar, the solar years are grouped in fifty-two-year cycles. The Maya gave each year in the cycle a specific name, and regarded each as having its own special quality. This methodology is similar in some ways to the Chinese twelve-year cycle of animals, in which people who are born in a given

year supposedly share similar qualities that are reflected in their personality and character.

- **The Phase of Venus.** The cycle of the planet Venus is divided into four main periods, used as calendar markers. The phase in which a person is born can offer insights into social values and his or her role in society.

The system works as follows: First, the twenty named days repeat endlessly, as does our seven-day planetary week (inherited from the civilizations of the Ancient Near East). Each named day functions much like a zodiac sign, in that it symbolizes an archetypal concept that appears to be deeply imprinted in the psyche of any person born on that day. This interpretation is much like the Western zodiac approach except that the signs change daily. The unit of twenty days appears to function much like a biorhythm—a cycle of twenty days, in which one of the days is personal.

Days are also grouped into units of thirteen days. These units take on the name of the day-sign (one of the twenty named days) that begins the period. After thirteen cycles of the twenty named days, and twenty cycles of the thirteen-day periods, exactly 260 days have elapsed, and the interplay of thirteen and twenty begins again. As a result, 260 basic personality types are possible in this system because any birth is located in one of the twenty named days, and also within one of the thirteen-day periods.

The Mayan Calendar is a brilliant intellectual creation from a numerological perspective and continues to fascinate the archaeologists and astronomers who study it. What makes the system truly impressive is that it appears to have captured something about human personality as well. Before exploring the many-faceted calendar, however, it is important to understand something about the culture that created it.

CULTURE AND HISTORY OF THE MAYA

The Maya are a distinct culture that originated and still live in the southern parts of Mexico, all of Guatemala and Belize, and the western portions of Honduras and El Salvador. The ancient Maya are known for their hieroglyphic writing, their accomplishments in mathematics and astronomy, their monumental architectural structures, their art, and their cosmology, among other achievements. Mayan civilization developed over the course of several millennia and flourished at about the same time as the later Roman Empire and the early Byzantine and Islamic civilizations. For nearly all of their history, the Maya were a culture of mainly autonomous cities and villages that shared related languages and customs. They traded among themselves and formed dynastic alliances, and they also fought bitterly with each other. Until the arrival of the Spanish, however, the Maya were rarely disturbed by outside civilizations such as the Toltecs or Aztecs. Today, as many as six million Maya live in the same regions as their ancestors did and continue to practice many of their traditional ways in spite of constant pressure from religious and commercial institutions that strive to force Western views on them.

Mayan history, which spans over three millennia, has been divided into three major periods. During the Preclassic period (1800 BC to AD 250) many core components of Mayan culture were created. One of these components is the Mayan calendar, which was based on highly sophisticated astronomical observations applied in an astrological manner. Another component is hieroglyphic writing, the only true writing of the New World. Also during this period, the Maya built large ceremonial centers consisting of spectacular architectural constructions decorated with paintings and sculptures. It is now thought that some of the earliest Mayan centers were located near the Pacific coast. The ancient ceremonial center of Izapa in this region shows much sophistication at what was otherwise an early time for such architecture. The influence of the even more ancient Olmec peoples is found here as well, and some archaeologists have speculated that the coastal location suggests possible contacts with peoples from South America. Later, Preclassic Mayan centers were established farther inland, in Belize and Guatemala.

The Classic period of the Maya is dated from AD 250 to 925. This middle period was the time of the Maya's greatest achievements in astronomy, architecture, and cosmology. All major events were dated in the overall framework of The Long Count, which was being used in the late Preclassic period, as early as the first century BC. The Long Count is a 5,125-year cycle incorporating many smaller blocks of time utilized by the Mayans, including the 260-day Mayan year and the trecenas. Wars and dynastic histories were recorded in stone; the names of many rulers and their offspring, the dates of the births, ascensions to the throne, and deaths are now common knowledge. Because of these inscribed records, dynasties in Copan, Tikal, and other areas are now known in great detail.

Huge ceremonial centers were built during this period and in many ways they functioned like cities. These centers were for religious rituals, for trade, and for learning. Around AD 400, the influence of the huge Mexican center Teotihuacán began to be evident throughout the larger cultural region of Mesoamerica.

The Classic Maya reached their zenith around AD 700. After that, fewer centers were built, and by 800 most of them had collapsed. The cause of this sudden decline of one of the world's greatest civilizations is not fully understood. Certainly population pressures, deforestation, the degradation of soil, land erosion, and most likely a change to a warmer and dryer climate played a role. By the end of the Classic period, only a few centers in northern Yucatan, such as Uxmal and Chichen Itza, were still functioning.

The Postclassic period (AD 925 to 1697) was a time of smaller-scale building projects, many of which featured fortifications, and of more defensive alliances among groups. In about 980–990, Toltec peoples from Mexico invaded Yucatan, influencing the Itza, a dominant Mayan lineage. A great leader called Kulkucan (Quetzalcoatl) may have led the invasion, and the result was the introduction of new architectural and artistic styles. About 1275, Mayapan emerged as a center of power for the Itza, but clashes among its rulers led to its decline. The Spanish arrived in Yucatan in 1517, and by 1541 they had gained control of the region around Merida. Meanwhile, the Itza had earlier moved South to Lake Peten in Guatemala where they founded a new capital, Tayasal. This new capital was not taken by the Spanish until 1697. Since that time, the Maya have revolted against the Spanish many times. In recent times, the Sandanista uprising in Chiapas could be said to be yet another instance of the Maya resisting post-Colonial domination. The authors encourage readers to learn more about the plight of the modern Maya and their culture.

UNDERSTANDING THE CALENDAR

How do we know what we do about the tzolkin? First, inscriptions and glyphs have been found in stone stelae and in ancient books called codices (plural of "codex") that show its use and structure. Second, the tzolkin is still in use today in remote areas of Guatemala and Mexico, maintained by an oral tradition. Ethnologists have reported on this contemporary use of the astrological calendar. Third, although the Spanish friars enthusiastically destroyed every written record that might perpetuate the indigenous traditions, they also reported on these matters so as to better identify them for further destruction by their successors. Some of these writings have survived, and they serve as useful, though uncomprehending, guides to the astrological traditions.

The calendar sequence of 260 days had nothing to do with the seasons. Instead, the count of days embodied astronomical cycles and possibly some important biological rhythms, including the length of human gestation. The count was kept faithfully and consistently for centuries throughout Mesoamerica. When it was 1-Imix in Tulum, it was 1-Imix in Tula. A few dates recorded in both Mesoamerican and European calendars shortly after the Conquest are consistent with contemporary day counts from day-keepers in remote sections of Mexico and Guatemala, so it is possible to determine the current day-signs. The correlation of calendars is known with great certainty, but this fact has not stopped certain New Age writers from promoting their own ideas on this matter.

Because many readers will be familiar with the Western approach to astrology, the authors will draw many comparisons between it and the Mayan system in this book. The best-known component of Western astrology is the twelve-sign zodiac, essentially a twelve-fold symbolic map of the seasonal cycle. Aries begins the process with self-interest, energy, and vigor, and Pisces ends it in universalism and meltdown. Each sign represents a stage along the cycle of life. Anyone who has studied and applied it will know that it really works, though that validity has been difficult to demonstrate statistically as of yet. However, the real key to understanding the symbolism of both the zodiac and the Mayan 260-day astrological calendar lies in an understanding of the most basic, astronomically derived spatial and temporal frames of reference—the four directions.

THE MAYAN CALENDAR AND THE FOUR DIRECTIONS

Astrology has deep roots in what might be termed directional symbolism. In many ancient cosmological systems, the four directions typically

Cosmogram from the cover of the Fejervary-Mayer codex*

form the cornerstones of the known universe, and they play an important role in religious ritual as well. The link to astrology has to do with the fact that the sun's daily and annual motion defines the four directions. The sun, or more accurately the rotation of the earth and the location of the sunrises and sunsets during the year, establishes a four-fold, seasonal structure of the year. The sun rises in the east, sets in the west, reaches its northernmost rise and set in summer and its southernmost in winter.

The nature of each of these solar locations in the diurnal and seasonal cycles of the northern hemisphere suggests specific qualities that

*A cosmogram is a two-dimensional drawing of the cosmos in which ancient peoples depicted the four directions, the gods, and other important symbols in specific levels and sequences.

have become associated with each of the four directions. In general, east, where the sun rises and begins the day, suggests emergence. West is where the sun goes down and merges with the earth. The power of the north dominates during winter in the northern hemisphere, seeming to push the sun to the south, while the reverse is true during summer when the sun rides high towards the north in the sky. In many traditions, north was connected with the problems and practicalities of life while south suggested the elements of social and emotional life.

The zodiac in Western astrology appears to be founded on the four directions, which may also be the basis of the four elements—fire, earth, air, and water. This relationship is also reflected in the basic quadrant form of the horoscope. Directional symbolism, with essentially the same meanings as in the four elements of astrology, is also found in Vedic and Chinese astrology, and also in many divination systems including Tarot and the I Ching.

The directional symbolism used in Mayan astrology is applied to the sequence of day-signs. The concepts that correspond to each direction are as follows:

DIRECTION	ACTIVITY	PROCESS	REALM	POWER
East	initiation	emergence	individual	creativity
North	separation	sacrifice	objective	materialization
West	cooperation	adjustment	collective	communication
South	connection	feeling	subjective	emotion

In Mesoamerican astrology, each of the twenty day-signs is linked with one of the four directions in a consistent order: first day—east; second day—north; third day—west; and fourth day—south. Beginning with the fifth day, this order repeats five times, making five cycles, or stages, of the four directions in each twenty-day period. The authors believe that the symbolism of each direction is a strong factor in the personality dynamics of those born under them. For example, all the day-signs linked to the east are quite powerful and often dominating, while those linked to the west are adaptive and compromising. Many of the twenty key symbols of the Maya are named in a way not unlike the Western zodiac signs. Some of the signs are named for plants (grass, reed) and more of them for animals (including reptiles, birds, and mammals). Other signs are named for natural forces such as wind and rain. This naming reflects the close connection between humans and the natural environment at the time the system was created.

Each day of a twenty-day period is named, and each name is packed with symbolic meaning. Together the signs form a personality matrix that makes the models of personality taught in modern psychology seem quite limited. People appear to be influenced by these signs from the moment of their birth. Below is a listing of the twenty day-signs and their directional linkages. These signs are the classic Yucatec Mayan names with rough English translations. The authors recommend that this table be committed to memory, as the signs and their corresponding directions form the foundation of much of Mayan astrology.

DAY-SIGNS, STAGES, AND DIRECTIONAL LINKAGES

	EAST	NORTH	WEST	SOUTH
1st stage	Imix (crocodile)	Ik (wind)	Akbal (night)	Kan (corn)
2nd stage	Chicchan (serpent)	Cimi (owl, skull)	Manik (deer)	Lamat (rabbit)
3rd stage	Muluc (water)	Oc (dog)	Chuen (monkey)	Eb (broom)
4th stage	Ben (reed)	Ix (jaguar)	Men (eagle)	Cib (vulture)
5th stage	Caban (movement)	Etz'nab (flint knife)	Cauac (storm)	Ahau (lord)

The sequence of the twenty signs is not haphazard. A series of symbols moving from basic to complex describes forces of nature and forms of manifestation. The twenty named days themselves are a component within the larger 260-day calendar; thirteen repetitions occur within this framework. Like the Western zodiac and other symbol systems, the tzolkin contains within it a number of fascinating symmetries. The calendar divides into fourths (sixty-five-day segments) and fifths (fifty-two-day segments). The count meshes with the 365-day calendar perfectly every 52 years, when it has repeated 73 times. It also meshes with the Venus synodic cycle every 104 years. (A synodic cycle is the period of time it takes for a body in the solar system to return to the same position relative to the Sun as seen from Earth.) Venus's cycle repeats every 584 days. In 104 years (2 x 52) there are 146 repeats of the 260-day tzolkin and 65 Venus synodic cycles.

What makes the tzolkin potentially useful is its simple requirements (birth date only, in most cases) and its ability to accurately delineate personality patterns and life issues. Unlike Western astrology, which requires accurate birth times and the processing of numerous planetary placements and configurations, the 260-day calendar does not require any particular technical expertise. Anyone with a good understanding of the day-signs will be in possession of a powerful diagnostic tool. As with Western astrology, birth signs are only symbols of one's proper cosmic orientation and potential; they are not meant to indicate limits on what one can do in life. Astrology is, in the modern age, a tool for individual growth, not a science of fatalism.

HOW TO USE THIS BOOK

Chapters 1 through 5 in part 1 explain the symbolism, logic, and meaning of the five primary components of the Mayan system. In these chapters you will also find delineations of the individual personality profiles associated with each day-sign, trecena, Night Lord, year, and phase of Venus. The authors have assembled a simple geometric grid on which to chart the particular data that apply to an individual's date of birth for each of these components. Chapter 6 explains how to set up and use this chart to do readings. It provides sample charts and readings for well-known personalities to help familiarize the reader with how to fit all the pieces together.

In part 2, the scope of our revival of Mayan astrology widens to include topics of interest to serious followers of Western astrology as well as the Mayan system. Chapter 7 adds a dynamic dimension to Mayan astrology, explaining a fundamental rhythm that runs through the tzolkin and impacts both the world and each individual. Chapter 8 considers the katun cycle of the Maya, which is a kind of world astrology and also the basis of Mayan prophecies. Chapter 9 explores the structure of the Mayan Calendar in greater depth and discusses some of the controversies surrounding its interpretation. Chapter 10 presents a method devised by the authors for creating a chart that displays relevant planetary positions for an individual, using the tzolkin as the reference grid in much the same way as the zodiac is used in Western astrology.

NOTES ON PRONUNCIATION

Mayan names and words are basically transcriptions of the Mayan language into Old Spanish. Most words are pronounced as they would be read in Spanish with a few exceptions. One of these is the x, which is pronounced "sh." Another is the c, which is pronounced hard (as in "cat"). Here are some examples.

> Imix – *ee-MISH*
> tzolkin – *zol-KEEN*
> katun – *kah-TUNE*
> Ahau – *ah-HAW*
> Cib – *keeb*
> Muluc – *moo-LUKE*

"MAYA" OR "MAYAN?"

One final note: In most scientific publications, the word "Mayan" is used only to refer to the language of the Maya. All other contexts utilize the word "Maya." Examples would be Maya architecture, Maya weaving, Maya cosmology, and Maya astronomy. Convention, at least convention within the framework of those who do the most serious and responsible work in regard to the study of the Maya, suggests that "Maya Astrology" is the proper expression of this book's topic. However, in the popular press the term "Mayan Calendar" has become widely used, establishing the convention of using "Mayan" as the adjective form. To facilitate ease of pronunciation and consistency with common usage, therefore, in this text the authors will use the term "Mayan" in all references when the word serves as an adjective, and the word "Maya" when the word refers to the people themselves.

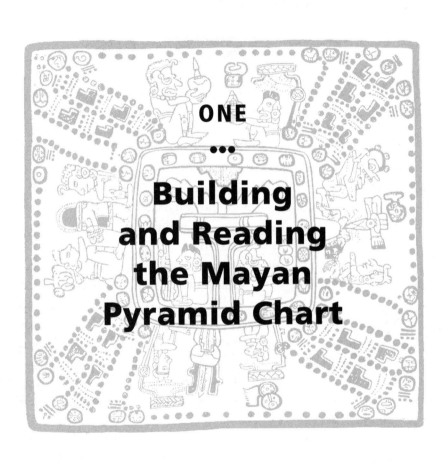

ONE

•••

Building
and Reading
the Mayan
Pyramid Chart

ONE
THE SUN AND
THE DAY-SIGNS

In this chapter you will find descriptions of the twenty day-signs used by the Maya and by other Mesoamerican peoples. Like the signs of the Western zodiac, these day-signs reveal important components of personality and destiny. They describe an individual's primary motivations, personal style, and role in the social world.

The day is a unit of time that is derived from observation of the regular daily cycle of the sun as seen from any point on the earth. Today we know that it is the rotation of the earth that causes the sun to appear to move through the sky and then pass under the earth, only to rise again the next day. Still, from the perspective of an Earth-bound observer, it is the motion of the sun that establishes the basic twenty-four-hour rhythm of time as we know it. Our clocks and calendars are based on the sun's daily and yearly motions, and hundreds of rhythms in our body are attuned to them as well. These circadian (*circa* = about, *dia* = day) rhythms are found in nearly all organisms and are used to maintain a balance among all the different life processes. In the larger sense, our lives depend on the sun—for nourishment through the foods we eat, and for a myriad of internal biochemical rhythms, including the sleep cycle. Using the sun-derived unit of time called the day as the basis of an astrological and divinatory system makes good sense. In fact, the Maya used the term *kin* as a reference to the sun, the day, and to time itself.

After many years of observations, the authors believe that the transition from one day-sign to the next becomes effective about the time of

14

sunset. This means that persons born at 9 p.m. on January 1st would look to January 2nd in the tables to locate their day-sign. Customs and historical records of the Maya also tend to support sunset being an important transition point between named days.

The table below summarizes the twenty day-signs, and includes the names and meanings of the signs in both the Mayan and Aztec systems.

NUMBER OF DAY IN SEQUENCE	CLASSIC MAYAN NAME	MEANING	AZTEC NAME	MEANING
1	Imix	Earth dragon	Cipactli	crocodile
2	Ik	air, life	Ehecatl	wind
3	Akbal	night, darkness	Cali	house
4	Kan	corn, ripe	Cuetzpallin	lizard
5	Chicchan	serpent	Coatl	serpent
6	Cimi	death, owl	Miquiztli	death
7	Manik	grasp, deer	Mazatl	deer
8	Lamat	Venus	Tochtli	rabbit
9	Muluc	water, rain	Atl	water
10	Oc	dog	Itzcuintli	dog
11	Chuen	monkey	Ozomatli	monkey
12	Eb	tooth, jaw	Malinalli	grass
13	Ben	reed, cane	Acatl	reed
14	Ix	jaguar, magician	Ocelotl	jaguar
15	Men	eagle	Cuauhtli	eagle
16	Cib	vulture, ancestor	Cozcacuauhtli	vulture
17	Caban	force, earth	Ollin	motion, earthquake
18	Etz'nab	flint knife	Tecpatl	flint knife
19	Cauac	storm, rain	Quiahuitl	rain
20	Ahau	lord	Xochitl	flower

The day-sign itself appears to function like a combination of the Sun and the Ascendant in Western astrology, describing the characteristics that the self takes in the world, as well as many of one's primary motivations. The thirteen-day period functions like the Moon-sign, as we will see in chapter 2. The cycling of the twenty-day-signs also incorporates the four directions. Each direction occurs a total of five times during the cycle, and it is the eastern direction that appears to set the tone for five major sequences or stages. To the authors, these stages suggest an evolutionary sequence contained within the twenty days. Imix begins the first stage and appears to symbolize physical and emotional-territorial foundations upon which the next three signs elaborate. The first four day-signs are indeed very physical and fundamental, relating to birth, life, and reproduction. The next sequence, beginning with Chicchan, suggests the rising of consciousness out of these roots and the challenges of social living, including cooperation and competition. Muluc begins a sequence that suggests the evolution of emotions and feelings to better navigate and explore the world and the potentials of being. The authors believe that Ben, a day-sign of intellect and the process of learning and knowing, denotes a theme that is continued to some extent in the three day-signs that follow it. Finally, Caban and the last three day-signs suggest the effects of rising consciousness on the world and the need to come to terms with them.

PERSONALITY PROFILES OF THE DAY-SIGNS

The rest of this chapter delineates the personal characteristics attributable to each of the twenty day-signs. Each entry begins with the name of the day-sign and its directional complement, as well as a short summary of the Mayan symbolism associated with that day-sign. This is followed by a general profile of the personality characteristics for that day-sign, a brief description of the life situations likely to challenge people born under that sign, and finally a suggested approach to those areas of difficulty.

The modern delineations presented here are based on comparisons of many persons born under each day-sign as well as interpretations of Mayan and Aztec symbolism. They were developed by Bruce Scofield in the late 1980s and have proven to be accurate and revealing indicators for hundreds of people who have applied them since.

The Mayan glyphs for the twenty signs are shown in the chart on the opposite page.

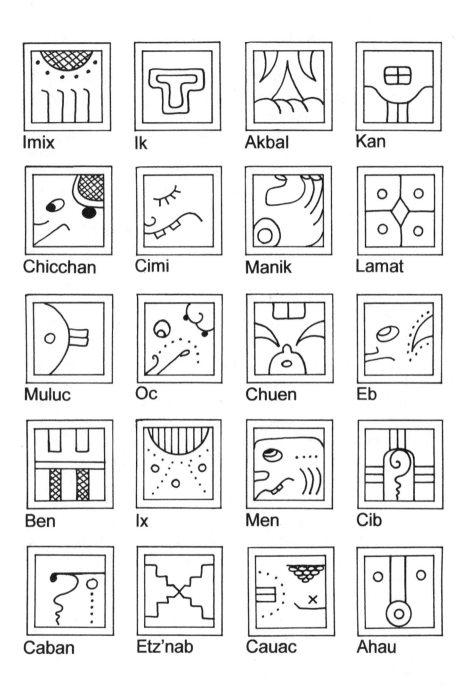

Mayan glyphs for the twenty day-signs

In addition to individual personal profiles, the day-signs offer insight into relationships. Every fourth day, signs of the same direction arise, and in between, signs of the other directions arise. Such patterns suggest the basis for compatibility between signs. While it is true that day-signs linked to the same direction will have much in common, they may not in all cases be the most compatible. Signs of opposite directions—e.g., Imix (East) and Manik (West)—may be more complementary and just as likely to figure in the establishment of a long-term relationship. Such a pattern may be particularly true for day-signs of opposite directions that are also "opposite" each other in the entire twenty-day sequence when the sequence is seen as a wheel. For example, Chuen (West) is not only the opposite direction of Imix (East), but it is ten days ahead of Imix, i.e., halfway through the twenty-day sequence.

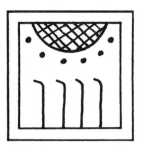

Imix—East

Symbolism: The Mayan name, Imix (ee-MISH) or Imox, is a word that the authors believe refers to the earth god and consequently to Earth itself. The Mayan glyph for the day has been compared to a woman's nipple, a symbol of nourishment. Imix also has connections with the ceiba tree, a giant tree usually found growing in the old town plazas, that symbolizes growth from deep within the earth (from its core, to be exact).

Personality: Imix types are often constantly at work, usually trying to maintain the integrity of their world. They are energetic, rigid, creative, and initiating. They have intense emotional power and a need to be deeply involved in whatever they do, a need that must be used creatively or it may become a source of problems in relationships. Imix types have strong nurturing instincts, are quite sensitive, and require privacy. They are not always comfortable sharing feelings. They are protective and dominating in a parental way and often struggle psychologically with the voice of an internalized critical parent. Persons born under Imix can be assertive and even aggressive in some ways. Many feel rejected by their families or parents, and in compensation, seek group friendships that make up for this loss. Some become founders of businesses, organizations or associations. They relate to the world around them through their feelings and not their intellect. This causes them to be quite reactive to any changes taking place around them, and they often rush in to keep the "dam from breaking," so-to-speak. This reactive nature is probably behind their tendency to initiate activities. They are often found breaking new ground or starting projects from scratch. When motivated, the Imix type will work incessantly until emotional security has been restored and stabilized. When they do achieve emotional security, however, they may become extremely lazy and even lethargic.

Challenge: To accept themselves completely and to become free from feelings of rejection by parents or other authority figures; to join with others on terms that are shared by the others; to refrain from being judgmental.

Solution: Founding a business or creating a home. Learning to be independent.

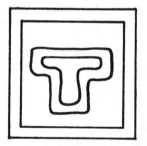

Ik—North

Symbolism: The Mayan name Ik (eek) means wind, breath, and life, suggesting a concept like "the breath of life." The glyph for this day-sign, which usually included a "T" design, had associations with a god of rains as well as wind. Rains are needed to germinate seeds and stimulate life, and this "coming to life" may be the meaning the Maya intended.

Personality: Ik types are communicative, mental, agile, clever, and multifaceted. They have a tendency to do many things, to be a "jack of all trades but master of none." They tend to be idealistic and romantic, fashion-conscious or artistic, and somewhat non-committal or indecisive. They seem to have problems with issues of responsibility, obligation, and commitment, these being their greatest challenges. Ik types are thinking constantly, and this characteristic intrudes upon their awareness of the intense emotional realities within and around them. To others, they seem very much alive and alert. To themselves, they feel confused and uncertain as to the specific information on which they should act. Learning, speaking, reading, and other forms of mental communication appeal to them. Not a few Ik have tried their hand at writing in one form or another. A conversation with one born on this day-sign is always interesting and stimulating. However, breadth, not depth, is their forte. Wind types are clever and very intelligent when it comes to learning. They enjoy playing many roles in life but do not seek out leadership positions, in fact, service seems to come more easily to them.

Challenge: To deal with fears about responsibility and obligations; to accept commitments; to learn to be decisive.

Solution: To seek education; to gain mastery of language and verbal expression.

Akbal—West

Symbolism: Akbal (ahk-BAL) is the Mayan name for this day-sign, which means darkness or night. Another Mayan name for this day-sign is Uotan, meaning heart, which had associations with Earth gods and the drum. The glyph for Akbal may signify an animal of the underworld, perhaps the jaguar.

Personality: Akbal types are often powerful and tend to project an imposing or attractive presence on the world around them. Their personal power may be exerted in subtle ways, but it is always something others must contend with. In many cases, this power is completely legitimate, as when the person is a teacher, leader, or healer. They are logical, organized, and capable of deep thought, but they tend to be conservative in many matters. Patience, endurance, and hard work seem to come naturally to those born under the day-sign Akbal. Security, both mental and physical, is a major issue for those born under this day-sign. The physical security that a home, house, building, or other structure represents may be a focus in life, or the emotional security that family ties offer may draw intense interest. Science and math, or other systems of knowledge (including occultism, magic, and astrology), often interest the Akbal-born because those subjects aid the person in organizing practical matters of life. Traditions appeal to them and they have a great respect for history. Those born under Akbal take a structural approach to life. The more organized their lives are, the more they will feel secure and in control. If it takes ten years or more to achieve a goal of organization, then Akbal people will tough it out. Because Akbal types work so hard on seeing and understanding things in specific ways, they can develop mental inertia. As a result, a change for them requires a near overhaul of the logical framework that they have constructed, and they may resist such changes. Outsiders may see this characteristic as reliability and constancy, others may see it as stubbornness.

Challenge: Mental rigidity and problems with sharing; loss of control.

Solution: Becoming a builder of systems; stabilizing the foundations of whatever is done.

Kan—South

Symbolism: The Maya called this day Kan (kahn), which suggests corn and ripeness. The highly stylized glyph for the day does not offer much of a clue, though young maize plants are shown growing from the Kan glyph in the codices. The Kan glyph, often painted yellow, is also found in the codices near offerings of food, which suggests that corn, the most important food of the Maya, was simply a reference to that which sustains life.

Personality: Kan types are ready for life in the social world and are often interested in leadership and performance. They are active, dynamic, sexual, and influential. They hold themselves to high standards. Self-esteem is important to them, and they are often attracted to attention-getting activities. Persons born under Kan will often be found doing work that is creative or performance-oriented. It is a day-sign of leadership, or at least leadership where a personal performance is necessary. What is noteworthy is that these people thoroughly enjoy such situations, and they are generally very competent, and sometimes outstanding, at what they do. They often have a reputation for being different or deviating from the status quo. They have a strong drive toward independence and freedom from entanglements. Those born under the day-sign Kan are usually quite individualistic. They will compromise only under extreme pressure, and they may harbor resentment if forced to comply. Kan types often attract attention by being different, but they may be too involved in their own interests to be seriously concerned about what other people think of them. This allows them to eventually become extremely individualized and highly specialized persons. These people generally lead creative and productive lives and maintain stable, though usually somewhat unconventional, relationships with those of the opposite sex. Sexuality and relations with the opposite sex, however, can be a challenge for them as they sometimes struggle with self-esteen issues. Down deep, Kan people are very serious about the quality of their lives.

Challenge: To become a balanced individual; to become comfortable with the world of attraction and courtship.

Solution: Engaging in activities in which performance is evaluated; sweating the details.

Chicchan—East

Symbolism: To the Maya, Chicchan (chee-CHAHN) suggested the celestial serpents, located at the four quarters and linked to rainfall. The glyph itself suggests the head or scales of a snake, and in the codices, it is linked to a serpent god.

Personality: Chicchan is a strong-willed, powerful, and charismatic day-sign. Chicchan types can be quite dramatic and are usually regarded by others as having "sex appeal." They are quite intelligent and usually well informed, but tend to become fanatical about one subject or another. Death and sex fascinate them, and they can become obsessive about these matters. The emotional power of those born under this sign is remarkable. They are often found prancing around one stage or another or attracting attention indirectly by lurking suspiciously in the shadows. Leadership comes naturally to them in part due to their ability to grab and hold the attention of others. They are quite strong physically and mentally, and are capable of living under very stressful conditions. On the other hand, failure to nurture themselves adequately is a common weakness of these types. Natives of Chicchan are intelligent but also extremist in many ways. They have strong emotions or personal powers that affect others deeply. They have such strong emotional reactions that they sometimes explode with anger, causing great upheavals in relationships. When these powerful emotional energies are harnessed, Chicchan types can be quite constructive and creative, pouring out products or performances without any apparent rest. Indeed, they are capable of saving the world.

Challenge: To experience powerful transformations consciously; to generate energy for the benefit of all involved.

Solution: To seek to learn and to develop a deep understanding of life.

Cimi—North

Symbolism: Cimi (kee-MEE), the Mayan word for this day, comes from the root word for death. The glyph for the day is clearly a skull, the skull of the death god. The owl, a night bird as well as an omen of death, was also linked to this day, as was the underworld.

Personality: Cimi types tend to be security conscious, materialistic, sacrificing, accepting of change, and helpful. They are not often confident leaders and will more often comfortably accept a secondary role or position. Tradition appeals to them, and since they have a strong faith, so does religion. Often those born under this sign are unsure of where their life is headed, and faith or instinct are all they can go on. They are materialistic, very concerned with domestic security, and may have an interest in real estate, or perhaps work with homes or houses in some way. They have an interest and concern for the community and politics and are concerned with what is happening in the world or their neighborhood. They like to feel that they can do something about it. They cooperate well with others and rarely allow their egos to get in the way of progress toward the collective goals in which they believe. Those Cimi who make politics a career will often associate themselves with powerful allies, even with those more powerful than themselves. Cimi types take all kinds of responsibilities very seriously. Obligations to others, and a sense of duty, tend to dominate their lives. Because Cimi types are usually polite and hesitant to speak their true feelings, they tend to give in to others more often than may be necessary or even reasonable.

Challenge: To have faith; not to be a victim; not to feel obliged to make too many sacrifices.

Solution: To become truly useful to society and the world around them.

Manik—West

Symbolism: The Mayan name for this day, Manik (mah-NEEK), does not translate easily and is, unfortunately, not useful as a clue to the symbolism of this day-sign. The glyph itself, which appears to be a hand in a grasping position, is not suggestive of anything in particular either.

Personality: The Manik type is peaceful, generous, cooperative, artistic, and inspiring. While they are generally placid people, they can also be very bold in speaking up for what they feel to be right. They can be mentally powerful and, as one would expect, are not easily convinced or swayed from their intellectual positions. Manik people need companionship. For these natives, community and family are of great importance, but so is their freedom to follow their nomadic instincts. Manik is a sign of participation in the community. Those born under it are often deeply involved with family traditions, and in some cases, socio-political traditions. Family or community may be such a strong issue that crucial life decisions are often based completely on these elements. Manik types are also very sensual, artistic, and even eccentric. Their aesthetic sense is usually highly developed, and they often dabble in one or another of the arts. Those born on this day-sign are very sensual and sexually inclined, yet are also quite intuitive and very sensitive to the needs and concerns of other beings.

Challenge: To be free, independent and secure in relationships.

Solution: To accept and be comfortable with their own individuality, no matter what strange characteristics it may entail.

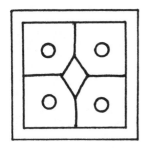

Lamat—South

Symbolism: The Mayan word Lamat (la-MAHT) referred to the planet Venus, the "great star." The glyph for this day was the sign for the planet Venus itself, and in some variations is a celestial dragon with markings signifying Venus. Drunkenness is suggested by this symbolism also, because the Mayan conception of Venus included the notion of inebriation.

Personality: Lamat is energetic, busy, nervous, quick, and playful. Those born under it are moving constantly and are always busy with something. They are intelligent, but somewhat paranoid, and can at times be self-destructive. They usually appreciate a good fight. Lamat is a sign of cleverness, games, and competition, and it produces people with active minds who must always be doing something. Intellectual challenges such as debating, arguing, and deal-making appeal to them. Many are drawn into the business world where competitiveness and cleverness are assets. They also have a great need for physical activity and are sometimes known for their nervous bodily movements. Some exercise; others dance. But all Lamats need to keep moving about. These are people who can do enormous amounts of work in very little time and not seem to be tired for it. They have a great fondness for music and humor, but they can also be argumentative, working against their own best interests at times. Many born on Lamat are performers or entertainers. They can be quite egocentric, but they are not as confident of their abilities as one would think. Their capacity for subtlety of mind causes them to be interested in details, mysteries, intelligence-gathering work, psychology, and the occult. They tend to be suspicious of every new person they meet, though once they know you they can be very loyal friends.

Challenge: To keep themselves under control so as to be able to finish things.

Solution: To carefully select friends and lovers and to avoid extremes and excesses.

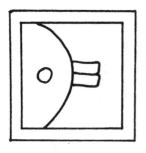

Muluc—East

Symbolism: The Mayan name for this day, Muluc (moo-LUKE) appears to refer to water, though it may also refer to jade, a symbol for water, suggesting that it was precious, as well as green and blue. The glyph itself is probably that of the head of a fish.

Personality: Muluc is emotional, imaginative, psychic, romantic, and fantasy prone. Some born on Muluc have a natural flair for the public life as a performer—and they can be capable of transferring their strong emotions to the audience. Many become successful performers or artists, while others associate themselves indirectly with show business or romantic lifestyles. Persons born under this sign struggle with powerful emotions and urges, and they have the ability to dominate others by expressing their strong feelings. In some cases, these people are very deep emotionally, have a strong sexual nature, or are interested in things that are sometimes considered normal in primitive societies but uncouth in modern life. Their strong feelings often lead to compulsive and addictive behaviors, or on the positive side, they lead toward the emotion-driven achievement of goals. People born under this day-sign are inclined to take risks, which can sometimes lead to great success and unforeseen opportunities. They are great dreamers and are sometimes psychic. For many, this intense connection with the subconscious manifests as creative, artistic ability and vision. This day-sign has an extremist quality that can lead to great success—these people are not moderates.

Muluc confers a strong and independent mind that can solve problems intuitively. They may have problems with responsibilities, however, a characteristic that is traceable to their childhood experiences. With good parental role models, they will find success later in life more easily.

Challenge: To handle self-control and responsibility issues.

Solution: To seek consistency and persistence, which will help to control and focus the emotions and support leadership endeavors.

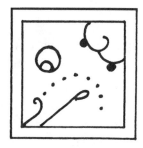

Oc—North

Symbolism: The Mayan name for this day-sign, Oc (oke) means dog. In the codices, the dog is often shown holding a torch, perhaps referring to the Mayan myth in which the dog brings fire to humans. In some depictions of this day-sign, the dog's ear is emphasized by its being torn-off, mangled, or diseased. The dog, one of the most loyal of domesticated animals, was probably used to symbolize guidance, loyalty, and companionship—probable themes of this sign.

Personality: Oc is a cooperative, loyal, and helpful day-sign. Consistency and commitment characterize persons born under it. They have a strong group instinct and will stick by their allies in times of trouble. They are good team players, usually very creative, and strive patiently to fill authoritative positions. They instinctively know where they and others stand in the social ranking of any given situation, and this understanding allows them to be patient and to wait their turn for leadership. They know how to inspire loyalty in others because they have such a good understanding of it themselves. They also like to roam, but not too far from their territory. Oc enjoy short-distance travel—what they can do with a car or a boat. They enjoy monitoring their territory and have a strong interest in their neighborhoods. They require much variety in life and find the arts, especially music, rewarding. They approach their art form as a craft to be learned and mastered, and they are often technique-conscious. They may also be creative in the social and political arenas. Their father, or a father figure, often makes a strong impression on them, and they may either benefit through him or struggle over power issues and independence. For Oc, life is about achieving emotional maturity, and it is often through understanding the father, and authority in general, that this goal is achieved.

Challenge: Lack of emotional maturity; father-related/authority issues.

Solution: To learn patience followed by acceptance of direction from others, when it is needed.

Chuen—West

Symbolism: The Mayan name for this day-sign, Chuen (chew-EN) translates as artisan or craftsman. Among the Quiche Maya, the name for this day is Batz, which is the term for monkey, particularly howling monkey. The glyphs for the sign are very stylized, though some appear to show the head of a monkey. Like the Aztecs, the Maya linked this sign with the arts and the crafts.

Personality: Chuen types are frequently attention-getting, artistic, clever, and demonstrative. They are often found working, or at least interested, in the performing or communicative arts. They seek attention from others and are quick learners, interested in everything around them. Actors, artists, musicians, designers, and writers make up an unusually large percentage of people born on this day. They also make good teachers and salespersons. It is the cultivation and development of the personality that is the core issue for Chuen. Although they are socially active, they often struggle in close intimate relationships, needing the contact but wishing for more variety. They enjoy "playing the field," which is just another way of getting attention. This distance in relationships may be appealing to others, and it adds to the mystery of their character. Their sexual drives are strong and motivate them toward relationships, but commitment is their greatest challenge. Chuen is communicative and curious, like a monkey, and people born under this sign learn at a fast pace. Mentally, they can handle details, but they excel at generalities. Leadership positions come naturally. By nature, they are not followers and therefore the choice is either independence or leadership. This need to be the center of attention may be a response to a deep social insecurity.

Challenge: To stay with one thing long enough to become good at it; to actualize their creative potentials in ways that are not debilitating to themselves and that won't result in distancing them from close companions.

Solution: To apply creativity; to be artistic and to explore the secrets of nature.

Eb—South

Symbolism: Eb (abe) does not translate easily. The glyph combines the symbols for death and water, which has led some to conclude that it symbolized harmful rains and mildew. E, the Quiche Maya name for Eb, means tooth, and in their tradition the day is considered favorable for getting good advice and for praying.

Personality: The Eb type tends to be relaxed, courteous, practical, careful, and helpful. They tend to be pleasant people who enjoy good company and who best relate to others casually. They are generous and giving persons who usually expect nothing in return. Relationships are very important to them and are often the centerpiece of their lives. This need conditions them to make sacrifices for others. Eb types are often perceived as ambitious and hard-working. They are intensely practical, they know how to solve problems, they don't hesitate to get going when needed, and they do good work. They will compete with others, but prefer peace to conflict. Persons born under Eb may appear easy-going and compromising, but they are also easily distressed and are known to hide deep hurts and feelings. Eb types are often quite sensitive, are sometimes emotionally fragile, and are easily hurt by rejection or criticism. They tend to hold on to feelings of anger and resentment and often use hard work as a means to constructively ventilate those feelings. While they are slow to get going, Eb people are quite persistent and will finish a job or achieve a goal. They are very practical and capable of solving problems; many become designers or engineers of some kind. In general, this is a conservative day-sign that seeks peace with the world.

Challenge: To avoid poisoning themselves by suppressing anger.

Solution: To let others know how they feel.

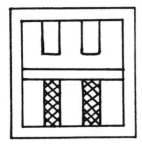

Ben—East

Symbolism: To the Maya, this day-sign, Ben (bane) appears to have symbolized the development of both the maize plant and man. The word Ben does not seem to refer to any particular plant or deity. Some researchers have thought that the sign probably referred to the standing corn stalk—as opposed to ripe corn—or perhaps to a reed or cane. The glyph is highly stylized, though in some variants a link with vegetation appears to be present. Some people have suggested that the glyph refers to a mat made of reeds, representing a kind of weaving.

Personality: Ben types are often popular, knowledgeable, accomplished, and competent, with strong opinions. They are often highly regarded by others for their talent or expertise. In some cases they are simply way ahead of their competitors, or have made their mark on the field in which they work. In other cases, it is just a matter of general competency—the ability to excel at whatever it is they decide to do. They are fighters for moral or ethical principles and are quick to take on challenges. At worst, they are opinionated. These people will "stick to their guns" when under fire, keep a "stiff upper lip" when in trouble and, like a reed or cane stalk, remain firm in tense situations. They can be intellectually rigid and prone to argue, however. These people have a militant side, and although they don't deliberately seek conflict, they seem to thrive in it. Persons born under Ben are usually popular and social, having deep knowledge of human nature. For some, this quality brings them well-deserved fame; for others, it brings respect and recognition from their peers. Although Ben types have enemies, even their enemies respect Ben's successful ways. People born under the Ben sign are ambitious and clear about their goals and intentions.

Challenge: Being opinionated or holding rigid attitudes.

Solution: To understand human nature; to apply social skills.

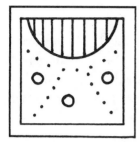

Ix—North

Symbolism: The Mayan name for this day, Ix (eesh), probably refers to the earth god or to a magician. The Quiche Maya name, Balam, definitely means jaguar throughout the Mayan region. The connection here is that the jaguar is an animal of the underworld, of the earth. The Mayan glyph is stylized, but it appears to show the spots of this animal.

Personality: Ix types can be private, sensitive, intelligent, and psychic. They have an inborn sense of strategy and make good planners and investigators. Ix types may be aggressive but they will generally avoid direct confrontations. They will fight to make a point, though they usually do so in somewhat indirect ways. Some are cryptic communicators. They are not fearful of becoming entangled with other people's lives. Ix types tend to become deeply involved with others on many levels, and they will base their security needs on these relationships. When things turn sour, they find themselves caught up in a network of ties and obligations that are difficult to throw off easily and quickly. This tendency leaves a lot of unfinished business and opportunities to process what has happened, which may yield deep spiritual insights. Ix types make good healers and consultants. They are inclined to be concerned with religion or spirituality, and they often display various kinds of psychic abilities. They are very sensitive in general and can read people intuitively. When this psychic ability is combined with their tendency to become deeply involved in human relationships, what emerges is essentially an identity as doctor or counselor. At their very best, Ix types are healers and confessors and as such provide a necessary service to humanity.

Challenge: To sort out complex and entangled human relationships; to purify one's social life.

Solution: To develop healing and counseling skills.

Men—West

Symbolism: The Maya called this day Men (mane), the root word for the verb "to make" or "to do." The glyph for the day is that of a head with dots in a line behind the eyes, which has been suggested to be evidence that the sign represented the old moon deity. This goddess is drawn with a headdress and shield of eagle feathers. An eagle's claw is also her symbol. This Mayan goddess was the patroness of weaving and other female activities. In this case, however, the day-sign's symbolism doesn't match the personality type very well.

Personality: Men types are independent, ambitious, and escapist. They can be scientific, technically inclined, critical, and exacting, and they frequently have an interest, or background, in philosophy, science, or the more technical aspects of their chosen field. Men types are usually a bit ahead of their time in their thinking, and they tend to be experimental in many areas of life. They are perfectionists with exacting, critical minds that require challenges. Making plans and layouts is particularly appealing to them. Persons born under this sign are typically perfectionists capable of handling much detail. Men types are often unconventional in significant ways; they have their own set of rules in life that develop from their own unique perspective on things. They can be driven, yet they also enjoy a good escape now and then. They would probably just take off for parts unknown, but they usually have complex relationship entanglements to handle, so they don't. On a more positive level, many Men types are concerned with making the world a better place, and they only appear to be escapist to others. Those born under Men are usually popular and well-liked, which is interesting since they are the ones who tend to frequently bend the rules as understood by others. They will compete when necessary, and can be very serious about such things, but they usually try to avoid it. Competition with themselves is more their style and is perhaps the basis of their personal ambitions.

Challenge: To create a lifestyle that offers both freedom and companionship.

Solution: To gain a deeper knowledge of human nature.

Cib—South

Symbolism: This day-sign, called Cib (keeb) by the Maya, appears to refer to a small insect, possibly the bee. The Bacabs (the personified four directions in Mayan cosmology) were bee-keepers. The Maya held a general belief that the dead return to the earth in the form of insects. The glyph itself probably represents a shell, a symbol worn by some of the Bacabs. Jaguar features appear in some of the glyphs, as well, suggesting darkness and night.

Personality: Cib is a serious, wise, deep, realistic, and pragmatic day-sign. Some Cib types are philosophical about life, others sing the blues. These people have a sense of limits and fatality that makes them seem ultra-realistic and pragmatic. They know nonsense when they see it but will give credit where it is due. Some are hardened to life, and most are status conscious and have very high standards. Most have an excellent sense of judgment, are extremely competent at what they do, yet are critical of how others do the same thing. Some have a tendency to downplay the apparent feelings of others. Although they have to work hard in life, or they may be deprived in some way, they still make progress. They tend to ask, Why should others be held to a different standard? Cib types are sensitive to authority and hierarchy, often driven to seek high positions, and they sometimes become the victims of those already so positioned. Those born under Cib are acutely conscious of their social or political status at any given moment. For most Cib types, this characteristic means that they are self-conscious when around people who can judge them in some way, and they fear rejection. Although most Cib types maintain their authority and high position relative to others, many are victims. They face the authority issues that are central to this day-sign from the other side. Some are simply taken advantage of; some are even beaten and abused. In certain cases, this abuse is more a social issue, in which the majority rejects what the Cib type believes in. It is in giving advice that many Cib types excel. Their challenges in life, and their acute awareness of what works and what doesn't in society, give them the ability to make good judgments for others.

Challenge: To overcome self-consciousness and personal insecurities.

Solution: To excel in one's career.

Caban—East

Symbolism: The Mayan name for this day, Caban (ka-BANE) means Earth, and there are associations of this day with earthquakes. The Mayan glyph of the day includes a curving line that may represent a lock of hair of the young moon goddess, who is also the goddess of Earth. The Maya considered this day good for matchmaking, medicine, and commerce.

Personality: Caban types are mentally active, rationalizing, clever but practical. They tend to believe that the world is ultimately reducible to logic and that rational solutions are the only solutions. They can be brilliant engineers or strategists who pioneer new solutions to stubborn problems. For some, however, this capacity to rationalize everything they perceive leads to inaccurate judgments and poor choices. Caban types are usually liberal and progressive. Their intense thinking often leads to views that are based on abstractions or unrealized ideals. Many Caban personalities have a great sense of humor. This may be due to the sharpness of their minds and their ability to make practical use of their insights into human nature. Strong convictions are found in those born under this day-sign. They are fiercely independent and stubborn persons who can't stand being told what to do, and they frequently pay the price for this trait in their close relationships. As leaders, they are usually regarded as progressive and possibly a bit threatening to followers of the status quo. Caban types tend to seek out leadership positions or solo positions, possibly because they know how hard it is for them to follow the path of another.

Challenge: To hold one's life together according to a reasonable plan.

Solution: To become more flexible, tolerant, and patient.

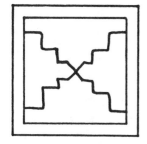

Etz'nab—North

Symbolism: The Mayan name Etz'nab (ets-NOB) translates as something like "knife" or "sharp implement." The glyph for the sign may indicate a blade, and the same design was frequently found depicted on the tips of spears.

Personality: Those born under Etz'nab are social, but also often practical, mechanically inclined, and well coordinated. Family life, parties, group events, love affairs, and partnerships can become very important, and sometimes even obsessive, to those born under this day-sign. They simply can't help being excited when around others. Their ideas about how relationships should be maintained may be in direct conflict with their own needs, which they tend to downplay and, on some level, they are angry about this trait. For the most part, they are polite, compromising, and self-sacrificing people, but when pushed, they tend to have hot tempers. While they will avoid a conflict by repressing their feelings for a time, when finally pushed too far, they will explode with pent-up rage, or at least say things that others wouldn't expect them to say. They are often extremely interested in the more technical aspects of what they do, and they have a good head for detail. They are adept at solving mechanical problems, working with tools or even mastering finger coordination for a musical instrument. These are people who thoroughly enjoy sharing a discussion on some technical subject with others. The great weakness of those born under Etz'nab is their vanity. They can be very self-absorbed both in their work and in regard to their appearance. The great strength of this day-sign is the level of personal sacrifice it bestows. Etz'nab people, for whatever psychological reason, will put their own interests aside in order to meet the needs of others who, hopefully, appreciate such gestures.

Challenge: The tendency to choose self-interest over self-sacrifice or to solve other people's problems.

Solution: To share and to let others take leadership.

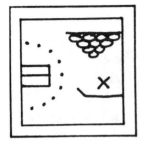

Cauac—West

Symbolism: The Mayan name for this day was Cauac (cow-AHK), which means storm, thunder, and rain. The glyph appears to contain clouds and symbols that also appear on drawings of the celestial dragons, which bring rains and storms. The Guatemalan name for this day, Ayotl, means turtle. The day-sign is linked with rain as this animal, as well as the frog, are depicted as coming down with the rain.

Personality: Positively, Cauac is a youthful, restless, friendly, helpful, and compassionate day-sign. Such people are multifaceted and often accomplished in several areas. One of the most obvious characteristics of this friendly day-sign is their youthfulness. Cauac people often choose careers that involve them with children, or they may occasionally just act like children. Those born under this sign are often mentally active and talkative. They are good learners and often become teachers or counselors. A concern for the welfare of others, especially the public, is common in those born under Cauac. They have a strong intuition and can improvise when in a tight spot. Cauac types are more inclined to imitate than to innovate. They respect tradition and the forms created by those who came before them, whether in art, science, or business. Those born under Cauac generally have an interest in the deeper meanings of life. Many are drawn to the study or practice of religion, spirituality, or philosophy. They are often found working in the medical or psychological fields. The cleansing and healing process has a special importance for those born under this day-sign. Many born under Cauac become doctors or healers of some sort. Their natural instincts to protect and nurture, combined with excellent intuition, technical aptitude, and a mind capable of grasping details, makes them well-suited for such work.

Challenge: To develop the ability to teach and to heal.

Solution: To study under a master.

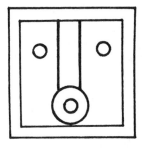

Ahau—South

Symbolism: The Mayan name for this day-sign was Ahau (ah-HAW), which means lord or chief. The glyph for the day is sometimes a four-petaled flower though it also appears as a face. To the Maya, the flower was a symbol of the lord or sun, and this was its day.

Personality: Ahau types are loving, devoted, artistic, dreamy, and romantic. They can be loyal friends and lovers, but often suffer in relationships because of unrealistic expectations. They are extremely devoted to others, including friends and lovers, and are hurt badly when they are left for another. Ahau types have a beautiful vision of what life, and most importantly what life with another, can be. In some cases, an obsession with the future and with some kind of ultimate perfection generates illusions, fuels unrealistic expectations, and brings about disappointments. In other cases, Ahau types will live a life dedicated to an ideal, and they will accomplish much, sometimes changing the world in the process. Art and beauty draw the interest of those born under this day-sign. Many become successful artists, writers, or craftspeople who produce decorative, aesthetically pleasing products. Ahau types are generally intelligent and hard-working, but they can also be stubborn and uncompromising. One major problem is their unwillingness to compromise their ideals. Ahau types are determined people who would rather not participate than have to accept a less-than-perfect situation. Ahau is a sign that needs to combine realism and idealism, and when this compromise is able to be made, their doors will open to a more perfect world.

Challenge: To handle disappointments due to unrealistic expectations; to accept a world that is not up to their hopes and wishes; to tolerate unfairness in others.

Solution: To keep life simple and to appreciate the little things.

TWO

THE MOON AND
THE TRECENA

Contained within the 260-day astrological calendar used by the Maya are twenty blocks of thirteen days called *trecenas*. They indicate general qualities of the personality similar to those described by the moon in Western astrology. These qualities are receptivity, reaction, instinctive response, and emotional connections with family, community, and society at large.

The moon played an important role in mythology and folklore in ancient Mexico. In the West, the moon has long been associated with the feminine aspects of life, and this relationship was also true for the Maya. For example, the Mayan moon was linked with the goddess Ix Chel, "Lady Rainbow," who was the wife of Itzam, the supreme god. She was a goddess of the woman's world of weaving, childbirth, and healing.

The moon also played an important role in ancient Mayan astrology. Mayan astrologers no doubt noticed how quickly the moon moves through the stars across the night sky. In one day the moon's position relative to the background stars moves as far as the sun's in thirteen days. It takes the moon about twenty-seven to twenty-eight days to pass through the 360 degrees of the zodiac. At that rate, it covers about thirteen degrees of the zodiac in one day. The sun moves at the rate of about one degree of the zodiac per day, so it takes about thirteen days to cover the same distance as the moon does in a single day. The moon also cycles with the sun thirteen times in one year. From new moon to new moon is about twnety-nine days, and roughly thirteen of these cycles match the yearly cycle of the sun through the zodiac. These are two major reasons why the number thirteen came to be the most powerful number in ancient Mexican astrology.

The Mayan tzolkin had twenty "weeks" of thirteen days, a total of 260 days. The twenty thirteen-day weeks, known in Spanish as the trecenas (meaning thirteenths), appear to be lunar in nature. They represent the time taken for the sun to match the moon's daily travel. Ancient codices and inscriptions indicated that each of the twenty thirteen-day periods had a specific meaning that was generated by the named solar day (the day-sign) that began the period. These "first days" are numbered 1, followed by the name of the day. Like the day-signs, each of these periods was ruled by a specific deity.

The trecenas appear to correlate with the public trends of the world. News events, both local and global, tend to reflect the nature of whatever thirteen-day period is currently active. For example, when the period called 1-Ben occurs, people with strong and rigid opinions make news. During 1-Cib, a sign of politics, we often hear stories of complex political maneuvering in Washington, D.C., and elsewhere. Close observers will notice that persons described by a specific thirteen-day period will often make news during its thirteen-day span of influence. Also, certain kinds of activities tend to proliferate, or at least become public knowledge, in some trecena periods but not in others. Ancient Mesoamerican astrologers used this astrological calendar when choosing the best times to do things, a process called electional astrology in the West.

The trecena not only offers a description of current trends, but also serves as an index of personality. A birth occurring during a thirteen-day period is strongly influenced by that trecena. In fact, this effect was one of the main interpretations of the trecenas in ancient Mexico. These thirteen-day periods were indicators of character and destiny that also said something about a person's connection to family, community, or even nation.

The order of the trecenas does not follow that of the twenty day-signs. For example, thirteen days after the beginning of the trecena called 1-Imix, the day-sign Ix begins the next trecena and is the next to have the number 1 as a prefix. Another thirteen signs ahead (using the day-sign sequence as a continuous loop) is Manik, which will begin the next trecena and have the number 1 as its prefix.

You can see how all twenty day-signs cycle as trecenas through the 260 days of the astrological calendar by turning to table 1 on page 125. A birth will always occur within one of these thirteen-day trecenas. This placement means that each birth is designated not only by a day-sign, but also by its position within a thirteen-day period. For example, the day 3-Ben is the third day in the trecena that began with the day 1-Chuen. A person born on the third day of the trecena 1-Chuen has Ben as their day-sign. Ben describes the solar or dominant personality, which in this case would be strong, dominating, intellectual, and crusading. But lurking beneath the dominant personality are the more instinctive (lunar) behavior patterns described by Chuen. Subconsciously, a person born under this combination would seek attention and adulation. The combination, a sign of the East (Ben) and one of the West (Chuen), might also produce a person torn between self-interest and compromise, and that person might find resolution in dramatic performances that meet the needs of others. The harnessing of self-interest and aggressiveness to the need for attention and contact with others through a career or recreational activity would appear to be a practical resolution of this conflict.

DELINEATIONS OF THE TRECENAS

1-Imix

Personal: Beneath the 1-Imix surface personality is an emotional power-house. These people have strong creative urges and feel an instinctive need to nurture others. For many, this need is actually the reflection of a desire to have a family to protect, although this need can also be met through pets and friends. Those born during this period can be emotionally domi-nating, in an unconscious way, and others may have problems with this personality characteristic.

Societal: The Imix trecena is a time when people struggle for security. Tribal bonds are intensified and nationalism, schools, children, and fam-ily issues are often in the news. Creativity is enhanced during this period, a time that traditionally was ruled by the creator god/goddess of the ancient Mexicans.

1-Ix

Personal: Beneath the 1-Ix surface personality is a challenged commu-nicator, a person who struggles with self-control, a person who is an explorer of the human condition. Critical events occurring in Ix people's lives, such as deaths or other powerful transformations, may cause them

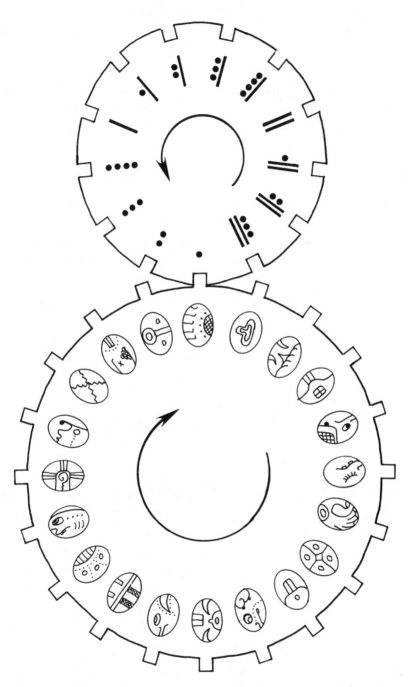

The cycles of thirteen trecenas (represented by the Mayan number symbols in the top wheel) and twenty days (represented in the bottom wheel by their day signs) can be seen as gears that mesh to produce the 260-day year.

to turn inward and keep their feelings and thoughts to themselves. People born during the Ix trecena need to be realistic about responsibilities and not shirk from them or take on too many.

Societal: Control over passions is often the issue during this period. Reckless and prideful behaviors create problems and make news, but solutions are found through psychological and technical insights.

1-Manik

Personal: Beneath the 1-Manik surface personality is a person who struggles with issues of freedom versus security. Manik people display an urge to take off for parts unknown, but they also demonstrate a desire for the security of home and family. Because the struggle with this conflict leads people to discover unique solutions, they often become innovators or creators of a somewhat unconventional personal lifestyle. Frequently, they have unusual interests of an investigative or searching nature.

Societal: In ancient times, when might and power ruled, Manik was said to be a time of peaceful, even timid, behaviors. Today, it appears that sensitivity to others, and the equality of the sexes, are important themes in the news.

1-Ahau

Personal: Beneath the 1-Ahau surface personality lies a self that is romantic and attracted to a glamorous lifestyle. Such a person may find success in a life in fashion or as a performer or public personality. The greatest weakness of Ahau people is in matters of relationship. In this area they tend to be idealistic and can often make poor choices that lead to problems.

Societal: 1-Ahau is a good time for demonstrating commitment to an ideal. It is a time of social progress and settling scores. People tend to respond to their feelings more during its influence, making it a fine time for religion and the arts.

1-Ben

Personal: Beneath the 1-Ben surface personality is a person who seeks constant self-improvement. Such people have a strong need to persuade others, to conquer their enemies, and to achieve their objectives. While they make good teachers and role models, they also have a tendency to be somewhat self-righteous and overconfident of their own opinions.

Societal: Ben is a time for making rulings, judgments, and decrees, settling treaties, promoting ideas, airing opinions, and debating policies. In ancient times it was considered an unfortunate period, probably because having people express their own ideas was not acceptable in a tightly controlled society.

1-Cimi

Personal: Beneath the 1-Cimi surface personality is a person with a strong commitment to the community. Cimi people will sacrifice time for others, though they are often not sure just why it is that they do so. They have an extremely strong sense of tradition and are attracted to history and antiquities. They are ultimately down-to-earth people with deep concern for preservation of the family, community, and nation.

Societal: This trecena is one of the periods ruled by the moon itself. Its patron deity was Teccizcatl, the self-sacrificer who actually became the moon when the present age was created. It is a time when people display devotion and dedication to collective causes and populist leaders. It is a powerful time for the common people.

1-Cauac

Personal: Beneath the 1-Cauac surface personality lies a self that can become too dependent on others. Such people have a strong need to feel that they are part of a family. They also have an independent streak that causes them to need time alone, apart from the world. In this respect, they experience many internal contradictions.

Societal: In ancient times, the Cauac period was feared and was considered unfortunate. It was said to be a time when sorcerers were born and demons came to earth. Typically, crashes, bombings, and military or corporate takeovers make the news during this period. One of the more positive trends experienced during this time is a sense of openness to nature and to the mysteries of the universe.

1-Eb

Personal: Conflicting social needs influence the behavior of those born during the Eb trecena. One part of an Eb personality is the inclination to work to please others; the other Eb tendency is to feel resentment about the compromises that they are expected to make in those efforts. Eb types have an interest in the deep, dark recesses of the world and in the psyches of other people. They may do well in a career that allows them to legitimately explore such areas.

Societal: Healing rifts and settling differences between individuals and nations, and health/illness issues often arise during this period. It is a time for healing and understanding. The general tendency during the period is for nurturing and healing events to occur. Women or women's issues are also prominent in this trecena.

1-Chicchan

Personal: Beneath the 1-Chicchan surface personality is a person who struggles with powerful inner conflicts. This internal wrestling often leads the person to take committed positions on issues. When Chicchan people get going, they play hardball. Others may find them a bit fanatical at times, or at least somewhat extreme. Chicchans know intuitively what they have to do in life, even though they may not be able to express those inclinations logically.

Societal: The Chicchan trecena favors merchants and warriors. It is a good time for traveling, for launching an expedition, or for going boldly where none have gone before. In ancient Mexico, soldiers marched to distant battles during these periods. Chicchan's influence today inspires confrontations and daring discoveries. Revelations of secrecy also make the news during these times.

1-Etz'nab

Personal: Beneath the 1-Etz'nab surface personality is a person who seeks powerful and transformative experiences. Such people are willing to go the distance in order to stimulate changes in themselves and others. They tend to be restless, and possibly a bit unstable, but they are persistent and quite devoted to their life callings. At times, they will take risks that may even be life-threatening, or are attracted to others who do so.

Societal: Demonstrations of competency occur during this period. It was once considered to be a time when skillful leaders emerged, or were born, and this attribute still holds true today. Etz'nab is a good time for making tough choices and decisions, which is often reflected in the activities of leaders.

1-Chuen

Personal: Beneath the 1-Chuen surface personality is a strong need to be in the limelight, or at least to gain the attention of the public. People born in this trecena are instinctively attracted to activities like teaching, performance, and presentations of all kinds. They love to play and usually have several hobbies in which they engage when they are not working.

Societal: This is a favorable time for artists, musicians, dancers, and other creative types. Likewise, it is a time that favors creative activities. It is also a time of posturing and drama in politics. Traditionally, a second theme of this period has to do with the diagnosis and healing of disease.

1-Kan

Personal: Beneath the 1-Kan surface personality are found strong needs for recognition. The reactive self is creatively alive and seeks outlets for this energy, sometimes in the sexual arena. Kan people are often leaders at an early age. Others admire them for their confidence and willingness to take a stand.

Societal: According to ancient Mexican sources, this period was one of the more positive ones. It favors youth and also great performances.

People born at this time are said to be lucky and are able to prosper without employing much effort. There is a premature side to the Kan influence, however, in that in spite of all the show, strong actions taken during this time tend to fail.

1-Caban

Personal: Beneath the 1-Caban surface personality is a dreamer. Caban people have a fertile imagination and often find ways to make fantasy pay off for themselves. They may excel at one of the arts, or at least have a great appreciation for the arts. The Cabans' greatest asset is the ability to find ways to practically apply their ideas, bridging the gap from fantasy to fact.

Societal: This period was deemed to be a serious one, and said to be favorable only for those who did their penances. Today Caban is a time when political conditions become destabilized. It is a time when changes and reforms are in the works, when boundaries shift and change.

1-Oc

Personal: Beneath the 1-Oc surface personality are people who are very consistent in belief and loyalty. They will continue with a single program or activity for years. Although they can be an inspiration to others, they can also be extremely stubborn. Once they are committed to their own lifestyles, no matter how unconventional, they are dedicated for life.

Societal: In ancient times, this period was considered quite fortunate. It was seen as a time when successful people were born. This attribute still is the case today, making Oc a good time for celebrations and cooperation.

1-Akbal

Personal: Beneath the 1-Akbal surface personality is a deep need for very secure foundations. These security needs may be intellectual, as in science or religion, or they may be material, as in possession of valuables. Whether or not such persons seek mental or economic security, they are usually people with high standards to meet and uphold.

Societal: The Akbal period was said to be a time of trouble and vice. Secret financial dealings, spy cases, group paranoia, and other similar things have been known to come to light during this time. It's probably a good time to come clean with the truth and not to hide anything.

1-Cib

Personal: Beneath the 1-Cib surface personality is a person of strong will, not easily convinced by others. Such people have high standards and tend to hold themselves "above-it-all" and beyond criticism. They have a deep fear of rejection and are often troubled by guilt. Both of these proclivities have a strong effect on the Cib person's sense of self-worth. Although most Cib people are quite talented or at least knowledgeable—and as a result have much to offer to the world—in some cases, they feel overshadowed in life by others.

Societal: This is a time of tough decisions and of being tested, which is easy for those who are realistic and self-controlled, but can be painful or challenging for the sensitive or weak. Cib is a time of hard-ball politics. During this period, people realize what is real and what is not. Some people get depressed; others get to work.

1-Muluc

Personal: Beneath the 1-Muluc surface personality is a strong will propelled by powerful, irrational urges. These people do things in life without a rational explanation, just because they feel they have to do them. They find it necessary to keep themselves under control much of the time, or they may risk offending others who don't understand them. They would be well advised to choose their friends very carefully for this reason.

Societal: It seems that in ancient times, the Muluc period was considered difficult, if not just plain unfortunate. It appears today, however, that Muluc is a time when people must deal both with the messy aspects of life and also with their own negative emotions. Those who are most unstable emotionally will be affected the most. There is a need for group healing, for acceptance of change by the group during Muluc.

1-Ik

Personal: Beneath the 1-Ik surface personality is a strong need to communicate. For some, this urge or interest may lead to a life of teaching or performing. Those born during this period are carriers of ideas; they are people with a message to get across. They will always be instinctively drawn towards activities that will meet such needs.

Societal: Ik is a fickle and restless period during which spiritual, strange, and even unstable people make the news or influence events. It is a time when external control is weak, experiments are undertaken, and barriers are destroyed.

1-Men

Personal: Beneath the 1-Men surface personality is a person with powerful faculties of discrimination. Men people know the differences between things, know how to express such distinctions, and are often outstanding at articulating their emotions and expressing their feelings through creative or artistic projects. They are also somewhat psychic and find that their unconscious is their best friend, once they know how to listen to it.

Societal: Men is a time that favors self-interest. Rash decisions and actions, usually proven later to be problematic, are often in the news. Men types think a lot and talk about details, but few are able to see the big picture.

1-Lamat

Personal: Beneath the 1-Lamat surface personality is a competitor and fighter. This aspect of character may not always be apparent to others until they get to know the Lamat-born person well. Lamats secretly love a confrontation and will take risks in life in order to create conflict. These people prefer a life of competitive challenges rather than one of routine, and they should try to meet those needs in non-destructive ways. such as through running a business.

Societal: Lamat is a positive, productive period, a time when the public is moved or very enthusiastic about something. Popular heroes make the news at this time.

THREE

THE LORDS OF
THE NIGHT

A constantly repeating cycle of nine deities was recorded on many Mayan inscriptions and in nearly all the astrological codices. They are commonly called the Lords of the Night, or in Mayan, *Bolon ti ku,* which translates as "nine of them." These ruling divinities were gods of the underworld, gods that humanity had to contend with in order to find everlasting life. Some researchers believe, however, that the nine-day sequence refers only to nighttime, when the gods of the underworld were dominant. On inscriptions, these deities are often listed next to the tzolkin dates, and they are also found on inscriptions that list the phases of the moon. It has been suggested that the Lords of the Night were connected with the lunar month, which is close to three cycles of nine.

Compared to the twenty day-signs or the trecenas, not much is known about the Lords of the Night. It is not even known whether these nine deities ruled only partial hours of the days or nights, or perhaps full days or nights. The Mayan scholar Eduard Seler thought they ruled a series of nocturnal hours in which the length of the night was divided into ninths, and in which each of those segments was ruled by one of the special deities. Other researchers have postulated that the deities designated a sequence of nine days and nights in the same way that the seven planets give their names to the Western week, which is the approach taken here.

The authors suspect that, like the tzolkin, the nine Lords of the Night were a basic component of Mesoamerican astrology and that the known Aztec deities are a key to understanding the role of the Mayan lords. The Aztec lords appear to be in a sequence that is parallel to that of the Maya, even though we don't know all the Mayan names. Mayan Lord of the Night 4 is thought to have been an agricultural deity—and, interestingly, the Aztec list has Cinteotl, the corn goddess, at the fourth position. Scholars do know that the Maya had these lords tagged to the Long Count and that on August 11, 3114 BC, the first day of the Long Count, the ninth lord was ruler. By starting from this date, the nine-day cycle can simply be run parallel to the day-signs to determine the Lord of the Night for any given day in the Western calendar. The Night Lord designations in table 1 at the end of this book were determined in this manner.

The Lords of the Night are equivalent to the Lords of Death of the *Popol Vuh,* one of the most important Mayan texts to have survived the destruction perpetuated by Christian friars. This account of Mayan creation mythology was found in Guatemala long after the Spanish Conquest, and it has been an exceptional window into the thoughts and beliefs of the Pre-Conquest Maya. It is a tale of hero twins who some believe represent the sun and moon, others the sun and Venus. These twins were ball players, athletes of a game that was played by every major Mesoamerican culture. In the game, a large rubber ball was passed between players, who used their hips to direct the ball. Ball game stadiums are found throughout the lands of the Maya; the one at Chichen Itza is as big as a football field.

The *Popul Vuh* tells the story of how the twins avenged their father's death, which took place at the hands of the underworld-dwelling Lords of Death. As the story goes, the twins ventured underground and, after enduring a number of ordeals, beat the Lords of Death at their own sacred ball game. In the process, the twins became immortal.

The Lords of the Night rule the underworld, which might itself be equated with the world of the unconscious. These gods are the ones who must be defeated in order for humanity to rise above the primitive animal/human condition and attain immortality. It might be said that the message of the *Popul Vuh* is that mastery of the primordial impulses of the reptilian brain are the key to transformation, immortality, and peace in the world as we know it.

Exactly what each of the Lords of the Night actually means in terms of individual personality or destiny is yet another matter. In the opinion of the authors, the Lord that rules over a particular day has an effect on at least some aspects of personality for those born on that day. And whenever the Lord of the Night and the day-sign are similar in nature (as they are, for example, in Ix and Lord 8), the reinforcement of personality traits is quite pronounced. It is possible that the specific Lord for a particular day may predict something about a person's darker side and inner tendencies, or perhaps say something about a person's unconscious life in general.

Both the Mixtec Fejervary-Mayer Codex and the Mayan Madrid Codex contain cosmograms that locate the nine Lords of the Night directionally, at least in terms of East and West. These two positions are occupied by G-2/G-3 and G-6/G-7, respectively. While G-4/G-5 and G-8/G-9 appear to be in the North and South sides of the diagram, they may actually be representing above and below. Finally, G-1 is in the center. Other possible schemes for the directions are to have G-1 begin the series, ruling the East, G-2 the North, G-3 the West and G-4 the South. This process would continue for another cycle and then G-9 would rule the East. We have chosen to use the Fejervary-Mayer scheme based on our observations that those born under G-9 are often exceptionally powerful people who do not necessarily initiate, which would be typical of the direction East, but who tend to exert control over others in their social worlds.

In the Mayan codices and inscriptions, the glyph for G-9 appears far more frequently than those of the others. The reason for this is that G-9 occurs on all tun endings, a tun being a 360-day period that is evenly divided by the number 9. The 260-day count is not evenly divided by 9; in fact, a full nine cycles of the tzolkin must run before the same Lord of the Night comes up on the last day. One interesting permutation involving the tzolkin and the nine Lords has been recognized in the Dresden Codex. Nine cycles of the 260-day count is equal to 2,340 days. Dividing this figure by 20 equals 117 days (very close to the synodic cycle of Mercury). Dividing 117 days by nine equals 13 days. Dividing 2,340 days by 13 equals 180 days, which itself divided by 9 equals twenty. If nothing else, these mathematical correlations show how complex the inner workings of Mayan astro-numerology can be, and also how central the role of nine is in at least this portion of the scheme.

The pattern of cycling nine times can be seen on a larger scale. The calendar round of fifty-two years or seventy-three tzolkin, known as the Mesoamerican century, amounts to 18,980 days. This figure is not divisible by 9. It requires nine full standard calendar rounds before the same Lord of the Night is located on the ending date. This cycle of nine fifty-two-year rounds, or 468 years, is the basis of the nine "hells" that supposedly began in 1519, the year Cortes arrived in Mexico, which many Mexicans count as the beginning of their downfall. The period ended in 1987 at the time of the Harmonic Convergence—a spiritual event based largely on the Mayan Calendar that took place around the world, celebrating the dawn of a supposedly new era. The authors have concluded that the cycle of nine Lords of the Night is a symbolic cycle of some sort with possibly some astrological value, but we are far from knowing exactly how it was applied.

Most of the Mayan names of the Lords are lost; today, Mayan scholars list the Lords by number, i.e., G-1, G-2, etc. The nine Mayan Lords have been identified in codices and inscriptions, and possible meanings have been proposed but none can be confirmed. However, a complete Aztec list exists of nine deities that are also considered to be nocturnal, and much more is known about this list than about the Mayan deities of the night. The Toltec and Aztec Lords of the Night do have names and known mythologies which are believed to be parallel to their Mayan counterparts, as shown in the table below.

MAYAN LORD	DOMAIN	AZTEC LORD	MYTHOLOGY	DIRECTION
G-1	water	Xiuhtecutli	fire god	Center
G-2	rain	Itzli	sacrificial knife	East
G-3	rain	Pilzintechutli	sun god	East
G-4	corn	Cinteotl	corn god	North
G-5	earth	Miclantecutli	death god	North
G-6	youth	Chalchiuhtlicue	jade water goddess	West
G-7	jaguar	Tlazolteotl	confession goddess	West
G-8	conch	Tepeyollotl	jaguar god	South
G-9	night	Tlaloc	rain god	South

The following delineations of personal characteristics attributable to those born under each Lord of the Night are based on anecdotal evidence and comparisons with Western-style horoscopes. The authors based these calculations on a continuous cycling of the nine Lords, with G-9 linked to major period endings in the context of the Long Count. Further observation needs to be done, however, to corroborate these insights.

G-1

This powerful lord rules the Center. Persons born under it tend to be direct, assertive, and even combative toward others. As a result of this intensity, they tend to experience strong, forceful events in their lives. They are often driven by very basic or primal needs. Leadership is one of their greatest challenges; they must learn to utilize leadership skills. G-1 people can quickly move to the center of things, but once there, they are not sure that others will follow them. If they don't learn to be more sensitive to how others perceive them and develop an understanding of social norms, they will lose followers. G-1 types want to be where the action is, and their contribution of energy and enthusiasm is usually vital to the groups in which they participate. Father-related issues often play into a G-1's leadership dysfunction. Having a distant or abusive father sometimes results in inadequate training for leadership. Sometimes even a good paternal relationship can cause stress for a G-1, who then tries to reach real or perceived high standards. In either case, an understanding of the father is probably very important to a G-1's self-understanding. The dark side displayed by these people has to do with uncontrollable urges to put oneself first. G-1's general personality traits are similar to those of Mars in Western astrology.

G-2 (East)

These types are dedicated to their work regardless of whether they are employees, run their own businesses, do volunteer work, or merely do work around their own homes. G-2's sense of responsibility is quite high. Others may perceive them as obsessive and compulsive and inclined to do more than needs to be done. G-2 people are hard workers, stubborn and often quite thorough about attending to details. Personal sacrifice comes naturally to them and one of their most basic reactions in any situation is to stand aside for others who assert themselves. G-2s are ambivalent about being the boss, and they maneuver themselves into jobs or situations where they can take orders from above. Most people see them as polite, accommodating, considerate, and respectful. An important life lesson for G-2 types lies in making their personal sacrifices meaningful. Another lesson comes from learning to focus their tremendous capacity for giving. Their dark side lies in excessive self-denial. Many of those born under this influence have strong Neptune placements in their Western birth charts. Neptune is a planet that represents loss of self and a willingness to make a personal sacrifice.

G-3 (East)

Many born under this Lord seem to have a strong need for respect from others. They are serious people who are occasionally insecure, but they often occupy a prominent position in life, or at least feel that they should be publicly recognized for their actions. Some people born under G-3 project this need onto others; they may associate with or be married to a person who is powerful in the outside world. They have high expectations for themselves and often for others, and they work hard to achieve their goals. In doing so they may neglect relationships, or may simply make pragmatic choices in this area in order to accomplish their tasks. This dedication can lead to a lopsided emotional life and can occasionally raise questions in the minds of others about a G-3 person's basic motivations. G-3 types seek the limelight and recognition for their accomplishments, but they may work under the shadow of another person, such as a father or another authority figure. They see value in apprenticing and learning from their elders. One of their tasks in life is to learn how to be an authority in their own right. This need is something that G-3s meet through earning it, rather than by acquiring it through association. Their strength lies in their persistence and dedication to greater learning and improvement. Their dark side lies in their internalized, critical parent, the voice that judges. Sun/Saturn combinations are the Western astrological correlation for this lord.

G-4 (North)

Some people born under the influence of this Lord are teachers, some are healers, and some are over-protective parents. Most seem to have a nervous disposition and a need to talk. They are intense guardians of one thing or another: other people, children, pets. Youth is often a fixation for them; they are drawn to children and perhaps even work with them in some capacity. Their nurturing instincts are quite strong, and they need to find healthy outlets to express this urge. Their darker side lies in understanding that their nurturing influence can become a detriment in many ways. The communication skills of G-4 types make them excellent teachers. They can be very creative with their thinking, a quality that lends itself to art and writing. On the darker side, they think or talk incessantly and often struggle with ways to turn off their minds. By working as a teacher or communicator, they may be able to turn this tendency into positive activity. G-4 types have a tendency to scatter their energies and this inclination may lead to being a "jack of all trades but master of none." Mercury is usually strong in the charts of those who are born under this lord, as is an emphasized twelfth house.

G-5 (North)

This Lord is positioned at the midpoint of the series of nine. A person under the influence of G-5 seeks to be at the center of a group and will sometimes use others to get there. One of G-5's greatest challenges is to act from their true centers and not to use or be used by others. People born under the influence of this lord become deeply involved in relation-ships but, for the most part, also struggle with them. They are sensitive people and they tend to be touchy about a number of things, including their own expectations. Because they seek perfection, they are sensitive to disappointments, and often need to develop more realistic expectations and avoid putting the burden of relationship failures on others. Idealis-tic and compromising by nature, G-5 types are rarely content with the choices they have made. Their dark side includes a tendency to hold dis-torted opinions or to have over-inflated expectations of others. At their worst, they can be blamers, blind to the reality that they are the cause of their own problems. Recognizing this pattern can be a tremendous step forward in a G-5's spiritual progress. These types need to be with oth-ers who are stable and helpful, and avoid those who could worsen their fears. They also need to be accepting of others. It is in their own beliefs about relationships that both their problems and their solutions lie. A prominent moon, an emphasized seventh house, and Scorpio/Pluto are found in the charts of those born here.

G-6 (West)

Persons born under this Lord seem to be self-controlled, practical, traditional, and markedly entrepreneurial. They often create a self-sufficient kind of lifestyle or career and may be self-employed. They have a strong desire to build things and are very hard workers. Their work is rarely of a solitary nature; more often than not, they deal directly with the public, perhaps as a consultant or counselor. They take responsibility for themselves and are very self-reliant, but this makes other people less important for them in the process of achieving happiness. They are strongly motivated by fame and worldly success, and they hold themselves to high standards of performance. They are driven to success in the world because they strive to be accepted by others. Their drive for independence and approval is part of a quest for self-worth. This inner insecurity is their dark side, and they need to ask why they drive themselves so hard. They are sensitive to the rhythms and nuances of life and may develop a special interest in and respect for the feminine side of life. Overall, however, their intentions are good and others recognize this fact. Mars and Saturn are often prominent in their charts, along with the sign Leo.

G-7 (West)

Persons born under this lord are strongly motivated by relationships; they like to partner, and they enjoy working with the public. Many born on this day are excellent consultants, teachers, or healers. They like the finer things of life, or at least have more than a casual appreciation for quality, and they deeply enjoy music or art. G-7 types want to be in control of their outer world because their inner world is not so controllable. Their level of sexual desire is very strong, and they often feel a need to repress such urges so as not to disturb their social life. Some bury themselves in work in an attempt to deny these deeper urges. This repressive approach doesn't always work, and impulsive behaviors may result in social disturbances that can wound them deeply. Even thoughts may make a G-7 feel guilty. Sometimes these types will apply a kind of self-inflicted punishment in order to make amends. At their best, they will find ways to creatively explore their deeper urges through art or through various healing modalities. This process may lead them to become a healer of others. The common astrological signatures found in charts of those born on this day are a strong Venus/Libra emphasis and also the sign Virgo.

G-8 (South)

Those born here tend to have over-stimulated minds and are often obsessive talkers, in some cases being counselors or psychologists. They are complex people who learn to face the inner world and who know how to get to the center of things. They are drawn to the deeper, darker sides of life, and are sometimes caught up in struggles with negative thoughts—their own or those of others. This tendency means a G-8 might choose a career as a psychotherapist or an investigator. This type reacts to stimuli very quickly, perhaps over-reacting some of the time. G-8 people are very clever, quick of mind, and fast on their feet. This facility may be a boon in situations where decisiveness is valued, but it can cause trouble under more controlled conditions. Their need to talk is strong, and their powerful intellect is best used for research or investigation. One of their challenges is that they need to learn how to study effectively. In addition, they need to be physically active by walking, running, or riding. The planet Mercury, the sign Gemini, and an emphasized ninth house are commonly found in the charts of those born here.

G-9 (South)

People born under this Lord are usually strong, independent characters, stubborn and sometimes a little antagonistic. They are so self-sufficient that others often interpret this response as a rejection. Their independent nature makes it difficult for them to sustain relationships. They are hard workers who prefer to do things by themselves, and they don't want much help. In part, it's their lack of patience that motivates them to do things by themselves. Others sometimes see this as forceful or rejecting behavior. This particular trait is their darker side, and to balance it they need to cultivate compassion for those who are different. Those born under G-9 value privacy and desire time alone. They are known to accumulate things, usually collections or things of value. They enjoy things from the past or things originating from the sea. Spending time in nature is a healing experience for them and, as a result, they need to make the effort to get into the natural world from time to time. Those born on this day tend to have an emphasis of water signs in their charts as well as a prominent Mars influence.

FOUR

THE YEARS AND
THE YEARBEARERS

In ancient Mesoamerica, each solar year was given a name and was thought to have its own distinct qualities that would influence anyone born in that year. Most Mayan calendars named each year for the day-sign on which it began. If 13-Ben fell on "New Year's Day" in the Mayan calendar, then that year was named 13-Ben. In one 365-day solar year, the twenty day-signs cycle eighteen times, with five days left over. This rotation means that every year is named for a sign five places ahead of the previous year's sign in the twenty-day count, and only four signs are utilized in the rotation. After four years, the first of the four signs again falls on the day that begins the new year (4 x 5 = 20). These four signs are called the yearbearers, the signs that bear the weight, or carry the year. Because they are spaced five signs apart, each one of the four is ruled by a different direction. These annual directions cycle every four years: from East, to North, to West, and then to South.

Interpreting the yearbearers is challenging because a lack of consensus has existed (even in pre-Conquest times) about which set of four yearbearers actually ruled the years. Many calendars with different sets of yearbearers were used by the Classic and Postclassic Maya. Today's Quiche Maya, however, use the set used by the Classic Maya—Caban (East), Ik (North), Manik (West), and Eb (South). Further, because the year was a quarter-day longer than 365 days, the first day of the new year gradually moved ahead in the seasons. One custom in ancient

Mesoamerica was to establish the year's beginning around a solstice or equinox and then to make a full twenty-day adjustment, like a leap year, every eighty-three years. Following this formula meant that the beginning of the year would stay near the equinox or solstice, but would only fall precisely on it approximately every eighty-three years.

Four cycles of thirteen solar years make up a fifty-two-year calendar round, which is sometimes referred to as the Mesoamerican century. According to the Quiche tradition, the year's name is followed by the number from one to thirteen that corresponds to its place in that sequence.

It appears that the Maya delineated a four-year cycle, each fourth of which had a specific meaning known to us only in the form of weather and agricultural conditions that were predicted. But as to what other meanings were assigned to the years, and the larger significance of the four-year cycle, we can only speculate. One possibility is that the synodic cycle of Venus played a role in this four-year cycle since every four years, Earth, Venus, and the sun align in similar ways on the same day of the year. Other four- and eight-year cycles have also been found in nature by cycle researchers that include precipitation, fish abundance, and sugar prices. How these are related is not exactly clear, but they do follow an 8-year cycle of highs and lows.

A four-year cycle could have been intended to mirror the seasons. From a symbolic point of view, significant connections are evident between the cycle of the day and the seasonal cycle of the year. At dawn, the sun rises in the East and brings with it the emergence of light and the start of the day. When the sun crosses vernal equinox, it rises due East and marks the initiation of the spring season, a time of new life and the point at which the days become longer than the nights. At noon, the sun is at its highest and brightest point in the sky during the day. When the sun is at the summer solstice—the longest day of the year in the northern hemisphere—it rises and sets at its northernmost point in the yearly cycle, where it spends more time above the horizon than below it. Sunset marks the end of the day and the beginning of the night. At the autumnal equinox, the sun sets due West and marks the point at which the nights become longer than the days. At midnight, the sun is at the lowest point beneath the horizon and no light reaches the part of Earth experiencing night. At the winter solstice, the shortest day of the year in the northern hemisphere, the sun rises and sets at its southernmost position, where it spends the least amount of time above the horizon in the yearly cycle.

It is interesting to note that the Olympics and United States presidential elections have come to be held every four years—in the year that is ruled by the east, according to the Quiche Maya and Classic Maya. Further, the Chinese cycle of twelve years correlates with this pattern if the twelve signs of the zodiac are superimposed on that cycle. The year ruled by Rat is thought by some to correlate with Aries. If this is so, then three of the four-year cycles within the twelve-year Chinese cycle begin with a fire sign that correlates with the Quiche Caban or Earthquake, a sign of the East. Considering these synchronicities, the authors have based their interpretation of the years on the system used by the Quiche Maya and Classic Maya.

Delineations of the Years

As with many components of Mayan astrology, the application and astrological value of this four-year cycle cannot be ascertained. The first question to be considered is when the year begins. The Quiche Maya year started in March, early in the month. The Postclassic Maya year started in July, but this marker was a moving starting point based on the fact that the Mayan calendar lost one day every four years. As described in the table calculation notes on page 319 the authors have chosen to utilize the Classic "Tikal" calendar (as described by Munro Edmonson in *The Book of the Year*) as the basis for assigning the yearbearers in this book's astrological scheme. This calendar is the system found in the *Dresden Codex,* and it served as the primary civil calendar of the Eastern Maya from the first century on.

An interpretation of the years should begin by considering traditional lore. Below is a list of Quiche Maya and Aztec notions about the years and their directional rulers.

DIRECTION	QUICHE	AZTEC
East	creative/mental	fertile/abundant
North	violent weather	barren/dry/cold
West	wild/losses/illness	cloudy/evil
South	good business/health	variable

Clearly, general agreement exists between these two systems. Years ruled by the East and South are regarded as more positive than those ruled by the North and West. This belief is in keeping with the general, even worldwide, notions about the directions themselves, where East is spring, North is winter, West is autumn, and South is summer. In the northern hemisphere, spring and summer are seasons to look forward to, especially for people who live close to the land, and fall and winter bring darkness and hardship. The following delineations of the meanings of the years are speculations and they reflect both traditional ideas and the authors' general observations. As these periods are quite long, descriptions should be interpreted as applying in only very general ways. Each year is like a mini-generation with a distinct overall character—something like the general group personality observed by teachers in each wave of students passing through a school system.

Not everyone exhibits the qualities of the year under which they were born; such characteristics are more prevalent in the collective identity. Certain individuals who embody the qualities of a specific year, however, may operate in that year with high visibility in the world and serve as focal points of the symbolism.

Years Ruled by the East

The East is the direction that symbolizes the energy behind the "coming into existence" of something. For those born during a year ruled by the East, life itself is an opportunity to demonstrate self-worth and to celebrate individual existence. These years are ones of firsts and new beginnings. Most people born in these years, and especially those who rise to prominence, are self-starters and activists. They tend to be competitive and self-involved. They work hard at being progressive, often standing at the forefront of any movement they are a part of. In world events, these years include bold initiatives. They are times when the world moves forward into uncharted territory or gathers to celebrate the power of creativity.

Years Ruled by the North

The North is where living things must invent ingenious survival tactics in order to make life worth living. A difficult environment stimulates intelligent adaptation. Correspondingly, those born during a North year are, in a general sense, adept at finding ways to preserve themselves. They don't seek to dominate their physical or social environment; they find ways to adjust to it, modify it, and work with it. North years are years of problems, challenges, and difficulties, and Northern types are fit to survive. Most people born in these years tend to be more mentally focused and rational, and are often distracted from the emotional realities around them. They are precise and exacting, and are good problem solvers. In world events, the North year is one of crisis. It is a time when people meet and handle obstacles, a time when problems that challenge forward momentum occur.

Years Ruled by the West

The West is a direction that is symbolic of both transition and merging, a point of balance between two worlds. In a general sense, those born during these years stride along boundaries, one foot in the past and one in the future. One foot is planted in their own individual concerns, the other in the concerns of the social world around them. The energy of West years is one of balance. West years are a time of cooperation and interaction. Connecting with others is a challenge for those born during these years. Skillfulness in dealing with people, diplomacy, and counseling abilities are the strong points of people born in years ruled by the West; indecisiveness is their weak point. In world events, a West-dominated year is characterized by meetings, alliances, and agreements. For those born in these years, success comes through coalition building and understanding.

Years Ruled by the South

The South is a region characterized by the triumph of life over nature. The South is where the uncontrolled growth of the jungle overcomes even the mountains. Accordingly, the southern direction symbolizes the power and energies of non-rational feelings and emotions. Those born during a year of the South are strongly motivated by feelings and emotions, at least in a general sense. These years are ones of closure and completion. The feelings and emotions of those born during these years have more influence over personal choices than do the feelings of those born during North years. This wave of people, especially those with higher public profiles, can appear emotionally complex to others, or they can be perceived as being over-reactive. In world events, these are years when the emotions of leaders (and the irrational need to be important) lead us into complex situations that are not easily resolved.

FIVE

THE PLANET VENUS

Next to the sun, Venus was the most important astronomical body to the Mayan and other Mesoamerican cultures. The planet was feared, but its cycle was valued as a guide to the optimum timing of actions and as a calendar marker.

This cycle was embedded in several astrological and calendrical time periods that are found inscribed on Mayan monuments. The Venus cycle was divided into four main periods delineated in the ancient codices. The authors believe that knowledge of the influence of these four periods is vital in understanding how a person functions in society.

The Maya timed important political events by the cycle of Venus, including changes of leadership. They even used it to calculate the best time for battles and sacrifices. Even though our society perceives warfare and sacrifice to be bloody and uncivilized activities, during ancient times those actions were actually a ritualized part of civilized life. Consider the possibility that ritualized warfare was perceived by the Maya as a calculated way to vent hostile emotions—necessary actions for the preservation of their culture. In this sense, Venus is the civilizer that regulates the animalistic and destructive urges in humanity. Mesoamerican astrologers might say that, in order to perpetuate civilized social life, humanity needs to ventilate according to this planet's schedule.

The meaning of the planet Venus in Mesoamerican astrology differs, at least on the surface, from its meaning in Western and in Vedic astrology. First, Venus in this tradition is male. Most students and practitioners of astrology have learned to see Venus as a feminine symbol, the archetype of the Goddess as feminine lover. However, in ancient

Mexico, Venus was associated in symbol and myth with the man-god Quetzalcoatl (Nahua or Aztec) or Kukulcan (Maya). The historic myth of Quetzalcoatl, a legend that entered Yucatan during the Postclassic period, is a story about social ideals, impeccability, fornication, and the fall from grace. The myth speaks of the quest for a higher and purer level of living, and also of human frailty and the sins of the flesh. Some writers who have studied Mesoamerican civilization have linked the Quetzalcoatl myth with the notion of civilization itself, addressing both society's creation as well as its destruction. Others have focused primarily on the historic Toltec ruler or rulers who wore the title of Quetzalcoatl. Like the myths of the planetary gods of the ancient Near Eastern and Mediterranean civilizations, the Mexican Quetzalcoatl stories vary somewhat in content, but they do offer some deep insights into the symbolism surrounding Venus.

In brief, the myth goes as follows: Quetzalcoatl was conceived and born miraculously after his mother swallowed a piece of jade—a virgin birth. He eventually assumed kingship of a perfect empire. Over time, he became obsessed with his own ritualistic spiritual practices and lost contact with the real world beyond his city. Meanwhile, strange and socially destabilizing events—some of a sexual nature—began to occur in his kingdom, and the populace began to sense that something was wrong. One day, evil sorcerers infiltrated Quetzalcoatl's compound and held a mirror to his face. Quetzalcoatl's appearance had been transformed through severe spiritual practices to such a significant degree that he recoiled from the sight of himself and was easily persuaded by the sorcerers to let them beautify him. Later, these sorcerers enticed him to take five cups of the alcoholic beverage *pulque*. Quetzalcoatl downed the drinks and became intoxicated. Dancing followed, and he called for his sister to join him in the wildness of the moment. The next morning, he awoke to find that he had committed sexual sins with his sister. Having broken one of the most important moral laws, the taboo against incest, he renounced his throne, left the city, and slowly made his way to the East. Upon his arrival at the seacoast, he sailed into the rising sun on a raft—or, in some versions of the myth, built a funeral pyre and immolated himself. At his death in the fire, he became the planet Venus.

The events of the Quetzalcoatl myth were associated by the ancient Mayans with components of the astronomical cycle of Venus. Venus orbits the sun once every 225 days, and that period is called its sidereal cycle. Earthbound observers cannot see this cycle, but they can observe a 584-day cycle between successive appearances as either a morning or evening star. During this 584-day period—the synodic cycle—Venus actually makes two conjunctions with the sun. One of those is the inferior conjunction that occurs when Venus passes between Earth and the sun. This passage is the closest to Earth and it occurs while Venus is in retrograde, or moving backward relative to the zodiac. The inferior conjunction is short, lasting only a few days, because Venus is moving in retrograde while the sun is moving forward against the zodiac. Venus and the sun thus pass each other, moving in opposite directions, a movement that increases their angular separation at a rate of about two degrees per day. The superior conjunction occurs when Venus is farthest from Earth with the sun positioned between Venus and Earth. At the superior conjunction, Venus and the sun advance in the zodiac at nearly the same speed. At this conjunction, it takes weeks for Venus to pass the sun and gain some angular distance ahead of it.

In pre-Columbian times, Mesoamerican astrologers divided the synodic cycle of Venus into four primary parts: inferior conjunction, morning star, superior conjunction, and evening star. They began Venus's 584-day cycle with the brief inferior conjunction, specifically with the first appearance of Venus after this invisible event. Just a few days after the inferior conjunction, Venus makes its first appearance in the East as a morning star. At this first appearance, called the heliacal rising, Venus was regarded as a dangerous omen, and ritual precautions were taken to deflect its power to strike down those in high places. This phase correlated with the arrival of the god Quetzalcoatl on Earth. As a god on Earth, Quetzalcoatl committed the sins of drunkeness and incest with his sister. He sinned at some point during Venus's morning-star phase, perhaps when Venus was reaching its greatest elongation, or greatest distance from the sun. At the superior conjunction, Quetzalcoatl judged himself, or was judged by the gods. During Venus's evening-star phase, Quetzalcoatl stepped down and walked the earth as a mortal, obeying moral laws, until his sacrifice at the inferior conjunction, during which he became a god again.

Skeptics of astrology often compare the Mesoamerican astrological Venus with the Western astrological Mars, implying that astrology is completely internal to the culture that creates it. That assumption may be true on the surface, but as we will see, there is no disagreement over the fundamental astrological properties of Venus in both Meso-american and Western astrology. The ancient Mesoamerican scripting correlates well with the great Western astrologer Dane Rudhyar's observations on the distinctions between Venus as a morning or evening star in natal charts. Rudhyar said that as a morning star, Venus signified the "projection of individual vision and purpose upon life." Venus in its evening-star phase, according to Rudhyar, signifies the projection of a more collective vision and purpose. Combining these ideas, the authors maintain that Venus, as a morning star, may indicate a tendency to follow one's own instinctive urges, which can then lead to tensions with the dominant social paradigm within which the individual operates and functions. Social "sins" are committed during this phase. Venus as evening star may indicate a tendency to follow the guidelines of human social conduct that are embraced by society. Here, a humbled Venus follows the laws, just as Quetzalcoatl did after recognizing the error of his ways.

These distinctions seem to be quite valid when applied to well-known personalities. Individuals such as Hugh Hefner, Woody Allen, and Isadora Duncan were born when Venus was a morning star and near greatest elongation from the sun (about 43–47 degrees). They belong to a group of people who are, or were, clearly pushing against social norms in their actions and behaviors. In contrast, individuals born during the evening-star phase take no chances. Some examples of those born during Venus's greatest elongation in the evening star phase are Walt Disney, Mia Farrow, and Augustus Caesar. These people might be considered "pillars of society" in that they reinforced traditional values in their actions and deeds.

The inferior and superior conjunctions are quite distinct from each other in their effects on human behavior. The inferior conjunction marks the time when Quetzalcoatl was born on Earth, and was noted in the Mayan codices as having a "striking" effect. The people noted that Venus's appearance in this phase coincided with downfalls of leaders and other social upsets. In the *Dresden Codex*, Venus is portrayed as the Toltec male deity Tlahuitzcalpantecuhtli who strikes and spears his victims. Newsworthy events occurring at, or just after, the inferior conjunction are often characterized by impulsive human errors that lead to a leveling or crash of some sort. Some events that have occurred at this point in the 584-day cycle are the Watergate arrests that led to the downfall of

Richard Nixon, the downing of the Korean 007 airline by the Russians, the sacking of Russian leader Mikhail Gorbachev, and the election of 1994 when a large portion of Congress was ousted and replaced with inexperienced, agenda-driven Republicans. The most dramatic manifestation of the inferior conjunction (and the heliacal rising of Venus a few days later) in recent memory occurred in January of 1998. The myth of Quetzalcoat's downfall via sexual misconduct was echoed by President Clinton and a White House intern. Life was imitating myth.

The inferior conjunction is quite brief (in comparison with the entire Venus/sun synodic cycle) and therefore fewer people are born during this phase. The *Dresden Codex* labels this phase as North. Many more people are likely to be born during the period of the superior conjunction, which lasts for weeks. This point in the cycle is when Venus/Quetzalcoatl grapples with issues of morality and is judged by the gods. Well known personalities born during this phase are Charles Manson, Howard Stern, and Billy Graham, in whose lives issues of morality have been most prominent.

Astronomically, the approximate observable length of each phase is as follows: eight days for inferior conjunction, a period when Venus disappears from our view as it passes between the earth and the sun; 263 days as morning star, when Venus rises before the sun and is visible just before dawn; 50 days for superior conjunction, a longer period of invisibility when Venus passes on the far side of the sun; and 263 days as evening star, when Venus rises after the sun and is visible just after sunset. The conjunction periods are centered on the actual point when the astronomical event occurs, so the dates encompassing the inferior conjunction phase, for example, which comprise an eight day period, are the four days before and the four days after the exact moment that Venus passes is front of the sun.

The Maya, however, did not use the actual astronomical periods used in modern times. They used periods that were more in phase with the lunar cycle, presumably for ease of calculation relative to other aspects of their calendar. The authors have chosen to continue that tradition and to denote Venus's phases using these Mayan "canonical" periods: 8 days for the inferior conjunction, 236 days for the morning phase, 90 days for the superior conjunction, and 250 days for the evening phase. Table 3 on page 307 shows the Mayan phases of Venus as they correlate to specific birth dates. Delineations of the four Mayan phases are as follows.

Inferior Conjunction—North

Because this phase of Venus lasts just eight days, only one in seventy-three people will be born during it. Those born during this period have very strong feelings and intuitions and are often attracted to activities or occupations that can be considered risky. At times, they may be headstrong, upsetting others in the process and putting themselves into embarrassing situations. These people are naturally creative. They need to cultivate patience and restraint in order to realize their best ideas. They tend to be intense about sexuality, swinging from one extreme to another, from excess to abstinence. Their relationship needs are strong, but so is their need for freedom. In close relationships, they usually overpower their partner.

Morning Star—East

This phase, which spans 236 days, follows the inferior conjunction and precedes the superior conjunction phase. Persons born during it are like the inferior conjunction types in that they might be described as having youthful emotions and feelings. They are interested in the world and in other people and go out to meet them. They act first, evaluate later. Their warmth of feeling and willingness to join in with others makes them popular, unless others reject some of their more radical social initiatives. Ultimately, it is their feelings that move them to action and these feelings also allow them to make instant evaluations. Underneath it all, they are individuals who test society's limits. Their personal vision drives their sense of purpose and motivations in life. But, in their enthusiasm for life, they may occasionally make some serious mistakes. They need to remember to consider others' perspectives before acting on their instincts and putting their emotional energy into action. These creative people respond to a deep and very personal voice. In some cases, the rules of society may severely limit their initiatives, resulting in experiences of defeat and disillusionment. Positively, and with persistence, these people may eventually succeed in impressing something of themselves onto the world, changing it for the better. All of the above is especially true for those born at the greatest elongation, when Venus is farthest from the sun, about two months after the inferior conjunction.

Superior Conjunction—South

It appears that persons born in this ninety-day phase have something of a struggle in life. Getting what they want is a real challenge for them. In the area of relationships, major emotional problems arise, typically having to do with power and dominance. Those born in this phase struggle hard over what is right and what is wrong. Although they desire peace in the world as well as in their own relationships, this peace is not easy for them to come by. In order to move ahead in life, these people need to learn the lessons of defeat; experiencing a loss can lead to a spiritual breakthrough, not just to a loss of ego. They also have a dark side to their personality that they find difficult to suppress. Their desire for power is strong and this desire pushes them to climb to great heights in life. Sexuality and violence are two themes that can draw their attention, particularly in movies and literature. The darker side of human life is as important to those influenced by the South as is the lighter side. Such people need to face the darkness within themselves and befriend it, not stifle or alienate it.

Evening Star—West

Following the superior conjunction, Venus spends 250 days as an evening star. For people born during this period, feelings and emotions arise after an action has been taken. In making judgments, which they usually do very well, they evaluate what has happened against the background of society's rules and values. They instinctively understand the power, and perhaps the correctness, of the world as it is and has been. Their vision is one that has probably been strongly influenced by tradition. One positive manifestation of evening-star Venus is that those born in this phase may become successful, consciously or unconsciously, due to the fact that they personify certain family and traditional values. In extreme cases, they become heroes, because they represent what their society believes in. Through embracing tradition and cultural definitions of reality, these people achieve emotional satisfaction and success in life. The above is particularly true when Venus is at its greatest elongation, about two months before the inferior conjunction.

For the Astronomically Inclined

For those readers who have an interest in astronomy, the "Phenomena" column in table 3 (page 307) also lists the approximate dates (based on Greenwich time) of six Venus phenomena. Descriptions of these astronomical events are included below.

Inferior conjunction: Venus, Earth, and the sun are aligned, with Venus between the earth and sun at its closest point to the earth. Venus is in retrograde, that is, it appears to be moving backward against the zodiac. After this point, Venus moves to the west of the sun and becomes a morning star, meaning that it will rise and set before the sun. The time of the first visibility of Venus in the morning sky after inferior conjunction, when it rises just before the sun, is called its heliacal rising. Depending on the position of Venus in its orbit, this will occur from one to five days after inferior conjunction. This time was regarded by the Maya as a time of great danger, when the rays from the newly visible Venus would strike down certain individuals. The exact nature of its effect depended on the trecena in which the rising occurred and other astrological factors.

Stationary Direct: Venus reverses its retrograde motion and begins to move forward through the zodiac. About two weeks after this date, Venus reaches it maximum brilliancy as a morning star, becoming the third brightest object in the sky (after the sun and moon).

Maximum Western Elongation: Venus has reached its maximum distance west of the sun (45 to 47 degrees).

Superior Conjunction: Venus, Earth, and the sun are aligned, and Venus is on the opposite side of the sun from the earth. It is at its farthest possible distance from Earth. After this point, Venus moves to the east of the sun, and after a few weeks of invisibility, becomes an evening star (meaning that it rises and sets after the sun).

Maximum Eastern Elongation: Venus has reached its maximum distance east of the sun (45 to 47 degrees).

Stationary Retrograde: At this point, from the perspective of Earth, Venus appears to stop in its forward motion and begins a period when it seems to be moving backwards (retrograde) through the zodiac. About two weeks before this date, Venus reaches it maximum brilliance as an evening star.

SIX

PUTTING IT TOGETHER: INDIVIDUAL MAYAN CHARTS

In this chapter we present a simple geometric grid in the shape of a pyramid for charting the personal information derived from the five components of Mayan astrology that we have described in chapters 2 through 5. This chart serves to organize the day-sign, trecena, Night Lord, year, and phase of Venus in terms of their hierarchy in the reading and their patterns of directionality (east, west, etc.).

A blank Mayan pyramid chart is provided at the end of this chapter. Feel free to reproduce it and use it for your own work with Mayan astrology. Sample charts and readings in the next section of this chapter illustrate how the information gathered from the five components can be synthesized for an in-depth reading.

SETTING UP THE CHART

Our Mayan chart is a three-tiered pyramid viewed from above. Each of the four sides of the pyramid faces one of the four directions. In cosmograms found in the surviving codices, east is always at the top, north to the left, west at the bottom, and south on the right. Our chart conforms to this Mesoamerican custom. Each component of a person's personal data should be written into the chart in the space facing its associated direction. For example, a person born on a day for which the Night

Lord, trecena, and day-sign are all associated with the east would write the names and numbers of these in the top three spaces in the pyramid.

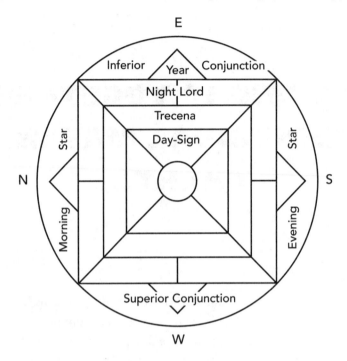

Mayan pyramid chart with key

To set up the chart for a reading, first turn to table 2 on page 306 to find the Mayan New Year's day that precedes the birth date, along with its corresponding direction. Record the number for the Mayan year in the outer level of the pyramid—its offset base—on the side that corresponds with its direction (at the top for east, right for south, etc.).

For a person born January 31, 2004, for example, table 2 shows that the Mayan year in which that date falls began on April 5, 2003. In the Year column for this day, the value is "5-South," meaning that this person was born in a year ruled by the South. (Note: see Table Calculation Notes on page 319 for a discussion of the method used to ascertain the Mayan calendar correlations for the tables in part 3.)

Next, find the individual's ruling Night Lord in table 1 to the far right of the date of birth, in the column labeled "L." Since the first Lord rules the center, anyone ruled by that Lord will need to place it on the central opening at the top of the pyramid. The other Lords may be noted in the corners of the lower pyramid level facing the appropriate directions. (Note: each side has two partitions. To locate your Night Lord in the right partition, count each partition beginning with the top right as G-2, G-3, etc., moving counter-clockwise.) For the aforementioned person born January 31, 2004, the Lord of the Night is G-2, which would be written in the top right section of the lowest level of the pyramid.

The second level of the pyramid concerns the trecena. The directional complement to each thirteen-day period determines where the trecena of birth is registered in the pyramid chart. To find the trecena, first find the birth date in table 1, then search backward through the preceding dates until you locate the tzolkin date in bold type that begins with the number 1. This number and name is the trecena, or birth "week." Its directional complement is found by locating the day the trecena is named for in the table of day-signs on page 124, preceding table 1. So, once again for our hypothetical person born on January 31, 2004, the trecena is 1-Manik. This would be noted on the bottom side of the second level, because it is a sign of the west.

The third and top level of the pyramid is for recording the person's day-sign, found immediately to the right of the date of birth in table 1. The directional quality of the day-sign, which can also be found in the table of day-signs mentioned above, determines its placement in the quartered summit of the pyramid. The day-sign for our 1/31/04 birthdate is 7-Ben, a sign of the east, so it would be noted in the top part of the upper level of the pyramid.

The phase of Venus can be noted using either the Mayan glyph of the cross and four dots (the symbol of the day-sign Lamat, which has connections to Venus—see page 25), or a simple five-pointed star. It is placed within the outer circle that surrounds the pyramid. Venus at inferior conjunction is placed in the North, morning star in the East, superior conjunction in the South, and evening star in the West. To find the phase in which Venus was located when a person was born, turn to table 3 and find the date that precedes the birth date.

Once again, using our January 31, 2004 birthdate, the Mayan phase of Venus preceding this date was "evening star," which began on September 27, 2003. This particular phase ran from September 27, 2003 to June 5, 2004, when Venus entered its inferior conjunction phase. Therefore, this person is considered to be born in the evening star phase.

A NOTE ABOUT BIRTH TIME

The issue of exactly when a tzolkin day begins has been the subject of much discussion among the authors and users of this system. The authors have found that someone born an hour or two before midnight (daylight savings time accounted for) generally has the characteristics of the day-sign for the next day. In some cases it seems that persons born as early as just after sunset are best described by the next day-sign, or a combination of two day-signs. So if you find that a day-sign description for someone born between sunset and midnight does not appear to fit that person, look up the information (in table 1) for the next day to get a description of the next day-sign and Night Lord.

READING THE MAYAN CHART

Now that you have recorded all the specific personal astrological data, you are ready to look at the corresponding descriptions to do an in-depth reading.

Begin the reading with a discussion of the day-sign, the element in the chart that is most conscious and most central to identity. This sign is the crown of the persona, the form through which the individual speaks to the world. It is the *tonal* of Carlos Casteneda, the form that the self takes so that it can be recognized and sustained. Descriptions of the individual day-sign qualities begin on page 14.

Next, discuss the trecena. The trecena is descriptive of instinctive behaviors that are reflected in the desires, interests, and responses of the individual. They may not be conscious factors in personality, themes that individuals know to be a part of themselves, but they may be perfectly obvious to others. This level may be that of the *nagual* of Carlos Casteneda, the unformed impulse that drives one forward. The trecena descriptions begin on page 38.

Now consider the influence of the Night Lords. It may be that those born during the night are more responsive to this set of symbols, but the authors assume that these symbols mean something to everyone. They represent a kind of inherited or genetic impulse, a drive that is deep and one that represents an extension of the parental ancestry. Night Lord descriptions begin on page 49.

Now think about what has been revealed by the day-sign, trecena, and Night Lord, and attempt to blend all three. Pay particular attention to any patterns of directionality. If all three influences face in one direction, that is a strong indicator of a personality that is focused in one specific way. In contrast, when the indicators are in opposing directions, it suggests internal tension as well as the need for a conscious balancing of self and persona.

Next, consider the direction of the year and what it indicates about the place of the person in a social frame of reference. Finally, integrate Venus into the reading as an indicator of socio-sexual qualities—needs, desires, and behaviors. The descriptions of the years begin on page 58, and the Venus phases on page 64. After completing an assessment of these five points, you may wish to calculate the burner dates (see chapter 7 beginning on page 88) and discuss how they may reflect the cycles of the personality.

SAMPLE READINGS FOR WELL-KNOWN PERSONALITIES

Reading the five key personal data points in the Mayan chart requires the use of a consistent methodology and much practice. The following sample readings can give you a sense of how to interpret all of the components as they apply to a specific person.

President George W. Bush (7/6/1946)

Day-Sign: 13-Chicchan
Trecena: 1-Ben
Year: 13-West
Night Lord: G-7
Venus Phase: Evening Star

President George W. Bush was born on the day-sign 13-Chicchan. His is a secretive day-sign, suggestive of someone who is able to control those around him with charisma and drive. This sign is not a moderate one; it is a powerful sign that leans toward extremes, and those born under it are inclined to demonstrate their power. President Bush's trecena is 1-Ben, a powerful period that causes those under its influence to need to be correct and respected. His instincts are those of a warrior who

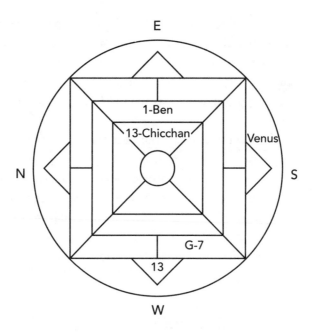

Mayan chart for George W. Bush

seeks to conquer the enemy and spread his own truth. The challenge for those influenced by 1-Ben is to not become absorbed in a single view of the truth, which can lead to self-righteousness and overconfidence. Still this sign of the East is dynamic and takes the initiative. The combination of both trecena and day-sign being of the East suggests a dominating persona that overcomes obstacles and doesn't look back. President Bush was born in a year ruled by the West, a direction suggestive of a strong need to belong and to participate in society. His basic nature, operating within society, is to relate to others and to receive acceptance, and so he has learned to be diplomatic and to negotiate agreements. His primary challenge is to learn to build coalitions with others who may not agree with him.

The deeper subconscious is shown by the Night Lord, which for Bush is G-7. His close relationship with his wife and with Condoleezza Rice indicates a strong partnership orientation. He also desires to work closely with the public, even when large segments of the population reject him. Bush is motivated by aesthetics, comforts, and material security. He has strong urges, which he strives to repress and conceal, and these can get him into trouble for which he has to repent. He is motivated by security, and has even created a cabinet position with this word in its title. For Bush, Venus is an evening star, another indication of the power of others in Bush's chart. Venus's position suggests that Bush instinctively conforms to established social norms; he does not rock the boat and he even imposes traditional views on others. It is inconceivable for him to imagine that alternative ways of living with others are viable; he only sees value in the old ways and feels that they must be preserved.

Altogether, George W. Bush's Mayan chart describes a powerful individual who is driven to a position of power, but who is also partnered closely with the people around him. If these others have good intentions, then Bush is able to bring decisive leadership to the world and a crusader-like zeal to whatever he chooses to do. He is conservative and very social, but he does not reveal much about himself. Those who know him best know that he has a very strong character, with strong opinions and an intense sense of right and wrong.

Princess Diana (7/1/1961)

Day-Sign: 1-Cauac
Trecena: 1-Cauac
Year: 2-North
Night Lord: G-9
Venus Phase: Morning Star

Princess Diana was born on the first day of the trecena Cauac, and therefore under the day-sign Cauac. Her trecena and day-sign being one and the same, her individual personality became merged with her subconscious and reactive personality. Her instincts and feelings were probably very strong and she dedicated herself to social causes that made her a powerful public personage, almost a goddess. As a day-sign, Cauac projects youthfulness and compassion. It confers a complex but multifaceted personality and inclines one toward the healing professions. Diana was concerned for the less fortunate, and in other circumstances might have become a nurse or doctor.

Diana was born in the year 2-North. In the larger sense, Diana was driven to solve problems. She was a doer, and she sought solutions to social problems, but she also made mistakes along the way. Her needs

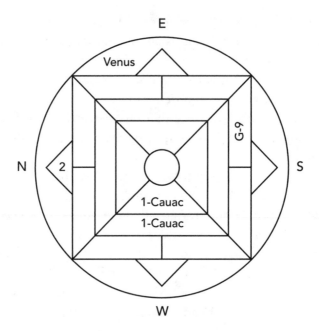

Mayan chart for Princess Diana

forced her to become more conscious of her interactions with others to the point of feeling awkward and not always accepted. The fact that she was born in a north year implies that, once she became strong enough, she would find a larger social destiny that involved the kind of problem solving associated with the north direction.

The ninth Lord of the Night was effective on Diana's birthday and this influence probably added to her already strong independent streak, possibly increasing the parts of her personality that could be said to be antagonistic. People born under this Night Lord are fighters and hard workers. They are often very direct with others and consequently not always successful in maintaining balanced relationships. Diana was inclined to go her own way, on her own terms, and this approach wasn't always approved of by others. Further, Venus was a morning star at her birth, a position that inclined Diana toward a social life full of risks. She could never accept the traditional rules of social interaction, and she found herself continually pushing the social envelope, right up until her death. Diana was a person who extended social boundaries through her unconventional behaviors, and she paid a price as she did so.

Christopher Reeve (9/25/1952)

Day-Sign: 11-Etz'nab
Trecena: 1-Lamat
Year: 6-East
Night Lord: G-3
Venus Phase: Evening Star

The day-sign 11-Etz'nab suggests that Christopher Reeve was a very practical person who was well-coordinated and skillful. It also suggests a life of personal sacrifice. Etz'nab is a social sign and it is also somewhat vain. Those born under this day-sign find that it is necessary to exercise a certain amount of personal restraint in most social situations, even to the point of repressing their instincts. Sooner or later, this internal pressure will release itself—productively through creative work, or negatively in the form of social difficulties or through a crisis or an accident. Reeve did have to work at his relationships, and he did learn the art of sharing and self-sacrifice. The trecena of his birth was 1-Lamat, a suggestion that his instincts drew him toward exciting and potentially risky situations. Lamat is an active sign that can't sit still, and Reeve was

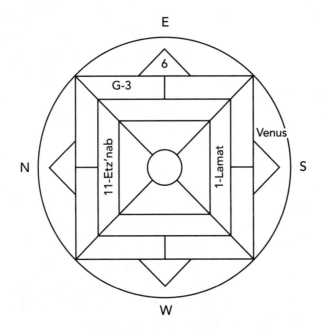

Mayan chart for Christopher Reeve

involved in several sports, as well as a career in acting, until his accident. Lamat is also known to be somewhat self-destructive, and it challenges the ability of a person born under its influence to be in control of his or her behaviors. Reeve's instincts were powerful and impulsive, and he required outlets for this drive. He did drive himself hard both before and after his accident. The year of Christopher Reeve's birth was a year of the East, an indicator of a deep personal drive, a general need to move forward in life, and the specific need to take risks along the way. The eastern direction suggests self-involvement and self-initiative. There is no question that Reeve had to make adjustments in his life, and he handled those adjustments creatively. Perhaps his "Superman" identity could be related to this fundamental component of his Mayan chart.

Born under the third Night Lord, Reeve was actually a deeply serious and dedicated person, with a strong sense of responsibility. This Lord inclines one to seek popular acceptance, and it is an appropriate indicator of a person who will become engaged in show business. It is a serious Night Lord, though, and those born under it generally take life very much as it is and try to make their sacrifices meaningful. His Evening Star birth made Reeve quite conventional in relationships. Once he realized that his relationship problems were of his own doing, he entered therapy and worked on changing himself in this regard. The result was a good marriage, but this outcome was the natural result of Reeve's acceptance of the status quo rules of social engagement. Venus as an evening star does not rock the boat; it steadies it. In his relationships, then, Reeve was no reformer.

Oprah Winfrey (1/29/1954)

Day-Sign: 8-Muluc
Trecena: 1-Ik
Year: 7-North
Night Lord: G-8
Venus Phase: Superior Conjunction

Born under the day-sign Muluc, Oprah is a natural performer and has captured the public in ways few have. She relates emotionally to her audience, whether in person or via television. Her emotional intensity is not diminished by broadcasting; she uses her medium effectively to get her messages

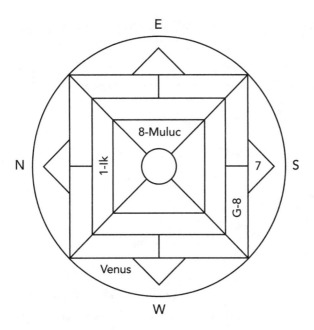

Mayan chart for Oprah Winfrey

across. She has brought topics to her audience that were previously not considered appropriate and is obviously not afraid of taking risks. This characteristic has been a key component of her success as a public figure. Her struggle with her weight is a sign that she experiences compulsive and addictive behaviors, but her will is strong, and she has transformed herself several times. There is no question that she is a dominant personality; her influence, especially on what books people read, is enormous. Her trecena, 1-Ik, suggests that she has a strong need to communicate and indeed she does, verbally and through her reading recommendations. Oprah is essentially a teacher/performer and she has many messages to convey to others on many topics. Like others born during a North year, Oprah relies on her quick mind and intellectual abilities to help her navigate her world. She brings information and ideas to her audience.

Oprah was born under the eighth Night Lord. She is a talker, in some ways more a counselor or group psychologist. She is a complex person not afraid to face her inner world, and she knows how to get to the center of things. She reacts very quickly to stimuli, and she is fast on her feet. Venus was at its superior conjunction at her birth, exact to within a day, indicating that Oprah is emotionally deep and very concerned with right and wrong. She is interested in human problems, including sexual problems, and she brings these topics into public awareness through her television show. As a result, many people have become more comfortable talking about topics that might have been taboo in the past.

Bob Dylan (5/24/1941)

Day-Sign: 3-Cib
Trecena: 1-Ix
Year: 8-North
Night Lord: G-1
Venus Phase: Evening Star

The day-sign Cib is one of the more serious and self-conscious signs that projects the image of a wise and realistic person. Many have regarded Bob Dylan in this way, as the spokesman of a generation, as a prophet, and so on. Dylan is very pragmatic and tough, and this feature comes out in many of his songs (e.g., "A Hard Rain's Gonna Fall"), some of which involve putdowns of others or political criticism. Dylan doesn't try to be funny very often, but when he does, some hidden or deeper meaning is usually behind the humor. Sometimes, it isn't even clear to what extent he is joking. He knows exactly what he likes and doesn't like, a common characteristic of Cib types. Another Cib issue has to do with authority and one's stance towards it. Dylan has largely avoided the political limelight—but he has managed to maintain an authoritative image as a voice of the counterculture. Cib types can be remote. For the most part, Dylan has lived a private life in spite of his immense popularity, so the public knows little about him. On a more instinctive and reactive level, Dylan is influenced by 1-Ix, the sign of the cryptic communicator. Whether or not he has self-control issues, he is an explorer of the human condition, and he lives his life more inwardly than outwardly. Born in a north year, Dylan expresses the mental detachment associated with that direction, and that sense of detachment is apparent in his songs (which feature more words than notes).

The first Night Lord reigned when Bob Dylan was born. This influence suggests that Dylan is a very tough person who is out for himself, who understands power intimately. He is also direct and combative

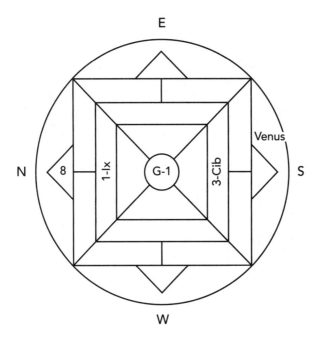

Mayan chart for Bob Dylan

in his song lyrics and many of his songs come from very basic human emotions that deal with pecking orders and sex, though these attitudes are disguised in his creative use of words (such as in his songs, "Like a Rolling Stone" and "Lay Lady Lay"). Venus was an evening star at Dylan's birth, suggesting that he is not really challenging the status quo in his life and art, but is instead reinforcing it. His lifestyle hasn't caused an uproar, and he hasn't advocated any sort of rebellion or revolution, though many have interpreted his music to suggest that outcome. Dylan writes and sings about the realities of life and love as they are, not as they might be. Dylan isn't so radical after all; he has been a reflector of changes rather than an agitator like John Lennon, who was born during the morning star phase of Venus.

East

North

South

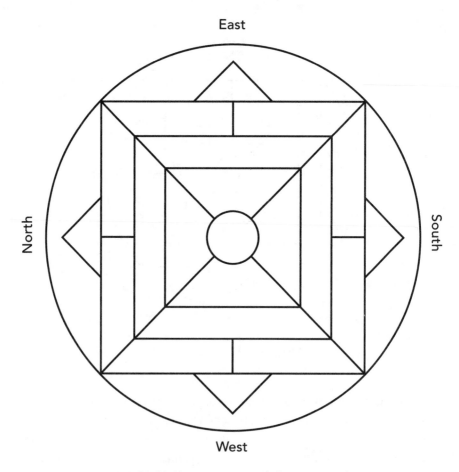

West

Use this blank Mayan pyramid chart to record
information for individual readings

TWO

•••

Further Studies in Mayan Astrology

SEVEN

THE BURNER DAYS

The ancient Maya kept track of a sixty-five-day rhythm that, as we shall see, served as a kind of collective biorhythm. The 260-day astrological calendar was traditionally divided into four sixty-five-day periods with four key day-signs standing at the boundaries of these periods. Each of these four days was considered a time to work out group karma, to purify the community, and to focus attention on the need for greater social cohesion. Days of preparation were made for each "burner day"—so named because of the rituals associated with them, which culminated with a fire-walking ceremony that is still performed in some Mayan communities.

The four burner dates in the 260-day astrological calendar are the Mayan days 4-Oc, 4-Men, 4-Ahau, and 4-Chicchan. In English, these names translate to Dog, Eagle, Lord/Flower, and Serpent, and they correspond respectively to the directions north, west, south, and east. The four directions in Mesoamerican astrology are much like the four elements in Western astrology; they designate fundamental qualities. The correspondences are east/fire, north/earth, west/air, and south/water. Because burner dates occur every sixty-five days, they cycle independently of the solar year and won't occur on the same Western calendar date each year.

After studying these dates for many years, the authors have concluded that the burner dates could be more than just an obscure ritual of an ancient civilization. Correlating the dates of important world events with the Mayan calendar, it is clear that they almost always occur or reach a crescendo near these days. The evidence strongly suggests that

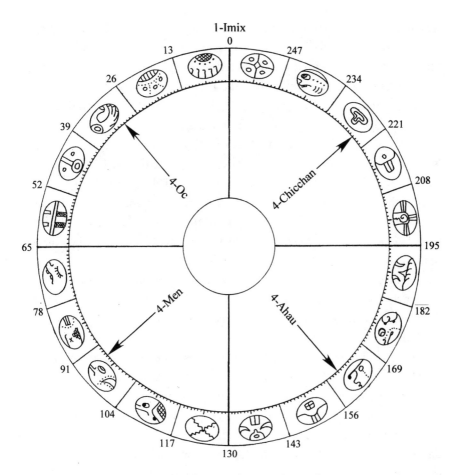

The burner dates in the 260-day tzolkin

the burner dates are crisis points during which a collective ventilation of suppressed energies, or a kind of reconciliation with the past, occurs. Furthermore, the authors have found that one's day-sign and three other days spaced one quarter through the 260-day calendar can serve as personal burner days—days of peak personal energy and experience.

It became obvious to the authors and to others not only that these burner dates correlated with significant news events, but that the events themselves shared certain features. Many of the events have come in the form of a national frenzy of some sort. Some of those major events include such things as important elections, a significant pre-election debate, and the death of leaders. Critical points are often reached in wars, when such actions as hostage takings (motivated by chronic, unjust treatment of an indigenous population) have occurred. National purges or cleansing have also occurred at the time of burner dates, such as when Hillary Clinton appeared in court to defend herself and the President in the Whitewater scandal and when the French government admitted that its behavior toward the Jews during WWII was unconscionable. The Peruvian hostage crisis began and ended near burner dates. In China, these dates coincided with the death of Communist Party leader Deng Xiaoping and the annexation of Hong Kong to China in 1997. In 2004, Ronald Reagan died on the day before a burner day, unleashing a week-long series of funerary rituals. Interestingly, the arrest of O. J. Simpson happened two days before the burner date of June 19, 1994. His trial then became a national spectacle in which racial tensions were driven daily into the conscious part of the collective mind.

In short, it does appear as if these dates have something to do with large groups of people and the ventilation of and coming to terms with emotionally charged issues that are necessary for group integration.

The persistent coincidence of the burner dates with specific kinds of world events suggests to the authors that the Maya had discovered something very important. Having found the burner dates to be crisis points, the Maya deliberately orchestrated emotional purging for their society through planned rituals. They vented their tensions ritualistically, and in conformity with a natural cycle they had observed—a sixty-five-day collective biorhythm. Through this approach, the Maya probably maintained a high level of group health and integrity.

The actual Mayan ritual for the burner dates ran roughly as follows: Twenty days prior to the arrival of each burner date, leaders would draw attention to the coming date by lighting ritual fires. On or near the actual burner date, some sort of group ritual—such as fire-walking or a giant bonfire—was held, bringing the entire community together. Rituals twenty days afterward would provide a re-acclimation to "regular" life. In this way, the Maya vented tensions and kept the group psychically intact at the same time. This approach brings to mind an episode from the television series M*A*S*H, when frustrations in the camp rose so high that the doctors and enlisted men spontaneously started a bonfire, throwing furniture and everything else into it. The group then stood around this night fire in total silence, watching the flames. Everyone felt better after this event. Anyone who has gone camping knows the power of a group campfire to bring people together and share feelings.

To fully understand the astronomical mechanics behind the burner dates, we must turn to the 260-day astrological calendar. Dividing the 260-day count by four, the number of the four directions, produces four sixty-five-day burner periods. If we begin this division with what is usually considered the first day of the 260-day count, 1-Imix (Crocodile), then the next point, sixty-five days later, will be 1-Cimi (Death), then 1-Chuen (Monkey), and finally 1-Cib (Vulture). But the ancient Mayan tradition of the burner dates does not start with the first date of the 260-day count; it begins with the 160th, the day 4-Ahau (Lord/Flower). Why? No one knows for sure, but August 11, 3114 BC was the day that the Long Count (the Mayan Calendar) "rested," and a new age began. Intervals of sixty-five days from this point in the 260-day count give 4-Chicchan (Serpent), 4-Oc (Dog), and 4-Men (Eagle) as the other three burner dates.

Starting the 260-day astrological calendar with 1-Imix and quartering it establishes a quadrant framework, and the traditional burner days that stem from the resting day of the Long Count stand very close to the midpoints of each of these quadrants. In fact, they are just three days off from being exactly at each quadrant's center. This attention to midpoints is similar to Western astrology's 15th degree of the fixed signs, the midpoints of the Cardinal points. Because four sixty-five-day periods equals 260-days, the burner rhythm is a kind of spiking of equidistant points within the framework of a cycle that is the key to all of Mesoamerican astrology. Again, compare this rhythm to the arrival of the semi-cardinal points in the solar calendar year, the points that coincide with the ancient Celtic holidays of Lammas, Beltane, Candlemas, and Samhain.

In Mesoamerican astrology, Venus was the planet involved with regulation of human desire, which is a prerequisite to the process of civilization. If the burner dates have something to do with Venus, then maybe these are dates when groups need to bring their anti-social feelings to the surface, a prerequisite to a higher order of collective integration. Another possible meaning of the burner days is that they represent parts of ourselves that we humans need to integrate from time to time. In this sense, our day-sign is the dominant personality, but the other three signs complete us in some important way.

The burner dates in Mayan astrology illustrate how collectively structured their society must have been. The way the Maya utilized the burner dates is similar to the strategy of a teacher who takes an entire class outdoors at a scheduled time for recess, rather than allowing individual students to jump up out of their seats whenever they wish. The Maya attuned themselves through ritual practices to a natural cycle based on astronomical realities. In our modern world of unchecked individualism, people go off the deep end every day of the year. We do have a few holidays when people collectively vent, like the Fourth of July, St. Patrick's Day (the unofficial rite of spring), and Superbowl Sunday. But for the most part, ours is a weakly integrated society of individuals and, except for the sanitized rituals of officially sanctioned religions, we keep clear of collective events. Most of our holidays are family days, not community ritual days.

But what of the individual need to vent internal pressures? The authors have found that individuals have personal burner dates that function much like the collective ones described above. Beginning with the date in the 260-day astrological calendar on which one was born, intervals of sixty-five days seem to correlate with a need for a personal release of internal tensions. We have found that the week or so preceding one of these points is a period of build-up, and that tension then releases on, or a few days before, the critical date. We have observed that people who plan an intense event of some sort to focus the energy building in them prior to these dates—such as a good physical workout or an active group gathering—can profit from such concentration. Perhaps the world would be a safer place if individuals focused their personal tensions every sixty-five days in some such constructive ritual.

Calculation of one's burner days is simple. The first burner day is one's day-sign, which comes up every 260 days. The second burner date is sixty-five days later and five signs ahead in the order of the day-signs. It has the same number attached to it as the date-of-birth day-sign. For example, if your day-sign is 3-Imix, then the next burner day is five signs ahead, Cimi, specifically 3-Cimi. Notice that your day-sign is a sign of the East, but this burner day is a sign of the North. The next burner day will be the day-sign five more signs ahead and opposite your own, which in this example is Chuen, specifically 3-Chuen. Note that this is a sign of the West. The fourth burner date will be five day-signs ahead, Cib, a sign of the South, specifically 3-Cib. You can find your own four burner days, all spaced sixty-five days apart, using table 1 starting on page 125.

EIGHT

THE CYCLE OF THE THIRTEEN KATUNS

What is popularly known as the Mayan Calendar is what archaeologists, anthropologists, and archaeoastronomers call the Long Count. The Long Count is a large segment of time—1/5 of the approximately 26,000-year cycle of the astronomical event known as the precession of the equinoxes, which will be explained in chapter 9. The Long Count has a definite starting and ending point; it began on August 11, 3114 BC and it ends on December 21, 2012 AD. The Long Count's span of 5,125 solar years was divided by the ancient Maya into thirteenths, twentieths, and 260ths. The thirteenths spanned 394 years and were called baktuns. The 260ths spanned 19.7 years and were called katuns. The twentieths of the Long Count were groups of thirteen katuns, or 256 years, sometimes referred to as the Short Count. This latter grouping had a long prophetic tradition and is the main topic of this chapter.

The katun was extremely important in both ritual and politics and was thought to designate larger shifts in history. Still used by the Mayans, this cycle of 7,200 days measures just under twenty years (19.7 years), which is very close to the cycle of Jupiter and Saturn conjunctions (19.86 years). Katuns are subdivided into twenty sets of 360-day units called tuns. (It is thought that 360 days, rather than 365 days, was used as a value for the year for computing purposes.) Thirteen katuns, a period of 260 tuns, make a full Short Count cycle and each katun is seen as describing the characteristics of an entire generation.

The Short Count's 256-year cycle of thirteen katuns was clearly a Mayan prophecy cycle; each of the thirteen katuns had a specific "fate" attached to it. The Maya believed that the arrival of each of the katuns brought its particular fate to the world every 256 years. We know about this belief from surviving records, including the books of "Chilam Balam" (jaguar priest) from various regions that were written after the Spanish conquest of Yucatan. The manner of distinguishing these thirteen katuns from each other requires an understanding of the tzolkin.

Each of the thirteen katuns in the cycle is indicated by a number from one to thirteen and the name Ahau. The reason for this designation was that each katun ends with the last day in the 260-day calendar, the day Ahau. The first day, therefore, of any given katun always falls on the day Imix, which follows Ahau and is the first of the twenty day-signs. Because twenty is one factor in the length of a katun cycle (7200 days = 20 x 360), each katun always ends on a day with the same name in the 260-day calendar, though not on the same number. Ahau is also the day on which the entire Short Count cycle ends—or, from the perspective of the Maya, the day on which it reaches completion.

The katuns did not follow each other in numerical order. Any given katun in the cycle was always followed by a katun that was numbered two less. For example, katun 10-Ahau was followed by katun 8-Ahau. This relationship can be seen more clearly on the katun wheel shown on page 95. This diagram is from a book about the Maya, *Relacion de las Cosas de Yucatan* (Account of Things in Yucatan), written shortly after the Conquest by Friar Diego de Landa. The diagram shows the cycle of the katuns and should be read in a clockwise direction. The katun from which the cycle was said to begin was katun 11-Ahau. The clockwise sequence of katuns begins under the cross at the top with katun 11-Ahau, followed by katun 9-Ahau, katun 7-Ahau, etc. The thirteen face glyphs are for the day-sign Ahau; the numbers are in both Roman numerals and in the Mayan language. The words in the center translate as "They call this count in their language Vazlazonkatun which is to say the revolving of the katuns."

Essentially, the cycle of thirteen katuns was, for the Maya, a kind of mundane astrology of the society and its history, not an astrology of the individual. In the several books of Chilam Balam, the influences of the thirteen katuns are stated, usually as a description of historical events that occurred during previous cycles. It becomes clear to the reader,

Katun wheel showing the cycle of the thirteen katuns

however, that the Maya always expected history to repeat itself and it is also obvious that the ancient Maya were not optimistic about their fate. Most of these fates are negative, but then this perspective may have been a reflection of how difficult life was in their time.

The following delineations for the katuns are a composite taken from the Book of Chilam Balam of Chumayel, the Codex Perez, and the Book of Chilam Balam of Mani.

Katun 11-Ahau

Apparently food is scarce during this katun and invading foreigners disperse the population. This katun brings an end to traditional rule, with no successors. Since this katun is the first one, it always opens up a new era. For example, during the span of this katun, the Spanish began their takeover of Yucatan and imposed Christianity on the natives.

Katun 9-Ahau

This period is one of corrupt government, when the ruler abuses his people and commits misdeeds. Rulers are so bad in this time that they wind up losing some of their power to the priests. Carnal sin and adultery are practiced openly—by rulers and others—during this katun, and wars are waged. It is also known as the katun of "the forcible withdrawal of the hand," an enigmatic phrase whose meaning is unclear.

Katun 7-Ahau

This time is apparently one of social excess, including extremes in drinking and adultery. It is a low point in the history of society. Governments stoop to their lowest levels of corruption in this katun. The "bud of the flower," an allusion to eroticism, is said to sprout during this katun.

Katun 5-Ahau

During this katun of misfortune, rulers and their subjects separate; the people lose faith in their leaders. Leaders may be harshly treated, even hung. This period brings an abundance of snakes, a great famine, and fewer than usual births.

Katun 3-Ahau

This katun brings changes and calamities such as droughts and wars. The people become homeless and society disintegrates.

Katun 1-Ahau

This katun brings even worse troubles, weak rulers, and destruction. Governments fall apart due to rivalries. This katun may be the time of a great war, after which some degreee of brotherhood will return.

Katun 12-Ahau

After a long period of crisis, war, and disintegration, this katun is a positive one. During this period, governments and rulers are wise. Poor men become rich and there is abundance in the land. Friendship and peace return for six good years, followed by six bad ones.

Katun 10-Ahau

Although this katun is a holy one, trouble returns to the land once again. This katun brings drought and famine; it is a time of foreign occupation, reform of the calendar by outsiders, and sadness.

Katun 8-Ahau

This period may be the worst of the katuns. Both Chichen Itza and Mayapan, the two great ruling cities of Yucatan, were destroyed during this period. The texts speak of demolition and destruction among the governors, and much fighting. But it is also a time that brings an end to greed. It is the katun of "settling down in a new place."

Katun 6-Ahau

This is a time of corrupt or inept and deceptive government. It is also a time of starvation and famine. (Note: the Mayan prophecy for katun 6-Ahau comes down to us in particularly abbreviated form and we can't be sure how it may have been understood centuries ago by Mayan astrologers.)

Katun 4-Ahau

Scarcities of corn and squash occur during this katun, a calamity that leads to extensive mortality. It was during this katun that the settlement of Chichen Itza occurred, when the man-god Kukulcan (one of the names for Quetzalcoatl) arrived. This katun is a time of remembering and recording knowledge.

Katun 2-Ahau

For half of this katun, food will be in good supply; for half of it, misfortunes will occur. This katun brings the end of authoritative order. It is a time of uniting for a cause.

Katun 13-Ahau

Total collapse occurs, and everything is lost. This katun is the time of the judgment of God. Epidemics, plagues and then famines take place. Governments are lost to foreigners. Wise men and prophets disappear.

Of the thirteen katuns, only one, 12-Ahau, has a positive reading. And only in katuns 4-Ahau and 2-Ahau are disastrous events at least partially balanced by positive occurrences. This bleakness, no doubt, is a reflection of the difficulties of life during those times. Determining the astrological value in the cycle of katuns is a work in progress—we will have to find it through observation of the events that occur in each one. Here are the dates of katuns during the past 1,000 years:

KATUN	FIRST WESTERN YEARS OF THIS CYCLE				
13-Ahau	1007	1263	1520	1776	2032
11-Ahau	1027	1283	1539	1796	2052
9-Ahau	1046	1303	1559	1815	
7-Ahau	1066	1322	1579	1835	
5-Ahau	1086	1342	1598	1855	
3-Ahau	1106	1362	1618	1874	
1-Ahau	1125	1382	1638	1894	
12-Ahau	1145	1401	1658	1914	
10-Ahau	1165	1421	1677	1934	
8-Ahau	1185	1441	1697	1953	
6-Ahau	1204	1460	1717	1973	
4-Ahau	1224	1480	1736	1993	
2-Ahau	1244	1500	1756	2012	

The table shows that we have recently lived through katun 6-Ahau: 1973–1993. During this period, the prophecy suggests bad or deceptive government and starvation. Those two decades were a time of deceptive government, at least in the United States, if one considers the Water-gate and Iran/Contra scandals. Those twenty years were also the time of acute famines in Africa and the fall of the Soviet Union. The last time this katun occurred was between 1717 and 1736. During this period, Russia became a major European power, and the "South Sea Bubble," a major business failure, caused a financial panic. In those same years, in England, the old and young "Pretenders" continued to claim the throne. During the 1460–1480 katun 6-Ahau, rulership of England was fought over by rival families, Spain was unified by marriage between the Aragon and Castile families, the Spanish Inquisition was established, and Lorenzo the Magnificent, a clever statesman from Italy's Medici family, ruled Florence alone. Finally, during katun 6-Ahau, from 1204 to 1224, a Mayan revolt at Chichen Itza led to the establishment of a new capital at Mayapan, Genghis Khan extended his Asian empire, and the Magna Carta was forced on the king of England by his subjects.

And what of the present katun in which we are living, katun 4-Ahau? According to the Mayan inscriptions, the katun began on 4/6/1993 and it will end with the entire Long Count/creation epoch on 12/21/2012. If this katun follows the prophecy scheme of the cycle of the 13 katuns listed above, we can expect scarcities as well as the arrival of great leaders. This katun is also a time of "remembering knowledge and writing it down." In the past, this katun coincided with a measure of stability in the world and also with significant advances in communication and information storage. For example, katun 4-Ahau lasted from 1224 to 1244. During this time, Frederick II took Jerusalem, but he took it diplomatically. The next time this katun occurred was between 1480 and 1500. This period was one of great voyages and discoveries, and of relatively stable politics, which made those explorations possible. This period also saw important advances in printing. Katun 4-Ahau next came up between 1736 and 1756. Interest-ingly, it was during this period that the first encyclopedia was published. The 1740–1748 War of the Austrian Succession brought a settlement of territories and a measure of stability. A number of political alliances were formed during this time, as well. Power bases kept shifting, but disorder did not erupt in any significant ways. The same may eventually be said about the katun from 1993 to 2012. The establishment of the European Union marks a milestone in Europe's long history and the arrival of the internet during this katun has coincided with the prophecy of "remember-ing knowledge and writing it down."

Finally, the present Long Count/creation epoch of the Maya comes to an end on December 21st (the winter solstice), in 2012. What will the katun that begins this new era be like? The Maya regarded katun 2-Ahau as half good and half bad, a time of uniting for a cause, but also as the katun during which came the "end of the word of God." And what does that mean? It is true that in previous 2-Ahau katuns, great religious or ideological crises took place. Between 1500 and 1520, the Aztecs were conquered and forced to convert to Christianity; in 1517, Martin Luther started the Protestant Reformation; and 256 years later, between 1756 and 1776, the ideals of liberty and the rights of countries and individuals became a growing trend and this movement led to the American colonies declaring independence from England. One could say that a new era was indeed dawning, although it took a few more katuns before it could stand on its own two feet. Quite possibly some of our most taken-for-granted beliefs, secular and religious, will begin to lose cohesiveness and credibility after 2012, paving the way for a genuinely new age. If the Maya were right, expect enormous changes to begin in 2012 and to culminate with katun 13-Ahau, which starts in 2032.

The katuns allowed the Maya to schedule their rituals and organize their lives around predictable structures. The katuns gave the Maya a means to anticipate the future, and find meaning in what would otherwise seem like random events. Like a fractal wave, the Maya saw history as replicating itself on differing scales: the 260 katuns of the Long Count mimic the 260 days of the tzolkin, as do the 260 tuns of the Short Count.

NINE

DISPELLING MYTHS ABOUT THE MAYAN CALENDAR

We hear the term "Mayan calendar" often these days, usually in association with its 2012 "end date," or maybe linked with some sort of prophecy put forth by modern prophets of both Native American and Anglo heritage. There are many who believe that the Mayan calendar—or as those who actually study the subject call it, the Long Count—is a way of reckoning where we, as humans on planet Earth, are located in the path of our collective destiny. This may be a helpful way of understanding it for some and there may be some truth in it. Others look at it as a map to the end of the world. This perspective, so much like Armageddon in Christianity, is not helpful to anyone. The one thing that is clear, however, is that very few people truly understand what this calendar is all about.

In this chapter, we take a close look at the Long Count and show that it is essentially the tzolkin on a vast scale in which katuns of 20 years in length are the "days" of a creation epoch. This refutes some popular ideas about the Mayan calendar, including the notion that the end of the current Long Count marks the "end of days" and the assertion that it will usher in a new era for humanity orchestrated by some higher intelligence. Further, we argue that the Long Count is more than a calendar; it is the largest piece of the system of astrology created by the Maya. The Long Count is therefore best understood as a kind of astrology, complementary to but not necessarily superior to Western astrology.

Since the 1970s, the published results of archaeoastronomical research on Maya astronomy has stimulated popular interest in this subject, though the astrological component has not been officially endorsed by the academic community. Interest in the Mayan calendar intensified in August of 1987, when a half million or so people prayed for the Earth in what was called the Harmonic Convergence. Artist and visionary José Argüelles was one of the promoters of this event, and some of his imaginative logic justifying the timing can be found in his book *The Mayan Factor*. Although most people probably knew that the Harmonic Convergence had something to do with the Mayan calendar running out or reaching its end point, I don't think very many people really understood the complex rationale behind the event. However, the Harmonic Convergence was a success in many ways. It spurred an interest in Native American prophecy and symbolism and spawned several global meditations for peace since that time.

THE MAYAN CALENDAR BANDWAGON

Some researchers have argued that the Mayan calendar maps out the evolution of human consciousness. Their theory is based on the scope of significant events that occurred within the 5,125-year span of the Long Count. This period encompasses most of human oral and written history. In fact, ancient history nearly everywhere starts around 3000 BC. This was the time of the building of the first pyramids and the establishment of the Old Kingdom—the first pinnacle of Egyptian civilization. At this time, the first writing was done in Sumeria, and the first structures at Stonehenge were put into place. The Kali Yuga, the calendrical system that maps out ages in Hindu cosmology, began at this time as well.

There are also many people who believe, we think mistakenly, that 2012 marks the "end of days" and will usher in a kind of apocalypse. It is indeed true that the Long Count is approaching its end date—it will do so on December 21, 2012. To grasp the real significance of this turning of the ages requires an understanding of all the symbolic components of Mayan astrology.

CYCLICAL VERSUS LINEAR TIME

Symbolic and divinatory systems like astrology were among humanity's first attempts to frame an understanding of the process of life in a way that could be transmitted to succeeding generations. Cultures on nearly every part of our planet created symbol systems that gave meaning to the predictable cycles observed in the world around them, many of which were so successful that they have survived into present times. In ancient Mesopotamia, the Sumerians, Babylonians, and Chaldeans (and later the Greeks and Romans) established a body of knowledge based on the effects and qualities of the visible planets, on our cosmic environment, on human life. This tradition is known to us as astrology. In ancient China, an astrological system based on the numbers 12 and 60, both figures related to the cycles of Jupiter, was developed. In ancient India, Vedic astrology, with its emphasis on the moon and its movements, was born. While those Eastern traditions were influenced to some extent by Mesopotamian astrology, both stand today as subjects in their own right with their own history and interpretive techniques. These systems, based on natural phemomena and offering a holistic view of people and society, meet human needs that are not addressed by the dominant institutions of our time. In fact, these astronomically based symbol systems continue to function as psychological roadmaps for persons interested in self-knowledge, personal growth, and spiritual development.

Unlike these other astrological traditions, Mesoamerican astrology seems to have developed in complete isolation from the rest of the world. The Maya, Toltec, and Aztec civilizations of ancient Mesoamerica (Mexico and Central America) found their own unique way of relating human life and natural phenomena to the rhythms of the sky. The Olmec, one of the earliest cultures in the Americas and contemporaries of the ancient Greeks, left evidence of a symbol system using numbers and days. Later, the Maya, Toltec, and Aztec civilizations continued this tradition until the Spanish Conquest. While it is true that much of the astrology of Ancient America has been lost, native Maya daykeepers in Guatemala and Mexico have kept portions of it alive as an oral tradition, and the fragments gleaned from the ruins by archaeologists offer clues as to its original structure.

A key to understanding the Mayan system lies in the fractal-like relationship between cycles, especially that of the 260-day sequence and the Long Count. The Long Count shares three elements with the Western calendar: (1) a means of grouping large periods of time, (2) a base date, and (3) an astrological component. From the counting of moons in the Paleolithic era to the modern definition of the second, created by fractioning the Earth's orbit around the sun, astronomy has been the backbone of our calendars and time-keeping systems. In the Western calendar, time is grouped into solar years, decades, centuries, and millennia. We organize time according to the solar year in multiples of the number ten, a good number to use if one counts on fingers. The base date of the Western calendar is what is thought to be the date of Christ's birth. Dates before that date are labeled BC, dates after are AD. The astrological component of the Western calendar is found in the seven-day planetary week (days are named for planets) and the twelve months that roughly correlate with the twelve signs of the zodiac.

In the Long Count, as in the tzolkin, time is grouped into multiples of the numbers twenty (fingers and toes) and also thirteen. An even more fundamental difference between the systems, however, is in their conceptualization of time itself. In Western calendars and perceptions time is linear, something that moves perpetually forward and is always understood in relationship to—being "before" or "after"—a given starting point on a straight line. Extra significance is thought to occur when a multiple of ten is crossed, like the year 2000. In the Long Count, time moves forward as well as cyclically—perpetually repeating a specific sequence of patterns that can be observed and predicted.

Between the starting point, or base date, of the Long Count on August 11, 3114 BC and the end date of December 21, 2012 is a span of 5,125.37 years or exactly 1,872,000 days. There are therefore a finite number of days that occur between the base date and the end date, and these days are grouped in several blocks of time that cycle simultaneously. As we've seen in previous chapters, one fundamental time unit used by the Maya—the tun—measures 360 days and approximates the solar year. 5,200 tuns make up the Long Count. Another fundamental time unit is the katun, a period equal to twenty tuns (20 × 360 = 7,200 days or 19.71 years). As we have seen, the Maya regarded the katun as a major historic time period, a generation marker of sorts. Interestingly, a katun is very close (within fifty-four days) to the mean synodic cycle of Jupiter and Saturn, which is 19.86 years. It is very probable that the katun represents the Jupiter/Saturn synodic cycle, rounded off just as the 365.24 days of the year are rounded off to 360 degrees of the zodiac.

There are 260 katuns in the Long Count (7200 x 260 = 1,872,000 days). The baktun, a period of 144,000 days or 394 years, subsumes twenty katuns. And exactly thirteen baktuns are in the Long Count. Because each baktun contains twenty katuns, each baktun is also related to the cycle of Jupiter and Saturn's conjunctions. The table below illustrates the alignment of the subunits of the Long Count with the cycle of Jupiter and Saturn.

1 solar year = 365.24 days	1 tun = 360 days = 0.99 years
1 Jupiter/Saturn conjunction = 19.86 years	1 katun = 20 tuns = 19.71 years
20 Jupiter/Saturn conjunctions = 397 years	1 baktun = 20 katuns = 394 years

The Long Count is also a larger version of the 260-day astrological calendar, which is itself based on astronomical cycles. Consider the following:

1. The length of Venus's appearance as a morning star or evening star = 263 days.
2. Nine twenty-nine-day synodic cycles of the moon = 261 days.
3. The interval of time between one of the sun's intersections with the path of the moon and its return to the same intersection = 346.62 days. Half of that interval, 173.31 days, is called the eclipse half year. Three of these rounds off to 520 days, or 2 x 260.
4. The synodic cycle of Mars is 780 days. One third of this figure = 260 days.
5. Twenty synodic cycles of Mercury (about 117 days) is equivalent to nine cycles of 260 days or 2,340 days.
6. Four synodic cycles of Venus (584 days) equals nine cycles of 260 days.
7. Three synodic cycles of Mars (780 days) exactly equals nine cycles of 260 days.

The correlations of the 260-day tzolkin with planetary periods that are multiples and fractions of its length is suggestive of resonance, a special kind of linkage that binds two or more cycles together in time.

The Maya used these resonances as a means for extremely accurate long-range calculations without resorting to fractions. In fact, it is often claimed that the Mayan year was more accurate than the Western year, a result of the Maya's recognition of this resonance between astronomical cycles and the tzolkin.

Clearly, the 260-day count incorporates real sky rhythms and will therefore always be synchronized to a large degree with certain aspects of the changing sky. Was this delineation of time for calendrical computation purposes only? The evidence from the archaeological record and the oral tradition suggests otherwise—the Mayan use of time was unquestionably in large part astrological. The symbolism associated with the tzolkin, resonant with the planets and embedded within a complex organization of longer astronomically-based time units, suggests an astrological system.

The 260 days of the tzolkin also resonate with human biological rhythms. The native Maya believed that 260 days was the length of human gestation, and it seems reasonable to infer that the Maya intended the conception day-sign and the birth day-sign to be the same. All of the above suggests that, for the Maya, time was a master key that linked heaven and earth.

MEASURES OF TIME
OR MARKERS OF CHANGE?

While the Western calendar is anchored to an earthly event—the year that Jesus was allegedly born—it measures time utilizing a week of seven days that are named for planets. This seven-day week, a quarter of the lunar cycle, is actually an astrological remnant of the pre-Christian Near East. In that tradition, the day itself and also the planetary hours (divisions of the day) were thought to have an astrological quality. Seven planetary rulerships were believed to cycle during each 24-hour period and the hour that began each day at dawn gave its planetary name to that day. At various times in the history of Western astrology, the planetary hours were used to predict propitious times for various activities, to read the destiny of a newborn, and to evaluate the nature of the new year itself. The planetary hours are a remnant of a kind of astrology that uses blocks of time as "signs," very much like the Mesoamerican day-signs, though in a seven-day framework. In contrast, nearly all of

Western astrology since the Greeks uses blocks of space that hold symbolic meaning, such as signs, houses, and aspects. The Mesoamerican astrological tradition is built on a structure of blocks of time that function like the spatial signs of Western astrology.

One would expect the Long Count's divisions into blocks of 260 katuns and thirteen baktuns to have some kind of astrological value, since they resonate with the Jupiter-Saturn cycle. Given that Western astrology, and probably Chinese astrology, as well, used these planets as primary markers of historical change, it seems logical that the Long Count could also function as an accurate time-grid for mapping the start and end of historically significant shifts. But would-be historians, be warned. Finding events to match the divisions of the Long Count is very different from arriving at a deep understanding of history and then attempting to perceive a pattern. For example, the last baktun of the Long Count began in 1618. Certain authors have pointed to that time as the beginning of materialistic science. It is true that the scientific revolution was in full swing then. But most historians see the scientific revolution as a process that began decades earlier, and some even place it in the late Middle Ages.

As regards the prediction of historical shifts or cycles, certain New Age writers focusing on the Mayan calendar are touting it as far superior to Western astrology without knowing very much about the latter subject. Further, such writers are often disparaging of Western astrology, assuming it has nothing of consequence to offer in regard to understanding world history, or even the evolution of consciousness. Many writers on the Mayan calendar are uninformed when it comes to the larger body of astrological tradition.

The baktun appears to be a reasonably good historical marker, but Western astrology has plenty of methodology that draws similar grids over history. The Great Mutation Cycle of Jupiter and Saturn of about 800 years (794 to be exact) marks the shifting of Jupiter/Saturn conjunctions into Fire signs. It has been one of the premier astrological chronocrators of human and Earth history. The last Great Mutation occurred in 1603, and the pioneering astronomer Johannes Kepler himself wondered what kind of new age it would bring, knowing that 800 years earlier, Charlemagne restored the Holy Roman Empire and 800 years before that Christ walked the Earth.

THE TZOLKIN AS A FRACTAL
OF THE LONG COUNT

Since 260 katuns make up the Long Count, the day unit of the 260-day astrological calendar can be correlated with the katun unit of the Long Count. In other words, we can say that the tzolkin is a fractal, or microcosm, of the Long Count. If the tzolkin is astrological, then can we say the same of the Long Count? Astrology is the symbolic mapping of astronomical cycles to reveal predictable patterns of natural phenomena and human character and destiny. Astrology creates a grid through which one can perceive patterns in nature and human life that are not so clearly apparent from other perspectives. The Long Count is such a grid. As we have seen, its structure is based on planetary cycles—Jupiter-Saturn conjunctions. And we shall now see it is also based on variations in the Earth's orbit which result in the astronomical phemonenon known as the precession of the equinoxes.

The 5,125-year period of the Long Count is only one fifth of a much larger cycle, the cycle of the precession of the equinoxes. In a single, full orbit of the sun, the earth rotates on its axis 365.24 times. At the same time, the Earth's axis is wobbling like a top in such a way that if the crown of the planet were extended into space, over the course of about 25,770 years it would describe a cone. This wobbling also translates into the movement of the equinoxes, the points where the Earth's extended equator intersects the Earth's orbital plane. The equinoxes move backwards against the constellations, or precess, at a rate of about 1 degree every 72 years. If we take the precession cycle of 25,770 years and divide it by 12, we get astrological ages of about 2,148 years. This classification into specific ages is one of Western astrology's ways of delineating long periods of historical time. According to that framework, many people believe that we are now approaching the "Age of Aquarius."

Now if we take that mean precession cycle of 25,770 years and divide it by 5, we get 5,154 years. This figure is remarkably close to the 5,125-year span of the Long Count. Considering the fact that the figure given for precession is a mean figure and that the actual value may vary by two or three hundred years, this number was an extremely accurate reading of astronomical motion by the Maya. It is much closer than the figures for precession given by Plato and those encoded in the Great Pyramid. Both Mayan and Aztec cosmology tell of five great ages, the present age being the fifth. Further, the Maya had time periods much larger than the Long Count itself, extending time far beyond the boundaries of ancient Western cultures.

This information suggests that the Long Count is simply a one-fifth segment of the precession cycle, and that in Mayan cosmology time existed before 3114 BC and will exist after 2012. It seems reasonable, then, to regard the beginning and ending of the Long Count as transition points of the larger precession cycle and not as absolute originations or terminations.

Given the simple technology available to them, the ancient Mesoamerican astronomers did some amazing work. Not only did they measure the length of the precession cycle, but they also apparently anchored it with a remarkable alignment, the meeting of the winter solstice sun (not the vernal equinox that is used in Western astrology) with the band of the Milky Way. Since our galaxy is shaped like a disk, we can draw an equator-like plane through the Milky Way and mark where it intersects the ecliptic, the plane of the Earth's orbit around the sun.

Mayan cosmology was very night-sky oriented and the Milky Way, specifically the dark band that runs inside it in the vicinity of the ecliptic, figured prominently in Mayan mythology. This dark band was seen as the road to the underworld, the place of origins and the home of the gods. It was in the late 1980s and early 1990s that a few astrology-friendly independent writers and researchers, including Raymond Mardyks and John Major Jenkins, were the first to suggest that the Long Count was more than simply a long string of numbers. They believed that it marked the precession of the winter solstice sun over the galactic equator. It now appears that the Maya—or possibly their predecessors—calculated *in advance* when the winter solstice point would pass through the dark band in the Milky Way in 2012, and then projected the Long Count backward, arriving at its base date in 3114 BC. (John Major Jenkins, whose writings on this subject the authors highly recommend, makes a good case for this calculation having occurred in Izapa, an ancient city near the Pacific coast at the Mexican/Guatemalan border.)

BEGINNINGS AND ENDINGS

A crucial element in any theory addressing the Long Count's purpose or meaning is the determination of the count's base date—its starting date.

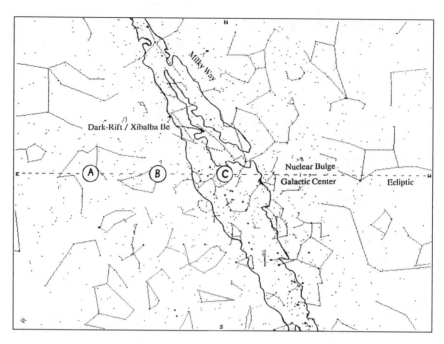

The position of the winter solstice sun relative to the dark band of the Milky Way (A) 5000 years ago, (B) 2000 years ago, and (C) in 2012. Illustration from *Maya Cosmogenesis 2012*, courtesy of John Major Jenkins.

In order for us to know when key events occurred, or will occur, relative to the 260-day count or the Long Count, we must have a method of correlating them with the Western calendar. One way of correlating the 260-day astrological calendar or the Long Count with an event recorded in the civil calendar is to link it to a Julian date. Historians and astronomers have numbered the days in the Western calendar as far back as several millennia before the Common Era (AD), each day having its own unique Julian number.

The 260-day tzolkin may have originated as far back as 2,500 years ago. It is thought that the Long Count of the Maya originated perhaps 500 years later. Both counts appear to have run continuously without interruption since their beginnings. If we know the Julian date of an event, and we have our calendars linked to this system, then we can correlate dates back and forth between calendars.

For nearly a century, researchers struggled with the precise location in time of the Long Count's base date. During the 1970s and 1980s, a majority of investigators in several fields came to accept a correlation that is supported by the available evidence. Known as the Goodman-Martinez-Thompson correlation, or the G.M.T., it is named for the three men who settled on the same Julian date number for the base date of the Long Count, Julian day 584,283. This correlation is backed up by ancient stone inscriptions, historical records, astronomical data, and the oral tradition of the most conservative Maya in Guatemala. Today, nearly all researchers have accepted Julian Day 584,283, which corresponds to August 11, 3114 BC, to be the base date for the Long Count.

Despite the wide acceptance of this established date, some of the most popular theories about the Mayan calendar disregard it. The artist and writer José Argüelles, one of the people associated with the Harmonic Convergence of 1987 and Dreamspell (an oracular game based on the Mayan calendar) has promoted some very controversial ideas about this aspect of Mayan culture. In his 1987 book *The Mayan Factor,* Argüelles explains his belief that the Mayan Calendar is a kind of holographic code that times the passage of Earth with its human passengers through a beam emanating from the galactic center. This galactic synchronization will then mark a transition point in the evolution of consciousness and will usher in a new Solar Age. While this idea is an intriguing one, Argüelles' calendar correlation has led to much confusion on this issue. Argüelles and the followers of his writings and users of his product Dreamspell use a correlation that now differs from the G.M.T. correlation by seven weeks. Between 2004 and 2008, it will differ by one day less because it ignores leap year and thus loses one day every four years. Every day counted to the ancient Maya; no days were ever dropped.

In this book, we consider the cornerstone of Mesoamerican astrology to be the 260-day astrological calendar and the Long Count, with its 260 katuns, as simply a large-scale version of the 260-day astrological count. Within the context of the Long Count, the thirteen baktuns mark off historic time as listed below, each one containing twenty katuns, each of which could be interpreted as a day-sign. The baktun can be seen as a round-figure approximation of twenty Jupiter/Saturn conjunctions.

Baktun 1 – 3114 BC to 2720
Baktun 2 – 2720 to 2325
Baktun 3 – 2325 to 1931
Baktun 4 – 1931 to 1537

Baktun 5 – 1537 to 1143
Baktun 6 – 1143 to 748
Baktun 7 – 748 to 354
Baktun 8 – 354 BC to AD 40
Baktun 9 – 40 to 434
Baktun 10 – 434 to 829
Baktun 11 – 829 to 1223
Baktun 12 – 1223 to 1617
Baktun 13 – 1617 to 2012

Each of the thirteen baktuns in the Long Count contains twenty katuns. The last katun of each baktun corresponds to the last day-sign of the twenty-day count, and the last katun of the entire Long Count can be seen as corresponding with the last day of the entire 260-day astrological calendar, which is the day 13-Ahau. This relationship supports interpretation of the Long Count as simply a large scale version of the tzolkin, rather than a countdown of some sort.

But the katuns can be organized in another way in the Long Count. We know for sure that the Maya also counted katuns in groups of thirteen, a period of 256 years sometimes called the Short Count (see discussion in chapter 8). This cycle length has astronomical counterparts. For example, thirteen mean Jupiter/Saturn conjunctions is 258 years, and twice the mean Pluto/Uranus cycle is 255 years. Does this relationship make the Short Count astrological? Astrologers know that Pluto/Uranus conjunctions pack a big punch, and this is especially true when they combine with the Jupiter/Saturn conjunctions as they do at the end of each Short Count cycle. Many serious scholars of the Maya think that this katun cycle was the real Mayan prophecy cycle. The cycle appears to correlate with historical events, but this fact could just as easily be attributed to the Jupiter/Saturn cycle. We are currently in the last katun of the entire Long Count which correlates symbolically with the last day-sign (Ahau) of the last trecena (1-Lamat).

There is no reason why the sequence of katuns should end in 2012, as postulated by proponents of the "end of days" scenarios. Remember that each katun is named for the day it ends on, which is always Ahau. But each katun also begins with the day Imix, the first of the 20 day-signs. It turns out that the katun that begins in 2052 and ends in 2072 will begin with the first day of the 260-day count, the day-sign 1-Imix.

Although the 260-day calendar is thought to be a continuous process that can begin at any point within it, 1-Imix is considered the starting point, the point of initiation. Imix, the sign of creation, symbolizes the crack in the cosmic egg, the bursting forth of energy moving from one world to another, and the generative and creative forces that rule the Earth. The sign is also concerned with nourishment and sustenance and suggests the need to care for our offspring and our surroundings; our lives depend on our relationship to our environment. In terms of the order of katuns, the period beginning with 2052 would be a likely candidate for the inception of a new age.

The 2012 end date of the Long Count is both the terminal point of the current fifth part of the precessional cycle and, in the context of the Mesoamerican five-stage creation cosmology, the terminal point of the entire 25,770-year cycle itself. Just as happened at the time of the turning of the millennium a few years ago, prognostications abound as to what will happen. We don't think this time passage marks the end of days. The truth is that December 21, 2012, marks the beginning of a new phase in the precession of the winter solstice, but only if you accept that the dark band in the Milky Way constitutes the most important anchor point in the entire cycle. If you are looking for the moment when the solstice point aligns exactly with the galactic equatorial plane itself (which is what most modern astrologers would look for) then look behind you. This alignment occurred during 1998–1999.

As the position of the winter solstice sun moves backward along the ecliptic, it crosses the line defining the galactic equator over the course of about thirty-six years. This occurs because the disk of the sun measures about one half degree of longitude and, given the rate of precession of about 1 degree per 72 years, some part of the sun will cover this node for half that time. So the solstice sun's initial and final contact points are actually around 1980 and 2116. And because the angle of intersection of the ecliptic and galactic equator is about 61 degrees, this relationship extends the period of solar contact with the equator by about another five years on each side. So, truth be told, the exact alignment has already occurred. Were the Maya wrong in using the dark band as the winter solstice sun's target as it passes through the Milky Way?

The Maya were definitely concerned with this dark zone that is visible on a clear night far away from light pollution. In their cosmology, this dark band was the origin point of the creation, the pathway to the gods who dwelled in the underworld called Xibalba. Contact of the solstice with this point would seem extremely significant given the Maya's cosmology and mythology. And it turns out that their calculations were fairly accurate, so the "end date" still stands. But what does it all mean?

Here we enter Mayan calendar central, literally and figuratively. First, keep in mind that the academic researchers have nothing to say about this matter. They will only point out that the Long Count reaches completion at this time and that the next cycle then begins. After all, the Maya did have longer periods than the Long Count so they must have expected time to continue. The indigenous people, however, dropped the Long Count ages ago, so we don't have a solid, extant oral tradition on this topic. Some indigenous Maya have issued prophecies of end times, but these may not be Long Count prophecies. It is likely that some of these predictions have been influenced by American New Age interpretations of their ancestor's calendar. This lack of, and possible distortion of, a Native tradition has left the barn door open to interpretations that are based primarily on personal beliefs.

For example, if you believe that there is a divine plan behind the evolution of consciousness, then you could see the Mayan calendar as a time grid that reveals the intelligent process of creation that is making the world we experience. In other words, the Long Count is evidence of intelligent design and also a means by which humans can attune themselves to the cosmic junction just ahead of us in 2012. One could say the same thing about Western or Hindu astrology. Such explanations are only the beginning of diverse interpretations of the Long Count. They leave us free to imagine that the alignment of the solstice sun with either the galactic equator (which has already happened), the galactic center (which won't ever happen but which will be closest to happening in about two centuries), or the dark band of the Road to Xibalba (which is happening now), will coincide with or trigger a major event. Perhaps we will witness the unleashing of a galactic beam of consciousness from the center of the galaxy directly onto us humans on earth, which will somehow lead us to join our space brothers in a new world of evolved consciousness and interstellar peace. But probably not. Many other variations on this sort of prophecy, some with astonishing details, can be found in the steadily growing literature of the Mayan calendar.

The foundations for these concepts are open to question. First of all, many writers on this subject tend to talk about the Mayan calendar, but they base much of their judgments on what we know from the Aztecs. So it's not just the Mayan calendar, but a blending of Mesoamerican cosmologies that has seeded these visionary perspectives. Second, as we have already pointed out, these writers typically dismiss Western astrology and hesitate to actually identify the Mayan calendar as an astrological system, but that conclusion is hard to avoid. Yet, ultimately, these writers actually promote a kind of astrological hierarchy, with the Mayan Calendar at the top—because it promotes the "evolution of consciousness"—and Western astrology at the bottom because, as they say, it is materialistic and based on the wrong numerology.

Third, in their research these writers find the supporting documentation they need in history in order to support their theory. Fourth, ideas of a golden age, end times, and transcendent utopias are all part of a phenomenon called millennialism or millennarianism, which has been going on for, as it turns out, millennia. Humans, often driven by religious beliefs, tend to become agitated when calendars cross boundaries. Most of the New Age literature on the Mayan calendar falls into this category and is a manifestation of people's much larger frustration with the way society is evolving. The end-date of the Mayan calendar won't save us. We have big problems to solve right now. We need to face them the best way each and every one of us can.

We're not suggesting that the Long Count is just another calendar. We are saying that it is a remarkable creation of Mayan culture, and that it is also a kind of astrology that offers another way of measuring symbolic time. Some of its parameters are intriguing, especially its origin date around 3100 BC—which is, without a doubt, a tremendously important time in history. Also intriguing is the midpoint of the Long Count at 551 BC, which was approximately the time when Pythagoras, Buddha, Lao Tzu, and many other wise people lived. Again, it is indeed possible that the Long Count describes history with some degree of accuracy because it resonates with the Jupiter/Saturn cycle of conjunctions, which other astrologically-minded cultures also thought was the key to long-term time-based analysis. The ending of the Long Count close to the passage of the winter solstice over the galactic equator is also interesting, and it provides evidence that the Maya were excellent astronomers.

So it is possible that the Long Count is symbolically descriptive of the passage of waves of history of varying lengths. We would encourage historically minded people to take a closer look. But let's not forget that cycles of the outer planets are also known, in the astrological tradition, to be representative of significant historical patterns. Both Mayan and Western astrology offer intriguing material for an analysis of history on the basis of recurring cycles.

Is the Mayan way better than the Western way?

Anyone paying attention to the world these days may conclude that we are racing at high speed toward a wall. Whether it be 2012 or 2036, or any other date in the next fifty years for that matter, we are going to pay a price for how we've been choosing to live. Our consciousness will have to change to prevent any number of crises, and furthermore, it will have to change by admitting to ourselves that we humans are soiling our own nest. We have become self-absorbed lemmings dumping our garbage on billions of other life forms that are supporting our existence. We absolutely must make a shift from a linear, short-term profit mode of thinking to a non-linear grasp of our interconnectedness with our own environment. In the authors' view, the "transformation of consciousness" is principally a matter of humans learning to stop defining everything in terms of "humanness." Sadly, that change is improbable; we humans are so self-absorbed that nothing else seems to exist for us. What we can say is that the Maya may have managed to call attention to perhaps the greatest wake-up call for humanity since the beginning of the previous glacial period. And that's pretty impressive.

TEN

A MAYAN PLANETARY
HOROSCOPE

When Western astrologers measure a planet's position, they do so by using a spatial background called the zodiac, which represents the twelve constellations that the sun appears to cross in the course of a year. This chapter presents a method devised by the authors for creating a horoscope that displays relevant planetary positions for an individual, using the tzolkin as the reference grid in much the same way as the zodiac is used in Western astrology. The position of planets within their synodic cycles with the sun at any given time can be plotted forward or backward on this grid.

In Mayan astrology, planetary movement is measured in terms of the age of the planet's synodic cycle, which is its cycle with the sun. For example, the first quarter of the moon's cycle is described in Western astrology as being a square between the moon and sun. In Mesoamerican astrology, the same thing would be described in terms of the "age" of the moon, which in this case would be seven days or one-quarter of the way through its cycle with the sun. Consider Venus, which has a 584-day synodic cycle. A person born when Venus is 45 degrees ahead of the sun might be born about sixty days into the 584-day Venus cycle.

The first horoscopes in Western astrology were simply lists that reported such things as "the sun is in the Scales," "Venus is in the claws of the Scorpion," "Mars is at the Bull's eye," and "the moon is in Aries." Not much later (as early as about AD 200), the Maya were inscribing astrological data on monuments called stelae. Dates of important events, along with planetary information, were recorded on these stone monuments. Dates were given first in terms of the distance in time (the number of days, and groups of days) from a specific time-anchor located in 3114 BC, the birth of the Long Count. This data is called the Initial Series. Additional information about the age of the moon, and other planetary tidbits, are found in what is called the Supplementary Series.

Aside from the Initial Series listings, no known Mayan horoscope exists. But if there was one, it would be a logical extension of the way the system recorded planetary movement before the Spanish Conquest. One possible method for creating such a diagram would involve a time-based analysis of the synodic periods of the planets. In Western astrology, the sun is used to define the space of the zodiac, which then becomes the measure of other features such as aspects and houses. Mayan astrology places a birth, or an event, within the context of on-going sun-based time. The sun is a good choice for a workable and objective measure of time.

Using a listing of planetary conjunctions (including the moon's) with the sun, one can determine the number of days that have elapsed since the previous conjunction of each planet with the sun. This figure can then be divided by the synodic period of each planet. Next, this decimal can be multiplied by 260 to arrive at the position of the planet within the 260-degree Mesoamerican grid.

Example: The synodic cycle of sun and moon is 29.5 days. Suppose an event, like a birth, occurred five days after the new moon (the start of the synodic period). Dividing 5 by 29.5 gives us 0.169. When this figure is multiplied by 260, the result is 44, or the day-sign within the tzolkin that corresponds to that portion of the synodic cycle. This same process can be done for all the other planets. The synodic periods of the planets measured in days are:

Moon—29.5	Saturn—378.1
Mercury—115.9	Uranus—369.7
Venus—583.9	Neptune—367.5
Mars—780	Pluto—366.7
Jupiter—398.9	

We have designed a format for creating individual Mayan horoscopes using this method to plot planetary positions. The illustration on page 120 demonstrates how this horoscope works, using birth data for Bill Clinton as an example (a blank Mayan planetary horoscope is provided for your use at the end of this chapter). The astronomical data required to construct a chart such as this can be found in any astronomical ephemeris. The calculations can be done with a calculator by noting the previous conjunctions of the planets with the sun and the length of each synodic cycle. Far easier is to use a computer program like one being designed by Astrolabe Software (www.alabe.com).

You will notice a ring of twenty signs with numbers at their cusps on the outside of the sample horoscope. These are the signs of the trecenas that establish the order of the 260-day Mesoamerican astrological cycle. As we have seen, the trecenas are thirteen-day periods, somewhat lunar in nature.

To plot an individual's birth data, names or symbols for the planets are placed on the wheel in proportion to their "age" at the time of the person's birth. For example, Bill Clinton's natal moon is at the third quarter, so it is located about ³/₄ through the wheel near the end of the trecena Cib, a sign of hard-ball politics—strongly suggesting that the feminine principle, expressed by himself and also by the significant females in his life, is realistic and very strong. Mercury was located fairly early in its 116-day synodic cycle and in the trecena Ahau, a sign that has social and diplomatic qualities. Venus was located in the fourth quarter of its 584-day synodic cycle and so is located fairly close to the moon, but in a different trecena. Between Venus and the moon are Mars and Jupiter, suggesting that Clinton's emotional life and dealings with the feminine are subject to strong impulses characterized by the sign Muluc, the trecena in which three of these planets are located. Muluc also implies a tendency to run emotional risks.

The day-sign should be noted in the top portion of the central square of the horoscope. The Night Lord should be shown in the left portion of this square, the year in the bottom portion, and the trecena in the right portion.

Notice the circle with the letters DS in it that is located at point 109 in the trecena Chicchan. This is Clinton's day-sign, which happens to be 5-Muluc, the fifth day of the trecena 1-Chicchan. The day-sign (DS) is the key to all of Mesoamerican Astrology and it appears to have both solar

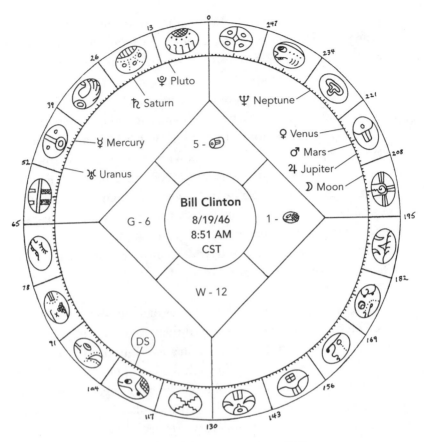

Mayan planetary horoscope for Bill Clinton

and ascendant-like qualities. Carlos Casteneda's teacher Don Juan told him that the world was composed of two things, the tonal and the nagual. The tonal is the form that things take; the nagual is that unknown element behind the form. A person's day-sign is the form that the individual takes in this world, the mask of the self that lies behind it.

Since the DS moves ahead every day, completing the circle in 260 days, it acts like a trigger point, activating the planetary positions it passes during the course of its cycle. The DS is also subject to "transits" from the planets—contacts between the moving planets of the present and the static planetary positions at birth. For example, Mars was at a point in its 780-day synodic cycle that corresponds to Clinton's transiting point in November of 1994, the month of the Republican election victory. According to our calculations, Mars actually entered the trecena

1-Serpent, in which Clinton's day-sign is located, on November 2nd and ran over his DS on the 13th. Mars was running opposite this point in its synodic cycle in December 1995, when the president was in the midst of battling over the budget with Congress. These sorts of transits also work well for the natal planetary positions.

Planetary positions in this system can also be progressed at a rate of a day-for-a-year, as is done in Western and Vedic astrology. The positions of the planets the day after the birth correspond to the conditions of life at age 1 year. Two days after birth corresponds to age 2 years, and so on. Horoscopes can also be compared for couples or partners to show striking correlations and reveal compatibility or the lack of it.

The Mayan planetary horoscope presented here is a completely original methodology, but one that is based on the fundamental principles of ancient Mayan astrology. The authors believe that if Mayan astrology had been allowed to progress, and had not been destroyed by intolerant priests and friars, it may have eventually evolved into a system similar to this one. We have offered this concluding chapter to the reader as a window into the amazing possibilities of Mayan astrology. Perhaps in the future, Mayan astrology will be both restored and advanced in ways like those described in this chapter, and will once again serve to illuminate the unique qualities and possibilities of every individual.

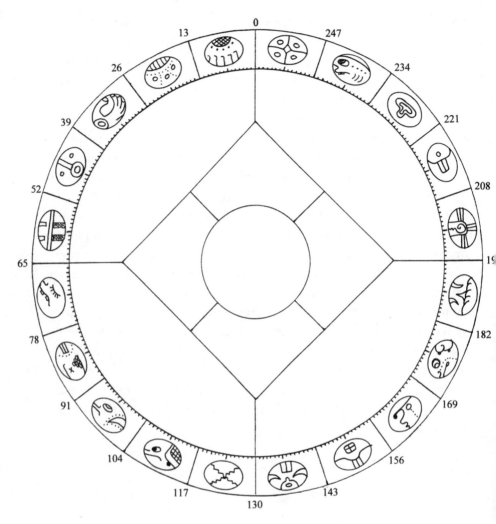

Use this blank Mayan planetary horoscope to record
data for individual readings

THREE

•••

The Mayan Almanac
1920–2020

DAY-SIGNS AND DIRECTIONAL LINKAGES

EAST	NORTH	WEST	SOUTH
Imix (crocodile)	Ik (wind)	Akbal (night)	Kan (corn)
Chicchan (serpent)	Cimi (owl, skull)	Manik (deer)	Lamat (rabbit)
Muluc (water)	Oc (dog)	Chuen (monkey)	Eb (broom)
Ben (reed)	Ix (jaguar)	Men (eagle)	Cib (vulture)
Caban (movement)	Etz'nab (flint knife)	Cauac (storm)	Ahau (lord)

TABLE ONE

THE TZOLKIN DAY-SIGNS, TRECENAS, AND LORDS OF THE NIGHT

Date	Day-Sign	L	Date	Day-Sign	L	Date	Day-Sign	L
Dec 31 1919	1-Imix	7	Feb 28 1920	8-Ahau	3	Apr 27 1920	2-Cauac	8
Jan 1 1920	2-Ik	8	Feb 29 1920	9-Imix	4	Apr 28 1920	3-Ahau	9
Jan 2 1920	3-Akbal	9	Mar 1 1920	10-Ik	5	Apr 29 1920	4-Imix	1
Jan 3 1920	4-Kan	1	Mar 2 1920	11-Akbal	6	Apr 30 1920	5-Ik	2
Jan 4 1920	5-Chicchan	2	Mar 3 1920	12-Kan	7	May 1 1920	6-Akbal	3
Jan 5 1920	6-Cimi	3	Mar 4 1920	13-Chicchan	8	May 2 1920	7-Kan	4
Jan 6 1920	7-Manik	4	Mar 5 1920	1-Cimi	9	May 3 1920	8-Chicchan	5
Jan 7 1920	8-Lamat	5	Mar 6 1920	2-Manik	1	May 4 1920	9-Cimi	6
Jan 8 1920	9-Muluc	6	Mar 7 1920	3-Lamat	2	May 5 1920	10-Manik	7
Jan 9 1920	10-Oc	7	Mar 8 1920	4-Muluc	3	May 6 1920	11-Lamat	8
Jan 10 1920	11-Chuen	8	Mar 9 1920	5-Oc	4	May 7 1920	12-Muluc	9
Jan 11 1920	12-Eb	9	Mar 10 1920	6-Chuen	5	May 8 1920	13-Oc	1
Jan 12 1920	13-Ben	1	Mar 11 1920	7-Eb	6	May 9 1920	1-Chuen	2
Jan 13 1920	1-Ix	2	Mar 12 1920	8-Ben	7	May 10 1920	2-Eb	3
Jan 14 1920	2-Men	3	Mar 13 1920	9-Ix	8	May 11 1920	3-Ben	4
Jan 15 1920	3-Cib	4	Mar 14 1920	10-Men	9	May 12 1920	4-Ix	5
Jan 16 1920	4-Caban	5	Mar 15 1920	11-Cib	1	May 13 1920	5-Men	6
Jan 17 1920	5-Etz'nab	6	Mar 16 1920	12-Caban	2	May 14 1920	6-Cib	7
Jan 18 1920	6-Cauac	7	Mar 17 1920	13-Etz'nab	3	May 15 1920	7-Caban	8
Jan 19 1920	7-Ahau	8	Mar 18 1920	1-Cauac	4	May 16 1920	8-Etz'nab	9
Jan 20 1920	8-Imix	9	Mar 19 1920	2-Ahau	5	May 17 1920	9-Cauac	1
Jan 21 1920	9-Ik	1	Mar 20 1920	3-Imix	6	May 18 1920	10-Ahau	2
Jan 22 1920	10-Akbal	2	Mar 21 1920	4-Ik	7	May 19 1920	11-Imix	3
Jan 23 1920	11-Kan	3	Mar 22 1920	5-Akbal	8	May 20 1920	12-Ik	4
Jan 24 1920	12-Chicchan	4	Mar 23 1920	6-Kan	9	May 21 1920	13-Akbal	5
Jan 25 1920	13-Cimi	5	Mar 24 1920	7-Chicchan	1	May 22 1920	1-Kan	6
Jan 26 1920	1-Manik	6	Mar 25 1920	8-Cimi	2	May 23 1920	2-Chicchan	7
Jan 27 1920	2-Lamat	7	Mar 26 1920	9-Manik	3	May 24 1920	3-Cimi	8
Jan 28 1920	3-Muluc	8	Mar 27 1920	10-Lamat	4	May 25 1920	4-Manik	9
Jan 29 1920	4-Oc	9	Mar 28 1920	11-Muluc	5	May 26 1920	5-Lamat	1
Jan 30 1920	5-Chuen	1	Mar 29 1920	12-Oc	6	May 27 1920	6-Muluc	2
Jan 31 1920	6-Eb	2	Mar 30 1920	13-Chuen	7	May 28 1920	7-Oc	3
Feb 1 1920	7-Ben	3	Mar 31 1920	1-Eb	8	May 29 1920	8-Chuen	4
Feb 2 1920	8-Ix	4	Apr 1 1920	2-Ben	9	May 30 1920	9-Eb	5
Feb 3 1920	9-Men	5	Apr 2 1920	3-Ix	1	May 31 1920	10-Ben	6
Feb 4 1920	10-Cib	6	Apr 3 1920	4-Men	2	Jun 1 1920	11-Ix	7
Feb 5 1920	11-Caban	7	Apr 4 1920	5-Cib	3	Jun 2 1920	12-Men	8
Feb 6 1920	12-Etz'nab	8	Apr 5 1920	6-Caban	4	Jun 3 1920	13-Cib	9
Feb 7 1920	13-Cauac	9	Apr 6 1920	7-Etz'nab	5	Jun 4 1920	1-Caban	1
Feb 8 1920	1-Ahau	1	Apr 7 1920	8-Cauac	6	Jun 5 1920	2-Etz'nab	2
Feb 9 1920	2-Imix	2	Apr 8 1920	9-Ahau	7	Jun 6 1920	3-Cauac	3
Feb 10 1920	3-Ik	3	Apr 9 1920	10-Imix	8	Jun 7 1920	4-Ahau	4
Feb 11 1920	4-Akbal	4	Apr 10 1920	11-Ik	9	Jun 8 1920	5-Imix	5
Feb 12 1920	5-Kan	5	Apr 11 1920	12-Akbal	1	Jun 9 1920	6-Ik	6
Feb 13 1920	6-Chicchan	6	Apr 12 1920	13-Kan	2	Jun 10 1920	7-Akbal	7
Feb 14 1920	7-Cimi	7	Apr 13 1920	1-Chicchan	3	Jun 11 1920	8-Kan	8
Feb 15 1920	8-Manik	8	Apr 14 1920	2-Cimi	4	Jun 12 1920	9-Chicchan	9
Feb 16 1920	9-Lamat	9	Apr 15 1920	3-Manik	5	Jun 13 1920	10-Cimi	1
Feb 17 1920	10-Muluc	1	Apr 16 1920	4-Lamat	6	Jun 14 1920	11-Manik	2
Feb 18 1920	11-Oc	2	Apr 17 1920	5-Muluc	7	Jun 15 1920	12-Lamat	3
Feb 19 1920	12-Chuen	3	Apr 18 1920	6-Oc	8	Jun 16 1920	13-Muluc	4
Feb 20 1920	13-Eb	4	Apr 19 1920	7-Chuen	9	Jun 17 1920	1-Oc	5
Feb 21 1920	1-Ben	5	Apr 20 1920	8-Eb	1	Jun 18 1920	2-Chuen	6
Feb 22 1920	2-Ix	6	Apr 21 1920	9-Ben	2	Jun 19 1920	3-Eb	7
Feb 23 1920	3-Men	7	Apr 22 1920	10-Ix	3	Jun 20 1920	4-Ben	8
Feb 24 1920	4-Cib	8	Apr 23 1920	11-Men	4	Jun 21 1920	5-Ix	9
Feb 25 1920	5-Caban	9	Apr 24 1920	12-Cib	5	Jun 22 1920	6-Men	1
Feb 26 1920	6-Etz'nab	1	Apr 25 1920	13-Caban	6	Jun 23 1920	7-Cib	2
Feb 27 1920	7-Cauac	2	Apr 26 1920	1-Etz'nab	7	Jun 24 1920	8-Caban	3

Date	Day-Sign	L
Jun 25 1920	9-Etz'nab	4
Jun 26 1920	10-Cauac	5
Jun 27 1920	11-Ahau	6
Jun 28 1920	12-Imix	7
Jun 29 1920	13-Ik	8
Jun 30 1920	1-Akbal	9
Jul 1 1920	2-Kan	1
Jul 2 1920	3-Chicchan	2
Jul 3 1920	4-Cimi	3
Jul 4 1920	5-Manik	4
Jul 5 1920	6-Lamat	5
Jul 6 1920	7-Muluc	6
Jul 7 1920	8-Oc	7
Jul 8 1920	9-Chuen	8
Jul 9 1920	10-Eb	9
Jul 10 1920	11-Ben	1
Jul 11 1920	12-Ix	2
Jul 12 1920	13-Men	3
Jul 13 1920	1-Cib	4
Jul 14 1920	2-Caban	5
Jul 15 1920	3-Etz'nab	6
Jul 16 1920	4-Cauac	7
Jul 17 1920	5-Ahau	8
Jul 18 1920	6-Imix	9
Jul 19 1920	7-Ik	1
Jul 20 1920	8-Akbal	2
Jul 21 1920	9-Kan	3
Jul 22 1920	10-Chicchan	4
Jul 23 1920	11-Cimi	5
Jul 24 1920	12-Manik	6
Jul 25 1920	13-Lamat	7
Jul 26 1920	1-Muluc	8
Jul 27 1920	2-Oc	9
Jul 28 1920	3-Chuen	1
Jul 29 1920	4-Eb	2
Jul 30 1920	5-Ben	3
Jul 31 1920	6-Ix	4
Aug 1 1920	7-Men	5
Aug 2 1920	8-Cib	6
Aug 3 1920	9-Caban	7
Aug 4 1920	10-Etz'nab	8
Aug 5 1920	11-Cauac	9
Aug 6 1920	12-Ahau	1
Aug 7 1920	13-Imix	2
Aug 8 1920	1-Ik	3
Aug 9 1920	2-Akbal	4
Aug 10 1920	3-Kan	5
Aug 11 1920	4-Chicchan	6
Aug 12 1920	5-Cimi	7
Aug 13 1920	6-Manik	8
Aug 14 1920	7-Lamat	9
Aug 15 1920	8-Muluc	1
Aug 16 1920	9-Oc	2
Aug 17 1920	10-Chuen	3
Aug 18 1920	11-Eb	4
Aug 19 1920	12-Ben	5
Aug 20 1920	13-Ix	6
Aug 21 1920	1-Men	7
Aug 22 1920	2-Cib	8
Aug 23 1920	3-Caban	9
Aug 24 1920	4-Etz'nab	1
Aug 25 1920	5-Cauac	2
Aug 26 1920	6-Ahau	3
Aug 27 1920	7-Imix	4
Aug 28 1920	8-Ik	5
Aug 29 1920	9-Akbal	6
Aug 30 1920	10-Kan	7
Aug 31 1920	11-Chicchan	8

Date	Day-Sign	L
Sep 1 1920	12-Cimi	9
Sep 2 1920	13-Manik	1
Sep 3 1920	1-Lamat	2
Sep 4 1920	2-Muluc	3
Sep 5 1920	3-Oc	4
Sep 6 1920	4-Chuen	5
Sep 7 1920	5-Eb	6
Sep 8 1920	6-Ben	7
Sep 9 1920	7-Ix	8
Sep 10 1920	8-Men	9
Sep 11 1920	9-Cib	1
Sep 12 1920	10-Caban	2
Sep 13 1920	11-Etz'nab	3
Sep 14 1920	12-Cauac	4
Sep 15 1920	13-Ahau	5
Sep 16 1920	1-Imix	6
Sep 17 1920	2-Ik	7
Sep 18 1920	3-Akbal	8
Sep 19 1920	4-Kan	9
Sep 20 1920	5-Chicchan	1
Sep 21 1920	6-Cimi	2
Sep 22 1920	7-Manik	3
Sep 23 1920	8-Lamat	4
Sep 24 1920	9-Muluc	5
Sep 25 1920	10-Oc	6
Sep 26 1920	11-Chuen	7
Sep 27 1920	12-Eb	8
Sep 28 1920	13-Ben	9
Sep 29 1920	1-Ix	1
Sep 30 1920	2-Men	2
Oct 1 1920	3-Cib	3
Oct 2 1920	4-Caban	4
Oct 3 1920	5-Etz'nab	5
Oct 4 1920	6-Cauac	6
Oct 5 1920	7-Ahau	7
Oct 6 1920	8-Imix	8
Oct 7 1920	9-Ik	9
Oct 8 1920	10-Akbal	1
Oct 9 1920	11-Kan	2
Oct 10 1920	12-Chicchan	3
Oct 11 1920	13-Cimi	4
Oct 12 1920	1-Manik	5
Oct 13 1920	2-Lamat	6
Oct 14 1920	3-Muluc	7
Oct 15 1920	4-Oc	8
Oct 16 1920	5-Chuen	9
Oct 17 1920	6-Eb	1
Oct 18 1920	7-Ben	2
Oct 19 1920	8-Ix	3
Oct 20 1920	9-Men	4
Oct 21 1920	10-Cib	5
Oct 22 1920	11-Caban	6
Oct 23 1920	12-Etz'nab	7
Oct 24 1920	13-Cauac	8
Oct 25 1920	1-Ahau	9
Oct 26 1920	2-Imix	1
Oct 27 1920	3-Ik	2
Oct 28 1920	4-Akbal	3
Oct 29 1920	5-Kan	4
Oct 30 1920	6-Chicchan	5
Oct 31 1920	7-Cimi	6
Nov 1 1920	8-Manik	7
Nov 2 1920	9-Lamat	8
Nov 3 1920	10-Muluc	9
Nov 4 1920	11-Oc	1
Nov 5 1920	12-Chuen	2
Nov 6 1920	13-Eb	3
Nov 7 1920	1-Ben	4

Date	Day-Sign	L
Nov 8 1920	2-Ix	5
Nov 9 1920	3-Men	6
Nov 10 1920	4-Cib	7
Nov 11 1920	5-Caban	8
Nov 12 1920	6-Etz'nab	9
Nov 13 1920	7-Cauac	1
Nov 14 1920	8-Ahau	2
Nov 15 1920	9-Imix	3
Nov 16 1920	10-Ik	4
Nov 17 1920	11-Akbal	5
Nov 18 1920	12-Kan	6
Nov 19 1920	13-Chicchan	7
Nov 20 1920	1-Cimi	8
Nov 21 1920	2-Manik	9
Nov 22 1920	3-Lamat	1
Nov 23 1920	4-Muluc	2
Nov 24 1920	5-Oc	3
Nov 25 1920	6-Chuen	4
Nov 26 1920	7-Eb	5
Nov 27 1920	8-Ben	6
Nov 28 1920	9-Ix	7
Nov 29 1920	10-Men	8
Nov 30 1920	11-Cib	9
Dec 1 1920	12-Caban	1
Dec 2 1920	13-Etz'nab	2
Dec 3 1920	1-Cauac	3
Dec 4 1920	2-Ahau	4
Dec 5 1920	3-Imix	5
Dec 6 1920	4-Ik	6
Dec 7 1920	5-Akbal	7
Dec 8 1920	6-Kan	8
Dec 9 1920	7-Chicchan	9
Dec 10 1920	8-Cimi	1
Dec 11 1920	9-Manik	2
Dec 12 1920	10-Lamat	3
Dec 13 1920	11-Muluc	4
Dec 14 1920	12-Oc	5
Dec 15 1920	13-Chuen	6
Dec 16 1920	1-Eb	7
Dec 17 1920	2-Ben	8
Dec 18 1920	3-Ix	9
Dec 19 1920	4-Men	1
Dec 20 1920	5-Cib	2
Dec 21 1920	6-Caban	3
Dec 22 1920	7-Etz'nab	4
Dec 23 1920	8-Cauac	5
Dec 24 1920	9-Ahau	6
Dec 25 1920	10-Imix	7
Dec 26 1920	11-Ik	8
Dec 27 1920	12-Akbal	9
Dec 28 1920	13-Kan	1
Dec 29 1920	1-Chicchan	2
Dec 30 1920	2-Cimi	3
Dec 31 1920	3-Manik	4
Jan 1 1921	4-Lamat	5
Jan 2 1921	5-Muluc	6
Jan 3 1921	6-Oc	7
Jan 4 1921	7-Chuen	8
Jan 5 1921	8-Eb	9
Jan 6 1921	9-Ben	1
Jan 7 1921	10-Ix	2
Jan 8 1921	11-Men	3
Jan 9 1921	12-Cib	4
Jan 10 1921	13-Caban	5
Jan 11 1921	1-Etz'nab	6
Jan 12 1921	2-Cauac	7
Jan 13 1921	3-Ahau	8
Jan 14 1921	4-Imix	9

Date	Day-Sign	L
Jan 15 1921	5-Ik	1
Jan 16 1921	6-Akbal	2
Jan 17 1921	7-Kan	3
Jan 18 1921	8-Chicchan	4
Jan 19 1921	9-Cimi	5
Jan 20 1921	10-Manik	6
Jan 21 1921	11-Lamat	7
Jan 22 1921	12-Muluc	8
Jan 23 1921	13-Oc	9
Jan 24 1921	1-Chuen	1
Jan 25 1921	2-Eb	2
Jan 26 1921	3-Ben	3
Jan 27 1921	4-Ix	4
Jan 28 1921	5-Men	5
Jan 29 1921	6-Cib	6
Jan 30 1921	7-Caban	7
Jan 31 1921	8-Etz'nab	8
Feb 1 1921	9-Cauac	9
Feb 2 1921	10-Ahau	1
Feb 3 1921	11-Imix	2
Feb 4 1921	12-Ik	3
Feb 5 1921	13-Akbal	4
Feb 6 1921	1-Kan	5
Feb 7 1921	2-Chicchan	6
Feb 8 1921	3-Cimi	7
Feb 9 1921	4-Manik	8
Feb 10 1921	5-Lamat	9
Feb 11 1921	6-Muluc	1
Feb 12 1921	7-Oc	2
Feb 13 1921	8-Chuen	3
Feb 14 1921	9-Eb	4
Feb 15 1921	10-Ben	5
Feb 16 1921	11-Ix	6
Feb 17 1921	12-Men	7
Feb 18 1921	13-Cib	8
Feb 19 1921	1-Caban	9
Feb 20 1921	2-Etz'nab	1
Feb 21 1921	3-Cauac	2
Feb 22 1921	4-Ahau	3
Feb 23 1921	5-Imix	4
Feb 24 1921	6-Ik	5
Feb 25 1921	7-Akbal	6
Feb 26 1921	8-Kan	7
Feb 27 1921	9-Chicchan	8
Feb 28 1921	10-Cimi	9
Mar 1 1921	11-Manik	1
Mar 2 1921	12-Lamat	2
Mar 3 1921	13-Muluc	3
Mar 4 1921	1-Oc	4
Mar 5 1921	2-Chuen	5
Mar 6 1921	3-Eb	6
Mar 7 1921	4-Ben	7
Mar 8 1921	5-Ix	8
Mar 9 1921	6-Men	9
Mar 10 1921	7-Cib	1
Mar 11 1921	8-Caban	2
Mar 12 1921	9-Etz'nab	3
Mar 13 1921	10-Cauac	4
Mar 14 1921	11-Ahau	5
Mar 15 1921	12-Imix	6
Mar 16 1921	13-Ik	7
Mar 17 1921	1-Akbal	8
Mar 18 1921	2-Kan	9
Mar 19 1921	3-Chicchan	1
Mar 20 1921	4-Cimi	2
Mar 21 1921	5-Manik	3
Mar 22 1921	6-Lamat	4
Mar 23 1921	7-Muluc	5

Date	Day-Sign	L
Mar 24 1921	8-Oc	6
Mar 25 1921	9-Chuen	7
Mar 26 1921	10-Eb	8
Mar 27 1921	11-Ben	9
Mar 28 1921	12-Ix	1
Mar 29 1921	13-Men	2
Mar 30 1921	1-Cib	3
Mar 31 1921	2-Caban	4
Apr 1 1921	3-Etz'nab	5
Apr 2 1921	4-Cauac	6
Apr 3 1921	5-Ahau	7
Apr 4 1921	6-Imix	8
Apr 5 1921	7-Ik	9
Apr 6 1921	8-Akbal	1
Apr 7 1921	9-Kan	2
Apr 8 1921	10-Chicchan	3
Apr 9 1921	11-Cimi	4
Apr 10 1921	12-Manik	5
Apr 11 1921	13-Lamat	6
Apr 12 1921	1-Muluc	7
Apr 13 1921	2-Oc	8
Apr 14 1921	3-Chuen	9
Apr 15 1921	4-Eb	1
Apr 16 1921	5-Ben	2
Apr 17 1921	6-Ix	3
Apr 18 1921	7-Men	4
Apr 19 1921	8-Cib	5
Apr 20 1921	9-Caban	6
Apr 21 1921	10-Etz'nab	7
Apr 22 1921	11-Cauac	8
Apr 23 1921	12-Ahau	9
Apr 24 1921	13-Imix	1
Apr 25 1921	1-Ik	2
Apr 26 1921	2-Akbal	3
Apr 27 1921	3-Kan	4
Apr 28 1921	4-Chicchan	5
Apr 29 1921	5-Cimi	6
Apr 30 1921	6-Manik	7
May 1 1921	7-Lamat	8
May 2 1921	8-Muluc	9
May 3 1921	9-Oc	1
May 4 1921	10-Chuen	2
May 5 1921	11-Eb	3
May 6 1921	12-Ben	4
May 7 1921	13-Ix	5
May 8 1921	1-Men	6
May 9 1921	2-Cib	7
May 10 1921	3-Caban	8
May 11 1921	4-Etz'nab	9
May 12 1921	5-Cauac	1
May 13 1921	6-Ahau	2
May 14 1921	7-Imix	3
May 15 1921	8-Ik	4
May 16 1921	9-Akbal	5
May 17 1921	10-Kan	6
May 18 1921	11-Chicchan	7
May 19 1921	12-Cimi	8
May 20 1921	13-Manik	9
May 21 1921	1-Lamat	1
May 22 1921	2-Muluc	2
May 23 1921	3-Oc	3
May 24 1921	4-Chuen	4
May 25 1921	5-Eb	5
May 26 1921	6-Ben	6
May 27 1921	7-Ix	7
May 28 1921	8-Men	8
May 29 1921	9-Cib	9
May 30 1921	10-Caban	1

Date	Day-Sign	L
May 31 1921	11-Etz'nab	2
Jun 1 1921	12-Cauac	3
Jun 2 1921	13-Ahau	4
Jun 3 1921	1-Imix	5
Jun 4 1921	2-Ik	6
Jun 5 1921	3-Akbal	7
Jun 6 1921	4-Kan	8
Jun 7 1921	5-Chicchan	9
Jun 8 1921	6-Cimi	1
Jun 9 1921	7-Manik	2
Jun 10 1921	8-Lamat	3
Jun 11 1921	9-Muluc	4
Jun 12 1921	10-Oc	5
Jun 13 1921	11-Chuen	6
Jun 14 1921	12-Eb	7
Jun 15 1921	13-Ben	8
Jun 16 1921	1-Ix	9
Jun 17 1921	2-Men	1
Jun 18 1921	3-Cib	2
Jun 19 1921	4-Caban	3
Jun 20 1921	5-Etz'nab	4
Jun 21 1921	6-Cauac	5
Jun 22 1921	7-Ahau	6
Jun 23 1921	8-Imix	7
Jun 24 1921	9-Ik	8
Jun 25 1921	10-Akbal	9
Jun 26 1921	11-Kan	1
Jun 27 1921	12-Chicchan	2
Jun 28 1921	13-Cimi	3
Jun 29 1921	1-Manik	4
Jun 30 1921	2-Lamat	5
Jul 1 1921	3-Muluc	6
Jul 2 1921	4-Oc	7
Jul 3 1921	5-Chuen	8
Jul 4 1921	6-Eb	9
Jul 5 1921	7-Ben	1
Jul 6 1921	8-Ix	2
Jul 7 1921	9-Men	3
Jul 8 1921	10-Cib	4
Jul 9 1921	11-Caban	5
Jul 10 1921	12-Etz'nab	6
Jul 11 1921	13-Cauac	7
Jul 12 1921	1-Ahau	8
Jul 13 1921	2-Imix	9
Jul 14 1921	3-Ik	1
Jul 15 1921	4-Akbal	2
Jul 16 1921	5-Kan	3
Jul 17 1921	6-Chicchan	4
Jul 18 1921	7-Cimi	5
Jul 19 1921	8-Manik	6
Jul 20 1921	9-Lamat	7
Jul 21 1921	10-Muluc	8
Jul 22 1921	11-Oc	9
Jul 23 1921	12-Chuen	1
Jul 24 1921	13-Eb	2
Jul 25 1921	1-Ben	3
Jul 26 1921	2-Ix	4
Jul 27 1921	3-Men	5
Jul 28 1921	4-Cib	6
Jul 29 1921	5-Caban	7
Jul 30 1921	6-Etz'nab	8
Jul 31 1921	7-Cauac	9
Aug 1 1921	8-Ahau	1
Aug 2 1921	9-Imix	2
Aug 3 1921	10-Ik	3
Aug 4 1921	11-Akbal	4
Aug 5 1921	12-Kan	5
Aug 6 1921	13-Chicchan	6

Date	Day-Sign	L	Date	Day-Sign	L	Date	Day-Sign	L
Aug 7 1921	1-Cimi	7	Oct 14 1921	4-Ix	3	Dec 21 1921	7-Ik	8
Aug 8 1921	2-Manik	8	Oct 15 1921	5-Men	4	Dec 22 1921	8-Akbal	9
Aug 9 1921	3-Lamat	9	Oct 16 1921	6-Cib	5	Dec 23 1921	9-Kan	1
Aug 10 1921	4-Muluc	1	Oct 17 1921	7-Caban	6	Dec 24 1921	10-Chicchan	2
Aug 11 1921	5-Oc	2	Oct 18 1921	8-Etz'nab	7	Dec 25 1921	11-Cimi	3
Aug 12 1921	6-Chuen	3	Oct 19 1921	9-Cauac	8	Dec 26 1921	12-Manik	4
Aug 13 1921	7-Eb	4	Oct 20 1921	10-Ahau	9	Dec 27 1921	13-Lamat	5
Aug 14 1921	8-Ben	5	Oct 21 1921	11-Imix	1	Dec 28 1921	1-Muluc	6
Aug 15 1921	9-Ix	6	Oct 22 1921	12-Ik	2	Dec 29 1921	2-Oc	7
Aug 16 1921	10-Men	7	Oct 23 1921	13-Akbal	3	Dec 30 1921	3-Chuen	8
Aug 17 1921	11-Cib	8	Oct 24 1921	1-Kan	4	Dec 31 1921	4-Eb	9
Aug 18 1921	12-Caban	9	Oct 25 1921	2-Chicchan	5	Jan 1 1922	5-Ben	1
Aug 19 1921	13-Etz'nab	1	Oct 26 1921	3-Cimi	6	Jan 2 1922	6-Ix	2
Aug 20 1921	1-Cauac	2	Oct 27 1921	4-Manik	7	Jan 3 1922	7-Men	3
Aug 21 1921	2-Ahau	3	Oct 28 1921	5-Lamat	8	Jan 4 1922	8-Cib	4
Aug 22 1921	3-Imix	4	Oct 29 1921	6-Muluc	9	Jan 5 1922	9-Caban	5
Aug 23 1921	4-Ik	5	Oct 30 1921	7-Oc	1	Jan 6 1922	10-Etz'nab	6
Aug 24 1921	5-Akbal	6	Oct 31 1921	8-Chuen	2	Jan 7 1922	11-Cauac	7
Aug 25 1921	6-Kan	7	Nov 1 1921	9-Eb	3	Jan 8 1922	12-Ahau	8
Aug 26 1921	7-Chicchan	8	Nov 2 1921	10-Ben	4	Jan 9 1922	13-Imix	9
Aug 27 1921	8-Cimi	9	Nov 3 1921	11-Ix	5	Jan 10 1922	1-Ik	1
Aug 28 1921	9-Manik	1	Nov 4 1921	12-Men	6	Jan 11 1922	2-Akbal	2
Aug 29 1921	10-Lamat	2	Nov 5 1921	13-Cib	7	Jan 12 1922	3-Kan	3
Aug 30 1921	11-Muluc	3	Nov 6 1921	1-Caban	8	Jan 13 1922	4-Chicchan	4
Aug 31 1921	12-Oc	4	Nov 7 1921	2-Etz'nab	9	Jan 14 1922	5-Cimi	5
Sep 1 1921	13-Chuen	5	Nov 8 1921	3-Cauac	1	Jan 15 1922	6-Manik	6
Sep 2 1921	1-Eb	6	Nov 9 1921	4-Ahau	2	Jan 16 1922	7-Lamat	7
Sep 3 1921	2-Ben	7	Nov 10 1921	5-Imix	3	Jan 17 1922	8-Muluc	8
Sep 4 1921	3-Ix	8	Nov 11 1921	6-Ik	4	Jan 18 1922	9-Oc	9
Sep 5 1921	4-Men	9	Nov 12 1921	7-Akbal	5	Jan 19 1922	10-Chuen	1
Sep 6 1921	5-Cib	1	Nov 13 1921	8-Kan	6	Jan 20 1922	11-Eb	2
Sep 7 1921	6-Caban	2	Nov 14 1921	9-Chicchan	7	Jan 21 1922	12-Ben	3
Sep 8 1921	7-Etz'nab	3	Nov 15 1921	10-Cimi	8	Jan 22 1922	13-Ix	4
Sep 9 1921	8-Cauac	4	Nov 16 1921	11-Manik	9	Jan 23 1922	1-Men	5
Sep 10 1921	9-Ahau	5	Nov 17 1921	12-Lamat	1	Jan 24 1922	2-Cib	6
Sep 11 1921	10-Imix	6	Nov 18 1921	13-Muluc	2	Jan 25 1922	3-Caban	7
Sep 12 1921	11-Ik	7	Nov 19 1921	1-Oc	3	Jan 26 1922	4-Etz'nab	8
Sep 13 1921	12-Akbal	8	Nov 20 1921	2-Chuen	4	Jan 27 1922	5-Cauac	9
Sep 14 1921	13-Kan	9	Nov 21 1921	3-Eb	5	Jan 28 1922	6-Ahau	1
Sep 15 1921	1-Chicchan	1	Nov 22 1921	4-Ben	6	Jan 29 1922	7-Imix	2
Sep 16 1921	2-Cimi	2	Nov 23 1921	5-Ix	7	Jan 30 1922	8-Ik	3
Sep 17 1921	3-Manik	3	Nov 24 1921	6-Men	8	Jan 31 1922	9-Akbal	4
Sep 18 1921	4-Lamat	4	Nov 25 1921	7-Cib	9	Feb 1 1922	10-Kan	5
Sep 19 1921	5-Muluc	5	Nov 26 1921	8-Caban	1	Feb 2 1922	11-Chicchan	6
Sep 20 1921	6-Oc	6	Nov 27 1921	9-Etz'nab	2	Feb 3 1922	12-Cimi	7
Sep 21 1921	7-Chuen	7	Nov 28 1921	10-Cauac	3	Feb 4 1922	13-Manik	8
Sep 22 1921	8-Eb	8	Nov 29 1921	11-Ahau	4	Feb 5 1922	1-Lamat	9
Sep 23 1921	9-Ben	9	Nov 30 1921	12-Imix	5	Feb 6 1922	2-Muluc	1
Sep 24 1921	10-Ix	1	Dec 1 1921	13-Ik	6	Feb 7 1922	3-Oc	2
Sep 25 1921	11-Men	2	Dec 2 1921	1-Akbal	7	Feb 8 1922	4-Chuen	3
Sep 26 1921	12-Cib	3	Dec 3 1921	2-Kan	8	Feb 9 1922	5-Eb	4
Sep 27 1921	13-Caban	4	Dec 4 1921	3-Chicchan	9	Feb 10 1922	6-Ben	5
Sep 28 1921	1-Etz'nab	5	Dec 5 1921	4-Cimi	1	Feb 11 1922	7-Ix	6
Sep 29 1921	2-Cauac	6	Dec 6 1921	5-Manik	2	Feb 12 1922	8-Men	7
Sep 30 1921	3-Ahau	7	Dec 7 1921	6-Lamat	3	Feb 13 1922	9-Cib	8
Oct 1 1921	4-Imix	8	Dec 8 1921	7-Muluc	4	Feb 14 1922	10-Caban	9
Oct 2 1921	5-Ik	9	Dec 9 1921	8-Oc	5	Feb 15 1922	11-Etz'nab	1
Oct 3 1921	6-Akbal	1	Dec 10 1921	9-Chuen	6	Feb 16 1922	12-Cauac	2
Oct 4 1921	7-Kan	2	Dec 11 1921	10-Eb	7	Feb 17 1922	13-Ahau	3
Oct 5 1921	8-Chicchan	3	Dec 12 1921	11-Ben	8	Feb 18 1922	1-Imix	4
Oct 6 1921	9-Cimi	4	Dec 13 1921	12-Ix	9	Feb 19 1922	2-Ik	5
Oct 7 1921	10-Manik	5	Dec 14 1921	13-Men	1	Feb 20 1922	3-Akbal	6
Oct 8 1921	11-Lamat	6	Dec 15 1921	1-Cib	2	Feb 21 1922	4-Kan	7
Oct 9 1921	12-Muluc	7	Dec 16 1921	2-Caban	3	Feb 22 1922	5-Chicchan	8
Oct 10 1921	13-Oc	8	Dec 17 1921	3-Etz'nab	4	Feb 23 1922	6-Cimi	9
Oct 11 1921	1-Chuen	9	Dec 18 1921	4-Cauac	5	Feb 24 1922	7-Manik	1
Oct 12 1921	2-Eb	1	Dec 19 1921	5-Ahau	6	Feb 25 1922	8-Lamat	2
Oct 13 1921	3-Ben	2	Dec 20 1921	6-Imix	7	Feb 26 1922	9-Muluc	3

Date	Day-Sign	L	Date	Day-Sign	L	Date	Day-Sign	L
Feb 27 1922	10-Oc	4	May 6 1922	13-Etz'nab	9	Jul 13 1922	3-Cimi	5
Feb 28 1922	11-Chuen	5	May 7 1922	**1-Cauac**	1	Jul 14 1922	4-Manik	6
Mar 1 1922	12-Eb	6	May 8 1922	2-Ahau	2	Jul 15 1922	5-Lamat	7
Mar 2 1922	13-Ben	7	May 9 1922	3-*Imix*	3	Jul 16 1922	6-Muluc	8
Mar 3 1922	**1-Ix**	8	May 10 1922	4-Ik	4	Jul 17 1922	7-Oc	9
Mar 4 1922	2-Men	9	May 11 1922	5-Akbal	5	Jul 18 1922	8-Chuen	1
Mar 5 1922	3-Cib	1	May 12 1922	6-Kan	6	Jul 19 1922	9-Eb	2
Mar 6 1922	4-Caban	2	May 13 1922	7-Chicchan	7	Jul 20 1922	10-Ben	3
Mar 7 1922	5-Etz'nab	3	May 14 1922	8-Cimi	8	Jul 21 1922	11-Ix	4
Mar 8 1922	6-Cauac	4	May 15 1922	9-Manik	9	Jul 22 1922	12-Men	5
Mar 9 1922	7-Ahau	5	May 16 1922	10-Lamat	1	Jul 23 1922	13-Cib	6
Mar 10 1922	8-*Imix*	6	May 17 1922	11-Muluc	2	Jul 24 1922	**1-Caban**	7
Mar 11 1922	9-Ik	7	May 18 1922	12-Oc	3	Jul 25 1922	2-Etz'nab	8
Mar 12 1922	10-Akbal	8	May 19 1922	13-Chuen	4	Jul 26 1922	3-Cauac	9
Mar 13 1922	11-Kan	9	May 20 1922	**1-Eb**	5	Jul 27 1922	4-Ahau	1
Mar 14 1922	12-Chicchan	1	May 21 1922	2-Ben	6	Jul 28 1922	5-*Imix*	2
Mar 15 1922	13-Cimi	2	May 22 1922	3-Ix	7	Jul 29 1922	6-Ik	3
Mar 16 1922	**1-Manik**	3	May 23 1922	4-Men	8	Jul 30 1922	7-Akbal	4
Mar 17 1922	2-Lamat	4	May 24 1922	5-Cib	9	Jul 31 1922	8-Kan	5
Mar 18 1922	3-Muluc	5	May 25 1922	6-Caban	1	Aug 1 1922	9-Chicchan	6
Mar 19 1922	4-Oc	6	May 26 1922	7-Etz'nab	2	Aug 2 1922	10-Cimi	7
Mar 20 1922	5-Chuen	7	May 27 1922	8-Cauac	3	Aug 3 1922	11-Manik	8
Mar 21 1922	6-Eb	8	May 28 1922	9-Ahau	4	Aug 4 1922	12-Lamat	9
Mar 22 1922	7-Ben	9	May 29 1922	10-*Imix*	5	Aug 5 1922	13-Muluc	1
Mar 23 1922	8-Ix	1	May 30 1922	11-Ik	6	Aug 6 1922	**1-Oc**	2
Mar 24 1922	9-Men	2	May 31 1922	12-Akbal	7	Aug 7 1922	2-Chuen	3
Mar 25 1922	10-Cib	3	Jun 1 1922	13-Kan	8	Aug 8 1922	3-Eb	4
Mar 26 1922	11-Caban	4	Jun 2 1922	**1-Chicchan**	9	Aug 9 1922	4-Ben	5
Mar 27 1922	12-Etz'nab	5	Jun 3 1922	2-Cimi	1	Aug 10 1922	5-Ix	6
Mar 28 1922	13-Cauac	6	Jun 4 1922	3-Manik	2	Aug 11 1922	6-Men	7
Mar 29 1922	**1-Ahau**	7	Jun 5 1922	4-Lamat	3	Aug 12 1922	7-Cib	8
Mar 30 1922	2-*Imix*	8	Jun 6 1922	5-Muluc	4	Aug 13 1922	8-Caban	9
Mar 31 1922	3-Ik	9	Jun 7 1922	6-Oc	5	Aug 14 1922	9-Etz'nab	1
Apr 1 1922	4-Akbal	1	Jun 8 1922	7-Chuen	6	Aug 15 1922	10-Cauac	2
Apr 2 1922	5-Kan	2	Jun 9 1922	8-Eb	7	Aug 16 1922	11-Ahau	3
Apr 3 1922	6-Chicchan	3	Jun 10 1922	9-Ben	8	Aug 17 1922	12-*Imix*	4
Apr 4 1922	7-Cimi	4	Jun 11 1922	10-Ix	9	Aug 18 1922	13-Ik	5
Apr 5 1922	8-Manik	5	Jun 12 1922	11-Men	1	Aug 19 1922	**1-Akbal**	6
Apr 6 1922	9-Lamat	6	Jun 13 1922	12-Cib	2	Aug 20 1922	2-Kan	7
Apr 7 1922	10-Muluc	7	Jun 14 1922	13-Caban	3	Aug 21 1922	3-Chicchan	8
Apr 8 1922	11-Oc	8	Jun 15 1922	**1-Etz'nab**	4	Aug 22 1922	4-Cimi	9
Apr 9 1922	12-Chuen	9	Jun 16 1922	2-Cauac	5	Aug 23 1922	5-Manik	1
Apr 10 1922	13-Eb	1	Jun 17 1922	3-Ahau	6	Aug 24 1922	6-Lamat	2
Apr 11 1922	**1-Ben**	2	Jun 18 1922	4-*Imix*	7	Aug 25 1922	7-Muluc	3
Apr 12 1922	2-Ix	3	Jun 19 1922	5-Ik	8	Aug 26 1922	8-Oc	4
Apr 13 1922	3-Men	4	Jun 20 1922	6-Akbal	9	Aug 27 1922	9-Chuen	5
Apr 14 1922	4-Cib	5	Jun 21 1922	7-Kan	1	Aug 28 1922	10-Eb	6
Apr 15 1922	5-Caban	6	Jun 22 1922	8-Chicchan	2	Aug 29 1922	11-Ben	7
Apr 16 1922	6-Etz'nab	7	Jun 23 1922	9-Cimi	3	Aug 30 1922	12-Ix	8
Apr 17 1922	7-Cauac	8	Jun 24 1922	10-Manik	4	Aug 31 1922	13-Men	9
Apr 18 1922	8-Ahau	9	Jun 25 1922	11-Lamat	5	Sep 1 1922	**1-Cib**	1
Apr 19 1922	9-*Imix*	1	Jun 26 1922	12-Muluc	6	Sep 2 1922	2-Caban	2
Apr 20 1922	10-Ik	2	Jun 27 1922	13-Oc	7	Sep 3 1922	3-Etz'nab	3
Apr 21 1922	11-Akbal	3	Jun 28 1922	**1-Chuen**	8	Sep 4 1922	4-Cauac	4
Apr 22 1922	12-Kan	4	Jun 29 1922	2-Eb	9	Sep 5 1922	5-Ahau	5
Apr 23 1922	13-Chicchan	5	Jun 30 1922	3-Ben	1	Sep 6 1922	6-*Imix*	6
Apr 24 1922	**1-Cimi**	6	Jul 1 1922	4-Ix	2	Sep 7 1922	7-Ik	7
Apr 25 1922	2-Manik	7	Jul 2 1922	5-Men	3	Sep 8 1922	8-Akbal	8
Apr 26 1922	3-Lamat	8	Jul 3 1922	6-Cib	4	Sep 9 1922	9-Kan	9
Apr 27 1922	4-Muluc	9	Jul 4 1922	7-Caban	5	Sep 10 1922	10-Chicchan	1
Apr 28 1922	5-Oc	1	Jul 5 1922	8-Etz'nab	6	Sep 11 1922	11-Cimi	2
Apr 29 1922	6-Chuen	2	Jul 6 1922	9-Cauac	7	Sep 12 1922	12-Manik	3
Apr 30 1922	7-Eb	3	Jul 7 1922	10-Ahau	8	Sep 13 1922	13-Lamat	4
May 1 1922	8-Ben	4	Jul 8 1922	11-*Imix*	9	Sep 14 1922	**1-Muluc**	5
May 2 1922	9-Ix	5	Jul 9 1922	12-Ik	1	Sep 15 1922	2-Oc	6
May 3 1922	10-Men	6	Jul 10 1922	13-Akbal	2	Sep 16 1922	3-Chuen	7
May 4 1922	11-Cib	7	Jul 11 1922	**1-Kan**	3	Sep 17 1922	4-Eb	8
May 5 1922	12-Caban	8	Jul 12 1922	2-Chicchan	4	Sep 18 1922	5-Ben	9

Date	Day-Sign	L	Date	Day-Sign	L	Date	Day-Sign	L
Sep 19 1922	6-Ix	1	Nov 26 1922	9-Ik	6	Feb 2 1923	12-Oc	2
Sep 20 1922	7-Men	2	Nov 27 1922	10-Akbal	7	Feb 3 1923	13-Chuen	3
Sep 21 1922	8-Cib	3	Nov 28 1922	11-Kan	8	Feb 4 1923	**1-Eb**	4
Sep 22 1922	9-Caban	4	Nov 29 1922	12-Chicchan	9	Feb 5 1923	2-Ben	5
Sep 23 1922	10-Etz'nab	5	Nov 30 1922	13-Cimi	1	Feb 6 1923	3-Ix	6
Sep 24 1922	11-Cauac	6	Dec 1 1922	**1-Manik**	2	Feb 7 1923	4-Men	7
Sep 25 1922	12-Ahau	7	Dec 2 1922	2-Lamat	3	Feb 8 1923	5-Cib	8
Sep 26 1922	*13-Imix*	8	Dec 3 1922	3-Muluc	4	Feb 9 1923	6-Caban	9
Sep 27 1922	**1-Ik**	9	Dec 4 1922	4-Oc	5	Feb 10 1923	7-Etz'nab	1
Sep 28 1922	2-Akbal	1	Dec 5 1922	5-Chuen	6	Feb 11 1923	8-Cauac	2
Sep 29 1922	3-Kan	2	Dec 6 1922	6-Eb	7	Feb 12 1923	9-Ahau	3
Sep 30 1922	4-Chicchan	3	Dec 7 1922	7-Ben	8	Feb 13 1923	*10-Imix*	4
Oct 1 1922	5-Cimi	4	Dec 8 1922	8-Ix	9	Feb 14 1923	11-Ik	5
Oct 2 1922	6-Manik	5	Dec 9 1922	9-Men	1	Feb 15 1923	12-Akbal	6
Oct 3 1922	7-Lamat	6	Dec 10 1922	10-Cib	2	Feb 16 1923	13-Kan	7
Oct 4 1922	8-Muluc	7	Dec 11 1922	11-Caban	3	Feb 17 1923	**1-Chicchan**	8
Oct 5 1922	9-Oc	8	Dec 12 1922	12-Etz'nab	4	Feb 18 1923	2-Cimi	9
Oct 6 1922	10-Chuen	9	Dec 13 1922	13-Cauac	5	Feb 19 1923	3-Manik	1
Oct 7 1922	11-Eb	1	Dec 14 1922	**1-Ahau**	6	Feb 20 1923	4-Lamat	2
Oct 8 1922	12-Ben	2	Dec 15 1922	*2-Imix*	7	Feb 21 1923	5-Muluc	3
Oct 9 1922	13-Ix	3	Dec 16 1922	3-Ik	8	Feb 22 1923	6-Oc	4
Oct 10 1922	**1-Men**	4	Dec 17 1922	4-Akbal	9	Feb 23 1923	7-Chuen	5
Oct 11 1922	2-Cib	5	Dec 18 1922	5-Kan	1	Feb 24 1923	8-Eb	6
Oct 12 1922	3-Caban	6	Dec 19 1922	6-Chicchan	2	Feb 25 1923	9-Ben	7
Oct 13 1922	4-Etz'nab	7	Dec 20 1922	7-Cimi	3	Feb 26 1923	10-Ix	8
Oct 14 1922	5-Cauac	8	Dec 21 1922	8-Manik	4	Feb 27 1923	11-Men	9
Oct 15 1922	6-Ahau	9	Dec 22 1922	9-Lamat	5	Feb 28 1923	12-Cib	1
Oct 16 1922	7-Imix	1	Dec 23 1922	10-Muluc	6	Mar 1 1923	13-Caban	2
Oct 17 1922	8-Ik	2	Dec 24 1922	11-Oc	7	Mar 2 1923	**1-Etz'nab**	3
Oct 18 1922	9-Akbal	3	Dec 25 1922	12-Chuen	8	Mar 3 1923	2-Cauac	4
Oct 19 1922	10-Kan	4	Dec 26 1922	13-Eb	9	Mar 4 1923	3-Ahau	5
Oct 20 1922	11-Chicchan	5	Dec 27 1922	**1-Ben**	1	Mar 5 1923	*4-Imix*	6
Oct 21 1922	12-Cimi	6	Dec 28 1922	2-Ix	2	Mar 6 1923	5-Ik	7
Oct 22 1922	13-Manik	7	Dec 29 1922	3-Men	3	Mar 7 1923	6-Akbal	8
Oct 23 1922	**1-Lamat**	8	Dec 30 1922	4-Cib	4	Mar 8 1923	7-Kan	9
Oct 24 1922	2-Muluc	9	Dec 31 1922	5-Caban	5	Mar 9 1923	8-Chicchan	1
Oct 25 1922	3-Oc	1	Jan 1 1923	6-Etz'nab	6	Mar 10 1923	9-Cimi	2
Oct 26 1922	4-Chuen	2	Jan 2 1923	7-Cauac	7	Mar 11 1923	10-Manik	3
Oct 27 1922	5-Eb	3	Jan 3 1923	8-Ahau	8	Mar 12 1923	11-Lamat	4
Oct 28 1922	6-Ben	4	Jan 4 1923	*9-Imix*	9	Mar 13 1923	12-Muluc	5
Oct 29 1922	7-Ix	5	Jan 5 1923	10-Ik	1	Mar 14 1923	13-Oc	6
Oct 30 1922	8-Men	6	Jan 6 1923	11-Akbal	2	Mar 15 1923	**1-Chuen**	7
Oct 31 1922	9-Cib	7	Jan 7 1923	12-Kan	3	Mar 16 1923	2-Eb	8
Nov 1 1922	10-Caban	8	Jan 8 1923	13-Chicchan	4	Mar 17 1923	3-Ben	9
Nov 2 1922	11-Etz'nab	9	Jan 9 1923	**1-Cimi**	5	Mar 18 1923	4-Ix	1
Nov 3 1922	12-Cauac	1	Jan 10 1923	2-Manik	6	Mar 19 1923	5-Men	2
Nov 4 1922	13-Ahau	2	Jan 11 1923	3-Lamat	7	Mar 20 1923	6-Cib	3
Nov 5 1922	**1-Imix**	3	Jan 12 1923	4-Muluc	8	Mar 21 1923	7-Caban	4
Nov 6 1922	2-Ik	4	Jan 13 1923	5-Oc	9	Mar 22 1923	8-Etz'nab	5
Nov 7 1922	3-Akbal	5	Jan 14 1923	6-Chuen	1	Mar 23 1923	9-Cauac	6
Nov 8 1922	4-Kan	6	Jan 15 1923	7-Eb	2	Mar 24 1923	10-Ahau	7
Nov 9 1922	5-Chicchan	7	Jan 16 1923	8-Ben	3	Mar 25 1923	*11-Imix*	8
Nov 10 1922	6-Cimi	8	Jan 17 1923	9-Ix	4	Mar 26 1923	12-Ik	9
Nov 11 1922	7-Manik	9	Jan 18 1923	10-Men	5	Mar 27 1923	13-Akbal	1
Nov 12 1922	8-Lamat	1	Jan 19 1923	11-Cib	6	Mar 28 1923	**1-Kan**	2
Nov 13 1922	9-Muluc	2	Jan 20 1923	12-Caban	7	Mar 29 1923	2-Chicchan	3
Nov 14 1922	10-Oc	3	Jan 21 1923	13-Etz'nab	8	Mar 30 1923	3-Cimi	4
Nov 15 1922	11-Chuen	4	Jan 22 1923	**1-Cauac**	9	Mar 31 1923	4-Manik	5
Nov 16 1922	12-Eb	5	Jan 23 1923	2-Ahau	1	Apr 1 1923	5-Lamat	6
Nov 17 1922	13-Ben	6	Jan 24 1923	*3-Imix*	2	Apr 2 1923	6-Muluc	7
Nov 18 1922	**1-Ix**	7	Jan 25 1923	4-Ik	3	Apr 3 1923	7-Oc	8
Nov 19 1922	2-Men	8	Jan 26 1923	5-Akbal	4	Apr 4 1923	8-Chuen	9
Nov 20 1922	3-Cib	9	Jan 27 1923	6-Kan	5	Apr 5 1923	9-Eb	1
Nov 21 1922	4-Caban	1	Jan 28 1923	7-Chicchan	6	Apr 6 1923	10-Ben	2
Nov 22 1922	5-Etz'nab	2	Jan 29 1923	8-Cimi	7	Apr 7 1923	11-Ix	3
Nov 23 1922	6-Cauac	3	Jan 30 1923	9-Manik	8	Apr 8 1923	12-Men	4
Nov 24 1922	7-Ahau	4	Jan 31 1923	10-Lamat	9	Apr 9 1923	13-Cib	5
Nov 25 1922	*8-Imix*	5	Feb 1 1923	11-Muluc	1	Apr 10 1923	**1-Caban**	6

Date	Day-Sign	L
Apr 11 1923	2-Etz'nab	7
Apr 12 1923	3-Cauac	8
Apr 13 1923	4-Ahau	9
Apr 14 1923	5-*Imix*	1
Apr 15 1923	6-Ik	2
Apr 16 1923	7-Akbal	3
Apr 17 1923	8-Kan	4
Apr 18 1923	9-Chicchan	5
Apr 19 1923	10-Cimi	6
Apr 20 1923	11-Manik	7
Apr 21 1923	12-Lamat	8
Apr 22 1923	13-Muluc	9
Apr 23 1923	**1-Oc**	1
Apr 24 1923	2-Chuen	2
Apr 25 1923	3-Eb	3
Apr 26 1923	4-Ben	4
Apr 27 1923	5-Ix	5
Apr 28 1923	6-Men	6
Apr 29 1923	7-Cib	7
Apr 30 1923	8-Caban	8
May 1 1923	9-Etz'nab	9
May 2 1923	10-Cauac	1
May 3 1923	11-Ahau	2
May 4 1923	12-*Imix*	3
May 5 1923	13-Ik	4
May 6 1923	**1-Akbal**	5
May 7 1923	2-Kan	6
May 8 1923	3-Chicchan	7
May 9 1923	4-Cimi	8
May 10 1923	5-Manik	9
May 11 1923	6-Lamat	1
May 12 1923	7-Muluc	2
May 13 1923	8-Oc	3
May 14 1923	9-Chuen	4
May 15 1923	10-Eb	5
May 16 1923	11-Ben	6
May 17 1923	12-Ix	7
May 18 1923	13-Men	8
May 19 1923	**1-Cib**	9
May 20 1923	2-Caban	1
May 21 1923	3-Etz'nab	2
May 22 1923	4-Cauac	3
May 23 1923	5-Ahau	4
May 24 1923	6-*Imix*	5
May 25 1923	7-Ik	6
May 26 1923	8-Akbal	7
May 27 1923	9-Kan	8
May 28 1923	10-Chicchan	9
May 29 1923	11-Cimi	1
May 30 1923	12-Manik	2
May 31 1923	13-Lamat	3
Jun 1 1923	**1-Muluc**	4
Jun 2 1923	2-Oc	5
Jun 3 1923	3-Chuen	6
Jun 4 1923	4-Eb	7
Jun 5 1923	5-Ben	8
Jun 6 1923	6-Ix	9
Jun 7 1923	7-Men	1
Jun 8 1923	8-Cib	2
Jun 9 1923	9-Caban	3
Jun 10 1923	10-Etz'nab	4
Jun 11 1923	11-Cauac	5
Jun 12 1923	12-Ahau	6
Jun 13 1923	13-*Imix*	7
Jun 14 1923	**1-Ik**	8
Jun 15 1923	2-Akbal	9
Jun 16 1923	3-Kan	1
Jun 17 1923	4-Chicchan	2

Date	Day-Sign	L
Jun 18 1923	5-Cimi	3
Jun 19 1923	6-Manik	4
Jun 20 1923	7-Lamat	5
Jun 21 1923	8-Muluc	6
Jun 22 1923	9-Oc	7
Jun 23 1923	10-Chuen	8
Jun 24 1923	11-Eb	9
Jun 25 1923	12-Ben	1
Jun 26 1923	13-Ix	2
Jun 27 1923	**1-Men**	3
Jun 28 1923	2-Cib	4
Jun 29 1923	3-Caban	5
Jun 30 1923	4-Etz'nab	6
Jul 1 1923	5-Cauac	7
Jul 2 1923	6-Ahau	8
Jul 3 1923	7-*Imix*	9
Jul 4 1923	8-Ik	1
Jul 5 1923	9-Akbal	2
Jul 6 1923	10-Kan	3
Jul 7 1923	11-Chicchan	4
Jul 8 1923	12-Cimi	5
Jul 9 1923	13-Manik	6
Jul 10 1923	**1-Lamat**	7
Jul 11 1923	2-Muluc	8
Jul 12 1923	3-Oc	9
Jul 13 1923	4-Chuen	1
Jul 14 1923	5-Eb	2
Jul 15 1923	6-Ben	3
Jul 16 1923	7-Ix	4
Jul 17 1923	8-Men	5
Jul 18 1923	9-Cib	6
Jul 19 1923	10-Caban	7
Jul 20 1923	11-Etz'nab	8
Jul 21 1923	12-Cauac	9
Jul 22 1923	13-Ahau	1
Jul 23 1923	**1-Imix**	2
Jul 24 1923	2-Ik	3
Jul 25 1923	3-Akbal	4
Jul 26 1923	4-Kan	5
Jul 27 1923	5-Chicchan	6
Jul 28 1923	6-Cimi	7
Jul 29 1923	7-Manik	8
Jul 30 1923	8-Lamat	9
Jul 31 1923	9-Muluc	1
Aug 1 1923	10-Oc	2
Aug 2 1923	11-Chuen	3
Aug 3 1923	12-Eb	4
Aug 4 1923	13-Ben	5
Aug 5 1923	**1-Ix**	6
Aug 6 1923	2-Men	7
Aug 7 1923	3-Cib	8
Aug 8 1923	4-Caban	9
Aug 9 1923	5-Etz'nab	1
Aug 10 1923	6-Cauac	2
Aug 11 1923	7-Ahau	3
Aug 12 1923	8-*Imix*	4
Aug 13 1923	9-Ik	5
Aug 14 1923	10-Akbal	6
Aug 15 1923	11-Kan	7
Aug 16 1923	12-Chicchan	8
Aug 17 1923	13-Cimi	9
Aug 18 1923	**1-Manik**	1
Aug 19 1923	2-Lamat	2
Aug 20 1923	3-Muluc	3
Aug 21 1923	4-Oc	4
Aug 22 1923	5-Chuen	5
Aug 23 1923	6-Eb	6
Aug 24 1923	7-Ben	7

Date	Day-Sign	L
Aug 25 1923	8-Ix	8
Aug 26 1923	9-Men	9
Aug 27 1923	10-Cib	1
Aug 28 1923	11-Caban	2
Aug 29 1923	12-Etz'nab	3
Aug 30 1923	13-Cauac	4
Aug 31 1923	**1-Ahau**	5
Sep 1 1923	2-*Imix*	6
Sep 2 1923	3-Ik	7
Sep 3 1923	4-Akbal	8
Sep 4 1923	5-Kan	9
Sep 5 1923	6-Chicchan	1
Sep 6 1923	7-Cimi	2
Sep 7 1923	8-Manik	3
Sep 8 1923	9-Lamat	4
Sep 9 1923	10-Muluc	5
Sep 10 1923	11-Oc	6
Sep 11 1923	12-Chuen	7
Sep 12 1923	13-Eb	8
Sep 13 1923	**1-Ben**	9
Sep 14 1923	2-Ix	1
Sep 15 1923	3-Men	2
Sep 16 1923	4-Cib	3
Sep 17 1923	5-Caban	4
Sep 18 1923	6-Etz'nab	5
Sep 19 1923	7-Cauac	6
Sep 20 1923	8-Ahau	7
Sep 21 1923	9-*Imix*	8
Sep 22 1923	10-Ik	9
Sep 23 1923	11-Akbal	1
Sep 24 1923	12-Kan	2
Sep 25 1923	13-Chicchan	3
Sep 26 1923	**1-Cimi**	4
Sep 27 1923	2-Manik	5
Sep 28 1923	3-Lamat	6
Sep 29 1923	4-Muluc	7
Sep 30 1923	5-Oc	8
Oct 1 1923	6-Chuen	9
Oct 2 1923	7-Eb	1
Oct 3 1923	8-Ben	2
Oct 4 1923	9-Ix	3
Oct 5 1923	10-Men	4
Oct 6 1923	11-Cib	5
Oct 7 1923	12-Caban	6
Oct 8 1923	13-Etz'nab	7
Oct 9 1923	**1-Cauac**	8
Oct 10 1923	2-Ahau	9
Oct 11 1923	3-*Imix*	1
Oct 12 1923	4-Ik	2
Oct 13 1923	5-Akbal	3
Oct 14 1923	6-Kan	4
Oct 15 1923	7-Chicchan	5
Oct 16 1923	8-Cimi	6
Oct 17 1923	9-Manik	7
Oct 18 1923	10-Lamat	8
Oct 19 1923	11-Muluc	9
Oct 20 1923	12-Oc	1
Oct 21 1923	13-Chuen	2
Oct 22 1923	**1-Eb**	3
Oct 23 1923	2-Ben	4
Oct 24 1923	3-Ix	5
Oct 25 1923	4-Men	6
Oct 26 1923	5-Cib	7
Oct 27 1923	6-Caban	8
Oct 28 1923	7-Etz'nab	9
Oct 29 1923	8-Cauac	1
Oct 30 1923	9-Ahau	2
Oct 31 1923	10-*Imix*	3

Date	Day-Sign	L
Nov 1 1923	11-Ik	4
Nov 2 1923	12-Akbal	5
Nov 3 1923	13-Kan	6
Nov 4 1923	**1-Chicchan**	7
Nov 5 1923	2-Cimi	8
Nov 6 1923	3-Manik	9
Nov 7 1923	4-Lamat	1
Nov 8 1923	5-Muluc	2
Nov 9 1923	6-Oc	3
Nov 10 1923	7-Chuen	4
Nov 11 1923	8-Eb	5
Nov 12 1923	9-Ben	6
Nov 13 1923	10-Ix	7
Nov 14 1923	11-Men	8
Nov 15 1923	12-Cib	9
Nov 16 1923	13-Caban	1
Nov 17 1923	**1-Etz'nab**	2
Nov 18 1923	2-Cauac	3
Nov 19 1923	3-Ahau	4
Nov 20 1923	*4-Imix*	5
Nov 21 1923	5-Ik	6
Nov 22 1923	6-Akbal	7
Nov 23 1923	7-Kan	8
Nov 24 1923	8-Chicchan	9
Nov 25 1923	9-Cimi	1
Nov 26 1923	10-Manik	2
Nov 27 1923	11-Lamat	3
Nov 28 1923	12-Muluc	4
Nov 29 1923	13-Oc	5
Nov 30 1923	**1-Chuen**	6
Dec 1 1923	2-Eb	7
Dec 2 1923	3-Ben	8
Dec 3 1923	4-Ix	9
Dec 4 1923	5-Men	1
Dec 5 1923	6-Cib	2
Dec 6 1923	7-Caban	3
Dec 7 1923	8-Etz'nab	4
Dec 8 1923	9-Cauac	5
Dec 9 1923	10-Ahau	6
Dec 10 1923	*11-Imix*	7
Dec 11 1923	12-Ik	8
Dec 12 1923	13-Akbal	9
Dec 13 1923	**1-Kan**	1
Dec 14 1923	2-Chicchan	2
Dec 15 1923	3-Cimi	3
Dec 16 1923	4-Manik	4
Dec 17 1923	5-Lamat	5
Dec 18 1923	6-Muluc	6
Dec 19 1923	7-Oc	7
Dec 20 1923	8-Chuen	8
Dec 21 1923	9-Eb	9
Dec 22 1923	10-Ben	1
Dec 23 1923	11-Ix	2
Dec 24 1923	12-Men	3
Dec 25 1923	13-Cib	4
Dec 26 1923	**1-Caban**	5
Dec 27 1923	2-Etz'nab	6
Dec 28 1923	3-Cauac	7
Dec 29 1923	4-Ahau	8
Dec 30 1923	*5-Imix*	9
Dec 31 1923	6-Ik	1
Jan 1 1924	7-Akbal	2
Jan 2 1924	8-Kan	3
Jan 3 1924	9-Chicchan	4
Jan 4 1924	10-Cimi	5
Jan 5 1924	11-Manik	6
Jan 6 1924	12-Lamat	7
Jan 7 1924	13-Muluc	8

Date	Day-Sign	L
Jan 8 1924	**1-Oc**	9
Jan 9 1924	2-Chuen	1
Jan 10 1924	3-Eb	2
Jan 11 1924	4-Ben	3
Jan 12 1924	5-Ix	4
Jan 13 1924	6-Men	5
Jan 14 1924	7-Cib	6
Jan 15 1924	8-Caban	7
Jan 16 1924	9-Etz'nab	8
Jan 17 1924	10-Cauac	9
Jan 18 1924	11-Ahau	1
Jan 19 1924	*12-Imix*	2
Jan 20 1924	13-Ik	3
Jan 21 1924	**1-Akbal**	4
Jan 22 1924	2-Kan	5
Jan 23 1924	3-Chicchan	6
Jan 24 1924	4-Cimi	7
Jan 25 1924	5-Manik	8
Jan 26 1924	6-Lamat	9
Jan 27 1924	7-Muluc	1
Jan 28 1924	8-Oc	2
Jan 29 1924	9-Chuen	3
Jan 30 1924	10-Eb	4
Jan 31 1924	11-Ben	5
Feb 1 1924	12-Ix	6
Feb 2 1924	13-Men	7
Feb 3 1924	**1-Cib**	8
Feb 4 1924	2-Caban	9
Feb 5 1924	3-Etz'nab	1
Feb 6 1924	4-Cauac	2
Feb 7 1924	5-Ahau	3
Feb 8 1924	*6-Imix*	4
Feb 9 1924	7-Ik	5
Feb 10 1924	8-Akbal	6
Feb 11 1924	9-Kan	7
Feb 12 1924	10-Chicchan	8
Feb 13 1924	11-Cimi	9
Feb 14 1924	12-Manik	1
Feb 15 1924	13-Lamat	2
Feb 16 1924	**1-Muluc**	3
Feb 17 1924	2-Oc	4
Feb 18 1924	3-Chuen	5
Feb 19 1924	4-Eb	6
Feb 20 1924	5-Ben	7
Feb 21 1924	6-Ix	8
Feb 22 1924	7-Men	9
Feb 23 1924	8-Cib	1
Feb 24 1924	9-Caban	2
Feb 25 1924	10-Etz'nab	3
Feb 26 1924	11-Cauac	4
Feb 27 1924	12-Ahau	5
Feb 28 1924	*13-Imix*	6
Feb 29 1924	**1-Ik**	7
Mar 1 1924	2-Akbal	8
Mar 2 1924	3-Kan	9
Mar 3 1924	4-Chicchan	1
Mar 4 1924	5-Cimi	2
Mar 5 1924	6-Manik	3
Mar 6 1924	7-Lamat	4
Mar 7 1924	8-Muluc	5
Mar 8 1924	9-Oc	6
Mar 9 1924	10-Chuen	7
Mar 10 1924	11-Eb	8
Mar 11 1924	12-Ben	9
Mar 12 1924	13-Ix	1
Mar 13 1924	**1-Men**	2
Mar 14 1924	2-Cib	3
Mar 15 1924	3-Caban	4

Date	Day-Sign	L
Mar 16 1924	4-Etz'nab	5
Mar 17 1924	5-Cauac	6
Mar 18 1924	6-Ahau	7
Mar 19 1924	*7-Imix*	8
Mar 20 1924	8-Ik	9
Mar 21 1924	9-Akbal	1
Mar 22 1924	10-Kan	2
Mar 23 1924	11-Chicchan	3
Mar 24 1924	12-Cimi	4
Mar 25 1924	13-Manik	5
Mar 26 1924	**1-Lamat**	6
Mar 27 1924	2-Muluc	7
Mar 28 1924	3-Oc	8
Mar 29 1924	4-Chuen	9
Mar 30 1924	5-Eb	1
Mar 31 1924	6-Ben	2
Apr 1 1924	7-Ix	3
Apr 2 1924	8-Men	4
Apr 3 1924	9-Cib	5
Apr 4 1924	10-Caban	6
Apr 5 1924	11-Etz'nab	7
Apr 6 1924	12-Cauac	8
Apr 7 1924	13-Ahau	9
Apr 8 1924	**1-Imix**	1
Apr 9 1924	2-Ik	2
Apr 10 1924	3-Akbal	3
Apr 11 1924	4-Kan	4
Apr 12 1924	5-Chicchan	5
Apr 13 1924	6-Cimi	6
Apr 14 1924	7-Manik	7
Apr 15 1924	8-Lamat	8
Apr 16 1924	9-Muluc	9
Apr 17 1924	10-Oc	1
Apr 18 1924	11-Chuen	2
Apr 19 1924	12-Eb	3
Apr 20 1924	13-Ben	4
Apr 21 1924	**1-Ix**	5
Apr 22 1924	2-Men	6
Apr 23 1924	3-Cib	7
Apr 24 1924	4-Caban	8
Apr 25 1924	5-Etz'nab	9
Apr 26 1924	6-Cauac	1
Apr 27 1924	7-Ahau	2
Apr 28 1924	*8-Imix*	3
Apr 29 1924	9-Ik	4
Apr 30 1924	10-Akbal	5
May 1 1924	11-Kan	6
May 2 1924	12-Chicchan	7
May 3 1924	13-Cimi	8
May 4 1924	**1-Manik**	9
May 5 1924	2-Lamat	1
May 6 1924	3-Muluc	2
May 7 1924	4-Oc	3
May 8 1924	5-Chuen	4
May 9 1924	6-Eb	5
May 10 1924	7-Ben	6
May 11 1924	8-Ix	7
May 12 1924	9-Men	8
May 13 1924	10-Cib	9
May 14 1924	11-Caban	1
May 15 1924	12-Etz'nab	2
May 16 1924	13-Cauac	3
May 17 1924	**1-Ahau**	4
May 18 1924	*2-Imix*	5
May 19 1924	3-Ik	6
May 20 1924	4-Akbal	7
May 21 1924	5-Kan	8
May 22 1924	6-Chicchan	9

Date	Day-Sign	L
May 23 1924	7-Cimi	1
May 24 1924	8-Manik	2
May 25 1924	9-Lamat	3
May 26 1924	10-Muluc	4
May 27 1924	11-Oc	5
May 28 1924	12-Chuen	6
May 29 1924	13-Eb	7
May 30 1924	**1-Ben**	8
May 31 1924	2-Ix	9
Jun 1 1924	3-Men	1
Jun 2 1924	4-Cib	2
Jun 3 1924	5-Caban	3
Jun 4 1924	6-Etz'nab	4
Jun 5 1924	7-Cauac	5
Jun 6 1924	8-Ahau	6
Jun 7 1924	*9-Imix*	7
Jun 8 1924	10-Ik	8
Jun 9 1924	11-Akbal	9
Jun 10 1924	12-Kan	1
Jun 11 1924	13-Chicchan	2
Jun 12 1924	**1-Cimi**	3
Jun 13 1924	2-Manik	4
Jun 14 1924	3-Lamat	5
Jun 15 1924	4-Muluc	6
Jun 16 1924	5-Oc	7
Jun 17 1924	6-Chuen	8
Jun 18 1924	7-Eb	9
Jun 19 1924	8-Ben	1
Jun 20 1924	9-Ix	2
Jun 21 1924	10-Men	3
Jun 22 1924	11-Cib	4
Jun 23 1924	12-Caban	5
Jun 24 1924	13-Etz'nab	6
Jun 25 1924	**1-Cauac**	7
Jun 26 1924	2-Ahau	8
Jun 27 1924	*3-Imix*	9
Jun 28 1924	4-Ik	1
Jun 29 1924	5-Akbal	2
Jun 30 1924	6-Kan	3
Jul 1 1924	7-Chicchan	4
Jul 2 1924	8-Cimi	5
Jul 3 1924	9-Manik	6
Jul 4 1924	10-Lamat	7
Jul 5 1924	11-Muluc	8
Jul 6 1924	12-Oc	9
Jul 7 1924	13-Chuen	1
Jul 8 1924	**1-Eb**	2
Jul 9 1924	2-Ben	3
Jul 10 1924	3-Ix	4
Jul 11 1924	4-Men	5
Jul 12 1924	5-Cib	6
Jul 13 1924	6-Caban	7
Jul 14 1924	7-Etz'nab	8
Jul 15 1924	8-Cauac	9
Jul 16 1924	9-Ahau	1
Jul 17 1924	*10-Imix*	2
Jul 18 1924	11-Ik	3
Jul 19 1924	12-Akbal	4
Jul 20 1924	13-Kan	5
Jul 21 1924	**1-Chicchan**	6
Jul 22 1924	2-Cimi	7
Jul 23 1924	3-Manik	8
Jul 24 1924	4-Lamat	9
Jul 25 1924	5-Muluc	1
Jul 26 1924	6-Oc	2
Jul 27 1924	7-Chuen	3
Jul 28 1924	8-Eb	4
Jul 29 1924	9-Ben	5

Date	Day-Sign	L
Jul 30 1924	10-Ix	6
Jul 31 1924	11-Men	7
Aug 1 1924	12-Cib	8
Aug 2 1924	13-Caban	9
Aug 3 1924	**1-Etz'nab**	1
Aug 4 1924	2-Cauac	2
Aug 5 1924	3-Ahau	3
Aug 6 1924	*4-Imix*	4
Aug 7 1924	5-Ik	5
Aug 8 1924	6-Akbal	6
Aug 9 1924	7-Kan	7
Aug 10 1924	8-Chicchan	8
Aug 11 1924	9-Cimi	9
Aug 12 1924	10-Manik	1
Aug 13 1924	11-Lamat	2
Aug 14 1924	12-Muluc	3
Aug 15 1924	13-Oc	4
Aug 16 1924	**1-Chuen**	5
Aug 17 1924	2-Eb	6
Aug 18 1924	3-Ben	7
Aug 19 1924	4-Ix	8
Aug 20 1924	5-Men	9
Aug 21 1924	6-Cib	1
Aug 22 1924	7-Caban	2
Aug 23 1924	8-Etz'nab	3
Aug 24 1924	9-Cauac	4
Aug 25 1924	10-Ahau	5
Aug 26 1924	*11-Imix*	6
Aug 27 1924	12-Ik	7
Aug 28 1924	13-Akbal	8
Aug 29 1924	**1-Kan**	9
Aug 30 1924	2-Chicchan	1
Aug 31 1924	3-Cimi	2
Sep 1 1924	4-Manik	3
Sep 2 1924	5-Lamat	4
Sep 3 1924	6-Muluc	5
Sep 4 1924	7-Oc	6
Sep 5 1924	8-Chuen	7
Sep 6 1924	9-Eb	8
Sep 7 1924	10-Ben	9
Sep 8 1924	11-Ix	1
Sep 9 1924	12-Men	2
Sep 10 1924	13-Cib	3
Sep 11 1924	**1-Caban**	4
Sep 12 1924	2-Etz'nab	5
Sep 13 1924	3-Cauac	6
Sep 14 1924	4-Ahau	7
Sep 15 1924	*5-Imix*	8
Sep 16 1924	6-Ik	9
Sep 17 1924	7-Akbal	1
Sep 18 1924	8-Kan	2
Sep 19 1924	9-Chicchan	3
Sep 20 1924	10-Cimi	4
Sep 21 1924	11-Manik	5
Sep 22 1924	12-Lamat	6
Sep 23 1924	13-Muluc	7
Sep 24 1924	**1-Oc**	8
Sep 25 1924	2-Chuen	9
Sep 26 1924	3-Eb	1
Sep 27 1924	4-Ben	2
Sep 28 1924	5-Ix	3
Sep 29 1924	6-Men	4
Sep 30 1924	7-Cib	5
Oct 1 1924	8-Caban	6
Oct 2 1924	9-Etz'nab	7
Oct 3 1924	10-Cauac	8
Oct 4 1924	11-Ahau	9
Oct 5 1924	*12-Imix*	1

Date	Day-Sign	L
Oct 6 1924	13-Ik	2
Oct 7 1924	**1-Akbal**	3
Oct 8 1924	2-Kan	4
Oct 9 1924	3-Chicchan	5
Oct 10 1924	4-Cimi	6
Oct 11 1924	5-Manik	7
Oct 12 1924	6-Lamat	8
Oct 13 1924	7-Muluc	9
Oct 14 1924	8-Oc	1
Oct 15 1924	9-Chuen	2
Oct 16 1924	10-Eb	3
Oct 17 1924	11-Ben	4
Oct 18 1924	12-Ix	5
Oct 19 1924	13-Men	6
Oct 20 1924	**1-Cib**	7
Oct 21 1924	2-Caban	8
Oct 22 1924	3-Etz'nab	9
Oct 23 1924	4-Cauac	1
Oct 24 1924	5-Ahau	2
Oct 25 1924	*6-Imix*	3
Oct 26 1924	7-Ik	4
Oct 27 1924	8-Akbal	5
Oct 28 1924	9-Kan	6
Oct 29 1924	10-Chicchan	7
Oct 30 1924	11-Cimi	8
Oct 31 1924	12-Manik	9
Nov 1 1924	13-Lamat	1
Nov 2 1924	**1-Muluc**	2
Nov 3 1924	2-Oc	3
Nov 4 1924	3-Chuen	4
Nov 5 1924	4-Eb	5
Nov 6 1924	5-Ben	6
Nov 7 1924	6-Ix	7
Nov 8 1924	7-Men	8
Nov 9 1924	8-Cib	9
Nov 10 1924	9-Caban	1
Nov 11 1924	10-Etz'nab	2
Nov 12 1924	11-Cauac	3
Nov 13 1924	12-Ahau	4
Nov 14 1924	*13-Imix*	5
Nov 15 1924	**1-Ik**	6
Nov 16 1924	2-Akbal	7
Nov 17 1924	3-Kan	8
Nov 18 1924	4-Chicchan	9
Nov 19 1924	5-Cimi	1
Nov 20 1924	6-Manik	2
Nov 21 1924	7-Lamat	3
Nov 22 1924	8-Muluc	4
Nov 23 1924	9-Oc	5
Nov 24 1924	10-Chuen	6
Nov 25 1924	11-Eb	7
Nov 26 1924	12-Ben	8
Nov 27 1924	13-Ix	9
Nov 28 1924	**1-Men**	1
Nov 29 1924	2-Cib	2
Nov 30 1924	3-Caban	3
Dec 1 1924	4-Etz'nab	4
Dec 2 1924	5-Cauac	5
Dec 3 1924	6-Ahau	6
Dec 4 1924	*7-Imix*	7
Dec 5 1924	8-Ik	8
Dec 6 1924	9-Akbal	9
Dec 7 1924	10-Kan	1
Dec 8 1924	11-Chicchan	2
Dec 9 1924	12-Cimi	3
Dec 10 1924	13-Manik	4
Dec 11 1924	**1-Lamat**	5
Dec 12 1924	2-Muluc	6

Date	Day-Sign	L	Date	Day-Sign	L	Date	Day-Sign	L
Dec 13 1924	3-Oc	7	Feb 19 1925	6-Etz'nab	3	Apr 28 1925	9-Cimi	8
Dec 14 1924	4-Chuen	8	Feb 20 1925	7-Cauac	4	Apr 29 1925	10-Manik	9
Dec 15 1924	5-Eb	9	Feb 21 1925	8-Ahau	5	Apr 30 1925	11-Lamat	1
Dec 16 1924	6-Ben	1	Feb 22 1925	9-Imix	6	May 1 1925	12-Muluc	2
Dec 17 1924	7-Ix	2	Feb 23 1925	10-Ik	7	May 2 1925	13-Oc	3
Dec 18 1924	8-Men	3	Feb 24 1925	11-Akbal	8	May 3 1925	1-Chuen	4
Dec 19 1924	9-Cib	4	Feb 25 1925	12-Kan	9	May 4 1925	2-Eb	5
Dec 20 1924	10-Caban	5	Feb 26 1925	13-Chicchan	1	May 5 1925	3-Ben	6
Dec 21 1924	11-Etz'nab	6	Feb 27 1925	1-Cimi	2	May 6 1925	4-Ix	7
Dec 22 1924	12-Cauac	7	Feb 28 1925	2-Manik	3	May 7 1925	5-Men	8
Dec 23 1924	13-Ahau	8	Mar 1 1925	3-Lamat	4	May 8 1925	6-Cib	9
Dec 24 1924	1-Imix	9	Mar 2 1925	4-Muluc	5	May 9 1925	7-Caban	1
Dec 25 1924	2-Ik	1	Mar 3 1925	5-Oc	6	May 10 1925	8-Etz'nab	2
Dec 26 1924	3-Akbal	2	Mar 4 1925	6-Chuen	7	May 11 1925	9-Cauac	3
Dec 27 1924	4-Kan	3	Mar 5 1925	7-Eb	8	May 12 1925	10-Ahau	4
Dec 28 1924	5-Chicchan	4	Mar 6 1925	8-Ben	9	May 13 1925	11-Imix	5
Dec 29 1924	6-Cimi	5	Mar 7 1925	9-Ix	1	May 14 1925	12-Ik	6
Dec 30 1924	7-Manik	6	Mar 8 1925	10-Men	2	May 15 1925	13-Akbal	7
Dec 31 1924	8-Lamat	7	Mar 9 1925	11-Cib	3	May 16 1925	1-Kan	8
Jan 1 1925	9-Muluc	8	Mar 10 1925	12-Caban	4	May 17 1925	2-Chicchan	9
Jan 2 1925	10-Oc	9	Mar 11 1925	13-Etz'nab	5	May 18 1925	3-Cimi	1
Jan 3 1925	11-Chuen	1	Mar 12 1925	1-Cauac	6	May 19 1925	4-Manik	2
Jan 4 1925	12-Eb	2	Mar 13 1925	2-Ahau	7	May 20 1925	5-Lamat	3
Jan 5 1925	13-Ben	3	Mar 14 1925	3-Imix	8	May 21 1925	6-Muluc	4
Jan 6 1925	1-Ix	4	Mar 15 1925	4-Ik	9	May 22 1925	7-Oc	5
Jan 7 1925	2-Men	5	Mar 16 1925	5-Akbal	1	May 23 1925	8-Chuen	6
Jan 8 1925	3-Cib	6	Mar 17 1925	6-Kan	2	May 24 1925	9-Eb	7
Jan 9 1925	4-Caban	7	Mar 18 1925	7-Chicchan	3	May 25 1925	10-Ben	8
Jan 10 1925	5-Etz'nab	8	Mar 19 1925	8-Cimi	4	May 26 1925	11-Ix	9
Jan 11 1925	6-Cauac	9	Mar 20 1925	9-Manik	5	May 27 1925	12-Men	1
Jan 12 1925	7-Ahau	1	Mar 21 1925	10-Lamat	6	May 28 1925	13-Cib	2
Jan 13 1925	8-Imix	2	Mar 22 1925	11-Muluc	7	May 29 1925	1-Caban	3
Jan 14 1925	9-Ik	3	Mar 23 1925	12-Oc	8	May 30 1925	2-Etz'nab	4
Jan 15 1925	10-Akbal	4	Mar 24 1925	13-Chuen	9	May 31 1925	3-Cauac	5
Jan 16 1925	11-Kan	5	Mar 25 1925	1-Eb	1	Jun 1 1925	4-Ahau	6
Jan 17 1925	12-Chicchan	6	Mar 26 1925	2-Ben	2	Jun 2 1925	5-Imix	7
Jan 18 1925	13-Cimi	7	Mar 27 1925	3-Ix	3	Jun 3 1925	6-Ik	8
Jan 19 1925	1-Manik	8	Mar 28 1925	4-Men	4	Jun 4 1925	7-Akbal	9
Jan 20 1925	2-Lamat	9	Mar 29 1925	5-Cib	5	Jun 5 1925	8-Kan	1
Jan 21 1925	3-Muluc	1	Mar 30 1925	6-Caban	6	Jun 6 1925	9-Chicchan	2
Jan 22 1925	4-Oc	2	Mar 31 1925	7-Etz'nab	7	Jun 7 1925	10-Cimi	3
Jan 23 1925	5-Chuen	3	Apr 1 1925	8-Cauac	8	Jun 8 1925	11-Manik	4
Jan 24 1925	6-Eb	4	Apr 2 1925	9-Ahau	9	Jun 9 1925	12-Lamat	5
Jan 25 1925	7-Ben	5	Apr 3 1925	10-Imix	1	Jun 10 1925	13-Muluc	6
Jan 26 1925	8-Ix	6	Apr 4 1925	11-Ik	2	Jun 11 1925	1-Oc	7
Jan 27 1925	9-Men	7	Apr 5 1925	12-Akbal	3	Jun 12 1925	2-Chuen	8
Jan 28 1925	10-Cib	8	Apr 6 1925	13-Kan	4	Jun 13 1925	3-Eb	9
Jan 29 1925	11-Caban	9	Apr 7 1925	1-Chicchan	5	Jun 14 1925	4-Ben	1
Jan 30 1925	12-Etz'nab	1	Apr 8 1925	2-Cimi	6	Jun 15 1925	5-Ix	2
Jan 31 1925	13-Cauac	2	Apr 9 1925	3-Manik	7	Jun 16 1925	6-Men	3
Feb 1 1925	1-Ahau	3	Apr 10 1925	4-Lamat	8	Jun 17 1925	7-Cib	4
Feb 2 1925	2-Imix	4	Apr 11 1925	5-Muluc	9	Jun 18 1925	8-Caban	5
Feb 3 1925	3-Ik	5	Apr 12 1925	6-Oc	1	Jun 19 1925	9-Etz'nab	6
Feb 4 1925	4-Akbal	6	Apr 13 1925	7-Chuen	2	Jun 20 1925	10-Cauac	7
Feb 5 1925	5-Kan	7	Apr 14 1925	8-Eb	3	Jun 21 1925	11-Ahau	8
Feb 6 1925	6-Chicchan	8	Apr 15 1925	9-Ben	4	Jun 22 1925	12-Imix	9
Feb 7 1925	7-Cimi	9	Apr 16 1925	10-Ix	5	Jun 23 1925	13-Ik	1
Feb 8 1925	8-Manik	1	Apr 17 1925	11-Men	6	Jun 24 1925	1-Akbal	2
Feb 9 1925	9-Lamat	2	Apr 18 1925	12-Cib	7	Jun 25 1925	2-Kan	3
Feb 10 1925	10-Muluc	3	Apr 19 1925	13-Caban	8	Jun 26 1925	3-Chicchan	4
Feb 11 1925	11-Oc	4	Apr 20 1925	1-Etz'nab	9	Jun 27 1925	4-Cimi	5
Feb 12 1925	12-Chuen	5	Apr 21 1925	2-Cauac	1	Jun 28 1925	5-Manik	6
Feb 13 1925	13-Eb	6	Apr 22 1925	3-Ahau	2	Jun 29 1925	6-Lamat	7
Feb 14 1925	1-Ben	7	Apr 23 1925	4-Imix	3	Jun 30 1925	7-Muluc	8
Feb 15 1925	2-Ix	8	Apr 24 1925	5-Ik	4	Jul 1 1925	8-Oc	9
Feb 16 1925	3-Men	9	Apr 25 1925	6-Akbal	5	Jul 2 1925	9-Chuen	1
Feb 17 1925	4-Cib	1	Apr 26 1925	7-Kan	6	Jul 3 1925	10-Eb	2
Feb 18 1925	5-Caban	2	Apr 27 1925	8-Chicchan	7	Jul 4 1925	11-Ben	3

Date	Day-Sign	L	Date	Day-Sign	L	Date	Day-Sign	L
Jul 5 1925	12-Ix	4	Sep 11 1925	2-Ik	9	Nov 18 1925	5-Oc	5
Jul 6 1925	13-Men	5	Sep 12 1925	3-Akbal	1	Nov 19 1925	6-Chuen	6
Jul 7 1925	**1-Cib**	6	Sep 13 1925	4-Kan	2	Nov 20 1925	7-Eb	7
Jul 8 1925	2-Caban	7	Sep 14 1925	5-Chicchan	3	Nov 21 1925	8-Ben	8
Jul 9 1925	3-Etz'nab	8	Sep 15 1925	6-Cimi	4	Nov 22 1925	9-Ix	9
Jul 10 1925	4-Cauac	9	Sep 16 1925	7-Manik	5	Nov 23 1925	10-Men	1
Jul 11 1925	5-Ahau	1	Sep 17 1925	8-Lamat	6	Nov 24 1925	11-Cib	2
Jul 12 1925	*6-Imix*	2	Sep 18 1925	9-Muluc	7	Nov 25 1925	12-Caban	3
Jul 13 1925	7-Ik	3	Sep 19 1925	10-Oc	8	Nov 26 1925	13-Etz'nab	4
Jul 14 1925	8-Akbal	4	Sep 20 1925	11-Chuen	9	Nov 27 1925	**1-Cauac**	5
Jul 15 1925	9-Kan	5	Sep 21 1925	12-Eb	1	Nov 28 1925	2-Ahau	6
Jul 16 1925	10-Chicchan	6	Sep 22 1925	13-Ben	2	Nov 29 1925	*3-Imix*	7
Jul 17 1925	11-Cimi	7	Sep 23 1925	**1-Ix**	3	Nov 30 1925	4-Ik	8
Jul 18 1925	12-Manik	8	Sep 24 1925	2-Men	4	Dec 1 1925	5-Akbal	9
Jul 19 1925	13-Lamat	9	Sep 25 1925	3-Cib	5	Dec 2 1925	6-Kan	1
Jul 20 1925	**1-Muluc**	1	Sep 26 1925	4-Caban	6	Dec 3 1925	7-Chicchan	2
Jul 21 1925	2-Oc	2	Sep 27 1925	5-Etz'nab	7	Dec 4 1925	8-Cimi	3
Jul 22 1925	3-Chuen	3	Sep 28 1925	6-Cauac	8	Dec 5 1925	9-Manik	4
Jul 23 1925	4-Eb	4	Sep 29 1925	7-Ahau	9	Dec 6 1925	10-Lamat	5
Jul 24 1925	5-Ben	5	Sep 30 1925	*8-Imix*	1	Dec 7 1925	11-Muluc	6
Jul 25 1925	6-Ix	6	Oct 1 1925	9-Ik	2	Dec 8 1925	12-Oc	7
Jul 26 1925	7-Men	7	Oct 2 1925	10-Akbal	3	Dec 9 1925	13-Chuen	8
Jul 27 1925	8-Cib	8	Oct 3 1925	11-Kan	4	Dec 10 1925	**1-Eb**	9
Jul 28 1925	9-Caban	9	Oct 4 1925	12-Chicchan	5	Dec 11 1925	2-Ben	1
Jul 29 1925	10-Etz'nab	1	Oct 5 1925	13-Cimi	6	Dec 12 1925	3-Ix	2
Jul 30 1925	11-Cauac	2	Oct 6 1925	**1-Manik**	7	Dec 13 1925	4-Men	3
Jul 31 1925	12-Ahau	3	Oct 7 1925	2-Lamat	8	Dec 14 1925	5-Cib	4
Aug 1 1925	*13-Imix*	4	Oct 8 1925	3-Muluc	9	Dec 15 1925	6-Caban	5
Aug 2 1925	**1-Ik**	5	Oct 9 1925	4-Oc	1	Dec 16 1925	7-Etz'nab	6
Aug 3 1925	2-Akbal	6	Oct 10 1925	5-Chuen	2	Dec 17 1925	8-Cauac	7
Aug 4 1925	3-Kan	7	Oct 11 1925	6-Eb	3	Dec 18 1925	9-Ahau	8
Aug 5 1925	4-Chicchan	8	Oct 12 1925	7-Ben	4	Dec 19 1925	*10-Imix*	9
Aug 6 1925	5-Cimi	9	Oct 13 1925	8-Ix	5	Dec 20 1925	11-Ik	1
Aug 7 1925	6-Manik	1	Oct 14 1925	9-Men	6	Dec 21 1925	12-Akbal	2
Aug 8 1925	7-Lamat	2	Oct 15 1925	10-Cib	7	Dec 22 1925	13-Kan	3
Aug 9 1925	8-Muluc	3	Oct 16 1925	11-Caban	8	Dec 23 1925	**1-Chicchan**	4
Aug 10 1925	9-Oc	4	Oct 17 1925	12-Etz'nab	9	Dec 24 1925	2-Cimi	5
Aug 11 1925	10-Chuen	5	Oct 18 1925	13-Cauac	1	Dec 25 1925	3-Manik	6
Aug 12 1925	11-Eb	6	Oct 19 1925	**1-Ahau**	2	Dec 26 1925	4-Lamat	7
Aug 13 1925	12-Ben	7	Oct 20 1925	*2-Imix*	3	Dec 27 1925	5-Muluc	8
Aug 14 1925	13-Ix	8	Oct 21 1925	3-Ik	4	Dec 28 1925	6-Oc	9
Aug 15 1925	**1-Men**	9	Oct 22 1925	4-Akbal	5	Dec 29 1925	7-Chuen	1
Aug 16 1925	2-Cib	1	Oct 23 1925	5-Kan	6	Dec 30 1925	8-Eb	2
Aug 17 1925	3-Caban	2	Oct 24 1925	6-Chicchan	7	Dec 31 1925	9-Ben	3
Aug 18 1925	4-Etz'nab	3	Oct 25 1925	7-Cimi	8	Jan 1 1926	10-Ix	4
Aug 19 1925	5-Cauac	4	Oct 26 1925	8-Manik	9	Jan 2 1926	11-Men	5
Aug 20 1925	6-Ahau	5	Oct 27 1925	9-Lamat	1	Jan 3 1926	12-Cib	6
Aug 21 1925	*7-Imix*	6	Oct 28 1925	10-Muluc	2	Jan 4 1926	13-Caban	7
Aug 22 1925	8-Ik	7	Oct 29 1925	11-Oc	3	Jan 5 1926	**1-Etz'nab**	8
Aug 23 1925	9-Akbal	8	Oct 30 1925	12-Chuen	4	Jan 6 1926	2-Cauac	9
Aug 24 1925	10-Kan	9	Oct 31 1925	13-Eb	5	Jan 7 1926	3-Ahau	1
Aug 25 1925	11-Chicchan	1	Nov 1 1925	**1-Ben**	6	Jan 8 1926	*4-Imix*	2
Aug 26 1925	12-Cimi	2	Nov 2 1925	2-Ix	7	Jan 9 1926	5-Ik	3
Aug 27 1925	13-Manik	3	Nov 3 1925	3-Men	8	Jan 10 1926	6-Akbal	4
Aug 28 1925	**1-Lamat**	4	Nov 4 1925	4-Cib	9	Jan 11 1926	7-Kan	5
Aug 29 1925	2-Muluc	5	Nov 5 1925	5-Caban	1	Jan 12 1926	8-Chicchan	6
Aug 30 1925	3-Oc	6	Nov 6 1925	6-Etz'nab	2	Jan 13 1926	9-Cimi	7
Aug 31 1925	4-Chuen	7	Nov 7 1925	7-Cauac	3	Jan 14 1926	10-Manik	8
Sep 1 1925	5-Eb	8	Nov 8 1925	8-Ahau	4	Jan 15 1926	11-Lamat	9
Sep 2 1925	6-Ben	9	Nov 9 1925	*9-Imix*	5	Jan 16 1926	12-Muluc	1
Sep 3 1925	7-Ix	1	Nov 10 1925	10-Ik	6	Jan 17 1926	13-Oc	2
Sep 4 1925	8-Men	2	Nov 11 1925	11-Akbal	7	Jan 18 1926	**1-Chuen**	3
Sep 5 1925	9-Cib	3	Nov 12 1925	12-Kan	8	Jan 19 1926	2-Eb	4
Sep 6 1925	10-Caban	4	Nov 13 1925	13-Chicchan	9	Jan 20 1926	3-Ben	5
Sep 7 1925	11-Etz'nab	5	Nov 14 1925	**1-Cimi**	1	Jan 21 1926	4-Ix	6
Sep 8 1925	12-Cauac	6	Nov 15 1925	2-Manik	2	Jan 22 1926	5-Men	7
Sep 9 1925	13-Ahau	7	Nov 16 1925	3-Lamat	3	Jan 23 1926	6-Cib	8
Sep 10 1925	**1-Imix**	8	Nov 17 1925	4-Muluc	4	Jan 24 1926	7-Caban	9

Date	Day-Sign	L		Date	Day-Sign	L		Date	Day-Sign	L
Jan 25 1926	8-Etz'nab	1		Apr 3 1926	11-Cimi	6		Jun 10 1926	**1-Ix**	2
Jan 26 1926	9-Cauac	2		Apr 4 1926	12-Manik	7		Jun 11 1926	2-Men	3
Jan 27 1926	10-Ahau	3		Apr 5 1926	13-Lamat	8		Jun 12 1926	3-Cib	4
Jan 28 1926	*11-Imix*	4		Apr 6 1926	**1-Muluc**	9		Jun 13 1926	4-Caban	5
Jan 29 1926	12-Ik	5		Apr 7 1926	2-Oc	1		Jun 14 1926	5-Etz'nab	6
Jan 30 1926	13-Akbal	6		Apr 8 1926	3-Chuen	2		Jun 15 1926	6-Cauac	7
Jan 31 1926	**1-Kan**	7		Apr 9 1926	4-Eb	3		Jun 16 1926	7-Ahau	8
Feb 1 1926	2-Chicchan	8		Apr 10 1926	5-Ben	4		Jun 17 1926	*8-Imix*	9
Feb 2 1926	3-Cimi	9		Apr 11 1926	6-Ix	5		Jun 18 1926	9-Ik	1
Feb 3 1926	4-Manik	1		Apr 12 1926	7-Men	6		Jun 19 1926	10-Akbal	2
Feb 4 1926	5-Lamat	2		Apr 13 1926	8-Cib	7		Jun 20 1926	11-Kan	3
Feb 5 1926	6-Muluc	3		Apr 14 1926	9-Caban	8		Jun 21 1926	12-Chicchan	4
Feb 6 1926	7-Oc	4		Apr 15 1926	10-Etz'nab	9		Jun 22 1926	13-Cimi	5
Feb 7 1926	8-Chuen	5		Apr 16 1926	11-Cauac	1		Jun 23 1926	**1-Manik**	6
Feb 8 1926	9-Eb	6		Apr 17 1926	12-Ahau	2		Jun 24 1926	2-Lamat	7
Feb 9 1926	10-Ben	7		Apr 18 1926	*13-Imix*	3		Jun 25 1926	3-Muluc	8
Feb 10 1926	11-Ix	8		Apr 19 1926	**1-Ik**	4		Jun 26 1926	4-Oc	9
Feb 11 1926	12-Men	9		Apr 20 1926	2-Akbal	5		Jun 27 1926	5-Chuen	1
Feb 12 1926	13-Cib	1		Apr 21 1926	3-Kan	6		Jun 28 1926	6-Eb	2
Feb 13 1926	**1-Caban**	2		Apr 22 1926	4-Chicchan	7		Jun 29 1926	7-Ben	3
Feb 14 1926	2-Etz'nab	3		Apr 23 1926	5-Cimi	8		Jun 30 1926	8-Ix	4
Feb 15 1926	3-Cauac	4		Apr 24 1926	6-Manik	9		Jul 1 1926	9-Men	5
Feb 16 1926	4-Ahau	5		Apr 25 1926	7-Lamat	1		Jul 2 1926	10-Cib	6
Feb 17 1926	*5-Imix*	6		Apr 26 1926	8-Muluc	2		Jul 3 1926	11-Caban	7
Feb 18 1926	6-Ik	7		Apr 27 1926	9-Oc	3		Jul 4 1926	12-Etz'nab	8
Feb 19 1926	7-Akbal	8		Apr 28 1926	10-Chuen	4		Jul 5 1926	13-Cauac	9
Feb 20 1926	8-Kan	9		Apr 29 1926	11-Eb	5		Jul 6 1926	**1-Ahau**	1
Feb 21 1926	9-Chicchan	1		Apr 30 1926	12-Ben	6		Jul 7 1926	*2-Imix*	2
Feb 22 1926	10-Cimi	2		May 1 1926	13-Ix	7		Jul 8 1926	3-Ik	3
Feb 23 1926	11-Manik	3		May 2 1926	**1-Men**	8		Jul 9 1926	4-Akbal	4
Feb 24 1926	12-Lamat	4		May 3 1926	2-Cib	9		Jul 10 1926	5-Kan	5
Feb 25 1926	13-Muluc	5		May 4 1926	3-Caban	1		Jul 11 1926	6-Chicchan	6
Feb 26 1926	**1-Oc**	6		May 5 1926	4-Etz'nab	2		Jul 12 1926	7-Cimi	7
Feb 27 1926	2-Chuen	7		May 6 1926	5-Cauac	3		Jul 13 1926	8-Manik	8
Feb 28 1926	3-Eb	8		May 7 1926	6-Ahau	4		Jul 14 1926	9-Lamat	9
Mar 1 1926	4-Ben	9		May 8 1926	*7-Imix*	5		Jul 15 1926	10-Muluc	1
Mar 2 1926	5-Ix	1		May 9 1926	8-Ik	6		Jul 16 1926	11-Oc	2
Mar 3 1926	6-Men	2		May 10 1926	9-Akbal	7		Jul 17 1926	12-Chuen	3
Mar 4 1926	7-Cib	3		May 11 1926	10-Kan	8		Jul 18 1926	13-Eb	4
Mar 5 1926	8-Caban	4		May 12 1926	11-Chicchan	9		Jul 19 1926	**1-Ben**	5
Mar 6 1926	9-Etz'nab	5		May 13 1926	12-Cimi	1		Jul 20 1926	2-Ix	6
Mar 7 1926	10-Cauac	6		May 14 1926	13-Manik	2		Jul 21 1926	3-Men	7
Mar 8 1926	11-Ahau	7		May 15 1926	**1-Lamat**	3		Jul 22 1926	4-Cib	8
Mar 9 1926	*12-Imix*	8		May 16 1926	2-Muluc	4		Jul 23 1926	5-Caban	9
Mar 10 1926	13-Ik	9		May 17 1926	3-Oc	5		Jul 24 1926	6-Etz'nab	1
Mar 11 1926	**1-Akbal**	1		May 18 1926	4-Chuen	6		Jul 25 1926	7-Cauac	2
Mar 12 1926	2-Kan	2		May 19 1926	5-Eb	7		Jul 26 1926	8-Ahau	3
Mar 13 1926	3-Chicchan	3		May 20 1926	6-Ben	8		Jul 27 1926	*9-Imix*	4
Mar 14 1926	4-Cimi	4		May 21 1926	7-Ix	9		Jul 28 1926	10-Ik	5
Mar 15 1926	5-Manik	5		May 22 1926	8-Men	1		Jul 29 1926	11-Akbal	6
Mar 16 1926	6-Lamat	6		May 23 1926	9-Cib	2		Jul 30 1926	12-Kan	7
Mar 17 1926	7-Muluc	7		May 24 1926	10-Caban	3		Jul 31 1926	13-Chicchan	8
Mar 18 1926	8-Oc	8		May 25 1926	11-Etz'nab	4		Aug 1 1926	**1-Cimi**	9
Mar 19 1926	9-Chuen	9		May 26 1926	12-Cauac	5		Aug 2 1926	2-Manik	1
Mar 20 1926	10-Eb	1		May 27 1926	13-Ahau	6		Aug 3 1926	3-Lamat	2
Mar 21 1926	11-Ben	2		May 28 1926	**1-Imix**	7		Aug 4 1926	4-Muluc	3
Mar 22 1926	12-Ix	3		May 29 1926	2-Ik	8		Aug 5 1926	5-Oc	4
Mar 23 1926	13-Men	4		May 30 1926	3-Akbal	9		Aug 6 1926	6-Chuen	5
Mar 24 1926	**1-Cib**	5		May 31 1926	4-Kan	1		Aug 7 1926	7-Eb	6
Mar 25 1926	2-Caban	6		Jun 1 1926	5-Chicchan	2		Aug 8 1926	8-Ben	7
Mar 26 1926	3-Etz'nab	7		Jun 2 1926	6-Cimi	3		Aug 9 1926	9-Ix	8
Mar 27 1926	4-Cauac	8		Jun 3 1926	7-Manik	4		Aug 10 1926	10-Men	9
Mar 28 1926	5-Ahau	9		Jun 4 1926	8-Lamat	5		Aug 11 1926	11-Cib	1
Mar 29 1926	*6-Imix*	1		Jun 5 1926	9-Muluc	6		Aug 12 1926	12-Caban	2
Mar 30 1926	7-Ik	2		Jun 6 1926	10-Oc	7		Aug 13 1926	13-Etz'nab	3
Mar 31 1926	8-Akbal	3		Jun 7 1926	11-Chuen	8		Aug 14 1926	**1-Cauac**	4
Apr 1 1926	9-Kan	4		Jun 8 1926	12-Eb	9		Aug 15 1926	2-Ahau	5
Apr 2 1926	10-Chicchan	5		Jun 9 1926	13-Ben	1		Aug 16 1926	*3-Imix*	6

Date	Day-Sign	L	Date	Day-Sign	L	Date	Day-Sign	L
Aug 17 1926	4-Ik	7	Oct 24 1926	7-Oc	3	Dec 31 1926	10-Etz'nab	8
Aug 18 1926	5-Akbal	8	Oct 25 1926	8-Chuen	4	Jan 1 1927	11-Cauac	9
Aug 19 1926	6-Kan	9	Oct 26 1926	9-Eb	5	Jan 2 1927	12-Ahau	1
Aug 20 1926	7-Chicchan	1	Oct 27 1926	10-Ben	6	Jan 3 1927	13-Imix	2
Aug 21 1926	8-Cimi	2	Oct 28 1926	11-Ix	7	Jan 4 1927	1-Ik	3
Aug 22 1926	9-Manik	3	Oct 29 1926	12-Men	8	Jan 5 1927	2-Akbal	4
Aug 23 1926	10-Lamat	4	Oct 30 1926	13-Cib	9	Jan 6 1927	3-Kan	5
Aug 24 1926	11-Muluc	5	Oct 31 1926	1-Caban	1	Jan 7 1927	4-Chicchan	6
Aug 25 1926	12-Oc	6	Nov 1 1926	2-Etz'nab	2	Jan 8 1927	5-Cimi	7
Aug 26 1926	13-Chuen	7	Nov 2 1926	3-Cauac	3	Jan 9 1927	6-Manik	8
Aug 27 1926	1-Eb	8	Nov 3 1926	4-Ahau	4	Jan 10 1927	7-Lamat	9
Aug 28 1926	2-Ben	9	Nov 4 1926	5-Imix	5	Jan 11 1927	8-Muluc	1
Aug 29 1926	3-Ix	1	Nov 5 1926	6-Ik	6	Jan 12 1927	9-Oc	2
Aug 30 1926	4-Men	2	Nov 6 1926	7-Akbal	7	Jan 13 1927	10-Chuen	3
Aug 31 1926	5-Cib	3	Nov 7 1926	8-Kan	8	Jan 14 1927	11-Eb	4
Sep 1 1926	6-Caban	4	Nov 8 1926	9-Chicchan	9	Jan 15 1927	12-Ben	5
Sep 2 1926	7-Etz'nab	5	Nov 9 1926	10-Cimi	1	Jan 16 1927	13-Ix	6
Sep 3 1926	8-Cauac	6	Nov 10 1926	11-Manik	2	Jan 17 1927	1-Men	7
Sep 4 1926	9-Ahau	7	Nov 11 1926	12-Lamat	3	Jan 18 1927	2-Cib	8
Sep 5 1926	10-Imix	8	Nov 12 1926	13-Muluc	4	Jan 19 1927	3-Caban	9
Sep 6 1926	11-Ik	9	Nov 13 1926	1-Oc	5	Jan 20 1927	4-Etz'nab	1
Sep 7 1926	12-Akbal	1	Nov 14 1926	2-Chuen	6	Jan 21 1927	5-Cauac	2
Sep 8 1926	13-Kan	2	Nov 15 1926	3-Eb	7	Jan 22 1927	6-Ahau	3
Sep 9 1926	1-Chicchan	3	Nov 16 1926	4-Ben	8	Jan 23 1927	7-Imix	4
Sep 10 1926	2-Cimi	4	Nov 17 1926	5-Ix	9	Jan 24 1927	8-Ik	5
Sep 11 1926	3-Manik	5	Nov 18 1926	6-Men	1	Jan 25 1927	9-Akbal	6
Sep 12 1926	4-Lamat	6	Nov 19 1926	7-Cib	2	Jan 26 1927	10-Kan	7
Sep 13 1926	5-Muluc	7	Nov 20 1926	8-Caban	3	Jan 27 1927	11-Chicchan	8
Sep 14 1926	6-Oc	8	Nov 21 1926	9-Etz'nab	4	Jan 28 1927	12-Cimi	9
Sep 15 1926	7-Chuen	9	Nov 22 1926	10-Cauac	5	Jan 29 1927	13-Manik	1
Sep 16 1926	8-Eb	1	Nov 23 1926	11-Ahau	6	Jan 30 1927	1-Lamat	2
Sep 17 1926	9-Ben	2	Nov 24 1926	12-Imix	7	Jan 31 1927	2-Muluc	3
Sep 18 1926	10-Ix	3	Nov 25 1926	13-Ik	8	Feb 1 1927	3-Oc	4
Sep 19 1926	11-Men	4	Nov 26 1926	1-Akbal	9	Feb 2 1927	4-Chuen	5
Sep 20 1926	12-Cib	5	Nov 27 1926	2-Kan	1	Feb 3 1927	5-Eb	6
Sep 21 1926	13-Caban	6	Nov 28 1926	3-Chicchan	2	Feb 4 1927	6-Ben	7
Sep 22 1926	1-Etz'nab	7	Nov 29 1926	4-Cimi	3	Feb 5 1927	7-Ix	8
Sep 23 1926	2-Cauac	8	Nov 30 1926	5-Manik	4	Feb 6 1927	8-Men	9
Sep 24 1926	3-Ahau	9	Dec 1 1926	6-Lamat	5	Feb 7 1927	9-Cib	1
Sep 25 1926	4-Imix	1	Dec 2 1926	7-Muluc	6	Feb 8 1927	10-Caban	2
Sep 26 1926	5-Ik	2	Dec 3 1926	8-Oc	7	Feb 9 1927	11-Etz'nab	3
Sep 27 1926	6-Akbal	3	Dec 4 1926	9-Chuen	8	Feb 10 1927	12-Cauac	4
Sep 28 1926	7-Kan	4	Dec 5 1926	10-Eb	9	Feb 11 1927	13-Ahau	5
Sep 29 1926	8-Chicchan	5	Dec 6 1926	11-Ben	1	Feb 12 1927	1-Imix	6
Sep 30 1926	9-Cimi	6	Dec 7 1926	12-Ix	2	Feb 13 1927	2-Ik	7
Oct 1 1926	10-Manik	7	Dec 8 1926	13-Men	3	Feb 14 1927	3-Akbal	8
Oct 2 1926	11-Lamat	8	Dec 9 1926	1-Cib	4	Feb 15 1927	4-Kan	9
Oct 3 1926	12-Muluc	9	Dec 10 1926	2-Caban	5	Feb 16 1927	5-Chicchan	1
Oct 4 1926	13-Oc	1	Dec 11 1926	3-Etz'nab	6	Feb 17 1927	6-Cimi	2
Oct 5 1926	1-Chuen	2	Dec 12 1926	4-Cauac	7	Feb 18 1927	7-Manik	3
Oct 6 1926	2-Eb	3	Dec 13 1926	5-Ahau	8	Feb 19 1927	8-Lamat	4
Oct 7 1926	3-Ben	4	Dec 14 1926	6-Imix	9	Feb 20 1927	9-Muluc	5
Oct 8 1926	4-Ix	5	Dec 15 1926	7-Ik	1	Feb 21 1927	10-Oc	6
Oct 9 1926	5-Men	6	Dec 16 1926	8-Akbal	2	Feb 22 1927	11-Chuen	7
Oct 10 1926	6-Cib	7	Dec 17 1926	9-Kan	3	Feb 23 1927	12-Eb	8
Oct 11 1926	7-Caban	8	Dec 18 1926	10-Chicchan	4	Feb 24 1927	13-Ben	9
Oct 12 1926	8-Etz'nab	9	Dec 19 1926	11-Cimi	5	Feb 25 1927	1-Ix	1
Oct 13 1926	9-Cauac	1	Dec 20 1926	12-Manik	6	Feb 26 1927	2-Men	2
Oct 14 1926	10-Ahau	2	Dec 21 1926	13-Lamat	7	Feb 27 1927	3-Cib	3
Oct 15 1926	11-Imix	3	Dec 22 1926	1-Muluc	8	Feb 28 1927	4-Caban	4
Oct 16 1926	12-Ik	4	Dec 23 1926	2-Oc	9	Mar 1 1927	5-Etz'nab	5
Oct 17 1926	13-Akbal	5	Dec 24 1926	3-Chuen	1	Mar 2 1927	6-Cauac	6
Oct 18 1926	1-Kan	6	Dec 25 1926	4-Eb	2	Mar 3 1927	7-Ahau	7
Oct 19 1926	2-Chicchan	7	Dec 26 1926	5-Ben	3	Mar 4 1927	8-Imix	8
Oct 20 1926	3-Cimi	8	Dec 27 1926	6-Ix	4	Mar 5 1927	9-Ik	9
Oct 21 1926	4-Manik	9	Dec 28 1926	7-Men	5	Mar 6 1927	10-Akbal	1
Oct 22 1926	5-Lamat	1	Dec 29 1926	8-Cib	6	Mar 7 1927	11-Kan	2
Oct 23 1926	6-Muluc	2	Dec 30 1926	9-Caban	7	Mar 8 1927	12-Chicchan	3

Date	Day-Sign	L	Date	Day-Sign	L	Date	Day-Sign	L
Mar 9 1927	13-Cimi	4	May 16 1927	3-Ix	9	Jul 23 1927	6-Ik	5
Mar 10 1927	**1-Manik**	5	May 17 1927	4-Men	1	Jul 24 1927	7-Akbal	6
Mar 11 1927	2-Lamat	6	May 18 1927	5-Cib	2	Jul 25 1927	8-Kan	7
Mar 12 1927	3-Muluc	7	May 19 1927	6-Caban	3	Jul 26 1927	9-Chicchan	8
Mar 13 1927	4-Oc	8	May 20 1927	7-Etz'nab	4	Jul 27 1927	10-Cimi	9
Mar 14 1927	5-Chuen	9	May 21 1927	8-Cauac	5	Jul 28 1927	11-Manik	1
Mar 15 1927	6-Eb	1	May 22 1927	9-Ahau	6	Jul 29 1927	12-Lamat	2
Mar 16 1927	7-Ben	2	May 23 1927	*10-Imix*	7	Jul 30 1927	13-Muluc	3
Mar 17 1927	8-Ix	3	May 24 1927	11-Ik	8	Jul 31 1927	**1-Oc**	4
Mar 18 1927	9-Men	4	May 25 1927	12-Akbal	9	Aug 1 1927	2-Chuen	5
Mar 19 1927	10-Cib	5	May 26 1927	13-Kan	1	Aug 2 1927	3-Eb	6
Mar 20 1927	11-Caban	6	May 27 1927	**1-Chicchan**	2	Aug 3 1927	4-Ben	7
Mar 21 1927	12-Etz'nab	7	May 28 1927	2-Cimi	3	Aug 4 1927	5-Ix	8
Mar 22 1927	13-Cauac	8	May 29 1927	3-Manik	4	Aug 5 1927	6-Men	9
Mar 23 1927	**1-Ahau**	9	May 30 1927	4-Lamat	5	Aug 6 1927	7-Cib	1
Mar 24 1927	*2-Imix*	1	May 31 1927	5-Muluc	6	Aug 7 1927	8-Caban	2
Mar 25 1927	3-Ik	2	Jun 1 1927	6-Oc	7	Aug 8 1927	9-Etz'nab	3
Mar 26 1927	4-Akbal	3	Jun 2 1927	7-Chuen	8	Aug 9 1927	10-Cauac	4
Mar 27 1927	5-Kan	4	Jun 3 1927	8-Eb	9	Aug 10 1927	11-Ahau	5
Mar 28 1927	6-Chicchan	5	Jun 4 1927	9-Ben	1	Aug 11 1927	*12-Imix*	6
Mar 29 1927	7-Cimi	6	Jun 5 1927	10-Ix	2	Aug 12 1927	13-Ik	7
Mar 30 1927	8-Manik	7	Jun 6 1927	11-Men	3	Aug 13 1927	**1-Akbal**	8
Mar 31 1927	9-Lamat	8	Jun 7 1927	12-Cib	4	Aug 14 1927	2-Kan	9
Apr 1 1927	10-Muluc	9	Jun 8 1927	13-Caban	5	Aug 15 1927	3-Chicchan	1
Apr 2 1927	11-Oc	1	Jun 9 1927	**1-Etz'nab**	6	Aug 16 1927	4-Cimi	2
Apr 3 1927	12-Chuen	2	Jun 10 1927	2-Cauac	7	Aug 17 1927	5-Manik	3
Apr 4 1927	13-Eb	3	Jun 11 1927	3-Ahau	8	Aug 18 1927	6-Lamat	4
Apr 5 1927	**1-Ben**	4	Jun 12 1927	*4-Imix*	9	Aug 19 1927	7-Muluc	5
Apr 6 1927	2-Ix	5	Jun 13 1927	5-Ik	1	Aug 20 1927	8-Oc	6
Apr 7 1927	3-Men	6	Jun 14 1927	6-Akbal	2	Aug 21 1927	9-Chuen	7
Apr 8 1927	4-Cib	7	Jun 15 1927	7-Kan	3	Aug 22 1927	10-Eb	8
Apr 9 1927	5-Caban	8	Jun 16 1927	8-Chicchan	4	Aug 23 1927	11-Ben	9
Apr 10 1927	6-Etz'nab	9	Jun 17 1927	9-Cimi	5	Aug 24 1927	12-Ix	1
Apr 11 1927	7-Cauac	1	Jun 18 1927	10-Manik	6	Aug 25 1927	13-Men	2
Apr 12 1927	8-Ahau	2	Jun 19 1927	11-Lamat	7	Aug 26 1927	**1-Cib**	3
Apr 13 1927	*9-Imix*	3	Jun 20 1927	12-Muluc	8	Aug 27 1927	2-Caban	4
Apr 14 1927	10-Ik	4	Jun 21 1927	13-Oc	9	Aug 28 1927	3-Etz'nab	5
Apr 15 1927	11-Akbal	5	Jun 22 1927	**1-Chuen**	1	Aug 29 1927	4-Cauac	6
Apr 16 1927	12-Kan	6	Jun 23 1927	2-Eb	2	Aug 30 1927	5-Ahau	7
Apr 17 1927	13-Chicchan	7	Jun 24 1927	3-Ben	3	Aug 31 1927	*6-Imix*	8
Apr 18 1927	**1-Cimi**	8	Jun 25 1927	4-Ix	4	Sep 1 1927	7-Ik	9
Apr 19 1927	2-Manik	9	Jun 26 1927	5-Men	5	Sep 2 1927	8-Akbal	1
Apr 20 1927	3-Lamat	1	Jun 27 1927	6-Cib	6	Sep 3 1927	9-Kan	2
Apr 21 1927	4-Muluc	2	Jun 28 1927	7-Caban	7	Sep 4 1927	10-Chicchan	3
Apr 22 1927	5-Oc	3	Jun 29 1927	8-Etz'nab	8	Sep 5 1927	11-Cimi	4
Apr 23 1927	6-Chuen	4	Jun 30 1927	9-Cauac	9	Sep 6 1927	12-Manik	5
Apr 24 1927	7-Eb	5	Jul 1 1927	10-Ahau	1	Sep 7 1927	13-Lamat	6
Apr 25 1927	8-Ben	6	Jul 2 1927	*11-Imix*	2	Sep 8 1927	**1-Muluc**	7
Apr 26 1927	9-Ix	7	Jul 3 1927	12-Ik	3	Sep 9 1927	2-Oc	8
Apr 27 1927	10-Men	8	Jul 4 1927	13-Akbal	4	Sep 10 1927	3-Chuen	9
Apr 28 1927	11-Cib	9	Jul 5 1927	**1-Kan**	5	Sep 11 1927	4-Eb	1
Apr 29 1927	12-Caban	1	Jul 6 1927	2-Chicchan	6	Sep 12 1927	5-Ben	2
Apr 30 1927	13-Etz'nab	2	Jul 7 1927	3-Cimi	7	Sep 13 1927	6-Ix	3
May 1 1927	**1-Cauac**	3	Jul 8 1927	4-Manik	8	Sep 14 1927	7-Men	4
May 2 1927	2-Ahau	4	Jul 9 1927	5-Lamat	9	Sep 15 1927	8-Cib	5
May 3 1927	*3-Imix*	5	Jul 10 1927	6-Muluc	1	Sep 16 1927	9-Caban	6
May 4 1927	4-Ik	6	Jul 11 1927	7-Oc	2	Sep 17 1927	10-Etz'nab	7
May 5 1927	5-Akbal	7	Jul 12 1927	8-Chuen	3	Sep 18 1927	11-Cauac	8
May 6 1927	6-Kan	8	Jul 13 1927	9-Eb	4	Sep 19 1927	12-Ahau	9
May 7 1927	7-Chicchan	9	Jul 14 1927	10-Ben	5	Sep 20 1927	*13-Imix*	1
May 8 1927	8-Cimi	1	Jul 15 1927	11-Ix	6	Sep 21 1927	**1-Ik**	2
May 9 1927	9-Manik	2	Jul 16 1927	12-Men	7	Sep 22 1927	2-Akbal	3
May 10 1927	10-Lamat	3	Jul 17 1927	13-Cib	8	Sep 23 1927	3-Kan	4
May 11 1927	11-Muluc	4	Jul 18 1927	**1-Caban**	9	Sep 24 1927	4-Chicchan	5
May 12 1927	12-Oc	5	Jul 19 1927	2-Etz'nab	1	Sep 25 1927	5-Cimi	6
May 13 1927	13-Chuen	6	Jul 20 1927	3-Cauac	2	Sep 26 1927	6-Manik	7
May 14 1927	**1-Eb**	7	Jul 21 1927	4-Ahau	3	Sep 27 1927	7-Lamat	8
May 15 1927	2-Ben	8	Jul 22 1927	*5-Imix*	4	Sep 28 1927	8-Muluc	9

Date	Day-Sign	L
Sep 29 1927	9-Oc	1
Sep 30 1927	10-Chuen	2
Oct 1 1927	11-Eb	3
Oct 2 1927	12-Ben	4
Oct 3 1927	13-Ix	5
Oct 4 1927	1-Men	6
Oct 5 1927	2-Cib	7
Oct 6 1927	3-Caban	8
Oct 7 1927	4-Etz'nab	9
Oct 8 1927	5-Cauac	1
Oct 9 1927	6-Ahau	2
Oct 10 1927	7-Imix	3
Oct 11 1927	8-Ik	4
Oct 12 1927	9-Akbal	5
Oct 13 1927	10-Kan	6
Oct 14 1927	11-Chicchan	7
Oct 15 1927	12-Cimi	8
Oct 16 1927	13-Manik	9
Oct 17 1927	1-Lamat	1
Oct 18 1927	2-Muluc	2
Oct 19 1927	3-Oc	3
Oct 20 1927	4-Chuen	4
Oct 21 1927	5-Eb	5
Oct 22 1927	6-Ben	6
Oct 23 1927	7-Ix	7
Oct 24 1927	8-Men	8
Oct 25 1927	9-Cib	9
Oct 26 1927	10-Caban	1
Oct 27 1927	11-Etz'nab	2
Oct 28 1927	12-Cauac	3
Oct 29 1927	13-Ahau	4
Oct 30 1927	1-Imix	5
Oct 31 1927	2-Ik	6
Nov 1 1927	3-Akbal	7
Nov 2 1927	4-Kan	8
Nov 3 1927	5-Chicchan	9
Nov 4 1927	6-Cimi	1
Nov 5 1927	7-Manik	2
Nov 6 1927	8-Lamat	3
Nov 7 1927	9-Muluc	4
Nov 8 1927	10-Oc	5
Nov 9 1927	11-Chuen	6
Nov 10 1927	12-Eb	7
Nov 11 1927	13-Ben	8
Nov 12 1927	1-Ix	9
Nov 13 1927	2-Men	1
Nov 14 1927	3-Cib	2
Nov 15 1927	4-Caban	3
Nov 16 1927	5-Etz'nab	4
Nov 17 1927	6-Cauac	5
Nov 18 1927	7-Ahau	6
Nov 19 1927	8-Imix	7
Nov 20 1927	9-Ik	8
Nov 21 1927	10-Akbal	9
Nov 22 1927	11-Kan	1
Nov 23 1927	12-Chicchan	2
Nov 24 1927	13-Cimi	3
Nov 25 1927	1-Manik	4
Nov 26 1927	2-Lamat	5
Nov 27 1927	3-Muluc	6
Nov 28 1927	4-Oc	7
Nov 29 1927	5-Chuen	8
Nov 30 1927	6-Eb	9
Dec 1 1927	7-Ben	1
Dec 2 1927	8-Ix	2
Dec 3 1927	9-Men	3
Dec 4 1927	10-Cib	4
Dec 5 1927	11-Caban	5

Date	Day-Sign	L
Dec 6 1927	12-Etz'nab	6
Dec 7 1927	13-Cauac	7
Dec 8 1927	1-Ahau	8
Dec 9 1927	2-Imix	9
Dec 10 1927	3-Ik	1
Dec 11 1927	4-Akbal	2
Dec 12 1927	5-Kan	3
Dec 13 1927	6-Chicchan	4
Dec 14 1927	7-Cimi	5
Dec 15 1927	8-Manik	6
Dec 16 1927	9-Lamat	7
Dec 17 1927	10-Muluc	8
Dec 18 1927	11-Oc	9
Dec 19 1927	12-Chuen	1
Dec 20 1927	13-Eb	2
Dec 21 1927	1-Ben	3
Dec 22 1927	2-Ix	4
Dec 23 1927	3-Men	5
Dec 24 1927	4-Cib	6
Dec 25 1927	5-Caban	7
Dec 26 1927	6-Etz'nab	8
Dec 27 1927	7-Cauac	9
Dec 28 1927	8-Ahau	1
Dec 29 1927	9-Imix	2
Dec 30 1927	10-Ik	3
Dec 31 1927	11-Akbal	4
Jan 1 1928	12-Kan	5
Jan 2 1928	13-Chicchan	6
Jan 3 1928	1-Cimi	7
Jan 4 1928	2-Manik	8
Jan 5 1928	3-Lamat	9
Jan 6 1928	4-Muluc	1
Jan 7 1928	5-Oc	2
Jan 8 1928	6-Chuen	3
Jan 9 1928	7-Eb	4
Jan 10 1928	8-Ben	5
Jan 11 1928	9-Ix	6
Jan 12 1928	10-Men	7
Jan 13 1928	11-Cib	8
Jan 14 1928	12-Caban	9
Jan 15 1928	13-Etz'nab	1
Jan 16 1928	1-Cauac	2
Jan 17 1928	2-Ahau	3
Jan 18 1928	3-Imix	4
Jan 19 1928	4-Ik	5
Jan 20 1928	5-Akbal	6
Jan 21 1928	6-Kan	7
Jan 22 1928	7-Chicchan	8
Jan 23 1928	8-Cimi	9
Jan 24 1928	9-Manik	1
Jan 25 1928	10-Lamat	2
Jan 26 1928	11-Muluc	3
Jan 27 1928	12-Oc	4
Jan 28 1928	13-Chuen	5
Jan 29 1928	1-Eb	6
Jan 30 1928	2-Ben	7
Jan 31 1928	3-Ix	8
Feb 1 1928	4-Men	9
Feb 2 1928	5-Cib	1
Feb 3 1928	6-Caban	2
Feb 4 1928	7-Etz'nab	3
Feb 5 1928	8-Cauac	4
Feb 6 1928	9-Ahau	5
Feb 7 1928	10-Imix	6
Feb 8 1928	11-Ik	7
Feb 9 1928	12-Akbal	8
Feb 10 1928	13-Kan	9
Feb 11 1928	1-Chicchan	1

Date	Day-Sign	L
Feb 12 1928	2-Cimi	2
Feb 13 1928	3-Manik	3
Feb 14 1928	4-Lamat	4
Feb 15 1928	5-Muluc	5
Feb 16 1928	6-Oc	6
Feb 17 1928	7-Chuen	7
Feb 18 1928	8-Eb	8
Feb 19 1928	9-Ben	9
Feb 20 1928	10-Ix	1
Feb 21 1928	11-Men	2
Feb 22 1928	12-Cib	3
Feb 23 1928	13-Caban	4
Feb 24 1928	1-Etz'nab	5
Feb 25 1928	2-Cauac	6
Feb 26 1928	3-Ahau	7
Feb 27 1928	4-Imix	8
Feb 28 1928	5-Ik	9
Feb 29 1928	6-Akbal	1
Mar 1 1928	7-Kan	2
Mar 2 1928	8-Chicchan	3
Mar 3 1928	9-Cimi	4
Mar 4 1928	10-Manik	5
Mar 5 1928	11-Lamat	6
Mar 6 1928	12-Muluc	7
Mar 7 1928	13-Oc	8
Mar 8 1928	1-Chuen	9
Mar 9 1928	2-Eb	1
Mar 10 1928	3-Ben	2
Mar 11 1928	4-Ix	3
Mar 12 1928	5-Men	4
Mar 13 1928	6-Cib	5
Mar 14 1928	7-Caban	6
Mar 15 1928	8-Etz'nab	7
Mar 16 1928	9-Cauac	8
Mar 17 1928	10-Ahau	9
Mar 18 1928	11-Imix	1
Mar 19 1928	12-Ik	2
Mar 20 1928	13-Akbal	3
Mar 21 1928	1-Kan	4
Mar 22 1928	2-Chicchan	5
Mar 23 1928	3-Cimi	6
Mar 24 1928	4-Manik	7
Mar 25 1928	5-Lamat	8
Mar 26 1928	6-Muluc	9
Mar 27 1928	7-Oc	1
Mar 28 1928	8-Chuen	2
Mar 29 1928	9-Eb	3
Mar 30 1928	10-Ben	4
Mar 31 1928	11-Ix	5
Apr 1 1928	12-Men	6
Apr 2 1928	13-Cib	7
Apr 3 1928	1-Caban	8
Apr 4 1928	2-Etz'nab	9
Apr 5 1928	3-Cauac	1
Apr 6 1928	4-Ahau	2
Apr 7 1928	5-Imix	3
Apr 8 1928	6-Ik	4
Apr 9 1928	7-Akbal	5
Apr 10 1928	8-Kan	6
Apr 11 1928	9-Chicchan	7
Apr 12 1928	10-Cimi	8
Apr 13 1928	11-Manik	9
Apr 14 1928	12-Lamat	1
Apr 15 1928	13-Muluc	2
Apr 16 1928	1-Oc	3
Apr 17 1928	2-Chuen	4
Apr 18 1928	3-Eb	5
Apr 19 1928	4-Ben	6

Date	Day-Sign	L		Date	Day-Sign	L		Date	Day-Sign	L
Apr 20 1928	5-Ix	7		Jun 27 1928	8-Ik	3		Sep 3 1928	11-Oc	8
Apr 21 1928	6-Men	8		Jun 28 1928	9-Akbal	4		Sep 4 1928	12-Chuen	9
Apr 22 1928	7-Cib	9		Jun 29 1928	10-Kan	5		Sep 5 1928	13-Eb	1
Apr 23 1928	8-Caban	1		Jun 30 1928	11-Chicchan	6		Sep 6 1928	**1-Ben**	2
Apr 24 1928	9-Etz'nab	2		Jul 1 1928	12-Cimi	7		Sep 7 1928	2-Ix	3
Apr 25 1928	10-Cauac	3		Jul 2 1928	13-Manik	8		Sep 8 1928	3-Men	4
Apr 26 1928	11-Ahau	4		Jul 3 1928	**1-Lamat**	9		Sep 9 1928	4-Cib	5
Apr 27 1928	*12-Imix*	5		Jul 4 1928	2-Muluc	1		Sep 10 1928	5-Caban	6
Apr 28 1928	13-Ik	6		Jul 5 1928	3-Oc	2		Sep 11 1928	6-Etz'nab	7
Apr 29 1928	**1-Akbal**	7		Jul 6 1928	4-Chuen	3		Sep 12 1928	7-Cauac	8
Apr 30 1928	2-Kan	8		Jul 7 1928	5-Eb	4		Sep 13 1928	8-Ahau	9
May 1 1928	3-Chicchan	9		Jul 8 1928	6-Ben	5		Sep 14 1928	*9-Imix*	1
May 2 1928	4-Cimi	1		Jul 9 1928	7-Ix	6		Sep 15 1928	10-Ik	2
May 3 1928	5-Manik	2		Jul 10 1928	8-Men	7		Sep 16 1928	11-Akbal	3
May 4 1928	6-Lamat	3		Jul 11 1928	9-Cib	8		Sep 17 1928	12-Kan	4
May 5 1928	7-Muluc	4		Jul 12 1928	10-Caban	9		Sep 18 1928	13-Chicchan	5
May 6 1928	8-Oc	5		Jul 13 1928	11-Etz'nab	1		Sep 19 1928	**1-Cimi**	6
May 7 1928	9-Chuen	6		Jul 14 1928	12-Cauac	2		Sep 20 1928	2-Manik	7
May 8 1928	10-Eb	7		Jul 15 1928	13-Ahau	3		Sep 21 1928	3-Lamat	8
May 9 1928	11-Ben	8		Jul 16 1928	**1-Imix**	4		Sep 22 1928	4-Muluc	9
May 10 1928	12-Ix	9		Jul 17 1928	2-Ik	5		Sep 23 1928	5-Oc	1
May 11 1928	13-Men	1		Jul 18 1928	3-Akbal	6		Sep 24 1928	6-Chuen	2
May 12 1928	**1-Cib**	2		Jul 19 1928	4-Kan	7		Sep 25 1928	7-Eb	3
May 13 1928	2-Caban	3		Jul 20 1928	5-Chicchan	8		Sep 26 1928	8-Ben	4
May 14 1928	3-Etz'nab	4		Jul 21 1928	6-Cimi	9		Sep 27 1928	9-Ix	5
May 15 1928	4-Cauac	5		Jul 22 1928	7-Manik	1		Sep 28 1928	10-Men	6
May 16 1928	5-Ahau	6		Jul 23 1928	8-Lamat	2		Sep 29 1928	11-Cib	7
May 17 1928	*6-Imix*	7		Jul 24 1928	9-Muluc	3		Sep 30 1928	12-Caban	8
May 18 1928	7-Ik	8		Jul 25 1928	10-Oc	4		Oct 1 1928	13-Etz'nab	9
May 19 1928	8-Akbal	9		Jul 26 1928	11-Chuen	5		Oct 2 1928	**1-Cauac**	1
May 20 1928	9-Kan	1		Jul 27 1928	12-Eb	6		Oct 3 1928	2-Ahau	2
May 21 1928	10-Chicchan	2		Jul 28 1928	13-Ben	7		Oct 4 1928	*3-Imix*	3
May 22 1928	11-Cimi	3		Jul 29 1928	**1-Ix**	8		Oct 5 1928	4-Ik	4
May 23 1928	12-Manik	4		Jul 30 1928	2-Men	9		Oct 6 1928	5-Akbal	5
May 24 1928	13-Lamat	5		Jul 31 1928	3-Cib	1		Oct 7 1928	6-Kan	6
May 25 1928	**1-Muluc**	6		Aug 1 1928	4-Caban	2		Oct 8 1928	7-Chicchan	7
May 26 1928	2-Oc	7		Aug 2 1928	5-Etz'nab	3		Oct 9 1928	8-Cimi	8
May 27 1928	3-Chuen	8		Aug 3 1928	6-Cauac	4		Oct 10 1928	9-Manik	9
May 28 1928	4-Eb	9		Aug 4 1928	7-Ahau	5		Oct 11 1928	10-Lamat	1
May 29 1928	5-Ben	1		Aug 5 1928	*8-Imix*	6		Oct 12 1928	11-Muluc	2
May 30 1928	6-Ix	2		Aug 6 1928	9-Ik	7		Oct 13 1928	12-Oc	3
May 31 1928	7-Men	3		Aug 7 1928	10-Akbal	8		Oct 14 1928	13-Chuen	4
Jun 1 1928	8-Cib	4		Aug 8 1928	11-Kan	9		Oct 15 1928	**1-Eb**	5
Jun 2 1928	9-Caban	5		Aug 9 1928	12-Chicchan	1		Oct 16 1928	2-Ben	6
Jun 3 1928	10-Etz'nab	6		Aug 10 1928	13-Cimi	2		Oct 17 1928	3-Ix	7
Jun 4 1928	11-Cauac	7		Aug 11 1928	**1-Manik**	3		Oct 18 1928	4-Men	8
Jun 5 1928	12-Ahau	8		Aug 12 1928	2-Lamat	4		Oct 19 1928	5-Cib	9
Jun 6 1928	*13-Imix*	9		Aug 13 1928	3-Muluc	5		Oct 20 1928	6-Caban	1
Jun 7 1928	**1-Ik**	1		Aug 14 1928	4-Oc	6		Oct 21 1928	7-Etz'nab	2
Jun 8 1928	2-Akbal	2		Aug 15 1928	5-Chuen	7		Oct 22 1928	8-Cauac	3
Jun 9 1928	3-Kan	3		Aug 16 1928	6-Eb	8		Oct 23 1928	9-Ahau	4
Jun 10 1928	4-Chicchan	4		Aug 17 1928	7-Ben	9		Oct 24 1928	*10-Imix*	5
Jun 11 1928	5-Cimi	5		Aug 18 1928	8-Ix	1		Oct 25 1928	11-Ik	6
Jun 12 1928	6-Manik	6		Aug 19 1928	9-Men	2		Oct 26 1928	12-Akbal	7
Jun 13 1928	7-Lamat	7		Aug 20 1928	10-Cib	3		Oct 27 1928	13-Kan	8
Jun 14 1928	8-Muluc	8		Aug 21 1928	11-Caban	4		Oct 28 1928	**1-Chicchan**	9
Jun 15 1928	9-Oc	9		Aug 22 1928	12-Etz'nab	5		Oct 29 1928	2-Cimi	1
Jun 16 1928	10-Chuen	1		Aug 23 1928	13-Cauac	6		Oct 30 1928	3-Manik	2
Jun 17 1928	11-Eb	2		Aug 24 1928	**1-Ahau**	7		Oct 31 1928	4-Lamat	3
Jun 18 1928	12-Ben	3		Aug 25 1928	*2-Imix*	8		Nov 1 1928	5-Muluc	4
Jun 19 1928	13-Ix	4		Aug 26 1928	3-Ik	9		Nov 2 1928	6-Oc	5
Jun 20 1928	**1-Men**	5		Aug 27 1928	4-Akbal	1		Nov 3 1928	7-Chuen	6
Jun 21 1928	2-Cib	6		Aug 28 1928	5-Kan	2		Nov 4 1928	8-Eb	7
Jun 22 1928	3-Caban	7		Aug 29 1928	6-Chicchan	3		Nov 5 1928	9-Ben	8
Jun 23 1928	4-Etz'nab	8		Aug 30 1928	7-Cimi	4		Nov 6 1928	10-Ix	9
Jun 24 1928	5-Cauac	9		Aug 31 1928	8-Manik	5		Nov 7 1928	11-Men	1
Jun 25 1928	6-Ahau	1		Sep 1 1928	9-Lamat	6		Nov 8 1928	12-Cib	2
Jun 26 1928	*7-Imix*	2		Sep 2 1928	10-Muluc	7		Nov 9 1928	13-Caban	3

Date	Day-Sign	L
Nov 10 1928	**1-Etz'nab**	4
Nov 11 1928	2-Cauac	5
Nov 12 1928	3-Ahau	6
Nov 13 1928	*4-Imix*	7
Nov 14 1928	5-Ik	8
Nov 15 1928	6-Akbal	9
Nov 16 1928	7-Kan	1
Nov 17 1928	8-Chicchan	2
Nov 18 1928	9-Cimi	3
Nov 19 1928	10-Manik	4
Nov 20 1928	11-Lamat	5
Nov 21 1928	12-Muluc	6
Nov 22 1928	13-Oc	7
Nov 23 1928	**1-Chuen**	8
Nov 24 1928	2-Eb	9
Nov 25 1928	3-Ben	1
Nov 26 1928	4-Ix	2
Nov 27 1928	5-Men	3
Nov 28 1928	6-Cib	4
Nov 29 1928	7-Caban	5
Nov 30 1928	8-Etz'nab	6
Dec 1 1928	9-Cauac	7
Dec 2 1928	10-Ahau	8
Dec 3 1928	*11-Imix*	9
Dec 4 1928	12-Ik	1
Dec 5 1928	13-Akbal	2
Dec 6 1928	**1-Kan**	3
Dec 7 1928	2-Chicchan	4
Dec 8 1928	3-Cimi	5
Dec 9 1928	4-Manik	6
Dec 10 1928	5-Lamat	7
Dec 11 1928	6-Muluc	8
Dec 12 1928	7-Oc	9
Dec 13 1928	8-Chuen	1
Dec 14 1928	9-Eb	2
Dec 15 1928	10-Ben	3
Dec 16 1928	11-Ix	4
Dec 17 1928	12-Men	5
Dec 18 1928	13-Cib	6
Dec 19 1928	**1-Caban**	7
Dec 20 1928	2-Etz'nab	8
Dec 21 1928	3-Cauac	9
Dec 22 1928	4-Ahau	1
Dec 23 1928	*5-Imix*	2
Dec 24 1928	6-Ik	3
Dec 25 1928	7-Akbal	4
Dec 26 1928	8-Kan	5
Dec 27 1928	9-Chicchan	6
Dec 28 1928	10-Cimi	7
Dec 29 1928	11-Manik	8
Dec 30 1928	12-Lamat	9
Dec 31 1928	13-Muluc	1
Jan 1 1929	**1-Oc**	2
Jan 2 1929	2-Chuen	3
Jan 3 1929	3-Eb	4
Jan 4 1929	4-Ben	5
Jan 5 1929	5-Ix	6
Jan 6 1929	6-Men	7
Jan 7 1929	7-Cib	8
Jan 8 1929	8-Caban	9
Jan 9 1929	9-Etz'nab	1
Jan 10 1929	10-Cauac	2
Jan 11 1929	11-Ahau	3
Jan 12 1929	*12-Imix*	4
Jan 13 1929	13-Ik	5
Jan 14 1929	**1-Akbal**	6
Jan 15 1929	2-Kan	7
Jan 16 1929	3-Chicchan	8

Date	Day-Sign	L
Jan 17 1929	4-Cimi	9
Jan 18 1929	5-Manik	1
Jan 19 1929	6-Lamat	2
Jan 20 1929	7-Muluc	3
Jan 21 1929	8-Oc	4
Jan 22 1929	9-Chuen	5
Jan 23 1929	10-Eb	6
Jan 24 1929	11-Ben	7
Jan 25 1929	12-Ix	8
Jan 26 1929	13-Men	9
Jan 27 1929	**1-Cib**	1
Jan 28 1929	2-Caban	2
Jan 29 1929	3-Etz'nab	3
Jan 30 1929	4-Cauac	4
Jan 31 1929	5-Ahau	5
Feb 1 1929	*6-Imix*	6
Feb 2 1929	7-Ik	7
Feb 3 1929	8-Akbal	8
Feb 4 1929	9-Kan	9
Feb 5 1929	10-Chicchan	1
Feb 6 1929	11-Cimi	2
Feb 7 1929	12-Manik	3
Feb 8 1929	13-Lamat	4
Feb 9 1929	**1-Muluc**	5
Feb 10 1929	2-Oc	6
Feb 11 1929	3-Chuen	7
Feb 12 1929	4-Eb	8
Feb 13 1929	5-Ben	9
Feb 14 1929	6-Ix	1
Feb 15 1929	7-Men	2
Feb 16 1929	8-Cib	3
Feb 17 1929	9-Caban	4
Feb 18 1929	10-Etz'nab	5
Feb 19 1929	11-Cauac	6
Feb 20 1929	12-Ahau	7
Feb 21 1929	*13-Imix*	8
Feb 22 1929	**1-Ik**	9
Feb 23 1929	2-Akbal	1
Feb 24 1929	3-Kan	2
Feb 25 1929	4-Chicchan	3
Feb 26 1929	5-Cimi	4
Feb 27 1929	6-Manik	5
Feb 28 1929	7-Lamat	6
Mar 1 1929	8-Muluc	7
Mar 2 1929	9-Oc	8
Mar 3 1929	10-Chuen	9
Mar 4 1929	11-Eb	1
Mar 5 1929	12-Ben	2
Mar 6 1929	13-Ix	3
Mar 7 1929	**1-Men**	4
Mar 8 1929	2-Cib	5
Mar 9 1929	3-Caban	6
Mar 10 1929	4-Etz'nab	7
Mar 11 1929	5-Cauac	8
Mar 12 1929	6-Ahau	9
Mar 13 1929	*7-Imix*	1
Mar 14 1929	8-Ik	2
Mar 15 1929	9-Akbal	3
Mar 16 1929	10-Kan	4
Mar 17 1929	11-Chicchan	5
Mar 18 1929	12-Cimi	6
Mar 19 1929	13-Manik	7
Mar 20 1929	**1-Lamat**	8
Mar 21 1929	2-Muluc	9
Mar 22 1929	3-Oc	1
Mar 23 1929	4-Chuen	2
Mar 24 1929	5-Eb	3
Mar 25 1929	6-Ben	4

Date	Day-Sign	L
Mar 26 1929	7-Ix	5
Mar 27 1929	8-Men	6
Mar 28 1929	9-Cib	7
Mar 29 1929	10-Caban	8
Mar 30 1929	11-Etz'nab	9
Mar 31 1929	12-Cauac	1
Apr 1 1929	13-Ahau	2
Apr 2 1929	**1-Imix**	3
Apr 3 1929	2-Ik	4
Apr 4 1929	3-Akbal	5
Apr 5 1929	4-Kan	6
Apr 6 1929	5-Chicchan	7
Apr 7 1929	6-Cimi	8
Apr 8 1929	7-Manik	9
Apr 9 1929	8-Lamat	1
Apr 10 1929	9-Muluc	2
Apr 11 1929	10-Oc	3
Apr 12 1929	11-Chuen	4
Apr 13 1929	12-Eb	5
Apr 14 1929	13-Ben	6
Apr 15 1929	**1-Ix**	7
Apr 16 1929	2-Men	8
Apr 17 1929	3-Cib	9
Apr 18 1929	4-Caban	1
Apr 19 1929	5-Etz'nab	2
Apr 20 1929	6-Cauac	3
Apr 21 1929	7-Ahau	4
Apr 22 1929	*8-Imix*	5
Apr 23 1929	9-Ik	6
Apr 24 1929	10-Akbal	7
Apr 25 1929	11-Kan	8
Apr 26 1929	12-Chicchan	9
Apr 27 1929	13-Cimi	1
Apr 28 1929	**1-Manik**	2
Apr 29 1929	2-Lamat	3
Apr 30 1929	3-Muluc	4
May 1 1929	4-Oc	5
May 2 1929	5-Chuen	6
May 3 1929	6-Eb	7
May 4 1929	7-Ben	8
May 5 1929	8-Ix	9
May 6 1929	9-Men	1
May 7 1929	10-Cib	2
May 8 1929	11-Caban	3
May 9 1929	12-Etz'nab	4
May 10 1929	13-Cauac	5
May 11 1929	**1-Ahau**	6
May 12 1929	*2-Imix*	7
May 13 1929	3-Ik	8
May 14 1929	4-Akbal	9
May 15 1929	5-Kan	1
May 16 1929	6-Chicchan	2
May 17 1929	7-Cimi	3
May 18 1929	8-Manik	4
May 19 1929	9-Lamat	5
May 20 1929	10-Muluc	6
May 21 1929	11-Oc	7
May 22 1929	12-Chuen	8
May 23 1929	13-Eb	9
May 24 1929	**1-Ben**	1
May 25 1929	2-Ix	2
May 26 1929	3-Men	3
May 27 1929	4-Cib	4
May 28 1929	5-Caban	5
May 29 1929	6-Etz'nab	6
May 30 1929	7-Cauac	7
May 31 1929	8-Ahau	8
Jun 1 1929	*9-Imix*	9

Date	Day-Sign	L
Jun 2 1929	10-Ik	1
Jun 3 1929	11-Akbal	2
Jun 4 1929	12-Kan	3
Jun 5 1929	13-Chicchan	4
Jun 6 1929	**1-Cimi**	5
Jun 7 1929	2-Manik	6
Jun 8 1929	3-Lamat	7
Jun 9 1929	4-Muluc	8
Jun 10 1929	5-Oc	9
Jun 11 1929	6-Chuen	1
Jun 12 1929	7-Eb	2
Jun 13 1929	8-Ben	3
Jun 14 1929	9-Ix	4
Jun 15 1929	10-Men	5
Jun 16 1929	11-Cib	6
Jun 17 1929	12-Caban	7
Jun 18 1929	13-Etz'nab	8
Jun 19 1929	**1-Cauac**	9
Jun 20 1929	2-Ahau	1
Jun 21 1929	*3-Imix*	2
Jun 22 1929	4-Ik	3
Jun 23 1929	5-Akbal	4
Jun 24 1929	6-Kan	5
Jun 25 1929	7-Chicchan	6
Jun 26 1929	8-Cimi	7
Jun 27 1929	9-Manik	8
Jun 28 1929	10-Lamat	9
Jun 29 1929	11-Muluc	1
Jun 30 1929	12-Oc	2
Jul 1 1929	13-Chuen	3
Jul 2 1929	**1-Eb**	4
Jul 3 1929	2-Ben	5
Jul 4 1929	3-Ix	6
Jul 5 1929	4-Men	7
Jul 6 1929	5-Cib	8
Jul 7 1929	6-Caban	9
Jul 8 1929	7-Etz'nab	1
Jul 9 1929	8-Cauac	2
Jul 10 1929	9-Ahau	3
Jul 11 1929	*10-Imix*	4
Jul 12 1929	11-Ik	5
Jul 13 1929	12-Akbal	6
Jul 14 1929	13-Kan	7
Jul 15 1929	**1-Chicchan**	8
Jul 16 1929	2-Cimi	9
Jul 17 1929	3-Manik	1
Jul 18 1929	4-Lamat	2
Jul 19 1929	5-Muluc	3
Jul 20 1929	6-Oc	4
Jul 21 1929	7-Chuen	5
Jul 22 1929	8-Eb	6
Jul 23 1929	9-Ben	7
Jul 24 1929	10-Ix	8
Jul 25 1929	11-Men	9
Jul 26 1929	12-Cib	1
Jul 27 1929	13-Caban	2
Jul 28 1929	**1-Etz'nab**	3
Jul 29 1929	2-Cauac	4
Jul 30 1929	3-Ahau	5
Jul 31 1929	*4-Imix*	6
Aug 1 1929	5-Ik	7
Aug 2 1929	6-Akbal	8
Aug 3 1929	7-Kan	9
Aug 4 1929	8-Chicchan	1
Aug 5 1929	9-Cimi	2
Aug 6 1929	10-Manik	3
Aug 7 1929	11-Lamat	4
Aug 8 1929	12-Muluc	5

Date	Day-Sign	L
Aug 9 1929	13-Oc	6
Aug 10 1929	**1-Chuen**	7
Aug 11 1929	2-Eb	8
Aug 12 1929	3-Ben	9
Aug 13 1929	4-Ix	1
Aug 14 1929	5-Men	2
Aug 15 1929	6-Cib	3
Aug 16 1929	7-Caban	4
Aug 17 1929	8-Etz'nab	5
Aug 18 1929	9-Cauac	6
Aug 19 1929	10-Ahau	7
Aug 20 1929	*11-Imix*	8
Aug 21 1929	12-Ik	9
Aug 22 1929	13-Akbal	1
Aug 23 1929	**1-Kan**	2
Aug 24 1929	2-Chicchan	3
Aug 25 1929	3-Cimi	4
Aug 26 1929	4-Manik	5
Aug 27 1929	5-Lamat	6
Aug 28 1929	6-Muluc	7
Aug 29 1929	7-Oc	8
Aug 30 1929	8-Chuen	9
Aug 31 1929	9-Eb	1
Sep 1 1929	10-Ben	2
Sep 2 1929	11-Ix	3
Sep 3 1929	12-Men	4
Sep 4 1929	13-Cib	5
Sep 5 1929	**1-Caban**	6
Sep 6 1929	2-Etz'nab	7
Sep 7 1929	3-Cauac	8
Sep 8 1929	4-Ahau	9
Sep 9 1929	*5-Imix*	1
Sep 10 1929	6-Ik	2
Sep 11 1929	7-Akbal	3
Sep 12 1929	8-Kan	4
Sep 13 1929	9-Chicchan	5
Sep 14 1929	10-Cimi	6
Sep 15 1929	11-Manik	7
Sep 16 1929	12-Lamat	8
Sep 17 1929	13-Muluc	9
Sep 18 1929	**1-Oc**	1
Sep 19 1929	2-Chuen	2
Sep 20 1929	3-Eb	3
Sep 21 1929	4-Ben	4
Sep 22 1929	5-Ix	5
Sep 23 1929	6-Men	6
Sep 24 1929	7-Cib	7
Sep 25 1929	8-Caban	8
Sep 26 1929	9-Etz'nab	9
Sep 27 1929	10-Cauac	1
Sep 28 1929	11-Ahau	2
Sep 29 1929	*12-Imix*	3
Sep 30 1929	13-Ik	4
Oct 1 1929	**1-Akbal**	5
Oct 2 1929	2-Kan	6
Oct 3 1929	3-Chicchan	7
Oct 4 1929	4-Cimi	8
Oct 5 1929	5-Manik	9
Oct 6 1929	6-Lamat	1
Oct 7 1929	7-Muluc	2
Oct 8 1929	8-Oc	3
Oct 9 1929	9-Chuen	4
Oct 10 1929	10-Eb	5
Oct 11 1929	11-Ben	6
Oct 12 1929	12-Ix	7
Oct 13 1929	13-Men	8
Oct 14 1929	**1-Cib**	9
Oct 15 1929	2-Caban	1

Date	Day-Sign	L
Oct 16 1929	3-Etz'nab	2
Oct 17 1929	4-Cauac	3
Oct 18 1929	5-Ahau	4
Oct 19 1929	*6-Imix*	5
Oct 20 1929	7-Ik	6
Oct 21 1929	8-Akbal	7
Oct 22 1929	9-Kan	8
Oct 23 1929	10-Chicchan	9
Oct 24 1929	11-Cimi	1
Oct 25 1929	12-Manik	2
Oct 26 1929	13-Lamat	3
Oct 27 1929	**1-Muluc**	4
Oct 28 1929	2-Oc	5
Oct 29 1929	3-Chuen	6
Oct 30 1929	4-Eb	7
Oct 31 1929	5-Ben	8
Nov 1 1929	6-Ix	9
Nov 2 1929	7-Men	1
Nov 3 1929	8-Cib	2
Nov 4 1929	9-Caban	3
Nov 5 1929	10-Etz'nab	4
Nov 6 1929	11-Cauac	5
Nov 7 1929	12-Ahau	6
Nov 8 1929	*13-Imix*	7
Nov 9 1929	**1-Ik**	8
Nov 10 1929	2-Akbal	9
Nov 11 1929	3-Kan	1
Nov 12 1929	4-Chicchan	2
Nov 13 1929	5-Cimi	3
Nov 14 1929	6-Manik	4
Nov 15 1929	7-Lamat	5
Nov 16 1929	8-Muluc	6
Nov 17 1929	9-Oc	7
Nov 18 1929	10-Chuen	8
Nov 19 1929	11-Eb	9
Nov 20 1929	12-Ben	1
Nov 21 1929	13-Ix	2
Nov 22 1929	**1-Men**	3
Nov 23 1929	2-Cib	4
Nov 24 1929	3-Caban	5
Nov 25 1929	4-Etz'nab	6
Nov 26 1929	5-Cauac	7
Nov 27 1929	6-Ahau	8
Nov 28 1929	*7-Imix*	9
Nov 29 1929	8-Ik	1
Nov 30 1929	9-Akbal	2
Dec 1 1929	10-Kan	3
Dec 2 1929	11-Chicchan	4
Dec 3 1929	12-Cimi	5
Dec 4 1929	13-Manik	6
Dec 5 1929	**1-Lamat**	7
Dec 6 1929	2-Muluc	8
Dec 7 1929	3-Oc	9
Dec 8 1929	4-Chuen	1
Dec 9 1929	5-Eb	2
Dec 10 1929	6-Ben	3
Dec 11 1929	7-Ix	4
Dec 12 1929	8-Men	5
Dec 13 1929	9-Cib	6
Dec 14 1929	10-Caban	7
Dec 15 1929	11-Etz'nab	8
Dec 16 1929	12-Cauac	9
Dec 17 1929	13-Ahau	1
Dec 18 1929	**1-Imix**	2
Dec 19 1929	2-Ik	3
Dec 20 1929	3-Akbal	4
Dec 21 1929	4-Kan	5
Dec 22 1929	5-Chicchan	6

Date	Day-Sign	L	Date	Day-Sign	L	Date	Day-Sign	L
Dec 23 1929	6-Cimi	7	Mar 1 1930	9-Ix	3	May 8 1930	12-Ik	8
Dec 24 1929	7-Manik	8	Mar 2 1930	10-Men	4	May 9 1930	13-Akbal	9
Dec 25 1929	8-Lamat	9	Mar 3 1930	11-Cib	5	May 10 1930	1-Kan	1
Dec 26 1929	9-Muluc	1	Mar 4 1930	12-Caban	6	May 11 1930	2-Chicchan	2
Dec 27 1929	10-Oc	2	Mar 5 1930	13-Etz'nab	7	May 12 1930	3-Cimi	3
Dec 28 1929	11-Chuen	3	Mar 6 1930	1-Cauac	8	May 13 1930	4-Manik	4
Dec 29 1929	12-Eb	4	Mar 7 1930	2-Ahau	9	May 14 1930	5-Lamat	5
Dec 30 1929	13-Ben	5	Mar 8 1930	3-Imix	1	May 15 1930	6-Muluc	6
Dec 31 1929	1-Ix	6	Mar 9 1930	4-Ik	2	May 16 1930	7-Oc	7
Jan 1 1930	2-Men	7	Mar 10 1930	5-Akbal	3	May 17 1930	8-Chuen	8
Jan 2 1930	3-Cib	8	Mar 11 1930	6-Kan	4	May 18 1930	9-Eb	9
Jan 3 1930	4-Caban	9	Mar 12 1930	7-Chicchan	5	May 19 1930	10-Ben	1
Jan 4 1930	5-Etz'nab	1	Mar 13 1930	8-Cimi	6	May 20 1930	11-Ix	2
Jan 5 1930	6-Cauac	2	Mar 14 1930	9-Manik	7	May 21 1930	12-Men	3
Jan 6 1930	7-Ahau	3	Mar 15 1930	10-Lamat	8	May 22 1930	13-Cib	4
Jan 7 1930	8-Imix	4	Mar 16 1930	11-Muluc	9	May 23 1930	1-Caban	5
Jan 8 1930	9-Ik	5	Mar 17 1930	12-Oc	1	May 24 1930	2-Etz'nab	6
Jan 9 1930	10-Akbal	6	Mar 18 1930	13-Chuen	2	May 25 1930	3-Cauac	7
Jan 10 1930	11-Kan	7	Mar 19 1930	1-Eb	3	May 26 1930	4-Ahau	8
Jan 11 1930	12-Chicchan	8	Mar 20 1930	2-Ben	4	May 27 1930	5-Imix	9
Jan 12 1930	13-Cimi	9	Mar 21 1930	3-Ix	5	May 28 1930	6-Ik	1
Jan 13 1930	1-Manik	1	Mar 22 1930	4-Men	6	May 29 1930	7-Akbal	2
Jan 14 1930	2-Lamat	2	Mar 23 1930	5-Cib	7	May 30 1930	8-Kan	3
Jan 15 1930	3-Muluc	3	Mar 24 1930	6-Caban	8	May 31 1930	9-Chicchan	4
Jan 16 1930	4-Oc	4	Mar 25 1930	7-Etz'nab	9	Jun 1 1930	10-Cimi	5
Jan 17 1930	5-Chuen	5	Mar 26 1930	8-Cauac	1	Jun 2 1930	11-Manik	6
Jan 18 1930	6-Eb	6	Mar 27 1930	9-Ahau	2	Jun 3 1930	12-Lamat	7
Jan 19 1930	7-Ben	7	Mar 28 1930	10-Imix	3	Jun 4 1930	13-Muluc	8
Jan 20 1930	8-Ix	8	Mar 29 1930	11-Ik	4	Jun 5 1930	1-Oc	9
Jan 21 1930	9-Men	9	Mar 30 1930	12-Akbal	5	Jun 6 1930	2-Chuen	1
Jan 22 1930	10-Cib	1	Mar 31 1930	13-Kan	6	Jun 7 1930	3-Eb	2
Jan 23 1930	11-Caban	2	Apr 1 1930	1-Chicchan	7	Jun 8 1930	4-Ben	3
Jan 24 1930	12-Etz'nab	3	Apr 2 1930	2-Cimi	8	Jun 9 1930	5-Ix	4
Jan 25 1930	13-Cauac	4	Apr 3 1930	3-Manik	9	Jun 10 1930	6-Men	5
Jan 26 1930	1-Ahau	5	Apr 4 1930	4-Lamat	1	Jun 11 1930	7-Cib	6
Jan 27 1930	2-Imix	6	Apr 5 1930	5-Muluc	2	Jun 12 1930	8-Caban	7
Jan 28 1930	3-Ik	7	Apr 6 1930	6-Oc	3	Jun 13 1930	9-Etz'nab	8
Jan 29 1930	4-Akbal	8	Apr 7 1930	7-Chuen	4	Jun 14 1930	10-Cauac	9
Jan 30 1930	5-Kan	9	Apr 8 1930	8-Eb	5	Jun 15 1930	11-Ahau	1
Jan 31 1930	6-Chicchan	1	Apr 9 1930	9-Ben	6	Jun 16 1930	12-Imix	2
Feb 1 1930	7-Cimi	2	Apr 10 1930	10-Ix	7	Jun 17 1930	13-Ik	3
Feb 2 1930	8-Manik	3	Apr 11 1930	11-Men	8	Jun 18 1930	1-Akbal	4
Feb 3 1930	9-Lamat	4	Apr 12 1930	12-Cib	9	Jun 19 1930	2-Kan	5
Feb 4 1930	10-Muluc	5	Apr 13 1930	13-Caban	1	Jun 20 1930	3-Chicchan	6
Feb 5 1930	11-Oc	6	Apr 14 1930	1-Etz'nab	2	Jun 21 1930	4-Cimi	7
Feb 6 1930	12-Chuen	7	Apr 15 1930	2-Cauac	3	Jun 22 1930	5-Manik	8
Feb 7 1930	13-Eb	8	Apr 16 1930	3-Ahau	4	Jun 23 1930	6-Lamat	9
Feb 8 1930	1-Ben	9	Apr 17 1930	4-Imix	5	Jun 24 1930	7-Muluc	1
Feb 9 1930	2-Ix	1	Apr 18 1930	5-Ik	6	Jun 25 1930	8-Oc	2
Feb 10 1930	3-Men	2	Apr 19 1930	6-Akbal	7	Jun 26 1930	9-Chuen	3
Feb 11 1930	4-Cib	3	Apr 20 1930	7-Kan	8	Jun 27 1930	10-Eb	4
Feb 12 1930	5-Caban	4	Apr 21 1930	8-Chicchan	9	Jun 28 1930	11-Ben	5
Feb 13 1930	6-Etz'nab	5	Apr 22 1930	9-Cimi	1	Jun 29 1930	12-Ix	6
Feb 14 1930	7-Cauac	6	Apr 23 1930	10-Manik	2	Jun 30 1930	13-Men	7
Feb 15 1930	8-Ahau	7	Apr 24 1930	11-Lamat	3	Jul 1 1930	1-Cib	8
Feb 16 1930	9-Imix	8	Apr 25 1930	12-Muluc	4	Jul 2 1930	2-Caban	9
Feb 17 1930	10-Ik	9	Apr 26 1930	13-Oc	5	Jul 3 1930	3-Etz'nab	1
Feb 18 1930	11-Akbal	1	Apr 27 1930	1-Chuen	6	Jul 4 1930	4-Cauac	2
Feb 19 1930	12-Kan	2	Apr 28 1930	2-Eb	7	Jul 5 1930	5-Ahau	3
Feb 20 1930	13-Chicchan	3	Apr 29 1930	3-Ben	8	Jul 6 1930	6-Imix	4
Feb 21 1930	1-Cimi	4	Apr 30 1930	4-Ix	9	Jul 7 1930	7-Ik	5
Feb 22 1930	2-Manik	5	May 1 1930	5-Men	1	Jul 8 1930	8-Akbal	6
Feb 23 1930	3-Lamat	6	May 2 1930	6-Cib	2	Jul 9 1930	9-Kan	7
Feb 24 1930	4-Muluc	7	May 3 1930	7-Caban	3	Jul 10 1930	10-Chicchan	8
Feb 25 1930	5-Oc	8	May 4 1930	8-Etz'nab	4	Jul 11 1930	11-Cimi	9
Feb 26 1930	6-Chuen	9	May 5 1930	9-Cauac	5	Jul 12 1930	12-Manik	1
Feb 27 1930	7-Eb	1	May 6 1930	10-Ahau	6	Jul 13 1930	13-Lamat	2
Feb 28 1930	8-Ben	2	May 7 1930	11-Imix	7	Jul 14 1930	1-Muluc	3

Date	Day-Sign	L	Date	Day-Sign	L	Date	Day-Sign	L
Jul 15 1930	2-Oc	4	Sep 21 1930	5-Etz'nab	9	Nov 28 1930	8-Cimi	5
Jul 16 1930	3-Chuen	5	Sep 22 1930	6-Cauac	1	Nov 29 1930	9-Manik	6
Jul 17 1930	4-Eb	6	Sep 23 1930	7-Ahau	2	Nov 30 1930	10-Lamat	7
Jul 18 1930	5-Ben	7	Sep 24 1930	*8-Imix*	3	Dec 1 1930	11-Muluc	8
Jul 19 1930	6-Ix	8	Sep 25 1930	9-Ik	4	Dec 2 1930	12-Oc	9
Jul 20 1930	7-Men	9	Sep 26 1930	10-Akbal	5	Dec 3 1930	13-Chuen	1
Jul 21 1930	8-Cib	1	Sep 27 1930	11-Kan	6	Dec 4 1930	**1-Eb**	2
Jul 22 1930	9-Caban	2	Sep 28 1930	12-Chicchan	7	Dec 5 1930	2-Ben	3
Jul 23 1930	10-Etz'nab	3	Sep 29 1930	13-Cimi	8	Dec 6 1930	3-Ix	4
Jul 24 1930	11-Cauac	4	Sep 30 1930	**1-Manik**	9	Dec 7 1930	4-Men	5
Jul 25 1930	12-Ahau	5	Oct 1 1930	2-Lamat	1	Dec 8 1930	5-Cib	6
Jul 26 1930	*13-Imix*	6	Oct 2 1930	3-Muluc	2	Dec 9 1930	6-Caban	7
Jul 27 1930	**1-Ik**	7	Oct 3 1930	4-Oc	3	Dec 10 1930	7-Etz'nab	8
Jul 28 1930	2-Akbal	8	Oct 4 1930	5-Chuen	4	Dec 11 1930	8-Cauac	9
Jul 29 1930	3-Kan	9	Oct 5 1930	6-Eb	5	Dec 12 1930	9-Ahau	1
Jul 30 1930	4-Chicchan	1	Oct 6 1930	7-Ben	6	Dec 13 1930	*10-Imix*	2
Jul 31 1930	5-Cimi	2	Oct 7 1930	8-Ix	7	Dec 14 1930	11-Ik	3
Aug 1 1930	6-Manik	3	Oct 8 1930	9-Men	8	Dec 15 1930	12-Akbal	4
Aug 2 1930	7-Lamat	4	Oct 9 1930	10-Cib	9	Dec 16 1930	13-Kan	5
Aug 3 1930	8-Muluc	5	Oct 10 1930	11-Caban	1	Dec 17 1930	**1-Chicchan**	6
Aug 4 1930	9-Oc	6	Oct 11 1930	12-Etz'nab	2	Dec 18 1930	2-Cimi	7
Aug 5 1930	10-Chuen	7	Oct 12 1930	13-Cauac	3	Dec 19 1930	3-Manik	8
Aug 6 1930	11-Eb	8	Oct 13 1930	**1-Ahau**	4	Dec 20 1930	4-Lamat	9
Aug 7 1930	12-Ben	9	Oct 14 1930	*2-Imix*	5	Dec 21 1930	5-Muluc	1
Aug 8 1930	13-Ix	1	Oct 15 1930	3-Ik	6	Dec 22 1930	6-Oc	2
Aug 9 1930	**1-Men**	2	Oct 16 1930	4-Akbal	7	Dec 23 1930	7-Chuen	3
Aug 10 1930	2-Cib	3	Oct 17 1930	5-Kan	8	Dec 24 1930	8-Eb	4
Aug 11 1930	3-Caban	4	Oct 18 1930	6-Chicchan	9	Dec 25 1930	9-Ben	5
Aug 12 1930	4-Etz'nab	5	Oct 19 1930	7-Cimi	1	Dec 26 1930	10-Ix	6
Aug 13 1930	5-Cauac	6	Oct 20 1930	8-Manik	2	Dec 27 1930	11-Men	7
Aug 14 1930	6-Ahau	7	Oct 21 1930	9-Lamat	3	Dec 28 1930	12-Cib	8
Aug 15 1930	*7-Imix*	8	Oct 22 1930	10-Muluc	4	Dec 29 1930	13-Caban	9
Aug 16 1930	8-Ik	9	Oct 23 1930	11-Oc	5	Dec 30 1930	**1-Etz'nab**	1
Aug 17 1930	9-Akbal	1	Oct 24 1930	12-Chuen	6	Dec 31 1930	2-Cauac	2
Aug 18 1930	10-Kan	2	Oct 25 1930	13-Eb	7	Jan 1 1931	3-Ahau	3
Aug 19 1930	11-Chicchan	3	Oct 26 1930	**1-Ben**	8	Jan 2 1931	*4-Imix*	4
Aug 20 1930	12-Cimi	4	Oct 27 1930	2-Ix	9	Jan 3 1931	5-Ik	5
Aug 21 1930	13-Manik	5	Oct 28 1930	3-Men	1	Jan 4 1931	6-Akbal	6
Aug 22 1930	**1-Lamat**	6	Oct 29 1930	4-Cib	2	Jan 5 1931	7-Kan	7
Aug 23 1930	2-Muluc	7	Oct 30 1930	5-Caban	3	Jan 6 1931	8-Chicchan	8
Aug 24 1930	3-Oc	8	Oct 31 1930	6-Etz'nab	4	Jan 7 1931	9-Cimi	9
Aug 25 1930	4-Chuen	9	Nov 1 1930	7-Cauac	5	Jan 8 1931	10-Manik	1
Aug 26 1930	5-Eb	1	Nov 2 1930	8-Ahau	6	Jan 9 1931	11-Lamat	2
Aug 27 1930	6-Ben	2	Nov 3 1930	*9-Imix*	7	Jan 10 1931	12-Muluc	3
Aug 28 1930	7-Ix	3	Nov 4 1930	10-Ik	8	Jan 11 1931	13-Oc	4
Aug 29 1930	8-Men	4	Nov 5 1930	11-Akbal	9	Jan 12 1931	**1-Chuen**	5
Aug 30 1930	9-Cib	5	Nov 6 1930	12-Kan	1	Jan 13 1931	2-Eb	6
Aug 31 1930	10-Caban	6	Nov 7 1930	13-Chicchan	2	Jan 14 1931	3-Ben	7
Sep 1 1930	11-Etz'nab	7	Nov 8 1930	**1-Cimi**	3	Jan 15 1931	4-Ix	8
Sep 2 1930	12-Cauac	8	Nov 9 1930	2-Manik	4	Jan 16 1931	5-Men	9
Sep 3 1930	13-Ahau	9	Nov 10 1930	3-Lamat	5	Jan 17 1931	6-Cib	1
Sep 4 1930	**1-Imix**	1	Nov 11 1930	4-Muluc	6	Jan 18 1931	7-Caban	2
Sep 5 1930	2-Ik	2	Nov 12 1930	5-Oc	7	Jan 19 1931	8-Etz'nab	3
Sep 6 1930	3-Akbal	3	Nov 13 1930	6-Chuen	8	Jan 20 1931	9-Cauac	4
Sep 7 1930	4-Kan	4	Nov 14 1930	7-Eb	9	Jan 21 1931	10-Ahau	5
Sep 8 1930	5-Chicchan	5	Nov 15 1930	8-Ben	1	Jan 22 1931	*11-Imix*	6
Sep 9 1930	6-Cimi	6	Nov 16 1930	9-Ix	2	Jan 23 1931	12-Ik	7
Sep 10 1930	7-Manik	7	Nov 17 1930	10-Men	3	Jan 24 1931	13-Akbal	8
Sep 11 1930	8-Lamat	8	Nov 18 1930	11-Cib	4	Jan 25 1931	**1-Kan**	9
Sep 12 1930	9-Muluc	9	Nov 19 1930	12-Caban	5	Jan 26 1931	2-Chicchan	1
Sep 13 1930	10-Oc	1	Nov 20 1930	13-Etz'nab	6	Jan 27 1931	3-Cimi	2
Sep 14 1930	11-Chuen	2	Nov 21 1930	**1-Cauac**	7	Jan 28 1931	4-Manik	3
Sep 15 1930	12-Eb	3	Nov 22 1930	2-Ahau	8	Jan 29 1931	5-Lamat	4
Sep 16 1930	13-Ben	4	Nov 23 1930	*3-Imix*	9	Jan 30 1931	6-Muluc	5
Sep 17 1930	**1-Ix**	5	Nov 24 1930	4-Ik	1	Jan 31 1931	7-Oc	6
Sep 18 1930	2-Men	6	Nov 25 1930	5-Akbal	2	Feb 1 1931	8-Chuen	7
Sep 19 1930	3-Cib	7	Nov 26 1930	6-Kan	3	Feb 2 1931	9-Eb	8
Sep 20 1930	4-Caban	8	Nov 27 1930	7-Chicchan	4	Feb 3 1931	10-Ben	9

Date	Day-Sign	L	Date	Day-Sign	L	Date	Day-Sign	L
Feb 4 1931	11-Ix	1	Apr 13 1931	**1-Ik**	6	Jun 20 1931	4-Oc	2
Feb 5 1931	12-Men	2	Apr 14 1931	2-Akbal	7	Jun 21 1931	5-Chuen	3
Feb 6 1931	13-Cib	3	Apr 15 1931	3-Kan	8	Jun 22 1931	6-Eb	4
Feb 7 1931	**1-Caban**	4	Apr 16 1931	4-Chicchan	9	Jun 23 1931	7-Ben	5
Feb 8 1931	2-Etz'nab	5	Apr 17 1931	5-Cimi	1	Jun 24 1931	8-Ix	6
Feb 9 1931	3-Cauac	6	Apr 18 1931	6-Manik	2	Jun 25 1931	9-Men	7
Feb 10 1931	4-Ahau	7	Apr 19 1931	7-Lamat	3	Jun 26 1931	10-Cib	8
Feb 11 1931	5-*Imix*	8	Apr 20 1931	8-Muluc	4	Jun 27 1931	11-Caban	9
Feb 12 1931	6-Ik	9	Apr 21 1931	9-Oc	5	Jun 28 1931	12-Etz'nab	1
Feb 13 1931	7-Akbal	1	Apr 22 1931	10-Chuen	6	Jun 29 1931	13-Cauac	2
Feb 14 1931	8-Kan	2	Apr 23 1931	11-Eb	7	Jun 30 1931	**1-Ahau**	3
Feb 15 1931	9-Chicchan	3	Apr 24 1931	12-Ben	8	Jul 1 1931	2-*Imix*	4
Feb 16 1931	10-Cimi	4	Apr 25 1931	13-Ix	9	Jul 2 1931	3-Ik	5
Feb 17 1931	11-Manik	5	Apr 26 1931	**1-Men**	1	Jul 3 1931	4-Akbal	6
Feb 18 1931	12-Lamat	6	Apr 27 1931	2-Cib	2	Jul 4 1931	5-Kan	7
Feb 19 1931	13-Muluc	7	Apr 28 1931	3-Caban	3	Jul 5 1931	6-Chicchan	8
Feb 20 1931	**1-Oc**	8	Apr 29 1931	4-Etz'nab	4	Jul 6 1931	7-Cimi	9
Feb 21 1931	2-Chuen	9	Apr 30 1931	5-Cauac	5	Jul 7 1931	8-Manik	1
Feb 22 1931	3-Eb	1	May 1 1931	6-Ahau	6	Jul 8 1931	9-Lamat	2
Feb 23 1931	4-Ben	2	May 2 1931	7-*Imix*	7	Jul 9 1931	10-Muluc	3
Feb 24 1931	5-Ix	3	May 3 1931	8-Ik	8	Jul 10 1931	11-Oc	4
Feb 25 1931	6-Men	4	May 4 1931	9-Akbal	9	Jul 11 1931	12-Chuen	5
Feb 26 1931	7-Cib	5	May 5 1931	10-Kan	1	Jul 12 1931	13-Eb	6
Feb 27 1931	8-Caban	6	May 6 1931	11-Chicchan	2	Jul 13 1931	**1-Ben**	7
Feb 28 1931	9-Etz'nab	7	May 7 1931	12-Cimi	3	Jul 14 1931	2-Ix	8
Mar 1 1931	10-Cauac	8	May 8 1931	13-Manik	4	Jul 15 1931	3-Men	9
Mar 2 1931	11-Ahau	9	May 9 1931	**1-Lamat**	5	Jul 16 1931	4-Cib	1
Mar 3 1931	12-*Imix*	1	May 10 1931	2-Muluc	6	Jul 17 1931	5-Caban	2
Mar 4 1931	13-Ik	2	May 11 1931	3-Oc	7	Jul 18 1931	6-Etz'nab	3
Mar 5 1931	**1-Akbal**	3	May 12 1931	4-Chuen	8	Jul 19 1931	7-Cauac	4
Mar 6 1931	2-Kan	4	May 13 1931	5-Eb	9	Jul 20 1931	8-Ahau	5
Mar 7 1931	3-Chicchan	5	May 14 1931	6-Ben	1	Jul 21 1931	9-*Imix*	6
Mar 8 1931	4-Cimi	6	May 15 1931	7-Ix	2	Jul 22 1931	10-Ik	7
Mar 9 1931	5-Manik	7	May 16 1931	8-Men	3	Jul 23 1931	11-Akbal	8
Mar 10 1931	6-Lamat	8	May 17 1931	9-Cib	4	Jul 24 1931	12-Kan	9
Mar 11 1931	7-Muluc	9	May 18 1931	10-Caban	5	Jul 25 1931	13-Chicchan	1
Mar 12 1931	8-Oc	1	May 19 1931	11-Etz'nab	6	Jul 26 1931	**1-Cimi**	2
Mar 13 1931	9-Chuen	2	May 20 1931	12-Cauac	7	Jul 27 1931	2-Manik	3
Mar 14 1931	10-Eb	3	May 21 1931	13-Ahau	8	Jul 28 1931	3-Lamat	4
Mar 15 1931	11-Ben	4	May 22 1931	**1-Imix**	9	Jul 29 1931	4-Muluc	5
Mar 16 1931	12-Ix	5	May 23 1931	2-Ik	1	Jul 30 1931	5-Oc	6
Mar 17 1931	13-Men	6	May 24 1931	3-Akbal	2	Jul 31 1931	6-Chuen	7
Mar 18 1931	**1-Cib**	7	May 25 1931	4-Kan	3	Aug 1 1931	7-Eb	8
Mar 19 1931	2-Caban	8	May 26 1931	5-Chicchan	4	Aug 2 1931	8-Ben	9
Mar 20 1931	3-Etz'nab	9	May 27 1931	6-Cimi	5	Aug 3 1931	9-Ix	1
Mar 21 1931	4-Cauac	1	May 28 1931	7-Manik	6	Aug 4 1931	10-Men	2
Mar 22 1931	5-Ahau	2	May 29 1931	8-Lamat	7	Aug 5 1931	11-Cib	3
Mar 23 1931	6-*Imix*	3	May 30 1931	9-Muluc	8	Aug 6 1931	12-Caban	4
Mar 24 1931	7-Ik	4	May 31 1931	10-Oc	9	Aug 7 1931	13-Etz'nab	5
Mar 25 1931	8-Akbal	5	Jun 1 1931	11-Chuen	1	Aug 8 1931	**1-Cauac**	6
Mar 26 1931	9-Kan	6	Jun 2 1931	12-Eb	2	Aug 9 1931	2-Ahau	7
Mar 27 1931	10-Chicchan	7	Jun 3 1931	13-Ben	3	Aug 10 1931	3-*Imix*	8
Mar 28 1931	11-Cimi	8	Jun 4 1931	**1-Ix**	4	Aug 11 1931	4-Ik	9
Mar 29 1931	12-Manik	9	Jun 5 1931	2-Men	5	Aug 12 1931	5-Akbal	1
Mar 30 1931	13-Lamat	1	Jun 6 1931	3-Cib	6	Aug 13 1931	6-Kan	2
Mar 31 1931	**1-Muluc**	2	Jun 7 1931	4-Caban	7	Aug 14 1931	7-Chicchan	3
Apr 1 1931	2-Oc	3	Jun 8 1931	5-Etz'nab	8	Aug 15 1931	8-Cimi	4
Apr 2 1931	3-Chuen	4	Jun 9 1931	6-Cauac	9	Aug 16 1931	9-Manik	5
Apr 3 1931	4-Eb	5	Jun 10 1931	7-Ahau	1	Aug 17 1931	10-Lamat	6
Apr 4 1931	5-Ben	6	Jun 11 1931	8-*Imix*	2	Aug 18 1931	11-Muluc	7
Apr 5 1931	6-Ix	7	Jun 12 1931	9-Ik	3	Aug 19 1931	12-Oc	8
Apr 6 1931	7-Men	8	Jun 13 1931	10-Akbal	4	Aug 20 1931	13-Chuen	9
Apr 7 1931	8-Cib	9	Jun 14 1931	11-Kan	5	Aug 21 1931	**1-Eb**	1
Apr 8 1931	9-Caban	1	Jun 15 1931	12-Chicchan	6	Aug 22 1931	2-Ben	2
Apr 9 1931	10-Etz'nab	2	Jun 16 1931	13-Cimi	7	Aug 23 1931	3-Ix	3
Apr 10 1931	11-Cauac	3	Jun 17 1931	**1-Manik**	8	Aug 24 1931	4-Men	4
Apr 11 1931	12-Ahau	4	Jun 18 1931	2-Lamat	9	Aug 25 1931	5-Cib	5
Apr 12 1931	13-*Imix*	5	Jun 19 1931	3-Muluc	1	Aug 26 1931	6-Caban	6

Date	Day-Sign	L
Aug 27 1931	7-Etz'nab	7
Aug 28 1931	8-Cauac	8
Aug 29 1931	9-Ahau	9
Aug 30 1931	*10-Imix*	1
Aug 31 1931	11-Ik	2
Sep 1 1931	12-Akbal	3
Sep 2 1931	13-Kan	4
Sep 3 1931	**1-Chicchan**	5
Sep 4 1931	2-Cimi	6
Sep 5 1931	3-Manik	7
Sep 6 1931	4-Lamat	8
Sep 7 1931	5-Muluc	9
Sep 8 1931	6-Oc	1
Sep 9 1931	7-Chuen	2
Sep 10 1931	8-Eb	3
Sep 11 1931	9-Ben	4
Sep 12 1931	10-Ix	5
Sep 13 1931	11-Men	6
Sep 14 1931	12-Cib	7
Sep 15 1931	13-Caban	8
Sep 16 1931	**1-Etz'nab**	9
Sep 17 1931	2-Cauac	1
Sep 18 1931	3-Ahau	2
Sep 19 1931	*4-Imix*	3
Sep 20 1931	5-Ik	4
Sep 21 1931	6-Akbal	5
Sep 22 1931	7-Kan	6
Sep 23 1931	8-Chicchan	7
Sep 24 1931	9-Cimi	8
Sep 25 1931	10-Manik	9
Sep 26 1931	11-Lamat	1
Sep 27 1931	12-Muluc	2
Sep 28 1931	13-Oc	3
Sep 29 1931	**1-Chuen**	4
Sep 30 1931	2-Eb	5
Oct 1 1931	3-Ben	6
Oct 2 1931	4-Ix	7
Oct 3 1931	5-Men	8
Oct 4 1931	6-Cib	9
Oct 5 1931	7-Caban	1
Oct 6 1931	8-Etz'nab	2
Oct 7 1931	9-Cauac	3
Oct 8 1931	10-Ahau	4
Oct 9 1931	*11-Imix*	5
Oct 10 1931	12-Ik	6
Oct 11 1931	13-Akbal	7
Oct 12 1931	**1-Kan**	8
Oct 13 1931	2-Chicchan	9
Oct 14 1931	3-Cimi	1
Oct 15 1931	4-Manik	2
Oct 16 1931	5-Lamat	3
Oct 17 1931	6-Muluc	4
Oct 18 1931	7-Oc	5
Oct 19 1931	8-Chuen	6
Oct 20 1931	9-Eb	7
Oct 21 1931	10-Ben	8
Oct 22 1931	11-Ix	9
Oct 23 1931	12-Men	1
Oct 24 1931	13-Cib	2
Oct 25 1931	**1-Caban**	3
Oct 26 1931	2-Etz'nab	4
Oct 27 1931	3-Cauac	5
Oct 28 1931	4-Ahau	6
Oct 29 1931	*5-Imix*	7
Oct 30 1931	6-Ik	8
Oct 31 1931	7-Akbal	9
Nov 1 1931	8-Kan	1
Nov 2 1931	9-Chicchan	2

Date	Day-Sign	L
Nov 3 1931	10-Cimi	3
Nov 4 1931	11-Manik	4
Nov 5 1931	12-Lamat	5
Nov 6 1931	13-Muluc	6
Nov 7 1931	**1-Oc**	7
Nov 8 1931	2-Chuen	8
Nov 9 1931	3-Eb	9
Nov 10 1931	4-Ben	1
Nov 11 1931	5-Ix	2
Nov 12 1931	6-Men	3
Nov 13 1931	7-Cib	4
Nov 14 1931	8-Caban	5
Nov 15 1931	9-Etz'nab	6
Nov 16 1931	10-Cauac	7
Nov 17 1931	11-Ahau	8
Nov 18 1931	*12-Imix*	9
Nov 19 1931	13-Ik	1
Nov 20 1931	**1-Akbal**	2
Nov 21 1931	2-Kan	3
Nov 22 1931	3-Chicchan	4
Nov 23 1931	4-Cimi	5
Nov 24 1931	5-Manik	6
Nov 25 1931	6-Lamat	7
Nov 26 1931	7-Muluc	8
Nov 27 1931	8-Oc	9
Nov 28 1931	9-Chuen	1
Nov 29 1931	10-Eb	2
Nov 30 1931	11-Ben	3
Dec 1 1931	12-Ix	4
Dec 2 1931	13-Men	5
Dec 3 1931	**1-Cib**	6
Dec 4 1931	2-Caban	7
Dec 5 1931	3-Etz'nab	8
Dec 6 1931	4-Cauac	9
Dec 7 1931	5-Ahau	1
Dec 8 1931	*6-Imix*	2
Dec 9 1931	7-Ik	3
Dec 10 1931	8-Akbal	4
Dec 11 1931	9-Kan	5
Dec 12 1931	10-Chicchan	6
Dec 13 1931	11-Cimi	7
Dec 14 1931	12-Manik	8
Dec 15 1931	13-Lamat	9
Dec 16 1931	**1-Muluc**	1
Dec 17 1931	2-Oc	2
Dec 18 1931	3-Chuen	3
Dec 19 1931	4-Eb	4
Dec 20 1931	5-Ben	5
Dec 21 1931	6-Ix	6
Dec 22 1931	7-Men	7
Dec 23 1931	8-Cib	8
Dec 24 1931	9-Caban	9
Dec 25 1931	10-Etz'nab	1
Dec 26 1931	11-Cauac	2
Dec 27 1931	12-Ahau	3
Dec 28 1931	*13-Imix*	4
Dec 29 1931	**1-Ik**	5
Dec 30 1931	2-Akbal	6
Dec 31 1931	3-Kan	7
Jan 1 1932	4-Chicchan	8
Jan 2 1932	5-Cimi	9
Jan 3 1932	6-Manik	1
Jan 4 1932	7-Lamat	2
Jan 5 1932	8-Muluc	3
Jan 6 1932	9-Oc	4
Jan 7 1932	10-Chuen	5
Jan 8 1932	11-Eb	6
Jan 9 1932	12-Ben	7

Date	Day-Sign	L
Jan 10 1932	13-Ix	8
Jan 11 1932	**1-Men**	9
Jan 12 1932	2-Cib	1
Jan 13 1932	3-Caban	2
Jan 14 1932	4-Etz'nab	3
Jan 15 1932	5-Cauac	4
Jan 16 1932	6-Ahau	5
Jan 17 1932	*7-Imix*	6
Jan 18 1932	8-Ik	7
Jan 19 1932	9-Akbal	8
Jan 20 1932	10-Kan	9
Jan 21 1932	11-Chicchan	1
Jan 22 1932	12-Cimi	2
Jan 23 1932	13-Manik	3
Jan 24 1932	**1-Lamat**	4
Jan 25 1932	2-Muluc	5
Jan 26 1932	3-Oc	6
Jan 27 1932	4-Chuen	7
Jan 28 1932	5-Eb	8
Jan 29 1932	6-Ben	9
Jan 30 1932	7-Ix	1
Jan 31 1932	8-Men	2
Feb 1 1932	9-Cib	3
Feb 2 1932	10-Caban	4
Feb 3 1932	11-Etz'nab	5
Feb 4 1932	12-Cauac	6
Feb 5 1932	13-Ahau	7
Feb 6 1932	**1-Imix**	8
Feb 7 1932	2-Ik	9
Feb 8 1932	3-Akbal	1
Feb 9 1932	4-Kan	2
Feb 10 1932	5-Chicchan	3
Feb 11 1932	6-Cimi	4
Feb 12 1932	7-Manik	5
Feb 13 1932	8-Lamat	6
Feb 14 1932	9-Muluc	7
Feb 15 1932	10-Oc	8
Feb 16 1932	11-Chuen	9
Feb 17 1932	12-Eb	1
Feb 18 1932	13-Ben	2
Feb 19 1932	**1-Ix**	3
Feb 20 1932	2-Men	4
Feb 21 1932	3-Cib	5
Feb 22 1932	4-Caban	6
Feb 23 1932	5-Etz'nab	7
Feb 24 1932	6-Cauac	8
Feb 25 1932	7-Ahau	9
Feb 26 1932	*8-Imix*	1
Feb 27 1932	9-Ik	2
Feb 28 1932	10-Akbal	3
Feb 29 1932	11-Kan	4
Mar 1 1932	12-Chicchan	5
Mar 2 1932	13-Cimi	6
Mar 3 1932	**1-Manik**	7
Mar 4 1932	2-Lamat	8
Mar 5 1932	3-Muluc	9
Mar 6 1932	4-Oc	1
Mar 7 1932	5-Chuen	2
Mar 8 1932	6-Eb	3
Mar 9 1932	7-Ben	4
Mar 10 1932	8-Ix	5
Mar 11 1932	9-Men	6
Mar 12 1932	10-Cib	7
Mar 13 1932	11-Caban	8
Mar 14 1932	12-Etz'nab	9
Mar 15 1932	13-Cauac	1
Mar 16 1932	**1-Ahau**	2
Mar 17 1932	*2-Imix*	3

Date	Day-Sign	L
Mar 18 1932	3-Ik	4
Mar 19 1932	4-Akbal	5
Mar 20 1932	5-Kan	6
Mar 21 1932	6-Chicchan	7
Mar 22 1932	7-Cimi	8
Mar 23 1932	8-Manik	9
Mar 24 1932	9-Lamat	1
Mar 25 1932	10-Muluc	2
Mar 26 1932	11-Oc	3
Mar 27 1932	12-Chuen	4
Mar 28 1932	13-Eb	5
Mar 29 1932	**1-Ben**	6
Mar 30 1932	2-Ix	7
Mar 31 1932	3-Men	8
Apr 1 1932	4-Cib	9
Apr 2 1932	5-Caban	1
Apr 3 1932	6-Etz'nab	2
Apr 4 1932	7-Cauac	3
Apr 5 1932	8-Ahau	4
Apr 6 1932	*9-Imix*	5
Apr 7 1932	10-Ik	6
Apr 8 1932	11-Akbal	7
Apr 9 1932	12-Kan	8
Apr 10 1932	13-Chicchan	9
Apr 11 1932	**1-Cimi**	1
Apr 12 1932	2-Manik	2
Apr 13 1932	3-Lamat	3
Apr 14 1932	4-Muluc	4
Apr 15 1932	5-Oc	5
Apr 16 1932	6-Chuen	6
Apr 17 1932	7-Eb	7
Apr 18 1932	8-Ben	8
Apr 19 1932	9-Ix	9
Apr 20 1932	10-Men	1
Apr 21 1932	11-Cib	2
Apr 22 1932	12-Caban	3
Apr 23 1932	13-Etz'nab	4
Apr 24 1932	**1-Cauac**	5
Apr 25 1932	2-Ahau	6
Apr 26 1932	*3-Imix*	7
Apr 27 1932	4-Ik	8
Apr 28 1932	5-Akbal	9
Apr 29 1932	6-Kan	1
Apr 30 1932	7-Chicchan	2
May 1 1932	8-Cimi	3
May 2 1932	9-Manik	4
May 3 1932	10-Lamat	5
May 4 1932	11-Muluc	6
May 5 1932	12-Oc	7
May 6 1932	13-Chuen	8
May 7 1932	**1-Eb**	9
May 8 1932	2-Ben	1
May 9 1932	3-Ix	2
May 10 1932	4-Men	3
May 11 1932	5-Cib	4
May 12 1932	6-Caban	5
May 13 1932	7-Etz'nab	6
May 14 1932	8-Cauac	7
May 15 1932	9-Ahau	8
May 16 1932	*10-Imix*	9
May 17 1932	11-Ik	1
May 18 1932	12-Akbal	2
May 19 1932	13-Kan	3
May 20 1932	**1-Chicchan**	4
May 21 1932	2-Cimi	5
May 22 1932	3-Manik	6
May 23 1932	4-Lamat	7
May 24 1932	5-Muluc	8

Date	Day-Sign	L
May 25 1932	6-Oc	9
May 26 1932	7-Chuen	1
May 27 1932	8-Eb	2
May 28 1932	9-Ben	3
May 29 1932	10-Ix	4
May 30 1932	11-Men	5
May 31 1932	12-Cib	6
Jun 1 1932	13-Caban	7
Jun 2 1932	**1-Etz'nab**	8
Jun 3 1932	2-Cauac	9
Jun 4 1932	3-Ahau	1
Jun 5 1932	*4-Imix*	2
Jun 6 1932	5-Ik	3
Jun 7 1932	6-Akbal	4
Jun 8 1932	7-Kan	5
Jun 9 1932	8-Chicchan	6
Jun 10 1932	9-Cimi	7
Jun 11 1932	10-Manik	8
Jun 12 1932	11-Lamat	9
Jun 13 1932	12-Muluc	1
Jun 14 1932	13-Oc	2
Jun 15 1932	**1-Chuen**	3
Jun 16 1932	2-Eb	4
Jun 17 1932	3-Ben	5
Jun 18 1932	4-Ix	6
Jun 19 1932	5-Men	7
Jun 20 1932	6-Cib	8
Jun 21 1932	7-Caban	9
Jun 22 1932	8-Etz'nab	1
Jun 23 1932	9-Cauac	2
Jun 24 1932	10-Ahau	3
Jun 25 1932	*11-Imix*	4
Jun 26 1932	12-Ik	5
Jun 27 1932	13-Akbal	6
Jun 28 1932	**1-Kan**	7
Jun 29 1932	2-Chicchan	8
Jun 30 1932	3-Cimi	9
Jul 1 1932	4-Manik	1
Jul 2 1932	5-Lamat	2
Jul 3 1932	6-Muluc	3
Jul 4 1932	7-Oc	4
Jul 5 1932	8-Chuen	5
Jul 6 1932	9-Eb	6
Jul 7 1932	10-Ben	7
Jul 8 1932	11-Ix	8
Jul 9 1932	12-Men	9
Jul 10 1932	13-Cib	1
Jul 11 1932	**1-Caban**	2
Jul 12 1932	2-Etz'nab	3
Jul 13 1932	3-Cauac	4
Jul 14 1932	4-Ahau	5
Jul 15 1932	*5-Imix*	6
Jul 16 1932	6-Ik	7
Jul 17 1932	7-Akbal	8
Jul 18 1932	8-Kan	9
Jul 19 1932	9-Chicchan	1
Jul 20 1932	10-Cimi	2
Jul 21 1932	11-Manik	3
Jul 22 1932	12-Lamat	4
Jul 23 1932	13-Muluc	5
Jul 24 1932	**1-Oc**	6
Jul 25 1932	2-Chuen	7
Jul 26 1932	3-Eb	8
Jul 27 1932	4-Ben	9
Jul 28 1932	5-Ix	1
Jul 29 1932	6-Men	2
Jul 30 1932	7-Cib	3
Jul 31 1932	8-Caban	4

Date	Day-Sign	L
Aug 1 1932	9-Etz'nab	5
Aug 2 1932	10-Cauac	6
Aug 3 1932	11-Ahau	7
Aug 4 1932	*12-Imix*	8
Aug 5 1932	13-Ik	9
Aug 6 1932	**1-Akbal**	1
Aug 7 1932	2-Kan	2
Aug 8 1932	3-Chicchan	3
Aug 9 1932	4-Cimi	4
Aug 10 1932	5-Manik	5
Aug 11 1932	6-Lamat	6
Aug 12 1932	7-Muluc	7
Aug 13 1932	8-Oc	8
Aug 14 1932	9-Chuen	9
Aug 15 1932	10-Eb	1
Aug 16 1932	11-Ben	2
Aug 17 1932	12-Ix	3
Aug 18 1932	13-Men	4
Aug 19 1932	**1-Cib**	5
Aug 20 1932	2-Caban	6
Aug 21 1932	3-Etz'nab	7
Aug 22 1932	4-Cauac	8
Aug 23 1932	5-Ahau	9
Aug 24 1932	*6-Imix*	1
Aug 25 1932	7-Ik	2
Aug 26 1932	8-Akbal	3
Aug 27 1932	9-Kan	4
Aug 28 1932	10-Chicchan	5
Aug 29 1932	11-Cimi	6
Aug 30 1932	12-Manik	7
Aug 31 1932	13-Lamat	8
Sep 1 1932	**1-Muluc**	9
Sep 2 1932	2-Oc	1
Sep 3 1932	3-Chuen	2
Sep 4 1932	4-Eb	3
Sep 5 1932	5-Ben	4
Sep 6 1932	6-Ix	5
Sep 7 1932	7-Men	6
Sep 8 1932	8-Cib	7
Sep 9 1932	9-Caban	8
Sep 10 1932	10-Etz'nab	9
Sep 11 1932	11-Cauac	1
Sep 12 1932	12-Ahau	2
Sep 13 1932	*13-Imix*	3
Sep 14 1932	**1-Ik**	4
Sep 15 1932	2-Akbal	5
Sep 16 1932	3-Kan	6
Sep 17 1932	4-Chicchan	7
Sep 18 1932	5-Cimi	8
Sep 19 1932	6-Manik	9
Sep 20 1932	7-Lamat	1
Sep 21 1932	8-Muluc	2
Sep 22 1932	9-Oc	3
Sep 23 1932	10-Chuen	4
Sep 24 1932	11-Eb	5
Sep 25 1932	12-Ben	6
Sep 26 1932	13-Ix	7
Sep 27 1932	**1-Men**	8
Sep 28 1932	2-Cib	9
Sep 29 1932	3-Caban	1
Sep 30 1932	4-Etz'nab	2
Oct 1 1932	5-Cauac	3
Oct 2 1932	6-Ahau	4
Oct 3 1932	*7-Imix*	5
Oct 4 1932	8-Ik	6
Oct 5 1932	9-Akbal	7
Oct 6 1932	10-Kan	8
Oct 7 1932	11-Chicchan	9

Date	Day-Sign	L
Oct 8 1932	12-Cimi	1
Oct 9 1932	13-Manik	2
Oct 10 1932	1-Lamat	3
Oct 11 1932	2-Muluc	4
Oct 12 1932	3-Oc	5
Oct 13 1932	4-Chuen	6
Oct 14 1932	5-Eb	7
Oct 15 1932	6-Ben	8
Oct 16 1932	7-Ix	9
Oct 17 1932	8-Men	1
Oct 18 1932	9-Cib	2
Oct 19 1932	10-Caban	3
Oct 20 1932	11-Etz'nab	4
Oct 21 1932	12-Cauac	5
Oct 22 1932	13-Ahau	6
Oct 23 1932	1-Imix	7
Oct 24 1932	2-Ik	8
Oct 25 1932	3-Akbal	9
Oct 26 1932	4-Kan	1
Oct 27 1932	5-Chicchan	2
Oct 28 1932	6-Cimi	3
Oct 29 1932	7-Manik	4
Oct 30 1932	8-Lamat	5
Oct 31 1932	9-Muluc	6
Nov 1 1932	10-Oc	7
Nov 2 1932	11-Chuen	8
Nov 3 1932	12-Eb	9
Nov 4 1932	13-Ben	1
Nov 5 1932	1-Ix	2
Nov 6 1932	2-Men	3
Nov 7 1932	3-Cib	4
Nov 8 1932	4-Caban	5
Nov 9 1932	5-Etz'nab	6
Nov 10 1932	6-Cauac	7
Nov 11 1932	7-Ahau	8
Nov 12 1932	8-Imix	9
Nov 13 1932	9-Ik	1
Nov 14 1932	10-Akbal	2
Nov 15 1932	11-Kan	3
Nov 16 1932	12-Chicchan	4
Nov 17 1932	13-Cimi	5
Nov 18 1932	1-Manik	6
Nov 19 1932	2-Lamat	7
Nov 20 1932	3-Muluc	8
Nov 21 1932	4-Oc	9
Nov 22 1932	5-Chuen	1
Nov 23 1932	6-Eb	2
Nov 24 1932	7-Ben	3
Nov 25 1932	8-Ix	4
Nov 26 1932	9-Men	5
Nov 27 1932	10-Cib	6
Nov 28 1932	11-Caban	7
Nov 29 1932	12-Etz'nab	8
Nov 30 1932	13-Cauac	9
Dec 1 1932	1-Ahau	1
Dec 2 1932	2-Imix	2
Dec 3 1932	3-Ik	3
Dec 4 1932	4-Akbal	4
Dec 5 1932	5-Kan	5
Dec 6 1932	6-Chicchan	6
Dec 7 1932	7-Cimi	7
Dec 8 1932	8-Manik	8
Dec 9 1932	9-Lamat	9
Dec 10 1932	10-Muluc	1
Dec 11 1932	11-Oc	2
Dec 12 1932	12-Chuen	3
Dec 13 1932	13-Eb	4
Dec 14 1932	1-Ben	5

Date	Day-Sign	L
Dec 15 1932	2-Ix	6
Dec 16 1932	3-Men	7
Dec 17 1932	4-Cib	8
Dec 18 1932	5-Caban	9
Dec 19 1932	6-Etz'nab	1
Dec 20 1932	7-Cauac	2
Dec 21 1932	8-Ahau	3
Dec 22 1932	9-Imix	4
Dec 23 1932	10-Ik	5
Dec 24 1932	11-Akbal	6
Dec 25 1932	12-Kan	7
Dec 26 1932	13-Chicchan	8
Dec 27 1932	1-Cimi	9
Dec 28 1932	2-Manik	1
Dec 29 1932	3-Lamat	2
Dec 30 1932	4-Muluc	3
Dec 31 1932	5-Oc	4
Jan 1 1933	6-Chuen	5
Jan 2 1933	7-Eb	6
Jan 3 1933	8-Ben	7
Jan 4 1933	9-Ix	8
Jan 5 1933	10-Men	9
Jan 6 1933	11-Cib	1
Jan 7 1933	12-Caban	2
Jan 8 1933	13-Etz'nab	3
Jan 9 1933	1-Cauac	4
Jan 10 1933	2-Ahau	5
Jan 11 1933	3-Imix	6
Jan 12 1933	4-Ik	7
Jan 13 1933	5-Akbal	8
Jan 14 1933	6-Kan	9
Jan 15 1933	7-Chicchan	1
Jan 16 1933	8-Cimi	2
Jan 17 1933	9-Manik	3
Jan 18 1933	10-Lamat	4
Jan 19 1933	11-Muluc	5
Jan 20 1933	12-Oc	6
Jan 21 1933	13-Chuen	7
Jan 22 1933	1-Eb	8
Jan 23 1933	2-Ben	9
Jan 24 1933	3-Ix	1
Jan 25 1933	4-Men	2
Jan 26 1933	5-Cib	3
Jan 27 1933	6-Caban	4
Jan 28 1933	7-Etz'nab	5
Jan 29 1933	8-Cauac	6
Jan 30 1933	9-Ahau	7
Jan 31 1933	10-Imix	8
Feb 1 1933	11-Ik	9
Feb 2 1933	12-Akbal	1
Feb 3 1933	13-Kan	2
Feb 4 1933	1-Chicchan	3
Feb 5 1933	2-Cimi	4
Feb 6 1933	3-Manik	5
Feb 7 1933	4-Lamat	6
Feb 8 1933	5-Muluc	7
Feb 9 1933	6-Oc	8
Feb 10 1933	7-Chuen	9
Feb 11 1933	8-Eb	1
Feb 12 1933	9-Ben	2
Feb 13 1933	10-Ix	3
Feb 14 1933	11-Men	4
Feb 15 1933	12-Cib	5
Feb 16 1933	13-Caban	6
Feb 17 1933	1-Etz'nab	7
Feb 18 1933	2-Cauac	8
Feb 19 1933	3-Ahau	9
Feb 20 1933	4-Imix	1

Date	Day-Sign	L
Feb 21 1933	5-Ik	2
Feb 22 1933	6-Akbal	3
Feb 23 1933	7-Kan	4
Feb 24 1933	8-Chicchan	5
Feb 25 1933	9-Cimi	6
Feb 26 1933	10-Manik	7
Feb 27 1933	11-Lamat	8
Feb 28 1933	12-Muluc	9
Mar 1 1933	13-Oc	1
Mar 2 1933	1-Chuen	2
Mar 3 1933	2-Eb	3
Mar 4 1933	3-Ben	4
Mar 5 1933	4-Ix	5
Mar 6 1933	5-Men	6
Mar 7 1933	6-Cib	7
Mar 8 1933	7-Caban	8
Mar 9 1933	8-Etz'nab	9
Mar 10 1933	9-Cauac	1
Mar 11 1933	10-Ahau	2
Mar 12 1933	11-Imix	3
Mar 13 1933	12-Ik	4
Mar 14 1933	13-Akbal	5
Mar 15 1933	1-Kan	6
Mar 16 1933	2-Chicchan	7
Mar 17 1933	3-Cimi	8
Mar 18 1933	4-Manik	9
Mar 19 1933	5-Lamat	1
Mar 20 1933	6-Muluc	2
Mar 21 1933	7-Oc	3
Mar 22 1933	8-Chuen	4
Mar 23 1933	9-Eb	5
Mar 24 1933	10-Ben	6
Mar 25 1933	11-Ix	7
Mar 26 1933	12-Men	8
Mar 27 1933	13-Cib	9
Mar 28 1933	1-Caban	1
Mar 29 1933	2-Etz'nab	2
Mar 30 1933	3-Cauac	3
Mar 31 1933	4-Ahau	4
Apr 1 1933	5-Imix	5
Apr 2 1933	6-Ik	6
Apr 3 1933	7-Akbal	7
Apr 4 1933	8-Kan	8
Apr 5 1933	9-Chicchan	9
Apr 6 1933	10-Cimi	1
Apr 7 1933	11-Manik	2
Apr 8 1933	12-Lamat	3
Apr 9 1933	13-Muluc	4
Apr 10 1933	1-Oc	5
Apr 11 1933	2-Chuen	6
Apr 12 1933	3-Eb	7
Apr 13 1933	4-Ben	8
Apr 14 1933	5-Ix	9
Apr 15 1933	6-Men	1
Apr 16 1933	7-Cib	2
Apr 17 1933	8-Caban	3
Apr 18 1933	9-Etz'nab	4
Apr 19 1933	10-Cauac	5
Apr 20 1933	11-Ahau	6
Apr 21 1933	12-Imix	7
Apr 22 1933	13-Ik	8
Apr 23 1933	1-Akbal	9
Apr 24 1933	2-Kan	1
Apr 25 1933	3-Chicchan	2
Apr 26 1933	4-Cimi	3
Apr 27 1933	5-Manik	4
Apr 28 1933	6-Lamat	5
Apr 29 1933	7-Muluc	6

Date	Day-Sign	L	Date	Day-Sign	L	Date	Day-Sign	L
Apr 30 1933	8-Oc	7	Jul 7 1933	11-Etz'nab	3	Sep 13 1933	1-Cimi	8
May 1 1933	9-Chuen	8	Jul 8 1933	12-Cauac	4	Sep 14 1933	2-Manik	9
May 2 1933	10-Eb	9	Jul 9 1933	13-Ahau	5	Sep 15 1933	3-Lamat	1
May 3 1933	11-Ben	1	Jul 10 1933	1-Imix	6	Sep 16 1933	4-Muluc	2
May 4 1933	12-Ix	2	Jul 11 1933	2-Ik	7	Sep 17 1933	5-Oc	3
May 5 1933	13-Men	3	Jul 12 1933	3-Akbal	8	Sep 18 1933	6-Chuen	4
May 6 1933	1-Cib	4	Jul 13 1933	4-Kan	9	Sep 19 1933	7-Eb	5
May 7 1933	2-Caban	5	Jul 14 1933	5-Chicchan	1	Sep 20 1933	8-Ben	6
May 8 1933	3-Etz'nab	6	Jul 15 1933	6-Cimi	2	Sep 21 1933	9-Ix	7
May 9 1933	4-Cauac	7	Jul 16 1933	7-Manik	3	Sep 22 1933	10-Men	8
May 10 1933	5-Ahau	8	Jul 17 1933	8-Lamat	4	Sep 23 1933	11-Cib	9
May 11 1933	6-Imix	9	Jul 18 1933	9-Muluc	5	Sep 24 1933	12-Caban	1
May 12 1933	7-Ik	1	Jul 19 1933	10-Oc	6	Sep 25 1933	13-Etz'nab	2
May 13 1933	8-Akbal	2	Jul 20 1933	11-Chuen	7	Sep 26 1933	1-Cauac	3
May 14 1933	9-Kan	3	Jul 21 1933	12-Eb	8	Sep 27 1933	2-Ahau	4
May 15 1933	10-Chicchan	4	Jul 22 1933	13-Ben	9	Sep 28 1933	3-Imix	5
May 16 1933	11-Cimi	5	Jul 23 1933	1-Ix	1	Sep 29 1933	4-Ik	6
May 17 1933	12-Manik	6	Jul 24 1933	2-Men	2	Sep 30 1933	5-Akbal	7
May 18 1933	13-Lamat	7	Jul 25 1933	3-Cib	3	Oct 1 1933	6-Kan	8
May 19 1933	1-Muluc	8	Jul 26 1933	4-Caban	4	Oct 2 1933	7-Chicchan	9
May 20 1933	2-Oc	9	Jul 27 1933	5-Etz'nab	5	Oct 3 1933	8-Cimi	1
May 21 1933	3-Chuen	1	Jul 28 1933	6-Cauac	6	Oct 4 1933	9-Manik	2
May 22 1933	4-Eb	2	Jul 29 1933	7-Ahau	7	Oct 5 1933	10-Lamat	3
May 23 1933	5-Ben	3	Jul 30 1933	8-Imix	8	Oct 6 1933	11-Muluc	4
May 24 1933	6-Ix	4	Jul 31 1933	9-Ik	9	Oct 7 1933	12-Oc	5
May 25 1933	7-Men	5	Aug 1 1933	10-Akbal	1	Oct 8 1933	13-Chuen	6
May 26 1933	8-Cib	6	Aug 2 1933	11-Kan	2	Oct 9 1933	1-Eb	7
May 27 1933	9-Caban	7	Aug 3 1933	12-Chicchan	3	Oct 10 1933	2-Ben	8
May 28 1933	10-Etz'nab	8	Aug 4 1933	13-Cimi	4	Oct 11 1933	3-Ix	9
May 29 1933	11-Cauac	9	Aug 5 1933	1-Manik	5	Oct 12 1933	4-Men	1
May 30 1933	12-Ahau	1	Aug 6 1933	2-Lamat	6	Oct 13 1933	5-Cib	2
May 31 1933	13-Imix	2	Aug 7 1933	3-Muluc	7	Oct 14 1933	6-Caban	3
Jun 1 1933	1-Ik	3	Aug 8 1933	4-Oc	8	Oct 15 1933	7-Etz'nab	4
Jun 2 1933	2-Akbal	4	Aug 9 1933	5-Chuen	9	Oct 16 1933	8-Cauac	5
Jun 3 1933	3-Kan	5	Aug 10 1933	6-Eb	1	Oct 17 1933	9-Ahau	6
Jun 4 1933	4-Chicchan	6	Aug 11 1933	7-Ben	2	Oct 18 1933	10-Imix	7
Jun 5 1933	5-Cimi	7	Aug 12 1933	8-Ix	3	Oct 19 1933	11-Ik	8
Jun 6 1933	6-Manik	8	Aug 13 1933	9-Men	4	Oct 20 1933	12-Akbal	9
Jun 7 1933	7-Lamat	9	Aug 14 1933	10-Cib	5	Oct 21 1933	13-Kan	1
Jun 8 1933	8-Muluc	1	Aug 15 1933	11-Caban	6	Oct 22 1933	1-Chicchan	2
Jun 9 1933	9-Oc	2	Aug 16 1933	12-Etz'nab	7	Oct 23 1933	2-Cimi	3
Jun 10 1933	10-Chuen	3	Aug 17 1933	13-Cauac	8	Oct 24 1933	3-Manik	4
Jun 11 1933	11-Eb	4	Aug 18 1933	1-Ahau	9	Oct 25 1933	4-Lamat	5
Jun 12 1933	12-Ben	5	Aug 19 1933	2-Imix	1	Oct 26 1933	5-Muluc	6
Jun 13 1933	13-Ix	6	Aug 20 1933	3-Ik	2	Oct 27 1933	6-Oc	7
Jun 14 1933	1-Men	7	Aug 21 1933	4-Akbal	3	Oct 28 1933	7-Chuen	8
Jun 15 1933	2-Cib	8	Aug 22 1933	5-Kan	4	Oct 29 1933	8-Eb	9
Jun 16 1933	3-Caban	9	Aug 23 1933	6-Chicchan	5	Oct 30 1933	9-Ben	1
Jun 17 1933	4-Etz'nab	1	Aug 24 1933	7-Cimi	6	Oct 31 1933	10-Ix	2
Jun 18 1933	5-Cauac	2	Aug 25 1933	8-Manik	7	Nov 1 1933	11-Men	3
Jun 19 1933	6-Ahau	3	Aug 26 1933	9-Lamat	8	Nov 2 1933	12-Cib	4
Jun 20 1933	7-Imix	4	Aug 27 1933	10-Muluc	9	Nov 3 1933	13-Caban	5
Jun 21 1933	8-Ik	5	Aug 28 1933	11-Oc	1	Nov 4 1933	1-Etz'nab	6
Jun 22 1933	9-Akbal	6	Aug 29 1933	12-Chuen	2	Nov 5 1933	2-Cauac	7
Jun 23 1933	10-Kan	7	Aug 30 1933	13-Eb	3	Nov 6 1933	3-Ahau	8
Jun 24 1933	11-Chicchan	8	Aug 31 1933	1-Ben	4	Nov 7 1933	4-Imix	9
Jun 25 1933	12-Cimi	9	Sep 1 1933	2-Ix	5	Nov 8 1933	5-Ik	1
Jun 26 1933	13-Manik	1	Sep 2 1933	3-Men	6	Nov 9 1933	6-Akbal	2
Jun 27 1933	1-Lamat	2	Sep 3 1933	4-Cib	7	Nov 10 1933	7-Kan	3
Jun 28 1933	2-Muluc	3	Sep 4 1933	5-Caban	8	Nov 11 1933	8-Chicchan	4
Jun 29 1933	3-Oc	4	Sep 5 1933	6-Etz'nab	9	Nov 12 1933	9-Cimi	5
Jun 30 1933	4-Chuen	5	Sep 6 1933	7-Cauac	1	Nov 13 1933	10-Manik	6
Jul 1 1933	5-Eb	6	Sep 7 1933	8-Ahau	2	Nov 14 1933	11-Lamat	7
Jul 2 1933	6-Ben	7	Sep 8 1933	9-Imix	3	Nov 15 1933	12-Muluc	8
Jul 3 1933	7-Ix	8	Sep 9 1933	10-Ik	4	Nov 16 1933	13-Oc	9
Jul 4 1933	8-Men	9	Sep 10 1933	11-Akbal	5	Nov 17 1933	1-Chuen	1
Jul 5 1933	9-Cib	1	Sep 11 1933	12-Kan	6	Nov 18 1933	2-Eb	2
Jul 6 1933	10-Caban	2	Sep 12 1933	13-Chicchan	7	Nov 19 1933	3-Ben	3

Date	Day-Sign	L	Date	Day-Sign	L	Date	Day-Sign	L
Nov 20 1933	4-Ix	4	Jan 27 1934	7-Ik	9	Apr 5 1934	10-Oc	5
Nov 21 1933	5-Men	5	Jan 28 1934	8-Akbal	1	Apr 6 1934	11-Chuen	6
Nov 22 1933	6-Cib	6	Jan 29 1934	9-Kan	2	Apr 7 1934	12-Eb	7
Nov 23 1933	7-Caban	7	Jan 30 1934	10-Chicchan	3	Apr 8 1934	13-Ben	8
Nov 24 1933	8-Etz'nab	8	Jan 31 1934	11-Cimi	4	Apr 9 1934	**1-Ix**	9
Nov 25 1933	9-Cauac	9	Feb 1 1934	12-Manik	5	Apr 10 1934	2-Men	1
Nov 26 1933	10-Ahau	1	Feb 2 1934	13-Lamat	6	Apr 11 1934	3-Cib	2
Nov 27 1933	*11-Imix*	2	Feb 3 1934	**1-Muluc**	7	Apr 12 1934	4-Caban	3
Nov 28 1933	12-Ik	3	Feb 4 1934	2-Oc	8	Apr 13 1934	5-Etz'nab	4
Nov 29 1933	13-Akbal	4	Feb 5 1934	3-Chuen	9	Apr 14 1934	6-Cauac	5
Nov 30 1933	**1-Kan**	5	Feb 6 1934	4-Eb	1	Apr 15 1934	7-Ahau	6
Dec 1 1933	2-Chicchan	6	Feb 7 1934	5-Ben	2	Apr 16 1934	*8-Imix*	7
Dec 2 1933	3-Cimi	7	Feb 8 1934	6-Ix	3	Apr 17 1934	9-Ik	8
Dec 3 1933	4-Manik	8	Feb 9 1934	7-Men	4	Apr 18 1934	10-Akbal	9
Dec 4 1933	5-Lamat	9	Feb 10 1934	8-Cib	5	Apr 19 1934	11-Kan	1
Dec 5 1933	6-Muluc	1	Feb 11 1934	9-Caban	6	Apr 20 1934	12-Chicchan	2
Dec 6 1933	7-Oc	2	Feb 12 1934	10-Etz'nab	7	Apr 21 1934	13-Cimi	3
Dec 7 1933	8-Chuen	3	Feb 13 1934	11-Cauac	8	Apr 22 1934	**1-Manik**	4
Dec 8 1933	9-Eb	4	Feb 14 1934	12-Ahau	9	Apr 23 1934	2-Lamat	5
Dec 9 1933	10-Ben	5	Feb 15 1934	*13-Imix*	1	Apr 24 1934	3-Muluc	6
Dec 10 1933	11-Ix	6	Feb 16 1934	**1-Ik**	2	Apr 25 1934	4-Oc	7
Dec 11 1933	12-Men	7	Feb 17 1934	2-Akbal	3	Apr 26 1934	5-Chuen	8
Dec 12 1933	13-Cib	8	Feb 18 1934	3-Kan	4	Apr 27 1934	6-Eb	9
Dec 13 1933	**1-Caban**	9	Feb 19 1934	4-Chicchan	5	Apr 28 1934	7-Ben	1
Dec 14 1933	2-Etz'nab	1	Feb 20 1934	5-Cimi	6	Apr 29 1934	8-Ix	2
Dec 15 1933	3-Cauac	2	Feb 21 1934	6-Manik	7	Apr 30 1934	9-Men	3
Dec 16 1933	4-Ahau	3	Feb 22 1934	7-Lamat	8	May 1 1934	10-Cib	4
Dec 17 1933	*5-Imix*	4	Feb 23 1934	8-Muluc	9	May 2 1934	11-Caban	5
Dec 18 1933	6-Ik	5	Feb 24 1934	9-Oc	1	May 3 1934	12-Etz'nab	6
Dec 19 1933	7-Akbal	6	Feb 25 1934	10-Chuen	2	May 4 1934	13-Cauac	7
Dec 20 1933	8-Kan	7	Feb 26 1934	11-Eb	3	May 5 1934	**1-Ahau**	8
Dec 21 1933	9-Chicchan	8	Feb 27 1934	12-Ben	4	May 6 1934	*2-Imix*	9
Dec 22 1933	10-Cimi	9	Feb 28 1934	13-Ix	5	May 7 1934	3-Ik	1
Dec 23 1933	11-Manik	1	Mar 1 1934	**1-Men**	6	May 8 1934	4-Akbal	2
Dec 24 1933	12-Lamat	2	Mar 2 1934	2-Cib	7	May 9 1934	5-Kan	3
Dec 25 1933	13-Muluc	3	Mar 3 1934	3-Caban	8	May 10 1934	6-Chicchan	4
Dec 26 1933	**1-Oc**	4	Mar 4 1934	4-Etz'nab	9	May 11 1934	7-Cimi	5
Dec 27 1933	2-Chuen	5	Mar 5 1934	5-Cauac	1	May 12 1934	8-Manik	6
Dec 28 1933	3-Eb	6	Mar 6 1934	6-Ahau	2	May 13 1934	9-Lamat	7
Dec 29 1933	4-Ben	7	Mar 7 1934	*7-Imix*	3	May 14 1934	10-Muluc	8
Dec 30 1933	5-Ix	8	Mar 8 1934	8-Ik	4	May 15 1934	11-Oc	9
Dec 31 1933	6-Men	9	Mar 9 1934	9-Akbal	5	May 16 1934	12-Chuen	1
Jan 1 1934	7-Cib	1	Mar 10 1934	10-Kan	6	May 17 1934	13-Eb	2
Jan 2 1934	8-Caban	2	Mar 11 1934	11-Chicchan	7	May 18 1934	**1-Ben**	3
Jan 3 1934	9-Etz'nab	3	Mar 12 1934	12-Cimi	8	May 19 1934	2-Ix	4
Jan 4 1934	10-Cauac	4	Mar 13 1934	13-Manik	9	May 20 1934	3-Men	5
Jan 5 1934	11-Ahau	5	Mar 14 1934	**1-Lamat**	1	May 21 1934	4-Cib	6
Jan 6 1934	*12-Imix*	6	Mar 15 1934	2-Muluc	2	May 22 1934	5-Caban	7
Jan 7 1934	13-Ik	7	Mar 16 1934	3-Oc	3	May 23 1934	6-Etz'nab	8
Jan 8 1934	**1-Akbal**	8	Mar 17 1934	4-Chuen	4	May 24 1934	7-Cauac	9
Jan 9 1934	2-Kan	9	Mar 18 1934	5-Eb	5	May 25 1934	8-Ahau	1
Jan 10 1934	3-Chicchan	1	Mar 19 1934	6-Ben	6	May 26 1934	*9-Imix*	2
Jan 11 1934	4-Cimi	2	Mar 20 1934	7-Ix	7	May 27 1934	10-Ik	3
Jan 12 1934	5-Manik	3	Mar 21 1934	8-Men	8	May 28 1934	11-Akbal	4
Jan 13 1934	6-Lamat	4	Mar 22 1934	9-Cib	9	May 29 1934	12-Kan	5
Jan 14 1934	7-Muluc	5	Mar 23 1934	10-Caban	1	May 30 1934	13-Chicchan	6
Jan 15 1934	8-Oc	6	Mar 24 1934	11-Etz'nab	2	May 31 1934	**1-Cimi**	7
Jan 16 1934	9-Chuen	7	Mar 25 1934	12-Cauac	3	Jun 1 1934	2-Manik	8
Jan 17 1934	10-Eb	8	Mar 26 1934	13-Ahau	4	Jun 2 1934	3-Lamat	9
Jan 18 1934	11-Ben	9	Mar 27 1934	**1-Imix**	5	Jun 3 1934	4-Muluc	1
Jan 19 1934	12-Ix	1	Mar 28 1934	2-Ik	6	Jun 4 1934	5-Oc	2
Jan 20 1934	13-Men	2	Mar 29 1934	3-Akbal	7	Jun 5 1934	6-Chuen	3
Jan 21 1934	**1-Cib**	3	Mar 30 1934	4-Kan	8	Jun 6 1934	7-Eb	4
Jan 22 1934	2-Caban	4	Mar 31 1934	5-Chicchan	9	Jun 7 1934	8-Ben	5
Jan 23 1934	3-Etz'nab	5	Apr 1 1934	6-Cimi	1	Jun 8 1934	9-Ix	6
Jan 24 1934	4-Cauac	6	Apr 2 1934	7-Manik	2	Jun 9 1934	10-Men	7
Jan 25 1934	5-Ahau	7	Apr 3 1934	8-Lamat	3	Jun 10 1934	11-Cib	8
Jan 26 1934	*6-Imix*	8	Apr 4 1934	9-Muluc	4	Jun 11 1934	12-Caban	9

Date	Day-Sign	L	Date	Day-Sign	L	Date	Day-Sign	L
Jun 12 1934	13-Etz'nab	1	Aug 19 1934	3-Cimi	6	Oct 26 1934	6-Ix	2
Jun 13 1934	1-Cauac	2	Aug 20 1934	4-Manik	7	Oct 27 1934	7-Men	3
Jun 14 1934	2-Ahau	3	Aug 21 1934	5-Lamat	8	Oct 28 1934	8-Cib	4
Jun 15 1934	3-Imix	4	Aug 22 1934	6-Muluc	9	Oct 29 1934	9-Caban	5
Jun 16 1934	4-Ik	5	Aug 23 1934	7-Oc	1	Oct 30 1934	10-Etz'nab	6
Jun 17 1934	5-Akbal	6	Aug 24 1934	8-Chuen	2	Oct 31 1934	11-Cauac	7
Jun 18 1934	6-Kan	7	Aug 25 1934	9-Eb	3	Nov 1 1934	12-Ahau	8
Jun 19 1934	7-Chicchan	8	Aug 26 1934	10-Ben	4	Nov 2 1934	13-Imix	9
Jun 20 1934	8-Cimi	9	Aug 27 1934	11-Ix	5	Nov 3 1934	1-Ik	1
Jun 21 1934	9-Manik	1	Aug 28 1934	12-Men	6	Nov 4 1934	2-Akbal	2
Jun 22 1934	10-Lamat	2	Aug 29 1934	13-Cib	7	Nov 5 1934	3-Kan	3
Jun 23 1934	11-Muluc	3	Aug 30 1934	1-Caban	8	Nov 6 1934	4-Chicchan	4
Jun 24 1934	12-Oc	4	Aug 31 1934	2-Etz'nab	9	Nov 7 1934	5-Cimi	5
Jun 25 1934	13-Chuen	5	Sep 1 1934	3-Cauac	1	Nov 8 1934	6-Manik	6
Jun 26 1934	1-Eb	6	Sep 2 1934	4-Ahau	2	Nov 9 1934	7-Lamat	7
Jun 27 1934	2-Ben	7	Sep 3 1934	5-Imix	3	Nov 10 1934	8-Muluc	8
Jun 28 1934	3-Ix	8	Sep 4 1934	6-Ik	4	Nov 11 1934	9-Oc	9
Jun 29 1934	4-Men	9	Sep 5 1934	7-Akbal	5	Nov 12 1934	10-Chuen	1
Jun 30 1934	5-Cib	1	Sep 6 1934	8-Kan	6	Nov 13 1934	11-Eb	2
Jul 1 1934	6-Caban	2	Sep 7 1934	9-Chicchan	7	Nov 14 1934	12-Ben	3
Jul 2 1934	7-Etz'nab	3	Sep 8 1934	10-Cimi	8	Nov 15 1934	13-Ix	4
Jul 3 1934	8-Cauac	4	Sep 9 1934	11-Manik	9	Nov 16 1934	1-Men	5
Jul 4 1934	9-Ahau	5	Sep 10 1934	12-Lamat	1	Nov 17 1934	2-Cib	6
Jul 5 1934	10-Imix	6	Sep 11 1934	13-Muluc	2	Nov 18 1934	3-Caban	7
Jul 6 1934	11-Ik	7	Sep 12 1934	1-Oc	3	Nov 19 1934	4-Etz'nab	8
Jul 7 1934	12-Akbal	8	Sep 13 1934	2-Chuen	4	Nov 20 1934	5-Cauac	9
Jul 8 1934	13-Kan	9	Sep 14 1934	3-Eb	5	Nov 21 1934	6-Ahau	1
Jul 9 1934	1-Chicchan	1	Sep 15 1934	4-Ben	6	Nov 22 1934	7-Imix	2
Jul 10 1934	2-Cimi	2	Sep 16 1934	5-Ix	7	Nov 23 1934	8-Ik	3
Jul 11 1934	3-Manik	3	Sep 17 1934	6-Men	8	Nov 24 1934	9-Akbal	4
Jul 12 1934	4-Lamat	4	Sep 18 1934	7-Cib	9	Nov 25 1934	10-Kan	5
Jul 13 1934	5-Muluc	5	Sep 19 1934	8-Caban	1	Nov 26 1934	11-Chicchan	6
Jul 14 1934	6-Oc	6	Sep 20 1934	9-Etz'nab	2	Nov 27 1934	12-Cimi	7
Jul 15 1934	7-Chuen	7	Sep 21 1934	10-Cauac	3	Nov 28 1934	13-Manik	8
Jul 16 1934	8-Eb	8	Sep 22 1934	11-Ahau	4	Nov 29 1934	1-Lamat	9
Jul 17 1934	9-Ben	9	Sep 23 1934	12-Imix	5	Nov 30 1934	2-Muluc	1
Jul 18 1934	10-Ix	1	Sep 24 1934	13-Ik	6	Dec 1 1934	3-Oc	2
Jul 19 1934	11-Men	2	Sep 25 1934	1-Akbal	7	Dec 2 1934	4-Chuen	3
Jul 20 1934	12-Cib	3	Sep 26 1934	2-Kan	8	Dec 3 1934	5-Eb	4
Jul 21 1934	13-Caban	4	Sep 27 1934	3-Chicchan	9	Dec 4 1934	6-Ben	5
Jul 22 1934	1-Etz'nab	5	Sep 28 1934	4-Cimi	1	Dec 5 1934	7-Ix	6
Jul 23 1934	2-Cauac	6	Sep 29 1934	5-Manik	2	Dec 6 1934	8-Men	7
Jul 24 1934	3-Ahau	7	Sep 30 1934	6-Lamat	3	Dec 7 1934	9-Cib	8
Jul 25 1934	4-Imix	8	Oct 1 1934	7-Muluc	4	Dec 8 1934	10-Caban	9
Jul 26 1934	5-Ik	9	Oct 2 1934	8-Oc	5	Dec 9 1934	11-Etz'nab	1
Jul 27 1934	6-Akbal	1	Oct 3 1934	9-Chuen	6	Dec 10 1934	12-Cauac	2
Jul 28 1934	7-Kan	2	Oct 4 1934	10-Eb	7	Dec 11 1934	13-Ahau	3
Jul 29 1934	8-Chicchan	3	Oct 5 1934	11-Ben	8	Dec 12 1934	1-Imix	4
Jul 30 1934	9-Cimi	4	Oct 6 1934	12-Ix	9	Dec 13 1934	2-Ik	5
Jul 31 1934	10-Manik	5	Oct 7 1934	13-Men	1	Dec 14 1934	3-Akbal	6
Aug 1 1934	11-Lamat	6	Oct 8 1934	1-Cib	2	Dec 15 1934	4-Kan	7
Aug 2 1934	12-Muluc	7	Oct 9 1934	2-Caban	3	Dec 16 1934	5-Chicchan	8
Aug 3 1934	13-Oc	8	Oct 10 1934	3-Etz'nab	4	Dec 17 1934	6-Cimi	9
Aug 4 1934	1-Chuen	9	Oct 11 1934	4-Cauac	5	Dec 18 1934	7-Manik	1
Aug 5 1934	2-Eb	1	Oct 12 1934	5-Ahau	6	Dec 19 1934	8-Lamat	2
Aug 6 1934	3-Ben	2	Oct 13 1934	6-Imix	7	Dec 20 1934	9-Muluc	3
Aug 7 1934	4-Ix	3	Oct 14 1934	7-Ik	8	Dec 21 1934	10-Oc	4
Aug 8 1934	5-Men	4	Oct 15 1934	8-Akbal	9	Dec 22 1934	11-Chuen	5
Aug 9 1934	6-Cib	5	Oct 16 1934	9-Kan	1	Dec 23 1934	12-Eb	6
Aug 10 1934	7-Caban	6	Oct 17 1934	10-Chicchan	2	Dec 24 1934	13-Ben	7
Aug 11 1934	8-Etz'nab	7	Oct 18 1934	11-Cimi	3	Dec 25 1934	1-Ix	8
Aug 12 1934	9-Cauac	8	Oct 19 1934	12-Manik	4	Dec 26 1934	2-Men	9
Aug 13 1934	10-Ahau	9	Oct 20 1934	13-Lamat	5	Dec 27 1934	3-Cib	1
Aug 14 1934	11-Imix	1	Oct 21 1934	1-Muluc	6	Dec 28 1934	4-Caban	2
Aug 15 1934	12-Ik	2	Oct 22 1934	2-Oc	7	Dec 29 1934	5-Etz'nab	3
Aug 16 1934	13-Akbal	3	Oct 23 1934	3-Chuen	8	Dec 30 1934	6-Cauac	4
Aug 17 1934	1-Kan	4	Oct 24 1934	4-Eb	9	Dec 31 1934	7-Ahau	5
Aug 18 1934	2-Chicchan	5	Oct 25 1934	5-Ben	1	Jan 1 1935	8-Imix	6

Date	Day-Sign	L
Jan 2 1935	9-Ik	7
Jan 3 1935	10-Akbal	8
Jan 4 1935	11-Kan	9
Jan 5 1935	12-Chicchan	1
Jan 6 1935	13-Cimi	2
Jan 7 1935	**1-Manik**	3
Jan 8 1935	2-Lamat	4
Jan 9 1935	3-Muluc	5
Jan 10 1935	4-Oc	6
Jan 11 1935	5-Chuen	7
Jan 12 1935	6-Eb	8
Jan 13 1935	7-Ben	9
Jan 14 1935	8-Ix	1
Jan 15 1935	9-Men	2
Jan 16 1935	10-Cib	3
Jan 17 1935	11-Caban	4
Jan 18 1935	12-Etz'nab	5
Jan 19 1935	13-Cauac	6
Jan 20 1935	**1-Ahau**	7
Jan 21 1935	2-*Imix*	8
Jan 22 1935	3-Ik	9
Jan 23 1935	4-Akbal	1
Jan 24 1935	5-Kan	2
Jan 25 1935	6-Chicchan	3
Jan 26 1935	7-Cimi	4
Jan 27 1935	8-Manik	5
Jan 28 1935	9-Lamat	6
Jan 29 1935	10-Muluc	7
Jan 30 1935	11-Oc	8
Jan 31 1935	12-Chuen	9
Feb 1 1935	13-Eb	1
Feb 2 1935	**1-Ben**	2
Feb 3 1935	2-Ix	3
Feb 4 1935	3-Men	4
Feb 5 1935	4-Cib	5
Feb 6 1935	5-Caban	6
Feb 7 1935	6-Etz'nab	7
Feb 8 1935	7-Cauac	8
Feb 9 1935	8-Ahau	9
Feb 10 1935	9-*Imix*	1
Feb 11 1935	10-Ik	2
Feb 12 1935	11-Akbal	3
Feb 13 1935	12-Kan	4
Feb 14 1935	13-Chicchan	5
Feb 15 1935	**1-Cimi**	6
Feb 16 1935	2-Manik	7
Feb 17 1935	3-Lamat	8
Feb 18 1935	4-Muluc	9
Feb 19 1935	5-Oc	1
Feb 20 1935	6-Chuen	2
Feb 21 1935	7-Eb	3
Feb 22 1935	8-Ben	4
Feb 23 1935	9-Ix	5
Feb 24 1935	10-Men	6
Feb 25 1935	11-Cib	7
Feb 26 1935	12-Caban	8
Feb 27 1935	13-Etz'nab	9
Feb 28 1935	**1-Cauac**	1
Mar 1 1935	2-Ahau	2
Mar 2 1935	3-*Imix*	3
Mar 3 1935	4-Ik	4
Mar 4 1935	5-Akbal	5
Mar 5 1935	6-Kan	6
Mar 6 1935	7-Chicchan	7
Mar 7 1935	8-Cimi	8
Mar 8 1935	9-Manik	9
Mar 9 1935	10-Lamat	1
Mar 10 1935	11-Muluc	2

Date	Day-Sign	L
Mar 11 1935	12-Oc	3
Mar 12 1935	13-Chuen	4
Mar 13 1935	**1-Eb**	5
Mar 14 1935	2-Ben	6
Mar 15 1935	3-Ix	7
Mar 16 1935	4-Men	8
Mar 17 1935	5-Cib	9
Mar 18 1935	6-Caban	1
Mar 19 1935	7-Etz'nab	2
Mar 20 1935	8-Cauac	3
Mar 21 1935	9-Ahau	4
Mar 22 1935	10-*Imix*	5
Mar 23 1935	11-Ik	6
Mar 24 1935	12-Akbal	7
Mar 25 1935	13-Kan	8
Mar 26 1935	**1-Chicchan**	9
Mar 27 1935	2-Cimi	1
Mar 28 1935	3-Manik	2
Mar 29 1935	4-Lamat	3
Mar 30 1935	5-Muluc	4
Mar 31 1935	6-Oc	5
Apr 1 1935	7-Chuen	6
Apr 2 1935	8-Eb	7
Apr 3 1935	9-Ben	8
Apr 4 1935	10-Ix	9
Apr 5 1935	11-Men	1
Apr 6 1935	12-Cib	2
Apr 7 1935	13-Caban	3
Apr 8 1935	**1-Etz'nab**	4
Apr 9 1935	2-Cauac	5
Apr 10 1935	3-Ahau	6
Apr 11 1935	4-*Imix*	7
Apr 12 1935	5-Ik	8
Apr 13 1935	6-Akbal	9
Apr 14 1935	7-Kan	1
Apr 15 1935	8-Chicchan	2
Apr 16 1935	9-Cimi	3
Apr 17 1935	10-Manik	4
Apr 18 1935	11-Lamat	5
Apr 19 1935	12-Muluc	6
Apr 20 1935	13-Oc	7
Apr 21 1935	**1-Chuen**	8
Apr 22 1935	2-Eb	9
Apr 23 1935	3-Ben	1
Apr 24 1935	4-Ix	2
Apr 25 1935	5-Men	3
Apr 26 1935	6-Cib	4
Apr 27 1935	7-Caban	5
Apr 28 1935	8-Etz'nab	6
Apr 29 1935	9-Cauac	7
Apr 30 1935	10-Ahau	8
May 1 1935	11-*Imix*	9
May 2 1935	12-Ik	1
May 3 1935	13-Akbal	2
May 4 1935	**1-Kan**	3
May 5 1935	2-Chicchan	4
May 6 1935	3-Cimi	5
May 7 1935	4-Manik	6
May 8 1935	5-Lamat	7
May 9 1935	6-Muluc	8
May 10 1935	7-Oc	9
May 11 1935	8-Chuen	1
May 12 1935	9-Eb	2
May 13 1935	10-Ben	3
May 14 1935	11-Ix	4
May 15 1935	12-Men	5
May 16 1935	13-Cib	6
May 17 1935	**1-Caban**	7

Date	Day-Sign	L
May 18 1935	2-Etz'nab	8
May 19 1935	3-Cauac	9
May 20 1935	4-Ahau	1
May 21 1935	5-*Imix*	2
May 22 1935	6-Ik	3
May 23 1935	7-Akbal	4
May 24 1935	8-Kan	5
May 25 1935	9-Chicchan	6
May 26 1935	10-Cimi	7
May 27 1935	11-Manik	8
May 28 1935	12-Lamat	9
May 29 1935	13-Muluc	1
May 30 1935	**1-Oc**	2
May 31 1935	2-Chuen	3
Jun 1 1935	3-Eb	4
Jun 2 1935	4-Ben	5
Jun 3 1935	5-Ix	6
Jun 4 1935	6-Men	7
Jun 5 1935	7-Cib	8
Jun 6 1935	8-Caban	9
Jun 7 1935	9-Etz'nab	1
Jun 8 1935	10-Cauac	2
Jun 9 1935	11-Ahau	3
Jun 10 1935	12-*Imix*	4
Jun 11 1935	13-Ik	5
Jun 12 1935	**1-Akbal**	6
Jun 13 1935	2-Kan	7
Jun 14 1935	3-Chicchan	8
Jun 15 1935	4-Cimi	9
Jun 16 1935	5-Manik	1
Jun 17 1935	6-Lamat	2
Jun 18 1935	7-Muluc	3
Jun 19 1935	8-Oc	4
Jun 20 1935	9-Chuen	5
Jun 21 1935	10-Eb	6
Jun 22 1935	11-Ben	7
Jun 23 1935	12-Ix	8
Jun 24 1935	13-Men	9
Jun 25 1935	**1-Cib**	1
Jun 26 1935	2-Caban	2
Jun 27 1935	3-Etz'nab	3
Jun 28 1935	4-Cauac	4
Jun 29 1935	5-Ahau	5
Jun 30 1935	6-*Imix*	6
Jul 1 1935	7-Ik	7
Jul 2 1935	8-Akbal	8
Jul 3 1935	9-Kan	9
Jul 4 1935	10-Chicchan	1
Jul 5 1935	11-Cimi	2
Jul 6 1935	12-Manik	3
Jul 7 1935	13-Lamat	4
Jul 8 1935	**1-Muluc**	5
Jul 9 1935	2-Oc	6
Jul 10 1935	3-Chuen	7
Jul 11 1935	4-Eb	8
Jul 12 1935	5-Ben	9
Jul 13 1935	6-Ix	1
Jul 14 1935	7-Men	2
Jul 15 1935	8-Cib	3
Jul 16 1935	9-Caban	4
Jul 17 1935	10-Etz'nab	5
Jul 18 1935	11-Cauac	6
Jul 19 1935	12-Ahau	7
Jul 20 1935	13-*Imix*	8
Jul 21 1935	**1-Ik**	9
Jul 22 1935	2-Akbal	1
Jul 23 1935	3-Kan	2
Jul 24 1935	4-Chicchan	3

Date	Day-Sign	L		Date	Day-Sign	L		Date	Day-Sign	L
Jul 25 1935	5-Cimi	4		Oct 1 1935	8-Ix	9		Dec 8 1935	11-Ik	5
Jul 26 1935	6-Manik	5		Oct 2 1935	9-Men	1		Dec 9 1935	12-Akbal	6
Jul 27 1935	7-Lamat	6		Oct 3 1935	10-Cib	2		Dec 10 1935	13-Kan	7
Jul 28 1935	8-Muluc	7		Oct 4 1935	11-Caban	3		Dec 11 1935	**1-Chicchan**	8
Jul 29 1935	9-Oc	8		Oct 5 1935	12-Etz'nab	4		Dec 12 1935	2-Cimi	9
Jul 30 1935	10-Chuen	9		Oct 6 1935	13-Cauac	5		Dec 13 1935	3-Manik	1
Jul 31 1935	11-Eb	1		Oct 7 1935	**1-Ahau**	6		Dec 14 1935	4-Lamat	2
Aug 1 1935	12-Ben	2		Oct 8 1935	*2-Imix*	7		Dec 15 1935	5-Muluc	3
Aug 2 1935	13-Ix	3		Oct 9 1935	3-Ik	8		Dec 16 1935	6-Oc	4
Aug 3 1935	**1-Men**	4		Oct 10 1935	4-Akbal	9		Dec 17 1935	7-Chuen	5
Aug 4 1935	2-Cib	5		Oct 11 1935	5-Kan	1		Dec 18 1935	8-Eb	6
Aug 5 1935	3-Caban	6		Oct 12 1935	6-Chicchan	2		Dec 19 1935	9-Ben	7
Aug 6 1935	4-Etz'nab	7		Oct 13 1935	7-Cimi	3		Dec 20 1935	10-Ix	8
Aug 7 1935	5-Cauac	8		Oct 14 1935	8-Manik	4		Dec 21 1935	11-Men	9
Aug 8 1935	6-Ahau	9		Oct 15 1935	9-Lamat	5		Dec 22 1935	12-Cib	1
Aug 9 1935	*7-Imix*	1		Oct 16 1935	10-Muluc	6		Dec 23 1935	13-Caban	2
Aug 10 1935	8-Ik	2		Oct 17 1935	11-Oc	7		Dec 24 1935	**1-Etz'nab**	3
Aug 11 1935	9-Akbal	3		Oct 18 1935	12-Chuen	8		Dec 25 1935	2-Cauac	4
Aug 12 1935	10-Kan	4		Oct 19 1935	13-Eb	9		Dec 26 1935	3-Ahau	5
Aug 13 1935	11-Chicchan	5		Oct 20 1935	**1-Ben**	1		Dec 27 1935	*4-Imix*	6
Aug 14 1935	12-Cimi	6		Oct 21 1935	2-Ix	2		Dec 28 1935	5-Ik	7
Aug 15 1935	13-Manik	7		Oct 22 1935	3-Men	3		Dec 29 1935	6-Akbal	8
Aug 16 1935	**1-Lamat**	8		Oct 23 1935	4-Cib	4		Dec 30 1935	7-Kan	9
Aug 17 1935	2-Muluc	9		Oct 24 1935	5-Caban	5		Dec 31 1935	8-Chicchan	1
Aug 18 1935	3-Oc	1		Oct 25 1935	6-Etz'nab	6		Jan 1 1936	9-Cimi	2
Aug 19 1935	4-Chuen	2		Oct 26 1935	7-Cauac	7		Jan 2 1936	10-Manik	3
Aug 20 1935	5-Eb	3		Oct 27 1935	8-Ahau	8		Jan 3 1936	11-Lamat	4
Aug 21 1935	6-Ben	4		Oct 28 1935	*9-Imix*	9		Jan 4 1936	12-Muluc	5
Aug 22 1935	7-Ix	5		Oct 29 1935	10-Ik	1		Jan 5 1936	13-Oc	6
Aug 23 1935	8-Men	6		Oct 30 1935	11-Akbal	2		Jan 6 1936	**1-Chuen**	7
Aug 24 1935	9-Cib	7		Oct 31 1935	12-Kan	3		Jan 7 1936	2-Eb	8
Aug 25 1935	10-Caban	8		Nov 1 1935	13-Chicchan	4		Jan 8 1936	3-Ben	9
Aug 26 1935	11-Etz'nab	9		Nov 2 1935	**1-Cimi**	5		Jan 9 1936	4-Ix	1
Aug 27 1935	12-Cauac	1		Nov 3 1935	2-Manik	6		Jan 10 1936	5-Men	2
Aug 28 1935	13-Ahau	2		Nov 4 1935	3-Lamat	7		Jan 11 1936	6-Cib	3
Aug 29 1935	**1-Imix**	3		Nov 5 1935	4-Muluc	8		Jan 12 1936	7-Caban	4
Aug 30 1935	2-Ik	4		Nov 6 1935	5-Oc	9		Jan 13 1936	8-Etz'nab	5
Aug 31 1935	3-Akbal	5		Nov 7 1935	6-Chuen	1		Jan 14 1936	9-Cauac	6
Sep 1 1935	4-Kan	6		Nov 8 1935	7-Eb	2		Jan 15 1936	10-Ahau	7
Sep 2 1935	5-Chicchan	7		Nov 9 1935	8-Ben	3		Jan 16 1936	*11-Imix*	8
Sep 3 1935	6-Cimi	8		Nov 10 1935	9-Ix	4		Jan 17 1936	12-Ik	9
Sep 4 1935	7-Manik	9		Nov 11 1935	10-Men	5		Jan 18 1936	13-Akbal	1
Sep 5 1935	8-Lamat	1		Nov 12 1935	11-Cib	6		Jan 19 1936	**1-Kan**	2
Sep 6 1935	9-Muluc	2		Nov 13 1935	12-Caban	7		Jan 20 1936	2-Chicchan	3
Sep 7 1935	10-Oc	3		Nov 14 1935	13-Etz'nab	8		Jan 21 1936	3-Cimi	4
Sep 8 1935	11-Chuen	4		Nov 15 1935	**1-Cauac**	9		Jan 22 1936	4-Manik	5
Sep 9 1935	12-Eb	5		Nov 16 1935	2-Ahau	1		Jan 23 1936	5-Lamat	6
Sep 10 1935	13-Ben	6		Nov 17 1935	*3-Imix*	2		Jan 24 1936	6-Muluc	7
Sep 11 1935	**1-Ix**	7		Nov 18 1935	4-Ik	3		Jan 25 1936	7-Oc	8
Sep 12 1935	2-Men	8		Nov 19 1935	5-Akbal	4		Jan 26 1936	8-Chuen	9
Sep 13 1935	3-Cib	9		Nov 20 1935	6-Kan	5		Jan 27 1936	9-Eb	1
Sep 14 1935	4-Caban	1		Nov 21 1935	7-Chicchan	6		Jan 28 1936	10-Ben	2
Sep 15 1935	5-Etz'nab	2		Nov 22 1935	8-Cimi	7		Jan 29 1936	11-Ix	3
Sep 16 1935	6-Cauac	3		Nov 23 1935	9-Manik	8		Jan 30 1936	12-Men	4
Sep 17 1935	7-Ahau	4		Nov 24 1935	10-Lamat	9		Jan 31 1936	13-Cib	5
Sep 18 1935	*8-Imix*	5		Nov 25 1935	11-Muluc	1		Feb 1 1936	**1-Caban**	6
Sep 19 1935	9-Ik	6		Nov 26 1935	12-Oc	2		Feb 2 1936	2-Etz'nab	7
Sep 20 1935	10-Akbal	7		Nov 27 1935	13-Chuen	3		Feb 3 1936	3-Cauac	8
Sep 21 1935	11-Kan	8		Nov 28 1935	**1-Eb**	4		Feb 4 1936	4-Ahau	9
Sep 22 1935	12-Chicchan	9		Nov 29 1935	2-Ben	5		Feb 5 1936	*5-Imix*	1
Sep 23 1935	13-Cimi	1		Nov 30 1935	3-Ix	6		Feb 6 1936	6-Ik	2
Sep 24 1935	**1-Manik**	2		Dec 1 1935	4-Men	7		Feb 7 1936	7-Akbal	3
Sep 25 1935	2-Lamat	3		Dec 2 1935	5-Cib	8		Feb 8 1936	8-Kan	4
Sep 26 1935	3-Muluc	4		Dec 3 1935	6-Caban	9		Feb 9 1936	9-Chicchan	5
Sep 27 1935	4-Oc	5		Dec 4 1935	7-Etz'nab	1		Feb 10 1936	10-Cimi	6
Sep 28 1935	5-Chuen	6		Dec 5 1935	8-Cauac	2		Feb 11 1936	11-Manik	7
Sep 29 1935	6-Eb	7		Dec 6 1935	9-Ahau	3		Feb 12 1936	12-Lamat	8
Sep 30 1935	7-Ben	8		Dec 7 1935	*10-Imix*	4		Feb 13 1936	13-Muluc	9

Date	Day-Sign	L
Feb 14 1936	1-Oc	1
Feb 15 1936	2-Chuen	2
Feb 16 1936	3-Eb	3
Feb 17 1936	4-Ben	4
Feb 18 1936	5-Ix	5
Feb 19 1936	6-Men	6
Feb 20 1936	7-Cib	7
Feb 21 1936	8-Caban	8
Feb 22 1936	9-Etz'nab	9
Feb 23 1936	10-Cauac	1
Feb 24 1936	11-Ahau	2
Feb 25 1936	12-Imix	3
Feb 26 1936	13-Ik	4
Feb 27 1936	1-Akbal	5
Feb 28 1936	2-Kan	6
Feb 29 1936	3-Chicchan	7
Mar 1 1936	4-Cimi	8
Mar 2 1936	5-Manik	9
Mar 3 1936	6-Lamat	1
Mar 4 1936	7-Muluc	2
Mar 5 1936	8-Oc	3
Mar 6 1936	9-Chuen	4
Mar 7 1936	10-Eb	5
Mar 8 1936	11-Ben	6
Mar 9 1936	12-Ix	7
Mar 10 1936	13-Men	8
Mar 11 1936	1-Cib	9
Mar 12 1936	2-Caban	1
Mar 13 1936	3-Etz'nab	2
Mar 14 1936	4-Cauac	3
Mar 15 1936	5-Ahau	4
Mar 16 1936	6-Imix	5
Mar 17 1936	7-Ik	6
Mar 18 1936	8-Akbal	7
Mar 19 1936	9-Kan	8
Mar 20 1936	10-Chicchan	9
Mar 21 1936	11-Cimi	1
Mar 22 1936	12-Manik	2
Mar 23 1936	13-Lamat	3
Mar 24 1936	1-Muluc	4
Mar 25 1936	2-Oc	5
Mar 26 1936	3-Chuen	6
Mar 27 1936	4-Eb	7
Mar 28 1936	5-Ben	8
Mar 29 1936	6-Ix	9
Mar 30 1936	7-Men	1
Mar 31 1936	8-Cib	2
Apr 1 1936	9-Caban	3
Apr 2 1936	10-Etz'nab	4
Apr 3 1936	11-Cauac	5
Apr 4 1936	12-Ahau	6
Apr 5 1936	13-Imix	7
Apr 6 1936	1-Ik	8
Apr 7 1936	2-Akbal	9
Apr 8 1936	3-Kan	1
Apr 9 1936	4-Chicchan	2
Apr 10 1936	5-Cimi	3
Apr 11 1936	6-Manik	4
Apr 12 1936	7-Lamat	5
Apr 13 1936	8-Muluc	6
Apr 14 1936	9-Oc	7
Apr 15 1936	10-Chuen	8
Apr 16 1936	11-Eb	9
Apr 17 1936	12-Ben	1
Apr 18 1936	13-Ix	2
Apr 19 1936	1-Men	3
Apr 20 1936	2-Cib	4
Apr 21 1936	3-Caban	5
Apr 22 1936	4-Etz'nab	6
Apr 23 1936	5-Cauac	7
Apr 24 1936	6-Ahau	8
Apr 25 1936	7-Imix	9
Apr 26 1936	8-Ik	1
Apr 27 1936	9-Akbal	2
Apr 28 1936	10-Kan	3
Apr 29 1936	11-Chicchan	4
Apr 30 1936	12-Cimi	5
May 1 1936	13-Manik	6
May 2 1936	1-Lamat	7
May 3 1936	2-Muluc	8
May 4 1936	3-Oc	9
May 5 1936	4-Chuen	1
May 6 1936	5-Eb	2
May 7 1936	6-Ben	3
May 8 1936	7-Ix	4
May 9 1936	8-Men	5
May 10 1936	9-Cib	6
May 11 1936	10-Caban	7
May 12 1936	11-Etz'nab	8
May 13 1936	12-Cauac	9
May 14 1936	13-Ahau	1
May 15 1936	1-Imix	2
May 16 1936	2-Ik	3
May 17 1936	3-Akbal	4
May 18 1936	4-Kan	5
May 19 1936	5-Chicchan	6
May 20 1936	6-Cimi	7
May 21 1936	7-Manik	8
May 22 1936	8-Lamat	9
May 23 1936	9-Muluc	1
May 24 1936	10-Oc	2
May 25 1936	11-Chuen	3
May 26 1936	12-Eb	4
May 27 1936	13-Ben	5
May 28 1936	1-Ix	6
May 29 1936	2-Men	7
May 30 1936	3-Cib	8
May 31 1936	4-Caban	9
Jun 1 1936	5-Etz'nab	1
Jun 2 1936	6-Cauac	2
Jun 3 1936	7-Ahau	3
Jun 4 1936	8-Imix	4
Jun 5 1936	9-Ik	5
Jun 6 1936	10-Akbal	6
Jun 7 1936	11-Kan	7
Jun 8 1936	12-Chicchan	8
Jun 9 1936	13-Cimi	9
Jun 10 1936	1-Manik	1
Jun 11 1936	2-Lamat	2
Jun 12 1936	3-Muluc	3
Jun 13 1936	4-Oc	4
Jun 14 1936	5-Chuen	5
Jun 15 1936	6-Eb	6
Jun 16 1936	7-Ben	7
Jun 17 1936	8-Ik	8
Jun 18 1936	9-Men	9
Jun 19 1936	10-Cib	1
Jun 20 1936	11-Caban	2
Jun 21 1936	12-Etz'nab	3
Jun 22 1936	13-Cauac	4
Jun 23 1936	1-Ahau	5
Jun 24 1936	2-Imix	6
Jun 25 1936	3-Ik	7
Jun 26 1936	4-Akbal	8
Jun 27 1936	5-Kan	9
Jun 28 1936	6-Chicchan	1
Jun 29 1936	7-Cimi	2
Jun 30 1936	8-Manik	3
Jul 1 1936	9-Lamat	4
Jul 2 1936	10-Muluc	5
Jul 3 1936	11-Oc	6
Jul 4 1936	12-Chuen	7
Jul 5 1936	13-Eb	8
Jul 6 1936	1-Ben	9
Jul 7 1936	2-Ix	1
Jul 8 1936	3-Men	2
Jul 9 1936	4-Cib	3
Jul 10 1936	5-Caban	4
Jul 11 1936	6-Etz'nab	5
Jul 12 1936	7-Cauac	6
Jul 13 1936	8-Ahau	7
Jul 14 1936	9-Imix	8
Jul 15 1936	10-Ik	9
Jul 16 1936	11-Akbal	1
Jul 17 1936	12-Kan	2
Jul 18 1936	13-Chicchan	3
Jul 19 1936	1-Cimi	4
Jul 20 1936	2-Manik	5
Jul 21 1936	3-Lamat	6
Jul 22 1936	4-Muluc	7
Jul 23 1936	5-Oc	8
Jul 24 1936	6-Chuen	9
Jul 25 1936	7-Eb	1
Jul 26 1936	8-Ben	2
Jul 27 1936	9-Ix	3
Jul 28 1936	10-Men	4
Jul 29 1936	11-Cib	5
Jul 30 1936	12-Caban	6
Jul 31 1936	13-Etz'nab	7
Aug 1 1936	1-Cauac	8
Aug 2 1936	2-Ahau	9
Aug 3 1936	3-Imix	1
Aug 4 1936	4-Ik	2
Aug 5 1936	5-Akbal	3
Aug 6 1936	6-Kan	4
Aug 7 1936	7-Chicchan	5
Aug 8 1936	8-Cimi	6
Aug 9 1936	9-Manik	7
Aug 10 1936	10-Lamat	8
Aug 11 1936	11-Muluc	9
Aug 12 1936	12-Oc	1
Aug 13 1936	13-Chuen	2
Aug 14 1936	1-Eb	3
Aug 15 1936	2-Ben	4
Aug 16 1936	3-Ix	5
Aug 17 1936	4-Men	6
Aug 18 1936	5-Cib	7
Aug 19 1936	6-Caban	8
Aug 20 1936	7-Etz'nab	9
Aug 21 1936	8-Cauac	1
Aug 22 1936	9-Ahau	2
Aug 23 1936	10-Imix	3
Aug 24 1936	11-Ik	4
Aug 25 1936	12-Akbal	5
Aug 26 1936	13-Kan	6
Aug 27 1936	1-Chicchan	7
Aug 28 1936	2-Cimi	8
Aug 29 1936	3-Manik	9
Aug 30 1936	4-Lamat	1
Aug 31 1936	5-Muluc	2
Sep 1 1936	6-Oc	3
Sep 2 1936	7-Chuen	4
Sep 3 1936	8-Eb	5
Sep 4 1936	9-Ben	6

Date	Day-Sign	L
Sep 5 1936	10-Ix	7
Sep 6 1936	11-Men	8
Sep 7 1936	12-Cib	9
Sep 8 1936	13-Caban	1
Sep 9 1936	1-Etz'nab	2
Sep 10 1936	2-Cauac	3
Sep 11 1936	3-Ahau	4
Sep 12 1936	4-Imix	5
Sep 13 1936	5-Ik	6
Sep 14 1936	6-Akbal	7
Sep 15 1936	7-Kan	8
Sep 16 1936	8-Chicchan	9
Sep 17 1936	9-Cimi	1
Sep 18 1936	10-Manik	2
Sep 19 1936	11-Lamat	3
Sep 20 1936	12-Muluc	4
Sep 21 1936	13-Oc	5
Sep 22 1936	1-Chuen	6
Sep 23 1936	2-Eb	7
Sep 24 1936	3-Ben	8
Sep 25 1936	4-Ix	9
Sep 26 1936	5-Men	1
Sep 27 1936	6-Cib	2
Sep 28 1936	7-Caban	3
Sep 29 1936	8-Etz'nab	4
Sep 30 1936	9-Cauac	5
Oct 1 1936	10-Ahau	6
Oct 2 1936	11-Imix	7
Oct 3 1936	12-Ik	8
Oct 4 1936	13-Akbal	9
Oct 5 1936	1-Kan	1
Oct 6 1936	2-Chicchan	2
Oct 7 1936	3-Cimi	3
Oct 8 1936	4-Manik	4
Oct 9 1936	5-Lamat	5
Oct 10 1936	6-Muluc	6
Oct 11 1936	7-Oc	7
Oct 12 1936	8-Chuen	8
Oct 13 1936	9-Eb	9
Oct 14 1936	10-Ben	1
Oct 15 1936	11-Ix	2
Oct 16 1936	12-Men	3
Oct 17 1936	13-Cib	4
Oct 18 1936	1-Caban	5
Oct 19 1936	2-Etz'nab	6
Oct 20 1936	3-Cauac	7
Oct 21 1936	4-Ahau	8
Oct 22 1936	5-Imix	9
Oct 23 1936	6-Ik	1
Oct 24 1936	7-Akbal	2
Oct 25 1936	8-Kan	3
Oct 26 1936	9-Chicchan	4
Oct 27 1936	10-Cimi	5
Oct 28 1936	11-Manik	6
Oct 29 1936	12-Lamat	7
Oct 30 1936	13-Muluc	8
Oct 31 1936	1-Oc	9
Nov 1 1936	2-Chuen	1
Nov 2 1936	3-Eb	2
Nov 3 1936	4-Ben	3
Nov 4 1936	5-Ix	4
Nov 5 1936	6-Men	5
Nov 6 1936	7-Cib	6
Nov 7 1936	8-Caban	7
Nov 8 1936	9-Etz'nab	8
Nov 9 1936	10-Cauac	9
Nov 10 1936	11-Ahau	1
Nov 11 1936	12-Imix	2

Date	Day-Sign	L
Nov 12 1936	13-Ik	3
Nov 13 1936	1-Akbal	4
Nov 14 1936	2-Kan	5
Nov 15 1936	3-Chicchan	6
Nov 16 1936	4-Cimi	7
Nov 17 1936	5-Manik	8
Nov 18 1936	6-Lamat	9
Nov 19 1936	7-Muluc	1
Nov 20 1936	8-Oc	2
Nov 21 1936	9-Chuen	3
Nov 22 1936	10-Eb	4
Nov 23 1936	11-Ben	5
Nov 24 1936	12-Ix	6
Nov 25 1936	13-Men	7
Nov 26 1936	1-Cib	8
Nov 27 1936	2-Caban	9
Nov 28 1936	3-Etz'nab	1
Nov 29 1936	4-Cauac	2
Nov 30 1936	5-Ahau	3
Dec 1 1936	6-Imix	4
Dec 2 1936	7-Ik	5
Dec 3 1936	8-Akbal	6
Dec 4 1936	9-Kan	7
Dec 5 1936	10-Chicchan	8
Dec 6 1936	11-Cimi	9
Dec 7 1936	12-Manik	1
Dec 8 1936	13-Lamat	2
Dec 9 1936	1-Muluc	3
Dec 10 1936	2-Oc	4
Dec 11 1936	3-Chuen	5
Dec 12 1936	4-Eb	6
Dec 13 1936	5-Ben	7
Dec 14 1936	6-Ix	8
Dec 15 1936	7-Men	9
Dec 16 1936	8-Cib	1
Dec 17 1936	9-Caban	2
Dec 18 1936	10-Etz'nab	3
Dec 19 1936	11-Cauac	4
Dec 20 1936	12-Ahau	5
Dec 21 1936	13-Imix	6
Dec 22 1936	1-Ik	7
Dec 23 1936	2-Akbal	8
Dec 24 1936	3-Kan	9
Dec 25 1936	4-Chicchan	1
Dec 26 1936	5-Cimi	2
Dec 27 1936	6-Manik	3
Dec 28 1936	7-Lamat	4
Dec 29 1936	8-Muluc	5
Dec 30 1936	9-Oc	6
Dec 31 1936	10-Chuen	7
Jan 1 1937	11-Eb	8
Jan 2 1937	12-Ben	9
Jan 3 1937	13-Ix	1
Jan 4 1937	1-Men	2
Jan 5 1937	2-Cib	3
Jan 6 1937	3-Caban	4
Jan 7 1937	4-Etz'nab	5
Jan 8 1937	5-Cauac	6
Jan 9 1937	6-Ahau	7
Jan 10 1937	7-Imix	8
Jan 11 1937	8-Ik	9
Jan 12 1937	9-Akbal	1
Jan 13 1937	10-Kan	2
Jan 14 1937	11-Chicchan	3
Jan 15 1937	12-Cimi	4
Jan 16 1937	13-Manik	5
Jan 17 1937	1-Lamat	6
Jan 18 1937	2-Muluc	7

Date	Day-Sign	L
Jan 19 1937	3-Oc	8
Jan 20 1937	4-Chuen	9
Jan 21 1937	5-Eb	1
Jan 22 1937	6-Ben	2
Jan 23 1937	7-Ix	3
Jan 24 1937	8-Men	4
Jan 25 1937	9-Cib	5
Jan 26 1937	10-Caban	6
Jan 27 1937	11-Etz'nab	7
Jan 28 1937	12-Cauac	8
Jan 29 1937	13-Ahau	9
Jan 30 1937	1-Imix	1
Jan 31 1937	2-Ik	2
Feb 1 1937	3-Akbal	3
Feb 2 1937	4-Kan	4
Feb 3 1937	5-Chicchan	5
Feb 4 1937	6-Cimi	6
Feb 5 1937	7-Manik	7
Feb 6 1937	8-Lamat	8
Feb 7 1937	9-Muluc	9
Feb 8 1937	10-Oc	1
Feb 9 1937	11-Chuen	2
Feb 10 1937	12-Eb	3
Feb 11 1937	13-Ben	4
Feb 12 1937	1-Ix	5
Feb 13 1937	2-Men	6
Feb 14 1937	3-Cib	7
Feb 15 1937	4-Caban	8
Feb 16 1937	5-Etz'nab	9
Feb 17 1937	6-Cauac	1
Feb 18 1937	7-Ahau	2
Feb 19 1937	8-Imix	3
Feb 20 1937	9-Ik	4
Feb 21 1937	10-Akbal	5
Feb 22 1937	11-Kan	6
Feb 23 1937	12-Chicchan	7
Feb 24 1937	13-Cimi	8
Feb 25 1937	1-Manik	9
Feb 26 1937	2-Lamat	1
Feb 27 1937	3-Muluc	2
Feb 28 1937	4-Oc	3
Mar 1 1937	5-Chuen	4
Mar 2 1937	6-Eb	5
Mar 3 1937	7-Ben	6
Mar 4 1937	8-Ix	7
Mar 5 1937	9-Men	8
Mar 6 1937	10-Cib	9
Mar 7 1937	11-Caban	1
Mar 8 1937	12-Etz'nab	2
Mar 9 1937	13-Cauac	3
Mar 10 1937	1-Ahau	4
Mar 11 1937	2-Imix	5
Mar 12 1937	3-Ik	6
Mar 13 1937	4-Akbal	7
Mar 14 1937	5-Kan	8
Mar 15 1937	6-Chicchan	9
Mar 16 1937	7-Cimi	1
Mar 17 1937	8-Manik	2
Mar 18 1937	9-Lamat	3
Mar 19 1937	10-Muluc	4
Mar 20 1937	11-Oc	5
Mar 21 1937	12-Chuen	6
Mar 22 1937	13-Eb	7
Mar 23 1937	1-Ben	8
Mar 24 1937	2-Ix	9
Mar 25 1937	3-Men	1
Mar 26 1937	4-Cib	2
Mar 27 1937	5-Caban	3

Date	Day-Sign	L	Date	Day-Sign	L	Date	Day-Sign	L
Mar 28 1937	6-Etz'nab	4	Jun 4 1937	9-Cimi	9	Aug 11 1937	12-Ix	5
Mar 29 1937	7-Cauac	5	Jun 5 1937	10-Manik	1	Aug 12 1937	13-Men	6
Mar 30 1937	8-Ahau	6	Jun 6 1937	11-Lamat	2	Aug 13 1937	1-Cib	7
Mar 31 1937	9-Imix	7	Jun 7 1937	12-Muluc	3	Aug 14 1937	2-Caban	8
Apr 1 1937	10-Ik	8	Jun 8 1937	13-Oc	4	Aug 15 1937	3-Etz'nab	9
Apr 2 1937	11-Akbal	9	Jun 9 1937	1-Chuen	5	Aug 16 1937	4-Cauac	1
Apr 3 1937	12-Kan	1	Jun 10 1937	2-Eb	6	Aug 17 1937	5-Ahau	2
Apr 4 1937	13-Chicchan	2	Jun 11 1937	3-Ben	7	Aug 18 1937	6-Imix	3
Apr 5 1937	1-Cimi	3	Jun 12 1937	4-Ix	8	Aug 19 1937	7-Ik	4
Apr 6 1937	2-Manik	4	Jun 13 1937	5-Men	9	Aug 20 1937	8-Akbal	5
Apr 7 1937	3-Lamat	5	Jun 14 1937	6-Cib	1	Aug 21 1937	9-Kan	6
Apr 8 1937	4-Muluc	6	Jun 15 1937	7-Caban	2	Aug 22 1937	10-Chicchan	7
Apr 9 1937	5-Oc	7	Jun 16 1937	8-Etz'nab	3	Aug 23 1937	11-Cimi	8
Apr 10 1937	6-Chuen	8	Jun 17 1937	9-Cauac	4	Aug 24 1937	12-Manik	9
Apr 11 1937	7-Eb	9	Jun 18 1937	10-Ahau	5	Aug 25 1937	13-Lamat	1
Apr 12 1937	8-Ben	1	Jun 19 1937	11-Imix	6	Aug 26 1937	1-Muluc	2
Apr 13 1937	9-Ix	2	Jun 20 1937	12-Ik	7	Aug 27 1937	2-Oc	3
Apr 14 1937	10-Men	3	Jun 21 1937	13-Akbal	8	Aug 28 1937	3-Chuen	4
Apr 15 1937	11-Cib	4	Jun 22 1937	1-Kan	9	Aug 29 1937	4-Eb	5
Apr 16 1937	12-Caban	5	Jun 23 1937	2-Chicchan	1	Aug 30 1937	5-Ben	6
Apr 17 1937	13-Etz'nab	6	Jun 24 1937	3-Cimi	2	Aug 31 1937	6-Ix	7
Apr 18 1937	1-Cauac	7	Jun 25 1937	4-Manik	3	Sep 1 1937	7-Men	8
Apr 19 1937	2-Ahau	8	Jun 26 1937	5-Lamat	4	Sep 2 1937	8-Cib	9
Apr 20 1937	3-Imix	9	Jun 27 1937	6-Muluc	5	Sep 3 1937	9-Caban	1
Apr 21 1937	4-Ik	1	Jun 28 1937	7-Oc	6	Sep 4 1937	10-Etz'nab	2
Apr 22 1937	5-Akbal	2	Jun 29 1937	8-Chuen	7	Sep 5 1937	11-Cauac	3
Apr 23 1937	6-Kan	3	Jun 30 1937	9-Eb	8	Sep 6 1937	12-Ahau	4
Apr 24 1937	7-Chicchan	4	Jul 1 1937	10-Ben	9	Sep 7 1937	13-Imix	5
Apr 25 1937	8-Cimi	5	Jul 2 1937	11-Ix	1	Sep 8 1937	1-Ik	6
Apr 26 1937	9-Manik	6	Jul 3 1937	12-Men	2	Sep 9 1937	2-Akbal	7
Apr 27 1937	10-Lamat	7	Jul 4 1937	13-Cib	3	Sep 10 1937	3-Kan	8
Apr 28 1937	11-Muluc	8	Jul 5 1937	1-Caban	4	Sep 11 1937	4-Chicchan	9
Apr 29 1937	12-Oc	9	Jul 6 1937	2-Etz'nab	5	Sep 12 1937	5-Cimi	1
Apr 30 1937	13-Chuen	1	Jul 7 1937	3-Cauac	6	Sep 13 1937	6-Manik	2
May 1 1937	1-Eb	2	Jul 8 1937	4-Ahau	7	Sep 14 1937	7-Lamat	3
May 2 1937	2-Ben	3	Jul 9 1937	5-Imix	8	Sep 15 1937	8-Muluc	4
May 3 1937	3-Ix	4	Jul 10 1937	6-Ik	9	Sep 16 1937	9-Oc	5
May 4 1937	4-Men	5	Jul 11 1937	7-Akbal	1	Sep 17 1937	10-Chuen	6
May 5 1937	5-Cib	6	Jul 12 1937	8-Kan	2	Sep 18 1937	11-Eb	7
May 6 1937	6-Caban	7	Jul 13 1937	9-Chicchan	3	Sep 19 1937	12-Ben	8
May 7 1937	7-Etz'nab	8	Jul 14 1937	10-Cimi	4	Sep 20 1937	13-Ix	9
May 8 1937	8-Cauac	9	Jul 15 1937	11-Manik	5	Sep 21 1937	1-Men	1
May 9 1937	9-Ahau	1	Jul 16 1937	12-Lamat	6	Sep 22 1937	2-Cib	2
May 10 1937	10-Imix	2	Jul 17 1937	13-Muluc	7	Sep 23 1937	3-Caban	3
May 11 1937	11-Ik	3	Jul 18 1937	1-Oc	8	Sep 24 1937	4-Etz'nab	4
May 12 1937	12-Akbal	4	Jul 19 1937	2-Chuen	9	Sep 25 1937	5-Cauac	5
May 13 1937	13-Kan	5	Jul 20 1937	3-Eb	1	Sep 26 1937	6-Ahau	6
May 14 1937	1-Chicchan	6	Jul 21 1937	4-Ben	2	Sep 27 1937	7-Imix	7
May 15 1937	2-Cimi	7	Jul 22 1937	5-Ix	3	Sep 28 1937	8-Ik	8
May 16 1937	3-Manik	8	Jul 23 1937	6-Men	4	Sep 29 1937	9-Akbal	9
May 17 1937	4-Lamat	9	Jul 24 1937	7-Cib	5	Sep 30 1937	10-Kan	1
May 18 1937	5-Muluc	1	Jul 25 1937	8-Caban	6	Oct 1 1937	11-Chicchan	2
May 19 1937	6-Oc	2	Jul 26 1937	9-Etz'nab	7	Oct 2 1937	12-Cimi	3
May 20 1937	7-Chuen	3	Jul 27 1937	10-Cauac	8	Oct 3 1937	13-Manik	4
May 21 1937	8-Eb	4	Jul 28 1937	11-Ahau	9	Oct 4 1937	1-Lamat	5
May 22 1937	9-Ben	5	Jul 29 1937	12-Imix	1	Oct 5 1937	2-Muluc	6
May 23 1937	10-Ix	6	Jul 30 1937	13-Ik	2	Oct 6 1937	3-Oc	7
May 24 1937	11-Men	7	Jul 31 1937	1-Akbal	3	Oct 7 1937	4-Chuen	8
May 25 1937	12-Cib	8	Aug 1 1937	2-Kan	4	Oct 8 1937	5-Eb	9
May 26 1937	13-Caban	9	Aug 2 1937	3-Chicchan	5	Oct 9 1937	6-Ben	1
May 27 1937	1-Etz'nab	1	Aug 3 1937	4-Cimi	6	Oct 10 1937	7-Ix	2
May 28 1937	2-Cauac	2	Aug 4 1937	5-Manik	7	Oct 11 1937	8-Men	3
May 29 1937	3-Ahau	3	Aug 5 1937	6-Lamat	8	Oct 12 1937	9-Cib	4
May 30 1937	4-Imix	4	Aug 6 1937	7-Muluc	9	Oct 13 1937	10-Caban	5
May 31 1937	5-Ik	5	Aug 7 1937	8-Oc	1	Oct 14 1937	11-Etz'nab	6
Jun 1 1937	6-Akbal	6	Aug 8 1937	9-Chuen	2	Oct 15 1937	12-Cauac	7
Jun 2 1937	7-Kan	7	Aug 9 1937	10-Eb	3	Oct 16 1937	13-Ahau	8
Jun 3 1937	8-Chicchan	8	Aug 10 1937	11-Ben	4	Oct 17 1937	1-Imix	9

Date	Day-Sign	L
Oct 18 1937	2-Ik	1
Oct 19 1937	3-Akbal	2
Oct 20 1937	4-Kan	3
Oct 21 1937	5-Chicchan	4
Oct 22 1937	6-Cimi	5
Oct 23 1937	7-Manik	6
Oct 24 1937	8-Lamat	7
Oct 25 1937	9-Muluc	8
Oct 26 1937	10-Oc	9
Oct 27 1937	11-Chuen	1
Oct 28 1937	12-Eb	2
Oct 29 1937	13-Ben	3
Oct 30 1937	**1-Ik**	4
Oct 31 1937	2-Men	5
Nov 1 1937	3-Cib	6
Nov 2 1937	4-Caban	7
Nov 3 1937	5-Etz'nab	8
Nov 4 1937	6-Cauac	9
Nov 5 1937	7-Ahau	1
Nov 6 1937	*8-Imix*	2
Nov 7 1937	9-Ik	3
Nov 8 1937	10-Akbal	4
Nov 9 1937	11-Kan	5
Nov 10 1937	12-Chicchan	6
Nov 11 1937	13-Cimi	7
Nov 12 1937	**1-Manik**	8
Nov 13 1937	2-Lamat	9
Nov 14 1937	3-Muluc	1
Nov 15 1937	4-Oc	2
Nov 16 1937	5-Chuen	3
Nov 17 1937	6-Eb	4
Nov 18 1937	7-Ben	5
Nov 19 1937	8-Ix	6
Nov 20 1937	9-Men	7
Nov 21 1937	10-Cib	8
Nov 22 1937	11-Caban	9
Nov 23 1937	12-Etz'nab	1
Nov 24 1937	13-Cauac	2
Nov 25 1937	**1-Ahau**	3
Nov 26 1937	*2-Imix*	4
Nov 27 1937	3-Ik	5
Nov 28 1937	4-Akbal	6
Nov 29 1937	5-Kan	7
Nov 30 1937	6-Chicchan	8
Dec 1 1937	7-Cimi	9
Dec 2 1937	8-Manik	1
Dec 3 1937	9-Lamat	2
Dec 4 1937	10-Muluc	3
Dec 5 1937	11-Oc	4
Dec 6 1937	12-Chuen	5
Dec 7 1937	13-Eb	6
Dec 8 1937	**1-Ben**	7
Dec 9 1937	2-Ix	8
Dec 10 1937	3-Men	9
Dec 11 1937	4-Cib	1
Dec 12 1937	5-Caban	2
Dec 13 1937	6-Etz'nab	3
Dec 14 1937	7-Cauac	4
Dec 15 1937	8-Ahau	5
Dec 16 1937	*9-Imix*	6
Dec 17 1937	10-Ik	7
Dec 18 1937	11-Akbal	8
Dec 19 1937	12-Kan	9
Dec 20 1937	13-Chicchan	1
Dec 21 1937	**1-Cimi**	2
Dec 22 1937	2-Manik	3
Dec 23 1937	3-Lamat	4
Dec 24 1937	4-Muluc	5

Date	Day-Sign	L
Dec 25 1937	5-Oc	6
Dec 26 1937	6-Chuen	7
Dec 27 1937	7-Eb	8
Dec 28 1937	8-Ben	9
Dec 29 1937	9-Ix	1
Dec 30 1937	10-Men	2
Dec 31 1937	11-Cib	3
Jan 1 1938	12-Caban	4
Jan 2 1938	13-Etz'nab	5
Jan 3 1938	**1-Cauac**	6
Jan 4 1938	2-Ahau	7
Jan 5 1938	*3-Imix*	8
Jan 6 1938	4-Ik	9
Jan 7 1938	5-Akbal	1
Jan 8 1938	6-Kan	2
Jan 9 1938	7-Chicchan	3
Jan 10 1938	8-Cimi	4
Jan 11 1938	9-Manik	5
Jan 12 1938	10-Lamat	6
Jan 13 1938	11-Muluc	7
Jan 14 1938	12-Oc	8
Jan 15 1938	13-Chuen	9
Jan 16 1938	**1-Eb**	1
Jan 17 1938	2-Ben	2
Jan 18 1938	3-Ix	3
Jan 19 1938	4-Men	4
Jan 20 1938	5-Cib	5
Jan 21 1938	6-Caban	6
Jan 22 1938	7-Etz'nab	7
Jan 23 1938	8-Cauac	8
Jan 24 1938	9-Ahau	9
Jan 25 1938	*10-Imix*	1
Jan 26 1938	11-Ik	2
Jan 27 1938	12-Akbal	3
Jan 28 1938	13-Kan	4
Jan 29 1938	**1-Chicchan**	5
Jan 30 1938	2-Cimi	6
Jan 31 1938	3-Manik	7
Feb 1 1938	4-Lamat	8
Feb 2 1938	5-Muluc	9
Feb 3 1938	6-Oc	1
Feb 4 1938	7-Chuen	2
Feb 5 1938	8-Eb	3
Feb 6 1938	9-Ben	4
Feb 7 1938	10-Ix	5
Feb 8 1938	11-Men	6
Feb 9 1938	12-Cib	7
Feb 10 1938	13-Caban	8
Feb 11 1938	**1-Etz'nab**	9
Feb 12 1938	2-Cauac	1
Feb 13 1938	3-Ahau	2
Feb 14 1938	*4-Imix*	3
Feb 15 1938	5-Ik	4
Feb 16 1938	6-Akbal	5
Feb 17 1938	7-Kan	6
Feb 18 1938	8-Chicchan	7
Feb 19 1938	9-Cimi	8
Feb 20 1938	10-Manik	9
Feb 21 1938	11-Lamat	1
Feb 22 1938	12-Muluc	2
Feb 23 1938	13-Oc	3
Feb 24 1938	**1-Chuen**	4
Feb 25 1938	2-Eb	5
Feb 26 1938	3-Ben	6
Feb 27 1938	4-Ix	7
Feb 28 1938	5-Men	8
Mar 1 1938	6-Cib	9
Mar 2 1938	7-Caban	1

Date	Day-Sign	L
Mar 3 1938	8-Etz'nab	2
Mar 4 1938	9-Cauac	3
Mar 5 1938	10-Ahau	4
Mar 6 1938	*11-Imix*	5
Mar 7 1938	12-Ik	6
Mar 8 1938	13-Akbal	7
Mar 9 1938	**1-Kan**	8
Mar 10 1938	2-Chicchan	9
Mar 11 1938	3-Cimi	1
Mar 12 1938	4-Manik	2
Mar 13 1938	5-Lamat	3
Mar 14 1938	6-Muluc	4
Mar 15 1938	7-Oc	5
Mar 16 1938	8-Chuen	6
Mar 17 1938	9-Eb	7
Mar 18 1938	10-Ben	8
Mar 19 1938	11-Ix	9
Mar 20 1938	12-Men	1
Mar 21 1938	13-Cib	2
Mar 22 1938	**1-Caban**	3
Mar 23 1938	2-Etz'nab	4
Mar 24 1938	3-Cauac	5
Mar 25 1938	4-Ahau	6
Mar 26 1938	*5-Imix*	7
Mar 27 1938	6-Ik	8
Mar 28 1938	7-Akbal	9
Mar 29 1938	8-Kan	1
Mar 30 1938	9-Chicchan	2
Mar 31 1938	10-Cimi	3
Apr 1 1938	11-Manik	4
Apr 2 1938	12-Lamat	5
Apr 3 1938	13-Muluc	6
Apr 4 1938	**1-Oc**	7
Apr 5 1938	2-Chuen	8
Apr 6 1938	3-Eb	9
Apr 7 1938	4-Ben	1
Apr 8 1938	5-Ix	2
Apr 9 1938	6-Men	3
Apr 10 1938	7-Cib	4
Apr 11 1938	8-Caban	5
Apr 12 1938	9-Etz'nab	6
Apr 13 1938	10-Cauac	7
Apr 14 1938	11-Ahau	8
Apr 15 1938	*12-Imix*	9
Apr 16 1938	13-Ik	1
Apr 17 1938	**1-Akbal**	2
Apr 18 1938	2-Kan	3
Apr 19 1938	3-Chicchan	4
Apr 20 1938	4-Cimi	5
Apr 21 1938	5-Manik	6
Apr 22 1938	6-Lamat	7
Apr 23 1938	7-Muluc	8
Apr 24 1938	8-Oc	9
Apr 25 1938	9-Chuen	1
Apr 26 1938	10-Eb	2
Apr 27 1938	11-Ben	3
Apr 28 1938	12-Ix	4
Apr 29 1938	13-Men	5
Apr 30 1938	**1-Cib**	6
May 1 1938	2-Caban	7
May 2 1938	3-Etz'nab	8
May 3 1938	4-Cauac	9
May 4 1938	5-Ahau	1
May 5 1938	*6-Imix*	2
May 6 1938	7-Ik	3
May 7 1938	8-Akbal	4
May 8 1938	9-Kan	5
May 9 1938	10-Chicchan	6

Date	Day-Sign	L	Date	Day-Sign	L	Date	Day-Sign	L
May 10 1938	11-Cimi	7	Jul 17 1938	1-Ix	3	Sep 23 1938	4-Ik	8
May 11 1938	12-Manik	8	Jul 18 1938	2-Men	4	Sep 24 1938	5-Akbal	9
May 12 1938	13-Lamat	9	Jul 19 1938	3-Cib	5	Sep 25 1938	6-Kan	1
May 13 1938	1-Muluc	1	Jul 20 1938	4-Caban	6	Sep 26 1938	7-Chicchan	2
May 14 1938	2-Oc	2	Jul 21 1938	5-Etz'nab	7	Sep 27 1938	8-Cimi	3
May 15 1938	3-Chuen	3	Jul 22 1938	6-Cauac	8	Sep 28 1938	9-Manik	4
May 16 1938	4-Eb	4	Jul 23 1938	7-Ahau	9	Sep 29 1938	10-Lamat	5
May 17 1938	5-Ben	5	Jul 24 1938	8-Imix	1	Sep 30 1938	11-Muluc	6
May 18 1938	6-Ix	6	Jul 25 1938	9-Ik	2	Oct 1 1938	12-Oc	7
May 19 1938	7-Men	7	Jul 26 1938	10-Akbal	3	Oct 2 1938	13-Chuen	8
May 20 1938	8-Cib	8	Jul 27 1938	11-Kan	4	Oct 3 1938	1-Eb	9
May 21 1938	9-Caban	9	Jul 28 1938	12-Chicchan	5	Oct 4 1938	2-Ben	1
May 22 1938	10-Etz'nab	1	Jul 29 1938	13-Cimi	6	Oct 5 1938	3-Ix	2
May 23 1938	11-Cauac	2	Jul 30 1938	1-Manik	7	Oct 6 1938	4-Men	3
May 24 1938	12-Ahau	3	Jul 31 1938	2-Lamat	8	Oct 7 1938	5-Cib	4
May 25 1938	13-Imix	4	Aug 1 1938	3-Muluc	9	Oct 8 1938	6-Caban	5
May 26 1938	1-Ik	5	Aug 2 1938	4-Oc	1	Oct 9 1938	7-Etz'nab	6
May 27 1938	2-Akbal	6	Aug 3 1938	5-Chuen	2	Oct 10 1938	8-Cauac	7
May 28 1938	3-Kan	7	Aug 4 1938	6-Eb	3	Oct 11 1938	9-Ahau	8
May 29 1938	4-Chicchan	8	Aug 5 1938	7-Ben	4	Oct 12 1938	10-Imix	9
May 30 1938	5-Cimi	9	Aug 6 1938	8-Ix	5	Oct 13 1938	11-Ik	1
May 31 1938	6-Manik	1	Aug 7 1938	9-Men	6	Oct 14 1938	12-Akbal	2
Jun 1 1938	7-Lamat	2	Aug 8 1938	10-Cib	7	Oct 15 1938	13-Kan	3
Jun 2 1938	8-Muluc	3	Aug 9 1938	11-Caban	8	Oct 16 1938	1-Chicchan	4
Jun 3 1938	9-Oc	4	Aug 10 1938	12-Etz'nab	9	Oct 17 1938	2-Cimi	5
Jun 4 1938	10-Chuen	5	Aug 11 1938	13-Cauac	1	Oct 18 1938	3-Manik	6
Jun 5 1938	11-Eb	6	Aug 12 1938	1-Ahau	2	Oct 19 1938	4-Lamat	7
Jun 6 1938	12-Ben	7	Aug 13 1938	2-Imix	3	Oct 20 1938	5-Muluc	8
Jun 7 1938	13-Ix	8	Aug 14 1938	3-Ik	4	Oct 21 1938	6-Oc	9
Jun 8 1938	1-Men	9	Aug 15 1938	4-Akbal	5	Oct 22 1938	7-Chuen	1
Jun 9 1938	2-Cib	1	Aug 16 1938	5-Kan	6	Oct 23 1938	8-Eb	2
Jun 10 1938	3-Caban	2	Aug 17 1938	6-Chicchan	7	Oct 24 1938	9-Ben	3
Jun 11 1938	4-Etz'nab	3	Aug 18 1938	7-Cimi	8	Oct 25 1938	10-Ix	4
Jun 12 1938	5-Cauac	4	Aug 19 1938	8-Manik	9	Oct 26 1938	11-Men	5
Jun 13 1938	6-Ahau	5	Aug 20 1938	9-Lamat	1	Oct 27 1938	12-Cib	6
Jun 14 1938	7-Imix	6	Aug 21 1938	10-Muluc	2	Oct 28 1938	13-Caban	7
Jun 15 1938	8-Ik	7	Aug 22 1938	11-Oc	3	Oct 29 1938	1-Etz'nab	8
Jun 16 1938	9-Akbal	8	Aug 23 1938	12-Chuen	4	Oct 30 1938	2-Cauac	9
Jun 17 1938	10-Kan	9	Aug 24 1938	13-Eb	5	Oct 31 1938	3-Ahau	1
Jun 18 1938	11-Chicchan	1	Aug 25 1938	1-Ben	6	Nov 1 1938	4-Imix	2
Jun 19 1938	12-Cimi	2	Aug 26 1938	2-Ix	7	Nov 2 1938	5-Ik	3
Jun 20 1938	13-Manik	3	Aug 27 1938	3-Men	8	Nov 3 1938	6-Akbal	4
Jun 21 1938	1-Lamat	4	Aug 28 1938	4-Cib	9	Nov 4 1938	7-Kan	5
Jun 22 1938	2-Muluc	5	Aug 29 1938	5-Caban	1	Nov 5 1938	8-Chicchan	6
Jun 23 1938	3-Oc	6	Aug 30 1938	6-Etz'nab	2	Nov 6 1938	9-Cimi	7
Jun 24 1938	4-Chuen	7	Aug 31 1938	7-Cauac	3	Nov 7 1938	10-Manik	8
Jun 25 1938	5-Eb	8	Sep 1 1938	8-Ahau	4	Nov 8 1938	11-Lamat	9
Jun 26 1938	6-Ben	9	Sep 2 1938	9-Imix	5	Nov 9 1938	12-Muluc	1
Jun 27 1938	7-Ix	1	Sep 3 1938	10-Ik	6	Nov 10 1938	13-Oc	2
Jun 28 1938	8-Men	2	Sep 4 1938	11-Akbal	7	Nov 11 1938	1-Chuen	3
Jun 29 1938	9-Cib	3	Sep 5 1938	12-Kan	8	Nov 12 1938	2-Eb	4
Jun 30 1938	10-Caban	4	Sep 6 1938	13-Chicchan	9	Nov 13 1938	3-Ben	5
Jul 1 1938	11-Etz'nab	5	Sep 7 1938	1-Cimi	1	Nov 14 1938	4-Ix	6
Jul 2 1938	12-Cauac	6	Sep 8 1938	2-Manik	2	Nov 15 1938	5-Men	7
Jul 3 1938	13-Ahau	7	Sep 9 1938	3-Lamat	3	Nov 16 1938	6-Cib	8
Jul 4 1938	1-Imix	8	Sep 10 1938	4-Muluc	4	Nov 17 1938	7-Caban	9
Jul 5 1938	2-Ik	9	Sep 11 1938	5-Oc	5	Nov 18 1938	8-Etz'nab	1
Jul 6 1938	3-Akbal	1	Sep 12 1938	6-Chuen	6	Nov 19 1938	9-Cauac	2
Jul 7 1938	4-Kan	2	Sep 13 1938	7-Eb	7	Nov 20 1938	10-Ahau	3
Jul 8 1938	5-Chicchan	3	Sep 14 1938	8-Ben	8	Nov 21 1938	11-Imix	4
Jul 9 1938	6-Cimi	4	Sep 15 1938	9-Ix	9	Nov 22 1938	12-Ik	5
Jul 10 1938	7-Manik	5	Sep 16 1938	10-Men	1	Nov 23 1938	13-Akbal	6
Jul 11 1938	8-Lamat	6	Sep 17 1938	11-Cib	2	Nov 24 1938	1-Kan	7
Jul 12 1938	9-Muluc	7	Sep 18 1938	12-Caban	3	Nov 25 1938	2-Chicchan	8
Jul 13 1938	10-Oc	8	Sep 19 1938	13-Etz'nab	4	Nov 26 1938	3-Cimi	9
Jul 14 1938	11-Chuen	9	Sep 20 1938	1-Cauac	5	Nov 27 1938	4-Manik	1
Jul 15 1938	12-Eb	1	Sep 21 1938	2-Ahau	6	Nov 28 1938	5-Lamat	2
Jul 16 1938	13-Ben	2	Sep 22 1938	3-Imix	7	Nov 29 1938	6-Muluc	3

Date	Day-Sign	L
Nov 30 1938	7-Oc	4
Dec 1 1938	8-Chuen	5
Dec 2 1938	9-Eb	6
Dec 3 1938	10-Ben	7
Dec 4 1938	11-Ix	8
Dec 5 1938	12-Men	9
Dec 6 1938	13-Cib	1
Dec 7 1938	1-Caban	2
Dec 8 1938	2-Etz'nab	3
Dec 9 1938	3-Cauac	4
Dec 10 1938	4-Ahau	5
Dec 11 1938	5-Imix	6
Dec 12 1938	6-Ik	7
Dec 13 1938	7-Akbal	8
Dec 14 1938	8-Kan	9
Dec 15 1938	9-Chicchan	1
Dec 16 1938	10-Cimi	2
Dec 17 1938	11-Manik	3
Dec 18 1938	12-Lamat	4
Dec 19 1938	13-Muluc	5
Dec 20 1938	1-Oc	6
Dec 21 1938	2-Chuen	7
Dec 22 1938	3-Eb	8
Dec 23 1938	4-Ben	9
Dec 24 1938	5-Ix	1
Dec 25 1938	6-Men	2
Dec 26 1938	7-Cib	3
Dec 27 1938	8-Caban	4
Dec 28 1938	9-Etz'nab	5
Dec 29 1938	10-Cauac	6
Dec 30 1938	11-Ahau	7
Dec 31 1938	12-Imix	8
Jan 1 1939	13-Ik	9
Jan 2 1939	1-Akbal	1
Jan 3 1939	2-Kan	2
Jan 4 1939	3-Chicchan	3
Jan 5 1939	4-Cimi	4
Jan 6 1939	5-Manik	5
Jan 7 1939	6-Lamat	6
Jan 8 1939	7-Muluc	7
Jan 9 1939	8-Oc	8
Jan 10 1939	9-Chuen	9
Jan 11 1939	10-Eb	1
Jan 12 1939	11-Ben	2
Jan 13 1939	12-Ix	3
Jan 14 1939	13-Men	4
Jan 15 1939	1-Cib	5
Jan 16 1939	2-Caban	6
Jan 17 1939	3-Etz'nab	7
Jan 18 1939	4-Cauac	8
Jan 19 1939	5-Ahau	9
Jan 20 1939	6-Imix	1
Jan 21 1939	7-Ik	2
Jan 22 1939	8-Akbal	3
Jan 23 1939	9-Kan	4
Jan 24 1939	10-Chicchan	5
Jan 25 1939	11-Cimi	6
Jan 26 1939	12-Manik	7
Jan 27 1939	13-Lamat	8
Jan 28 1939	1-Muluc	9
Jan 29 1939	2-Oc	1
Jan 30 1939	3-Chuen	2
Jan 31 1939	4-Eb	3
Feb 1 1939	5-Ben	4
Feb 2 1939	6-Ix	5
Feb 3 1939	7-Men	6
Feb 4 1939	8-Cib	7
Feb 5 1939	9-Caban	8

Date	Day-Sign	L
Feb 6 1939	10-Etz'nab	9
Feb 7 1939	11-Cauac	1
Feb 8 1939	12-Ahau	2
Feb 9 1939	13-Imix	3
Feb 10 1939	1-Ik	4
Feb 11 1939	2-Akbal	5
Feb 12 1939	3-Kan	6
Feb 13 1939	4-Chicchan	7
Feb 14 1939	5-Cimi	8
Feb 15 1939	6-Manik	9
Feb 16 1939	7-Lamat	1
Feb 17 1939	8-Muluc	2
Feb 18 1939	9-Oc	3
Feb 19 1939	10-Chuen	4
Feb 20 1939	11-Eb	5
Feb 21 1939	12-Ben	6
Feb 22 1939	13-Ix	7
Feb 23 1939	1-Men	8
Feb 24 1939	2-Cib	9
Feb 25 1939	3-Caban	1
Feb 26 1939	4-Etz'nab	2
Feb 27 1939	5-Cauac	3
Feb 28 1939	6-Ahau	4
Mar 1 1939	7-Imix	5
Mar 2 1939	8-Ik	6
Mar 3 1939	9-Akbal	7
Mar 4 1939	10-Kan	8
Mar 5 1939	11-Chicchan	9
Mar 6 1939	12-Cimi	1
Mar 7 1939	13-Manik	2
Mar 8 1939	1-Lamat	3
Mar 9 1939	2-Muluc	4
Mar 10 1939	3-Oc	5
Mar 11 1939	4-Chuen	6
Mar 12 1939	5-Eb	7
Mar 13 1939	6-Ben	8
Mar 14 1939	7-Ix	9
Mar 15 1939	8-Men	1
Mar 16 1939	9-Cib	2
Mar 17 1939	10-Caban	3
Mar 18 1939	11-Etz'nab	4
Mar 19 1939	12-Cauac	5
Mar 20 1939	13-Ahau	6
Mar 21 1939	1-Imix	7
Mar 22 1939	2-Ik	8
Mar 23 1939	3-Akbal	9
Mar 24 1939	4-Kan	1
Mar 25 1939	5-Chicchan	2
Mar 26 1939	6-Cimi	3
Mar 27 1939	7-Manik	4
Mar 28 1939	8-Lamat	5
Mar 29 1939	9-Muluc	6
Mar 30 1939	10-Oc	7
Mar 31 1939	11-Chuen	8
Apr 1 1939	12-Eb	9
Apr 2 1939	13-Ben	1
Apr 3 1939	1-Ix	2
Apr 4 1939	2-Men	3
Apr 5 1939	3-Cib	4
Apr 6 1939	4-Caban	5
Apr 7 1939	5-Etz'nab	6
Apr 8 1939	6-Cauac	7
Apr 9 1939	7-Ahau	8
Apr 10 1939	8-Imix	9
Apr 11 1939	9-Ik	1
Apr 12 1939	10-Akbal	2
Apr 13 1939	11-Kan	3
Apr 14 1939	12-Chicchan	4

Date	Day-Sign	L
Apr 15 1939	13-Cimi	5
Apr 16 1939	1-Manik	6
Apr 17 1939	2-Lamat	7
Apr 18 1939	3-Muluc	8
Apr 19 1939	4-Oc	9
Apr 20 1939	5-Chuen	1
Apr 21 1939	6-Eb	2
Apr 22 1939	7-Ben	3
Apr 23 1939	8-Ix	4
Apr 24 1939	9-Men	5
Apr 25 1939	10-Cib	6
Apr 26 1939	11-Caban	7
Apr 27 1939	12-Etz'nab	8
Apr 28 1939	13-Cauac	9
Apr 29 1939	1-Ahau	1
Apr 30 1939	2-Imix	2
May 1 1939	3-Ik	3
May 2 1939	4-Akbal	4
May 3 1939	5-Kan	5
May 4 1939	6-Chicchan	6
May 5 1939	7-Cimi	7
May 6 1939	8-Manik	8
May 7 1939	9-Lamat	9
May 8 1939	10-Muluc	1
May 9 1939	11-Oc	2
May 10 1939	12-Chuen	3
May 11 1939	13-Eb	4
May 12 1939	1-Ben	5
May 13 1939	2-Ix	6
May 14 1939	3-Men	7
May 15 1939	4-Cib	8
May 16 1939	5-Caban	9
May 17 1939	6-Etz'nab	1
May 18 1939	7-Cauac	2
May 19 1939	8-Ahau	3
May 20 1939	9-Imix	4
May 21 1939	10-Ik	5
May 22 1939	11-Akbal	6
May 23 1939	12-Kan	7
May 24 1939	13-Chicchan	8
May 25 1939	1-Cimi	9
May 26 1939	2-Manik	1
May 27 1939	3-Lamat	2
May 28 1939	4-Muluc	3
May 29 1939	5-Oc	4
May 30 1939	6-Chuen	5
May 31 1939	7-Eb	6
Jun 1 1939	8-Ben	7
Jun 2 1939	9-Ix	8
Jun 3 1939	10-Men	9
Jun 4 1939	11-Cib	1
Jun 5 1939	12-Caban	2
Jun 6 1939	13-Etz'nab	3
Jun 7 1939	1-Cauac	4
Jun 8 1939	2-Ahau	5
Jun 9 1939	3-Imix	6
Jun 10 1939	4-Ik	7
Jun 11 1939	5-Akbal	8
Jun 12 1939	6-Kan	9
Jun 13 1939	7-Chicchan	1
Jun 14 1939	8-Cimi	2
Jun 15 1939	9-Manik	3
Jun 16 1939	10-Lamat	4
Jun 17 1939	11-Muluc	5
Jun 18 1939	12-Oc	6
Jun 19 1939	13-Chuen	7
Jun 20 1939	1-Eb	8
Jun 21 1939	2-Ben	9

Date	Day-Sign	L	Date	Day-Sign	L	Date	Day-Sign	L
Jun 22 1939	3-Ix	1	Aug 29 1939	6-Ik	6	Nov 5 1939	9-Oc	2
Jun 23 1939	4-Men	2	Aug 30 1939	7-Akbal	7	Nov 6 1939	10-Chuen	3
Jun 24 1939	5-Cib	3	Aug 31 1939	8-Kan	8	Nov 7 1939	11-Eb	4
Jun 25 1939	6-Caban	4	Sep 1 1939	9-Chicchan	9	Nov 8 1939	12-Ben	5
Jun 26 1939	7-Etz'nab	5	Sep 2 1939	10-Cimi	1	Nov 9 1939	13-Ix	6
Jun 27 1939	8-Cauac	6	Sep 3 1939	11-Manik	2	Nov 10 1939	1-Men	7
Jun 28 1939	9-Ahau	7	Sep 4 1939	12-Lamat	3	Nov 11 1939	2-Cib	8
Jun 29 1939	10-Imix	8	Sep 5 1939	13-Muluc	4	Nov 12 1939	3-Caban	9
Jun 30 1939	11-Ik	9	Sep 6 1939	1-Oc	5	Nov 13 1939	4-Etz'nab	1
Jul 1 1939	12-Akbal	1	Sep 7 1939	2-Chuen	6	Nov 14 1939	5-Cauac	2
Jul 2 1939	13-Kan	2	Sep 8 1939	3-Eb	7	Nov 15 1939	6-Ahau	3
Jul 3 1939	1-Chicchan	3	Sep 9 1939	4-Ben	8	Nov 16 1939	7-Imix	4
Jul 4 1939	2-Cimi	4	Sep 10 1939	5-Ix	9	Nov 17 1939	8-Ik	5
Jul 5 1939	3-Manik	5	Sep 11 1939	6-Men	1	Nov 18 1939	9-Akbal	6
Jul 6 1939	4-Lamat	6	Sep 12 1939	7-Cib	2	Nov 19 1939	10-Kan	7
Jul 7 1939	5-Muluc	7	Sep 13 1939	8-Caban	3	Nov 20 1939	11-Chicchan	8
Jul 8 1939	6-Oc	8	Sep 14 1939	9-Etz'nab	4	Nov 21 1939	12-Cimi	9
Jul 9 1939	7-Chuen	9	Sep 15 1939	10-Cauac	5	Nov 22 1939	13-Manik	1
Jul 10 1939	8-Eb	1	Sep 16 1939	11-Ahau	6	Nov 23 1939	1-Lamat	2
Jul 11 1939	9-Ben	2	Sep 17 1939	12-Imix	7	Nov 24 1939	2-Muluc	3
Jul 12 1939	10-Ix	3	Sep 18 1939	13-Ik	8	Nov 25 1939	3-Oc	4
Jul 13 1939	11-Men	4	Sep 19 1939	1-Akbal	9	Nov 26 1939	4-Chuen	5
Jul 14 1939	12-Cib	5	Sep 20 1939	2-Kan	1	Nov 27 1939	5-Eb	6
Jul 15 1939	13-Caban	6	Sep 21 1939	3-Chicchan	2	Nov 28 1939	6-Ben	7
Jul 16 1939	1-Etz'nab	7	Sep 22 1939	4-Cimi	3	Nov 29 1939	7-Ix	8
Jul 17 1939	2-Cauac	8	Sep 23 1939	5-Manik	4	Nov 30 1939	8-Men	9
Jul 18 1939	3-Ahau	9	Sep 24 1939	6-Lamat	5	Dec 1 1939	9-Cib	1
Jul 19 1939	4-Imix	1	Sep 25 1939	7-Muluc	6	Dec 2 1939	10-Caban	2
Jul 20 1939	5-Ik	2	Sep 26 1939	8-Oc	7	Dec 3 1939	11-Etz'nab	3
Jul 21 1939	6-Akbal	3	Sep 27 1939	9-Chuen	8	Dec 4 1939	12-Cauac	4
Jul 22 1939	7-Kan	4	Sep 28 1939	10-Eb	9	Dec 5 1939	13-Ahau	5
Jul 23 1939	8-Chicchan	5	Sep 29 1939	11-Ben	1	Dec 6 1939	1-Imix	6
Jul 24 1939	9-Cimi	6	Sep 30 1939	12-Ix	2	Dec 7 1939	2-Ik	7
Jul 25 1939	10-Manik	7	Oct 1 1939	13-Men	3	Dec 8 1939	3-Akbal	8
Jul 26 1939	11-Lamat	8	Oct 2 1939	1-Cib	4	Dec 9 1939	4-Kan	9
Jul 27 1939	12-Muluc	9	Oct 3 1939	2-Caban	5	Dec 10 1939	5-Chicchan	1
Jul 28 1939	13-Oc	1	Oct 4 1939	3-Etz'nab	6	Dec 11 1939	6-Cimi	2
Jul 29 1939	1-Chuen	2	Oct 5 1939	4-Cauac	7	Dec 12 1939	7-Manik	3
Jul 30 1939	2-Eb	3	Oct 6 1939	5-Ahau	8	Dec 13 1939	8-Lamat	4
Jul 31 1939	3-Ben	4	Oct 7 1939	6-Imix	9	Dec 14 1939	9-Muluc	5
Aug 1 1939	4-Ix	5	Oct 8 1939	7-Ik	1	Dec 15 1939	10-Oc	6
Aug 2 1939	5-Men	6	Oct 9 1939	8-Akbal	2	Dec 16 1939	11-Chuen	7
Aug 3 1939	6-Cib	7	Oct 10 1939	9-Kan	3	Dec 17 1939	12-Eb	8
Aug 4 1939	7-Caban	8	Oct 11 1939	10-Chicchan	4	Dec 18 1939	13-Ben	9
Aug 5 1939	8-Etz'nab	9	Oct 12 1939	11-Cimi	5	Dec 19 1939	1-Ix	1
Aug 6 1939	9-Cauac	1	Oct 13 1939	12-Manik	6	Dec 20 1939	2-Men	2
Aug 7 1939	10-Ahau	2	Oct 14 1939	13-Lamat	7	Dec 21 1939	3-Cib	3
Aug 8 1939	11-Imix	3	Oct 15 1939	1-Muluc	8	Dec 22 1939	4-Caban	4
Aug 9 1939	12-Ik	4	Oct 16 1939	2-Oc	9	Dec 23 1939	5-Etz'nab	5
Aug 10 1939	13-Akbal	5	Oct 17 1939	3-Chuen	1	Dec 24 1939	6-Cauac	6
Aug 11 1939	1-Kan	6	Oct 18 1939	4-Eb	2	Dec 25 1939	7-Ahau	7
Aug 12 1939	2-Chicchan	7	Oct 19 1939	5-Ben	3	Dec 26 1939	8-Imix	8
Aug 13 1939	3-Cimi	8	Oct 20 1939	6-Ix	4	Dec 27 1939	9-Ik	9
Aug 14 1939	4-Manik	9	Oct 21 1939	7-Men	5	Dec 28 1939	10-Akbal	1
Aug 15 1939	5-Lamat	1	Oct 22 1939	8-Cib	6	Dec 29 1939	11-Kan	2
Aug 16 1939	6-Muluc	2	Oct 23 1939	9-Caban	7	Dec 30 1939	12-Chicchan	3
Aug 17 1939	7-Oc	3	Oct 24 1939	10-Etz'nab	8	Dec 31 1939	13-Cimi	4
Aug 18 1939	8-Chuen	4	Oct 25 1939	11-Cauac	9	Jan 1 1940	1-Manik	5
Aug 19 1939	9-Eb	5	Oct 26 1939	12-Ahau	1	Jan 2 1940	2-Lamat	6
Aug 20 1939	10-Ben	6	Oct 27 1939	13-Imix	2	Jan 3 1940	3-Muluc	7
Aug 21 1939	11-Ix	7	Oct 28 1939	1-Ik	3	Jan 4 1940	4-Oc	8
Aug 22 1939	12-Men	8	Oct 29 1939	2-Akbal	4	Jan 5 1940	5-Chuen	9
Aug 23 1939	13-Cib	9	Oct 30 1939	3-Kan	5	Jan 6 1940	6-Eb	1
Aug 24 1939	1-Caban	1	Oct 31 1939	4-Chicchan	6	Jan 7 1940	7-Ben	2
Aug 25 1939	2-Etz'nab	2	Nov 1 1939	5-Cimi	7	Jan 8 1940	8-Ix	3
Aug 26 1939	3-Cauac	3	Nov 2 1939	6-Manik	8	Jan 9 1940	9-Men	4
Aug 27 1939	4-Ahau	4	Nov 3 1939	7-Lamat	9	Jan 10 1940	10-Cib	5
Aug 28 1939	5-Imix	5	Nov 4 1939	8-Muluc	1	Jan 11 1940	11-Caban	6

Date	Day-Sign	L	Date	Day-Sign	L	Date	Day-Sign	L
Jan 12 1940	12-Etz'nab	7	Mar 20 1940	2-Cimi	3	May 27 1940	5-Ix	8
Jan 13 1940	13-Cauac	8	Mar 21 1940	3-Manik	4	May 28 1940	6-Men	9
Jan 14 1940	**1-Ahau**	9	Mar 22 1940	4-Lamat	5	May 29 1940	7-Cib	1
Jan 15 1940	*2-Imix*	1	Mar 23 1940	5-Muluc	6	May 30 1940	8-Caban	2
Jan 16 1940	3-Ik	2	Mar 24 1940	6-Oc	7	May 31 1940	9-Etz'nab	3
Jan 17 1940	4-Akbal	3	Mar 25 1940	7-Chuen	8	Jun 1 1940	10-Cauac	4
Jan 18 1940	5-Kan	4	Mar 26 1940	8-Eb	9	Jun 2 1940	11-Ahau	5
Jan 19 1940	6-Chicchan	5	Mar 27 1940	9-Ben	1	Jun 3 1940	*12-Imix*	6
Jan 20 1940	7-Cimi	6	Mar 28 1940	10-Ix	2	Jun 4 1940	13-Ik	7
Jan 21 1940	8-Manik	7	Mar 29 1940	11-Men	3	Jun 5 1940	**1-Akbal**	8
Jan 22 1940	9-Lamat	8	Mar 30 1940	12-Cib	4	Jun 6 1940	2-Kan	9
Jan 23 1940	10-Muluc	9	Mar 31 1940	13-Caban	5	Jun 7 1940	3-Chicchan	1
Jan 24 1940	11-Oc	1	Apr 1 1940	**1-Etz'nab**	6	Jun 8 1940	4-Cimi	2
Jan 25 1940	12-Chuen	2	Apr 2 1940	2-Cauac	7	Jun 9 1940	5-Manik	3
Jan 26 1940	13-Eb	3	Apr 3 1940	3-Ahau	8	Jun 10 1940	6-Lamat	4
Jan 27 1940	**1-Ben**	4	Apr 4 1940	*4-Imix*	9	Jun 11 1940	7-Muluc	5
Jan 28 1940	2-Ix	5	Apr 5 1940	5-Ik	1	Jun 12 1940	8-Oc	6
Jan 29 1940	3-Men	6	Apr 6 1940	6-Akbal	2	Jun 13 1940	9-Chuen	7
Jan 30 1940	4-Cib	7	Apr 7 1940	7-Kan	3	Jun 14 1940	10-Eb	8
Jan 31 1940	5-Caban	8	Apr 8 1940	8-Chicchan	4	Jun 15 1940	11-Ben	9
Feb 1 1940	6-Etz'nab	9	Apr 9 1940	9-Cimi	5	Jun 16 1940	12-Ix	1
Feb 2 1940	7-Cauac	1	Apr 10 1940	10-Manik	6	Jun 17 1940	13-Men	2
Feb 3 1940	8-Ahau	2	Apr 11 1940	11-Lamat	7	Jun 18 1940	**1-Cib**	3
Feb 4 1940	*9-Imix*	3	Apr 12 1940	12-Muluc	8	Jun 19 1940	2-Caban	4
Feb 5 1940	10-Ik	4	Apr 13 1940	13-Oc	9	Jun 20 1940	3-Etz'nab	5
Feb 6 1940	11-Akbal	5	Apr 14 1940	**1-Chuen**	1	Jun 21 1940	4-Cauac	6
Feb 7 1940	12-Kan	6	Apr 15 1940	2-Eb	2	Jun 22 1940	5-Ahau	7
Feb 8 1940	13-Chicchan	7	Apr 16 1940	3-Ben	3	Jun 23 1940	*6-Imix*	8
Feb 9 1940	**1-Cimi**	8	Apr 17 1940	4-Ix	4	Jun 24 1940	7-Ik	9
Feb 10 1940	2-Manik	9	Apr 18 1940	5-Men	5	Jun 25 1940	8-Akbal	1
Feb 11 1940	3-Lamat	1	Apr 19 1940	6-Cib	6	Jun 26 1940	9-Kan	2
Feb 12 1940	4-Muluc	2	Apr 20 1940	7-Caban	7	Jun 27 1940	10-Chicchan	3
Feb 13 1940	5-Oc	3	Apr 21 1940	8-Etz'nab	8	Jun 28 1940	11-Cimi	4
Feb 14 1940	6-Chuen	4	Apr 22 1940	9-Cauac	9	Jun 29 1940	12-Manik	5
Feb 15 1940	7-Eb	5	Apr 23 1940	10-Ahau	1	Jun 30 1940	13-Lamat	6
Feb 16 1940	8-Ben	6	Apr 24 1940	*11-Imix*	2	Jul 1 1940	**1-Muluc**	7
Feb 17 1940	9-Ix	7	Apr 25 1940	12-Ik	3	Jul 2 1940	2-Oc	8
Feb 18 1940	10-Men	8	Apr 26 1940	13-Akbal	4	Jul 3 1940	3-Chuen	9
Feb 19 1940	11-Cib	9	Apr 27 1940	**1-Kan**	5	Jul 4 1940	4-Eb	1
Feb 20 1940	12-Caban	1	Apr 28 1940	2-Chicchan	6	Jul 5 1940	5-Ben	2
Feb 21 1940	13-Etz'nab	2	Apr 29 1940	3-Cimi	7	Jul 6 1940	6-Ix	3
Feb 22 1940	**1-Cauac**	3	Apr 30 1940	4-Manik	8	Jul 7 1940	7-Men	4
Feb 23 1940	2-Ahau	4	May 1 1940	5-Lamat	9	Jul 8 1940	8-Cib	5
Feb 24 1940	*3-Imix*	5	May 2 1940	6-Muluc	1	Jul 9 1940	9-Caban	6
Feb 25 1940	4-Ik	6	May 3 1940	7-Oc	2	Jul 10 1940	10-Etz'nab	7
Feb 26 1940	5-Akbal	7	May 4 1940	8-Chuen	3	Jul 11 1940	11-Cauac	8
Feb 27 1940	6-Kan	8	May 5 1940	9-Eb	4	Jul 12 1940	12-Ahau	9
Feb 28 1940	7-Chicchan	9	May 6 1940	10-Ben	5	Jul 13 1940	*13-Imix*	1
Feb 29 1940	8-Cimi	1	May 7 1940	11-Ix	6	Jul 14 1940	**1-Ik**	2
Mar 1 1940	9-Manik	2	May 8 1940	12-Men	7	Jul 15 1940	2-Akbal	3
Mar 2 1940	10-Lamat	3	May 9 1940	13-Cib	8	Jul 16 1940	3-Kan	4
Mar 3 1940	11-Muluc	4	May 10 1940	**1-Caban**	9	Jul 17 1940	4-Chicchan	5
Mar 4 1940	12-Oc	5	May 11 1940	2-Etz'nab	1	Jul 18 1940	5-Cimi	6
Mar 5 1940	13-Chuen	6	May 12 1940	3-Cauac	2	Jul 19 1940	6-Manik	7
Mar 6 1940	**1-Eb**	7	May 13 1940	4-Ahau	3	Jul 20 1940	7-Lamat	8
Mar 7 1940	2-Ben	8	May 14 1940	*5-Imix*	4	Jul 21 1940	8-Muluc	9
Mar 8 1940	3-Ix	9	May 15 1940	6-Ik	5	Jul 22 1940	9-Oc	1
Mar 9 1940	4-Men	1	May 16 1940	7-Akbal	6	Jul 23 1940	10-Chuen	2
Mar 10 1940	5-Cib	2	May 17 1940	8-Kan	7	Jul 24 1940	11-Eb	3
Mar 11 1940	6-Caban	3	May 18 1940	9-Chicchan	8	Jul 25 1940	12-Ben	4
Mar 12 1940	7-Etz'nab	4	May 19 1940	10-Cimi	9	Jul 26 1940	13-Ix	5
Mar 13 1940	8-Cauac	5	May 20 1940	11-Manik	1	Jul 27 1940	**1-Men**	6
Mar 14 1940	9-Ahau	6	May 21 1940	12-Lamat	2	Jul 28 1940	2-Cib	7
Mar 15 1940	*10-Imix*	7	May 22 1940	13-Muluc	3	Jul 29 1940	3-Caban	8
Mar 16 1940	11-Ik	8	May 23 1940	**1-Oc**	4	Jul 30 1940	4-Etz'nab	9
Mar 17 1940	12-Akbal	9	May 24 1940	2-Chuen	5	Jul 31 1940	5-Cauac	1
Mar 18 1940	13-Kan	1	May 25 1940	3-Eb	6	Aug 1 1940	6-Ahau	2
Mar 19 1940	**1-Chicchan**	2	May 26 1940	4-Ben	7	Aug 2 1940	*7-Imix*	3

Date	Day-Sign	L
Aug 3 1940	8-Ik	4
Aug 4 1940	9-Akbal	5
Aug 5 1940	10-Kan	6
Aug 6 1940	11-Chicchan	7
Aug 7 1940	12-Cimi	8
Aug 8 1940	13-Manik	9
Aug 9 1940	1-Lamat	1
Aug 10 1940	2-Muluc	2
Aug 11 1940	3-Oc	3
Aug 12 1940	4-Chuen	4
Aug 13 1940	5-Eb	5
Aug 14 1940	6-Ben	6
Aug 15 1940	7-Ix	7
Aug 16 1940	8-Men	8
Aug 17 1940	9-Cib	9
Aug 18 1940	10-Caban	1
Aug 19 1940	11-Etz'nab	2
Aug 20 1940	12-Cauac	3
Aug 21 1940	13-Ahau	4
Aug 22 1940	1-Imix	5
Aug 23 1940	2-Ik	6
Aug 24 1940	3-Akbal	7
Aug 25 1940	4-Kan	8
Aug 26 1940	5-Chicchan	9
Aug 27 1940	6-Cimi	1
Aug 28 1940	7-Manik	2
Aug 29 1940	8-Lamat	3
Aug 30 1940	9-Muluc	4
Aug 31 1940	10-Oc	5
Sep 1 1940	11-Chuen	6
Sep 2 1940	12-Eb	7
Sep 3 1940	13-Ben	8
Sep 4 1940	1-Ix	9
Sep 5 1940	2-Men	1
Sep 6 1940	3-Cib	2
Sep 7 1940	4-Caban	3
Sep 8 1940	5-Etz'nab	4
Sep 9 1940	6-Cauac	5
Sep 10 1940	7-Ahau	6
Sep 11 1940	8-Imix	7
Sep 12 1940	9-Ik	8
Sep 13 1940	10-Akbal	9
Sep 14 1940	11-Kan	1
Sep 15 1940	12-Chicchan	2
Sep 16 1940	13-Cimi	3
Sep 17 1940	1-Manik	4
Sep 18 1940	2-Lamat	5
Sep 19 1940	3-Muluc	6
Sep 20 1940	4-Oc	7
Sep 21 1940	5-Chuen	8
Sep 22 1940	6-Eb	9
Sep 23 1940	7-Ben	1
Sep 24 1940	8-Ix	2
Sep 25 1940	9-Men	3
Sep 26 1940	10-Cib	4
Sep 27 1940	11-Caban	5
Sep 28 1940	12-Etz'nab	6
Sep 29 1940	13-Cauac	7
Sep 30 1940	1-Ahau	8
Oct 1 1940	2-Imix	9
Oct 2 1940	3-Ik	1
Oct 3 1940	4-Akbal	2
Oct 4 1940	5-Kan	3
Oct 5 1940	6-Chicchan	4
Oct 6 1940	7-Cimi	5
Oct 7 1940	8-Manik	6
Oct 8 1940	9-Lamat	7
Oct 9 1940	10-Muluc	8

Date	Day-Sign	L
Oct 10 1940	11-Oc	9
Oct 11 1940	12-Chuen	1
Oct 12 1940	13-Eb	2
Oct 13 1940	1-Ben	3
Oct 14 1940	2-Ix	4
Oct 15 1940	3-Men	5
Oct 16 1940	4-Cib	6
Oct 17 1940	5-Caban	7
Oct 18 1940	6-Etz'nab	8
Oct 19 1940	7-Cauac	9
Oct 20 1940	8-Ahau	1
Oct 21 1940	9-Imix	2
Oct 22 1940	10-Ik	3
Oct 23 1940	11-Akbal	4
Oct 24 1940	12-Kan	5
Oct 25 1940	13-Chicchan	6
Oct 26 1940	1-Cimi	7
Oct 27 1940	2-Manik	8
Oct 28 1940	3-Lamat	9
Oct 29 1940	4-Muluc	1
Oct 30 1940	5-Oc	2
Oct 31 1940	6-Chuen	3
Nov 1 1940	7-Eb	4
Nov 2 1940	8-Ben	5
Nov 3 1940	9-Ix	6
Nov 4 1940	10-Men	7
Nov 5 1940	11-Cib	8
Nov 6 1940	12-Caban	9
Nov 7 1940	13-Etz'nab	1
Nov 8 1940	1-Cauac	2
Nov 9 1940	2-Ahau	3
Nov 10 1940	3-Imix	4
Nov 11 1940	4-Ik	5
Nov 12 1940	5-Akbal	6
Nov 13 1940	6-Kan	7
Nov 14 1940	7-Chicchan	8
Nov 15 1940	8-Cimi	9
Nov 16 1940	9-Manik	1
Nov 17 1940	10-Lamat	2
Nov 18 1940	11-Muluc	3
Nov 19 1940	12-Oc	4
Nov 20 1940	13-Chuen	5
Nov 21 1940	1-Eb	6
Nov 22 1940	2-Ben	7
Nov 23 1940	3-Ix	8
Nov 24 1940	4-Men	9
Nov 25 1940	5-Cib	1
Nov 26 1940	6-Caban	2
Nov 27 1940	7-Etz'nab	3
Nov 28 1940	8-Cauac	4
Nov 29 1940	9-Ahau	5
Nov 30 1940	10-Imix	6
Dec 1 1940	11-Ik	7
Dec 2 1940	12-Akbal	8
Dec 3 1940	13-Kan	9
Dec 4 1940	1-Chicchan	1
Dec 5 1940	2-Cimi	2
Dec 6 1940	3-Manik	3
Dec 7 1940	4-Lamat	4
Dec 8 1940	5-Muluc	5
Dec 9 1940	6-Oc	6
Dec 10 1940	7-Chuen	7
Dec 11 1940	8-Eb	8
Dec 12 1940	9-Ben	9
Dec 13 1940	10-Ix	1
Dec 14 1940	11-Men	2
Dec 15 1940	12-Cib	3
Dec 16 1940	13-Caban	4

Date	Day-Sign	L
Dec 17 1940	1-Etz'nab	5
Dec 18 1940	2-Cauac	6
Dec 19 1940	3-Ahau	7
Dec 20 1940	4-Imix	8
Dec 21 1940	5-Ik	9
Dec 22 1940	6-Akbal	1
Dec 23 1940	7-Kan	2
Dec 24 1940	8-Chicchan	3
Dec 25 1940	9-Cimi	4
Dec 26 1940	10-Manik	5
Dec 27 1940	11-Lamat	6
Dec 28 1940	12-Muluc	7
Dec 29 1940	13-Oc	8
Dec 30 1940	1-Chuen	9
Dec 31 1940	2-Eb	1
Jan 1 1941	3-Ben	2
Jan 2 1941	4-Ix	3
Jan 3 1941	5-Men	4
Jan 4 1941	6-Cib	5
Jan 5 1941	7-Caban	6
Jan 6 1941	8-Etz'nab	7
Jan 7 1941	9-Cauac	8
Jan 8 1941	10-Ahau	9
Jan 9 1941	11-Imix	1
Jan 10 1941	12-Ik	2
Jan 11 1941	13-Akbal	3
Jan 12 1941	1-Kan	4
Jan 13 1941	2-Chicchan	5
Jan 14 1941	3-Cimi	6
Jan 15 1941	4-Manik	7
Jan 16 1941	5-Lamat	8
Jan 17 1941	6-Muluc	9
Jan 18 1941	7-Oc	1
Jan 19 1941	8-Chuen	2
Jan 20 1941	9-Eb	3
Jan 21 1941	10-Ben	4
Jan 22 1941	11-Ix	5
Jan 23 1941	12-Men	6
Jan 24 1941	13-Cib	7
Jan 25 1941	1-Caban	8
Jan 26 1941	2-Etz'nab	9
Jan 27 1941	3-Cauac	1
Jan 28 1941	4-Ahau	2
Jan 29 1941	5-Imix	3
Jan 30 1941	6-Ik	4
Jan 31 1941	7-Akbal	5
Feb 1 1941	8-Kan	6
Feb 2 1941	9-Chicchan	7
Feb 3 1941	10-Cimi	8
Feb 4 1941	11-Manik	9
Feb 5 1941	12-Lamat	1
Feb 6 1941	13-Muluc	2
Feb 7 1941	1-Oc	3
Feb 8 1941	2-Chuen	4
Feb 9 1941	3-Eb	5
Feb 10 1941	4-Ben	6
Feb 11 1941	5-Ix	7
Feb 12 1941	6-Men	8
Feb 13 1941	7-Cib	9
Feb 14 1941	8-Caban	1
Feb 15 1941	9-Etz'nab	2
Feb 16 1941	10-Cauac	3
Feb 17 1941	11-Ahau	4
Feb 18 1941	12-Imix	5
Feb 19 1941	13-Ik	6
Feb 20 1941	1-Akbal	7
Feb 21 1941	2-Kan	8
Feb 22 1941	3-Chicchan	9

Date	Day-Sign	L
Feb 23 1941	4-Cimi	1
Feb 24 1941	5-Manik	2
Feb 25 1941	6-Lamat	3
Feb 26 1941	7-Muluc	4
Feb 27 1941	8-Oc	5
Feb 28 1941	9-Chuen	6
Mar 1 1941	10-Eb	7
Mar 2 1941	11-Ben	8
Mar 3 1941	12-Ix	9
Mar 4 1941	13-Men	1
Mar 5 1941	**1-Cib**	2
Mar 6 1941	2-Caban	3
Mar 7 1941	3-Etz'nab	4
Mar 8 1941	4-Cauac	5
Mar 9 1941	5-Ahau	6
Mar 10 1941	*6-Imix*	7
Mar 11 1941	7-Ik	8
Mar 12 1941	8-Akbal	9
Mar 13 1941	9-Kan	1
Mar 14 1941	10-Chicchan	2
Mar 15 1941	11-Cimi	3
Mar 16 1941	12-Manik	4
Mar 17 1941	13-Lamat	5
Mar 18 1941	**1-Muluc**	6
Mar 19 1941	2-Oc	7
Mar 20 1941	3-Chuen	8
Mar 21 1941	4-Eb	9
Mar 22 1941	5-Ben	1
Mar 23 1941	6-Ix	2
Mar 24 1941	7-Men	3
Mar 25 1941	8-Cib	4
Mar 26 1941	9-Caban	5
Mar 27 1941	10-Etz'nab	6
Mar 28 1941	11-Cauac	7
Mar 29 1941	12-Ahau	8
Mar 30 1941	*13-Imix*	9
Mar 31 1941	**1-Ik**	1
Apr 1 1941	2-Akbal	2
Apr 2 1941	3-Kan	3
Apr 3 1941	4-Chicchan	4
Apr 4 1941	5-Cimi	5
Apr 5 1941	6-Manik	6
Apr 6 1941	7-Lamat	7
Apr 7 1941	8-Muluc	8
Apr 8 1941	9-Oc	9
Apr 9 1941	10-Chuen	1
Apr 10 1941	11-Eb	2
Apr 11 1941	12-Ben	3
Apr 12 1941	13-Ix	4
Apr 13 1941	**1-Men**	5
Apr 14 1941	2-Cib	6
Apr 15 1941	3-Caban	7
Apr 16 1941	4-Etz'nab	8
Apr 17 1941	5-Cauac	9
Apr 18 1941	6-Ahau	1
Apr 19 1941	*7-Imix*	2
Apr 20 1941	8-Ik	3
Apr 21 1941	9-Akbal	4
Apr 22 1941	10-Kan	5
Apr 23 1941	11-Chicchan	6
Apr 24 1941	12-Cimi	7
Apr 25 1941	13-Manik	8
Apr 26 1941	**1-Lamat**	9
Apr 27 1941	2-Muluc	1
Apr 28 1941	3-Oc	2
Apr 29 1941	4-Chuen	3
Apr 30 1941	5-Eb	4
May 1 1941	6-Ben	5

Date	Day-Sign	L
May 2 1941	7-Ix	6
May 3 1941	8-Men	7
May 4 1941	9-Cib	8
May 5 1941	10-Caban	9
May 6 1941	11-Etz'nab	1
May 7 1941	12-Cauac	2
May 8 1941	13-Ahau	3
May 9 1941	**1-Imix**	4
May 10 1941	2-Ik	5
May 11 1941	3-Akbal	6
May 12 1941	4-Kan	7
May 13 1941	5-Chicchan	8
May 14 1941	6-Cimi	9
May 15 1941	7-Manik	1
May 16 1941	8-Lamat	2
May 17 1941	9-Muluc	3
May 18 1941	10-Oc	4
May 19 1941	11-Chuen	5
May 20 1941	12-Eb	6
May 21 1941	13-Ben	7
May 22 1941	**1-Ix**	8
May 23 1941	2-Men	9
May 24 1941	3-Cib	1
May 25 1941	4-Caban	2
May 26 1941	5-Etz'nab	3
May 27 1941	6-Cauac	4
May 28 1941	7-Ahau	5
May 29 1941	*8-Imix*	6
May 30 1941	9-Ik	7
May 31 1941	10-Akbal	8
Jun 1 1941	11-Kan	9
Jun 2 1941	12-Chicchan	1
Jun 3 1941	13-Cimi	2
Jun 4 1941	**1-Manik**	3
Jun 5 1941	2-Lamat	4
Jun 6 1941	3-Muluc	5
Jun 7 1941	4-Oc	6
Jun 8 1941	5-Chuen	7
Jun 9 1941	6-Eb	8
Jun 10 1941	7-Ben	9
Jun 11 1941	8-Ix	1
Jun 12 1941	9-Men	2
Jun 13 1941	10-Cib	3
Jun 14 1941	11-Caban	4
Jun 15 1941	12-Etz'nab	5
Jun 16 1941	13-Cauac	6
Jun 17 1941	**1-Ahau**	7
Jun 18 1941	*2-Imix*	8
Jun 19 1941	3-Ik	9
Jun 20 1941	4-Akbal	1
Jun 21 1941	5-Kan	2
Jun 22 1941	6-Chicchan	3
Jun 23 1941	7-Cimi	4
Jun 24 1941	8-Manik	5
Jun 25 1941	9-Lamat	6
Jun 26 1941	10-Muluc	7
Jun 27 1941	11-Oc	8
Jun 28 1941	12-Chuen	9
Jun 29 1941	13-Eb	1
Jun 30 1941	**1-Ben**	2
Jul 1 1941	2-Ix	3
Jul 2 1941	3-Men	4
Jul 3 1941	4-Cib	5
Jul 4 1941	5-Caban	6
Jul 5 1941	6-Etz'nab	7
Jul 6 1941	7-Cauac	8
Jul 7 1941	8-Ahau	9
Jul 8 1941	*9-Imix*	1

Date	Day-Sign	L
Jul 9 1941	10-Ik	2
Jul 10 1941	11-Akbal	3
Jul 11 1941	12-Kan	4
Jul 12 1941	13-Chicchan	5
Jul 13 1941	**1-Cimi**	6
Jul 14 1941	2-Manik	7
Jul 15 1941	3-Lamat	8
Jul 16 1941	4-Muluc	9
Jul 17 1941	5-Oc	1
Jul 18 1941	6-Chuen	2
Jul 19 1941	7-Eb	3
Jul 20 1941	8-Ben	4
Jul 21 1941	9-Ix	5
Jul 22 1941	10-Men	6
Jul 23 1941	11-Cib	7
Jul 24 1941	12-Caban	8
Jul 25 1941	13-Etz'nab	9
Jul 26 1941	**1-Cauac**	1
Jul 27 1941	2-Ahau	2
Jul 28 1941	*3-Imix*	3
Jul 29 1941	4-Ik	4
Jul 30 1941	5-Akbal	5
Jul 31 1941	6-Kan	6
Aug 1 1941	7-Chicchan	7
Aug 2 1941	8-Cimi	8
Aug 3 1941	9-Manik	9
Aug 4 1941	10-Lamat	1
Aug 5 1941	11-Muluc	2
Aug 6 1941	12-Oc	3
Aug 7 1941	13-Chuen	4
Aug 8 1941	**1-Eb**	5
Aug 9 1941	2-Ben	6
Aug 10 1941	3-Ix	7
Aug 11 1941	4-Men	8
Aug 12 1941	5-Cib	9
Aug 13 1941	6-Caban	1
Aug 14 1941	7-Etz'nab	2
Aug 15 1941	8-Cauac	3
Aug 16 1941	9-Ahau	4
Aug 17 1941	*10-Imix*	5
Aug 18 1941	11-Ik	6
Aug 19 1941	12-Akbal	7
Aug 20 1941	13-Kan	8
Aug 21 1941	**1-Chicchan**	9
Aug 22 1941	2-Cimi	1
Aug 23 1941	3-Manik	2
Aug 24 1941	4-Lamat	3
Aug 25 1941	5-Muluc	4
Aug 26 1941	6-Oc	5
Aug 27 1941	7-Chuen	6
Aug 28 1941	8-Eb	7
Aug 29 1941	9-Ben	8
Aug 30 1941	10-Ix	9
Aug 31 1941	11-Men	1
Sep 1 1941	12-Cib	2
Sep 2 1941	13-Caban	3
Sep 3 1941	**1-Etz'nab**	4
Sep 4 1941	2-Cauac	5
Sep 5 1941	3-Ahau	6
Sep 6 1941	*4-Imix*	7
Sep 7 1941	5-Ik	8
Sep 8 1941	6-Akbal	9
Sep 9 1941	7-Kan	1
Sep 10 1941	8-Chicchan	2
Sep 11 1941	9-Cimi	3
Sep 12 1941	10-Manik	4
Sep 13 1941	11-Lamat	5
Sep 14 1941	12-Muluc	6

Date	Day-Sign	L	Date	Day-Sign	L	Date	Day-Sign	L
Sep 15 1941	13-Oc	7	Nov 22 1941	3-Etz'nab	3	Jan 29 1942	6-Cimi	8
Sep 16 1941	1-Chuen	8	Nov 23 1941	4-Cauac	4	Jan 30 1942	7-Manik	9
Sep 17 1941	2-Eb	9	Nov 24 1941	5-Ahau	5	Jan 31 1942	8-Lamat	1
Sep 18 1941	3-Ben	1	Nov 25 1941	6-Imix	6	Feb 1 1942	9-Muluc	2
Sep 19 1941	4-Ix	2	Nov 26 1941	7-Ik	7	Feb 2 1942	10-Oc	3
Sep 20 1941	5-Men	3	Nov 27 1941	8-Akbal	8	Feb 3 1942	11-Chuen	4
Sep 21 1941	6-Cib	4	Nov 28 1941	9-Kan	9	Feb 4 1942	12-Eb	5
Sep 22 1941	7-Caban	5	Nov 29 1941	10-Chicchan	1	Feb 5 1942	13-Ben	6
Sep 23 1941	8-Etz'nab	6	Nov 30 1941	11-Cimi	2	Feb 6 1942	1-Ix	7
Sep 24 1941	9-Cauac	7	Dec 1 1941	12-Manik	3	Feb 7 1942	2-Men	8
Sep 25 1941	10-Ahau	8	Dec 2 1941	13-Lamat	4	Feb 8 1942	3-Cib	9
Sep 26 1941	11-Imix	9	Dec 3 1941	1-Muluc	5	Feb 9 1942	4-Caban	1
Sep 27 1941	12-Ik	1	Dec 4 1941	2-Oc	6	Feb 10 1942	5-Etz'nab	2
Sep 28 1941	13-Akbal	2	Dec 5 1941	3-Chuen	7	Feb 11 1942	6-Cauac	3
Sep 29 1941	1-Kan	3	Dec 6 1941	4-Eb	8	Feb 12 1942	7-Ahau	4
Sep 30 1941	2-Chicchan	4	Dec 7 1941	5-Ben	9	Feb 13 1942	8-Imix	5
Oct 1 1941	3-Cimi	5	Dec 8 1941	6-Ix	1	Feb 14 1942	9-Ik	6
Oct 2 1941	4-Manik	6	Dec 9 1941	7-Men	2	Feb 15 1942	10-Akbal	7
Oct 3 1941	5-Lamat	7	Dec 10 1941	8-Cib	3	Feb 16 1942	11-Kan	8
Oct 4 1941	6-Muluc	8	Dec 11 1941	9-Caban	4	Feb 17 1942	12-Chicchan	9
Oct 5 1941	7-Oc	9	Dec 12 1941	10-Etz'nab	5	Feb 18 1942	13-Cimi	1
Oct 6 1941	8-Chuen	1	Dec 13 1941	11-Cauac	6	Feb 19 1942	1-Manik	2
Oct 7 1941	9-Eb	2	Dec 14 1941	12-Ahau	7	Feb 20 1942	2-Lamat	3
Oct 8 1941	10-Ben	3	Dec 15 1941	13-Imix	8	Feb 21 1942	3-Muluc	4
Oct 9 1941	11-Ix	4	Dec 16 1941	1-Ik	9	Feb 22 1942	4-Oc	5
Oct 10 1941	12-Men	5	Dec 17 1941	2-Akbal	1	Feb 23 1942	5-Chuen	6
Oct 11 1941	13-Cib	6	Dec 18 1941	3-Kan	2	Feb 24 1942	6-Eb	7
Oct 12 1941	1-Caban	7	Dec 19 1941	4-Chicchan	3	Feb 25 1942	7-Ben	8
Oct 13 1941	2-Etz'nab	8	Dec 20 1941	5-Cimi	4	Feb 26 1942	8-Ix	9
Oct 14 1941	3-Cauac	9	Dec 21 1941	6-Manik	5	Feb 27 1942	9-Men	1
Oct 15 1941	4-Ahau	1	Dec 22 1941	7-Lamat	6	Feb 28 1942	10-Cib	2
Oct 16 1941	5-Imix	2	Dec 23 1941	8-Muluc	7	Mar 1 1942	11-Caban	3
Oct 17 1941	6-Ik	3	Dec 24 1941	9-Oc	8	Mar 2 1942	12-Etz'nab	4
Oct 18 1941	7-Akbal	4	Dec 25 1941	10-Chuen	9	Mar 3 1942	13-Cauac	5
Oct 19 1941	8-Kan	5	Dec 26 1941	11-Eb	1	Mar 4 1942	1-Ahau	6
Oct 20 1941	9-Chicchan	6	Dec 27 1941	12-Ben	2	Mar 5 1942	2-Imix	7
Oct 21 1941	10-Cimi	7	Dec 28 1941	13-Ix	3	Mar 6 1942	3-Ik	8
Oct 22 1941	11-Manik	8	Dec 29 1941	1-Men	4	Mar 7 1942	4-Akbal	9
Oct 23 1941	12-Lamat	9	Dec 30 1941	2-Cib	5	Mar 8 1942	5-Kan	1
Oct 24 1941	13-Muluc	1	Dec 31 1941	3-Caban	6	Mar 9 1942	6-Chicchan	2
Oct 25 1941	1-Oc	2	Jan 1 1942	4-Etz'nab	7	Mar 10 1942	7-Cimi	3
Oct 26 1941	2-Chuen	3	Jan 2 1942	5-Cauac	8	Mar 11 1942	8-Manik	4
Oct 27 1941	3-Eb	4	Jan 3 1942	6-Ahau	9	Mar 12 1942	9-Lamat	5
Oct 28 1941	4-Ben	5	Jan 4 1942	7-Imix	1	Mar 13 1942	10-Muluc	6
Oct 29 1941	5-Ix	6	Jan 5 1942	8-Ik	2	Mar 14 1942	11-Oc	7
Oct 30 1941	6-Men	7	Jan 6 1942	9-Akbal	3	Mar 15 1942	12-Chuen	8
Oct 31 1941	7-Cib	8	Jan 7 1942	10-Kan	4	Mar 16 1942	13-Eb	9
Nov 1 1941	8-Caban	9	Jan 8 1942	11-Chicchan	5	Mar 17 1942	1-Ben	1
Nov 2 1941	9-Etz'nab	1	Jan 9 1942	12-Cimi	6	Mar 18 1942	2-Ix	2
Nov 3 1941	10-Cauac	2	Jan 10 1942	13-Manik	7	Mar 19 1942	3-Men	3
Nov 4 1941	11-Ahau	3	Jan 11 1942	1-Lamat	8	Mar 20 1942	4-Cib	4
Nov 5 1941	12-Imix	4	Jan 12 1942	2-Muluc	9	Mar 21 1942	5-Caban	5
Nov 6 1941	13-Ik	5	Jan 13 1942	3-Oc	1	Mar 22 1942	6-Etz'nab	6
Nov 7 1941	1-Akbal	6	Jan 14 1942	4-Chuen	2	Mar 23 1942	7-Cauac	7
Nov 8 1941	2-Kan	7	Jan 15 1942	5-Eb	3	Mar 24 1942	8-Ahau	8
Nov 9 1941	3-Chicchan	8	Jan 16 1942	6-Ben	4	Mar 25 1942	9-Imix	9
Nov 10 1941	4-Cimi	9	Jan 17 1942	7-Ix	5	Mar 26 1942	10-Ik	1
Nov 11 1941	5-Manik	1	Jan 18 1942	8-Men	6	Mar 27 1942	11-Akbal	2
Nov 12 1941	6-Lamat	2	Jan 19 1942	9-Cib	7	Mar 28 1942	12-Kan	3
Nov 13 1941	7-Muluc	3	Jan 20 1942	10-Caban	8	Mar 29 1942	13-Chicchan	4
Nov 14 1941	8-Oc	4	Jan 21 1942	11-Etz'nab	9	Mar 30 1942	1-Cimi	5
Nov 15 1941	9-Chuen	5	Jan 22 1942	12-Cauac	1	Mar 31 1942	2-Manik	6
Nov 16 1941	10-Eb	6	Jan 23 1942	13-Ahau	2	Apr 1 1942	3-Lamat	7
Nov 17 1941	11-Ben	7	Jan 24 1942	1-Imix	3	Apr 2 1942	4-Muluc	8
Nov 18 1941	12-Ix	8	Jan 25 1942	2-Ik	4	Apr 3 1942	5-Oc	9
Nov 19 1941	13-Men	9	Jan 26 1942	3-Akbal	5	Apr 4 1942	6-Chuen	1
Nov 20 1941	1-Cib	1	Jan 27 1942	4-Kan	6	Apr 5 1942	7-Eb	2
Nov 21 1941	2-Caban	2	Jan 28 1942	5-Chicchan	7	Apr 6 1942	8-Ben	3

Date	Day-Sign	L	Date	Day-Sign	L	Date	Day-Sign	L
Apr 7 1942	9-Ix	4	Jun 14 1942	12-Ik	9	Aug 21 1942	2-Oc	5
Apr 8 1942	10-Men	5	Jun 15 1942	13-Akbal	1	Aug 22 1942	3-Chuen	6
Apr 9 1942	11-Cib	6	Jun 16 1942	**1-Kan**	2	Aug 23 1942	4-Eb	7
Apr 10 1942	12-Caban	7	Jun 17 1942	2-Chicchan	3	Aug 24 1942	5-Ben	8
Apr 11 1942	13-Etz'nab	8	Jun 18 1942	3-Cimi	4	Aug 25 1942	6-Ix	9
Apr 12 1942	**1-Cauac**	9	Jun 19 1942	4-Manik	5	Aug 26 1942	7-Men	1
Apr 13 1942	2-Ahau	1	Jun 20 1942	5-Lamat	6	Aug 27 1942	8-Cib	2
Apr 14 1942	3-*Imix*	2	Jun 21 1942	6-Muluc	7	Aug 28 1942	9-Caban	3
Apr 15 1942	4-Ik	3	Jun 22 1942	7-Oc	8	Aug 29 1942	10-Etz'nab	4
Apr 16 1942	5-Akbal	4	Jun 23 1942	8-Chuen	9	Aug 30 1942	11-Cauac	5
Apr 17 1942	6-Kan	5	Jun 24 1942	9-Eb	1	Aug 31 1942	12-Ahau	6
Apr 18 1942	7-Chicchan	6	Jun 25 1942	10-Ben	2	Sep 1 1942	13-*Imix*	7
Apr 19 1942	8-Cimi	7	Jun 26 1942	11-Ix	3	Sep 2 1942	**1-Ik**	8
Apr 20 1942	9-Manik	8	Jun 27 1942	12-Men	4	Sep 3 1942	2-Akbal	9
Apr 21 1942	10-Lamat	9	Jun 28 1942	13-Cib	5	Sep 4 1942	3-Kan	1
Apr 22 1942	11-Muluc	1	Jun 29 1942	**1-Caban**	6	Sep 5 1942	4-Chicchan	2
Apr 23 1942	12-Oc	2	Jun 30 1942	2-Etz'nab	7	Sep 6 1942	5-Cimi	3
Apr 24 1942	13-Chuen	3	Jul 1 1942	3-Cauac	8	Sep 7 1942	6-Manik	4
Apr 25 1942	**1-Eb**	4	Jul 2 1942	4-Ahau	9	Sep 8 1942	7-Lamat	5
Apr 26 1942	2-Ben	5	Jul 3 1942	5-*Imix*	1	Sep 9 1942	8-Muluc	6
Apr 27 1942	3-Ix	6	Jul 4 1942	6-Ik	2	Sep 10 1942	9-Oc	7
Apr 28 1942	4-Men	7	Jul 5 1942	7-Akbal	3	Sep 11 1942	10-Chuen	8
Apr 29 1942	5-Cib	8	Jul 6 1942	8-Kan	4	Sep 12 1942	11-Eb	9
Apr 30 1942	6-Caban	9	Jul 7 1942	9-Chicchan	5	Sep 13 1942	12-Ben	1
May 1 1942	7-Etz'nab	1	Jul 8 1942	10-Cimi	6	Sep 14 1942	13-Ix	2
May 2 1942	8-Cauac	2	Jul 9 1942	11-Manik	7	Sep 15 1942	**1-Men**	3
May 3 1942	9-Ahau	3	Jul 10 1942	12-Lamat	8	Sep 16 1942	2-Cib	4
May 4 1942	10-*Imix*	4	Jul 11 1942	13-Muluc	9	Sep 17 1942	3-Caban	5
May 5 1942	11-Ik	5	Jul 12 1942	**1-Oc**	1	Sep 18 1942	4-Etz'nab	6
May 6 1942	12-Akbal	6	Jul 13 1942	2-Chuen	2	Sep 19 1942	5-Cauac	7
May 7 1942	13-Kan	7	Jul 14 1942	3-Eb	3	Sep 20 1942	6-Ahau	8
May 8 1942	**1-Chicchan**	8	Jul 15 1942	4-Ben	4	Sep 21 1942	7-*Imix*	9
May 9 1942	2-Cimi	9	Jul 16 1942	5-Ix	5	Sep 22 1942	8-Ik	1
May 10 1942	3-Manik	1	Jul 17 1942	6-Men	6	Sep 23 1942	9-Akbal	2
May 11 1942	4-Lamat	2	Jul 18 1942	7-Cib	7	Sep 24 1942	10-Kan	3
May 12 1942	5-Muluc	3	Jul 19 1942	8-Caban	8	Sep 25 1942	11-Chicchan	4
May 13 1942	6-Oc	4	Jul 20 1942	9-Etz'nab	9	Sep 26 1942	12-Cimi	5
May 14 1942	7-Chuen	5	Jul 21 1942	10-Cauac	1	Sep 27 1942	13-Manik	6
May 15 1942	8-Eb	6	Jul 22 1942	11-Ahau	2	Sep 28 1942	**1-Lamat**	7
May 16 1942	9-Ben	7	Jul 23 1942	12-*Imix*	3	Sep 29 1942	2-Muluc	8
May 17 1942	10-Ix	8	Jul 24 1942	13-Ik	4	Sep 30 1942	3-Oc	9
May 18 1942	11-Men	9	Jul 25 1942	**1-Akbal**	5	Oct 1 1942	4-Chuen	1
May 19 1942	12-Cib	1	Jul 26 1942	2-Kan	6	Oct 2 1942	5-Eb	2
May 20 1942	13-Caban	2	Jul 27 1942	3-Chicchan	7	Oct 3 1942	6-Ben	3
May 21 1942	**1-Etz'nab**	3	Jul 28 1942	4-Cimi	8	Oct 4 1942	7-Ix	4
May 22 1942	2-Cauac	4	Jul 29 1942	5-Manik	9	Oct 5 1942	8-Men	5
May 23 1942	3-Ahau	5	Jul 30 1942	6-Lamat	1	Oct 6 1942	9-Cib	6
May 24 1942	4-*Imix*	6	Jul 31 1942	7-Muluc	2	Oct 7 1942	10-Caban	7
May 25 1942	5-Ik	7	Aug 1 1942	8-Oc	3	Oct 8 1942	11-Etz'nab	8
May 26 1942	6-Akbal	8	Aug 2 1942	9-Chuen	4	Oct 9 1942	12-Cauac	9
May 27 1942	7-Kan	9	Aug 3 1942	10-Eb	5	Oct 10 1942	13-Ahau	1
May 28 1942	8-Chicchan	1	Aug 4 1942	11-Ben	6	Oct 11 1942	**1-Imix**	2
May 29 1942	9-Cimi	2	Aug 5 1942	12-Ix	7	Oct 12 1942	2-Ik	3
May 30 1942	10-Manik	3	Aug 6 1942	13-Men	8	Oct 13 1942	3-Akbal	4
May 31 1942	11-Lamat	4	Aug 7 1942	**1-Cib**	9	Oct 14 1942	4-Kan	5
Jun 1 1942	12-Muluc	5	Aug 8 1942	2-Caban	1	Oct 15 1942	5-Chicchan	6
Jun 2 1942	13-Oc	6	Aug 9 1942	3-Etz'nab	2	Oct 16 1942	6-Cimi	7
Jun 3 1942	**1-Chuen**	7	Aug 10 1942	4-Cauac	3	Oct 17 1942	7-Manik	8
Jun 4 1942	2-Eb	8	Aug 11 1942	5-Ahau	4	Oct 18 1942	8-Lamat	9
Jun 5 1942	3-Ben	9	Aug 12 1942	6-*Imix*	5	Oct 19 1942	9-Muluc	1
Jun 6 1942	4-Ix	1	Aug 13 1942	7-Ik	6	Oct 20 1942	10-Oc	2
Jun 7 1942	5-Men	2	Aug 14 1942	8-Akbal	7	Oct 21 1942	11-Chuen	3
Jun 8 1942	6-Cib	3	Aug 15 1942	9-Kan	8	Oct 22 1942	12-Eb	4
Jun 9 1942	7-Caban	4	Aug 16 1942	10-Chicchan	9	Oct 23 1942	13-Ben	5
Jun 10 1942	8-Etz'nab	5	Aug 17 1942	11-Cimi	1	Oct 24 1942	**1-Ix**	6
Jun 11 1942	9-Cauac	6	Aug 18 1942	12-Manik	2	Oct 25 1942	2-Men	7
Jun 12 1942	10-Ahau	7	Aug 19 1942	13-Lamat	3	Oct 26 1942	3-Cib	8
Jun 13 1942	11-*Imix*	8	Aug 20 1942	**1-Muluc**	4	Oct 27 1942	4-Caban	9

Date	Day-Sign	L	Date	Day-Sign	L	Date	Day-Sign	L
Oct 28 1942	5-Etz'nab	1	Jan 4 1943	8-Cimi	6	Mar 13 1943	11-Ix	2
Oct 29 1942	6-Cauac	2	Jan 5 1943	9-Manik	7	Mar 14 1943	12-Men	3
Oct 30 1942	7-Ahau	3	Jan 6 1943	10-Lamat	8	Mar 15 1943	13-Cib	4
Oct 31 1942	8-*Imix*	4	Jan 7 1943	11-Muluc	9	Mar 16 1943	**1-Caban**	5
Nov 1 1942	9-Ik	5	Jan 8 1943	12-Oc	1	Mar 17 1943	2-Etz'nab	6
Nov 2 1942	10-Akbal	6	Jan 9 1943	13-Chuen	2	Mar 18 1943	3-Cauac	7
Nov 3 1942	11-Kan	7	Jan 10 1943	**1-Eb**	3	Mar 19 1943	4-Ahau	8
Nov 4 1942	12-Chicchan	8	Jan 11 1943	2-Ben	4	Mar 20 1943	5-*Imix*	9
Nov 5 1942	13-Cimi	9	Jan 12 1943	3-Ix	5	Mar 21 1943	6-Ik	1
Nov 6 1942	**1-Manik**	1	Jan 13 1943	4-Men	6	Mar 22 1943	7-Akbal	2
Nov 7 1942	2-Lamat	2	Jan 14 1943	5-Cib	7	Mar 23 1943	8-Kan	3
Nov 8 1942	3-Muluc	3	Jan 15 1943	6-Caban	8	Mar 24 1943	9-Chicchan	4
Nov 9 1942	4-Oc	4	Jan 16 1943	7-Etz'nab	9	Mar 25 1943	10-Cimi	5
Nov 10 1942	5-Chuen	5	Jan 17 1943	8-Cauac	1	Mar 26 1943	11-Manik	6
Nov 11 1942	6-Eb	6	Jan 18 1943	9-Ahau	2	Mar 27 1943	12-Lamat	7
Nov 12 1942	7-Ben	7	Jan 19 1943	10-*Imix*	3	Mar 28 1943	13-Muluc	8
Nov 13 1942	8-Ix	8	Jan 20 1943	11-Ik	4	Mar 29 1943	**1-Oc**	9
Nov 14 1942	9-Men	9	Jan 21 1943	12-Akbal	5	Mar 30 1943	2-Chuen	1
Nov 15 1942	10-Cib	1	Jan 22 1943	13-Kan	6	Mar 31 1943	3-Eb	2
Nov 16 1942	11-Caban	2	Jan 23 1943	**1-Chicchan**	7	Apr 1 1943	4-Ben	3
Nov 17 1942	12-Etz'nab	3	Jan 24 1943	2-Cimi	8	Apr 2 1943	5-Ix	4
Nov 18 1942	13-Cauac	4	Jan 25 1943	3-Manik	9	Apr 3 1943	6-Men	5
Nov 19 1942	**1-Ahau**	5	Jan 26 1943	4-Lamat	1	Apr 4 1943	7-Cib	6
Nov 20 1942	2-*Imix*	6	Jan 27 1943	5-Muluc	2	Apr 5 1943	8-Caban	7
Nov 21 1942	3-Ik	7	Jan 28 1943	6-Oc	3	Apr 6 1943	9-Etz'nab	8
Nov 22 1942	4-Akbal	8	Jan 29 1943	7-Chuen	4	Apr 7 1943	10-Cauac	9
Nov 23 1942	5-Kan	9	Jan 30 1943	8-Eb	5	Apr 8 1943	11-Ahau	1
Nov 24 1942	6-Chicchan	1	Jan 31 1943	9-Ben	6	Apr 9 1943	12-*Imix*	2
Nov 25 1942	7-Cimi	2	Feb 1 1943	10-Ix	7	Apr 10 1943	13-Ik	3
Nov 26 1942	8-Manik	3	Feb 2 1943	11-Men	8	Apr 11 1943	**1-Akbal**	4
Nov 27 1942	9-Lamat	4	Feb 3 1943	12-Cib	9	Apr 12 1943	2-Kan	5
Nov 28 1942	10-Muluc	5	Feb 4 1943	13-Caban	1	Apr 13 1943	3-Chicchan	6
Nov 29 1942	11-Oc	6	Feb 5 1943	**1-Etz'nab**	2	Apr 14 1943	4-Cimi	7
Nov 30 1942	12-Chuen	7	Feb 6 1943	2-Cauac	3	Apr 15 1943	5-Manik	8
Dec 1 1942	13-Eb	8	Feb 7 1943	3-Ahau	4	Apr 16 1943	6-Lamat	9
Dec 2 1942	**1-Ben**	9	Feb 8 1943	4-*Imix*	5	Apr 17 1943	7-Muluc	1
Dec 3 1942	2-Ix	1	Feb 9 1943	5-Ik	6	Apr 18 1943	8-Oc	2
Dec 4 1942	3-Men	2	Feb 10 1943	6-Akbal	7	Apr 19 1943	9-Chuen	3
Dec 5 1942	4-Cib	3	Feb 11 1943	7-Kan	8	Apr 20 1943	10-Eb	4
Dec 6 1942	5-Caban	4	Feb 12 1943	8-Chicchan	9	Apr 21 1943	11-Ben	5
Dec 7 1942	6-Etz'nab	5	Feb 13 1943	9-Cimi	1	Apr 22 1943	12-Ix	6
Dec 8 1942	7-Cauac	6	Feb 14 1943	10-Manik	2	Apr 23 1943	13-Men	7
Dec 9 1942	8-Ahau	7	Feb 15 1943	11-Lamat	3	Apr 24 1943	**1-Cib**	8
Dec 10 1942	9-*Imix*	8	Feb 16 1943	12-Muluc	4	Apr 25 1943	2-Caban	9
Dec 11 1942	10-Ik	9	Feb 17 1943	13-Oc	5	Apr 26 1943	3-Etz'nab	1
Dec 12 1942	11-Akbal	1	Feb 18 1943	**1-Chuen**	6	Apr 27 1943	4-Cauac	2
Dec 13 1942	12-Kan	2	Feb 19 1943	2-Eb	7	Apr 28 1943	5-Ahau	3
Dec 14 1942	13-Chicchan	3	Feb 20 1943	3-Ben	8	Apr 29 1943	6-*Imix*	4
Dec 15 1942	**1-Cimi**	4	Feb 21 1943	4-Ix	9	Apr 30 1943	7-Ik	5
Dec 16 1942	2-Manik	5	Feb 22 1943	5-Men	1	May 1 1943	8-Akbal	6
Dec 17 1942	3-Lamat	6	Feb 23 1943	6-Cib	2	May 2 1943	9-Kan	7
Dec 18 1942	4-Muluc	7	Feb 24 1943	7-Caban	3	May 3 1943	10-Chicchan	8
Dec 19 1942	5-Oc	8	Feb 25 1943	8-Etz'nab	4	May 4 1943	11-Cimi	9
Dec 20 1942	6-Chuen	9	Feb 26 1943	9-Cauac	5	May 5 1943	12-Manik	1
Dec 21 1942	7-Eb	1	Feb 27 1943	10-Ahau	6	May 6 1943	13-Lamat	2
Dec 22 1942	8-Ben	2	Feb 28 1943	11-*Imix*	7	May 7 1943	**1-Muluc**	3
Dec 23 1942	9-Ix	3	Mar 1 1943	12-Ik	8	May 8 1943	2-Oc	4
Dec 24 1942	10-Men	4	Mar 2 1943	13-Akbal	9	May 9 1943	3-Chuen	5
Dec 25 1942	11-Cib	5	Mar 3 1943	**1-Kan**	1	May 10 1943	4-Eb	6
Dec 26 1942	12-Caban	6	Mar 4 1943	2-Chicchan	2	May 11 1943	5-Ben	7
Dec 27 1942	13-Etz'nab	7	Mar 5 1943	3-Cimi	3	May 12 1943	6-Ix	8
Dec 28 1942	**1-Cauac**	8	Mar 6 1943	4-Manik	4	May 13 1943	7-Men	9
Dec 29 1942	2-Ahau	9	Mar 7 1943	5-Lamat	5	May 14 1943	8-Cib	1
Dec 30 1942	3-*Imix*	1	Mar 8 1943	6-Muluc	6	May 15 1943	9-Caban	2
Dec 31 1942	4-Ik	2	Mar 9 1943	7-Oc	7	May 16 1943	10-Etz'nab	3
Jan 1 1943	5-Akbal	3	Mar 10 1943	8-Chuen	8	May 17 1943	11-Cauac	4
Jan 2 1943	6-Kan	4	Mar 11 1943	9-Eb	9	May 18 1943	12-Ahau	5
Jan 3 1943	7-Chicchan	5	Mar 12 1943	10-Ben	1	May 19 1943	13-*Imix*	6

Date	Day-Sign	L	Date	Day-Sign	L	Date	Day-Sign	L
May 20 1943	**1-Ik**	7	Jul 27 1943	4-Oc	3	Oct 3 1943	7-Etz'nab	8
May 21 1943	2-Akbal	8	Jul 28 1943	5-Chuen	4	Oct 4 1943	8-Cauac	9
May 22 1943	3-Kan	9	Jul 29 1943	6-Eb	5	Oct 5 1943	9-Ahau	1
May 23 1943	4-Chicchan	1	Jul 30 1943	7-Ben	6	Oct 6 1943	*10-Imix*	2
May 24 1943	5-Cimi	2	Jul 31 1943	8-Ix	7	Oct 7 1943	11-Ik	3
May 25 1943	6-Manik	3	Aug 1 1943	9-Men	8	Oct 8 1943	12-Akbal	4
May 26 1943	7-Lamat	4	Aug 2 1943	10-Cib	9	Oct 9 1943	13-Kan	5
May 27 1943	8-Muluc	5	Aug 3 1943	11-Caban	1	Oct 10 1943	**1-Chicchan**	6
May 28 1943	9-Oc	6	Aug 4 1943	12-Etz'nab	2	Oct 11 1943	2-Cimi	7
May 29 1943	10-Chuen	7	Aug 5 1943	13-Cauac	3	Oct 12 1943	3-Manik	8
May 30 1943	11-Eb	8	Aug 6 1943	**1-Ahau**	4	Oct 13 1943	4-Lamat	9
May 31 1943	12-Ben	9	Aug 7 1943	*2-Imix*	5	Oct 14 1943	5-Muluc	1
Jun 1 1943	13-Ix	1	Aug 8 1943	3-Ik	6	Oct 15 1943	6-Oc	2
Jun 2 1943	**1-Men**	2	Aug 9 1943	4-Akbal	7	Oct 16 1943	7-Chuen	3
Jun 3 1943	2-Cib	3	Aug 10 1943	5-Kan	8	Oct 17 1943	8-Eb	4
Jun 4 1943	3-Caban	4	Aug 11 1943	6-Chicchan	9	Oct 18 1943	9-Ben	5
Jun 5 1943	4-Etz'nab	5	Aug 12 1943	7-Cimi	1	Oct 19 1943	10-Ix	6
Jun 6 1943	5-Cauac	6	Aug 13 1943	8-Manik	2	Oct 20 1943	11-Men	7
Jun 7 1943	6-Ahau	7	Aug 14 1943	9-Lamat	3	Oct 21 1943	12-Cib	8
Jun 8 1943	*7-Imix*	8	Aug 15 1943	10-Muluc	4	Oct 22 1943	13-Caban	9
Jun 9 1943	8-Ik	9	Aug 16 1943	11-Oc	5	Oct 23 1943	**1-Etz'nab**	1
Jun 10 1943	9-Akbal	1	Aug 17 1943	12-Chuen	6	Oct 24 1943	2-Cauac	2
Jun 11 1943	10-Kan	2	Aug 18 1943	13-Eb	7	Oct 25 1943	3-Ahau	3
Jun 12 1943	11-Chicchan	3	Aug 19 1943	**1-Ben**	8	Oct 26 1943	*4-Imix*	4
Jun 13 1943	12-Cimi	4	Aug 20 1943	2-Ix	9	Oct 27 1943	5-Ik	5
Jun 14 1943	13-Manik	5	Aug 21 1943	3-Men	1	Oct 28 1943	6-Akbal	6
Jun 15 1943	**1-Lamat**	6	Aug 22 1943	4-Cib	2	Oct 29 1943	7-Kan	7
Jun 16 1943	2-Muluc	7	Aug 23 1943	5-Caban	3	Oct 30 1943	8-Chicchan	8
Jun 17 1943	3-Oc	8	Aug 24 1943	6-Etz'nab	4	Oct 31 1943	9-Cimi	9
Jun 18 1943	4-Chuen	9	Aug 25 1943	7-Cauac	5	Nov 1 1943	10-Manik	1
Jun 19 1943	5-Eb	1	Aug 26 1943	8-Ahau	6	Nov 2 1943	11-Lamat	2
Jun 20 1943	6-Ben	2	Aug 27 1943	*9-Imix*	7	Nov 3 1943	12-Muluc	3
Jun 21 1943	7-Ix	3	Aug 28 1943	10-Ik	8	Nov 4 1943	13-Oc	4
Jun 22 1943	8-Men	4	Aug 29 1943	11-Akbal	9	Nov 5 1943	**1-Chuen**	5
Jun 23 1943	9-Cib	5	Aug 30 1943	12-Kan	1	Nov 6 1943	2-Eb	6
Jun 24 1943	10-Caban	6	Aug 31 1943	13-Chicchan	2	Nov 7 1943	3-Ben	7
Jun 25 1943	11-Etz'nab	7	Sep 1 1943	**1-Cimi**	3	Nov 8 1943	4-Ix	8
Jun 26 1943	12-Cauac	8	Sep 2 1943	2-Manik	4	Nov 9 1943	5-Men	9
Jun 27 1943	13-Ahau	9	Sep 3 1943	3-Lamat	5	Nov 10 1943	6-Cib	1
Jun 28 1943	**1-Imix**	1	Sep 4 1943	4-Muluc	6	Nov 11 1943	7-Caban	2
Jun 29 1943	2-Ik	2	Sep 5 1943	5-Oc	7	Nov 12 1943	8-Etz'nab	3
Jun 30 1943	3-Akbal	3	Sep 6 1943	6-Chuen	8	Nov 13 1943	9-Cauac	4
Jul 1 1943	4-Kan	4	Sep 7 1943	7-Eb	9	Nov 14 1943	10-Ahau	5
Jul 2 1943	5-Chicchan	5	Sep 8 1943	8-Ben	1	Nov 15 1943	*11-Imix*	6
Jul 3 1943	6-Cimi	6	Sep 9 1943	9-Ix	2	Nov 16 1943	12-Ik	7
Jul 4 1943	7-Manik	7	Sep 10 1943	10-Men	3	Nov 17 1943	13-Akbal	8
Jul 5 1943	8-Lamat	8	Sep 11 1943	11-Cib	4	Nov 18 1943	**1-Kan**	9
Jul 6 1943	9-Muluc	9	Sep 12 1943	12-Caban	5	Nov 19 1943	2-Chicchan	1
Jul 7 1943	10-Oc	1	Sep 13 1943	13-Etz'nab	6	Nov 20 1943	3-Cimi	2
Jul 8 1943	11-Chuen	2	Sep 14 1943	**1-Cauac**	7	Nov 21 1943	4-Manik	3
Jul 9 1943	12-Eb	3	Sep 15 1943	2-Ahau	8	Nov 22 1943	5-Lamat	4
Jul 10 1943	13-Ben	4	Sep 16 1943	*3-Imix*	9	Nov 23 1943	6-Muluc	5
Jul 11 1943	**1-Ix**	5	Sep 17 1943	4-Ik	1	Nov 24 1943	7-Oc	6
Jul 12 1943	2-Men	6	Sep 18 1943	5-Akbal	2	Nov 25 1943	8-Chuen	7
Jul 13 1943	3-Cib	7	Sep 19 1943	6-Kan	3	Nov 26 1943	9-Eb	8
Jul 14 1943	4-Caban	8	Sep 20 1943	7-Chicchan	4	Nov 27 1943	10-Ben	9
Jul 15 1943	5-Etz'nab	9	Sep 21 1943	8-Cimi	5	Nov 28 1943	11-Ix	1
Jul 16 1943	6-Cauac	1	Sep 22 1943	9-Manik	6	Nov 29 1943	12-Men	2
Jul 17 1943	7-Ahau	2	Sep 23 1943	10-Lamat	7	Nov 30 1943	13-Cib	3
Jul 18 1943	*8-Imix*	3	Sep 24 1943	11-Muluc	8	Dec 1 1943	**1-Caban**	4
Jul 19 1943	9-Ik	4	Sep 25 1943	12-Oc	9	Dec 2 1943	2-Etz'nab	5
Jul 20 1943	10-Akbal	5	Sep 26 1943	13-Chuen	1	Dec 3 1943	3-Cauac	6
Jul 21 1943	11-Kan	6	Sep 27 1943	**1-Eb**	2	Dec 4 1943	4-Ahau	7
Jul 22 1943	12-Chicchan	7	Sep 28 1943	2-Ben	3	Dec 5 1943	*5-Imix*	8
Jul 23 1943	13-Cimi	8	Sep 29 1943	3-Ix	4	Dec 6 1943	6-Ik	9
Jul 24 1943	**1-Manik**	9	Sep 30 1943	4-Men	5	Dec 7 1943	7-Akbal	1
Jul 25 1943	2-Lamat	1	Oct 1 1943	5-Cib	6	Dec 8 1943	8-Kan	2
Jul 26 1943	3-Muluc	2	Oct 2 1943	6-Caban	7	Dec 9 1943	9-Chicchan	3

Date	Day-Sign	L
Dec 10 1943	10-Cimi	4
Dec 11 1943	11-Manik	5
Dec 12 1943	12-Lamat	6
Dec 13 1943	13-Muluc	7
Dec 14 1943	**1-Oc**	8
Dec 15 1943	2-Chuen	9
Dec 16 1943	3-Eb	1
Dec 17 1943	4-Ben	2
Dec 18 1943	5-Ix	3
Dec 19 1943	6-Men	4
Dec 20 1943	7-Cib	5
Dec 21 1943	8-Caban	6
Dec 22 1943	9-Etz'nab	7
Dec 23 1943	10-Cauac	8
Dec 24 1943	11-Ahau	9
Dec 25 1943	*12-Imix*	1
Dec 26 1943	13-Ik	2
Dec 27 1943	**1-Akbal**	3
Dec 28 1943	2-Kan	4
Dec 29 1943	3-Chicchan	5
Dec 30 1943	4-Cimi	6
Dec 31 1943	5-Manik	7
Jan 1 1944	6-Lamat	8
Jan 2 1944	7-Muluc	9
Jan 3 1944	8-Oc	1
Jan 4 1944	9-Chuen	2
Jan 5 1944	10-Eb	3
Jan 6 1944	11-Ben	4
Jan 7 1944	12-Ix	5
Jan 8 1944	13-Men	6
Jan 9 1944	**1-Cib**	7
Jan 10 1944	2-Caban	8
Jan 11 1944	3-Etz'nab	9
Jan 12 1944	4-Cauac	1
Jan 13 1944	5-Ahau	2
Jan 14 1944	*6-Imix*	3
Jan 15 1944	7-Ik	4
Jan 16 1944	8-Akbal	5
Jan 17 1944	9-Kan	6
Jan 18 1944	10-Chicchan	7
Jan 19 1944	11-Cimi	8
Jan 20 1944	12-Manik	9
Jan 21 1944	13-Lamat	1
Jan 22 1944	**1-Muluc**	2
Jan 23 1944	2-Oc	3
Jan 24 1944	3-Chuen	4
Jan 25 1944	4-Eb	5
Jan 26 1944	5-Ben	6
Jan 27 1944	6-Ix	7
Jan 28 1944	7-Men	8
Jan 29 1944	8-Cib	9
Jan 30 1944	9-Caban	1
Jan 31 1944	10-Etz'nab	2
Feb 1 1944	11-Cauac	3
Feb 2 1944	12-Ahau	4
Feb 3 1944	*13-Imix*	5
Feb 4 1944	**1-Ik**	6
Feb 5 1944	2-Akbal	7
Feb 6 1944	3-Kan	8
Feb 7 1944	4-Chicchan	9
Feb 8 1944	5-Cimi	1
Feb 9 1944	6-Manik	2
Feb 10 1944	7-Lamat	3
Feb 11 1944	8-Muluc	4
Feb 12 1944	9-Oc	5
Feb 13 1944	10-Chuen	6
Feb 14 1944	11-Eb	7
Feb 15 1944	12-Ben	8

Date	Day-Sign	L
Feb 16 1944	13-Ix	9
Feb 17 1944	**1-Men**	1
Feb 18 1944	2-Cib	2
Feb 19 1944	3-Caban	3
Feb 20 1944	4-Etz'nab	4
Feb 21 1944	5-Cauac	5
Feb 22 1944	6-Ahau	6
Feb 23 1944	*7-Imix*	7
Feb 24 1944	8-Ik	8
Feb 25 1944	9-Akbal	9
Feb 26 1944	10-Kan	1
Feb 27 1944	11-Chicchan	2
Feb 28 1944	12-Cimi	3
Feb 29 1944	13-Manik	4
Mar 1 1944	**1-Lamat**	5
Mar 2 1944	2-Muluc	6
Mar 3 1944	3-Oc	7
Mar 4 1944	4-Chuen	8
Mar 5 1944	5-Eb	9
Mar 6 1944	6-Ben	1
Mar 7 1944	7-Ix	2
Mar 8 1944	8-Men	3
Mar 9 1944	9-Cib	4
Mar 10 1944	10-Caban	5
Mar 11 1944	11-Etz'nab	6
Mar 12 1944	12-Cauac	7
Mar 13 1944	13-Ahau	8
Mar 14 1944	**1-Imix**	9
Mar 15 1944	2-Ik	1
Mar 16 1944	3-Akbal	2
Mar 17 1944	4-Kan	3
Mar 18 1944	5-Chicchan	4
Mar 19 1944	6-Cimi	5
Mar 20 1944	7-Manik	6
Mar 21 1944	8-Lamat	7
Mar 22 1944	9-Muluc	8
Mar 23 1944	10-Oc	9
Mar 24 1944	11-Chuen	1
Mar 25 1944	12-Eb	2
Mar 26 1944	13-Ben	3
Mar 27 1944	**1-Ix**	4
Mar 28 1944	2-Men	5
Mar 29 1944	3-Cib	6
Mar 30 1944	4-Caban	7
Mar 31 1944	5-Etz'nab	8
Apr 1 1944	6-Cauac	9
Apr 2 1944	7-Ahau	1
Apr 3 1944	*8-Imix*	2
Apr 4 1944	9-Ik	3
Apr 5 1944	10-Akbal	4
Apr 6 1944	11-Kan	5
Apr 7 1944	12-Chicchan	6
Apr 8 1944	13-Cimi	7
Apr 9 1944	**1-Manik**	8
Apr 10 1944	2-Lamat	9
Apr 11 1944	3-Muluc	1
Apr 12 1944	4-Oc	2
Apr 13 1944	5-Chuen	3
Apr 14 1944	6-Eb	4
Apr 15 1944	7-Ben	5
Apr 16 1944	8-Ix	6
Apr 17 1944	9-Men	7
Apr 18 1944	10-Cib	8
Apr 19 1944	11-Caban	9
Apr 20 1944	12-Etz'nab	1
Apr 21 1944	13-Cauac	2
Apr 22 1944	**1-Ahau**	3
Apr 23 1944	*2-Imix*	4

Date	Day-Sign	L
Apr 24 1944	3-Ik	5
Apr 25 1944	4-Akbal	6
Apr 26 1944	5-Kan	7
Apr 27 1944	6-Chicchan	8
Apr 28 1944	7-Cimi	9
Apr 29 1944	8-Manik	1
Apr 30 1944	9-Lamat	2
May 1 1944	10-Muluc	3
May 2 1944	11-Oc	4
May 3 1944	12-Chuen	5
May 4 1944	13-Eb	6
May 5 1944	**1-Ben**	7
May 6 1944	2-Ix	8
May 7 1944	3-Men	9
May 8 1944	4-Cib	1
May 9 1944	5-Caban	2
May 10 1944	6-Etz'nab	3
May 11 1944	7-Cauac	4
May 12 1944	8-Ahau	5
May 13 1944	*9-Imix*	6
May 14 1944	10-Ik	7
May 15 1944	11-Akbal	8
May 16 1944	12-Kan	9
May 17 1944	13-Chicchan	1
May 18 1944	**1-Cimi**	2
May 19 1944	2-Manik	3
May 20 1944	3-Lamat	4
May 21 1944	4-Muluc	5
May 22 1944	5-Oc	6
May 23 1944	6-Chuen	7
May 24 1944	7-Eb	8
May 25 1944	8-Ben	9
May 26 1944	9-Ix	1
May 27 1944	10-Men	2
May 28 1944	11-Cib	3
May 29 1944	12-Caban	4
May 30 1944	13-Etz'nab	5
May 31 1944	**1-Cauac**	6
Jun 1 1944	2-Ahau	7
Jun 2 1944	*3-Imix*	8
Jun 3 1944	4-Ik	9
Jun 4 1944	5-Akbal	1
Jun 5 1944	6-Kan	2
Jun 6 1944	7-Chicchan	3
Jun 7 1944	8-Cimi	4
Jun 8 1944	9-Manik	5
Jun 9 1944	10-Lamat	6
Jun 10 1944	11-Muluc	7
Jun 11 1944	12-Oc	8
Jun 12 1944	13-Chuen	9
Jun 13 1944	**1-Eb**	1
Jun 14 1944	2-Ben	2
Jun 15 1944	3-Ix	3
Jun 16 1944	4-Men	4
Jun 17 1944	5-Cib	5
Jun 18 1944	6-Caban	6
Jun 19 1944	7-Etz'nab	7
Jun 20 1944	8-Cauac	8
Jun 21 1944	9-Ahau	9
Jun 22 1944	*10-Imix*	1
Jun 23 1944	11-Ik	2
Jun 24 1944	12-Akbal	3
Jun 25 1944	13-Kan	4
Jun 26 1944	**1-Chicchan**	5
Jun 27 1944	2-Cimi	6
Jun 28 1944	3-Manik	7
Jun 29 1944	4-Lamat	8
Jun 30 1944	5-Muluc	9

Date	Day-Sign	L
Jul 1 1944	6-Oc	1
Jul 2 1944	7-Chuen	2
Jul 3 1944	8-Eb	3
Jul 4 1944	9-Ben	4
Jul 5 1944	10-Ix	5
Jul 6 1944	11-Men	6
Jul 7 1944	12-Cib	7
Jul 8 1944	13-Caban	8
Jul 9 1944	1-Etz'nab	9
Jul 10 1944	2-Cauac	1
Jul 11 1944	3-Ahau	2
Jul 12 1944	4-Imix	3
Jul 13 1944	5-Ik	4
Jul 14 1944	6-Akbal	5
Jul 15 1944	7-Kan	6
Jul 16 1944	8-Chicchan	7
Jul 17 1944	9-Cimi	8
Jul 18 1944	10-Manik	9
Jul 19 1944	11-Lamat	1
Jul 20 1944	12-Muluc	2
Jul 21 1944	13-Oc	3
Jul 22 1944	1-Chuen	4
Jul 23 1944	2-Eb	5
Jul 24 1944	3-Ben	6
Jul 25 1944	4-Ix	7
Jul 26 1944	5-Men	8
Jul 27 1944	6-Cib	9
Jul 28 1944	7-Caban	1
Jul 29 1944	8-Etz'nab	2
Jul 30 1944	9-Cauac	3
Jul 31 1944	10-Ahau	4
Aug 1 1944	11-Imix	5
Aug 2 1944	12-Ik	6
Aug 3 1944	13-Akbal	7
Aug 4 1944	1-Kan	8
Aug 5 1944	2-Chicchan	9
Aug 6 1944	3-Cimi	1
Aug 7 1944	4-Manik	2
Aug 8 1944	5-Lamat	3
Aug 9 1944	6-Muluc	4
Aug 10 1944	7-Oc	5
Aug 11 1944	8-Chuen	6
Aug 12 1944	9-Eb	7
Aug 13 1944	10-Ben	8
Aug 14 1944	11-Ix	9
Aug 15 1944	12-Men	1
Aug 16 1944	13-Cib	2
Aug 17 1944	1-Caban	3
Aug 18 1944	2-Etz'nab	4
Aug 19 1944	3-Cauac	5
Aug 20 1944	4-Ahau	6
Aug 21 1944	5-Imix	7
Aug 22 1944	6-Ik	8
Aug 23 1944	7-Akbal	9
Aug 24 1944	8-Kan	1
Aug 25 1944	9-Chicchan	2
Aug 26 1944	10-Cimi	3
Aug 27 1944	11-Manik	4
Aug 28 1944	12-Lamat	5
Aug 29 1944	13-Muluc	6
Aug 30 1944	1-Oc	7
Aug 31 1944	2-Chuen	8
Sep 1 1944	3-Eb	9
Sep 2 1944	4-Ben	1
Sep 3 1944	5-Ix	2
Sep 4 1944	6-Men	3
Sep 5 1944	7-Cib	4
Sep 6 1944	8-Caban	5

Date	Day-Sign	L
Sep 7 1944	9-Etz'nab	6
Sep 8 1944	10-Cauac	7
Sep 9 1944	11-Ahau	8
Sep 10 1944	12-Imix	9
Sep 11 1944	13-Ik	1
Sep 12 1944	1-Akbal	2
Sep 13 1944	2-Kan	3
Sep 14 1944	3-Chicchan	4
Sep 15 1944	4-Cimi	5
Sep 16 1944	5-Manik	6
Sep 17 1944	6-Lamat	7
Sep 18 1944	7-Muluc	8
Sep 19 1944	8-Oc	9
Sep 20 1944	9-Chuen	1
Sep 21 1944	10-Eb	2
Sep 22 1944	11-Ben	3
Sep 23 1944	12-Ix	4
Sep 24 1944	13-Men	5
Sep 25 1944	1-Cib	6
Sep 26 1944	2-Caban	7
Sep 27 1944	3-Etz'nab	8
Sep 28 1944	4-Cauac	9
Sep 29 1944	5-Ahau	1
Sep 30 1944	6-Imix	2
Oct 1 1944	7-Ik	3
Oct 2 1944	8-Akbal	4
Oct 3 1944	9-Kan	5
Oct 4 1944	10-Chicchan	6
Oct 5 1944	11-Cimi	7
Oct 6 1944	12-Manik	8
Oct 7 1944	13-Lamat	9
Oct 8 1944	1-Muluc	1
Oct 9 1944	2-Oc	2
Oct 10 1944	3-Chuen	3
Oct 11 1944	4-Eb	4
Oct 12 1944	5-Ben	5
Oct 13 1944	6-Ix	6
Oct 14 1944	7-Men	7
Oct 15 1944	8-Cib	8
Oct 16 1944	9-Caban	9
Oct 17 1944	10-Etz'nab	1
Oct 18 1944	11-Cauac	2
Oct 19 1944	12-Ahau	3
Oct 20 1944	13-Imix	4
Oct 21 1944	1-Ik	5
Oct 22 1944	2-Akbal	6
Oct 23 1944	3-Kan	7
Oct 24 1944	4-Chicchan	8
Oct 25 1944	5-Cimi	9
Oct 26 1944	6-Manik	1
Oct 27 1944	7-Lamat	2
Oct 28 1944	8-Muluc	3
Oct 29 1944	9-Oc	4
Oct 30 1944	10-Chuen	5
Oct 31 1944	11-Eb	6
Nov 1 1944	12-Ben	7
Nov 2 1944	13-Ix	8
Nov 3 1944	1-Men	9
Nov 4 1944	2-Cib	1
Nov 5 1944	3-Caban	2
Nov 6 1944	4-Etz'nab	3
Nov 7 1944	5-Cauac	4
Nov 8 1944	6-Ahau	5
Nov 9 1944	7-Imix	6
Nov 10 1944	8-Ik	7
Nov 11 1944	9-Akbal	8
Nov 12 1944	10-Kan	9
Nov 13 1944	11-Chicchan	1

Date	Day-Sign	L
Nov 14 1944	12-Cimi	2
Nov 15 1944	13-Manik	3
Nov 16 1944	1-Lamat	4
Nov 17 1944	2-Muluc	5
Nov 18 1944	3-Oc	6
Nov 19 1944	4-Chuen	7
Nov 20 1944	5-Eb	8
Nov 21 1944	6-Ben	9
Nov 22 1944	7-Ix	1
Nov 23 1944	8-Men	2
Nov 24 1944	9-Cib	3
Nov 25 1944	10-Caban	4
Nov 26 1944	11-Etz'nab	5
Nov 27 1944	12-Cauac	6
Nov 28 1944	13-Ahau	7
Nov 29 1944	1-Imix	8
Nov 30 1944	2-Ik	9
Dec 1 1944	3-Akbal	1
Dec 2 1944	4-Kan	2
Dec 3 1944	5-Chicchan	3
Dec 4 1944	6-Cimi	4
Dec 5 1944	7-Manik	5
Dec 6 1944	8-Lamat	6
Dec 7 1944	9-Muluc	7
Dec 8 1944	10-Oc	8
Dec 9 1944	11-Chuen	9
Dec 10 1944	12-Eb	1
Dec 11 1944	13-Ben	2
Dec 12 1944	1-Ix	3
Dec 13 1944	2-Men	4
Dec 14 1944	3-Cib	5
Dec 15 1944	4-Caban	6
Dec 16 1944	5-Etz'nab	7
Dec 17 1944	6-Cauac	8
Dec 18 1944	7-Ahau	9
Dec 19 1944	8-Imix	1
Dec 20 1944	9-Ik	2
Dec 21 1944	10-Akbal	3
Dec 22 1944	11-Kan	4
Dec 23 1944	12-Chicchan	5
Dec 24 1944	13-Cimi	6
Dec 25 1944	1-Manik	7
Dec 26 1944	2-Lamat	8
Dec 27 1944	3-Muluc	9
Dec 28 1944	4-Oc	1
Dec 29 1944	5-Chuen	2
Dec 30 1944	6-Eb	3
Dec 31 1944	7-Ben	4
Jan 1 1945	8-Ix	5
Jan 2 1945	9-Men	6
Jan 3 1945	10-Cib	7
Jan 4 1945	11-Caban	8
Jan 5 1945	12-Etz'nab	9
Jan 6 1945	13-Cauac	1
Jan 7 1945	1-Ahau	2
Jan 8 1945	2-Imix	3
Jan 9 1945	3-Ik	4
Jan 10 1945	4-Akbal	5
Jan 11 1945	5-Kan	6
Jan 12 1945	6-Chicchan	7
Jan 13 1945	7-Cimi	8
Jan 14 1945	8-Manik	9
Jan 15 1945	9-Lamat	1
Jan 16 1945	10-Muluc	2
Jan 17 1945	11-Oc	3
Jan 18 1945	12-Chuen	4
Jan 19 1945	13-Eb	5
Jan 20 1945	1-Ben	6

Date	Day-Sign	L		Date	Day-Sign	L		Date	Day-Sign	L
Jan 21 1945	2-Ix	7		Mar 30 1945	5-Ik	3		Jun 6 1945	8-Oc	8
Jan 22 1945	3-Men	8		Mar 31 1945	6-Akbal	4		Jun 7 1945	9-Chuen	9
Jan 23 1945	4-Cib	9		Apr 1 1945	7-Kan	5		Jun 8 1945	10-Eb	1
Jan 24 1945	5-Caban	1		Apr 2 1945	8-Chicchan	6		Jun 9 1945	11-Ben	2
Jan 25 1945	6-Etz'nab	2		Apr 3 1945	9-Cimi	7		Jun 10 1945	12-Ix	3
Jan 26 1945	7-Cauac	3		Apr 4 1945	10-Manik	8		Jun 11 1945	13-Men	4
Jan 27 1945	8-Ahau	4		Apr 5 1945	11-Lamat	9		Jun 12 1945	**1-Cib**	5
Jan 28 1945	9-Imix	5		Apr 6 1945	12-Muluc	1		Jun 13 1945	2-Caban	6
Jan 29 1945	10-Ik	6		Apr 7 1945	13-Oc	2		Jun 14 1945	3-Etz'nab	7
Jan 30 1945	11-Akbal	7		Apr 8 1945	**1-Chuen**	3		Jun 15 1945	4-Cauac	8
Jan 31 1945	12-Kan	8		Apr 9 1945	2-Eb	4		Jun 16 1945	5-Ahau	9
Feb 1 1945	13-Chicchan	9		Apr 10 1945	3-Ben	5		Jun 17 1945	6-Imix	1
Feb 2 1945	**1-Cimi**	1		Apr 11 1945	4-Ix	6		Jun 18 1945	7-Ik	2
Feb 3 1945	2-Manik	2		Apr 12 1945	5-Men	7		Jun 19 1945	8-Akbal	3
Feb 4 1945	3-Lamat	3		Apr 13 1945	6-Cib	8		Jun 20 1945	9-Kan	4
Feb 5 1945	4-Muluc	4		Apr 14 1945	7-Caban	9		Jun 21 1945	10-Chicchan	5
Feb 6 1945	5-Oc	5		Apr 15 1945	8-Etz'nab	1		Jun 22 1945	11-Cimi	6
Feb 7 1945	6-Chuen	6		Apr 16 1945	9-Cauac	2		Jun 23 1945	12-Manik	7
Feb 8 1945	7-Eb	7		Apr 17 1945	10-Ahau	3		Jun 24 1945	13-Lamat	8
Feb 9 1945	8-Ben	8		Apr 18 1945	11-Imix	4		Jun 25 1945	**1-Muluc**	9
Feb 10 1945	9-Ix	9		Apr 19 1945	12-Ik	5		Jun 26 1945	2-Oc	1
Feb 11 1945	10-Men	1		Apr 20 1945	13-Akbal	6		Jun 27 1945	3-Chuen	2
Feb 12 1945	11-Cib	2		Apr 21 1945	**1-Kan**	7		Jun 28 1945	4-Eb	3
Feb 13 1945	12-Caban	3		Apr 22 1945	2-Chicchan	8		Jun 29 1945	5-Ben	4
Feb 14 1945	13-Etz'nab	4		Apr 23 1945	3-Cimi	9		Jun 30 1945	6-Ix	5
Feb 15 1945	**1-Cauac**	5		Apr 24 1945	4-Manik	1		Jul 1 1945	7-Men	6
Feb 16 1945	2-Ahau	6		Apr 25 1945	5-Lamat	2		Jul 2 1945	8-Cib	7
Feb 17 1945	3-Imix	7		Apr 26 1945	6-Muluc	3		Jul 3 1945	9-Caban	8
Feb 18 1945	4-Ik	8		Apr 27 1945	7-Oc	4		Jul 4 1945	10-Etz'nab	9
Feb 19 1945	5-Akbal	9		Apr 28 1945	8-Chuen	5		Jul 5 1945	11-Cauac	1
Feb 20 1945	6-Kan	1		Apr 29 1945	9-Eb	6		Jul 6 1945	12-Ahau	2
Feb 21 1945	7-Chicchan	2		Apr 30 1945	10-Ben	7		Jul 7 1945	13-Imix	3
Feb 22 1945	8-Cimi	3		May 1 1945	11-Ix	8		Jul 8 1945	**1-Ik**	4
Feb 23 1945	9-Manik	4		May 2 1945	12-Men	9		Jul 9 1945	2-Akbal	5
Feb 24 1945	10-Lamat	5		May 3 1945	13-Cib	1		Jul 10 1945	3-Kan	6
Feb 25 1945	11-Muluc	6		May 4 1945	**1-Caban**	2		Jul 11 1945	4-Chicchan	7
Feb 26 1945	12-Oc	7		May 5 1945	2-Etz'nab	3		Jul 12 1945	5-Cimi	8
Feb 27 1945	13-Chuen	8		May 6 1945	3-Cauac	4		Jul 13 1945	6-Manik	9
Feb 28 1945	**1-Eb**	9		May 7 1945	4-Ahau	5		Jul 14 1945	7-Lamat	1
Mar 1 1945	2-Ben	1		May 8 1945	5-Imix	6		Jul 15 1945	8-Muluc	2
Mar 2 1945	3-Ix	2		May 9 1945	6-Ik	7		Jul 16 1945	9-Oc	3
Mar 3 1945	4-Men	3		May 10 1945	7-Akbal	8		Jul 17 1945	10-Chuen	4
Mar 4 1945	5-Cib	4		May 11 1945	8-Kan	9		Jul 18 1945	11-Eb	5
Mar 5 1945	6-Caban	5		May 12 1945	9-Chicchan	1		Jul 19 1945	12-Ben	6
Mar 6 1945	7-Etz'nab	6		May 13 1945	10-Cimi	2		Jul 20 1945	13-Ix	7
Mar 7 1945	8-Cauac	7		May 14 1945	11-Manik	3		Jul 21 1945	**1-Men**	8
Mar 8 1945	9-Ahau	8		May 15 1945	12-Lamat	4		Jul 22 1945	2-Cib	9
Mar 9 1945	10-Imix	9		May 16 1945	13-Muluc	5		Jul 23 1945	3-Caban	1
Mar 10 1945	11-Ik	1		May 17 1945	**1-Oc**	6		Jul 24 1945	4-Etz'nab	2
Mar 11 1945	12-Akbal	2		May 18 1945	2-Chuen	7		Jul 25 1945	5-Cauac	3
Mar 12 1945	13-Kan	3		May 19 1945	3-Eb	8		Jul 26 1945	6-Ahau	4
Mar 13 1945	**1-Chicchan**	4		May 20 1945	4-Ben	9		Jul 27 1945	7-Imix	5
Mar 14 1945	2-Cimi	5		May 21 1945	5-Ix	1		Jul 28 1945	8-Ik	6
Mar 15 1945	3-Manik	6		May 22 1945	6-Men	2		Jul 29 1945	9-Akbal	7
Mar 16 1945	4-Lamat	7		May 23 1945	7-Cib	3		Jul 30 1945	10-Kan	8
Mar 17 1945	5-Muluc	8		May 24 1945	8-Caban	4		Jul 31 1945	11-Chicchan	9
Mar 18 1945	6-Oc	9		May 25 1945	9-Etz'nab	5		Aug 1 1945	12-Cimi	1
Mar 19 1945	7-Chuen	1		May 26 1945	10-Cauac	6		Aug 2 1945	13-Manik	2
Mar 20 1945	8-Eb	2		May 27 1945	11-Ahau	7		Aug 3 1945	**1-Lamat**	3
Mar 21 1945	9-Ben	3		May 28 1945	12-Imix	8		Aug 4 1945	2-Muluc	4
Mar 22 1945	10-Ix	4		May 29 1945	13-Ik	9		Aug 5 1945	3-Oc	5
Mar 23 1945	11-Men	5		May 30 1945	**1-Akbal**	1		Aug 6 1945	4-Chuen	6
Mar 24 1945	12-Cib	6		May 31 1945	2-Kan	2		Aug 7 1945	5-Eb	7
Mar 25 1945	13-Caban	7		Jun 1 1945	3-Chicchan	3		Aug 8 1945	6-Ben	8
Mar 26 1945	**1-Etz'nab**	8		Jun 2 1945	4-Cimi	4		Aug 9 1945	7-Ix	9
Mar 27 1945	2-Cauac	9		Jun 3 1945	5-Manik	5		Aug 10 1945	8-Men	1
Mar 28 1945	3-Ahau	1		Jun 4 1945	6-Lamat	6		Aug 11 1945	9-Cib	2
Mar 29 1945	4-Imix	2		Jun 5 1945	7-Muluc	7		Aug 12 1945	10-Caban	3

Date	Day-Sign	L		Date	Day-Sign	L		Date	Day-Sign	L
Aug 13 1945	11-Etz'nab	4		Oct 20 1945	1-Cimi	9		Dec 27 1945	4-Ix	5
Aug 14 1945	12-Cauac	5		Oct 21 1945	2-Manik	1		Dec 28 1945	5-Men	6
Aug 15 1945	13-Ahau	6		Oct 22 1945	3-Lamat	2		Dec 29 1945	6-Cib	7
Aug 16 1945	1-Imix	7		Oct 23 1945	4-Muluc	3		Dec 30 1945	7-Caban	8
Aug 17 1945	2-Ik	8		Oct 24 1945	5-Oc	4		Dec 31 1945	8-Etz'nab	9
Aug 18 1945	3-Akbal	9		Oct 25 1945	6-Chuen	5		Jan 1 1946	9-Cauac	1
Aug 19 1945	4-Kan	1		Oct 26 1945	7-Eb	6		Jan 2 1946	10-Ahau	2
Aug 20 1945	5-Chicchan	2		Oct 27 1945	8-Ben	7		Jan 3 1946	11-Imix	3
Aug 21 1945	6-Cimi	3		Oct 28 1945	9-Ix	8		Jan 4 1946	12-Ik	4
Aug 22 1945	7-Manik	4		Oct 29 1945	10-Men	9		Jan 5 1946	13-Akbal	5
Aug 23 1945	8-Lamat	5		Oct 30 1945	11-Cib	1		Jan 6 1946	1-Kan	6
Aug 24 1945	9-Muluc	6		Oct 31 1945	12-Caban	2		Jan 7 1946	2-Chicchan	7
Aug 25 1945	10-Oc	7		Nov 1 1945	13-Etz'nab	3		Jan 8 1946	3-Cimi	8
Aug 26 1945	11-Chuen	8		Nov 2 1945	1-Cauac	4		Jan 9 1946	4-Manik	9
Aug 27 1945	12-Eb	9		Nov 3 1945	2-Ahau	5		Jan 10 1946	5-Lamat	1
Aug 28 1945	13-Ben	1		Nov 4 1945	3-Imix	6		Jan 11 1946	6-Muluc	2
Aug 29 1945	1-Ix	2		Nov 5 1945	4-Ik	7		Jan 12 1946	7-Oc	3
Aug 30 1945	2-Men	3		Nov 6 1945	5-Akbal	8		Jan 13 1946	8-Chuen	4
Aug 31 1945	3-Cib	4		Nov 7 1945	6-Kan	9		Jan 14 1946	9-Eb	5
Sep 1 1945	4-Caban	5		Nov 8 1945	7-Chicchan	1		Jan 15 1946	10-Ben	6
Sep 2 1945	5-Etz'nab	6		Nov 9 1945	8-Cimi	2		Jan 16 1946	11-Ix	7
Sep 3 1945	6-Cauac	7		Nov 10 1945	9-Manik	3		Jan 17 1946	12-Men	8
Sep 4 1945	7-Ahau	8		Nov 11 1945	10-Lamat	4		Jan 18 1946	13-Cib	9
Sep 5 1945	8-Imix	9		Nov 12 1945	11-Muluc	5		Jan 19 1946	1-Caban	1
Sep 6 1945	9-Ik	1		Nov 13 1945	12-Oc	6		Jan 20 1946	2-Etz'nab	2
Sep 7 1945	10-Akbal	2		Nov 14 1945	13-Chuen	7		Jan 21 1946	3-Cauac	3
Sep 8 1945	11-Kan	3		Nov 15 1945	1-Eb	8		Jan 22 1946	4-Ahau	4
Sep 9 1945	12-Chicchan	4		Nov 16 1945	2-Ben	9		Jan 23 1946	5-Imix	5
Sep 10 1945	13-Cimi	5		Nov 17 1945	3-Ix	1		Jan 24 1946	6-Ik	6
Sep 11 1945	1-Manik	6		Nov 18 1945	4-Men	2		Jan 25 1946	7-Akbal	7
Sep 12 1945	2-Lamat	7		Nov 19 1945	5-Cib	3		Jan 26 1946	8-Kan	8
Sep 13 1945	3-Muluc	8		Nov 20 1945	6-Caban	4		Jan 27 1946	9-Chicchan	9
Sep 14 1945	4-Oc	9		Nov 21 1945	7-Etz'nab	5		Jan 28 1946	10-Cimi	1
Sep 15 1945	5-Chuen	1		Nov 22 1945	8-Cauac	6		Jan 29 1946	11-Manik	2
Sep 16 1945	6-Eb	2		Nov 23 1945	9-Ahau	7		Jan 30 1946	12-Lamat	3
Sep 17 1945	7-Ben	3		Nov 24 1945	10-Imix	8		Jan 31 1946	13-Muluc	4
Sep 18 1945	8-Ik	4		Nov 25 1945	11-Ik	9		Feb 1 1946	1-Oc	5
Sep 19 1945	9-Men	5		Nov 26 1945	12-Akbal	1		Feb 2 1946	2-Chuen	6
Sep 20 1945	10-Cib	6		Nov 27 1945	13-Kan	2		Feb 3 1946	3-Eb	7
Sep 21 1945	11-Caban	7		Nov 28 1945	1-Chicchan	3		Feb 4 1946	4-Ben	8
Sep 22 1945	12-Etz'nab	8		Nov 29 1945	2-Cimi	4		Feb 5 1946	5-Ix	9
Sep 23 1945	13-Cauac	9		Nov 30 1945	3-Manik	5		Feb 6 1946	6-Men	1
Sep 24 1945	1-Ahau	1		Dec 1 1945	4-Lamat	6		Feb 7 1946	7-Cib	2
Sep 25 1945	2-Imix	2		Dec 2 1945	5-Muluc	7		Feb 8 1946	8-Caban	3
Sep 26 1945	3-Ik	3		Dec 3 1945	6-Oc	8		Feb 9 1946	9-Etz'nab	4
Sep 27 1945	4-Akbal	4		Dec 4 1945	7-Chuen	9		Feb 10 1946	10-Cauac	5
Sep 28 1945	5-Kan	5		Dec 5 1945	8-Eb	1		Feb 11 1946	11-Ahau	6
Sep 29 1945	6-Chicchan	6		Dec 6 1945	9-Ben	2		Feb 12 1946	12-Imix	7
Sep 30 1945	7-Cimi	7		Dec 7 1945	10-Ix	3		Feb 13 1946	13-Ik	8
Oct 1 1945	8-Manik	8		Dec 8 1945	11-Men	4		Feb 14 1946	1-Akbal	9
Oct 2 1945	9-Lamat	9		Dec 9 1945	12-Cib	5		Feb 15 1946	2-Kan	1
Oct 3 1945	10-Muluc	1		Dec 10 1945	13-Caban	6		Feb 16 1946	3-Chicchan	2
Oct 4 1945	11-Oc	2		Dec 11 1945	1-Etz'nab	7		Feb 17 1946	4-Cimi	3
Oct 5 1945	12-Chuen	3		Dec 12 1945	2-Cauac	8		Feb 18 1946	5-Manik	4
Oct 6 1945	13-Eb	4		Dec 13 1945	3-Ahau	9		Feb 19 1946	6-Lamat	5
Oct 7 1945	1-Ben	5		Dec 14 1945	4-Imix	1		Feb 20 1946	7-Muluc	6
Oct 8 1945	2-Ix	6		Dec 15 1945	5-Ik	2		Feb 21 1946	8-Oc	7
Oct 9 1945	3-Men	7		Dec 16 1945	6-Akbal	3		Feb 22 1946	9-Chuen	8
Oct 10 1945	4-Cib	8		Dec 17 1945	7-Kan	4		Feb 23 1946	10-Eb	9
Oct 11 1945	5-Caban	9		Dec 18 1945	8-Chicchan	5		Feb 24 1946	11-Ben	1
Oct 12 1945	6-Etz'nab	1		Dec 19 1945	9-Cimi	6		Feb 25 1946	12-Ix	2
Oct 13 1945	7-Cauac	2		Dec 20 1945	10-Manik	7		Feb 26 1946	13-Men	3
Oct 14 1945	8-Ahau	3		Dec 21 1945	11-Lamat	8		Feb 27 1946	1-Cib	4
Oct 15 1945	9-Imix	4		Dec 22 1945	12-Muluc	9		Feb 28 1946	2-Caban	5
Oct 16 1945	10-Ik	5		Dec 23 1945	13-Oc	1		Mar 1 1946	3-Etz'nab	6
Oct 17 1945	11-Akbal	6		Dec 24 1945	1-Chuen	2		Mar 2 1946	4-Cauac	7
Oct 18 1945	12-Kan	7		Dec 25 1945	2-Eb	3		Mar 3 1946	5-Ahau	8
Oct 19 1945	13-Chicchan	8		Dec 26 1945	3-Ben	4		Mar 4 1946	6-Imix	9

Date	Day-Sign	L	Date	Day-Sign	L	Date	Day-Sign	L
Mar 5 1946	7-Ik	1	May 12 1946	10-Oc	6	Jul 19 1946	13-Etz'nab	2
Mar 6 1946	8-Akbal	2	May 13 1946	11-Chuen	7	Jul 20 1946	**1-Cauac**	3
Mar 7 1946	9-Kan	3	May 14 1946	12-Eb	8	Jul 21 1946	2-Ahau	4
Mar 8 1946	10-Chicchan	4	May 15 1946	13-Ben	9	Jul 22 1946	*3-Imix*	5
Mar 9 1946	11-Cimi	5	May 16 1946	**1-Ix**	1	Jul 23 1946	4-Ik	6
Mar 10 1946	12-Manik	6	May 17 1946	2-Men	2	Jul 24 1946	5-Akbal	7
Mar 11 1946	13-Lamat	7	May 18 1946	3-Cib	3	Jul 25 1946	6-Kan	8
Mar 12 1946	**1-Muluc**	8	May 19 1946	4-Caban	4	Jul 26 1946	7-Chicchan	9
Mar 13 1946	2-Oc	9	May 20 1946	5-Etz'nab	5	Jul 27 1946	8-Cimi	1
Mar 14 1946	3-Chuen	1	May 21 1946	6-Cauac	6	Jul 28 1946	9-Manik	2
Mar 15 1946	4-Eb	2	May 22 1946	7-Ahau	7	Jul 29 1946	10-Lamat	3
Mar 16 1946	5-Ben	3	May 23 1946	*8-Imix*	8	Jul 30 1946	11-Muluc	4
Mar 17 1946	6-Ix	4	May 24 1946	9-Ik	9	Jul 31 1946	12-Oc	5
Mar 18 1946	7-Men	5	May 25 1946	10-Akbal	1	Aug 1 1946	13-Chuen	6
Mar 19 1946	8-Cib	6	May 26 1946	11-Kan	2	Aug 2 1946	**1-Eb**	7
Mar 20 1946	9-Caban	7	May 27 1946	12-Chicchan	3	Aug 3 1946	2-Ben	8
Mar 21 1946	10-Etz'nab	8	May 28 1946	13-Cimi	4	Aug 4 1946	3-Ix	9
Mar 22 1946	11-Cauac	9	May 29 1946	**1-Manik**	5	Aug 5 1946	4-Men	1
Mar 23 1946	12-Ahau	1	May 30 1946	2-Lamat	6	Aug 6 1946	5-Cib	2
Mar 24 1946	*13-Imix*	2	May 31 1946	3-Muluc	7	Aug 7 1946	6-Caban	3
Mar 25 1946	**1-Ik**	3	Jun 1 1946	4-Oc	8	Aug 8 1946	7-Etz'nab	4
Mar 26 1946	2-Akbal	4	Jun 2 1946	5-Chuen	9	Aug 9 1946	8-Cauac	5
Mar 27 1946	3-Kan	5	Jun 3 1946	6-Eb	1	Aug 10 1946	9-Ahau	6
Mar 28 1946	4-Chicchan	6	Jun 4 1946	7-Ben	2	Aug 11 1946	*10-Imix*	7
Mar 29 1946	5-Cimi	7	Jun 5 1946	8-Ix	3	Aug 12 1946	11-Ik	8
Mar 30 1946	6-Manik	8	Jun 6 1946	9-Men	4	Aug 13 1946	12-Akbal	9
Mar 31 1946	7-Lamat	9	Jun 7 1946	10-Cib	5	Aug 14 1946	13-Kan	1
Apr 1 1946	8-Muluc	1	Jun 8 1946	11-Caban	6	Aug 15 1946	**1-Chicchan**	2
Apr 2 1946	9-Oc	2	Jun 9 1946	12-Etz'nab	7	Aug 16 1946	2-Cimi	3
Apr 3 1946	10-Chuen	3	Jun 10 1946	13-Cauac	8	Aug 17 1946	3-Manik	4
Apr 4 1946	11-Eb	4	Jun 11 1946	**1-Ahau**	9	Aug 18 1946	4-Lamat	5
Apr 5 1946	12-Ben	5	Jun 12 1946	*2-Imix*	1	Aug 19 1946	5-Muluc	6
Apr 6 1946	13-Ix	6	Jun 13 1946	3-Ik	2	Aug 20 1946	6-Oc	7
Apr 7 1946	**1-Men**	7	Jun 14 1946	4-Akbal	3	Aug 21 1946	7-Chuen	8
Apr 8 1946	2-Cib	8	Jun 15 1946	5-Kan	4	Aug 22 1946	8-Eb	9
Apr 9 1946	3-Caban	9	Jun 16 1946	6-Chicchan	5	Aug 23 1946	9-Ben	1
Apr 10 1946	4-Etz'nab	1	Jun 17 1946	7-Cimi	6	Aug 24 1946	10-Ix	2
Apr 11 1946	5-Cauac	2	Jun 18 1946	8-Manik	7	Aug 25 1946	11-Men	3
Apr 12 1946	6-Ahau	3	Jun 19 1946	9-Lamat	8	Aug 26 1946	12-Cib	4
Apr 13 1946	*7-Imix*	4	Jun 20 1946	10-Muluc	9	Aug 27 1946	13-Caban	5
Apr 14 1946	8-Ik	5	Jun 21 1946	11-Oc	1	Aug 28 1946	**1-Etz'nab**	6
Apr 15 1946	9-Akbal	6	Jun 22 1946	12-Chuen	2	Aug 29 1946	2-Cauac	7
Apr 16 1946	10-Kan	7	Jun 23 1946	13-Eb	3	Aug 30 1946	3-Ahau	8
Apr 17 1946	11-Chicchan	8	Jun 24 1946	**1-Ben**	4	Aug 31 1946	*4-Imix*	9
Apr 18 1946	12-Cimi	9	Jun 25 1946	2-Ix	5	Sep 1 1946	5-Ik	1
Apr 19 1946	13-Manik	1	Jun 26 1946	3-Men	6	Sep 2 1946	6-Akbal	2
Apr 20 1946	**1-Lamat**	2	Jun 27 1946	4-Cib	7	Sep 3 1946	7-Kan	3
Apr 21 1946	2-Muluc	3	Jun 28 1946	5-Caban	8	Sep 4 1946	8-Chicchan	4
Apr 22 1946	3-Oc	4	Jun 29 1946	6-Etz'nab	9	Sep 5 1946	9-Cimi	5
Apr 23 1946	4-Chuen	5	Jun 30 1946	7-Cauac	1	Sep 6 1946	10-Manik	6
Apr 24 1946	5-Eb	6	Jul 1 1946	8-Ahau	2	Sep 7 1946	11-Lamat	7
Apr 25 1946	6-Ben	7	Jul 2 1946	*9-Imix*	3	Sep 8 1946	12-Muluc	8
Apr 26 1946	7-Ix	8	Jul 3 1946	10-Ik	4	Sep 9 1946	13-Oc	9
Apr 27 1946	8-Men	9	Jul 4 1946	11-Akbal	5	Sep 10 1946	**1-Chuen**	1
Apr 28 1946	9-Cib	1	Jul 5 1946	12-Kan	6	Sep 11 1946	2-Eb	2
Apr 29 1946	10-Caban	2	Jul 6 1946	13-Chicchan	7	Sep 12 1946	3-Ben	3
Apr 30 1946	11-Etz'nab	3	Jul 7 1946	**1-Cimi**	8	Sep 13 1946	4-Ix	4
May 1 1946	12-Cauac	4	Jul 8 1946	2-Manik	9	Sep 14 1946	5-Men	5
May 2 1946	13-Ahau	5	Jul 9 1946	3-Lamat	1	Sep 15 1946	6-Cib	6
May 3 1946	**1-Imix**	6	Jul 10 1946	4-Muluc	2	Sep 16 1946	7-Caban	7
May 4 1946	2-Ik	7	Jul 11 1946	5-Oc	3	Sep 17 1946	8-Etz'nab	8
May 5 1946	3-Akbal	8	Jul 12 1946	6-Chuen	4	Sep 18 1946	9-Cauac	9
May 6 1946	4-Kan	9	Jul 13 1946	7-Eb	5	Sep 19 1946	10-Ahau	1
May 7 1946	5-Chicchan	1	Jul 14 1946	8-Ben	6	Sep 20 1946	*11-Imix*	2
May 8 1946	6-Cimi	2	Jul 15 1946	9-Ix	7	Sep 21 1946	12-Ik	3
May 9 1946	7-Manik	3	Jul 16 1946	10-Men	8	Sep 22 1946	13-Akbal	4
May 10 1946	8-Lamat	4	Jul 17 1946	11-Cib	9	Sep 23 1946	**1-Kan**	5
May 11 1946	9-Muluc	5	Jul 18 1946	12-Caban	1	Sep 24 1946	2-Chicchan	6

Date	Day-Sign	L	Date	Day-Sign	L	Date	Day-Sign	L
Sep 25 1946	3-Cimi	7	Dec 2 1946	6-Ix	3	Feb 8 1947	9-Ik	8
Sep 26 1946	4-Manik	8	Dec 3 1946	7-Men	4	Feb 9 1947	10-Akbal	9
Sep 27 1946	5-Lamat	9	Dec 4 1946	8-Cib	5	Feb 10 1947	11-Kan	1
Sep 28 1946	6-Muluc	1	Dec 5 1946	9-Caban	6	Feb 11 1947	12-Chicchan	2
Sep 29 1946	7-Oc	2	Dec 6 1946	10-Etz'nab	7	Feb 12 1947	13-Cimi	3
Sep 30 1946	8-Chuen	3	Dec 7 1946	11-Cauac	8	Feb 13 1947	1-Manik	4
Oct 1 1946	9-Eb	4	Dec 8 1946	12-Ahau	9	Feb 14 1947	2-Lamat	5
Oct 2 1946	10-Ben	5	Dec 9 1946	13-Imix	1	Feb 15 1947	3-Muluc	6
Oct 3 1946	11-Ix	6	Dec 10 1946	1-Ik	2	Feb 16 1947	4-Oc	7
Oct 4 1946	12-Men	7	Dec 11 1946	2-Akbal	3	Feb 17 1947	5-Chuen	8
Oct 5 1946	13-Cib	8	Dec 12 1946	3-Kan	4	Feb 18 1947	6-Eb	9
Oct 6 1946	1-Caban	9	Dec 13 1946	4-Chicchan	5	Feb 19 1947	7-Ben	1
Oct 7 1946	2-Etz'nab	1	Dec 14 1946	5-Cimi	6	Feb 20 1947	8-Ix	2
Oct 8 1946	3-Cauac	2	Dec 15 1946	6-Manik	7	Feb 21 1947	9-Men	3
Oct 9 1946	4-Ahau	3	Dec 16 1946	7-Lamat	8	Feb 22 1947	10-Cib	4
Oct 10 1946	5-Imix	4	Dec 17 1946	8-Muluc	9	Feb 23 1947	11-Caban	5
Oct 11 1946	6-Ik	5	Dec 18 1946	9-Oc	1	Feb 24 1947	12-Etz'nab	6
Oct 12 1946	7-Akbal	6	Dec 19 1946	10-Chuen	2	Feb 25 1947	13-Cauac	7
Oct 13 1946	8-Kan	7	Dec 20 1946	11-Eb	3	Feb 26 1947	1-Ahau	8
Oct 14 1946	9-Chicchan	8	Dec 21 1946	12-Ben	4	Feb 27 1947	2-Imix	9
Oct 15 1946	10-Cimi	9	Dec 22 1946	13-Ix	5	Feb 28 1947	3-Ik	1
Oct 16 1946	11-Manik	1	Dec 23 1946	1-Men	6	Mar 1 1947	4-Akbal	2
Oct 17 1946	12-Lamat	2	Dec 24 1946	2-Cib	7	Mar 2 1947	5-Kan	3
Oct 18 1946	13-Muluc	3	Dec 25 1946	3-Caban	8	Mar 3 1947	6-Chicchan	4
Oct 19 1946	1-Oc	4	Dec 26 1946	4-Etz'nab	9	Mar 4 1947	7-Cimi	5
Oct 20 1946	2-Chuen	5	Dec 27 1946	5-Cauac	1	Mar 5 1947	8-Manik	6
Oct 21 1946	3-Eb	6	Dec 28 1946	6-Ahau	2	Mar 6 1947	9-Lamat	7
Oct 22 1946	4-Ben	7	Dec 29 1946	7-Imix	3	Mar 7 1947	10-Muluc	8
Oct 23 1946	5-Ix	8	Dec 30 1946	8-Ik	4	Mar 8 1947	11-Oc	9
Oct 24 1946	6-Men	9	Dec 31 1946	9-Akbal	5	Mar 9 1947	12-Chuen	1
Oct 25 1946	7-Cib	1	Jan 1 1947	10-Kan	6	Mar 10 1947	13-Eb	2
Oct 26 1946	8-Caban	2	Jan 2 1947	11-Chicchan	7	Mar 11 1947	1-Ben	3
Oct 27 1946	9-Etz'nab	3	Jan 3 1947	12-Cimi	8	Mar 12 1947	2-Ix	4
Oct 28 1946	10-Cauac	4	Jan 4 1947	13-Manik	9	Mar 13 1947	3-Men	5
Oct 29 1946	11-Ahau	5	Jan 5 1947	1-Lamat	1	Mar 14 1947	4-Cib	6
Oct 30 1946	12-Imix	6	Jan 6 1947	2-Muluc	2	Mar 15 1947	5-Caban	7
Oct 31 1946	13-Ik	7	Jan 7 1947	3-Oc	3	Mar 16 1947	6-Etz'nab	8
Nov 1 1946	1-Akbal	8	Jan 8 1947	4-Chuen	4	Mar 17 1947	7-Cauac	9
Nov 2 1946	2-Kan	9	Jan 9 1947	5-Eb	5	Mar 18 1947	8-Ahau	1
Nov 3 1946	3-Chicchan	1	Jan 10 1947	6-Ben	6	Mar 19 1947	9-Imix	2
Nov 4 1946	4-Cimi	2	Jan 11 1947	7-Ix	7	Mar 20 1947	10-Ik	3
Nov 5 1946	5-Manik	3	Jan 12 1947	8-Men	8	Mar 21 1947	11-Akbal	4
Nov 6 1946	6-Lamat	4	Jan 13 1947	9-Cib	9	Mar 22 1947	12-Kan	5
Nov 7 1946	7-Muluc	5	Jan 14 1947	10-Caban	1	Mar 23 1947	13-Chicchan	6
Nov 8 1946	8-Oc	6	Jan 15 1947	11-Etz'nab	2	Mar 24 1947	1-Cimi	7
Nov 9 1946	9-Chuen	7	Jan 16 1947	12-Cauac	3	Mar 25 1947	2-Manik	8
Nov 10 1946	10-Eb	8	Jan 17 1947	13-Ahau	4	Mar 26 1947	3-Lamat	9
Nov 11 1946	11-Ben	9	Jan 18 1947	1-Imix	5	Mar 27 1947	4-Muluc	1
Nov 12 1946	12-Ix	1	Jan 19 1947	2-Ik	6	Mar 28 1947	5-Oc	2
Nov 13 1946	13-Men	2	Jan 20 1947	3-Akbal	7	Mar 29 1947	6-Chuen	3
Nov 14 1946	1-Cib	3	Jan 21 1947	4-Kan	8	Mar 30 1947	7-Eb	4
Nov 15 1946	2-Caban	4	Jan 22 1947	5-Chicchan	9	Mar 31 1947	8-Ben	5
Nov 16 1946	3-Etz'nab	5	Jan 23 1947	6-Cimi	1	Apr 1 1947	9-Ix	6
Nov 17 1946	4-Cauac	6	Jan 24 1947	7-Manik	2	Apr 2 1947	10-Men	7
Nov 18 1946	5-Ahau	7	Jan 25 1947	8-Lamat	3	Apr 3 1947	11-Cib	8
Nov 19 1946	6-Imix	8	Jan 26 1947	9-Muluc	4	Apr 4 1947	12-Caban	9
Nov 20 1946	7-Ik	9	Jan 27 1947	10-Oc	5	Apr 5 1947	13-Etz'nab	1
Nov 21 1946	8-Akbal	1	Jan 28 1947	11-Chuen	6	Apr 6 1947	1-Cauac	2
Nov 22 1946	9-Kan	2	Jan 29 1947	12-Eb	7	Apr 7 1947	2-Ahau	3
Nov 23 1946	10-Chicchan	3	Jan 30 1947	13-Ben	8	Apr 8 1947	3-Imix	4
Nov 24 1946	11-Cimi	4	Jan 31 1947	1-Ix	9	Apr 9 1947	4-Ik	5
Nov 25 1946	12-Manik	5	Feb 1 1947	2-Men	1	Apr 10 1947	5-Akbal	6
Nov 26 1946	13-Lamat	6	Feb 2 1947	3-Cib	2	Apr 11 1947	6-Kan	7
Nov 27 1946	1-Muluc	7	Feb 3 1947	4-Caban	3	Apr 12 1947	7-Chicchan	8
Nov 28 1946	2-Oc	8	Feb 4 1947	5-Etz'nab	4	Apr 13 1947	8-Cimi	9
Nov 29 1946	3-Chuen	9	Feb 5 1947	6-Cauac	5	Apr 14 1947	9-Manik	1
Nov 30 1946	4-Eb	1	Feb 6 1947	7-Ahau	6	Apr 15 1947	10-Lamat	2
Dec 1 1946	5-Ben	2	Feb 7 1947	8-Imix	7	Apr 16 1947	11-Muluc	3

Date	Day-Sign	L		Date	Day-Sign	L		Date	Day-Sign	L
Apr 17 1947	12-Oc	4		Jun 24 1947	2-Etz'nab	9		Aug 31 1947	5-Cimi	5
Apr 18 1947	13-Chuen	5		Jun 25 1947	3-Cauac	1		Sep 1 1947	6-Manik	6
Apr 19 1947	**1-Eb**	6		Jun 26 1947	4-Ahau	2		Sep 2 1947	7-Lamat	7
Apr 20 1947	2-Ben	7		Jun 27 1947	5-*Imix*	3		Sep 3 1947	8-Muluc	8
Apr 21 1947	3-Ix	8		Jun 28 1947	6-Ik	4		Sep 4 1947	9-Oc	9
Apr 22 1947	4-Men	9		Jun 29 1947	7-Akbal	5		Sep 5 1947	10-Chuen	1
Apr 23 1947	5-Cib	1		Jun 30 1947	8-Kan	6		Sep 6 1947	11-Eb	2
Apr 24 1947	6-Caban	2		Jul 1 1947	9-Chicchan	7		Sep 7 1947	12-Ben	3
Apr 25 1947	7-Etz'nab	3		Jul 2 1947	10-Cimi	8		Sep 8 1947	13-Ix	4
Apr 26 1947	8-Cauac	4		Jul 3 1947	11-Manik	9		Sep 9 1947	**1-Men**	5
Apr 27 1947	9-Ahau	5		Jul 4 1947	12-Lamat	1		Sep 10 1947	2-Cib	6
Apr 28 1947	10-*Imix*	6		Jul 5 1947	13-Muluc	2		Sep 11 1947	3-Caban	7
Apr 29 1947	11-Ik	7		Jul 6 1947	**1-Oc**	3		Sep 12 1947	4-Etz'nab	8
Apr 30 1947	12-Akbal	8		Jul 7 1947	2-Chuen	4		Sep 13 1947	5-Cauac	9
May 1 1947	13-Kan	9		Jul 8 1947	3-Eb	5		Sep 14 1947	6-Ahau	1
May 2 1947	**1-Chicchan**	1		Jul 9 1947	4-Ben	6		Sep 15 1947	7-*Imix*	2
May 3 1947	2-Cimi	2		Jul 10 1947	5-Ix	7		Sep 16 1947	8-Ik	3
May 4 1947	3-Manik	3		Jul 11 1947	6-Men	8		Sep 17 1947	9-Akbal	4
May 5 1947	4-Lamat	4		Jul 12 1947	7-Cib	9		Sep 18 1947	10-Kan	5
May 6 1947	5-Muluc	5		Jul 13 1947	8-Caban	1		Sep 19 1947	11-Chicchan	6
May 7 1947	6-Oc	6		Jul 14 1947	9-Etz'nab	2		Sep 20 1947	12-Cimi	7
May 8 1947	7-Chuen	7		Jul 15 1947	10-Cauac	3		Sep 21 1947	13-Manik	8
May 9 1947	8-Eb	8		Jul 16 1947	11-Ahau	4		Sep 22 1947	**1-Lamat**	9
May 10 1947	9-Ben	9		Jul 17 1947	12-*Imix*	5		Sep 23 1947	2-Muluc	1
May 11 1947	10-Ix	1		Jul 18 1947	13-Ik	6		Sep 24 1947	3-Oc	2
May 12 1947	11-Men	2		Jul 19 1947	**1-Akbal**	7		Sep 25 1947	4-Chuen	3
May 13 1947	12-Cib	3		Jul 20 1947	2-Kan	8		Sep 26 1947	5-Eb	4
May 14 1947	13-Caban	4		Jul 21 1947	3-Chicchan	9		Sep 27 1947	6-Ben	5
May 15 1947	**1-Etz'nab**	5		Jul 22 1947	4-Cimi	1		Sep 28 1947	7-Ix	6
May 16 1947	2-Cauac	6		Jul 23 1947	5-Manik	2		Sep 29 1947	8-Men	7
May 17 1947	3-Ahau	7		Jul 24 1947	6-Lamat	3		Sep 30 1947	9-Cib	8
May 18 1947	4-*Imix*	8		Jul 25 1947	7-Muluc	4		Oct 1 1947	10-Caban	9
May 19 1947	5-Ik	9		Jul 26 1947	8-Oc	5		Oct 2 1947	11-Etz'nab	1
May 20 1947	6-Akbal	1		Jul 27 1947	9-Chuen	6		Oct 3 1947	12-Cauac	2
May 21 1947	7-Kan	2		Jul 28 1947	10-Eb	7		Oct 4 1947	13-Ahau	3
May 22 1947	8-Chicchan	3		Jul 29 1947	11-Ben	8		Oct 5 1947	**1-Imix**	4
May 23 1947	9-Cimi	4		Jul 30 1947	12-Ix	9		Oct 6 1947	2-Ik	5
May 24 1947	10-Manik	5		Jul 31 1947	13-Men	1		Oct 7 1947	3-Akbal	6
May 25 1947	11-Lamat	6		Aug 1 1947	**1-Cib**	2		Oct 8 1947	4-Kan	7
May 26 1947	12-Muluc	7		Aug 2 1947	2-Caban	3		Oct 9 1947	5-Chicchan	8
May 27 1947	13-Oc	8		Aug 3 1947	3-Etz'nab	4		Oct 10 1947	6-Cimi	9
May 28 1947	**1-Chuen**	9		Aug 4 1947	4-Cauac	5		Oct 11 1947	7-Manik	1
May 29 1947	2-Eb	1		Aug 5 1947	5-Ahau	6		Oct 12 1947	8-Lamat	2
May 30 1947	3-Ben	2		Aug 6 1947	6-*Imix*	7		Oct 13 1947	9-Muluc	3
May 31 1947	4-Ix	3		Aug 7 1947	7-Ik	8		Oct 14 1947	10-Oc	4
Jun 1 1947	5-Men	4		Aug 8 1947	8-Akbal	9		Oct 15 1947	11-Chuen	5
Jun 2 1947	6-Cib	5		Aug 9 1947	9-Kan	1		Oct 16 1947	12-Eb	6
Jun 3 1947	7-Caban	6		Aug 10 1947	10-Chicchan	2		Oct 17 1947	13-Ben	7
Jun 4 1947	8-Etz'nab	7		Aug 11 1947	11-Cimi	3		Oct 18 1947	**1-Ix**	8
Jun 5 1947	9-Cauac	8		Aug 12 1947	12-Manik	4		Oct 19 1947	2-Men	9
Jun 6 1947	10-Ahau	9		Aug 13 1947	13-Lamat	5		Oct 20 1947	3-Cib	1
Jun 7 1947	11-*Imix*	1		Aug 14 1947	**1-Muluc**	6		Oct 21 1947	4-Caban	2
Jun 8 1947	12-Ik	2		Aug 15 1947	2-Oc	7		Oct 22 1947	5-Etz'nab	3
Jun 9 1947	13-Akbal	3		Aug 16 1947	3-Chuen	8		Oct 23 1947	6-Cauac	4
Jun 10 1947	**1-Kan**	4		Aug 17 1947	4-Eb	9		Oct 24 1947	7-Ahau	5
Jun 11 1947	2-Chicchan	5		Aug 18 1947	5-Ben	1		Oct 25 1947	8-*Imix*	6
Jun 12 1947	3-Cimi	6		Aug 19 1947	6-Ix	2		Oct 26 1947	9-Ik	7
Jun 13 1947	4-Manik	7		Aug 20 1947	7-Men	3		Oct 27 1947	10-Akbal	8
Jun 14 1947	5-Lamat	8		Aug 21 1947	8-Cib	4		Oct 28 1947	11-Kan	9
Jun 15 1947	6-Muluc	9		Aug 22 1947	9-Caban	5		Oct 29 1947	12-Chicchan	1
Jun 16 1947	7-Oc	1		Aug 23 1947	10-Etz'nab	6		Oct 30 1947	13-Cimi	2
Jun 17 1947	8-Chuen	2		Aug 24 1947	11-Cauac	7		Oct 31 1947	**1-Manik**	3
Jun 18 1947	9-Eb	3		Aug 25 1947	12-Ahau	8		Nov 1 1947	2-Lamat	4
Jun 19 1947	10-Ben	4		Aug 26 1947	13-*Imix*	9		Nov 2 1947	3-Muluc	5
Jun 20 1947	11-Ix	5		Aug 27 1947	**1-Ik**	1		Nov 3 1947	4-Oc	6
Jun 21 1947	12-Men	6		Aug 28 1947	2-Akbal	2		Nov 4 1947	5-Chuen	7
Jun 22 1947	13-Cib	7		Aug 29 1947	3-Kan	3		Nov 5 1947	6-Eb	8
Jun 23 1947	**1-Caban**	8		Aug 30 1947	4-Chicchan	4		Nov 6 1947	7-Ben	9

Date	Day-Sign	L	Date	Day-Sign	L	Date	Day-Sign	L
Nov 7 1947	8-Ix	1	Jan 14 1948	11-Ik	6	Mar 22 1948	1-Oc	2
Nov 8 1947	9-Men	2	Jan 15 1948	12-Akbal	7	Mar 23 1948	2-Chuen	3
Nov 9 1947	10-Cib	3	Jan 16 1948	13-Kan	8	Mar 24 1948	3-Eb	4
Nov 10 1947	11-Caban	4	Jan 17 1948	1-Chicchan	9	Mar 25 1948	4-Ben	5
Nov 11 1947	12-Etz'nab	5	Jan 18 1948	2-Cimi	1	Mar 26 1948	5-Ix	6
Nov 12 1947	13-Cauac	6	Jan 19 1948	3-Manik	2	Mar 27 1948	6-Men	7
Nov 13 1947	1-Ahau	7	Jan 20 1948	4-Lamat	3	Mar 28 1948	7-Cib	8
Nov 14 1947	2-Imix	8	Jan 21 1948	5-Muluc	4	Mar 29 1948	8-Caban	9
Nov 15 1947	3-Ik	9	Jan 22 1948	6-Oc	5	Mar 30 1948	9-Etz'nab	1
Nov 16 1947	4-Akbal	1	Jan 23 1948	7-Chuen	6	Mar 31 1948	10-Cauac	2
Nov 17 1947	5-Kan	2	Jan 24 1948	8-Eb	7	Apr 1 1948	11-Ahau	3
Nov 18 1947	6-Chicchan	3	Jan 25 1948	9-Ben	8	Apr 2 1948	12-Imix	4
Nov 19 1947	7-Cimi	4	Jan 26 1948	10-Ix	9	Apr 3 1948	13-Ik	5
Nov 20 1947	8-Manik	5	Jan 27 1948	11-Men	1	Apr 4 1948	1-Akbal	6
Nov 21 1947	9-Lamat	6	Jan 28 1948	12-Cib	2	Apr 5 1948	2-Kan	7
Nov 22 1947	10-Muluc	7	Jan 29 1948	13-Caban	3	Apr 6 1948	3-Chicchan	8
Nov 23 1947	11-Oc	8	Jan 30 1948	1-Etz'nab	4	Apr 7 1948	4-Cimi	9
Nov 24 1947	12-Chuen	9	Jan 31 1948	2-Cauac	5	Apr 8 1948	5-Manik	1
Nov 25 1947	13-Eb	1	Feb 1 1948	3-Ahau	6	Apr 9 1948	6-Lamat	2
Nov 26 1947	1-Ben	2	Feb 2 1948	4-Imix	7	Apr 10 1948	7-Muluc	3
Nov 27 1947	2-Ix	3	Feb 3 1948	5-Ik	8	Apr 11 1948	8-Oc	4
Nov 28 1947	3-Men	4	Feb 4 1948	6-Akbal	9	Apr 12 1948	9-Chuen	5
Nov 29 1947	4-Cib	5	Feb 5 1948	7-Kan	1	Apr 13 1948	10-Eb	6
Nov 30 1947	5-Caban	6	Feb 6 1948	8-Chicchan	2	Apr 14 1948	11-Ben	7
Dec 1 1947	6-Etz'nab	7	Feb 7 1948	9-Cimi	3	Apr 15 1948	12-Ix	8
Dec 2 1947	7-Cauac	8	Feb 8 1948	10-Manik	4	Apr 16 1948	13-Men	9
Dec 3 1947	8-Ahau	9	Feb 9 1948	11-Lamat	5	Apr 17 1948	1-Cib	1
Dec 4 1947	9-Imix	1	Feb 10 1948	12-Muluc	6	Apr 18 1948	2-Caban	2
Dec 5 1947	10-Ik	2	Feb 11 1948	13-Oc	7	Apr 19 1948	3-Etz'nab	3
Dec 6 1947	11-Akbal	3	Feb 12 1948	1-Chuen	8	Apr 20 1948	4-Cauac	4
Dec 7 1947	12-Kan	4	Feb 13 1948	2-Eb	9	Apr 21 1948	5-Ahau	5
Dec 8 1947	13-Chicchan	5	Feb 14 1948	3-Ben	1	Apr 22 1948	6-Imix	6
Dec 9 1947	1-Cimi	6	Feb 15 1948	4-Ix	2	Apr 23 1948	7-Ik	7
Dec 10 1947	2-Manik	7	Feb 16 1948	5-Men	3	Apr 24 1948	8-Akbal	8
Dec 11 1947	3-Lamat	8	Feb 17 1948	6-Cib	4	Apr 25 1948	9-Kan	9
Dec 12 1947	4-Muluc	9	Feb 18 1948	7-Caban	5	Apr 26 1948	10-Chicchan	1
Dec 13 1947	5-Oc	1	Feb 19 1948	8-Etz'nab	6	Apr 27 1948	11-Cimi	2
Dec 14 1947	6-Chuen	2	Feb 20 1948	9-Cauac	7	Apr 28 1948	12-Manik	3
Dec 15 1947	7-Eb	3	Feb 21 1948	10-Ahau	8	Apr 29 1948	13-Lamat	4
Dec 16 1947	8-Ben	4	Feb 22 1948	11-Imix	9	Apr 30 1948	1-Muluc	5
Dec 17 1947	9-Ix	5	Feb 23 1948	12-Ik	1	May 1 1948	2-Oc	6
Dec 18 1947	10-Men	6	Feb 24 1948	13-Akbal	2	May 2 1948	3-Chuen	7
Dec 19 1947	11-Cib	7	Feb 25 1948	1-Kan	3	May 3 1948	4-Eb	8
Dec 20 1947	12-Caban	8	Feb 26 1948	2-Chicchan	4	May 4 1948	5-Ben	9
Dec 21 1947	13-Etz'nab	9	Feb 27 1948	3-Cimi	5	May 5 1948	6-Ix	1
Dec 22 1947	1-Cauac	1	Feb 28 1948	4-Manik	6	May 6 1948	7-Men	2
Dec 23 1947	2-Ahau	2	Feb 29 1948	5-Lamat	7	May 7 1948	8-Cib	3
Dec 24 1947	3-Imix	3	Mar 1 1948	6-Muluc	8	May 8 1948	9-Caban	4
Dec 25 1947	4-Ik	4	Mar 2 1948	7-Oc	9	May 9 1948	10-Etz'nab	5
Dec 26 1947	5-Akbal	5	Mar 3 1948	8-Chuen	1	May 10 1948	11-Cauac	6
Dec 27 1947	6-Kan	6	Mar 4 1948	9-Eb	2	May 11 1948	12-Ahau	7
Dec 28 1947	7-Chicchan	7	Mar 5 1948	10-Ben	3	May 12 1948	13-Imix	8
Dec 29 1947	8-Cimi	8	Mar 6 1948	11-Ix	4	May 13 1948	1-Ik	9
Dec 30 1947	9-Manik	9	Mar 7 1948	12-Men	5	May 14 1948	2-Akbal	1
Dec 31 1947	10-Lamat	1	Mar 8 1948	13-Cib	6	May 15 1948	3-Kan	2
Jan 1 1948	11-Muluc	2	Mar 9 1948	1-Caban	7	May 16 1948	4-Chicchan	3
Jan 2 1948	12-Oc	3	Mar 10 1948	2-Etz'nab	8	May 17 1948	5-Cimi	4
Jan 3 1948	13-Chuen	4	Mar 11 1948	3-Cauac	9	May 18 1948	6-Manik	5
Jan 4 1948	1-Eb	5	Mar 12 1948	4-Ahau	1	May 19 1948	7-Lamat	6
Jan 5 1948	2-Ben	6	Mar 13 1948	5-Imix	2	May 20 1948	8-Muluc	7
Jan 6 1948	3-Ix	7	Mar 14 1948	6-Ik	3	May 21 1948	9-Oc	8
Jan 7 1948	4-Men	8	Mar 15 1948	7-Akbal	4	May 22 1948	10-Chuen	9
Jan 8 1948	5-Cib	9	Mar 16 1948	8-Kan	5	May 23 1948	11-Eb	1
Jan 9 1948	6-Caban	1	Mar 17 1948	9-Chicchan	6	May 24 1948	12-Ben	2
Jan 10 1948	7-Etz'nab	2	Mar 18 1948	10-Cimi	7	May 25 1948	13-Ix	3
Jan 11 1948	8-Cauac	3	Mar 19 1948	11-Manik	8	May 26 1948	1-Men	4
Jan 12 1948	9-Ahau	4	Mar 20 1948	12-Lamat	9	May 27 1948	2-Cib	5
Jan 13 1948	10-Imix	5	Mar 21 1948	13-Muluc	1	May 28 1948	3-Caban	6

Date	Day-Sign	L	Date	Day-Sign	L	Date	Day-Sign	L
May 29 1948	4-Etz'nab	7	Aug 5 1948	7-Cimi	3	Oct 12 1948	10-Ix	8
May 30 1948	5-Cauac	8	Aug 6 1948	8-Manik	4	Oct 13 1948	11-Men	9
May 31 1948	6-Ahau	9	Aug 7 1948	9-Lamat	5	Oct 14 1948	12-Cib	1
Jun 1 1948	7-*Imix*	1	Aug 8 1948	10-Muluc	6	Oct 15 1948	13-Caban	2
Jun 2 1948	8-Ik	2	Aug 9 1948	11-Oc	7	Oct 16 1948	**1-Etz'nab**	3
Jun 3 1948	9-Akbal	3	Aug 10 1948	12-Chuen	8	Oct 17 1948	2-Cauac	4
Jun 4 1948	10-Kan	4	Aug 11 1948	13-Eb	9	Oct 18 1948	3-Ahau	5
Jun 5 1948	11-Chicchan	5	Aug 12 1948	**1-Ben**	1	Oct 19 1948	*4-Imix*	6
Jun 6 1948	12-Cimi	6	Aug 13 1948	2-Ix	2	Oct 20 1948	5-Ik	7
Jun 7 1948	13-Manik	7	Aug 14 1948	3-Men	3	Oct 21 1948	6-Akbal	8
Jun 8 1948	**1-Lamat**	8	Aug 15 1948	4-Cib	4	Oct 22 1948	7-Kan	9
Jun 9 1948	2-Muluc	9	Aug 16 1948	5-Caban	5	Oct 23 1948	8-Chicchan	1
Jun 10 1948	3-Oc	1	Aug 17 1948	6-Etz'nab	6	Oct 24 1948	9-Cimi	2
Jun 11 1948	4-Chuen	2	Aug 18 1948	7-Cauac	7	Oct 25 1948	10-Manik	3
Jun 12 1948	5-Eb	3	Aug 19 1948	8-Ahau	8	Oct 26 1948	11-Lamat	4
Jun 13 1948	6-Ben	4	Aug 20 1948	*9-Imix*	9	Oct 27 1948	12-Muluc	5
Jun 14 1948	7-Ix	5	Aug 21 1948	10-Ik	1	Oct 28 1948	13-Oc	6
Jun 15 1948	8-Men	6	Aug 22 1948	11-Akbal	2	Oct 29 1948	**1-Chuen**	7
Jun 16 1948	9-Cib	7	Aug 23 1948	12-Kan	3	Oct 30 1948	2-Eb	8
Jun 17 1948	10-Caban	8	Aug 24 1948	13-Chicchan	4	Oct 31 1948	3-Ben	9
Jun 18 1948	11-Etz'nab	9	Aug 25 1948	**1-Cimi**	5	Nov 1 1948	4-Ix	1
Jun 19 1948	12-Cauac	1	Aug 26 1948	2-Manik	6	Nov 2 1948	5-Men	2
Jun 20 1948	13-Ahau	2	Aug 27 1948	3-Lamat	7	Nov 3 1948	6-Cib	3
Jun 21 1948	**1-Imix**	3	Aug 28 1948	4-Muluc	8	Nov 4 1948	7-Caban	4
Jun 22 1948	2-Ik	4	Aug 29 1948	5-Oc	9	Nov 5 1948	8-Etz'nab	5
Jun 23 1948	3-Akbal	5	Aug 30 1948	6-Chuen	1	Nov 6 1948	9-Cauac	6
Jun 24 1948	4-Kan	6	Aug 31 1948	7-Eb	2	Nov 7 1948	10-Ahau	7
Jun 25 1948	5-Chicchan	7	Sep 1 1948	8-Ben	3	Nov 8 1948	*11-Imix*	8
Jun 26 1948	6-Cimi	8	Sep 2 1948	9-Ix	4	Nov 9 1948	12-Ik	9
Jun 27 1948	7-Manik	9	Sep 3 1948	10-Men	5	Nov 10 1948	13-Akbal	1
Jun 28 1948	8-Lamat	1	Sep 4 1948	11-Cib	6	Nov 11 1948	**1-Kan**	2
Jun 29 1948	9-Muluc	2	Sep 5 1948	12-Caban	7	Nov 12 1948	2-Chicchan	3
Jun 30 1948	10-Oc	3	Sep 6 1948	13-Etz'nab	8	Nov 13 1948	3-Cimi	4
Jul 1 1948	11-Chuen	4	Sep 7 1948	**1-Cauac**	9	Nov 14 1948	4-Manik	5
Jul 2 1948	12-Eb	5	Sep 8 1948	2-Ahau	1	Nov 15 1948	5-Lamat	6
Jul 3 1948	13-Ben	6	Sep 9 1948	*3-Imix*	2	Nov 16 1948	6-Muluc	7
Jul 4 1948	**1-Ix**	7	Sep 10 1948	4-Ik	3	Nov 17 1948	7-Oc	8
Jul 5 1948	2-Men	8	Sep 11 1948	5-Akbal	4	Nov 18 1948	8-Chuen	9
Jul 6 1948	3-Cib	9	Sep 12 1948	6-Kan	5	Nov 19 1948	9-Eb	1
Jul 7 1948	4-Caban	1	Sep 13 1948	7-Chicchan	6	Nov 20 1948	10-Ben	2
Jul 8 1948	5-Etz'nab	2	Sep 14 1948	8-Cimi	7	Nov 21 1948	11-Ix	3
Jul 9 1948	6-Cauac	3	Sep 15 1948	9-Manik	8	Nov 22 1948	12-Men	4
Jul 10 1948	7-Ahau	4	Sep 16 1948	10-Lamat	9	Nov 23 1948	13-Cib	5
Jul 11 1948	8-*Imix*	5	Sep 17 1948	11-Muluc	1	Nov 24 1948	**1-Caban**	6
Jul 12 1948	9-Ik	6	Sep 18 1948	12-Oc	2	Nov 25 1948	2-Etz'nab	7
Jul 13 1948	10-Akbal	7	Sep 19 1948	13-Chuen	3	Nov 26 1948	3-Cauac	8
Jul 14 1948	11-Kan	8	Sep 20 1948	**1-Eb**	4	Nov 27 1948	4-Ahau	9
Jul 15 1948	12-Chicchan	9	Sep 21 1948	2-Ben	5	Nov 28 1948	*5-Imix*	1
Jul 16 1948	13-Cimi	1	Sep 22 1948	3-Ix	6	Nov 29 1948	6-Ik	2
Jul 17 1948	**1-Manik**	2	Sep 23 1948	4-Men	7	Nov 30 1948	7-Akbal	3
Jul 18 1948	2-Lamat	3	Sep 24 1948	5-Cib	8	Dec 1 1948	8-Kan	4
Jul 19 1948	3-Muluc	4	Sep 25 1948	6-Caban	9	Dec 2 1948	9-Chicchan	5
Jul 20 1948	4-Oc	5	Sep 26 1948	7-Etz'nab	1	Dec 3 1948	10-Cimi	6
Jul 21 1948	5-Chuen	6	Sep 27 1948	8-Cauac	2	Dec 4 1948	11-Manik	7
Jul 22 1948	6-Eb	7	Sep 28 1948	9-Ahau	3	Dec 5 1948	12-Lamat	8
Jul 23 1948	7-Ben	8	Sep 29 1948	*10-Imix*	4	Dec 6 1948	13-Muluc	9
Jul 24 1948	8-Ix	9	Sep 30 1948	11-Ik	5	Dec 7 1948	**1-Oc**	1
Jul 25 1948	9-Men	1	Oct 1 1948	12-Akbal	6	Dec 8 1948	2-Chuen	2
Jul 26 1948	10-Cib	2	Oct 2 1948	13-Kan	7	Dec 9 1948	3-Eb	3
Jul 27 1948	11-Caban	3	Oct 3 1948	**1-Chicchan**	8	Dec 10 1948	4-Ben	4
Jul 28 1948	12-Etz'nab	4	Oct 4 1948	2-Cimi	9	Dec 11 1948	5-Ix	5
Jul 29 1948	13-Cauac	5	Oct 5 1948	3-Manik	1	Dec 12 1948	6-Men	6
Jul 30 1948	**1-Ahau**	6	Oct 6 1948	4-Lamat	2	Dec 13 1948	7-Cib	7
Jul 31 1948	2-*Imix*	7	Oct 7 1948	5-Muluc	3	Dec 14 1948	8-Caban	8
Aug 1 1948	3-Ik	8	Oct 8 1948	6-Oc	4	Dec 15 1948	9-Etz'nab	9
Aug 2 1948	4-Akbal	9	Oct 9 1948	7-Chuen	5	Dec 16 1948	10-Cauac	1
Aug 3 1948	5-Kan	1	Oct 10 1948	8-Eb	6	Dec 17 1948	11-Ahau	2
Aug 4 1948	6-Chicchan	2	Oct 11 1948	9-Ben	7	Dec 18 1948	*12-Imix*	3

Date	Day-Sign	L
Dec 19 1948	13-Ik	4
Dec 20 1948	1-Akbal	5
Dec 21 1948	2-Kan	6
Dec 22 1948	3-Chicchan	7
Dec 23 1948	4-Cimi	8
Dec 24 1948	5-Manik	9
Dec 25 1948	6-Lamat	1
Dec 26 1948	7-Muluc	2
Dec 27 1948	8-Oc	3
Dec 28 1948	9-Chuen	4
Dec 29 1948	10-Eb	5
Dec 30 1948	11-Ben	6
Dec 31 1948	12-Ix	7
Jan 1 1949	13-Men	8
Jan 2 1949	1-Cib	9
Jan 3 1949	2-Caban	1
Jan 4 1949	3-Etz'nab	2
Jan 5 1949	4-Cauac	3
Jan 6 1949	5-Ahau	4
Jan 7 1949	6-Imix	5
Jan 8 1949	7-Ik	6
Jan 9 1949	8-Akbal	7
Jan 10 1949	9-Kan	8
Jan 11 1949	10-Chicchan	9
Jan 12 1949	11-Cimi	1
Jan 13 1949	12-Manik	2
Jan 14 1949	13-Lamat	3
Jan 15 1949	1-Muluc	4
Jan 16 1949	2-Oc	5
Jan 17 1949	3-Chuen	6
Jan 18 1949	4-Eb	7
Jan 19 1949	5-Ben	8
Jan 20 1949	6-Ix	9
Jan 21 1949	7-Men	1
Jan 22 1949	8-Cib	2
Jan 23 1949	9-Caban	3
Jan 24 1949	10-Etz'nab	4
Jan 25 1949	11-Cauac	5
Jan 26 1949	12-Ahau	6
Jan 27 1949	13-Imix	7
Jan 28 1949	1-Ik	8
Jan 29 1949	2-Akbal	9
Jan 30 1949	3-Kan	1
Jan 31 1949	4-Chicchan	2
Feb 1 1949	5-Cimi	3
Feb 2 1949	6-Manik	4
Feb 3 1949	7-Lamat	5
Feb 4 1949	8-Muluc	6
Feb 5 1949	9-Oc	7
Feb 6 1949	10-Chuen	8
Feb 7 1949	11-Eb	9
Feb 8 1949	12-Ben	1
Feb 9 1949	13-Ix	2
Feb 10 1949	1-Men	3
Feb 11 1949	2-Cib	4
Feb 12 1949	3-Caban	5
Feb 13 1949	4-Etz'nab	6
Feb 14 1949	5-Cauac	7
Feb 15 1949	6-Ahau	8
Feb 16 1949	7-Imix	9
Feb 17 1949	8-Ik	1
Feb 18 1949	9-Akbal	2
Feb 19 1949	10-Kan	3
Feb 20 1949	11-Chicchan	4
Feb 21 1949	12-Cimi	5
Feb 22 1949	13-Manik	6
Feb 23 1949	1-Lamat	7
Feb 24 1949	2-Muluc	8

Date	Day-Sign	L
Feb 25 1949	3-Oc	9
Feb 26 1949	4-Chuen	1
Feb 27 1949	5-Eb	2
Feb 28 1949	6-Ben	3
Mar 1 1949	7-Ix	4
Mar 2 1949	8-Men	5
Mar 3 1949	9-Cib	6
Mar 4 1949	10-Caban	7
Mar 5 1949	11-Etz'nab	8
Mar 6 1949	12-Cauac	9
Mar 7 1949	13-Ahau	1
Mar 8 1949	1-Imix	2
Mar 9 1949	2-Ik	3
Mar 10 1949	3-Akbal	4
Mar 11 1949	4-Kan	5
Mar 12 1949	5-Chicchan	6
Mar 13 1949	6-Cimi	7
Mar 14 1949	7-Manik	8
Mar 15 1949	8-Lamat	9
Mar 16 1949	9-Muluc	1
Mar 17 1949	10-Oc	2
Mar 18 1949	11-Chuen	3
Mar 19 1949	12-Eb	4
Mar 20 1949	13-Ben	5
Mar 21 1949	1-Ix	6
Mar 22 1949	2-Men	7
Mar 23 1949	3-Cib	8
Mar 24 1949	4-Caban	9
Mar 25 1949	5-Etz'nab	1
Mar 26 1949	6-Cauac	2
Mar 27 1949	7-Ahau	3
Mar 28 1949	8-Imix	4
Mar 29 1949	9-Ik	5
Mar 30 1949	10-Akbal	6
Mar 31 1949	11-Kan	7
Apr 1 1949	12-Chicchan	8
Apr 2 1949	13-Cimi	9
Apr 3 1949	1-Manik	1
Apr 4 1949	2-Lamat	2
Apr 5 1949	3-Muluc	3
Apr 6 1949	4-Oc	4
Apr 7 1949	5-Chuen	5
Apr 8 1949	6-Eb	6
Apr 9 1949	7-Ben	7
Apr 10 1949	8-Ix	8
Apr 11 1949	9-Men	9
Apr 12 1949	10-Cib	1
Apr 13 1949	11-Caban	2
Apr 14 1949	12-Etz'nab	3
Apr 15 1949	13-Cauac	4
Apr 16 1949	1-Ahau	5
Apr 17 1949	2-Imix	6
Apr 18 1949	3-Ik	7
Apr 19 1949	4-Akbal	8
Apr 20 1949	5-Kan	9
Apr 21 1949	6-Chicchan	1
Apr 22 1949	7-Cimi	2
Apr 23 1949	8-Manik	3
Apr 24 1949	9-Lamat	4
Apr 25 1949	10-Muluc	5
Apr 26 1949	11-Oc	6
Apr 27 1949	12-Chuen	7
Apr 28 1949	13-Eb	8
Apr 29 1949	1-Ben	9
Apr 30 1949	2-Ix	1
May 1 1949	3-Men	2
May 2 1949	4-Cib	3
May 3 1949	5-Caban	4

Date	Day-Sign	L
May 4 1949	6-Etz'nab	5
May 5 1949	7-Cauac	6
May 6 1949	8-Ahau	7
May 7 1949	9-Imix	8
May 8 1949	10-Ik	9
May 9 1949	11-Akbal	1
May 10 1949	12-Kan	2
May 11 1949	13-Chicchan	3
May 12 1949	1-Cimi	4
May 13 1949	2-Manik	5
May 14 1949	3-Lamat	6
May 15 1949	4-Muluc	7
May 16 1949	5-Oc	8
May 17 1949	6-Chuen	9
May 18 1949	7-Eb	1
May 19 1949	8-Ben	2
May 20 1949	9-Ix	3
May 21 1949	10-Men	4
May 22 1949	11-Cib	5
May 23 1949	12-Caban	6
May 24 1949	13-Etz'nab	7
May 25 1949	1-Cauac	8
May 26 1949	2-Ahau	9
May 27 1949	3-Imix	1
May 28 1949	4-Ik	2
May 29 1949	5-Akbal	3
May 30 1949	6-Kan	4
May 31 1949	7-Chicchan	5
Jun 1 1949	8-Cimi	6
Jun 2 1949	9-Manik	7
Jun 3 1949	10-Lamat	8
Jun 4 1949	11-Muluc	9
Jun 5 1949	12-Oc	1
Jun 6 1949	13-Chuen	2
Jun 7 1949	1-Eb	3
Jun 8 1949	2-Ben	4
Jun 9 1949	3-Ix	5
Jun 10 1949	4-Men	6
Jun 11 1949	5-Cib	7
Jun 12 1949	6-Caban	8
Jun 13 1949	7-Etz'nab	9
Jun 14 1949	8-Cauac	1
Jun 15 1949	9-Ahau	2
Jun 16 1949	10-Imix	3
Jun 17 1949	11-Ik	4
Jun 18 1949	12-Akbal	5
Jun 19 1949	13-Kan	6
Jun 20 1949	1-Chicchan	7
Jun 21 1949	2-Cimi	8
Jun 22 1949	3-Manik	9
Jun 23 1949	4-Lamat	1
Jun 24 1949	5-Muluc	2
Jun 25 1949	6-Oc	3
Jun 26 1949	7-Chuen	4
Jun 27 1949	8-Eb	5
Jun 28 1949	9-Ben	6
Jun 29 1949	10-Ix	7
Jun 30 1949	11-Men	8
Jul 1 1949	12-Cib	9
Jul 2 1949	13-Caban	1
Jul 3 1949	1-Etz'nab	2
Jul 4 1949	2-Cauac	3
Jul 5 1949	3-Ahau	4
Jul 6 1949	4-Imix	5
Jul 7 1949	5-Ik	6
Jul 8 1949	6-Akbal	7
Jul 9 1949	7-Kan	8
Jul 10 1949	8-Chicchan	9

Date	Day-Sign	L
Jul 11 1949	9-Cimi	1
Jul 12 1949	10-Manik	2
Jul 13 1949	11-Lamat	3
Jul 14 1949	12-Muluc	4
Jul 15 1949	13-Oc	5
Jul 16 1949	1-Chuen	6
Jul 17 1949	2-Eb	7
Jul 18 1949	3-Ben	8
Jul 19 1949	4-Ix	9
Jul 20 1949	5-Men	1
Jul 21 1949	6-Cib	2
Jul 22 1949	7-Caban	3
Jul 23 1949	8-Etz'nab	4
Jul 24 1949	9-Cauac	5
Jul 25 1949	10-Ahau	6
Jul 26 1949	11-Imix	7
Jul 27 1949	12-Ik	8
Jul 28 1949	13-Akbal	9
Jul 29 1949	1-Kan	1
Jul 30 1949	2-Chicchan	2
Jul 31 1949	3-Cimi	3
Aug 1 1949	4-Manik	4
Aug 2 1949	5-Lamat	5
Aug 3 1949	6-Muluc	6
Aug 4 1949	7-Oc	7
Aug 5 1949	8-Chuen	8
Aug 6 1949	9-Eb	9
Aug 7 1949	10-Ben	1
Aug 8 1949	11-Ix	2
Aug 9 1949	12-Men	3
Aug 10 1949	13-Cib	4
Aug 11 1949	1-Caban	5
Aug 12 1949	2-Etz'nab	6
Aug 13 1949	3-Cauac	7
Aug 14 1949	4-Ahau	8
Aug 15 1949	5-Imix	9
Aug 16 1949	6-Ik	1
Aug 17 1949	7-Akbal	2
Aug 18 1949	8-Kan	3
Aug 19 1949	9-Chicchan	4
Aug 20 1949	10-Cimi	5
Aug 21 1949	11-Manik	6
Aug 22 1949	12-Lamat	7
Aug 23 1949	13-Muluc	8
Aug 24 1949	1-Oc	9
Aug 25 1949	2-Chuen	1
Aug 26 1949	3-Eb	2
Aug 27 1949	4-Ben	3
Aug 28 1949	5-Ix	4
Aug 29 1949	6-Men	5
Aug 30 1949	7-Cib	6
Aug 31 1949	8-Caban	7
Sep 1 1949	9-Etz'nab	8
Sep 2 1949	10-Cauac	9
Sep 3 1949	11-Ahau	1
Sep 4 1949	12-Imix	2
Sep 5 1949	13-Ik	3
Sep 6 1949	1-Akbal	4
Sep 7 1949	2-Kan	5
Sep 8 1949	3-Chicchan	6
Sep 9 1949	4-Cimi	7
Sep 10 1949	5-Manik	8
Sep 11 1949	6-Lamat	9
Sep 12 1949	7-Muluc	1
Sep 13 1949	8-Oc	2
Sep 14 1949	9-Chuen	3
Sep 15 1949	10-Eb	4
Sep 16 1949	11-Ben	5

Date	Day-Sign	L
Sep 17 1949	12-Ix	6
Sep 18 1949	13-Men	7
Sep 19 1949	1-Cib	8
Sep 20 1949	2-Caban	9
Sep 21 1949	3-Etz'nab	1
Sep 22 1949	4-Cauac	2
Sep 23 1949	5-Ahau	3
Sep 24 1949	6-Imix	4
Sep 25 1949	7-Ik	5
Sep 26 1949	8-Akbal	6
Sep 27 1949	9-Kan	7
Sep 28 1949	10-Chicchan	8
Sep 29 1949	11-Cimi	9
Sep 30 1949	12-Manik	1
Oct 1 1949	13-Akbal	2
Oct 2 1949	1-Muluc	3
Oct 3 1949	2-Oc	4
Oct 4 1949	3-Chuen	5
Oct 5 1949	4-Eb	6
Oct 6 1949	5-Ben	7
Oct 7 1949	6-Ix	8
Oct 8 1949	7-Men	9
Oct 9 1949	8-Cib	1
Oct 10 1949	9-Caban	2
Oct 11 1949	10-Etz'nab	3
Oct 12 1949	11-Cauac	4
Oct 13 1949	12-Ahau	5
Oct 14 1949	13-Imix	6
Oct 15 1949	1-Ik	7
Oct 16 1949	2-Akbal	8
Oct 17 1949	3-Kan	9
Oct 18 1949	4-Chicchan	1
Oct 19 1949	5-Cimi	2
Oct 20 1949	6-Manik	3
Oct 21 1949	7-Lamat	4
Oct 22 1949	8-Muluc	5
Oct 23 1949	9-Oc	6
Oct 24 1949	10-Chuen	7
Oct 25 1949	11-Eb	8
Oct 26 1949	12-Ben	9
Oct 27 1949	13-Ix	1
Oct 28 1949	1-Men	2
Oct 29 1949	2-Cib	3
Oct 30 1949	3-Caban	4
Oct 31 1949	4-Etz'nab	5
Nov 1 1949	5-Cauac	6
Nov 2 1949	6-Ahau	7
Nov 3 1949	7-Imix	8
Nov 4 1949	8-Ik	9
Nov 5 1949	9-Akbal	1
Nov 6 1949	10-Kan	2
Nov 7 1949	11-Chicchan	3
Nov 8 1949	12-Cimi	4
Nov 9 1949	13-Manik	5
Nov 10 1949	1-Lamat	6
Nov 11 1949	2-Muluc	7
Nov 12 1949	3-Oc	8
Nov 13 1949	4-Chuen	9
Nov 14 1949	5-Eb	1
Nov 15 1949	6-Ben	2
Nov 16 1949	7-Ix	3
Nov 17 1949	8-Men	4
Nov 18 1949	9-Cib	5
Nov 19 1949	10-Caban	6
Nov 20 1949	11-Etz'nab	7
Nov 21 1949	12-Cauac	8
Nov 22 1949	13-Ahau	9
Nov 23 1949	1-Imix	1

Date	Day-Sign	L
Nov 24 1949	2-Ik	2
Nov 25 1949	3-Akbal	3
Nov 26 1949	4-Kan	4
Nov 27 1949	5-Chicchan	5
Nov 28 1949	6-Cimi	6
Nov 29 1949	7-Manik	7
Nov 30 1949	8-Lamat	8
Dec 1 1949	9-Muluc	9
Dec 2 1949	10-Oc	1
Dec 3 1949	11-Chuen	2
Dec 4 1949	12-Eb	3
Dec 5 1949	13-Ben	4
Dec 6 1949	1-Ix	5
Dec 7 1949	2-Men	6
Dec 8 1949	3-Cib	7
Dec 9 1949	4-Caban	8
Dec 10 1949	5-Etz'nab	9
Dec 11 1949	6-Cauac	1
Dec 12 1949	7-Ahau	2
Dec 13 1949	8-Imix	3
Dec 14 1949	9-Ik	4
Dec 15 1949	10-Akbal	5
Dec 16 1949	11-Kan	6
Dec 17 1949	12-Chicchan	7
Dec 18 1949	13-Cimi	8
Dec 19 1949	1-Manik	9
Dec 20 1949	2-Lamat	1
Dec 21 1949	3-Muluc	2
Dec 22 1949	4-Oc	3
Dec 23 1949	5-Chuen	4
Dec 24 1949	6-Eb	5
Dec 25 1949	7-Ben	6
Dec 26 1949	8-Ix	7
Dec 27 1949	9-Men	8
Dec 28 1949	10-Cib	9
Dec 29 1949	11-Caban	1
Dec 30 1949	12-Etz'nab	2
Dec 31 1949	13-Cauac	3
Jan 1 1950	1-Ahau	4
Jan 2 1950	2-Imix	5
Jan 3 1950	3-Ik	6
Jan 4 1950	4-Akbal	7
Jan 5 1950	5-Kan	8
Jan 6 1950	6-Chicchan	9
Jan 7 1950	7-Cimi	1
Jan 8 1950	8-Manik	2
Jan 9 1950	9-Lamat	3
Jan 10 1950	10-Muluc	4
Jan 11 1950	11-Oc	5
Jan 12 1950	12-Chuen	6
Jan 13 1950	13-Eb	7
Jan 14 1950	1-Ben	8
Jan 15 1950	2-Ix	9
Jan 16 1950	3-Men	1
Jan 17 1950	4-Cib	2
Jan 18 1950	5-Caban	3
Jan 19 1950	6-Etz'nab	4
Jan 20 1950	7-Cauac	5
Jan 21 1950	8-Ahau	6
Jan 22 1950	9-Imix	7
Jan 23 1950	10-Ik	8
Jan 24 1950	11-Akbal	9
Jan 25 1950	12-Kan	1
Jan 26 1950	13-Chicchan	2
Jan 27 1950	1-Cimi	3
Jan 28 1950	2-Manik	4
Jan 29 1950	3-Lamat	5
Jan 30 1950	4-Muluc	6

Date	Day-Sign	L	Date	Day-Sign	L	Date	Day-Sign	L
Jan 31 1950	5-Oc	7	Apr 9 1950	8-Etz'nab	3	Jun 16 1950	11-Cimi	8
Feb 1 1950	6-Chuen	8	Apr 10 1950	9-Cauac	4	Jun 17 1950	12-Manik	9
Feb 2 1950	7-Eb	9	Apr 11 1950	10-Ahau	5	Jun 18 1950	13-Lamat	1
Feb 3 1950	8-Ben	1	Apr 12 1950	*11-Imix*	6	Jun 19 1950	**1-Muluc**	2
Feb 4 1950	9-Ix	2	Apr 13 1950	12-Ik	7	Jun 20 1950	2-Oc	3
Feb 5 1950	10-Men	3	Apr 14 1950	13-Akbal	8	Jun 21 1950	3-Chuen	4
Feb 6 1950	11-Cib	4	Apr 15 1950	**1-Kan**	9	Jun 22 1950	4-Eb	5
Feb 7 1950	12-Caban	5	Apr 16 1950	2-Chicchan	1	Jun 23 1950	5-Ben	6
Feb 8 1950	13-Etz'nab	6	Apr 17 1950	3-Cimi	2	Jun 24 1950	6-Ix	7
Feb 9 1950	**1-Cauac**	7	Apr 18 1950	4-Manik	3	Jun 25 1950	7-Men	8
Feb 10 1950	2-Ahau	8	Apr 19 1950	5-Lamat	4	Jun 26 1950	8-Cib	9
Feb 11 1950	*3-Imix*	9	Apr 20 1950	6-Muluc	5	Jun 27 1950	9-Caban	1
Feb 12 1950	4-Ik	1	Apr 21 1950	7-Oc	6	Jun 28 1950	10-Etz'nab	2
Feb 13 1950	5-Akbal	2	Apr 22 1950	8-Chuen	7	Jun 29 1950	11-Cauac	3
Feb 14 1950	6-Kan	3	Apr 23 1950	9-Eb	8	Jun 30 1950	12-Ahau	4
Feb 15 1950	7-Chicchan	4	Apr 24 1950	10-Ben	9	Jul 1 1950	*13-Imix*	5
Feb 16 1950	8-Cimi	5	Apr 25 1950	11-Ix	1	Jul 2 1950	**1-Ik**	6
Feb 17 1950	9-Manik	6	Apr 26 1950	12-Men	2	Jul 3 1950	2-Akbal	7
Feb 18 1950	10-Lamat	7	Apr 27 1950	13-Cib	3	Jul 4 1950	3-Kan	8
Feb 19 1950	11-Muluc	8	Apr 28 1950	**1-Caban**	4	Jul 5 1950	4-Chicchan	9
Feb 20 1950	12-Oc	9	Apr 29 1950	2-Etz'nab	5	Jul 6 1950	5-Cimi	1
Feb 21 1950	13-Chuen	1	Apr 30 1950	3-Cauac	6	Jul 7 1950	6-Manik	2
Feb 22 1950	**1-Eb**	2	May 1 1950	4-Ahau	7	Jul 8 1950	7-Lamat	3
Feb 23 1950	2-Ben	3	May 2 1950	*5-Imix*	8	Jul 9 1950	8-Muluc	4
Feb 24 1950	3-Ix	4	May 3 1950	6-Ik	9	Jul 10 1950	9-Oc	5
Feb 25 1950	4-Men	5	May 4 1950	7-Akbal	1	Jul 11 1950	10-Chuen	6
Feb 26 1950	5-Cib	6	May 5 1950	8-Kan	2	Jul 12 1950	11-Eb	7
Feb 27 1950	6-Caban	7	May 6 1950	9-Chicchan	3	Jul 13 1950	12-Ben	8
Feb 28 1950	7-Etz'nab	8	May 7 1950	10-Cimi	4	Jul 14 1950	13-Ix	9
Mar 1 1950	8-Cauac	9	May 8 1950	11-Manik	5	Jul 15 1950	**1-Men**	1
Mar 2 1950	9-Ahau	1	May 9 1950	12-Lamat	6	Jul 16 1950	2-Cib	2
Mar 3 1950	*10-Imix*	2	May 10 1950	13-Muluc	7	Jul 17 1950	3-Caban	3
Mar 4 1950	11-Ik	3	May 11 1950	**1-Oc**	8	Jul 18 1950	4-Etz'nab	4
Mar 5 1950	12-Akbal	4	May 12 1950	2-Chuen	9	Jul 19 1950	5-Cauac	5
Mar 6 1950	13-Kan	5	May 13 1950	3-Eb	1	Jul 20 1950	6-Ahau	6
Mar 7 1950	**1-Chicchan**	6	May 14 1950	4-Ben	2	Jul 21 1950	*7-Imix*	7
Mar 8 1950	2-Cimi	7	May 15 1950	5-Ix	3	Jul 22 1950	8-Ik	8
Mar 9 1950	3-Manik	8	May 16 1950	6-Men	4	Jul 23 1950	9-Akbal	9
Mar 10 1950	4-Lamat	9	May 17 1950	7-Cib	5	Jul 24 1950	10-Kan	1
Mar 11 1950	5-Muluc	1	May 18 1950	8-Caban	6	Jul 25 1950	11-Chicchan	2
Mar 12 1950	6-Oc	2	May 19 1950	9-Etz'nab	7	Jul 26 1950	12-Cimi	3
Mar 13 1950	7-Chuen	3	May 20 1950	10-Cauac	8	Jul 27 1950	13-Manik	4
Mar 14 1950	8-Eb	4	May 21 1950	11-Ahau	9	Jul 28 1950	**1-Lamat**	5
Mar 15 1950	9-Ben	5	May 22 1950	*12-Imix*	1	Jul 29 1950	2-Muluc	6
Mar 16 1950	10-Ix	6	May 23 1950	13-Ik	2	Jul 30 1950	3-Oc	7
Mar 17 1950	11-Men	7	May 24 1950	**1-Akbal**	3	Jul 31 1950	4-Chuen	8
Mar 18 1950	12-Cib	8	May 25 1950	2-Kan	4	Aug 1 1950	5-Eb	9
Mar 19 1950	13-Caban	9	May 26 1950	3-Chicchan	5	Aug 2 1950	6-Ben	1
Mar 20 1950	**1-Etz'nab**	1	May 27 1950	4-Cimi	6	Aug 3 1950	7-Ix	2
Mar 21 1950	2-Cauac	2	May 28 1950	5-Manik	7	Aug 4 1950	8-Men	3
Mar 22 1950	3-Ahau	3	May 29 1950	6-Lamat	8	Aug 5 1950	9-Cib	4
Mar 23 1950	*4-Imix*	4	May 30 1950	7-Muluc	9	Aug 6 1950	10-Caban	5
Mar 24 1950	5-Ik	5	May 31 1950	8-Oc	1	Aug 7 1950	11-Etz'nab	6
Mar 25 1950	6-Akbal	6	Jun 1 1950	9-Chuen	2	Aug 8 1950	12-Cauac	7
Mar 26 1950	7-Kan	7	Jun 2 1950	10-Eb	3	Aug 9 1950	13-Ahau	8
Mar 27 1950	8-Chicchan	8	Jun 3 1950	11-Ben	4	Aug 10 1950	***1-Imix***	9
Mar 28 1950	9-Cimi	9	Jun 4 1950	12-Ix	5	Aug 11 1950	2-Ik	1
Mar 29 1950	10-Manik	1	Jun 5 1950	13-Men	6	Aug 12 1950	3-Akbal	2
Mar 30 1950	11-Lamat	2	Jun 6 1950	**1-Cib**	7	Aug 13 1950	4-Kan	3
Mar 31 1950	12-Muluc	3	Jun 7 1950	2-Caban	8	Aug 14 1950	5-Chicchan	4
Apr 1 1950	13-Oc	4	Jun 8 1950	3-Etz'nab	9	Aug 15 1950	6-Cimi	5
Apr 2 1950	**1-Chuen**	5	Jun 9 1950	4-Cauac	1	Aug 16 1950	7-Manik	6
Apr 3 1950	2-Eb	6	Jun 10 1950	5-Ahau	2	Aug 17 1950	8-Lamat	7
Apr 4 1950	3-Ben	7	Jun 11 1950	*6-Imix*	3	Aug 18 1950	9-Muluc	8
Apr 5 1950	4-Ix	8	Jun 12 1950	7-Ik	4	Aug 19 1950	10-Oc	9
Apr 6 1950	5-Men	9	Jun 13 1950	8-Akbal	5	Aug 20 1950	11-Chuen	1
Apr 7 1950	6-Cib	1	Jun 14 1950	9-Kan	6	Aug 21 1950	12-Eb	2
Apr 8 1950	7-Caban	2	Jun 15 1950	10-Chicchan	7	Aug 22 1950	13-Ben	3

Date	Day-Sign	L
Aug 23 1950	1-Ix	4
Aug 24 1950	2-Men	5
Aug 25 1950	3-Cib	6
Aug 26 1950	4-Caban	7
Aug 27 1950	5-Etz'nab	8
Aug 28 1950	6-Cauac	9
Aug 29 1950	7-Ahau	1
Aug 30 1950	8-Imix	2
Aug 31 1950	9-Ik	3
Sep 1 1950	10-Akbal	4
Sep 2 1950	11-Kan	5
Sep 3 1950	12-Chicchan	6
Sep 4 1950	13-Cimi	7
Sep 5 1950	1-Manik	8
Sep 6 1950	2-Lamat	9
Sep 7 1950	3-Muluc	1
Sep 8 1950	4-Oc	2
Sep 9 1950	5-Chuen	3
Sep 10 1950	6-Eb	4
Sep 11 1950	7-Ben	5
Sep 12 1950	8-Ix	6
Sep 13 1950	9-Men	7
Sep 14 1950	10-Cib	8
Sep 15 1950	11-Caban	9
Sep 16 1950	12-Etz'nab	1
Sep 17 1950	13-Cauac	2
Sep 18 1950	1-Ahau	3
Sep 19 1950	2-Imix	4
Sep 20 1950	3-Ik	5
Sep 21 1950	4-Akbal	6
Sep 22 1950	5-Kan	7
Sep 23 1950	6-Chicchan	8
Sep 24 1950	7-Cimi	9
Sep 25 1950	8-Manik	1
Sep 26 1950	9-Lamat	2
Sep 27 1950	10-Muluc	3
Sep 28 1950	11-Oc	4
Sep 29 1950	12-Chuen	5
Sep 30 1950	13-Eb	6
Oct 1 1950	1-Ben	7
Oct 2 1950	2-Ix	8
Oct 3 1950	3-Men	9
Oct 4 1950	4-Cib	1
Oct 5 1950	5-Caban	2
Oct 6 1950	6-Etz'nab	3
Oct 7 1950	7-Cauac	4
Oct 8 1950	8-Ahau	5
Oct 9 1950	9-Imix	6
Oct 10 1950	10-Ik	7
Oct 11 1950	11-Akbal	8
Oct 12 1950	12-Kan	9
Oct 13 1950	13-Chicchan	1
Oct 14 1950	1-Cimi	2
Oct 15 1950	2-Manik	3
Oct 16 1950	3-Lamat	4
Oct 17 1950	4-Muluc	5
Oct 18 1950	5-Oc	6
Oct 19 1950	6-Chuen	7
Oct 20 1950	7-Eb	8
Oct 21 1950	8-Ben	9
Oct 22 1950	9-Ix	1
Oct 23 1950	10-Men	2
Oct 24 1950	11-Cib	3
Oct 25 1950	12-Caban	4
Oct 26 1950	13-Etz'nab	5
Oct 27 1950	1-Cauac	6
Oct 28 1950	2-Ahau	7
Oct 29 1950	3-Imix	8

Date	Day-Sign	L
Oct 30 1950	4-Ik	9
Oct 31 1950	5-Akbal	1
Nov 1 1950	6-Kan	2
Nov 2 1950	7-Chicchan	3
Nov 3 1950	8-Cimi	4
Nov 4 1950	9-Manik	5
Nov 5 1950	10-Lamat	6
Nov 6 1950	11-Muluc	7
Nov 7 1950	12-Oc	8
Nov 8 1950	13-Chuen	9
Nov 9 1950	1-Eb	1
Nov 10 1950	2-Ben	2
Nov 11 1950	3-Ix	3
Nov 12 1950	4-Men	4
Nov 13 1950	5-Cib	5
Nov 14 1950	6-Caban	6
Nov 15 1950	7-Etz'nab	7
Nov 16 1950	8-Cauac	8
Nov 17 1950	9-Ahau	9
Nov 18 1950	10-Imix	1
Nov 19 1950	11-Ik	2
Nov 20 1950	12-Akbal	3
Nov 21 1950	13-Kan	4
Nov 22 1950	1-Chicchan	5
Nov 23 1950	2-Cimi	6
Nov 24 1950	3-Manik	7
Nov 25 1950	4-Lamat	8
Nov 26 1950	5-Muluc	9
Nov 27 1950	6-Oc	1
Nov 28 1950	7-Chuen	2
Nov 29 1950	8-Eb	3
Nov 30 1950	9-Ben	4
Dec 1 1950	10-Ix	5
Dec 2 1950	11-Men	6
Dec 3 1950	12-Cib	7
Dec 4 1950	13-Caban	8
Dec 5 1950	1-Etz'nab	9
Dec 6 1950	2-Cauac	1
Dec 7 1950	3-Ahau	2
Dec 8 1950	4-Imix	3
Dec 9 1950	5-Ik	4
Dec 10 1950	6-Akbal	5
Dec 11 1950	7-Kan	6
Dec 12 1950	8-Chicchan	7
Dec 13 1950	9-Cimi	8
Dec 14 1950	10-Manik	9
Dec 15 1950	11-Lamat	1
Dec 16 1950	12-Muluc	2
Dec 17 1950	13-Oc	3
Dec 18 1950	1-Chuen	4
Dec 19 1950	2-Eb	5
Dec 20 1950	3-Ben	6
Dec 21 1950	4-Ix	7
Dec 22 1950	5-Men	8
Dec 23 1950	6-Cib	9
Dec 24 1950	7-Caban	1
Dec 25 1950	8-Etz'nab	2
Dec 26 1950	9-Cauac	3
Dec 27 1950	10-Ahau	4
Dec 28 1950	11-Imix	5
Dec 29 1950	12-Ik	6
Dec 30 1950	13-Akbal	7
Dec 31 1950	1-Kan	8
Jan 1 1951	2-Chicchan	9
Jan 2 1951	3-Cimi	1
Jan 3 1951	4-Manik	2
Jan 4 1951	5-Lamat	3
Jan 5 1951	6-Muluc	4

Date	Day-Sign	L
Jan 6 1951	7-Oc	5
Jan 7 1951	8-Chuen	6
Jan 8 1951	9-Eb	7
Jan 9 1951	10-Ben	8
Jan 10 1951	11-Ix	9
Jan 11 1951	12-Men	1
Jan 12 1951	13-Cib	2
Jan 13 1951	1-Caban	3
Jan 14 1951	2-Etz'nab	4
Jan 15 1951	3-Cauac	5
Jan 16 1951	4-Ahau	6
Jan 17 1951	5-Imix	7
Jan 18 1951	6-Ik	8
Jan 19 1951	7-Akbal	9
Jan 20 1951	8-Kan	1
Jan 21 1951	9-Chicchan	2
Jan 22 1951	10-Cimi	3
Jan 23 1951	11-Manik	4
Jan 24 1951	12-Lamat	5
Jan 25 1951	13-Muluc	6
Jan 26 1951	1-Oc	7
Jan 27 1951	2-Chuen	8
Jan 28 1951	3-Eb	9
Jan 29 1951	4-Ben	1
Jan 30 1951	5-Ix	2
Jan 31 1951	6-Men	3
Feb 1 1951	7-Cib	4
Feb 2 1951	8-Caban	5
Feb 3 1951	9-Etz'nab	6
Feb 4 1951	10-Cauac	7
Feb 5 1951	11-Ahau	8
Feb 6 1951	12-Imix	9
Feb 7 1951	13-Ik	1
Feb 8 1951	1-Akbal	2
Feb 9 1951	2-Kan	3
Feb 10 1951	3-Chicchan	4
Feb 11 1951	4-Cimi	5
Feb 12 1951	5-Manik	6
Feb 13 1951	6-Lamat	7
Feb 14 1951	7-Muluc	8
Feb 15 1951	8-Oc	9
Feb 16 1951	9-Chuen	1
Feb 17 1951	10-Eb	2
Feb 18 1951	11-Ben	3
Feb 19 1951	12-Ix	4
Feb 20 1951	13-Men	5
Feb 21 1951	1-Cib	6
Feb 22 1951	2-Caban	7
Feb 23 1951	3-Etz'nab	8
Feb 24 1951	4-Cauac	9
Feb 25 1951	5-Ahau	1
Feb 26 1951	6-Imix	2
Feb 27 1951	7-Ik	3
Feb 28 1951	8-Akbal	4
Mar 1 1951	9-Kan	5
Mar 2 1951	10-Chicchan	6
Mar 3 1951	11-Cimi	7
Mar 4 1951	12-Manik	8
Mar 5 1951	13-Lamat	9
Mar 6 1951	1-Muluc	1
Mar 7 1951	2-Oc	2
Mar 8 1951	3-Chuen	3
Mar 9 1951	4-Eb	4
Mar 10 1951	5-Ben	5
Mar 11 1951	6-Ix	6
Mar 12 1951	7-Men	7
Mar 13 1951	8-Cib	8
Mar 14 1951	9-Caban	9

Date	Day-Sign	L
Mar 15 1951	10-Etz'nab	1
Mar 16 1951	11-Cauac	2
Mar 17 1951	12-Ahau	3
Mar 18 1951	13-Imix	4
Mar 19 1951	1-Ik	5
Mar 20 1951	2-Akbal	6
Mar 21 1951	3-Kan	7
Mar 22 1951	4-Chicchan	8
Mar 23 1951	5-Cimi	9
Mar 24 1951	6-Manik	1
Mar 25 1951	7-Lamat	2
Mar 26 1951	8-Muluc	3
Mar 27 1951	9-Oc	4
Mar 28 1951	10-Chuen	5
Mar 29 1951	11-Eb	6
Mar 30 1951	12-Ben	7
Mar 31 1951	13-Ix	8
Apr 1 1951	1-Men	9
Apr 2 1951	2-Cib	1
Apr 3 1951	3-Caban	2
Apr 4 1951	4-Etz'nab	3
Apr 5 1951	5-Cauac	4
Apr 6 1951	6-Ahau	5
Apr 7 1951	7-Imix	6
Apr 8 1951	8-Ik	7
Apr 9 1951	9-Akbal	8
Apr 10 1951	10-Kan	9
Apr 11 1951	11-Chicchan	1
Apr 12 1951	12-Cimi	2
Apr 13 1951	13-Manik	3
Apr 14 1951	1-Lamat	4
Apr 15 1951	2-Muluc	5
Apr 16 1951	3-Oc	6
Apr 17 1951	4-Chuen	7
Apr 18 1951	5-Eb	8
Apr 19 1951	6-Ben	9
Apr 20 1951	7-Ix	1
Apr 21 1951	8-Men	2
Apr 22 1951	9-Cib	3
Apr 23 1951	10-Caban	4
Apr 24 1951	11-Etz'nab	5
Apr 25 1951	12-Cauac	6
Apr 26 1951	13-Ahau	7
Apr 27 1951	1-Imix	8
Apr 28 1951	2-Ik	9
Apr 29 1951	3-Akbal	1
Apr 30 1951	4-Kan	2
May 1 1951	5-Chicchan	3
May 2 1951	6-Cimi	4
May 3 1951	7-Manik	5
May 4 1951	8-Lamat	6
May 5 1951	9-Muluc	7
May 6 1951	10-Oc	8
May 7 1951	11-Chuen	9
May 8 1951	12-Eb	1
May 9 1951	13-Ben	2
May 10 1951	1-Ix	3
May 11 1951	2-Men	4
May 12 1951	3-Cib	5
May 13 1951	4-Caban	6
May 14 1951	5-Etz'nab	7
May 15 1951	6-Cauac	8
May 16 1951	7-Ahau	9
May 17 1951	8-Imix	1
May 18 1951	9-Ik	2
May 19 1951	10-Akbal	3
May 20 1951	11-Kan	4
May 21 1951	12-Chicchan	5

Date	Day-Sign	L
May 22 1951	13-Cimi	6
May 23 1951	1-Manik	7
May 24 1951	2-Lamat	8
May 25 1951	3-Muluc	9
May 26 1951	4-Oc	1
May 27 1951	5-Chuen	2
May 28 1951	6-Eb	3
May 29 1951	7-Ben	4
May 30 1951	8-Ix	5
May 31 1951	9-Men	6
Jun 1 1951	10-Cib	7
Jun 2 1951	11-Caban	8
Jun 3 1951	12-Etz'nab	9
Jun 4 1951	13-Cauac	1
Jun 5 1951	1-Ahau	2
Jun 6 1951	2-Imix	3
Jun 7 1951	3-Ik	4
Jun 8 1951	4-Akbal	5
Jun 9 1951	5-Kan	6
Jun 10 1951	6-Chicchan	7
Jun 11 1951	7-Cimi	8
Jun 12 1951	8-Manik	9
Jun 13 1951	9-Lamat	1
Jun 14 1951	10-Muluc	2
Jun 15 1951	11-Oc	3
Jun 16 1951	12-Chuen	4
Jun 17 1951	13-Eb	5
Jun 18 1951	1-Ben	6
Jun 19 1951	2-Ix	7
Jun 20 1951	3-Men	8
Jun 21 1951	4-Cib	9
Jun 22 1951	5-Caban	1
Jun 23 1951	6-Etz'nab	2
Jun 24 1951	7-Cauac	3
Jun 25 1951	8-Ahau	4
Jun 26 1951	9-Imix	5
Jun 27 1951	10-Ik	6
Jun 28 1951	11-Akbal	7
Jun 29 1951	12-Kan	8
Jun 30 1951	13-Chicchan	9
Jul 1 1951	1-Cimi	1
Jul 2 1951	2-Manik	2
Jul 3 1951	3-Lamat	3
Jul 4 1951	4-Muluc	4
Jul 5 1951	5-Oc	5
Jul 6 1951	6-Chuen	6
Jul 7 1951	7-Eb	7
Jul 8 1951	8-Ben	8
Jul 9 1951	9-Ix	9
Jul 10 1951	10-Men	1
Jul 11 1951	11-Cib	2
Jul 12 1951	12-Caban	3
Jul 13 1951	13-Etz'nab	4
Jul 14 1951	1-Cauac	5
Jul 15 1951	2-Ahau	6
Jul 16 1951	3-Imix	7
Jul 17 1951	4-Ik	8
Jul 18 1951	5-Akbal	9
Jul 19 1951	6-Kan	1
Jul 20 1951	7-Chicchan	2
Jul 21 1951	8-Cimi	3
Jul 22 1951	9-Manik	4
Jul 23 1951	10-Lamat	5
Jul 24 1951	11-Muluc	6
Jul 25 1951	12-Oc	7
Jul 26 1951	13-Chuen	8
Jul 27 1951	1-Eb	9
Jul 28 1951	2-Ben	1

Date	Day-Sign	L
Jul 29 1951	3-Ix	2
Jul 30 1951	4-Men	3
Jul 31 1951	5-Cib	4
Aug 1 1951	6-Caban	5
Aug 2 1951	7-Etz'nab	6
Aug 3 1951	8-Cauac	7
Aug 4 1951	9-Ahau	8
Aug 5 1951	10-Imix	9
Aug 6 1951	11-Ik	1
Aug 7 1951	12-Akbal	2
Aug 8 1951	13-Kan	3
Aug 9 1951	1-Chicchan	4
Aug 10 1951	2-Cimi	5
Aug 11 1951	3-Manik	6
Aug 12 1951	4-Lamat	7
Aug 13 1951	5-Muluc	8
Aug 14 1951	6-Oc	9
Aug 15 1951	7-Chuen	1
Aug 16 1951	8-Eb	2
Aug 17 1951	9-Ben	3
Aug 18 1951	10-Ix	4
Aug 19 1951	11-Men	5
Aug 20 1951	12-Cib	6
Aug 21 1951	13-Caban	7
Aug 22 1951	1-Etz'nab	8
Aug 23 1951	2-Cauac	9
Aug 24 1951	3-Ahau	1
Aug 25 1951	4-Imix	2
Aug 26 1951	5-Ik	3
Aug 27 1951	6-Akbal	4
Aug 28 1951	7-Kan	5
Aug 29 1951	8-Chicchan	6
Aug 30 1951	9-Cimi	7
Aug 31 1951	10-Manik	8
Sep 1 1951	11-Lamat	9
Sep 2 1951	12-Muluc	1
Sep 3 1951	13-Oc	2
Sep 4 1951	1-Chuen	3
Sep 5 1951	2-Eb	4
Sep 6 1951	3-Ben	5
Sep 7 1951	4-Ix	6
Sep 8 1951	5-Men	7
Sep 9 1951	6-Cib	8
Sep 10 1951	7-Caban	9
Sep 11 1951	8-Etz'nab	1
Sep 12 1951	9-Cauac	2
Sep 13 1951	10-Ahau	3
Sep 14 1951	11-Imix	4
Sep 15 1951	12-Ik	5
Sep 16 1951	13-Akbal	6
Sep 17 1951	1-Kan	7
Sep 18 1951	2-Chicchan	8
Sep 19 1951	3-Cimi	9
Sep 20 1951	4-Manik	1
Sep 21 1951	5-Lamat	2
Sep 22 1951	6-Muluc	3
Sep 23 1951	7-Oc	4
Sep 24 1951	8-Chuen	5
Sep 25 1951	9-Eb	6
Sep 26 1951	10-Ben	7
Sep 27 1951	11-Ix	8
Sep 28 1951	12-Men	9
Sep 29 1951	13-Cib	1
Sep 30 1951	1-Caban	2
Oct 1 1951	2-Etz'nab	3
Oct 2 1951	3-Cauac	4
Oct 3 1951	4-Ahau	5
Oct 4 1951	5-Imix	6

Date	Day-Sign	L		Date	Day-Sign	L		Date	Day-Sign	L
Oct 5 1951	6-Ik	7		Dec 12 1951	9-Oc	3		Feb 18 1952	12-Etz'nab	8
Oct 6 1951	7-Akbal	8		Dec 13 1951	10-Chuen	4		Feb 19 1952	13-Cauac	9
Oct 7 1951	8-Kan	9		Dec 14 1951	11-Eb	5		Feb 20 1952	1-Ahau	1
Oct 8 1951	9-Chicchan	1		Dec 15 1951	12-Ben	6		Feb 21 1952	2-Imix	2
Oct 9 1951	10-Cimi	2		Dec 16 1951	13-Ix	7		Feb 22 1952	3-Ik	3
Oct 10 1951	11-Manik	3		Dec 17 1951	1-Men	8		Feb 23 1952	4-Akbal	4
Oct 11 1951	12-Lamat	4		Dec 18 1951	2-Cib	9		Feb 24 1952	5-Kan	5
Oct 12 1951	13-Muluc	5		Dec 19 1951	3-Caban	1		Feb 25 1952	6-Chicchan	6
Oct 13 1951	1-Oc	6		Dec 20 1951	4-Etz'nab	2		Feb 26 1952	7-Cimi	7
Oct 14 1951	2-Chuen	7		Dec 21 1951	5-Cauac	3		Feb 27 1952	8-Manik	8
Oct 15 1951	3-Eb	8		Dec 22 1951	6-Ahau	4		Feb 28 1952	9-Lamat	9
Oct 16 1951	4-Ben	9		Dec 23 1951	7-Imix	5		Feb 29 1952	10-Muluc	1
Oct 17 1951	5-Ix	1		Dec 24 1951	8-Ik	6		Mar 1 1952	11-Oc	2
Oct 18 1951	6-Men	2		Dec 25 1951	9-Akbal	7		Mar 2 1952	12-Chuen	3
Oct 19 1951	7-Cib	3		Dec 26 1951	10-Kan	8		Mar 3 1952	13-Eb	4
Oct 20 1951	8-Caban	4		Dec 27 1951	11-Chicchan	9		Mar 4 1952	1-Ben	5
Oct 21 1951	9-Etz'nab	5		Dec 28 1951	12-Cimi	1		Mar 5 1952	2-Ix	6
Oct 22 1951	10-Cauac	6		Dec 29 1951	13-Manik	2		Mar 6 1952	3-Men	7
Oct 23 1951	11-Ahau	7		Dec 30 1951	1-Lamat	3		Mar 7 1952	4-Cib	8
Oct 24 1951	12-Imix	8		Dec 31 1951	2-Muluc	4		Mar 8 1952	5-Caban	9
Oct 25 1951	13-Ik	9		Jan 1 1952	3-Oc	5		Mar 9 1952	6-Etz'nab	1
Oct 26 1951	1-Akbal	1		Jan 2 1952	4-Chuen	6		Mar 10 1952	7-Cauac	2
Oct 27 1951	2-Kan	2		Jan 3 1952	5-Eb	7		Mar 11 1952	8-Ahau	3
Oct 28 1951	3-Chicchan	3		Jan 4 1952	6-Ben	8		Mar 12 1952	9-Imix	4
Oct 29 1951	4-Cimi	4		Jan 5 1952	7-Ix	9		Mar 13 1952	10-Ik	5
Oct 30 1951	5-Manik	5		Jan 6 1952	8-Men	1		Mar 14 1952	11-Akbal	6
Oct 31 1951	6-Lamat	6		Jan 7 1952	9-Cib	2		Mar 15 1952	12-Kan	7
Nov 1 1951	7-Muluc	7		Jan 8 1952	10-Caban	3		Mar 16 1952	13-Chicchan	8
Nov 2 1951	8-Oc	8		Jan 9 1952	11-Etz'nab	4		Mar 17 1952	1-Cimi	9
Nov 3 1951	9-Chuen	9		Jan 10 1952	12-Cauac	5		Mar 18 1952	2-Manik	1
Nov 4 1951	10-Eb	1		Jan 11 1952	13-Ahau	6		Mar 19 1952	3-Lamat	2
Nov 5 1951	11-Ben	2		Jan 12 1952	1-Imix	7		Mar 20 1952	4-Muluc	3
Nov 6 1951	12-Ix	3		Jan 13 1952	2-Ik	8		Mar 21 1952	5-Oc	4
Nov 7 1951	13-Men	4		Jan 14 1952	3-Akbal	9		Mar 22 1952	6-Chuen	5
Nov 8 1951	1-Cib	5		Jan 15 1952	4-Kan	1		Mar 23 1952	7-Eb	6
Nov 9 1951	2-Caban	6		Jan 16 1952	5-Chicchan	2		Mar 24 1952	8-Ben	7
Nov 10 1951	3-Etz'nab	7		Jan 17 1952	6-Cimi	3		Mar 25 1952	9-Ix	8
Nov 11 1951	4-Cauac	8		Jan 18 1952	7-Manik	4		Mar 26 1952	10-Men	9
Nov 12 1951	5-Ahau	9		Jan 19 1952	8-Lamat	5		Mar 27 1952	11-Cib	1
Nov 13 1951	6-Imix	1		Jan 20 1952	9-Muluc	6		Mar 28 1952	12-Caban	2
Nov 14 1951	7-Ik	2		Jan 21 1952	10-Oc	7		Mar 29 1952	13-Etz'nab	3
Nov 15 1951	8-Akbal	3		Jan 22 1952	11-Chuen	8		Mar 30 1952	1-Cauac	4
Nov 16 1951	9-Kan	4		Jan 23 1952	12-Eb	9		Mar 31 1952	2-Ahau	5
Nov 17 1951	10-Chicchan	5		Jan 24 1952	13-Ben	1		Apr 1 1952	3-Imix	6
Nov 18 1951	11-Cimi	6		Jan 25 1952	1-Ix	2		Apr 2 1952	4-Ik	7
Nov 19 1951	12-Manik	7		Jan 26 1952	2-Men	3		Apr 3 1952	5-Akbal	8
Nov 20 1951	13-Lamat	8		Jan 27 1952	3-Cib	4		Apr 4 1952	6-Kan	9
Nov 21 1951	1-Muluc	9		Jan 28 1952	4-Caban	5		Apr 5 1952	7-Chicchan	1
Nov 22 1951	2-Oc	1		Jan 29 1952	5-Etz'nab	6		Apr 6 1952	8-Cimi	2
Nov 23 1951	3-Chuen	2		Jan 30 1952	6-Cauac	7		Apr 7 1952	9-Manik	3
Nov 24 1951	4-Eb	3		Jan 31 1952	7-Ahau	8		Apr 8 1952	10-Lamat	4
Nov 25 1951	5-Ben	4		Feb 1 1952	8-Imix	9		Apr 9 1952	11-Muluc	5
Nov 26 1951	6-Ix	5		Feb 2 1952	9-Ik	1		Apr 10 1952	12-Oc	6
Nov 27 1951	7-Men	6		Feb 3 1952	10-Akbal	2		Apr 11 1952	13-Chuen	7
Nov 28 1951	8-Cib	7		Feb 4 1952	11-Kan	3		Apr 12 1952	1-Eb	8
Nov 29 1951	9-Caban	8		Feb 5 1952	12-Chicchan	4		Apr 13 1952	2-Ben	9
Nov 30 1951	10-Etz'nab	9		Feb 6 1952	13-Cimi	5		Apr 14 1952	3-Ix	1
Dec 1 1951	11-Cauac	1		Feb 7 1952	1-Manik	6		Apr 15 1952	4-Men	2
Dec 2 1951	12-Ahau	2		Feb 8 1952	2-Lamat	7		Apr 16 1952	5-Cib	3
Dec 3 1951	13-Imix	3		Feb 9 1952	3-Muluc	8		Apr 17 1952	6-Caban	4
Dec 4 1951	1-Ik	4		Feb 10 1952	4-Oc	9		Apr 18 1952	7-Etz'nab	5
Dec 5 1951	2-Akbal	5		Feb 11 1952	5-Chuen	1		Apr 19 1952	8-Cauac	6
Dec 6 1951	3-Kan	6		Feb 12 1952	6-Eb	2		Apr 20 1952	9-Ahau	7
Dec 7 1951	4-Chicchan	7		Feb 13 1952	7-Ben	3		Apr 21 1952	10-Imix	8
Dec 8 1951	5-Cimi	8		Feb 14 1952	8-Ix	4		Apr 22 1952	11-Ik	9
Dec 9 1951	6-Manik	9		Feb 15 1952	9-Men	5		Apr 23 1952	12-Akbal	1
Dec 10 1951	7-Lamat	1		Feb 16 1952	10-Cib	6		Apr 24 1952	13-Kan	2
Dec 11 1951	8-Muluc	2		Feb 17 1952	11-Caban	7		Apr 25 1952	1-Chicchan	3

Date	Day-Sign	L
Apr 26 1952	2-Cimi	4
Apr 27 1952	3-Manik	5
Apr 28 1952	4-Lamat	6
Apr 29 1952	5-Muluc	7
Apr 30 1952	6-Oc	8
May 1 1952	7-Chuen	9
May 2 1952	8-Eb	1
May 3 1952	9-Ben	2
May 4 1952	10-Ix	3
May 5 1952	11-Men	4
May 6 1952	12-Cib	5
May 7 1952	13-Caban	6
May 8 1952	1-Etz'nab	7
May 9 1952	2-Cauac	8
May 10 1952	3-Ahau	9
May 11 1952	4-Imix	1
May 12 1952	5-Ik	2
May 13 1952	6-Akbal	3
May 14 1952	7-Kan	4
May 15 1952	8-Chicchan	5
May 16 1952	9-Cimi	6
May 17 1952	10-Manik	7
May 18 1952	11-Lamat	8
May 19 1952	12-Muluc	9
May 20 1952	13-Oc	1
May 21 1952	1-Chuen	2
May 22 1952	2-Eb	3
May 23 1952	3-Ben	4
May 24 1952	4-Ix	5
May 25 1952	5-Men	6
May 26 1952	6-Cib	7
May 27 1952	7-Caban	8
May 28 1952	8-Etz'nab	9
May 29 1952	9-Cauac	1
May 30 1952	10-Ahau	2
May 31 1952	11-Imix	3
Jun 1 1952	12-Ik	4
Jun 2 1952	13-Akbal	5
Jun 3 1952	1-Kan	6
Jun 4 1952	2-Chicchan	7
Jun 5 1952	3-Cimi	8
Jun 6 1952	4-Manik	9
Jun 7 1952	5-Lamat	1
Jun 8 1952	6-Muluc	2
Jun 9 1952	7-Oc	3
Jun 10 1952	8-Chuen	4
Jun 11 1952	9-Eb	5
Jun 12 1952	10-Ben	6
Jun 13 1952	11-Ix	7
Jun 14 1952	12-Men	8
Jun 15 1952	13-Cib	9
Jun 16 1952	1-Caban	1
Jun 17 1952	2-Etz'nab	2
Jun 18 1952	3-Cauac	3
Jun 19 1952	4-Ahau	4
Jun 20 1952	5-Imix	5
Jun 21 1952	6-Ik	6
Jun 22 1952	7-Akbal	7
Jun 23 1952	8-Kan	8
Jun 24 1952	9-Chicchan	9
Jun 25 1952	10-Cimi	1
Jun 26 1952	11-Manik	2
Jun 27 1952	12-Lamat	3
Jun 28 1952	13-Muluc	4
Jun 29 1952	1-Oc	5
Jun 30 1952	2-Chuen	6
Jul 1 1952	3-Eb	7
Jul 2 1952	4-Ben	8

Date	Day-Sign	L
Jul 3 1952	5-Ix	9
Jul 4 1952	6-Men	1
Jul 5 1952	7-Cib	2
Jul 6 1952	8-Caban	3
Jul 7 1952	9-Etz'nab	4
Jul 8 1952	10-Cauac	5
Jul 9 1952	11-Ahau	6
Jul 10 1952	12-Imix	7
Jul 11 1952	13-Ik	8
Jul 12 1952	1-Akbal	9
Jul 13 1952	2-Kan	1
Jul 14 1952	3-Chicchan	2
Jul 15 1952	4-Cimi	3
Jul 16 1952	5-Manik	4
Jul 17 1952	6-Lamat	5
Jul 18 1952	7-Muluc	6
Jul 19 1952	8-Oc	7
Jul 20 1952	9-Chuen	8
Jul 21 1952	10-Eb	9
Jul 22 1952	11-Ben	1
Jul 23 1952	12-Ix	2
Jul 24 1952	13-Men	3
Jul 25 1952	1-Cib	4
Jul 26 1952	2-Caban	5
Jul 27 1952	3-Etz'nab	6
Jul 28 1952	4-Cauac	7
Jul 29 1952	5-Ahau	8
Jul 30 1952	6-Imix	9
Jul 31 1952	7-Ik	1
Aug 1 1952	8-Akbal	2
Aug 2 1952	9-Kan	3
Aug 3 1952	10-Chicchan	4
Aug 4 1952	11-Cimi	5
Aug 5 1952	12-Manik	6
Aug 6 1952	13-Lamat	7
Aug 7 1952	1-Muluc	8
Aug 8 1952	2-Oc	9
Aug 9 1952	3-Chuen	1
Aug 10 1952	4-Eb	2
Aug 11 1952	5-Ben	3
Aug 12 1952	6-Ix	4
Aug 13 1952	7-Men	5
Aug 14 1952	8-Cib	6
Aug 15 1952	9-Caban	7
Aug 16 1952	10-Etz'nab	8
Aug 17 1952	11-Cauac	9
Aug 18 1952	12-Ahau	1
Aug 19 1952	13-Imix	2
Aug 20 1952	1-Ik	3
Aug 21 1952	2-Akbal	4
Aug 22 1952	3-Kan	5
Aug 23 1952	4-Chicchan	6
Aug 24 1952	5-Cimi	7
Aug 25 1952	6-Manik	8
Aug 26 1952	7-Lamat	9
Aug 27 1952	8-Muluc	1
Aug 28 1952	9-Oc	2
Aug 29 1952	10-Chuen	3
Aug 30 1952	11-Eb	4
Aug 31 1952	12-Ben	5
Sep 1 1952	13-Ix	6
Sep 2 1952	1-Men	7
Sep 3 1952	2-Cib	8
Sep 4 1952	3-Caban	9
Sep 5 1952	4-Etz'nab	1
Sep 6 1952	5-Cauac	2
Sep 7 1952	6-Ahau	3
Sep 8 1952	7-Imix	4

Date	Day-Sign	L
Sep 9 1952	8-Ik	5
Sep 10 1952	9-Akbal	6
Sep 11 1952	10-Kan	7
Sep 12 1952	11-Chicchan	8
Sep 13 1952	12-Cimi	9
Sep 14 1952	13-Manik	1
Sep 15 1952	1-Lamat	2
Sep 16 1952	2-Muluc	3
Sep 17 1952	3-Oc	4
Sep 18 1952	4-Chuen	5
Sep 19 1952	5-Eb	6
Sep 20 1952	6-Ben	7
Sep 21 1952	7-Ix	8
Sep 22 1952	8-Men	9
Sep 23 1952	9-Cib	1
Sep 24 1952	10-Caban	2
Sep 25 1952	11-Etz'nab	3
Sep 26 1952	12-Cauac	4
Sep 27 1952	13-Ahau	5
Sep 28 1952	1-Imix	6
Sep 29 1952	2-Ik	7
Sep 30 1952	3-Akbal	8
Oct 1 1952	4-Kan	9
Oct 2 1952	5-Chicchan	1
Oct 3 1952	6-Cimi	2
Oct 4 1952	7-Manik	3
Oct 5 1952	8-Lamat	4
Oct 6 1952	9-Muluc	5
Oct 7 1952	10-Oc	6
Oct 8 1952	11-Chuen	7
Oct 9 1952	12-Eb	8
Oct 10 1952	13-Ben	9
Oct 11 1952	1-Ix	1
Oct 12 1952	2-Men	2
Oct 13 1952	3-Cib	3
Oct 14 1952	4-Caban	4
Oct 15 1952	5-Etz'nab	5
Oct 16 1952	6-Cauac	6
Oct 17 1952	7-Ahau	7
Oct 18 1952	8-Imix	8
Oct 19 1952	9-Ik	9
Oct 20 1952	10-Akbal	1
Oct 21 1952	11-Kan	2
Oct 22 1952	12-Chicchan	3
Oct 23 1952	13-Cimi	4
Oct 24 1952	1-Manik	5
Oct 25 1952	2-Lamat	6
Oct 26 1952	3-Muluc	7
Oct 27 1952	4-Oc	8
Oct 28 1952	5-Chuen	9
Oct 29 1952	6-Eb	1
Oct 30 1952	7-Ben	2
Oct 31 1952	8-Ix	3
Nov 1 1952	9-Men	4
Nov 2 1952	10-Cib	5
Nov 3 1952	11-Caban	6
Nov 4 1952	12-Etz'nab	7
Nov 5 1952	13-Cauac	8
Nov 6 1952	1-Ahau	9
Nov 7 1952	2-Imix	1
Nov 8 1952	3-Ik	2
Nov 9 1952	4-Akbal	3
Nov 10 1952	5-Kan	4
Nov 11 1952	6-Chicchan	5
Nov 12 1952	7-Cimi	6
Nov 13 1952	8-Manik	7
Nov 14 1952	9-Lamat	8
Nov 15 1952	10-Muluc	9

Date	Day-Sign	L
Nov 16 1952	11-Oc	1
Nov 17 1952	12-Chuen	2
Nov 18 1952	13-Eb	3
Nov 19 1952	**1-Ben**	4
Nov 20 1952	2-Ix	5
Nov 21 1952	3-Men	6
Nov 22 1952	4-Cib	7
Nov 23 1952	5-Caban	8
Nov 24 1952	6-Etz'nab	9
Nov 25 1952	7-Cauac	1
Nov 26 1952	8-Ahau	2
Nov 27 1952	9-*Imix*	3
Nov 28 1952	10-Ik	4
Nov 29 1952	11-Akbal	5
Nov 30 1952	12-Kan	6
Dec 1 1952	13-Chicchan	7
Dec 2 1952	**1-Cimi**	8
Dec 3 1952	2-Manik	9
Dec 4 1952	3-Lamat	1
Dec 5 1952	4-Muluc	2
Dec 6 1952	5-Oc	3
Dec 7 1952	6-Chuen	4
Dec 8 1952	7-Eb	5
Dec 9 1952	8-Ben	6
Dec 10 1952	9-Ix	7
Dec 11 1952	10-Men	8
Dec 12 1952	11-Cib	9
Dec 13 1952	12-Caban	1
Dec 14 1952	13-Etz'nab	2
Dec 15 1952	**1-Cauac**	3
Dec 16 1952	2-Ahau	4
Dec 17 1952	3-*Imix*	5
Dec 18 1952	4-Ik	6
Dec 19 1952	5-Akbal	7
Dec 20 1952	6-Kan	8
Dec 21 1952	7-Chicchan	9
Dec 22 1952	8-Cimi	1
Dec 23 1952	9-Manik	2
Dec 24 1952	10-Lamat	3
Dec 25 1952	11-Muluc	4
Dec 26 1952	12-Oc	5
Dec 27 1952	13-Chuen	6
Dec 28 1952	**1-Eb**	7
Dec 29 1952	2-Ben	8
Dec 30 1952	3-Ix	9
Dec 31 1952	4-Men	1
Jan 1 1953	5-Cib	2
Jan 2 1953	6-Caban	3
Jan 3 1953	7-Etz'nab	4
Jan 4 1953	8-Cauac	5
Jan 5 1953	9-Ahau	6
Jan 6 1953	10-*Imix*	7
Jan 7 1953	11-Ik	8
Jan 8 1953	12-Akbal	9
Jan 9 1953	13-Kan	1
Jan 10 1953	**1-Chicchan**	2
Jan 11 1953	2-Cimi	3
Jan 12 1953	3-Manik	4
Jan 13 1953	4-Lamat	5
Jan 14 1953	5-Muluc	6
Jan 15 1953	6-Oc	7
Jan 16 1953	7-Chuen	8
Jan 17 1953	8-Eb	9
Jan 18 1953	9-Ben	1
Jan 19 1953	10-Ix	2
Jan 20 1953	11-Men	3
Jan 21 1953	12-Cib	4
Jan 22 1953	13-Caban	5

Date	Day-Sign	L
Jan 23 1953	**1-Etz'nab**	6
Jan 24 1953	2-Cauac	7
Jan 25 1953	3-Ahau	8
Jan 26 1953	4-*Imix*	9
Jan 27 1953	5-Ik	1
Jan 28 1953	6-Akbal	2
Jan 29 1953	7-Kan	3
Jan 30 1953	8-Chicchan	4
Jan 31 1953	9-Cimi	5
Feb 1 1953	10-Manik	6
Feb 2 1953	11-Lamat	7
Feb 3 1953	12-Muluc	8
Feb 4 1953	13-Oc	9
Feb 5 1953	**1-Chuen**	1
Feb 6 1953	2-Eb	2
Feb 7 1953	3-Ben	3
Feb 8 1953	4-Ix	4
Feb 9 1953	5-Men	5
Feb 10 1953	6-Cib	6
Feb 11 1953	7-Caban	7
Feb 12 1953	8-Etz'nab	8
Feb 13 1953	9-Cauac	9
Feb 14 1953	10-Ahau	1
Feb 15 1953	11-*Imix*	2
Feb 16 1953	12-Ik	3
Feb 17 1953	13-Akbal	4
Feb 18 1953	**1-Kan**	5
Feb 19 1953	2-Chicchan	6
Feb 20 1953	3-Cimi	7
Feb 21 1953	4-Manik	8
Feb 22 1953	5-Lamat	9
Feb 23 1953	6-Muluc	1
Feb 24 1953	7-Oc	2
Feb 25 1953	8-Chuen	3
Feb 26 1953	9-Eb	4
Feb 27 1953	10-Ben	5
Feb 28 1953	11-Ix	6
Mar 1 1953	12-Men	7
Mar 2 1953	13-Cib	8
Mar 3 1953	**1-Caban**	9
Mar 4 1953	2-Etz'nab	1
Mar 5 1953	3-Cauac	2
Mar 6 1953	4-Ahau	3
Mar 7 1953	5-*Imix*	4
Mar 8 1953	6-Ik	5
Mar 9 1953	7-Akbal	6
Mar 10 1953	8-Kan	7
Mar 11 1953	9-Chicchan	8
Mar 12 1953	10-Cimi	9
Mar 13 1953	11-Manik	1
Mar 14 1953	12-Lamat	2
Mar 15 1953	13-Muluc	3
Mar 16 1953	**1-Oc**	4
Mar 17 1953	2-Chuen	5
Mar 18 1953	3-Eb	6
Mar 19 1953	4-Ben	7
Mar 20 1953	5-Ix	8
Mar 21 1953	6-Men	9
Mar 22 1953	7-Cib	1
Mar 23 1953	8-Caban	2
Mar 24 1953	9-Etz'nab	3
Mar 25 1953	10-Cauac	4
Mar 26 1953	11-Ahau	5
Mar 27 1953	12-*Imix*	6
Mar 28 1953	13-Ik	7
Mar 29 1953	**1-Akbal**	8
Mar 30 1953	2-Kan	9
Mar 31 1953	3-Chicchan	1

Date	Day-Sign	L
Apr 1 1953	4-Cimi	2
Apr 2 1953	5-Manik	3
Apr 3 1953	6-Lamat	4
Apr 4 1953	7-Muluc	5
Apr 5 1953	8-Oc	6
Apr 6 1953	9-Chuen	7
Apr 7 1953	10-Eb	8
Apr 8 1953	11-Ben	9
Apr 9 1953	12-Ix	1
Apr 10 1953	13-Men	2
Apr 11 1953	**1-Cib**	3
Apr 12 1953	2-Caban	4
Apr 13 1953	3-Etz'nab	5
Apr 14 1953	4-Cauac	6
Apr 15 1953	5-Ahau	7
Apr 16 1953	6-*Imix*	8
Apr 17 1953	7-Ik	9
Apr 18 1953	8-Akbal	1
Apr 19 1953	9-Kan	2
Apr 20 1953	10-Chicchan	3
Apr 21 1953	11-Cimi	4
Apr 22 1953	12-Manik	5
Apr 23 1953	13-Lamat	6
Apr 24 1953	**1-Muluc**	7
Apr 25 1953	2-Oc	8
Apr 26 1953	3-Chuen	9
Apr 27 1953	4-Eb	1
Apr 28 1953	5-Ben	2
Apr 29 1953	6-Ix	3
Apr 30 1953	7-Men	4
May 1 1953	8-Cib	5
May 2 1953	9-Caban	6
May 3 1953	10-Etz'nab	7
May 4 1953	11-Cauac	8
May 5 1953	12-Ahau	9
May 6 1953	13-*Imix*	1
May 7 1953	**1-Ik**	2
May 8 1953	2-Akbal	3
May 9 1953	3-Kan	4
May 10 1953	4-Chicchan	5
May 11 1953	5-Cimi	6
May 12 1953	6-Manik	7
May 13 1953	7-Lamat	8
May 14 1953	8-Muluc	9
May 15 1953	9-Oc	1
May 16 1953	10-Chuen	2
May 17 1953	11-Eb	3
May 18 1953	12-Ben	4
May 19 1953	13-Ix	5
May 20 1953	**1-Men**	6
May 21 1953	2-Cib	7
May 22 1953	3-Caban	8
May 23 1953	4-Etz'nab	9
May 24 1953	5-Cauac	1
May 25 1953	6-Ahau	2
May 26 1953	7-*Imix*	3
May 27 1953	8-Ik	4
May 28 1953	9-Akbal	5
May 29 1953	10-Kan	6
May 30 1953	11-Chicchan	7
May 31 1953	12-Cimi	8
Jun 1 1953	13-Manik	9
Jun 2 1953	**1-Lamat**	1
Jun 3 1953	2-Muluc	2
Jun 4 1953	3-Oc	3
Jun 5 1953	4-Chuen	4
Jun 6 1953	5-Eb	5
Jun 7 1953	6-Ben	6

Date	Day-Sign	L	Date	Day-Sign	L	Date	Day-Sign	L
Jun 8 1953	7-Ix	7	Aug 15 1953	10-Ik	3	Oct 22 1953	13-Oc	8
Jun 9 1953	8-Men	8	Aug 16 1953	11-Akbal	4	Oct 23 1953	**1-Chuen**	9
Jun 10 1953	9-Cib	9	Aug 17 1953	12-Kan	5	Oct 24 1953	2-Eb	1
Jun 11 1953	10-Caban	1	Aug 18 1953	13-Chicchan	6	Oct 25 1953	3-Ben	2
Jun 12 1953	11-Etz'nab	2	Aug 19 1953	**1-Cimi**	7	Oct 26 1953	4-Ix	3
Jun 13 1953	12-Cauac	3	Aug 20 1953	2-Manik	8	Oct 27 1953	5-Men	4
Jun 14 1953	13-Ahau	4	Aug 21 1953	3-Lamat	9	Oct 28 1953	6-Cib	5
Jun 15 1953	**1-Imix**	5	Aug 22 1953	4-Muluc	1	Oct 29 1953	7-Caban	6
Jun 16 1953	2-Ik	6	Aug 23 1953	5-Oc	2	Oct 30 1953	8-Etz'nab	7
Jun 17 1953	3-Akbal	7	Aug 24 1953	6-Chuen	3	Oct 31 1953	9-Cauac	8
Jun 18 1953	4-Kan	8	Aug 25 1953	7-Eb	4	Nov 1 1953	10-Ahau	9
Jun 19 1953	5-Chicchan	9	Aug 26 1953	8-Ben	5	Nov 2 1953	11-*Imix*	1
Jun 20 1953	6-Cimi	1	Aug 27 1953	9-Ix	6	Nov 3 1953	12-Ik	2
Jun 21 1953	7-Manik	2	Aug 28 1953	10-Men	7	Nov 4 1953	13-Akbal	3
Jun 22 1953	8-Lamat	3	Aug 29 1953	11-Cib	8	Nov 5 1953	**1-Kan**	4
Jun 23 1953	9-Muluc	4	Aug 30 1953	12-Caban	9	Nov 6 1953	2-Chicchan	5
Jun 24 1953	10-Oc	5	Aug 31 1953	13-Etz'nab	1	Nov 7 1953	3-Cimi	6
Jun 25 1953	11-Chuen	6	Sep 1 1953	**1-Cauac**	2	Nov 8 1953	4-Manik	7
Jun 26 1953	12-Eb	7	Sep 2 1953	2-Ahau	3	Nov 9 1953	5-Lamat	8
Jun 27 1953	13-Ben	8	Sep 3 1953	3-*Imix*	4	Nov 10 1953	6-Muluc	9
Jun 28 1953	**1-Ix**	9	Sep 4 1953	4-Ik	5	Nov 11 1953	7-Oc	1
Jun 29 1953	2-Men	1	Sep 5 1953	5-Akbal	6	Nov 12 1953	8-Chuen	2
Jun 30 1953	3-Cib	2	Sep 6 1953	6-Kan	7	Nov 13 1953	9-Eb	3
Jul 1 1953	4-Caban	3	Sep 7 1953	7-Chicchan	8	Nov 14 1953	10-Ben	4
Jul 2 1953	5-Etz'nab	4	Sep 8 1953	8-Cimi	9	Nov 15 1953	11-Ix	5
Jul 3 1953	6-Cauac	5	Sep 9 1953	9-Manik	1	Nov 16 1953	12-Men	6
Jul 4 1953	7-Ahau	6	Sep 10 1953	10-Lamat	2	Nov 17 1953	13-Cib	7
Jul 5 1953	8-*Imix*	7	Sep 11 1953	11-Muluc	3	Nov 18 1953	**1-Caban**	8
Jul 6 1953	9-Ik	8	Sep 12 1953	12-Oc	4	Nov 19 1953	2-Etz'nab	9
Jul 7 1953	10-Akbal	9	Sep 13 1953	13-Chuen	5	Nov 20 1953	3-Cauac	1
Jul 8 1953	11-Kan	1	Sep 14 1953	**1-Eb**	6	Nov 21 1953	4-Ahau	2
Jul 9 1953	12-Chicchan	2	Sep 15 1953	2-Ben	7	Nov 22 1953	5-*Imix*	3
Jul 10 1953	13-Cimi	3	Sep 16 1953	3-Ix	8	Nov 23 1953	6-Ik	4
Jul 11 1953	**1-Manik**	4	Sep 17 1953	4-Men	9	Nov 24 1953	7-Akbal	5
Jul 12 1953	2-Lamat	5	Sep 18 1953	5-Cib	1	Nov 25 1953	8-Kan	6
Jul 13 1953	3-Muluc	6	Sep 19 1953	6-Caban	2	Nov 26 1953	9-Chicchan	7
Jul 14 1953	4-Oc	7	Sep 20 1953	7-Etz'nab	3	Nov 27 1953	10-Cimi	8
Jul 15 1953	5-Chuen	8	Sep 21 1953	8-Cauac	4	Nov 28 1953	11-Manik	9
Jul 16 1953	6-Eb	9	Sep 22 1953	9-Ahau	5	Nov 29 1953	12-Lamat	1
Jul 17 1953	7-Ben	1	Sep 23 1953	10-*Imix*	6	Nov 30 1953	13-Muluc	2
Jul 18 1953	8-Ix	2	Sep 24 1953	11-Ik	7	Dec 1 1953	**1-Oc**	3
Jul 19 1953	9-Men	3	Sep 25 1953	12-Akbal	8	Dec 2 1953	2-Chuen	4
Jul 20 1953	10-Cib	4	Sep 26 1953	13-Kan	9	Dec 3 1953	3-Eb	5
Jul 21 1953	11-Caban	5	Sep 27 1953	**1-Chicchan**	1	Dec 4 1953	4-Ben	6
Jul 22 1953	12-Etz'nab	6	Sep 28 1953	2-Cimi	2	Dec 5 1953	5-Ix	7
Jul 23 1953	13-Cauac	7	Sep 29 1953	3-Manik	3	Dec 6 1953	6-Men	8
Jul 24 1953	**1-Ahau**	8	Sep 30 1953	4-Lamat	4	Dec 7 1953	7-Cib	9
Jul 25 1953	2-*Imix*	9	Oct 1 1953	5-Muluc	5	Dec 8 1953	8-Caban	1
Jul 26 1953	3-Ik	1	Oct 2 1953	6-Oc	6	Dec 9 1953	9-Etz'nab	2
Jul 27 1953	4-Akbal	2	Oct 3 1953	7-Chuen	7	Dec 10 1953	10-Cauac	3
Jul 28 1953	5-Kan	3	Oct 4 1953	8-Eb	8	Dec 11 1953	11-Ahau	4
Jul 29 1953	6-Chicchan	4	Oct 5 1953	9-Ben	9	Dec 12 1953	12-*Imix*	5
Jul 30 1953	7-Cimi	5	Oct 6 1953	10-Ix	1	Dec 13 1953	13-Ik	6
Jul 31 1953	8-Manik	6	Oct 7 1953	11-Men	2	Dec 14 1953	**1-Akbal**	7
Aug 1 1953	9-Lamat	7	Oct 8 1953	12-Cib	3	Dec 15 1953	2-Kan	8
Aug 2 1953	10-Muluc	8	Oct 9 1953	13-Caban	4	Dec 16 1953	3-Chicchan	9
Aug 3 1953	11-Oc	9	Oct 10 1953	**1-Etz'nab**	5	Dec 17 1953	4-Cimi	1
Aug 4 1953	12-Chuen	1	Oct 11 1953	2-Cauac	6	Dec 18 1953	5-Manik	2
Aug 5 1953	13-Eb	2	Oct 12 1953	3-Ahau	7	Dec 19 1953	6-Lamat	3
Aug 6 1953	**1-Ben**	3	Oct 13 1953	4-*Imix*	8	Dec 20 1953	7-Muluc	4
Aug 7 1953	2-Ix	4	Oct 14 1953	5-Ik	9	Dec 21 1953	8-Oc	5
Aug 8 1953	3-Men	5	Oct 15 1953	6-Akbal	1	Dec 22 1953	9-Chuen	6
Aug 9 1953	4-Cib	6	Oct 16 1953	7-Kan	2	Dec 23 1953	10-Eb	7
Aug 10 1953	5-Caban	7	Oct 17 1953	8-Chicchan	3	Dec 24 1953	11-Ben	8
Aug 11 1953	6-Etz'nab	8	Oct 18 1953	9-Cimi	4	Dec 25 1953	12-Ix	9
Aug 12 1953	7-Cauac	9	Oct 19 1953	10-Manik	5	Dec 26 1953	13-Men	1
Aug 13 1953	8-Ahau	1	Oct 20 1953	11-Lamat	6	Dec 27 1953	**1-Cib**	2
Aug 14 1953	9-*Imix*	2	Oct 21 1953	12-Muluc	7	Dec 28 1953	2-Caban	3

Date	Day-Sign	L
Dec 29 1953	3-Etz'nab	4
Dec 30 1953	4-Cauac	5
Dec 31 1953	5-Ahau	6
Jan 1 1954	6-Imix	7
Jan 2 1954	7-Ik	8
Jan 3 1954	8-Akbal	9
Jan 4 1954	9-Kan	1
Jan 5 1954	10-Chicchan	2
Jan 6 1954	11-Cimi	3
Jan 7 1954	12-Manik	4
Jan 8 1954	13-Lamat	5
Jan 9 1954	1-Muluc	6
Jan 10 1954	2-Oc	7
Jan 11 1954	3-Chuen	8
Jan 12 1954	4-Eb	9
Jan 13 1954	5-Ben	1
Jan 14 1954	6-Ix	2
Jan 15 1954	7-Men	3
Jan 16 1954	8-Cib	4
Jan 17 1954	9-Caban	5
Jan 18 1954	10-Etz'nab	6
Jan 19 1954	11-Cauac	7
Jan 20 1954	12-Ahau	8
Jan 21 1954	13-Imix	9
Jan 22 1954	1-Ik	1
Jan 23 1954	2-Akbal	2
Jan 24 1954	3-Kan	3
Jan 25 1954	4-Chicchan	4
Jan 26 1954	5-Cimi	5
Jan 27 1954	6-Manik	6
Jan 28 1954	7-Lamat	7
Jan 29 1954	8-Muluc	8
Jan 30 1954	9-Oc	9
Jan 31 1954	10-Chuen	1
Feb 1 1954	11-Eb	2
Feb 2 1954	12-Ben	3
Feb 3 1954	13-Ix	4
Feb 4 1954	1-Men	5
Feb 5 1954	2-Cib	6
Feb 6 1954	3-Caban	7
Feb 7 1954	4-Etz'nab	8
Feb 8 1954	5-Cauac	9
Feb 9 1954	6-Ahau	1
Feb 10 1954	7-Imix	2
Feb 11 1954	8-Ik	3
Feb 12 1954	9-Akbal	4
Feb 13 1954	10-Kan	5
Feb 14 1954	11-Chicchan	6
Feb 15 1954	12-Cimi	7
Feb 16 1954	13-Manik	8
Feb 17 1954	1-Lamat	9
Feb 18 1954	2-Muluc	1
Feb 19 1954	3-Oc	2
Feb 20 1954	4-Chuen	3
Feb 21 1954	5-Eb	4
Feb 22 1954	6-Ben	5
Feb 23 1954	7-Ix	6
Feb 24 1954	8-Men	7
Feb 25 1954	9-Cib	8
Feb 26 1954	10-Caban	9
Feb 27 1954	11-Etz'nab	1
Feb 28 1954	12-Cauac	2
Mar 1 1954	13-Ahau	3
Mar 2 1954	1-Imix	4
Mar 3 1954	2-Ik	5
Mar 4 1954	3-Akbal	6
Mar 5 1954	4-Kan	7
Mar 6 1954	5-Chicchan	8
Mar 7 1954	6-Cimi	9
Mar 8 1954	7-Manik	1
Mar 9 1954	8-Lamat	2
Mar 10 1954	9-Muluc	3
Mar 11 1954	10-Oc	4
Mar 12 1954	11-Chuen	5
Mar 13 1954	12-Eb	6
Mar 14 1954	13-Ben	7
Mar 15 1954	1-Ix	8
Mar 16 1954	2-Men	9
Mar 17 1954	3-Cib	1
Mar 18 1954	4-Caban	2
Mar 19 1954	5-Etz'nab	3
Mar 20 1954	6-Cauac	4
Mar 21 1954	7-Ahau	5
Mar 22 1954	8-Imix	6
Mar 23 1954	9-Ik	7
Mar 24 1954	10-Akbal	8
Mar 25 1954	11-Kan	9
Mar 26 1954	12-Chicchan	1
Mar 27 1954	13-Cimi	2
Mar 28 1954	1-Manik	3
Mar 29 1954	2-Lamat	4
Mar 30 1954	3-Muluc	5
Mar 31 1954	4-Oc	6
Apr 1 1954	5-Chuen	7
Apr 2 1954	6-Eb	8
Apr 3 1954	7-Ben	9
Apr 4 1954	8-Ix	1
Apr 5 1954	9-Men	2
Apr 6 1954	10-Cib	3
Apr 7 1954	11-Caban	4
Apr 8 1954	12-Etz'nab	5
Apr 9 1954	13-Cauac	6
Apr 10 1954	1-Ahau	7
Apr 11 1954	2-Imix	8
Apr 12 1954	3-Ik	9
Apr 13 1954	4-Akbal	1
Apr 14 1954	5-Kan	2
Apr 15 1954	6-Chicchan	3
Apr 16 1954	7-Cimi	4
Apr 17 1954	8-Manik	5
Apr 18 1954	9-Lamat	6
Apr 19 1954	10-Muluc	7
Apr 20 1954	11-Oc	8
Apr 21 1954	12-Chuen	9
Apr 22 1954	13-Eb	1
Apr 23 1954	1-Ben	2
Apr 24 1954	2-Ix	3
Apr 25 1954	3-Men	4
Apr 26 1954	4-Cib	5
Apr 27 1954	5-Caban	6
Apr 28 1954	6-Etz'nab	7
Apr 29 1954	7-Cauac	8
Apr 30 1954	8-Ahau	9
May 1 1954	9-Imix	1
May 2 1954	10-Ik	2
May 3 1954	11-Akbal	3
May 4 1954	12-Kan	4
May 5 1954	13-Chicchan	5
May 6 1954	1-Cimi	6
May 7 1954	2-Manik	7
May 8 1954	3-Lamat	8
May 9 1954	4-Muluc	9
May 10 1954	5-Oc	1
May 11 1954	6-Chuen	2
May 12 1954	7-Eb	3
May 13 1954	8-Ben	4
May 14 1954	9-Ix	5
May 15 1954	10-Men	6
May 16 1954	11-Cib	7
May 17 1954	12-Caban	8
May 18 1954	13-Etz'nab	9
May 19 1954	1-Cauac	1
May 20 1954	2-Ahau	2
May 21 1954	3-Imix	3
May 22 1954	4-Ik	4
May 23 1954	5-Akbal	5
May 24 1954	6-Kan	6
May 25 1954	7-Chicchan	7
May 26 1954	8-Cimi	8
May 27 1954	9-Manik	9
May 28 1954	10-Lamat	1
May 29 1954	11-Muluc	2
May 30 1954	12-Oc	3
May 31 1954	13-Chuen	4
Jun 1 1954	1-Eb	5
Jun 2 1954	2-Ben	6
Jun 3 1954	3-Ix	7
Jun 4 1954	4-Men	8
Jun 5 1954	5-Cib	9
Jun 6 1954	6-Caban	1
Jun 7 1954	7-Etz'nab	2
Jun 8 1954	8-Cauac	3
Jun 9 1954	9-Ahau	4
Jun 10 1954	10-Imix	5
Jun 11 1954	11-Ik	6
Jun 12 1954	12-Akbal	7
Jun 13 1954	13-Kan	8
Jun 14 1954	1-Chicchan	9
Jun 15 1954	2-Cimi	1
Jun 16 1954	3-Manik	2
Jun 17 1954	4-Lamat	3
Jun 18 1954	5-Muluc	4
Jun 19 1954	6-Oc	5
Jun 20 1954	7-Chuen	6
Jun 21 1954	8-Eb	7
Jun 22 1954	9-Ben	8
Jun 23 1954	10-Ix	9
Jun 24 1954	11-Men	1
Jun 25 1954	12-Cib	2
Jun 26 1954	13-Caban	3
Jun 27 1954	1-Etz'nab	4
Jun 28 1954	2-Cauac	5
Jun 29 1954	3-Ahau	6
Jun 30 1954	4-Imix	7
Jul 1 1954	5-Ik	8
Jul 2 1954	6-Akbal	9
Jul 3 1954	7-Kan	1
Jul 4 1954	8-Chicchan	2
Jul 5 1954	9-Cimi	3
Jul 6 1954	10-Manik	4
Jul 7 1954	11-Lamat	5
Jul 8 1954	12-Muluc	6
Jul 9 1954	13-Oc	7
Jul 10 1954	1-Chuen	8
Jul 11 1954	2-Eb	9
Jul 12 1954	3-Ben	1
Jul 13 1954	4-Ix	2
Jul 14 1954	5-Men	3
Jul 15 1954	6-Cib	4
Jul 16 1954	7-Caban	5
Jul 17 1954	8-Etz'nab	6
Jul 18 1954	9-Cauac	7
Jul 19 1954	10-Ahau	8
Jul 20 1954	11-Imix	9

Date	Day-Sign	L
Jul 21 1954	12-Ik	1
Jul 22 1954	13-Akbal	2
Jul 23 1954	**1-Kan**	3
Jul 24 1954	2-Chicchan	4
Jul 25 1954	3-Cimi	5
Jul 26 1954	4-Manik	6
Jul 27 1954	5-Lamat	7
Jul 28 1954	6-Muluc	8
Jul 29 1954	7-Oc	9
Jul 30 1954	8-Chuen	1
Jul 31 1954	9-Eb	2
Aug 1 1954	10-Ben	3
Aug 2 1954	11-Ix	4
Aug 3 1954	12-Men	5
Aug 4 1954	13-Cib	6
Aug 5 1954	**1-Caban**	7
Aug 6 1954	2-Etz'nab	8
Aug 7 1954	3-Cauac	9
Aug 8 1954	4-Ahau	1
Aug 9 1954	*5-Imix*	2
Aug 10 1954	6-Ik	3
Aug 11 1954	7-Akbal	4
Aug 12 1954	8-Kan	5
Aug 13 1954	9-Chicchan	6
Aug 14 1954	10-Cimi	7
Aug 15 1954	11-Manik	8
Aug 16 1954	12-Lamat	9
Aug 17 1954	13-Muluc	1
Aug 18 1954	**1-Oc**	2
Aug 19 1954	2-Chuen	3
Aug 20 1954	3-Eb	4
Aug 21 1954	4-Ben	5
Aug 22 1954	5-Ix	6
Aug 23 1954	6-Men	7
Aug 24 1954	7-Cib	8
Aug 25 1954	8-Caban	9
Aug 26 1954	9-Etz'nab	1
Aug 27 1954	10-Cauac	2
Aug 28 1954	11-Ahau	3
Aug 29 1954	*12-Imix*	4
Aug 30 1954	13-Ik	5
Aug 31 1954	**1-Akbal**	6
Sep 1 1954	2-Kan	7
Sep 2 1954	3-Chicchan	8
Sep 3 1954	4-Cimi	9
Sep 4 1954	5-Manik	1
Sep 5 1954	6-Lamat	2
Sep 6 1954	7-Muluc	3
Sep 7 1954	8-Oc	4
Sep 8 1954	9-Chuen	5
Sep 9 1954	10-Eb	6
Sep 10 1954	11-Ben	7
Sep 11 1954	12-Ix	8
Sep 12 1954	13-Men	9
Sep 13 1954	**1-Cib**	1
Sep 14 1954	2-Caban	2
Sep 15 1954	3-Etz'nab	3
Sep 16 1954	4-Cauac	4
Sep 17 1954	5-Ahau	5
Sep 18 1954	*6-Imix*	6
Sep 19 1954	7-Ik	7
Sep 20 1954	8-Akbal	8
Sep 21 1954	9-Kan	9
Sep 22 1954	10-Chicchan	1
Sep 23 1954	11-Cimi	2
Sep 24 1954	12-Manik	3
Sep 25 1954	13-Lamat	4
Sep 26 1954	**1-Muluc**	5

Date	Day-Sign	L
Sep 27 1954	2-Oc	6
Sep 28 1954	3-Chuen	7
Sep 29 1954	4-Eb	8
Sep 30 1954	5-Ben	9
Oct 1 1954	6-Ix	1
Oct 2 1954	7-Men	2
Oct 3 1954	8-Cib	3
Oct 4 1954	9-Caban	4
Oct 5 1954	10-Etz'nab	5
Oct 6 1954	11-Cauac	6
Oct 7 1954	12-Ahau	7
Oct 8 1954	*13-Imix*	8
Oct 9 1954	**1-Ik**	9
Oct 10 1954	2-Akbal	1
Oct 11 1954	3-Kan	2
Oct 12 1954	4-Chicchan	3
Oct 13 1954	5-Cimi	4
Oct 14 1954	6-Manik	5
Oct 15 1954	7-Lamat	6
Oct 16 1954	8-Muluc	7
Oct 17 1954	9-Oc	8
Oct 18 1954	10-Chuen	9
Oct 19 1954	11-Eb	1
Oct 20 1954	12-Ben	2
Oct 21 1954	13-Ix	3
Oct 22 1954	**1-Men**	4
Oct 23 1954	2-Cib	5
Oct 24 1954	3-Caban	6
Oct 25 1954	4-Etz'nab	7
Oct 26 1954	5-Cauac	8
Oct 27 1954	6-Ahau	9
Oct 28 1954	*7-Imix*	1
Oct 29 1954	8-Ik	2
Oct 30 1954	9-Akbal	3
Oct 31 1954	10-Kan	4
Nov 1 1954	11-Chicchan	5
Nov 2 1954	12-Cimi	6
Nov 3 1954	13-Manik	7
Nov 4 1954	**1-Lamat**	8
Nov 5 1954	2-Muluc	9
Nov 6 1954	3-Oc	1
Nov 7 1954	4-Chuen	2
Nov 8 1954	5-Eb	3
Nov 9 1954	6-Ben	4
Nov 10 1954	7-Ix	5
Nov 11 1954	8-Men	6
Nov 12 1954	9-Cib	7
Nov 13 1954	10-Caban	8
Nov 14 1954	11-Etz'nab	9
Nov 15 1954	12-Cauac	1
Nov 16 1954	13-Ahau	2
Nov 17 1954	**1-Imix**	3
Nov 18 1954	2-Ik	4
Nov 19 1954	3-Akbal	5
Nov 20 1954	4-Kan	6
Nov 21 1954	5-Chicchan	7
Nov 22 1954	6-Cimi	8
Nov 23 1954	7-Manik	9
Nov 24 1954	8-Lamat	1
Nov 25 1954	9-Muluc	2
Nov 26 1954	10-Oc	3
Nov 27 1954	11-Chuen	4
Nov 28 1954	12-Eb	5
Nov 29 1954	13-Ben	6
Nov 30 1954	**1-Ix**	7
Dec 1 1954	2-Men	8
Dec 2 1954	3-Cib	9
Dec 3 1954	4-Caban	1

Date	Day-Sign	L
Dec 4 1954	5-Etz'nab	2
Dec 5 1954	6-Cauac	3
Dec 6 1954	7-Ahau	4
Dec 7 1954	*8-Imix*	5
Dec 8 1954	9-Ik	6
Dec 9 1954	10-Akbal	7
Dec 10 1954	11-Kan	8
Dec 11 1954	12-Chicchan	9
Dec 12 1954	13-Cimi	1
Dec 13 1954	**1-Manik**	2
Dec 14 1954	2-Lamat	3
Dec 15 1954	3-Muluc	4
Dec 16 1954	4-Oc	5
Dec 17 1954	5-Chuen	6
Dec 18 1954	6-Eb	7
Dec 19 1954	7-Ben	8
Dec 20 1954	8-Ix	9
Dec 21 1954	9-Men	1
Dec 22 1954	10-Cib	2
Dec 23 1954	11-Caban	3
Dec 24 1954	12-Etz'nab	4
Dec 25 1954	13-Cauac	5
Dec 26 1954	**1-Ahau**	6
Dec 27 1954	*2-Imix*	7
Dec 28 1954	3-Ik	8
Dec 29 1954	4-Akbal	9
Dec 30 1954	5-Kan	1
Dec 31 1954	6-Chicchan	2
Jan 1 1955	7-Cimi	3
Jan 2 1955	8-Manik	4
Jan 3 1955	9-Lamat	5
Jan 4 1955	10-Muluc	6
Jan 5 1955	11-Oc	7
Jan 6 1955	12-Chuen	8
Jan 7 1955	13-Eb	9
Jan 8 1955	**1-Ben**	1
Jan 9 1955	2-Ix	2
Jan 10 1955	3-Men	3
Jan 11 1955	4-Cib	4
Jan 12 1955	5-Caban	5
Jan 13 1955	6-Etz'nab	6
Jan 14 1955	7-Cauac	7
Jan 15 1955	8-Ahau	8
Jan 16 1955	*9-Imix*	9
Jan 17 1955	10-Ik	1
Jan 18 1955	11-Akbal	2
Jan 19 1955	12-Kan	3
Jan 20 1955	13-Chicchan	4
Jan 21 1955	**1-Cimi**	5
Jan 22 1955	2-Manik	6
Jan 23 1955	3-Lamat	7
Jan 24 1955	4-Muluc	8
Jan 25 1955	5-Oc	9
Jan 26 1955	6-Chuen	1
Jan 27 1955	7-Eb	2
Jan 28 1955	8-Ben	3
Jan 29 1955	9-Ix	4
Jan 30 1955	10-Men	5
Jan 31 1955	11-Cib	6
Feb 1 1955	12-Caban	7
Feb 2 1955	13-Etz'nab	8
Feb 3 1955	**1-Cauac**	9
Feb 4 1955	2-Ahau	1
Feb 5 1955	*3-Imix*	2
Feb 6 1955	4-Ik	3
Feb 7 1955	5-Akbal	4
Feb 8 1955	6-Kan	5
Feb 9 1955	7-Chicchan	6

Date	Day-Sign	L
Feb 10 1955	8-Cimi	7
Feb 11 1955	9-Manik	8
Feb 12 1955	10-Lamat	9
Feb 13 1955	11-Muluc	1
Feb 14 1955	12-Oc	2
Feb 15 1955	13-Chuen	3
Feb 16 1955	1-Eb	4
Feb 17 1955	2-Ben	5
Feb 18 1955	3-Ix	6
Feb 19 1955	4-Men	7
Feb 20 1955	5-Cib	8
Feb 21 1955	6-Caban	9
Feb 22 1955	7-Etz'nab	1
Feb 23 1955	8-Cauac	2
Feb 24 1955	9-Ahau	3
Feb 25 1955	10-Imix	4
Feb 26 1955	11-Ik	5
Feb 27 1955	12-Akbal	6
Feb 28 1955	13-Kan	7
Mar 1 1955	1-Chicchan	8
Mar 2 1955	2-Cimi	9
Mar 3 1955	3-Manik	1
Mar 4 1955	4-Lamat	2
Mar 5 1955	5-Muluc	3
Mar 6 1955	6-Oc	4
Mar 7 1955	7-Chuen	5
Mar 8 1955	8-Eb	6
Mar 9 1955	9-Ben	7
Mar 10 1955	10-Ix	8
Mar 11 1955	11-Men	9
Mar 12 1955	12-Cib	1
Mar 13 1955	13-Caban	2
Mar 14 1955	1-Etz'nab	3
Mar 15 1955	2-Cauac	4
Mar 16 1955	3-Ahau	5
Mar 17 1955	4-Imix	6
Mar 18 1955	5-Ik	7
Mar 19 1955	6-Akbal	8
Mar 20 1955	7-Kan	9
Mar 21 1955	8-Chicchan	1
Mar 22 1955	9-Cimi	2
Mar 23 1955	10-Manik	3
Mar 24 1955	11-Lamat	4
Mar 25 1955	12-Muluc	5
Mar 26 1955	13-Oc	6
Mar 27 1955	1-Chuen	7
Mar 28 1955	2-Eb	8
Mar 29 1955	3-Ben	9
Mar 30 1955	4-Ix	1
Mar 31 1955	5-Men	2
Apr 1 1955	6-Cib	3
Apr 2 1955	7-Caban	4
Apr 3 1955	8-Etz'nab	5
Apr 4 1955	9-Cauac	6
Apr 5 1955	10-Ahau	7
Apr 6 1955	11-Imix	8
Apr 7 1955	12-Ik	9
Apr 8 1955	13-Akbal	1
Apr 9 1955	1-Kan	2
Apr 10 1955	2-Chicchan	3
Apr 11 1955	3-Cimi	4
Apr 12 1955	4-Manik	5
Apr 13 1955	5-Lamat	6
Apr 14 1955	6-Muluc	7
Apr 15 1955	7-Oc	8
Apr 16 1955	8-Chuen	9
Apr 17 1955	9-Eb	1
Apr 18 1955	10-Ben	2

Date	Day-Sign	L
Apr 19 1955	11-Ix	3
Apr 20 1955	12-Men	4
Apr 21 1955	13-Cib	5
Apr 22 1955	1-Caban	6
Apr 23 1955	2-Etz'nab	7
Apr 24 1955	3-Cauac	8
Apr 25 1955	4-Ahau	9
Apr 26 1955	5-Imix	1
Apr 27 1955	6-Ik	2
Apr 28 1955	7-Akbal	3
Apr 29 1955	8-Kan	4
Apr 30 1955	9-Chicchan	5
May 1 1955	10-Cimi	6
May 2 1955	11-Manik	7
May 3 1955	12-Lamat	8
May 4 1955	13-Muluc	9
May 5 1955	1-Oc	1
May 6 1955	2-Chuen	2
May 7 1955	3-Eb	3
May 8 1955	4-Ben	4
May 9 1955	5-Ix	5
May 10 1955	6-Men	6
May 11 1955	7-Cib	7
May 12 1955	8-Caban	8
May 13 1955	9-Etz'nab	9
May 14 1955	10-Cauac	1
May 15 1955	11-Ahau	2
May 16 1955	12-Imix	3
May 17 1955	13-Ik	4
May 18 1955	1-Akbal	5
May 19 1955	2-Kan	6
May 20 1955	3-Chicchan	7
May 21 1955	4-Cimi	8
May 22 1955	5-Manik	9
May 23 1955	6-Lamat	1
May 24 1955	7-Muluc	2
May 25 1955	8-Oc	3
May 26 1955	9-Chuen	4
May 27 1955	10-Eb	5
May 28 1955	11-Ben	6
May 29 1955	12-Ix	7
May 30 1955	13-Men	8
May 31 1955	1-Cib	9
Jun 1 1955	2-Caban	1
Jun 2 1955	3-Etz'nab	2
Jun 3 1955	4-Cauac	3
Jun 4 1955	5-Ahau	4
Jun 5 1955	6-Imix	5
Jun 6 1955	7-Ik	6
Jun 7 1955	8-Akbal	7
Jun 8 1955	9-Kan	8
Jun 9 1955	10-Chicchan	9
Jun 10 1955	11-Cimi	1
Jun 11 1955	12-Manik	2
Jun 12 1955	13-Lamat	3
Jun 13 1955	1-Muluc	4
Jun 14 1955	2-Oc	5
Jun 15 1955	3-Chuen	6
Jun 16 1955	4-Eb	7
Jun 17 1955	5-Ben	8
Jun 18 1955	6-Ix	9
Jun 19 1955	7-Men	1
Jun 20 1955	8-Cib	2
Jun 21 1955	9-Caban	3
Jun 22 1955	10-Etz'nab	4
Jun 23 1955	11-Cauac	5
Jun 24 1955	12-Ahau	6
Jun 25 1955	13-Imix	7

Date	Day-Sign	L
Jun 26 1955	1-Ik	8
Jun 27 1955	2-Akbal	9
Jun 28 1955	3-Kan	1
Jun 29 1955	4-Chicchan	2
Jun 30 1955	5-Cimi	3
Jul 1 1955	6-Manik	4
Jul 2 1955	7-Lamat	5
Jul 3 1955	8-Muluc	6
Jul 4 1955	9-Oc	7
Jul 5 1955	10-Chuen	8
Jul 6 1955	11-Eb	9
Jul 7 1955	12-Ben	1
Jul 8 1955	13-Ix	2
Jul 9 1955	1-Men	3
Jul 10 1955	2-Cib	4
Jul 11 1955	3-Caban	5
Jul 12 1955	4-Etz'nab	6
Jul 13 1955	5-Cauac	7
Jul 14 1955	6-Ahau	8
Jul 15 1955	7-Imix	9
Jul 16 1955	8-Ik	1
Jul 17 1955	9-Akbal	2
Jul 18 1955	10-Kan	3
Jul 19 1955	11-Chicchan	4
Jul 20 1955	12-Cimi	5
Jul 21 1955	13-Manik	6
Jul 22 1955	1-Lamat	7
Jul 23 1955	2-Muluc	8
Jul 24 1955	3-Oc	9
Jul 25 1955	4-Chuen	1
Jul 26 1955	5-Eb	2
Jul 27 1955	6-Ben	3
Jul 28 1955	7-Ix	4
Jul 29 1955	8-Men	5
Jul 30 1955	9-Cib	6
Jul 31 1955	10-Caban	7
Aug 1 1955	11-Etz'nab	8
Aug 2 1955	12-Cauac	9
Aug 3 1955	13-Ahau	1
Aug 4 1955	1-Imix	2
Aug 5 1955	2-Ik	3
Aug 6 1955	3-Akbal	4
Aug 7 1955	4-Kan	5
Aug 8 1955	5-Chicchan	6
Aug 9 1955	6-Cimi	7
Aug 10 1955	7-Manik	8
Aug 11 1955	8-Lamat	9
Aug 12 1955	9-Muluc	1
Aug 13 1955	10-Oc	2
Aug 14 1955	11-Chuen	3
Aug 15 1955	12-Eb	4
Aug 16 1955	13-Ben	5
Aug 17 1955	1-Ix	6
Aug 18 1955	2-Men	7
Aug 19 1955	3-Cib	8
Aug 20 1955	4-Caban	9
Aug 21 1955	5-Etz'nab	1
Aug 22 1955	6-Cauac	2
Aug 23 1955	7-Ahau	3
Aug 24 1955	8-Imix	4
Aug 25 1955	9-Ik	5
Aug 26 1955	10-Akbal	6
Aug 27 1955	11-Kan	7
Aug 28 1955	12-Chicchan	8
Aug 29 1955	13-Cimi	9
Aug 30 1955	1-Manik	1
Aug 31 1955	2-Lamat	2
Sep 1 1955	3-Muluc	3

Date	Day-Sign	L	Date	Day-Sign	L	Date	Day-Sign	L
Sep 2 1955	4-Oc	4	Nov 9 1955	7-Etz'nab	9	Jan 16 1956	10-Cimi	5
Sep 3 1955	5-Chuen	5	Nov 10 1955	8-Cauac	1	Jan 17 1956	11-Manik	6
Sep 4 1955	6-Eb	6	Nov 11 1955	9-Ahau	2	Jan 18 1956	12-Lamat	7
Sep 5 1955	7-Ben	7	Nov 12 1955	10-*Imix*	3	Jan 19 1956	13-Muluc	8
Sep 6 1955	8-Ix	8	Nov 13 1955	11-Ik	4	Jan 20 1956	**1-Oc**	9
Sep 7 1955	9-Men	9	Nov 14 1955	12-Akbal	5	Jan 21 1956	2-Chuen	1
Sep 8 1955	10-Cib	1	Nov 15 1955	13-Kan	6	Jan 22 1956	3-Eb	2
Sep 9 1955	11-Caban	2	Nov 16 1955	**1-Chicchan**	7	Jan 23 1956	4-Ben	3
Sep 10 1955	12-Etz'nab	3	Nov 17 1955	2-Cimi	8	Jan 24 1956	5-Ix	4
Sep 11 1955	13-Cauac	4	Nov 18 1955	3-Manik	9	Jan 25 1956	6-Men	5
Sep 12 1955	**1-Ahau**	5	Nov 19 1955	4-Lamat	1	Jan 26 1956	7-Cib	6
Sep 13 1955	2-*Imix*	6	Nov 20 1955	5-Muluc	2	Jan 27 1956	8-Caban	7
Sep 14 1955	3-Ik	7	Nov 21 1955	6-Oc	3	Jan 28 1956	9-Etz'nab	8
Sep 15 1955	4-Akbal	8	Nov 22 1955	7-Chuen	4	Jan 29 1956	10-Cauac	9
Sep 16 1955	5-Kan	9	Nov 23 1955	8-Eb	5	Jan 30 1956	11-Ahau	1
Sep 17 1955	6-Chicchan	1	Nov 24 1955	9-Ben	6	Jan 31 1956	12-*Imix*	2
Sep 18 1955	7-Cimi	2	Nov 25 1955	10-Ix	7	Feb 1 1956	13-Ik	3
Sep 19 1955	8-Manik	3	Nov 26 1955	11-Men	8	Feb 2 1956	**1-Akbal**	4
Sep 20 1955	9-Lamat	4	Nov 27 1955	12-Cib	9	Feb 3 1956	2-Kan	5
Sep 21 1955	10-Muluc	5	Nov 28 1955	13-Caban	1	Feb 4 1956	3-Chicchan	6
Sep 22 1955	11-Oc	6	Nov 29 1955	**1-Etz'nab**	2	Feb 5 1956	4-Cimi	7
Sep 23 1955	12-Chuen	7	Nov 30 1955	2-Cauac	3	Feb 6 1956	5-Manik	8
Sep 24 1955	13-Eb	8	Dec 1 1955	3-Ahau	4	Feb 7 1956	6-Lamat	9
Sep 25 1955	**1-Ben**	9	Dec 2 1955	4-*Imix*	5	Feb 8 1956	7-Muluc	1
Sep 26 1955	2-Ix	1	Dec 3 1955	5-Ik	6	Feb 9 1956	8-Oc	2
Sep 27 1955	3-Men	2	Dec 4 1955	6-Akbal	7	Feb 10 1956	9-Chuen	3
Sep 28 1955	4-Cib	3	Dec 5 1955	7-Kan	8	Feb 11 1956	10-Eb	4
Sep 29 1955	5-Caban	4	Dec 6 1955	8-Chicchan	9	Feb 12 1956	11-Ben	5
Sep 30 1955	6-Etz'nab	5	Dec 7 1955	9-Cimi	1	Feb 13 1956	12-Ix	6
Oct 1 1955	7-Cauac	6	Dec 8 1955	10-Manik	2	Feb 14 1956	13-Men	7
Oct 2 1955	8-Ahau	7	Dec 9 1955	11-Lamat	3	Feb 15 1956	**1-Cib**	8
Oct 3 1955	9-*Imix*	8	Dec 10 1955	12-Muluc	4	Feb 16 1956	2-Caban	9
Oct 4 1955	10-Ik	9	Dec 11 1955	13-Oc	5	Feb 17 1956	3-Etz'nab	1
Oct 5 1955	11-Akbal	1	Dec 12 1955	**1-Chuen**	6	Feb 18 1956	4-Cauac	2
Oct 6 1955	12-Kan	2	Dec 13 1955	2-Eb	7	Feb 19 1956	5-Ahau	3
Oct 7 1955	13-Chicchan	3	Dec 14 1955	3-Ben	8	Feb 20 1956	6-*Imix*	4
Oct 8 1955	**1-Cimi**	4	Dec 15 1955	4-Ix	9	Feb 21 1956	7-Ik	5
Oct 9 1955	2-Manik	5	Dec 16 1955	5-Men	1	Feb 22 1956	8-Akbal	6
Oct 10 1955	3-Lamat	6	Dec 17 1955	6-Cib	2	Feb 23 1956	9-Kan	7
Oct 11 1955	4-Muluc	7	Dec 18 1955	7-Caban	3	Feb 24 1956	10-Chicchan	8
Oct 12 1955	5-Oc	8	Dec 19 1955	8-Etz'nab	4	Feb 25 1956	11-Cimi	9
Oct 13 1955	6-Chuen	9	Dec 20 1955	9-Cauac	5	Feb 26 1956	12-Manik	1
Oct 14 1955	7-Eb	1	Dec 21 1955	10-Ahau	6	Feb 27 1956	13-Lamat	2
Oct 15 1955	8-Ben	2	Dec 22 1955	11-*Imix*	7	Feb 28 1956	**1-Muluc**	3
Oct 16 1955	9-Ix	3	Dec 23 1955	12-Ik	8	Feb 29 1956	2-Oc	4
Oct 17 1955	10-Men	4	Dec 24 1955	13-Akbal	9	Mar 1 1956	3-Chuen	5
Oct 18 1955	11-Cib	5	Dec 25 1955	**1-Kan**	1	Mar 2 1956	4-Eb	6
Oct 19 1955	12-Caban	6	Dec 26 1955	2-Chicchan	2	Mar 3 1956	5-Ben	7
Oct 20 1955	13-Etz'nab	7	Dec 27 1955	3-Cimi	3	Mar 4 1956	6-Ix	8
Oct 21 1955	**1-Cauac**	8	Dec 28 1955	4-Manik	4	Mar 5 1956	7-Men	9
Oct 22 1955	2-Ahau	9	Dec 29 1955	5-Lamat	5	Mar 6 1956	8-Cib	1
Oct 23 1955	3-*Imix*	1	Dec 30 1955	6-Muluc	6	Mar 7 1956	9-Caban	2
Oct 24 1955	4-Ik	2	Dec 31 1955	7-Oc	7	Mar 8 1956	10-Etz'nab	3
Oct 25 1955	5-Akbal	3	Jan 1 1956	8-Chuen	8	Mar 9 1956	11-Cauac	4
Oct 26 1955	6-Kan	4	Jan 2 1956	9-Eb	9	Mar 10 1956	12-Ahau	5
Oct 27 1955	7-Chicchan	5	Jan 3 1956	10-Ben	1	Mar 11 1956	13-*Imix*	6
Oct 28 1955	8-Cimi	6	Jan 4 1956	11-Ix	2	Mar 12 1956	**1-Ik**	7
Oct 29 1955	9-Manik	7	Jan 5 1956	12-Men	3	Mar 13 1956	2-Akbal	8
Oct 30 1955	10-Lamat	8	Jan 6 1956	13-Cib	4	Mar 14 1956	3-Kan	9
Oct 31 1955	11-Muluc	9	Jan 7 1956	**1-Caban**	5	Mar 15 1956	4-Chicchan	1
Nov 1 1955	12-Oc	1	Jan 8 1956	2-Etz'nab	6	Mar 16 1956	5-Cimi	2
Nov 2 1955	13-Chuen	2	Jan 9 1956	3-Cauac	7	Mar 17 1956	6-Manik	3
Nov 3 1955	**1-Eb**	3	Jan 10 1956	4-Ahau	8	Mar 18 1956	7-Lamat	4
Nov 4 1955	2-Ben	4	Jan 11 1956	5-*Imix*	9	Mar 19 1956	8-Muluc	5
Nov 5 1955	3-Ix	5	Jan 12 1956	6-Ik	1	Mar 20 1956	9-Oc	6
Nov 6 1955	4-Men	6	Jan 13 1956	7-Akbal	2	Mar 21 1956	10-Chuen	7
Nov 7 1955	5-Cib	7	Jan 14 1956	8-Kan	3	Mar 22 1956	11-Eb	8
Nov 8 1955	6-Caban	8	Jan 15 1956	9-Chicchan	4	Mar 23 1956	12-Ben	9

Date	Day-Sign	L	Date	Day-Sign	L	Date	Day-Sign	L
Mar 24 1956	13-Ix	1	May 31 1956	3-Ik	6	Aug 7 1956	6-Oc	2
Mar 25 1956	**1-Men**	2	Jun 1 1956	4-Akbal	7	Aug 8 1956	7-Chuen	3
Mar 26 1956	2-Cib	3	Jun 2 1956	5-Kan	8	Aug 9 1956	8-Eb	4
Mar 27 1956	3-Caban	4	Jun 3 1956	6-Chicchan	9	Aug 10 1956	9-Ben	5
Mar 28 1956	4-Etz'nab	5	Jun 4 1956	7-Cimi	1	Aug 11 1956	10-Ix	6
Mar 29 1956	5-Cauac	6	Jun 5 1956	8-Manik	2	Aug 12 1956	11-Men	7
Mar 30 1956	6-Ahau	7	Jun 6 1956	9-Lamat	3	Aug 13 1956	12-Cib	8
Mar 31 1956	7-*Imix*	8	Jun 7 1956	10-Muluc	4	Aug 14 1956	13-Caban	9
Apr 1 1956	8-Ik	9	Jun 8 1956	11-Oc	5	Aug 15 1956	**1-Etz'nab**	1
Apr 2 1956	9-Akbal	1	Jun 9 1956	12-Chuen	6	Aug 16 1956	2-Cauac	2
Apr 3 1956	10-Kan	2	Jun 10 1956	13-Eb	7	Aug 17 1956	3-Ahau	3
Apr 4 1956	11-Chicchan	3	Jun 11 1956	**1-Ben**	8	Aug 18 1956	4-*Imix*	4
Apr 5 1956	12-Cimi	4	Jun 12 1956	2-Ix	9	Aug 19 1956	5-Ik	5
Apr 6 1956	13-Manik	5	Jun 13 1956	3-Men	1	Aug 20 1956	6-Akbal	6
Apr 7 1956	**1-Lamat**	6	Jun 14 1956	4-Cib	2	Aug 21 1956	7-Kan	7
Apr 8 1956	2-Muluc	7	Jun 15 1956	5-Caban	3	Aug 22 1956	8-Chicchan	8
Apr 9 1956	3-Oc	8	Jun 16 1956	6-Etz'nab	4	Aug 23 1956	9-Cimi	9
Apr 10 1956	4-Chuen	9	Jun 17 1956	7-Cauac	5	Aug 24 1956	10-Manik	1
Apr 11 1956	5-Eb	1	Jun 18 1956	8-Ahau	6	Aug 25 1956	11-Lamat	2
Apr 12 1956	6-Ben	2	Jun 19 1956	9-*Imix*	7	Aug 26 1956	12-Muluc	3
Apr 13 1956	7-Ix	3	Jun 20 1956	10-Ik	8	Aug 27 1956	13-Oc	4
Apr 14 1956	8-Men	4	Jun 21 1956	11-Akbal	9	Aug 28 1956	**1-Chuen**	5
Apr 15 1956	9-Cib	5	Jun 22 1956	12-Kan	1	Aug 29 1956	2-Eb	6
Apr 16 1956	10-Caban	6	Jun 23 1956	13-Chicchan	2	Aug 30 1956	3-Ben	7
Apr 17 1956	11-Etz'nab	7	Jun 24 1956	**1-Cimi**	3	Aug 31 1956	4-Ix	8
Apr 18 1956	12-Cauac	8	Jun 25 1956	2-Manik	4	Sep 1 1956	5-Men	9
Apr 19 1956	13-Ahau	9	Jun 26 1956	3-Lamat	5	Sep 2 1956	6-Cib	1
Apr 20 1956	**1-Imix**	1	Jun 27 1956	4-Muluc	6	Sep 3 1956	7-Caban	2
Apr 21 1956	2-Ik	2	Jun 28 1956	5-Oc	7	Sep 4 1956	8-Etz'nab	3
Apr 22 1956	3-Akbal	3	Jun 29 1956	6-Chuen	8	Sep 5 1956	9-Cauac	4
Apr 23 1956	4-Kan	4	Jun 30 1956	7-Eb	9	Sep 6 1956	10-Ahau	5
Apr 24 1956	5-Chicchan	5	Jul 1 1956	8-Ben	1	Sep 7 1956	11-*Imix*	6
Apr 25 1956	6-Cimi	6	Jul 2 1956	9-Ix	2	Sep 8 1956	12-Ik	7
Apr 26 1956	7-Manik	7	Jul 3 1956	10-Men	3	Sep 9 1956	13-Akbal	8
Apr 27 1956	8-Lamat	8	Jul 4 1956	11-Cib	4	Sep 10 1956	**1-Kan**	9
Apr 28 1956	9-Muluc	9	Jul 5 1956	12-Caban	5	Sep 11 1956	2-Chicchan	1
Apr 29 1956	10-Oc	1	Jul 6 1956	13-Etz'nab	6	Sep 12 1956	3-Cimi	2
Apr 30 1956	11-Chuen	2	Jul 7 1956	**1-Cauac**	7	Sep 13 1956	4-Manik	3
May 1 1956	12-Eb	3	Jul 8 1956	2-Ahau	8	Sep 14 1956	5-Lamat	4
May 2 1956	13-Ben	4	Jul 9 1956	3-*Imix*	9	Sep 15 1956	6-Muluc	5
May 3 1956	**1-Ix**	5	Jul 10 1956	4-Ik	1	Sep 16 1956	7-Oc	6
May 4 1956	2-Men	6	Jul 11 1956	5-Akbal	2	Sep 17 1956	8-Chuen	7
May 5 1956	3-Cib	7	Jul 12 1956	6-Kan	3	Sep 18 1956	9-Eb	8
May 6 1956	4-Caban	8	Jul 13 1956	7-Chicchan	4	Sep 19 1956	10-Ben	9
May 7 1956	5-Etz'nab	9	Jul 14 1956	8-Cimi	5	Sep 20 1956	11-Ix	1
May 8 1956	6-Cauac	1	Jul 15 1956	9-Manik	6	Sep 21 1956	12-Men	2
May 9 1956	7-Ahau	2	Jul 16 1956	10-Lamat	7	Sep 22 1956	13-Cib	3
May 10 1956	8-*Imix*	3	Jul 17 1956	11-Muluc	8	Sep 23 1956	**1-Caban**	4
May 11 1956	9-Ik	4	Jul 18 1956	12-Oc	9	Sep 24 1956	2-Etz'nab	5
May 12 1956	10-Akbal	5	Jul 19 1956	13-Chuen	1	Sep 25 1956	3-Cauac	6
May 13 1956	11-Kan	6	Jul 20 1956	**1-Eb**	2	Sep 26 1956	4-Ahau	7
May 14 1956	12-Chicchan	7	Jul 21 1956	2-Ben	3	Sep 27 1956	5-*Imix*	8
May 15 1956	13-Cimi	8	Jul 22 1956	3-Ix	4	Sep 28 1956	6-Ik	9
May 16 1956	**1-Manik**	9	Jul 23 1956	4-Men	5	Sep 29 1956	7-Akbal	1
May 17 1956	2-Lamat	1	Jul 24 1956	5-Cib	6	Sep 30 1956	8-Kan	2
May 18 1956	3-Muluc	2	Jul 25 1956	6-Caban	7	Oct 1 1956	9-Chicchan	3
May 19 1956	4-Oc	3	Jul 26 1956	7-Etz'nab	8	Oct 2 1956	10-Cimi	4
May 20 1956	5-Chuen	4	Jul 27 1956	8-Cauac	9	Oct 3 1956	11-Manik	5
May 21 1956	6-Eb	5	Jul 28 1956	9-Ahau	1	Oct 4 1956	12-Lamat	6
May 22 1956	7-Ben	6	Jul 29 1956	10-*Imix*	2	Oct 5 1956	13-Muluc	7
May 23 1956	8-Ix	7	Jul 30 1956	11-Ik	3	Oct 6 1956	**1-Oc**	8
May 24 1956	9-Men	8	Jul 31 1956	12-Akbal	4	Oct 7 1956	2-Chuen	9
May 25 1956	10-Cib	9	Aug 1 1956	13-Kan	5	Oct 8 1956	3-Eb	1
May 26 1956	11-Caban	1	Aug 2 1956	**1-Chicchan**	6	Oct 9 1956	4-Ben	2
May 27 1956	12-Etz'nab	2	Aug 3 1956	2-Cimi	7	Oct 10 1956	5-Ix	3
May 28 1956	13-Cauac	3	Aug 4 1956	3-Manik	8	Oct 11 1956	6-Men	4
May 29 1956	**1-Ahau**	4	Aug 5 1956	4-Lamat	9	Oct 12 1956	7-Cib	5
May 30 1956	2-*Imix*	5	Aug 6 1956	5-Muluc	1	Oct 13 1956	8-Caban	6

Date	Day-Sign	L	Date	Day-Sign	L	Date	Day-Sign	L
Oct 14 1956	9-Etz'nab	7	Dec 21 1956	12-Cimi	3	Feb 27 1957	2-Ix	8
Oct 15 1956	10-Cauac	8	Dec 22 1956	13-Manik	4	Feb 28 1957	3-Men	9
Oct 16 1956	11-Ahau	9	Dec 23 1956	1-Lamat	5	Mar 1 1957	4-Cib	1
Oct 17 1956	12-Imix	1	Dec 24 1956	2-Muluc	6	Mar 2 1957	5-Caban	2
Oct 18 1956	13-Ik	2	Dec 25 1956	3-Oc	7	Mar 3 1957	6-Etz'nab	3
Oct 19 1956	1-Akbal	3	Dec 26 1956	4-Chuen	8	Mar 4 1957	7-Cauac	4
Oct 20 1956	2-Kan	4	Dec 27 1956	5-Eb	9	Mar 5 1957	8-Ahau	5
Oct 21 1956	3-Chiccan	5	Dec 28 1956	6-Ben	1	Mar 6 1957	9-Imix	6
Oct 22 1956	4-Cimi	6	Dec 29 1956	7-Ix	2	Mar 7 1957	10-Ik	7
Oct 23 1956	5-Manik	7	Dec 30 1956	8-Men	3	Mar 8 1957	11-Akbal	8
Oct 24 1956	6-Lamat	8	Dec 31 1956	9-Cib	4	Mar 9 1957	12-Kan	9
Oct 25 1956	7-Muluc	9	Jan 1 1957	10-Caban	5	Mar 10 1957	13-Chiccan	1
Oct 26 1956	8-Oc	1	Jan 2 1957	11-Etz'nab	6	Mar 11 1957	1-Cimi	2
Oct 27 1956	9-Chuen	2	Jan 3 1957	12-Cauac	7	Mar 12 1957	2-Manik	3
Oct 28 1956	10-Eb	3	Jan 4 1957	13-Ahau	8	Mar 13 1957	3-Lamat	4
Oct 29 1956	11-Ben	4	Jan 5 1957	1-Imix	9	Mar 14 1957	4-Muluc	5
Oct 30 1956	12-Ix	5	Jan 6 1957	2-Ik	1	Mar 15 1957	5-Oc	6
Oct 31 1956	13-Men	6	Jan 7 1957	3-Akbal	2	Mar 16 1957	6-Chuen	7
Nov 1 1956	1-Cib	7	Jan 8 1957	4-Kan	3	Mar 17 1957	7-Eb	8
Nov 2 1956	2-Caban	8	Jan 9 1957	5-Chiccan	4	Mar 18 1957	8-Ben	9
Nov 3 1956	3-Etz'nab	9	Jan 10 1957	6-Cimi	5	Mar 19 1957	9-Ix	1
Nov 4 1956	4-Cauac	1	Jan 11 1957	7-Manik	6	Mar 20 1957	10-Men	2
Nov 5 1956	5-Ahau	2	Jan 12 1957	8-Lamat	7	Mar 21 1957	11-Cib	3
Nov 6 1956	6-Imix	3	Jan 13 1957	9-Muluc	8	Mar 22 1957	12-Caban	4
Nov 7 1956	7-Ik	4	Jan 14 1957	10-Oc	9	Mar 23 1957	13-Etz'nab	5
Nov 8 1956	8-Akbal	5	Jan 15 1957	11-Chuen	1	Mar 24 1957	1-Cauac	6
Nov 9 1956	9-Kan	6	Jan 16 1957	12-Eb	2	Mar 25 1957	2-Ahau	7
Nov 10 1956	10-Chicchan	7	Jan 17 1957	13-Ben	3	Mar 26 1957	3-Imix	8
Nov 11 1956	11-Cimi	8	Jan 18 1957	1-Ix	4	Mar 27 1957	4-Ik	9
Nov 12 1956	12-Manik	9	Jan 19 1957	2-Men	5	Mar 28 1957	5-Akbal	1
Nov 13 1956	13-Lamat	1	Jan 20 1957	3-Cib	6	Mar 29 1957	6-Kan	2
Nov 14 1956	1-Muluc	2	Jan 21 1957	4-Caban	7	Mar 30 1957	7-Chicchan	3
Nov 15 1956	2-Oc	3	Jan 22 1957	5-Etz'nab	8	Mar 31 1957	8-Cimi	4
Nov 16 1956	3-Chuen	4	Jan 23 1957	6-Cauac	9	Apr 1 1957	9-Manik	5
Nov 17 1956	4-Eb	5	Jan 24 1957	7-Ahau	1	Apr 2 1957	10-Lamat	6
Nov 18 1956	5-Ben	6	Jan 25 1957	8-Imix	2	Apr 3 1957	11-Muluc	7
Nov 19 1956	6-Ix	7	Jan 26 1957	9-Ik	3	Apr 4 1957	12-Oc	8
Nov 20 1956	7-Men	8	Jan 27 1957	10-Akbal	4	Apr 5 1957	13-Chuen	9
Nov 21 1956	8-Cib	9	Jan 28 1957	11-Kan	5	Apr 6 1957	1-Eb	1
Nov 22 1956	9-Caban	1	Jan 29 1957	12-Chicchan	6	Apr 7 1957	2-Ben	2
Nov 23 1956	10-Etz'nab	2	Jan 30 1957	13-Cimi	7	Apr 8 1957	3-Ix	3
Nov 24 1956	11-Cauac	3	Jan 31 1957	1-Manik	8	Apr 9 1957	4-Men	4
Nov 25 1956	12-Ahau	4	Feb 1 1957	2-Lamat	9	Apr 10 1957	5-Cib	5
Nov 26 1956	13-Imix	5	Feb 2 1957	3-Muluc	1	Apr 11 1957	6-Caban	6
Nov 27 1956	1-Ik	6	Feb 3 1957	4-Oc	2	Apr 12 1957	7-Etz'nab	7
Nov 28 1956	2-Akbal	7	Feb 4 1957	5-Chuen	3	Apr 13 1957	8-Cauac	8
Nov 29 1956	3-Kan	8	Feb 5 1957	6-Eb	4	Apr 14 1957	9-Ahau	9
Nov 30 1956	4-Chicchan	9	Feb 6 1957	7-Ben	5	Apr 15 1957	10-Imix	1
Dec 1 1956	5-Cimi	1	Feb 7 1957	8-Ix	6	Apr 16 1957	11-Ik	2
Dec 2 1956	6-Manik	2	Feb 8 1957	9-Men	7	Apr 17 1957	12-Akbal	3
Dec 3 1956	7-Lamat	3	Feb 9 1957	10-Cib	8	Apr 18 1957	13-Kan	4
Dec 4 1956	8-Muluc	4	Feb 10 1957	11-Caban	9	Apr 19 1957	1-Chicchan	5
Dec 5 1956	9-Oc	5	Feb 11 1957	12-Etz'nab	1	Apr 20 1957	2-Cimi	6
Dec 6 1956	10-Chuen	6	Feb 12 1957	13-Cauac	2	Apr 21 1957	3-Manik	7
Dec 7 1956	11-Eb	7	Feb 13 1957	1-Ahau	3	Apr 22 1957	4-Lamat	8
Dec 8 1956	12-Ben	8	Feb 14 1957	2-Imix	4	Apr 23 1957	5-Muluc	9
Dec 9 1956	13-Ix	9	Feb 15 1957	3-Ik	5	Apr 24 1957	6-Oc	1
Dec 10 1956	1-Men	1	Feb 16 1957	4-Akbal	6	Apr 25 1957	7-Chuen	2
Dec 11 1956	2-Cib	2	Feb 17 1957	5-Kan	7	Apr 26 1957	8-Eb	3
Dec 12 1956	3-Caban	3	Feb 18 1957	6-Chicchan	8	Apr 27 1957	9-Ben	4
Dec 13 1956	4-Etz'nab	4	Feb 19 1957	7-Cimi	9	Apr 28 1957	10-Ix	5
Dec 14 1956	5-Cauac	5	Feb 20 1957	8-Manik	1	Apr 29 1957	11-Men	6
Dec 15 1956	6-Ahau	6	Feb 21 1957	9-Lamat	2	Apr 30 1957	12-Cib	7
Dec 16 1956	7-Imix	7	Feb 22 1957	10-Muluc	3	May 1 1957	13-Caban	8
Dec 17 1956	8-Ik	8	Feb 23 1957	11-Oc	4	May 2 1957	1-Etz'nab	9
Dec 18 1956	9-Akbal	9	Feb 24 1957	12-Chuen	5	May 3 1957	2-Cauac	1
Dec 19 1956	10-Kan	1	Feb 25 1957	13-Eb	6	May 4 1957	3-Ahau	2
Dec 20 1956	11-Chicchan	2	Feb 26 1957	1-Ben	7	May 5 1957	4-Imix	3

Date	Day-Sign	L
May 6 1957	5-Ik	4
May 7 1957	6-Akbal	5
May 8 1957	7-Kan	6
May 9 1957	8-Chicchan	7
May 10 1957	9-Cimi	8
May 11 1957	10-Manik	9
May 12 1957	11-Lamat	1
May 13 1957	12-Muluc	2
May 14 1957	13-Oc	3
May 15 1957	1-Chuen	4
May 16 1957	2-Eb	5
May 17 1957	3-Ben	6
May 18 1957	4-Ix	7
May 19 1957	5-Men	8
May 20 1957	6-Cib	9
May 21 1957	7-Caban	1
May 22 1957	8-Etz'nab	2
May 23 1957	9-Cauac	3
May 24 1957	10-Ahau	4
May 25 1957	11-Imix	5
May 26 1957	12-Ik	6
May 27 1957	13-Akbal	7
May 28 1957	1-Kan	8
May 29 1957	2-Chicchan	9
May 30 1957	3-Cimi	1
May 31 1957	4-Manik	2
Jun 1 1957	5-Lamat	3
Jun 2 1957	6-Muluc	4
Jun 3 1957	7-Oc	5
Jun 4 1957	8-Chuen	6
Jun 5 1957	9-Eb	7
Jun 6 1957	10-Ben	8
Jun 7 1957	11-Ix	9
Jun 8 1957	12-Men	1
Jun 9 1957	13-Cib	2
Jun 10 1957	1-Caban	3
Jun 11 1957	2-Etz'nab	4
Jun 12 1957	3-Cauac	5
Jun 13 1957	4-Ahau	6
Jun 14 1957	5-Imix	7
Jun 15 1957	6-Ik	8
Jun 16 1957	7-Akbal	9
Jun 17 1957	8-Kan	1
Jun 18 1957	9-Chicchan	2
Jun 19 1957	10-Cimi	3
Jun 20 1957	11-Manik	4
Jun 21 1957	12-Lamat	5
Jun 22 1957	13-Muluc	6
Jun 23 1957	1-Oc	7
Jun 24 1957	2-Chuen	8
Jun 25 1957	3-Eb	9
Jun 26 1957	4-Ben	1
Jun 27 1957	5-Ix	2
Jun 28 1957	6-Men	3
Jun 29 1957	7-Cib	4
Jun 30 1957	8-Caban	5
Jul 1 1957	9-Etz'nab	6
Jul 2 1957	10-Cauac	7
Jul 3 1957	11-Ahau	8
Jul 4 1957	12-Imix	9
Jul 5 1957	13-Ik	1
Jul 6 1957	1-Akbal	2
Jul 7 1957	2-Kan	3
Jul 8 1957	3-Chicchan	4
Jul 9 1957	4-Cimi	5
Jul 10 1957	5-Manik	6
Jul 11 1957	6-Lamat	7
Jul 12 1957	7-Muluc	8

Date	Day-Sign	L
Jul 13 1957	8-Oc	9
Jul 14 1957	9-Chuen	1
Jul 15 1957	10-Eb	2
Jul 16 1957	11-Ben	3
Jul 17 1957	12-Ix	4
Jul 18 1957	13-Men	5
Jul 19 1957	1-Cib	6
Jul 20 1957	2-Caban	7
Jul 21 1957	3-Etz'nab	8
Jul 22 1957	4-Cauac	9
Jul 23 1957	5-Ahau	1
Jul 24 1957	6-Imix	2
Jul 25 1957	7-Ik	3
Jul 26 1957	8-Akbal	4
Jul 27 1957	9-Kan	5
Jul 28 1957	10-Chicchan	6
Jul 29 1957	11-Cimi	7
Jul 30 1957	12-Manik	8
Jul 31 1957	13-Lamat	9
Aug 1 1957	1-Muluc	1
Aug 2 1957	2-Oc	2
Aug 3 1957	3-Chuen	3
Aug 4 1957	4-Eb	4
Aug 5 1957	5-Ben	5
Aug 6 1957	6-Ix	6
Aug 7 1957	7-Men	7
Aug 8 1957	8-Cib	8
Aug 9 1957	9-Caban	9
Aug 10 1957	10-Etz'nab	1
Aug 11 1957	11-Cauac	2
Aug 12 1957	12-Ahau	3
Aug 13 1957	13-Imix	4
Aug 14 1957	1-Ik	5
Aug 15 1957	2-Akbal	6
Aug 16 1957	3-Kan	7
Aug 17 1957	4-Chicchan	8
Aug 18 1957	5-Cimi	9
Aug 19 1957	6-Manik	1
Aug 20 1957	7-Lamat	2
Aug 21 1957	8-Muluc	3
Aug 22 1957	9-Oc	4
Aug 23 1957	10-Chuen	5
Aug 24 1957	11-Eb	6
Aug 25 1957	12-Ben	7
Aug 26 1957	13-Ix	8
Aug 27 1957	1-Men	9
Aug 28 1957	2-Cib	1
Aug 29 1957	3-Caban	2
Aug 30 1957	4-Etz'nab	3
Aug 31 1957	5-Cauac	4
Sep 1 1957	6-Ahau	5
Sep 2 1957	7-Imix	6
Sep 3 1957	8-Ik	7
Sep 4 1957	9-Akbal	8
Sep 5 1957	10-Kan	9
Sep 6 1957	11-Chicchan	1
Sep 7 1957	12-Cimi	2
Sep 8 1957	13-Manik	3
Sep 9 1957	1-Lamat	4
Sep 10 1957	2-Muluc	5
Sep 11 1957	3-Oc	6
Sep 12 1957	4-Chuen	7
Sep 13 1957	5-Eb	8
Sep 14 1957	6-Ben	9
Sep 15 1957	7-Ix	1
Sep 16 1957	8-Men	2
Sep 17 1957	9-Cib	3
Sep 18 1957	10-Caban	4

Date	Day-Sign	L
Sep 19 1957	11-Etz'nab	5
Sep 20 1957	12-Cauac	6
Sep 21 1957	13-Ahau	7
Sep 22 1957	1-Imix	8
Sep 23 1957	2-Ik	9
Sep 24 1957	3-Akbal	1
Sep 25 1957	4-Kan	2
Sep 26 1957	5-Chicchan	3
Sep 27 1957	6-Cimi	4
Sep 28 1957	7-Manik	5
Sep 29 1957	8-Lamat	6
Sep 30 1957	9-Muluc	7
Oct 1 1957	10-Oc	8
Oct 2 1957	11-Chuen	9
Oct 3 1957	12-Eb	1
Oct 4 1957	13-Ben	2
Oct 5 1957	1-Ix	3
Oct 6 1957	2-Men	4
Oct 7 1957	3-Cib	5
Oct 8 1957	4-Caban	6
Oct 9 1957	5-Etz'nab	7
Oct 10 1957	6-Cauac	8
Oct 11 1957	7-Ahau	9
Oct 12 1957	8-Imix	1
Oct 13 1957	9-Ik	2
Oct 14 1957	10-Akbal	3
Oct 15 1957	11-Kan	4
Oct 16 1957	12-Chicchan	5
Oct 17 1957	13-Cimi	6
Oct 18 1957	1-Manik	7
Oct 19 1957	2-Lamat	8
Oct 20 1957	3-Muluc	9
Oct 21 1957	4-Oc	1
Oct 22 1957	5-Chuen	2
Oct 23 1957	6-Eb	3
Oct 24 1957	7-Ben	4
Oct 25 1957	8-Ix	5
Oct 26 1957	9-Men	6
Oct 27 1957	10-Cib	7
Oct 28 1957	11-Caban	8
Oct 29 1957	12-Etz'nab	9
Oct 30 1957	13-Cauac	1
Oct 31 1957	1-Ahau	2
Nov 1 1957	2-Imix	3
Nov 2 1957	3-Ik	4
Nov 3 1957	4-Akbal	5
Nov 4 1957	5-Kan	6
Nov 5 1957	6-Chicchan	7
Nov 6 1957	7-Cimi	8
Nov 7 1957	8-Manik	9
Nov 8 1957	9-Lamat	1
Nov 9 1957	10-Muluc	2
Nov 10 1957	11-Oc	3
Nov 11 1957	12-Chuen	4
Nov 12 1957	13-Eb	5
Nov 13 1957	1-Ben	6
Nov 14 1957	2-Ix	7
Nov 15 1957	3-Men	8
Nov 16 1957	4-Cib	9
Nov 17 1957	5-Caban	1
Nov 18 1957	6-Etz'nab	2
Nov 19 1957	7-Cauac	3
Nov 20 1957	8-Ahau	4
Nov 21 1957	9-Imix	5
Nov 22 1957	10-Ik	6
Nov 23 1957	11-Akbal	7
Nov 24 1957	12-Kan	8
Nov 25 1957	13-Chicchan	9

Date	Day-Sign	L
Nov 26 1957	1-Cimi	1
Nov 27 1957	2-Manik	2
Nov 28 1957	3-Lamat	3
Nov 29 1957	4-Muluc	4
Nov 30 1957	5-Oc	5
Dec 1 1957	6-Chuen	6
Dec 2 1957	7-Eb	7
Dec 3 1957	8-Ben	8
Dec 4 1957	9-Ix	9
Dec 5 1957	10-Men	1
Dec 6 1957	11-Cib	2
Dec 7 1957	12-Caban	3
Dec 8 1957	13-Etz'nab	4
Dec 9 1957	1-Cauac	5
Dec 10 1957	2-Ahau	6
Dec 11 1957	3-Imix	7
Dec 12 1957	4-Ik	8
Dec 13 1957	5-Akbal	9
Dec 14 1957	6-Kan	1
Dec 15 1957	7-Chicchan	2
Dec 16 1957	8-Cimi	3
Dec 17 1957	9-Manik	4
Dec 18 1957	10-Lamat	5
Dec 19 1957	11-Muluc	6
Dec 20 1957	12-Oc	7
Dec 21 1957	13-Chuen	8
Dec 22 1957	1-Eb	9
Dec 23 1957	2-Ben	1
Dec 24 1957	3-Ix	2
Dec 25 1957	4-Men	3
Dec 26 1957	5-Cib	4
Dec 27 1957	6-Caban	5
Dec 28 1957	7-Etz'nab	6
Dec 29 1957	8-Cauac	7
Dec 30 1957	9-Ahau	8
Dec 31 1957	10-Imix	9
Jan 1 1958	11-Ik	1
Jan 2 1958	12-Akbal	2
Jan 3 1958	13-Kan	3
Jan 4 1958	1-Chicchan	4
Jan 5 1958	2-Cimi	5
Jan 6 1958	3-Manik	6
Jan 7 1958	4-Lamat	7
Jan 8 1958	5-Muluc	8
Jan 9 1958	6-Oc	9
Jan 10 1958	7-Chuen	1
Jan 11 1958	8-Eb	2
Jan 12 1958	9-Ben	3
Jan 13 1958	10-Ix	4
Jan 14 1958	11-Men	5
Jan 15 1958	12-Cib	6
Jan 16 1958	13-Caban	7
Jan 17 1958	1-Etz'nab	8
Jan 18 1958	2-Cauac	9
Jan 19 1958	3-Ahau	1
Jan 20 1958	4-Imix	2
Jan 21 1958	5-Ik	3
Jan 22 1958	6-Akbal	4
Jan 23 1958	7-Kan	5
Jan 24 1958	8-Chicchan	6
Jan 25 1958	9-Cimi	7
Jan 26 1958	10-Manik	8
Jan 27 1958	11-Lamat	9
Jan 28 1958	12-Muluc	1
Jan 29 1958	13-Oc	2
Jan 30 1958	1-Chuen	3
Jan 31 1958	2-Eb	4
Feb 1 1958	3-Ben	5

Date	Day-Sign	L
Feb 2 1958	4-Ix	6
Feb 3 1958	5-Men	7
Feb 4 1958	6-Cib	8
Feb 5 1958	7-Caban	9
Feb 6 1958	8-Etz'nab	1
Feb 7 1958	9-Cauac	2
Feb 8 1958	10-Ahau	3
Feb 9 1958	11-Imix	4
Feb 10 1958	12-Ik	5
Feb 11 1958	13-Akbal	6
Feb 12 1958	1-Kan	7
Feb 13 1958	2-Chicchan	8
Feb 14 1958	3-Cimi	9
Feb 15 1958	4-Manik	1
Feb 16 1958	5-Lamat	2
Feb 17 1958	6-Muluc	3
Feb 18 1958	7-Oc	4
Feb 19 1958	8-Chuen	5
Feb 20 1958	9-Eb	6
Feb 21 1958	10-Ben	7
Feb 22 1958	11-Ix	8
Feb 23 1958	12-Men	9
Feb 24 1958	13-Cib	1
Feb 25 1958	1-Caban	2
Feb 26 1958	2-Etz'nab	3
Feb 27 1958	3-Cauac	4
Feb 28 1958	4-Ahau	5
Mar 1 1958	5-Imix	6
Mar 2 1958	6-Ik	7
Mar 3 1958	7-Akbal	8
Mar 4 1958	8-Kan	9
Mar 5 1958	9-Chicchan	1
Mar 6 1958	10-Cimi	2
Mar 7 1958	11-Manik	3
Mar 8 1958	12-Lamat	4
Mar 9 1958	13-Muluc	5
Mar 10 1958	1-Oc	6
Mar 11 1958	2-Chuen	7
Mar 12 1958	3-Eb	8
Mar 13 1958	4-Ben	9
Mar 14 1958	5-Ix	1
Mar 15 1958	6-Men	2
Mar 16 1958	7-Cib	3
Mar 17 1958	8-Caban	4
Mar 18 1958	9-Etz'nab	5
Mar 19 1958	10-Cauac	6
Mar 20 1958	11-Ahau	7
Mar 21 1958	12-Imix	8
Mar 22 1958	13-Ik	9
Mar 23 1958	1-Akbal	1
Mar 24 1958	2-Kan	2
Mar 25 1958	3-Chicchan	3
Mar 26 1958	4-Cimi	4
Mar 27 1958	5-Manik	5
Mar 28 1958	6-Lamat	6
Mar 29 1958	7-Muluc	7
Mar 30 1958	8-Oc	8
Mar 31 1958	9-Chuen	9
Apr 1 1958	10-Eb	1
Apr 2 1958	11-Ben	2
Apr 3 1958	12-Ix	3
Apr 4 1958	13-Men	4
Apr 5 1958	1-Cib	5
Apr 6 1958	2-Caban	6
Apr 7 1958	3-Etz'nab	7
Apr 8 1958	4-Cauac	8
Apr 9 1958	5-Ahau	9
Apr 10 1958	6-Imix	1

Date	Day-Sign	L
Apr 11 1958	7-Ik	2
Apr 12 1958	8-Akbal	3
Apr 13 1958	9-Kan	4
Apr 14 1958	10-Chicchan	5
Apr 15 1958	11-Cimi	6
Apr 16 1958	12-Manik	7
Apr 17 1958	13-Lamat	8
Apr 18 1958	1-Muluc	9
Apr 19 1958	2-Oc	1
Apr 20 1958	3-Chuen	2
Apr 21 1958	4-Eb	3
Apr 22 1958	5-Ben	4
Apr 23 1958	6-Ix	5
Apr 24 1958	7-Men	6
Apr 25 1958	8-Cib	7
Apr 26 1958	9-Caban	8
Apr 27 1958	10-Etz'nab	9
Apr 28 1958	11-Cauac	1
Apr 29 1958	12-Ahau	2
Apr 30 1958	13-Imix	3
May 1 1958	1-Ik	4
May 2 1958	2-Akbal	5
May 3 1958	3-Kan	6
May 4 1958	4-Chicchan	7
May 5 1958	5-Cimi	8
May 6 1958	6-Manik	9
May 7 1958	7-Lamat	1
May 8 1958	8-Muluc	2
May 9 1958	9-Oc	3
May 10 1958	10-Chuen	4
May 11 1958	11-Eb	5
May 12 1958	12-Ben	6
May 13 1958	13-Ix	7
May 14 1958	1-Men	8
May 15 1958	2-Cib	9
May 16 1958	3-Caban	1
May 17 1958	4-Etz'nab	2
May 18 1958	5-Cauac	3
May 19 1958	6-Ahau	4
May 20 1958	7-Imix	5
May 21 1958	8-Ik	6
May 22 1958	9-Akbal	7
May 23 1958	10-Kan	8
May 24 1958	11-Chicchan	9
May 25 1958	12-Cimi	1
May 26 1958	13-Manik	2
May 27 1958	1-Lamat	3
May 28 1958	2-Muluc	4
May 29 1958	3-Oc	5
May 30 1958	4-Chuen	6
May 31 1958	5-Eb	7
Jun 1 1958	6-Ben	8
Jun 2 1958	7-Ix	9
Jun 3 1958	8-Men	1
Jun 4 1958	9-Cib	2
Jun 5 1958	10-Caban	3
Jun 6 1958	11-Etz'nab	4
Jun 7 1958	12-Cauac	5
Jun 8 1958	13-Ahau	6
Jun 9 1958	1-Imix	7
Jun 10 1958	2-Ik	8
Jun 11 1958	3-Akbal	9
Jun 12 1958	4-Kan	1
Jun 13 1958	5-Chicchan	2
Jun 14 1958	6-Cimi	3
Jun 15 1958	7-Manik	4
Jun 16 1958	8-Lamat	5
Jun 17 1958	9-Muluc	6

Date	Day-Sign	L	Date	Day-Sign	L	Date	Day-Sign	L
Jun 18 1958	10-Oc	7	Aug 25 1958	13-Etz'nab	3	Nov 1 1958	3-Cimi	8
Jun 19 1958	11-Chuen	8	Aug 26 1958	1-Cauac	4	Nov 2 1958	4-Manik	9
Jun 20 1958	12-Eb	9	Aug 27 1958	2-Ahau	5	Nov 3 1958	5-Lamat	1
Jun 21 1958	13-Ben	1	Aug 28 1958	3-Imix	6	Nov 4 1958	6-Muluc	2
Jun 22 1958	1-Ix	2	Aug 29 1958	4-Ik	7	Nov 5 1958	7-Oc	3
Jun 23 1958	2-Men	3	Aug 30 1958	5-Akbal	8	Nov 6 1958	8-Chuen	4
Jun 24 1958	3-Cib	4	Aug 31 1958	6-Kan	9	Nov 7 1958	9-Eb	5
Jun 25 1958	4-Caban	5	Sep 1 1958	7-Chicchan	1	Nov 8 1958	10-Ben	6
Jun 26 1958	5-Etz'nab	6	Sep 2 1958	8-Cimi	2	Nov 9 1958	11-Ix	7
Jun 27 1958	6-Cauac	7	Sep 3 1958	9-Manik	3	Nov 10 1958	12-Men	8
Jun 28 1958	7-Ahau	8	Sep 4 1958	10-Lamat	4	Nov 11 1958	13-Cib	9
Jun 29 1958	8-Imix	9	Sep 5 1958	11-Muluc	5	Nov 12 1958	1-Caban	1
Jun 30 1958	9-Ik	1	Sep 6 1958	12-Oc	6	Nov 13 1958	2-Etz'nab	2
Jul 1 1958	10-Akbal	2	Sep 7 1958	13-Chuen	7	Nov 14 1958	3-Cauac	3
Jul 2 1958	11-Kan	3	Sep 8 1958	1-Eb	8	Nov 15 1958	4-Ahau	4
Jul 3 1958	12-Chicchan	4	Sep 9 1958	2-Ben	9	Nov 16 1958	5-Imix	5
Jul 4 1958	13-Cimi	5	Sep 10 1958	3-Ix	1	Nov 17 1958	6-Ik	6
Jul 5 1958	1-Manik	6	Sep 11 1958	4-Men	2	Nov 18 1958	7-Akbal	7
Jul 6 1958	2-Lamat	7	Sep 12 1958	5-Cib	3	Nov 19 1958	8-Kan	8
Jul 7 1958	3-Muluc	8	Sep 13 1958	6-Caban	4	Nov 20 1958	9-Chicchan	9
Jul 8 1958	4-Oc	9	Sep 14 1958	7-Etz'nab	5	Nov 21 1958	10-Cimi	1
Jul 9 1958	5-Chuen	1	Sep 15 1958	8-Cauac	6	Nov 22 1958	11-Manik	2
Jul 10 1958	6-Eb	2	Sep 16 1958	9-Ahau	7	Nov 23 1958	12-Lamat	3
Jul 11 1958	7-Ben	3	Sep 17 1958	10-Imix	8	Nov 24 1958	13-Muluc	4
Jul 12 1958	8-Ix	4	Sep 18 1958	11-Ik	9	Nov 25 1958	1-Oc	5
Jul 13 1958	9-Men	5	Sep 19 1958	12-Akbal	1	Nov 26 1958	2-Chuen	6
Jul 14 1958	10-Cib	6	Sep 20 1958	13-Kan	2	Nov 27 1958	3-Eb	7
Jul 15 1958	11-Caban	7	Sep 21 1958	1-Chicchan	3	Nov 28 1958	4-Ben	8
Jul 16 1958	12-Etz'nab	8	Sep 22 1958	2-Cimi	4	Nov 29 1958	5-Ix	9
Jul 17 1958	13-Cauac	9	Sep 23 1958	3-Manik	5	Nov 30 1958	6-Men	1
Jul 18 1958	1-Ahau	1	Sep 24 1958	4-Lamat	6	Dec 1 1958	7-Cib	2
Jul 19 1958	2-Imix	2	Sep 25 1958	5-Muluc	7	Dec 2 1958	8-Caban	3
Jul 20 1958	3-Ik	3	Sep 26 1958	6-Oc	8	Dec 3 1958	9-Etz'nab	4
Jul 21 1958	4-Akbal	4	Sep 27 1958	7-Chuen	9	Dec 4 1958	10-Cauac	5
Jul 22 1958	5-Kan	5	Sep 28 1958	8-Eb	1	Dec 5 1958	11-Ahau	6
Jul 23 1958	6-Chicchan	6	Sep 29 1958	9-Ben	2	Dec 6 1958	12-Imix	7
Jul 24 1958	7-Cimi	7	Sep 30 1958	10-Ix	3	Dec 7 1958	13-Ik	8
Jul 25 1958	8-Manik	8	Oct 1 1958	11-Men	4	Dec 8 1958	1-Akbal	9
Jul 26 1958	9-Lamat	9	Oct 2 1958	12-Cib	5	Dec 9 1958	2-Kan	1
Jul 27 1958	10-Muluc	1	Oct 3 1958	13-Caban	6	Dec 10 1958	3-Chicchan	2
Jul 28 1958	11-Oc	2	Oct 4 1958	1-Etz'nab	7	Dec 11 1958	4-Cimi	3
Jul 29 1958	12-Chuen	3	Oct 5 1958	2-Cauac	8	Dec 12 1958	5-Manik	4
Jul 30 1958	13-Eb	4	Oct 6 1958	3-Ahau	9	Dec 13 1958	6-Lamat	5
Jul 31 1958	1-Ben	5	Oct 7 1958	4-Imix	1	Dec 14 1958	7-Muluc	6
Aug 1 1958	2-Ix	6	Oct 8 1958	5-Ik	2	Dec 15 1958	8-Oc	7
Aug 2 1958	3-Men	7	Oct 9 1958	6-Akbal	3	Dec 16 1958	9-Chuen	8
Aug 3 1958	4-Cib	8	Oct 10 1958	7-Kan	4	Dec 17 1958	10-Eb	9
Aug 4 1958	5-Caban	9	Oct 11 1958	8-Chicchan	5	Dec 18 1958	11-Ben	1
Aug 5 1958	6-Etz'nab	1	Oct 12 1958	9-Cimi	6	Dec 19 1958	12-Ix	2
Aug 6 1958	7-Cauac	2	Oct 13 1958	10-Manik	7	Dec 20 1958	13-Men	3
Aug 7 1958	8-Ahau	3	Oct 14 1958	11-Lamat	8	Dec 21 1958	1-Cib	4
Aug 8 1958	9-Imix	4	Oct 15 1958	12-Muluc	9	Dec 22 1958	2-Caban	5
Aug 9 1958	10-Ik	5	Oct 16 1958	13-Oc	1	Dec 23 1958	3-Etz'nab	6
Aug 10 1958	11-Akbal	6	Oct 17 1958	1-Chuen	2	Dec 24 1958	4-Cauac	7
Aug 11 1958	12-Kan	7	Oct 18 1958	2-Eb	3	Dec 25 1958	5-Ahau	8
Aug 12 1958	13-Chicchan	8	Oct 19 1958	3-Ben	4	Dec 26 1958	6-Imix	9
Aug 13 1958	1-Cimi	9	Oct 20 1958	4-Ix	5	Dec 27 1958	7-Ik	1
Aug 14 1958	2-Manik	1	Oct 21 1958	5-Men	6	Dec 28 1958	8-Akbal	2
Aug 15 1958	3-Lamat	2	Oct 22 1958	6-Cib	7	Dec 29 1958	9-Kan	3
Aug 16 1958	4-Muluc	3	Oct 23 1958	7-Caban	8	Dec 30 1958	10-Chicchan	4
Aug 17 1958	5-Oc	4	Oct 24 1958	8-Etz'nab	9	Dec 31 1958	11-Cimi	5
Aug 18 1958	6-Chuen	5	Oct 25 1958	9-Cauac	1	Jan 1 1959	12-Manik	6
Aug 19 1958	7-Eb	6	Oct 26 1958	10-Ahau	2	Jan 2 1959	13-Lamat	7
Aug 20 1958	8-Ben	7	Oct 27 1958	11-Imix	3	Jan 3 1959	1-Muluc	8
Aug 21 1958	9-Ix	8	Oct 28 1958	12-Ik	4	Jan 4 1959	2-Oc	9
Aug 22 1958	10-Men	9	Oct 29 1958	13-Akbal	5	Jan 5 1959	3-Chuen	1
Aug 23 1958	11-Cib	1	Oct 30 1958	1-Kan	6	Jan 6 1959	4-Eb	2
Aug 24 1958	12-Caban	2	Oct 31 1958	2-Chicchan	7	Jan 7 1959	5-Ben	3

Date	Day-Sign	L	Date	Day-Sign	L	Date	Day-Sign	L
Jan 8 1959	6-Ix	4	Mar 17 1959	9-Ik	9	May 24 1959	12-Oc	5
Jan 9 1959	7-Men	5	Mar 18 1959	10-Akbal	1	May 25 1959	13-Chuen	6
Jan 10 1959	8-Cib	6	Mar 19 1959	11-Kan	2	May 26 1959	1-Eb	7
Jan 11 1959	9-Caban	7	Mar 20 1959	12-Chicchan	3	May 27 1959	2-Ben	8
Jan 12 1959	10-Etz'nab	8	Mar 21 1959	13-Cimi	4	May 28 1959	3-Ix	9
Jan 13 1959	11-Cauac	9	Mar 22 1959	1-Manik	5	May 29 1959	4-Men	1
Jan 14 1959	12-Ahau	1	Mar 23 1959	2-Lamat	6	May 30 1959	5-Cib	2
Jan 15 1959	13-Imix	2	Mar 24 1959	3-Muluc	7	May 31 1959	6-Caban	3
Jan 16 1959	1-Ik	3	Mar 25 1959	4-Oc	8	Jun 1 1959	7-Etz'nab	4
Jan 17 1959	2-Akbal	4	Mar 26 1959	5-Chuen	9	Jun 2 1959	8-Cauac	5
Jan 18 1959	3-Kan	5	Mar 27 1959	6-Eb	1	Jun 3 1959	9-Ahau	6
Jan 19 1959	4-Chicchan	6	Mar 28 1959	7-Ben	2	Jun 4 1959	10-Imix	7
Jan 20 1959	5-Cimi	7	Mar 29 1959	8-Ix	3	Jun 5 1959	11-Ik	8
Jan 21 1959	6-Manik	8	Mar 30 1959	9-Men	4	Jun 6 1959	12-Akbal	9
Jan 22 1959	7-Lamat	9	Mar 31 1959	10-Cib	5	Jun 7 1959	13-Kan	1
Jan 23 1959	8-Muluc	1	Apr 1 1959	11-Caban	6	Jun 8 1959	1-Chicchan	2
Jan 24 1959	9-Oc	2	Apr 2 1959	12-Etz'nab	7	Jun 9 1959	2-Cimi	3
Jan 25 1959	10-Chuen	3	Apr 3 1959	13-Cauac	8	Jun 10 1959	3-Manik	4
Jan 26 1959	11-Eb	4	Apr 4 1959	1-Ahau	9	Jun 11 1959	4-Lamat	5
Jan 27 1959	12-Ben	5	Apr 5 1959	2-Imix	1	Jun 12 1959	5-Muluc	6
Jan 28 1959	13-Ix	6	Apr 6 1959	3-Ik	2	Jun 13 1959	6-Oc	7
Jan 29 1959	1-Men	7	Apr 7 1959	4-Akbal	3	Jun 14 1959	7-Chuen	8
Jan 30 1959	2-Cib	8	Apr 8 1959	5-Kan	4	Jun 15 1959	8-Eb	9
Jan 31 1959	3-Caban	9	Apr 9 1959	6-Chicchan	5	Jun 16 1959	9-Ben	1
Feb 1 1959	4-Etz'nab	1	Apr 10 1959	7-Cimi	6	Jun 17 1959	10-Ix	2
Feb 2 1959	5-Cauac	2	Apr 11 1959	8-Manik	7	Jun 18 1959	11-Men	3
Feb 3 1959	6-Ahau	3	Apr 12 1959	9-Lamat	8	Jun 19 1959	12-Cib	4
Feb 4 1959	7-Imix	4	Apr 13 1959	10-Muluc	9	Jun 20 1959	13-Caban	5
Feb 5 1959	8-Ik	5	Apr 14 1959	11-Oc	1	Jun 21 1959	1-Etz'nab	6
Feb 6 1959	9-Akbal	6	Apr 15 1959	12-Chuen	2	Jun 22 1959	2-Cauac	7
Feb 7 1959	10-Kan	7	Apr 16 1959	13-Eb	3	Jun 23 1959	3-Ahau	8
Feb 8 1959	11-Chicchan	8	Apr 17 1959	1-Ben	4	Jun 24 1959	4-Imix	9
Feb 9 1959	12-Cimi	9	Apr 18 1959	2-Ix	5	Jun 25 1959	5-Ik	1
Feb 10 1959	13-Manik	1	Apr 19 1959	3-Men	6	Jun 26 1959	6-Akbal	2
Feb 11 1959	1-Lamat	2	Apr 20 1959	4-Cib	7	Jun 27 1959	7-Kan	3
Feb 12 1959	2-Muluc	3	Apr 21 1959	5-Caban	8	Jun 28 1959	8-Chicchan	4
Feb 13 1959	3-Oc	4	Apr 22 1959	6-Etz'nab	9	Jun 29 1959	9-Cimi	5
Feb 14 1959	4-Chuen	5	Apr 23 1959	7-Cauac	1	Jun 30 1959	10-Manik	6
Feb 15 1959	5-Eb	6	Apr 24 1959	8-Ahau	2	Jul 1 1959	11-Lamat	7
Feb 16 1959	6-Ben	7	Apr 25 1959	9-Imix	3	Jul 2 1959	12-Muluc	8
Feb 17 1959	7-Ix	8	Apr 26 1959	10-Ik	4	Jul 3 1959	13-Oc	9
Feb 18 1959	8-Men	9	Apr 27 1959	11-Akbal	5	Jul 4 1959	1-Chuen	1
Feb 19 1959	9-Cib	1	Apr 28 1959	12-Kan	6	Jul 5 1959	2-Eb	2
Feb 20 1959	10-Caban	2	Apr 29 1959	13-Chicchan	7	Jul 6 1959	3-Ben	3
Feb 21 1959	11-Etz'nab	3	Apr 30 1959	1-Cimi	8	Jul 7 1959	4-Ix	4
Feb 22 1959	12-Cauac	4	May 1 1959	2-Manik	9	Jul 8 1959	5-Men	5
Feb 23 1959	13-Ahau	5	May 2 1959	3-Lamat	1	Jul 9 1959	6-Cib	6
Feb 24 1959	1-Imix	6	May 3 1959	4-Muluc	2	Jul 10 1959	7-Caban	7
Feb 25 1959	2-Ik	7	May 4 1959	5-Oc	3	Jul 11 1959	8-Etz'nab	8
Feb 26 1959	3-Akbal	8	May 5 1959	6-Chuen	4	Jul 12 1959	9-Cauac	9
Feb 27 1959	4-Kan	9	May 6 1959	7-Eb	5	Jul 13 1959	10-Ahau	1
Feb 28 1959	5-Chicchan	1	May 7 1959	8-Ben	6	Jul 14 1959	11-Imix	2
Mar 1 1959	6-Cimi	2	May 8 1959	9-Ix	7	Jul 15 1959	12-Ik	3
Mar 2 1959	7-Manik	3	May 9 1959	10-Men	8	Jul 16 1959	13-Akbal	4
Mar 3 1959	8-Lamat	4	May 10 1959	11-Cib	9	Jul 17 1959	1-Kan	5
Mar 4 1959	9-Muluc	5	May 11 1959	12-Caban	1	Jul 18 1959	2-Chicchan	6
Mar 5 1959	10-Oc	6	May 12 1959	13-Etz'nab	2	Jul 19 1959	3-Cimi	7
Mar 6 1959	11-Chuen	7	May 13 1959	1-Cauac	3	Jul 20 1959	4-Manik	8
Mar 7 1959	12-Eb	8	May 14 1959	2-Ahau	4	Jul 21 1959	5-Lamat	9
Mar 8 1959	13-Ben	9	May 15 1959	3-Imix	5	Jul 22 1959	6-Muluc	1
Mar 9 1959	1-Ix	1	May 16 1959	4-Ik	6	Jul 23 1959	7-Oc	2
Mar 10 1959	2-Men	2	May 17 1959	5-Akbal	7	Jul 24 1959	8-Chuen	3
Mar 11 1959	3-Cib	3	May 18 1959	6-Kan	8	Jul 25 1959	9-Eb	4
Mar 12 1959	4-Caban	4	May 19 1959	7-Chicchan	9	Jul 26 1959	10-Ben	5
Mar 13 1959	5-Etz'nab	5	May 20 1959	8-Cimi	1	Jul 27 1959	11-Ix	6
Mar 14 1959	6-Cauac	6	May 21 1959	9-Manik	2	Jul 28 1959	12-Men	7
Mar 15 1959	7-Ahau	7	May 22 1959	10-Lamat	3	Jul 29 1959	13-Cib	8
Mar 16 1959	8-Imix	8	May 23 1959	11-Muluc	4	Jul 30 1959	1-Caban	9

Date	Day-Sign	L		Date	Day-Sign	L		Date	Day-Sign	L
Jul 31 1959	2-Etz'nab	1		Oct 7 1959	5-Cimi	6		Dec 14 1959	8-Ix	2
Aug 1 1959	3-Cauac	2		Oct 8 1959	6-Manik	7		Dec 15 1959	9-Men	3
Aug 2 1959	4-Ahau	3		Oct 9 1959	7-Lamat	8		Dec 16 1959	10-Cib	4
Aug 3 1959	5-Imix	4		Oct 10 1959	8-Muluc	9		Dec 17 1959	11-Caban	5
Aug 4 1959	6-Ik	5		Oct 11 1959	9-Oc	1		Dec 18 1959	12-Etz'nab	6
Aug 5 1959	7-Akbal	6		Oct 12 1959	10-Chuen	2		Dec 19 1959	13-Cauac	7
Aug 6 1959	8-Kan	7		Oct 13 1959	11-Eb	3		Dec 20 1959	1-Ahau	8
Aug 7 1959	9-Chicchan	8		Oct 14 1959	12-Ben	4		Dec 21 1959	2-Imix	9
Aug 8 1959	10-Cimi	9		Oct 15 1959	13-Ix	5		Dec 22 1959	3-Ik	1
Aug 9 1959	11-Manik	1		Oct 16 1959	1-Men	6		Dec 23 1959	4-Akbal	2
Aug 10 1959	12-Lamat	2		Oct 17 1959	2-Cib	7		Dec 24 1959	5-Kan	3
Aug 11 1959	13-Muluc	3		Oct 18 1959	3-Caban	8		Dec 25 1959	6-Chicchan	4
Aug 12 1959	1-Oc	4		Oct 19 1959	4-Etz'nab	9		Dec 26 1959	7-Cimi	5
Aug 13 1959	2-Chuen	5		Oct 20 1959	5-Cauac	1		Dec 27 1959	8-Manik	6
Aug 14 1959	3-Eb	6		Oct 21 1959	6-Ahau	2		Dec 28 1959	9-Lamat	7
Aug 15 1959	4-Ben	7		Oct 22 1959	7-Imix	3		Dec 29 1959	10-Muluc	8
Aug 16 1959	5-Ix	8		Oct 23 1959	8-Ik	4		Dec 30 1959	11-Oc	9
Aug 17 1959	6-Men	9		Oct 24 1959	9-Akbal	5		Dec 31 1959	12-Chuen	1
Aug 18 1959	7-Cib	1		Oct 25 1959	10-Kan	6		Jan 1 1960	13-Eb	2
Aug 19 1959	8-Caban	2		Oct 26 1959	11-Chicchan	7		Jan 2 1960	1-Ben	3
Aug 20 1959	9-Etz'nab	3		Oct 27 1959	12-Cimi	8		Jan 3 1960	2-Ix	4
Aug 21 1959	10-Cauac	4		Oct 28 1959	13-Manik	9		Jan 4 1960	3-Men	5
Aug 22 1959	11-Ahau	5		Oct 29 1959	1-Lamat	1		Jan 5 1960	4-Cib	6
Aug 23 1959	12-Imix	6		Oct 30 1959	2-Muluc	2		Jan 6 1960	5-Caban	7
Aug 24 1959	13-Ik	7		Oct 31 1959	3-Oc	3		Jan 7 1960	6-Etz'nab	8
Aug 25 1959	1-Akbal	8		Nov 1 1959	4-Chuen	4		Jan 8 1960	7-Cauac	9
Aug 26 1959	2-Kan	9		Nov 2 1959	5-Eb	5		Jan 9 1960	8-Ahau	1
Aug 27 1959	3-Chicchan	1		Nov 3 1959	6-Ben	6		Jan 10 1960	9-Imix	2
Aug 28 1959	4-Cimi	2		Nov 4 1959	7-Ix	7		Jan 11 1960	10-Ik	3
Aug 29 1959	5-Manik	3		Nov 5 1959	8-Men	8		Jan 12 1960	11-Akbal	4
Aug 30 1959	6-Lamat	4		Nov 6 1959	9-Cib	9		Jan 13 1960	12-Kan	5
Aug 31 1959	7-Muluc	5		Nov 7 1959	10-Caban	1		Jan 14 1960	13-Chicchan	6
Sep 1 1959	8-Oc	6		Nov 8 1959	11-Etz'nab	2		Jan 15 1960	1-Cimi	7
Sep 2 1959	9-Chuen	7		Nov 9 1959	12-Cauac	3		Jan 16 1960	2-Manik	8
Sep 3 1959	10-Eb	8		Nov 10 1959	13-Ahau	4		Jan 17 1960	3-Lamat	9
Sep 4 1959	11-Ben	9		Nov 11 1959	1-Imix	5		Jan 18 1960	4-Muluc	1
Sep 5 1959	12-Ix	1		Nov 12 1959	2-Ik	6		Jan 19 1960	5-Oc	2
Sep 6 1959	13-Men	2		Nov 13 1959	3-Akbal	7		Jan 20 1960	6-Chuen	3
Sep 7 1959	1-Cib	3		Nov 14 1959	4-Kan	8		Jan 21 1960	7-Eb	4
Sep 8 1959	2-Caban	4		Nov 15 1959	5-Chicchan	9		Jan 22 1960	8-Ben	5
Sep 9 1959	3-Etz'nab	5		Nov 16 1959	6-Cimi	1		Jan 23 1960	9-Ix	6
Sep 10 1959	4-Cauac	6		Nov 17 1959	7-Manik	2		Jan 24 1960	10-Men	7
Sep 11 1959	5-Ahau	7		Nov 18 1959	8-Lamat	3		Jan 25 1960	11-Cib	8
Sep 12 1959	6-Imix	8		Nov 19 1959	9-Muluc	4		Jan 26 1960	12-Caban	9
Sep 13 1959	7-Ik	9		Nov 20 1959	10-Oc	5		Jan 27 1960	13-Etz'nab	1
Sep 14 1959	8-Akbal	1		Nov 21 1959	11-Chuen	6		Jan 28 1960	1-Cauac	2
Sep 15 1959	9-Kan	2		Nov 22 1959	12-Eb	7		Jan 29 1960	2-Ahau	3
Sep 16 1959	10-Chicchan	3		Nov 23 1959	13-Ben	8		Jan 30 1960	3-Imix	4
Sep 17 1959	11-Cimi	4		Nov 24 1959	1-Ix	9		Jan 31 1960	4-Ik	5
Sep 18 1959	12-Manik	5		Nov 25 1959	2-Men	1		Feb 1 1960	5-Akbal	6
Sep 19 1959	13-Lamat	6		Nov 26 1959	3-Cib	2		Feb 2 1960	6-Kan	7
Sep 20 1959	1-Muluc	7		Nov 27 1959	4-Caban	3		Feb 3 1960	7-Chicchan	8
Sep 21 1959	2-Oc	8		Nov 28 1959	5-Etz'nab	4		Feb 4 1960	8-Cimi	9
Sep 22 1959	3-Chuen	9		Nov 29 1959	6-Cauac	5		Feb 5 1960	9-Manik	1
Sep 23 1959	4-Eb	1		Nov 30 1959	7-Ahau	6		Feb 6 1960	10-Lamat	2
Sep 24 1959	5-Ben	2		Dec 1 1959	8-Imix	7		Feb 7 1960	11-Muluc	3
Sep 25 1959	6-Ix	3		Dec 2 1959	9-Ik	8		Feb 8 1960	12-Oc	4
Sep 26 1959	7-Men	4		Dec 3 1959	10-Akbal	9		Feb 9 1960	13-Chuen	5
Sep 27 1959	8-Cib	5		Dec 4 1959	11-Kan	1		Feb 10 1960	1-Eb	6
Sep 28 1959	9-Caban	6		Dec 5 1959	12-Chicchan	2		Feb 11 1960	2-Ben	7
Sep 29 1959	10-Etz'nab	7		Dec 6 1959	13-Cimi	3		Feb 12 1960	3-Ix	8
Sep 30 1959	11-Cauac	8		Dec 7 1959	1-Manik	4		Feb 13 1960	4-Men	9
Oct 1 1959	12-Ahau	9		Dec 8 1959	2-Lamat	5		Feb 14 1960	5-Cib	1
Oct 2 1959	13-Imix	1		Dec 9 1959	3-Muluc	6		Feb 15 1960	6-Caban	2
Oct 3 1959	1-Ik	2		Dec 10 1959	4-Oc	7		Feb 16 1960	7-Etz'nab	3
Oct 4 1959	2-Akbal	3		Dec 11 1959	5-Chuen	8		Feb 17 1960	8-Cauac	4
Oct 5 1959	3-Kan	4		Dec 12 1959	6-Eb	9		Feb 18 1960	9-Ahau	5
Oct 6 1959	4-Chicchan	5		Dec 13 1959	7-Ben	1		Feb 19 1960	10-Imix	6

Date	Day-Sign	L
Feb 20 1960	11-Ik	7
Feb 21 1960	12-Akbal	8
Feb 22 1960	13-Kan	9
Feb 23 1960	**1-Chicchan**	1
Feb 24 1960	2-Cimi	2
Feb 25 1960	3-Manik	3
Feb 26 1960	4-Lamat	4
Feb 27 1960	5-Muluc	5
Feb 28 1960	6-Oc	6
Feb 29 1960	7-Chuen	7
Mar 1 1960	8-Eb	8
Mar 2 1960	9-Ben	9
Mar 3 1960	10-Ix	1
Mar 4 1960	11-Men	2
Mar 5 1960	12-Cib	3
Mar 6 1960	13-Caban	4
Mar 7 1960	**1-Etz'nab**	5
Mar 8 1960	2-Cauac	6
Mar 9 1960	3-Ahau	7
Mar 10 1960	*4-Imix*	8
Mar 11 1960	5-Ik	9
Mar 12 1960	6-Akbal	1
Mar 13 1960	7-Kan	2
Mar 14 1960	8-Chicchan	3
Mar 15 1960	9-Cimi	4
Mar 16 1960	10-Manik	5
Mar 17 1960	11-Lamat	6
Mar 18 1960	12-Muluc	7
Mar 19 1960	13-Oc	8
Mar 20 1960	**1-Chuen**	9
Mar 21 1960	2-Eb	1
Mar 22 1960	3-Ben	2
Mar 23 1960	4-Ix	3
Mar 24 1960	5-Men	4
Mar 25 1960	6-Cib	5
Mar 26 1960	7-Caban	6
Mar 27 1960	8-Etz'nab	7
Mar 28 1960	9-Cauac	8
Mar 29 1960	10-Ahau	9
Mar 30 1960	*11-Imix*	1
Mar 31 1960	12-Ik	2
Apr 1 1960	13-Akbal	3
Apr 2 1960	**1-Kan**	4
Apr 3 1960	2-Chicchan	5
Apr 4 1960	3-Cimi	6
Apr 5 1960	4-Manik	7
Apr 6 1960	5-Lamat	8
Apr 7 1960	6-Muluc	9
Apr 8 1960	7-Oc	1
Apr 9 1960	8-Chuen	2
Apr 10 1960	9-Eb	3
Apr 11 1960	10-Ben	4
Apr 12 1960	11-Ix	5
Apr 13 1960	12-Men	6
Apr 14 1960	13-Cib	7
Apr 15 1960	**1-Caban**	8
Apr 16 1960	2-Etz'nab	9
Apr 17 1960	3-Cauac	1
Apr 18 1960	4-Ahau	2
Apr 19 1960	*5-Imix*	3
Apr 20 1960	6-Ik	4
Apr 21 1960	7-Akbal	5
Apr 22 1960	8-Kan	6
Apr 23 1960	9-Chicchan	7
Apr 24 1960	10-Cimi	8
Apr 25 1960	11-Manik	9
Apr 26 1960	12-Lamat	1
Apr 27 1960	13-Muluc	2

Date	Day-Sign	L
Apr 28 1960	**1-Oc**	3
Apr 29 1960	2-Chuen	4
Apr 30 1960	3-Eb	5
May 1 1960	4-Ben	6
May 2 1960	5-Ix	7
May 3 1960	6-Men	8
May 4 1960	7-Cib	9
May 5 1960	8-Caban	1
May 6 1960	9-Etz'nab	2
May 7 1960	10-Cauac	3
May 8 1960	11-Ahau	4
May 9 1960	*12-Imix*	5
May 10 1960	13-Ik	6
May 11 1960	**1-Akbal**	7
May 12 1960	2-Kan	8
May 13 1960	3-Chicchan	9
May 14 1960	4-Cimi	1
May 15 1960	5-Manik	2
May 16 1960	6-Lamat	3
May 17 1960	7-Muluc	4
May 18 1960	8-Oc	5
May 19 1960	9-Chuen	6
May 20 1960	10-Eb	7
May 21 1960	11-Ben	8
May 22 1960	12-Ix	9
May 23 1960	13-Men	1
May 24 1960	**1-Cib**	2
May 25 1960	2-Caban	3
May 26 1960	3-Etz'nab	4
May 27 1960	4-Cauac	5
May 28 1960	5-Ahau	6
May 29 1960	*6-Imix*	7
May 30 1960	7-Ik	8
May 31 1960	8-Akbal	9
Jun 1 1960	9-Kan	1
Jun 2 1960	10-Chicchan	2
Jun 3 1960	11-Cimi	3
Jun 4 1960	12-Manik	4
Jun 5 1960	13-Lamat	5
Jun 6 1960	**1-Muluc**	6
Jun 7 1960	2-Oc	7
Jun 8 1960	3-Chuen	8
Jun 9 1960	4-Eb	9
Jun 10 1960	5-Ben	1
Jun 11 1960	6-Ix	2
Jun 12 1960	7-Men	3
Jun 13 1960	8-Cib	4
Jun 14 1960	9-Caban	5
Jun 15 1960	10-Etz'nab	6
Jun 16 1960	11-Cauac	7
Jun 17 1960	12-Ahau	8
Jun 18 1960	*13-Imix*	9
Jun 19 1960	**1-Ik**	1
Jun 20 1960	2-Akbal	2
Jun 21 1960	3-Kan	3
Jun 22 1960	4-Chicchan	4
Jun 23 1960	5-Cimi	5
Jun 24 1960	6-Manik	6
Jun 25 1960	7-Lamat	7
Jun 26 1960	8-Muluc	8
Jun 27 1960	9-Oc	9
Jun 28 1960	10-Chuen	1
Jun 29 1960	11-Eb	2
Jun 30 1960	12-Ben	3
Jul 1 1960	13-Ix	4
Jul 2 1960	**1-Men**	5
Jul 3 1960	2-Cib	6
Jul 4 1960	3-Caban	7

Date	Day-Sign	L
Jul 5 1960	4-Etz'nab	8
Jul 6 1960	5-Cauac	9
Jul 7 1960	6-Ahau	1
Jul 8 1960	*7-Imix*	2
Jul 9 1960	8-Ik	3
Jul 10 1960	9-Akbal	4
Jul 11 1960	10-Kan	5
Jul 12 1960	11-Chicchan	6
Jul 13 1960	12-Cimi	7
Jul 14 1960	13-Manik	8
Jul 15 1960	**1-Lamat**	9
Jul 16 1960	2-Muluc	1
Jul 17 1960	3-Oc	2
Jul 18 1960	4-Chuen	3
Jul 19 1960	5-Eb	4
Jul 20 1960	6-Ben	5
Jul 21 1960	7-Ix	6
Jul 22 1960	8-Men	7
Jul 23 1960	9-Cib	8
Jul 24 1960	10-Caban	9
Jul 25 1960	11-Etz'nab	1
Jul 26 1960	12-Cauac	2
Jul 27 1960	13-Ahau	3
Jul 28 1960	**1-Imix**	4
Jul 29 1960	2-Ik	5
Jul 30 1960	3-Akbal	6
Jul 31 1960	4-Kan	7
Aug 1 1960	5-Chicchan	8
Aug 2 1960	6-Cimi	9
Aug 3 1960	7-Manik	1
Aug 4 1960	8-Lamat	2
Aug 5 1960	9-Muluc	3
Aug 6 1960	10-Oc	4
Aug 7 1960	11-Chuen	5
Aug 8 1960	12-Eb	6
Aug 9 1960	13-Ben	7
Aug 10 1960	**1-Ix**	8
Aug 11 1960	2-Men	9
Aug 12 1960	3-Cib	1
Aug 13 1960	4-Caban	2
Aug 14 1960	5-Etz'nab	3
Aug 15 1960	6-Cauac	4
Aug 16 1960	7-Ahau	5
Aug 17 1960	*8-Imix*	6
Aug 18 1960	9-Ik	7
Aug 19 1960	10-Akbal	8
Aug 20 1960	11-Kan	9
Aug 21 1960	12-Chicchan	1
Aug 22 1960	13-Cimi	2
Aug 23 1960	**1-Manik**	3
Aug 24 1960	2-Lamat	4
Aug 25 1960	3-Muluc	5
Aug 26 1960	4-Oc	6
Aug 27 1960	5-Chuen	7
Aug 28 1960	6-Eb	8
Aug 29 1960	7-Ben	9
Aug 30 1960	8-Ix	1
Aug 31 1960	9-Men	2
Sep 1 1960	10-Cib	3
Sep 2 1960	11-Caban	4
Sep 3 1960	12-Etz'nab	5
Sep 4 1960	13-Cauac	6
Sep 5 1960	**1-Ahau**	7
Sep 6 1960	*2-Imix*	8
Sep 7 1960	3-Ik	9
Sep 8 1960	4-Akbal	1
Sep 9 1960	5-Kan	2
Sep 10 1960	6-Chicchan	3

Date	Day-Sign	L
Sep 11 1960	7-Cimi	4
Sep 12 1960	8-Manik	5
Sep 13 1960	9-Lamat	6
Sep 14 1960	10-Muluc	7
Sep 15 1960	11-Oc	8
Sep 16 1960	12-Chuen	9
Sep 17 1960	13-Eb	1
Sep 18 1960	**1-Ben**	2
Sep 19 1960	2-Ix	3
Sep 20 1960	3-Men	4
Sep 21 1960	4-Cib	5
Sep 22 1960	5-Caban	6
Sep 23 1960	6-Etz'nab	7
Sep 24 1960	7-Cauac	8
Sep 25 1960	8-Ahau	9
Sep 26 1960	*9-Imix*	1
Sep 27 1960	10-Ik	2
Sep 28 1960	11-Akbal	3
Sep 29 1960	12-Kan	4
Sep 30 1960	13-Chicchan	5
Oct 1 1960	**1-Cimi**	6
Oct 2 1960	2-Manik	7
Oct 3 1960	3-Lamat	8
Oct 4 1960	4-Muluc	9
Oct 5 1960	5-Oc	1
Oct 6 1960	6-Chuen	2
Oct 7 1960	7-Eb	3
Oct 8 1960	8-Ben	4
Oct 9 1960	9-Ix	5
Oct 10 1960	10-Men	6
Oct 11 1960	11-Cib	7
Oct 12 1960	12-Caban	8
Oct 13 1960	13-Etz'nab	9
Oct 14 1960	**1-Cauac**	1
Oct 15 1960	2-Ahau	2
Oct 16 1960	*3-Imix*	3
Oct 17 1960	4-Ik	4
Oct 18 1960	5-Akbal	5
Oct 19 1960	6-Kan	6
Oct 20 1960	7-Chicchan	7
Oct 21 1960	8-Cimi	8
Oct 22 1960	9-Manik	9
Oct 23 1960	10-Lamat	1
Oct 24 1960	11-Muluc	2
Oct 25 1960	12-Oc	3
Oct 26 1960	13-Chuen	4
Oct 27 1960	**1-Eb**	5
Oct 28 1960	2-Ben	6
Oct 29 1960	3-Ix	7
Oct 30 1960	4-Men	8
Oct 31 1960	5-Cib	9
Nov 1 1960	6-Caban	1
Nov 2 1960	7-Etz'nab	2
Nov 3 1960	8-Cauac	3
Nov 4 1960	9-Ahau	4
Nov 5 1960	*10-Imix*	5
Nov 6 1960	11-Ik	6
Nov 7 1960	12-Akbal	7
Nov 8 1960	13-Kan	8
Nov 9 1960	**1-Chicchan**	9
Nov 10 1960	2-Cimi	1
Nov 11 1960	3-Manik	2
Nov 12 1960	4-Lamat	3
Nov 13 1960	5-Muluc	4
Nov 14 1960	6-Oc	5
Nov 15 1960	7-Chuen	6
Nov 16 1960	8-Eb	7
Nov 17 1960	9-Ben	8

Date	Day-Sign	L
Nov 18 1960	10-Ix	9
Nov 19 1960	11-Men	1
Nov 20 1960	12-Cib	2
Nov 21 1960	13-Caban	3
Nov 22 1960	**1-Etz'nab**	4
Nov 23 1960	2-Cauac	5
Nov 24 1960	3-Ahau	6
Nov 25 1960	*4-Imix*	7
Nov 26 1960	5-Ik	8
Nov 27 1960	6-Akbal	9
Nov 28 1960	7-Kan	1
Nov 29 1960	8-Chicchan	2
Nov 30 1960	9-Cimi	3
Dec 1 1960	10-Manik	4
Dec 2 1960	11-Lamat	5
Dec 3 1960	12-Muluc	6
Dec 4 1960	13-Oc	7
Dec 5 1960	**1-Chuen**	8
Dec 6 1960	2-Eb	9
Dec 7 1960	3-Ben	1
Dec 8 1960	4-Ix	2
Dec 9 1960	5-Men	3
Dec 10 1960	6-Cib	4
Dec 11 1960	7-Caban	5
Dec 12 1960	8-Etz'nab	6
Dec 13 1960	9-Cauac	7
Dec 14 1960	10-Ahau	8
Dec 15 1960	*11-Imix*	9
Dec 16 1960	12-Ik	1
Dec 17 1960	13-Akbal	2
Dec 18 1960	**1-Kan**	3
Dec 19 1960	2-Chicchan	4
Dec 20 1960	3-Cimi	5
Dec 21 1960	4-Manik	6
Dec 22 1960	5-Lamat	7
Dec 23 1960	6-Muluc	8
Dec 24 1960	7-Oc	9
Dec 25 1960	8-Chuen	1
Dec 26 1960	9-Eb	2
Dec 27 1960	10-Ben	3
Dec 28 1960	11-Ix	4
Dec 29 1960	12-Men	5
Dec 30 1960	13-Cib	6
Dec 31 1960	**1-Caban**	7
Jan 1 1961	2-Etz'nab	8
Jan 2 1961	3-Cauac	9
Jan 3 1961	4-Ahau	1
Jan 4 1961	*5-Imix*	2
Jan 5 1961	6-Ik	3
Jan 6 1961	7-Akbal	4
Jan 7 1961	8-Kan	5
Jan 8 1961	9-Chicchan	6
Jan 9 1961	10-Cimi	7
Jan 10 1961	11-Manik	8
Jan 11 1961	12-Lamat	9
Jan 12 1961	13-Muluc	1
Jan 13 1961	**1-Oc**	2
Jan 14 1961	2-Chuen	3
Jan 15 1961	3-Eb	4
Jan 16 1961	4-Ben	5
Jan 17 1961	5-Ix	6
Jan 18 1961	6-Men	7
Jan 19 1961	7-Cib	8
Jan 20 1961	8-Caban	9
Jan 21 1961	9-Etz'nab	1
Jan 22 1961	10-Cauac	2
Jan 23 1961	11-Ahau	3
Jan 24 1961	*12-Imix*	4

Date	Day-Sign	L
Jan 25 1961	13-Ik	5
Jan 26 1961	**1-Akbal**	6
Jan 27 1961	2-Kan	7
Jan 28 1961	3-Chicchan	8
Jan 29 1961	4-Cimi	9
Jan 30 1961	5-Manik	1
Jan 31 1961	6-Lamat	2
Feb 1 1961	7-Muluc	3
Feb 2 1961	8-Oc	4
Feb 3 1961	9-Chuen	5
Feb 4 1961	10-Eb	6
Feb 5 1961	11-Ben	7
Feb 6 1961	12-Ix	8
Feb 7 1961	13-Men	9
Feb 8 1961	**1-Cib**	1
Feb 9 1961	2-Caban	2
Feb 10 1961	3-Etz'nab	3
Feb 11 1961	4-Cauac	4
Feb 12 1961	5-Ahau	5
Feb 13 1961	*6-Imix*	6
Feb 14 1961	7-Ik	7
Feb 15 1961	8-Akbal	8
Feb 16 1961	9-Kan	9
Feb 17 1961	10-Chicchan	1
Feb 18 1961	11-Cimi	2
Feb 19 1961	12-Manik	3
Feb 20 1961	13-Lamat	4
Feb 21 1961	**1-Muluc**	5
Feb 22 1961	2-Oc	6
Feb 23 1961	3-Chuen	7
Feb 24 1961	4-Eb	8
Feb 25 1961	5-Ben	9
Feb 26 1961	6-Ix	1
Feb 27 1961	7-Men	2
Feb 28 1961	8-Cib	3
Mar 1 1961	9-Caban	4
Mar 2 1961	10-Etz'nab	5
Mar 3 1961	11-Cauac	6
Mar 4 1961	12-Ahau	7
Mar 5 1961	*13-Imix*	8
Mar 6 1961	**1-Ik**	9
Mar 7 1961	2-Akbal	1
Mar 8 1961	3-Kan	2
Mar 9 1961	4-Chicchan	3
Mar 10 1961	5-Cimi	4
Mar 11 1961	6-Manik	5
Mar 12 1961	7-Lamat	6
Mar 13 1961	8-Muluc	7
Mar 14 1961	9-Oc	8
Mar 15 1961	10-Chuen	9
Mar 16 1961	11-Eb	1
Mar 17 1961	12-Ben	2
Mar 18 1961	13-Ix	3
Mar 19 1961	**1-Men**	4
Mar 20 1961	2-Cib	5
Mar 21 1961	3-Caban	6
Mar 22 1961	4-Etz'nab	7
Mar 23 1961	5-Cauac	8
Mar 24 1961	6-Ahau	9
Mar 25 1961	*7-Imix*	1
Mar 26 1961	8-Ik	2
Mar 27 1961	9-Akbal	3
Mar 28 1961	10-Kan	4
Mar 29 1961	11-Chicchan	5
Mar 30 1961	12-Cimi	6
Mar 31 1961	13-Manik	7
Apr 1 1961	**1-Lamat**	8
Apr 2 1961	2-Muluc	9

Date	Day-Sign	L	Date	Day-Sign	L	Date	Day-Sign	L
Apr 3 1961	3-Oc	1	Jun 10 1961	6-Etz'nab	6	Aug 17 1961	9-Cimi	2
Apr 4 1961	4-Chuen	2	Jun 11 1961	7-Cauac	7	Aug 18 1961	10-Manik	3
Apr 5 1961	5-Eb	3	Jun 12 1961	8-Ahau	8	Aug 19 1961	11-Lamat	4
Apr 6 1961	6-Ben	4	Jun 13 1961	9-Imix	9	Aug 20 1961	12-Muluc	5
Apr 7 1961	7-Ix	5	Jun 14 1961	10-Ik	1	Aug 21 1961	13-Oc	6
Apr 8 1961	8-Men	6	Jun 15 1961	11-Akbal	2	Aug 22 1961	**1-Chuen**	7
Apr 9 1961	9-Cib	7	Jun 16 1961	12-Kan	3	Aug 23 1961	2-Eb	8
Apr 10 1961	10-Caban	8	Jun 17 1961	13-Chicchan	4	Aug 24 1961	3-Ben	9
Apr 11 1961	11-Etz'nab	9	Jun 18 1961	**1-Cimi**	5	Aug 25 1961	4-Ix	1
Apr 12 1961	12-Cauac	1	Jun 19 1961	2-Manik	6	Aug 26 1961	5-Men	2
Apr 13 1961	13-Ahau	2	Jun 20 1961	3-Lamat	7	Aug 27 1961	6-Cib	3
Apr 14 1961	**1-Imix**	3	Jun 21 1961	4-Muluc	8	Aug 28 1961	7-Caban	4
Apr 15 1961	2-Ik	4	Jun 22 1961	5-Oc	9	Aug 29 1961	8-Etz'nab	5
Apr 16 1961	3-Akbal	5	Jun 23 1961	6-Chuen	1	Aug 30 1961	9-Cauac	6
Apr 17 1961	4-Kan	6	Jun 24 1961	7-Eb	2	Aug 31 1961	10-Ahau	7
Apr 18 1961	5-Chicchan	7	Jun 25 1961	8-Ben	3	Sep 1 1961	11-Imix	8
Apr 19 1961	6-Cimi	8	Jun 26 1961	9-Ix	4	Sep 2 1961	12-Ik	9
Apr 20 1961	7-Manik	9	Jun 27 1961	10-Men	5	Sep 3 1961	13-Akbal	1
Apr 21 1961	8-Lamat	1	Jun 28 1961	11-Cib	6	Sep 4 1961	**1-Kan**	2
Apr 22 1961	9-Muluc	2	Jun 29 1961	12-Caban	7	Sep 5 1961	2-Chicchan	3
Apr 23 1961	10-Oc	3	Jun 30 1961	13-Etz'nab	8	Sep 6 1961	3-Cimi	4
Apr 24 1961	11-Chuen	4	Jul 1 1961	**1-Cauac**	9	Sep 7 1961	4-Manik	5
Apr 25 1961	12-Eb	5	Jul 2 1961	2-Ahau	1	Sep 8 1961	5-Lamat	6
Apr 26 1961	13-Ben	6	Jul 3 1961	3-Imix	2	Sep 9 1961	6-Muluc	7
Apr 27 1961	**1-Ix**	7	Jul 4 1961	4-Ik	3	Sep 10 1961	7-Oc	8
Apr 28 1961	2-Men	8	Jul 5 1961	5-Akbal	4	Sep 11 1961	8-Chuen	9
Apr 29 1961	3-Cib	9	Jul 6 1961	6-Kan	5	Sep 12 1961	9-Eb	1
Apr 30 1961	4-Caban	1	Jul 7 1961	7-Chicchan	6	Sep 13 1961	10-Ben	2
May 1 1961	5-Etz'nab	2	Jul 8 1961	8-Cimi	7	Sep 14 1961	11-Ix	3
May 2 1961	6-Cauac	3	Jul 9 1961	9-Manik	8	Sep 15 1961	12-Men	4
May 3 1961	7-Ahau	4	Jul 10 1961	10-Lamat	9	Sep 16 1961	13-Cib	5
May 4 1961	8-Imix	5	Jul 11 1961	11-Muluc	1	Sep 17 1961	**1-Caban**	6
May 5 1961	9-Ik	6	Jul 12 1961	12-Oc	2	Sep 18 1961	2-Etz'nab	7
May 6 1961	10-Akbal	7	Jul 13 1961	13-Chuen	3	Sep 19 1961	3-Cauac	8
May 7 1961	11-Kan	8	Jul 14 1961	**1-Eb**	4	Sep 20 1961	4-Ahau	9
May 8 1961	12-Chicchan	9	Jul 15 1961	2-Ben	5	Sep 21 1961	5-Imix	1
May 9 1961	13-Cimi	1	Jul 16 1961	3-Ix	6	Sep 22 1961	6-Ik	2
May 10 1961	**1-Manik**	2	Jul 17 1961	4-Men	7	Sep 23 1961	7-Akbal	3
May 11 1961	2-Lamat	3	Jul 18 1961	5-Cib	8	Sep 24 1961	8-Kan	4
May 12 1961	3-Muluc	4	Jul 19 1961	6-Caban	9	Sep 25 1961	9-Chicchan	5
May 13 1961	4-Oc	5	Jul 20 1961	7-Etz'nab	1	Sep 26 1961	10-Cimi	6
May 14 1961	5-Chuen	6	Jul 21 1961	8-Cauac	2	Sep 27 1961	11-Manik	7
May 15 1961	6-Eb	7	Jul 22 1961	9-Ahau	3	Sep 28 1961	12-Lamat	8
May 16 1961	7-Ben	8	Jul 23 1961	10-Imix	4	Sep 29 1961	13-Muluc	9
May 17 1961	8-Ix	9	Jul 24 1961	11-Ik	5	Sep 30 1961	**1-Oc**	1
May 18 1961	9-Men	1	Jul 25 1961	12-Akbal	6	Oct 1 1961	2-Chuen	2
May 19 1961	10-Cib	2	Jul 26 1961	13-Kan	7	Oct 2 1961	3-Eb	3
May 20 1961	11-Caban	3	Jul 27 1961	**1-Chicchan**	8	Oct 3 1961	4-Ben	4
May 21 1961	12-Etz'nab	4	Jul 28 1961	2-Cimi	9	Oct 4 1961	5-Ix	5
May 22 1961	13-Cauac	5	Jul 29 1961	3-Manik	1	Oct 5 1961	6-Men	6
May 23 1961	**1-Ahau**	6	Jul 30 1961	4-Lamat	2	Oct 6 1961	7-Cib	7
May 24 1961	2-Imix	7	Jul 31 1961	5-Muluc	3	Oct 7 1961	8-Caban	8
May 25 1961	3-Ik	8	Aug 1 1961	6-Oc	4	Oct 8 1961	9-Etz'nab	9
May 26 1961	4-Akbal	9	Aug 2 1961	7-Chuen	5	Oct 9 1961	10-Cauac	1
May 27 1961	5-Kan	1	Aug 3 1961	8-Eb	6	Oct 10 1961	11-Ahau	2
May 28 1961	6-Chicchan	2	Aug 4 1961	9-Ben	7	Oct 11 1961	12-Imix	3
May 29 1961	7-Cimi	3	Aug 5 1961	10-Ix	8	Oct 12 1961	13-Ik	4
May 30 1961	8-Manik	4	Aug 6 1961	11-Men	9	Oct 13 1961	**1-Akbal**	5
May 31 1961	9-Lamat	5	Aug 7 1961	12-Cib	1	Oct 14 1961	2-Kan	6
Jun 1 1961	10-Muluc	6	Aug 8 1961	13-Caban	2	Oct 15 1961	3-Chicchan	7
Jun 2 1961	11-Oc	7	Aug 9 1961	**1-Etz'nab**	3	Oct 16 1961	4-Cimi	8
Jun 3 1961	12-Chuen	8	Aug 10 1961	2-Cauac	4	Oct 17 1961	5-Manik	9
Jun 4 1961	13-Eb	9	Aug 11 1961	3-Ahau	5	Oct 18 1961	6-Lamat	1
Jun 5 1961	**1-Ben**	1	Aug 12 1961	4-Imix	6	Oct 19 1961	7-Muluc	2
Jun 6 1961	2-Ix	2	Aug 13 1961	5-Ik	7	Oct 20 1961	8-Oc	3
Jun 7 1961	3-Men	3	Aug 14 1961	6-Akbal	8	Oct 21 1961	9-Chuen	4
Jun 8 1961	4-Cib	4	Aug 15 1961	7-Kan	9	Oct 22 1961	10-Eb	5
Jun 9 1961	5-Caban	5	Aug 16 1961	8-Chicchan	1	Oct 23 1961	11-Ben	6

Date	Day-Sign	L
Oct 24 1961	12-Ix	7
Oct 25 1961	13-Men	8
Oct 26 1961	1-Cib	9
Oct 27 1961	2-Caban	1
Oct 28 1961	3-Etz'nab	2
Oct 29 1961	4-Cauac	3
Oct 30 1961	5-Ahau	4
Oct 31 1961	6-Imix	5
Nov 1 1961	7-Ik	6
Nov 2 1961	8-Akbal	7
Nov 3 1961	9-Kan	8
Nov 4 1961	10-Chicchan	9
Nov 5 1961	11-Cimi	1
Nov 6 1961	12-Manik	2
Nov 7 1961	13-Lamat	3
Nov 8 1961	1-Muluc	4
Nov 9 1961	2-Oc	5
Nov 10 1961	3-Chuen	6
Nov 11 1961	4-Eb	7
Nov 12 1961	5-Ben	8
Nov 13 1961	6-Ix	9
Nov 14 1961	7-Men	1
Nov 15 1961	8-Cib	2
Nov 16 1961	9-Caban	3
Nov 17 1961	10-Etz'nab	4
Nov 18 1961	11-Cauac	5
Nov 19 1961	12-Ahau	6
Nov 20 1961	13-Imix	7
Nov 21 1961	1-Ik	8
Nov 22 1961	2-Akbal	9
Nov 23 1961	3-Kan	1
Nov 24 1961	4-Chicchan	2
Nov 25 1961	5-Cimi	3
Nov 26 1961	6-Manik	4
Nov 27 1961	7-Lamat	5
Nov 28 1961	8-Muluc	6
Nov 29 1961	9-Oc	7
Nov 30 1961	10-Chuen	8
Dec 1 1961	11-Eb	9
Dec 2 1961	12-Ben	1
Dec 3 1961	13-Ix	2
Dec 4 1961	1-Men	3
Dec 5 1961	2-Cib	4
Dec 6 1961	3-Caban	5
Dec 7 1961	4-Etz'nab	6
Dec 8 1961	5-Cauac	7
Dec 9 1961	6-Ahau	8
Dec 10 1961	7-Imix	9
Dec 11 1961	8-Ik	1
Dec 12 1961	9-Akbal	2
Dec 13 1961	10-Kan	3
Dec 14 1961	11-Chicchan	4
Dec 15 1961	12-Cimi	5
Dec 16 1961	13-Manik	6
Dec 17 1961	1-Lamat	7
Dec 18 1961	2-Muluc	8
Dec 19 1961	3-Oc	9
Dec 20 1961	4-Chuen	1
Dec 21 1961	5-Eb	2
Dec 22 1961	6-Ben	3
Dec 23 1961	7-Ix	4
Dec 24 1961	8-Men	5
Dec 25 1961	9-Cib	6
Dec 26 1961	10-Caban	7
Dec 27 1961	11-Etz'nab	8
Dec 28 1961	12-Cauac	9
Dec 29 1961	13-Ahau	1
Dec 30 1961	1-Imix	2

Date	Day-Sign	L
Dec 31 1961	2-Ik	3
Jan 1 1962	3-Akbal	4
Jan 2 1962	4-Kan	5
Jan 3 1962	5-Chicchan	6
Jan 4 1962	6-Cimi	7
Jan 5 1962	7-Manik	8
Jan 6 1962	8-Lamat	9
Jan 7 1962	9-Muluc	1
Jan 8 1962	10-Oc	2
Jan 9 1962	11-Chuen	3
Jan 10 1962	12-Eb	4
Jan 11 1962	13-Ben	5
Jan 12 1962	1-Ix	6
Jan 13 1962	2-Men	7
Jan 14 1962	3-Cib	8
Jan 15 1962	4-Caban	9
Jan 16 1962	5-Etz'nab	1
Jan 17 1962	6-Cauac	2
Jan 18 1962	7-Ahau	3
Jan 19 1962	8-Imix	4
Jan 20 1962	9-Ik	5
Jan 21 1962	10-Akbal	6
Jan 22 1962	11-Kan	7
Jan 23 1962	12-Chicchan	8
Jan 24 1962	13-Cimi	9
Jan 25 1962	1-Manik	1
Jan 26 1962	2-Lamat	2
Jan 27 1962	3-Muluc	3
Jan 28 1962	4-Oc	4
Jan 29 1962	5-Chuen	5
Jan 30 1962	6-Eb	6
Jan 31 1962	7-Ben	7
Feb 1 1962	8-Ix	8
Feb 2 1962	9-Men	9
Feb 3 1962	10-Cib	1
Feb 4 1962	11-Caban	2
Feb 5 1962	12-Etz'nab	3
Feb 6 1962	13-Cauac	4
Feb 7 1962	1-Ahau	5
Feb 8 1962	2-Imix	6
Feb 9 1962	3-Ik	7
Feb 10 1962	4-Akbal	8
Feb 11 1962	5-Kan	9
Feb 12 1962	6-Chicchan	1
Feb 13 1962	7-Cimi	2
Feb 14 1962	8-Manik	3
Feb 15 1962	9-Lamat	4
Feb 16 1962	10-Muluc	5
Feb 17 1962	11-Oc	6
Feb 18 1962	12-Chuen	7
Feb 19 1962	13-Eb	8
Feb 20 1962	1-Ben	9
Feb 21 1962	2-Ix	1
Feb 22 1962	3-Men	2
Feb 23 1962	4-Cib	3
Feb 24 1962	5-Caban	4
Feb 25 1962	6-Etz'nab	5
Feb 26 1962	7-Cauac	6
Feb 27 1962	8-Ahau	7
Feb 28 1962	9-Imix	8
Mar 1 1962	10-Ik	9
Mar 2 1962	11-Akbal	1
Mar 3 1962	12-Kan	2
Mar 4 1962	13-Chicchan	3
Mar 5 1962	1-Cimi	4
Mar 6 1962	2-Manik	5
Mar 7 1962	3-Lamat	6
Mar 8 1962	4-Muluc	7

Date	Day-Sign	L
Mar 9 1962	5-Oc	8
Mar 10 1962	6-Chuen	9
Mar 11 1962	7-Eb	1
Mar 12 1962	8-Ben	2
Mar 13 1962	9-Ix	3
Mar 14 1962	10-Men	4
Mar 15 1962	11-Cib	5
Mar 16 1962	12-Caban	6
Mar 17 1962	13-Etz'nab	7
Mar 18 1962	1-Cauac	8
Mar 19 1962	2-Ahau	9
Mar 20 1962	3-Imix	1
Mar 21 1962	4-Ik	2
Mar 22 1962	5-Akbal	3
Mar 23 1962	6-Kan	4
Mar 24 1962	7-Chicchan	5
Mar 25 1962	8-Cimi	6
Mar 26 1962	9-Manik	7
Mar 27 1962	10-Lamat	8
Mar 28 1962	11-Muluc	9
Mar 29 1962	12-Oc	1
Mar 30 1962	13-Chuen	2
Mar 31 1962	1-Eb	3
Apr 1 1962	2-Ben	4
Apr 2 1962	3-Ix	5
Apr 3 1962	4-Men	6
Apr 4 1962	5-Cib	7
Apr 5 1962	6-Caban	8
Apr 6 1962	7-Etz'nab	9
Apr 7 1962	8-Cauac	1
Apr 8 1962	9-Ahau	2
Apr 9 1962	10-Imix	3
Apr 10 1962	11-Ik	4
Apr 11 1962	12-Akbal	5
Apr 12 1962	13-Kan	6
Apr 13 1962	1-Chicchan	7
Apr 14 1962	2-Cimi	8
Apr 15 1962	3-Manik	9
Apr 16 1962	4-Lamat	1
Apr 17 1962	5-Muluc	2
Apr 18 1962	6-Oc	3
Apr 19 1962	7-Chuen	4
Apr 20 1962	8-Eb	5
Apr 21 1962	9-Ben	6
Apr 22 1962	10-Ix	7
Apr 23 1962	11-Men	8
Apr 24 1962	12-Cib	9
Apr 25 1962	13-Caban	1
Apr 26 1962	1-Etz'nab	2
Apr 27 1962	2-Cauac	3
Apr 28 1962	3-Ahau	4
Apr 29 1962	4-Imix	5
Apr 30 1962	5-Ik	6
May 1 1962	6-Akbal	7
May 2 1962	7-Kan	8
May 3 1962	8-Chicchan	9
May 4 1962	9-Cimi	1
May 5 1962	10-Manik	2
May 6 1962	11-Lamat	3
May 7 1962	12-Muluc	4
May 8 1962	13-Oc	5
May 9 1962	1-Chuen	6
May 10 1962	2-Eb	7
May 11 1962	3-Ben	8
May 12 1962	4-Ix	9
May 13 1962	5-Men	1
May 14 1962	6-Cib	2
May 15 1962	7-Caban	3

Date	Day-Sign	L	Date	Day-Sign	L	Date	Day-Sign	L
May 16 1962	8-Etz'nab	4	Jul 23 1962	11-Cimi	9	Sep 29 1962	**1-Ix**	5
May 17 1962	9-Cauac	5	Jul 24 1962	12-Manik	1	Sep 30 1962	2-Men	6
May 18 1962	10-Ahau	6	Jul 25 1962	13-Lamat	2	Oct 1 1962	3-Cib	7
May 19 1962	*11-Imix*	7	Jul 26 1962	**1-Muluc**	3	Oct 2 1962	4-Caban	8
May 20 1962	12-Ik	8	Jul 27 1962	2-Oc	4	Oct 3 1962	5-Etz'nab	9
May 21 1962	13-Akbal	9	Jul 28 1962	3-Chuen	5	Oct 4 1962	6-Cauac	1
May 22 1962	**1-Kan**	1	Jul 29 1962	4-Eb	6	Oct 5 1962	7-Ahau	2
May 23 1962	2-Chicchan	2	Jul 30 1962	5-Ben	7	Oct 6 1962	*8-Imix*	3
May 24 1962	3-Cimi	3	Jul 31 1962	6-Ix	8	Oct 7 1962	9-Ik	4
May 25 1962	4-Manik	4	Aug 1 1962	7-Men	9	Oct 8 1962	10-Akbal	5
May 26 1962	5-Lamat	5	Aug 2 1962	8-Cib	1	Oct 9 1962	11-Kan	6
May 27 1962	6-Muluc	6	Aug 3 1962	9-Caban	2	Oct 10 1962	12-Chicchan	7
May 28 1962	7-Oc	7	Aug 4 1962	10-Etz'nab	3	Oct 11 1962	13-Cimi	8
May 29 1962	8-Chuen	8	Aug 5 1962	11-Cauac	4	Oct 12 1962	**1-Manik**	9
May 30 1962	9-Eb	9	Aug 6 1962	12-Ahau	5	Oct 13 1962	2-Lamat	1
May 31 1962	10-Ben	1	Aug 7 1962	*13-Imix*	6	Oct 14 1962	3-Muluc	2
Jun 1 1962	11-Ix	2	Aug 8 1962	**1-Ik**	7	Oct 15 1962	4-Oc	3
Jun 2 1962	12-Men	3	Aug 9 1962	2-Akbal	8	Oct 16 1962	5-Chuen	4
Jun 3 1962	13-Cib	4	Aug 10 1962	3-Kan	9	Oct 17 1962	6-Eb	5
Jun 4 1962	**1-Caban**	5	Aug 11 1962	4-Chicchan	1	Oct 18 1962	7-Ben	6
Jun 5 1962	2-Etz'nab	6	Aug 12 1962	5-Cimi	2	Oct 19 1962	8-Ix	7
Jun 6 1962	3-Cauac	7	Aug 13 1962	6-Manik	3	Oct 20 1962	9-Men	8
Jun 7 1962	4-Ahau	8	Aug 14 1962	7-Lamat	4	Oct 21 1962	10-Cib	9
Jun 8 1962	*5-Imix*	9	Aug 15 1962	8-Muluc	5	Oct 22 1962	11-Caban	1
Jun 9 1962	6-Ik	1	Aug 16 1962	9-Oc	6	Oct 23 1962	12-Etz'nab	2
Jun 10 1962	7-Akbal	2	Aug 17 1962	10-Chuen	7	Oct 24 1962	13-Cauac	3
Jun 11 1962	8-Kan	3	Aug 18 1962	11-Eb	8	Oct 25 1962	**1-Ahau**	4
Jun 12 1962	9-Chicchan	4	Aug 19 1962	12-Ben	9	Oct 26 1962	*2-Imix*	5
Jun 13 1962	10-Cimi	5	Aug 20 1962	13-Ix	1	Oct 27 1962	3-Ik	6
Jun 14 1962	11-Manik	6	Aug 21 1962	**1-Men**	2	Oct 28 1962	4-Akbal	7
Jun 15 1962	12-Lamat	7	Aug 22 1962	2-Cib	3	Oct 29 1962	5-Kan	8
Jun 16 1962	13-Muluc	8	Aug 23 1962	3-Caban	4	Oct 30 1962	6-Chicchan	9
Jun 17 1962	**1-Oc**	9	Aug 24 1962	4-Etz'nab	5	Oct 31 1962	7-Cimi	1
Jun 18 1962	2-Chuen	1	Aug 25 1962	5-Cauac	6	Nov 1 1962	8-Manik	2
Jun 19 1962	3-Eb	2	Aug 26 1962	6-Ahau	7	Nov 2 1962	9-Lamat	3
Jun 20 1962	4-Ben	3	Aug 27 1962	*7-Imix*	8	Nov 3 1962	10-Muluc	4
Jun 21 1962	5-Ix	4	Aug 28 1962	8-Ik	9	Nov 4 1962	11-Oc	5
Jun 22 1962	6-Men	5	Aug 29 1962	9-Akbal	1	Nov 5 1962	12-Chuen	6
Jun 23 1962	7-Cib	6	Aug 30 1962	10-Kan	2	Nov 6 1962	13-Eb	7
Jun 24 1962	8-Caban	7	Aug 31 1962	11-Chicchan	3	Nov 7 1962	**1-Ben**	8
Jun 25 1962	9-Etz'nab	8	Sep 1 1962	12-Cimi	4	Nov 8 1962	2-Ix	9
Jun 26 1962	10-Cauac	9	Sep 2 1962	13-Manik	5	Nov 9 1962	3-Men	1
Jun 27 1962	11-Ahau	1	Sep 3 1962	**1-Lamat**	6	Nov 10 1962	4-Cib	2
Jun 28 1962	*12-Imix*	2	Sep 4 1962	2-Muluc	7	Nov 11 1962	5-Caban	3
Jun 29 1962	13-Ik	3	Sep 5 1962	3-Oc	8	Nov 12 1962	6-Etz'nab	4
Jun 30 1962	**1-Akbal**	4	Sep 6 1962	4-Chuen	9	Nov 13 1962	7-Cauac	5
Jul 1 1962	2-Kan	5	Sep 7 1962	5-Eb	1	Nov 14 1962	8-Ahau	6
Jul 2 1962	3-Chicchan	6	Sep 8 1962	6-Ben	2	Nov 15 1962	*9-Imix*	7
Jul 3 1962	4-Cimi	7	Sep 9 1962	7-Ix	3	Nov 16 1962	10-Ik	8
Jul 4 1962	5-Manik	8	Sep 10 1962	8-Men	4	Nov 17 1962	11-Akbal	9
Jul 5 1962	6-Lamat	9	Sep 11 1962	9-Cib	5	Nov 18 1962	12-Kan	1
Jul 6 1962	7-Muluc	1	Sep 12 1962	10-Caban	6	Nov 19 1962	13-Chicchan	2
Jul 7 1962	8-Oc	2	Sep 13 1962	11-Etz'nab	7	Nov 20 1962	**1-Cimi**	3
Jul 8 1962	9-Chuen	3	Sep 14 1962	12-Cauac	8	Nov 21 1962	2-Manik	4
Jul 9 1962	10-Eb	4	Sep 15 1962	13-Ahau	9	Nov 22 1962	3-Lamat	5
Jul 10 1962	11-Ben	5	Sep 16 1962	**1-Imix**	1	Nov 23 1962	4-Muluc	6
Jul 11 1962	12-Ix	6	Sep 17 1962	2-Ik	2	Nov 24 1962	5-Oc	7
Jul 12 1962	13-Men	7	Sep 18 1962	3-Akbal	3	Nov 25 1962	6-Chuen	8
Jul 13 1962	**1-Cib**	8	Sep 19 1962	4-Kan	4	Nov 26 1962	7-Eb	9
Jul 14 1962	2-Caban	9	Sep 20 1962	5-Chicchan	5	Nov 27 1962	8-Ben	1
Jul 15 1962	3-Etz'nab	1	Sep 21 1962	6-Cimi	6	Nov 28 1962	9-Ix	2
Jul 16 1962	4-Cauac	2	Sep 22 1962	7-Manik	7	Nov 29 1962	10-Men	3
Jul 17 1962	5-Ahau	3	Sep 23 1962	8-Lamat	8	Nov 30 1962	11-Cib	4
Jul 18 1962	*6-Imix*	4	Sep 24 1962	9-Muluc	9	Dec 1 1962	12-Caban	5
Jul 19 1962	7-Ik	5	Sep 25 1962	10-Oc	1	Dec 2 1962	13-Etz'nab	6
Jul 20 1962	8-Akbal	6	Sep 26 1962	11-Chuen	2	Dec 3 1962	**1-Cauac**	7
Jul 21 1962	9-Kan	7	Sep 27 1962	12-Eb	3	Dec 4 1962	2-Ahau	8
Jul 22 1962	10-Chicchan	8	Sep 28 1962	13-Ben	4	Dec 5 1962	*3-Imix*	9

Date	Day-Sign	L
Dec 6 1962	4-Ik	1
Dec 7 1962	5-Akbal	2
Dec 8 1962	6-Kan	3
Dec 9 1962	7-Chicchan	4
Dec 10 1962	8-Cimi	5
Dec 11 1962	9-Manik	6
Dec 12 1962	10-Lamat	7
Dec 13 1962	11-Muluc	8
Dec 14 1962	12-Oc	9
Dec 15 1962	13-Chuen	1
Dec 16 1962	1-Eb	2
Dec 17 1962	2-Ben	3
Dec 18 1962	3-Ix	4
Dec 19 1962	4-Men	5
Dec 20 1962	5-Cib	6
Dec 21 1962	6-Caban	7
Dec 22 1962	7-Etz'nab	8
Dec 23 1962	8-Cauac	9
Dec 24 1962	9-Ahau	1
Dec 25 1962	10-Imix	2
Dec 26 1962	11-Ik	3
Dec 27 1962	12-Akbal	4
Dec 28 1962	13-Kan	5
Dec 29 1962	1-Chicchan	6
Dec 30 1962	2-Cimi	7
Dec 31 1962	3-Manik	8
Jan 1 1963	4-Lamat	9
Jan 2 1963	5-Muluc	1
Jan 3 1963	6-Oc	2
Jan 4 1963	7-Chuen	3
Jan 5 1963	8-Eb	4
Jan 6 1963	9-Ben	5
Jan 7 1963	10-Ix	6
Jan 8 1963	11-Men	7
Jan 9 1963	12-Cib	8
Jan 10 1963	13-Caban	9
Jan 11 1963	1-Etz'nab	1
Jan 12 1963	2-Cauac	2
Jan 13 1963	3-Ahau	3
Jan 14 1963	4-Imix	4
Jan 15 1963	5-Ik	5
Jan 16 1963	6-Akbal	6
Jan 17 1963	7-Kan	7
Jan 18 1963	8-Chicchan	8
Jan 19 1963	9-Cimi	9
Jan 20 1963	10-Manik	1
Jan 21 1963	11-Lamat	2
Jan 22 1963	12-Muluc	3
Jan 23 1963	13-Oc	4
Jan 24 1963	1-Chuen	5
Jan 25 1963	2-Eb	6
Jan 26 1963	3-Ben	7
Jan 27 1963	4-Ix	8
Jan 28 1963	5-Men	9
Jan 29 1963	6-Cib	1
Jan 30 1963	7-Caban	2
Jan 31 1963	8-Etz'nab	3
Feb 1 1963	9-Cauac	4
Feb 2 1963	10-Ahau	5
Feb 3 1963	11-Imix	6
Feb 4 1963	12-Ik	7
Feb 5 1963	13-Akbal	8
Feb 6 1963	1-Kan	9
Feb 7 1963	2-Chicchan	1
Feb 8 1963	3-Cimi	2
Feb 9 1963	4-Manik	3
Feb 10 1963	5-Lamat	4
Feb 11 1963	6-Muluc	5

Date	Day-Sign	L
Feb 12 1963	7-Oc	6
Feb 13 1963	8-Chuen	7
Feb 14 1963	9-Eb	8
Feb 15 1963	10-Ben	9
Feb 16 1963	11-Ix	1
Feb 17 1963	12-Men	2
Feb 18 1963	13-Cib	3
Feb 19 1963	1-Caban	4
Feb 20 1963	2-Etz'nab	5
Feb 21 1963	3-Cauac	6
Feb 22 1963	4-Ahau	7
Feb 23 1963	5-Imix	8
Feb 24 1963	6-Ik	9
Feb 25 1963	7-Akbal	1
Feb 26 1963	8-Kan	2
Feb 27 1963	9-Chicchan	3
Feb 28 1963	10-Cimi	4
Mar 1 1963	11-Manik	5
Mar 2 1963	12-Lamat	6
Mar 3 1963	13-Muluc	7
Mar 4 1963	1-Oc	8
Mar 5 1963	2-Chuen	9
Mar 6 1963	3-Eb	1
Mar 7 1963	4-Ben	2
Mar 8 1963	5-Ix	3
Mar 9 1963	6-Men	4
Mar 10 1963	7-Cib	5
Mar 11 1963	8-Caban	6
Mar 12 1963	9-Etz'nab	7
Mar 13 1963	10-Cauac	8
Mar 14 1963	11-Ahau	9
Mar 15 1963	12-Imix	1
Mar 16 1963	13-Ik	2
Mar 17 1963	1-Akbal	3
Mar 18 1963	2-Kan	4
Mar 19 1963	3-Chicchan	5
Mar 20 1963	4-Cimi	6
Mar 21 1963	5-Manik	7
Mar 22 1963	6-Lamat	8
Mar 23 1963	7-Muluc	9
Mar 24 1963	8-Oc	1
Mar 25 1963	9-Chuen	2
Mar 26 1963	10-Eb	3
Mar 27 1963	11-Ben	4
Mar 28 1963	12-Ix	5
Mar 29 1963	13-Men	6
Mar 30 1963	1-Cib	7
Mar 31 1963	2-Caban	8
Apr 1 1963	3-Etz'nab	9
Apr 2 1963	4-Cauac	1
Apr 3 1963	5-Ahau	2
Apr 4 1963	6-Imix	3
Apr 5 1963	7-Ik	4
Apr 6 1963	8-Akbal	5
Apr 7 1963	9-Kan	6
Apr 8 1963	10-Chicchan	7
Apr 9 1963	11-Cimi	8
Apr 10 1963	12-Manik	9
Apr 11 1963	13-Lamat	1
Apr 12 1963	1-Muluc	2
Apr 13 1963	2-Oc	3
Apr 14 1963	3-Chuen	4
Apr 15 1963	4-Eb	5
Apr 16 1963	5-Ben	6
Apr 17 1963	6-Ix	7
Apr 18 1963	7-Men	8
Apr 19 1963	8-Cib	9
Apr 20 1963	9-Caban	1

Date	Day-Sign	L
Apr 21 1963	10-Etz'nab	2
Apr 22 1963	11-Cauac	3
Apr 23 1963	12-Ahau	4
Apr 24 1963	13-Imix	5
Apr 25 1963	1-Ik	6
Apr 26 1963	2-Akbal	7
Apr 27 1963	3-Kan	8
Apr 28 1963	4-Chicchan	9
Apr 29 1963	5-Cimi	1
Apr 30 1963	6-Manik	2
May 1 1963	7-Lamat	3
May 2 1963	8-Muluc	4
May 3 1963	9-Oc	5
May 4 1963	10-Chuen	6
May 5 1963	11-Eb	7
May 6 1963	12-Ben	8
May 7 1963	13-Ix	9
May 8 1963	1-Men	1
May 9 1963	2-Cib	2
May 10 1963	3-Caban	3
May 11 1963	4-Etz'nab	4
May 12 1963	5-Cauac	5
May 13 1963	6-Ahau	6
May 14 1963	7-Imix	7
May 15 1963	8-Ik	8
May 16 1963	9-Akbal	9
May 17 1963	10-Kan	1
May 18 1963	11-Chicchan	2
May 19 1963	12-Cimi	3
May 20 1963	13-Manik	4
May 21 1963	1-Lamat	5
May 22 1963	2-Muluc	6
May 23 1963	3-Oc	7
May 24 1963	4-Chuen	8
May 25 1963	5-Eb	9
May 26 1963	6-Ben	1
May 27 1963	7-Ix	2
May 28 1963	8-Men	3
May 29 1963	9-Cib	4
May 30 1963	10-Caban	5
May 31 1963	11-Etz'nab	6
Jun 1 1963	12-Cauac	7
Jun 2 1963	13-Ahau	8
Jun 3 1963	1-Imix	9
Jun 4 1963	2-Ik	1
Jun 5 1963	3-Akbal	2
Jun 6 1963	4-Kan	3
Jun 7 1963	5-Chicchan	4
Jun 8 1963	6-Cimi	5
Jun 9 1963	7-Manik	6
Jun 10 1963	8-Lamat	7
Jun 11 1963	9-Muluc	8
Jun 12 1963	10-Oc	9
Jun 13 1963	11-Chuen	1
Jun 14 1963	12-Eb	2
Jun 15 1963	13-Ben	3
Jun 16 1963	1-Ix	4
Jun 17 1963	2-Men	5
Jun 18 1963	3-Cib	6
Jun 19 1963	4-Caban	7
Jun 20 1963	5-Etz'nab	8
Jun 21 1963	6-Cauac	9
Jun 22 1963	7-Ahau	1
Jun 23 1963	8-Imix	2
Jun 24 1963	9-Ik	3
Jun 25 1963	10-Akbal	4
Jun 26 1963	11-Kan	5
Jun 27 1963	12-Chicchan	6

Date	Day-Sign	L	Date	Day-Sign	L	Date	Day-Sign	L
Jun 28 1963	13-Cimi	7	Sep 4 1963	3-Ix	3	Nov 11 1963	6-Ik	8
Jun 29 1963	**1-Manik**	8	Sep 5 1963	4-Men	4	Nov 12 1963	7-Akbal	9
Jun 30 1963	2-Lamat	9	Sep 6 1963	5-Cib	5	Nov 13 1963	8-Kan	1
Jul 1 1963	3-Muluc	1	Sep 7 1963	6-Caban	6	Nov 14 1963	9-Chicchan	2
Jul 2 1963	4-Oc	2	Sep 8 1963	7-Etz'nab	7	Nov 15 1963	10-Cimi	3
Jul 3 1963	5-Chuen	3	Sep 9 1963	8-Cauac	8	Nov 16 1963	11-Manik	4
Jul 4 1963	6-Eb	4	Sep 10 1963	9-Ahau	9	Nov 17 1963	12-Lamat	5
Jul 5 1963	7-Ben	5	Sep 11 1963	10-*Imix*	1	Nov 18 1963	13-Muluc	6
Jul 6 1963	8-Ix	6	Sep 12 1963	11-Ik	2	Nov 19 1963	**1-Oc**	7
Jul 7 1963	9-Men	7	Sep 13 1963	12-Akbal	3	Nov 20 1963	2-Chuen	8
Jul 8 1963	10-Cib	8	Sep 14 1963	13-Kan	4	Nov 21 1963	3-Eb	9
Jul 9 1963	11-Caban	9	Sep 15 1963	**1-Chicchan**	5	Nov 22 1963	4-Ben	1
Jul 10 1963	12-Etz'nab	1	Sep 16 1963	2-Cimi	6	Nov 23 1963	5-Ix	2
Jul 11 1963	13-Cauac	2	Sep 17 1963	3-Manik	7	Nov 24 1963	6-Men	3
Jul 12 1963	**1-Ahau**	3	Sep 18 1963	4-Lamat	8	Nov 25 1963	7-Cib	4
Jul 13 1963	2-*Imix*	4	Sep 19 1963	5-Muluc	9	Nov 26 1963	8-Caban	5
Jul 14 1963	3-Ik	5	Sep 20 1963	6-Oc	1	Nov 27 1963	9-Etz'nab	6
Jul 15 1963	4-Akbal	6	Sep 21 1963	7-Chuen	2	Nov 28 1963	10-Cauac	7
Jul 16 1963	5-Kan	7	Sep 22 1963	8-Eb	3	Nov 29 1963	11-Ahau	8
Jul 17 1963	6-Chicchan	8	Sep 23 1963	9-Ben	4	Nov 30 1963	12-*Imix*	9
Jul 18 1963	7-Cimi	9	Sep 24 1963	10-Ix	5	Dec 1 1963	13-Ik	1
Jul 19 1963	8-Manik	1	Sep 25 1963	11-Men	6	Dec 2 1963	**1-Akbal**	2
Jul 20 1963	9-Lamat	2	Sep 26 1963	12-Cib	7	Dec 3 1963	2-Kan	3
Jul 21 1963	10-Muluc	3	Sep 27 1963	13-Caban	8	Dec 4 1963	3-Chicchan	4
Jul 22 1963	11-Oc	4	Sep 28 1963	**1-Etz'nab**	9	Dec 5 1963	4-Cimi	5
Jul 23 1963	12-Chuen	5	Sep 29 1963	2-Cauac	1	Dec 6 1963	5-Manik	6
Jul 24 1963	13-Eb	6	Sep 30 1963	3-Ahau	2	Dec 7 1963	6-Lamat	7
Jul 25 1963	**1-Ben**	7	Oct 1 1963	4-*Imix*	3	Dec 8 1963	7-Muluc	8
Jul 26 1963	2-Ix	8	Oct 2 1963	5-Ik	4	Dec 9 1963	8-Oc	9
Jul 27 1963	3-Men	9	Oct 3 1963	6-Akbal	5	Dec 10 1963	9-Chuen	1
Jul 28 1963	4-Cib	1	Oct 4 1963	7-Kan	6	Dec 11 1963	10-Eb	2
Jul 29 1963	5-Caban	2	Oct 5 1963	8-Chicchan	7	Dec 12 1963	11-Ben	3
Jul 30 1963	6-Etz'nab	3	Oct 6 1963	9-Cimi	8	Dec 13 1963	12-Ix	4
Jul 31 1963	7-Cauac	4	Oct 7 1963	10-Manik	9	Dec 14 1963	13-Men	5
Aug 1 1963	8-Ahau	5	Oct 8 1963	11-Lamat	1	Dec 15 1963	**1-Cib**	6
Aug 2 1963	9-*Imix*	6	Oct 9 1963	12-Muluc	2	Dec 16 1963	2-Caban	7
Aug 3 1963	10-Ik	7	Oct 10 1963	13-Oc	3	Dec 17 1963	3-Etz'nab	8
Aug 4 1963	11-Akbal	8	Oct 11 1963	**1-Chuen**	4	Dec 18 1963	4-Cauac	9
Aug 5 1963	12-Kan	9	Oct 12 1963	2-Eb	5	Dec 19 1963	5-Ahau	1
Aug 6 1963	13-Chicchan	1	Oct 13 1963	3-Ben	6	Dec 20 1963	6-*Imix*	2
Aug 7 1963	**1-Cimi**	2	Oct 14 1963	4-Ix	7	Dec 21 1963	7-Ik	3
Aug 8 1963	2-Manik	3	Oct 15 1963	5-Men	8	Dec 22 1963	8-Akbal	4
Aug 9 1963	3-Lamat	4	Oct 16 1963	6-Cib	9	Dec 23 1963	9-Kan	5
Aug 10 1963	4-Muluc	5	Oct 17 1963	7-Caban	1	Dec 24 1963	10-Chicchan	6
Aug 11 1963	5-Oc	6	Oct 18 1963	8-Etz'nab	2	Dec 25 1963	11-Cimi	7
Aug 12 1963	6-Chuen	7	Oct 19 1963	9-Cauac	3	Dec 26 1963	12-Manik	8
Aug 13 1963	7-Eb	8	Oct 20 1963	10-Ahau	4	Dec 27 1963	13-Lamat	9
Aug 14 1963	8-Ben	9	Oct 21 1963	11-*Imix*	5	Dec 28 1963	**1-Muluc**	1
Aug 15 1963	9-Ix	1	Oct 22 1963	12-Ik	6	Dec 29 1963	2-Oc	2
Aug 16 1963	10-Men	2	Oct 23 1963	13-Akbal	7	Dec 30 1963	3-Chuen	3
Aug 17 1963	11-Cib	3	Oct 24 1963	**1-Kan**	8	Dec 31 1963	4-Eb	4
Aug 18 1963	12-Caban	4	Oct 25 1963	2-Chicchan	9	Jan 1 1964	5-Ben	5
Aug 19 1963	13-Etz'nab	5	Oct 26 1963	3-Cimi	1	Jan 2 1964	6-Ix	6
Aug 20 1963	**1-Cauac**	6	Oct 27 1963	4-Manik	2	Jan 3 1964	7-Men	7
Aug 21 1963	2-Ahau	7	Oct 28 1963	5-Lamat	3	Jan 4 1964	8-Cib	8
Aug 22 1963	3-*Imix*	8	Oct 29 1963	6-Muluc	4	Jan 5 1964	9-Caban	9
Aug 23 1963	4-Ik	9	Oct 30 1963	7-Oc	5	Jan 6 1964	10-Etz'nab	1
Aug 24 1963	5-Akbal	1	Oct 31 1963	8-Chuen	6	Jan 7 1964	11-Cauac	2
Aug 25 1963	6-Kan	2	Nov 1 1963	9-Eb	7	Jan 8 1964	12-Ahau	3
Aug 26 1963	7-Chicchan	3	Nov 2 1963	10-Ben	8	Jan 9 1964	13-*Imix*	4
Aug 27 1963	8-Cimi	4	Nov 3 1963	11-Ix	9	Jan 10 1964	**1-Ik**	5
Aug 28 1963	9-Manik	5	Nov 4 1963	12-Men	1	Jan 11 1964	2-Akbal	6
Aug 29 1963	10-Lamat	6	Nov 5 1963	13-Cib	2	Jan 12 1964	3-Kan	7
Aug 30 1963	11-Muluc	7	Nov 6 1963	**1-Caban**	3	Jan 13 1964	4-Chicchan	8
Aug 31 1963	12-Oc	8	Nov 7 1963	2-Etz'nab	4	Jan 14 1964	5-Cimi	9
Sep 1 1963	13-Chuen	9	Nov 8 1963	3-Cauac	5	Jan 15 1964	6-Manik	1
Sep 2 1963	**1-Eb**	1	Nov 9 1963	4-Ahau	6	Jan 16 1964	7-Lamat	2
Sep 3 1963	2-Ben	2	Nov 10 1963	5-*Imix*	7	Jan 17 1964	8-Muluc	3

Date	Day-Sign	L	Date	Day-Sign	L	Date	Day-Sign	L
Jan 18 1964	9-Oc	4	Mar 26 1964	12-Etz'nab	9	Jun 2 1964	2-Cimi	5
Jan 19 1964	10-Chuen	5	Mar 27 1964	13-Cauac	1	Jun 3 1964	3-Manik	6
Jan 20 1964	11-Eb	6	Mar 28 1964	**1-Ahau**	2	Jun 4 1964	4-Lamat	7
Jan 21 1964	12-Ben	7	Mar 29 1964	*2-Imix*	3	Jun 5 1964	5-Muluc	8
Jan 22 1964	13-Ix	8	Mar 30 1964	3-Ik	4	Jun 6 1964	6-Oc	9
Jan 23 1964	**1-Men**	9	Mar 31 1964	4-Akbal	5	Jun 7 1964	7-Chuen	1
Jan 24 1964	2-Cib	1	Apr 1 1964	5-Kan	6	Jun 8 1964	8-Eb	2
Jan 25 1964	3-Caban	2	Apr 2 1964	6-Chicchan	7	Jun 9 1964	9-Ben	3
Jan 26 1964	4-Etz'nab	3	Apr 3 1964	7-Cimi	8	Jun 10 1964	10-Ix	4
Jan 27 1964	5-Cauac	4	Apr 4 1964	8-Manik	9	Jun 11 1964	11-Men	5
Jan 28 1964	6-Ahau	5	Apr 5 1964	9-Lamat	1	Jun 12 1964	12-Cib	6
Jan 29 1964	*7-Imix*	6	Apr 6 1964	10-Muluc	2	Jun 13 1964	13-Caban	7
Jan 30 1964	8-Ik	7	Apr 7 1964	11-Oc	3	Jun 14 1964	**1-Etz'nab**	8
Jan 31 1964	9-Akbal	8	Apr 8 1964	12-Chuen	4	Jun 15 1964	2-Cauac	9
Feb 1 1964	10-Kan	9	Apr 9 1964	13-Eb	5	Jun 16 1964	3-Ahau	1
Feb 2 1964	11-Chicchan	1	Apr 10 1964	**1-Ben**	6	Jun 17 1964	*4-Imix*	2
Feb 3 1964	12-Cimi	2	Apr 11 1964	2-Ix	7	Jun 18 1964	5-Ik	3
Feb 4 1964	13-Manik	3	Apr 12 1964	3-Men	8	Jun 19 1964	6-Akbal	4
Feb 5 1964	**1-Lamat**	4	Apr 13 1964	4-Cib	9	Jun 20 1964	7-Kan	5
Feb 6 1964	2-Muluc	5	Apr 14 1964	5-Caban	1	Jun 21 1964	8-Chicchan	6
Feb 7 1964	3-Oc	6	Apr 15 1964	6-Etz'nab	2	Jun 22 1964	9-Cimi	7
Feb 8 1964	4-Chuen	7	Apr 16 1964	7-Cauac	3	Jun 23 1964	10-Manik	8
Feb 9 1964	5-Eb	8	Apr 17 1964	8-Ahau	4	Jun 24 1964	11-Lamat	9
Feb 10 1964	6-Ben	9	Apr 18 1964	*9-Imix*	5	Jun 25 1964	12-Muluc	1
Feb 11 1964	7-Ix	1	Apr 19 1964	10-Ik	6	Jun 26 1964	13-Oc	2
Feb 12 1964	8-Men	2	Apr 20 1964	11-Akbal	7	Jun 27 1964	**1-Chuen**	3
Feb 13 1964	9-Cib	3	Apr 21 1964	12-Kan	8	Jun 28 1964	2-Eb	4
Feb 14 1964	10-Caban	4	Apr 22 1964	13-Chicchan	9	Jun 29 1964	3-Ben	5
Feb 15 1964	11-Etz'nab	5	Apr 23 1964	**1-Cimi**	1	Jun 30 1964	4-Ix	6
Feb 16 1964	12-Cauac	6	Apr 24 1964	2-Manik	2	Jul 1 1964	5-Men	7
Feb 17 1964	13-Ahau	7	Apr 25 1964	3-Lamat	3	Jul 2 1964	6-Cib	8
Feb 18 1964	**1-Imix**	8	Apr 26 1964	4-Muluc	4	Jul 3 1964	7-Caban	9
Feb 19 1964	2-Ik	9	Apr 27 1964	5-Oc	5	Jul 4 1964	8-Etz'nab	1
Feb 20 1964	3-Akbal	1	Apr 28 1964	6-Chuen	6	Jul 5 1964	9-Cauac	2
Feb 21 1964	4-Kan	2	Apr 29 1964	7-Eb	7	Jul 6 1964	10-Ahau	3
Feb 22 1964	5-Chicchan	3	Apr 30 1964	8-Ben	8	Jul 7 1964	*11-Imix*	4
Feb 23 1964	6-Cimi	4	May 1 1964	9-Ix	9	Jul 8 1964	12-Ik	5
Feb 24 1964	7-Manik	5	May 2 1964	10-Men	1	Jul 9 1964	13-Akbal	6
Feb 25 1964	8-Lamat	6	May 3 1964	11-Cib	2	Jul 10 1964	**1-Kan**	7
Feb 26 1964	9-Muluc	7	May 4 1964	12-Caban	3	Jul 11 1964	2-Chicchan	8
Feb 27 1964	10-Oc	8	May 5 1964	13-Etz'nab	4	Jul 12 1964	3-Cimi	9
Feb 28 1964	11-Chuen	9	May 6 1964	**1-Cauac**	5	Jul 13 1964	4-Manik	1
Feb 29 1964	12-Eb	1	May 7 1964	2-Ahau	6	Jul 14 1964	5-Lamat	2
Mar 1 1964	13-Ben	2	May 8 1964	*3-Imix*	7	Jul 15 1964	6-Muluc	3
Mar 2 1964	**1-Ix**	3	May 9 1964	4-Ik	8	Jul 16 1964	7-Oc	4
Mar 3 1964	2-Men	4	May 10 1964	5-Akbal	9	Jul 17 1964	8-Chuen	5
Mar 4 1964	3-Cib	5	May 11 1964	6-Kan	1	Jul 18 1964	9-Eb	6
Mar 5 1964	4-Caban	6	May 12 1964	7-Chicchan	2	Jul 19 1964	10-Ben	7
Mar 6 1964	5-Etz'nab	7	May 13 1964	8-Cimi	3	Jul 20 1964	11-Ix	8
Mar 7 1964	6-Cauac	8	May 14 1964	9-Manik	4	Jul 21 1964	12-Men	9
Mar 8 1964	7-Ahau	9	May 15 1964	10-Lamat	5	Jul 22 1964	13-Cib	1
Mar 9 1964	*8-Imix*	1	May 16 1964	11-Muluc	6	Jul 23 1964	**1-Caban**	2
Mar 10 1964	9-Ik	2	May 17 1964	12-Oc	7	Jul 24 1964	2-Etz'nab	3
Mar 11 1964	10-Akbal	3	May 18 1964	13-Chuen	8	Jul 25 1964	3-Cauac	4
Mar 12 1964	11-Kan	4	May 19 1964	**1-Eb**	9	Jul 26 1964	4-Ahau	5
Mar 13 1964	12-Chicchan	5	May 20 1964	2-Ben	1	Jul 27 1964	*5-Imix*	6
Mar 14 1964	13-Cimi	6	May 21 1964	3-Ix	2	Jul 28 1964	6-Ik	7
Mar 15 1964	**1-Manik**	7	May 22 1964	4-Men	3	Jul 29 1964	7-Akbal	8
Mar 16 1964	2-Lamat	8	May 23 1964	5-Cib	4	Jul 30 1964	8-Kan	9
Mar 17 1964	3-Muluc	9	May 24 1964	6-Caban	5	Jul 31 1964	9-Chicchan	1
Mar 18 1964	4-Oc	1	May 25 1964	7-Etz'nab	6	Aug 1 1964	10-Cimi	2
Mar 19 1964	5-Chuen	2	May 26 1964	8-Cauac	7	Aug 2 1964	11-Manik	3
Mar 20 1964	6-Eb	3	May 27 1964	9-Ahau	8	Aug 3 1964	12-Lamat	4
Mar 21 1964	7-Ben	4	May 28 1964	*10-Imix*	9	Aug 4 1964	13-Muluc	5
Mar 22 1964	8-Ix	5	May 29 1964	11-Ik	1	Aug 5 1964	**1-Oc**	6
Mar 23 1964	9-Men	6	May 30 1964	12-Akbal	2	Aug 6 1964	2-Chuen	7
Mar 24 1964	10-Cib	7	May 31 1964	13-Kan	3	Aug 7 1964	3-Eb	8
Mar 25 1964	11-Caban	8	Jun 1 1964	**1-Chicchan**	4	Aug 8 1964	4-Ben	9

Date	Day-Sign	L	Date	Day-Sign	L	Date	Day-Sign	L
Aug 9 1964	5-Ix	1	Oct 16 1964	8-Ik	6	Dec 23 1964	11-Oc	2
Aug 10 1964	6-Men	2	Oct 17 1964	9-Akbal	7	Dec 24 1964	12-Chuen	3
Aug 11 1964	7-Cib	3	Oct 18 1964	10-Kan	8	Dec 25 1964	13-Eb	4
Aug 12 1964	8-Caban	4	Oct 19 1964	11-Chicchan	9	Dec 26 1964	**1-Ben**	5
Aug 13 1964	9-Etz'nab	5	Oct 20 1964	12-Cimi	1	Dec 27 1964	2-Ix	6
Aug 14 1964	10-Cauac	6	Oct 21 1964	13-Manik	2	Dec 28 1964	3-Men	7
Aug 15 1964	11-Ahau	7	Oct 22 1964	**1-Lamat**	3	Dec 29 1964	4-Cib	8
Aug 16 1964	*12-Imix*	8	Oct 23 1964	2-Muluc	4	Dec 30 1964	5-Caban	9
Aug 17 1964	13-Ik	9	Oct 24 1964	3-Oc	5	Dec 31 1964	6-Etz'nab	1
Aug 18 1964	**1-Akbal**	1	Oct 25 1964	4-Chuen	6	Jan 1 1965	7-Cauac	2
Aug 19 1964	2-Kan	2	Oct 26 1964	5-Eb	7	Jan 2 1965	8-Ahau	3
Aug 20 1964	3-Chicchan	3	Oct 27 1964	6-Ben	8	Jan 3 1965	*9-Imix*	4
Aug 21 1964	4-Cimi	4	Oct 28 1964	7-Ix	9	Jan 4 1965	10-Ik	5
Aug 22 1964	5-Manik	5	Oct 29 1964	8-Men	1	Jan 5 1965	11-Akbal	6
Aug 23 1964	6-Lamat	6	Oct 30 1964	9-Cib	2	Jan 6 1965	12-Kan	7
Aug 24 1964	7-Muluc	7	Oct 31 1964	10-Caban	3	Jan 7 1965	13-Chicchan	8
Aug 25 1964	8-Oc	8	Nov 1 1964	11-Etz'nab	4	Jan 8 1965	**1-Cimi**	9
Aug 26 1964	9-Chuen	9	Nov 2 1964	12-Cauac	5	Jan 9 1965	2-Manik	1
Aug 27 1964	10-Eb	1	Nov 3 1964	13-Ahau	6	Jan 10 1965	3-Lamat	2
Aug 28 1964	11-Ben	2	Nov 4 1964	**1-Imix**	7	Jan 11 1965	4-Muluc	3
Aug 29 1964	12-Ix	3	Nov 5 1964	2-Ik	8	Jan 12 1965	5-Oc	4
Aug 30 1964	13-Men	4	Nov 6 1964	3-Akbal	9	Jan 13 1965	6-Chuen	5
Aug 31 1964	**1-Cib**	5	Nov 7 1964	4-Kan	1	Jan 14 1965	7-Eb	6
Sep 1 1964	2-Caban	6	Nov 8 1964	5-Chicchan	2	Jan 15 1965	8-Ben	7
Sep 2 1964	3-Etz'nab	7	Nov 9 1964	6-Cimi	3	Jan 16 1965	9-Ix	8
Sep 3 1964	4-Cauac	8	Nov 10 1964	7-Manik	4	Jan 17 1965	10-Men	9
Sep 4 1964	5-Ahau	9	Nov 11 1964	8-Lamat	5	Jan 18 1965	11-Cib	1
Sep 5 1964	*6-Imix*	1	Nov 12 1964	9-Muluc	6	Jan 19 1965	12-Caban	2
Sep 6 1964	7-Ik	2	Nov 13 1964	10-Oc	7	Jan 20 1965	13-Etz'nab	3
Sep 7 1964	8-Akbal	3	Nov 14 1964	11-Chuen	8	Jan 21 1965	**1-Cauac**	4
Sep 8 1964	9-Kan	4	Nov 15 1964	12-Eb	9	Jan 22 1965	2-Ahau	5
Sep 9 1964	10-Chicchan	5	Nov 16 1964	13-Ben	1	Jan 23 1965	*3-Imix*	6
Sep 10 1964	11-Cimi	6	Nov 17 1964	**1-Ix**	2	Jan 24 1965	4-Ik	7
Sep 11 1964	12-Manik	7	Nov 18 1964	2-Men	3	Jan 25 1965	5-Akbal	8
Sep 12 1964	13-Lamat	8	Nov 19 1964	3-Cib	4	Jan 26 1965	6-Kan	9
Sep 13 1964	**1-Muluc**	9	Nov 20 1964	4-Caban	5	Jan 27 1965	7-Chicchan	1
Sep 14 1964	2-Oc	1	Nov 21 1964	5-Etz'nab	6	Jan 28 1965	8-Cimi	2
Sep 15 1964	3-Chuen	2	Nov 22 1964	6-Cauac	7	Jan 29 1965	9-Manik	3
Sep 16 1964	4-Eb	3	Nov 23 1964	7-Ahau	8	Jan 30 1965	10-Lamat	4
Sep 17 1964	5-Ben	4	Nov 24 1964	*8-Imix*	9	Jan 31 1965	11-Muluc	5
Sep 18 1964	6-Ix	5	Nov 25 1964	9-Ik	1	Feb 1 1965	12-Oc	6
Sep 19 1964	7-Men	6	Nov 26 1964	10-Akbal	2	Feb 2 1965	13-Chuen	7
Sep 20 1964	8-Cib	7	Nov 27 1964	11-Kan	3	Feb 3 1965	**1-Eb**	8
Sep 21 1964	9-Caban	8	Nov 28 1964	12-Chicchan	4	Feb 4 1965	2-Ben	9
Sep 22 1964	10-Etz'nab	9	Nov 29 1964	13-Cimi	5	Feb 5 1965	3-Ix	1
Sep 23 1964	11-Cauac	1	Nov 30 1964	**1-Manik**	6	Feb 6 1965	4-Men	2
Sep 24 1964	12-Ahau	2	Dec 1 1964	2-Lamat	7	Feb 7 1965	5-Cib	3
Sep 25 1964	*13-Imix*	3	Dec 2 1964	3-Muluc	8	Feb 8 1965	6-Caban	4
Sep 26 1964	**1-Ik**	4	Dec 3 1964	4-Oc	9	Feb 9 1965	7-Etz'nab	5
Sep 27 1964	2-Akbal	5	Dec 4 1964	5-Chuen	1	Feb 10 1965	8-Cauac	6
Sep 28 1964	3-Kan	6	Dec 5 1964	6-Eb	2	Feb 11 1965	9-Ahau	7
Sep 29 1964	4-Chicchan	7	Dec 6 1964	7-Ben	3	Feb 12 1965	*10-Imix*	8
Sep 30 1964	5-Cimi	8	Dec 7 1964	8-Ix	4	Feb 13 1965	11-Ik	9
Oct 1 1964	6-Manik	9	Dec 8 1964	9-Men	5	Feb 14 1965	12-Akbal	1
Oct 2 1964	7-Lamat	1	Dec 9 1964	10-Cib	6	Feb 15 1965	13-Kan	2
Oct 3 1964	8-Muluc	2	Dec 10 1964	11-Caban	7	Feb 16 1965	**1-Chicchan**	3
Oct 4 1964	9-Oc	3	Dec 11 1964	12-Etz'nab	8	Feb 17 1965	2-Cimi	4
Oct 5 1964	10-Chuen	4	Dec 12 1964	13-Cauac	9	Feb 18 1965	3-Manik	5
Oct 6 1964	11-Eb	5	Dec 13 1964	**1-Ahau**	1	Feb 19 1965	4-Lamat	6
Oct 7 1964	12-Ben	6	Dec 14 1964	*2-Imix*	2	Feb 20 1965	5-Muluc	7
Oct 8 1964	13-Ix	7	Dec 15 1964	3-Ik	3	Feb 21 1965	6-Oc	8
Oct 9 1964	**1-Men**	8	Dec 16 1964	4-Akbal	4	Feb 22 1965	7-Chuen	9
Oct 10 1964	2-Cib	9	Dec 17 1964	5-Kan	5	Feb 23 1965	8-Eb	1
Oct 11 1964	3-Caban	1	Dec 18 1964	6-Chicchan	6	Feb 24 1965	9-Ben	2
Oct 12 1964	4-Etz'nab	2	Dec 19 1964	7-Cimi	7	Feb 25 1965	10-Ix	3
Oct 13 1964	5-Cauac	3	Dec 20 1964	8-Manik	8	Feb 26 1965	11-Men	4
Oct 14 1964	6-Ahau	4	Dec 21 1964	9-Lamat	9	Feb 27 1965	12-Cib	5
Oct 15 1964	*7-Imix*	5	Dec 22 1964	10-Muluc	1	Feb 28 1965	13-Caban	6

Date	Day-Sign	L	Date	Day-Sign	L	Date	Day-Sign	L
Mar 1 1965	1-Etz'nab	7	May 8 1965	4-Cimi	3	Jul 15 1965	7-Ix	8
Mar 2 1965	2-Cauac	8	May 9 1965	5-Manik	4	Jul 16 1965	8-Men	9
Mar 3 1965	3-Ahau	9	May 10 1965	6-Lamat	5	Jul 17 1965	9-Cib	1
Mar 4 1965	4-Imix	1	May 11 1965	7-Muluc	6	Jul 18 1965	10-Caban	2
Mar 5 1965	5-Ik	2	May 12 1965	8-Oc	7	Jul 19 1965	11-Etz'nab	3
Mar 6 1965	6-Akbal	3	May 13 1965	9-Chuen	8	Jul 20 1965	12-Cauac	4
Mar 7 1965	7-Kan	4	May 14 1965	10-Eb	9	Jul 21 1965	13-Ahau	5
Mar 8 1965	8-Chicchan	5	May 15 1965	11-Ben	1	Jul 22 1965	1-Imix	6
Mar 9 1965	9-Cimi	6	May 16 1965	12-Ix	2	Jul 23 1965	2-Ik	7
Mar 10 1965	10-Manik	7	May 17 1965	13-Men	3	Jul 24 1965	3-Akbal	8
Mar 11 1965	11-Lamat	8	May 18 1965	1-Cib	4	Jul 25 1965	4-Kan	9
Mar 12 1965	12-Muluc	9	May 19 1965	2-Caban	5	Jul 26 1965	5-Chicchan	1
Mar 13 1965	13-Oc	1	May 20 1965	3-Etz'nab	6	Jul 27 1965	6-Cimi	2
Mar 14 1965	1-Chuen	2	May 21 1965	4-Cauac	7	Jul 28 1965	7-Manik	3
Mar 15 1965	2-Eb	3	May 22 1965	5-Ahau	8	Jul 29 1965	8-Lamat	4
Mar 16 1965	3-Ben	4	May 23 1965	6-Imix	9	Jul 30 1965	9-Muluc	5
Mar 17 1965	4-Ix	5	May 24 1965	7-Ik	1	Jul 31 1965	10-Oc	6
Mar 18 1965	5-Men	6	May 25 1965	8-Akbal	2	Aug 1 1965	11-Chuen	7
Mar 19 1965	6-Cib	7	May 26 1965	9-Kan	3	Aug 2 1965	12-Eb	8
Mar 20 1965	7-Caban	8	May 27 1965	10-Chicchan	4	Aug 3 1965	13-Ben	9
Mar 21 1965	8-Etz'nab	9	May 28 1965	11-Cimi	5	Aug 4 1965	1-Ix	1
Mar 22 1965	9-Cauac	1	May 29 1965	12-Manik	6	Aug 5 1965	2-Men	2
Mar 23 1965	10-Ahau	2	May 30 1965	13-Lamat	7	Aug 6 1965	3-Cib	3
Mar 24 1965	11-Imix	3	May 31 1965	1-Muluc	8	Aug 7 1965	4-Caban	4
Mar 25 1965	12-Ik	4	Jun 1 1965	2-Oc	9	Aug 8 1965	5-Etz'nab	5
Mar 26 1965	13-Akbal	5	Jun 2 1965	3-Chuen	1	Aug 9 1965	6-Cauac	6
Mar 27 1965	1-Kan	6	Jun 3 1965	4-Eb	2	Aug 10 1965	7-Ahau	7
Mar 28 1965	2-Chicchan	7	Jun 4 1965	5-Ben	3	Aug 11 1965	8-Imix	8
Mar 29 1965	3-Cimi	8	Jun 5 1965	6-Ix	4	Aug 12 1965	9-Ik	9
Mar 30 1965	4-Manik	9	Jun 6 1965	7-Men	5	Aug 13 1965	10-Akbal	1
Mar 31 1965	5-Lamat	1	Jun 7 1965	8-Cib	6	Aug 14 1965	11-Kan	2
Apr 1 1965	6-Muluc	2	Jun 8 1965	9-Caban	7	Aug 15 1965	12-Chicchan	3
Apr 2 1965	7-Oc	3	Jun 9 1965	10-Etz'nab	8	Aug 16 1965	13-Cimi	4
Apr 3 1965	8-Chuen	4	Jun 10 1965	11-Cauac	9	Aug 17 1965	1-Manik	5
Apr 4 1965	9-Eb	5	Jun 11 1965	12-Ahau	1	Aug 18 1965	2-Lamat	6
Apr 5 1965	10-Ben	6	Jun 12 1965	13-Imix	2	Aug 19 1965	3-Muluc	7
Apr 6 1965	11-Ix	7	Jun 13 1965	1-Ik	3	Aug 20 1965	4-Oc	8
Apr 7 1965	12-Men	8	Jun 14 1965	2-Akbal	4	Aug 21 1965	5-Chuen	9
Apr 8 1965	13-Cib	9	Jun 15 1965	3-Kan	5	Aug 22 1965	6-Eb	1
Apr 9 1965	1-Caban	1	Jun 16 1965	4-Chicchan	6	Aug 23 1965	7-Ben	2
Apr 10 1965	2-Etz'nab	2	Jun 17 1965	5-Cimi	7	Aug 24 1965	8-Ix	3
Apr 11 1965	3-Cauac	3	Jun 18 1965	6-Manik	8	Aug 25 1965	9-Men	4
Apr 12 1965	4-Ahau	4	Jun 19 1965	7-Lamat	9	Aug 26 1965	10-Cib	5
Apr 13 1965	5-Imix	5	Jun 20 1965	8-Muluc	1	Aug 27 1965	11-Caban	6
Apr 14 1965	6-Ik	6	Jun 21 1965	9-Oc	2	Aug 28 1965	12-Etz'nab	7
Apr 15 1965	7-Akbal	7	Jun 22 1965	10-Chuen	3	Aug 29 1965	13-Cauac	8
Apr 16 1965	8-Kan	8	Jun 23 1965	11-Eb	4	Aug 30 1965	1-Ahau	9
Apr 17 1965	9-Chicchan	9	Jun 24 1965	12-Ben	5	Aug 31 1965	2-Imix	1
Apr 18 1965	10-Cimi	1	Jun 25 1965	13-Ix	6	Sep 1 1965	3-Ik	2
Apr 19 1965	11-Manik	2	Jun 26 1965	1-Men	7	Sep 2 1965	4-Akbal	3
Apr 20 1965	12-Lamat	3	Jun 27 1965	2-Cib	8	Sep 3 1965	5-Kan	4
Apr 21 1965	13-Muluc	4	Jun 28 1965	3-Caban	9	Sep 4 1965	6-Chicchan	5
Apr 22 1965	1-Oc	5	Jun 29 1965	4-Etz'nab	1	Sep 5 1965	7-Cimi	6
Apr 23 1965	2-Chuen	6	Jun 30 1965	5-Cauac	2	Sep 6 1965	8-Manik	7
Apr 24 1965	3-Eb	7	Jul 1 1965	6-Ahau	3	Sep 7 1965	9-Lamat	8
Apr 25 1965	4-Ben	8	Jul 2 1965	7-Imix	4	Sep 8 1965	10-Muluc	9
Apr 26 1965	5-Ix	9	Jul 3 1965	8-Ik	5	Sep 9 1965	11-Oc	1
Apr 27 1965	6-Men	1	Jul 4 1965	9-Akbal	6	Sep 10 1965	12-Chuen	2
Apr 28 1965	7-Cib	2	Jul 5 1965	10-Kan	7	Sep 11 1965	13-Eb	3
Apr 29 1965	8-Caban	3	Jul 6 1965	11-Chicchan	8	Sep 12 1965	1-Ben	4
Apr 30 1965	9-Etz'nab	4	Jul 7 1965	12-Cimi	9	Sep 13 1965	2-Ix	5
May 1 1965	10-Cauac	5	Jul 8 1965	13-Manik	1	Sep 14 1965	3-Men	6
May 2 1965	11-Ahau	6	Jul 9 1965	1-Lamat	2	Sep 15 1965	4-Cib	7
May 3 1965	12-Imix	7	Jul 10 1965	2-Muluc	3	Sep 16 1965	5-Caban	8
May 4 1965	13-Ik	8	Jul 11 1965	3-Oc	4	Sep 17 1965	6-Etz'nab	9
May 5 1965	1-Akbal	9	Jul 12 1965	4-Chuen	5	Sep 18 1965	7-Cauac	1
May 6 1965	2-Kan	1	Jul 13 1965	5-Eb	6	Sep 19 1965	8-Ahau	2
May 7 1965	3-Chicchan	2	Jul 14 1965	6-Ben	7	Sep 20 1965	9-Imix	3

Date	Day-Sign	L	Date	Day-Sign	L	Date	Day-Sign	L
Sep 21 1965	10-Ik	4	Nov 28 1965	13-Oc	9	Feb 4 1966	3-Etz'nab	5
Sep 22 1965	11-Akbal	5	Nov 29 1965	**1-Chuen**	1	Feb 5 1966	4-Cauac	6
Sep 23 1965	12-Kan	6	Nov 30 1965	2-Eb	2	Feb 6 1966	5-Ahau	7
Sep 24 1965	13-Chicchan	7	Dec 1 1965	3-Ben	3	Feb 7 1966	*6-Imix*	8
Sep 25 1965	**1-Cimi**	8	Dec 2 1965	4-Ix	4	Feb 8 1966	7-Ik	9
Sep 26 1965	2-Manik	9	Dec 3 1965	5-Men	5	Feb 9 1966	8-Akbal	1
Sep 27 1965	3-Lamat	1	Dec 4 1965	6-Cib	6	Feb 10 1966	9-Kan	2
Sep 28 1965	4-Muluc	2	Dec 5 1965	7-Caban	7	Feb 11 1966	10-Chicchan	3
Sep 29 1965	5-Oc	3	Dec 6 1965	8-Etz'nab	8	Feb 12 1966	11-Cimi	4
Sep 30 1965	6-Chuen	4	Dec 7 1965	9-Cauac	9	Feb 13 1966	12-Manik	5
Oct 1 1965	7-Eb	5	Dec 8 1965	10-Ahau	1	Feb 14 1966	13-Lamat	6
Oct 2 1965	8-Ben	6	Dec 9 1965	*11-Imix*	2	Feb 15 1966	**1-Muluc**	7
Oct 3 1965	9-Ix	7	Dec 10 1965	12-Ik	3	Feb 16 1966	2-Oc	8
Oct 4 1965	10-Men	8	Dec 11 1965	13-Akbal	4	Feb 17 1966	3-Chuen	9
Oct 5 1965	11-Cib	9	Dec 12 1965	**1-Kan**	5	Feb 18 1966	4-Eb	1
Oct 6 1965	12-Caban	1	Dec 13 1965	2-Chicchan	6	Feb 19 1966	5-Ben	2
Oct 7 1965	13-Etz'nab	2	Dec 14 1965	3-Cimi	7	Feb 20 1966	6-Ix	3
Oct 8 1965	**1-Cauac**	3	Dec 15 1965	4-Manik	8	Feb 21 1966	7-Men	4
Oct 9 1965	2-Ahau	4	Dec 16 1965	5-Lamat	9	Feb 22 1966	8-Cib	5
Oct 10 1965	*3-Imix*	5	Dec 17 1965	6-Muluc	1	Feb 23 1966	9-Caban	6
Oct 11 1965	4-Ik	6	Dec 18 1965	7-Oc	2	Feb 24 1966	10-Etz'nab	7
Oct 12 1965	5-Akbal	7	Dec 19 1965	8-Chuen	3	Feb 25 1966	11-Cauac	8
Oct 13 1965	6-Kan	8	Dec 20 1965	9-Eb	4	Feb 26 1966	12-Ahau	9
Oct 14 1965	7-Chicchan	9	Dec 21 1965	10-Ben	5	Feb 27 1966	*13-Imix*	1
Oct 15 1965	8-Cimi	1	Dec 22 1965	11-Ix	6	Feb 28 1966	**1-Ik**	2
Oct 16 1965	9-Manik	2	Dec 23 1965	12-Men	7	Mar 1 1966	2-Akbal	3
Oct 17 1965	10-Lamat	3	Dec 24 1965	13-Cib	8	Mar 2 1966	3-Kan	4
Oct 18 1965	11-Muluc	4	Dec 25 1965	**1-Caban**	9	Mar 3 1966	4-Chicchan	5
Oct 19 1965	12-Oc	5	Dec 26 1965	2-Etz'nab	1	Mar 4 1966	5-Cimi	6
Oct 20 1965	13-Chuen	6	Dec 27 1965	3-Cauac	2	Mar 5 1966	6-Manik	7
Oct 21 1965	**1-Eb**	7	Dec 28 1965	4-Ahau	3	Mar 6 1966	7-Lamat	8
Oct 22 1965	2-Ben	8	Dec 29 1965	*5-Imix*	4	Mar 7 1966	8-Muluc	9
Oct 23 1965	3-Ix	9	Dec 30 1965	6-Ik	5	Mar 8 1966	9-Oc	1
Oct 24 1965	4-Men	1	Dec 31 1965	7-Akbal	6	Mar 9 1966	10-Chuen	2
Oct 25 1965	5-Cib	2	Jan 1 1966	8-Kan	7	Mar 10 1966	11-Eb	3
Oct 26 1965	6-Caban	3	Jan 2 1966	9-Chicchan	8	Mar 11 1966	12-Ben	4
Oct 27 1965	7-Etz'nab	4	Jan 3 1966	10-Cimi	9	Mar 12 1966	13-Ix	5
Oct 28 1965	8-Cauac	5	Jan 4 1966	11-Manik	1	Mar 13 1966	**1-Men**	6
Oct 29 1965	9-Ahau	6	Jan 5 1966	12-Lamat	2	Mar 14 1966	2-Cib	7
Oct 30 1965	*10-Imix*	7	Jan 6 1966	13-Muluc	3	Mar 15 1966	3-Caban	8
Oct 31 1965	11-Ik	8	Jan 7 1966	**1-Oc**	4	Mar 16 1966	4-Etz'nab	9
Nov 1 1965	12-Akbal	9	Jan 8 1966	2-Chuen	5	Mar 17 1966	5-Cauac	1
Nov 2 1965	13-Kan	1	Jan 9 1966	3-Eb	6	Mar 18 1966	6-Ahau	2
Nov 3 1965	**1-Chicchan**	2	Jan 10 1966	4-Ben	7	Mar 19 1966	*7-Imix*	3
Nov 4 1965	2-Cimi	3	Jan 11 1966	5-Ix	8	Mar 20 1966	8-Ik	4
Nov 5 1965	3-Manik	4	Jan 12 1966	6-Men	9	Mar 21 1966	9-Akbal	5
Nov 6 1965	4-Lamat	5	Jan 13 1966	7-Cib	1	Mar 22 1966	10-Kan	6
Nov 7 1965	5-Muluc	6	Jan 14 1966	8-Caban	2	Mar 23 1966	11-Chicchan	7
Nov 8 1965	6-Oc	7	Jan 15 1966	9-Etz'nab	3	Mar 24 1966	12-Cimi	8
Nov 9 1965	7-Chuen	8	Jan 16 1966	10-Cauac	4	Mar 25 1966	13-Manik	9
Nov 10 1965	8-Eb	9	Jan 17 1966	11-Ahau	5	Mar 26 1966	**1-Lamat**	1
Nov 11 1965	9-Ben	1	Jan 18 1966	*12-Imix*	6	Mar 27 1966	2-Muluc	2
Nov 12 1965	10-Ix	2	Jan 19 1966	13-Ik	7	Mar 28 1966	3-Oc	3
Nov 13 1965	11-Men	3	Jan 20 1966	**1-Akbal**	8	Mar 29 1966	4-Chuen	4
Nov 14 1965	12-Cib	4	Jan 21 1966	2-Kan	9	Mar 30 1966	5-Eb	5
Nov 15 1965	13-Caban	5	Jan 22 1966	3-Chicchan	1	Mar 31 1966	6-Ben	6
Nov 16 1965	**1-Etz'nab**	6	Jan 23 1966	4-Cimi	2	Apr 1 1966	7-Ix	7
Nov 17 1965	2-Cauac	7	Jan 24 1966	5-Manik	3	Apr 2 1966	8-Men	8
Nov 18 1965	3-Ahau	8	Jan 25 1966	6-Lamat	4	Apr 3 1966	9-Cib	9
Nov 19 1965	*4-Imix*	9	Jan 26 1966	7-Muluc	5	Apr 4 1966	10-Caban	1
Nov 20 1965	5-Ik	1	Jan 27 1966	8-Oc	6	Apr 5 1966	11-Etz'nab	2
Nov 21 1965	6-Akbal	2	Jan 28 1966	9-Chuen	7	Apr 6 1966	12-Cauac	3
Nov 22 1965	7-Kan	3	Jan 29 1966	10-Eb	8	Apr 7 1966	13-Ahau	4
Nov 23 1965	8-Chicchan	4	Jan 30 1966	11-Ben	9	Apr 8 1966	**1-Imix**	5
Nov 24 1965	9-Cimi	5	Jan 31 1966	12-Ix	1	Apr 9 1966	2-Ik	6
Nov 25 1965	10-Manik	6	Feb 1 1966	13-Men	2	Apr 10 1966	3-Akbal	7
Nov 26 1965	11-Lamat	7	Feb 2 1966	**1-Cib**	3	Apr 11 1966	4-Kan	8
Nov 27 1965	12-Muluc	8	Feb 3 1966	2-Caban	4	Apr 12 1966	5-Chicchan	9

Date	Day-Sign	L	Date	Day-Sign	L	Date	Day-Sign	L
Apr 13 1966	6-Cimi	1	Jun 20 1966	9-Ix	6	Aug 27 1966	12-Ik	2
Apr 14 1966	7-Manik	2	Jun 21 1966	10-Men	7	Aug 28 1966	13-Akbal	3
Apr 15 1966	8-Lamat	3	Jun 22 1966	11-Cib	8	Aug 29 1966	**1-Kan**	4
Apr 16 1966	9-Muluc	4	Jun 23 1966	12-Caban	9	Aug 30 1966	2-Chicchan	5
Apr 17 1966	10-Oc	5	Jun 24 1966	13-Etz'nab	1	Aug 31 1966	3-Cimi	6
Apr 18 1966	11-Chuen	6	Jun 25 1966	**1-Cauac**	2	Sep 1 1966	4-Manik	7
Apr 19 1966	12-Eb	7	Jun 26 1966	2-Ahau	3	Sep 2 1966	5-Lamat	8
Apr 20 1966	13-Ben	8	Jun 27 1966	*3-Imix*	4	Sep 3 1966	6-Muluc	9
Apr 21 1966	**1-Ix**	9	Jun 28 1966	4-Ik	5	Sep 4 1966	7-Oc	1
Apr 22 1966	2-Men	1	Jun 29 1966	5-Akbal	6	Sep 5 1966	8-Chuen	2
Apr 23 1966	3-Cib	2	Jun 30 1966	6-Kan	7	Sep 6 1966	9-Eb	3
Apr 24 1966	4-Caban	3	Jul 1 1966	7-Chicchan	8	Sep 7 1966	10-Ben	4
Apr 25 1966	5-Etz'nab	4	Jul 2 1966	8-Cimi	9	Sep 8 1966	11-Ix	5
Apr 26 1966	6-Cauac	5	Jul 3 1966	9-Manik	1	Sep 9 1966	12-Men	6
Apr 27 1966	7-Ahau	6	Jul 4 1966	10-Lamat	2	Sep 10 1966	13-Cib	7
Apr 28 1966	*8-Imix*	7	Jul 5 1966	11-Muluc	3	Sep 11 1966	**1-Caban**	8
Apr 29 1966	9-Ik	8	Jul 6 1966	12-Oc	4	Sep 12 1966	2-Etz'nab	9
Apr 30 1966	10-Akbal	9	Jul 7 1966	13-Chuen	5	Sep 13 1966	3-Cauac	1
May 1 1966	11-Kan	1	Jul 8 1966	**1-Eb**	6	Sep 14 1966	4-Ahau	2
May 2 1966	12-Chicchan	2	Jul 9 1966	2-Ben	7	Sep 15 1966	*5-Imix*	3
May 3 1966	13-Cimi	3	Jul 10 1966	3-Ix	8	Sep 16 1966	6-Ik	4
May 4 1966	**1-Manik**	4	Jul 11 1966	4-Men	9	Sep 17 1966	7-Akbal	5
May 5 1966	2-Lamat	5	Jul 12 1966	5-Cib	1	Sep 18 1966	8-Kan	6
May 6 1966	3-Muluc	6	Jul 13 1966	6-Caban	2	Sep 19 1966	9-Chicchan	7
May 7 1966	4-Oc	7	Jul 14 1966	7-Etz'nab	3	Sep 20 1966	10-Cimi	8
May 8 1966	5-Chuen	8	Jul 15 1966	8-Cauac	4	Sep 21 1966	11-Manik	9
May 9 1966	6-Eb	9	Jul 16 1966	9-Ahau	5	Sep 22 1966	12-Lamat	1
May 10 1966	7-Ben	1	Jul 17 1966	*10-Imix*	6	Sep 23 1966	13-Muluc	2
May 11 1966	8-Ix	2	Jul 18 1966	11-Ik	7	Sep 24 1966	**1-Oc**	3
May 12 1966	9-Men	3	Jul 19 1966	12-Akbal	8	Sep 25 1966	2-Chuen	4
May 13 1966	10-Cib	4	Jul 20 1966	13-Kan	9	Sep 26 1966	3-Eb	5
May 14 1966	11-Caban	5	Jul 21 1966	**1-Chicchan**	1	Sep 27 1966	4-Ben	6
May 15 1966	12-Etz'nab	6	Jul 22 1966	2-Cimi	2	Sep 28 1966	5-Ix	7
May 16 1966	13-Cauac	7	Jul 23 1966	3-Manik	3	Sep 29 1966	6-Men	8
May 17 1966	**1-Ahau**	8	Jul 24 1966	4-Lamat	4	Sep 30 1966	7-Cib	9
May 18 1966	*2-Imix*	9	Jul 25 1966	5-Muluc	5	Oct 1 1966	8-Caban	1
May 19 1966	3-Ik	1	Jul 26 1966	6-Oc	6	Oct 2 1966	9-Etz'nab	2
May 20 1966	4-Akbal	2	Jul 27 1966	7-Chuen	7	Oct 3 1966	10-Cauac	3
May 21 1966	5-Kan	3	Jul 28 1966	8-Eb	8	Oct 4 1966	11-Ahau	4
May 22 1966	6-Chicchan	4	Jul 29 1966	9-Ben	9	Oct 5 1966	*12-Imix*	5
May 23 1966	7-Cimi	5	Jul 30 1966	10-Ix	1	Oct 6 1966	13-Ik	6
May 24 1966	8-Manik	6	Jul 31 1966	11-Men	2	Oct 7 1966	**1-Akbal**	7
May 25 1966	9-Lamat	7	Aug 1 1966	12-Cib	3	Oct 8 1966	2-Kan	8
May 26 1966	10-Muluc	8	Aug 2 1966	13-Caban	4	Oct 9 1966	3-Chicchan	9
May 27 1966	11-Oc	9	Aug 3 1966	**1-Etz'nab**	5	Oct 10 1966	4-Cimi	1
May 28 1966	12-Chuen	1	Aug 4 1966	2-Cauac	6	Oct 11 1966	5-Manik	2
May 29 1966	13-Eb	2	Aug 5 1966	3-Ahau	7	Oct 12 1966	6-Lamat	3
May 30 1966	**1-Ben**	3	Aug 6 1966	*4-Imix*	8	Oct 13 1966	7-Muluc	4
May 31 1966	2-Ix	4	Aug 7 1966	5-Ik	9	Oct 14 1966	8-Oc	5
Jun 1 1966	3-Men	5	Aug 8 1966	6-Akbal	1	Oct 15 1966	9-Chuen	6
Jun 2 1966	4-Cib	6	Aug 9 1966	7-Kan	2	Oct 16 1966	10-Eb	7
Jun 3 1966	5-Caban	7	Aug 10 1966	8-Chicchan	3	Oct 17 1966	11-Ben	8
Jun 4 1966	6-Etz'nab	8	Aug 11 1966	9-Cimi	4	Oct 18 1966	12-Ix	9
Jun 5 1966	7-Cauac	9	Aug 12 1966	10-Manik	5	Oct 19 1966	13-Men	1
Jun 6 1966	8-Ahau	1	Aug 13 1966	11-Lamat	6	Oct 20 1966	**1-Cib**	2
Jun 7 1966	*9-Imix*	2	Aug 14 1966	12-Muluc	7	Oct 21 1966	2-Caban	3
Jun 8 1966	10-Ik	3	Aug 15 1966	13-Oc	8	Oct 22 1966	3-Etz'nab	4
Jun 9 1966	11-Akbal	4	Aug 16 1966	**1-Chuen**	9	Oct 23 1966	4-Cauac	5
Jun 10 1966	12-Kan	5	Aug 17 1966	2-Eb	1	Oct 24 1966	5-Ahau	6
Jun 11 1966	13-Chicchan	6	Aug 18 1966	3-Ben	2	Oct 25 1966	*6-Imix*	7
Jun 12 1966	**1-Cimi**	7	Aug 19 1966	4-Ix	3	Oct 26 1966	7-Ik	8
Jun 13 1966	2-Manik	8	Aug 20 1966	5-Men	4	Oct 27 1966	8-Akbal	9
Jun 14 1966	3-Lamat	9	Aug 21 1966	6-Cib	5	Oct 28 1966	9-Kan	1
Jun 15 1966	4-Muluc	1	Aug 22 1966	7-Caban	6	Oct 29 1966	10-Chicchan	2
Jun 16 1966	5-Oc	2	Aug 23 1966	8-Etz'nab	7	Oct 30 1966	11-Cimi	3
Jun 17 1966	6-Chuen	3	Aug 24 1966	9-Cauac	8	Oct 31 1966	12-Manik	4
Jun 18 1966	7-Eb	4	Aug 25 1966	10-Ahau	9	Nov 1 1966	13-Lamat	5
Jun 19 1966	8-Ben	5	Aug 26 1966	*11-Imix*	1	Nov 2 1966	**1-Muluc**	6

Date	Day-Sign	L		Date	Day-Sign	L		Date	Day-Sign	L
Nov 3 1966	2-Oc	7		Jan 10 1967	5-Etz'nab	3		Mar 19 1967	8-Cimi	8
Nov 4 1966	3-Chuen	8		Jan 11 1967	6-Cauac	4		Mar 20 1967	9-Manik	9
Nov 5 1966	4-Eb	9		Jan 12 1967	7-Ahau	5		Mar 21 1967	10-Lamat	1
Nov 6 1966	5-Ben	1		Jan 13 1967	8-Imix	6		Mar 22 1967	11-Muluc	2
Nov 7 1966	6-Ix	2		Jan 14 1967	9-Ik	7		Mar 23 1967	12-Oc	3
Nov 8 1966	7-Men	3		Jan 15 1967	10-Akbal	8		Mar 24 1967	13-Chuen	4
Nov 9 1966	8-Cib	4		Jan 16 1967	11-Kan	9				
Nov 10 1966	9-Caban	5		Jan 17 1967	12-Chicchan	1		Mar 25 1967	1-Eb	5
Nov 11 1966	10-Etz'nab	6		Jan 18 1967	13-Cimi	2		Mar 26 1967	2-Ben	6
Nov 12 1966	11-Cauac	7						Mar 27 1967	3-Ix	7
Nov 13 1966	12-Ahau	8		Jan 19 1967	1-Manik	3		Mar 28 1967	4-Men	8
Nov 14 1966	13-Imix	9		Jan 20 1967	2-Lamat	4		Mar 29 1967	5-Cib	9
				Jan 21 1967	3-Muluc	5		Mar 30 1967	6-Caban	1
Nov 15 1966	1-Ik	1		Jan 22 1967	4-Oc	6		Mar 31 1967	7-Etz'nab	2
Nov 16 1966	2-Akbal	2		Jan 23 1967	5-Chuen	7		Apr 1 1967	8-Cauac	3
Nov 17 1966	3-Kan	3		Jan 24 1967	6-Eb	8		Apr 2 1967	9-Ahau	4
Nov 18 1966	4-Chicchan	4		Jan 25 1967	7-Ben	9		Apr 3 1967	10-Imix	5
Nov 19 1966	5-Cimi	5		Jan 26 1967	8-Ix	1		Apr 4 1967	11-Ik	6
Nov 20 1966	6-Manik	6		Jan 27 1967	9-Men	2		Apr 5 1967	12-Akbal	7
Nov 21 1966	7-Lamat	7		Jan 28 1967	10-Cib	3		Apr 6 1967	13-Kan	8
Nov 22 1966	8-Muluc	8		Jan 29 1967	11-Caban	4				
Nov 23 1966	9-Oc	9		Jan 30 1967	12-Etz'nab	5		Apr 7 1967	1-Chicchan	9
Nov 24 1966	10-Chuen	1		Jan 31 1967	13-Cauac	6		Apr 8 1967	2-Cimi	1
Nov 25 1966	11-Eb	2						Apr 9 1967	3-Manik	2
Nov 26 1966	12-Ben	3		Feb 1 1967	1-Ahau	7		Apr 10 1967	4-Lamat	3
Nov 27 1966	13-Ix	4		Feb 2 1967	2-Imix	8		Apr 11 1967	5-Muluc	4
				Feb 3 1967	3-Ik	9		Apr 12 1967	6-Oc	5
Nov 28 1966	1-Men	5		Feb 4 1967	4-Akbal	1		Apr 13 1967	7-Chuen	6
Nov 29 1966	2-Cib	6		Feb 5 1967	5-Kan	2		Apr 14 1967	8-Eb	7
Nov 30 1966	3-Caban	7		Feb 6 1967	6-Chicchan	3		Apr 15 1967	9-Ben	8
Dec 1 1966	4-Etz'nab	8		Feb 7 1967	7-Cimi	4		Apr 16 1967	10-Ix	9
Dec 2 1966	5-Cauac	9		Feb 8 1967	8-Manik	5		Apr 17 1967	11-Men	1
Dec 3 1966	6-Ahau	1		Feb 9 1967	9-Lamat	6		Apr 18 1967	12-Cib	2
Dec 4 1966	7-Imix	2		Feb 10 1967	10-Muluc	7		Apr 19 1967	13-Caban	3
Dec 5 1966	8-Ik	3		Feb 11 1967	11-Oc	8				
Dec 6 1966	9-Akbal	4		Feb 12 1967	12-Chuen	9		Apr 20 1967	1-Etz'nab	4
Dec 7 1966	10-Kan	5		Feb 13 1967	13-Eb	1		Apr 21 1967	2-Cauac	5
Dec 8 1966	11-Chicchan	6						Apr 22 1967	3-Ahau	6
Dec 9 1966	12-Cimi	7		Feb 14 1967	1-Ben	2		Apr 23 1967	4-Imix	7
Dec 10 1966	13-Manik	8		Feb 15 1967	2-Ix	3		Apr 24 1967	5-Ik	8
				Feb 16 1967	3-Men	4		Apr 25 1967	6-Akbal	9
Dec 11 1966	1-Lamat	9		Feb 17 1967	4-Cib	5		Apr 26 1967	7-Kan	1
Dec 12 1966	2-Muluc	1		Feb 18 1967	5-Caban	6		Apr 27 1967	8-Chicchan	2
Dec 13 1966	3-Oc	2		Feb 19 1967	6-Etz'nab	7		Apr 28 1967	9-Cimi	3
Dec 14 1966	4-Chuen	3		Feb 20 1967	7-Cauac	8		Apr 29 1967	10-Manik	4
Dec 15 1966	5-Eb	4		Feb 21 1967	8-Ahau	9		Apr 30 1967	11-Lamat	5
Dec 16 1966	6-Ben	5		Feb 22 1967	9-Imix	1		May 1 1967	12-Muluc	6
Dec 17 1966	7-Ix	6		Feb 23 1967	10-Ik	2		May 2 1967	13-Oc	7
Dec 18 1966	8-Men	7		Feb 24 1967	11-Akbal	3				
Dec 19 1966	9-Cib	8		Feb 25 1967	12-Kan	4		May 3 1967	1-Chuen	8
Dec 20 1966	10-Caban	9		Feb 26 1967	13-Chicchan	5		May 4 1967	2-Eb	9
Dec 21 1966	11-Etz'nab	1						May 5 1967	3-Ben	1
Dec 22 1966	12-Cauac	2		Feb 27 1967	1-Cimi	6		May 6 1967	4-Ix	2
Dec 23 1966	13-Ahau	3		Feb 28 1967	2-Manik	7		May 7 1967	5-Men	3
				Mar 1 1967	3-Lamat	8		May 8 1967	6-Cib	4
Dec 24 1966	1-Imix	4		Mar 2 1967	4-Muluc	9		May 9 1967	7-Caban	5
Dec 25 1966	2-Ik	5		Mar 3 1967	5-Oc	1		May 10 1967	8-Etz'nab	6
Dec 26 1966	3-Akbal	6		Mar 4 1967	6-Chuen	2		May 11 1967	9-Cauac	7
Dec 27 1966	4-Kan	7		Mar 5 1967	7-Eb	3		May 12 1967	10-Ahau	8
Dec 28 1966	5-Chicchan	8		Mar 6 1967	8-Ben	4		May 13 1967	11-Imix	9
Dec 29 1966	6-Cimi	9		Mar 7 1967	9-Ix	5		May 14 1967	12-Ik	1
Dec 30 1966	7-Manik	1		Mar 8 1967	10-Men	6		May 15 1967	13-Akbal	2
Dec 31 1966	8-Lamat	2		Mar 9 1967	11-Cib	7				
Jan 1 1967	9-Muluc	3		Mar 10 1967	12-Caban	8		May 16 1967	1-Kan	3
Jan 2 1967	10-Oc	4		Mar 11 1967	13-Etz'nab	9		May 17 1967	2-Chicchan	4
Jan 3 1967	11-Chuen	5						May 18 1967	3-Cimi	5
Jan 4 1967	12-Eb	6		Mar 12 1967	1-Cauac	1		May 19 1967	4-Manik	6
Jan 5 1967	13-Ben	7		Mar 13 1967	2-Ahau	2		May 20 1967	5-Lamat	7
				Mar 14 1967	3-Imix	3		May 21 1967	6-Muluc	8
Jan 6 1967	1-Ix	8		Mar 15 1967	4-Ik	4		May 22 1967	7-Oc	9
Jan 7 1967	2-Men	9		Mar 16 1967	5-Akbal	5		May 23 1967	8-Chuen	1
Jan 8 1967	3-Cib	1		Mar 17 1967	6-Kan	6		May 24 1967	9-Eb	2
Jan 9 1967	4-Caban	2		Mar 18 1967	7-Chicchan	7		May 25 1967	10-Ben	3

Date	Day-Sign	L
May 26 1967	11-Ix	4
May 27 1967	12-Men	5
May 28 1967	13-Cib	6
May 29 1967	1-Caban	7
May 30 1967	2-Etz'nab	8
May 31 1967	3-Cauac	9
Jun 1 1967	4-Ahau	1
Jun 2 1967	5-Imix	2
Jun 3 1967	6-Ik	3
Jun 4 1967	7-Akbal	4
Jun 5 1967	8-Kan	5
Jun 6 1967	9-Chicchan	6
Jun 7 1967	10-Cimi	7
Jun 8 1967	11-Manik	8
Jun 9 1967	12-Lamat	9
Jun 10 1967	13-Muluc	1
Jun 11 1967	1-Oc	2
Jun 12 1967	2-Chuen	3
Jun 13 1967	3-Eb	4
Jun 14 1967	4-Ben	5
Jun 15 1967	5-Ix	6
Jun 16 1967	6-Men	7
Jun 17 1967	7-Cib	8
Jun 18 1967	8-Caban	9
Jun 19 1967	9-Etz'nab	1
Jun 20 1967	10-Cauac	2
Jun 21 1967	11-Ahau	3
Jun 22 1967	12-Imix	4
Jun 23 1967	13-Ik	5
Jun 24 1967	1-Akbal	6
Jun 25 1967	2-Kan	7
Jun 26 1967	3-Chicchan	8
Jun 27 1967	4-Cimi	9
Jun 28 1967	5-Manik	1
Jun 29 1967	6-Lamat	2
Jun 30 1967	7-Muluc	3
Jul 1 1967	8-Oc	4
Jul 2 1967	9-Chuen	5
Jul 3 1967	10-Eb	6
Jul 4 1967	11-Ben	7
Jul 5 1967	12-Ix	8
Jul 6 1967	13-Men	9
Jul 7 1967	1-Cib	1
Jul 8 1967	2-Caban	2
Jul 9 1967	3-Etz'nab	3
Jul 10 1967	4-Cauac	4
Jul 11 1967	5-Ahau	5
Jul 12 1967	6-Imix	6
Jul 13 1967	7-Ik	7
Jul 14 1967	8-Akbal	8
Jul 15 1967	9-Kan	9
Jul 16 1967	10-Chicchan	1
Jul 17 1967	11-Cimi	2
Jul 18 1967	12-Manik	3
Jul 19 1967	13-Lamat	4
Jul 20 1967	1-Muluc	5
Jul 21 1967	2-Oc	6
Jul 22 1967	3-Chuen	7
Jul 23 1967	4-Eb	8
Jul 24 1967	5-Ben	9
Jul 25 1967	6-Ix	1
Jul 26 1967	7-Men	2
Jul 27 1967	8-Cib	3
Jul 28 1967	9-Caban	4
Jul 29 1967	10-Etz'nab	5
Jul 30 1967	11-Cauac	6
Jul 31 1967	12-Ahau	7
Aug 1 1967	13-Imix	8

Date	Day-Sign	L
Aug 2 1967	1-Ik	9
Aug 3 1967	2-Akbal	1
Aug 4 1967	3-Kan	2
Aug 5 1967	4-Chicchan	3
Aug 6 1967	5-Cimi	4
Aug 7 1967	6-Manik	5
Aug 8 1967	7-Lamat	6
Aug 9 1967	8-Muluc	7
Aug 10 1967	9-Oc	8
Aug 11 1967	10-Chuen	9
Aug 12 1967	11-Eb	1
Aug 13 1967	12-Ben	2
Aug 14 1967	13-Ix	3
Aug 15 1967	1-Men	4
Aug 16 1967	2-Cib	5
Aug 17 1967	3-Caban	6
Aug 18 1967	4-Etz'nab	7
Aug 19 1967	5-Cauac	8
Aug 20 1967	6-Ahau	9
Aug 21 1967	7-Imix	1
Aug 22 1967	8-Ik	2
Aug 23 1967	9-Akbal	3
Aug 24 1967	10-Kan	4
Aug 25 1967	11-Chicchan	5
Aug 26 1967	12-Cimi	6
Aug 27 1967	13-Manik	7
Aug 28 1967	1-Lamat	8
Aug 29 1967	2-Muluc	9
Aug 30 1967	3-Oc	1
Aug 31 1967	4-Chuen	2
Sep 1 1967	5-Eb	3
Sep 2 1967	6-Ben	4
Sep 3 1967	7-Ix	5
Sep 4 1967	8-Men	6
Sep 5 1967	9-Cib	7
Sep 6 1967	10-Caban	8
Sep 7 1967	11-Etz'nab	9
Sep 8 1967	12-Cauac	1
Sep 9 1967	13-Ahau	2
Sep 10 1967	1-Imix	3
Sep 11 1967	2-Ik	4
Sep 12 1967	3-Akbal	5
Sep 13 1967	4-Kan	6
Sep 14 1967	5-Chicchan	7
Sep 15 1967	6-Cimi	8
Sep 16 1967	7-Manik	9
Sep 17 1967	8-Lamat	1
Sep 18 1967	9-Muluc	2
Sep 19 1967	10-Oc	3
Sep 20 1967	11-Chuen	4
Sep 21 1967	12-Eb	5
Sep 22 1967	13-Ben	6
Sep 23 1967	1-Ix	7
Sep 24 1967	2-Men	8
Sep 25 1967	3-Cib	9
Sep 26 1967	4-Caban	1
Sep 27 1967	5-Etz'nab	2
Sep 28 1967	6-Cauac	3
Sep 29 1967	7-Ahau	4
Sep 30 1967	8-Imix	5
Oct 1 1967	9-Ik	6
Oct 2 1967	10-Akbal	7
Oct 3 1967	11-Kan	8
Oct 4 1967	12-Chicchan	9
Oct 5 1967	13-Cimi	1
Oct 6 1967	1-Manik	2
Oct 7 1967	2-Lamat	3
Oct 8 1967	3-Muluc	4

Date	Day-Sign	L
Oct 9 1967	4-Oc	5
Oct 10 1967	5-Chuen	6
Oct 11 1967	6-Eb	7
Oct 12 1967	7-Ben	8
Oct 13 1967	8-Ix	9
Oct 14 1967	9-Men	1
Oct 15 1967	10-Cib	2
Oct 16 1967	11-Caban	3
Oct 17 1967	12-Etz'nab	4
Oct 18 1967	13-Cauac	5
Oct 19 1967	1-Ahau	6
Oct 20 1967	2-Imix	7
Oct 21 1967	3-Ik	8
Oct 22 1967	4-Akbal	9
Oct 23 1967	5-Kan	1
Oct 24 1967	6-Chicchan	2
Oct 25 1967	7-Cimi	3
Oct 26 1967	8-Manik	4
Oct 27 1967	9-Lamat	5
Oct 28 1967	10-Muluc	6
Oct 29 1967	11-Oc	7
Oct 30 1967	12-Chuen	8
Oct 31 1967	13-Eb	9
Nov 1 1967	1-Ben	1
Nov 2 1967	2-Ix	2
Nov 3 1967	3-Men	3
Nov 4 1967	4-Cib	4
Nov 5 1967	5-Caban	5
Nov 6 1967	6-Etz'nab	6
Nov 7 1967	7-Cauac	7
Nov 8 1967	8-Ahau	8
Nov 9 1967	9-Imix	9
Nov 10 1967	10-Ik	1
Nov 11 1967	11-Akbal	2
Nov 12 1967	12-Kan	3
Nov 13 1967	13-Chicchan	4
Nov 14 1967	1-Cimi	5
Nov 15 1967	2-Manik	6
Nov 16 1967	3-Lamat	7
Nov 17 1967	4-Muluc	8
Nov 18 1967	5-Oc	9
Nov 19 1967	6-Chuen	1
Nov 20 1967	7-Eb	2
Nov 21 1967	8-Ben	3
Nov 22 1967	9-Ix	4
Nov 23 1967	10-Men	5
Nov 24 1967	11-Cib	6
Nov 25 1967	12-Caban	7
Nov 26 1967	13-Etz'nab	8
Nov 27 1967	1-Cauac	9
Nov 28 1967	2-Ahau	1
Nov 29 1967	3-Imix	2
Nov 30 1967	4-Ik	3
Dec 1 1967	5-Akbal	4
Dec 2 1967	6-Kan	5
Dec 3 1967	7-Chicchan	6
Dec 4 1967	8-Cimi	7
Dec 5 1967	9-Manik	8
Dec 6 1967	10-Lamat	9
Dec 7 1967	11-Muluc	1
Dec 8 1967	12-Oc	2
Dec 9 1967	13-Chuen	3
Dec 10 1967	1-Eb	4
Dec 11 1967	2-Ben	5
Dec 12 1967	3-Ix	6
Dec 13 1967	4-Men	7
Dec 14 1967	5-Cib	8
Dec 15 1967	6-Caban	9

Date	Day-Sign	L
Dec 16 1967	7-Etz'nab	1
Dec 17 1967	8-Cauac	2
Dec 18 1967	9-Ahau	3
Dec 19 1967	10-Imix	4
Dec 20 1967	11-Ik	5
Dec 21 1967	12-Akbal	6
Dec 22 1967	13-Kan	7
Dec 23 1967	1-Chicchan	8
Dec 24 1967	2-Cimi	9
Dec 25 1967	3-Manik	1
Dec 26 1967	4-Lamat	2
Dec 27 1967	5-Muluc	3
Dec 28 1967	6-Oc	4
Dec 29 1967	7-Chuen	5
Dec 30 1967	8-Eb	6
Dec 31 1967	9-Ben	7
Jan 1 1968	10-Ix	8
Jan 2 1968	11-Men	9
Jan 3 1968	12-Cib	1
Jan 4 1968	13-Caban	2
Jan 5 1968	1-Etz'nab	3
Jan 6 1968	2-Cauac	4
Jan 7 1968	3-Ahau	5
Jan 8 1968	4-Imix	6
Jan 9 1968	5-Ik	7
Jan 10 1968	6-Akbal	8
Jan 11 1968	7-Kan	9
Jan 12 1968	8-Chicchan	1
Jan 13 1968	9-Cimi	2
Jan 14 1968	10-Manik	3
Jan 15 1968	11-Lamat	4
Jan 16 1968	12-Muluc	5
Jan 17 1968	13-Oc	6
Jan 18 1968	1-Chuen	7
Jan 19 1968	2-Eb	8
Jan 20 1968	3-Ben	9
Jan 21 1968	4-Ix	1
Jan 22 1968	5-Men	2
Jan 23 1968	6-Cib	3
Jan 24 1968	7-Caban	4
Jan 25 1968	8-Etz'nab	5
Jan 26 1968	9-Cauac	6
Jan 27 1968	10-Ahau	7
Jan 28 1968	11-Imix	8
Jan 29 1968	12-Ik	9
Jan 30 1968	13-Akbal	1
Jan 31 1968	1-Kan	2
Feb 1 1968	2-Chicchan	3
Feb 2 1968	3-Cimi	4
Feb 3 1968	4-Manik	5
Feb 4 1968	5-Lamat	6
Feb 5 1968	6-Muluc	7
Feb 6 1968	7-Oc	8
Feb 7 1968	8-Chuen	9
Feb 8 1968	9-Eb	1
Feb 9 1968	10-Ben	2
Feb 10 1968	11-Ix	3
Feb 11 1968	12-Men	4
Feb 12 1968	13-Cib	5
Feb 13 1968	1-Caban	6
Feb 14 1968	2-Etz'nab	7
Feb 15 1968	3-Cauac	8
Feb 16 1968	4-Ahau	9
Feb 17 1968	5-Imix	1
Feb 18 1968	6-Ik	2
Feb 19 1968	7-Akbal	3
Feb 20 1968	8-Kan	4
Feb 21 1968	9-Chicchan	5

Date	Day-Sign	L
Feb 22 1968	10-Cimi	6
Feb 23 1968	11-Manik	7
Feb 24 1968	12-Lamat	8
Feb 25 1968	13-Muluc	9
Feb 26 1968	1-Oc	1
Feb 27 1968	2-Chuen	2
Feb 28 1968	3-Eb	3
Feb 29 1968	4-Ben	4
Mar 1 1968	5-Ix	5
Mar 2 1968	6-Men	6
Mar 3 1968	7-Cib	7
Mar 4 1968	8-Caban	8
Mar 5 1968	9-Etz'nab	9
Mar 6 1968	10-Cauac	1
Mar 7 1968	11-Ahau	2
Mar 8 1968	12-Imix	3
Mar 9 1968	13-Ik	4
Mar 10 1968	1-Akbal	5
Mar 11 1968	2-Kan	6
Mar 12 1968	3-Chicchan	7
Mar 13 1968	4-Cimi	8
Mar 14 1968	5-Manik	9
Mar 15 1968	6-Lamat	1
Mar 16 1968	7-Muluc	2
Mar 17 1968	8-Oc	3
Mar 18 1968	9-Chuen	4
Mar 19 1968	10-Eb	5
Mar 20 1968	11-Ben	6
Mar 21 1968	12-Ix	7
Mar 22 1968	13-Men	8
Mar 23 1968	1-Cib	9
Mar 24 1968	2-Caban	1
Mar 25 1968	3-Etz'nab	2
Mar 26 1968	4-Cauac	3
Mar 27 1968	5-Ahau	4
Mar 28 1968	6-Imix	5
Mar 29 1968	7-Ik	6
Mar 30 1968	8-Akbal	7
Mar 31 1968	9-Kan	8
Apr 1 1968	10-Chicchan	9
Apr 2 1968	11-Cimi	1
Apr 3 1968	12-Manik	2
Apr 4 1968	13-Lamat	3
Apr 5 1968	1-Muluc	4
Apr 6 1968	2-Oc	5
Apr 7 1968	3-Chuen	6
Apr 8 1968	4-Eb	7
Apr 9 1968	5-Ben	8
Apr 10 1968	6-Ix	9
Apr 11 1968	7-Men	1
Apr 12 1968	8-Cib	2
Apr 13 1968	9-Caban	3
Apr 14 1968	10-Etz'nab	4
Apr 15 1968	11-Cauac	5
Apr 16 1968	12-Ahau	6
Apr 17 1968	13-Imix	7
Apr 18 1968	1-Ik	8
Apr 19 1968	2-Akbal	9
Apr 20 1968	3-Kan	1
Apr 21 1968	4-Chicchan	2
Apr 22 1968	5-Cimi	3
Apr 23 1968	6-Manik	4
Apr 24 1968	7-Lamat	5
Apr 25 1968	8-Muluc	6
Apr 26 1968	9-Oc	7
Apr 27 1968	10-Chuen	8
Apr 28 1968	11-Eb	9
Apr 29 1968	12-Ben	1

Date	Day-Sign	L
Apr 30 1968	13-Ix	2
May 1 1968	1-Men	3
May 2 1968	2-Cib	4
May 3 1968	3-Caban	5
May 4 1968	4-Etz'nab	6
May 5 1968	5-Cauac	7
May 6 1968	6-Ahau	8
May 7 1968	7-Imix	9
May 8 1968	8-Ik	1
May 9 1968	9-Akbal	2
May 10 1968	10-Kan	3
May 11 1968	11-Chicchan	4
May 12 1968	12-Cimi	5
May 13 1968	13-Manik	6
May 14 1968	1-Lamat	7
May 15 1968	2-Muluc	8
May 16 1968	3-Oc	9
May 17 1968	4-Chuen	1
May 18 1968	5-Eb	2
May 19 1968	6-Ben	3
May 20 1968	7-Ix	4
May 21 1968	8-Men	5
May 22 1968	9-Cib	6
May 23 1968	10-Caban	7
May 24 1968	11-Etz'nab	8
May 25 1968	12-Cauac	9
May 26 1968	13-Ahau	1
May 27 1968	1-Imix	2
May 28 1968	2-Ik	3
May 29 1968	3-Akbal	4
May 30 1968	4-Kan	5
May 31 1968	5-Chicchan	6
Jun 1 1968	6-Cimi	7
Jun 2 1968	7-Manik	8
Jun 3 1968	8-Lamat	9
Jun 4 1968	9-Muluc	1
Jun 5 1968	10-Oc	2
Jun 6 1968	11-Chuen	3
Jun 7 1968	12-Eb	4
Jun 8 1968	13-Ben	5
Jun 9 1968	1-Ix	6
Jun 10 1968	2-Men	7
Jun 11 1968	3-Cib	8
Jun 12 1968	4-Caban	9
Jun 13 1968	5-Etz'nab	1
Jun 14 1968	6-Cauac	2
Jun 15 1968	7-Ahau	3
Jun 16 1968	8-Imix	4
Jun 17 1968	9-Ik	5
Jun 18 1968	10-Akbal	6
Jun 19 1968	11-Kan	7
Jun 20 1968	12-Chicchan	8
Jun 21 1968	13-Cimi	9
Jun 22 1968	1-Manik	1
Jun 23 1968	2-Lamat	2
Jun 24 1968	3-Muluc	3
Jun 25 1968	4-Oc	4
Jun 26 1968	5-Chuen	5
Jun 27 1968	6-Eb	6
Jun 28 1968	7-Ben	7
Jun 29 1968	8-Ix	8
Jun 30 1968	9-Men	9
Jul 1 1968	10-Cib	1
Jul 2 1968	11-Caban	2
Jul 3 1968	12-Etz'nab	3
Jul 4 1968	13-Cauac	4
Jul 5 1968	1-Ahau	5
Jul 6 1968	2-Imix	6

Date	Day-Sign	L	Date	Day-Sign	L	Date	Day-Sign	L
Jul 7 1968	3-Ik	7	Sep 13 1968	6-Oc	3	Nov 20 1968	9-Etz'nab	8
Jul 8 1968	4-Akbal	8	Sep 14 1968	7-Chuen	4	Nov 21 1968	10-Cauac	9
Jul 9 1968	5-Kan	9	Sep 15 1968	8-Eb	5	Nov 22 1968	11-Ahau	1
Jul 10 1968	6-Chicchan	1	Sep 16 1968	9-Ben	6	Nov 23 1968	12-*Imix*	2
Jul 11 1968	7-Cimi	2	Sep 17 1968	10-Ix	7	Nov 24 1968	13-Ik	3
Jul 12 1968	8-Manik	3	Sep 18 1968	11-Men	8	Nov 25 1968	**1-Akbal**	4
Jul 13 1968	9-Lamat	4	Sep 19 1968	12-Cib	9	Nov 26 1968	2-Kan	5
Jul 14 1968	10-Muluc	5	Sep 20 1968	13-Caban	1	Nov 27 1968	3-Chicchan	6
Jul 15 1968	11-Oc	6	Sep 21 1968	**1-Etz'nab**	2	Nov 28 1968	4-Cimi	7
Jul 16 1968	12-Chuen	7	Sep 22 1968	2-Cauac	3	Nov 29 1968	5-Manik	8
Jul 17 1968	13-Eb	8	Sep 23 1968	3-Ahau	4	Nov 30 1968	6-Lamat	9
Jul 18 1968	**1-Ben**	9	Sep 24 1968	4-*Imix*	5	Dec 1 1968	7-Muluc	1
Jul 19 1968	2-Ix	1	Sep 25 1968	5-Ik	6	Dec 2 1968	8-Oc	2
Jul 20 1968	3-Men	2	Sep 26 1968	6-Akbal	7	Dec 3 1968	9-Chuen	3
Jul 21 1968	4-Cib	3	Sep 27 1968	7-Kan	8	Dec 4 1968	10-Eb	4
Jul 22 1968	5-Caban	4	Sep 28 1968	8-Chicchan	9	Dec 5 1968	11-Ben	5
Jul 23 1968	6-Etz'nab	5	Sep 29 1968	9-Cimi	1	Dec 6 1968	12-Ix	6
Jul 24 1968	7-Cauac	6	Sep 30 1968	10-Manik	2	Dec 7 1968	13-Men	7
Jul 25 1968	8-Ahau	7	Oct 1 1968	11-Lamat	3	Dec 8 1968	**1-Cib**	8
Jul 26 1968	9-*Imix*	8	Oct 2 1968	12-Muluc	4	Dec 9 1968	2-Caban	9
Jul 27 1968	10-Ik	9	Oct 3 1968	13-Oc	5	Dec 10 1968	3-Etz'nab	1
Jul 28 1968	11-Akbal	1	Oct 4 1968	**1-Chuen**	6	Dec 11 1968	4-Cauac	2
Jul 29 1968	12-Kan	2	Oct 5 1968	2-Eb	7	Dec 12 1968	5-Ahau	3
Jul 30 1968	13-Chicchan	3	Oct 6 1968	3-Ben	8	Dec 13 1968	6-*Imix*	4
Jul 31 1968	**1-Cimi**	4	Oct 7 1968	4-Ix	9	Dec 14 1968	7-Ik	5
Aug 1 1968	2-Manik	5	Oct 8 1968	5-Men	1	Dec 15 1968	8-Akbal	6
Aug 2 1968	3-Lamat	6	Oct 9 1968	6-Cib	2	Dec 16 1968	9-Kan	7
Aug 3 1968	4-Muluc	7	Oct 10 1968	7-Caban	3	Dec 17 1968	10-Chicchan	8
Aug 4 1968	5-Oc	8	Oct 11 1968	8-Etz'nab	4	Dec 18 1968	11-Cimi	9
Aug 5 1968	6-Chuen	9	Oct 12 1968	9-Cauac	5	Dec 19 1968	12-Manik	1
Aug 6 1968	7-Eb	1	Oct 13 1968	10-Ahau	6	Dec 20 1968	13-Lamat	2
Aug 7 1968	8-Ben	2	Oct 14 1968	11-*Imix*	7	Dec 21 1968	**1-Muluc**	3
Aug 8 1968	9-Ix	3	Oct 15 1968	12-Ik	8	Dec 22 1968	2-Oc	4
Aug 9 1968	10-Men	4	Oct 16 1968	13-Akbal	9	Dec 23 1968	3-Chuen	5
Aug 10 1968	11-Cib	5	Oct 17 1968	**1-Kan**	1	Dec 24 1968	4-Eb	6
Aug 11 1968	12-Caban	6	Oct 18 1968	2-Chicchan	2	Dec 25 1968	5-Ben	7
Aug 12 1968	13-Etz'nab	7	Oct 19 1968	3-Cimi	3	Dec 26 1968	6-Ix	8
Aug 13 1968	**1-Cauac**	8	Oct 20 1968	4-Manik	4	Dec 27 1968	7-Men	9
Aug 14 1968	2-Ahau	9	Oct 21 1968	5-Lamat	5	Dec 28 1968	8-Cib	1
Aug 15 1968	3-*Imix*	1	Oct 22 1968	6-Muluc	6	Dec 29 1968	9-Caban	2
Aug 16 1968	4-Ik	2	Oct 23 1968	7-Oc	7	Dec 30 1968	10-Etz'nab	3
Aug 17 1968	5-Akbal	3	Oct 24 1968	8-Chuen	8	Dec 31 1968	11-Cauac	4
Aug 18 1968	6-Kan	4	Oct 25 1968	9-Eb	9	Jan 1 1969	12-Ahau	5
Aug 19 1968	7-Chicchan	5	Oct 26 1968	10-Ben	1	Jan 2 1969	13-*Imix*	6
Aug 20 1968	8-Cimi	6	Oct 27 1968	11-Ix	2	Jan 3 1969	**1-Ik**	7
Aug 21 1968	9-Manik	7	Oct 28 1968	12-Men	3	Jan 4 1969	2-Akbal	8
Aug 22 1968	10-Lamat	8	Oct 29 1968	13-Cib	4	Jan 5 1969	3-Kan	9
Aug 23 1968	11-Muluc	9	Oct 30 1968	**1-Caban**	5	Jan 6 1969	4-Chicchan	1
Aug 24 1968	12-Oc	1	Oct 31 1968	2-Etz'nab	6	Jan 7 1969	5-Cimi	2
Aug 25 1968	13-Chuen	2	Nov 1 1968	3-Cauac	7	Jan 8 1969	6-Manik	3
Aug 26 1968	**1-Eb**	3	Nov 2 1968	4-Ahau	8	Jan 9 1969	7-Lamat	4
Aug 27 1968	2-Ben	4	Nov 3 1968	5-*Imix*	9	Jan 10 1969	8-Muluc	5
Aug 28 1968	3-Ix	5	Nov 4 1968	6-Ik	1	Jan 11 1969	9-Oc	6
Aug 29 1968	4-Men	6	Nov 5 1968	7-Akbal	2	Jan 12 1969	10-Chuen	7
Aug 30 1968	5-Cib	7	Nov 6 1968	8-Kan	3	Jan 13 1969	11-Eb	8
Aug 31 1968	6-Caban	8	Nov 7 1968	9-Chicchan	4	Jan 14 1969	12-Ben	9
Sep 1 1968	7-Etz'nab	9	Nov 8 1968	10-Cimi	5	Jan 15 1969	13-Ix	1
Sep 2 1968	8-Cauac	1	Nov 9 1968	11-Manik	6	Jan 16 1969	**1-Men**	2
Sep 3 1968	9-Ahau	2	Nov 10 1968	12-Lamat	7	Jan 17 1969	2-Cib	3
Sep 4 1968	10-*Imix*	3	Nov 11 1968	13-Muluc	8	Jan 18 1969	3-Caban	4
Sep 5 1968	11-Ik	4	Nov 12 1968	**1-Oc**	9	Jan 19 1969	4-Etz'nab	5
Sep 6 1968	12-Akbal	5	Nov 13 1968	2-Chuen	1	Jan 20 1969	5-Cauac	6
Sep 7 1968	13-Kan	6	Nov 14 1968	3-Eb	2	Jan 21 1969	6-Ahau	7
Sep 8 1968	**1-Chicchan**	7	Nov 15 1968	4-Ben	3	Jan 22 1969	7-*Imix*	8
Sep 9 1968	2-Cimi	8	Nov 16 1968	5-Ix	4	Jan 23 1969	8-Ik	9
Sep 10 1968	3-Manik	9	Nov 17 1968	6-Men	5	Jan 24 1969	9-Akbal	1
Sep 11 1968	4-Lamat	1	Nov 18 1968	7-Cib	6	Jan 25 1969	10-Kan	2
Sep 12 1968	5-Muluc	2	Nov 19 1968	8-Caban	7	Jan 26 1969	11-Chicchan	3

Date	Day-Sign	L	Date	Day-Sign	L	Date	Day-Sign	L
Jan 27 1969	12-Cimi	4	Apr 5 1969	2-Ix	9	Jun 12 1969	5-Ik	5
Jan 28 1969	13-Manik	5	Apr 6 1969	3-Men	1	Jun 13 1969	6-Akbal	6
Jan 29 1969	1-Lamat	6	Apr 7 1969	4-Cib	2	Jun 14 1969	7-Kan	7
Jan 30 1969	2-Muluc	7	Apr 8 1969	5-Caban	3	Jun 15 1969	8-Chicchan	8
Jan 31 1969	3-Oc	8	Apr 9 1969	6-Etz'nab	4	Jun 16 1969	9-Cimi	9
Feb 1 1969	4-Chuen	9	Apr 10 1969	7-Cauac	5	Jun 17 1969	10-Manik	1
Feb 2 1969	5-Eb	1	Apr 11 1969	8-Ahau	6	Jun 18 1969	11-Lamat	2
Feb 3 1969	6-Ben	2	Apr 12 1969	9-Imix	7	Jun 19 1969	12-Muluc	3
Feb 4 1969	7-Ix	3	Apr 13 1969	10-Ik	8	Jun 20 1969	13-Oc	4
Feb 5 1969	8-Men	4	Apr 14 1969	11-Akbal	9	Jun 21 1969	1-Chuen	5
Feb 6 1969	9-Cib	5	Apr 15 1969	12-Kan	1	Jun 22 1969	2-Eb	6
Feb 7 1969	10-Caban	6	Apr 16 1969	13-Chicchan	2	Jun 23 1969	3-Ben	7
Feb 8 1969	11-Etz'nab	7	Apr 17 1969	1-Cimi	3	Jun 24 1969	4-Ix	8
Feb 9 1969	12-Cauac	8	Apr 18 1969	2-Manik	4	Jun 25 1969	5-Men	9
Feb 10 1969	13-Ahau	9	Apr 19 1969	3-Lamat	5	Jun 26 1969	6-Cib	1
Feb 11 1969	1-Imix	1	Apr 20 1969	4-Muluc	6	Jun 27 1969	7-Caban	2
Feb 12 1969	2-Ik	2	Apr 21 1969	5-Oc	7	Jun 28 1969	8-Etz'nab	3
Feb 13 1969	3-Akbal	3	Apr 22 1969	6-Chuen	8	Jun 29 1969	9-Cauac	4
Feb 14 1969	4-Kan	4	Apr 23 1969	7-Eb	9	Jun 30 1969	10-Ahau	5
Feb 15 1969	5-Chicchan	5	Apr 24 1969	8-Ben	1	Jul 1 1969	11-Imix	6
Feb 16 1969	6-Cimi	6	Apr 25 1969	9-Ix	2	Jul 2 1969	12-Ik	7
Feb 17 1969	7-Manik	7	Apr 26 1969	10-Men	3	Jul 3 1969	13-Akbal	8
Feb 18 1969	8-Lamat	8	Apr 27 1969	11-Cib	4	Jul 4 1969	1-Kan	9
Feb 19 1969	9-Muluc	9	Apr 28 1969	12-Caban	5	Jul 5 1969	2-Chicchan	1
Feb 20 1969	10-Oc	1	Apr 29 1969	13-Etz'nab	6	Jul 6 1969	3-Cimi	2
Feb 21 1969	11-Chuen	2	Apr 30 1969	1-Cauac	7	Jul 7 1969	4-Manik	3
Feb 22 1969	12-Eb	3	May 1 1969	2-Ahau	8	Jul 8 1969	5-Lamat	4
Feb 23 1969	13-Ben	4	May 2 1969	3-Imix	9	Jul 9 1969	6-Muluc	5
Feb 24 1969	1-Ix	5	May 3 1969	4-Ik	1	Jul 10 1969	7-Oc	6
Feb 25 1969	2-Men	6	May 4 1969	5-Akbal	2	Jul 11 1969	8-Chuen	7
Feb 26 1969	3-Cib	7	May 5 1969	6-Kan	3	Jul 12 1969	9-Eb	8
Feb 27 1969	4-Caban	8	May 6 1969	7-Chicchan	4	Jul 13 1969	10-Ben	9
Feb 28 1969	5-Etz'nab	9	May 7 1969	8-Cimi	5	Jul 14 1969	11-Ix	1
Mar 1 1969	6-Cauac	1	May 8 1969	9-Manik	6	Jul 15 1969	12-Men	2
Mar 2 1969	7-Ahau	2	May 9 1969	10-Lamat	7	Jul 16 1969	13-Cib	3
Mar 3 1969	8-Imix	3	May 10 1969	11-Muluc	8	Jul 17 1969	1-Caban	4
Mar 4 1969	9-Ik	4	May 11 1969	12-Oc	9	Jul 18 1969	2-Etz'nab	5
Mar 5 1969	10-Akbal	5	May 12 1969	13-Chuen	1	Jul 19 1969	3-Cauac	6
Mar 6 1969	11-Kan	6	May 13 1969	1-Eb	2	Jul 20 1969	4-Ahau	7
Mar 7 1969	12-Chicchan	7	May 14 1969	2-Ben	3	Jul 21 1969	5-Imix	8
Mar 8 1969	13-Cimi	8	May 15 1969	3-Ix	4	Jul 22 1969	6-Ik	9
Mar 9 1969	1-Manik	9	May 16 1969	4-Men	5	Jul 23 1969	7-Akbal	1
Mar 10 1969	2-Lamat	1	May 17 1969	5-Cib	6	Jul 24 1969	8-Kan	2
Mar 11 1969	3-Muluc	2	May 18 1969	6-Caban	7	Jul 25 1969	9-Chicchan	3
Mar 12 1969	4-Oc	3	May 19 1969	7-Etz'nab	8	Jul 26 1969	10-Cimi	4
Mar 13 1969	5-Chuen	4	May 20 1969	8-Cauac	9	Jul 27 1969	11-Manik	5
Mar 14 1969	6-Eb	5	May 21 1969	9-Ahau	1	Jul 28 1969	12-Lamat	6
Mar 15 1969	7-Ben	6	May 22 1969	10-Imix	2	Jul 29 1969	13-Muluc	7
Mar 16 1969	8-Ix	7	May 23 1969	11-Ik	3	Jul 30 1969	1-Oc	8
Mar 17 1969	9-Men	8	May 24 1969	12-Akbal	4	Jul 31 1969	2-Chuen	9
Mar 18 1969	10-Cib	9	May 25 1969	13-Kan	5	Aug 1 1969	3-Eb	1
Mar 19 1969	11-Caban	1	May 26 1969	1-Chicchan	6	Aug 2 1969	4-Ben	2
Mar 20 1969	12-Etz'nab	2	May 27 1969	2-Cimi	7	Aug 3 1969	5-Ix	3
Mar 21 1969	13-Cauac	3	May 28 1969	3-Manik	8	Aug 4 1969	6-Men	4
Mar 22 1969	1-Ahau	4	May 29 1969	4-Lamat	9	Aug 5 1969	7-Cib	5
Mar 23 1969	2-Imix	5	May 30 1969	5-Muluc	1	Aug 6 1969	8-Caban	6
Mar 24 1969	3-Ik	6	May 31 1969	6-Oc	2	Aug 7 1969	9-Etz'nab	7
Mar 25 1969	4-Akbal	7	Jun 1 1969	7-Chuen	3	Aug 8 1969	10-Cauac	8
Mar 26 1969	5-Kan	8	Jun 2 1969	8-Eb	4	Aug 9 1969	11-Ahau	9
Mar 27 1969	6-Chicchan	9	Jun 3 1969	9-Ben	5	Aug 10 1969	12-Imix	1
Mar 28 1969	7-Cimi	1	Jun 4 1969	10-Ix	6	Aug 11 1969	13-Ik	2
Mar 29 1969	8-Manik	2	Jun 5 1969	11-Men	7	Aug 12 1969	1-Akbal	3
Mar 30 1969	9-Lamat	3	Jun 6 1969	12-Cib	8	Aug 13 1969	2-Kan	4
Mar 31 1969	10-Muluc	4	Jun 7 1969	13-Caban	9	Aug 14 1969	3-Chicchan	5
Apr 1 1969	11-Oc	5	Jun 8 1969	1-Etz'nab	1	Aug 15 1969	4-Cimi	6
Apr 2 1969	12-Chuen	6	Jun 9 1969	2-Cauac	2	Aug 16 1969	5-Manik	7
Apr 3 1969	13-Eb	7	Jun 10 1969	3-Ahau	3	Aug 17 1969	6-Lamat	8
Apr 4 1969	1-Ben	8	Jun 11 1969	4-Imix	4	Aug 18 1969	7-Muluc	9

Date	Day-Sign	L
Aug 19 1969	8-Oc	1
Aug 20 1969	9-Chuen	2
Aug 21 1969	10-Eb	3
Aug 22 1969	11-Ben	4
Aug 23 1969	12-Ix	5
Aug 24 1969	13-Men	6
Aug 25 1969	1-Cib	7
Aug 26 1969	2-Caban	8
Aug 27 1969	3-Etz'nab	9
Aug 28 1969	4-Cauac	1
Aug 29 1969	5-Ahau	2
Aug 30 1969	6-Imix	3
Aug 31 1969	7-Ik	4
Sep 1 1969	8-Akbal	5
Sep 2 1969	9-Kan	6
Sep 3 1969	10-Chicchan	7
Sep 4 1969	11-Cimi	8
Sep 5 1969	12-Manik	9
Sep 6 1969	13-Lamat	1
Sep 7 1969	1-Muluc	2
Sep 8 1969	2-Oc	3
Sep 9 1969	3-Chuen	4
Sep 10 1969	4-Eb	5
Sep 11 1969	5-Ben	6
Sep 12 1969	6-Ix	7
Sep 13 1969	7-Men	8
Sep 14 1969	8-Cib	9
Sep 15 1969	9-Caban	1
Sep 16 1969	10-Etz'nab	2
Sep 17 1969	11-Cauac	3
Sep 18 1969	12-Ahau	4
Sep 19 1969	13-Imix	5
Sep 20 1969	1-Ik	6
Sep 21 1969	2-Akbal	7
Sep 22 1969	3-Kan	8
Sep 23 1969	4-Chicchan	9
Sep 24 1969	5-Cimi	1
Sep 25 1969	6-Manik	2
Sep 26 1969	7-Lamat	3
Sep 27 1969	8-Muluc	4
Sep 28 1969	9-Oc	5
Sep 29 1969	10-Chuen	6
Sep 30 1969	11-Eb	7
Oct 1 1969	12-Ben	8
Oct 2 1969	13-Ix	9
Oct 3 1969	1-Men	1
Oct 4 1969	2-Cib	2
Oct 5 1969	3-Caban	3
Oct 6 1969	4-Etz'nab	4
Oct 7 1969	5-Cauac	5
Oct 8 1969	6-Ahau	6
Oct 9 1969	7-Imix	7
Oct 10 1969	8-Ik	8
Oct 11 1969	9-Akbal	9
Oct 12 1969	10-Kan	1
Oct 13 1969	11-Chicchan	2
Oct 14 1969	12-Cimi	3
Oct 15 1969	13-Manik	4
Oct 16 1969	1-Lamat	5
Oct 17 1969	2-Muluc	6
Oct 18 1969	3-Oc	7
Oct 19 1969	4-Chuen	8
Oct 20 1969	5-Eb	9
Oct 21 1969	6-Ben	1
Oct 22 1969	7-Ix	2
Oct 23 1969	8-Men	3
Oct 24 1969	9-Cib	4
Oct 25 1969	10-Caban	5

Date	Day-Sign	L
Oct 26 1969	11-Etz'nab	6
Oct 27 1969	12-Cauac	7
Oct 28 1969	13-Ahau	8
Oct 29 1969	1-Imix	9
Oct 30 1969	2-Ik	1
Oct 31 1969	3-Akbal	2
Nov 1 1969	4-Kan	3
Nov 2 1969	5-Chicchan	4
Nov 3 1969	6-Cimi	5
Nov 4 1969	7-Manik	6
Nov 5 1969	8-Lamat	7
Nov 6 1969	9-Muluc	8
Nov 7 1969	10-Oc	9
Nov 8 1969	11-Chuen	1
Nov 9 1969	12-Eb	2
Nov 10 1969	13-Ben	3
Nov 11 1969	1-Ix	4
Nov 12 1969	2-Men	5
Nov 13 1969	3-Cib	6
Nov 14 1969	4-Caban	7
Nov 15 1969	5-Etz'nab	8
Nov 16 1969	6-Cauac	9
Nov 17 1969	7-Ahau	1
Nov 18 1969	8-Imix	2
Nov 19 1969	9-Ik	3
Nov 20 1969	10-Akbal	4
Nov 21 1969	11-Kan	5
Nov 22 1969	12-Chicchan	6
Nov 23 1969	13-Cimi	7
Nov 24 1969	1-Manik	8
Nov 25 1969	2-Lamat	9
Nov 26 1969	3-Muluc	1
Nov 27 1969	4-Oc	2
Nov 28 1969	5-Chuen	3
Nov 29 1969	6-Eb	4
Nov 30 1969	7-Ben	5
Dec 1 1969	8-Ix	6
Dec 2 1969	9-Men	7
Dec 3 1969	10-Cib	8
Dec 4 1969	11-Caban	9
Dec 5 1969	12-Etz'nab	1
Dec 6 1969	13-Cauac	2
Dec 7 1969	1-Ahau	3
Dec 8 1969	2-Imix	4
Dec 9 1969	3-Ik	5
Dec 10 1969	4-Akbal	6
Dec 11 1969	5-Kan	7
Dec 12 1969	6-Chicchan	8
Dec 13 1969	7-Cimi	9
Dec 14 1969	8-Manik	1
Dec 15 1969	9-Lamat	2
Dec 16 1969	10-Muluc	3
Dec 17 1969	11-Oc	4
Dec 18 1969	12-Chuen	5
Dec 19 1969	13-Eb	6
Dec 20 1969	1-Ben	7
Dec 21 1969	2-Ix	8
Dec 22 1969	3-Men	9
Dec 23 1969	4-Cib	1
Dec 24 1969	5-Caban	2
Dec 25 1969	6-Etz'nab	3
Dec 26 1969	7-Cauac	4
Dec 27 1969	8-Ahau	5
Dec 28 1969	9-Imix	6
Dec 29 1969	10-Ik	7
Dec 30 1969	11-Akbal	8
Dec 31 1969	12-Kan	9
Jan 1 1970	13-Chicchan	1

Date	Day-Sign	L
Jan 2 1970	1-Cimi	2
Jan 3 1970	2-Manik	3
Jan 4 1970	3-Lamat	4
Jan 5 1970	4-Muluc	5
Jan 6 1970	5-Oc	6
Jan 7 1970	6-Chuen	7
Jan 8 1970	7-Eb	8
Jan 9 1970	8-Ben	9
Jan 10 1970	9-Ix	1
Jan 11 1970	10-Men	2
Jan 12 1970	11-Cib	3
Jan 13 1970	12-Caban	4
Jan 14 1970	13-Etz'nab	5
Jan 15 1970	1-Cauac	6
Jan 16 1970	2-Ahau	7
Jan 17 1970	3-Imix	8
Jan 18 1970	4-Ik	9
Jan 19 1970	5-Akbal	1
Jan 20 1970	6-Kan	2
Jan 21 1970	7-Chicchan	3
Jan 22 1970	8-Cimi	4
Jan 23 1970	9-Manik	5
Jan 24 1970	10-Lamat	6
Jan 25 1970	11-Muluc	7
Jan 26 1970	12-Oc	8
Jan 27 1970	13-Chuen	9
Jan 28 1970	1-Eb	1
Jan 29 1970	2-Ben	2
Jan 30 1970	3-Ix	3
Jan 31 1970	4-Men	4
Feb 1 1970	5-Cib	5
Feb 2 1970	6-Caban	6
Feb 3 1970	7-Etz'nab	7
Feb 4 1970	8-Cauac	8
Feb 5 1970	9-Ahau	9
Feb 6 1970	10-Imix	1
Feb 7 1970	11-Ik	2
Feb 8 1970	12-Akbal	3
Feb 9 1970	13-Kan	4
Feb 10 1970	1-Chicchan	5
Feb 11 1970	2-Cimi	6
Feb 12 1970	3-Manik	7
Feb 13 1970	4-Lamat	8
Feb 14 1970	5-Muluc	9
Feb 15 1970	6-Oc	1
Feb 16 1970	7-Chuen	2
Feb 17 1970	8-Eb	3
Feb 18 1970	9-Ben	4
Feb 19 1970	10-Ix	5
Feb 20 1970	11-Men	6
Feb 21 1970	12-Cib	7
Feb 22 1970	13-Caban	8
Feb 23 1970	1-Etz'nab	9
Feb 24 1970	2-Cauac	1
Feb 25 1970	3-Ahau	2
Feb 26 1970	4-Imix	3
Feb 27 1970	5-Ik	4
Feb 28 1970	6-Akbal	5
Mar 1 1970	7-Kan	6
Mar 2 1970	8-Chicchan	7
Mar 3 1970	9-Cimi	8
Mar 4 1970	10-Manik	9
Mar 5 1970	11-Lamat	1
Mar 6 1970	12-Muluc	2
Mar 7 1970	13-Oc	3
Mar 8 1970	1-Chuen	4
Mar 9 1970	2-Eb	5
Mar 10 1970	3-Ben	6

Date	Day-Sign	L
Mar 11 1970	4-Ix	7
Mar 12 1970	5-Men	8
Mar 13 1970	6-Cib	9
Mar 14 1970	7-Caban	1
Mar 15 1970	8-Etz'nab	2
Mar 16 1970	9-Cauac	3
Mar 17 1970	10-Ahau	4
Mar 18 1970	11-Imix	5
Mar 19 1970	12-Ik	6
Mar 20 1970	13-Akbal	7
Mar 21 1970	1-Kan	8
Mar 22 1970	2-Chicchan	9
Mar 23 1970	3-Cimi	1
Mar 24 1970	4-Manik	2
Mar 25 1970	5-Lamat	3
Mar 26 1970	6-Muluc	4
Mar 27 1970	7-Oc	5
Mar 28 1970	8-Chuen	6
Mar 29 1970	9-Eb	7
Mar 30 1970	10-Ben	8
Mar 31 1970	11-Ix	9
Apr 1 1970	12-Men	1
Apr 2 1970	13-Cib	2
Apr 3 1970	1-Caban	3
Apr 4 1970	2-Etz'nab	4
Apr 5 1970	3-Cauac	5
Apr 6 1970	4-Ahau	6
Apr 7 1970	5-Imix	7
Apr 8 1970	6-Ik	8
Apr 9 1970	7-Akbal	9
Apr 10 1970	8-Kan	1
Apr 11 1970	9-Chicchan	2
Apr 12 1970	10-Cimi	3
Apr 13 1970	11-Manik	4
Apr 14 1970	12-Lamat	5
Apr 15 1970	13-Muluc	6
Apr 16 1970	1-Oc	7
Apr 17 1970	2-Chuen	8
Apr 18 1970	3-Eb	9
Apr 19 1970	4-Ben	1
Apr 20 1970	5-Ix	2
Apr 21 1970	6-Men	3
Apr 22 1970	7-Cib	4
Apr 23 1970	8-Caban	5
Apr 24 1970	9-Etz'nab	6
Apr 25 1970	10-Cauac	7
Apr 26 1970	11-Ahau	8
Apr 27 1970	12-Imix	9
Apr 28 1970	13-Ik	1
Apr 29 1970	1-Akbal	2
Apr 30 1970	2-Kan	3
May 1 1970	3-Chicchan	4
May 2 1970	4-Cimi	5
May 3 1970	5-Manik	6
May 4 1970	6-Lamat	7
May 5 1970	7-Muluc	8
May 6 1970	8-Oc	9
May 7 1970	9-Chuen	1
May 8 1970	10-Eb	2
May 9 1970	11-Ben	3
May 10 1970	12-Ix	4
May 11 1970	13-Men	5
May 12 1970	1-Cib	6
May 13 1970	2-Caban	7
May 14 1970	3-Etz'nab	8
May 15 1970	4-Cauac	9
May 16 1970	5-Ahau	1
May 17 1970	6-Imix	2

Date	Day-Sign	L
May 18 1970	7-Ik	3
May 19 1970	8-Akbal	4
May 20 1970	9-Kan	5
May 21 1970	10-Chicchan	6
May 22 1970	11-Cimi	7
May 23 1970	12-Manik	8
May 24 1970	13-Lamat	9
May 25 1970	1-Muluc	1
May 26 1970	2-Oc	2
May 27 1970	3-Chuen	3
May 28 1970	4-Eb	4
May 29 1970	5-Ben	5
May 30 1970	6-Ix	6
May 31 1970	7-Men	7
Jun 1 1970	8-Cib	8
Jun 2 1970	9-Caban	9
Jun 3 1970	10-Etz'nab	1
Jun 4 1970	11-Cauac	2
Jun 5 1970	12-Ahau	3
Jun 6 1970	13-Imix	4
Jun 7 1970	1-Ik	5
Jun 8 1970	2-Akbal	6
Jun 9 1970	3-Kan	7
Jun 10 1970	4-Chicchan	8
Jun 11 1970	5-Cimi	9
Jun 12 1970	6-Manik	1
Jun 13 1970	7-Lamat	2
Jun 14 1970	8-Muluc	3
Jun 15 1970	9-Oc	4
Jun 16 1970	10-Chuen	5
Jun 17 1970	11-Eb	6
Jun 18 1970	12-Ben	7
Jun 19 1970	13-Ix	8
Jun 20 1970	1-Men	9
Jun 21 1970	2-Cib	1
Jun 22 1970	3-Caban	2
Jun 23 1970	4-Etz'nab	3
Jun 24 1970	5-Cauac	4
Jun 25 1970	6-Ahau	5
Jun 26 1970	7-Imix	6
Jun 27 1970	8-Ik	7
Jun 28 1970	9-Akbal	8
Jun 29 1970	10-Kan	9
Jun 30 1970	11-Chicchan	1
Jul 1 1970	12-Cimi	2
Jul 2 1970	13-Manik	3
Jul 3 1970	1-Lamat	4
Jul 4 1970	2-Muluc	5
Jul 5 1970	3-Oc	6
Jul 6 1970	4-Chuen	7
Jul 7 1970	5-Eb	8
Jul 8 1970	6-Ben	9
Jul 9 1970	7-Ix	1
Jul 10 1970	8-Men	2
Jul 11 1970	9-Cib	3
Jul 12 1970	10-Caban	4
Jul 13 1970	11-Etz'nab	5
Jul 14 1970	12-Cauac	6
Jul 15 1970	13-Ahau	7
Jul 16 1970	1-Imix	8
Jul 17 1970	2-Ik	9
Jul 18 1970	3-Akbal	1
Jul 19 1970	4-Kan	2
Jul 20 1970	5-Chicchan	3
Jul 21 1970	6-Cimi	4
Jul 22 1970	7-Manik	5
Jul 23 1970	8-Lamat	6
Jul 24 1970	9-Muluc	7

Date	Day-Sign	L
Jul 25 1970	10-Oc	8
Jul 26 1970	11-Chuen	9
Jul 27 1970	12-Eb	1
Jul 28 1970	13-Ben	2
Jul 29 1970	1-Ix	3
Jul 30 1970	2-Men	4
Jul 31 1970	3-Cib	5
Aug 1 1970	4-Caban	6
Aug 2 1970	5-Etz'nab	7
Aug 3 1970	6-Cauac	8
Aug 4 1970	7-Ahau	9
Aug 5 1970	8-Imix	1
Aug 6 1970	9-Ik	2
Aug 7 1970	10-Akbal	3
Aug 8 1970	11-Kan	4
Aug 9 1970	12-Chicchan	5
Aug 10 1970	13-Cimi	6
Aug 11 1970	1-Manik	7
Aug 12 1970	2-Lamat	8
Aug 13 1970	3-Muluc	9
Aug 14 1970	4-Oc	1
Aug 15 1970	5-Chuen	2
Aug 16 1970	6-Eb	3
Aug 17 1970	7-Ben	4
Aug 18 1970	8-Ix	5
Aug 19 1970	9-Men	6
Aug 20 1970	10-Cib	7
Aug 21 1970	11-Caban	8
Aug 22 1970	12-Etz'nab	9
Aug 23 1970	13-Cauac	1
Aug 24 1970	1-Ahau	2
Aug 25 1970	2-Imix	3
Aug 26 1970	3-Ik	4
Aug 27 1970	4-Akbal	5
Aug 28 1970	5-Kan	6
Aug 29 1970	6-Chicchan	7
Aug 30 1970	7-Cimi	8
Aug 31 1970	8-Manik	9
Sep 1 1970	9-Lamat	1
Sep 2 1970	10-Muluc	2
Sep 3 1970	11-Oc	3
Sep 4 1970	12-Chuen	4
Sep 5 1970	13-Eb	5
Sep 6 1970	1-Ben	6
Sep 7 1970	2-Ix	7
Sep 8 1970	3-Men	8
Sep 9 1970	4-Cib	9
Sep 10 1970	5-Caban	1
Sep 11 1970	6-Etz'nab	2
Sep 12 1970	7-Cauac	3
Sep 13 1970	8-Ahau	4
Sep 14 1970	9-Imix	5
Sep 15 1970	10-Ik	6
Sep 16 1970	11-Akbal	7
Sep 17 1970	12-Kan	8
Sep 18 1970	13-Chicchan	9
Sep 19 1970	1-Cimi	1
Sep 20 1970	2-Manik	2
Sep 21 1970	3-Lamat	3
Sep 22 1970	4-Muluc	4
Sep 23 1970	5-Oc	5
Sep 24 1970	6-Chuen	6
Sep 25 1970	7-Eb	7
Sep 26 1970	8-Ben	8
Sep 27 1970	9-Ix	9
Sep 28 1970	10-Men	1
Sep 29 1970	11-Cib	2
Sep 30 1970	12-Caban	3

Date	Day-Sign	L	Date	Day-Sign	L	Date	Day-Sign	L
Oct 1 1970	13-Etz'nab	4	Dec 8 1970	3-Cimi	9	Feb 14 1971	6-Ix	5
Oct 2 1970	1-Cauac	5	Dec 9 1970	4-Manik	1	Feb 15 1971	7-Men	6
Oct 3 1970	2-Ahau	6	Dec 10 1970	5-Lamat	2	Feb 16 1971	8-Cib	7
Oct 4 1970	3-Imix	7	Dec 11 1970	6-Muluc	3	Feb 17 1971	9-Caban	8
Oct 5 1970	4-Ik	8	Dec 12 1970	7-Oc	4	Feb 18 1971	10-Etz'nab	9
Oct 6 1970	5-Akbal	9	Dec 13 1970	8-Chuen	5	Feb 19 1971	11-Cauac	1
Oct 7 1970	6-Kan	1	Dec 14 1970	9-Eb	6	Feb 20 1971	12-Ahau	2
Oct 8 1970	7-Chicchan	2	Dec 15 1970	10-Ben	7	Feb 21 1971	13-Imix	3
Oct 9 1970	8-Cimi	3	Dec 16 1970	11-Ix	8	Feb 22 1971	1-Ik	4
Oct 10 1970	9-Manik	4	Dec 17 1970	12-Men	9	Feb 23 1971	2-Akbal	5
Oct 11 1970	10-Lamat	5	Dec 18 1970	13-Cib	1	Feb 24 1971	3-Kan	6
Oct 12 1970	11-Muluc	6	Dec 19 1970	1-Caban	2	Feb 25 1971	4-Chicchan	7
Oct 13 1970	12-Oc	7	Dec 20 1970	2-Etz'nab	3	Feb 26 1971	5-Cimi	8
Oct 14 1970	13-Chuen	8	Dec 21 1970	3-Cauac	4	Feb 27 1971	6-Manik	9
Oct 15 1970	1-Eb	9	Dec 22 1970	4-Ahau	5	Feb 28 1971	7-Lamat	1
Oct 16 1970	2-Ben	1	Dec 23 1970	5-Imix	6	Mar 1 1971	8-Muluc	2
Oct 17 1970	3-Ix	2	Dec 24 1970	6-Ik	7	Mar 2 1971	9-Oc	3
Oct 18 1970	4-Men	3	Dec 25 1970	7-Akbal	8	Mar 3 1971	10-Chuen	4
Oct 19 1970	5-Cib	4	Dec 26 1970	8-Kan	9	Mar 4 1971	11-Eb	5
Oct 20 1970	6-Caban	5	Dec 27 1970	9-Chicchan	1	Mar 5 1971	12-Ben	6
Oct 21 1970	7-Etz'nab	6	Dec 28 1970	10-Cimi	2	Mar 6 1971	13-Ix	7
Oct 22 1970	8-Cauac	7	Dec 29 1970	11-Manik	3	Mar 7 1971	1-Men	8
Oct 23 1970	9-Ahau	8	Dec 30 1970	12-Lamat	4	Mar 8 1971	2-Cib	9
Oct 24 1970	10-Imix	9	Dec 31 1970	13-Muluc	5	Mar 9 1971	3-Caban	1
Oct 25 1970	11-Ik	1	Jan 1 1971	1-Oc	6	Mar 10 1971	4-Etz'nab	2
Oct 26 1970	12-Akbal	2	Jan 2 1971	2-Chuen	7	Mar 11 1971	5-Cauac	3
Oct 27 1970	13-Kan	3	Jan 3 1971	3-Eb	8	Mar 12 1971	6-Ahau	4
Oct 28 1970	1-Chicchan	4	Jan 4 1971	4-Ben	9	Mar 13 1971	7-Imix	5
Oct 29 1970	2-Cimi	5	Jan 5 1971	5-Ix	1	Mar 14 1971	8-Ik	6
Oct 30 1970	3-Manik	6	Jan 6 1971	6-Men	2	Mar 15 1971	9-Akbal	7
Oct 31 1970	4-Lamat	7	Jan 7 1971	7-Cib	3	Mar 16 1971	10-Kan	8
Nov 1 1970	5-Muluc	8	Jan 8 1971	8-Caban	4	Mar 17 1971	11-Chicchan	9
Nov 2 1970	6-Oc	9	Jan 9 1971	9-Etz'nab	5	Mar 18 1971	12-Cimi	1
Nov 3 1970	7-Chuen	1	Jan 10 1971	10-Cauac	6	Mar 19 1971	13-Manik	2
Nov 4 1970	8-Eb	2	Jan 11 1971	11-Ahau	7	Mar 20 1971	1-Lamat	3
Nov 5 1970	9-Ben	3	Jan 12 1971	12-Imix	8	Mar 21 1971	2-Muluc	4
Nov 6 1970	10-Ix	4	Jan 13 1971	13-Ik	9	Mar 22 1971	3-Oc	5
Nov 7 1970	11-Men	5	Jan 14 1971	1-Akbal	1	Mar 23 1971	4-Chuen	6
Nov 8 1970	12-Cib	6	Jan 15 1971	2-Kan	2	Mar 24 1971	5-Eb	7
Nov 9 1970	13-Caban	7	Jan 16 1971	3-Chicchan	3	Mar 25 1971	6-Ben	8
Nov 10 1970	1-Etz'nab	8	Jan 17 1971	4-Cimi	4	Mar 26 1971	7-Ix	9
Nov 11 1970	2-Cauac	9	Jan 18 1971	5-Manik	5	Mar 27 1971	8-Men	1
Nov 12 1970	3-Ahau	1	Jan 19 1971	6-Lamat	6	Mar 28 1971	9-Cib	2
Nov 13 1970	4-Imix	2	Jan 20 1971	7-Muluc	7	Mar 29 1971	10-Caban	3
Nov 14 1970	5-Ik	3	Jan 21 1971	8-Oc	8	Mar 30 1971	11-Etz'nab	4
Nov 15 1970	6-Akbal	4	Jan 22 1971	9-Chuen	9	Mar 31 1971	12-Cauac	5
Nov 16 1970	7-Kan	5	Jan 23 1971	10-Eb	1	Apr 1 1971	13-Ahau	6
Nov 17 1970	8-Chicchan	6	Jan 24 1971	11-Ben	2	Apr 2 1971	1-Imix	7
Nov 18 1970	9-Cimi	7	Jan 25 1971	12-Ix	3	Apr 3 1971	2-Ik	8
Nov 19 1970	10-Manik	8	Jan 26 1971	13-Men	4	Apr 4 1971	3-Akbal	9
Nov 20 1970	11-Lamat	9	Jan 27 1971	1-Cib	5	Apr 5 1971	4-Kan	1
Nov 21 1970	12-Muluc	1	Jan 28 1971	2-Caban	6	Apr 6 1971	5-Chicchan	2
Nov 22 1970	13-Oc	2	Jan 29 1971	3-Etz'nab	7	Apr 7 1971	6-Cimi	3
Nov 23 1970	1-Chuen	3	Jan 30 1971	4-Cauac	8	Apr 8 1971	7-Manik	4
Nov 24 1970	2-Eb	4	Jan 31 1971	5-Ahau	9	Apr 9 1971	8-Lamat	5
Nov 25 1970	3-Ben	5	Feb 1 1971	6-Imix	1	Apr 10 1971	9-Muluc	6
Nov 26 1970	4-Ix	6	Feb 2 1971	7-Ik	2	Apr 11 1971	10-Oc	7
Nov 27 1970	5-Men	7	Feb 3 1971	8-Akbal	3	Apr 12 1971	11-Chuen	8
Nov 28 1970	6-Cib	8	Feb 4 1971	9-Kan	4	Apr 13 1971	12-Eb	9
Nov 29 1970	7-Caban	9	Feb 5 1971	10-Chicchan	5	Apr 14 1971	13-Ben	1
Nov 30 1970	8-Etz'nab	1	Feb 6 1971	11-Cimi	6	Apr 15 1971	1-Ix	2
Dec 1 1970	9-Cauac	2	Feb 7 1971	12-Manik	7	Apr 16 1971	2-Men	3
Dec 2 1970	10-Ahau	3	Feb 8 1971	13-Lamat	8	Apr 17 1971	3-Cib	4
Dec 3 1970	11-Imix	4	Feb 9 1971	1-Muluc	9	Apr 18 1971	4-Caban	5
Dec 4 1970	12-Ik	5	Feb 10 1971	2-Oc	1	Apr 19 1971	5-Etz'nab	6
Dec 5 1970	13-Akbal	6	Feb 11 1971	3-Chuen	2	Apr 20 1971	6-Cauac	7
Dec 6 1970	1-Kan	7	Feb 12 1971	4-Eb	3	Apr 21 1971	7-Ahau	8
Dec 7 1970	2-Chicchan	8	Feb 13 1971	5-Ben	4	Apr 22 1971	8-Imix	9

Date	Day-Sign	L	Date	Day-Sign	L	Date	Day-Sign	L
Apr 23 1971	9-Ik	1	Jun 30 1971	12-Oc	6	Sep 6 1971	2-Etz'nab	2
Apr 24 1971	10-Akbal	2	Jul 1 1971	13-Chuen	7	Sep 7 1971	3-Cauac	3
Apr 25 1971	11-Kan	3	Jul 2 1971	1-Eb	8	Sep 8 1971	4-Ahau	4
Apr 26 1971	12-Chicchan	4	Jul 3 1971	2-Ben	9	Sep 9 1971	5-Imix	5
Apr 27 1971	13-Cimi	5	Jul 4 1971	3-Ix	1	Sep 10 1971	6-Ik	6
Apr 28 1971	1-Manik	6	Jul 5 1971	4-Men	2	Sep 11 1971	7-Akbal	7
Apr 29 1971	2-Lamat	7	Jul 6 1971	5-Cib	3	Sep 12 1971	8-Kan	8
Apr 30 1971	3-Muluc	8	Jul 7 1971	6-Caban	4	Sep 13 1971	9-Chicchan	9
May 1 1971	4-Oc	9	Jul 8 1971	7-Etz'nab	5	Sep 14 1971	10-Cimi	1
May 2 1971	5-Chuen	1	Jul 9 1971	8-Cauac	6	Sep 15 1971	11-Manik	2
May 3 1971	6-Eb	2	Jul 10 1971	9-Ahau	7	Sep 16 1971	12-Lamat	3
May 4 1971	7-Ben	3	Jul 11 1971	10-Imix	8	Sep 17 1971	13-Muluc	4
May 5 1971	8-Ix	4	Jul 12 1971	11-Ik	9	Sep 18 1971	1-Oc	5
May 6 1971	9-Men	5	Jul 13 1971	12-Akbal	1	Sep 19 1971	2-Chuen	6
May 7 1971	10-Cib	6	Jul 14 1971	13-Kan	2	Sep 20 1971	3-Eb	7
May 8 1971	11-Caban	7	Jul 15 1971	1-Chicchan	3	Sep 21 1971	4-Ben	8
May 9 1971	12-Etz'nab	8	Jul 16 1971	2-Cimi	4	Sep 22 1971	5-Ix	9
May 10 1971	13-Cauac	9	Jul 17 1971	3-Manik	5	Sep 23 1971	6-Men	1
May 11 1971	1-Ahau	1	Jul 18 1971	4-Lamat	6	Sep 24 1971	7-Cib	2
May 12 1971	2-Imix	2	Jul 19 1971	5-Muluc	7	Sep 25 1971	8-Caban	3
May 13 1971	3-Ik	3	Jul 20 1971	6-Oc	8	Sep 26 1971	9-Etz'nab	4
May 14 1971	4-Akbal	4	Jul 21 1971	7-Chuen	9	Sep 27 1971	10-Cauac	5
May 15 1971	5-Kan	5	Jul 22 1971	8-Eb	1	Sep 28 1971	11-Ahau	6
May 16 1971	6-Chicchan	6	Jul 23 1971	9-Ben	2	Sep 29 1971	12-Imix	7
May 17 1971	7-Cimi	7	Jul 24 1971	10-Ix	3	Sep 30 1971	13-Ik	8
May 18 1971	8-Manik	8	Jul 25 1971	11-Men	4	Oct 1 1971	1-Akbal	9
May 19 1971	9-Lamat	9	Jul 26 1971	12-Cib	5	Oct 2 1971	2-Kan	1
May 20 1971	10-Muluc	1	Jul 27 1971	13-Caban	6	Oct 3 1971	3-Chicchan	2
May 21 1971	11-Oc	2	Jul 28 1971	1-Etz'nab	7	Oct 4 1971	4-Cimi	3
May 22 1971	12-Chuen	3	Jul 29 1971	2-Cauac	8	Oct 5 1971	5-Manik	4
May 23 1971	13-Eb	4	Jul 30 1971	3-Ahau	9	Oct 6 1971	6-Lamat	5
May 24 1971	1-Ben	5	Jul 31 1971	4-Imix	1	Oct 7 1971	7-Muluc	6
May 25 1971	2-Ix	6	Aug 1 1971	5-Ik	2	Oct 8 1971	8-Oc	7
May 26 1971	3-Men	7	Aug 2 1971	6-Akbal	3	Oct 9 1971	9-Chuen	8
May 27 1971	4-Cib	8	Aug 3 1971	7-Kan	4	Oct 10 1971	10-Eb	9
May 28 1971	5-Caban	9	Aug 4 1971	8-Chicchan	5	Oct 11 1971	11-Ben	1
May 29 1971	6-Etz'nab	1	Aug 5 1971	9-Cimi	6	Oct 12 1971	12-Ix	2
May 30 1971	7-Cauac	2	Aug 6 1971	10-Manik	7	Oct 13 1971	13-Men	3
May 31 1971	8-Ahau	3	Aug 7 1971	11-Lamat	8	Oct 14 1971	1-Cib	4
Jun 1 1971	9-Imix	4	Aug 8 1971	12-Muluc	9	Oct 15 1971	2-Caban	5
Jun 2 1971	10-Ik	5	Aug 9 1971	13-Oc	1	Oct 16 1971	3-Etz'nab	6
Jun 3 1971	11-Akbal	6	Aug 10 1971	1-Chuen	2	Oct 17 1971	4-Cauac	7
Jun 4 1971	12-Kan	7	Aug 11 1971	2-Eb	3	Oct 18 1971	5-Ahau	8
Jun 5 1971	13-Chicchan	8	Aug 12 1971	3-Ben	4	Oct 19 1971	6-Imix	9
Jun 6 1971	1-Cimi	9	Aug 13 1971	4-Ix	5	Oct 20 1971	7-Ik	1
Jun 7 1971	2-Manik	1	Aug 14 1971	5-Men	6	Oct 21 1971	8-Akbal	2
Jun 8 1971	3-Lamat	2	Aug 15 1971	6-Cib	7	Oct 22 1971	9-Kan	3
Jun 9 1971	4-Muluc	3	Aug 16 1971	7-Caban	8	Oct 23 1971	10-Chicchan	4
Jun 10 1971	5-Oc	4	Aug 17 1971	8-Etz'nab	9	Oct 24 1971	11-Cimi	5
Jun 11 1971	6-Chuen	5	Aug 18 1971	9-Cauac	1	Oct 25 1971	12-Manik	6
Jun 12 1971	7-Eb	6	Aug 19 1971	10-Ahau	2	Oct 26 1971	13-Lamat	7
Jun 13 1971	8-Ben	7	Aug 20 1971	11-Imix	3	Oct 27 1971	1-Muluc	8
Jun 14 1971	9-Ix	8	Aug 21 1971	12-Ik	4	Oct 28 1971	2-Oc	9
Jun 15 1971	10-Men	9	Aug 22 1971	13-Akbal	5	Oct 29 1971	3-Chuen	1
Jun 16 1971	11-Cib	1	Aug 23 1971	1-Kan	6	Oct 30 1971	4-Eb	2
Jun 17 1971	12-Caban	2	Aug 24 1971	2-Chicchan	7	Oct 31 1971	5-Ben	3
Jun 18 1971	13-Etz'nab	3	Aug 25 1971	3-Cimi	8	Nov 1 1971	6-Ix	4
Jun 19 1971	1-Cauac	4	Aug 26 1971	4-Manik	9	Nov 2 1971	7-Men	5
Jun 20 1971	2-Ahau	5	Aug 27 1971	5-Lamat	1	Nov 3 1971	8-Cib	6
Jun 21 1971	3-Imix	6	Aug 28 1971	6-Muluc	2	Nov 4 1971	9-Caban	7
Jun 22 1971	4-Ik	7	Aug 29 1971	7-Oc	3	Nov 5 1971	10-Etz'nab	8
Jun 23 1971	5-Akbal	8	Aug 30 1971	8-Chuen	4	Nov 6 1971	11-Cauac	9
Jun 24 1971	6-Kan	9	Aug 31 1971	9-Eb	5	Nov 7 1971	12-Ahau	1
Jun 25 1971	7-Chicchan	1	Sep 1 1971	10-Ben	6	Nov 8 1971	13-Imix	2
Jun 26 1971	8-Cimi	2	Sep 2 1971	11-Ix	7	Nov 9 1971	1-Ik	3
Jun 27 1971	9-Manik	3	Sep 3 1971	12-Men	8	Nov 10 1971	2-Akbal	4
Jun 28 1971	10-Lamat	4	Sep 4 1971	13-Cib	9	Nov 11 1971	3-Kan	5
Jun 29 1971	11-Muluc	5	Sep 5 1971	1-Caban	1	Nov 12 1971	4-Chicchan	6

Date	Day-Sign	L
Nov 13 1971	5-Cimi	7
Nov 14 1971	6-Manik	8
Nov 15 1971	7-Lamat	9
Nov 16 1971	8-Muluc	1
Nov 17 1971	9-Oc	2
Nov 18 1971	10-Chuen	3
Nov 19 1971	11-Eb	4
Nov 20 1971	12-Ben	5
Nov 21 1971	13-Ix	6
Nov 22 1971	**1-Men**	7
Nov 23 1971	2-Cib	8
Nov 24 1971	3-Caban	9
Nov 25 1971	4-Etz'nab	1
Nov 26 1971	5-Cauac	2
Nov 27 1971	6-Ahau	3
Nov 28 1971	*7-Imix*	4
Nov 29 1971	8-Ik	5
Nov 30 1971	9-Akbal	6
Dec 1 1971	10-Kan	7
Dec 2 1971	11-Chicchan	8
Dec 3 1971	12-Cimi	9
Dec 4 1971	13-Manik	1
Dec 5 1971	**1-Lamat**	2
Dec 6 1971	2-Muluc	3
Dec 7 1971	3-Oc	4
Dec 8 1971	4-Chuen	5
Dec 9 1971	5-Eb	6
Dec 10 1971	6-Ben	7
Dec 11 1971	7-Ix	8
Dec 12 1971	8-Men	9
Dec 13 1971	9-Cib	1
Dec 14 1971	10-Caban	2
Dec 15 1971	11-Etz'nab	3
Dec 16 1971	12-Cauac	4
Dec 17 1971	13-Ahau	5
Dec 18 1971	**1-Imix**	6
Dec 19 1971	2-Ik	7
Dec 20 1971	3-Akbal	8
Dec 21 1971	4-Kan	9
Dec 22 1971	5-Chicchan	1
Dec 23 1971	6-Cimi	2
Dec 24 1971	7-Manik	3
Dec 25 1971	8-Lamat	4
Dec 26 1971	9-Muluc	5
Dec 27 1971	10-Oc	6
Dec 28 1971	11-Chuen	7
Dec 29 1971	12-Eb	8
Dec 30 1971	13-Ben	9
Dec 31 1971	**1-Ix**	1
Jan 1 1972	2-Men	2
Jan 2 1972	3-Cib	3
Jan 3 1972	4-Caban	4
Jan 4 1972	5-Etz'nab	5
Jan 5 1972	6-Cauac	6
Jan 6 1972	7-Ahau	7
Jan 7 1972	*8-Imix*	8
Jan 8 1972	9-Ik	9
Jan 9 1972	10-Akbal	1
Jan 10 1972	11-Kan	2
Jan 11 1972	12-Chicchan	3
Jan 12 1972	13-Cimi	4
Jan 13 1972	**1-Manik**	5
Jan 14 1972	2-Lamat	6
Jan 15 1972	3-Muluc	7
Jan 16 1972	4-Oc	8
Jan 17 1972	5-Chuen	9
Jan 18 1972	6-Eb	1
Jan 19 1972	7-Ben	2

Date	Day-Sign	L
Jan 20 1972	8-Ix	3
Jan 21 1972	9-Men	4
Jan 22 1972	10-Cib	5
Jan 23 1972	11-Caban	6
Jan 24 1972	12-Etz'nab	7
Jan 25 1972	13-Cauac	8
Jan 26 1972	**1-Ahau**	9
Jan 27 1972	*2-Imix*	1
Jan 28 1972	3-Ik	2
Jan 29 1972	4-Akbal	3
Jan 30 1972	5-Kan	4
Jan 31 1972	6-Chicchan	5
Feb 1 1972	7-Cimi	6
Feb 2 1972	8-Manik	7
Feb 3 1972	9-Lamat	8
Feb 4 1972	10-Muluc	9
Feb 5 1972	11-Oc	1
Feb 6 1972	12-Chuen	2
Feb 7 1972	13-Eb	3
Feb 8 1972	**1-Ben**	4
Feb 9 1972	2-Ix	5
Feb 10 1972	3-Men	6
Feb 11 1972	4-Cib	7
Feb 12 1972	5-Caban	8
Feb 13 1972	6-Etz'nab	9
Feb 14 1972	7-Cauac	1
Feb 15 1972	8-Ahau	2
Feb 16 1972	*9-Imix*	3
Feb 17 1972	10-Ik	4
Feb 18 1972	11-Akbal	5
Feb 19 1972	12-Kan	6
Feb 20 1972	13-Chicchan	7
Feb 21 1972	**1-Cimi**	8
Feb 22 1972	2-Manik	9
Feb 23 1972	3-Lamat	1
Feb 24 1972	4-Muluc	2
Feb 25 1972	5-Oc	3
Feb 26 1972	6-Chuen	4
Feb 27 1972	7-Eb	5
Feb 28 1972	8-Ben	6
Feb 29 1972	9-Ix	7
Mar 1 1972	10-Men	8
Mar 2 1972	11-Cib	9
Mar 3 1972	12-Caban	1
Mar 4 1972	13-Etz'nab	2
Mar 5 1972	**1-Cauac**	3
Mar 6 1972	2-Ahau	4
Mar 7 1972	*3-Imix*	5
Mar 8 1972	4-Ik	6
Mar 9 1972	5-Akbal	7
Mar 10 1972	6-Kan	8
Mar 11 1972	7-Chicchan	9
Mar 12 1972	8-Cimi	1
Mar 13 1972	9-Manik	2
Mar 14 1972	10-Lamat	3
Mar 15 1972	11-Muluc	4
Mar 16 1972	12-Oc	5
Mar 17 1972	13-Chuen	6
Mar 18 1972	**1-Eb**	7
Mar 19 1972	2-Ben	8
Mar 20 1972	3-Ix	9
Mar 21 1972	4-Men	1
Mar 22 1972	5-Cib	2
Mar 23 1972	6-Caban	3
Mar 24 1972	7-Etz'nab	4
Mar 25 1972	8-Cauac	5
Mar 26 1972	9-Ahau	6
Mar 27 1972	*10-Imix*	7

Date	Day-Sign	L
Mar 28 1972	11-Ik	8
Mar 29 1972	12-Akbal	9
Mar 30 1972	13-Kan	1
Mar 31 1972	**1-Chicchan**	2
Apr 1 1972	2-Cimi	3
Apr 2 1972	3-Manik	4
Apr 3 1972	4-Lamat	5
Apr 4 1972	5-Muluc	6
Apr 5 1972	6-Oc	7
Apr 6 1972	7-Chuen	8
Apr 7 1972	8-Eb	9
Apr 8 1972	9-Ben	1
Apr 9 1972	10-Ix	2
Apr 10 1972	11-Men	3
Apr 11 1972	12-Cib	4
Apr 12 1972	13-Caban	5
Apr 13 1972	**1-Etz'nab**	6
Apr 14 1972	2-Cauac	7
Apr 15 1972	3-Ahau	8
Apr 16 1972	*4-Imix*	9
Apr 17 1972	5-Ik	1
Apr 18 1972	6-Akbal	2
Apr 19 1972	7-Kan	3
Apr 20 1972	8-Chicchan	4
Apr 21 1972	9-Cimi	5
Apr 22 1972	10-Manik	6
Apr 23 1972	11-Lamat	7
Apr 24 1972	12-Muluc	8
Apr 25 1972	13-Oc	9
Apr 26 1972	**1-Chuen**	1
Apr 27 1972	2-Eb	2
Apr 28 1972	3-Ben	3
Apr 29 1972	4-Ix	4
Apr 30 1972	5-Men	5
May 1 1972	6-Cib	6
May 2 1972	7-Caban	7
May 3 1972	8-Etz'nab	8
May 4 1972	9-Cauac	9
May 5 1972	10-Ahau	1
May 6 1972	*11-Imix*	2
May 7 1972	12-Ik	3
May 8 1972	13-Akbal	4
May 9 1972	**1-Kan**	5
May 10 1972	2-Chicchan	6
May 11 1972	3-Cimi	7
May 12 1972	4-Manik	8
May 13 1972	5-Lamat	9
May 14 1972	6-Muluc	1
May 15 1972	7-Oc	2
May 16 1972	8-Chuen	3
May 17 1972	9-Eb	4
May 18 1972	10-Ben	5
May 19 1972	11-Ix	6
May 20 1972	12-Men	7
May 21 1972	13-Cib	8
May 22 1972	**1-Caban**	9
May 23 1972	2-Etz'nab	1
May 24 1972	3-Cauac	2
May 25 1972	4-Ahau	3
May 26 1972	*5-Imix*	4
May 27 1972	6-Ik	5
May 28 1972	7-Akbal	6
May 29 1972	8-Kan	7
May 30 1972	9-Chicchan	8
May 31 1972	10-Cimi	9
Jun 1 1972	11-Manik	1
Jun 2 1972	12-Lamat	2
Jun 3 1972	13-Muluc	3

Date	Day-Sign	L
Jun 4 1972	1-Oc	4
Jun 5 1972	2-Chuen	5
Jun 6 1972	3-Eb	6
Jun 7 1972	4-Ben	7
Jun 8 1972	5-Ix	8
Jun 9 1972	6-Men	9
Jun 10 1972	7-Cib	1
Jun 11 1972	8-Caban	2
Jun 12 1972	9-Etz'nab	3
Jun 13 1972	10-Cauac	4
Jun 14 1972	11-Ahau	5
Jun 15 1972	12-Imix	6
Jun 16 1972	13-Ik	7
Jun 17 1972	1-Akbal	8
Jun 18 1972	2-Kan	9
Jun 19 1972	3-Chicchan	1
Jun 20 1972	4-Cimi	2
Jun 21 1972	5-Manik	3
Jun 22 1972	6-Lamat	4
Jun 23 1972	7-Muluc	5
Jun 24 1972	8-Oc	6
Jun 25 1972	9-Chuen	7
Jun 26 1972	10-Eb	8
Jun 27 1972	11-Ben	9
Jun 28 1972	12-Ix	1
Jun 29 1972	13-Men	2
Jun 30 1972	1-Cib	3
Jul 1 1972	2-Caban	4
Jul 2 1972	3-Etz'nab	5
Jul 3 1972	4-Cauac	6
Jul 4 1972	5-Ahau	7
Jul 5 1972	6-Imix	8
Jul 6 1972	7-Ik	9
Jul 7 1972	8-Akbal	1
Jul 8 1972	9-Kan	2
Jul 9 1972	10-Chicchan	3
Jul 10 1972	11-Cimi	4
Jul 11 1972	12-Manik	5
Jul 12 1972	13-Lamat	6
Jul 13 1972	1-Muluc	7
Jul 14 1972	2-Oc	8
Jul 15 1972	3-Chuen	9
Jul 16 1972	4-Eb	1
Jul 17 1972	5-Ben	2
Jul 18 1972	6-Ix	3
Jul 19 1972	7-Men	4
Jul 20 1972	8-Cib	5
Jul 21 1972	9-Caban	6
Jul 22 1972	10-Etz'nab	7
Jul 23 1972	11-Cauac	8
Jul 24 1972	12-Ahau	9
Jul 25 1972	13-Imix	1
Jul 26 1972	1-Ik	2
Jul 27 1972	2-Akbal	3
Jul 28 1972	3-Kan	4
Jul 29 1972	4-Chicchan	5
Jul 30 1972	5-Cimi	6
Jul 31 1972	6-Manik	7
Aug 1 1972	7-Lamat	8
Aug 2 1972	8-Muluc	9
Aug 3 1972	9-Oc	1
Aug 4 1972	10-Chuen	2
Aug 5 1972	11-Eb	3
Aug 6 1972	12-Ben	4
Aug 7 1972	13-Ix	5
Aug 8 1972	1-Men	6
Aug 9 1972	2-Cib	7
Aug 10 1972	3-Caban	8

Date	Day-Sign	L
Aug 11 1972	4-Etz'nab	9
Aug 12 1972	5-Cauac	1
Aug 13 1972	6-Ahau	2
Aug 14 1972	7-Imix	3
Aug 15 1972	8-Ik	4
Aug 16 1972	9-Akbal	5
Aug 17 1972	10-Kan	6
Aug 18 1972	11-Chicchan	7
Aug 19 1972	12-Cimi	8
Aug 20 1972	13-Manik	9
Aug 21 1972	1-Lamat	1
Aug 22 1972	2-Muluc	2
Aug 23 1972	3-Oc	3
Aug 24 1972	4-Chuen	4
Aug 25 1972	5-Eb	5
Aug 26 1972	6-Ben	6
Aug 27 1972	7-Ix	7
Aug 28 1972	8-Men	8
Aug 29 1972	9-Cib	9
Aug 30 1972	10-Caban	1
Aug 31 1972	11-Etz'nab	2
Sep 1 1972	12-Cauac	3
Sep 2 1972	13-Ahau	4
Sep 3 1972	1-Imix	5
Sep 4 1972	2-Ik	6
Sep 5 1972	3-Akbal	7
Sep 6 1972	4-Kan	8
Sep 7 1972	5-Chicchan	9
Sep 8 1972	6-Cimi	1
Sep 9 1972	7-Manik	2
Sep 10 1972	8-Lamat	3
Sep 11 1972	9-Muluc	4
Sep 12 1972	10-Oc	5
Sep 13 1972	11-Chuen	6
Sep 14 1972	12-Eb	7
Sep 15 1972	13-Ben	8
Sep 16 1972	1-Ix	9
Sep 17 1972	2-Men	1
Sep 18 1972	3-Cib	2
Sep 19 1972	4-Caban	3
Sep 20 1972	5-Etz'nab	4
Sep 21 1972	6-Cauac	5
Sep 22 1972	7-Ahau	6
Sep 23 1972	8-Imix	7
Sep 24 1972	9-Ik	8
Sep 25 1972	10-Akbal	9
Sep 26 1972	11-Kan	1
Sep 27 1972	12-Chicchan	2
Sep 28 1972	13-Cimi	3
Sep 29 1972	1-Manik	4
Sep 30 1972	2-Lamat	5
Oct 1 1972	3-Muluc	6
Oct 2 1972	4-Oc	7
Oct 3 1972	5-Chuen	8
Oct 4 1972	6-Eb	9
Oct 5 1972	7-Ben	1
Oct 6 1972	8-Ix	2
Oct 7 1972	9-Men	3
Oct 8 1972	10-Cib	4
Oct 9 1972	11-Caban	5
Oct 10 1972	12-Etz'nab	6
Oct 11 1972	13-Cauac	7
Oct 12 1972	1-Ahau	8
Oct 13 1972	2-Imix	9
Oct 14 1972	3-Ik	1
Oct 15 1972	4-Akbal	2
Oct 16 1972	5-Kan	3
Oct 17 1972	6-Chicchan	4

Date	Day-Sign	L
Oct 18 1972	7-Cimi	5
Oct 19 1972	8-Manik	6
Oct 20 1972	9-Lamat	7
Oct 21 1972	10-Muluc	8
Oct 22 1972	11-Oc	9
Oct 23 1972	12-Chuen	1
Oct 24 1972	13-Eb	2
Oct 25 1972	1-Ben	3
Oct 26 1972	2-Ix	4
Oct 27 1972	3-Men	5
Oct 28 1972	4-Cib	6
Oct 29 1972	5-Caban	7
Oct 30 1972	6-Etz'nab	8
Oct 31 1972	7-Cauac	9
Nov 1 1972	8-Ahau	1
Nov 2 1972	9-Imix	2
Nov 3 1972	10-Ik	3
Nov 4 1972	11-Akbal	4
Nov 5 1972	12-Kan	5
Nov 6 1972	13-Chicchan	6
Nov 7 1972	1-Cimi	7
Nov 8 1972	2-Manik	8
Nov 9 1972	3-Lamat	9
Nov 10 1972	4-Muluc	1
Nov 11 1972	5-Oc	2
Nov 12 1972	6-Chuen	3
Nov 13 1972	7-Eb	4
Nov 14 1972	8-Ben	5
Nov 15 1972	9-Ix	6
Nov 16 1972	10-Men	7
Nov 17 1972	11-Cib	8
Nov 18 1972	12-Caban	9
Nov 19 1972	13-Etz'nab	1
Nov 20 1972	1-Cauac	2
Nov 21 1972	2-Ahau	3
Nov 22 1972	3-Imix	4
Nov 23 1972	4-Ik	5
Nov 24 1972	5-Akbal	6
Nov 25 1972	6-Kan	7
Nov 26 1972	7-Chicchan	8
Nov 27 1972	8-Cimi	9
Nov 28 1972	9-Manik	1
Nov 29 1972	10-Lamat	2
Nov 30 1972	11-Muluc	3
Dec 1 1972	12-Oc	4
Dec 2 1972	13-Chuen	5
Dec 3 1972	1-Eb	6
Dec 4 1972	2-Ben	7
Dec 5 1972	3-Ix	8
Dec 6 1972	4-Men	9
Dec 7 1972	5-Cib	1
Dec 8 1972	6-Caban	2
Dec 9 1972	7-Etz'nab	3
Dec 10 1972	8-Cauac	4
Dec 11 1972	9-Ahau	5
Dec 12 1972	10-Imix	6
Dec 13 1972	11-Ik	7
Dec 14 1972	12-Akbal	8
Dec 15 1972	13-Kan	9
Dec 16 1972	1-Chicchan	1
Dec 17 1972	2-Cimi	2
Dec 18 1972	3-Manik	3
Dec 19 1972	4-Lamat	4
Dec 20 1972	5-Muluc	5
Dec 21 1972	6-Oc	6
Dec 22 1972	7-Chuen	7
Dec 23 1972	8-Eb	8
Dec 24 1972	9-Ben	9

Date	Day-Sign	L
Dec 25 1972	10-Ix	1
Dec 26 1972	11-Men	2
Dec 27 1972	12-Cib	3
Dec 28 1972	13-Caban	4
Dec 29 1972	**1-Etz'nab**	5
Dec 30 1972	2-Cauac	6
Dec 31 1972	3-Ahau	7
Jan 1 1973	*4-Imix*	8
Jan 2 1973	5-Ik	9
Jan 3 1973	6-Akbal	1
Jan 4 1973	7-Kan	2
Jan 5 1973	8-Chicchan	3
Jan 6 1973	9-Cimi	4
Jan 7 1973	10-Manik	5
Jan 8 1973	11-Lamat	6
Jan 9 1973	12-Muluc	7
Jan 10 1973	13-Oc	8
Jan 11 1973	**1-Chuen**	9
Jan 12 1973	2-Eb	1
Jan 13 1973	3-Ben	2
Jan 14 1973	4-Ix	3
Jan 15 1973	5-Men	4
Jan 16 1973	6-Cib	5
Jan 17 1973	7-Caban	6
Jan 18 1973	8-Etz'nab	7
Jan 19 1973	9-Cauac	8
Jan 20 1973	10-Ahau	9
Jan 21 1973	*11-Imix*	1
Jan 22 1973	12-Ik	2
Jan 23 1973	13-Akbal	3
Jan 24 1973	**1-Kan**	4
Jan 25 1973	2-Chicchan	5
Jan 26 1973	3-Cimi	6
Jan 27 1973	4-Manik	7
Jan 28 1973	5-Lamat	8
Jan 29 1973	6-Muluc	9
Jan 30 1973	7-Oc	1
Jan 31 1973	8-Chuen	2
Feb 1 1973	9-Eb	3
Feb 2 1973	10-Ben	4
Feb 3 1973	11-Ix	5
Feb 4 1973	12-Men	6
Feb 5 1973	13-Cib	7
Feb 6 1973	**1-Caban**	8
Feb 7 1973	2-Etz'nab	9
Feb 8 1973	3-Cauac	1
Feb 9 1973	4-Ahau	2
Feb 10 1973	*5-Imix*	3
Feb 11 1973	6-Ik	4
Feb 12 1973	7-Akbal	5
Feb 13 1973	8-Kan	6
Feb 14 1973	9-Chicchan	7
Feb 15 1973	10-Cimi	8
Feb 16 1973	11-Manik	9
Feb 17 1973	12-Lamat	1
Feb 18 1973	13-Muluc	2
Feb 19 1973	**1-Oc**	3
Feb 20 1973	2-Chuen	4
Feb 21 1973	3-Eb	5
Feb 22 1973	4-Ben	6
Feb 23 1973	5-Ix	7
Feb 24 1973	6-Men	8
Feb 25 1973	7-Cib	9
Feb 26 1973	8-Caban	1
Feb 27 1973	9-Etz'nab	2
Feb 28 1973	10-Cauac	3
Mar 1 1973	11-Ahau	4
Mar 2 1973	*12-Imix*	5

Date	Day-Sign	L
Mar 3 1973	13-Ik	6
Mar 4 1973	**1-Akbal**	7
Mar 5 1973	2-Kan	8
Mar 6 1973	3-Chicchan	9
Mar 7 1973	4-Cimi	1
Mar 8 1973	5-Manik	2
Mar 9 1973	6-Lamat	3
Mar 10 1973	7-Muluc	4
Mar 11 1973	8-Oc	5
Mar 12 1973	9-Chuen	6
Mar 13 1973	10-Eb	7
Mar 14 1973	11-Ben	8
Mar 15 1973	12-Ix	9
Mar 16 1973	13-Men	1
Mar 17 1973	**1-Cib**	2
Mar 18 1973	2-Caban	3
Mar 19 1973	3-Etz'nab	4
Mar 20 1973	4-Cauac	5
Mar 21 1973	5-Ahau	6
Mar 22 1973	*6-Imix*	7
Mar 23 1973	7-Ik	8
Mar 24 1973	8-Akbal	9
Mar 25 1973	9-Kan	1
Mar 26 1973	10-Chicchan	2
Mar 27 1973	11-Cimi	3
Mar 28 1973	12-Manik	4
Mar 29 1973	13-Lamat	5
Mar 30 1973	**1-Muluc**	6
Mar 31 1973	2-Oc	7
Apr 1 1973	3-Chuen	8
Apr 2 1973	4-Eb	9
Apr 3 1973	5-Ben	1
Apr 4 1973	6-Ix	2
Apr 5 1973	7-Men	3
Apr 6 1973	8-Cib	4
Apr 7 1973	9-Caban	5
Apr 8 1973	10-Etz'nab	6
Apr 9 1973	11-Cauac	7
Apr 10 1973	12-Ahau	8
Apr 11 1973	*13-Imix*	9
Apr 12 1973	**1-Ik**	1
Apr 13 1973	2-Akbal	2
Apr 14 1973	3-Kan	3
Apr 15 1973	4-Chicchan	4
Apr 16 1973	5-Cimi	5
Apr 17 1973	6-Manik	6
Apr 18 1973	7-Lamat	7
Apr 19 1973	8-Muluc	8
Apr 20 1973	9-Oc	9
Apr 21 1973	10-Chuen	1
Apr 22 1973	11-Eb	2
Apr 23 1973	12-Ben	3
Apr 24 1973	13-Ix	4
Apr 25 1973	**1-Men**	5
Apr 26 1973	2-Cib	6
Apr 27 1973	3-Caban	7
Apr 28 1973	4-Etz'nab	8
Apr 29 1973	5-Cauac	9
Apr 30 1973	6-Ahau	1
May 1 1973	*7-Imix*	2
May 2 1973	8-Ik	3
May 3 1973	9-Akbal	4
May 4 1973	10-Kan	5
May 5 1973	11-Chicchan	6
May 6 1973	12-Cimi	7
May 7 1973	13-Manik	8
May 8 1973	**1-Lamat**	9
May 9 1973	2-Muluc	1

Date	Day-Sign	L
May 10 1973	3-Oc	2
May 11 1973	4-Chuen	3
May 12 1973	5-Eb	4
May 13 1973	6-Ben	5
May 14 1973	7-Ix	6
May 15 1973	8-Men	7
May 16 1973	9-Cib	8
May 17 1973	10-Caban	9
May 18 1973	11-Etz'nab	1
May 19 1973	12-Cauac	2
May 20 1973	13-Ahau	3
May 21 1973	**1-Imix**	4
May 22 1973	2-Ik	5
May 23 1973	3-Akbal	6
May 24 1973	4-Kan	7
May 25 1973	5-Chicchan	8
May 26 1973	6-Cimi	9
May 27 1973	7-Manik	1
May 28 1973	8-Lamat	2
May 29 1973	9-Muluc	3
May 30 1973	10-Oc	4
May 31 1973	11-Chuen	5
Jun 1 1973	12-Eb	6
Jun 2 1973	13-Ben	7
Jun 3 1973	**1-Ix**	8
Jun 4 1973	2-Men	9
Jun 5 1973	3-Cib	1
Jun 6 1973	4-Caban	2
Jun 7 1973	5-Etz'nab	3
Jun 8 1973	6-Cauac	4
Jun 9 1973	7-Ahau	5
Jun 10 1973	*8-Imix*	6
Jun 11 1973	9-Ik	7
Jun 12 1973	10-Akbal	8
Jun 13 1973	11-Kan	9
Jun 14 1973	12-Chicchan	1
Jun 15 1973	13-Cimi	2
Jun 16 1973	**1-Manik**	3
Jun 17 1973	2-Lamat	4
Jun 18 1973	3-Muluc	5
Jun 19 1973	4-Oc	6
Jun 20 1973	5-Chuen	7
Jun 21 1973	6-Eb	8
Jun 22 1973	7-Ben	9
Jun 23 1973	8-Ix	1
Jun 24 1973	9-Men	2
Jun 25 1973	10-Cib	3
Jun 26 1973	11-Caban	4
Jun 27 1973	12-Etz'nab	5
Jun 28 1973	13-Cauac	6
Jun 29 1973	**1-Ahau**	7
Jun 30 1973	*2-Imix*	8
Jul 1 1973	3-Ik	9
Jul 2 1973	4-Akbal	1
Jul 3 1973	5-Kan	2
Jul 4 1973	6-Chicchan	3
Jul 5 1973	7-Cimi	4
Jul 6 1973	8-Manik	5
Jul 7 1973	9-Lamat	6
Jul 8 1973	10-Muluc	7
Jul 9 1973	11-Oc	8
Jul 10 1973	12-Chuen	9
Jul 11 1973	13-Eb	1
Jul 12 1973	**1-Ben**	2
Jul 13 1973	2-Ix	3
Jul 14 1973	3-Men	4
Jul 15 1973	4-Cib	5
Jul 16 1973	5-Caban	6

Date	Day-Sign	L
Jul 17 1973	6-Etz'nab	7
Jul 18 1973	7-Cauac	8
Jul 19 1973	8-Ahau	9
Jul 20 1973	9-Imix	1
Jul 21 1973	10-Ik	2
Jul 22 1973	11-Akbal	3
Jul 23 1973	12-Kan	4
Jul 24 1973	13-Chicchan	5
Jul 25 1973	1-Cimi	6
Jul 26 1973	2-Manik	7
Jul 27 1973	3-Lamat	8
Jul 28 1973	4-Muluc	9
Jul 29 1973	5-Oc	1
Jul 30 1973	6-Chuen	2
Jul 31 1973	7-Eb	3
Aug 1 1973	8-Ben	4
Aug 2 1973	9-Ix	5
Aug 3 1973	10-Men	6
Aug 4 1973	11-Cib	7
Aug 5 1973	12-Caban	8
Aug 6 1973	13-Etz'nab	9
Aug 7 1973	1-Cauac	1
Aug 8 1973	2-Ahau	2
Aug 9 1973	3-Imix	3
Aug 10 1973	4-Ik	4
Aug 11 1973	5-Akbal	5
Aug 12 1973	6-Kan	6
Aug 13 1973	7-Chicchan	7
Aug 14 1973	8-Cimi	8
Aug 15 1973	9-Manik	9
Aug 16 1973	10-Lamat	1
Aug 17 1973	11-Muluc	2
Aug 18 1973	12-Oc	3
Aug 19 1973	13-Chuen	4
Aug 20 1973	1-Eb	5
Aug 21 1973	2-Ben	6
Aug 22 1973	3-Ix	7
Aug 23 1973	4-Men	8
Aug 24 1973	5-Cib	9
Aug 25 1973	6-Caban	1
Aug 26 1973	7-Etz'nab	2
Aug 27 1973	8-Cauac	3
Aug 28 1973	9-Ahau	4
Aug 29 1973	10-Imix	5
Aug 30 1973	11-Ik	6
Aug 31 1973	12-Akbal	7
Sep 1 1973	13-Kan	8
Sep 2 1973	1-Chicchan	9
Sep 3 1973	2-Cimi	1
Sep 4 1973	3-Manik	2
Sep 5 1973	4-Lamat	3
Sep 6 1973	5-Muluc	4
Sep 7 1973	6-Oc	5
Sep 8 1973	7-Chuen	6
Sep 9 1973	8-Eb	7
Sep 10 1973	9-Ben	8
Sep 11 1973	10-Ix	9
Sep 12 1973	11-Men	1
Sep 13 1973	12-Cib	2
Sep 14 1973	13-Caban	3
Sep 15 1973	1-Etz'nab	4
Sep 16 1973	2-Cauac	5
Sep 17 1973	3-Ahau	6
Sep 18 1973	4-Imix	7
Sep 19 1973	5-Ik	8
Sep 20 1973	6-Akbal	9
Sep 21 1973	7-Kan	1
Sep 22 1973	8-Chicchan	2

Date	Day-Sign	L
Sep 23 1973	9-Cimi	3
Sep 24 1973	10-Manik	4
Sep 25 1973	11-Lamat	5
Sep 26 1973	12-Muluc	6
Sep 27 1973	13-Oc	7
Sep 28 1973	1-Chuen	8
Sep 29 1973	2-Eb	9
Sep 30 1973	3-Ben	1
Oct 1 1973	4-Ix	2
Oct 2 1973	5-Men	3
Oct 3 1973	6-Cib	4
Oct 4 1973	7-Caban	5
Oct 5 1973	8-Etz'nab	6
Oct 6 1973	9-Cauac	7
Oct 7 1973	10-Ahau	8
Oct 8 1973	11-Imix	9
Oct 9 1973	12-Ik	1
Oct 10 1973	13-Akbal	2
Oct 11 1973	1-Kan	3
Oct 12 1973	2-Chicchan	4
Oct 13 1973	3-Cimi	5
Oct 14 1973	4-Manik	6
Oct 15 1973	5-Lamat	7
Oct 16 1973	6-Muluc	8
Oct 17 1973	7-Oc	9
Oct 18 1973	8-Chuen	1
Oct 19 1973	9-Eb	2
Oct 20 1973	10-Ben	3
Oct 21 1973	11-Ix	4
Oct 22 1973	12-Men	5
Oct 23 1973	13-Cib	6
Oct 24 1973	1-Caban	7
Oct 25 1973	2-Etz'nab	8
Oct 26 1973	3-Cauac	9
Oct 27 1973	4-Ahau	1
Oct 28 1973	5-Imix	2
Oct 29 1973	6-Ik	3
Oct 30 1973	7-Akbal	4
Oct 31 1973	8-Kan	5
Nov 1 1973	9-Chicchan	6
Nov 2 1973	10-Cimi	7
Nov 3 1973	11-Manik	8
Nov 4 1973	12-Lamat	9
Nov 5 1973	13-Muluc	1
Nov 6 1973	1-Oc	2
Nov 7 1973	2-Chuen	3
Nov 8 1973	3-Eb	4
Nov 9 1973	4-Ben	5
Nov 10 1973	5-Ix	6
Nov 11 1973	6-Men	7
Nov 12 1973	7-Cib	8
Nov 13 1973	8-Caban	9
Nov 14 1973	9-Etz'nab	1
Nov 15 1973	10-Cauac	2
Nov 16 1973	11-Ahau	3
Nov 17 1973	12-Imix	4
Nov 18 1973	13-Ik	5
Nov 19 1973	1-Akbal	6
Nov 20 1973	2-Kan	7
Nov 21 1973	3-Chicchan	8
Nov 22 1973	4-Cimi	9
Nov 23 1973	5-Manik	1
Nov 24 1973	6-Lamat	2
Nov 25 1973	7-Muluc	3
Nov 26 1973	8-Oc	4
Nov 27 1973	9-Chuen	5
Nov 28 1973	10-Eb	6
Nov 29 1973	11-Ben	7

Date	Day-Sign	L
Nov 30 1973	12-Ix	8
Dec 1 1973	13-Men	9
Dec 2 1973	1-Cib	1
Dec 3 1973	2-Caban	2
Dec 4 1973	3-Etz'nab	3
Dec 5 1973	4-Cauac	4
Dec 6 1973	5-Ahau	5
Dec 7 1973	6-Imix	6
Dec 8 1973	7-Ik	7
Dec 9 1973	8-Akbal	8
Dec 10 1973	9-Kan	9
Dec 11 1973	10-Chicchan	1
Dec 12 1973	11-Cimi	2
Dec 13 1973	12-Manik	3
Dec 14 1973	13-Lamat	4
Dec 15 1973	1-Muluc	5
Dec 16 1973	2-Oc	6
Dec 17 1973	3-Chuen	7
Dec 18 1973	4-Eb	8
Dec 19 1973	5-Ben	9
Dec 20 1973	6-Ix	1
Dec 21 1973	7-Men	2
Dec 22 1973	8-Cib	3
Dec 23 1973	9-Caban	4
Dec 24 1973	10-Etz'nab	5
Dec 25 1973	11-Cauac	6
Dec 26 1973	12-Ahau	7
Dec 27 1973	13-Imix	8
Dec 28 1973	1-Ik	9
Dec 29 1973	2-Akbal	1
Dec 30 1973	3-Kan	2
Dec 31 1973	4-Chicchan	3
Jan 1 1974	5-Cimi	4
Jan 2 1974	6-Manik	5
Jan 3 1974	7-Lamat	6
Jan 4 1974	8-Muluc	7
Jan 5 1974	9-Oc	8
Jan 6 1974	10-Chuen	9
Jan 7 1974	11-Eb	1
Jan 8 1974	12-Ben	2
Jan 9 1974	13-Ix	3
Jan 10 1974	1-Men	4
Jan 11 1974	2-Cib	5
Jan 12 1974	3-Caban	6
Jan 13 1974	4-Etz'nab	7
Jan 14 1974	5-Cauac	8
Jan 15 1974	6-Ahau	9
Jan 16 1974	7-Imix	1
Jan 17 1974	8-Ik	2
Jan 18 1974	9-Akbal	3
Jan 19 1974	10-Kan	4
Jan 20 1974	11-Chicchan	5
Jan 21 1974	12-Cimi	6
Jan 22 1974	13-Manik	7
Jan 23 1974	1-Lamat	8
Jan 24 1974	2-Muluc	9
Jan 25 1974	3-Oc	1
Jan 26 1974	4-Chuen	2
Jan 27 1974	5-Eb	3
Jan 28 1974	6-Ben	4
Jan 29 1974	7-Ix	5
Jan 30 1974	8-Men	6
Jan 31 1974	9-Cib	7
Feb 1 1974	10-Caban	8
Feb 2 1974	11-Etz'nab	9
Feb 3 1974	12-Cauac	1
Feb 4 1974	13-Ahau	2
Feb 5 1974	1-Imix	3

Date	Day-Sign	L	Date	Day-Sign	L	Date	Day-Sign	L
Feb 6 1974	2-Ik	4	Apr 15 1974	5-Oc	9	Jun 22 1974	8-Etz'nab	5
Feb 7 1974	3-Akbal	5	Apr 16 1974	6-Chuen	1	Jun 23 1974	9-Cauac	6
Feb 8 1974	4-Kan	6	Apr 17 1974	7-Eb	2	Jun 24 1974	10-Ahau	7
Feb 9 1974	5-Chicchan	7	Apr 18 1974	8-Ben	3	Jun 25 1974	11-*Imix*	8
Feb 10 1974	6-Cimi	8	Apr 19 1974	9-Ix	4	Jun 26 1974	12-Ik	9
Feb 11 1974	7-Manik	9	Apr 20 1974	10-Men	5	Jun 27 1974	13-Akbal	1
Feb 12 1974	8-Lamat	1	Apr 21 1974	11-Cib	6	Jun 28 1974	**1-Kan**	2
Feb 13 1974	9-Muluc	2	Apr 22 1974	12-Caban	7	Jun 29 1974	2-Chicchan	3
Feb 14 1974	10-Oc	3	Apr 23 1974	13-Etz'nab	8	Jun 30 1974	3-Cimi	4
Feb 15 1974	11-Chuen	4	Apr 24 1974	**1-Cauac**	9	Jul 1 1974	4-Manik	5
Feb 16 1974	12-Eb	5	Apr 25 1974	2-Ahau	1	Jul 2 1974	5-Lamat	6
Feb 17 1974	13-Ben	6	Apr 26 1974	3-*Imix*	2	Jul 3 1974	6-Muluc	7
Feb 18 1974	**1-Ix**	7	Apr 27 1974	4-Ik	3	Jul 4 1974	7-Oc	8
Feb 19 1974	2-Men	8	Apr 28 1974	5-Akbal	4	Jul 5 1974	8-Chuen	9
Feb 20 1974	3-Cib	9	Apr 29 1974	6-Kan	5	Jul 6 1974	9-Eb	1
Feb 21 1974	4-Caban	1	Apr 30 1974	7-Chicchan	6	Jul 7 1974	10-Ben	2
Feb 22 1974	5-Etz'nab	2	May 1 1974	8-Cimi	7	Jul 8 1974	11-Ix	3
Feb 23 1974	6-Cauac	3	May 2 1974	9-Manik	8	Jul 9 1974	12-Men	4
Feb 24 1974	7-Ahau	4	May 3 1974	10-Lamat	9	Jul 10 1974	13-Cib	5
Feb 25 1974	8-*Imix*	5	May 4 1974	11-Muluc	1	Jul 11 1974	**1-Caban**	6
Feb 26 1974	9-Ik	6	May 5 1974	12-Oc	2	Jul 12 1974	2-Etz'nab	7
Feb 27 1974	10-Akbal	7	May 6 1974	13-Chuen	3	Jul 13 1974	3-Cauac	8
Feb 28 1974	11-Kan	8	May 7 1974	**1-Eb**	4	Jul 14 1974	4-Ahau	9
Mar 1 1974	12-Chicchan	9	May 8 1974	2-Ben	5	Jul 15 1974	5-*Imix*	1
Mar 2 1974	13-Cimi	1	May 9 1974	3-Ix	6	Jul 16 1974	6-Ik	2
Mar 3 1974	**1-Manik**	2	May 10 1974	4-Men	7	Jul 17 1974	7-Akbal	3
Mar 4 1974	2-Lamat	3	May 11 1974	5-Cib	8	Jul 18 1974	8-Kan	4
Mar 5 1974	3-Muluc	4	May 12 1974	6-Caban	9	Jul 19 1974	9-Chicchan	5
Mar 6 1974	4-Oc	5	May 13 1974	7-Etz'nab	1	Jul 20 1974	10-Cimi	6
Mar 7 1974	5-Chuen	6	May 14 1974	8-Cauac	2	Jul 21 1974	11-Manik	7
Mar 8 1974	6-Eb	7	May 15 1974	9-Ahau	3	Jul 22 1974	12-Lamat	8
Mar 9 1974	7-Ben	8	May 16 1974	10-*Imix*	4	Jul 23 1974	13-Muluc	9
Mar 10 1974	8-Ix	9	May 17 1974	11-Ik	5	Jul 24 1974	**1-Oc**	1
Mar 11 1974	9-Men	1	May 18 1974	12-Akbal	6	Jul 25 1974	2-Chuen	2
Mar 12 1974	10-Cib	2	May 19 1974	13-Kan	7	Jul 26 1974	3-Eb	3
Mar 13 1974	11-Caban	3	May 20 1974	**1-Chicchan**	8	Jul 27 1974	4-Ben	4
Mar 14 1974	12-Etz'nab	4	May 21 1974	2-Cimi	9	Jul 28 1974	5-Ix	5
Mar 15 1974	13-Cauac	5	May 22 1974	3-Manik	1	Jul 29 1974	6-Men	6
Mar 16 1974	**1-Ahau**	6	May 23 1974	4-Lamat	2	Jul 30 1974	7-Cib	7
Mar 17 1974	2-*Imix*	7	May 24 1974	5-Muluc	3	Jul 31 1974	8-Caban	8
Mar 18 1974	3-Ik	8	May 25 1974	6-Oc	4	Aug 1 1974	9-Etz'nab	9
Mar 19 1974	4-Akbal	9	May 26 1974	7-Chuen	5	Aug 2 1974	10-Cauac	1
Mar 20 1974	5-Kan	1	May 27 1974	8-Eb	6	Aug 3 1974	11-Ahau	2
Mar 21 1974	6-Chicchan	2	May 28 1974	9-Ben	7	Aug 4 1974	12-*Imix*	3
Mar 22 1974	7-Cimi	3	May 29 1974	10-Ix	8	Aug 5 1974	13-Ik	4
Mar 23 1974	8-Manik	4	May 30 1974	11-Men	9	Aug 6 1974	**1-Akbal**	5
Mar 24 1974	9-Lamat	5	May 31 1974	12-Cib	1	Aug 7 1974	2-Kan	6
Mar 25 1974	10-Muluc	6	Jun 1 1974	13-Caban	2	Aug 8 1974	3-Chicchan	7
Mar 26 1974	11-Oc	7	Jun 2 1974	**1-Etz'nab**	3	Aug 9 1974	4-Cimi	8
Mar 27 1974	12-Chuen	8	Jun 3 1974	2-Cauac	4	Aug 10 1974	5-Manik	9
Mar 28 1974	13-Eb	9	Jun 4 1974	3-Ahau	5	Aug 11 1974	6-Lamat	1
Mar 29 1974	**1-Ben**	1	Jun 5 1974	4-*Imix*	6	Aug 12 1974	7-Muluc	2
Mar 30 1974	2-Ix	2	Jun 6 1974	5-Ik	7	Aug 13 1974	8-Oc	3
Mar 31 1974	3-Men	3	Jun 7 1974	6-Akbal	8	Aug 14 1974	9-Chuen	4
Apr 1 1974	4-Cib	4	Jun 8 1974	7-Kan	9	Aug 15 1974	10-Eb	5
Apr 2 1974	5-Caban	5	Jun 9 1974	8-Chicchan	1	Aug 16 1974	11-Ben	6
Apr 3 1974	6-Etz'nab	6	Jun 10 1974	9-Cimi	2	Aug 17 1974	12-Ix	7
Apr 4 1974	7-Cauac	7	Jun 11 1974	10-Manik	3	Aug 18 1974	13-Men	8
Apr 5 1974	8-Ahau	8	Jun 12 1974	11-Lamat	4	Aug 19 1974	**1-Cib**	9
Apr 6 1974	9-*Imix*	9	Jun 13 1974	12-Muluc	5	Aug 20 1974	2-Caban	1
Apr 7 1974	10-Ik	1	Jun 14 1974	13-Oc	6	Aug 21 1974	3-Etz'nab	2
Apr 8 1974	11-Akbal	2	Jun 15 1974	**1-Chuen**	7	Aug 22 1974	4-Cauac	3
Apr 9 1974	12-Kan	3	Jun 16 1974	2-Eb	8	Aug 23 1974	5-Ahau	4
Apr 10 1974	13-Chicchan	4	Jun 17 1974	3-Ben	9	Aug 24 1974	6-*Imix*	5
Apr 11 1974	**1-Cimi**	5	Jun 18 1974	4-Ix	1	Aug 25 1974	7-Ik	6
Apr 12 1974	2-Manik	6	Jun 19 1974	5-Men	2	Aug 26 1974	8-Akbal	7
Apr 13 1974	3-Lamat	7	Jun 20 1974	6-Cib	3	Aug 27 1974	9-Kan	8
Apr 14 1974	4-Muluc	8	Jun 21 1974	7-Caban	4	Aug 28 1974	10-Chicchan	9

Date	Day-Sign	L
Aug 29 1974	11-Cimi	1
Aug 30 1974	12-Manik	2
Aug 31 1974	13-Lamat	3
Sep 1 1974	1-Muluc	4
Sep 2 1974	2-Oc	5
Sep 3 1974	3-Chuen	6
Sep 4 1974	4-Eb	7
Sep 5 1974	5-Ben	8
Sep 6 1974	6-Ix	9
Sep 7 1974	7-Men	1
Sep 8 1974	8-Cib	2
Sep 9 1974	9-Caban	3
Sep 10 1974	10-Etz'nab	4
Sep 11 1974	11-Cauac	5
Sep 12 1974	12-Ahau	6
Sep 13 1974	13-Imix	7
Sep 14 1974	1-Ik	8
Sep 15 1974	2-Akbal	9
Sep 16 1974	3-Kan	1
Sep 17 1974	4-Chicchan	2
Sep 18 1974	5-Cimi	3
Sep 19 1974	6-Manik	4
Sep 20 1974	7-Lamat	5
Sep 21 1974	8-Muluc	6
Sep 22 1974	9-Oc	7
Sep 23 1974	10-Chuen	8
Sep 24 1974	11-Eb	9
Sep 25 1974	12-Ben	1
Sep 26 1974	13-Ix	2
Sep 27 1974	1-Men	3
Sep 28 1974	2-Cib	4
Sep 29 1974	3-Caban	5
Sep 30 1974	4-Etz'nab	6
Oct 1 1974	5-Cauac	7
Oct 2 1974	6-Ahau	8
Oct 3 1974	7-Imix	9
Oct 4 1974	8-Ik	1
Oct 5 1974	9-Akbal	2
Oct 6 1974	10-Kan	3
Oct 7 1974	11-Chicchan	4
Oct 8 1974	12-Cimi	5
Oct 9 1974	13-Manik	6
Oct 10 1974	1-Lamat	7
Oct 11 1974	2-Muluc	8
Oct 12 1974	3-Oc	9
Oct 13 1974	4-Chuen	1
Oct 14 1974	5-Eb	2
Oct 15 1974	6-Ben	3
Oct 16 1974	7-Ix	4
Oct 17 1974	8-Men	5
Oct 18 1974	9-Cib	6
Oct 19 1974	10-Caban	7
Oct 20 1974	11-Etz'nab	8
Oct 21 1974	12-Cauac	9
Oct 22 1974	13-Ahau	1
Oct 23 1974	1-Imix	2
Oct 24 1974	2-Ik	3
Oct 25 1974	3-Akbal	4
Oct 26 1974	4-Kan	5
Oct 27 1974	5-Chicchan	6
Oct 28 1974	6-Cimi	7
Oct 29 1974	7-Manik	8
Oct 30 1974	8-Lamat	9
Oct 31 1974	9-Muluc	1
Nov 1 1974	10-Oc	2
Nov 2 1974	11-Chuen	3
Nov 3 1974	12-Eb	4
Nov 4 1974	13-Ben	5

Date	Day-Sign	L
Nov 5 1974	1-Ix	6
Nov 6 1974	2-Men	7
Nov 7 1974	3-Cib	8
Nov 8 1974	4-Caban	9
Nov 9 1974	5-Etz'nab	1
Nov 10 1974	6-Cauac	2
Nov 11 1974	7-Ahau	3
Nov 12 1974	8-Imix	4
Nov 13 1974	9-Ik	5
Nov 14 1974	10-Akbal	6
Nov 15 1974	11-Kan	7
Nov 16 1974	12-Chicchan	8
Nov 17 1974	13-Cimi	9
Nov 18 1974	1-Manik	1
Nov 19 1974	2-Lamat	2
Nov 20 1974	3-Muluc	3
Nov 21 1974	4-Oc	4
Nov 22 1974	5-Chuen	5
Nov 23 1974	6-Eb	6
Nov 24 1974	7-Ben	7
Nov 25 1974	8-Ix	8
Nov 26 1974	9-Men	9
Nov 27 1974	10-Cib	1
Nov 28 1974	11-Caban	2
Nov 29 1974	12-Etz'nab	3
Nov 30 1974	13-Cauac	4
Dec 1 1974	1-Ahau	5
Dec 2 1974	2-Imix	6
Dec 3 1974	3-Ik	7
Dec 4 1974	4-Akbal	8
Dec 5 1974	5-Kan	9
Dec 6 1974	6-Chicchan	1
Dec 7 1974	7-Cimi	2
Dec 8 1974	8-Manik	3
Dec 9 1974	9-Lamat	4
Dec 10 1974	10-Muluc	5
Dec 11 1974	11-Oc	6
Dec 12 1974	12-Chuen	7
Dec 13 1974	13-Eb	8
Dec 14 1974	1-Ben	9
Dec 15 1974	2-Ix	1
Dec 16 1974	3-Men	2
Dec 17 1974	4-Cib	3
Dec 18 1974	5-Caban	4
Dec 19 1974	6-Etz'nab	5
Dec 20 1974	7-Cauac	6
Dec 21 1974	8-Ahau	7
Dec 22 1974	9-Imix	8
Dec 23 1974	10-Ik	9
Dec 24 1974	11-Akbal	1
Dec 25 1974	12-Kan	2
Dec 26 1974	13-Chicchan	3
Dec 27 1974	1-Cimi	4
Dec 28 1974	2-Manik	5
Dec 29 1974	3-Lamat	6
Dec 30 1974	4-Muluc	7
Dec 31 1974	5-Oc	8
Jan 1 1975	6-Chuen	9
Jan 2 1975	7-Eb	1
Jan 3 1975	8-Ben	2
Jan 4 1975	9-Ix	3
Jan 5 1975	10-Men	4
Jan 6 1975	11-Cib	5
Jan 7 1975	12-Caban	6
Jan 8 1975	13-Etz'nab	7
Jan 9 1975	1-Cauac	8
Jan 10 1975	2-Ahau	9
Jan 11 1975	3-Imix	1

Date	Day-Sign	L
Jan 12 1975	4-Ik	2
Jan 13 1975	5-Akbal	3
Jan 14 1975	6-Kan	4
Jan 15 1975	7-Chicchan	5
Jan 16 1975	8-Cimi	6
Jan 17 1975	9-Manik	7
Jan 18 1975	10-Lamat	8
Jan 19 1975	11-Muluc	9
Jan 20 1975	12-Oc	1
Jan 21 1975	13-Chuen	2
Jan 22 1975	1-Eb	3
Jan 23 1975	2-Ben	4
Jan 24 1975	3-Ix	5
Jan 25 1975	4-Men	6
Jan 26 1975	5-Cib	7
Jan 27 1975	6-Caban	8
Jan 28 1975	7-Etz'nab	9
Jan 29 1975	8-Cauac	1
Jan 30 1975	9-Ahau	2
Jan 31 1975	10-Imix	3
Feb 1 1975	11-Ik	4
Feb 2 1975	12-Akbal	5
Feb 3 1975	13-Kan	6
Feb 4 1975	1-Chicchan	7
Feb 5 1975	2-Cimi	8
Feb 6 1975	3-Manik	9
Feb 7 1975	4-Lamat	1
Feb 8 1975	5-Muluc	2
Feb 9 1975	6-Oc	3
Feb 10 1975	7-Chuen	4
Feb 11 1975	8-Eb	5
Feb 12 1975	9-Ben	6
Feb 13 1975	10-Ix	7
Feb 14 1975	11-Men	8
Feb 15 1975	12-Cib	9
Feb 16 1975	13-Caban	1
Feb 17 1975	1-Etz'nab	2
Feb 18 1975	2-Cauac	3
Feb 19 1975	3-Ahau	4
Feb 20 1975	4-Imix	5
Feb 21 1975	5-Ik	6
Feb 22 1975	6-Akbal	7
Feb 23 1975	7-Kan	8
Feb 24 1975	8-Chicchan	9
Feb 25 1975	9-Cimi	1
Feb 26 1975	10-Manik	2
Feb 27 1975	11-Lamat	3
Feb 28 1975	12-Muluc	4
Mar 1 1975	13-Oc	5
Mar 2 1975	1-Chuen	6
Mar 3 1975	2-Eb	7
Mar 4 1975	3-Ben	8
Mar 5 1975	4-Ix	9
Mar 6 1975	5-Men	1
Mar 7 1975	6-Cib	2
Mar 8 1975	7-Caban	3
Mar 9 1975	8-Etz'nab	4
Mar 10 1975	9-Cauac	5
Mar 11 1975	10-Ahau	6
Mar 12 1975	11-Imix	7
Mar 13 1975	12-Ik	8
Mar 14 1975	13-Akbal	9
Mar 15 1975	1-Kan	1
Mar 16 1975	2-Chicchan	2
Mar 17 1975	3-Cimi	3
Mar 18 1975	4-Manik	4
Mar 19 1975	5-Lamat	5
Mar 20 1975	6-Muluc	6

Date	Day-Sign	L	Date	Day-Sign	L	Date	Day-Sign	L
Mar 21 1975	7-Oc	7	May 28 1975	10-Etz'nab	3	Aug 4 1975	13-Cimi	8
Mar 22 1975	8-Chuen	8	May 29 1975	11-Cauac	4	Aug 5 1975	**1-Manik**	9
Mar 23 1975	9-Eb	9	May 30 1975	12-Ahau	5	Aug 6 1975	2-Lamat	1
Mar 24 1975	10-Ben	1	May 31 1975	*13-Imix*	6	Aug 7 1975	3-Muluc	2
Mar 25 1975	11-Ix	2	Jun 1 1975	**1-Ik**	7	Aug 8 1975	4-Oc	3
Mar 26 1975	12-Men	3	Jun 2 1975	2-Akbal	8	Aug 9 1975	5-Chuen	4
Mar 27 1975	13-Cib	4	Jun 3 1975	3-Kan	9	Aug 10 1975	6-Eb	5
Mar 28 1975	**1-Caban**	5	Jun 4 1975	4-Chicchan	1	Aug 11 1975	7-Ben	6
Mar 29 1975	2-Etz'nab	6	Jun 5 1975	5-Cimi	2	Aug 12 1975	8-Ix	7
Mar 30 1975	3-Cauac	7	Jun 6 1975	6-Manik	3	Aug 13 1975	9-Men	8
Mar 31 1975	4-Ahau	8	Jun 7 1975	7-Lamat	4	Aug 14 1975	10-Cib	9
Apr 1 1975	*5-Imix*	9	Jun 8 1975	8-Muluc	5	Aug 15 1975	11-Caban	1
Apr 2 1975	6-Ik	1	Jun 9 1975	9-Oc	6	Aug 16 1975	12-Etz'nab	2
Apr 3 1975	7-Akbal	2	Jun 10 1975	10-Chuen	7	Aug 17 1975	13-Cauac	3
Apr 4 1975	8-Kan	3	Jun 11 1975	11-Eb	8	Aug 18 1975	**1-Ahau**	4
Apr 5 1975	9-Chicchan	4	Jun 12 1975	12-Ben	9	Aug 19 1975	*2-Imix*	5
Apr 6 1975	10-Cimi	5	Jun 13 1975	13-Ix	1	Aug 20 1975	3-Ik	6
Apr 7 1975	11-Manik	6	Jun 14 1975	**1-Men**	2	Aug 21 1975	4-Akbal	7
Apr 8 1975	12-Lamat	7	Jun 15 1975	2-Cib	3	Aug 22 1975	5-Kan	8
Apr 9 1975	13-Muluc	8	Jun 16 1975	3-Caban	4	Aug 23 1975	6-Chicchan	9
Apr 10 1975	**1-Oc**	9	Jun 17 1975	4-Etz'nab	5	Aug 24 1975	7-Cimi	1
Apr 11 1975	2-Chuen	1	Jun 18 1975	5-Cauac	6	Aug 25 1975	8-Manik	2
Apr 12 1975	3-Eb	2	Jun 19 1975	6-Ahau	7	Aug 26 1975	9-Lamat	3
Apr 13 1975	4-Ben	3	Jun 20 1975	*7-Imix*	8	Aug 27 1975	10-Muluc	4
Apr 14 1975	5-Ix	4	Jun 21 1975	8-Ik	9	Aug 28 1975	11-Oc	5
Apr 15 1975	6-Men	5	Jun 22 1975	9-Akbal	1	Aug 29 1975	12-Chuen	6
Apr 16 1975	7-Cib	6	Jun 23 1975	10-Kan	2	Aug 30 1975	13-Eb	7
Apr 17 1975	8-Caban	7	Jun 24 1975	11-Chicchan	3	Aug 31 1975	**1-Ben**	8
Apr 18 1975	9-Etz'nab	8	Jun 25 1975	12-Cimi	4	Sep 1 1975	2-Ix	9
Apr 19 1975	10-Cauac	9	Jun 26 1975	13-Manik	5	Sep 2 1975	3-Men	1
Apr 20 1975	11-Ahau	1	Jun 27 1975	**1-Lamat**	6	Sep 3 1975	4-Cib	2
Apr 21 1975	*12-Imix*	2	Jun 28 1975	2-Muluc	7	Sep 4 1975	5-Caban	3
Apr 22 1975	13-Ik	3	Jun 29 1975	3-Oc	8	Sep 5 1975	6-Etz'nab	4
Apr 23 1975	**1-Akbal**	4	Jun 30 1975	4-Chuen	9	Sep 6 1975	7-Cauac	5
Apr 24 1975	2-Kan	5	Jul 1 1975	5-Eb	1	Sep 7 1975	8-Ahau	6
Apr 25 1975	3-Chicchan	6	Jul 2 1975	6-Ben	2	Sep 8 1975	*9-Imix*	7
Apr 26 1975	4-Cimi	7	Jul 3 1975	7-Ix	3	Sep 9 1975	10-Ik	8
Apr 27 1975	5-Manik	8	Jul 4 1975	8-Men	4	Sep 10 1975	11-Akbal	9
Apr 28 1975	6-Lamat	9	Jul 5 1975	9-Cib	5	Sep 11 1975	12-Kan	1
Apr 29 1975	7-Muluc	1	Jul 6 1975	10-Caban	6	Sep 12 1975	13-Chicchan	2
Apr 30 1975	8-Oc	2	Jul 7 1975	11-Etz'nab	7	Sep 13 1975	**1-Cimi**	3
May 1 1975	9-Chuen	3	Jul 8 1975	12-Cauac	8	Sep 14 1975	2-Manik	4
May 2 1975	10-Eb	4	Jul 9 1975	13-Ahau	9	Sep 15 1975	3-Lamat	5
May 3 1975	11-Ben	5	Jul 10 1975	**1-Imix**	1	Sep 16 1975	4-Muluc	6
May 4 1975	12-Ix	6	Jul 11 1975	2-Ik	2	Sep 17 1975	5-Oc	7
May 5 1975	13-Men	7	Jul 12 1975	3-Akbal	3	Sep 18 1975	6-Chuen	8
May 6 1975	**1-Cib**	8	Jul 13 1975	4-Kan	4	Sep 19 1975	7-Eb	9
May 7 1975	2-Caban	9	Jul 14 1975	5-Chicchan	5	Sep 20 1975	8-Ben	1
May 8 1975	3-Etz'nab	1	Jul 15 1975	6-Cimi	6	Sep 21 1975	9-Ix	2
May 9 1975	4-Cauac	2	Jul 16 1975	7-Manik	7	Sep 22 1975	10-Men	3
May 10 1975	5-Ahau	3	Jul 17 1975	8-Lamat	8	Sep 23 1975	11-Cib	4
May 11 1975	*6-Imix*	4	Jul 18 1975	9-Muluc	9	Sep 24 1975	12-Caban	5
May 12 1975	7-Ik	5	Jul 19 1975	10-Oc	1	Sep 25 1975	13-Etz'nab	6
May 13 1975	8-Akbal	6	Jul 20 1975	11-Chuen	2	Sep 26 1975	**1-Cauac**	7
May 14 1975	9-Kan	7	Jul 21 1975	12-Eb	3	Sep 27 1975	2-Ahau	8
May 15 1975	10-Chicchan	8	Jul 22 1975	13-Ben	4	Sep 28 1975	*3-Imix*	9
May 16 1975	11-Cimi	9	Jul 23 1975	**1-Ix**	5	Sep 29 1975	4-Ik	1
May 17 1975	12-Manik	1	Jul 24 1975	2-Men	6	Sep 30 1975	5-Akbal	2
May 18 1975	13-Lamat	2	Jul 25 1975	3-Cib	7	Oct 1 1975	6-Kan	3
May 19 1975	**1-Muluc**	3	Jul 26 1975	4-Caban	8	Oct 2 1975	7-Chicchan	4
May 20 1975	2-Oc	4	Jul 27 1975	5-Etz'nab	9	Oct 3 1975	8-Cimi	5
May 21 1975	3-Chuen	5	Jul 28 1975	6-Cauac	1	Oct 4 1975	9-Manik	6
May 22 1975	4-Eb	6	Jul 29 1975	7-Ahau	2	Oct 5 1975	10-Lamat	7
May 23 1975	5-Ben	7	Jul 30 1975	*8-Imix*	3	Oct 6 1975	11-Muluc	8
May 24 1975	6-Ix	8	Jul 31 1975	9-Ik	4	Oct 7 1975	12-Oc	9
May 25 1975	7-Men	9	Aug 1 1975	10-Akbal	5	Oct 8 1975	13-Chuen	1
May 26 1975	8-Cib	1	Aug 2 1975	11-Kan	6	Oct 9 1975	**1-Eb**	2
May 27 1975	9-Caban	2	Aug 3 1975	12-Chicchan	7	Oct 10 1975	2-Ben	3

Date	Day-Sign	L
Oct 11 1975	3-Ix	4
Oct 12 1975	4-Men	5
Oct 13 1975	5-Cib	6
Oct 14 1975	6-Caban	7
Oct 15 1975	7-Etz'nab	8
Oct 16 1975	8-Cauac	9
Oct 17 1975	9-Ahau	1
Oct 18 1975	10-Imix	2
Oct 19 1975	11-Ik	3
Oct 20 1975	12-Akbal	4
Oct 21 1975	13-Kan	5
Oct 22 1975	1-Chicchan	6
Oct 23 1975	2-Cimi	7
Oct 24 1975	3-Manik	8
Oct 25 1975	4-Lamat	9
Oct 26 1975	5-Muluc	1
Oct 27 1975	6-Oc	2
Oct 28 1975	7-Chuen	3
Oct 29 1975	8-Eb	4
Oct 30 1975	9-Ben	5
Oct 31 1975	10-Ix	6
Nov 1 1975	11-Men	7
Nov 2 1975	12-Cib	8
Nov 3 1975	13-Caban	9
Nov 4 1975	1-Etz'nab	1
Nov 5 1975	2-Cauac	2
Nov 6 1975	3-Ahau	3
Nov 7 1975	4-Imix	4
Nov 8 1975	5-Ik	5
Nov 9 1975	6-Akbal	6
Nov 10 1975	7-Kan	7
Nov 11 1975	8-Chicchan	8
Nov 12 1975	9-Cimi	9
Nov 13 1975	10-Manik	1
Nov 14 1975	11-Lamat	2
Nov 15 1975	12-Muluc	3
Nov 16 1975	13-Oc	4
Nov 17 1975	1-Chuen	5
Nov 18 1975	2-Eb	6
Nov 19 1975	3-Ben	7
Nov 20 1975	4-Ix	8
Nov 21 1975	5-Men	9
Nov 22 1975	6-Cib	1
Nov 23 1975	7-Caban	2
Nov 24 1975	8-Etz'nab	3
Nov 25 1975	9-Cauac	4
Nov 26 1975	10-Ahau	5
Nov 27 1975	11-Imix	6
Nov 28 1975	12-Ik	7
Nov 29 1975	13-Akbal	8
Nov 30 1975	1-Kan	9
Dec 1 1975	2-Chicchan	1
Dec 2 1975	3-Cimi	2
Dec 3 1975	4-Manik	3
Dec 4 1975	5-Lamat	4
Dec 5 1975	6-Muluc	5
Dec 6 1975	7-Oc	6
Dec 7 1975	8-Chuen	7
Dec 8 1975	9-Eb	8
Dec 9 1975	10-Ben	9
Dec 10 1975	11-Ix	1
Dec 11 1975	12-Men	2
Dec 12 1975	13-Cib	3
Dec 13 1975	1-Caban	4
Dec 14 1975	2-Etz'nab	5
Dec 15 1975	3-Cauac	6
Dec 16 1975	4-Ahau	7
Dec 17 1975	5-Imix	8

Date	Day-Sign	L
Dec 18 1975	6-Ik	9
Dec 19 1975	7-Akbal	1
Dec 20 1975	8-Kan	2
Dec 21 1975	9-Chicchan	3
Dec 22 1975	10-Cimi	4
Dec 23 1975	11-Manik	5
Dec 24 1975	12-Lamat	6
Dec 25 1975	13-Muluc	7
Dec 26 1975	1-Oc	8
Dec 27 1975	2-Chuen	9
Dec 28 1975	3-Eb	1
Dec 29 1975	4-Ben	2
Dec 30 1975	5-Ix	3
Dec 31 1975	6-Men	4
Jan 1 1976	7-Cib	5
Jan 2 1976	8-Caban	6
Jan 3 1976	9-Etz'nab	7
Jan 4 1976	10-Cauac	8
Jan 5 1976	11-Ahau	9
Jan 6 1976	12-Imix	1
Jan 7 1976	13-Ik	2
Jan 8 1976	1-Akbal	3
Jan 9 1976	2-Kan	4
Jan 10 1976	3-Chicchan	5
Jan 11 1976	4-Cimi	6
Jan 12 1976	5-Manik	7
Jan 13 1976	6-Lamat	8
Jan 14 1976	7-Muluc	9
Jan 15 1976	8-Oc	1
Jan 16 1976	9-Chuen	2
Jan 17 1976	10-Eb	3
Jan 18 1976	11-Ben	4
Jan 19 1976	12-Ix	5
Jan 20 1976	13-Men	6
Jan 21 1976	1-Cib	7
Jan 22 1976	2-Caban	8
Jan 23 1976	3-Etz'nab	9
Jan 24 1976	4-Cauac	1
Jan 25 1976	5-Ahau	2
Jan 26 1976	6-Imix	3
Jan 27 1976	7-Ik	4
Jan 28 1976	8-Akbal	5
Jan 29 1976	9-Kan	6
Jan 30 1976	10-Chicchan	7
Jan 31 1976	11-Cimi	8
Feb 1 1976	12-Manik	9
Feb 2 1976	13-Lamat	1
Feb 3 1976	1-Muluc	2
Feb 4 1976	2-Oc	3
Feb 5 1976	3-Chuen	4
Feb 6 1976	4-Eb	5
Feb 7 1976	5-Ben	6
Feb 8 1976	6-Ix	7
Feb 9 1976	7-Men	8
Feb 10 1976	8-Cib	9
Feb 11 1976	9-Caban	1
Feb 12 1976	10-Etz'nab	2
Feb 13 1976	11-Cauac	3
Feb 14 1976	12-Ahau	4
Feb 15 1976	13-Imix	5
Feb 16 1976	1-Ik	6
Feb 17 1976	2-Akbal	7
Feb 18 1976	3-Kan	8
Feb 19 1976	4-Chicchan	9
Feb 20 1976	5-Cimi	1
Feb 21 1976	6-Manik	2
Feb 22 1976	7-Lamat	3
Feb 23 1976	8-Muluc	4

Date	Day-Sign	L
Feb 24 1976	9-Oc	5
Feb 25 1976	10-Chuen	6
Feb 26 1976	11-Eb	7
Feb 27 1976	12-Ben	8
Feb 28 1976	13-Ix	9
Feb 29 1976	1-Men	1
Mar 1 1976	2-Cib	2
Mar 2 1976	3-Caban	3
Mar 3 1976	4-Etz'nab	4
Mar 4 1976	5-Cauac	5
Mar 5 1976	6-Ahau	6
Mar 6 1976	7-Imix	7
Mar 7 1976	8-Ik	8
Mar 8 1976	9-Akbal	9
Mar 9 1976	10-Kan	1
Mar 10 1976	11-Chicchan	2
Mar 11 1976	12-Cimi	3
Mar 12 1976	13-Manik	4
Mar 13 1976	1-Lamat	5
Mar 14 1976	2-Muluc	6
Mar 15 1976	3-Oc	7
Mar 16 1976	4-Chuen	8
Mar 17 1976	5-Eb	9
Mar 18 1976	6-Ben	1
Mar 19 1976	7-Ix	2
Mar 20 1976	8-Men	3
Mar 21 1976	9-Cib	4
Mar 22 1976	10-Caban	5
Mar 23 1976	11-Etz'nab	6
Mar 24 1976	12-Cauac	7
Mar 25 1976	13-Ahau	8
Mar 26 1976	1-Imix	9
Mar 27 1976	2-Ik	1
Mar 28 1976	3-Akbal	2
Mar 29 1976	4-Kan	3
Mar 30 1976	5-Chicchan	4
Mar 31 1976	6-Cimi	5
Apr 1 1976	7-Manik	6
Apr 2 1976	8-Lamat	7
Apr 3 1976	9-Muluc	8
Apr 4 1976	10-Oc	9
Apr 5 1976	11-Chuen	1
Apr 6 1976	12-Eb	2
Apr 7 1976	13-Ben	3
Apr 8 1976	1-Ix	4
Apr 9 1976	2-Men	5
Apr 10 1976	3-Cib	6
Apr 11 1976	4-Caban	7
Apr 12 1976	5-Etz'nab	8
Apr 13 1976	6-Cauac	9
Apr 14 1976	7-Ahau	1
Apr 15 1976	8-Imix	2
Apr 16 1976	9-Ik	3
Apr 17 1976	10-Akbal	4
Apr 18 1976	11-Kan	5
Apr 19 1976	12-Chicchan	6
Apr 20 1976	13-Cimi	7
Apr 21 1976	1-Manik	8
Apr 22 1976	2-Lamat	1
Apr 23 1976	3-Muluc	1
Apr 24 1976	4-Oc	2
Apr 25 1976	5-Chuen	3
Apr 26 1976	6-Eb	4
Apr 27 1976	7-Ben	5
Apr 28 1976	8-Ix	6
Apr 29 1976	9-Men	7
Apr 30 1976	10-Cib	8
May 1 1976	11-Caban	9

Date	Day-Sign	L
May 2 1976	12-Etz'nab	1
May 3 1976	13-Cauac	2
May 4 1976	**1-Ahau**	3
May 5 1976	2-*Imix*	4
May 6 1976	3-Ik	5
May 7 1976	4-Akbal	6
May 8 1976	5-Kan	7
May 9 1976	6-Chicchan	8
May 10 1976	7-Cimi	9
May 11 1976	8-Manik	1
May 12 1976	9-Lamat	2
May 13 1976	10-Muluc	3
May 14 1976	11-Oc	4
May 15 1976	12-Chuen	5
May 16 1976	13-Eb	6
May 17 1976	**1-Ben**	7
May 18 1976	2-Ix	8
May 19 1976	3-Men	9
May 20 1976	4-Cib	1
May 21 1976	5-Caban	2
May 22 1976	6-Etz'nab	3
May 23 1976	7-Cauac	4
May 24 1976	8-Ahau	5
May 25 1976	9-*Imix*	6
May 26 1976	10-Ik	7
May 27 1976	11-Akbal	8
May 28 1976	12-Kan	9
May 29 1976	13-Chicchan	1
May 30 1976	**1-Cimi**	2
May 31 1976	2-Manik	3
Jun 1 1976	3-Lamat	4
Jun 2 1976	4-Muluc	5
Jun 3 1976	5-Oc	6
Jun 4 1976	6-Chuen	7
Jun 5 1976	7-Eb	8
Jun 6 1976	8-Ben	9
Jun 7 1976	9-Ix	1
Jun 8 1976	10-Men	2
Jun 9 1976	11-Cib	3
Jun 10 1976	12-Caban	4
Jun 11 1976	13-Etz'nab	5
Jun 12 1976	**1-Cauac**	6
Jun 13 1976	2-Ahau	7
Jun 14 1976	3-*Imix*	8
Jun 15 1976	4-Ik	9
Jun 16 1976	5-Akbal	1
Jun 17 1976	6-Kan	2
Jun 18 1976	7-Chicchan	3
Jun 19 1976	8-Cimi	4
Jun 20 1976	9-Manik	5
Jun 21 1976	10-Lamat	6
Jun 22 1976	11-Muluc	7
Jun 23 1976	12-Oc	8
Jun 24 1976	13-Chuen	9
Jun 25 1976	**1-Eb**	1
Jun 26 1976	2-Ben	2
Jun 27 1976	3-Ix	3
Jun 28 1976	4-Men	4
Jun 29 1976	5-Cib	5
Jun 30 1976	6-Caban	6
Jul 1 1976	7-Etz'nab	7
Jul 2 1976	8-Cauac	8
Jul 3 1976	9-Ahau	9
Jul 4 1976	10-*Imix*	1
Jul 5 1976	11-Ik	2
Jul 6 1976	12-Akbal	3
Jul 7 1976	13-Kan	4
Jul 8 1976	**1-Chicchan**	5

Date	Day-Sign	L
Jul 9 1976	2-Cimi	6
Jul 10 1976	3-Manik	7
Jul 11 1976	4-Lamat	8
Jul 12 1976	5-Muluc	9
Jul 13 1976	6-Oc	1
Jul 14 1976	7-Chuen	2
Jul 15 1976	8-Eb	3
Jul 16 1976	9-Ben	4
Jul 17 1976	10-Ix	5
Jul 18 1976	11-Men	6
Jul 19 1976	12-Cib	7
Jul 20 1976	13-Caban	8
Jul 21 1976	**1-Etz'nab**	9
Jul 22 1976	2-Cauac	1
Jul 23 1976	3-Ahau	2
Jul 24 1976	4-*Imix*	3
Jul 25 1976	5-Ik	4
Jul 26 1976	6-Akbal	5
Jul 27 1976	7-Kan	6
Jul 28 1976	8-Chicchan	7
Jul 29 1976	9-Cimi	8
Jul 30 1976	10-Manik	9
Jul 31 1976	11-Lamat	1
Aug 1 1976	12-Muluc	2
Aug 2 1976	13-Oc	3
Aug 3 1976	**1-Chuen**	4
Aug 4 1976	2-Eb	5
Aug 5 1976	3-Ben	6
Aug 6 1976	4-Ix	7
Aug 7 1976	5-Men	8
Aug 8 1976	6-Cib	9
Aug 9 1976	7-Caban	1
Aug 10 1976	8-Etz'nab	2
Aug 11 1976	9-Cauac	3
Aug 12 1976	10-Ahau	4
Aug 13 1976	11-*Imix*	5
Aug 14 1976	12-Ik	6
Aug 15 1976	13-Akbal	7
Aug 16 1976	**1-Kan**	8
Aug 17 1976	2-Chicchan	9
Aug 18 1976	3-Cimi	1
Aug 19 1976	4-Manik	2
Aug 20 1976	5-Lamat	3
Aug 21 1976	6-Muluc	4
Aug 22 1976	7-Oc	5
Aug 23 1976	8-Chuen	6
Aug 24 1976	9-Eb	7
Aug 25 1976	10-Ben	8
Aug 26 1976	11-Ix	9
Aug 27 1976	12-Men	1
Aug 28 1976	13-Cib	2
Aug 29 1976	**1-Caban**	3
Aug 30 1976	2-Etz'nab	4
Aug 31 1976	3-Cauac	5
Sep 1 1976	4-Ahau	6
Sep 2 1976	5-*Imix*	7
Sep 3 1976	6-Ik	8
Sep 4 1976	7-Akbal	9
Sep 5 1976	8-Kan	1
Sep 6 1976	9-Chicchan	2
Sep 7 1976	10-Cimi	3
Sep 8 1976	11-Manik	4
Sep 9 1976	12-Lamat	5
Sep 10 1976	13-Muluc	6
Sep 11 1976	**1-Oc**	7
Sep 12 1976	2-Chuen	8
Sep 13 1976	3-Eb	9
Sep 14 1976	4-Ben	1

Date	Day-Sign	L
Sep 15 1976	5-Ix	2
Sep 16 1976	6-Men	3
Sep 17 1976	7-Cib	4
Sep 18 1976	8-Caban	5
Sep 19 1976	9-Etz'nab	6
Sep 20 1976	10-Cauac	7
Sep 21 1976	11-Ahau	8
Sep 22 1976	12-*Imix*	9
Sep 23 1976	13-Ik	1
Sep 24 1976	**1-Akbal**	2
Sep 25 1976	2-Kan	3
Sep 26 1976	3-Chicchan	4
Sep 27 1976	4-Cimi	5
Sep 28 1976	5-Manik	6
Sep 29 1976	6-Lamat	7
Sep 30 1976	7-Muluc	8
Oct 1 1976	8-Oc	9
Oct 2 1976	9-Chuen	1
Oct 3 1976	10-Eb	2
Oct 4 1976	11-Ben	3
Oct 5 1976	12-Ix	4
Oct 6 1976	13-Men	5
Oct 7 1976	**1-Cib**	6
Oct 8 1976	2-Caban	7
Oct 9 1976	3-Etz'nab	8
Oct 10 1976	4-Cauac	9
Oct 11 1976	5-Ahau	1
Oct 12 1976	6-*Imix*	2
Oct 13 1976	7-Ik	3
Oct 14 1976	8-Akbal	4
Oct 15 1976	9-Kan	5
Oct 16 1976	10-Chicchan	6
Oct 17 1976	11-Cimi	7
Oct 18 1976	12-Manik	8
Oct 19 1976	13-Lamat	9
Oct 20 1976	**1-Muluc**	1
Oct 21 1976	2-Oc	2
Oct 22 1976	3-Chuen	3
Oct 23 1976	4-Eb	4
Oct 24 1976	5-Ben	5
Oct 25 1976	6-Ix	6
Oct 26 1976	7-Men	7
Oct 27 1976	8-Cib	8
Oct 28 1976	9-Caban	9
Oct 29 1976	10-Etz'nab	1
Oct 30 1976	11-Cauac	2
Oct 31 1976	12-Ahau	3
Nov 1 1976	13-*Imix*	4
Nov 2 1976	**1-Ik**	5
Nov 3 1976	2-Akbal	6
Nov 4 1976	3-Kan	7
Nov 5 1976	4-Chicchan	8
Nov 6 1976	5-Cimi	9
Nov 7 1976	6-Manik	1
Nov 8 1976	7-Lamat	2
Nov 9 1976	8-Muluc	3
Nov 10 1976	9-Oc	4
Nov 11 1976	10-Chuen	5
Nov 12 1976	11-Eb	6
Nov 13 1976	12-Ben	7
Nov 14 1976	13-Ix	8
Nov 15 1976	**1-Men**	9
Nov 16 1976	2-Cib	1
Nov 17 1976	3-Caban	2
Nov 18 1976	4-Etz'nab	3
Nov 19 1976	5-Cauac	4
Nov 20 1976	6-Ahau	5
Nov 21 1976	7-*Imix*	6

Date	Day-Sign	L
Nov 22 1976	8-Ik	7
Nov 23 1976	9-Akbal	8
Nov 24 1976	10-Kan	9
Nov 25 1976	11-Chicchan	1
Nov 26 1976	12-Cimi	2
Nov 27 1976	13-Manik	3
Nov 28 1976	1-Lamat	4
Nov 29 1976	2-Muluc	5
Nov 30 1976	3-Oc	6
Dec 1 1976	4-Chuen	7
Dec 2 1976	5-Eb	8
Dec 3 1976	6-Ben	9
Dec 4 1976	7-Ix	1
Dec 5 1976	8-Men	2
Dec 6 1976	9-Cib	3
Dec 7 1976	10-Caban	4
Dec 8 1976	11-Etz'nab	5
Dec 9 1976	12-Cauac	6
Dec 10 1976	13-Ahau	7
Dec 11 1976	1-Imix	8
Dec 12 1976	2-Ik	9
Dec 13 1976	3-Akbal	1
Dec 14 1976	4-Kan	2
Dec 15 1976	5-Chicchan	3
Dec 16 1976	6-Cimi	4
Dec 17 1976	7-Manik	5
Dec 18 1976	8-Lamat	6
Dec 19 1976	9-Muluc	7
Dec 20 1976	10-Oc	8
Dec 21 1976	11-Chuen	9
Dec 22 1976	12-Eb	1
Dec 23 1976	13-Ben	2
Dec 24 1976	1-Ix	3
Dec 25 1976	2-Men	4
Dec 26 1976	3-Cib	5
Dec 27 1976	4-Caban	6
Dec 28 1976	5-Etz'nab	7
Dec 29 1976	6-Cauac	8
Dec 30 1976	7-Ahau	9
Dec 31 1976	8-Imix	1
Jan 1 1977	9-Ik	2
Jan 2 1977	10-Akbal	3
Jan 3 1977	11-Kan	4
Jan 4 1977	12-Chicchan	5
Jan 5 1977	13-Cimi	6
Jan 6 1977	1-Manik	7
Jan 7 1977	2-Lamat	8
Jan 8 1977	3-Muluc	9
Jan 9 1977	4-Oc	1
Jan 10 1977	5-Chuen	2
Jan 11 1977	6-Eb	3
Jan 12 1977	7-Ben	4
Jan 13 1977	8-Ix	5
Jan 14 1977	9-Men	6
Jan 15 1977	10-Cib	7
Jan 16 1977	11-Caban	8
Jan 17 1977	12-Etz'nab	9
Jan 18 1977	13-Cauac	1
Jan 19 1977	1-Ahau	2
Jan 20 1977	2-Imix	3
Jan 21 1977	3-Ik	4
Jan 22 1977	4-Akbal	5
Jan 23 1977	5-Kan	6
Jan 24 1977	6-Chicchan	7
Jan 25 1977	7-Cimi	8
Jan 26 1977	8-Manik	9
Jan 27 1977	9-Lamat	1
Jan 28 1977	10-Muluc	2

Date	Day-Sign	L
Jan 29 1977	11-Oc	3
Jan 30 1977	12-Chuen	4
Jan 31 1977	13-Eb	5
Feb 1 1977	1-Ben	6
Feb 2 1977	2-Ix	7
Feb 3 1977	3-Men	8
Feb 4 1977	4-Cib	9
Feb 5 1977	5-Caban	1
Feb 6 1977	6-Etz'nab	2
Feb 7 1977	7-Cauac	3
Feb 8 1977	8-Ahau	4
Feb 9 1977	9-Imix	5
Feb 10 1977	10-Ik	6
Feb 11 1977	11-Akbal	7
Feb 12 1977	12-Kan	8
Feb 13 1977	13-Chicchan	9
Feb 14 1977	1-Cimi	1
Feb 15 1977	2-Manik	2
Feb 16 1977	3-Lamat	3
Feb 17 1977	4-Muluc	4
Feb 18 1977	5-Oc	5
Feb 19 1977	6-Chuen	6
Feb 20 1977	7-Eb	7
Feb 21 1977	8-Ben	8
Feb 22 1977	9-Ix	9
Feb 23 1977	10-Men	1
Feb 24 1977	11-Cib	2
Feb 25 1977	12-Caban	3
Feb 26 1977	13-Etz'nab	4
Feb 27 1977	1-Cauac	5
Feb 28 1977	2-Ahau	6
Mar 1 1977	3-Imix	7
Mar 2 1977	4-Ik	8
Mar 3 1977	5-Akbal	9
Mar 4 1977	6-Kan	1
Mar 5 1977	7-Chicchan	2
Mar 6 1977	8-Cimi	3
Mar 7 1977	9-Manik	4
Mar 8 1977	10-Lamat	5
Mar 9 1977	11-Muluc	6
Mar 10 1977	12-Oc	7
Mar 11 1977	13-Chuen	8
Mar 12 1977	1-Eb	9
Mar 13 1977	2-Ben	1
Mar 14 1977	3-Ix	2
Mar 15 1977	4-Men	3
Mar 16 1977	5-Cib	4
Mar 17 1977	6-Caban	5
Mar 18 1977	7-Etz'nab	6
Mar 19 1977	8-Cauac	7
Mar 20 1977	9-Ahau	8
Mar 21 1977	10-Imix	9
Mar 22 1977	11-Ik	1
Mar 23 1977	12-Akbal	2
Mar 24 1977	13-Kan	3
Mar 25 1977	1-Chicchan	4
Mar 26 1977	2-Cimi	5
Mar 27 1977	3-Manik	6
Mar 28 1977	4-Lamat	7
Mar 29 1977	5-Muluc	8
Mar 30 1977	6-Oc	9
Mar 31 1977	7-Chuen	1
Apr 1 1977	8-Eb	2
Apr 2 1977	9-Ben	3
Apr 3 1977	10-Ix	4
Apr 4 1977	11-Men	5
Apr 5 1977	12-Cib	6
Apr 6 1977	13-Caban	7

Date	Day-Sign	L
Apr 7 1977	1-Etz'nab	8
Apr 8 1977	2-Cauac	9
Apr 9 1977	3-Ahau	1
Apr 10 1977	4-Imix	2
Apr 11 1977	5-Ik	3
Apr 12 1977	6-Akbal	4
Apr 13 1977	7-Kan	5
Apr 14 1977	8-Chicchan	6
Apr 15 1977	9-Cimi	7
Apr 16 1977	10-Manik	8
Apr 17 1977	11-Lamat	9
Apr 18 1977	12-Muluc	1
Apr 19 1977	13-Oc	2
Apr 20 1977	1-Chuen	3
Apr 21 1977	2-Eb	4
Apr 22 1977	3-Ben	5
Apr 23 1977	4-Ix	6
Apr 24 1977	5-Men	7
Apr 25 1977	6-Cib	8
Apr 26 1977	7-Caban	9
Apr 27 1977	8-Etz'nab	1
Apr 28 1977	9-Cauac	2
Apr 29 1977	10-Ahau	3
Apr 30 1977	11-Imix	4
May 1 1977	12-Ik	5
May 2 1977	13-Akbal	6
May 3 1977	1-Kan	7
May 4 1977	2-Chicchan	8
May 5 1977	3-Cimi	9
May 6 1977	4-Manik	1
May 7 1977	5-Lamat	2
May 8 1977	6-Muluc	3
May 9 1977	7-Oc	4
May 10 1977	8-Chuen	5
May 11 1977	9-Eb	6
May 12 1977	10-Ben	7
May 13 1977	11-Ix	8
May 14 1977	12-Men	9
May 15 1977	13-Cib	1
May 16 1977	1-Caban	2
May 17 1977	2-Etz'nab	3
May 18 1977	3-Cauac	4
May 19 1977	4-Ahau	5
May 20 1977	5-Imix	6
May 21 1977	6-Ik	7
May 22 1977	7-Akbal	8
May 23 1977	8-Kan	9
May 24 1977	9-Chicchan	1
May 25 1977	10-Cimi	2
May 26 1977	11-Manik	3
May 27 1977	12-Lamat	4
May 28 1977	13-Muluc	5
May 29 1977	1-Oc	6
May 30 1977	2-Chuen	7
May 31 1977	3-Eb	8
Jun 1 1977	4-Ben	9
Jun 2 1977	5-Ix	1
Jun 3 1977	6-Men	2
Jun 4 1977	7-Cib	3
Jun 5 1977	8-Caban	4
Jun 6 1977	9-Etz'nab	5
Jun 7 1977	10-Cauac	6
Jun 8 1977	11-Ahau	7
Jun 9 1977	12-Imix	8
Jun 10 1977	13-Ik	9
Jun 11 1977	1-Akbal	1
Jun 12 1977	2-Kan	2
Jun 13 1977	3-Chicchan	3

Date	Day-Sign	L
Jun 14 1977	4-Cimi	4
Jun 15 1977	5-Manik	5
Jun 16 1977	6-Lamat	6
Jun 17 1977	7-Muluc	7
Jun 18 1977	8-Oc	8
Jun 19 1977	9-Chuen	9
Jun 20 1977	10-Eb	1
Jun 21 1977	11-Ben	2
Jun 22 1977	12-Ix	3
Jun 23 1977	13-Men	4
Jun 24 1977	1-Cib	5
Jun 25 1977	2-Caban	6
Jun 26 1977	3-Etz'nab	7
Jun 27 1977	4-Cauac	8
Jun 28 1977	5-Ahau	9
Jun 29 1977	6-Imix	1
Jun 30 1977	7-Ik	2
Jul 1 1977	8-Akbal	3
Jul 2 1977	9-Kan	4
Jul 3 1977	10-Chicchan	5
Jul 4 1977	11-Cimi	6
Jul 5 1977	12-Manik	7
Jul 6 1977	13-Lamat	8
Jul 7 1977	1-Muluc	9
Jul 8 1977	2-Oc	1
Jul 9 1977	3-Chuen	2
Jul 10 1977	4-Eb	3
Jul 11 1977	5-Ben	4
Jul 12 1977	6-Ix	5
Jul 13 1977	7-Men	6
Jul 14 1977	8-Cib	7
Jul 15 1977	9-Caban	8
Jul 16 1977	10-Etz'nab	9
Jul 17 1977	11-Cauac	1
Jul 18 1977	12-Ahau	2
Jul 19 1977	13-Imix	3
Jul 20 1977	1-Ik	4
Jul 21 1977	2-Akbal	5
Jul 22 1977	3-Kan	6
Jul 23 1977	4-Chicchan	7
Jul 24 1977	5-Cimi	8
Jul 25 1977	6-Manik	9
Jul 26 1977	7-Lamat	1
Jul 27 1977	8-Muluc	2
Jul 28 1977	9-Oc	3
Jul 29 1977	10-Chuen	4
Jul 30 1977	11-Eb	5
Jul 31 1977	12-Ben	6
Aug 1 1977	13-Ix	7
Aug 2 1977	1-Men	8
Aug 3 1977	2-Cib	9
Aug 4 1977	3-Caban	1
Aug 5 1977	4-Etz'nab	2
Aug 6 1977	5-Cauac	3
Aug 7 1977	6-Ahau	4
Aug 8 1977	7-Imix	5
Aug 9 1977	8-Ik	6
Aug 10 1977	9-Akbal	7
Aug 11 1977	10-Kan	8
Aug 12 1977	11-Chicchan	9
Aug 13 1977	12-Cimi	1
Aug 14 1977	13-Manik	2
Aug 15 1977	1-Lamat	3
Aug 16 1977	2-Muluc	4
Aug 17 1977	3-Oc	5
Aug 18 1977	4-Chuen	6
Aug 19 1977	5-Eb	7
Aug 20 1977	6-Ben	8

Date	Day-Sign	L
Aug 21 1977	7-Ix	9
Aug 22 1977	8-Men	1
Aug 23 1977	9-Cib	2
Aug 24 1977	10-Caban	3
Aug 25 1977	11-Etz'nab	4
Aug 26 1977	12-Cauac	5
Aug 27 1977	13-Ahau	6
Aug 28 1977	1-Imix	7
Aug 29 1977	2-Ik	8
Aug 30 1977	3-Akbal	9
Aug 31 1977	4-Kan	1
Sep 1 1977	5-Chicchan	2
Sep 2 1977	6-Cimi	3
Sep 3 1977	7-Manik	4
Sep 4 1977	8-Lamat	5
Sep 5 1977	9-Muluc	6
Sep 6 1977	10-Oc	7
Sep 7 1977	11-Chuen	8
Sep 8 1977	12-Eb	9
Sep 9 1977	13-Ben	1
Sep 10 1977	1-Ix	2
Sep 11 1977	2-Men	3
Sep 12 1977	3-Cib	4
Sep 13 1977	4-Caban	5
Sep 14 1977	5-Etz'nab	6
Sep 15 1977	6-Cauac	7
Sep 16 1977	7-Ahau	8
Sep 17 1977	8-Imix	9
Sep 18 1977	9-Ik	1
Sep 19 1977	10-Akbal	2
Sep 20 1977	11-Kan	3
Sep 21 1977	12-Chicchan	4
Sep 22 1977	13-Cimi	5
Sep 23 1977	1-Manik	6
Sep 24 1977	2-Lamat	7
Sep 25 1977	3-Muluc	8
Sep 26 1977	4-Oc	9
Sep 27 1977	5-Chuen	1
Sep 28 1977	6-Eb	2
Sep 29 1977	7-Ben	3
Sep 30 1977	8-Ix	4
Oct 1 1977	9-Men	5
Oct 2 1977	10-Cib	6
Oct 3 1977	11-Caban	7
Oct 4 1977	12-Etz'nab	8
Oct 5 1977	13-Cauac	9
Oct 6 1977	1-Ahau	1
Oct 7 1977	2-Imix	2
Oct 8 1977	3-Ik	3
Oct 9 1977	4-Akbal	4
Oct 10 1977	5-Kan	5
Oct 11 1977	6-Chicchan	6
Oct 12 1977	7-Cimi	7
Oct 13 1977	8-Manik	8
Oct 14 1977	9-Lamat	9
Oct 15 1977	10-Muluc	1
Oct 16 1977	11-Oc	2
Oct 17 1977	12-Chuen	3
Oct 18 1977	13-Eb	4
Oct 19 1977	1-Ben	5
Oct 20 1977	2-Ix	6
Oct 21 1977	3-Men	7
Oct 22 1977	4-Cib	8
Oct 23 1977	5-Caban	9
Oct 24 1977	6-Etz'nab	1
Oct 25 1977	7-Cauac	2
Oct 26 1977	8-Ahau	3
Oct 27 1977	9-Imix	4

Date	Day-Sign	L
Oct 28 1977	10-Ik	5
Oct 29 1977	11-Akbal	6
Oct 30 1977	12-Kan	7
Oct 31 1977	13-Chicchan	8
Nov 1 1977	1-Cimi	9
Nov 2 1977	2-Manik	1
Nov 3 1977	3-Lamat	2
Nov 4 1977	4-Muluc	3
Nov 5 1977	5-Oc	4
Nov 6 1977	6-Chuen	5
Nov 7 1977	7-Eb	6
Nov 8 1977	8-Ben	7
Nov 9 1977	9-Ix	8
Nov 10 1977	10-Men	9
Nov 11 1977	11-Cib	1
Nov 12 1977	12-Caban	2
Nov 13 1977	13-Etz'nab	3
Nov 14 1977	1-Cauac	4
Nov 15 1977	2-Ahau	5
Nov 16 1977	3-Imix	6
Nov 17 1977	4-Ik	7
Nov 18 1977	5-Akbal	8
Nov 19 1977	6-Kan	9
Nov 20 1977	7-Chicchan	1
Nov 21 1977	8-Cimi	2
Nov 22 1977	9-Manik	3
Nov 23 1977	10-Lamat	4
Nov 24 1977	11-Muluc	5
Nov 25 1977	12-Oc	6
Nov 26 1977	13-Chuen	7
Nov 27 1977	1-Eb	8
Nov 28 1977	2-Ben	9
Nov 29 1977	3-Ix	1
Nov 30 1977	4-Men	2
Dec 1 1977	5-Cib	3
Dec 2 1977	6-Caban	4
Dec 3 1977	7-Etz'nab	5
Dec 4 1977	8-Cauac	6
Dec 5 1977	9-Ahau	7
Dec 6 1977	10-Imix	8
Dec 7 1977	11-Ik	9
Dec 8 1977	12-Akbal	1
Dec 9 1977	13-Kan	2
Dec 10 1977	1-Chicchan	3
Dec 11 1977	2-Cimi	4
Dec 12 1977	3-Manik	5
Dec 13 1977	4-Lamat	6
Dec 14 1977	5-Muluc	7
Dec 15 1977	6-Oc	8
Dec 16 1977	7-Chuen	9
Dec 17 1977	8-Eb	1
Dec 18 1977	9-Ben	2
Dec 19 1977	10-Ix	3
Dec 20 1977	11-Men	4
Dec 21 1977	12-Cib	5
Dec 22 1977	13-Caban	6
Dec 23 1977	1-Etz'nab	7
Dec 24 1977	2-Cauac	8
Dec 25 1977	3-Ahau	9
Dec 26 1977	4-Imix	1
Dec 27 1977	5-Ik	2
Dec 28 1977	6-Akbal	3
Dec 29 1977	7-Kan	4
Dec 30 1977	8-Chicchan	5
Dec 31 1977	9-Cimi	6
Jan 1 1978	10-Manik	7
Jan 2 1978	11-Lamat	8
Jan 3 1978	12-Muluc	9

Date	Day-Sign	L
Jan 4 1978	13-Oc	1
Jan 5 1978	**1-Chuen**	2
Jan 6 1978	2-Eb	3
Jan 7 1978	3-Ben	4
Jan 8 1978	4-Ix	5
Jan 9 1978	5-Men	6
Jan 10 1978	6-Cib	7
Jan 11 1978	7-Caban	8
Jan 12 1978	8-Etz'nab	9
Jan 13 1978	9-Cauac	1
Jan 14 1978	10-Ahau	2
Jan 15 1978	*11-Imix*	3
Jan 16 1978	12-Ik	4
Jan 17 1978	13-Akbal	5
Jan 18 1978	**1-Kan**	6
Jan 19 1978	2-Chicchan	7
Jan 20 1978	3-Cimi	8
Jan 21 1978	4-Manik	9
Jan 22 1978	5-Lamat	1
Jan 23 1978	6-Muluc	2
Jan 24 1978	7-Oc	3
Jan 25 1978	8-Chuen	4
Jan 26 1978	9-Eb	5
Jan 27 1978	10-Ben	6
Jan 28 1978	11-Ix	7
Jan 29 1978	12-Men	8
Jan 30 1978	13-Cib	9
Jan 31 1978	**1-Caban**	1
Feb 1 1978	2-Etz'nab	2
Feb 2 1978	3-Cauac	3
Feb 3 1978	4-Ahau	4
Feb 4 1978	*5-Imix*	5
Feb 5 1978	6-Ik	6
Feb 6 1978	7-Akbal	7
Feb 7 1978	8-Kan	8
Feb 8 1978	9-Chicchan	9
Feb 9 1978	10-Cimi	1
Feb 10 1978	11-Manik	2
Feb 11 1978	12-Lamat	3
Feb 12 1978	13-Muluc	4
Feb 13 1978	**1-Oc**	5
Feb 14 1978	2-Chuen	6
Feb 15 1978	3-Eb	7
Feb 16 1978	4-Ben	8
Feb 17 1978	5-Ix	9
Feb 18 1978	6-Men	1
Feb 19 1978	7-Cib	2
Feb 20 1978	8-Caban	3
Feb 21 1978	9-Etz'nab	4
Feb 22 1978	10-Cauac	5
Feb 23 1978	11-Ahau	6
Feb 24 1978	*12-Imix*	7
Feb 25 1978	13-Ik	8
Feb 26 1978	**1-Akbal**	9
Feb 27 1978	2-Kan	1
Feb 28 1978	3-Chicchan	2
Mar 1 1978	4-Cimi	3
Mar 2 1978	5-Manik	4
Mar 3 1978	6-Lamat	5
Mar 4 1978	7-Muluc	6
Mar 5 1978	8-Oc	7
Mar 6 1978	9-Chuen	8
Mar 7 1978	10-Eb	9
Mar 8 1978	11-Ben	1
Mar 9 1978	12-Ix	2
Mar 10 1978	13-Men	3
Mar 11 1978	**1-Cib**	4
Mar 12 1978	2-Caban	5

Date	Day-Sign	L
Mar 13 1978	3-Etz'nab	6
Mar 14 1978	4-Cauac	7
Mar 15 1978	5-Ahau	8
Mar 16 1978	*6-Imix*	9
Mar 17 1978	7-Ik	1
Mar 18 1978	8-Akbal	2
Mar 19 1978	9-Kan	3
Mar 20 1978	10-Chicchan	4
Mar 21 1978	11-Cimi	5
Mar 22 1978	12-Manik	6
Mar 23 1978	13-Lamat	7
Mar 24 1978	**1-Muluc**	8
Mar 25 1978	2-Oc	9
Mar 26 1978	3-Chuen	1
Mar 27 1978	4-Eb	2
Mar 28 1978	5-Ben	3
Mar 29 1978	6-Ix	4
Mar 30 1978	7-Men	5
Mar 31 1978	8-Cib	6
Apr 1 1978	9-Caban	7
Apr 2 1978	10-Etz'nab	8
Apr 3 1978	11-Cauac	9
Apr 4 1978	12-Ahau	1
Apr 5 1978	*13-Imix*	2
Apr 6 1978	**1-Ik**	3
Apr 7 1978	2-Akbal	4
Apr 8 1978	3-Kan	5
Apr 9 1978	4-Chicchan	6
Apr 10 1978	5-Cimi	7
Apr 11 1978	6-Manik	8
Apr 12 1978	7-Lamat	9
Apr 13 1978	8-Muluc	1
Apr 14 1978	9-Oc	2
Apr 15 1978	10-Chuen	3
Apr 16 1978	11-Eb	4
Apr 17 1978	12-Ben	5
Apr 18 1978	13-Ix	6
Apr 19 1978	**1-Men**	7
Apr 20 1978	2-Cib	8
Apr 21 1978	3-Caban	9
Apr 22 1978	4-Etz'nab	1
Apr 23 1978	5-Cauac	2
Apr 24 1978	6-Ahau	3
Apr 25 1978	*7-Imix*	4
Apr 26 1978	8-Ik	5
Apr 27 1978	9-Akbal	6
Apr 28 1978	10-Kan	7
Apr 29 1978	11-Chicchan	8
Apr 30 1978	12-Cimi	9
May 1 1978	13-Manik	1
May 2 1978	**1-Lamat**	2
May 3 1978	2-Muluc	3
May 4 1978	3-Oc	4
May 5 1978	4-Chuen	5
May 6 1978	5-Eb	6
May 7 1978	6-Ben	7
May 8 1978	7-Ix	8
May 9 1978	8-Men	9
May 10 1978	9-Cib	1
May 11 1978	10-Caban	2
May 12 1978	11-Etz'nab	3
May 13 1978	12-Cauac	4
May 14 1978	13-Ahau	5
May 15 1978	**1-Imix**	6
May 16 1978	2-Ik	7
May 17 1978	3-Akbal	8
May 18 1978	4-Kan	9
May 19 1978	5-Chicchan	1

Date	Day-Sign	L
May 20 1978	6-Cimi	2
May 21 1978	7-Manik	3
May 22 1978	8-Lamat	4
May 23 1978	9-Muluc	5
May 24 1978	10-Oc	6
May 25 1978	11-Chuen	7
May 26 1978	12-Eb	8
May 27 1978	13-Ben	9
May 28 1978	**1-Ix**	1
May 29 1978	2-Men	2
May 30 1978	3-Cib	3
May 31 1978	4-Caban	4
Jun 1 1978	5-Etz'nab	5
Jun 2 1978	6-Cauac	6
Jun 3 1978	7-Ahau	7
Jun 4 1978	*8-Imix*	8
Jun 5 1978	9-Ik	9
Jun 6 1978	10-Akbal	1
Jun 7 1978	11-Kan	2
Jun 8 1978	12-Chicchan	3
Jun 9 1978	13-Cimi	4
Jun 10 1978	**1-Manik**	5
Jun 11 1978	2-Lamat	6
Jun 12 1978	3-Muluc	7
Jun 13 1978	4-Oc	8
Jun 14 1978	5-Chuen	9
Jun 15 1978	6-Eb	1
Jun 16 1978	7-Ben	2
Jun 17 1978	8-Ix	3
Jun 18 1978	9-Men	4
Jun 19 1978	10-Cib	5
Jun 20 1978	11-Caban	6
Jun 21 1978	12-Etz'nab	7
Jun 22 1978	13-Cauac	8
Jun 23 1978	**1-Ahau**	9
Jun 24 1978	*2-Imix*	1
Jun 25 1978	3-Ik	2
Jun 26 1978	4-Akbal	3
Jun 27 1978	5-Kan	4
Jun 28 1978	6-Chicchan	5
Jun 29 1978	7-Cimi	6
Jun 30 1978	8-Manik	7
Jul 1 1978	9-Lamat	8
Jul 2 1978	10-Muluc	9
Jul 3 1978	11-Oc	1
Jul 4 1978	12-Chuen	2
Jul 5 1978	13-Eb	3
Jul 6 1978	**1-Ben**	4
Jul 7 1978	2-Ix	5
Jul 8 1978	3-Men	6
Jul 9 1978	4-Cib	7
Jul 10 1978	5-Caban	8
Jul 11 1978	6-Etz'nab	9
Jul 12 1978	7-Cauac	1
Jul 13 1978	8-Ahau	2
Jul 14 1978	*9-Imix*	3
Jul 15 1978	10-Ik	4
Jul 16 1978	11-Akbal	5
Jul 17 1978	12-Kan	6
Jul 18 1978	13-Chicchan	7
Jul 19 1978	**1-Cimi**	8
Jul 20 1978	2-Manik	9
Jul 21 1978	3-Lamat	1
Jul 22 1978	4-Muluc	2
Jul 23 1978	5-Oc	3
Jul 24 1978	6-Chuen	4
Jul 25 1978	7-Eb	5
Jul 26 1978	8-Ben	6

Date	Day-Sign	L
Jul 27 1978	9-Ix	7
Jul 28 1978	10-Men	8
Jul 29 1978	11-Cib	9
Jul 30 1978	12-Caban	1
Jul 31 1978	13-Etz'nab	2
Aug 1 1978	**1-Cauac**	3
Aug 2 1978	2-Ahau	4
Aug 3 1978	*3-Imix*	5
Aug 4 1978	4-Ik	6
Aug 5 1978	5-Akbal	7
Aug 6 1978	6-Kan	8
Aug 7 1978	7-Chicchan	9
Aug 8 1978	8-Cimi	1
Aug 9 1978	9-Manik	2
Aug 10 1978	10-Lamat	3
Aug 11 1978	11-Muluc	4
Aug 12 1978	12-Oc	5
Aug 13 1978	13-Chuen	6
Aug 14 1978	**1-Eb**	7
Aug 15 1978	2-Ben	8
Aug 16 1978	3-Ix	9
Aug 17 1978	4-Men	1
Aug 18 1978	5-Cib	2
Aug 19 1978	6-Caban	3
Aug 20 1978	7-Etz'nab	4
Aug 21 1978	8-Cauac	5
Aug 22 1978	9-Ahau	6
Aug 23 1978	*10-Imix*	7
Aug 24 1978	11-Ik	8
Aug 25 1978	12-Akbal	9
Aug 26 1978	13-Kan	1
Aug 27 1978	**1-Chicchan**	2
Aug 28 1978	2-Cimi	3
Aug 29 1978	3-Manik	4
Aug 30 1978	4-Lamat	5
Aug 31 1978	5-Muluc	6
Sep 1 1978	6-Oc	7
Sep 2 1978	7-Chuen	8
Sep 3 1978	8-Eb	9
Sep 4 1978	9-Ben	1
Sep 5 1978	10-Ix	2
Sep 6 1978	11-Men	3
Sep 7 1978	12-Cib	4
Sep 8 1978	13-Caban	5
Sep 9 1978	**1-Etz'nab**	6
Sep 10 1978	2-Cauac	7
Sep 11 1978	3-Ahau	8
Sep 12 1978	*4-Imix*	9
Sep 13 1978	5-Ik	1
Sep 14 1978	6-Akbal	2
Sep 15 1978	7-Kan	3
Sep 16 1978	8-Chicchan	4
Sep 17 1978	9-Cimi	5
Sep 18 1978	10-Manik	6
Sep 19 1978	11-Lamat	7
Sep 20 1978	12-Muluc	8
Sep 21 1978	13-Oc	9
Sep 22 1978	**1-Chuen**	1
Sep 23 1978	2-Eb	2
Sep 24 1978	3-Ben	3
Sep 25 1978	4-Ix	4
Sep 26 1978	5-Men	5
Sep 27 1978	6-Cib	6
Sep 28 1978	7-Caban	7
Sep 29 1978	8-Etz'nab	8
Sep 30 1978	9-Cauac	9
Oct 1 1978	10-Ahau	1
Oct 2 1978	*11-Imix*	2

Date	Day-Sign	L
Oct 3 1978	12-Ik	3
Oct 4 1978	13-Akbal	4
Oct 5 1978	**1-Kan**	5
Oct 6 1978	2-Chicchan	6
Oct 7 1978	3-Cimi	7
Oct 8 1978	4-Manik	8
Oct 9 1978	5-Lamat	9
Oct 10 1978	6-Muluc	1
Oct 11 1978	7-Oc	2
Oct 12 1978	8-Chuen	3
Oct 13 1978	9-Eb	4
Oct 14 1978	10-Ben	5
Oct 15 1978	11-Ix	6
Oct 16 1978	12-Men	7
Oct 17 1978	13-Cib	8
Oct 18 1978	**1-Caban**	9
Oct 19 1978	2-Etz'nab	1
Oct 20 1978	3-Cauac	2
Oct 21 1978	4-Ahau	3
Oct 22 1978	*5-Imix*	4
Oct 23 1978	6-Ik	5
Oct 24 1978	7-Akbal	6
Oct 25 1978	8-Kan	7
Oct 26 1978	9-Chicchan	8
Oct 27 1978	10-Cimi	9
Oct 28 1978	11-Manik	1
Oct 29 1978	12-Lamat	2
Oct 30 1978	13-Muluc	3
Oct 31 1978	**1-Oc**	4
Nov 1 1978	2-Chuen	5
Nov 2 1978	3-Eb	6
Nov 3 1978	4-Ben	7
Nov 4 1978	5-Ix	8
Nov 5 1978	6-Men	9
Nov 6 1978	7-Cib	1
Nov 7 1978	8-Caban	2
Nov 8 1978	9-Etz'nab	3
Nov 9 1978	10-Cauac	4
Nov 10 1978	11-Ahau	5
Nov 11 1978	*12-Imix*	6
Nov 12 1978	13-Ik	7
Nov 13 1978	**1-Akbal**	8
Nov 14 1978	2-Kan	9
Nov 15 1978	3-Chicchan	1
Nov 16 1978	4-Cimi	2
Nov 17 1978	5-Manik	3
Nov 18 1978	6-Lamat	4
Nov 19 1978	7-Muluc	5
Nov 20 1978	8-Oc	6
Nov 21 1978	9-Chuen	7
Nov 22 1978	10-Eb	8
Nov 23 1978	11-Ben	9
Nov 24 1978	12-Ix	1
Nov 25 1978	13-Men	2
Nov 26 1978	**1-Cib**	3
Nov 27 1978	2-Caban	4
Nov 28 1978	3-Etz'nab	5
Nov 29 1978	4-Cauac	6
Nov 30 1978	5-Ahau	7
Dec 1 1978	*6-Imix*	8
Dec 2 1978	7-Ik	9
Dec 3 1978	8-Akbal	1
Dec 4 1978	9-Kan	2
Dec 5 1978	10-Chicchan	3
Dec 6 1978	11-Cimi	4
Dec 7 1978	12-Manik	5
Dec 8 1978	13-Lamat	6
Dec 9 1978	**1-Muluc**	7

Date	Day-Sign	L
Dec 10 1978	2-Oc	8
Dec 11 1978	3-Chuen	9
Dec 12 1978	4-Eb	1
Dec 13 1978	5-Ben	2
Dec 14 1978	6-Ix	3
Dec 15 1978	7-Men	4
Dec 16 1978	8-Cib	5
Dec 17 1978	9-Caban	6
Dec 18 1978	10-Etz'nab	7
Dec 19 1978	11-Cauac	8
Dec 20 1978	12-Ahau	9
Dec 21 1978	*13-Imix*	1
Dec 22 1978	**1-Ik**	2
Dec 23 1978	2-Akbal	3
Dec 24 1978	3-Kan	4
Dec 25 1978	4-Chicchan	5
Dec 26 1978	5-Cimi	6
Dec 27 1978	6-Manik	7
Dec 28 1978	7-Lamat	8
Dec 29 1978	8-Muluc	9
Dec 30 1978	9-Oc	1
Dec 31 1978	10-Chuen	2
Jan 1 1979	11-Eb	3
Jan 2 1979	12-Ben	4
Jan 3 1979	13-Ix	5
Jan 4 1979	**1-Men**	6
Jan 5 1979	2-Cib	7
Jan 6 1979	3-Caban	8
Jan 7 1979	4-Etz'nab	9
Jan 8 1979	5-Cauac	1
Jan 9 1979	6-Ahau	2
Jan 10 1979	*7-Imix*	3
Jan 11 1979	8-Ik	4
Jan 12 1979	9-Akbal	5
Jan 13 1979	10-Kan	6
Jan 14 1979	11-Chicchan	7
Jan 15 1979	12-Cimi	8
Jan 16 1979	13-Manik	9
Jan 17 1979	**1-Lamat**	1
Jan 18 1979	2-Muluc	2
Jan 19 1979	3-Oc	3
Jan 20 1979	4-Chuen	4
Jan 21 1979	5-Eb	5
Jan 22 1979	6-Ben	6
Jan 23 1979	7-Ix	7
Jan 24 1979	8-Men	8
Jan 25 1979	9-Cib	9
Jan 26 1979	10-Caban	1
Jan 27 1979	11-Etz'nab	2
Jan 28 1979	12-Cauac	3
Jan 29 1979	13-Ahau	4
Jan 30 1979	**1-Imix**	5
Jan 31 1979	2-Ik	6
Feb 1 1979	3-Akbal	7
Feb 2 1979	4-Kan	8
Feb 3 1979	5-Chicchan	9
Feb 4 1979	6-Cimi	1
Feb 5 1979	7-Manik	2
Feb 6 1979	8-Lamat	3
Feb 7 1979	9-Muluc	4
Feb 8 1979	10-Oc	5
Feb 9 1979	11-Chuen	6
Feb 10 1979	12-Eb	7
Feb 11 1979	13-Ben	8
Feb 12 1979	**1-Ix**	9
Feb 13 1979	2-Men	1
Feb 14 1979	3-Cib	2
Feb 15 1979	4-Caban	3

Date	Day-Sign	L	Date	Day-Sign	L	Date	Day-Sign	L
Feb 16 1979	5-Etz'nab	4	Apr 25 1979	8-Cimi	9	Jul 2 1979	11-Ix	5
Feb 17 1979	6-Cauac	5	Apr 26 1979	9-Manik	1	Jul 3 1979	12-Men	6
Feb 18 1979	7-Ahau	6	Apr 27 1979	10-Lamat	2	Jul 4 1979	13-Cib	7
Feb 19 1979	8-Imix	7	Apr 28 1979	11-Muluc	3	Jul 5 1979	1-Caban	8
Feb 20 1979	9-Ik	8	Apr 29 1979	12-Oc	4	Jul 6 1979	2-Etz'nab	9
Feb 21 1979	10-Akbal	9	Apr 30 1979	13-Chuen	5	Jul 7 1979	3-Cauac	1
Feb 22 1979	11-Kan	1	May 1 1979	1-Eb	6	Jul 8 1979	4-Ahau	2
Feb 23 1979	12-Chicchan	2	May 2 1979	2-Ben	7	Jul 9 1979	5-Imix	3
Feb 24 1979	13-Cimi	3	May 3 1979	3-Ix	8	Jul 10 1979	6-Ik	4
Feb 25 1979	1-Manik	4	May 4 1979	4-Men	9	Jul 11 1979	7-Akbal	5
Feb 26 1979	2-Lamat	5	May 5 1979	5-Cib	1	Jul 12 1979	8-Kan	6
Feb 27 1979	3-Muluc	6	May 6 1979	6-Caban	2	Jul 13 1979	9-Chicchan	7
Feb 28 1979	4-Oc	7	May 7 1979	7-Etz'nab	3	Jul 14 1979	10-Cimi	8
Mar 1 1979	5-Chuen	8	May 8 1979	8-Cauac	4	Jul 15 1979	11-Manik	9
Mar 2 1979	6-Eb	9	May 9 1979	9-Ahau	5	Jul 16 1979	12-Lamat	1
Mar 3 1979	7-Ben	1	May 10 1979	10-Imix	6	Jul 17 1979	13-Muluc	2
Mar 4 1979	8-Ix	2	May 11 1979	11-Ik	7	Jul 18 1979	1-Oc	3
Mar 5 1979	9-Men	3	May 12 1979	12-Akbal	8	Jul 19 1979	2-Chuen	4
Mar 6 1979	10-Cib	4	May 13 1979	13-Kan	9	Jul 20 1979	3-Eb	5
Mar 7 1979	11-Caban	5	May 14 1979	1-Chicchan	1	Jul 21 1979	4-Ben	6
Mar 8 1979	12-Etz'nab	6	May 15 1979	2-Cimi	2	Jul 22 1979	5-Ix	7
Mar 9 1979	13-Cauac	7	May 16 1979	3-Manik	3	Jul 23 1979	6-Men	8
Mar 10 1979	1-Ahau	8	May 17 1979	4-Lamat	4	Jul 24 1979	7-Cib	9
Mar 11 1979	2-Imix	9	May 18 1979	5-Muluc	5	Jul 25 1979	8-Caban	1
Mar 12 1979	3-Ik	1	May 19 1979	6-Oc	6	Jul 26 1979	9-Etz'nab	2
Mar 13 1979	4-Akbal	2	May 20 1979	7-Chuen	7	Jul 27 1979	10-Cauac	3
Mar 14 1979	5-Kan	3	May 21 1979	8-Eb	8	Jul 28 1979	11-Ahau	4
Mar 15 1979	6-Chicchan	4	May 22 1979	9-Ben	9	Jul 29 1979	12-Imix	5
Mar 16 1979	7-Cimi	5	May 23 1979	10-Ix	1	Jul 30 1979	13-Ik	6
Mar 17 1979	8-Manik	6	May 24 1979	11-Men	2	Jul 31 1979	1-Akbal	7
Mar 18 1979	9-Lamat	7	May 25 1979	12-Cib	3	Aug 1 1979	2-Kan	8
Mar 19 1979	10-Muluc	8	May 26 1979	13-Caban	4	Aug 2 1979	3-Chicchan	9
Mar 20 1979	11-Oc	9	May 27 1979	1-Etz'nab	5	Aug 3 1979	4-Cimi	1
Mar 21 1979	12-Chuen	1	May 28 1979	2-Cauac	6	Aug 4 1979	5-Manik	2
Mar 22 1979	13-Eb	2	May 29 1979	3-Ahau	7	Aug 5 1979	6-Lamat	3
Mar 23 1979	1-Ben	3	May 30 1979	4-Imix	8	Aug 6 1979	7-Muluc	4
Mar 24 1979	2-Ix	4	May 31 1979	5-Ik	9	Aug 7 1979	8-Oc	5
Mar 25 1979	3-Men	5	Jun 1 1979	6-Akbal	1	Aug 8 1979	9-Chuen	6
Mar 26 1979	4-Cib	6	Jun 2 1979	7-Kan	2	Aug 9 1979	10-Eb	7
Mar 27 1979	5-Caban	7	Jun 3 1979	8-Chicchan	3	Aug 10 1979	11-Ben	8
Mar 28 1979	6-Etz'nab	8	Jun 4 1979	9-Cimi	4	Aug 11 1979	12-Ix	9
Mar 29 1979	7-Cauac	9	Jun 5 1979	10-Manik	5	Aug 12 1979	13-Men	1
Mar 30 1979	8-Ahau	1	Jun 6 1979	11-Lamat	6	Aug 13 1979	1-Cib	2
Mar 31 1979	9-Imix	2	Jun 7 1979	12-Muluc	7	Aug 14 1979	2-Caban	3
Apr 1 1979	10-Ik	3	Jun 8 1979	13-Oc	8	Aug 15 1979	3-Etz'nab	4
Apr 2 1979	11-Akbal	4	Jun 9 1979	1-Chuen	9	Aug 16 1979	4-Cauac	5
Apr 3 1979	12-Kan	5	Jun 10 1979	2-Eb	1	Aug 17 1979	5-Ahau	6
Apr 4 1979	13-Chicchan	6	Jun 11 1979	3-Ben	2	Aug 18 1979	6-Imix	7
Apr 5 1979	1-Cimi	7	Jun 12 1979	4-Ix	3	Aug 19 1979	7-Ik	8
Apr 6 1979	2-Manik	8	Jun 13 1979	5-Men	4	Aug 20 1979	8-Akbal	9
Apr 7 1979	3-Lamat	9	Jun 14 1979	6-Cib	5	Aug 21 1979	9-Kan	1
Apr 8 1979	4-Muluc	1	Jun 15 1979	7-Caban	6	Aug 22 1979	10-Chicchan	2
Apr 9 1979	5-Oc	2	Jun 16 1979	8-Etz'nab	7	Aug 23 1979	11-Cimi	3
Apr 10 1979	6-Chuen	3	Jun 17 1979	9-Cauac	8	Aug 24 1979	12-Manik	4
Apr 11 1979	7-Eb	4	Jun 18 1979	10-Ahau	9	Aug 25 1979	13-Lamat	5
Apr 12 1979	8-Ben	5	Jun 19 1979	11-Imix	1	Aug 26 1979	1-Muluc	6
Apr 13 1979	9-Ix	6	Jun 20 1979	12-Ik	2	Aug 27 1979	2-Oc	7
Apr 14 1979	10-Men	7	Jun 21 1979	13-Akbal	3	Aug 28 1979	3-Chuen	8
Apr 15 1979	11-Cib	8	Jun 22 1979	1-Kan	4	Aug 29 1979	4-Eb	9
Apr 16 1979	12-Caban	9	Jun 23 1979	2-Chicchan	5	Aug 30 1979	5-Ben	1
Apr 17 1979	13-Etz'nab	1	Jun 24 1979	3-Cimi	6	Aug 31 1979	6-Ix	2
Apr 18 1979	1-Cauac	2	Jun 25 1979	4-Manik	7	Sep 1 1979	7-Men	3
Apr 19 1979	2-Ahau	3	Jun 26 1979	5-Lamat	8	Sep 2 1979	8-Cib	4
Apr 20 1979	3-Imix	4	Jun 27 1979	6-Muluc	9	Sep 3 1979	9-Caban	5
Apr 21 1979	4-Ik	5	Jun 28 1979	7-Oc	1	Sep 4 1979	10-Etz'nab	6
Apr 22 1979	5-Akbal	6	Jun 29 1979	8-Chuen	2	Sep 5 1979	11-Cauac	7
Apr 23 1979	6-Kan	7	Jun 30 1979	9-Eb	3	Sep 6 1979	12-Ahau	8
Apr 24 1979	7-Chicchan	8	Jul 1 1979	10-Ben	4	Sep 7 1979	13-Imix	9

Date	Day-Sign	L	Date	Day-Sign	L	Date	Day-Sign	L
Sep 8 1979	1-Ik	1	Nov 15 1979	4-Oc	6	Jan 22 1980	7-Etz'nab	2
Sep 9 1979	2-Akbal	2	Nov 16 1979	5-Chuen	7	Jan 23 1980	8-Cauac	3
Sep 10 1979	3-Kan	3	Nov 17 1979	6-Eb	8	Jan 24 1980	9-Ahau	4
Sep 11 1979	4-Chicchan	4	Nov 18 1979	7-Ben	9	Jan 25 1980	10-Imix	5
Sep 12 1979	5-Cimi	5	Nov 19 1979	8-Ix	1	Jan 26 1980	11-Ik	6
Sep 13 1979	6-Manik	6	Nov 20 1979	9-Men	2	Jan 27 1980	12-Akbal	7
Sep 14 1979	7-Lamat	7	Nov 21 1979	10-Cib	3	Jan 28 1980	13-Kan	8
Sep 15 1979	8-Muluc	8	Nov 22 1979	11-Caban	4	Jan 29 1980	1-Chicchan	9
Sep 16 1979	9-Oc	9	Nov 23 1979	12-Etz'nab	5	Jan 30 1980	2-Cimi	1
Sep 17 1979	10-Chuen	1	Nov 24 1979	13-Cauac	6	Jan 31 1980	3-Manik	2
Sep 18 1979	11-Eb	2	Nov 25 1979	1-Ahau	7	Feb 1 1980	4-Lamat	3
Sep 19 1979	12-Ben	3	Nov 26 1979	2-Imix	8	Feb 2 1980	5-Muluc	4
Sep 20 1979	13-Ix	4	Nov 27 1979	3-Ik	9	Feb 3 1980	6-Oc	5
Sep 21 1979	1-Men	5	Nov 28 1979	4-Akbal	1	Feb 4 1980	7-Chuen	6
Sep 22 1979	2-Cib	6	Nov 29 1979	5-Kan	2	Feb 5 1980	8-Eb	7
Sep 23 1979	3-Caban	7	Nov 30 1979	6-Chicchan	3	Feb 6 1980	9-Ben	8
Sep 24 1979	4-Etz'nab	8	Dec 1 1979	7-Cimi	4	Feb 7 1980	10-Ix	9
Sep 25 1979	5-Cauac	9	Dec 2 1979	8-Manik	5	Feb 8 1980	11-Men	1
Sep 26 1979	6-Ahau	1	Dec 3 1979	9-Lamat	6	Feb 9 1980	12-Cib	2
Sep 27 1979	7-Imix	2	Dec 4 1979	10-Muluc	7	Feb 10 1980	13-Caban	3
Sep 28 1979	8-Ik	3	Dec 5 1979	11-Oc	8	Feb 11 1980	1-Etz'nab	4
Sep 29 1979	9-Akbal	4	Dec 6 1979	12-Chuen	9	Feb 12 1980	2-Cauac	5
Sep 30 1979	10-Kan	5	Dec 7 1979	13-Eb	1	Feb 13 1980	3-Ahau	6
Oct 1 1979	11-Chicchan	6	Dec 8 1979	1-Ben	2	Feb 14 1980	4-Imix	7
Oct 2 1979	12-Cimi	7	Dec 9 1979	2-Ix	3	Feb 15 1980	5-Ik	8
Oct 3 1979	13-Manik	8	Dec 10 1979	3-Men	4	Feb 16 1980	6-Akbal	9
Oct 4 1979	1-Lamat	9	Dec 11 1979	4-Cib	5	Feb 17 1980	7-Kan	1
Oct 5 1979	2-Muluc	1	Dec 12 1979	5-Caban	6	Feb 18 1980	8-Chicchan	2
Oct 6 1979	3-Oc	2	Dec 13 1979	6-Etz'nab	7	Feb 19 1980	9-Cimi	3
Oct 7 1979	4-Chuen	3	Dec 14 1979	7-Cauac	8	Feb 20 1980	10-Manik	4
Oct 8 1979	5-Eb	4	Dec 15 1979	8-Ahau	9	Feb 21 1980	11-Lamat	5
Oct 9 1979	6-Ben	5	Dec 16 1979	9-Imix	1	Feb 22 1980	12-Muluc	6
Oct 10 1979	7-Ix	6	Dec 17 1979	10-Ik	2	Feb 23 1980	13-Oc	7
Oct 11 1979	8-Men	7	Dec 18 1979	11-Akbal	3	Feb 24 1980	1-Chuen	8
Oct 12 1979	9-Cib	8	Dec 19 1979	12-Kan	4	Feb 25 1980	2-Eb	9
Oct 13 1979	10-Caban	9	Dec 20 1979	13-Chicchan	5	Feb 26 1980	3-Ben	1
Oct 14 1979	11-Etz'nab	1	Dec 21 1979	1-Cimi	6	Feb 27 1980	4-Ix	2
Oct 15 1979	12-Cauac	2	Dec 22 1979	2-Manik	7	Feb 28 1980	5-Men	3
Oct 16 1979	13-Ahau	3	Dec 23 1979	3-Lamat	8	Feb 29 1980	6-Cib	4
Oct 17 1979	1-Imix	4	Dec 24 1979	4-Muluc	9	Mar 1 1980	7-Caban	5
Oct 18 1979	2-Ik	5	Dec 25 1979	5-Oc	1	Mar 2 1980	8-Etz'nab	6
Oct 19 1979	3-Akbal	6	Dec 26 1979	6-Chuen	2	Mar 3 1980	9-Cauac	7
Oct 20 1979	4-Kan	7	Dec 27 1979	7-Eb	3	Mar 4 1980	10-Ahau	8
Oct 21 1979	5-Chicchan	8	Dec 28 1979	8-Ben	4	Mar 5 1980	11-Imix	9
Oct 22 1979	6-Cimi	9	Dec 29 1979	9-Ix	5	Mar 6 1980	12-Ik	1
Oct 23 1979	7-Manik	1	Dec 30 1979	10-Men	6	Mar 7 1980	13-Akbal	2
Oct 24 1979	8-Lamat	2	Dec 31 1979	11-Cib	7	Mar 8 1980	1-Kan	3
Oct 25 1979	9-Muluc	3	Jan 1 1980	12-Caban	8	Mar 9 1980	2-Chicchan	4
Oct 26 1979	10-Oc	4	Jan 2 1980	13-Etz'nab	9	Mar 10 1980	3-Cimi	5
Oct 27 1979	11-Chuen	5	Jan 3 1980	1-Cauac	1	Mar 11 1980	4-Manik	6
Oct 28 1979	12-Eb	6	Jan 4 1980	2-Ahau	2	Mar 12 1980	5-Lamat	7
Oct 29 1979	13-Ben	7	Jan 5 1980	3-Imix	3	Mar 13 1980	6-Muluc	8
Oct 30 1979	1-Ix	8	Jan 6 1980	4-Ik	4	Mar 14 1980	7-Oc	9
Oct 31 1979	2-Men	9	Jan 7 1980	5-Akbal	5	Mar 15 1980	8-Chuen	1
Nov 1 1979	3-Cib	1	Jan 8 1980	6-Kan	6	Mar 16 1980	9-Eb	2
Nov 2 1979	4-Caban	2	Jan 9 1980	7-Chicchan	7	Mar 17 1980	10-Ben	3
Nov 3 1979	5-Etz'nab	3	Jan 10 1980	8-Cimi	8	Mar 18 1980	11-Ix	4
Nov 4 1979	6-Cauac	4	Jan 11 1980	9-Manik	9	Mar 19 1980	12-Men	5
Nov 5 1979	7-Ahau	5	Jan 12 1980	10-Lamat	1	Mar 20 1980	13-Cib	6
Nov 6 1979	8-Imix	6	Jan 13 1980	11-Muluc	2	Mar 21 1980	1-Caban	7
Nov 7 1979	9-Ik	7	Jan 14 1980	12-Oc	3	Mar 22 1980	2-Etz'nab	8
Nov 8 1979	10-Akbal	8	Jan 15 1980	13-Chuen	4	Mar 23 1980	3-Cauac	9
Nov 9 1979	11-Kan	9	Jan 16 1980	1-Eb	5	Mar 24 1980	4-Ahau	1
Nov 10 1979	12-Chicchan	1	Jan 17 1980	2-Ben	6	Mar 25 1980	5-Imix	2
Nov 11 1979	13-Cimi	2	Jan 18 1980	3-Ix	7	Mar 26 1980	6-Ik	3
Nov 12 1979	1-Manik	3	Jan 19 1980	4-Men	8	Mar 27 1980	7-Akbal	4
Nov 13 1979	2-Lamat	4	Jan 20 1980	5-Cib	9	Mar 28 1980	8-Kan	5
Nov 14 1979	3-Muluc	5	Jan 21 1980	6-Caban	1	Mar 29 1980	9-Chicchan	6

Date	Day-Sign	L	Date	Day-Sign	L	Date	Day-Sign	L
Mar 30 1980	10-Cimi	7	Jun 6 1980	13-Ix	3	Aug 13 1980	3-Ik	8
Mar 31 1980	11-Manik	8	Jun 7 1980	**1-Men**	4	Aug 14 1980	4-Akbal	9
Apr 1 1980	12-Lamat	9	Jun 8 1980	2-Cib	5	Aug 15 1980	5-Kan	1
Apr 2 1980	13-Muluc	1	Jun 9 1980	3-Caban	6	Aug 16 1980	6-Chicchan	2
Apr 3 1980	**1-Oc**	2	Jun 10 1980	4-Etz'nab	7	Aug 17 1980	7-Cimi	3
Apr 4 1980	2-Chuen	3	Jun 11 1980	5-Cauac	8	Aug 18 1980	8-Manik	4
Apr 5 1980	3-Eb	4	Jun 12 1980	6-Ahau	9	Aug 19 1980	9-Lamat	5
Apr 6 1980	4-Ben	5	Jun 13 1980	7-*Imix*	1	Aug 20 1980	10-Muluc	6
Apr 7 1980	5-Ix	6	Jun 14 1980	8-Ik	2	Aug 21 1980	11-Oc	7
Apr 8 1980	6-Men	7	Jun 15 1980	9-Akbal	3	Aug 22 1980	12-Chuen	8
Apr 9 1980	7-Cib	8	Jun 16 1980	10-Kan	4	Aug 23 1980	13-Eb	9
Apr 10 1980	8-Caban	9	Jun 17 1980	11-Chicchan	5	Aug 24 1980	**1-Ben**	1
Apr 11 1980	9-Etz'nab	1	Jun 18 1980	12-Cimi	6	Aug 25 1980	2-Ix	2
Apr 12 1980	10-Cauac	2	Jun 19 1980	13-Manik	7	Aug 26 1980	3-Men	3
Apr 13 1980	11-Ahau	3	Jun 20 1980	**1-Lamat**	8	Aug 27 1980	4-Cib	4
Apr 14 1980	12-*Imix*	4	Jun 21 1980	2-Muluc	9	Aug 28 1980	5-Caban	5
Apr 15 1980	13-Ik	5	Jun 22 1980	3-Oc	1	Aug 29 1980	6-Etz'nab	6
Apr 16 1980	**1-Akbal**	6	Jun 23 1980	4-Chuen	2	Aug 30 1980	7-Cauac	7
Apr 17 1980	2-Kan	7	Jun 24 1980	5-Eb	3	Aug 31 1980	8-Ahau	8
Apr 18 1980	3-Chicchan	8	Jun 25 1980	6-Ben	4	Sep 1 1980	9-*Imix*	9
Apr 19 1980	4-Cimi	9	Jun 26 1980	7-Ix	5	Sep 2 1980	10-Ik	1
Apr 20 1980	5-Manik	1	Jun 27 1980	8-Men	6	Sep 3 1980	11-Akbal	2
Apr 21 1980	6-Lamat	2	Jun 28 1980	9-Cib	7	Sep 4 1980	12-Kan	3
Apr 22 1980	7-Muluc	3	Jun 29 1980	10-Caban	8	Sep 5 1980	13-Chicchan	4
Apr 23 1980	8-Oc	4	Jun 30 1980	11-Etz'nab	9	Sep 6 1980	**1-Cimi**	5
Apr 24 1980	9-Chuen	5	Jul 1 1980	12-Cauac	1	Sep 7 1980	2-Manik	6
Apr 25 1980	10-Eb	6	Jul 2 1980	13-Ahau	2	Sep 8 1980	3-Lamat	7
Apr 26 1980	11-Ben	7	Jul 3 1980	**1-Imix**	3	Sep 9 1980	4-Muluc	8
Apr 27 1980	12-Ix	8	Jul 4 1980	2-Ik	4	Sep 10 1980	5-Oc	9
Apr 28 1980	13-Men	9	Jul 5 1980	3-Akbal	5	Sep 11 1980	6-Chuen	1
Apr 29 1980	**1-Cib**	1	Jul 6 1980	4-Kan	6	Sep 12 1980	7-Eb	2
Apr 30 1980	2-Caban	2	Jul 7 1980	5-Chicchan	7	Sep 13 1980	8-Ben	3
May 1 1980	3-Etz'nab	3	Jul 8 1980	6-Cimi	8	Sep 14 1980	9-Ix	4
May 2 1980	4-Cauac	4	Jul 9 1980	7-Manik	9	Sep 15 1980	10-Men	5
May 3 1980	5-Ahau	5	Jul 10 1980	8-Lamat	1	Sep 16 1980	11-Cib	6
May 4 1980	6-*Imix*	6	Jul 11 1980	9-Muluc	2	Sep 17 1980	12-Caban	7
May 5 1980	7-Ik	7	Jul 12 1980	10-Oc	3	Sep 18 1980	13-Etz'nab	8
May 6 1980	8-Akbal	8	Jul 13 1980	11-Chuen	4	Sep 19 1980	**1-Cauac**	9
May 7 1980	9-Kan	9	Jul 14 1980	12-Eb	5	Sep 20 1980	2-Ahau	1
May 8 1980	10-Chicchan	1	Jul 15 1980	13-Ben	6	Sep 21 1980	3-*Imix*	2
May 9 1980	11-Cimi	2	Jul 16 1980	**1-Ix**	7	Sep 22 1980	4-Ik	3
May 10 1980	12-Manik	3	Jul 17 1980	2-Men	8	Sep 23 1980	5-Akbal	4
May 11 1980	13-Lamat	4	Jul 18 1980	3-Cib	9	Sep 24 1980	6-Kan	5
May 12 1980	**1-Muluc**	5	Jul 19 1980	4-Caban	1	Sep 25 1980	7-Chicchan	6
May 13 1980	2-Oc	6	Jul 20 1980	5-Etz'nab	2	Sep 26 1980	8-Cimi	7
May 14 1980	3-Chuen	7	Jul 21 1980	6-Cauac	3	Sep 27 1980	9-Manik	8
May 15 1980	4-Eb	8	Jul 22 1980	7-Ahau	4	Sep 28 1980	10-Lamat	9
May 16 1980	5-Ben	9	Jul 23 1980	8-*Imix*	5	Sep 29 1980	11-Muluc	1
May 17 1980	6-Ix	1	Jul 24 1980	9-Ik	6	Sep 30 1980	12-Oc	2
May 18 1980	7-Men	2	Jul 25 1980	10-Akbal	7	Oct 1 1980	13-Chuen	3
May 19 1980	8-Cib	3	Jul 26 1980	11-Kan	8	Oct 2 1980	**1-Eb**	4
May 20 1980	9-Caban	4	Jul 27 1980	12-Chicchan	9	Oct 3 1980	2-Ben	5
May 21 1980	10-Etz'nab	5	Jul 28 1980	13-Cimi	1	Oct 4 1980	3-Ix	6
May 22 1980	11-Cauac	6	Jul 29 1980	**1-Manik**	2	Oct 5 1980	4-Men	7
May 23 1980	12-Ahau	7	Jul 30 1980	2-Lamat	3	Oct 6 1980	5-Cib	8
May 24 1980	13-*Imix*	8	Jul 31 1980	3-Muluc	4	Oct 7 1980	6-Caban	9
May 25 1980	**1-Ik**	9	Aug 1 1980	4-Oc	5	Oct 8 1980	7-Etz'nab	1
May 26 1980	2-Akbal	1	Aug 2 1980	5-Chuen	6	Oct 9 1980	8-Cauac	2
May 27 1980	3-Kan	2	Aug 3 1980	6-Eb	7	Oct 10 1980	9-Ahau	3
May 28 1980	4-Chicchan	3	Aug 4 1980	7-Ben	8	Oct 11 1980	10-*Imix*	4
May 29 1980	5-Cimi	4	Aug 5 1980	8-Ix	9	Oct 12 1980	11-Ik	5
May 30 1980	6-Manik	5	Aug 6 1980	9-Men	1	Oct 13 1980	12-Akbal	6
May 31 1980	7-Lamat	6	Aug 7 1980	10-Cib	2	Oct 14 1980	13-Kan	7
Jun 1 1980	8-Muluc	7	Aug 8 1980	11-Caban	3	Oct 15 1980	**1-Chicchan**	8
Jun 2 1980	9-Oc	8	Aug 9 1980	12-Etz'nab	4	Oct 16 1980	2-Cimi	9
Jun 3 1980	10-Chuen	9	Aug 10 1980	13-Cauac	5	Oct 17 1980	3-Manik	1
Jun 4 1980	11-Eb	1	Aug 11 1980	**1-Ahau**	6	Oct 18 1980	4-Lamat	2
Jun 5 1980	12-Ben	2	Aug 12 1980	2-*Imix*	7	Oct 19 1980	5-Muluc	3

Date	Day-Sign	L	Date	Day-Sign	L	Date	Day-Sign	L
Oct 20 1980	6-Oc	4	Dec 27 1980	9-Etz'nab	9	Mar 5 1981	12-Cimi	5
Oct 21 1980	7-Chuen	5	Dec 28 1980	10-Cauac	1	Mar 6 1981	13-Manik	6
Oct 22 1980	8-Eb	6	Dec 29 1980	11-Ahau	2	Mar 7 1981	1-Lamat	7
Oct 23 1980	9-Ben	7	Dec 30 1980	12-Imix	3	Mar 8 1981	2-Muluc	8
Oct 24 1980	10-Ix	8	Dec 31 1980	13-Ik	4	Mar 9 1981	3-Oc	9
Oct 25 1980	11-Men	9	Jan 1 1981	1-Akbal	5	Mar 10 1981	4-Chuen	1
Oct 26 1980	12-Cib	1	Jan 2 1981	2-Kan	6	Mar 11 1981	5-Eb	2
Oct 27 1980	13-Caban	2	Jan 3 1981	3-Chicchan	7	Mar 12 1981	6-Ben	3
Oct 28 1980	1-Etz'nab	3	Jan 4 1981	4-Cimi	8	Mar 13 1981	7-Ix	4
Oct 29 1980	2-Cauac	4	Jan 5 1981	5-Manik	9	Mar 14 1981	8-Men	5
Oct 30 1980	3-Ahau	5	Jan 6 1981	6-Lamat	1	Mar 15 1981	9-Cib	6
Oct 31 1980	4-Imix	6	Jan 7 1981	7-Muluc	2	Mar 16 1981	10-Caban	7
Nov 1 1980	5-Ik	7	Jan 8 1981	8-Oc	3	Mar 17 1981	11-Etz'nab	8
Nov 2 1980	6-Akbal	8	Jan 9 1981	9-Chuen	4	Mar 18 1981	12-Cauac	9
Nov 3 1980	7-Kan	9	Jan 10 1981	10-Eb	5	Mar 19 1981	13-Ahau	1
Nov 4 1980	8-Chicchan	1	Jan 11 1981	11-Ben	6	Mar 20 1981	1-Imix	2
Nov 5 1980	9-Cimi	2	Jan 12 1981	12-Ix	7	Mar 21 1981	2-Ik	3
Nov 6 1980	10-Manik	3	Jan 13 1981	13-Men	8	Mar 22 1981	3-Akbal	4
Nov 7 1980	11-Lamat	4	Jan 14 1981	1-Cib	9	Mar 23 1981	4-Kan	5
Nov 8 1980	12-Muluc	5	Jan 15 1981	2-Caban	1	Mar 24 1981	5-Chicchan	6
Nov 9 1980	13-Oc	6	Jan 16 1981	3-Etz'nab	2	Mar 25 1981	6-Cimi	7
Nov 10 1980	1-Chuen	7	Jan 17 1981	4-Cauac	3	Mar 26 1981	7-Manik	8
Nov 11 1980	2-Eb	8	Jan 18 1981	5-Ahau	4	Mar 27 1981	8-Lamat	9
Nov 12 1980	3-Ben	9	Jan 19 1981	6-Imix	5	Mar 28 1981	9-Muluc	1
Nov 13 1980	4-Ix	1	Jan 20 1981	7-Ik	6	Mar 29 1981	10-Oc	2
Nov 14 1980	5-Men	2	Jan 21 1981	8-Akbal	7	Mar 30 1981	11-Chuen	3
Nov 15 1980	6-Cib	3	Jan 22 1981	9-Kan	8	Mar 31 1981	12-Eb	4
Nov 16 1980	7-Caban	4	Jan 23 1981	10-Chicchan	9	Apr 1 1981	13-Ben	5
Nov 17 1980	8-Etz'nab	5	Jan 24 1981	11-Cimi	1	Apr 2 1981	1-Ix	6
Nov 18 1980	9-Cauac	6	Jan 25 1981	12-Manik	2	Apr 3 1981	2-Men	7
Nov 19 1980	10-Ahau	7	Jan 26 1981	13-Lamat	3	Apr 4 1981	3-Cib	8
Nov 20 1980	11-Imix	8	Jan 27 1981	1-Muluc	4	Apr 5 1981	4-Caban	9
Nov 21 1980	12-Ik	9	Jan 28 1981	2-Oc	5	Apr 6 1981	5-Etz'nab	1
Nov 22 1980	13-Akbal	1	Jan 29 1981	3-Chuen	6	Apr 7 1981	6-Cauac	2
Nov 23 1980	1-Kan	2	Jan 30 1981	4-Eb	7	Apr 8 1981	7-Ahau	3
Nov 24 1980	2-Chicchan	3	Jan 31 1981	5-Ben	8	Apr 9 1981	8-Imix	4
Nov 25 1980	3-Cimi	4	Feb 1 1981	6-Ix	9	Apr 10 1981	9-Ik	5
Nov 26 1980	4-Manik	5	Feb 2 1981	7-Men	1	Apr 11 1981	10-Akbal	6
Nov 27 1980	5-Lamat	6	Feb 3 1981	8-Cib	2	Apr 12 1981	11-Kan	7
Nov 28 1980	6-Muluc	7	Feb 4 1981	9-Caban	3	Apr 13 1981	12-Chicchan	8
Nov 29 1980	7-Oc	8	Feb 5 1981	10-Etz'nab	4	Apr 14 1981	13-Cimi	9
Nov 30 1980	8-Chuen	9	Feb 6 1981	11-Cauac	5	Apr 15 1981	1-Manik	1
Dec 1 1980	9-Eb	1	Feb 7 1981	12-Ahau	6	Apr 16 1981	2-Lamat	2
Dec 2 1980	10-Ben	2	Feb 8 1981	13-Imix	7	Apr 17 1981	3-Muluc	3
Dec 3 1980	11-Ix	3	Feb 9 1981	1-Ik	8	Apr 18 1981	4-Oc	4
Dec 4 1980	12-Men	4	Feb 10 1981	2-Akbal	9	Apr 19 1981	5-Chuen	5
Dec 5 1980	13-Cib	5	Feb 11 1981	3-Kan	1	Apr 20 1981	6-Eb	6
Dec 6 1980	1-Caban	6	Feb 12 1981	4-Chicchan	2	Apr 21 1981	7-Ben	7
Dec 7 1980	2-Etz'nab	7	Feb 13 1981	5-Cimi	3	Apr 22 1981	8-Ix	8
Dec 8 1980	3-Cauac	8	Feb 14 1981	6-Manik	4	Apr 23 1981	9-Men	9
Dec 9 1980	4-Ahau	9	Feb 15 1981	7-Lamat	5	Apr 24 1981	10-Cib	1
Dec 10 1980	5-Imix	1	Feb 16 1981	8-Muluc	6	Apr 25 1981	11-Caban	2
Dec 11 1980	6-Ik	2	Feb 17 1981	9-Oc	7	Apr 26 1981	12-Etz'nab	3
Dec 12 1980	7-Akbal	3	Feb 18 1981	10-Chuen	8	Apr 27 1981	13-Cauac	4
Dec 13 1980	8-Kan	4	Feb 19 1981	11-Eb	9	Apr 28 1981	1-Ahau	5
Dec 14 1980	9-Chicchan	5	Feb 20 1981	12-Ben	1	Apr 29 1981	2-Imix	6
Dec 15 1980	10-Cimi	6	Feb 21 1981	13-Ix	2	Apr 30 1981	3-Ik	7
Dec 16 1980	11-Manik	7	Feb 22 1981	1-Men	3	May 1 1981	4-Akbal	8
Dec 17 1980	12-Lamat	8	Feb 23 1981	2-Cib	4	May 2 1981	5-Kan	9
Dec 18 1980	13-Muluc	9	Feb 24 1981	3-Caban	5	May 3 1981	6-Chicchan	1
Dec 19 1980	1-Oc	1	Feb 25 1981	4-Etz'nab	6	May 4 1981	7-Cimi	2
Dec 20 1980	2-Chuen	2	Feb 26 1981	5-Cauac	7	May 5 1981	8-Manik	3
Dec 21 1980	3-Eb	3	Feb 27 1981	6-Ahau	8	May 6 1981	9-Lamat	4
Dec 22 1980	4-Ben	4	Feb 28 1981	7-Imix	9	May 7 1981	10-Muluc	5
Dec 23 1980	5-Ix	5	Mar 1 1981	8-Ik	1	May 8 1981	11-Oc	6
Dec 24 1980	6-Men	6	Mar 2 1981	9-Akbal	2	May 9 1981	12-Chuen	7
Dec 25 1980	7-Cib	7	Mar 3 1981	10-Kan	3	May 10 1981	13-Eb	8
Dec 26 1980	8-Caban	8	Mar 4 1981	11-Chicchan	4	May 11 1981	1-Ben	9

Date	Day-Sign	L		Date	Day-Sign	L		Date	Day-Sign	L
May 12 1981	2-Ix	1		Jul 19 1981	5-Ik	6		Sep 25 1981	8-Oc	2
May 13 1981	3-Men	2		Jul 20 1981	6-Akbal	7		Sep 26 1981	9-Chuen	3
May 14 1981	4-Cib	3		Jul 21 1981	7-Kan	8		Sep 27 1981	10-Eb	4
May 15 1981	5-Caban	4		Jul 22 1981	8-Chicchan	9		Sep 28 1981	11-Ben	5
May 16 1981	6-Etz'nab	5		Jul 23 1981	9-Cimi	1		Sep 29 1981	12-Ix	6
May 17 1981	7-Cauac	6		Jul 24 1981	10-Manik	2		Sep 30 1981	13-Men	7
May 18 1981	8-Ahau	7		Jul 25 1981	11-Lamat	3		Oct 1 1981	1-Cib	8
May 19 1981	9-Imix	8		Jul 26 1981	12-Muluc	4		Oct 2 1981	2-Caban	9
May 20 1981	10-Ik	9		Jul 27 1981	13-Oc	5		Oct 3 1981	3-Etz'nab	1
May 21 1981	11-Akbal	1		Jul 28 1981	1-Chuen	6		Oct 4 1981	4-Cauac	2
May 22 1981	12-Kan	2		Jul 29 1981	2-Eb	7		Oct 5 1981	5-Ahau	3
May 23 1981	13-Chicchan	3		Jul 30 1981	3-Ben	8		Oct 6 1981	6-Imix	4
May 24 1981	1-Cimi	4		Jul 31 1981	4-Ix	9		Oct 7 1981	7-!k	5
May 25 1981	2-Manik	5		Aug 1 1981	5-Men	1		Oct 8 1981	8-Akbal	6
May 26 1981	3-Lamat	6		Aug 2 1981	6-Cib	2		Oct 9 1981	9-Kan	7
May 27 1981	4-Muluc	7		Aug 3 1981	7-Caban	3		Oct 10 1981	10-Chicchan	8
May 28 1981	5-Oc	8		Aug 4 1981	8-Etz'nab	4		Oct 11 1981	11-Cimi	9
May 29 1981	6-Chuen	9		Aug 5 1981	9-Cauac	5		Oct 12 1981	12-Manik	1
May 30 1981	7-Eb	1		Aug 6 1981	10-Ahau	6		Oct 13 1981	13-Lamat	2
May 31 1981	8-Ben	2		Aug 7 1981	11-Imix	7		Oct 14 1981	1-Muluc	3
Jun 1 1981	9-Ix	3		Aug 8 1981	12-Ik	8		Oct 15 1981	2-Oc	4
Jun 2 1981	10-Men	4		Aug 9 1981	13-Akbal	9		Oct 16 1981	3-Chuen	5
Jun 3 1981	11-Cib	5		Aug 10 1981	1-Kan	1		Oct 17 1981	4-Eb	6
Jun 4 1981	12-Caban	6		Aug 11 1981	2-Chicchan	2		Oct 18 1981	5-Ben	7
Jun 5 1981	13-Etz'nab	7		Aug 12 1981	3-Cimi	3		Oct 19 1981	6-Ix	8
Jun 6 1981	1-Cauac	8		Aug 13 1981	4-Manik	4		Oct 20 1981	7-Men	9
Jun 7 1981	2-Ahau	9		Aug 14 1981	5-Lamat	5		Oct 21 1981	8-Cib	1
Jun 8 1981	3-Imix	1		Aug 15 1981	6-Muluc	6		Oct 22 1981	9-Caban	2
Jun 9 1981	4-Ik	2		Aug 16 1981	7-Oc	7		Oct 23 1981	10-Etz'nab	3
Jun 10 1981	5-Akbal	3		Aug 17 1981	8-Chuen	8		Oct 24 1981	11-Cauac	4
Jun 11 1981	6-Kan	4		Aug 18 1981	9-Eb	9		Oct 25 1981	12-Ahau	5
Jun 12 1981	7-Chicchan	5		Aug 19 1981	10-Ben	1		Oct 26 1981	13-Imix	6
Jun 13 1981	8-Cimi	6		Aug 20 1981	11-Ix	2		Oct 27 1981	1-Ik	7
Jun 14 1981	9-Manik	7		Aug 21 1981	12-Men	3		Oct 28 1981	2-Akbal	8
Jun 15 1981	10-Lamat	8		Aug 22 1981	13-Cib	4		Oct 29 1981	3-Kan	9
Jun 16 1981	11-Muluc	9		Aug 23 1981	1-Caban	5		Oct 30 1981	4-Chicchan	1
Jun 17 1981	12-Oc	1		Aug 24 1981	2-Etz'nab	6		Oct 31 1981	5-Cimi	2
Jun 18 1981	13-Chuen	2		Aug 25 1981	3-Cauac	7		Nov 1 1981	6-Manik	3
Jun 19 1981	1-Eb	3		Aug 26 1981	4-Ahau	8		Nov 2 1981	7-Lamat	4
Jun 20 1981	2-Ben	4		Aug 27 1981	5-Imix	9		Nov 3 1981	8-Muluc	5
Jun 21 1981	3-Ix	5		Aug 28 1981	6-Ik	1		Nov 4 1981	9-Oc	6
Jun 22 1981	4-Men	6		Aug 29 1981	7-Akbal	2		Nov 5 1981	10-Chuen	7
Jun 23 1981	5-Cib	7		Aug 30 1981	8-Kan	3		Nov 6 1981	11-Eb	8
Jun 24 1981	6-Caban	8		Aug 31 1981	9-Chicchan	4		Nov 7 1981	12-Ben	9
Jun 25 1981	7-Etz'nab	9		Sep 1 1981	10-Cimi	5		Nov 8 1981	13-Ix	1
Jun 26 1981	8-Cauac	1		Sep 2 1981	11-Manik	6		Nov 9 1981	1-Men	2
Jun 27 1981	9-Ahau	2		Sep 3 1981	12-Lamat	7		Nov 10 1981	2-Cib	3
Jun 28 1981	10-Imix	3		Sep 4 1981	13-Muluc	8		Nov 11 1981	3-Caban	4
Jun 29 1981	11-Ik	4		Sep 5 1981	1-Oc	9		Nov 12 1981	4-Etz'nab	5
Jun 30 1981	12-Akbal	5		Sep 6 1981	2-Chuen	1		Nov 13 1981	5-Cauac	6
Jul 1 1981	13-Kan	6		Sep 7 1981	3-Eb	2		Nov 14 1981	6-Ahau	7
Jul 2 1981	1-Chicchan	7		Sep 8 1981	4-Ben	3		Nov 15 1981	7-Imix	8
Jul 3 1981	2-Cimi	8		Sep 9 1981	5-Ix	4		Nov 16 1981	8-Ik	9
Jul 4 1981	3-Manik	9		Sep 10 1981	6-Men	5		Nov 17 1981	9-Akbal	1
Jul 5 1981	4-Lamat	1		Sep 11 1981	7-Cib	6		Nov 18 1981	10-Kan	2
Jul 6 1981	5-Muluc	2		Sep 12 1981	8-Caban	7		Nov 19 1981	11-Chicchan	3
Jul 7 1981	6-Oc	3		Sep 13 1981	9-Etz'nab	8		Nov 20 1981	12-Cimi	4
Jul 8 1981	7-Chuen	4		Sep 14 1981	10-Cauac	9		Nov 21 1981	13-Manik	5
Jul 9 1981	8-Eb	5		Sep 15 1981	11-Ahau	1		Nov 22 1981	1-Lamat	6
Jul 10 1981	9-Ben	6		Sep 16 1981	12-Imix	2		Nov 23 1981	2-Muluc	7
Jul 11 1981	10-Ix	7		Sep 17 1981	13-Ik	3		Nov 24 1981	3-Oc	8
Jul 12 1981	11-Men	8		Sep 18 1981	1-Akbal	4		Nov 25 1981	4-Chuen	9
Jul 13 1981	12-Cib	9		Sep 19 1981	2-Kan	5		Nov 26 1981	5-Eb	1
Jul 14 1981	13-Caban	1		Sep 20 1981	3-Chicchan	6		Nov 27 1981	6-Ben	2
Jul 15 1981	1-Etz'nab	2		Sep 21 1981	4-Cimi	7		Nov 28 1981	7-Ix	3
Jul 16 1981	2-Cauac	3		Sep 22 1981	5-Manik	8		Nov 29 1981	8-Men	4
Jul 17 1981	3-Ahau	4		Sep 23 1981	6-Lamat	9		Nov 30 1981	9-Cib	5
Jul 18 1981	4-Imix	5		Sep 24 1981	7-Muluc	1		Dec 1 1981	10-Caban	6

Date	Day-Sign	L	Date	Day-Sign	L	Date	Day-Sign	L
Dec 2 1981	11-Etz'nab	7	Feb 8 1982	1-Cimi	3	Apr 17 1982	4-Ix	8
Dec 3 1981	12-Cauac	8	Feb 9 1982	2-Manik	4	Apr 18 1982	5-Men	9
Dec 4 1981	13-Ahau	9	Feb 10 1982	3-Lamat	5	Apr 19 1982	6-Cib	1
Dec 5 1981	1-Imix	1	Feb 11 1982	4-Muluc	6	Apr 20 1982	7-Caban	2
Dec 6 1981	2-Ik	2	Feb 12 1982	5-Oc	7	Apr 21 1982	8-Etz'nab	3
Dec 7 1981	3-Akbal	3	Feb 13 1982	6-Chuen	8	Apr 22 1982	9-Cauac	4
Dec 8 1981	4-Kan	4	Feb 14 1982	7-Eb	9	Apr 23 1982	10-Ahau	5
Dec 9 1981	5-Chicchan	5	Feb 15 1982	8-Ben	1	Apr 24 1982	11-Imix	6
Dec 10 1981	6-Cimi	6	Feb 16 1982	9-Ix	2	Apr 25 1982	12-Ik	7
Dec 11 1981	7-Manik	7	Feb 17 1982	10-Men	3	Apr 26 1982	13-Akbal	8
Dec 12 1981	8-Lamat	8	Feb 18 1982	11-Cib	4	Apr 27 1982	1-Kan	9
Dec 13 1981	9-Muluc	9	Feb 19 1982	12-Caban	5	Apr 28 1982	2-Chicchan	1
Dec 14 1981	10-Oc	1	Feb 20 1982	13-Etz'nab	6	Apr 29 1982	3-Cimi	2
Dec 15 1981	11-Chuen	2	Feb 21 1982	1-Cauac	7	Apr 30 1982	4-Manik	3
Dec 16 1981	12-Eb	3	Feb 22 1982	2-Ahau	8	May 1 1982	5-Lamat	4
Dec 17 1981	13-Ben	4	Feb 23 1982	3-Imix	9	May 2 1982	6-Muluc	5
Dec 18 1981	1-Ix	5	Feb 24 1982	4-Ik	1	May 3 1982	7-Oc	6
Dec 19 1981	2-Men	6	Feb 25 1982	5-Akbal	2	May 4 1982	8-Chuen	7
Dec 20 1981	3-Cib	7	Feb 26 1982	6-Kan	3	May 5 1982	9-Eb	8
Dec 21 1981	4-Caban	8	Feb 27 1982	7-Chicchan	4	May 6 1982	10-Ben	9
Dec 22 1981	5-Etz'nab	9	Feb 28 1982	8-Cimi	5	May 7 1982	11-Ix	1
Dec 23 1981	6-Cauac	1	Mar 1 1982	9-Manik	6	May 8 1982	12-Men	2
Dec 24 1981	7-Ahau	2	Mar 2 1982	10-Lamat	7	May 9 1982	13-Cib	3
Dec 25 1981	8-Imix	3	Mar 3 1982	11-Muluc	8	May 10 1982	1-Caban	4
Dec 26 1981	9-Ik	4	Mar 4 1982	12-Oc	9	May 11 1982	2-Etz'nab	5
Dec 27 1981	10-Akbal	5	Mar 5 1982	13-Chuen	1	May 12 1982	3-Cauac	6
Dec 28 1981	11-Kan	6	Mar 6 1982	1-Eb	2	May 13 1982	4-Ahau	7
Dec 29 1981	12-Chicchan	7	Mar 7 1982	2-Ben	3	May 14 1982	5-Imix	8
Dec 30 1981	13-Cimi	8	Mar 8 1982	3-Ix	4	May 15 1982	6-Ik	9
Dec 31 1981	1-Manik	9	Mar 9 1982	4-Men	5	May 16 1982	7-Akbal	1
Jan 1 1982	2-Lamat	1	Mar 10 1982	5-Cib	6	May 17 1982	8-Kan	2
Jan 2 1982	3-Muluc	2	Mar 11 1982	6-Caban	7	May 18 1982	9-Chicchan	3
Jan 3 1982	4-Oc	3	Mar 12 1982	7-Etz'nab	8	May 19 1982	10-Cimi	4
Jan 4 1982	5-Chuen	4	Mar 13 1982	8-Cauac	9	May 20 1982	11-Manik	5
Jan 5 1982	6-Eb	5	Mar 14 1982	9-Ahau	1	May 21 1982	12-Lamat	6
Jan 6 1982	7-Ben	6	Mar 15 1982	10-Imix	2	May 22 1982	13-Muluc	7
Jan 7 1982	8-Ix	7	Mar 16 1982	11-Ik	3	May 23 1982	1-Oc	8
Jan 8 1982	9-Men	8	Mar 17 1982	12-Akbal	4	May 24 1982	2-Chuen	9
Jan 9 1982	10-Cib	9	Mar 18 1982	13-Kan	5	May 25 1982	3-Eb	1
Jan 10 1982	11-Caban	1	Mar 19 1982	1-Chicchan	6	May 26 1982	4-Ben	2
Jan 11 1982	12-Etz'nab	2	Mar 20 1982	2-Cimi	7	May 27 1982	5-Ix	3
Jan 12 1982	13-Cauac	3	Mar 21 1982	3-Manik	8	May 28 1982	6-Men	4
Jan 13 1982	1-Ahau	4	Mar 22 1982	4-Lamat	9	May 29 1982	7-Cib	5
Jan 14 1982	2-Imix	5	Mar 23 1982	5-Muluc	1	May 30 1982	8-Caban	6
Jan 15 1982	3-Ik	6	Mar 24 1982	6-Oc	2	May 31 1982	9-Etz'nab	7
Jan 16 1982	4-Akbal	7	Mar 25 1982	7-Chuen	3	Jun 1 1982	10-Cauac	8
Jan 17 1982	5-Kan	8	Mar 26 1982	8-Eb	4	Jun 2 1982	11-Ahau	9
Jan 18 1982	6-Chicchan	9	Mar 27 1982	9-Ben	5	Jun 3 1982	12-Imix	1
Jan 19 1982	7-Cimi	1	Mar 28 1982	10-Ix	6	Jun 4 1982	13-Ik	2
Jan 20 1982	8-Manik	2	Mar 29 1982	11-Men	7	Jun 5 1982	1-Akbal	3
Jan 21 1982	9-Lamat	3	Mar 30 1982	12-Cib	8	Jun 6 1982	2-Kan	4
Jan 22 1982	10-Muluc	4	Mar 31 1982	13-Caban	9	Jun 7 1982	3-Chicchan	5
Jan 23 1982	11-Oc	5	Apr 1 1982	1-Etz'nab	1	Jun 8 1982	4-Cimi	6
Jan 24 1982	12-Chuen	6	Apr 2 1982	2-Cauac	2	Jun 9 1982	5-Manik	7
Jan 25 1982	13-Eb	7	Apr 3 1982	3-Ahau	3	Jun 10 1982	6-Lamat	8
Jan 26 1982	1-Ben	8	Apr 4 1982	4-Imix	4	Jun 11 1982	7-Muluc	9
Jan 27 1982	2-Ix	9	Apr 5 1982	5-Ik	5	Jun 12 1982	8-Oc	1
Jan 28 1982	3-Men	1	Apr 6 1982	6-Akbal	6	Jun 13 1982	9-Chuen	2
Jan 29 1982	4-Cib	2	Apr 7 1982	7-Kan	7	Jun 14 1982	10-Eb	3
Jan 30 1982	5-Caban	3	Apr 8 1982	8-Chicchan	8	Jun 15 1982	11-Ben	4
Jan 31 1982	6-Etz'nab	4	Apr 9 1982	9-Cimi	9	Jun 16 1982	12-Ix	5
Feb 1 1982	7-Cauac	5	Apr 10 1982	10-Manik	1	Jun 17 1982	13-Men	6
Feb 2 1982	8-Ahau	6	Apr 11 1982	11-Lamat	2	Jun 18 1982	1-Cib	7
Feb 3 1982	9-Imix	7	Apr 12 1982	12-Muluc	3	Jun 19 1982	2-Caban	8
Feb 4 1982	10-Ik	8	Apr 13 1982	13-Oc	4	Jun 20 1982	3-Etz'nab	9
Feb 5 1982	11-Akbal	9	Apr 14 1982	1-Chuen	5	Jun 21 1982	4-Cauac	1
Feb 6 1982	12-Kan	1	Apr 15 1982	2-Eb	6	Jun 22 1982	5-Ahau	2
Feb 7 1982	13-Chicchan	2	Apr 16 1982	3-Ben	7	Jun 23 1982	6-Imix	3

Date	Day-Sign	L	Date	Day-Sign	L	Date	Day-Sign	L
Jun 24 1982	7-Ik	4	Aug 31 1982	10-Oc	9	Nov 7 1982	13-Etz'nab	5
Jun 25 1982	8-Akbal	5	Sep 1 1982	11-Chuen	1	Nov 8 1982	1-Cauac	6
Jun 26 1982	9-Kan	6	Sep 2 1982	12-Eb	2	Nov 9 1982	2-Ahau	7
Jun 27 1982	10-Chicchan	7	Sep 3 1982	13-Ben	3	Nov 10 1982	3-Imix	8
Jun 28 1982	11-Cimi	8	Sep 4 1982	1-Ix	4	Nov 11 1982	4-Ik	9
Jun 29 1982	12-Manik	9	Sep 5 1982	2-Men	5	Nov 12 1982	5-Akbal	1
Jun 30 1982	13-Lamat	1	Sep 6 1982	3-Cib	6	Nov 13 1982	6-Kan	2
Jul 1 1982	1-Muluc	2	Sep 7 1982	4-Caban	7	Nov 14 1982	7-Chicchan	3
Jul 2 1982	2-Oc	3	Sep 8 1982	5-Etz'nab	8	Nov 15 1982	8-Cimi	4
Jul 3 1982	3-Chuen	4	Sep 9 1982	6-Cauac	9	Nov 16 1982	9-Manik	5
Jul 4 1982	4-Eb	5	Sep 10 1982	7-Ahau	1	Nov 17 1982	10-Lamat	6
Jul 5 1982	5-Ben	6	Sep 11 1982	8-Imix	2	Nov 18 1982	11-Muluc	7
Jul 6 1982	6-Ix	7	Sep 12 1982	9-Ik	3	Nov 19 1982	12-Oc	8
Jul 7 1982	7-Men	8	Sep 13 1982	10-Akbal	4	Nov 20 1982	13-Chuen	9
Jul 8 1982	8-Cib	9	Sep 14 1982	11-Kan	5	Nov 21 1982	1-Eb	1
Jul 9 1982	9-Caban	1	Sep 15 1982	12-Chicchan	6	Nov 22 1982	2-Ben	2
Jul 10 1982	10-Etz'nab	2	Sep 16 1982	13-Cimi	7	Nov 23 1982	3-Ix	3
Jul 11 1982	11-Cauac	3	Sep 17 1982	1-Manik	8	Nov 24 1982	4-Men	4
Jul 12 1982	12-Ahau	4	Sep 18 1982	2-Lamat	9	Nov 25 1982	5-Cib	5
Jul 13 1982	13-Imix	5	Sep 19 1982	3-Muluc	1	Nov 26 1982	6-Caban	6
Jul 14 1982	1-Ik	6	Sep 20 1982	4-Oc	2	Nov 27 1982	7-Etz'nab	7
Jul 15 1982	2-Akbal	7	Sep 21 1982	5-Chuen	3	Nov 28 1982	8-Cauac	8
Jul 16 1982	3-Kan	8	Sep 22 1982	6-Eb	4	Nov 29 1982	9-Ahau	9
Jul 17 1982	4-Chicchan	9	Sep 23 1982	7-Ben	5	Nov 30 1982	10-Imix	1
Jul 18 1982	5-Cimi	1	Sep 24 1982	8-Ix	6	Dec 1 1982	11-Ik	2
Jul 19 1982	6-Manik	2	Sep 25 1982	9-Men	7	Dec 2 1982	12-Akbal	3
Jul 20 1982	7-Lamat	3	Sep 26 1982	10-Cib	8	Dec 3 1982	13-Kan	4
Jul 21 1982	8-Muluc	4	Sep 27 1982	11-Caban	9	Dec 4 1982	1-Chicchan	5
Jul 22 1982	9-Oc	5	Sep 28 1982	12-Etz'nab	1	Dec 5 1982	2-Cimi	6
Jul 23 1982	10-Chuen	6	Sep 29 1982	13-Cauac	2	Dec 6 1982	3-Manik	7
Jul 24 1982	11-Eb	7	Sep 30 1982	1-Ahau	3	Dec 7 1982	4-Lamat	8
Jul 25 1982	12-Ben	8	Oct 1 1982	2-Imix	4	Dec 8 1982	5-Muluc	9
Jul 26 1982	13-Ix	9	Oct 2 1982	3-Ik	5	Dec 9 1982	6-Oc	1
Jul 27 1982	1-Men	1	Oct 3 1982	4-Akbal	6	Dec 10 1982	7-Chuen	2
Jul 28 1982	2-Cib	2	Oct 4 1982	5-Kan	7	Dec 11 1982	8-Eb	3
Jul 29 1982	3-Caban	3	Oct 5 1982	6-Chicchan	8	Dec 12 1982	9-Ben	4
Jul 30 1982	4-Etz'nab	4	Oct 6 1982	7-Cimi	9	Dec 13 1982	10-Ix	5
Jul 31 1982	5-Cauac	5	Oct 7 1982	8-Manik	1	Dec 14 1982	11-Men	6
Aug 1 1982	6-Ahau	6	Oct 8 1982	9-Lamat	2	Dec 15 1982	12-Cib	7
Aug 2 1982	7-Imix	7	Oct 9 1982	10-Muluc	3	Dec 16 1982	13-Caban	8
Aug 3 1982	8-Ik	8	Oct 10 1982	11-Oc	4	Dec 17 1982	1-Etz'nab	9
Aug 4 1982	9-Akbal	9	Oct 11 1982	12-Chuen	5	Dec 18 1982	2-Cauac	1
Aug 5 1982	10-Kan	1	Oct 12 1982	13-Eb	6	Dec 19 1982	3-Ahau	2
Aug 6 1982	11-Chicchan	2	Oct 13 1982	1-Ben	7	Dec 20 1982	4-Imix	3
Aug 7 1982	12-Cimi	3	Oct 14 1982	2-Ix	8	Dec 21 1982	5-Ik	4
Aug 8 1982	13-Manik	4	Oct 15 1982	3-Men	9	Dec 22 1982	6-Akbal	5
Aug 9 1982	1-Lamat	5	Oct 16 1982	4-Cib	1	Dec 23 1982	7-Kan	6
Aug 10 1982	2-Muluc	6	Oct 17 1982	5-Caban	2	Dec 24 1982	8-Chicchan	7
Aug 11 1982	3-Oc	7	Oct 18 1982	6-Etz'nab	3	Dec 25 1982	9-Cimi	8
Aug 12 1982	4-Chuen	8	Oct 19 1982	7-Cauac	4	Dec 26 1982	10-Manik	9
Aug 13 1982	5-Eb	9	Oct 20 1982	8-Ahau	5	Dec 27 1982	11-Lamat	1
Aug 14 1982	6-Ben	1	Oct 21 1982	9-Imix	6	Dec 28 1982	12-Muluc	2
Aug 15 1982	7-Ix	2	Oct 22 1982	10-Ik	7	Dec 29 1982	13-Oc	3
Aug 16 1982	8-Men	3	Oct 23 1982	11-Akbal	8	Dec 30 1982	1-Chuen	4
Aug 17 1982	9-Cib	4	Oct 24 1982	12-Kan	9	Dec 31 1982	2-Eb	5
Aug 18 1982	10-Caban	5	Oct 25 1982	13-Chicchan	1	Jan 1 1983	3-Ben	6
Aug 19 1982	11-Etz'nab	6	Oct 26 1982	1-Cimi	2	Jan 2 1983	4-Ix	7
Aug 20 1982	12-Cauac	7	Oct 27 1982	2-Manik	3	Jan 3 1983	5-Men	8
Aug 21 1982	13-Ahau	8	Oct 28 1982	3-Lamat	4	Jan 4 1983	6-Cib	9
Aug 22 1982	1-Imix	9	Oct 29 1982	4-Muluc	5	Jan 5 1983	7-Caban	1
Aug 23 1982	2-Ik	1	Oct 30 1982	5-Oc	6	Jan 6 1983	8-Etz'nab	2
Aug 24 1982	3-Akbal	2	Oct 31 1982	6-Chuen	7	Jan 7 1983	9-Cauac	3
Aug 25 1982	4-Kan	3	Nov 1 1982	7-Eb	8	Jan 8 1983	10-Ahau	4
Aug 26 1982	5-Chicchan	4	Nov 2 1982	8-Ben	9	Jan 9 1983	11-Imix	5
Aug 27 1982	6-Cimi	5	Nov 3 1982	9-Ix	1	Jan 10 1983	12-Ik	6
Aug 28 1982	7-Manik	6	Nov 4 1982	10-Men	2	Jan 11 1983	13-Akbal	7
Aug 29 1982	8-Lamat	7	Nov 5 1982	11-Cib	3	Jan 12 1983	1-Kan	8
Aug 30 1982	9-Muluc	8	Nov 6 1982	12-Caban	4	Jan 13 1983	2-Chicchan	9

Date	Day-Sign	L	Date	Day-Sign	L	Date	Day-Sign	L
Jan 14 1983	3-Cimi	1	Mar 23 1983	6-Ix	6	May 30 1983	9-Ik	2
Jan 15 1983	4-Manik	2	Mar 24 1983	7-Men	7	May 31 1983	10-Akbal	3
Jan 16 1983	5-Lamat	3	Mar 25 1983	8-Cib	8	Jun 1 1983	11-Kan	4
Jan 17 1983	6-Muluc	4	Mar 26 1983	9-Caban	9	Jun 2 1983	12-Chicchan	5
Jan 18 1983	7-Oc	5	Mar 27 1983	10-Etz'nab	1	Jun 3 1983	13-Cimi	6
Jan 19 1983	8-Chuen	6	Mar 28 1983	11-Cauac	2	Jun 4 1983	1-Manik	7
Jan 20 1983	9-Eb	7	Mar 29 1983	12-Ahau	3	Jun 5 1983	2-Lamat	8
Jan 21 1983	10-Ben	8	Mar 30 1983	13-Imix	4	Jun 6 1983	3-Muluc	9
Jan 22 1983	11-Ix	9	Mar 31 1983	1-Ik	5	Jun 7 1983	4-Oc	1
Jan 23 1983	12-Men	1	Apr 1 1983	2-Akbal	6	Jun 8 1983	5-Chuen	2
Jan 24 1983	13-Cib	2	Apr 2 1983	3-Kan	7	Jun 9 1983	6-Eb	3
Jan 25 1983	1-Caban	3	Apr 3 1983	4-Chicchan	8	Jun 10 1983	7-Ben	4
Jan 26 1983	2-Etz'nab	4	Apr 4 1983	5-Cimi	9	Jun 11 1983	8-Ix	5
Jan 27 1983	3-Cauac	5	Apr 5 1983	6-Manik	1	Jun 12 1983	9-Men	6
Jan 28 1983	4-Ahau	6	Apr 6 1983	7-Lamat	2	Jun 13 1983	10-Cib	7
Jan 29 1983	5-Imix	7	Apr 7 1983	8-Muluc	3	Jun 14 1983	11-Caban	8
Jan 30 1983	6-Ik	8	Apr 8 1983	9-Oc	4	Jun 15 1983	12-Etz'nab	9
Jan 31 1983	7-Akbal	9	Apr 9 1983	10-Chuen	5	Jun 16 1983	13-Cauac	1
Feb 1 1983	8-Kan	1	Apr 10 1983	11-Eb	6	Jun 17 1983	1-Ahau	2
Feb 2 1983	9-Chicchan	2	Apr 11 1983	12-Ben	7	Jun 18 1983	2-Imix	3
Feb 3 1983	10-Cimi	3	Apr 12 1983	13-Ix	8	Jun 19 1983	3-Ik	4
Feb 4 1983	11-Manik	4	Apr 13 1983	1-Men	9	Jun 20 1983	4-Akbal	5
Feb 5 1983	12-Lamat	5	Apr 14 1983	2-Cib	1	Jun 21 1983	5-Kan	6
Feb 6 1983	13-Muluc	6	Apr 15 1983	3-Caban	2	Jun 22 1983	6-Chicchan	7
Feb 7 1983	1-Oc	7	Apr 16 1983	4-Etz'nab	3	Jun 23 1983	7-Cimi	8
Feb 8 1983	2-Chuen	8	Apr 17 1983	5-Cauac	4	Jun 24 1983	8-Manik	9
Feb 9 1983	3-Eb	9	Apr 18 1983	6-Ahau	5	Jun 25 1983	9-Lamat	1
Feb 10 1983	4-Ben	1	Apr 19 1983	7-Imix	6	Jun 26 1983	10-Muluc	2
Feb 11 1983	5-Ix	2	Apr 20 1983	8-Ik	7	Jun 27 1983	11-Oc	3
Feb 12 1983	6-Men	3	Apr 21 1983	9-Akbal	8	Jun 28 1983	12-Chuen	4
Feb 13 1983	7-Cib	4	Apr 22 1983	10-Kan	9	Jun 29 1983	13-Eb	5
Feb 14 1983	8-Caban	5	Apr 23 1983	11-Chicchan	1	Jun 30 1983	1-Ben	6
Feb 15 1983	9-Etz'nab	6	Apr 24 1983	12-Cimi	2	Jul 1 1983	2-Ix	7
Feb 16 1983	10-Cauac	7	Apr 25 1983	13-Manik	3	Jul 2 1983	3-Men	8
Feb 17 1983	11-Ahau	8	Apr 26 1983	1-Lamat	4	Jul 3 1983	4-Cib	9
Feb 18 1983	12-Imix	9	Apr 27 1983	2-Muluc	5	Jul 4 1983	5-Caban	1
Feb 19 1983	13-Ik	1	Apr 28 1983	3-Oc	6	Jul 5 1983	6-Etz'nab	2
Feb 20 1983	1-Akbal	2	Apr 29 1983	4-Chuen	7	Jul 6 1983	7-Cauac	3
Feb 21 1983	2-Kan	3	Apr 30 1983	5-Eb	8	Jul 7 1983	8-Ahau	4
Feb 22 1983	3-Chicchan	4	May 1 1983	6-Ben	9	Jul 8 1983	9-Imix	5
Feb 23 1983	4-Cimi	5	May 2 1983	7-Ix	1	Jul 9 1983	10-Ik	6
Feb 24 1983	5-Manik	6	May 3 1983	8-Men	2	Jul 10 1983	11-Akbal	7
Feb 25 1983	6-Lamat	7	May 4 1983	9-Cib	3	Jul 11 1983	12-Kan	8
Feb 26 1983	7-Muluc	8	May 5 1983	10-Caban	4	Jul 12 1983	13-Chicchan	9
Feb 27 1983	8-Oc	9	May 6 1983	11-Etz'nab	5	Jul 13 1983	1-Cimi	1
Feb 28 1983	9-Chuen	1	May 7 1983	12-Cauac	6	Jul 14 1983	2-Manik	2
Mar 1 1983	10-Eb	2	May 8 1983	13-Ahau	7	Jul 15 1983	3-Lamat	3
Mar 2 1983	11-Ben	3	May 9 1983	1-Imix	8	Jul 16 1983	4-Muluc	4
Mar 3 1983	12-Ix	4	May 10 1983	2-Ik	9	Jul 17 1983	5-Oc	5
Mar 4 1983	13-Men	5	May 11 1983	3-Akbal	1	Jul 18 1983	6-Chuen	6
Mar 5 1983	1-Cib	6	May 12 1983	4-Kan	2	Jul 19 1983	7-Eb	7
Mar 6 1983	2-Caban	7	May 13 1983	5-Chicchan	3	Jul 20 1983	8-Ben	8
Mar 7 1983	3-Etz'nab	8	May 14 1983	6-Cimi	4	Jul 21 1983	9-Ix	9
Mar 8 1983	4-Cauac	9	May 15 1983	7-Manik	5	Jul 22 1983	10-Men	1
Mar 9 1983	5-Ahau	1	May 16 1983	8-Lamat	6	Jul 23 1983	11-Cib	2
Mar 10 1983	6-Imix	2	May 17 1983	9-Muluc	7	Jul 24 1983	12-Caban	3
Mar 11 1983	7-Ik	3	May 18 1983	10-Oc	8	Jul 25 1983	13-Etz'nab	4
Mar 12 1983	8-Akbal	4	May 19 1983	11-Chuen	9	Jul 26 1983	1-Cauac	5
Mar 13 1983	9-Kan	5	May 20 1983	12-Eb	1	Jul 27 1983	2-Ahau	6
Mar 14 1983	10-Chicchan	6	May 21 1983	13-Ben	2	Jul 28 1983	3-Imix	7
Mar 15 1983	11-Cimi	7	May 22 1983	1-Ix	3	Jul 29 1983	4-Ik	8
Mar 16 1983	12-Manik	8	May 23 1983	2-Men	4	Jul 30 1983	5-Akbal	9
Mar 17 1983	13-Lamat	9	May 24 1983	3-Cib	5	Jul 31 1983	6-Kan	1
Mar 18 1983	1-Muluc	1	May 25 1983	4-Caban	6	Aug 1 1983	7-Chicchan	2
Mar 19 1983	2-Oc	2	May 26 1983	5-Etz'nab	7	Aug 2 1983	8-Cimi	3
Mar 20 1983	3-Chuen	3	May 27 1983	6-Cauac	8	Aug 3 1983	9-Manik	4
Mar 21 1983	4-Eb	4	May 28 1983	7-Ahau	9	Aug 4 1983	10-Lamat	5
Mar 22 1983	5-Ben	5	May 29 1983	8-Imix	1	Aug 5 1983	11-Muluc	6

Date	Day-Sign	L
Aug 6 1983	12-Oc	7
Aug 7 1983	13-Chuen	8
Aug 8 1983	1-Eb	9
Aug 9 1983	2-Ben	1
Aug 10 1983	3-Ix	2
Aug 11 1983	4-Men	3
Aug 12 1983	5-Cib	4
Aug 13 1983	6-Caban	5
Aug 14 1983	7-Etz'nab	6
Aug 15 1983	8-Cauac	7
Aug 16 1983	9-Ahau	8
Aug 17 1983	10-Imix	9
Aug 18 1983	11-Ik	1
Aug 19 1983	12-Akbal	2
Aug 20 1983	13-Kan	3
Aug 21 1983	1-Chicchan	4
Aug 22 1983	2-Cimi	5
Aug 23 1983	3-Manik	6
Aug 24 1983	4-Lamat	7
Aug 25 1983	5-Muluc	8
Aug 26 1983	6-Oc	9
Aug 27 1983	7-Chuen	1
Aug 28 1983	8-Eb	2
Aug 29 1983	9-Ben	3
Aug 30 1983	10-Ix	4
Aug 31 1983	11-Men	5
Sep 1 1983	12-Cib	6
Sep 2 1983	13-Caban	7
Sep 3 1983	1-Etz'nab	8
Sep 4 1983	2-Cauac	9
Sep 5 1983	3-Ahau	1
Sep 6 1983	4-Imix	2
Sep 7 1983	5-Ik	3
Sep 8 1983	6-Akbal	4
Sep 9 1983	7-Kan	5
Sep 10 1983	8-Chicchan	6
Sep 11 1983	9-Cimi	7
Sep 12 1983	10-Manik	8
Sep 13 1983	11-Lamat	9
Sep 14 1983	12-Muluc	1
Sep 15 1983	13-Oc	2
Sep 16 1983	1-Chuen	3
Sep 17 1983	2-Eb	4
Sep 18 1983	3-Ben	5
Sep 19 1983	4-Ix	6
Sep 20 1983	5-Men	7
Sep 21 1983	6-Cib	8
Sep 22 1983	7-Caban	9
Sep 23 1983	8-Etz'nab	1
Sep 24 1983	9-Cauac	2
Sep 25 1983	10-Ahau	3
Sep 26 1983	11-Imix	4
Sep 27 1983	12-Ik	5
Sep 28 1983	13-Akbal	6
Sep 29 1983	1-Kan	7
Sep 30 1983	2-Chicchan	8
Oct 1 1983	3-Cimi	9
Oct 2 1983	4-Manik	1
Oct 3 1983	5-Lamat	2
Oct 4 1983	6-Muluc	3
Oct 5 1983	7-Oc	4
Oct 6 1983	8-Chuen	5
Oct 7 1983	9-Eb	6
Oct 8 1983	10-Ben	7
Oct 9 1983	11-Ix	8
Oct 10 1983	12-Men	9
Oct 11 1983	13-Cib	1
Oct 12 1983	1-Caban	2

Date	Day-Sign	L
Oct 13 1983	2-Etz'nab	3
Oct 14 1983	3-Cauac	4
Oct 15 1983	4-Ahau	5
Oct 16 1983	5-Imix	6
Oct 17 1983	6-Ik	7
Oct 18 1983	7-Akbal	8
Oct 19 1983	8-Kan	9
Oct 20 1983	9-Chicchan	1
Oct 21 1983	10-Cimi	2
Oct 22 1983	11-Manik	3
Oct 23 1983	12-Lamat	4
Oct 24 1983	13-Muluc	5
Oct 25 1983	1-Oc	6
Oct 26 1983	2-Chuen	7
Oct 27 1983	3-Eb	8
Oct 28 1983	4-Ben	9
Oct 29 1983	5-Ix	1
Oct 30 1983	6-Men	2
Oct 31 1983	7-Cib	3
Nov 1 1983	8-Caban	4
Nov 2 1983	9-Etz'nab	5
Nov 3 1983	10-Cauac	6
Nov 4 1983	11-Ahau	7
Nov 5 1983	12-Imix	8
Nov 6 1983	13-Ik	9
Nov 7 1983	1-Akbal	1
Nov 8 1983	2-Kan	2
Nov 9 1983	3-Chicchan	3
Nov 10 1983	4-Cimi	4
Nov 11 1983	5-Manik	5
Nov 12 1983	6-Lamat	6
Nov 13 1983	7-Muluc	7
Nov 14 1983	8-Oc	8
Nov 15 1983	9-Chuen	9
Nov 16 1983	10-Eb	1
Nov 17 1983	11-Ben	2
Nov 18 1983	12-Ix	3
Nov 19 1983	13-Men	4
Nov 20 1983	1-Cib	5
Nov 21 1983	2-Caban	6
Nov 22 1983	3-Etz'nab	7
Nov 23 1983	4-Cauac	8
Nov 24 1983	5-Ahau	9
Nov 25 1983	6-Imix	1
Nov 26 1983	7-Ik	2
Nov 27 1983	8-Akbal	3
Nov 28 1983	9-Kan	4
Nov 29 1983	10-Chicchan	5
Nov 30 1983	11-Cimi	6
Dec 1 1983	12-Manik	7
Dec 2 1983	13-Lamat	8
Dec 3 1983	1-Muluc	9
Dec 4 1983	2-Oc	1
Dec 5 1983	3-Chuen	2
Dec 6 1983	4-Eb	3
Dec 7 1983	5-Ben	4
Dec 8 1983	6-Ix	5
Dec 9 1983	7-Men	6
Dec 10 1983	8-Cib	7
Dec 11 1983	9-Caban	8
Dec 12 1983	10-Etz'nab	9
Dec 13 1983	11-Cauac	1
Dec 14 1983	12-Ahau	2
Dec 15 1983	13-Imix	3
Dec 16 1983	1-Ik	4
Dec 17 1983	2-Akbal	5
Dec 18 1983	3-Kan	6
Dec 19 1983	4-Chicchan	7

Date	Day-Sign	L
Dec 20 1983	5-Cimi	8
Dec 21 1983	6-Manik	9
Dec 22 1983	7-Lamat	1
Dec 23 1983	8-Muluc	2
Dec 24 1983	9-Oc	3
Dec 25 1983	10-Chuen	4
Dec 26 1983	11-Eb	5
Dec 27 1983	12-Ben	6
Dec 28 1983	13-Ix	7
Dec 29 1983	1-Men	8
Dec 30 1983	2-Cib	9
Dec 31 1983	3-Caban	1
Jan 1 1984	4-Etz'nab	2
Jan 2 1984	5-Cauac	3
Jan 3 1984	6-Ahau	4
Jan 4 1984	7-Imix	5
Jan 5 1984	8-Ik	6
Jan 6 1984	9-Akbal	7
Jan 7 1984	10-Kan	8
Jan 8 1984	11-Chicchan	9
Jan 9 1984	12-Cimi	1
Jan 10 1984	13-Manik	2
Jan 11 1984	1-Lamat	3
Jan 12 1984	2-Muluc	4
Jan 13 1984	3-Oc	5
Jan 14 1984	4-Chuen	6
Jan 15 1984	5-Eb	7
Jan 16 1984	6-Ben	8
Jan 17 1984	7-Ix	9
Jan 18 1984	8-Men	1
Jan 19 1984	9-Cib	2
Jan 20 1984	10-Caban	3
Jan 21 1984	11-Etz'nab	4
Jan 22 1984	12-Cauac	5
Jan 23 1984	13-Ahau	6
Jan 24 1984	1-Imix	7
Jan 25 1984	2-Ik	8
Jan 26 1984	3-Akbal	9
Jan 27 1984	4-Kan	1
Jan 28 1984	5-Chicchan	2
Jan 29 1984	6-Cimi	3
Jan 30 1984	7-Manik	4
Jan 31 1984	8-Lamat	5
Feb 1 1984	9-Muluc	6
Feb 2 1984	10-Oc	7
Feb 3 1984	11-Chuen	8
Feb 4 1984	12-Eb	9
Feb 5 1984	13-Ben	1
Feb 6 1984	1-Ix	2
Feb 7 1984	2-Men	3
Feb 8 1984	3-Cib	4
Feb 9 1984	4-Caban	5
Feb 10 1984	5-Etz'nab	6
Feb 11 1984	6-Cauac	7
Feb 12 1984	7-Ahau	8
Feb 13 1984	8-Imix	9
Feb 14 1984	9-Ik	1
Feb 15 1984	10-Akbal	2
Feb 16 1984	11-Kan	3
Feb 17 1984	12-Chicchan	4
Feb 18 1984	13-Cimi	5
Feb 19 1984	1-Manik	6
Feb 20 1984	2-Lamat	7
Feb 21 1984	3-Muluc	8
Feb 22 1984	4-Oc	9
Feb 23 1984	5-Chuen	1
Feb 24 1984	6-Eb	2
Feb 25 1984	7-Ben	3

Date	Day-Sign	L
Feb 26 1984	8-Ix	4
Feb 27 1984	9-Men	5
Feb 28 1984	10-Cib	6
Feb 29 1984	11-Caban	7
Mar 1 1984	12-Etz'nab	8
Mar 2 1984	13-Cauac	9
Mar 3 1984	**1-Ahau**	1
Mar 4 1984	*2-Imix*	2
Mar 5 1984	3-Ik	3
Mar 6 1984	4-Akbal	4
Mar 7 1984	5-Kan	5
Mar 8 1984	6-Chicchan	6
Mar 9 1984	7-Cimi	7
Mar 10 1984	8-Manik	8
Mar 11 1984	9-Lamat	9
Mar 12 1984	10-Muluc	1
Mar 13 1984	11-Oc	2
Mar 14 1984	12-Chuen	3
Mar 15 1984	13-Eb	4
Mar 16 1984	**1-Ben**	5
Mar 17 1984	2-Ix	6
Mar 18 1984	3-Men	7
Mar 19 1984	4-Cib	8
Mar 20 1984	5-Caban	9
Mar 21 1984	6-Etz'nab	1
Mar 22 1984	7-Cauac	2
Mar 23 1984	8-Ahau	3
Mar 24 1984	*9-Imix*	4
Mar 25 1984	10-Ik	5
Mar 26 1984	11-Akbal	6
Mar 27 1984	12-Kan	7
Mar 28 1984	13-Chicchan	8
Mar 29 1984	**1-Cimi**	9
Mar 30 1984	2-Manik	1
Mar 31 1984	3-Lamat	2
Apr 1 1984	4-Muluc	3
Apr 2 1984	5-Oc	4
Apr 3 1984	6-Chuen	5
Apr 4 1984	7-Eb	6
Apr 5 1984	8-Ben	7
Apr 6 1984	9-Ix	8
Apr 7 1984	10-Men	9
Apr 8 1984	11-Cib	1
Apr 9 1984	12-Caban	2
Apr 10 1984	13-Etz'nab	3
Apr 11 1984	**1-Cauac**	4
Apr 12 1984	2-Ahau	5
Apr 13 1984	*3-Imix*	6
Apr 14 1984	4-Ik	7
Apr 15 1984	5-Akbal	8
Apr 16 1984	6-Kan	9
Apr 17 1984	7-Chicchan	1
Apr 18 1984	8-Cimi	2
Apr 19 1984	9-Manik	3
Apr 20 1984	10-Lamat	4
Apr 21 1984	11-Muluc	5
Apr 22 1984	12-Oc	6
Apr 23 1984	13-Chuen	7
Apr 24 1984	**1-Eb**	8
Apr 25 1984	2-Ben	9
Apr 26 1984	3-Ix	1
Apr 27 1984	4-Men	2
Apr 28 1984	5-Cib	3
Apr 29 1984	6-Caban	4
Apr 30 1984	7-Etz'nab	5
May 1 1984	8-Cauac	6
May 2 1984	9-Ahau	7
May 3 1984	*10-Imix*	8

Date	Day-Sign	L
May 4 1984	11-Ik	9
May 5 1984	12-Akbal	1
May 6 1984	13-Kan	2
May 7 1984	**1-Chicchan**	3
May 8 1984	2-Cimi	4
May 9 1984	3-Manik	5
May 10 1984	4-Lamat	6
May 11 1984	5-Muluc	7
May 12 1984	6-Oc	8
May 13 1984	7-Chuen	9
May 14 1984	8-Eb	1
May 15 1984	9-Ben	2
May 16 1984	10-Ix	3
May 17 1984	11-Men	4
May 18 1984	12-Cib	5
May 19 1984	13-Caban	6
May 20 1984	**1-Etz'nab**	7
May 21 1984	2-Cauac	8
May 22 1984	3-Ahau	9
May 23 1984	*4-Imix*	1
May 24 1984	5-Ik	2
May 25 1984	6-Akbal	3
May 26 1984	7-Kan	4
May 27 1984	8-Chicchan	5
May 28 1984	9-Cimi	6
May 29 1984	10-Manik	7
May 30 1984	11-Lamat	8
May 31 1984	12-Muluc	9
Jun 1 1984	13-Oc	1
Jun 2 1984	**1-Chuen**	2
Jun 3 1984	2-Eb	3
Jun 4 1984	3-Ben	4
Jun 5 1984	4-Ix	5
Jun 6 1984	5-Men	6
Jun 7 1984	6-Cib	7
Jun 8 1984	7-Caban	8
Jun 9 1984	8-Etz'nab	9
Jun 10 1984	9-Cauac	1
Jun 11 1984	10-Ahau	2
Jun 12 1984	*11-Imix*	3
Jun 13 1984	12-Ik	4
Jun 14 1984	13-Akbal	5
Jun 15 1984	**1-Kan**	6
Jun 16 1984	2-Chicchan	7
Jun 17 1984	3-Cimi	8
Jun 18 1984	4-Manik	9
Jun 19 1984	5-Lamat	1
Jun 20 1984	6-Muluc	2
Jun 21 1984	7-Oc	3
Jun 22 1984	8-Chuen	4
Jun 23 1984	9-Eb	5
Jun 24 1984	10-Ben	6
Jun 25 1984	11-Ix	7
Jun 26 1984	12-Men	8
Jun 27 1984	13-Cib	9
Jun 28 1984	**1-Caban**	1
Jun 29 1984	2-Etz'nab	2
Jun 30 1984	3-Cauac	3
Jul 1 1984	4-Ahau	4
Jul 2 1984	*5-Imix*	5
Jul 3 1984	6-Ik	6
Jul 4 1984	7-Akbal	7
Jul 5 1984	8-Kan	8
Jul 6 1984	9-Chicchan	9
Jul 7 1984	10-Cimi	1
Jul 8 1984	11-Manik	2
Jul 9 1984	12-Lamat	3
Jul 10 1984	13-Muluc	4

Date	Day-Sign	L
Jul 11 1984	**1-Oc**	5
Jul 12 1984	2-Chuen	6
Jul 13 1984	3-Eb	7
Jul 14 1984	4-Ben	8
Jul 15 1984	5-Ix	9
Jul 16 1984	6-Men	1
Jul 17 1984	7-Cib	2
Jul 18 1984	8-Caban	3
Jul 19 1984	9-Etz'nab	4
Jul 20 1984	10-Cauac	5
Jul 21 1984	11-Ahau	6
Jul 22 1984	*12-Imix*	7
Jul 23 1984	13-Ik	8
Jul 24 1984	**1-Akbal**	9
Jul 25 1984	2-Kan	1
Jul 26 1984	3-Chicchan	2
Jul 27 1984	4-Cimi	3
Jul 28 1984	5-Manik	4
Jul 29 1984	6-Lamat	5
Jul 30 1984	7-Muluc	6
Jul 31 1984	8-Oc	7
Aug 1 1984	9-Chuen	8
Aug 2 1984	10-Eb	9
Aug 3 1984	11-Ben	1
Aug 4 1984	12-Ix	2
Aug 5 1984	13-Men	3
Aug 6 1984	**1-Cib**	4
Aug 7 1984	2-Caban	5
Aug 8 1984	3-Etz'nab	6
Aug 9 1984	4-Cauac	7
Aug 10 1984	5-Ahau	8
Aug 11 1984	*6-Imix*	9
Aug 12 1984	7-Ik	1
Aug 13 1984	8-Akbal	2
Aug 14 1984	9-Kan	3
Aug 15 1984	10-Chicchan	4
Aug 16 1984	11-Cimi	5
Aug 17 1984	12-Manik	6
Aug 18 1984	13-Lamat	7
Aug 19 1984	**1-Muluc**	8
Aug 20 1984	2-Oc	9
Aug 21 1984	3-Chuen	1
Aug 22 1984	4-Eb	2
Aug 23 1984	5-Ben	3
Aug 24 1984	6-Ix	4
Aug 25 1984	7-Men	5
Aug 26 1984	8-Cib	6
Aug 27 1984	9-Caban	7
Aug 28 1984	10-Etz'nab	8
Aug 29 1984	11-Cauac	9
Aug 30 1984	12-Ahau	1
Aug 31 1984	*13-Imix*	2
Sep 1 1984	**1-Ik**	3
Sep 2 1984	2-Akbal	4
Sep 3 1984	3-Kan	5
Sep 4 1984	4-Chicchan	6
Sep 5 1984	5-Cimi	7
Sep 6 1984	6-Manik	8
Sep 7 1984	7-Lamat	9
Sep 8 1984	8-Muluc	1
Sep 9 1984	9-Oc	2
Sep 10 1984	10-Chuen	3
Sep 11 1984	11-Eb	4
Sep 12 1984	12-Ben	5
Sep 13 1984	13-Ix	6
Sep 14 1984	**1-Men**	7
Sep 15 1984	2-Cib	8
Sep 16 1984	3-Caban	9

Date	Day-Sign	L
Sep 17 1984	4-Etz'nab	1
Sep 18 1984	5-Cauac	2
Sep 19 1984	6-Ahau	3
Sep 20 1984	7-*Imix*	4
Sep 21 1984	8-Ik	5
Sep 22 1984	9-Akbal	6
Sep 23 1984	10-Kan	7
Sep 24 1984	11-Chicchan	8
Sep 25 1984	12-Cimi	9
Sep 26 1984	13-Manik	1
Sep 27 1984	**1-Lamat**	2
Sep 28 1984	2-Muluc	3
Sep 29 1984	3-Oc	4
Sep 30 1984	4-Chuen	5
Oct 1 1984	5-Eb	6
Oct 2 1984	6-Ben	7
Oct 3 1984	7-Ix	8
Oct 4 1984	8-Men	9
Oct 5 1984	9-Cib	1
Oct 6 1984	10-Caban	2
Oct 7 1984	11-Etz'nab	3
Oct 8 1984	12-Cauac	4
Oct 9 1984	13-Ahau	5
Oct 10 1984	**1-Imix**	6
Oct 11 1984	2-Ik	7
Oct 12 1984	3-Akbal	8
Oct 13 1984	4-Kan	9
Oct 14 1984	5-Chicchan	1
Oct 15 1984	6-Cimi	2
Oct 16 1984	7-Manik	3
Oct 17 1984	8-Lamat	4
Oct 18 1984	9-Muluc	5
Oct 19 1984	10-Oc	6
Oct 20 1984	11-Chuen	7
Oct 21 1984	12-Eb	8
Oct 22 1984	13-Ben	9
Oct 23 1984	**1-Ix**	1
Oct 24 1984	2-Men	2
Oct 25 1984	3-Cib	3
Oct 26 1984	4-Caban	4
Oct 27 1984	5-Etz'nab	5
Oct 28 1984	6-Cauac	6
Oct 29 1984	7-Ahau	7
Oct 30 1984	8-*Imix*	8
Oct 31 1984	9-Ik	9
Nov 1 1984	10-Akbal	1
Nov 2 1984	11-Kan	2
Nov 3 1984	12-Chicchan	3
Nov 4 1984	13-Cimi	4
Nov 5 1984	**1-Manik**	5
Nov 6 1984	2-Lamat	6
Nov 7 1984	3-Muluc	7
Nov 8 1984	4-Oc	8
Nov 9 1984	5-Chuen	9
Nov 10 1984	6-Eb	1
Nov 11 1984	7-Ben	2
Nov 12 1984	8-Ix	3
Nov 13 1984	9-Men	4
Nov 14 1984	10-Cib	5
Nov 15 1984	11-Caban	6
Nov 16 1984	12-Etz'nab	7
Nov 17 1984	13-Cauac	8
Nov 18 1984	**1-Ahau**	9
Nov 19 1984	2-*Imix*	1
Nov 20 1984	3-Ik	2
Nov 21 1984	4-Akbal	3
Nov 22 1984	5-Kan	4
Nov 23 1984	6-Chicchan	5

Date	Day-Sign	L
Nov 24 1984	7-Cimi	6
Nov 25 1984	8-Manik	7
Nov 26 1984	9-Lamat	8
Nov 27 1984	10-Muluc	9
Nov 28 1984	11-Oc	1
Nov 29 1984	12-Chuen	2
Nov 30 1984	13-Eb	3
Dec 1 1984	**1-Ben**	4
Dec 2 1984	2-Ix	5
Dec 3 1984	3-Men	6
Dec 4 1984	4-Cib	7
Dec 5 1984	5-Caban	8
Dec 6 1984	6-Etz'nab	9
Dec 7 1984	7-Cauac	1
Dec 8 1984	8-Ahau	2
Dec 9 1984	9-*Imix*	3
Dec 10 1984	10-Ik	4
Dec 11 1984	11-Akbal	5
Dec 12 1984	12-Kan	6
Dec 13 1984	13-Chicchan	7
Dec 14 1984	**1-Cimi**	8
Dec 15 1984	2-Manik	9
Dec 16 1984	3-Lamat	1
Dec 17 1984	4-Muluc	2
Dec 18 1984	5-Oc	3
Dec 19 1984	6-Chuen	4
Dec 20 1984	7-Eb	5
Dec 21 1984	8-Ben	6
Dec 22 1984	9-Ix	7
Dec 23 1984	10-Men	8
Dec 24 1984	11-Cib	9
Dec 25 1984	12-Caban	1
Dec 26 1984	13-Etz'nab	2
Dec 27 1984	**1-Cauac**	3
Dec 28 1984	2-Ahau	4
Dec 29 1984	3-*Imix*	5
Dec 30 1984	4-Ik	6
Dec 31 1984	5-Akbal	7
Jan 1 1985	6-Kan	8
Jan 2 1985	7-Chicchan	9
Jan 3 1985	8-Cimi	1
Jan 4 1985	9-Manik	2
Jan 5 1985	10-Lamat	3
Jan 6 1985	11-Muluc	4
Jan 7 1985	12-Oc	5
Jan 8 1985	13-Chuen	6
Jan 9 1985	**1-Eb**	7
Jan 10 1985	2-Ben	8
Jan 11 1985	3-Ix	9
Jan 12 1985	4-Men	1
Jan 13 1985	5-Cib	2
Jan 14 1985	6-Caban	3
Jan 15 1985	7-Etz'nab	4
Jan 16 1985	8-Cauac	5
Jan 17 1985	9-Ahau	6
Jan 18 1985	10-*Imix*	7
Jan 19 1985	11-Ik	8
Jan 20 1985	12-Akbal	9
Jan 21 1985	13-Kan	1
Jan 22 1985	**1-Chicchan**	2
Jan 23 1985	2-Cimi	3
Jan 24 1985	3-Manik	4
Jan 25 1985	4-Lamat	5
Jan 26 1985	5-Muluc	6
Jan 27 1985	6-Oc	7
Jan 28 1985	7-Chuen	8
Jan 29 1985	8-Eb	9
Jan 30 1985	9-Ben	1

Date	Day-Sign	L
Jan 31 1985	10-Ix	2
Feb 1 1985	11-Men	3
Feb 2 1985	12-Cib	4
Feb 3 1985	13-Caban	5
Feb 4 1985	**1-Etz'nab**	6
Feb 5 1985	2-Cauac	7
Feb 6 1985	3-Ahau	8
Feb 7 1985	4-*Imix*	9
Feb 8 1985	5-Ik	1
Feb 9 1985	6-Akbal	2
Feb 10 1985	7-Kan	3
Feb 11 1985	8-Chicchan	4
Feb 12 1985	9-Cimi	5
Feb 13 1985	10-Manik	6
Feb 14 1985	11-Lamat	7
Feb 15 1985	12-Muluc	8
Feb 16 1985	13-Oc	9
Feb 17 1985	**1-Chuen**	1
Feb 18 1985	2-Eb	2
Feb 19 1985	3-Ben	3
Feb 20 1985	4-Ix	4
Feb 21 1985	5-Men	5
Feb 22 1985	6-Cib	6
Feb 23 1985	7-Caban	7
Feb 24 1985	8-Etz'nab	8
Feb 25 1985	9-Cauac	9
Feb 26 1985	10-Ahau	1
Feb 27 1985	11-*Imix*	2
Feb 28 1985	12-Ik	3
Mar 1 1985	13-Akbal	4
Mar 2 1985	**1-Kan**	5
Mar 3 1985	2-Chicchan	6
Mar 4 1985	3-Cimi	7
Mar 5 1985	4-Manik	8
Mar 6 1985	5-Lamat	9
Mar 7 1985	6-Muluc	1
Mar 8 1985	7-Oc	2
Mar 9 1985	8-Chuen	3
Mar 10 1985	9-Eb	4
Mar 11 1985	10-Ben	5
Mar 12 1985	11-Ix	6
Mar 13 1985	12-Men	7
Mar 14 1985	13-Cib	8
Mar 15 1985	**1-Caban**	9
Mar 16 1985	2-Etz'nab	1
Mar 17 1985	3-Cauac	2
Mar 18 1985	4-Ahau	3
Mar 19 1985	5-*Imix*	4
Mar 20 1985	6-Ik	5
Mar 21 1985	7-Akbal	6
Mar 22 1985	8-Kan	7
Mar 23 1985	9-Chicchan	8
Mar 24 1985	10-Cimi	9
Mar 25 1985	11-Manik	1
Mar 26 1985	12-Lamat	2
Mar 27 1985	13-Muluc	3
Mar 28 1985	**1-Oc**	4
Mar 29 1985	2-Chuen	5
Mar 30 1985	3-Eb	6
Mar 31 1985	4-Ben	7
Apr 1 1985	5-Ix	8
Apr 2 1985	6-Men	9
Apr 3 1985	7-Cib	1
Apr 4 1985	8-Caban	2
Apr 5 1985	9-Etz'nab	3
Apr 6 1985	10-Cauac	4
Apr 7 1985	11-Ahau	5
Apr 8 1985	12-*Imix*	6

Date	Day-Sign	L
Apr 9 1985	13-Ik	7
Apr 10 1985	**1-Akbal**	8
Apr 11 1985	2-Kan	9
Apr 12 1985	3-Chicchan	1
Apr 13 1985	4-Cimi	2
Apr 14 1985	5-Manik	3
Apr 15 1985	6-Lamat	4
Apr 16 1985	7-Muluc	5
Apr 17 1985	8-Oc	6
Apr 18 1985	9-Chuen	7
Apr 19 1985	10-Eb	8
Apr 20 1985	11-Ben	9
Apr 21 1985	12-Ix	1
Apr 22 1985	13-Men	2
Apr 23 1985	**1-Cib**	3
Apr 24 1985	2-Caban	4
Apr 25 1985	3-Etz'nab	5
Apr 26 1985	4-Cauac	6
Apr 27 1985	5-Ahau	7
Apr 28 1985	*6-Imix*	8
Apr 29 1985	7-Ik	9
Apr 30 1985	8-Akbal	1
May 1 1985	9-Kan	2
May 2 1985	10-Chicchan	3
May 3 1985	11-Cimi	4
May 4 1985	12-Manik	5
May 5 1985	13-Lamat	6
May 6 1985	**1-Muluc**	7
May 7 1985	2-Oc	8
May 8 1985	3-Chuen	9
May 9 1985	4-Eb	1
May 10 1985	5-Ben	2
May 11 1985	6-Ix	3
May 12 1985	7-Men	4
May 13 1985	8-Cib	5
May 14 1985	9-Caban	6
May 15 1985	10-Etz'nab	7
May 16 1985	11-Cauac	8
May 17 1985	12-Ahau	9
May 18 1985	*13-Imix*	1
May 19 1985	**1-Ik**	2
May 20 1985	2-Akbal	3
May 21 1985	3-Kan	4
May 22 1985	4-Chicchan	5
May 23 1985	5-Cimi	6
May 24 1985	6-Manik	7
May 25 1985	7-Lamat	8
May 26 1985	8-Muluc	9
May 27 1985	9-Oc	1
May 28 1985	10-Chuen	2
May 29 1985	11-Eb	3
May 30 1985	12-Ben	4
May 31 1985	13-Ix	5
Jun 1 1985	**1-Men**	6
Jun 2 1985	2-Cib	7
Jun 3 1985	3-Caban	8
Jun 4 1985	4-Etz'nab	9
Jun 5 1985	5-Cauac	1
Jun 6 1985	6-Ahau	2
Jun 7 1985	*7-Imix*	3
Jun 8 1985	8-Ik	4
Jun 9 1985	9-Akbal	5
Jun 10 1985	10-Kan	6
Jun 11 1985	11-Chicchan	7
Jun 12 1985	12-Cimi	8
Jun 13 1985	13-Manik	9
Jun 14 1985	**1-Lamat**	1
Jun 15 1985	2-Muluc	2

Date	Day-Sign	L
Jun 16 1985	3-Oc	3
Jun 17 1985	4-Chuen	4
Jun 18 1985	5-Eb	5
Jun 19 1985	6-Ben	6
Jun 20 1985	7-Ix	7
Jun 21 1985	8-Men	8
Jun 22 1985	9-Cib	9
Jun 23 1985	10-Caban	1
Jun 24 1985	11-Etz'nab	2
Jun 25 1985	12-Cauac	3
Jun 26 1985	13-Ahau	4
Jun 27 1985	**1-Imix**	5
Jun 28 1985	2-Ik	6
Jun 29 1985	3-Akbal	7
Jun 30 1985	4-Kan	8
Jul 1 1985	5-Chicchan	9
Jul 2 1985	6-Cimi	1
Jul 3 1985	7-Manik	2
Jul 4 1985	8-Lamat	3
Jul 5 1985	9-Muluc	4
Jul 6 1985	10-Oc	5
Jul 7 1985	11-Chuen	6
Jul 8 1985	12-Eb	7
Jul 9 1985	13-Ben	8
Jul 10 1985	**1-Ix**	9
Jul 11 1985	2-Men	1
Jul 12 1985	3-Cib	2
Jul 13 1985	4-Caban	3
Jul 14 1985	5-Etz'nab	4
Jul 15 1985	6-Cauac	5
Jul 16 1985	7-Ahau	6
Jul 17 1985	*8-Imix*	7
Jul 18 1985	9-Ik	8
Jul 19 1985	10-Akbal	9
Jul 20 1985	11-Kan	1
Jul 21 1985	12-Chicchan	2
Jul 22 1985	13-Cib	3
Jul 23 1985	**1-Manik**	4
Jul 24 1985	2-Lamat	5
Jul 25 1985	3-Muluc	6
Jul 26 1985	4-Oc	7
Jul 27 1985	5-Chuen	8
Jul 28 1985	6-Eb	9
Jul 29 1985	7-Ben	1
Jul 30 1985	8-Ix	2
Jul 31 1985	9-Men	3
Aug 1 1985	10-Cib	4
Aug 2 1985	11-Caban	5
Aug 3 1985	12-Etz'nab	6
Aug 4 1985	13-Cauac	7
Aug 5 1985	**1-Ahau**	8
Aug 6 1985	*2-Imix*	9
Aug 7 1985	3-Ik	1
Aug 8 1985	4-Akbal	2
Aug 9 1985	5-Kan	3
Aug 10 1985	6-Chicchan	4
Aug 11 1985	7-Cimi	5
Aug 12 1985	8-Manik	6
Aug 13 1985	9-Lamat	7
Aug 14 1985	10-Muluc	8
Aug 15 1985	11-Oc	9
Aug 16 1985	12-Chuen	1
Aug 17 1985	13-Eb	2
Aug 18 1985	**1-Ben**	3
Aug 19 1985	2-Ix	4
Aug 20 1985	3-Men	5
Aug 21 1985	4-Cib	6
Aug 22 1985	5-Caban	7

Date	Day-Sign	L
Aug 23 1985	6-Etz'nab	8
Aug 24 1985	7-Cauac	9
Aug 25 1985	8-Ahau	1
Aug 26 1985	*9-Imix*	2
Aug 27 1985	10-Ik	3
Aug 28 1985	11-Akbal	4
Aug 29 1985	12-Kan	5
Aug 30 1985	13-Chicchan	6
Aug 31 1985	**1-Cimi**	7
Sep 1 1985	2-Manik	8
Sep 2 1985	3-Lamat	9
Sep 3 1985	4-Muluc	1
Sep 4 1985	5-Oc	2
Sep 5 1985	6-Chuen	3
Sep 6 1985	7-Eb	4
Sep 7 1985	8-Ben	5
Sep 8 1985	9-Ix	6
Sep 9 1985	10-Men	7
Sep 10 1985	11-Cib	8
Sep 11 1985	12-Caban	9
Sep 12 1985	13-Etz'nab	1
Sep 13 1985	**1-Cauac**	2
Sep 14 1985	2-Ahau	3
Sep 15 1985	*3-Imix*	4
Sep 16 1985	4-Ik	5
Sep 17 1985	5-Akbal	6
Sep 18 1985	6-Kan	7
Sep 19 1985	7-Chicchan	8
Sep 20 1985	8-Cimi	9
Sep 21 1985	9-Manik	1
Sep 22 1985	10-Lamat	2
Sep 23 1985	11-Muluc	3
Sep 24 1985	12-Oc	4
Sep 25 1985	13-Chuen	5
Sep 26 1985	**1-Eb**	6
Sep 27 1985	2-Ben	7
Sep 28 1985	3-Ix	8
Sep 29 1985	4-Men	9
Sep 30 1985	5-Cib	1
Oct 1 1985	6-Caban	2
Oct 2 1985	7-Etz'nab	3
Oct 3 1985	8-Cauac	4
Oct 4 1985	9-Ahau	5
Oct 5 1985	*10-Imix*	6
Oct 6 1985	11-Ik	7
Oct 7 1985	12-Akbal	8
Oct 8 1985	13-Kan	9
Oct 9 1985	**1-Chicchan**	1
Oct 10 1985	2-Cimi	2
Oct 11 1985	3-Manik	3
Oct 12 1985	4-Lamat	4
Oct 13 1985	5-Muluc	5
Oct 14 1985	6-Oc	6
Oct 15 1985	7-Chuen	7
Oct 16 1985	8-Eb	8
Oct 17 1985	9-Ben	9
Oct 18 1985	10-Ix	1
Oct 19 1985	11-Men	2
Oct 20 1985	12-Cib	3
Oct 21 1985	13-Caban	4
Oct 22 1985	**1-Etz'nab**	5
Oct 23 1985	2-Cauac	6
Oct 24 1985	3-Ahau	7
Oct 25 1985	*4-Imix*	8
Oct 26 1985	5-Ik	9
Oct 27 1985	6-Akbal	1
Oct 28 1985	7-Kan	2
Oct 29 1985	8-Chicchan	3

Date	Day-Sign	L
Oct 30 1985	9-Cimi	4
Oct 31 1985	10-Manik	5
Nov 1 1985	11-Lamat	6
Nov 2 1985	12-Muluc	7
Nov 3 1985	13-Oc	8
Nov 4 1985	**1-Chuen**	9
Nov 5 1985	2-Eb	1
Nov 6 1985	3-Ben	2
Nov 7 1985	4-Ix	3
Nov 8 1985	5-Men	4
Nov 9 1985	6-Cib	5
Nov 10 1985	7-Caban	6
Nov 11 1985	8-Etz'nab	7
Nov 12 1985	9-Cauac	8
Nov 13 1985	10-Ahau	9
Nov 14 1985	11-*Imix*	1
Nov 15 1985	12-Ik	2
Nov 16 1985	13-Akbal	3
Nov 17 1985	**1-Kan**	4
Nov 18 1985	2-Chicchan	5
Nov 19 1985	3-Cimi	6
Nov 20 1985	4-Manik	7
Nov 21 1985	5-Lamat	8
Nov 22 1985	6-Muluc	9
Nov 23 1985	7-Oc	1
Nov 24 1985	8-Chuen	2
Nov 25 1985	9-Eb	3
Nov 26 1985	10-Ben	4
Nov 27 1985	11-Ix	5
Nov 28 1985	12-Men	6
Nov 29 1985	13-Cib	7
Nov 30 1985	**1-Caban**	8
Dec 1 1985	2-Etz'nab	9
Dec 2 1985	3-Cauac	1
Dec 3 1985	4-Ahau	2
Dec 4 1985	5-*Imix*	3
Dec 5 1985	6-Ik	4
Dec 6 1985	7-Akbal	5
Dec 7 1985	8-Kan	6
Dec 8 1985	9-Chicchan	7
Dec 9 1985	10-Cimi	8
Dec 10 1985	11-Manik	9
Dec 11 1985	12-Lamat	1
Dec 12 1985	13-Muluc	2
Dec 13 1985	**1-Oc**	3
Dec 14 1985	2-Chuen	4
Dec 15 1985	3-Eb	5
Dec 16 1985	4-Ben	6
Dec 17 1985	5-Ix	7
Dec 18 1985	6-Men	8
Dec 19 1985	7-Cib	9
Dec 20 1985	8-Caban	1
Dec 21 1985	9-Etz'nab	2
Dec 22 1985	10-Cauac	3
Dec 23 1985	11-Ahau	4
Dec 24 1985	12-*Imix*	5
Dec 25 1985	13-Ik	6
Dec 26 1985	**1-Akbal**	7
Dec 27 1985	2-Kan	8
Dec 28 1985	3-Chicchan	9
Dec 29 1985	4-Cimi	1
Dec 30 1985	5-Manik	2
Dec 31 1985	6-Lamat	3
Jan 1 1986	7-Muluc	4
Jan 2 1986	8-Oc	5
Jan 3 1986	9-Chuen	6
Jan 4 1986	10-Eb	7
Jan 5 1986	11-Ben	8

Date	Day-Sign	L
Jan 6 1986	12-Ix	9
Jan 7 1986	13-Men	1
Jan 8 1986	**1-Cib**	2
Jan 9 1986	2-Caban	3
Jan 10 1986	3-Etz'nab	4
Jan 11 1986	4-Cauac	5
Jan 12 1986	5-Ahau	6
Jan 13 1986	6-*Imix*	7
Jan 14 1986	7-Ik	8
Jan 15 1986	8-Akbal	9
Jan 16 1986	9-Kan	1
Jan 17 1986	10-Chicchan	2
Jan 18 1986	11-Cimi	3
Jan 19 1986	12-Manik	4
Jan 20 1986	13-Lamat	5
Jan 21 1986	**1-Muluc**	6
Jan 22 1986	2-Oc	7
Jan 23 1986	3-Chuen	8
Jan 24 1986	4-Eb	9
Jan 25 1986	5-Ben	1
Jan 26 1986	6-Ix	2
Jan 27 1986	7-Men	3
Jan 28 1986	8-Cib	4
Jan 29 1986	9-Caban	5
Jan 30 1986	10-Etz'nab	6
Jan 31 1986	11-Cauac	7
Feb 1 1986	12-Ahau	8
Feb 2 1986	13-*Imix*	9
Feb 3 1986	**1-Ik**	1
Feb 4 1986	2-Akbal	2
Feb 5 1986	3-Kan	3
Feb 6 1986	4-Chicchan	4
Feb 7 1986	5-Cimi	5
Feb 8 1986	6-Manik	6
Feb 9 1986	7-Lamat	7
Feb 10 1986	8-Muluc	8
Feb 11 1986	9-Oc	9
Feb 12 1986	10-Chuen	1
Feb 13 1986	11-Eb	2
Feb 14 1986	12-Ben	3
Feb 15 1986	13-Ix	4
Feb 16 1986	**1-Men**	5
Feb 17 1986	2-Cib	6
Feb 18 1986	3-Caban	7
Feb 19 1986	4-Etz'nab	8
Feb 20 1986	5-Cauac	9
Feb 21 1986	6-Ahau	1
Feb 22 1986	7-*Imix*	2
Feb 23 1986	8-Ik	3
Feb 24 1986	9-Akbal	4
Feb 25 1986	10-Kan	5
Feb 26 1986	11-Chicchan	6
Feb 27 1986	12-Cimi	7
Feb 28 1986	13-Manik	8
Mar 1 1986	**1-Lamat**	9
Mar 2 1986	2-Muluc	1
Mar 3 1986	3-Oc	2
Mar 4 1986	4-Chuen	3
Mar 5 1986	5-Eb	4
Mar 6 1986	6-Ben	5
Mar 7 1986	7-Ix	6
Mar 8 1986	8-Men	7
Mar 9 1986	9-Cib	8
Mar 10 1986	10-Caban	9
Mar 11 1986	11-Etz'nab	1
Mar 12 1986	12-Cauac	2
Mar 13 1986	13-Ahau	3
Mar 14 1986	**1-Imix**	4

Date	Day-Sign	L
Mar 15 1986	2-Ik	5
Mar 16 1986	3-Akbal	6
Mar 17 1986	4-Kan	7
Mar 18 1986	5-Chicchan	8
Mar 19 1986	6-Cimi	9
Mar 20 1986	7-Manik	1
Mar 21 1986	8-Lamat	2
Mar 22 1986	9-Muluc	3
Mar 23 1986	10-Oc	4
Mar 24 1986	11-Chuen	5
Mar 25 1986	12-Eb	6
Mar 26 1986	13-Ben	7
Mar 27 1986	**1-Ix**	8
Mar 28 1986	2-Men	9
Mar 29 1986	3-Cib	1
Mar 30 1986	4-Caban	2
Mar 31 1986	5-Etz'nab	3
Apr 1 1986	6-Cauac	4
Apr 2 1986	7-Ahau	5
Apr 3 1986	8-*Imix*	6
Apr 4 1986	9-Ik	7
Apr 5 1986	10-Akbal	8
Apr 6 1986	11-Kan	9
Apr 7 1986	12-Chicchan	1
Apr 8 1986	13-Cimi	2
Apr 9 1986	**1-Manik**	3
Apr 10 1986	2-Lamat	4
Apr 11 1986	3-Muluc	5
Apr 12 1986	4-Oc	6
Apr 13 1986	5-Chuen	7
Apr 14 1986	6-Eb	8
Apr 15 1986	7-Ben	9
Apr 16 1986	8-Ix	1
Apr 17 1986	9-Men	2
Apr 18 1986	10-Cib	3
Apr 19 1986	11-Caban	4
Apr 20 1986	12-Etz'nab	5
Apr 21 1986	13-Cauac	6
Apr 22 1986	**1-Ahau**	7
Apr 23 1986	2-*Imix*	8
Apr 24 1986	3-Ik	9
Apr 25 1986	4-Akbal	1
Apr 26 1986	5-Kan	2
Apr 27 1986	6-Chicchan	3
Apr 28 1986	7-Cimi	4
Apr 29 1986	8-Manik	5
Apr 30 1986	9-Lamat	6
May 1 1986	10-Muluc	7
May 2 1986	11-Oc	8
May 3 1986	12-Chuen	9
May 4 1986	13-Eb	1
May 5 1986	**1-Ben**	2
May 6 1986	2-Ix	3
May 7 1986	3-Men	4
May 8 1986	4-Cib	5
May 9 1986	5-Caban	6
May 10 1986	6-Etz'nab	7
May 11 1986	7-Cauac	8
May 12 1986	8-Ahau	9
May 13 1986	9-*Imix*	1
May 14 1986	10-Ik	2
May 15 1986	11-Akbal	3
May 16 1986	12-Kan	4
May 17 1986	13-Chicchan	5
May 18 1986	**1-Cimi**	6
May 19 1986	2-Manik	7
May 20 1986	3-Lamat	8
May 21 1986	4-Muluc	9

Date	Day-Sign	L
May 22 1986	5-Oc	1
May 23 1986	6-Chuen	2
May 24 1986	7-Eb	3
May 25 1986	8-Ben	4
May 26 1986	9-Ix	5
May 27 1986	10-Men	6
May 28 1986	11-Cib	7
May 29 1986	12-Caban	8
May 30 1986	13-Etz'nab	9
May 31 1986	**1-Cauac**	1
Jun 1 1986	2-Ahau	2
Jun 2 1986	*3-Imix*	3
Jun 3 1986	4-Ik	4
Jun 4 1986	5-Akbal	5
Jun 5 1986	6-Kan	6
Jun 6 1986	7-Chicchan	7
Jun 7 1986	8-Cimi	8
Jun 8 1986	9-Manik	9
Jun 9 1986	10-Lamat	1
Jun 10 1986	11-Muluc	2
Jun 11 1986	12-Oc	3
Jun 12 1986	13-Chuen	4
Jun 13 1986	**1-Eb**	5
Jun 14 1986	2-Ben	6
Jun 15 1986	3-Ix	7
Jun 16 1986	4-Men	8
Jun 17 1986	5-Cib	9
Jun 18 1986	6-Caban	1
Jun 19 1986	7-Etz'nab	2
Jun 20 1986	8-Cauac	3
Jun 21 1986	9-Ahau	4
Jun 22 1986	*10-Imix*	5
Jun 23 1986	11-Ik	6
Jun 24 1986	12-Akbal	7
Jun 25 1986	13-Kan	8
Jun 26 1986	**1-Chicchan**	9
Jun 27 1986	2-Cimi	1
Jun 28 1986	3-Manik	2
Jun 29 1986	4-Lamat	3
Jun 30 1986	5-Muluc	4
Jul 1 1986	6-Oc	5
Jul 2 1986	7-Chuen	6
Jul 3 1986	8-Eb	7
Jul 4 1986	9-Ben	8
Jul 5 1986	10-Ix	9
Jul 6 1986	11-Men	1
Jul 7 1986	12-Cib	2
Jul 8 1986	13-Caban	3
Jul 9 1986	**1-Etz'nab**	4
Jul 10 1986	2-Cauac	5
Jul 11 1986	3-Ahau	6
Jul 12 1986	*4-Imix*	7
Jul 13 1986	5-Ik	8
Jul 14 1986	6-Akbal	9
Jul 15 1986	7-Kan	1
Jul 16 1986	8-Chicchan	2
Jul 17 1986	9-Cimi	3
Jul 18 1986	10-Manik	4
Jul 19 1986	11-Lamat	5
Jul 20 1986	12-Muluc	6
Jul 21 1986	13-Oc	7
Jul 22 1986	**1-Chuen**	8
Jul 23 1986	2-Eb	9
Jul 24 1986	3-Ben	1
Jul 25 1986	4-Ix	2
Jul 26 1986	5-Men	3
Jul 27 1986	6-Cib	4
Jul 28 1986	7-Caban	5

Date	Day-Sign	L
Jul 29 1986	8-Etz'nab	6
Jul 30 1986	9-Cauac	7
Jul 31 1986	10-Ahau	8
Aug 1 1986	*11-Imix*	9
Aug 2 1986	12-Ik	1
Aug 3 1986	13-Akbal	2
Aug 4 1986	**1-Kan**	3
Aug 5 1986	2-Chicchan	4
Aug 6 1986	3-Cimi	5
Aug 7 1986	4-Manik	6
Aug 8 1986	5-Lamat	7
Aug 9 1986	6-Muluc	8
Aug 10 1986	7-Oc	9
Aug 11 1986	8-Chuen	1
Aug 12 1986	9-Eb	2
Aug 13 1986	10-Ben	3
Aug 14 1986	11-Ix	4
Aug 15 1986	12-Men	5
Aug 16 1986	13-Cib	6
Aug 17 1986	**1-Caban**	7
Aug 18 1986	2-Etz'nab	8
Aug 19 1986	3-Cauac	9
Aug 20 1986	4-Ahau	1
Aug 21 1986	*5-Imix*	2
Aug 22 1986	6-Ik	3
Aug 23 1986	7-Akbal	4
Aug 24 1986	8-Kan	5
Aug 25 1986	9-Chicchan	6
Aug 26 1986	10-Cimi	7
Aug 27 1986	11-Manik	8
Aug 28 1986	12-Lamat	9
Aug 29 1986	13-Muluc	1
Aug 30 1986	**1-Oc**	2
Aug 31 1986	2-Chuen	3
Sep 1 1986	3-Eb	4
Sep 2 1986	4-Ben	5
Sep 3 1986	5-Ix	6
Sep 4 1986	6-Men	7
Sep 5 1986	7-Cib	8
Sep 6 1986	8-Caban	9
Sep 7 1986	9-Etz'nab	1
Sep 8 1986	10-Cauac	2
Sep 9 1986	11-Ahau	3
Sep 10 1986	*12-Imix*	4
Sep 11 1986	13-Ik	5
Sep 12 1986	**1-Akbal**	6
Sep 13 1986	2-Kan	7
Sep 14 1986	3-Chicchan	8
Sep 15 1986	4-Cimi	9
Sep 16 1986	5-Manik	1
Sep 17 1986	6-Lamat	2
Sep 18 1986	7-Muluc	3
Sep 19 1986	8-Oc	4
Sep 20 1986	9-Chuen	5
Sep 21 1986	10-Eb	6
Sep 22 1986	11-Ben	7
Sep 23 1986	12-Ix	8
Sep 24 1986	13-Men	9
Sep 25 1986	**1-Cib**	1
Sep 26 1986	2-Caban	2
Sep 27 1986	3-Etz'nab	3
Sep 28 1986	4-Cauac	4
Sep 29 1986	5-Ahau	5
Sep 30 1986	*6-Imix*	6
Oct 1 1986	7-Ik	7
Oct 2 1986	8-Akbal	8
Oct 3 1986	9-Kan	9
Oct 4 1986	10-Chicchan	1

Date	Day-Sign	L
Oct 5 1986	11-Cimi	2
Oct 6 1986	12-Manik	3
Oct 7 1986	13-Lamat	4
Oct 8 1986	**1-Muluc**	5
Oct 9 1986	2-Oc	6
Oct 10 1986	3-Chuen	7
Oct 11 1986	4-Eb	8
Oct 12 1986	5-Ben	9
Oct 13 1986	6-Ix	1
Oct 14 1986	7-Men	2
Oct 15 1986	8-Cib	3
Oct 16 1986	9-Caban	4
Oct 17 1986	10-Etz'nab	5
Oct 18 1986	11-Cauac	6
Oct 19 1986	12-Ahau	7
Oct 20 1986	*13-Imix*	8
Oct 21 1986	**1-Ik**	9
Oct 22 1986	2-Akbal	1
Oct 23 1986	3-Kan	2
Oct 24 1986	4-Chicchan	3
Oct 25 1986	5-Cimi	4
Oct 26 1986	6-Manik	5
Oct 27 1986	7-Lamat	6
Oct 28 1986	8-Muluc	7
Oct 29 1986	9-Oc	8
Oct 30 1986	10-Chuen	9
Oct 31 1986	11-Eb	1
Nov 1 1986	12-Ben	2
Nov 2 1986	13-Ix	3
Nov 3 1986	**1-Men**	4
Nov 4 1986	2-Cib	5
Nov 5 1986	3-Caban	6
Nov 6 1986	4-Etz'nab	7
Nov 7 1986	5-Cauac	8
Nov 8 1986	6-Ahau	9
Nov 9 1986	*7-Imix*	1
Nov 10 1986	8-Ik	2
Nov 11 1986	9-Akbal	3
Nov 12 1986	10-Kan	4
Nov 13 1986	11-Chicchan	5
Nov 14 1986	12-Cimi	6
Nov 15 1986	13-Manik	7
Nov 16 1986	**1-Lamat**	8
Nov 17 1986	2-Muluc	9
Nov 18 1986	3-Oc	1
Nov 19 1986	4-Chuen	2
Nov 20 1986	5-Eb	3
Nov 21 1986	6-Ben	4
Nov 22 1986	7-Ix	5
Nov 23 1986	8-Men	6
Nov 24 1986	9-Cib	7
Nov 25 1986	10-Caban	8
Nov 26 1986	11-Etz'nab	9
Nov 27 1986	12-Cauac	1
Nov 28 1986	13-Ahau	2
Nov 29 1986	**1-Imix**	3
Nov 30 1986	2-Ik	4
Dec 1 1986	3-Akbal	5
Dec 2 1986	4-Kan	6
Dec 3 1986	5-Chicchan	7
Dec 4 1986	6-Cimi	8
Dec 5 1986	7-Manik	9
Dec 6 1986	8-Lamat	1
Dec 7 1986	9-Muluc	2
Dec 8 1986	10-Oc	3
Dec 9 1986	11-Chuen	4
Dec 10 1986	12-Eb	5
Dec 11 1986	13-Ben	6

Date	Day-Sign	L	Date	Day-Sign	L	Date	Day-Sign	L
Dec 12 1986	1-Ix	7	Feb 18 1987	4-Ik	3	Apr 27 1987	7-Oc	8
Dec 13 1986	2-Men	8	Feb 19 1987	5-Akbal	4	Apr 28 1987	8-Chuen	9
Dec 14 1986	3-Cib	9	Feb 20 1987	6-Kan	5	Apr 29 1987	9-Eb	1
Dec 15 1986	4-Caban	1	Feb 21 1987	7-Chicchan	6	Apr 30 1987	10-Ben	2
Dec 16 1986	5-Etz'nab	2	Feb 22 1987	8-Cimi	7	May 1 1987	11-Ix	3
Dec 17 1986	6-Cauac	3	Feb 23 1987	9-Manik	8	May 2 1987	12-Men	4
Dec 18 1986	7-Ahau	4	Feb 24 1987	10-Lamat	9	May 3 1987	13-Cib	5
Dec 19 1986	8-Imix	5	Feb 25 1987	11-Muluc	1	May 4 1987	1-Caban	6
Dec 20 1986	9-Ik	6	Feb 26 1987	12-Oc	2	May 5 1987	2-Etz'nab	7
Dec 21 1986	10-Akbal	7	Feb 27 1987	13-Chuen	3	May 6 1987	3-Cauac	8
Dec 22 1986	11-Kan	8	Feb 28 1987	1-Eb	4	May 7 1987	4-Ahau	9
Dec 23 1986	12-Chicchan	9	Mar 1 1987	2-Ben	5	May 8 1987	5-Imix	1
Dec 24 1986	13-Cimi	1	Mar 2 1987	3-Ix	6	May 9 1987	6-Ik	2
Dec 25 1986	1-Manik	2	Mar 3 1987	4-Men	7	May 10 1987	7-Akbal	3
Dec 26 1986	2-Lamat	3	Mar 4 1987	5-Cib	8	May 11 1987	8-Kan	4
Dec 27 1986	3-Muluc	4	Mar 5 1987	6-Caban	9	May 12 1987	9-Chicchan	5
Dec 28 1986	4-Oc	5	Mar 6 1987	7-Etz'nab	1	May 13 1987	10-Cimi	6
Dec 29 1986	5-Chuen	6	Mar 7 1987	8-Cauac	2	May 14 1987	11-Manik	7
Dec 30 1986	6-Eb	7	Mar 8 1987	9-Ahau	3	May 15 1987	12-Lamat	8
Dec 31 1986	7-Ben	8	Mar 9 1987	10-Imix	4	May 16 1987	13-Muluc	9
Jan 1 1987	8-Ix	9	Mar 10 1987	11-Ik	5	May 17 1987	1-Oc	1
Jan 2 1987	9-Men	1	Mar 11 1987	12-Akbal	6	May 18 1987	2-Chuen	2
Jan 3 1987	10-Cib	2	Mar 12 1987	13-Kan	7	May 19 1987	3-Eb	3
Jan 4 1987	11-Caban	3	Mar 13 1987	1-Chicchan	8	May 20 1987	4-Ben	4
Jan 5 1987	12-Etz'nab	4	Mar 14 1987	2-Cimi	9	May 21 1987	5-Ix	5
Jan 6 1987	13-Cauac	5	Mar 15 1987	3-Manik	1	May 22 1987	6-Men	6
Jan 7 1987	1-Ahau	6	Mar 16 1987	4-Lamat	2	May 23 1987	7-Cib	7
Jan 8 1987	2-Imix	7	Mar 17 1987	5-Muluc	3	May 24 1987	8-Caban	8
Jan 9 1987	3-Ik	8	Mar 18 1987	6-Oc	4	May 25 1987	9-Etz'nab	9
Jan 10 1987	4-Akbal	9	Mar 19 1987	7-Chuen	5	May 26 1987	10-Cauac	1
Jan 11 1987	5-Kan	1	Mar 20 1987	8-Eb	6	May 27 1987	11-Ahau	2
Jan 12 1987	6-Chicchan	2	Mar 21 1987	9-Ben	7	May 28 1987	12-Imix	3
Jan 13 1987	7-Cimi	3	Mar 22 1987	10-Ix	8	May 29 1987	13-Ik	4
Jan 14 1987	8-Manik	4	Mar 23 1987	11-Men	9	May 30 1987	1-Akbal	5
Jan 15 1987	9-Lamat	5	Mar 24 1987	12-Cib	1	May 31 1987	2-Kan	6
Jan 16 1987	10-Muluc	6	Mar 25 1987	13-Caban	2	Jun 1 1987	3-Chicchan	7
Jan 17 1987	11-Oc	7	Mar 26 1987	1-Etz'nab	3	Jun 2 1987	4-Cimi	8
Jan 18 1987	12-Chuen	8	Mar 27 1987	2-Cauac	4	Jun 3 1987	5-Manik	9
Jan 19 1987	13-Eb	9	Mar 28 1987	3-Ahau	5	Jun 4 1987	6-Lamat	1
Jan 20 1987	1-Ben	1	Mar 29 1987	4-Imix	6	Jun 5 1987	7-Muluc	2
Jan 21 1987	2-Ix	2	Mar 30 1987	5-Ik	7	Jun 6 1987	8-Oc	3
Jan 22 1987	3-Men	3	Mar 31 1987	6-Akbal	8	Jun 7 1987	9-Chuen	4
Jan 23 1987	4-Cib	4	Apr 1 1987	7-Kan	9	Jun 8 1987	10-Eb	5
Jan 24 1987	5-Caban	5	Apr 2 1987	8-Chicchan	1	Jun 9 1987	11-Ben	6
Jan 25 1987	6-Etz'nab	6	Apr 3 1987	9-Cimi	2	Jun 10 1987	12-Ix	7
Jan 26 1987	7-Cauac	7	Apr 4 1987	10-Manik	3	Jun 11 1987	13-Men	8
Jan 27 1987	8-Ahau	8	Apr 5 1987	11-Lamat	4	Jun 12 1987	1-Cib	9
Jan 28 1987	9-Imix	9	Apr 6 1987	12-Muluc	5	Jun 13 1987	2-Caban	1
Jan 29 1987	10-Ik	1	Apr 7 1987	13-Oc	6	Jun 14 1987	3-Etz'nab	2
Jan 30 1987	11-Akbal	2	Apr 8 1987	1-Chuen	7	Jun 15 1987	4-Cauac	3
Jan 31 1987	12-Kan	3	Apr 9 1987	2-Eb	8	Jun 16 1987	5-Ahau	4
Feb 1 1987	13-Chicchan	4	Apr 10 1987	3-Ben	9	Jun 17 1987	6-Imix	5
Feb 2 1987	1-Cimi	5	Apr 11 1987	4-Ix	1	Jun 18 1987	7-Ik	6
Feb 3 1987	2-Manik	6	Apr 12 1987	5-Men	2	Jun 19 1987	8-Akbal	7
Feb 4 1987	3-Lamat	7	Apr 13 1987	6-Cib	3	Jun 20 1987	9-Kan	8
Feb 5 1987	4-Muluc	8	Apr 14 1987	7-Caban	4	Jun 21 1987	10-Chicchan	9
Feb 6 1987	5-Oc	9	Apr 15 1987	8-Etz'nab	5	Jun 22 1987	11-Cimi	1
Feb 7 1987	6-Chuen	1	Apr 16 1987	9-Cauac	6	Jun 23 1987	12-Manik	2
Feb 8 1987	7-Eb	2	Apr 17 1987	10-Ahau	7	Jun 24 1987	13-Lamat	3
Feb 9 1987	8-Ben	3	Apr 18 1987	11-Imix	8	Jun 25 1987	1-Muluc	4
Feb 10 1987	9-Ix	4	Apr 19 1987	12-Ik	9	Jun 26 1987	2-Oc	5
Feb 11 1987	10-Men	5	Apr 20 1987	13-Akbal	1	Jun 27 1987	3-Chuen	6
Feb 12 1987	11-Cib	6	Apr 21 1987	1-Kan	2	Jun 28 1987	4-Eb	7
Feb 13 1987	12-Caban	7	Apr 22 1987	2-Chicchan	3	Jun 29 1987	5-Ben	8
Feb 14 1987	13-Etz'nab	8	Apr 23 1987	3-Cimi	4	Jun 30 1987	6-Ix	9
Feb 15 1987	1-Cauac	9	Apr 24 1987	4-Manik	5	Jul 1 1987	7-Men	1
Feb 16 1987	2-Ahau	1	Apr 25 1987	5-Lamat	6	Jul 2 1987	8-Cib	2
Feb 17 1987	3-Imix	2	Apr 26 1987	6-Muluc	7	Jul 3 1987	9-Caban	3

Date	Day-Sign	L	Date	Day-Sign	L	Date	Day-Sign	L
Jul 4 1987	10-Etz'nab	4	Sep 10 1987	13-Cimi	9	Nov 17 1987	3-Ix	5
Jul 5 1987	11-Cauac	5	Sep 11 1987	**1-Manik**	1	Nov 18 1987	4-Men	6
Jul 6 1987	12-Ahau	6	Sep 12 1987	2-Lamat	2	Nov 19 1987	5-Cib	7
Jul 7 1987	*13-Imix*	7	Sep 13 1987	3-Muluc	3	Nov 20 1987	6-Caban	8
Jul 8 1987	**1-Ik**	8	Sep 14 1987	4-Oc	4	Nov 21 1987	7-Etz'nab	9
Jul 9 1987	2-Akbal	9	Sep 15 1987	5-Chuen	5	Nov 22 1987	8-Cauac	1
Jul 10 1987	3-Kan	1	Sep 16 1987	6-Eb	6	Nov 23 1987	9-Ahau	2
Jul 11 1987	4-Chicchan	2	Sep 17 1987	7-Ben	7	Nov 24 1987	*10-Imix*	3
Jul 12 1987	5-Cimi	3	Sep 18 1987	8-Ix	8	Nov 25 1987	11-Ik	4
Jul 13 1987	6-Manik	4	Sep 19 1987	9-Men	9	Nov 26 1987	12-Akbal	5
Jul 14 1987	7-Lamat	5	Sep 20 1987	10-Cib	1	Nov 27 1987	13-Kan	6
Jul 15 1987	8-Muluc	6	Sep 21 1987	11-Caban	2	Nov 28 1987	**1-Chicchan**	7
Jul 16 1987	9-Oc	7	Sep 22 1987	12-Etz'nab	3	Nov 29 1987	2-Cimi	8
Jul 17 1987	10-Chuen	8	Sep 23 1987	13-Cauac	4	Nov 30 1987	3-Manik	9
Jul 18 1987	11-Eb	9	Sep 24 1987	**1-Ahau**	5	Dec 1 1987	4-Lamat	1
Jul 19 1987	12-Ben	1	Sep 25 1987	*2-Imix*	6	Dec 2 1987	5-Muluc	2
Jul 20 1987	13-Ix	2	Sep 26 1987	3-Ik	7	Dec 3 1987	6-Oc	3
Jul 21 1987	**1-Men**	3	Sep 27 1987	4-Akbal	8	Dec 4 1987	7-Chuen	4
Jul 22 1987	2-Cib	4	Sep 28 1987	5-Kan	9	Dec 5 1987	8-Eb	5
Jul 23 1987	3-Caban	5	Sep 29 1987	6-Chicchan	1	Dec 6 1987	9-Ben	6
Jul 24 1987	4-Etz'nab	6	Sep 30 1987	7-Cimi	2	Dec 7 1987	10-Ix	7
Jul 25 1987	5-Cauac	7	Oct 1 1987	8-Manik	3	Dec 8 1987	11-Men	8
Jul 26 1987	6-Ahau	8	Oct 2 1987	9-Lamat	4	Dec 9 1987	12-Cib	9
Jul 27 1987	*7-Imix*	9	Oct 3 1987	10-Muluc	5	Dec 10 1987	13-Caban	1
Jul 28 1987	8-Ik	1	Oct 4 1987	11-Oc	6	Dec 11 1987	**1-Etz'nab**	2
Jul 29 1987	9-Akbal	2	Oct 5 1987	12-Chuen	7	Dec 12 1987	2-Cauac	3
Jul 30 1987	10-Kan	3	Oct 6 1987	13-Eb	8	Dec 13 1987	3-Ahau	4
Jul 31 1987	11-Chicchan	4	Oct 7 1987	**1-Ben**	9	Dec 14 1987	*4-Imix*	5
Aug 1 1987	12-Cimi	5	Oct 8 1987	2-Ix	1	Dec 15 1987	5-Ik	6
Aug 2 1987	13-Manik	6	Oct 9 1987	3-Men	2	Dec 16 1987	6-Akbal	7
Aug 3 1987	**1-Lamat**	7	Oct 10 1987	4-Cib	3	Dec 17 1987	7-Kan	8
Aug 4 1987	2-Muluc	8	Oct 11 1987	5-Caban	4	Dec 18 1987	8-Chicchan	9
Aug 5 1987	3-Oc	9	Oct 12 1987	6-Etz'nab	5	Dec 19 1987	9-Cimi	1
Aug 6 1987	4-Chuen	1	Oct 13 1987	7-Cauac	6	Dec 20 1987	10-Manik	2
Aug 7 1987	5-Eb	2	Oct 14 1987	8-Ahau	7	Dec 21 1987	11-Lamat	3
Aug 8 1987	6-Ben	3	Oct 15 1987	*9-Imix*	8	Dec 22 1987	12-Muluc	4
Aug 9 1987	7-Ix	4	Oct 16 1987	10-Ik	9	Dec 23 1987	13-Oc	5
Aug 10 1987	8-Men	5	Oct 17 1987	11-Akbal	1	Dec 24 1987	**1-Chuen**	6
Aug 11 1987	9-Cib	6	Oct 18 1987	12-Kan	2	Dec 25 1987	2-Eb	7
Aug 12 1987	10-Caban	7	Oct 19 1987	13-Chicchan	3	Dec 26 1987	3-Ben	8
Aug 13 1987	11-Etz'nab	8	Oct 20 1987	**1-Cimi**	4	Dec 27 1987	4-Ix	9
Aug 14 1987	12-Cauac	9	Oct 21 1987	2-Manik	5	Dec 28 1987	5-Men	1
Aug 15 1987	13-Ahau	1	Oct 22 1987	3-Lamat	6	Dec 29 1987	6-Cib	2
Aug 16 1987	**1-Imix**	2	Oct 23 1987	4-Muluc	7	Dec 30 1987	7-Caban	3
Aug 17 1987	2-Ik	3	Oct 24 1987	5-Oc	8	Dec 31 1987	8-Etz'nab	4
Aug 18 1987	3-Akbal	4	Oct 25 1987	6-Chuen	9	Jan 1 1988	9-Cauac	5
Aug 19 1987	4-Kan	5	Oct 26 1987	7-Eb	1	Jan 2 1988	10-Ahau	6
Aug 20 1987	5-Chicchan	6	Oct 27 1987	8-Ben	2	Jan 3 1988	*11-Imix*	7
Aug 21 1987	6-Cimi	7	Oct 28 1987	9-Ix	3	Jan 4 1988	12-Ik	8
Aug 22 1987	7-Manik	8	Oct 29 1987	10-Men	4	Jan 5 1988	13-Akbal	9
Aug 23 1987	8-Lamat	9	Oct 30 1987	11-Cib	5	Jan 6 1988	**1-Kan**	1
Aug 24 1987	9-Muluc	1	Oct 31 1987	12-Caban	6	Jan 7 1988	2-Chicchan	2
Aug 25 1987	10-Oc	2	Nov 1 1987	13-Etz'nab	7	Jan 8 1988	3-Cimi	3
Aug 26 1987	11-Chuen	3	Nov 2 1987	**1-Cauac**	8	Jan 9 1988	4-Manik	4
Aug 27 1987	12-Eb	4	Nov 3 1987	2-Ahau	9	Jan 10 1988	5-Lamat	5
Aug 28 1987	13-Ben	5	Nov 4 1987	*3-Imix*	1	Jan 11 1988	6-Muluc	6
Aug 29 1987	**1-Ix**	6	Nov 5 1987	4-Ik	2	Jan 12 1988	7-Oc	7
Aug 30 1987	2-Men	7	Nov 6 1987	5-Akbal	3	Jan 13 1988	8-Chuen	8
Aug 31 1987	3-Cib	8	Nov 7 1987	6-Kan	4	Jan 14 1988	9-Eb	9
Sep 1 1987	4-Caban	9	Nov 8 1987	7-Chicchan	5	Jan 15 1988	10-Ben	1
Sep 2 1987	5-Etz'nab	1	Nov 9 1987	8-Cimi	6	Jan 16 1988	11-Ix	2
Sep 3 1987	6-Cauac	2	Nov 10 1987	9-Manik	7	Jan 17 1988	12-Men	3
Sep 4 1987	7-Ahau	3	Nov 11 1987	10-Lamat	8	Jan 18 1988	13-Cib	4
Sep 5 1987	*8-Imix*	4	Nov 12 1987	11-Muluc	9	Jan 19 1988	**1-Caban**	5
Sep 6 1987	9-Ik	5	Nov 13 1987	12-Oc	1	Jan 20 1988	2-Etz'nab	6
Sep 7 1987	10-Akbal	6	Nov 14 1987	13-Chuen	2	Jan 21 1988	3-Cauac	7
Sep 8 1987	11-Kan	7	Nov 15 1987	**1-Eb**	3	Jan 22 1988	4-Ahau	8
Sep 9 1987	12-Chicchan	8	Nov 16 1987	2-Ben	4	Jan 23 1988	*5-Imix*	9

Date	Day-Sign	L
Jan 24 1988	6-Ik	1
Jan 25 1988	7-Akbal	2
Jan 26 1988	8-Kan	3
Jan 27 1988	9-Chicchan	4
Jan 28 1988	10-Cimi	5
Jan 29 1988	11-Manik	6
Jan 30 1988	12-Lamat	7
Jan 31 1988	13-Muluc	8
Feb 1 1988	**1-Oc**	9
Feb 2 1988	2-Chuen	1
Feb 3 1988	3-Eb	2
Feb 4 1988	4-Ben	3
Feb 5 1988	5-Ix	4
Feb 6 1988	6-Men	5
Feb 7 1988	7-Cib	6
Feb 8 1988	8-Caban	7
Feb 9 1988	9-Etz'nab	8
Feb 10 1988	10-Cauac	9
Feb 11 1988	11-Ahau	1
Feb 12 1988	*12-Imix*	2
Feb 13 1988	13-Ik	3
Feb 14 1988	**1-Akbal**	4
Feb 15 1988	2-Kan	5
Feb 16 1988	3-Chicchan	6
Feb 17 1988	4-Cimi	7
Feb 18 1988	5-Manik	8
Feb 19 1988	6-Lamat	9
Feb 20 1988	7-Muluc	1
Feb 21 1988	8-Oc	2
Feb 22 1988	9-Chuen	3
Feb 23 1988	10-Eb	4
Feb 24 1988	11-Ben	5
Feb 25 1988	12-Ix	6
Feb 26 1988	13-Men	7
Feb 27 1988	**1-Cib**	8
Feb 28 1988	2-Caban	9
Feb 29 1988	3-Etz'nab	1
Mar 1 1988	4-Cauac	2
Mar 2 1988	5-Ahau	3
Mar 3 1988	*6-Imix*	4
Mar 4 1988	7-Ik	5
Mar 5 1988	8-Akbal	6
Mar 6 1988	9-Kan	7
Mar 7 1988	10-Chicchan	8
Mar 8 1988	11-Cimi	9
Mar 9 1988	12-Manik	1
Mar 10 1988	13-Lamat	2
Mar 11 1988	**1-Muluc**	3
Mar 12 1988	2-Oc	4
Mar 13 1988	3-Chuen	5
Mar 14 1988	4-Eb	6
Mar 15 1988	5-Ben	7
Mar 16 1988	6-Ix	8
Mar 17 1988	7-Men	9
Mar 18 1988	8-Cib	1
Mar 19 1988	9-Caban	2
Mar 20 1988	10-Etz'nab	3
Mar 21 1988	11-Cauac	4
Mar 22 1988	12-Ahau	5
Mar 23 1988	*13-Imix*	6
Mar 24 1988	**1-Ik**	7
Mar 25 1988	2-Akbal	8
Mar 26 1988	3-Kan	9
Mar 27 1988	4-Chicchan	1
Mar 28 1988	5-Cimi	2
Mar 29 1988	6-Manik	3
Mar 30 1988	7-Lamat	4
Mar 31 1988	8-Muluc	5

Date	Day-Sign	L
Apr 1 1988	9-Oc	6
Apr 2 1988	10-Chuen	7
Apr 3 1988	11-Eb	8
Apr 4 1988	12-Ben	9
Apr 5 1988	13-Ix	1
Apr 6 1988	**1-Men**	2
Apr 7 1988	2-Cib	3
Apr 8 1988	3-Caban	4
Apr 9 1988	4-Etz'nab	5
Apr 10 1988	5-Cauac	6
Apr 11 1988	6-Ahau	7
Apr 12 1988	*7-Imix*	8
Apr 13 1988	8-Ik	9
Apr 14 1988	9-Akbal	1
Apr 15 1988	10-Kan	2
Apr 16 1988	11-Chicchan	3
Apr 17 1988	12-Cimi	4
Apr 18 1988	13-Manik	5
Apr 19 1988	**1-Lamat**	6
Apr 20 1988	2-Muluc	7
Apr 21 1988	3-Oc	8
Apr 22 1988	4-Chuen	9
Apr 23 1988	5-Eb	1
Apr 24 1988	6-Ben	2
Apr 25 1988	7-Ix	3
Apr 26 1988	8-Men	4
Apr 27 1988	9-Cib	5
Apr 28 1988	10-Caban	6
Apr 29 1988	11-Etz'nab	7
Apr 30 1988	12-Cauac	8
May 1 1988	13-Ahau	9
May 2 1988	**1-Imix**	1
May 3 1988	2-Ik	2
May 4 1988	3-Akbal	3
May 5 1988	4-Kan	4
May 6 1988	5-Chicchan	5
May 7 1988	6-Cimi	6
May 8 1988	7-Manik	7
May 9 1988	8-Lamat	8
May 10 1988	9-Muluc	9
May 11 1988	10-Oc	1
May 12 1988	11-Chuen	2
May 13 1988	12-Eb	3
May 14 1988	13-Ben	4
May 15 1988	**1-Ix**	5
May 16 1988	2-Men	6
May 17 1988	3-Cib	7
May 18 1988	4-Caban	8
May 19 1988	5-Etz'nab	9
May 20 1988	6-Cauac	1
May 21 1988	7-Ahau	2
May 22 1988	*8-Imix*	3
May 23 1988	9-Ik	4
May 24 1988	10-Akbal	5
May 25 1988	11-Kan	6
May 26 1988	12-Chicchan	7
May 27 1988	13-Cimi	8
May 28 1988	**1-Manik**	9
May 29 1988	2-Lamat	1
May 30 1988	3-Muluc	2
May 31 1988	4-Oc	3
Jun 1 1988	5-Chuen	4
Jun 2 1988	6-Eb	5
Jun 3 1988	7-Ben	6
Jun 4 1988	8-Ix	7
Jun 5 1988	9-Men	8
Jun 6 1988	10-Cib	9
Jun 7 1988	11-Caban	1

Date	Day-Sign	L
Jun 8 1988	12-Etz'nab	2
Jun 9 1988	13-Cauac	3
Jun 10 1988	**1-Ahau**	4
Jun 11 1988	*2-Imix*	5
Jun 12 1988	3-Ik	6
Jun 13 1988	4-Akbal	7
Jun 14 1988	5-Kan	8
Jun 15 1988	6-Chicchan	9
Jun 16 1988	7-Cimi	1
Jun 17 1988	8-Manik	2
Jun 18 1988	9-Lamat	3
Jun 19 1988	10-Muluc	4
Jun 20 1988	11-Oc	5
Jun 21 1988	12-Chuen	6
Jun 22 1988	13-Eb	7
Jun 23 1988	**1-Ben**	8
Jun 24 1988	2-Ix	9
Jun 25 1988	3-Men	1
Jun 26 1988	4-Cib	2
Jun 27 1988	5-Caban	3
Jun 28 1988	6-Etz'nab	4
Jun 29 1988	7-Cauac	5
Jun 30 1988	8-Ahau	6
Jul 1 1988	*9-Imix*	7
Jul 2 1988	10-Ik	8
Jul 3 1988	11-Akbal	9
Jul 4 1988	12-Kan	1
Jul 5 1988	13-Chicchan	2
Jul 6 1988	**1-Cimi**	3
Jul 7 1988	2-Manik	4
Jul 8 1988	3-Lamat	5
Jul 9 1988	4-Muluc	6
Jul 10 1988	5-Oc	7
Jul 11 1988	6-Chuen	8
Jul 12 1988	7-Eb	9
Jul 13 1988	8-Ben	1
Jul 14 1988	9-Ix	2
Jul 15 1988	10-Men	3
Jul 16 1988	11-Cib	4
Jul 17 1988	12-Caban	5
Jul 18 1988	13-Etz'nab	6
Jul 19 1988	**1-Cauac**	7
Jul 20 1988	2-Ahau	8
Jul 21 1988	*3-Imix*	9
Jul 22 1988	4-Ik	1
Jul 23 1988	5-Akbal	2
Jul 24 1988	6-Kan	3
Jul 25 1988	7-Chicchan	4
Jul 26 1988	8-Cimi	5
Jul 27 1988	9-Manik	6
Jul 28 1988	10-Lamat	7
Jul 29 1988	11-Muluc	8
Jul 30 1988	12-Oc	9
Jul 31 1988	13-Chuen	1
Aug 1 1988	**1-Eb**	2
Aug 2 1988	2-Ben	3
Aug 3 1988	3-Ix	4
Aug 4 1988	4-Men	5
Aug 5 1988	5-Cib	6
Aug 6 1988	6-Caban	7
Aug 7 1988	7-Etz'nab	8
Aug 8 1988	8-Cauac	9
Aug 9 1988	9-Ahau	1
Aug 10 1988	*10-Imix*	2
Aug 11 1988	11-Ik	3
Aug 12 1988	12-Akbal	4
Aug 13 1988	13-Kan	5
Aug 14 1988	**1-Chicchan**	6

Date	Day-Sign	L
Aug 15 1988	2-Cimi	7
Aug 16 1988	3-Manik	8
Aug 17 1988	4-Lamat	9
Aug 18 1988	5-Muluc	1
Aug 19 1988	6-Oc	2
Aug 20 1988	7-Chuen	3
Aug 21 1988	8-Eb	4
Aug 22 1988	9-Ben	5
Aug 23 1988	10-Ix	6
Aug 24 1988	11-Men	7
Aug 25 1988	12-Cib	8
Aug 26 1988	13-Caban	9
Aug 27 1988	**1-Etz'nab**	1
Aug 28 1988	2-Cauac	2
Aug 29 1988	3-Ahau	3
Aug 30 1988	*4-Imix*	4
Aug 31 1988	5-Ik	5
Sep 1 1988	6-Akbal	6
Sep 2 1988	7-Kan	7
Sep 3 1988	8-Chicchan	8
Sep 4 1988	9-Cimi	9
Sep 5 1988	10-Manik	1
Sep 6 1988	11-Lamat	2
Sep 7 1988	12-Muluc	3
Sep 8 1988	13-Oc	4
Sep 9 1988	**1-Chuen**	5
Sep 10 1988	2-Eb	6
Sep 11 1988	3-Ben	7
Sep 12 1988	4-Ix	8
Sep 13 1988	5-Men	9
Sep 14 1988	6-Cib	1
Sep 15 1988	7-Caban	2
Sep 16 1988	8-Etz'nab	3
Sep 17 1988	9-Cauac	4
Sep 18 1988	10-Ahau	5
Sep 19 1988	*11-Imix*	6
Sep 20 1988	12-Ik	7
Sep 21 1988	13-Akbal	8
Sep 22 1988	**1-Kan**	9
Sep 23 1988	2-Chicchan	1
Sep 24 1988	3-Cimi	2
Sep 25 1988	4-Manik	3
Sep 26 1988	5-Lamat	4
Sep 27 1988	6-Muluc	5
Sep 28 1988	7-Oc	6
Sep 29 1988	8-Chuen	7
Sep 30 1988	9-Eb	8
Oct 1 1988	10-Ben	9
Oct 2 1988	11-Ix	1
Oct 3 1988	12-Men	2
Oct 4 1988	13-Cib	3
Oct 5 1988	**1-Caban**	4
Oct 6 1988	2-Etz'nab	5
Oct 7 1988	3-Cauac	6
Oct 8 1988	4-Ahau	7
Oct 9 1988	*5-Imix*	8
Oct 10 1988	6-Ik	9
Oct 11 1988	7-Akbal	1
Oct 12 1988	8-Kan	2
Oct 13 1988	9-Chicchan	3
Oct 14 1988	10-Cimi	4
Oct 15 1988	11-Manik	5
Oct 16 1988	12-Lamat	6
Oct 17 1988	13-Muluc	7
Oct 18 1988	**1-Oc**	8
Oct 19 1988	2-Chuen	9
Oct 20 1988	3-Eb	1
Oct 21 1988	4-Ben	2
Oct 22 1988	5-Ix	3
Oct 23 1988	6-Men	4
Oct 24 1988	7-Cib	5
Oct 25 1988	8-Caban	6
Oct 26 1988	9-Etz'nab	7
Oct 27 1988	10-Cauac	8
Oct 28 1988	11-Ahau	9
Oct 29 1988	*12-Imix*	1
Oct 30 1988	13-Ik	2
Oct 31 1988	**1-Akbal**	3
Nov 1 1988	2-Kan	4
Nov 2 1988	3-Chicchan	5
Nov 3 1988	4-Cimi	6
Nov 4 1988	5-Manik	7
Nov 5 1988	6-Lamat	8
Nov 6 1988	7-Muluc	9
Nov 7 1988	8-Oc	1
Nov 8 1988	9-Chuen	2
Nov 9 1988	10-Eb	3
Nov 10 1988	11-Ben	4
Nov 11 1988	12-Ix	5
Nov 12 1988	13-Men	6
Nov 13 1988	**1-Cib**	7
Nov 14 1988	2-Caban	8
Nov 15 1988	3-Etz'nab	9
Nov 16 1988	4-Cauac	1
Nov 17 1988	5-Ahau	2
Nov 18 1988	*6-Imix*	3
Nov 19 1988	7-Ik	4
Nov 20 1988	8-Akbal	5
Nov 21 1988	9-Kan	6
Nov 22 1988	10-Chicchan	7
Nov 23 1988	11-Cimi	8
Nov 24 1988	12-Manik	9
Nov 25 1988	13-Lamat	1
Nov 26 1988	**1-Muluc**	2
Nov 27 1988	2-Oc	3
Nov 28 1988	3-Chuen	4
Nov 29 1988	4-Eb	5
Nov 30 1988	5-Ben	6
Dec 1 1988	6-Ix	7
Dec 2 1988	7-Men	8
Dec 3 1988	8-Cib	9
Dec 4 1988	9-Caban	1
Dec 5 1988	10-Etz'nab	2
Dec 6 1988	11-Cauac	3
Dec 7 1988	12-Ahau	4
Dec 8 1988	*13-Imix*	5
Dec 9 1988	**1-Ik**	6
Dec 10 1988	2-Akbal	7
Dec 11 1988	3-Kan	8
Dec 12 1988	4-Chicchan	9
Dec 13 1988	5-Cimi	1
Dec 14 1988	6-Manik	2
Dec 15 1988	7-Lamat	3
Dec 16 1988	8-Muluc	4
Dec 17 1988	9-Oc	5
Dec 18 1988	10-Chuen	6
Dec 19 1988	11-Eb	7
Dec 20 1988	12-Ben	8
Dec 21 1988	13-Ix	9
Dec 22 1988	**1-Men**	1
Dec 23 1988	2-Cib	2
Dec 24 1988	3-Caban	3
Dec 25 1988	4-Etz'nab	4
Dec 26 1988	5-Cauac	5
Dec 27 1988	6-Ahau	6
Dec 28 1988	*7-Imix*	7
Dec 29 1988	8-Ik	8
Dec 30 1988	9-Akbal	9
Dec 31 1988	10-Kan	1
Jan 1 1989	11-Chicchan	2
Jan 2 1989	12-Cimi	3
Jan 3 1989	13-Manik	4
Jan 4 1989	**1-Lamat**	5
Jan 5 1989	2-Muluc	6
Jan 6 1989	3-Oc	7
Jan 7 1989	4-Chuen	8
Jan 8 1989	5-Eb	9
Jan 9 1989	6-Ben	1
Jan 10 1989	7-Ix	2
Jan 11 1989	8-Men	3
Jan 12 1989	9-Cib	4
Jan 13 1989	10-Caban	5
Jan 14 1989	11-Etz'nab	6
Jan 15 1989	12-Cauac	7
Jan 16 1989	13-Ahau	8
Jan 17 1989	**1-Imix**	9
Jan 18 1989	2-Ik	1
Jan 19 1989	3-Akbal	2
Jan 20 1989	4-Kan	3
Jan 21 1989	5-Chicchan	4
Jan 22 1989	6-Cimi	5
Jan 23 1989	7-Manik	6
Jan 24 1989	8-Lamat	7
Jan 25 1989	9-Muluc	8
Jan 26 1989	10-Oc	9
Jan 27 1989	11-Chuen	1
Jan 28 1989	12-Eb	2
Jan 29 1989	13-Ben	3
Jan 30 1989	**1-Ix**	4
Jan 31 1989	2-Men	5
Feb 1 1989	3-Cib	6
Feb 2 1989	4-Caban	7
Feb 3 1989	5-Etz'nab	8
Feb 4 1989	6-Cauac	9
Feb 5 1989	7-Ahau	1
Feb 6 1989	*8-Imix*	2
Feb 7 1989	9-Ik	3
Feb 8 1989	10-Akbal	4
Feb 9 1989	11-Kan	5
Feb 10 1989	12-Chicchan	6
Feb 11 1989	13-Cimi	7
Feb 12 1989	**1-Manik**	8
Feb 13 1989	2-Lamat	9
Feb 14 1989	3-Muluc	1
Feb 15 1989	4-Oc	2
Feb 16 1989	5-Chuen	3
Feb 17 1989	6-Eb	4
Feb 18 1989	7-Ben	5
Feb 19 1989	8-Ix	6
Feb 20 1989	9-Men	7
Feb 21 1989	10-Cib	8
Feb 22 1989	11-Caban	9
Feb 23 1989	12-Etz'nab	1
Feb 24 1989	13-Cauac	2
Feb 25 1989	**1-Ahau**	3
Feb 26 1989	*2-Imix*	4
Feb 27 1989	3-Ik	5
Feb 28 1989	4-Akbal	6
Mar 1 1989	5-Kan	7
Mar 2 1989	6-Chicchan	8
Mar 3 1989	7-Cimi	9
Mar 4 1989	8-Manik	1
Mar 5 1989	9-Lamat	2
Mar 6 1989	10-Muluc	3

Date	Day-Sign	L
Mar 7 1989	11-Oc	4
Mar 8 1989	12-Chuen	5
Mar 9 1989	13-Eb	6
Mar 10 1989	1-Ben	7
Mar 11 1989	2-Ix	8
Mar 12 1989	3-Men	9
Mar 13 1989	4-Cib	1
Mar 14 1989	5-Caban	2
Mar 15 1989	6-Etz'nab	3
Mar 16 1989	7-Cauac	4
Mar 17 1989	8-Ahau	5
Mar 18 1989	9-Imix	6
Mar 19 1989	10-Ik	7
Mar 20 1989	11-Akbal	8
Mar 21 1989	12-Kan	9
Mar 22 1989	13-Chicchan	1
Mar 23 1989	1-Cimi	2
Mar 24 1989	2-Manik	3
Mar 25 1989	3-Lamat	4
Mar 26 1989	4-Muluc	5
Mar 27 1989	5-Oc	6
Mar 28 1989	6-Chuen	7
Mar 29 1989	7-Eb	8
Mar 30 1989	8-Ben	9
Mar 31 1989	9-Ix	1
Apr 1 1989	10-Men	2
Apr 2 1989	11-Cib	3
Apr 3 1989	12-Caban	4
Apr 4 1989	13-Etz'nab	5
Apr 5 1989	1-Cauac	6
Apr 6 1989	2-Ahau	7
Apr 7 1989	3-Imix	8
Apr 8 1989	4-Ik	9
Apr 9 1989	5-Akbal	1
Apr 10 1989	6-Kan	2
Apr 11 1989	7-Chicchan	3
Apr 12 1989	8-Cimi	4
Apr 13 1989	9-Manik	5
Apr 14 1989	10-Lamat	6
Apr 15 1989	11-Muluc	7
Apr 16 1989	12-Oc	8
Apr 17 1989	13-Chuen	9
Apr 18 1989	1-Eb	1
Apr 19 1989	2-Ben	2
Apr 20 1989	3-Ix	3
Apr 21 1989	4-Men	4
Apr 22 1989	5-Cib	5
Apr 23 1989	6-Caban	6
Apr 24 1989	7-Etz'nab	7
Apr 25 1989	8-Cauac	8
Apr 26 1989	9-Ahau	9
Apr 27 1989	10-Imix	1
Apr 28 1989	11-Ik	2
Apr 29 1989	12-Akbal	3
Apr 30 1989	13-Kan	4
May 1 1989	1-Chicchan	5
May 2 1989	2-Cimi	6
May 3 1989	3-Manik	7
May 4 1989	4-Lamat	8
May 5 1989	5-Muluc	9
May 6 1989	6-Oc	1
May 7 1989	7-Chuen	2
May 8 1989	8-Eb	3
May 9 1989	9-Ben	4
May 10 1989	10-Ix	5
May 11 1989	11-Men	6
May 12 1989	12-Cib	7
May 13 1989	13-Caban	8

Date	Day-Sign	L
May 14 1989	1-Etz'nab	9
May 15 1989	2-Cauac	1
May 16 1989	3-Ahau	2
May 17 1989	4-Imix	3
May 18 1989	5-Ik	4
May 19 1989	6-Akbal	5
May 20 1989	7-Kan	6
May 21 1989	8-Chicchan	7
May 22 1989	9-Cimi	8
May 23 1989	10-Manik	9
May 24 1989	11-Lamat	1
May 25 1989	12-Muluc	2
May 26 1989	13-Oc	3
May 27 1989	1-Chuen	4
May 28 1989	2-Eb	5
May 29 1989	3-Ben	6
May 30 1989	4-Ix	7
May 31 1989	5-Men	8
Jun 1 1989	6-Cib	9
Jun 2 1989	7-Caban	1
Jun 3 1989	8-Etz'nab	2
Jun 4 1989	9-Cauac	3
Jun 5 1989	10-Ahau	4
Jun 6 1989	11-Imix	5
Jun 7 1989	12-Ik	6
Jun 8 1989	13-Akbal	7
Jun 9 1989	1-Kan	8
Jun 10 1989	2-Chicchan	9
Jun 11 1989	3-Cimi	1
Jun 12 1989	4-Manik	2
Jun 13 1989	5-Lamat	3
Jun 14 1989	6-Muluc	4
Jun 15 1989	7-Oc	5
Jun 16 1989	8-Chuen	6
Jun 17 1989	9-Eb	7
Jun 18 1989	10-Ben	8
Jun 19 1989	11-Ix	9
Jun 20 1989	12-Men	1
Jun 21 1989	13-Cib	2
Jun 22 1989	1-Caban	3
Jun 23 1989	2-Etz'nab	4
Jun 24 1989	3-Cauac	5
Jun 25 1989	4-Ahau	6
Jun 26 1989	5-Imix	7
Jun 27 1989	6-Ik	8
Jun 28 1989	7-Akbal	9
Jun 29 1989	8-Kan	1
Jun 30 1989	9-Chicchan	2
Jul 1 1989	10-Cimi	3
Jul 2 1989	11-Manik	4
Jul 3 1989	12-Lamat	5
Jul 4 1989	13-Muluc	6
Jul 5 1989	1-Oc	7
Jul 6 1989	2-Chuen	8
Jul 7 1989	3-Eb	9
Jul 8 1989	4-Ben	1
Jul 9 1989	5-Ix	2
Jul 10 1989	6-Men	3
Jul 11 1989	7-Cib	4
Jul 12 1989	8-Caban	5
Jul 13 1989	9-Etz'nab	6
Jul 14 1989	10-Cauac	7
Jul 15 1989	11-Ahau	8
Jul 16 1989	12-Imix	9
Jul 17 1989	13-Ik	1
Jul 18 1989	1-Akbal	2
Jul 19 1989	2-Kan	3
Jul 20 1989	3-Chicchan	4

Date	Day-Sign	L
Jul 21 1989	4-Cimi	5
Jul 22 1989	5-Manik	6
Jul 23 1989	6-Lamat	7
Jul 24 1989	7-Muluc	8
Jul 25 1989	8-Oc	9
Jul 26 1989	9-Chuen	1
Jul 27 1989	10-Eb	2
Jul 28 1989	11-Ben	3
Jul 29 1989	12-Ix	4
Jul 30 1989	13-Men	5
Jul 31 1989	1-Cib	6
Aug 1 1989	2-Caban	7
Aug 2 1989	3-Etz'nab	8
Aug 3 1989	4-Cauac	9
Aug 4 1989	5-Ahau	1
Aug 5 1989	6-Imix	2
Aug 6 1989	7-Ik	3
Aug 7 1989	8-Akbal	4
Aug 8 1989	9-Kan	5
Aug 9 1989	10-Chicchan	6
Aug 10 1989	11-Cimi	7
Aug 11 1989	12-Manik	8
Aug 12 1989	13-Lamat	9
Aug 13 1989	1-Muluc	1
Aug 14 1989	2-Oc	2
Aug 15 1989	3-Chuen	3
Aug 16 1989	4-Eb	4
Aug 17 1989	5-Ben	5
Aug 18 1989	6-Ix	6
Aug 19 1989	7-Men	7
Aug 20 1989	8-Cib	8
Aug 21 1989	9-Caban	9
Aug 22 1989	10-Etz'nab	1
Aug 23 1989	11-Cauac	2
Aug 24 1989	12-Ahau	3
Aug 25 1989	13-Imix	4
Aug 26 1989	1-Ik	5
Aug 27 1989	2-Akbal	6
Aug 28 1989	3-Kan	7
Aug 29 1989	4-Chicchan	8
Aug 30 1989	5-Cimi	9
Aug 31 1989	6-Manik	1
Sep 1 1989	7-Lamat	2
Sep 2 1989	8-Muluc	3
Sep 3 1989	9-Oc	4
Sep 4 1989	10-Chuen	5
Sep 5 1989	11-Eb	6
Sep 6 1989	12-Ben	7
Sep 7 1989	13-Ix	8
Sep 8 1989	1-Men	9
Sep 9 1989	2-Cib	1
Sep 10 1989	3-Caban	2
Sep 11 1989	4-Etz'nab	3
Sep 12 1989	5-Cauac	4
Sep 13 1989	6-Ahau	5
Sep 14 1989	7-Imix	6
Sep 15 1989	8-Ik	7
Sep 16 1989	9-Akbal	8
Sep 17 1989	10-Kan	9
Sep 18 1989	11-Chicchan	1
Sep 19 1989	12-Cimi	2
Sep 20 1989	13-Manik	3
Sep 21 1989	1-Lamat	4
Sep 22 1989	2-Muluc	5
Sep 23 1989	3-Oc	6
Sep 24 1989	4-Chuen	7
Sep 25 1989	5-Eb	8
Sep 26 1989	6-Ben	9

Date	Day-Sign	L	Date	Day-Sign	L	Date	Day-Sign	L
Sep 27 1989	7-Ix	1	Dec 4 1989	10-Ik	6	Feb 10 1990	13-Oc	2
Sep 28 1989	8-Men	2	Dec 5 1989	11-Akbal	7	Feb 11 1990	1-Chuen	3
Sep 29 1989	9-Cib	3	Dec 6 1989	12-Kan	8	Feb 12 1990	2-Eb	4
Sep 30 1989	10-Caban	4	Dec 7 1989	13-Chicchan	9	Feb 13 1990	3-Ben	5
Oct 1 1989	11-Etz'nab	5	Dec 8 1989	1-Cimi	1	Feb 14 1990	4-Ix	6
Oct 2 1989	12-Cauac	6	Dec 9 1989	2-Manik	2	Feb 15 1990	5-Men	7
Oct 3 1989	13-Ahau	7	Dec 10 1989	3-Lamat	3	Feb 16 1990	6-Cib	8
Oct 4 1989	1-Imix	8	Dec 11 1989	4-Muluc	4	Feb 17 1990	7-Caban	9
Oct 5 1989	2-Ik	9	Dec 12 1989	5-Oc	5	Feb 18 1990	8-Etz'nab	1
Oct 6 1989	3-Akbal	1	Dec 13 1989	6-Chuen	6	Feb 19 1990	9-Cauac	2
Oct 7 1989	4-Kan	2	Dec 14 1989	7-Eb	7	Feb 20 1990	10-Ahau	3
Oct 8 1989	5-Chicchan	3	Dec 15 1989	8-Ben	8	Feb 21 1990	11-Imix	4
Oct 9 1989	6-Cimi	4	Dec 16 1989	9-Ix	9	Feb 22 1990	12-Ik	5
Oct 10 1989	7-Manik	5	Dec 17 1989	10-Men	1	Feb 23 1990	13-Akbal	6
Oct 11 1989	8-Lamat	6	Dec 18 1989	11-Cib	2	Feb 24 1990	1-Kan	7
Oct 12 1989	9-Muluc	7	Dec 19 1989	12-Caban	3	Feb 25 1990	2-Chicchan	8
Oct 13 1989	10-Oc	8	Dec 20 1989	13-Etz'nab	4	Feb 26 1990	3-Cimi	9
Oct 14 1989	11-Chuen	9	Dec 21 1989	1-Cauac	5	Feb 27 1990	4-Manik	1
Oct 15 1989	12-Eb	1	Dec 22 1989	2-Ahau	6	Feb 28 1990	5-Lamat	2
Oct 16 1989	13-Ben	2	Dec 23 1989	3-Imix	7	Mar 1 1990	6-Muluc	3
Oct 17 1989	1-Ix	3	Dec 24 1989	4-Ik	8	Mar 2 1990	7-Oc	4
Oct 18 1989	2-Men	4	Dec 25 1989	5-Akbal	9	Mar 3 1990	8-Chuen	5
Oct 19 1989	3-Cib	5	Dec 26 1989	6-Kan	1	Mar 4 1990	9-Eb	6
Oct 20 1989	4-Caban	6	Dec 27 1989	7-Chicchan	2	Mar 5 1990	10-Ben	7
Oct 21 1989	5-Etz'nab	7	Dec 28 1989	8-Cimi	3	Mar 6 1990	11-Ix	8
Oct 22 1989	6-Cauac	8	Dec 29 1989	9-Manik	4	Mar 7 1990	12-Men	9
Oct 23 1989	7-Ahau	9	Dec 30 1989	10-Lamat	5	Mar 8 1990	13-Cib	1
Oct 24 1989	8-Imix	1	Dec 31 1989	11-Muluc	6	Mar 9 1990	1-Caban	2
Oct 25 1989	9-Ik	2	Jan 1 1990	12-Oc	7	Mar 10 1990	2-Etz'nab	3
Oct 26 1989	10-Akbal	3	Jan 2 1990	13-Chuen	8	Mar 11 1990	3-Cauac	4
Oct 27 1989	11-Kan	4	Jan 3 1990	1-Eb	9	Mar 12 1990	4-Ahau	5
Oct 28 1989	12-Chicchan	5	Jan 4 1990	2-Ben	1	Mar 13 1990	5-Imix	6
Oct 29 1989	13-Cimi	6	Jan 5 1990	3-Ix	2	Mar 14 1990	6-Ik	7
Oct 30 1989	1-Manik	7	Jan 6 1990	4-Men	3	Mar 15 1990	7-Akbal	8
Oct 31 1989	2-Lamat	8	Jan 7 1990	5-Cib	4	Mar 16 1990	8-Kan	9
Nov 1 1989	3-Muluc	9	Jan 8 1990	6-Caban	5	Mar 17 1990	9-Chicchan	1
Nov 2 1989	4-Oc	1	Jan 9 1990	7-Etz'nab	6	Mar 18 1990	10-Cimi	2
Nov 3 1989	5-Chuen	2	Jan 10 1990	8-Cauac	7	Mar 19 1990	11-Manik	3
Nov 4 1989	6-Eb	3	Jan 11 1990	9-Ahau	8	Mar 20 1990	12-Lamat	4
Nov 5 1989	7-Ben	4	Jan 12 1990	10-Imix	9	Mar 21 1990	13-Muluc	5
Nov 6 1989	8-Ix	5	Jan 13 1990	11-Ik	1	Mar 22 1990	1-Oc	6
Nov 7 1989	9-Men	6	Jan 14 1990	12-Akbal	2	Mar 23 1990	2-Chuen	7
Nov 8 1989	10-Cib	7	Jan 15 1990	13-Kan	3	Mar 24 1990	3-Eb	8
Nov 9 1989	11-Caban	8	Jan 16 1990	1-Chicchan	4	Mar 25 1990	4-Ben	9
Nov 10 1989	12-Etz'nab	9	Jan 17 1990	2-Cimi	5	Mar 26 1990	5-Ix	1
Nov 11 1989	13-Cauac	1	Jan 18 1990	3-Manik	6	Mar 27 1990	6-Men	2
Nov 12 1989	1-Ahau	2	Jan 19 1990	4-Lamat	7	Mar 28 1990	7-Cib	3
Nov 13 1989	2-Imix	3	Jan 20 1990	5-Muluc	8	Mar 29 1990	8-Caban	4
Nov 14 1989	3-Ik	4	Jan 21 1990	6-Oc	9	Mar 30 1990	9-Etz'nab	5
Nov 15 1989	4-Akbal	5	Jan 22 1990	7-Chuen	1	Mar 31 1990	10-Cauac	6
Nov 16 1989	5-Kan	6	Jan 23 1990	8-Eb	2	Apr 1 1990	11-Ahau	7
Nov 17 1989	6-Chicchan	7	Jan 24 1990	9-Ben	3	Apr 2 1990	12-Imix	8
Nov 18 1989	7-Cimi	8	Jan 25 1990	10-Ix	4	Apr 3 1990	13-Ik	9
Nov 19 1989	8-Manik	9	Jan 26 1990	11-Men	5	Apr 4 1990	1-Akbal	1
Nov 20 1989	9-Lamat	1	Jan 27 1990	12-Cib	6	Apr 5 1990	2-Kan	2
Nov 21 1989	10-Muluc	2	Jan 28 1990	13-Caban	7	Apr 6 1990	3-Chicchan	3
Nov 22 1989	11-Oc	3	Jan 29 1990	1-Etz'nab	8	Apr 7 1990	4-Cimi	4
Nov 23 1989	12-Chuen	4	Jan 30 1990	2-Cauac	9	Apr 8 1990	5-Manik	5
Nov 24 1989	13-Eb	5	Jan 31 1990	3-Ahau	1	Apr 9 1990	6-Lamat	6
Nov 25 1989	1-Ben	6	Feb 1 1990	4-Imix	2	Apr 10 1990	7-Muluc	7
Nov 26 1989	2-Ix	7	Feb 2 1990	5-Ik	3	Apr 11 1990	8-Oc	8
Nov 27 1989	3-Men	8	Feb 3 1990	6-Akbal	4	Apr 12 1990	9-Chuen	9
Nov 28 1989	4-Cib	9	Feb 4 1990	7-Kan	5	Apr 13 1990	10-Eb	1
Nov 29 1989	5-Caban	1	Feb 5 1990	8-Chicchan	6	Apr 14 1990	11-Ben	2
Nov 30 1989	6-Etz'nab	2	Feb 6 1990	9-Cimi	7	Apr 15 1990	12-Ix	3
Dec 1 1989	7-Cauac	3	Feb 7 1990	10-Manik	8	Apr 16 1990	13-Men	4
Dec 2 1989	8-Ahau	4	Feb 8 1990	11-Lamat	9	Apr 17 1990	1-Cib	5
Dec 3 1989	9-Imix	5	Feb 9 1990	12-Muluc	1	Apr 18 1990	2-Caban	6

Date	Day-Sign	L	Date	Day-Sign	L	Date	Day-Sign	L
Apr 19 1990	3-Etz'nab	7	Jun 26 1990	6-Cimi	3	Sep 2 1990	9-Ix	8
Apr 20 1990	4-Cauac	8	Jun 27 1990	7-Manik	4	Sep 3 1990	10-Men	9
Apr 21 1990	5-Ahau	9	Jun 28 1990	8-Lamat	5	Sep 4 1990	11-Cib	1
Apr 22 1990	6-*Imix*	1	Jun 29 1990	9-Muluc	6	Sep 5 1990	12-Caban	2
Apr 23 1990	7-Ik	2	Jun 30 1990	10-Oc	7	Sep 6 1990	13-Etz'nab	3
Apr 24 1990	8-Akbal	3	Jul 1 1990	11-Chuen	8	Sep 7 1990	**1-Cauac**	4
Apr 25 1990	9-Kan	4	Jul 2 1990	12-Eb	9	Sep 8 1990	2-Ahau	5
Apr 26 1990	10-Chicchan	5	Jul 3 1990	13-Ben	1	Sep 9 1990	3-*Imix*	6
Apr 27 1990	11-Cimi	6	Jul 4 1990	**1-Ix**	2	Sep 10 1990	4-Ik	7
Apr 28 1990	12-Manik	7	Jul 5 1990	2-Men	3	Sep 11 1990	5-Akbal	8
Apr 29 1990	13-Lamat	8	Jul 6 1990	3-Cib	4	Sep 12 1990	6-Kan	9
Apr 30 1990	**1-Muluc**	9	Jul 7 1990	4-Caban	5	Sep 13 1990	7-Chicchan	1
May 1 1990	2-Oc	1	Jul 8 1990	5-Etz'nab	6	Sep 14 1990	8-Cimi	2
May 2 1990	3-Chuen	2	Jul 9 1990	6-Cauac	7	Sep 15 1990	9-Manik	3
May 3 1990	4-Eb	3	Jul 10 1990	7-Ahau	8	Sep 16 1990	10-Lamat	4
May 4 1990	5-Ben	4	Jul 11 1990	8-*Imix*	9	Sep 17 1990	11-Muluc	5
May 5 1990	6-Ix	5	Jul 12 1990	9-Ik	1	Sep 18 1990	12-Oc	6
May 6 1990	7-Men	6	Jul 13 1990	10-Akbal	2	Sep 19 1990	13-Chuen	7
May 7 1990	8-Cib	7	Jul 14 1990	11-Kan	3	Sep 20 1990	**1-Eb**	8
May 8 1990	9-Caban	8	Jul 15 1990	12-Chicchan	4	Sep 21 1990	2-Ben	9
May 9 1990	10-Etz'nab	9	Jul 16 1990	13-Cimi	5	Sep 22 1990	3-Ix	1
May 10 1990	11-Cauac	1	Jul 17 1990	**1-Manik**	6	Sep 23 1990	4-Men	2
May 11 1990	12-Ahau	2	Jul 18 1990	2-Lamat	7	Sep 24 1990	5-Cib	3
May 12 1990	13-*Imix*	3	Jul 19 1990	3-Muluc	8	Sep 25 1990	6-Caban	4
May 13 1990	**1-Ik**	4	Jul 20 1990	4-Oc	9	Sep 26 1990	7-Etz'nab	5
May 14 1990	2-Akbal	5	Jul 21 1990	5-Chuen	1	Sep 27 1990	8-Cauac	6
May 15 1990	3-Kan	6	Jul 22 1990	6-Eb	2	Sep 28 1990	9-Ahau	7
May 16 1990	4-Chicchan	7	Jul 23 1990	7-Ben	3	Sep 29 1990	10-*Imix*	8
May 17 1990	5-Cimi	8	Jul 24 1990	8-Ix	4	Sep 30 1990	11-Ik	9
May 18 1990	6-Manik	9	Jul 25 1990	9-Men	5	Oct 1 1990	12-Akbal	1
May 19 1990	7-Lamat	1	Jul 26 1990	10-Cib	6	Oct 2 1990	13-Kan	2
May 20 1990	8-Muluc	2	Jul 27 1990	11-Caban	7	Oct 3 1990	**1-Chicchan**	3
May 21 1990	9-Oc	3	Jul 28 1990	12-Etz'nab	8	Oct 4 1990	2-Cimi	4
May 22 1990	10-Chuen	4	Jul 29 1990	13-Cauac	9	Oct 5 1990	3-Manik	5
May 23 1990	11-Eb	5	Jul 30 1990	**1-Ahau**	1	Oct 6 1990	4-Lamat	6
May 24 1990	12-Ben	6	Jul 31 1990	2-*Imix*	2	Oct 7 1990	5-Muluc	7
May 25 1990	13-Ix	7	Aug 1 1990	3-Ik	3	Oct 8 1990	6-Oc	8
May 26 1990	**1-Men**	8	Aug 2 1990	4-Akbal	4	Oct 9 1990	7-Chuen	9
May 27 1990	2-Cib	9	Aug 3 1990	5-Kan	5	Oct 10 1990	8-Eb	1
May 28 1990	3-Caban	1	Aug 4 1990	6-Chicchan	6	Oct 11 1990	9-Ben	2
May 29 1990	4-Etz'nab	2	Aug 5 1990	7-Cimi	7	Oct 12 1990	10-Ix	3
May 30 1990	5-Cauac	3	Aug 6 1990	8-Manik	8	Oct 13 1990	11-Men	4
May 31 1990	6-Ahau	4	Aug 7 1990	9-Lamat	9	Oct 14 1990	12-Cib	5
Jun 1 1990	7-*Imix*	5	Aug 8 1990	10-Muluc	1	Oct 15 1990	13-Caban	6
Jun 2 1990	8-Ik	6	Aug 9 1990	11-Oc	2	Oct 16 1990	**1-Etz'nab**	7
Jun 3 1990	9-Akbal	7	Aug 10 1990	12-Chuen	3	Oct 17 1990	2-Cauac	8
Jun 4 1990	10-Kan	8	Aug 11 1990	13-Eb	4	Oct 18 1990	3-Ahau	9
Jun 5 1990	11-Chicchan	9	Aug 12 1990	**1-Ben**	5	Oct 19 1990	4-*Imix*	1
Jun 6 1990	12-Cimi	1	Aug 13 1990	2-Ix	6	Oct 20 1990	5-Ik	2
Jun 7 1990	13-Manik	2	Aug 14 1990	3-Men	7	Oct 21 1990	6-Akbal	3
Jun 8 1990	**1-Lamat**	3	Aug 15 1990	4-Cib	8	Oct 22 1990	7-Kan	4
Jun 9 1990	2-Muluc	4	Aug 16 1990	5-Caban	9	Oct 23 1990	8-Chicchan	5
Jun 10 1990	3-Oc	5	Aug 17 1990	6-Etz'nab	1	Oct 24 1990	9-Cimi	6
Jun 11 1990	4-Chuen	6	Aug 18 1990	7-Cauac	2	Oct 25 1990	10-Manik	7
Jun 12 1990	5-Eb	7	Aug 19 1990	8-Ahau	3	Oct 26 1990	11-Lamat	8
Jun 13 1990	6-Ben	8	Aug 20 1990	9-*Imix*	4	Oct 27 1990	12-Muluc	9
Jun 14 1990	7-Ix	9	Aug 21 1990	10-Ik	5	Oct 28 1990	13-Oc	1
Jun 15 1990	8-Men	1	Aug 22 1990	11-Akbal	6	Oct 29 1990	**1-Chuen**	2
Jun 16 1990	9-Cib	2	Aug 23 1990	12-Kan	7	Oct 30 1990	2-Eb	3
Jun 17 1990	10-Caban	3	Aug 24 1990	13-Chicchan	8	Oct 31 1990	3-Ben	4
Jun 18 1990	11-Etz'nab	4	Aug 25 1990	**1-Cimi**	9	Nov 1 1990	4-Ix	5
Jun 19 1990	12-Cauac	5	Aug 26 1990	2-Manik	1	Nov 2 1990	5-Men	6
Jun 20 1990	13-Ahau	6	Aug 27 1990	3-Lamat	2	Nov 3 1990	6-Cib	7
Jun 21 1990	**1-Imix**	7	Aug 28 1990	4-Muluc	3	Nov 4 1990	7-Caban	8
Jun 22 1990	2-Ik	8	Aug 29 1990	5-Oc	4	Nov 5 1990	8-Etz'nab	9
Jun 23 1990	3-Akbal	9	Aug 30 1990	6-Chuen	5	Nov 6 1990	9-Cauac	1
Jun 24 1990	4-Kan	1	Aug 31 1990	7-Eb	6	Nov 7 1990	10-Ahau	2
Jun 25 1990	5-Chicchan	2	Sep 1 1990	8-Ben	7	Nov 8 1990	11-*Imix*	3

Date	Day-Sign	L
Nov 9 1990	12-Ik	4
Nov 10 1990	13-Akbal	5
Nov 11 1990	**1-Kan**	6
Nov 12 1990	2-Chicchan	7
Nov 13 1990	3-Cimi	8
Nov 14 1990	4-Manik	9
Nov 15 1990	5-Lamat	1
Nov 16 1990	6-Muluc	2
Nov 17 1990	7-Oc	3
Nov 18 1990	8-Chuen	4
Nov 19 1990	9-Eb	5
Nov 20 1990	10-Ben	6
Nov 21 1990	11-Ix	7
Nov 22 1990	12-Men	8
Nov 23 1990	13-Cib	9
Nov 24 1990	**1-Caban**	1
Nov 25 1990	2-Etz'nab	2
Nov 26 1990	3-Cauac	3
Nov 27 1990	4-Ahau	4
Nov 28 1990	*5-Imix*	5
Nov 29 1990	6-Ik	6
Nov 30 1990	7-Akbal	7
Dec 1 1990	8-Kan	8
Dec 2 1990	9-Chicchan	9
Dec 3 1990	10-Cimi	1
Dec 4 1990	11-Manik	2
Dec 5 1990	12-Lamat	3
Dec 6 1990	13-Muluc	4
Dec 7 1990	**1-Oc**	5
Dec 8 1990	2-Chuen	6
Dec 9 1990	3-Eb	7
Dec 10 1990	4-Ben	8
Dec 11 1990	5-Ix	9
Dec 12 1990	6-Men	1
Dec 13 1990	7-Cib	2
Dec 14 1990	8-Caban	3
Dec 15 1990	9-Etz'nab	4
Dec 16 1990	10-Cauac	5
Dec 17 1990	11-Ahau	6
Dec 18 1990	*12-Imix*	7
Dec 19 1990	13-Ik	8
Dec 20 1990	**1-Akbal**	9
Dec 21 1990	2-Kan	1
Dec 22 1990	3-Chicchan	2
Dec 23 1990	4-Cimi	3
Dec 24 1990	5-Manik	4
Dec 25 1990	6-Lamat	5
Dec 26 1990	7-Muluc	6
Dec 27 1990	8-Oc	7
Dec 28 1990	9-Chuen	8
Dec 29 1990	10-Eb	9
Dec 30 1990	11-Ben	1
Dec 31 1990	12-Ix	2
Jan 1 1991	13-Men	3
Jan 2 1991	**1-Cib**	4
Jan 3 1991	2-Caban	5
Jan 4 1991	3-Etz'nab	6
Jan 5 1991	4-Cauac	7
Jan 6 1991	5-Ahau	8
Jan 7 1991	*6-Imix*	9
Jan 8 1991	7-Ik	1
Jan 9 1991	8-Akbal	2
Jan 10 1991	9-Kan	3
Jan 11 1991	10-Chicchan	4
Jan 12 1991	11-Cimi	5
Jan 13 1991	12-Manik	6
Jan 14 1991	13-Lamat	7
Jan 15 1991	**1-Muluc**	8

Date	Day-Sign	L
Jan 16 1991	2-Oc	9
Jan 17 1991	3-Chuen	1
Jan 18 1991	4-Eb	2
Jan 19 1991	5-Ben	3
Jan 20 1991	6-Ix	4
Jan 21 1991	7-Men	5
Jan 22 1991	8-Cib	6
Jan 23 1991	9-Caban	7
Jan 24 1991	10-Etz'nab	8
Jan 25 1991	11-Cauac	9
Jan 26 1991	12-Ahau	1
Jan 27 1991	*13-Imix*	2
Jan 28 1991	**1-Ik**	3
Jan 29 1991	2-Akbal	4
Jan 30 1991	3-Kan	5
Jan 31 1991	4-Chicchan	6
Feb 1 1991	5-Cimi	7
Feb 2 1991	6-Manik	8
Feb 3 1991	7-Lamat	9
Feb 4 1991	8-Muluc	1
Feb 5 1991	9-Oc	2
Feb 6 1991	10-Chuen	3
Feb 7 1991	11-Eb	4
Feb 8 1991	12-Ben	5
Feb 9 1991	13-Ix	6
Feb 10 1991	**1-Men**	7
Feb 11 1991	2-Cib	8
Feb 12 1991	3-Caban	9
Feb 13 1991	4-Etz'nab	1
Feb 14 1991	5-Cauac	2
Feb 15 1991	6-Ahau	3
Feb 16 1991	*7-Imix*	4
Feb 17 1991	8-Ik	5
Feb 18 1991	9-Akbal	6
Feb 19 1991	10-Kan	7
Feb 20 1991	11-Chicchan	8
Feb 21 1991	12-Cimi	9
Feb 22 1991	13-Manik	1
Feb 23 1991	**1-Lamat**	2
Feb 24 1991	2-Muluc	3
Feb 25 1991	3-Oc	4
Feb 26 1991	4-Chuen	5
Feb 27 1991	5-Eb	6
Feb 28 1991	6-Ben	7
Mar 1 1991	7-Ix	8
Mar 2 1991	8-Men	9
Mar 3 1991	9-Cib	1
Mar 4 1991	10-Caban	2
Mar 5 1991	11-Etz'nab	3
Mar 6 1991	12-Cauac	4
Mar 7 1991	13-Ahau	5
Mar 8 1991	**1-Imix**	6
Mar 9 1991	2-Ik	7
Mar 10 1991	3-Akbal	8
Mar 11 1991	4-Kan	9
Mar 12 1991	5-Chicchan	1
Mar 13 1991	6-Cimi	2
Mar 14 1991	7-Manik	3
Mar 15 1991	8-Lamat	4
Mar 16 1991	9-Muluc	5
Mar 17 1991	10-Oc	6
Mar 18 1991	11-Chuen	7
Mar 19 1991	12-Eb	8
Mar 20 1991	13-Ben	9
Mar 21 1991	**1-Ix**	1
Mar 22 1991	2-Men	2
Mar 23 1991	3-Cib	3
Mar 24 1991	4-Caban	4

Date	Day-Sign	L
Mar 25 1991	5-Etz'nab	5
Mar 26 1991	6-Cauac	6
Mar 27 1991	7-Ahau	7
Mar 28 1991	*8-Imix*	8
Mar 29 1991	9-Ik	9
Mar 30 1991	10-Akbal	1
Mar 31 1991	11-Kan	2
Apr 1 1991	12-Chicchan	3
Apr 2 1991	13-Cimi	4
Apr 3 1991	**1-Manik**	5
Apr 4 1991	2-Lamat	6
Apr 5 1991	3-Muluc	7
Apr 6 1991	4-Oc	8
Apr 7 1991	5-Chuen	9
Apr 8 1991	6-Eb	1
Apr 9 1991	7-Ben	2
Apr 10 1991	8-Ix	3
Apr 11 1991	9-Men	4
Apr 12 1991	10-Cib	5
Apr 13 1991	11-Caban	6
Apr 14 1991	12-Etz'nab	7
Apr 15 1991	13-Cauac	8
Apr 16 1991	**1-Ahau**	9
Apr 17 1991	*2-Imix*	1
Apr 18 1991	3-Ik	2
Apr 19 1991	4-Akbal	3
Apr 20 1991	5-Kan	4
Apr 21 1991	6-Chicchan	5
Apr 22 1991	7-Cimi	6
Apr 23 1991	8-Manik	7
Apr 24 1991	9-Lamat	8
Apr 25 1991	10-Muluc	9
Apr 26 1991	11-Oc	1
Apr 27 1991	12-Chuen	2
Apr 28 1991	13-Eb	3
Apr 29 1991	**1-Ben**	4
Apr 30 1991	2-Ix	5
May 1 1991	3-Men	6
May 2 1991	4-Cib	7
May 3 1991	5-Caban	8
May 4 1991	6-Etz'nab	9
May 5 1991	7-Cauac	1
May 6 1991	8-Ahau	2
May 7 1991	*9-Imix*	3
May 8 1991	10-Ik	4
May 9 1991	11-Akbal	5
May 10 1991	12-Kan	6
May 11 1991	13-Chicchan	7
May 12 1991	**1-Cimi**	8
May 13 1991	2-Manik	9
May 14 1991	3-Lamat	1
May 15 1991	4-Muluc	2
May 16 1991	5-Oc	3
May 17 1991	6-Chuen	4
May 18 1991	7-Eb	5
May 19 1991	8-Ben	6
May 20 1991	9-Ix	7
May 21 1991	10-Men	8
May 22 1991	11-Cib	9
May 23 1991	12-Caban	1
May 24 1991	13-Etz'nab	2
May 25 1991	**1-Cauac**	3
May 26 1991	2-Ahau	4
May 27 1991	*3-Imix*	5
May 28 1991	4-Ik	6
May 29 1991	5-Akbal	7
May 30 1991	6-Kan	8
May 31 1991	7-Chicchan	9

Date	Day-Sign	L
Jun 1 1991	8-Cimi	1
Jun 2 1991	9-Manik	2
Jun 3 1991	10-Lamat	3
Jun 4 1991	11-Muluc	4
Jun 5 1991	12-Oc	5
Jun 6 1991	13-Chuen	6
Jun 7 1991	**1-Eb**	7
Jun 8 1991	2-Ben	8
Jun 9 1991	3-Ix	9
Jun 10 1991	4-Men	1
Jun 11 1991	5-Cib	2
Jun 12 1991	6-Caban	3
Jun 13 1991	7-Etz'nab	4
Jun 14 1991	8-Cauac	5
Jun 15 1991	9-Ahau	6
Jun 16 1991	*10-Imix*	7
Jun 17 1991	11-Ik	8
Jun 18 1991	12-Akbal	9
Jun 19 1991	13-Kan	1
Jun 20 1991	**1-Chicchan**	2
Jun 21 1991	2-Cimi	3
Jun 22 1991	3-Manik	4
Jun 23 1991	4-Lamat	5
Jun 24 1991	5-Muluc	6
Jun 25 1991	6-Oc	7
Jun 26 1991	7-Chuen	8
Jun 27 1991	8-Eb	9
Jun 28 1991	9-Ben	1
Jun 29 1991	10-Ix	2
Jun 30 1991	11-Men	3
Jul 1 1991	12-Cib	4
Jul 2 1991	13-Caban	5
Jul 3 1991	**1-Etz'nab**	6
Jul 4 1991	2-Cauac	7
Jul 5 1991	3-Ahau	8
Jul 6 1991	*4-Imix*	9
Jul 7 1991	5-Ik	1
Jul 8 1991	6-Akbal	2
Jul 9 1991	7-Kan	3
Jul 10 1991	8-Chicchan	4
Jul 11 1991	9-Cimi	5
Jul 12 1991	10-Manik	6
Jul 13 1991	11-Lamat	7
Jul 14 1991	12-Muluc	8
Jul 15 1991	13-Oc	9
Jul 16 1991	**1-Chuen**	1
Jul 17 1991	2-Eb	2
Jul 18 1991	3-Ben	3
Jul 19 1991	4-Ix	4
Jul 20 1991	5-Men	5
Jul 21 1991	6-Cib	6
Jul 22 1991	7-Caban	7
Jul 23 1991	8-Etz'nab	8
Jul 24 1991	9-Cauac	9
Jul 25 1991	10-Ahau	1
Jul 26 1991	*11-Imix*	2
Jul 27 1991	12-Ik	3
Jul 28 1991	13-Akbal	4
Jul 29 1991	**1-Kan**	5
Jul 30 1991	2-Chicchan	6
Jul 31 1991	3-Cimi	7
Aug 1 1991	4-Manik	8
Aug 2 1991	5-Lamat	9
Aug 3 1991	6-Muluc	1
Aug 4 1991	7-Oc	2
Aug 5 1991	8-Chuen	3
Aug 6 1991	9-Eb	4
Aug 7 1991	10-Ben	5

Date	Day-Sign	L
Aug 8 1991	11-Ix	6
Aug 9 1991	12-Men	7
Aug 10 1991	13-Cib	8
Aug 11 1991	**1-Caban**	9
Aug 12 1991	2-Etz'nab	1
Aug 13 1991	3-Cauac	2
Aug 14 1991	4-Ahau	3
Aug 15 1991	*5-Imix*	4
Aug 16 1991	6-Ik	5
Aug 17 1991	7-Akbal	6
Aug 18 1991	8-Kan	7
Aug 19 1991	9-Chicchan	8
Aug 20 1991	10-Cimi	9
Aug 21 1991	11-Manik	1
Aug 22 1991	12-Lamat	2
Aug 23 1991	13-Muluc	3
Aug 24 1991	**1-Oc**	4
Aug 25 1991	2-Chuen	5
Aug 26 1991	3-Eb	6
Aug 27 1991	4-Ben	7
Aug 28 1991	5-Ix	8
Aug 29 1991	6-Men	9
Aug 30 1991	7-Cib	1
Aug 31 1991	8-Caban	2
Sep 1 1991	9-Etz'nab	3
Sep 2 1991	10-Cauac	4
Sep 3 1991	11-Ahau	5
Sep 4 1991	*12-Imix*	6
Sep 5 1991	13-Ik	7
Sep 6 1991	**1-Akbal**	8
Sep 7 1991	2-Kan	9
Sep 8 1991	3-Chicchan	1
Sep 9 1991	4-Cimi	2
Sep 10 1991	5-Manik	3
Sep 11 1991	6-Lamat	4
Sep 12 1991	7-Muluc	5
Sep 13 1991	8-Oc	6
Sep 14 1991	9-Chuen	7
Sep 15 1991	10-Eb	8
Sep 16 1991	11-Ben	9
Sep 17 1991	12-Ix	1
Sep 18 1991	13-Men	2
Sep 19 1991	**1-Cib**	3
Sep 20 1991	2-Caban	4
Sep 21 1991	3-Etz'nab	5
Sep 22 1991	4-Cauac	6
Sep 23 1991	5-Ahau	7
Sep 24 1991	*6-Imix*	8
Sep 25 1991	7-Ik	9
Sep 26 1991	8-Akbal	1
Sep 27 1991	9-Kan	2
Sep 28 1991	10-Chicchan	3
Sep 29 1991	11-Cimi	4
Sep 30 1991	12-Manik	5
Oct 1 1991	13-Lamat	6
Oct 2 1991	**1-Muluc**	7
Oct 3 1991	2-Oc	8
Oct 4 1991	3-Chuen	9
Oct 5 1991	4-Eb	1
Oct 6 1991	5-Ben	2
Oct 7 1991	6-Ix	3
Oct 8 1991	7-Men	4
Oct 9 1991	8-Cib	5
Oct 10 1991	9-Caban	6
Oct 11 1991	10-Etz'nab	7
Oct 12 1991	11-Cauac	8
Oct 13 1991	12-Ahau	9
Oct 14 1991	*13-Imix*	1

Date	Day-Sign	L
Oct 15 1991	**1-Ik**	2
Oct 16 1991	2-Akbal	3
Oct 17 1991	3-Kan	4
Oct 18 1991	4-Chicchan	5
Oct 19 1991	5-Cimi	6
Oct 20 1991	6-Manik	7
Oct 21 1991	7-Lamat	8
Oct 22 1991	8-Muluc	9
Oct 23 1991	9-Oc	1
Oct 24 1991	10-Chuen	2
Oct 25 1991	11-Eb	3
Oct 26 1991	12-Ben	4
Oct 27 1991	13-Ix	5
Oct 28 1991	**1-Men**	6
Oct 29 1991	2-Cib	7
Oct 30 1991	3-Caban	8
Oct 31 1991	4-Etz'nab	9
Nov 1 1991	5-Cauac	1
Nov 2 1991	6-Ahau	2
Nov 3 1991	*7-Imix*	3
Nov 4 1991	8-Ik	4
Nov 5 1991	9-Akbal	5
Nov 6 1991	10-Kan	6
Nov 7 1991	11-Chicchan	7
Nov 8 1991	12-Cimi	8
Nov 9 1991	13-Manik	9
Nov 10 1991	**1-Lamat**	1
Nov 11 1991	2-Muluc	2
Nov 12 1991	3-Oc	3
Nov 13 1991	4-Chuen	4
Nov 14 1991	5-Eb	5
Nov 15 1991	6-Ben	6
Nov 16 1991	7-Ix	7
Nov 17 1991	8-Men	8
Nov 18 1991	9-Cib	9
Nov 19 1991	10-Caban	1
Nov 20 1991	11-Etz'nab	2
Nov 21 1991	12-Cauac	3
Nov 22 1991	13-Ahau	4
Nov 23 1991	**1-Imix**	5
Nov 24 1991	2-Ik	6
Nov 25 1991	3-Akbal	7
Nov 26 1991	4-Kan	8
Nov 27 1991	5-Chicchan	9
Nov 28 1991	6-Cimi	1
Nov 29 1991	7-Manik	2
Nov 30 1991	8-Lamat	3
Dec 1 1991	9-Muluc	4
Dec 2 1991	10-Oc	5
Dec 3 1991	11-Chuen	6
Dec 4 1991	12-Eb	7
Dec 5 1991	13-Ben	8
Dec 6 1991	**1-Ix**	9
Dec 7 1991	2-Men	1
Dec 8 1991	3-Cib	2
Dec 9 1991	4-Caban	3
Dec 10 1991	5-Etz'nab	4
Dec 11 1991	6-Cauac	5
Dec 12 1991	7-Ahau	6
Dec 13 1991	*8-Imix*	7
Dec 14 1991	9-Ik	8
Dec 15 1991	10-Akbal	9
Dec 16 1991	11-Kan	1
Dec 17 1991	12-Chicchan	2
Dec 18 1991	13-Cimi	3
Dec 19 1991	**1-Manik**	4
Dec 20 1991	2-Lamat	5
Dec 21 1991	3-Muluc	6

Date	Day-Sign	L	Date	Day-Sign	L	Date	Day-Sign	L
Dec 22 1991	4-Oc	7	Feb 28 1992	7-Etz'nab	3	May 6 1992	10-Cimi	8
Dec 23 1991	5-Chuen	8	Feb 29 1992	8-Cauac	4	May 7 1992	11-Manik	9
Dec 24 1991	6-Eb	9	Mar 1 1992	9-Ahau	5	May 8 1992	12-Lamat	1
Dec 25 1991	7-Ben	1	Mar 2 1992	10-Imix	6	May 9 1992	13-Muluc	2
Dec 26 1991	8-Ix	2	Mar 3 1992	11-Ik	7	May 10 1992	1-Oc	3
Dec 27 1991	9-Men	3	Mar 4 1992	12-Akbal	8	May 11 1992	2-Chuen	4
Dec 28 1991	10-Cib	4	Mar 5 1992	13-Kan	9	May 12 1992	3-Eb	5
Dec 29 1991	11-Caban	5	Mar 6 1992	1-Chicchan	1	May 13 1992	4-Ben	6
Dec 30 1991	12-Etz'nab	6	Mar 7 1992	2-Cimi	2	May 14 1992	5-Ix	7
Dec 31 1991	13-Cauac	7	Mar 8 1992	3-Manik	3	May 15 1992	6-Men	8
Jan 1 1992	1-Ahau	8	Mar 9 1992	4-Lamat	4	May 16 1992	7-Cib	9
Jan 2 1992	2-Imix	9	Mar 10 1992	5-Muluc	5	May 17 1992	8-Caban	1
Jan 3 1992	3-Ik	1	Mar 11 1992	6-Oc	6	May 18 1992	9-Etz'nab	2
Jan 4 1992	4-Akbal	2	Mar 12 1992	7-Chuen	7	May 19 1992	10-Cauac	3
Jan 5 1992	5-Kan	3	Mar 13 1992	8-Eb	8	May 20 1992	11-Ahau	4
Jan 6 1992	6-Chicchan	4	Mar 14 1992	9-Ben	9	May 21 1992	12-Imix	5
Jan 7 1992	7-Cimi	5	Mar 15 1992	10-Ix	1	May 22 1992	13-Ik	6
Jan 8 1992	8-Manik	6	Mar 16 1992	11-Men	2	May 23 1992	1-Akbal	7
Jan 9 1992	9-Lamat	7	Mar 17 1992	12-Cib	3	May 24 1992	2-Kan	8
Jan 10 1992	10-Muluc	8	Mar 18 1992	13-Caban	4	May 25 1992	3-Chicchan	9
Jan 11 1992	11-Oc	9	Mar 19 1992	1-Etz'nab	5	May 26 1992	4-Cimi	1
Jan 12 1992	12-Chuen	1	Mar 20 1992	2-Cauac	6	May 27 1992	5-Manik	2
Jan 13 1992	13-Eb	2	Mar 21 1992	3-Ahau	7	May 28 1992	6-Lamat	3
Jan 14 1992	1-Ben	3	Mar 22 1992	4-Imix	8	May 29 1992	7-Muluc	4
Jan 15 1992	2-Ix	4	Mar 23 1992	5-Ik	9	May 30 1992	8-Oc	5
Jan 16 1992	3-Men	5	Mar 24 1992	6-Akbal	1	May 31 1992	9-Chuen	6
Jan 17 1992	4-Cib	6	Mar 25 1992	7-Kan	2	Jun 1 1992	10-Eb	7
Jan 18 1992	5-Caban	7	Mar 26 1992	8-Chicchan	3	Jun 2 1992	11-Ben	8
Jan 19 1992	6-Etz'nab	8	Mar 27 1992	9-Cimi	4	Jun 3 1992	12-Ix	9
Jan 20 1992	7-Cauac	9	Mar 28 1992	10-Manik	5	Jun 4 1992	13-Men	1
Jan 21 1992	8-Ahau	1	Mar 29 1992	11-Lamat	6	Jun 5 1992	1-Cib	2
Jan 22 1992	9-Imix	2	Mar 30 1992	12-Muluc	7	Jun 6 1992	2-Caban	3
Jan 23 1992	10-Ik	3	Mar 31 1992	13-Oc	8	Jun 7 1992	3-Etz'nab	4
Jan 24 1992	11-Akbal	4	Apr 1 1992	1-Chuen	9	Jun 8 1992	4-Cauac	5
Jan 25 1992	12-Kan	5	Apr 2 1992	2-Eb	1	Jun 9 1992	5-Ahau	6
Jan 26 1992	13-Chicchan	6	Apr 3 1992	3-Ben	2	Jun 10 1992	6-Imix	7
Jan 27 1992	1-Cimi	7	Apr 4 1992	4-Ix	3	Jun 11 1992	7-Ik	8
Jan 28 1992	2-Manik	8	Apr 5 1992	5-Men	4	Jun 12 1992	8-Akbal	9
Jan 29 1992	3-Lamat	9	Apr 6 1992	6-Cib	5	Jun 13 1992	9-Kan	1
Jan 30 1992	4-Muluc	1	Apr 7 1992	7-Caban	6	Jun 14 1992	10-Chicchan	2
Jan 31 1992	5-Oc	2	Apr 8 1992	8-Etz'nab	7	Jun 15 1992	11-Cimi	3
Feb 1 1992	6-Chuen	3	Apr 9 1992	9-Cauac	8	Jun 16 1992	12-Manik	4
Feb 2 1992	7-Eb	4	Apr 10 1992	10-Ahau	9	Jun 17 1992	13-Lamat	5
Feb 3 1992	8-Ben	5	Apr 11 1992	11-Imix	1	Jun 18 1992	1-Muluc	6
Feb 4 1992	9-Ix	6	Apr 12 1992	12-Ik	2	Jun 19 1992	2-Oc	7
Feb 5 1992	10-Men	7	Apr 13 1992	13-Akbal	3	Jun 20 1992	3-Chuen	8
Feb 6 1992	11-Cib	8	Apr 14 1992	1-Kan	4	Jun 21 1992	4-Eb	9
Feb 7 1992	12-Caban	9	Apr 15 1992	2-Chicchan	5	Jun 22 1992	5-Ben	1
Feb 8 1992	13-Etz'nab	1	Apr 16 1992	3-Cimi	6	Jun 23 1992	6-Ix	2
Feb 9 1992	1-Cauac	2	Apr 17 1992	4-Manik	7	Jun 24 1992	7-Men	3
Feb 10 1992	2-Ahau	3	Apr 18 1992	5-Lamat	8	Jun 25 1992	8-Cib	4
Feb 11 1992	3-Imix	4	Apr 19 1992	6-Muluc	9	Jun 26 1992	9-Caban	5
Feb 12 1992	4-Ik	5	Apr 20 1992	7-Oc	1	Jun 27 1992	10-Etz'nab	6
Feb 13 1992	5-Akbal	6	Apr 21 1992	8-Chuen	2	Jun 28 1992	11-Cauac	7
Feb 14 1992	6-Kan	7	Apr 22 1992	9-Eb	3	Jun 29 1992	12-Ahau	8
Feb 15 1992	7-Chicchan	8	Apr 23 1992	10-Ben	4	Jun 30 1992	13-Imix	9
Feb 16 1992	8-Cimi	9	Apr 24 1992	11-Ix	5	Jul 1 1992	1-Ik	1
Feb 17 1992	9-Manik	1	Apr 25 1992	12-Men	6	Jul 2 1992	2-Akbal	2
Feb 18 1992	10-Lamat	2	Apr 26 1992	13-Cib	7	Jul 3 1992	3-Kan	3
Feb 19 1992	11-Muluc	3	Apr 27 1992	1-Caban	8	Jul 4 1992	4-Chicchan	4
Feb 20 1992	12-Oc	4	Apr 28 1992	2-Etz'nab	9	Jul 5 1992	5-Cimi	5
Feb 21 1992	13-Chuen	5	Apr 29 1992	3-Cauac	1	Jul 6 1992	6-Manik	6
Feb 22 1992	1-Eb	6	Apr 30 1992	4-Ahau	2	Jul 7 1992	7-Lamat	7
Feb 23 1992	2-Ben	7	May 1 1992	5-Imix	3	Jul 8 1992	8-Muluc	8
Feb 24 1992	3-Ix	8	May 2 1992	6-Ik	4	Jul 9 1992	9-Oc	9
Feb 25 1992	4-Men	9	May 3 1992	7-Akbal	5	Jul 10 1992	10-Chuen	1
Feb 26 1992	5-Cib	1	May 4 1992	8-Kan	6	Jul 11 1992	11-Eb	2
Feb 27 1992	6-Caban	2	May 5 1992	9-Chicchan	7	Jul 12 1992	12-Ben	3

Date	Day-Sign	L	Date	Day-Sign	L	Date	Day-Sign	L
Jul 13 1992	13-Ix	4	Sep 19 1992	3-Ik	9	Nov 26 1992	6-Oc	5
Jul 14 1992	1-Men	5	Sep 20 1992	4-Akbal	1	Nov 27 1992	7-Chuen	6
Jul 15 1992	2-Cib	6	Sep 21 1992	5-Kan	2	Nov 28 1992	8-Eb	7
Jul 16 1992	3-Caban	7	Sep 22 1992	6-Chicchan	3	Nov 29 1992	9-Ben	8
Jul 17 1992	4-Etz'nab	8	Sep 23 1992	7-Cimi	4	Nov 30 1992	10-Ix	9
Jul 18 1992	5-Cauac	9	Sep 24 1992	8-Manik	5	Dec 1 1992	11-Men	1
Jul 19 1992	6-Ahau	1	Sep 25 1992	9-Lamat	6	Dec 2 1992	12-Cib	2
Jul 20 1992	7-Imix	2	Sep 26 1992	10-Muluc	7	Dec 3 1992	13-Caban	3
Jul 21 1992	8-Ik	3	Sep 27 1992	11-Oc	8	Dec 4 1992	1-Etz'nab	4
Jul 22 1992	9-Akbal	4	Sep 28 1992	12-Chuen	9	Dec 5 1992	2-Cauac	5
Jul 23 1992	10-Kan	5	Sep 29 1992	13-Eb	1	Dec 6 1992	3-Ahau	6
Jul 24 1992	11-Chicchan	6	Sep 30 1992	1-Ben	2	Dec 7 1992	4-Imix	7
Jul 25 1992	12-Cimi	7	Oct 1 1992	2-Ix	3	Dec 8 1992	5-Ik	8
Jul 26 1992	13-Manik	8	Oct 2 1992	3-Men	4	Dec 9 1992	6-Akbal	9
Jul 27 1992	1-Lamat	9	Oct 3 1992	4-Cib	5	Dec 10 1992	7-Kan	1
Jul 28 1992	2-Muluc	1	Oct 4 1992	5-Caban	6	Dec 11 1992	8-Chicchan	2
Jul 29 1992	3-Oc	2	Oct 5 1992	6-Etz'nab	7	Dec 12 1992	9-Cimi	3
Jul 30 1992	4-Chuen	3	Oct 6 1992	7-Cauac	8	Dec 13 1992	10-Manik	4
Jul 31 1992	5-Eb	4	Oct 7 1992	8-Ahau	9	Dec 14 1992	11-Lamat	5
Aug 1 1992	6-Ben	5	Oct 8 1992	9-Imix	1	Dec 15 1992	12-Muluc	6
Aug 2 1992	7-Ix	6	Oct 9 1992	10-Ik	2	Dec 16 1992	13-Oc	7
Aug 3 1992	8-Men	7	Oct 10 1992	11-Akbal	3	Dec 17 1992	1-Chuen	8
Aug 4 1992	9-Cib	8	Oct 11 1992	12-Kan	4	Dec 18 1992	2-Eb	9
Aug 5 1992	10-Caban	9	Oct 12 1992	13-Chicchan	5	Dec 19 1992	3-Ben	1
Aug 6 1992	11-Etz'nab	1	Oct 13 1992	1-Cimi	6	Dec 20 1992	4-Ix	2
Aug 7 1992	12-Cauac	2	Oct 14 1992	2-Manik	7	Dec 21 1992	5-Men	3
Aug 8 1992	13-Ahau	3	Oct 15 1992	3-Lamat	8	Dec 22 1992	6-Cib	4
Aug 9 1992	1-Imix	4	Oct 16 1992	4-Muluc	9	Dec 23 1992	7-Caban	5
Aug 10 1992	2-Ik	5	Oct 17 1992	5-Oc	1	Dec 24 1992	8-Etz'nab	6
Aug 11 1992	3-Akbal	6	Oct 18 1992	6-Chuen	2	Dec 25 1992	9-Cauac	7
Aug 12 1992	4-Kan	7	Oct 19 1992	7-Eb	3	Dec 26 1992	10-Ahau	8
Aug 13 1992	5-Chicchan	8	Oct 20 1992	8-Ben	4	Dec 27 1992	11-Imix	9
Aug 14 1992	6-Cimi	9	Oct 21 1992	9-Ix	5	Dec 28 1992	12-Ik	1
Aug 15 1992	7-Manik	1	Oct 22 1992	10-Men	6	Dec 29 1992	13-Akbal	2
Aug 16 1992	8-Lamat	2	Oct 23 1992	11-Cib	7	Dec 30 1992	1-Kan	3
Aug 17 1992	9-Muluc	3	Oct 24 1992	12-Caban	8	Dec 31 1992	2-Chicchan	4
Aug 18 1992	10-Oc	4	Oct 25 1992	13-Etz'nab	9	Jan 1 1993	3-Cimi	5
Aug 19 1992	11-Chuen	5	Oct 26 1992	1-Cauac	1	Jan 2 1993	4-Manik	6
Aug 20 1992	12-Eb	6	Oct 27 1992	2-Ahau	2	Jan 3 1993	5-Lamat	7
Aug 21 1992	13-Ben	7	Oct 28 1992	3-Imix	3	Jan 4 1993	6-Muluc	8
Aug 22 1992	1-Ix	8	Oct 29 1992	4-Ik	4	Jan 5 1993	7-Oc	9
Aug 23 1992	2-Men	9	Oct 30 1992	5-Akbal	5	Jan 6 1993	8-Chuen	1
Aug 24 1992	3-Cib	1	Oct 31 1992	6-Kan	6	Jan 7 1993	9-Eb	2
Aug 25 1992	4-Caban	2	Nov 1 1992	7-Chicchan	7	Jan 8 1993	10-Ben	3
Aug 26 1992	5-Etz'nab	3	Nov 2 1992	8-Cimi	8	Jan 9 1993	11-Ix	4
Aug 27 1992	6-Cauac	4	Nov 3 1992	9-Manik	9	Jan 10 1993	12-Men	5
Aug 28 1992	7-Ahau	5	Nov 4 1992	10-Lamat	1	Jan 11 1993	13-Cib	6
Aug 29 1992	8-Imix	6	Nov 5 1992	11-Muluc	2	Jan 12 1993	1-Caban	7
Aug 30 1992	9-Ik	7	Nov 6 1992	12-Oc	3	Jan 13 1993	2-Etz'nab	8
Aug 31 1992	10-Akbal	8	Nov 7 1992	13-Chuen	4	Jan 14 1993	3-Cauac	9
Sep 1 1992	11-Kan	9	Nov 8 1992	1-Eb	5	Jan 15 1993	4-Ahau	1
Sep 2 1992	12-Chicchan	1	Nov 9 1992	2-Ben	6	Jan 16 1993	5-Imix	2
Sep 3 1992	13-Cimi	2	Nov 10 1992	3-Ix	7	Jan 17 1993	6-Ik	3
Sep 4 1992	1-Manik	3	Nov 11 1992	4-Men	8	Jan 18 1993	7-Akbal	4
Sep 5 1992	2-Lamat	4	Nov 12 1992	5-Cib	9	Jan 19 1993	8-Kan	5
Sep 6 1992	3-Muluc	5	Nov 13 1992	6-Caban	1	Jan 20 1993	9-Chicchan	6
Sep 7 1992	4-Oc	6	Nov 14 1992	7-Etz'nab	2	Jan 21 1993	10-Cimi	7
Sep 8 1992	5-Chuen	7	Nov 15 1992	8-Cauac	3	Jan 22 1993	11-Manik	8
Sep 9 1992	6-Eb	8	Nov 16 1992	9-Ahau	4	Jan 23 1993	12-Lamat	9
Sep 10 1992	7-Ben	9	Nov 17 1992	10-Imix	5	Jan 24 1993	13-Muluc	1
Sep 11 1992	8-Ix	1	Nov 18 1992	11-Ik	6	Jan 25 1993	1-Oc	2
Sep 12 1992	9-Men	2	Nov 19 1992	12-Akbal	7	Jan 26 1993	2-Chuen	3
Sep 13 1992	10-Cib	3	Nov 20 1992	13-Kan	8	Jan 27 1993	3-Eb	4
Sep 14 1992	11-Caban	4	Nov 21 1992	1-Chicchan	9	Jan 28 1993	4-Ben	5
Sep 15 1992	12-Etz'nab	5	Nov 22 1992	2-Cimi	1	Jan 29 1993	5-Ix	6
Sep 16 1992	13-Cauac	6	Nov 23 1992	3-Manik	2	Jan 30 1993	6-Men	7
Sep 17 1992	1-Ahau	7	Nov 24 1992	4-Lamat	3	Jan 31 1993	7-Cib	8
Sep 18 1992	2-Imix	8	Nov 25 1992	5-Muluc	4	Feb 1 1993	8-Caban	9

Date	Day-Sign	L	Date	Day-Sign	L	Date	Day-Sign	L
Feb 2 1993	9-Etz'nab	1	Apr 11 1993	12-Cimi	6	Jun 18 1993	2-Ix	2
Feb 3 1993	10-Cauac	2	Apr 12 1993	13-Manik	7	Jun 19 1993	3-Men	3
Feb 4 1993	11-Ahau	3	Apr 13 1993	**1-Lamat**	8	Jun 20 1993	4-Cib	4
Feb 5 1993	*12-Imix*	4	Apr 14 1993	2-Muluc	9	Jun 21 1993	5-Caban	5
Feb 6 1993	13-Ik	5	Apr 15 1993	3-Oc	1	Jun 22 1993	6-Etz'nab	6
Feb 7 1993	**1-Akbal**	6	Apr 16 1993	4-Chuen	2	Jun 23 1993	7-Cauac	7
Feb 8 1993	2-Kan	7	Apr 17 1993	5-Eb	3	Jun 24 1993	8-Ahau	8
Feb 9 1993	3-Chicchan	8	Apr 18 1993	6-Ben	4	Jun 25 1993	*9-Imix*	9
Feb 10 1993	4-Cimi	9	Apr 19 1993	7-Ix	5	Jun 26 1993	10-Ik	1
Feb 11 1993	5-Manik	1	Apr 20 1993	8-Men	6	Jun 27 1993	11-Akbal	2
Feb 12 1993	6-Lamat	2	Apr 21 1993	9-Cib	7	Jun 28 1993	12-Kan	3
Feb 13 1993	7-Muluc	3	Apr 22 1993	10-Caban	8	Jun 29 1993	13-Chicchan	4
Feb 14 1993	8-Oc	4	Apr 23 1993	11-Etz'nab	9	Jun 30 1993	**1-Cimi**	5
Feb 15 1993	9-Chuen	5	Apr 24 1993	12-Cauac	1	Jul 1 1993	2-Manik	6
Feb 16 1993	10-Eb	6	Apr 25 1993	13-Ahau	2	Jul 2 1993	3-Lamat	7
Feb 17 1993	11-Ben	7	Apr 26 1993	**1-Imix**	3	Jul 3 1993	4-Muluc	8
Feb 18 1993	12-Ix	8	Apr 27 1993	2-Ik	4	Jul 4 1993	5-Oc	9
Feb 19 1993	13-Men	9	Apr 28 1993	3-Akbal	5	Jul 5 1993	6-Chuen	1
Feb 20 1993	**1-Cib**	1	Apr 29 1993	4-Kan	6	Jul 6 1993	7-Eb	2
Feb 21 1993	2-Caban	2	Apr 30 1993	5-Chicchan	7	Jul 7 1993	8-Ben	3
Feb 22 1993	3-Etz'nab	3	May 1 1993	6-Cimi	8	Jul 8 1993	9-Ix	4
Feb 23 1993	4-Cauac	4	May 2 1993	7-Manik	9	Jul 9 1993	10-Men	5
Feb 24 1993	5-Ahau	5	May 3 1993	8-Lamat	1	Jul 10 1993	11-Cib	6
Feb 25 1993	*6-Imix*	6	May 4 1993	9-Muluc	2	Jul 11 1993	12-Caban	7
Feb 26 1993	7-Ik	7	May 5 1993	10-Oc	3	Jul 12 1993	13-Etz'nab	8
Feb 27 1993	8-Akbal	8	May 6 1993	11-Chuen	4	Jul 13 1993	**1-Cauac**	9
Feb 28 1993	9-Kan	9	May 7 1993	12-Eb	5	Jul 14 1993	2-Ahau	1
Mar 1 1993	10-Chicchan	1	May 8 1993	13-Ben	6	Jul 15 1993	*3-Imix*	2
Mar 2 1993	11-Cimi	2	May 9 1993	**1-Ix**	7	Jul 16 1993	4-Ik	3
Mar 3 1993	12-Manik	3	May 10 1993	2-Men	8	Jul 17 1993	5-Akbal	4
Mar 4 1993	13-Lamat	4	May 11 1993	3-Cib	9	Jul 18 1993	6-Kan	5
Mar 5 1993	**1-Muluc**	5	May 12 1993	4-Caban	1	Jul 19 1993	7-Chicchan	6
Mar 6 1993	2-Oc	6	May 13 1993	5-Etz'nab	2	Jul 20 1993	8-Cimi	7
Mar 7 1993	3-Chuen	7	May 14 1993	6-Cauac	3	Jul 21 1993	9-Manik	8
Mar 8 1993	4-Eb	8	May 15 1993	7-Ahau	4	Jul 22 1993	10-Lamat	9
Mar 9 1993	5-Ben	9	May 16 1993	*8-Imix*	5	Jul 23 1993	11-Muluc	1
Mar 10 1993	6-Ix	1	May 17 1993	9-Ik	6	Jul 24 1993	12-Oc	2
Mar 11 1993	7-Men	2	May 18 1993	10-Akbal	7	Jul 25 1993	13-Chuen	3
Mar 12 1993	8-Cib	3	May 19 1993	11-Kan	8	Jul 26 1993	**1-Eb**	4
Mar 13 1993	9-Caban	4	May 20 1993	12-Chicchan	9	Jul 27 1993	2-Ben	5
Mar 14 1993	10-Etz'nab	5	May 21 1993	13-Cimi	1	Jul 28 1993	3-Ix	6
Mar 15 1993	11-Cauac	6	May 22 1993	**1-Manik**	2	Jul 29 1993	4-Men	7
Mar 16 1993	12-Ahau	7	May 23 1993	2-Lamat	3	Jul 30 1993	5-Cib	8
Mar 17 1993	*13-Imix*	8	May 24 1993	3-Muluc	4	Jul 31 1993	6-Caban	9
Mar 18 1993	**1-Ik**	9	May 25 1993	4-Oc	5	Aug 1 1993	7-Etz'nab	1
Mar 19 1993	2-Akbal	1	May 26 1993	5-Chuen	6	Aug 2 1993	8-Cauac	2
Mar 20 1993	3-Kan	2	May 27 1993	6-Eb	7	Aug 3 1993	9-Ahau	3
Mar 21 1993	4-Chicchan	3	May 28 1993	7-Ben	8	Aug 4 1993	*10-Imix*	4
Mar 22 1993	5-Cimi	4	May 29 1993	8-Ix	9	Aug 5 1993	11-Ik	5
Mar 23 1993	6-Manik	5	May 30 1993	9-Men	1	Aug 6 1993	12-Akbal	6
Mar 24 1993	7-Lamat	6	May 31 1993	10-Cib	2	Aug 7 1993	13-Kan	7
Mar 25 1993	8-Muluc	7	Jun 1 1993	11-Caban	3	Aug 8 1993	**1-Chicchan**	8
Mar 26 1993	9-Oc	8	Jun 2 1993	12-Etz'nab	4	Aug 9 1993	2-Cimi	9
Mar 27 1993	10-Chuen	9	Jun 3 1993	13-Cauac	5	Aug 10 1993	3-Manik	1
Mar 28 1993	11-Eb	1	Jun 4 1993	**1-Ahau**	6	Aug 11 1993	4-Lamat	2
Mar 29 1993	12-Ben	2	Jun 5 1993	*2-Imix*	7	Aug 12 1993	5-Muluc	3
Mar 30 1993	13-Ix	3	Jun 6 1993	3-Ik	8	Aug 13 1993	6-Oc	4
Mar 31 1993	**1-Men**	4	Jun 7 1993	4-Akbal	9	Aug 14 1993	7-Chuen	5
Apr 1 1993	2-Cib	5	Jun 8 1993	5-Kan	1	Aug 15 1993	8-Eb	6
Apr 2 1993	3-Caban	6	Jun 9 1993	6-Chicchan	2	Aug 16 1993	9-Ben	7
Apr 3 1993	4-Etz'nab	7	Jun 10 1993	7-Cimi	3	Aug 17 1993	10-Ix	8
Apr 4 1993	5-Cauac	8	Jun 11 1993	8-Manik	4	Aug 18 1993	11-Men	9
Apr 5 1993	6-Ahau	9	Jun 12 1993	9-Lamat	5	Aug 19 1993	12-Cib	1
Apr 6 1993	*7-Imix*	1	Jun 13 1993	10-Muluc	6	Aug 20 1993	13-Caban	2
Apr 7 1993	8-Ik	2	Jun 14 1993	11-Oc	7	Aug 21 1993	**1-Etz'nab**	3
Apr 8 1993	9-Akbal	3	Jun 15 1993	12-Chuen	8	Aug 22 1993	2-Cauac	4
Apr 9 1993	10-Kan	4	Jun 16 1993	13-Eb	9	Aug 23 1993	3-Ahau	5
Apr 10 1993	11-Chicchan	5	Jun 17 1993	**1-Ben**	1	Aug 24 1993	4-Imix	6

Date	Day-Sign	L	Date	Day-Sign	L	Date	Day-Sign	L
Aug 25 1993	5-Ik	7	Nov 1 1993	8-Oc	3	Jan 8 1994	11-Etz'nab	8
Aug 26 1993	6-Akbal	8	Nov 2 1993	9-Chuen	4	Jan 9 1994	12-Cauac	9
Aug 27 1993	7-Kan	9	Nov 3 1993	10-Eb	5	Jan 10 1994	13-Ahau	1
Aug 28 1993	8-Chicchan	1	Nov 4 1993	11-Ben	6	Jan 11 1994	1-Imix	2
Aug 29 1993	9-Cimi	2	Nov 5 1993	12-Ix	7	Jan 12 1994	2-Ik	3
Aug 30 1993	10-Manik	3	Nov 6 1993	13-Men	8	Jan 13 1994	3-Akbal	4
Aug 31 1993	11-Lamat	4	Nov 7 1993	1-Cib	9	Jan 14 1994	4-Kan	5
Sep 1 1993	12-Muluc	5	Nov 8 1993	2-Caban	1	Jan 15 1994	5-Chicchan	6
Sep 2 1993	13-Oc	6	Nov 9 1993	3-Etz'nab	2	Jan 16 1994	6-Cimi	7
Sep 3 1993	1-Chuen	7	Nov 10 1993	4-Cauac	3	Jan 17 1994	7-Manik	8
Sep 4 1993	2-Eb	8	Nov 11 1993	5-Ahau	4	Jan 18 1994	8-Lamat	9
Sep 5 1993	3-Ben	9	Nov 12 1993	6-Imix	5	Jan 19 1994	9-Muluc	1
Sep 6 1993	4-Ix	1	Nov 13 1993	7-Ik	6	Jan 20 1994	10-Oc	2
Sep 7 1993	5-Men	2	Nov 14 1993	8-Akbal	7	Jan 21 1994	11-Chuen	3
Sep 8 1993	6-Cib	3	Nov 15 1993	9-Kan	8	Jan 22 1994	12-Eb	4
Sep 9 1993	7-Caban	4	Nov 16 1993	10-Chicchan	9	Jan 23 1994	13-Ben	5
Sep 10 1993	8-Etz'nab	5	Nov 17 1993	11-Cimi	1	Jan 24 1994	1-Ix	6
Sep 11 1993	9-Cauac	6	Nov 18 1993	12-Manik	2	Jan 25 1994	2-Men	7
Sep 12 1993	10-Ahau	7	Nov 19 1993	13-Lamat	3	Jan 26 1994	3-Cib	8
Sep 13 1993	11-Imix	8	Nov 20 1993	1-Muluc	4	Jan 27 1994	4-Caban	9
Sep 14 1993	12-Ik	9	Nov 21 1993	2-Oc	5	Jan 28 1994	5-Etz'nab	1
Sep 15 1993	13-Akbal	1	Nov 22 1993	3-Chuen	6	Jan 29 1994	6-Cauac	2
Sep 16 1993	1-Kan	2	Nov 23 1993	4-Eb	7	Jan 30 1994	7-Ahau	3
Sep 17 1993	2-Chicchan	3	Nov 24 1993	5-Ben	8	Jan 31 1994	8-Imix	4
Sep 18 1993	3-Cimi	4	Nov 25 1993	6-Ix	9	Feb 1 1994	9-Ik	5
Sep 19 1993	4-Manik	5	Nov 26 1993	7-Men	1	Feb 2 1994	10-Akbal	6
Sep 20 1993	5-Lamat	6	Nov 27 1993	8-Cib	2	Feb 3 1994	11-Kan	7
Sep 21 1993	6-Muluc	7	Nov 28 1993	9-Caban	3	Feb 4 1994	12-Chicchan	8
Sep 22 1993	7-Oc	8	Nov 29 1993	10-Etz'nab	4	Feb 5 1994	13-Cimi	9
Sep 23 1993	8-Chuen	9	Nov 30 1993	11-Cauac	5	Feb 6 1994	1-Manik	1
Sep 24 1993	9-Eb	1	Dec 1 1993	12-Ahau	6	Feb 7 1994	2-Lamat	2
Sep 25 1993	10-Ben	2	Dec 2 1993	13-Imix	7	Feb 8 1994	3-Muluc	3
Sep 26 1993	11-Ix	3	Dec 3 1993	1-Ik	8	Feb 9 1994	4-Oc	4
Sep 27 1993	12-Men	4	Dec 4 1993	2-Akbal	9	Feb 10 1994	5-Chuen	5
Sep 28 1993	13-Cib	5	Dec 5 1993	3-Kan	1	Feb 11 1994	6-Eb	6
Sep 29 1993	1-Caban	6	Dec 6 1993	4-Chicchan	2	Feb 12 1994	7-Ben	7
Sep 30 1993	2-Etz'nab	7	Dec 7 1993	5-Cimi	3	Feb 13 1994	8-Ix	8
Oct 1 1993	3-Cauac	8	Dec 8 1993	6-Manik	4	Feb 14 1994	9-Men	9
Oct 2 1993	4-Ahau	9	Dec 9 1993	7-Lamat	5	Feb 15 1994	10-Cib	1
Oct 3 1993	5-Imix	1	Dec 10 1993	8-Muluc	6	Feb 16 1994	11-Caban	2
Oct 4 1993	6-Ik	2	Dec 11 1993	9-Oc	7	Feb 17 1994	12-Etz'nab	3
Oct 5 1993	7-Akbal	3	Dec 12 1993	10-Chuen	8	Feb 18 1994	13-Cauac	4
Oct 6 1993	8-Kan	4	Dec 13 1993	11-Eb	9	Feb 19 1994	1-Ahau	5
Oct 7 1993	9-Chicchan	5	Dec 14 1993	12-Ben	1	Feb 20 1994	2-Imix	6
Oct 8 1993	10-Cimi	6	Dec 15 1993	13-Ix	2	Feb 21 1994	3-Ik	7
Oct 9 1993	11-Manik	7	Dec 16 1993	1-Men	3	Feb 22 1994	4-Akbal	8
Oct 10 1993	12-Lamat	8	Dec 17 1993	2-Cib	4	Feb 23 1994	5-Kan	9
Oct 11 1993	13-Muluc	9	Dec 18 1993	3-Caban	5	Feb 24 1994	6-Chicchan	1
Oct 12 1993	1-Oc	1	Dec 19 1993	4-Etz'nab	6	Feb 25 1994	7-Cimi	2
Oct 13 1993	2-Chuen	2	Dec 20 1993	5-Cauac	7	Feb 26 1994	8-Manik	3
Oct 14 1993	3-Eb	3	Dec 21 1993	6-Ahau	8	Feb 27 1994	9-Lamat	4
Oct 15 1993	4-Ben	4	Dec 22 1993	7-Imix	9	Feb 28 1994	10-Muluc	5
Oct 16 1993	5-Ix	5	Dec 23 1993	8-Ik	1	Mar 1 1994	11-Oc	6
Oct 17 1993	6-Men	6	Dec 24 1993	9-Akbal	2	Mar 2 1994	12-Chuen	7
Oct 18 1993	7-Cib	7	Dec 25 1993	10-Kan	3	Mar 3 1994	13-Eb	8
Oct 19 1993	8-Caban	8	Dec 26 1993	11-Chicchan	4	Mar 4 1994	1-Ben	9
Oct 20 1993	9-Etz'nab	9	Dec 27 1993	12-Cimi	5	Mar 5 1994	2-Ix	1
Oct 21 1993	10-Cauac	1	Dec 28 1993	13-Manik	6	Mar 6 1994	3-Men	2
Oct 22 1993	11-Ahau	2	Dec 29 1993	1-Lamat	7	Mar 7 1994	4-Cib	3
Oct 23 1993	12-Imix	3	Dec 30 1993	2-Muluc	8	Mar 8 1994	5-Caban	4
Oct 24 1993	13-Ik	4	Dec 31 1993	3-Oc	9	Mar 9 1994	6-Etz'nab	5
Oct 25 1993	1-Akbal	5	Jan 1 1994	4-Chuen	1	Mar 10 1994	7-Cauac	6
Oct 26 1993	2-Kan	6	Jan 2 1994	5-Eb	2	Mar 11 1994	8-Ahau	7
Oct 27 1993	3-Chicchan	7	Jan 3 1994	6-Ben	3	Mar 12 1994	9-Imix	8
Oct 28 1993	4-Cimi	8	Jan 4 1994	7-Ix	4	Mar 13 1994	10-Ik	9
Oct 29 1993	5-Manik	9	Jan 5 1994	8-Men	5	Mar 14 1994	11-Akbal	1
Oct 30 1993	6-Lamat	1	Jan 6 1994	9-Cib	6	Mar 15 1994	12-Kan	2
Oct 31 1993	7-Muluc	2	Jan 7 1994	10-Caban	7	Mar 16 1994	13-Chicchan	3

Date	Day-Sign	L	Date	Day-Sign	L	Date	Day-Sign	L
Mar 17 1994	**1-Cimi**	4	May 24 1994	4-Ix	9	Jul 31 1994	7-Ik	5
Mar 18 1994	2-Manik	5	May 25 1994	5-Men	1	Aug 1 1994	8-Akbal	6
Mar 19 1994	3-Lamat	6	May 26 1994	6-Cib	2	Aug 2 1994	9-Kan	7
Mar 20 1994	4-Muluc	7	May 27 1994	7-Caban	3	Aug 3 1994	10-Chicchan	8
Mar 21 1994	5-Oc	8	May 28 1994	8-Etz'nab	4	Aug 4 1994	11-Cimi	9
Mar 22 1994	6-Chuen	9	May 29 1994	9-Cauac	5	Aug 5 1994	12-Manik	1
Mar 23 1994	7-Eb	1	May 30 1994	10-Ahau	6	Aug 6 1994	13-Lamat	2
Mar 24 1994	8-Ben	2	May 31 1994	*11-Imix*	7	Aug 7 1994	**1-Muluc**	3
Mar 25 1994	9-Ix	3	Jun 1 1994	12-Ik	8	Aug 8 1994	2-Oc	4
Mar 26 1994	10-Men	4	Jun 2 1994	13-Akbal	9	Aug 9 1994	3-Chuen	5
Mar 27 1994	11-Cib	5	Jun 3 1994	**1-Kan**	1	Aug 10 1994	4-Eb	6
Mar 28 1994	12-Caban	6	Jun 4 1994	2-Chicchan	2	Aug 11 1994	5-Ben	7
Mar 29 1994	13-Etz'nab	7	Jun 5 1994	3-Cimi	3	Aug 12 1994	6-Ix	8
Mar 30 1994	**1-Cauac**	8	Jun 6 1994	4-Manik	4	Aug 13 1994	7-Men	9
Mar 31 1994	2-Ahau	9	Jun 7 1994	5-Lamat	5	Aug 14 1994	8-Cib	1
Apr 1 1994	*3-Imix*	1	Jun 8 1994	6-Muluc	6	Aug 15 1994	9-Caban	2
Apr 2 1994	4-Ik	2	Jun 9 1994	7-Oc	7	Aug 16 1994	10-Etz'nab	3
Apr 3 1994	5-Akbal	3	Jun 10 1994	8-Chuen	8	Aug 17 1994	11-Cauac	4
Apr 4 1994	6-Kan	4	Jun 11 1994	9-Eb	9	Aug 18 1994	12-Ahau	5
Apr 5 1994	7-Chicchan	5	Jun 12 1994	10-Ben	1	Aug 19 1994	*13-Imix*	6
Apr 6 1994	8-Cimi	6	Jun 13 1994	11-Ix	2	Aug 20 1994	**1-Ik**	7
Apr 7 1994	9-Manik	7	Jun 14 1994	12-Men	3	Aug 21 1994	2-Akbal	8
Apr 8 1994	10-Lamat	8	Jun 15 1994	13-Cib	4	Aug 22 1994	3-Kan	9
Apr 9 1994	11-Muluc	9	Jun 16 1994	**1-Caban**	5	Aug 23 1994	4-Chicchan	1
Apr 10 1994	12-Oc	1	Jun 17 1994	2-Etz'nab	6	Aug 24 1994	5-Cimi	2
Apr 11 1994	13-Chuen	2	Jun 18 1994	3-Cauac	7	Aug 25 1994	6-Manik	3
Apr 12 1994	**1-Eb**	3	Jun 19 1994	4-Ahau	8	Aug 26 1994	7-Lamat	4
Apr 13 1994	2-Ben	4	Jun 20 1994	*5-Imix*	9	Aug 27 1994	8-Muluc	5
Apr 14 1994	3-Ix	5	Jun 21 1994	6-Ik	1	Aug 28 1994	9-Oc	6
Apr 15 1994	4-Men	6	Jun 22 1994	7-Akbal	2	Aug 29 1994	10-Chuen	7
Apr 16 1994	5-Cib	7	Jun 23 1994	8-Kan	3	Aug 30 1994	11-Eb	8
Apr 17 1994	6-Caban	8	Jun 24 1994	9-Chicchan	4	Aug 31 1994	12-Ben	9
Apr 18 1994	7-Etz'nab	9	Jun 25 1994	10-Cimi	5	Sep 1 1994	13-Ix	1
Apr 19 1994	8-Cauac	1	Jun 26 1994	11-Manik	6	Sep 2 1994	**1-Men**	2
Apr 20 1994	9-Ahau	2	Jun 27 1994	12-Lamat	7	Sep 3 1994	2-Cib	3
Apr 21 1994	*10-Imix*	3	Jun 28 1994	13-Muluc	8	Sep 4 1994	3-Caban	4
Apr 22 1994	11-Ik	4	Jun 29 1994	**1-Oc**	9	Sep 5 1994	4-Etz'nab	5
Apr 23 1994	12-Akbal	5	Jun 30 1994	2-Chuen	1	Sep 6 1994	5-Cauac	6
Apr 24 1994	13-Kan	6	Jul 1 1994	3-Eb	2	Sep 7 1994	6-Ahau	7
Apr 25 1994	**1-Chicchan**	7	Jul 2 1994	4-Ben	3	Sep 8 1994	*7-Imix*	8
Apr 26 1994	2-Cimi	8	Jul 3 1994	5-Ix	4	Sep 9 1994	8-Ik	9
Apr 27 1994	3-Manik	9	Jul 4 1994	6-Men	5	Sep 10 1994	9-Akbal	1
Apr 28 1994	4-Lamat	1	Jul 5 1994	7-Cib	6	Sep 11 1994	10-Kan	2
Apr 29 1994	5-Muluc	2	Jul 6 1994	8-Caban	7	Sep 12 1994	11-Chicchan	3
Apr 30 1994	6-Oc	3	Jul 7 1994	9-Etz'nab	8	Sep 13 1994	12-Cimi	4
May 1 1994	7-Chuen	4	Jul 8 1994	10-Cauac	9	Sep 14 1994	13-Manik	5
May 2 1994	8-Eb	5	Jul 9 1994	11-Ahau	1	Sep 15 1994	**1-Lamat**	6
May 3 1994	9-Ben	6	Jul 10 1994	*12-Imix*	2	Sep 16 1994	2-Muluc	7
May 4 1994	10-Ix	7	Jul 11 1994	13-Ik	3	Sep 17 1994	3-Oc	8
May 5 1994	11-Men	8	Jul 12 1994	**1-Akbal**	4	Sep 18 1994	4-Chuen	9
May 6 1994	12-Cib	9	Jul 13 1994	2-Kan	5	Sep 19 1994	5-Eb	1
May 7 1994	13-Caban	1	Jul 14 1994	3-Chicchan	6	Sep 20 1994	6-Ben	2
May 8 1994	**1-Etz'nab**	2	Jul 15 1994	4-Cimi	7	Sep 21 1994	7-Ix	3
May 9 1994	2-Cauac	3	Jul 16 1994	5-Manik	8	Sep 22 1994	8-Men	4
May 10 1994	3-Ahau	4	Jul 17 1994	6-Lamat	9	Sep 23 1994	9-Cib	5
May 11 1994	*4-Imix*	5	Jul 18 1994	7-Muluc	1	Sep 24 1994	10-Caban	6
May 12 1994	5-Ik	6	Jul 19 1994	8-Oc	2	Sep 25 1994	11-Etz'nab	7
May 13 1994	6-Akbal	7	Jul 20 1994	9-Chuen	3	Sep 26 1994	12-Cauac	8
May 14 1994	7-Kan	8	Jul 21 1994	10-Eb	4	Sep 27 1994	13-Ahau	9
May 15 1994	8-Chicchan	9	Jul 22 1994	11-Ben	5	Sep 28 1994	**1-Imix**	1
May 16 1994	9-Cimi	1	Jul 23 1994	12-Ix	6	Sep 29 1994	2-Ik	2
May 17 1994	10-Manik	2	Jul 24 1994	13-Men	7	Sep 30 1994	3-Akbal	3
May 18 1994	11-Lamat	3	Jul 25 1994	**1-Cib**	8	Oct 1 1994	4-Kan	4
May 19 1994	12-Muluc	4	Jul 26 1994	2-Caban	9	Oct 2 1994	5-Chicchan	5
May 20 1994	13-Oc	5	Jul 27 1994	3-Etz'nab	1	Oct 3 1994	6-Cimi	6
May 21 1994	**1-Chuen**	6	Jul 28 1994	4-Cauac	2	Oct 4 1994	7-Manik	7
May 22 1994	2-Eb	7	Jul 29 1994	5-Ahau	3	Oct 5 1994	8-Lamat	8
May 23 1994	3-Ben	8	Jul 30 1994	*6-Imix*	4	Oct 6 1994	9-Muluc	9

Date	Day-Sign	L
Oct 7 1994	10-Oc	1
Oct 8 1994	11-Chuen	2
Oct 9 1994	12-Eb	3
Oct 10 1994	13-Ben	4
Oct 11 1994	1-Ix	5
Oct 12 1994	2-Men	6
Oct 13 1994	3-Cib	7
Oct 14 1994	4-Caban	8
Oct 15 1994	5-Etz'nab	9
Oct 16 1994	6-Cauac	1
Oct 17 1994	7-Ahau	2
Oct 18 1994	8-Imix	3
Oct 19 1994	9-Ik	4
Oct 20 1994	10-Akbal	5
Oct 21 1994	11-Kan	6
Oct 22 1994	12-Chicchan	7
Oct 23 1994	13-Cimi	8
Oct 24 1994	1-Manik	9
Oct 25 1994	2-Lamat	1
Oct 26 1994	3-Muluc	2
Oct 27 1994	4-Oc	3
Oct 28 1994	5-Chuen	4
Oct 29 1994	6-Eb	5
Oct 30 1994	7-Ben	6
Oct 31 1994	8-Ix	7
Nov 1 1994	9-Men	8
Nov 2 1994	10-Cib	9
Nov 3 1994	11-Caban	1
Nov 4 1994	12-Etz'nab	2
Nov 5 1994	13-Cauac	3
Nov 6 1994	1-Ahau	4
Nov 7 1994	2-Imix	5
Nov 8 1994	3-Ik	6
Nov 9 1994	4-Akbal	7
Nov 10 1994	5-Kan	8
Nov 11 1994	6-Chicchan	9
Nov 12 1994	7-Cimi	1
Nov 13 1994	8-Manik	2
Nov 14 1994	9-Lamat	3
Nov 15 1994	10-Muluc	4
Nov 16 1994	11-Oc	5
Nov 17 1994	12-Chuen	6
Nov 18 1994	13-Eb	7
Nov 19 1994	1-Ben	8
Nov 20 1994	2-Ix	9
Nov 21 1994	3-Men	1
Nov 22 1994	4-Cib	2
Nov 23 1994	5-Caban	3
Nov 24 1994	6-Etz'nab	4
Nov 25 1994	7-Cauac	5
Nov 26 1994	8-Ahau	6
Nov 27 1994	9-Imix	7
Nov 28 1994	10-Ik	8
Nov 29 1994	11-Akbal	9
Nov 30 1994	12-Kan	1
Dec 1 1994	13-Chicchan	2
Dec 2 1994	1-Cimi	3
Dec 3 1994	2-Manik	4
Dec 4 1994	3-Lamat	5
Dec 5 1994	4-Muluc	6
Dec 6 1994	5-Oc	7
Dec 7 1994	6-Chuen	8
Dec 8 1994	7-Eb	9
Dec 9 1994	8-Ben	1
Dec 10 1994	9-Ix	2
Dec 11 1994	10-Men	3
Dec 12 1994	11-Cib	4
Dec 13 1994	12-Caban	5

Date	Day-Sign	L
Dec 14 1994	13-Etz'nab	6
Dec 15 1994	1-Cauac	7
Dec 16 1994	2-Ahau	8
Dec 17 1994	3-Imix	9
Dec 18 1994	4-Ik	1
Dec 19 1994	5-Akbal	2
Dec 20 1994	6-Kan	3
Dec 21 1994	7-Chicchan	4
Dec 22 1994	8-Cimi	5
Dec 23 1994	9-Manik	6
Dec 24 1994	10-Lamat	7
Dec 25 1994	11-Muluc	8
Dec 26 1994	12-Oc	9
Dec 27 1994	13-Chuen	1
Dec 28 1994	1-Eb	2
Dec 29 1994	2-Ben	3
Dec 30 1994	3-Ix	4
Dec 31 1994	4-Men	5
Jan 1 1995	5-Cib	6
Jan 2 1995	6-Caban	7
Jan 3 1995	7-Etz'nab	8
Jan 4 1995	8-Cauac	9
Jan 5 1995	9-Ahau	1
Jan 6 1995	10-Imix	2
Jan 7 1995	11-Ik	3
Jan 8 1995	12-Akbal	4
Jan 9 1995	13-Kan	5
Jan 10 1995	1-Chicchan	6
Jan 11 1995	2-Cimi	7
Jan 12 1995	3-Manik	8
Jan 13 1995	4-Lamat	9
Jan 14 1995	5-Muluc	1
Jan 15 1995	6-Oc	2
Jan 16 1995	7-Chuen	3
Jan 17 1995	8-Eb	4
Jan 18 1995	9-Ben	5
Jan 19 1995	10-Ix	6
Jan 20 1995	11-Men	7
Jan 21 1995	12-Cib	8
Jan 22 1995	13-Caban	9
Jan 23 1995	1-Etz'nab	1
Jan 24 1995	2-Cauac	2
Jan 25 1995	3-Ahau	3
Jan 26 1995	4-Imix	4
Jan 27 1995	5-Ik	5
Jan 28 1995	6-Akbal	6
Jan 29 1995	7-Kan	7
Jan 30 1995	8-Chicchan	8
Jan 31 1995	9-Cimi	9
Feb 1 1995	10-Manik	1
Feb 2 1995	11-Lamat	2
Feb 3 1995	12-Muluc	3
Feb 4 1995	13-Oc	4
Feb 5 1995	1-Chuen	5
Feb 6 1995	2-Eb	6
Feb 7 1995	3-Ben	7
Feb 8 1995	4-Ix	8
Feb 9 1995	5-Men	9
Feb 10 1995	6-Cib	1
Feb 11 1995	7-Caban	2
Feb 12 1995	8-Etz'nab	3
Feb 13 1995	9-Cauac	4
Feb 14 1995	10-Ahau	5
Feb 15 1995	11-Imix	6
Feb 16 1995	12-Ik	7
Feb 17 1995	13-Akbal	8
Feb 18 1995	1-Kan	9
Feb 19 1995	2-Chicchan	1

Date	Day-Sign	L
Feb 20 1995	3-Cimi	2
Feb 21 1995	4-Manik	3
Feb 22 1995	5-Lamat	4
Feb 23 1995	6-Muluc	5
Feb 24 1995	7-Oc	6
Feb 25 1995	8-Chuen	7
Feb 26 1995	9-Eb	8
Feb 27 1995	10-Ben	9
Feb 28 1995	11-Ix	1
Mar 1 1995	12-Men	2
Mar 2 1995	13-Cib	3
Mar 3 1995	1-Caban	4
Mar 4 1995	2-Etz'nab	5
Mar 5 1995	3-Cauac	6
Mar 6 1995	4-Ahau	7
Mar 7 1995	5-Imix	8
Mar 8 1995	6-Ik	9
Mar 9 1995	7-Akbal	1
Mar 10 1995	8-Kan	2
Mar 11 1995	9-Chicchan	3
Mar 12 1995	10-Cimi	4
Mar 13 1995	11-Manik	5
Mar 14 1995	12-Lamat	6
Mar 15 1995	13-Muluc	7
Mar 16 1995	1-Oc	8
Mar 17 1995	2-Chuen	9
Mar 18 1995	3-Eb	1
Mar 19 1995	4-Ben	2
Mar 20 1995	5-Ix	3
Mar 21 1995	6-Men	4
Mar 22 1995	7-Cib	5
Mar 23 1995	8-Caban	6
Mar 24 1995	9-Etz'nab	7
Mar 25 1995	10-Cauac	8
Mar 26 1995	11-Ahau	9
Mar 27 1995	12-Imix	1
Mar 28 1995	13-Ik	2
Mar 29 1995	1-Akbal	3
Mar 30 1995	2-Kan	4
Mar 31 1995	3-Chicchan	5
Apr 1 1995	4-Cimi	6
Apr 2 1995	5-Manik	7
Apr 3 1995	6-Lamat	8
Apr 4 1995	7-Muluc	9
Apr 5 1995	8-Oc	1
Apr 6 1995	9-Chuen	2
Apr 7 1995	10-Eb	3
Apr 8 1995	11-Ben	4
Apr 9 1995	12-Ix	5
Apr 10 1995	13-Men	6
Apr 11 1995	1-Cib	7
Apr 12 1995	2-Caban	8
Apr 13 1995	3-Etz'nab	9
Apr 14 1995	4-Cauac	1
Apr 15 1995	5-Ahau	2
Apr 16 1995	6-Imix	3
Apr 17 1995	7-Ik	4
Apr 18 1995	8-Akbal	5
Apr 19 1995	9-Kan	6
Apr 20 1995	10-Chicchan	7
Apr 21 1995	11-Cimi	8
Apr 22 1995	12-Manik	9
Apr 23 1995	13-Lamat	1
Apr 24 1995	1-Muluc	2
Apr 25 1995	2-Oc	3
Apr 26 1995	3-Chuen	4
Apr 27 1995	4-Eb	5
Apr 28 1995	5-Ben	6

Date	Day-Sign	L		Date	Day-Sign	L		Date	Day-Sign	L
Apr 29 1995	6-Ix	7		Jul 6 1995	9-Ik	3		Sep 12 1995	12-Oc	8
Apr 30 1995	7-Men	8		Jul 7 1995	10-Akbal	4		Sep 13 1995	13-Chuen	9
May 1 1995	8-Cib	9		Jul 8 1995	11-Kan	5		Sep 14 1995	**1-Eb**	1
May 2 1995	9-Caban	1		Jul 9 1995	12-Chicchan	6		Sep 15 1995	2-Ben	2
May 3 1995	10-Etz'nab	2		Jul 10 1995	13-Cimi	7		Sep 16 1995	3-Ix	3
May 4 1995	11-Cauac	3		Jul 11 1995	**1-Manik**	8		Sep 17 1995	4-Men	4
May 5 1995	12-Ahau	4		Jul 12 1995	2-Lamat	9		Sep 18 1995	5-Cib	5
May 6 1995	*13-Imix*	5		Jul 13 1995	3-Muluc	1		Sep 19 1995	6-Caban	6
May 7 1995	**1-Ik**	6		Jul 14 1995	4-Oc	2		Sep 20 1995	7-Etz'nab	7
May 8 1995	2-Akbal	7		Jul 15 1995	5-Chuen	3		Sep 21 1995	8-Cauac	8
May 9 1995	3-Kan	8		Jul 16 1995	6-Eb	4		Sep 22 1995	9-Ahau	9
May 10 1995	4-Chicchan	9		Jul 17 1995	7-Ben	5		Sep 23 1995	*10-Imix*	1
May 11 1995	5-Cimi	1		Jul 18 1995	8-Ix	6		Sep 24 1995	11-Ik	2
May 12 1995	6-Manik	2		Jul 19 1995	9-Men	7		Sep 25 1995	12-Akbal	3
May 13 1995	7-Lamat	3		Jul 20 1995	10-Cib	8		Sep 26 1995	13-Kan	4
May 14 1995	8-Muluc	4		Jul 21 1995	11-Caban	9		Sep 27 1995	**1-Chicchan**	5
May 15 1995	9-Oc	5		Jul 22 1995	12-Etz'nab	1		Sep 28 1995	2-Cimi	6
May 16 1995	10-Chuen	6		Jul 23 1995	13-Cauac	2		Sep 29 1995	3-Manik	7
May 17 1995	11-Eb	7		Jul 24 1995	**1-Ahau**	3		Sep 30 1995	4-Lamat	8
May 18 1995	12-Ben	8		Jul 25 1995	*2-Imix*	4		Oct 1 1995	5-Muluc	9
May 19 1995	13-Ix	9		Jul 26 1995	3-Ik	5		Oct 2 1995	6-Oc	1
May 20 1995	**1-Men**	1		Jul 27 1995	4-Akbal	6		Oct 3 1995	7-Chuen	2
May 21 1995	2-Cib	2		Jul 28 1995	5-Kan	7		Oct 4 1995	8-Eb	3
May 22 1995	3-Caban	3		Jul 29 1995	6-Chicchan	8		Oct 5 1995	9-Ben	4
May 23 1995	4-Etz'nab	4		Jul 30 1995	7-Cimi	9		Oct 6 1995	10-Ix	5
May 24 1995	5-Cauac	5		Jul 31 1995	8-Manik	1		Oct 7 1995	11-Men	6
May 25 1995	6-Ahau	6		Aug 1 1995	9-Lamat	2		Oct 8 1995	12-Cib	7
May 26 1995	*7-Imix*	7		Aug 2 1995	10-Muluc	3		Oct 9 1995	13-Caban	8
May 27 1995	8-Ik	8		Aug 3 1995	11-Oc	4		Oct 10 1995	**1-Etz'nab**	9
May 28 1995	9-Akbal	9		Aug 4 1995	12-Chuen	5		Oct 11 1995	2-Cauac	1
May 29 1995	10-Kan	1		Aug 5 1995	13-Eb	6		Oct 12 1995	3-Ahau	2
May 30 1995	11-Chicchan	2		Aug 6 1995	**1-Ben**	7		Oct 13 1995	*4-Imix*	3
May 31 1995	12-Cimi	3		Aug 7 1995	2-Ix	8		Oct 14 1995	5-Ik	4
Jun 1 1995	13-Manik	4		Aug 8 1995	3-Men	9		Oct 15 1995	6-Akbal	5
Jun 2 1995	**1-Lamat**	5		Aug 9 1995	4-Cib	1		Oct 16 1995	7-Kan	6
Jun 3 1995	2-Muluc	6		Aug 10 1995	5-Caban	2		Oct 17 1995	8-Chicchan	7
Jun 4 1995	3-Oc	7		Aug 11 1995	6-Etz'nab	3		Oct 18 1995	9-Cimi	8
Jun 5 1995	4-Chuen	8		Aug 12 1995	7-Cauac	4		Oct 19 1995	10-Manik	9
Jun 6 1995	5-Eb	9		Aug 13 1995	8-Ahau	5		Oct 20 1995	11-Lamat	1
Jun 7 1995	6-Ben	1		Aug 14 1995	*9-Imix*	6		Oct 21 1995	12-Muluc	2
Jun 8 1995	7-Ix	2		Aug 15 1995	10-Ik	7		Oct 22 1995	13-Oc	3
Jun 9 1995	8-Men	3		Aug 16 1995	11-Akbal	8		Oct 23 1995	**1-Chuen**	4
Jun 10 1995	9-Cib	4		Aug 17 1995	12-Kan	9		Oct 24 1995	2-Eb	5
Jun 11 1995	10-Caban	5		Aug 18 1995	13-Chicchan	1		Oct 25 1995	3-Ben	6
Jun 12 1995	11-Etz'nab	6		Aug 19 1995	**1-Cimi**	2		Oct 26 1995	4-Ix	7
Jun 13 1995	12-Cauac	7		Aug 20 1995	2-Manik	3		Oct 27 1995	5-Men	8
Jun 14 1995	13-Ahau	8		Aug 21 1995	3-Lamat	4		Oct 28 1995	6-Cib	9
Jun 15 1995	**1-Imix**	9		Aug 22 1995	4-Muluc	5		Oct 29 1995	7-Caban	1
Jun 16 1995	2-Ik	1		Aug 23 1995	5-Oc	6		Oct 30 1995	8-Etz'nab	2
Jun 17 1995	3-Akbal	2		Aug 24 1995	6-Chuen	7		Oct 31 1995	9-Cauac	3
Jun 18 1995	4-Kan	3		Aug 25 1995	7-Eb	8		Nov 1 1995	10-Ahau	4
Jun 19 1995	5-Chicchan	4		Aug 26 1995	8-Ben	9		Nov 2 1995	*11-Imix*	5
Jun 20 1995	6-Cimi	5		Aug 27 1995	9-Ix	1		Nov 3 1995	12-Ik	6
Jun 21 1995	7-Manik	6		Aug 28 1995	10-Men	2		Nov 4 1995	13-Akbal	7
Jun 22 1995	8-Lamat	7		Aug 29 1995	11-Cib	3		Nov 5 1995	**1-Kan**	8
Jun 23 1995	9-Muluc	8		Aug 30 1995	12-Caban	4		Nov 6 1995	2-Chicchan	9
Jun 24 1995	10-Oc	9		Aug 31 1995	13-Etz'nab	5		Nov 7 1995	3-Cimi	1
Jun 25 1995	11-Chuen	1		Sep 1 1995	**1-Cauac**	6		Nov 8 1995	4-Manik	2
Jun 26 1995	12-Eb	2		Sep 2 1995	2-Ahau	7		Nov 9 1995	5-Lamat	3
Jun 27 1995	13-Ben	3		Sep 3 1995	*3-Imix*	8		Nov 10 1995	6-Muluc	4
Jun 28 1995	**1-Ix**	4		Sep 4 1995	4-Ik	9		Nov 11 1995	7-Oc	5
Jun 29 1995	2-Men	5		Sep 5 1995	5-Akbal	1		Nov 12 1995	8-Chuen	6
Jun 30 1995	3-Cib	6		Sep 6 1995	6-Kan	2		Nov 13 1995	9-Eb	7
Jul 1 1995	4-Caban	7		Sep 7 1995	7-Chicchan	3		Nov 14 1995	10-Ben	8
Jul 2 1995	5-Etz'nab	8		Sep 8 1995	8-Cimi	4		Nov 15 1995	11-Ix	9
Jul 3 1995	6-Cauac	9		Sep 9 1995	9-Manik	5		Nov 16 1995	12-Men	1
Jul 4 1995	7-Ahau	1		Sep 10 1995	10-Lamat	6		Nov 17 1995	13-Cib	2
Jul 5 1995	*8-Imix*	2		Sep 11 1995	11-Muluc	7		Nov 18 1995	**1-Caban**	3

Date	Day-Sign	L
Nov 19 1995	2-Etz'nab	4
Nov 20 1995	3-Cauac	5
Nov 21 1995	4-Ahau	6
Nov 22 1995	5-*Imix*	7
Nov 23 1995	6-Ik	8
Nov 24 1995	7-Akbal	9
Nov 25 1995	8-Kan	1
Nov 26 1995	9-Chicchan	2
Nov 27 1995	10-Cimi	3
Nov 28 1995	11-Manik	4
Nov 29 1995	12-Lamat	5
Nov 30 1995	13-Muluc	6
Dec 1 1995	**1-Oc**	7
Dec 2 1995	2-Chuen	8
Dec 3 1995	3-Eb	9
Dec 4 1995	4-Ben	1
Dec 5 1995	5-Ix	2
Dec 6 1995	6-Men	3
Dec 7 1995	7-Cib	4
Dec 8 1995	8-Caban	5
Dec 9 1995	9-Etz'nab	6
Dec 10 1995	10-Cauac	7
Dec 11 1995	11-Ahau	8
Dec 12 1995	12-*Imix*	9
Dec 13 1995	13-Ik	1
Dec 14 1995	**1-Akbal**	2
Dec 15 1995	2-Kan	3
Dec 16 1995	3-Chicchan	4
Dec 17 1995	4-Cimi	5
Dec 18 1995	5-Manik	6
Dec 19 1995	6-Lamat	7
Dec 20 1995	7-Muluc	8
Dec 21 1995	8-Oc	9
Dec 22 1995	9-Chuen	1
Dec 23 1995	10-Eb	2
Dec 24 1995	11-Ben	3
Dec 25 1995	12-Ix	4
Dec 26 1995	13-Men	5
Dec 27 1995	**1-Cib**	6
Dec 28 1995	2-Caban	7
Dec 29 1995	3-Etz'nab	8
Dec 30 1995	4-Cauac	9
Dec 31 1995	5-Ahau	1
Jan 1 1996	6-*Imix*	2
Jan 2 1996	7-Ik	3
Jan 3 1996	8-Akbal	4
Jan 4 1996	9-Kan	5
Jan 5 1996	10-Chicchan	6
Jan 6 1996	11-Cimi	7
Jan 7 1996	12-Manik	8
Jan 8 1996	13-Lamat	9
Jan 9 1996	**1-Muluc**	1
Jan 10 1996	2-Oc	2
Jan 11 1996	3-Chuen	3
Jan 12 1996	4-Eb	4
Jan 13 1996	5-Ben	5
Jan 14 1996	6-Ix	6
Jan 15 1996	7-Men	7
Jan 16 1996	8-Cib	8
Jan 17 1996	9-Caban	9
Jan 18 1996	10-Etz'nab	1
Jan 19 1996	11-Cauac	2
Jan 20 1996	12-Ahau	3
Jan 21 1996	13-*Imix*	4
Jan 22 1996	**1-Ik**	5
Jan 23 1996	2-Akbal	6
Jan 24 1996	3-Kan	7
Jan 25 1996	4-Chicchan	8

Date	Day-Sign	L
Jan 26 1996	5-Cimi	9
Jan 27 1996	6-Manik	1
Jan 28 1996	7-Lamat	2
Jan 29 1996	8-Muluc	3
Jan 30 1996	9-Oc	4
Jan 31 1996	10-Chuen	5
Feb 1 1996	11-Eb	6
Feb 2 1996	12-Ben	7
Feb 3 1996	13-Ix	8
Feb 4 1996	**1-Men**	9
Feb 5 1996	2-Cib	1
Feb 6 1996	3-Caban	2
Feb 7 1996	4-Etz'nab	3
Feb 8 1996	5-Cauac	4
Feb 9 1996	6-Ahau	5
Feb 10 1996	7-*Imix*	6
Feb 11 1996	8-Ik	7
Feb 12 1996	9-Akbal	8
Feb 13 1996	10-Kan	9
Feb 14 1996	11-Chicchan	1
Feb 15 1996	12-Cimi	2
Feb 16 1996	13-Manik	3
Feb 17 1996	**1-Lamat**	4
Feb 18 1996	2-Muluc	5
Feb 19 1996	3-Oc	6
Feb 20 1996	4-Chuen	7
Feb 21 1996	5-Eb	8
Feb 22 1996	6-Ben	9
Feb 23 1996	7-Ix	1
Feb 24 1996	8-Men	2
Feb 25 1996	9-Cib	3
Feb 26 1996	10-Caban	4
Feb 27 1996	11-Etz'nab	5
Feb 28 1996	12-Cauac	6
Feb 29 1996	13-Ahau	7
Mar 1 1996	**1-Imix**	8
Mar 2 1996	2-Ik	9
Mar 3 1996	3-Akbal	1
Mar 4 1996	4-Kan	2
Mar 5 1996	5-Chicchan	3
Mar 6 1996	6-Cimi	4
Mar 7 1996	7-Manik	5
Mar 8 1996	8-Lamat	6
Mar 9 1996	9-Muluc	7
Mar 10 1996	10-Oc	8
Mar 11 1996	11-Chuen	9
Mar 12 1996	12-Eb	1
Mar 13 1996	13-Ben	2
Mar 14 1996	**1-Ix**	3
Mar 15 1996	2-Men	4
Mar 16 1996	3-Cib	5
Mar 17 1996	4-Caban	6
Mar 18 1996	5-Etz'nab	7
Mar 19 1996	6-Cauac	8
Mar 20 1996	7-Ahau	9
Mar 21 1996	8-*Imix*	1
Mar 22 1996	9-Ik	2
Mar 23 1996	10-Akbal	3
Mar 24 1996	11-Kan	4
Mar 25 1996	12-Chicchan	5
Mar 26 1996	13-Cimi	6
Mar 27 1996	**1-Manik**	7
Mar 28 1996	2-Lamat	8
Mar 29 1996	3-Muluc	9
Mar 30 1996	4-Oc	1
Mar 31 1996	5-Chuen	2
Apr 1 1996	6-Eb	3
Apr 2 1996	7-Ben	4

Date	Day-Sign	L
Apr 3 1996	8-Ix	5
Apr 4 1996	9-Men	6
Apr 5 1996	10-Cib	7
Apr 6 1996	11-Caban	8
Apr 7 1996	12-Etz'nab	9
Apr 8 1996	13-Cauac	1
Apr 9 1996	**1-Ahau**	2
Apr 10 1996	2-*Imix*	3
Apr 11 1996	3-Ik	4
Apr 12 1996	4-Akbal	5
Apr 13 1996	5-Kan	6
Apr 14 1996	6-Chicchan	7
Apr 15 1996	7-Cimi	8
Apr 16 1996	8-Manik	9
Apr 17 1996	9-Lamat	1
Apr 18 1996	10-Muluc	2
Apr 19 1996	11-Oc	3
Apr 20 1996	12-Chuen	4
Apr 21 1996	13-Eb	5
Apr 22 1996	**1-Ben**	6
Apr 23 1996	2-Ix	7
Apr 24 1996	3-Men	8
Apr 25 1996	4-Cib	9
Apr 26 1996	5-Caban	1
Apr 27 1996	6-Etz'nab	2
Apr 28 1996	7-Cauac	3
Apr 29 1996	8-Ahau	4
Apr 30 1996	9-*Imix*	5
May 1 1996	10-Ik	6
May 2 1996	11-Akbal	7
May 3 1996	12-Kan	8
May 4 1996	13-Chicchan	9
May 5 1996	**1-Cimi**	1
May 6 1996	2-Manik	2
May 7 1996	3-Lamat	3
May 8 1996	4-Muluc	4
May 9 1996	5-Oc	5
May 10 1996	6-Chuen	6
May 11 1996	7-Eb	7
May 12 1996	8-Ben	8
May 13 1996	9-Ix	9
May 14 1996	10-Men	1
May 15 1996	11-Cib	2
May 16 1996	12-Caban	3
May 17 1996	13-Etz'nab	4
May 18 1996	**1-Cauac**	5
May 19 1996	2-Ahau	6
May 20 1996	3-*Imix*	7
May 21 1996	4-Ik	8
May 22 1996	5-Akbal	9
May 23 1996	6-Kan	1
May 24 1996	7-Chicchan	2
May 25 1996	8-Cimi	3
May 26 1996	9-Manik	4
May 27 1996	10-Lamat	5
May 28 1996	11-Muluc	6
May 29 1996	12-Oc	7
May 30 1996	13-Chuen	8
May 31 1996	**1-Eb**	9
Jun 1 1996	2-Ben	1
Jun 2 1996	3-Ix	2
Jun 3 1996	4-Men	3
Jun 4 1996	5-Cib	4
Jun 5 1996	6-Caban	5
Jun 6 1996	7-Etz'nab	6
Jun 7 1996	8-Cauac	7
Jun 8 1996	9-Ahau	8
Jun 9 1996	10-*Imix*	9

Date	Day-Sign	L	Date	Day-Sign	L	Date	Day-Sign	L
Jun 10 1996	11-Ik	1	Aug 17 1996	**1-Oc**	6	Oct 24 1996	4-Etz'nab	2
Jun 11 1996	12-Akbal	2	Aug 18 1996	2-Chuen	7	Oct 25 1996	5-Cauac	3
Jun 12 1996	13-Kan	3	Aug 19 1996	3-Eb	8	Oct 26 1996	6-Ahau	4
Jun 13 1996	**1-Chicchan**	4	Aug 20 1996	4-Ben	9	Oct 27 1996	*7-Imix*	5
Jun 14 1996	2-Cimi	5	Aug 21 1996	5-Ix	1	Oct 28 1996	8-Ik	6
Jun 15 1996	3-Manik	6	Aug 22 1996	6-Men	2	Oct 29 1996	9-Akbal	7
Jun 16 1996	4-Lamat	7	Aug 23 1996	7-Cib	3	Oct 30 1996	10-Kan	8
Jun 17 1996	5-Muluc	8	Aug 24 1996	8-Caban	4	Oct 31 1996	11-Chicchan	9
Jun 18 1996	6-Oc	9	Aug 25 1996	9-Etz'nab	5	Nov 1 1996	12-Cimi	1
Jun 19 1996	7-Chuen	1	Aug 26 1996	10-Cauac	6	Nov 2 1996	13-Manik	2
Jun 20 1996	8-Eb	2	Aug 27 1996	11-Ahau	7	Nov 3 1996	**1-Lamat**	3
Jun 21 1996	9-Ben	3	Aug 28 1996	*12-Imix*	8	Nov 4 1996	2-Muluc	4
Jun 22 1996	10-Ix	4	Aug 29 1996	13-Ik	9	Nov 5 1996	3-Oc	5
Jun 23 1996	11-Men	5	Aug 30 1996	**1-Akbal**	1	Nov 6 1996	4-Chuen	6
Jun 24 1996	12-Cib	6	Aug 31 1996	2-Kan	2	Nov 7 1996	5-Eb	7
Jun 25 1996	13-Caban	7	Sep 1 1996	3-Chicchan	3	Nov 8 1996	6-Ben	8
Jun 26 1996	**1-Etz'nab**	8	Sep 2 1996	4-Cimi	4	Nov 9 1996	7-Ix	9
Jun 27 1996	2-Cauac	9	Sep 3 1996	5-Manik	5	Nov 10 1996	8-Men	1
Jun 28 1996	3-Ahau	1	Sep 4 1996	6-Lamat	6	Nov 11 1996	9-Cib	2
Jun 29 1996	*4-Imix*	2	Sep 5 1996	7-Muluc	7	Nov 12 1996	10-Caban	3
Jun 30 1996	5-Ik	3	Sep 6 1996	8-Oc	8	Nov 13 1996	11-Etz'nab	4
Jul 1 1996	6-Akbal	4	Sep 7 1996	9-Chuen	9	Nov 14 1996	12-Cauac	5
Jul 2 1996	7-Kan	5	Sep 8 1996	10-Eb	1	Nov 15 1996	13-Ahau	6
Jul 3 1996	8-Chicchan	6	Sep 9 1996	11-Ben	2	Nov 16 1996	**1-Imix**	7
Jul 4 1996	9-Cimi	7	Sep 10 1996	12-Ix	3	Nov 17 1996	2-Ik	8
Jul 5 1996	10-Manik	8	Sep 11 1996	13-Men	4	Nov 18 1996	3-Akbal	9
Jul 6 1996	11-Lamat	9	Sep 12 1996	**1-Cib**	5	Nov 19 1996	4-Kan	1
Jul 7 1996	12-Muluc	1	Sep 13 1996	2-Caban	6	Nov 20 1996	5-Chicchan	2
Jul 8 1996	13-Oc	2	Sep 14 1996	3-Etz'nab	7	Nov 21 1996	6-Cimi	3
Jul 9 1996	**1-Chuen**	3	Sep 15 1996	4-Cauac	8	Nov 22 1996	7-Manik	4
Jul 10 1996	2-Eb	4	Sep 16 1996	5-Ahau	9	Nov 23 1996	8-Lamat	5
Jul 11 1996	3-Ben	5	Sep 17 1996	*6-Imix*	1	Nov 24 1996	9-Muluc	6
Jul 12 1996	4-Ix	6	Sep 18 1996	7-Ik	2	Nov 25 1996	10-Oc	7
Jul 13 1996	5-Men	7	Sep 19 1996	8-Akbal	3	Nov 26 1996	11-Chuen	8
Jul 14 1996	6-Cib	8	Sep 20 1996	9-Kan	4	Nov 27 1996	12-Eb	9
Jul 15 1996	7-Caban	9	Sep 21 1996	10-Chicchan	5	Nov 28 1996	13-Ben	1
Jul 16 1996	8-Etz'nab	1	Sep 22 1996	11-Cimi	6	Nov 29 1996	**1-Ix**	2
Jul 17 1996	9-Cauac	2	Sep 23 1996	12-Manik	7	Nov 30 1996	2-Men	3
Jul 18 1996	10-Ahau	3	Sep 24 1996	13-Lamat	8	Dec 1 1996	3-Cib	4
Jul 19 1996	*11-Imix*	4	Sep 25 1996	**1-Muluc**	9	Dec 2 1996	4-Caban	5
Jul 20 1996	12-Ik	5	Sep 26 1996	2-Oc	1	Dec 3 1996	5-Etz'nab	6
Jul 21 1996	13-Akbal	6	Sep 27 1996	3-Chuen	2	Dec 4 1996	6-Cauac	7
Jul 22 1996	**1-Kan**	7	Sep 28 1996	4-Eb	3	Dec 5 1996	7-Ahau	8
Jul 23 1996	2-Chicchan	8	Sep 29 1996	5-Ben	4	Dec 6 1996	*8-Imix*	9
Jul 24 1996	3-Cimi	9	Sep 30 1996	6-Ix	5	Dec 7 1996	9-Ik	1
Jul 25 1996	4-Manik	1	Oct 1 1996	7-Men	6	Dec 8 1996	10-Akbal	2
Jul 26 1996	5-Lamat	2	Oct 2 1996	8-Cib	7	Dec 9 1996	11-Kan	3
Jul 27 1996	6-Muluc	3	Oct 3 1996	9-Caban	8	Dec 10 1996	12-Chicchan	4
Jul 28 1996	7-Oc	4	Oct 4 1996	10-Etz'nab	9	Dec 11 1996	13-Cimi	5
Jul 29 1996	8-Chuen	5	Oct 5 1996	11-Cauac	1	Dec 12 1996	**1-Manik**	6
Jul 30 1996	9-Eb	6	Oct 6 1996	12-Ahau	2	Dec 13 1996	2-Lamat	7
Jul 31 1996	10-Ben	7	Oct 7 1996	*13-Imix*	3	Dec 14 1996	3-Muluc	8
Aug 1 1996	11-Ix	8	Oct 8 1996	**1-Ik**	4	Dec 15 1996	4-Oc	9
Aug 2 1996	12-Men	9	Oct 9 1996	2-Akbal	5	Dec 16 1996	5-Chuen	1
Aug 3 1996	13-Cib	1	Oct 10 1996	3-Kan	6	Dec 17 1996	6-Eb	2
Aug 4 1996	**1-Caban**	2	Oct 11 1996	4-Chicchan	7	Dec 18 1996	7-Ben	3
Aug 5 1996	2-Etz'nab	3	Oct 12 1996	5-Cimi	8	Dec 19 1996	8-Ix	4
Aug 6 1996	3-Cauac	4	Oct 13 1996	6-Manik	9	Dec 20 1996	9-Men	5
Aug 7 1996	4-Ahau	5	Oct 14 1996	7-Lamat	1	Dec 21 1996	10-Cib	6
Aug 8 1996	*5-Imix*	6	Oct 15 1996	8-Muluc	2	Dec 22 1996	11-Caban	7
Aug 9 1996	6-Ik	7	Oct 16 1996	9-Oc	3	Dec 23 1996	12-Etz'nab	8
Aug 10 1996	7-Akbal	8	Oct 17 1996	10-Chuen	4	Dec 24 1996	13-Cauac	9
Aug 11 1996	8-Kan	9	Oct 18 1996	11-Eb	5	Dec 25 1996	**1-Ahau**	1
Aug 12 1996	9-Chicchan	1	Oct 19 1996	12-Ben	6	Dec 26 1996	*2-Imix*	2
Aug 13 1996	10-Cimi	2	Oct 20 1996	13-Ix	7	Dec 27 1996	3-Ik	3
Aug 14 1996	11-Manik	3	Oct 21 1996	**1-Men**	8	Dec 28 1996	4-Akbal	4
Aug 15 1996	12-Lamat	4	Oct 22 1996	2-Cib	9	Dec 29 1996	5-Kan	5
Aug 16 1996	13-Muluc	5	Oct 23 1996	3-Caban	1	Dec 30 1996	6-Chicchan	6

Date	Day-Sign	L
Dec 31 1996	7-Cimi	7
Jan 1 1997	8-Manik	8
Jan 2 1997	9-Lamat	9
Jan 3 1997	10-Muluc	1
Jan 4 1997	11-Oc	2
Jan 5 1997	12-Chuen	3
Jan 6 1997	13-Eb	4
Jan 7 1997	**1-Ben**	5
Jan 8 1997	2-Ix	6
Jan 9 1997	3-Men	7
Jan 10 1997	4-Cib	8
Jan 11 1997	5-Caban	9
Jan 12 1997	6-Etz'nab	1
Jan 13 1997	7-Cauac	2
Jan 14 1997	8-Ahau	3
Jan 15 1997	*9-Imix*	4
Jan 16 1997	10-Ik	5
Jan 17 1997	11-Akbal	6
Jan 18 1997	12-Kan	7
Jan 19 1997	13-Chicchan	8
Jan 20 1997	**1-Cimi**	9
Jan 21 1997	2-Manik	1
Jan 22 1997	3-Lamat	2
Jan 23 1997	4-Muluc	3
Jan 24 1997	5-Oc	4
Jan 25 1997	6-Chuen	5
Jan 26 1997	7-Eb	6
Jan 27 1997	8-Ben	7
Jan 28 1997	9-Ix	8
Jan 29 1997	10-Men	9
Jan 30 1997	11-Cib	1
Jan 31 1997	12-Caban	2
Feb 1 1997	13-Etz'nab	3
Feb 2 1997	**1-Cauac**	4
Feb 3 1997	2-Ahau	5
Feb 4 1997	*3-Imix*	6
Feb 5 1997	4-Ik	7
Feb 6 1997	5-Akbal	8
Feb 7 1997	6-Kan	9
Feb 8 1997	7-Chicchan	1
Feb 9 1997	8-Cimi	2
Feb 10 1997	9-Manik	3
Feb 11 1997	10-Lamat	4
Feb 12 1997	11-Muluc	5
Feb 13 1997	12-Oc	6
Feb 14 1997	13-Chuen	7
Feb 15 1997	**1-Eb**	8
Feb 16 1997	2-Ben	9
Feb 17 1997	3-Ix	1
Feb 18 1997	4-Men	2
Feb 19 1997	5-Cib	3
Feb 20 1997	6-Caban	4
Feb 21 1997	7-Etz'nab	5
Feb 22 1997	8-Cauac	6
Feb 23 1997	9-Ahau	7
Feb 24 1997	*10-Imix*	8
Feb 25 1997	11-Ik	9
Feb 26 1997	12-Akbal	1
Feb 27 1997	13-Kan	2
Feb 28 1997	**1-Chicchan**	3
Mar 1 1997	2-Cimi	4
Mar 2 1997	3-Manik	5
Mar 3 1997	4-Lamat	6
Mar 4 1997	5-Muluc	7
Mar 5 1997	6-Oc	8
Mar 6 1997	7-Chuen	9
Mar 7 1997	8-Eb	1
Mar 8 1997	9-Ben	2

Date	Day-Sign	L
Mar 9 1997	10-Ix	3
Mar 10 1997	11-Men	4
Mar 11 1997	12-Cib	5
Mar 12 1997	13-Caban	6
Mar 13 1997	**1-Etz'nab**	7
Mar 14 1997	2-Cauac	8
Mar 15 1997	3-Ahau	9
Mar 16 1997	*4-Imix*	1
Mar 17 1997	5-Ik	2
Mar 18 1997	6-Akbal	3
Mar 19 1997	7-Kan	4
Mar 20 1997	8-Chicchan	5
Mar 21 1997	9-Cimi	6
Mar 22 1997	10-Manik	7
Mar 23 1997	11-Lamat	8
Mar 24 1997	12-Muluc	9
Mar 25 1997	13-Oc	1
Mar 26 1997	**1-Chuen**	2
Mar 27 1997	2-Eb	3
Mar 28 1997	3-Ben	4
Mar 29 1997	4-Ix	5
Mar 30 1997	5-Men	6
Mar 31 1997	6-Cib	7
Apr 1 1997	7-Caban	8
Apr 2 1997	8-Etz'nab	9
Apr 3 1997	9-Cauac	1
Apr 4 1997	10-Ahau	2
Apr 5 1997	*11-Imix*	3
Apr 6 1997	12-Ik	4
Apr 7 1997	13-Akbal	5
Apr 8 1997	**1-Kan**	6
Apr 9 1997	2-Chicchan	7
Apr 10 1997	3-Cimi	8
Apr 11 1997	4-Manik	9
Apr 12 1997	5-Lamat	1
Apr 13 1997	6-Muluc	2
Apr 14 1997	7-Oc	3
Apr 15 1997	8-Chuen	4
Apr 16 1997	9-Eb	5
Apr 17 1997	10-Ben	6
Apr 18 1997	11-Ix	7
Apr 19 1997	12-Men	8
Apr 20 1997	13-Cib	9
Apr 21 1997	**1-Caban**	1
Apr 22 1997	2-Etz'nab	2
Apr 23 1997	3-Cauac	3
Apr 24 1997	4-Ahau	4
Apr 25 1997	*5-Imix*	5
Apr 26 1997	6-Ik	6
Apr 27 1997	7-Akbal	7
Apr 28 1997	8-Kan	8
Apr 29 1997	9-Chicchan	9
Apr 30 1997	10-Cimi	1
May 1 1997	11-Manik	2
May 2 1997	12-Lamat	3
May 3 1997	13-Muluc	4
May 4 1997	**1-Oc**	5
May 5 1997	2-Chuen	6
May 6 1997	3-Eb	7
May 7 1997	4-Ben	8
May 8 1997	5-Ix	9
May 9 1997	6-Men	1
May 10 1997	7-Cib	2
May 11 1997	8-Caban	3
May 12 1997	9-Etz'nab	4
May 13 1997	10-Cauac	5
May 14 1997	11-Ahau	6
May 15 1997	*12-Imix*	7

Date	Day-Sign	L
May 16 1997	13-Ik	8
May 17 1997	**1-Akbal**	9
May 18 1997	2-Kan	1
May 19 1997	3-Chicchan	2
May 20 1997	4-Cimi	3
May 21 1997	5-Manik	4
May 22 1997	6-Lamat	5
May 23 1997	7-Muluc	6
May 24 1997	8-Oc	7
May 25 1997	9-Chuen	8
May 26 1997	10-Eb	9
May 27 1997	11-Ben	1
May 28 1997	12-Ix	2
May 29 1997	13-Men	3
May 30 1997	**1-Cib**	4
May 31 1997	2-Caban	5
Jun 1 1997	3-Etz'nab	6
Jun 2 1997	4-Cauac	7
Jun 3 1997	5-Ahau	8
Jun 4 1997	*6-Imix*	9
Jun 5 1997	7-Ik	1
Jun 6 1997	8-Akbal	2
Jun 7 1997	9-Kan	3
Jun 8 1997	10-Chicchan	4
Jun 9 1997	11-Cimi	5
Jun 10 1997	12-Manik	6
Jun 11 1997	13-Lamat	7
Jun 12 1997	**1-Muluc**	8
Jun 13 1997	2-Oc	9
Jun 14 1997	3-Chuen	1
Jun 15 1997	4-Eb	2
Jun 16 1997	5-Ben	3
Jun 17 1997	6-Ix	4
Jun 18 1997	7-Men	5
Jun 19 1997	8-Cib	6
Jun 20 1997	9-Caban	7
Jun 21 1997	10-Etz'nab	8
Jun 22 1997	11-Cauac	9
Jun 23 1997	12-Ahau	1
Jun 24 1997	*13-Imix*	2
Jun 25 1997	**1-Ik**	3
Jun 26 1997	2-Akbal	4
Jun 27 1997	3-Kan	5
Jun 28 1997	4-Chicchan	6
Jun 29 1997	5-Cimi	7
Jun 30 1997	6-Manik	8
Jul 1 1997	7-Lamat	9
Jul 2 1997	8-Muluc	1
Jul 3 1997	9-Oc	2
Jul 4 1997	10-Chuen	3
Jul 5 1997	11-Eb	4
Jul 6 1997	12-Ben	5
Jul 7 1997	13-Ix	6
Jul 8 1997	**1-Men**	7
Jul 9 1997	2-Cib	8
Jul 10 1997	3-Caban	9
Jul 11 1997	4-Etz'nab	1
Jul 12 1997	5-Cauac	2
Jul 13 1997	6-Ahau	3
Jul 14 1997	*7-Imix*	4
Jul 15 1997	8-Ik	5
Jul 16 1997	9-Akbal	6
Jul 17 1997	10-Kan	7
Jul 18 1997	11-Chicchan	8
Jul 19 1997	12-Cimi	9
Jul 20 1997	13-Manik	1
Jul 21 1997	**1-Lamat**	2
Jul 22 1997	2-Muluc	3

Date	Day-Sign	L	Date	Day-Sign	L	Date	Day-Sign	L
Jul 23 1997	3-Oc	4	Sep 29 1997	6-Etz'nab	9	Dec 6 1997	9-Cimi	5
Jul 24 1997	4-Chuen	5	Sep 30 1997	7-Cauac	1	Dec 7 1997	10-Manik	6
Jul 25 1997	5-Eb	6	Oct 1 1997	8-Ahau	2	Dec 8 1997	11-Lamat	7
Jul 26 1997	6-Ben	7	Oct 2 1997	9-*Imix*	3	Dec 9 1997	12-Muluc	8
Jul 27 1997	7-Ix	8	Oct 3 1997	10-Ik	4	Dec 10 1997	13-Oc	9
Jul 28 1997	8-Men	9	Oct 4 1997	11-Akbal	5	Dec 11 1997	**1-Chuen**	1
Jul 29 1997	9-Cib	1	Oct 5 1997	12-Kan	6	Dec 12 1997	2-Eb	2
Jul 30 1997	10-Caban	2	Oct 6 1997	13-Chicchan	7	Dec 13 1997	3-Ben	3
Jul 31 1997	11-Etz'nab	3	Oct 7 1997	**1-Cimi**	8	Dec 14 1997	4-Ix	4
Aug 1 1997	12-Cauac	4	Oct 8 1997	2-Manik	9	Dec 15 1997	5-Men	5
Aug 2 1997	13-Ahau	5	Oct 9 1997	3-Lamat	1	Dec 16 1997	6-Cib	6
Aug 3 1997	**1-Imix**	6	Oct 10 1997	4-Muluc	2	Dec 17 1997	7-Caban	7
Aug 4 1997	2-Ik	7	Oct 11 1997	5-Oc	3	Dec 18 1997	8-Etz'nab	8
Aug 5 1997	3-Akbal	8	Oct 12 1997	6-Chuen	4	Dec 19 1997	9-Cauac	9
Aug 6 1997	4-Kan	9	Oct 13 1997	7-Eb	5	Dec 20 1997	10-Ahau	1
Aug 7 1997	5-Chicchan	1	Oct 14 1997	8-Ben	6	Dec 21 1997	11-*Imix*	2
Aug 8 1997	6-Cimi	2	Oct 15 1997	9-Ix	7	Dec 22 1997	12-Ik	3
Aug 9 1997	7-Manik	3	Oct 16 1997	10-Men	8	Dec 23 1997	13-Akbal	4
Aug 10 1997	8-Lamat	4	Oct 17 1997	11-Cib	9	Dec 24 1997	**1-Kan**	5
Aug 11 1997	9-Muluc	5	Oct 18 1997	12-Caban	1	Dec 25 1997	2-Chicchan	6
Aug 12 1997	10-Oc	6	Oct 19 1997	13-Etz'nab	2	Dec 26 1997	3-Cimi	7
Aug 13 1997	11-Chuen	7	Oct 20 1997	**1-Cauac**	3	Dec 27 1997	4-Manik	8
Aug 14 1997	12-Eb	8	Oct 21 1997	2-Ahau	4	Dec 28 1997	5-Lamat	9
Aug 15 1997	13-Ben	9	Oct 22 1997	3-*Imix*	5	Dec 29 1997	6-Muluc	1
Aug 16 1997	**1-Ix**	1	Oct 23 1997	4-Ik	6	Dec 30 1997	7-Oc	2
Aug 17 1997	2-Men	2	Oct 24 1997	5-Akbal	7	Dec 31 1997	8-Chuen	3
Aug 18 1997	3-Cib	3	Oct 25 1997	6-Kan	8	Jan 1 1998	9-Eb	4
Aug 19 1997	4-Caban	4	Oct 26 1997	7-Chicchan	9	Jan 2 1998	10-Ben	5
Aug 20 1997	5-Etz'nab	5	Oct 27 1997	8-Cimi	1	Jan 3 1998	11-Ix	6
Aug 21 1997	6-Cauac	6	Oct 28 1997	9-Manik	2	Jan 4 1998	12-Men	7
Aug 22 1997	7-Ahau	7	Oct 29 1997	10-Lamat	3	Jan 5 1998	13-Cib	8
Aug 23 1997	8-*Imix*	8	Oct 30 1997	11-Muluc	4	Jan 6 1998	**1-Caban**	9
Aug 24 1997	9-Ik	9	Oct 31 1997	12-Oc	5	Jan 7 1998	2-Etz'nab	1
Aug 25 1997	10-Akbal	1	Nov 1 1997	13-Chuen	6	Jan 8 1998	3-Cauac	2
Aug 26 1997	11-Kan	2	Nov 2 1997	**1-Eb**	7	Jan 9 1998	4-Ahau	3
Aug 27 1997	12-Chicchan	3	Nov 3 1997	2-Ben	8	Jan 10 1998	5-*Imix*	4
Aug 28 1997	13-Cimi	4	Nov 4 1997	3-Ix	9	Jan 11 1998	6-Ik	5
Aug 29 1997	**1-Manik**	5	Nov 5 1997	4-Men	1	Jan 12 1998	7-Akbal	6
Aug 30 1997	2-Lamat	6	Nov 6 1997	5-Cib	2	Jan 13 1998	8-Kan	7
Aug 31 1997	3-Muluc	7	Nov 7 1997	6-Caban	3	Jan 14 1998	9-Chicchan	8
Sep 1 1997	4-Oc	8	Nov 8 1997	7-Etz'nab	4	Jan 15 1998	10-Cimi	9
Sep 2 1997	5-Chuen	9	Nov 9 1997	8-Cauac	5	Jan 16 1998	11-Manik	1
Sep 3 1997	6-Eb	1	Nov 10 1997	9-Ahau	6	Jan 17 1998	12-Lamat	2
Sep 4 1997	7-Ben	2	Nov 11 1997	10-*Imix*	7	Jan 18 1998	13-Muluc	3
Sep 5 1997	8-Ix	3	Nov 12 1997	11-Ik	8	Jan 19 1998	**1-Oc**	4
Sep 6 1997	9-Men	4	Nov 13 1997	12-Akbal	9	Jan 20 1998	2-Chuen	5
Sep 7 1997	10-Cib	5	Nov 14 1997	13-Kan	1	Jan 21 1998	3-Eb	6
Sep 8 1997	11-Caban	6	Nov 15 1997	**1-Chicchan**	2	Jan 22 1998	4-Ben	7
Sep 9 1997	12-Etz'nab	7	Nov 16 1997	2-Cimi	3	Jan 23 1998	5-Ix	8
Sep 10 1997	13-Cauac	8	Nov 17 1997	3-Manik	4	Jan 24 1998	6-Men	9
Sep 11 1997	**1-Ahau**	9	Nov 18 1997	4-Lamat	5	Jan 25 1998	7-Cib	1
Sep 12 1997	2-*Imix*	1	Nov 19 1997	5-Muluc	6	Jan 26 1998	8-Caban	2
Sep 13 1997	3-Ik	2	Nov 20 1997	6-Oc	7	Jan 27 1998	9-Etz'nab	3
Sep 14 1997	4-Akbal	3	Nov 21 1997	7-Chuen	8	Jan 28 1998	10-Cauac	4
Sep 15 1997	5-Kan	4	Nov 22 1997	8-Eb	9	Jan 29 1998	11-Ahau	5
Sep 16 1997	6-Chicchan	5	Nov 23 1997	9-Ben	1	Jan 30 1998	12-*Imix*	6
Sep 17 1997	7-Cimi	6	Nov 24 1997	10-Ix	2	Jan 31 1998	13-Ik	7
Sep 18 1997	8-Manik	7	Nov 25 1997	11-Men	3	Feb 1 1998	**1-Akbal**	8
Sep 19 1997	9-Lamat	8	Nov 26 1997	12-Cib	4	Feb 2 1998	2-Kan	9
Sep 20 1997	10-Muluc	9	Nov 27 1997	13-Caban	5	Feb 3 1998	3-Chicchan	1
Sep 21 1997	11-Oc	1	Nov 28 1997	**1-Etz'nab**	6	Feb 4 1998	4-Cimi	2
Sep 22 1997	12-Chuen	2	Nov 29 1997	2-Cauac	7	Feb 5 1998	5-Manik	3
Sep 23 1997	13-Eb	3	Nov 30 1997	3-Ahau	8	Feb 6 1998	6-Lamat	4
Sep 24 1997	**1-Ben**	4	Dec 1 1997	4-*Imix*	9	Feb 7 1998	7-Muluc	5
Sep 25 1997	2-Ix	5	Dec 2 1997	5-Ik	1	Feb 8 1998	8-Oc	6
Sep 26 1997	3-Men	6	Dec 3 1997	6-Akbal	2	Feb 9 1998	9-Chuen	7
Sep 27 1997	4-Cib	7	Dec 4 1997	7-Kan	3	Feb 10 1998	10-Eb	8
Sep 28 1997	5-Caban	8	Dec 5 1997	8-Chicchan	4	Feb 11 1998	11-Ben	9

Date	Day-Sign	L	Date	Day-Sign	L	Date	Day-Sign	L
Feb 12 1998	12-Ix	1	Apr 21 1998	2-Ik	6	Jun 28 1998	5-Oc	2
Feb 13 1998	13-Men	2	Apr 22 1998	3-Akbal	7	Jun 29 1998	6-Chuen	3
Feb 14 1998	1-Cib	3	Apr 23 1998	4-Kan	8	Jun 30 1998	7-Eb	4
Feb 15 1998	2-Caban	4	Apr 24 1998	5-Chicchan	9	Jul 1 1998	8-Ben	5
Feb 16 1998	3-Etz'nab	5	Apr 25 1998	6-Cimi	1	Jul 2 1998	9-Ix	6
Feb 17 1998	4-Cauac	6	Apr 26 1998	7-Manik	2	Jul 3 1998	10-Men	7
Feb 18 1998	5-Ahau	7	Apr 27 1998	8-Lamat	3	Jul 4 1998	11-Cib	8
Feb 19 1998	6-Imix	8	Apr 28 1998	9-Muluc	4	Jul 5 1998	12-Caban	9
Feb 20 1998	7-Ik	9	Apr 29 1998	10-Oc	5	Jul 6 1998	13-Etz'nab	1
Feb 21 1998	8-Akbal	1	Apr 30 1998	11-Chuen	6	Jul 7 1998	1-Cauac	2
Feb 22 1998	9-Kan	2	May 1 1998	12-Eb	7	Jul 8 1998	2-Ahau	3
Feb 23 1998	10-Chicchan	3	May 2 1998	13-Ben	8	Jul 9 1998	3-Imix	4
Feb 24 1998	11-Cimi	4	May 3 1998	1-Ix	9	Jul 10 1998	4-Ik	5
Feb 25 1998	12-Manik	5	May 4 1998	2-Men	1	Jul 11 1998	5-Akbal	6
Feb 26 1998	13-Lamat	6	May 5 1998	3-Cib	2	Jul 12 1998	6-Kan	7
Feb 27 1998	1-Muluc	7	May 6 1998	4-Caban	3	Jul 13 1998	7-Chicchan	8
Feb 28 1998	2-Oc	8	May 7 1998	5-Etz'nab	4	Jul 14 1998	8-Cimi	9
Mar 1 1998	3-Chuen	9	May 8 1998	6-Cauac	5	Jul 15 1998	9-Manik	1
Mar 2 1998	4-Eb	1	May 9 1998	7-Ahau	6	Jul 16 1998	10-Lamat	2
Mar 3 1998	5-Ben	2	May 10 1998	8-Imix	7	Jul 17 1998	11-Muluc	3
Mar 4 1998	6-Ix	3	May 11 1998	9-Ik	8	Jul 18 1998	12-Oc	4
Mar 5 1998	7-Men	4	May 12 1998	10-Akbal	9	Jul 19 1998	13-Chuen	5
Mar 6 1998	8-Cib	5	May 13 1998	11-Kan	1	Jul 20 1998	1-Eb	6
Mar 7 1998	9-Caban	6	May 14 1998	12-Chicchan	2	Jul 21 1998	2-Ben	7
Mar 8 1998	10-Etz'nab	7	May 15 1998	13-Cimi	3	Jul 22 1998	3-Ix	8
Mar 9 1998	11-Cauac	8	May 16 1998	1-Manik	4	Jul 23 1998	4-Men	9
Mar 10 1998	12-Ahau	9	May 17 1998	2-Lamat	5	Jul 24 1998	5-Cib	1
Mar 11 1998	13-Imix	1	May 18 1998	3-Muluc	6	Jul 25 1998	6-Caban	2
Mar 12 1998	1-Ik	2	May 19 1998	4-Oc	7	Jul 26 1998	7-Etz'nab	3
Mar 13 1998	2-Akbal	3	May 20 1998	5-Chuen	8	Jul 27 1998	8-Cauac	4
Mar 14 1998	3-Kan	4	May 21 1998	6-Eb	9	Jul 28 1998	9-Ahau	5
Mar 15 1998	4-Chicchan	5	May 22 1998	7-Ben	1	Jul 29 1998	10-Imix	6
Mar 16 1998	5-Cimi	6	May 23 1998	8-Ix	2	Jul 30 1998	11-Ik	7
Mar 17 1998	6-Manik	7	May 24 1998	9-Men	3	Jul 31 1998	12-Akbal	8
Mar 18 1998	7-Lamat	8	May 25 1998	10-Cib	4	Aug 1 1998	13-Kan	9
Mar 19 1998	8-Muluc	9	May 26 1998	11-Caban	5	Aug 2 1998	1-Chicchan	1
Mar 20 1998	9-Oc	1	May 27 1998	12-Etz'nab	6	Aug 3 1998	2-Cimi	2
Mar 21 1998	10-Chuen	2	May 28 1998	13-Cauac	7	Aug 4 1998	3-Manik	3
Mar 22 1998	11-Eb	3	May 29 1998	1-Ahau	8	Aug 5 1998	4-Lamat	4
Mar 23 1998	12-Ben	4	May 30 1998	2-Imix	9	Aug 6 1998	5-Muluc	5
Mar 24 1998	13-Ix	5	May 31 1998	3-Ik	1	Aug 7 1998	6-Oc	6
Mar 25 1998	1-Men	6	Jun 1 1998	4-Akbal	2	Aug 8 1998	7-Chuen	7
Mar 26 1998	2-Cib	7	Jun 2 1998	5-Kan	3	Aug 9 1998	8-Eb	8
Mar 27 1998	3-Caban	8	Jun 3 1998	6-Chicchan	4	Aug 10 1998	9-Ben	9
Mar 28 1998	4-Etz'nab	9	Jun 4 1998	7-Cimi	5	Aug 11 1998	10-Ix	1
Mar 29 1998	5-Cauac	1	Jun 5 1998	8-Manik	6	Aug 12 1998	11-Men	2
Mar 30 1998	6-Ahau	2	Jun 6 1998	9-Lamat	7	Aug 13 1998	12-Cib	3
Mar 31 1998	7-Imix	3	Jun 7 1998	10-Muluc	8	Aug 14 1998	13-Caban	4
Apr 1 1998	8-Ik	4	Jun 8 1998	11-Oc	9	Aug 15 1998	1-Etz'nab	5
Apr 2 1998	9-Akbal	5	Jun 9 1998	12-Chuen	1	Aug 16 1998	2-Cauac	6
Apr 3 1998	10-Kan	6	Jun 10 1998	13-Eb	2	Aug 17 1998	3-Ahau	7
Apr 4 1998	11-Chicchan	7	Jun 11 1998	1-Ben	3	Aug 18 1998	4-Imix	8
Apr 5 1998	12-Cimi	8	Jun 12 1998	2-Ix	4	Aug 19 1998	5-Ik	9
Apr 6 1998	13-Manik	9	Jun 13 1998	3-Men	5	Aug 20 1998	6-Akbal	1
Apr 7 1998	1-Lamat	1	Jun 14 1998	4-Cib	6	Aug 21 1998	7-Kan	2
Apr 8 1998	2-Muluc	2	Jun 15 1998	5-Caban	7	Aug 22 1998	8-Chicchan	3
Apr 9 1998	3-Oc	3	Jun 16 1998	6-Etz'nab	8	Aug 23 1998	9-Cimi	4
Apr 10 1998	4-Chuen	4	Jun 17 1998	7-Cauac	9	Aug 24 1998	10-Manik	5
Apr 11 1998	5-Eb	5	Jun 18 1998	8-Ahau	1	Aug 25 1998	11-Lamat	6
Apr 12 1998	6-Ben	6	Jun 19 1998	9-Imix	2	Aug 26 1998	12-Muluc	7
Apr 13 1998	7-Ix	7	Jun 20 1998	10-Ik	3	Aug 27 1998	13-Oc	8
Apr 14 1998	8-Men	8	Jun 21 1998	11-Akbal	4	Aug 28 1998	1-Chuen	9
Apr 15 1998	9-Cib	9	Jun 22 1998	12-Kan	5	Aug 29 1998	2-Eb	1
Apr 16 1998	10-Caban	1	Jun 23 1998	13-Chicchan	6	Aug 30 1998	3-Ben	2
Apr 17 1998	11-Etz'nab	2	Jun 24 1998	1-Cimi	7	Aug 31 1998	4-Ix	3
Apr 18 1998	12-Cauac	3	Jun 25 1998	2-Manik	8	Sep 1 1998	5-Men	4
Apr 19 1998	13-Ahau	4	Jun 26 1998	3-Lamat	9	Sep 2 1998	6-Cib	5
Apr 20 1998	1-Imix	5	Jun 27 1998	4-Muluc	1	Sep 3 1998	7-Caban	6

Date	Day-Sign	L
Sep 4 1998	8-Etz'nab	7
Sep 5 1998	9-Cauac	8
Sep 6 1998	10-Ahau	9
Sep 7 1998	11-*Imix*	1
Sep 8 1998	12-Ik	2
Sep 9 1998	13-Akbal	3
Sep 10 1998	1-Kan	4
Sep 11 1998	2-Chicchan	5
Sep 12 1998	3-Cimi	6
Sep 13 1998	4-Manik	7
Sep 14 1998	5-Lamat	8
Sep 15 1998	6-Muluc	9
Sep 16 1998	7-Oc	1
Sep 17 1998	8-Chuen	2
Sep 18 1998	9-Eb	3
Sep 19 1998	10-Ben	4
Sep 20 1998	11-Ix	5
Sep 21 1998	12-Men	6
Sep 22 1998	13-Cib	7
Sep 23 1998	1-Caban	8
Sep 24 1998	2-Etz'nab	9
Sep 25 1998	3-Cauac	1
Sep 26 1998	4-Ahau	2
Sep 27 1998	5-*Imix*	3
Sep 28 1998	6-Ik	4
Sep 29 1998	7-Akbal	5
Sep 30 1998	8-Kan	6
Oct 1 1998	9-Chicchan	7
Oct 2 1998	10-Cimi	8
Oct 3 1998	11-Manik	9
Oct 4 1998	12-Lamat	1
Oct 5 1998	13-Muluc	2
Oct 6 1998	1-Oc	3
Oct 7 1998	2-Chuen	4
Oct 8 1998	3-Eb	5
Oct 9 1998	4-Ben	6
Oct 10 1998	5-Ix	7
Oct 11 1998	6-Men	8
Oct 12 1998	7-Cib	9
Oct 13 1998	8-Caban	1
Oct 14 1998	9-Etz'nab	2
Oct 15 1998	10-Cauac	3
Oct 16 1998	11-Ahau	4
Oct 17 1998	12-*Imix*	5
Oct 18 1998	13-Ik	6
Oct 19 1998	1-Akbal	7
Oct 20 1998	2-Kan	8
Oct 21 1998	3-Chicchan	9
Oct 22 1998	4-Cimi	1
Oct 23 1998	5-Manik	2
Oct 24 1998	6-Lamat	3
Oct 25 1998	7-Muluc	4
Oct 26 1998	8-Oc	5
Oct 27 1998	9-Chuen	6
Oct 28 1998	10-Eb	7
Oct 29 1998	11-Ben	8
Oct 30 1998	12-Ix	9
Oct 31 1998	13-Men	1
Nov 1 1998	1-Cib	2
Nov 2 1998	2-Caban	3
Nov 3 1998	3-Etz'nab	4
Nov 4 1998	4-Cauac	5
Nov 5 1998	5-Ahau	6
Nov 6 1998	6-*Imix*	7
Nov 7 1998	7-Ik	8
Nov 8 1998	8-Akbal	9
Nov 9 1998	9-Kan	1
Nov 10 1998	10-Chicchan	2

Date	Day-Sign	L
Nov 11 1998	11-Cimi	3
Nov 12 1998	12-Manik	4
Nov 13 1998	13-Lamat	5
Nov 14 1998	1-Muluc	6
Nov 15 1998	2-Oc	7
Nov 16 1998	3-Chuen	8
Nov 17 1998	4-Eb	9
Nov 18 1998	5-Ben	1
Nov 19 1998	6-Ix	2
Nov 20 1998	7-Men	3
Nov 21 1998	8-Cib	4
Nov 22 1998	9-Caban	5
Nov 23 1998	10-Etz'nab	6
Nov 24 1998	11-Cauac	7
Nov 25 1998	12-Ahau	8
Nov 26 1998	13-*Imix*	9
Nov 27 1998	1-Ik	1
Nov 28 1998	2-Akbal	2
Nov 29 1998	3-Kan	3
Nov 30 1998	4-Chicchan	4
Dec 1 1998	5-Cimi	5
Dec 2 1998	6-Manik	6
Dec 3 1998	7-Lamat	7
Dec 4 1998	8-Muluc	8
Dec 5 1998	9-Oc	9
Dec 6 1998	10-Chuen	1
Dec 7 1998	11-Eb	2
Dec 8 1998	12-Ben	3
Dec 9 1998	13-Ix	4
Dec 10 1998	1-Men	5
Dec 11 1998	2-Cib	6
Dec 12 1998	3-Caban	7
Dec 13 1998	4-Etz'nab	8
Dec 14 1998	5-Cauac	9
Dec 15 1998	6-Ahau	1
Dec 16 1998	7-*Imix*	2
Dec 17 1998	8-Ik	3
Dec 18 1998	9-Akbal	4
Dec 19 1998	10-Kan	5
Dec 20 1998	11-Chicchan	6
Dec 21 1998	12-Cimi	7
Dec 22 1998	13-Manik	8
Dec 23 1998	1-Lamat	9
Dec 24 1998	2-Muluc	1
Dec 25 1998	3-Oc	2
Dec 26 1998	4-Chuen	3
Dec 27 1998	5-Eb	4
Dec 28 1998	6-Ben	5
Dec 29 1998	7-Ix	6
Dec 30 1998	8-Men	7
Dec 31 1998	9-Cib	8
Jan 1 1999	10-Caban	9
Jan 2 1999	11-Etz'nab	1
Jan 3 1999	12-Cauac	2
Jan 4 1999	13-Ahau	3
Jan 5 1999	1-Imix	4
Jan 6 1999	2-Ik	5
Jan 7 1999	3-Akbal	6
Jan 8 1999	4-Kan	7
Jan 9 1999	5-Chicchan	8
Jan 10 1999	6-Cimi	9
Jan 11 1999	7-Manik	1
Jan 12 1999	8-Lamat	2
Jan 13 1999	9-Muluc	3
Jan 14 1999	10-Oc	4
Jan 15 1999	11-Chuen	5
Jan 16 1999	12-Eb	6
Jan 17 1999	13-Ben	7

Date	Day-Sign	L
Jan 18 1999	1-Ix	8
Jan 19 1999	2-Men	9
Jan 20 1999	3-Cib	1
Jan 21 1999	4-Caban	2
Jan 22 1999	5-Etz'nab	3
Jan 23 1999	6-Cauac	4
Jan 24 1999	7-Ahau	5
Jan 25 1999	8-*Imix*	6
Jan 26 1999	9-Ik	7
Jan 27 1999	10-Akbal	8
Jan 28 1999	11-Kan	9
Jan 29 1999	12-Chicchan	1
Jan 30 1999	13-Cimi	2
Jan 31 1999	1-Manik	3
Feb 1 1999	2-Lamat	4
Feb 2 1999	3-Muluc	5
Feb 3 1999	4-Oc	6
Feb 4 1999	5-Chuen	7
Feb 5 1999	6-Eb	8
Feb 6 1999	7-Ben	9
Feb 7 1999	8-Ix	1
Feb 8 1999	9-Men	2
Feb 9 1999	10-Cib	3
Feb 10 1999	11-Caban	4
Feb 11 1999	12-Etz'nab	5
Feb 12 1999	13-Cauac	6
Feb 13 1999	1-Ahau	7
Feb 14 1999	2-*Imix*	8
Feb 15 1999	3-Ik	9
Feb 16 1999	4-Akbal	1
Feb 17 1999	5-Kan	2
Feb 18 1999	6-Chicchan	3
Feb 19 1999	7-Cimi	4
Feb 20 1999	8-Manik	5
Feb 21 1999	9-Lamat	6
Feb 22 1999	10-Muluc	7
Feb 23 1999	11-Oc	8
Feb 24 1999	12-Chuen	9
Feb 25 1999	13-Eb	1
Feb 26 1999	1-Ben	2
Feb 27 1999	2-Ix	3
Feb 28 1999	3-Men	4
Mar 1 1999	4-Cib	5
Mar 2 1999	5-Caban	6
Mar 3 1999	6-Etz'nab	7
Mar 4 1999	7-Cauac	8
Mar 5 1999	8-Ahau	9
Mar 6 1999	9-*Imix*	1
Mar 7 1999	10-Ik	2
Mar 8 1999	11-Akbal	3
Mar 9 1999	12-Kan	4
Mar 10 1999	13-Chicchan	5
Mar 11 1999	1-Cimi	6
Mar 12 1999	2-Manik	7
Mar 13 1999	3-Lamat	8
Mar 14 1999	4-Muluc	9
Mar 15 1999	5-Oc	1
Mar 16 1999	6-Chuen	2
Mar 17 1999	7-Eb	3
Mar 18 1999	8-Ben	4
Mar 19 1999	9-Ix	5
Mar 20 1999	10-Men	6
Mar 21 1999	11-Cib	7
Mar 22 1999	12-Caban	8
Mar 23 1999	13-Etz'nab	9
Mar 24 1999	1-Cauac	1
Mar 25 1999	2-Ahau	2
Mar 26 1999	3-*Imix*	3

Date	Day-Sign	L	Date	Day-Sign	L	Date	Day-Sign	L
Mar 27 1999	4-Ik	4	Jun 3 1999	7-Oc	9	Aug 10 1999	10-Etz'nab	5
Mar 28 1999	5-Akbal	5	Jun 4 1999	8-Chuen	1	Aug 11 1999	11-Cauac	6
Mar 29 1999	6-Kan	6	Jun 5 1999	9-Eb	2	Aug 12 1999	12-Ahau	7
Mar 30 1999	7-Chicchan	7	Jun 6 1999	10-Ben	3	Aug 13 1999	*13-Imix*	8
Mar 31 1999	8-Cimi	8	Jun 7 1999	11-Ix	4	Aug 14 1999	**1-Ik**	9
Apr 1 1999	9-Manik	9	Jun 8 1999	12-Men	5	Aug 15 1999	2-Akbal	1
Apr 2 1999	10-Lamat	1	Jun 9 1999	13-Cib	6	Aug 16 1999	3-Kan	2
Apr 3 1999	11-Muluc	2	Jun 10 1999	**1-Caban**	7	Aug 17 1999	4-Chicchan	3
Apr 4 1999	12-Oc	3	Jun 11 1999	2-Etz'nab	8	Aug 18 1999	5-Cimi	4
Apr 5 1999	13-Chuen	4	Jun 12 1999	3-Cauac	9	Aug 19 1999	6-Manik	5
Apr 6 1999	**1-Eb**	5	Jun 13 1999	4-Ahau	1	Aug 20 1999	7-Lamat	6
Apr 7 1999	2-Ben	6	Jun 14 1999	*5-Imix*	2	Aug 21 1999	8-Muluc	7
Apr 8 1999	3-Ix	7	Jun 15 1999	6-Ik	3	Aug 22 1999	9-Oc	8
Apr 9 1999	4-Men	8	Jun 16 1999	7-Akbal	4	Aug 23 1999	10-Chuen	9
Apr 10 1999	5-Cib	9	Jun 17 1999	8-Kan	5	Aug 24 1999	11-Eb	1
Apr 11 1999	6-Caban	1	Jun 18 1999	9-Chicchan	6	Aug 25 1999	12-Ben	2
Apr 12 1999	7-Etz'nab	2	Jun 19 1999	10-Cimi	7	Aug 26 1999	13-Ix	3
Apr 13 1999	8-Cauac	3	Jun 20 1999	11-Manik	8	Aug 27 1999	**1-Men**	4
Apr 14 1999	9-Ahau	4	Jun 21 1999	12-Lamat	9	Aug 28 1999	2-Cib	5
Apr 15 1999	*10-Imix*	5	Jun 22 1999	13-Muluc	1	Aug 29 1999	3-Caban	6
Apr 16 1999	11-Ik	6	Jun 23 1999	**1-Oc**	2	Aug 30 1999	4-Etz'nab	7
Apr 17 1999	12-Akbal	7	Jun 24 1999	2-Chuen	3	Aug 31 1999	5-Cauac	8
Apr 18 1999	13-Kan	8	Jun 25 1999	3-Eb	4	Sep 1 1999	6-Ahau	9
Apr 19 1999	**1-Chicchan**	9	Jun 26 1999	4-Ben	5	Sep 2 1999	*7-Imix*	1
Apr 20 1999	2-Cimi	1	Jun 27 1999	5-Ix	6	Sep 3 1999	8-Ik	2
Apr 21 1999	3-Manik	2	Jun 28 1999	6-Men	7	Sep 4 1999	9-Akbal	3
Apr 22 1999	4-Lamat	3	Jun 29 1999	7-Cib	8	Sep 5 1999	10-Kan	4
Apr 23 1999	5-Muluc	4	Jun 30 1999	8-Caban	9	Sep 6 1999	11-Chicchan	5
Apr 24 1999	6-Oc	5	Jul 1 1999	9-Etz'nab	1	Sep 7 1999	12-Cimi	6
Apr 25 1999	7-Chuen	6	Jul 2 1999	10-Cauac	2	Sep 8 1999	13-Manik	7
Apr 26 1999	8-Eb	7	Jul 3 1999	11-Ahau	3	Sep 9 1999	**1-Lamat**	8
Apr 27 1999	9-Ben	8	Jul 4 1999	*12-Imix*	4	Sep 10 1999	2-Muluc	9
Apr 28 1999	10-Ix	9	Jul 5 1999	13-Ik	5	Sep 11 1999	3-Oc	1
Apr 29 1999	11-Men	1	Jul 6 1999	**1-Akbal**	6	Sep 12 1999	4-Chuen	2
Apr 30 1999	12-Cib	2	Jul 7 1999	2-Kan	7	Sep 13 1999	5-Eb	3
May 1 1999	13-Caban	3	Jul 8 1999	3-Chicchan	8	Sep 14 1999	6-Ben	4
May 2 1999	**1-Etz'nab**	4	Jul 9 1999	4-Cimi	9	Sep 15 1999	7-Ix	5
May 3 1999	2-Cauac	5	Jul 10 1999	5-Manik	1	Sep 16 1999	8-Men	6
May 4 1999	3-Ahau	6	Jul 11 1999	6-Lamat	2	Sep 17 1999	9-Cib	7
May 5 1999	*4-Imix*	7	Jul 12 1999	7-Muluc	3	Sep 18 1999	10-Caban	8
May 6 1999	5-Ik	8	Jul 13 1999	8-Oc	4	Sep 19 1999	11-Etz'nab	9
May 7 1999	6-Akbal	9	Jul 14 1999	9-Chuen	5	Sep 20 1999	12-Cauac	1
May 8 1999	7-Kan	1	Jul 15 1999	10-Eb	6	Sep 21 1999	13-Ahau	2
May 9 1999	8-Chicchan	2	Jul 16 1999	11-Ben	7	Sep 22 1999	**1-Imix**	3
May 10 1999	9-Cimi	3	Jul 17 1999	12-Ix	8	Sep 23 1999	2-Ik	4
May 11 1999	10-Manik	4	Jul 18 1999	13-Men	9	Sep 24 1999	3-Akbal	5
May 12 1999	11-Lamat	5	Jul 19 1999	**1-Cib**	1	Sep 25 1999	4-Kan	6
May 13 1999	12-Muluc	6	Jul 20 1999	2-Caban	2	Sep 26 1999	5-Chicchan	7
May 14 1999	13-Oc	7	Jul 21 1999	3-Etz'nab	3	Sep 27 1999	6-Cimi	8
May 15 1999	**1-Chuen**	8	Jul 22 1999	4-Cauac	4	Sep 28 1999	7-Manik	9
May 16 1999	2-Eb	9	Jul 23 1999	5-Ahau	5	Sep 29 1999	8-Lamat	1
May 17 1999	3-Ben	1	Jul 24 1999	*6-Imix*	6	Sep 30 1999	9-Muluc	2
May 18 1999	4-Ix	2	Jul 25 1999	7-Ix	7	Oct 1 1999	10-Oc	3
May 19 1999	5-Men	3	Jul 26 1999	8-Akbal	8	Oct 2 1999	11-Chuen	4
May 20 1999	6-Cib	4	Jul 27 1999	9-Kan	9	Oct 3 1999	12-Eb	5
May 21 1999	7-Caban	5	Jul 28 1999	10-Chicchan	1	Oct 4 1999	13-Ben	6
May 22 1999	8-Etz'nab	6	Jul 29 1999	11-Cimi	2	Oct 5 1999	**1-Ix**	7
May 23 1999	9-Cauac	7	Jul 30 1999	12-Manik	3	Oct 6 1999	2-Men	8
May 24 1999	10-Ahau	8	Jul 31 1999	13-Lamat	4	Oct 7 1999	3-Cib	9
May 25 1999	*11-Imix*	9	Aug 1 1999	**1-Muluc**	5	Oct 8 1999	4-Caban	1
May 26 1999	12-Ik	1	Aug 2 1999	2-Oc	6	Oct 9 1999	5-Etz'nab	2
May 27 1999	13-Akbal	2	Aug 3 1999	3-Chuen	7	Oct 10 1999	6-Cauac	3
May 28 1999	**1-Kan**	3	Aug 4 1999	4-Eb	8	Oct 11 1999	7-Ahau	4
May 29 1999	2-Chicchan	4	Aug 5 1999	5-Ben	9	Oct 12 1999	*8-Imix*	5
May 30 1999	3-Cimi	5	Aug 6 1999	6-Ix	1	Oct 13 1999	9-Ik	6
May 31 1999	4-Manik	6	Aug 7 1999	7-Men	2	Oct 14 1999	10-Akbal	7
Jun 1 1999	5-Lamat	7	Aug 8 1999	8-Cib	3	Oct 15 1999	11-Kan	8
Jun 2 1999	6-Muluc	8	Aug 9 1999	9-Caban	4	Oct 16 1999	12-Chicchan	9

Date	Day-Sign	L
Oct 17 1999	13-Cimi	1
Oct 18 1999	**1-Manik**	2
Oct 19 1999	2-Lamat	3
Oct 20 1999	3-Muluc	4
Oct 21 1999	4-Oc	5
Oct 22 1999	5-Chuen	6
Oct 23 1999	6-Eb	7
Oct 24 1999	7-Ben	8
Oct 25 1999	8-Ix	9
Oct 26 1999	9-Men	1
Oct 27 1999	10-Cib	2
Oct 28 1999	11-Caban	3
Oct 29 1999	12-Etz'nab	4
Oct 30 1999	13-Cauac	5
Oct 31 1999	**1-Ahau**	6
Nov 1 1999	2-*Imix*	7
Nov 2 1999	3-Ik	8
Nov 3 1999	4-Akbal	9
Nov 4 1999	5-Kan	1
Nov 5 1999	6-Chicchan	2
Nov 6 1999	7-Cimi	3
Nov 7 1999	8-Manik	4
Nov 8 1999	9-Lamat	5
Nov 9 1999	10-Muluc	6
Nov 10 1999	11-Oc	7
Nov 11 1999	12-Chuen	8
Nov 12 1999	13-Eb	9
Nov 13 1999	**1-Ben**	1
Nov 14 1999	2-Ix	2
Nov 15 1999	3-Men	3
Nov 16 1999	4-Cib	4
Nov 17 1999	5-Caban	5
Nov 18 1999	6-Etz'nab	6
Nov 19 1999	7-Cauac	7
Nov 20 1999	8-Ahau	8
Nov 21 1999	9-*Imix*	9
Nov 22 1999	10-Ik	1
Nov 23 1999	11-Akbal	2
Nov 24 1999	12-Kan	3
Nov 25 1999	13-Chicchan	4
Nov 26 1999	**1-Cimi**	5
Nov 27 1999	2-Manik	6
Nov 28 1999	3-Lamat	7
Nov 29 1999	4-Muluc	8
Nov 30 1999	5-Oc	9
Dec 1 1999	6-Chuen	1
Dec 2 1999	7-Eb	2
Dec 3 1999	8-Ben	3
Dec 4 1999	9-Ix	4
Dec 5 1999	10-Men	5
Dec 6 1999	11-Cib	6
Dec 7 1999	12-Caban	7
Dec 8 1999	13-Etz'nab	8
Dec 9 1999	**1-Cauac**	9
Dec 10 1999	2-Ahau	1
Dec 11 1999	3-*Imix*	2
Dec 12 1999	4-Ik	3
Dec 13 1999	5-Akbal	4
Dec 14 1999	6-Kan	5
Dec 15 1999	7-Chicchan	6
Dec 16 1999	8-Cimi	7
Dec 17 1999	9-Manik	8
Dec 18 1999	10-Lamat	9
Dec 19 1999	11-Muluc	1
Dec 20 1999	12-Oc	2
Dec 21 1999	13-Chuen	3
Dec 22 1999	**1-Eb**	4
Dec 23 1999	2-Ben	5

Date	Day-Sign	L
Dec 24 1999	3-Ix	6
Dec 25 1999	4-Men	7
Dec 26 1999	5-Cib	8
Dec 27 1999	6-Caban	9
Dec 28 1999	7-Etz'nab	1
Dec 29 1999	8-Cauac	2
Dec 30 1999	9-Ahau	3
Dec 31 1999	10-*Imix*	4
Jan 1 2000	11-Ik	5
Jan 2 2000	12-Akbal	6
Jan 3 2000	13-Kan	7
Jan 4 2000	**1-Chicchan**	8
Jan 5 2000	2-Cimi	9
Jan 6 2000	3-Manik	1
Jan 7 2000	4-Lamat	2
Jan 8 2000	5-Muluc	3
Jan 9 2000	6-Oc	4
Jan 10 2000	7-Chuen	5
Jan 11 2000	8-Eb	6
Jan 12 2000	9-Ben	7
Jan 13 2000	10-Ix	8
Jan 14 2000	11-Men	9
Jan 15 2000	12-Cib	1
Jan 16 2000	13-Caban	2
Jan 17 2000	**1-Etz'nab**	3
Jan 18 2000	2-Cauac	4
Jan 19 2000	3-Ahau	5
Jan 20 2000	4-*Imix*	6
Jan 21 2000	5-Ik	7
Jan 22 2000	6-Akbal	8
Jan 23 2000	7-Kan	9
Jan 24 2000	8-Chicchan	1
Jan 25 2000	9-Cimi	2
Jan 26 2000	10-Manik	3
Jan 27 2000	11-Lamat	4
Jan 28 2000	12-Muluc	5
Jan 29 2000	13-Oc	6
Jan 30 2000	**1-Chuen**	7
Jan 31 2000	2-Eb	8
Feb 1 2000	3-Ben	9
Feb 2 2000	4-Ix	1
Feb 3 2000	5-Men	2
Feb 4 2000	6-Cib	3
Feb 5 2000	7-Caban	4
Feb 6 2000	8-Etz'nab	5
Feb 7 2000	9-Cauac	6
Feb 8 2000	10-Ahau	7
Feb 9 2000	11-*Imix*	8
Feb 10 2000	12-Ik	9
Feb 11 2000	13-Akbal	1
Feb 12 2000	**1-Kan**	2
Feb 13 2000	2-Chicchan	3
Feb 14 2000	3-Cimi	4
Feb 15 2000	4-Manik	5
Feb 16 2000	5-Lamat	6
Feb 17 2000	6-Muluc	7
Feb 18 2000	7-Oc	8
Feb 19 2000	8-Chuen	9
Feb 20 2000	9-Eb	1
Feb 21 2000	10-Ben	2
Feb 22 2000	11-Ix	3
Feb 23 2000	12-Men	4
Feb 24 2000	13-Cib	5
Feb 25 2000	**1-Caban**	6
Feb 26 2000	2-Etz'nab	7
Feb 27 2000	3-Cauac	8
Feb 28 2000	4-Ahau	9
Feb 29 2000	5-*Imix*	1

Date	Day-Sign	L
Mar 1 2000	6-Ik	2
Mar 2 2000	7-Akbal	3
Mar 3 2000	8-Kan	4
Mar 4 2000	9-Chicchan	5
Mar 5 2000	10-Cimi	6
Mar 6 2000	11-Manik	7
Mar 7 2000	12-Lamat	8
Mar 8 2000	13-Muluc	9
Mar 9 2000	**1-Oc**	1
Mar 10 2000	2-Chuen	2
Mar 11 2000	3-Eb	3
Mar 12 2000	4-Ben	4
Mar 13 2000	5-Ix	5
Mar 14 2000	6-Men	6
Mar 15 2000	7-Cib	7
Mar 16 2000	8-Caban	8
Mar 17 2000	9-Etz'nab	9
Mar 18 2000	10-Cauac	1
Mar 19 2000	11-Ahau	2
Mar 20 2000	12-*Imix*	3
Mar 21 2000	13-Ik	4
Mar 22 2000	**1-Akbal**	5
Mar 23 2000	2-Kan	6
Mar 24 2000	3-Chicchan	7
Mar 25 2000	4-Cimi	8
Mar 26 2000	5-Manik	9
Mar 27 2000	6-Lamat	1
Mar 28 2000	7-Muluc	2
Mar 29 2000	8-Oc	3
Mar 30 2000	9-Chuen	4
Mar 31 2000	10-Eb	5
Apr 1 2000	11-Ben	6
Apr 2 2000	12-Ix	7
Apr 3 2000	13-Men	8
Apr 4 2000	**1-Cib**	9
Apr 5 2000	2-Caban	1
Apr 6 2000	3-Etz'nab	2
Apr 7 2000	4-Cauac	3
Apr 8 2000	5-Ahau	4
Apr 9 2000	6-*Imix*	5
Apr 10 2000	7-Ik	6
Apr 11 2000	8-Akbal	7
Apr 12 2000	9-Kan	8
Apr 13 2000	10-Chicchan	9
Apr 14 2000	11-Cimi	1
Apr 15 2000	12-Manik	2
Apr 16 2000	13-Lamat	3
Apr 17 2000	**1-Muluc**	4
Apr 18 2000	2-Oc	5
Apr 19 2000	3-Chuen	6
Apr 20 2000	4-Eb	7
Apr 21 2000	5-Ben	8
Apr 22 2000	6-Ix	9
Apr 23 2000	7-Men	1
Apr 24 2000	8-Cib	2
Apr 25 2000	9-Caban	3
Apr 26 2000	10-Etz'nab	4
Apr 27 2000	11-Cauac	5
Apr 28 2000	12-Ahau	6
Apr 29 2000	13-*Imix*	7
Apr 30 2000	**1-Ik**	8
May 1 2000	2-Akbal	9
May 2 2000	3-Kan	1
May 3 2000	4-Chicchan	2
May 4 2000	5-Cimi	3
May 5 2000	6-Manik	4
May 6 2000	7-Lamat	5
May 7 2000	8-Muluc	6

Date	Day-Sign	L
May 8 2000	9-Oc	7
May 9 2000	10-Chuen	8
May 10 2000	11-Eb	9
May 11 2000	12-Ben	1
May 12 2000	13-Ix	2
May 13 2000	1-Men	3
May 14 2000	2-Cib	4
May 15 2000	3-Caban	5
May 16 2000	4-Etz'nab	6
May 17 2000	5-Cauac	7
May 18 2000	6-Ahau	8
May 19 2000	7-Imix	9
May 20 2000	8-Ik	1
May 21 2000	9-Akbal	2
May 22 2000	10-Kan	3
May 23 2000	11-Chicchan	4
May 24 2000	12-Cimi	5
May 25 2000	13-Manik	6
May 26 2000	1-Lamat	7
May 27 2000	2-Muluc	8
May 28 2000	3-Oc	9
May 29 2000	4-Chuen	1
May 30 2000	5-Eb	2
May 31 2000	6-Ben	3
Jun 1 2000	7-Ix	4
Jun 2 2000	8-Men	5
Jun 3 2000	9-Cib	6
Jun 4 2000	10-Caban	7
Jun 5 2000	11-Etz'nab	8
Jun 6 2000	12-Cauac	9
Jun 7 2000	13-Ahau	1
Jun 8 2000	1-Imix	2
Jun 9 2000	2-Ik	3
Jun 10 2000	3-Akbal	4
Jun 11 2000	4-Kan	5
Jun 12 2000	5-Chicchan	6
Jun 13 2000	6-Cimi	7
Jun 14 2000	7-Manik	8
Jun 15 2000	8-Lamat	9
Jun 16 2000	9-Muluc	1
Jun 17 2000	10-Oc	2
Jun 18 2000	11-Chuen	3
Jun 19 2000	12-Eb	4
Jun 20 2000	13-Ben	5
Jun 21 2000	1-Ix	6
Jun 22 2000	2-Men	7
Jun 23 2000	3-Cib	8
Jun 24 2000	4-Caban	9
Jun 25 2000	5-Etz'nab	1
Jun 26 2000	6-Cauac	2
Jun 27 2000	7-Ahau	3
Jun 28 2000	8-Imix	4
Jun 29 2000	9-Ik	5
Jun 30 2000	10-Akbal	6
Jul 1 2000	11-Kan	7
Jul 2 2000	12-Chicchan	8
Jul 3 2000	13-Cimi	9
Jul 4 2000	1-Manik	1
Jul 5 2000	2-Lamat	2
Jul 6 2000	3-Muluc	3
Jul 7 2000	4-Oc	4
Jul 8 2000	5-Chuen	5
Jul 9 2000	6-Eb	6
Jul 10 2000	7-Ben	7
Jul 11 2000	8-Ix	8
Jul 12 2000	9-Men	9
Jul 13 2000	10-Cib	1
Jul 14 2000	11-Caban	2

Date	Day-Sign	L
Jul 15 2000	12-Etz'nab	3
Jul 16 2000	13-Cauac	4
Jul 17 2000	1-Ahau	5
Jul 18 2000	2-Imix	6
Jul 19 2000	3-Ik	7
Jul 20 2000	4-Akbal	8
Jul 21 2000	5-Kan	9
Jul 22 2000	6-Chicchan	1
Jul 23 2000	7-Cimi	2
Jul 24 2000	8-Manik	3
Jul 25 2000	9-Lamat	4
Jul 26 2000	10-Muluc	5
Jul 27 2000	11-Oc	6
Jul 28 2000	12-Chuen	7
Jul 29 2000	13-Eb	8
Jul 30 2000	1-Ben	9
Jul 31 2000	2-Ix	1
Aug 1 2000	3-Men	2
Aug 2 2000	4-Cib	3
Aug 3 2000	5-Caban	4
Aug 4 2000	6-Etz'nab	5
Aug 5 2000	7-Cauac	6
Aug 6 2000	8-Ahau	7
Aug 7 2000	9-Imix	8
Aug 8 2000	10-Ik	9
Aug 9 2000	11-Akbal	1
Aug 10 2000	12-Kan	2
Aug 11 2000	13-Chicchan	3
Aug 12 2000	1-Cimi	4
Aug 13 2000	2-Manik	5
Aug 14 2000	3-Lamat	6
Aug 15 2000	4-Muluc	7
Aug 16 2000	5-Oc	8
Aug 17 2000	6-Chuen	9
Aug 18 2000	7-Eb	1
Aug 19 2000	8-Ben	2
Aug 20 2000	9-Ix	3
Aug 21 2000	10-Men	4
Aug 22 2000	11-Cib	5
Aug 23 2000	12-Caban	6
Aug 24 2000	13-Etz'nab	7
Aug 25 2000	1-Cauac	8
Aug 26 2000	2-Ahau	9
Aug 27 2000	3-Imix	1
Aug 28 2000	4-Ik	2
Aug 29 2000	5-Akbal	3
Aug 30 2000	6-Kan	4
Aug 31 2000	7-Chicchan	5
Sep 1 2000	8-Cimi	6
Sep 2 2000	9-Manik	7
Sep 3 2000	10-Lamat	8
Sep 4 2000	11-Muluc	9
Sep 5 2000	12-Oc	1
Sep 6 2000	13-Chuen	2
Sep 7 2000	1-Eb	3
Sep 8 2000	2-Ben	4
Sep 9 2000	3-Ix	5
Sep 10 2000	4-Men	6
Sep 11 2000	5-Cib	7
Sep 12 2000	6-Caban	8
Sep 13 2000	7-Etz'nab	9
Sep 14 2000	8-Cauac	1
Sep 15 2000	9-Ahau	2
Sep 16 2000	10-Imix	3
Sep 17 2000	11-Ik	4
Sep 18 2000	12-Akbal	5
Sep 19 2000	13-Kan	6
Sep 20 2000	1-Chicchan	7

Date	Day-Sign	L
Sep 21 2000	2-Cimi	8
Sep 22 2000	3-Manik	9
Sep 23 2000	4-Lamat	1
Sep 24 2000	5-Muluc	2
Sep 25 2000	6-Oc	3
Sep 26 2000	7-Chuen	4
Sep 27 2000	8-Eb	5
Sep 28 2000	9-Ben	6
Sep 29 2000	10-Ix	7
Sep 30 2000	11-Men	8
Oct 1 2000	12-Cib	9
Oct 2 2000	13-Caban	1
Oct 3 2000	1-Etz'nab	2
Oct 4 2000	2-Cauac	3
Oct 5 2000	3-Ahau	4
Oct 6 2000	4-Imix	5
Oct 7 2000	5-Ik	6
Oct 8 2000	6-Akbal	7
Oct 9 2000	7-Kan	8
Oct 10 2000	8-Chicchan	9
Oct 11 2000	9-Cimi	1
Oct 12 2000	10-Manik	2
Oct 13 2000	11-Lamat	3
Oct 14 2000	12-Muluc	4
Oct 15 2000	13-Oc	5
Oct 16 2000	1-Chuen	6
Oct 17 2000	2-Eb	7
Oct 18 2000	3-Ben	8
Oct 19 2000	4-Ix	9
Oct 20 2000	5-Men	1
Oct 21 2000	6-Cib	2
Oct 22 2000	7-Caban	3
Oct 23 2000	8-Etz'nab	4
Oct 24 2000	9-Cauac	5
Oct 25 2000	10-Ahau	6
Oct 26 2000	11-Imix	7
Oct 27 2000	12-Ik	8
Oct 28 2000	13-Akbal	9
Oct 29 2000	1-Kan	1
Oct 30 2000	2-Chicchan	2
Oct 31 2000	3-Cimi	3
Nov 1 2000	4-Manik	4
Nov 2 2000	5-Lamat	5
Nov 3 2000	6-Muluc	6
Nov 4 2000	7-Oc	7
Nov 5 2000	8-Chuen	8
Nov 6 2000	9-Eb	9
Nov 7 2000	10-Ben	1
Nov 8 2000	11-Ix	2
Nov 9 2000	12-Men	3
Nov 10 2000	13-Cib	4
Nov 11 2000	1-Caban	5
Nov 12 2000	2-Etz'nab	6
Nov 13 2000	3-Cauac	7
Nov 14 2000	4-Ahau	8
Nov 15 2000	5-Imix	9
Nov 16 2000	6-Ik	1
Nov 17 2000	7-Akbal	2
Nov 18 2000	8-Kan	3
Nov 19 2000	9-Chicchan	4
Nov 20 2000	10-Cimi	5
Nov 21 2000	11-Manik	6
Nov 22 2000	12-Lamat	7
Nov 23 2000	13-Muluc	8
Nov 24 2000	1-Oc	9
Nov 25 2000	2-Chuen	1
Nov 26 2000	3-Eb	2
Nov 27 2000	4-Ben	3

Date	Day-Sign	L
Nov 28 2000	5-Ix	4
Nov 29 2000	6-Men	5
Nov 30 2000	7-Cib	6
Dec 1 2000	8-Caban	7
Dec 2 2000	9-Etz'nab	8
Dec 3 2000	10-Cauac	9
Dec 4 2000	11-Ahau	1
Dec 5 2000	12-Imix	2
Dec 6 2000	13-Ik	3
Dec 7 2000	1-Akbal	4
Dec 8 2000	2-Kan	5
Dec 9 2000	3-Chicchan	6
Dec 10 2000	4-Cimi	7
Dec 11 2000	5-Manik	8
Dec 12 2000	6-Lamat	9
Dec 13 2000	7-Muluc	1
Dec 14 2000	8-Oc	2
Dec 15 2000	9-Chuen	3
Dec 16 2000	10-Eb	4
Dec 17 2000	11-Ben	5
Dec 18 2000	12-Ix	6
Dec 19 2000	13-Men	7
Dec 20 2000	1-Cib	8
Dec 21 2000	2-Caban	9
Dec 22 2000	3-Etz'nab	1
Dec 23 2000	4-Cauac	2
Dec 24 2000	5-Ahau	3
Dec 25 2000	6-Imix	4
Dec 26 2000	7-Ik	5
Dec 27 2000	8-Akbal	6
Dec 28 2000	9-Kan	7
Dec 29 2000	10-Chicchan	8
Dec 30 2000	11-Cimi	9
Dec 31 2000	12-Manik	1
Jan 1 2001	13-Lamat	2
Jan 2 2001	1-Muluc	3
Jan 3 2001	2-Oc	4
Jan 4 2001	3-Chuen	5
Jan 5 2001	4-Eb	6
Jan 6 2001	5-Ben	7
Jan 7 2001	6-Ix	8
Jan 8 2001	7-Men	9
Jan 9 2001	8-Cib	1
Jan 10 2001	9-Caban	2
Jan 11 2001	10-Etz'nab	3
Jan 12 2001	11-Cauac	4
Jan 13 2001	12-Ahau	5
Jan 14 2001	13-Imix	6
Jan 15 2001	1-Ik	7
Jan 16 2001	2-Akbal	8
Jan 17 2001	3-Kan	9
Jan 18 2001	4-Chicchan	1
Jan 19 2001	5-Cimi	2
Jan 20 2001	6-Manik	3
Jan 21 2001	7-Lamat	4
Jan 22 2001	8-Muluc	5
Jan 23 2001	9-Oc	6
Jan 24 2001	10-Chuen	7
Jan 25 2001	11-Eb	8
Jan 26 2001	12-Ben	9
Jan 27 2001	13-Ix	1
Jan 28 2001	1-Men	2
Jan 29 2001	2-Cib	3
Jan 30 2001	3-Caban	4
Jan 31 2001	4-Etz'nab	5
Feb 1 2001	5-Cauac	6
Feb 2 2001	6-Ahau	7
Feb 3 2001	7-Imix	8

Date	Day-Sign	L
Feb 4 2001	8-Ik	9
Feb 5 2001	9-Akbal	1
Feb 6 2001	10-Kan	2
Feb 7 2001	11-Chicchan	3
Feb 8 2001	12-Cimi	4
Feb 9 2001	13-Manik	5
Feb 10 2001	1-Lamat	6
Feb 11 2001	2-Muluc	7
Feb 12 2001	3-Oc	8
Feb 13 2001	4-Chuen	9
Feb 14 2001	5-Eb	1
Feb 15 2001	6-Ben	2
Feb 16 2001	7-Ix	3
Feb 17 2001	8-Men	4
Feb 18 2001	9-Cib	5
Feb 19 2001	10-Caban	6
Feb 20 2001	11-Etz'nab	7
Feb 21 2001	12-Cauac	8
Feb 22 2001	13-Ahau	9
Feb 23 2001	1-Imix	1
Feb 24 2001	2-Ik	2
Feb 25 2001	3-Akbal	3
Feb 26 2001	4-Kan	4
Feb 27 2001	5-Chicchan	5
Feb 28 2001	6-Cimi	6
Mar 1 2001	7-Manik	7
Mar 2 2001	8-Lamat	8
Mar 3 2001	9-Muluc	9
Mar 4 2001	10-Oc	1
Mar 5 2001	11-Chuen	2
Mar 6 2001	12-Eb	3
Mar 7 2001	13-Ben	4
Mar 8 2001	1-Ix	5
Mar 9 2001	2-Men	6
Mar 10 2001	3-Cib	7
Mar 11 2001	4-Caban	8
Mar 12 2001	5-Etz'nab	9
Mar 13 2001	6-Cauac	1
Mar 14 2001	7-Ahau	2
Mar 15 2001	8-Imix	3
Mar 16 2001	9-Ik	4
Mar 17 2001	10-Akbal	5
Mar 18 2001	11-Kan	6
Mar 19 2001	12-Chicchan	7
Mar 20 2001	13-Cimi	8
Mar 21 2001	1-Manik	9
Mar 22 2001	2-Lamat	1
Mar 23 2001	3-Muluc	2
Mar 24 2001	4-Oc	3
Mar 25 2001	5-Chuen	4
Mar 26 2001	6-Eb	5
Mar 27 2001	7-Ben	6
Mar 28 2001	8-Ix	7
Mar 29 2001	9-Men	8
Mar 30 2001	10-Cib	9
Mar 31 2001	11-Caban	1
Apr 1 2001	12-Etz'nab	2
Apr 2 2001	13-Cauac	3
Apr 3 2001	1-Ahau	4
Apr 4 2001	2-Imix	5
Apr 5 2001	3-Ik	6
Apr 6 2001	4-Akbal	7
Apr 7 2001	5-Kan	8
Apr 8 2001	6-Chicchan	9
Apr 9 2001	7-Cimi	1
Apr 10 2001	8-Manik	2
Apr 11 2001	9-Lamat	3
Apr 12 2001	10-Muluc	4

Date	Day-Sign	L
Apr 13 2001	11-Oc	5
Apr 14 2001	12-Chuen	6
Apr 15 2001	13-Eb	7
Apr 16 2001	1-Ben	8
Apr 17 2001	2-Ix	9
Apr 18 2001	3-Men	1
Apr 19 2001	4-Cib	2
Apr 20 2001	5-Caban	3
Apr 21 2001	6-Etz'nab	4
Apr 22 2001	7-Cauac	5
Apr 23 2001	8-Ahau	6
Apr 24 2001	9-Imix	7
Apr 25 2001	10-Ik	8
Apr 26 2001	11-Akbal	9
Apr 27 2001	12-Kan	1
Apr 28 2001	13-Chicchan	2
Apr 29 2001	1-Cimi	3
Apr 30 2001	2-Manik	4
May 1 2001	3-Lamat	5
May 2 2001	4-Muluc	6
May 3 2001	5-Oc	7
May 4 2001	6-Chuen	8
May 5 2001	7-Eb	9
May 6 2001	8-Ben	1
May 7 2001	9-Ix	2
May 8 2001	10-Men	3
May 9 2001	11-Cib	4
May 10 2001	12-Caban	5
May 11 2001	13-Etz'nab	6
May 12 2001	1-Cauac	7
May 13 2001	2-Ahau	8
May 14 2001	3-Imix	9
May 15 2001	4-Ik	1
May 16 2001	5-Akbal	2
May 17 2001	6-Kan	3
May 18 2001	7-Chicchan	4
May 19 2001	8-Cimi	5
May 20 2001	9-Manik	6
May 21 2001	10-Lamat	7
May 22 2001	11-Muluc	8
May 23 2001	12-Oc	9
May 24 2001	13-Chuen	1
May 25 2001	1-Eb	2
May 26 2001	2-Ben	3
May 27 2001	3-Ix	4
May 28 2001	4-Men	5
May 29 2001	5-Cib	6
May 30 2001	6-Caban	7
May 31 2001	7-Etz'nab	8
Jun 1 2001	8-Cauac	9
Jun 2 2001	9-Ahau	1
Jun 3 2001	10-Imix	2
Jun 4 2001	11-Ik	3
Jun 5 2001	12-Akbal	4
Jun 6 2001	13-Kan	5
Jun 7 2001	1-Chicchan	6
Jun 8 2001	2-Cimi	7
Jun 9 2001	3-Manik	8
Jun 10 2001	4-Lamat	9
Jun 11 2001	5-Muluc	1
Jun 12 2001	6-Oc	2
Jun 13 2001	7-Chuen	3
Jun 14 2001	8-Eb	4
Jun 15 2001	9-Ben	5
Jun 16 2001	10-Ix	6
Jun 17 2001	11-Men	7
Jun 18 2001	12-Cib	8
Jun 19 2001	13-Caban	9

Date	Day-Sign	L	Date	Day-Sign	L	Date	Day-Sign	L
Jun 20 2001	1-Etz'nab	1	Aug 27 2001	4-Cimi	6	Nov 3 2001	7-Ix	2
Jun 21 2001	2-Cauac	2	Aug 28 2001	5-Manik	7	Nov 4 2001	8-Men	3
Jun 22 2001	3-Ahau	3	Aug 29 2001	6-Lamat	8	Nov 5 2001	9-Cib	4
Jun 23 2001	4-Imix	4	Aug 30 2001	7-Muluc	9	Nov 6 2001	10-Caban	5
Jun 24 2001	5-Ik	5	Aug 31 2001	8-Oc	1	Nov 7 2001	11-Etz'nab	6
Jun 25 2001	6-Akbal	6	Sep 1 2001	9-Chuen	2	Nov 8 2001	12-Cauac	7
Jun 26 2001	7-Kan	7	Sep 2 2001	10-Eb	3	Nov 9 2001	13-Ahau	8
Jun 27 2001	8-Chicchan	8	Sep 3 2001	11-Ben	4	Nov 10 2001	1-Imix	9
Jun 28 2001	9-Cimi	9	Sep 4 2001	12-Ix	5	Nov 11 2001	2-Ik	1
Jun 29 2001	10-Manik	1	Sep 5 2001	13-Men	6	Nov 12 2001	3-Akbal	2
Jun 30 2001	11-Lamat	2	Sep 6 2001	1-Cib	7	Nov 13 2001	4-Kan	3
Jul 1 2001	12-Muluc	3	Sep 7 2001	2-Caban	8	Nov 14 2001	5-Chicchan	4
Jul 2 2001	13-Oc	4	Sep 8 2001	3-Etz'nab	9	Nov 15 2001	6-Cimi	5
Jul 3 2001	1-Chuen	5	Sep 9 2001	4-Cauac	1	Nov 16 2001	7-Manik	6
Jul 4 2001	2-Eb	6	Sep 10 2001	5-Ahau	2	Nov 17 2001	8-Lamat	7
Jul 5 2001	3-Ben	7	Sep 11 2001	6-Imix	3	Nov 18 2001	9-Muluc	8
Jul 6 2001	4-Ix	8	Sep 12 2001	7-Ik	4	Nov 19 2001	10-Oc	9
Jul 7 2001	5-Men	9	Sep 13 2001	8-Akbal	5	Nov 20 2001	11-Chuen	1
Jul 8 2001	6-Cib	1	Sep 14 2001	9-Kan	6	Nov 21 2001	12-Eb	2
Jul 9 2001	7-Caban	2	Sep 15 2001	10-Chicchan	7	Nov 22 2001	13-Ben	3
Jul 10 2001	8-Etz'nab	3	Sep 16 2001	11-Cimi	8	Nov 23 2001	1-Ix	4
Jul 11 2001	9-Cauac	4	Sep 17 2001	12-Manik	9	Nov 24 2001	2-Men	5
Jul 12 2001	10-Ahau	5	Sep 18 2001	13-Lamat	1	Nov 25 2001	3-Cib	6
Jul 13 2001	11-Imix	6	Sep 19 2001	1-Muluc	2	Nov 26 2001	4-Caban	7
Jul 14 2001	12-Ik	7	Sep 20 2001	2-Oc	3	Nov 27 2001	5-Etz'nab	8
Jul 15 2001	13-Akbal	8	Sep 21 2001	3-Chuen	4	Nov 28 2001	6-Cauac	9
Jul 16 2001	1-Kan	9	Sep 22 2001	4-Eb	5	Nov 29 2001	7-Ahau	1
Jul 17 2001	2-Chicchan	1	Sep 23 2001	5-Ben	6	Nov 30 2001	8-Imix	2
Jul 18 2001	3-Cimi	2	Sep 24 2001	6-Ix	7	Dec 1 2001	9-Ik	3
Jul 19 2001	4-Manik	3	Sep 25 2001	7-Men	8	Dec 2 2001	10-Akbal	4
Jul 20 2001	5-Lamat	4	Sep 26 2001	8-Cib	9	Dec 3 2001	11-Kan	5
Jul 21 2001	6-Muluc	5	Sep 27 2001	9-Caban	1	Dec 4 2001	12-Chicchan	6
Jul 22 2001	7-Oc	6	Sep 28 2001	10-Etz'nab	2	Dec 5 2001	13-Cimi	7
Jul 23 2001	8-Chuen	7	Sep 29 2001	11-Cauac	3	Dec 6 2001	1-Manik	8
Jul 24 2001	9-Eb	8	Sep 30 2001	12-Ahau	4	Dec 7 2001	2-Lamat	9
Jul 25 2001	10-Ben	9	Oct 1 2001	13-Imix	5	Dec 8 2001	3-Muluc	1
Jul 26 2001	11-Ix	1	Oct 2 2001	1-Ik	6	Dec 9 2001	4-Oc	2
Jul 27 2001	12-Men	2	Oct 3 2001	2-Akbal	7	Dec 10 2001	5-Chuen	3
Jul 28 2001	13-Cib	3	Oct 4 2001	3-Kan	8	Dec 11 2001	6-Eb	4
Jul 29 2001	1-Caban	4	Oct 5 2001	4-Chicchan	9	Dec 12 2001	7-Ben	5
Jul 30 2001	2-Etz'nab	5	Oct 6 2001	5-Cimi	1	Dec 13 2001	8-Ix	6
Jul 31 2001	3-Cauac	6	Oct 7 2001	6-Manik	2	Dec 14 2001	9-Men	7
Aug 1 2001	4-Ahau	7	Oct 8 2001	7-Lamat	3	Dec 15 2001	10-Cib	8
Aug 2 2001	5-Imix	8	Oct 9 2001	8-Muluc	4	Dec 16 2001	11-Caban	9
Aug 3 2001	6-Ik	9	Oct 10 2001	9-Oc	5	Dec 17 2001	12-Etz'nab	1
Aug 4 2001	7-Akbal	1	Oct 11 2001	10-Chuen	6	Dec 18 2001	13-Cauac	2
Aug 5 2001	8-Kan	2	Oct 12 2001	11-Eb	7	Dec 19 2001	1-Ahau	3
Aug 6 2001	9-Chicchan	3	Oct 13 2001	12-Ben	8	Dec 20 2001	2-Imix	4
Aug 7 2001	10-Cimi	4	Oct 14 2001	13-Ix	9	Dec 21 2001	3-Ik	5
Aug 8 2001	11-Manik	5	Oct 15 2001	1-Men	1	Dec 22 2001	4-Akbal	6
Aug 9 2001	12-Lamat	6	Oct 16 2001	2-Cib	2	Dec 23 2001	5-Kan	7
Aug 10 2001	13-Muluc	7	Oct 17 2001	3-Caban	3	Dec 24 2001	6-Chicchan	8
Aug 11 2001	1-Oc	8	Oct 18 2001	4-Etz'nab	4	Dec 25 2001	7-Cimi	9
Aug 12 2001	2-Chuen	9	Oct 19 2001	5-Cauac	5	Dec 26 2001	8-Manik	1
Aug 13 2001	3-Eb	1	Oct 20 2001	6-Ahau	6	Dec 27 2001	9-Lamat	2
Aug 14 2001	4-Ben	2	Oct 21 2001	7-Imix	7	Dec 28 2001	10-Muluc	3
Aug 15 2001	5-Ix	3	Oct 22 2001	8-Ik	8	Dec 29 2001	11-Oc	4
Aug 16 2001	6-Men	4	Oct 23 2001	9-Akbal	9	Dec 30 2001	12-Chuen	5
Aug 17 2001	7-Cib	5	Oct 24 2001	10-Kan	1	Dec 31 2001	13-Eb	6
Aug 18 2001	8-Caban	6	Oct 25 2001	11-Chicchan	2	Jan 1 2002	1-Ben	7
Aug 19 2001	9-Etz'nab	7	Oct 26 2001	12-Cimi	3	Jan 2 2002	2-Ix	8
Aug 20 2001	10-Cauac	8	Oct 27 2001	13-Manik	4	Jan 3 2002	3-Men	9
Aug 21 2001	11-Ahau	9	Oct 28 2001	1-Lamat	5	Jan 4 2002	4-Cib	1
Aug 22 2001	12-Imix	1	Oct 29 2001	2-Muluc	6	Jan 5 2002	5-Caban	2
Aug 23 2001	13-Ik	2	Oct 30 2001	3-Oc	7	Jan 6 2002	6-Etz'nab	3
Aug 24 2001	1-Akbal	3	Oct 31 2001	4-Chuen	8	Jan 7 2002	7-Cauac	4
Aug 25 2001	2-Kan	4	Nov 1 2001	5-Eb	9	Jan 8 2002	8-Ahau	5
Aug 26 2001	3-Chicchan	5	Nov 2 2001	6-Ben	1	Jan 9 2002	9-Imix	6

Date	Day-Sign	L	Date	Day-Sign	L	Date	Day-Sign	L
Jan 10 2002	10-Ik	7	Mar 19 2002	13-Oc	3	May 26 2002	3-Etz'nab	8
Jan 11 2002	11-Akbal	8	Mar 20 2002	**1-Chuen**	4	May 27 2002	4-Cauac	9
Jan 12 2002	12-Kan	9	Mar 21 2002	2-Eb	5	May 28 2002	5-Ahau	1
Jan 13 2002	13-Chicchan	1	Mar 22 2002	3-Ben	6	May 29 2002	6-*Imix*	2
Jan 14 2002	**1-Cimi**	2	Mar 23 2002	4-Ix	7	May 30 2002	7-Ik	3
Jan 15 2002	2-Manik	3	Mar 24 2002	5-Men	8	May 31 2002	8-Akbal	4
Jan 16 2002	3-Lamat	4	Mar 25 2002	6-Cib	9	Jun 1 2002	9-Kan	5
Jan 17 2002	4-Muluc	5	Mar 26 2002	7-Caban	1	Jun 2 2002	10-Chicchan	6
Jan 18 2002	5-Oc	6	Mar 27 2002	8-Etz'nab	2	Jun 3 2002	11-Cimi	7
Jan 19 2002	6-Chuen	7	Mar 28 2002	9-Cauac	3	Jun 4 2002	12-Manik	8
Jan 20 2002	7-Eb	8	Mar 29 2002	10-Ahau	4	Jun 5 2002	13-Lamat	9
Jan 21 2002	8-Ben	9	Mar 30 2002	11-*Imix*	5	Jun 6 2002	**1-Muluc**	1
Jan 22 2002	9-Ix	1	Mar 31 2002	12-Ik	6	Jun 7 2002	2-Oc	2
Jan 23 2002	10-Men	2	Apr 1 2002	13-Akbal	7	Jun 8 2002	3-Chuen	3
Jan 24 2002	11-Cib	3	Apr 2 2002	**1-Kan**	8	Jun 9 2002	4-Eb	4
Jan 25 2002	12-Caban	4	Apr 3 2002	2-Chicchan	9	Jun 10 2002	5-Ben	5
Jan 26 2002	13-Etz'nab	5	Apr 4 2002	3-Cimi	1	Jun 11 2002	6-Ix	6
Jan 27 2002	**1-Cauac**	6	Apr 5 2002	4-Manik	2	Jun 12 2002	7-Men	7
Jan 28 2002	2-Ahau	7	Apr 6 2002	5-Lamat	3	Jun 13 2002	8-Cib	8
Jan 29 2002	3-*Imix*	8	Apr 7 2002	6-Muluc	4	Jun 14 2002	9-Caban	9
Jan 30 2002	4-Ik	9	Apr 8 2002	7-Oc	5	Jun 15 2002	10-Etz'nab	1
Jan 31 2002	5-Akbal	1	Apr 9 2002	8-Chuen	6	Jun 16 2002	11-Cauac	2
Feb 1 2002	6-Kan	2	Apr 10 2002	9-Eb	7	Jun 17 2002	12-Ahau	3
Feb 2 2002	7-Chicchan	3	Apr 11 2002	10-Ben	8	Jun 18 2002	13-*Imix*	4
Feb 3 2002	8-Cimi	4	Apr 12 2002	11-Ix	9	Jun 19 2002	**1-Ik**	5
Feb 4 2002	9-Manik	5	Apr 13 2002	12-Men	1	Jun 20 2002	2-Akbal	6
Feb 5 2002	10-Lamat	6	Apr 14 2002	13-Cib	2	Jun 21 2002	3-Kan	7
Feb 6 2002	11-Muluc	7	Apr 15 2002	**1-Caban**	3	Jun 22 2002	4-Chicchan	8
Feb 7 2002	12-Oc	8	Apr 16 2002	2-Etz'nab	4	Jun 23 2002	5-Cimi	9
Feb 8 2002	13-Chuen	9	Apr 17 2002	3-Cauac	5	Jun 24 2002	6-Manik	1
Feb 9 2002	**1-Eb**	1	Apr 18 2002	4-Ahau	6	Jun 25 2002	7-Lamat	2
Feb 10 2002	2-Ben	2	Apr 19 2002	5-*Imix*	7	Jun 26 2002	8-Muluc	3
Feb 11 2002	3-Ix	3	Apr 20 2002	6-Ik	8	Jun 27 2002	9-Oc	4
Feb 12 2002	4-Men	4	Apr 21 2002	7-Akbal	9	Jun 28 2002	10-Chuen	5
Feb 13 2002	5-Cib	5	Apr 22 2002	8-Kan	1	Jun 29 2002	11-Eb	6
Feb 14 2002	6-Caban	6	Apr 23 2002	9-Chicchan	2	Jun 30 2002	12-Ben	7
Feb 15 2002	7-Etz'nab	7	Apr 24 2002	10-Cimi	3	Jul 1 2002	13-Ix	8
Feb 16 2002	8-Cauac	8	Apr 25 2002	11-Manik	4	Jul 2 2002	**1-Men**	9
Feb 17 2002	9-Ahau	9	Apr 26 2002	12-Lamat	5	Jul 3 2002	2-Cib	1
Feb 18 2002	10-*Imix*	1	Apr 27 2002	13-Muluc	6	Jul 4 2002	3-Caban	2
Feb 19 2002	11-Ik	2	Apr 28 2002	**1-Oc**	7	Jul 5 2002	4-Etz'nab	3
Feb 20 2002	12-Akbal	3	Apr 29 2002	2-Chuen	8	Jul 6 2002	5-Cauac	4
Feb 21 2002	13-Kan	4	Apr 30 2002	3-Eb	9	Jul 7 2002	6-Ahau	5
Feb 22 2002	**1-Chicchan**	5	May 1 2002	4-Ben	1	Jul 8 2002	7-*Imix*	6
Feb 23 2002	2-Cimi	6	May 2 2002	5-Ix	2	Jul 9 2002	8-Ik	7
Feb 24 2002	3-Manik	7	May 3 2002	6-Men	3	Jul 10 2002	9-Akbal	8
Feb 25 2002	4-Lamat	8	May 4 2002	7-Cib	4	Jul 11 2002	10-Kan	9
Feb 26 2002	5-Muluc	9	May 5 2002	8-Caban	5	Jul 12 2002	11-Chicchan	1
Feb 27 2002	6-Oc	1	May 6 2002	9-Etz'nab	6	Jul 13 2002	12-Cimi	2
Feb 28 2002	7-Chuen	2	May 7 2002	10-Cauac	7	Jul 14 2002	13-Manik	3
Mar 1 2002	8-Eb	3	May 8 2002	11-Ahau	8	Jul 15 2002	**1-Lamat**	4
Mar 2 2002	9-Ben	4	May 9 2002	12-*Imix*	9	Jul 16 2002	2-Muluc	5
Mar 3 2002	10-Ix	5	May 10 2002	13-Ik	1	Jul 17 2002	3-Oc	6
Mar 4 2002	11-Men	6	May 11 2002	**1-Akbal**	2	Jul 18 2002	4-Chuen	7
Mar 5 2002	12-Cib	7	May 12 2002	2-Kan	3	Jul 19 2002	5-Eb	8
Mar 6 2002	13-Caban	8	May 13 2002	3-Chicchan	4	Jul 20 2002	6-Ben	9
Mar 7 2002	**1-Etz'nab**	9	May 14 2002	4-Cimi	5	Jul 21 2002	7-Ix	1
Mar 8 2002	2-Cauac	1	May 15 2002	5-Manik	6	Jul 22 2002	8-Men	2
Mar 9 2002	3-Ahau	2	May 16 2002	6-Lamat	7	Jul 23 2002	9-Cib	3
Mar 10 2002	4-*Imix*	3	May 17 2002	7-Muluc	8	Jul 24 2002	10-Caban	4
Mar 11 2002	5-Ik	4	May 18 2002	8-Oc	9	Jul 25 2002	11-Etz'nab	5
Mar 12 2002	6-Akbal	5	May 19 2002	9-Chuen	1	Jul 26 2002	12-Cauac	6
Mar 13 2002	7-Kan	6	May 20 2002	10-Eb	2	Jul 27 2002	13-Ahau	7
Mar 14 2002	8-Chicchan	7	May 21 2002	11-Ben	3	Jul 28 2002	**1-Imix**	8
Mar 15 2002	9-Cimi	8	May 22 2002	12-Ix	4	Jul 29 2002	2-Ik	9
Mar 16 2002	10-Manik	9	May 23 2002	13-Men	5	Jul 30 2002	3-Akbal	1
Mar 17 2002	11-Lamat	1	May 24 2002	**1-Cib**	6	Jul 31 2002	4-Kan	2
Mar 18 2002	12-Muluc	2	May 25 2002	2-Caban	7	Aug 1 2002	5-Chicchan	3

Date	Day-Sign	L	Date	Day-Sign	L	Date	Day-Sign	L
Aug 2 2002	6-Cimi	4	Oct 9 2002	9-Ix	9	Dec 16 2002	12-Ik	5
Aug 3 2002	7-Manik	5	Oct 10 2002	10-Men	1	Dec 17 2002	13-Akbal	6
Aug 4 2002	8-Lamat	6	Oct 11 2002	11-Cib	2	Dec 18 2002	**1-Kan**	7
Aug 5 2002	9-Muluc	7	Oct 12 2002	12-Caban	3	Dec 19 2002	2-Chicchan	8
Aug 6 2002	10-Oc	8	Oct 13 2002	13-Etz'nab	4	Dec 20 2002	3-Cimi	9
Aug 7 2002	11-Chuen	9	Oct 14 2002	**1-Cauac**	5	Dec 21 2002	4-Manik	1
Aug 8 2002	12-Eb	1	Oct 15 2002	2-Ahau	6	Dec 22 2002	5-Lamat	2
Aug 9 2002	13-Ben	2	Oct 16 2002	3-*Imix*	7	Dec 23 2002	6-Muluc	3
Aug 10 2002	**1-Ix**	3	Oct 17 2002	4-Ik	8	Dec 24 2002	7-Oc	4
Aug 11 2002	2-Men	4	Oct 18 2002	5-Akbal	9	Dec 25 2002	8-Chuen	5
Aug 12 2002	3-Cib	5	Oct 19 2002	6-Kan	1	Dec 26 2002	9-Eb	6
Aug 13 2002	4-Caban	6	Oct 20 2002	7-Chicchan	2	Dec 27 2002	10-Ben	7
Aug 14 2002	5-Etz'nab	7	Oct 21 2002	8-Cimi	3	Dec 28 2002	11-Ix	8
Aug 15 2002	6-Cauac	8	Oct 22 2002	9-Manik	4	Dec 29 2002	12-Men	9
Aug 16 2002	7-Ahau	9	Oct 23 2002	10-Lamat	5	Dec 30 2002	13-Cib	1
Aug 17 2002	8-*Imix*	1	Oct 24 2002	11-Muluc	6	Dec 31 2002	**1-Caban**	2
Aug 18 2002	9-Ik	2	Oct 25 2002	12-Oc	7	Jan 1 2003	2-Etz'nab	3
Aug 19 2002	10-Akbal	3	Oct 26 2002	13-Chuen	8	Jan 2 2003	3-Cauac	4
Aug 20 2002	11-Kan	4	Oct 27 2002	**1-Eb**	9	Jan 3 2003	4-Ahau	5
Aug 21 2002	12-Chicchan	5	Oct 28 2002	2-Ben	1	Jan 4 2003	5-*Imix*	6
Aug 22 2002	13-Cimi	6	Oct 29 2002	3-Ix	2	Jan 5 2003	6-Ik	7
Aug 23 2002	**1-Manik**	7	Oct 30 2002	4-Men	3	Jan 6 2003	7-Akbal	8
Aug 24 2002	2-Lamat	8	Oct 31 2002	5-Cib	4	Jan 7 2003	8-Kan	9
Aug 25 2002	3-Muluc	9	Nov 1 2002	6-Caban	5	Jan 8 2003	9-Chicchan	1
Aug 26 2002	4-Oc	1	Nov 2 2002	7-Etz'nab	6	Jan 9 2003	10-Cimi	2
Aug 27 2002	5-Chuen	2	Nov 3 2002	8-Cauac	7	Jan 10 2003	11-Manik	3
Aug 28 2002	6-Eb	3	Nov 4 2002	9-Ahau	8	Jan 11 2003	12-Lamat	4
Aug 29 2002	7-Ben	4	Nov 5 2002	10-*Imix*	9	Jan 12 2003	13-Muluc	5
Aug 30 2002	8-Ix	5	Nov 6 2002	11-Ik	1	Jan 13 2003	**1-Oc**	6
Aug 31 2002	9-Men	6	Nov 7 2002	12-Akbal	2	Jan 14 2003	2-Chuen	7
Sep 1 2002	10-Cib	7	Nov 8 2002	13-Kan	3	Jan 15 2003	3-Eb	8
Sep 2 2002	11-Caban	8	Nov 9 2002	**1-Chicchan**	4	Jan 16 2003	4-Ben	9
Sep 3 2002	12-Etz'nab	9	Nov 10 2002	2-Cimi	5	Jan 17 2003	5-Ix	1
Sep 4 2002	13-Cauac	1	Nov 11 2002	3-Manik	6	Jan 18 2003	6-Men	2
Sep 5 2002	**1-Ahau**	2	Nov 12 2002	4-Lamat	7	Jan 19 2003	7-Cib	3
Sep 6 2002	2-*Imix*	3	Nov 13 2002	5-Muluc	8	Jan 20 2003	8-Caban	4
Sep 7 2002	3-Ik	4	Nov 14 2002	6-Oc	9	Jan 21 2003	9-Etz'nab	5
Sep 8 2002	4-Akbal	5	Nov 15 2002	7-Chuen	1	Jan 22 2003	10-Cauac	6
Sep 9 2002	5-Kan	6	Nov 16 2002	8-Eb	2	Jan 23 2003	11-Ahau	7
Sep 10 2002	6-Chicchan	7	Nov 17 2002	9-Ben	3	Jan 24 2003	12-*Imix*	8
Sep 11 2002	7-Cimi	8	Nov 18 2002	10-Ix	4	Jan 25 2003	13-Ik	9
Sep 12 2002	8-Manik	9	Nov 19 2002	11-Men	5	Jan 26 2003	**1-Akbal**	1
Sep 13 2002	9-Lamat	1	Nov 20 2002	12-Cib	6	Jan 27 2003	2-Kan	2
Sep 14 2002	10-Muluc	2	Nov 21 2002	13-Caban	7	Jan 28 2003	3-Chicchan	3
Sep 15 2002	11-Oc	3	Nov 22 2002	**1-Etz'nab**	8	Jan 29 2003	4-Cimi	4
Sep 16 2002	12-Chuen	4	Nov 23 2002	2-Cauac	9	Jan 30 2003	5-Manik	5
Sep 17 2002	13-Eb	5	Nov 24 2002	3-Ahau	1	Jan 31 2003	6-Lamat	6
Sep 18 2002	**1-Ben**	6	Nov 25 2002	4-*Imix*	2	Feb 1 2003	7-Muluc	7
Sep 19 2002	2-Ix	7	Nov 26 2002	5-Ik	3	Feb 2 2003	8-Oc	8
Sep 20 2002	3-Men	8	Nov 27 2002	6-Akbal	4	Feb 3 2003	9-Chuen	9
Sep 21 2002	4-Cib	9	Nov 28 2002	7-Kan	5	Feb 4 2003	10-Eb	1
Sep 22 2002	5-Caban	1	Nov 29 2002	8-Chicchan	6	Feb 5 2003	11-Ben	2
Sep 23 2002	6-Etz'nab	2	Nov 30 2002	9-Cimi	7	Feb 6 2003	12-Ix	3
Sep 24 2002	7-Cauac	3	Dec 1 2002	10-Manik	8	Feb 7 2003	13-Men	4
Sep 25 2002	8-Ahau	4	Dec 2 2002	11-Lamat	9	Feb 8 2003	**1-Cib**	5
Sep 26 2002	9-*Imix*	5	Dec 3 2002	12-Muluc	1	Feb 9 2003	2-Caban	6
Sep 27 2002	10-Ik	6	Dec 4 2002	13-Oc	2	Feb 10 2003	3-Etz'nab	7
Sep 28 2002	11-Akbal	7	Dec 5 2002	**1-Chuen**	3	Feb 11 2003	4-Cauac	8
Sep 29 2002	12-Kan	8	Dec 6 2002	2-Eb	4	Feb 12 2003	5-Ahau	9
Sep 30 2002	13-Chicchan	9	Dec 7 2002	3-Ben	5	Feb 13 2003	6-*Imix*	1
Oct 1 2002	**1-Cimi**	1	Dec 8 2002	4-Ix	6	Feb 14 2003	7-Ik	2
Oct 2 2002	2-Manik	2	Dec 9 2002	5-Men	7	Feb 15 2003	8-Akbal	3
Oct 3 2002	3-Lamat	3	Dec 10 2002	6-Cib	8	Feb 16 2003	9-Kan	4
Oct 4 2002	4-Muluc	4	Dec 11 2002	7-Caban	9	Feb 17 2003	10-Chicchan	5
Oct 5 2002	5-Oc	5	Dec 12 2002	8-Etz'nab	1	Feb 18 2003	11-Cimi	6
Oct 6 2002	6-Chuen	6	Dec 13 2002	9-Cauac	2	Feb 19 2003	12-Manik	7
Oct 7 2002	7-Eb	7	Dec 14 2002	10-Ahau	3	Feb 20 2003	13-Lamat	8
Oct 8 2002	8-Ben	8	Dec 15 2002	11-*Imix*	4	Feb 21 2003	**1-Muluc**	9

Date	Day-Sign	L
Feb 22 2003	2-Oc	1
Feb 23 2003	3-Chuen	2
Feb 24 2003	4-Eb	3
Feb 25 2003	5-Ben	4
Feb 26 2003	6-Ix	5
Feb 27 2003	7-Men	6
Feb 28 2003	8-Cib	7
Mar 1 2003	9-Caban	8
Mar 2 2003	10-Etz'nab	9
Mar 3 2003	11-Cauac	1
Mar 4 2003	12-Ahau	2
Mar 5 2003	13-Imix	3
Mar 6 2003	1-Ik	4
Mar 7 2003	2-Akbal	5
Mar 8 2003	3-Kan	6
Mar 9 2003	4-Chicchan	7
Mar 10 2003	5-Cimi	8
Mar 11 2003	6-Manik	9
Mar 12 2003	7-Lamat	1
Mar 13 2003	8-Muluc	2
Mar 14 2003	9-Oc	3
Mar 15 2003	10-Chuen	4
Mar 16 2003	11-Eb	5
Mar 17 2003	12-Ben	6
Mar 18 2003	13-Ix	7
Mar 19 2003	1-Men	8
Mar 20 2003	2-Cib	9
Mar 21 2003	3-Caban	1
Mar 22 2003	4-Etz'nab	2
Mar 23 2003	5-Cauac	3
Mar 24 2003	6-Ahau	4
Mar 25 2003	7-Imix	5
Mar 26 2003	8-Ik	6
Mar 27 2003	9-Akbal	7
Mar 28 2003	10-Kan	8
Mar 29 2003	11-Chicchan	9
Mar 30 2003	12-Cimi	1
Mar 31 2003	13-Manik	2
Apr 1 2003	1-Lamat	3
Apr 2 2003	2-Muluc	4
Apr 3 2003	3-Oc	5
Apr 4 2003	4-Chuen	6
Apr 5 2003	5-Eb	7
Apr 6 2003	6-Ben	8
Apr 7 2003	7-Ix	9
Apr 8 2003	8-Men	1
Apr 9 2003	9-Cib	2
Apr 10 2003	10-Caban	3
Apr 11 2003	11-Etz'nab	4
Apr 12 2003	12-Cauac	5
Apr 13 2003	13-Ahau	6
Apr 14 2003	1-Imix	7
Apr 15 2003	2-Ik	8
Apr 16 2003	3-Akbal	9
Apr 17 2003	4-Kan	1
Apr 18 2003	5-Chicchan	2
Apr 19 2003	6-Cimi	3
Apr 20 2003	7-Manik	4
Apr 21 2003	8-Lamat	5
Apr 22 2003	9-Muluc	6
Apr 23 2003	10-Oc	7
Apr 24 2003	11-Chuen	8
Apr 25 2003	12-Eb	9
Apr 26 2003	13-Ben	1
Apr 27 2003	1-Ix	2
Apr 28 2003	2-Men	3
Apr 29 2003	3-Cib	4
Apr 30 2003	4-Caban	5

Date	Day-Sign	L
May 1 2003	5-Etz'nab	6
May 2 2003	6-Cauac	7
May 3 2003	7-Ahau	8
May 4 2003	8-Imix	9
May 5 2003	9-Ik	1
May 6 2003	10-Akbal	2
May 7 2003	11-Kan	3
May 8 2003	12-Chicchan	4
May 9 2003	13-Cimi	5
May 10 2003	1-Manik	6
May 11 2003	2-Lamat	7
May 12 2003	3-Muluc	8
May 13 2003	4-Oc	9
May 14 2003	5-Chuen	1
May 15 2003	6-Eb	2
May 16 2003	7-Ben	3
May 17 2003	8-Ix	4
May 18 2003	9-Men	5
May 19 2003	10-Cib	6
May 20 2003	11-Caban	7
May 21 2003	12-Etz'nab	8
May 22 2003	13-Cauac	9
May 23 2003	1-Ahau	1
May 24 2003	2-Imix	2
May 25 2003	3-Ik	3
May 26 2003	4-Akbal	4
May 27 2003	5-Kan	5
May 28 2003	6-Chicchan	6
May 29 2003	7-Cimi	7
May 30 2003	8-Manik	8
May 31 2003	9-Lamat	9
Jun 1 2003	10-Muluc	1
Jun 2 2003	11-Oc	2
Jun 3 2003	12-Chuen	3
Jun 4 2003	13-Eb	4
Jun 5 2003	1-Ben	5
Jun 6 2003	2-Ix	6
Jun 7 2003	3-Men	7
Jun 8 2003	4-Cib	8
Jun 9 2003	5-Caban	9
Jun 10 2003	6-Etz'nab	1
Jun 11 2003	7-Cauac	2
Jun 12 2003	8-Ahau	3
Jun 13 2003	9-Imix	4
Jun 14 2003	10-Ik	5
Jun 15 2003	11-Akbal	6
Jun 16 2003	12-Kan	7
Jun 17 2003	13-Chicchan	8
Jun 18 2003	1-Cimi	9
Jun 19 2003	2-Manik	1
Jun 20 2003	3-Lamat	2
Jun 21 2003	4-Muluc	3
Jun 22 2003	5-Oc	4
Jun 23 2003	6-Chuen	5
Jun 24 2003	7-Eb	6
Jun 25 2003	8-Ben	7
Jun 26 2003	9-Ix	8
Jun 27 2003	10-Men	9
Jun 28 2003	11-Cib	1
Jun 29 2003	12-Caban	2
Jun 30 2003	13-Etz'nab	3
Jul 1 2003	1-Cauac	4
Jul 2 2003	2-Ahau	5
Jul 3 2003	3-Imix	6
Jul 4 2003	4-Ik	7
Jul 5 2003	5-Akbal	8
Jul 6 2003	6-Kan	9
Jul 7 2003	7-Chicchan	1

Date	Day-Sign	L
Jul 8 2003	8-Cimi	2
Jul 9 2003	9-Manik	3
Jul 10 2003	10-Lamat	4
Jul 11 2003	11-Muluc	5
Jul 12 2003	12-Oc	6
Jul 13 2003	13-Chuen	7
Jul 14 2003	1-Eb	8
Jul 15 2003	2-Ben	9
Jul 16 2003	3-Ix	1
Jul 17 2003	4-Men	2
Jul 18 2003	5-Cib	3
Jul 19 2003	6-Caban	4
Jul 20 2003	7-Etz'nab	5
Jul 21 2003	8-Cauac	6
Jul 22 2003	9-Ahau	7
Jul 23 2003	10-Imix	8
Jul 24 2003	11-Ik	9
Jul 25 2003	12-Akbal	1
Jul 26 2003	13-Kan	2
Jul 27 2003	1-Chicchan	3
Jul 28 2003	2-Cimi	4
Jul 29 2003	3-Manik	5
Jul 30 2003	4-Lamat	6
Jul 31 2003	5-Muluc	7
Aug 1 2003	6-Oc	8
Aug 2 2003	7-Chuen	9
Aug 3 2003	8-Eb	1
Aug 4 2003	9-Ben	2
Aug 5 2003	10-Ix	3
Aug 6 2003	11-Men	4
Aug 7 2003	12-Cib	5
Aug 8 2003	13-Caban	6
Aug 9 2003	1-Etz'nab	7
Aug 10 2003	2-Cauac	8
Aug 11 2003	3-Ahau	9
Aug 12 2003	4-Imix	1
Aug 13 2003	5-Ik	2
Aug 14 2003	6-Akbal	3
Aug 15 2003	7-Kan	4
Aug 16 2003	8-Chicchan	5
Aug 17 2003	9-Cimi	6
Aug 18 2003	10-Manik	7
Aug 19 2003	11-Lamat	8
Aug 20 2003	12-Muluc	9
Aug 21 2003	13-Oc	1
Aug 22 2003	1-Chuen	2
Aug 23 2003	2-Eb	3
Aug 24 2003	3-Ben	4
Aug 25 2003	4-Ix	5
Aug 26 2003	5-Men	6
Aug 27 2003	6-Cib	7
Aug 28 2003	7-Caban	8
Aug 29 2003	8-Etz'nab	9
Aug 30 2003	9-Cauac	1
Aug 31 2003	10-Ahau	2
Sep 1 2003	11-Imix	3
Sep 2 2003	12-Ik	4
Sep 3 2003	13-Akbal	5
Sep 4 2003	1-Kan	6
Sep 5 2003	2-Chicchan	7
Sep 6 2003	3-Cimi	8
Sep 7 2003	4-Manik	9
Sep 8 2003	5-Lamat	1
Sep 9 2003	6-Muluc	2
Sep 10 2003	7-Oc	3
Sep 11 2003	8-Chuen	4
Sep 12 2003	9-Eb	5
Sep 13 2003	10-Ben	6

Date	Day-Sign	L
Sep 14 2003	11-Ix	7
Sep 15 2003	12-Men	8
Sep 16 2003	13-Cib	9
Sep 17 2003	**1-Caban**	1
Sep 18 2003	2-Etz'nab	2
Sep 19 2003	3-Cauac	3
Sep 20 2003	4-Ahau	4
Sep 21 2003	5-*Imix*	5
Sep 22 2003	6-Ik	6
Sep 23 2003	7-Akbal	7
Sep 24 2003	8-Kan	8
Sep 25 2003	9-Chicchan	9
Sep 26 2003	10-Cimi	1
Sep 27 2003	11-Manik	2
Sep 28 2003	12-Lamat	3
Sep 29 2003	13-Muluc	4
Sep 30 2003	**1-Oc**	5
Oct 1 2003	2-Chuen	6
Oct 2 2003	3-Eb	7
Oct 3 2003	4-*Ben*	8
Oct 4 2003	5-Ix	9
Oct 5 2003	6-Men	1
Oct 6 2003	7-Cib	2
Oct 7 2003	8-Caban	3
Oct 8 2003	9-Etz'nab	4
Oct 9 2003	10-Cauac	5
Oct 10 2003	11-Ahau	6
Oct 11 2003	12-*Imix*	7
Oct 12 2003	13-Ik	8
Oct 13 2003	**1-Akbal**	9
Oct 14 2003	2-Kan	1
Oct 15 2003	3-Chicchan	2
Oct 16 2003	4-Cimi	3
Oct 17 2003	5-Manik	4
Oct 18 2003	6-Lamat	5
Oct 19 2003	7-Muluc	6
Oct 20 2003	8-Oc	7
Oct 21 2003	9-Chuen	8
Oct 22 2003	10-Eb	9
Oct 23 2003	11-Ben	1
Oct 24 2003	12-Ix	2
Oct 25 2003	13-Men	3
Oct 26 2003	**1-Cib**	4
Oct 27 2003	2-Caban	5
Oct 28 2003	3-Etz'nab	6
Oct 29 2003	4-Cauac	7
Oct 30 2003	5-Ahau	8
Oct 31 2003	6-*Imix*	9
Nov 1 2003	7-Ik	1
Nov 2 2003	8-Akbal	2
Nov 3 2003	9-Kan	3
Nov 4 2003	10-Chicchan	4
Nov 5 2003	11-Cimi	5
Nov 6 2003	12-Manik	6
Nov 7 2003	13-Lamat	7
Nov 8 2003	**1-Muluc**	8
Nov 9 2003	2-Oc	9
Nov 10 2003	3-Chuen	1
Nov 11 2003	4-Eb	2
Nov 12 2003	5-Ben	3
Nov 13 2003	6-Ix	4
Nov 14 2003	7-Men	5
Nov 15 2003	8-Cib	6
Nov 16 2003	9-Caban	7
Nov 17 2003	10-Etz'nab	8
Nov 18 2003	11-Cauac	9
Nov 19 2003	12-Ahau	1
Nov 20 2003	13-*Imix*	2

Date	Day-Sign	L
Nov 21 2003	**1-Ik**	3
Nov 22 2003	2-Akbal	4
Nov 23 2003	3-Kan	5
Nov 24 2003	4-Chicchan	6
Nov 25 2003	5-Cimi	7
Nov 26 2003	6-Manik	8
Nov 27 2003	7-Lamat	9
Nov 28 2003	8-Muluc	1
Nov 29 2003	9-Oc	2
Nov 30 2003	10-Chuen	3
Dec 1 2003	11-Eb	4
Dec 2 2003	12-Ben	5
Dec 3 2003	13-Ix	6
Dec 4 2003	**1-Men**	7
Dec 5 2003	2-Cib	8
Dec 6 2003	3-Caban	9
Dec 7 2003	4-Etz'nab	1
Dec 8 2003	5-Cauac	2
Dec 9 2003	6-Ahau	3
Dec 10 2003	7-*Imix*	4
Dec 11 2003	8-Ik	5
Dec 12 2003	9-Akbal	6
Dec 13 2003	10-Kan	7
Dec 14 2003	11-Chicchan	8
Dec 15 2003	12-Cimi	9
Dec 16 2003	13-Manik	1
Dec 17 2003	**1-Lamat**	2
Dec 18 2003	2-Muluc	3
Dec 19 2003	3-Oc	4
Dec 20 2003	4-Chuen	5
Dec 21 2003	5-Eb	6
Dec 22 2003	6-Ben	7
Dec 23 2003	7-Ix	8
Dec 24 2003	8-Men	9
Dec 25 2003	9-Cib	1
Dec 26 2003	10-Caban	2
Dec 27 2003	11-Etz'nab	3
Dec 28 2003	12-Cauac	4
Dec 29 2003	13-Ahau	5
Dec 30 2003	**1-Imix**	6
Dec 31 2003	2-Ik	7
Jan 1 2004	3-Akbal	8
Jan 2 2004	4-Kan	9
Jan 3 2004	5-Chicchan	1
Jan 4 2004	6-Cimi	2
Jan 5 2004	7-Manik	3
Jan 6 2004	8-Lamat	4
Jan 7 2004	9-Muluc	5
Jan 8 2004	10-Oc	6
Jan 9 2004	11-Chuen	7
Jan 10 2004	12-Eb	8
Jan 11 2004	13-Ben	9
Jan 12 2004	**1-Ix**	1
Jan 13 2004	2-Men	2
Jan 14 2004	3-Cib	3
Jan 15 2004	4-Caban	4
Jan 16 2004	5-Etz'nab	5
Jan 17 2004	6-Cauac	6
Jan 18 2004	7-Ahau	7
Jan 19 2004	8-*Imix*	8
Jan 20 2004	9-Ik	9
Jan 21 2004	10-Akbal	1
Jan 22 2004	11-Kan	2
Jan 23 2004	12-Chicchan	3
Jan 24 2004	13-Cimi	4
Jan 25 2004	**1-Manik**	5
Jan 26 2004	2-Lamat	6
Jan 27 2004	3-Muluc	7

Date	Day-Sign	L
Jan 28 2004	4-Oc	8
Jan 29 2004	5-Chuen	9
Jan 30 2004	6-Eb	1
Jan 31 2004	7-Ben	2
Feb 1 2004	8-Ix	3
Feb 2 2004	9-Men	4
Feb 3 2004	10-Cib	5
Feb 4 2004	11-Caban	6
Feb 5 2004	12-Etz'nab	7
Feb 6 2004	13-Cauac	8
Feb 7 2004	**1-Ahau**	9
Feb 8 2004	2-*Imix*	1
Feb 9 2004	3-Ik	2
Feb 10 2004	4-Akbal	3
Feb 11 2004	5-Kan	4
Feb 12 2004	6-Chicchan	5
Feb 13 2004	7-Cimi	6
Feb 14 2004	8-Manik	7
Feb 15 2004	9-Lamat	8
Feb 16 2004	10-Muluc	9
Feb 17 2004	11-Oc	1
Feb 18 2004	12-Chuen	2
Feb 19 2004	13-Eb	3
Feb 20 2004	**1-Ben**	4
Feb 21 2004	2-Ix	5
Feb 22 2004	3-Men	6
Feb 23 2004	4-Cib	7
Feb 24 2004	5-Caban	8
Feb 25 2004	6-Etz'nab	9
Feb 26 2004	7-Cauac	1
Feb 27 2004	8-Ahau	2
Feb 28 2004	9-*Imix*	3
Feb 29 2004	10-Ik	4
Mar 1 2004	11-Akbal	5
Mar 2 2004	12-Kan	6
Mar 3 2004	13-Chicchan	7
Mar 4 2004	**1-Cimi**	8
Mar 5 2004	2-Manik	9
Mar 6 2004	3-Lamat	1
Mar 7 2004	4-Muluc	2
Mar 8 2004	5-Oc	3
Mar 9 2004	6-Chuen	4
Mar 10 2004	7-Eb	5
Mar 11 2004	8-Ben	6
Mar 12 2004	9-Ix	7
Mar 13 2004	10-Men	8
Mar 14 2004	11-Cib	9
Mar 15 2004	12-Caban	1
Mar 16 2004	13-Etz'nab	2
Mar 17 2004	**1-Cauac**	3
Mar 18 2004	2-Ahau	4
Mar 19 2004	3-*Imix*	5
Mar 20 2004	4-Ik	6
Mar 21 2004	5-Akbal	7
Mar 22 2004	6-Kan	8
Mar 23 2004	7-Chicchan	9
Mar 24 2004	8-Cimi	1
Mar 25 2004	9-Manik	2
Mar 26 2004	10-Lamat	3
Mar 27 2004	11-Muluc	4
Mar 28 2004	12-Oc	5
Mar 29 2004	13-Chuen	6
Mar 30 2004	**1-Eb**	7
Mar 31 2004	2-Ben	8
Apr 1 2004	3-Ik	9
Apr 2 2004	4-Men	1
Apr 3 2004	5-Cib	2
Apr 4 2004	6-Caban	3

Date	Day-Sign	L	Date	Day-Sign	L	Date	Day-Sign	L
Apr 5 2004	7-Etz'nab	4	Jun 12 2004	10-Cimi	9	Aug 19 2004	13-Ix	5
Apr 6 2004	8-Cauac	5	Jun 13 2004	11-Manik	1	Aug 20 2004	1-Men	6
Apr 7 2004	9-Ahau	6	Jun 14 2004	12-Lamat	2	Aug 21 2004	2-Cib	7
Apr 8 2004	10-Imix	7	Jun 15 2004	13-Muluc	3	Aug 22 2004	3-Caban	8
Apr 9 2004	11-Ik	8	Jun 16 2004	1-Oc	4	Aug 23 2004	4-Etz'nab	9
Apr 10 2004	12-Akbal	9	Jun 17 2004	2-Chuen	5	Aug 24 2004	5-Cauac	1
Apr 11 2004	13-Kan	1	Jun 18 2004	3-Eb	6	Aug 25 2004	6-Ahau	2
Apr 12 2004	1-Chicchan	2	Jun 19 2004	4-Ben	7	Aug 26 2004	7-Imix	3
Apr 13 2004	2-Cimi	3	Jun 20 2004	5-Ix	8	Aug 27 2004	8-Ik	4
Apr 14 2004	3-Manik	4	Jun 21 2004	6-Men	9	Aug 28 2004	9-Akbal	5
Apr 15 2004	4-Lamat	5	Jun 22 2004	7-Cib	1	Aug 29 2004	10-Kan	6
Apr 16 2004	5-Muluc	6	Jun 23 2004	8-Caban	2	Aug 30 2004	11-Chicchan	7
Apr 17 2004	6-Oc	7	Jun 24 2004	9-Etz'nab	3	Aug 31 2004	12-Cimi	8
Apr 18 2004	7-Chuen	8	Jun 25 2004	10-Cauac	4	Sep 1 2004	13-Manik	9
Apr 19 2004	8-Eb	9	Jun 26 2004	11-Ahau	5	Sep 2 2004	1-Lamat	1
Apr 20 2004	9-Ben	1	Jun 27 2004	12-Imix	6	Sep 3 2004	2-Muluc	2
Apr 21 2004	10-Ix	2	Jun 28 2004	13-Ik	7	Sep 4 2004	3-Oc	3
Apr 22 2004	11-Men	3	Jun 29 2004	1-Akbal	8	Sep 5 2004	4-Chuen	4
Apr 23 2004	12-Cib	4	Jun 30 2004	2-Kan	9	Sep 6 2004	5-Eb	5
Apr 24 2004	13-Caban	5	Jul 1 2004	3-Chicchan	1	Sep 7 2004	6-Ben	6
Apr 25 2004	1-Etz'nab	6	Jul 2 2004	4-Cimi	2	Sep 8 2004	7-Ix	7
Apr 26 2004	2-Cauac	7	Jul 3 2004	5-Manik	3	Sep 9 2004	8-Men	8
Apr 27 2004	3-Ahau	8	Jul 4 2004	6-Lamat	4	Sep 10 2004	9-Cib	9
Apr 28 2004	4-Imix	9	Jul 5 2004	7-Muluc	5	Sep 11 2004	10-Caban	1
Apr 29 2004	5-Ik	1	Jul 6 2004	8-Oc	6	Sep 12 2004	11-Etz'nab	2
Apr 30 2004	6-Akbal	2	Jul 7 2004	9-Chuen	7	Sep 13 2004	12-Cauac	3
May 1 2004	7-Kan	3	Jul 8 2004	10-Eb	8	Sep 14 2004	13-Ahau	4
May 2 2004	8-Chicchan	4	Jul 9 2004	11-Ben	9	Sep 15 2004	1-Imix	5
May 3 2004	9-Cimi	5	Jul 10 2004	12-Ix	1	Sep 16 2004	2-Ik	6
May 4 2004	10-Manik	6	Jul 11 2004	13-Men	2	Sep 17 2004	3-Akbal	7
May 5 2004	11-Lamat	7	Jul 12 2004	1-Cib	3	Sep 18 2004	4-Kan	8
May 6 2004	12-Muluc	8	Jul 13 2004	2-Caban	4	Sep 19 2004	5-Chicchan	9
May 7 2004	13-Oc	9	Jul 14 2004	3-Etz'nab	5	Sep 20 2004	6-Cimi	1
May 8 2004	1-Chuen	1	Jul 15 2004	4-Cauac	6	Sep 21 2004	7-Manik	2
May 9 2004	2-Eb	2	Jul 16 2004	5-Ahau	7	Sep 22 2004	8-Lamat	3
May 10 2004	3-Ben	3	Jul 17 2004	6-Imix	8	Sep 23 2004	9-Muluc	4
May 11 2004	4-Ix	4	Jul 18 2004	7-Ik	9	Sep 24 2004	10-Oc	5
May 12 2004	5-Men	5	Jul 19 2004	8-Akbal	1	Sep 25 2004	11-Chuen	6
May 13 2004	6-Cib	6	Jul 20 2004	9-Kan	2	Sep 26 2004	12-Eb	7
May 14 2004	7-Caban	7	Jul 21 2004	10-Chicchan	3	Sep 27 2004	13-Ben	8
May 15 2004	8-Etz'nab	8	Jul 22 2004	11-Cimi	4	Sep 28 2004	1-Ix	9
May 16 2004	9-Cauac	9	Jul 23 2004	12-Manik	5	Sep 29 2004	2-Men	1
May 17 2004	10-Ahau	1	Jul 24 2004	13-Lamat	6	Sep 30 2004	3-Cib	2
May 18 2004	11-Imix	2	Jul 25 2004	1-Muluc	7	Oct 1 2004	4-Caban	3
May 19 2004	12-Ik	3	Jul 26 2004	2-Oc	8	Oct 2 2004	5-Etz'nab	4
May 20 2004	13-Akbal	4	Jul 27 2004	3-Chuen	9	Oct 3 2004	6-Cauac	5
May 21 2004	1-Kan	5	Jul 28 2004	4-Eb	1	Oct 4 2004	7-Ahau	6
May 22 2004	2-Chicchan	6	Jul 29 2004	5-Ben	2	Oct 5 2004	8-Imix	7
May 23 2004	3-Cimi	7	Jul 30 2004	6-Ix	3	Oct 6 2004	9-Ik	8
May 24 2004	4-Manik	8	Jul 31 2004	7-Men	4	Oct 7 2004	10-Akbal	9
May 25 2004	5-Lamat	9	Aug 1 2004	8-Cib	5	Oct 8 2004	11-Kan	1
May 26 2004	6-Muluc	1	Aug 2 2004	9-Caban	6	Oct 9 2004	12-Chicchan	2
May 27 2004	7-Oc	2	Aug 3 2004	10-Etz'nab	7	Oct 10 2004	13-Cimi	3
May 28 2004	8-Chuen	3	Aug 4 2004	11-Cauac	8	Oct 11 2004	1-Manik	4
May 29 2004	9-Eb	4	Aug 5 2004	12-Ahau	9	Oct 12 2004	2-Lamat	5
May 30 2004	10-Ben	5	Aug 6 2004	13-Imix	1	Oct 13 2004	3-Muluc	6
May 31 2004	11-Ix	6	Aug 7 2004	1-Ik	2	Oct 14 2004	4-Oc	7
Jun 1 2004	12-Men	7	Aug 8 2004	2-Akbal	3	Oct 15 2004	5-Chuen	8
Jun 2 2004	13-Cib	8	Aug 9 2004	3-Kan	4	Oct 16 2004	6-Eb	9
Jun 3 2004	1-Caban	9	Aug 10 2004	4-Chicchan	5	Oct 17 2004	7-Ben	1
Jun 4 2004	2-Etz'nab	1	Aug 11 2004	5-Cimi	6	Oct 18 2004	8-Ix	2
Jun 5 2004	3-Cauac	2	Aug 12 2004	6-Manik	7	Oct 19 2004	9-Men	3
Jun 6 2004	4-Ahau	3	Aug 13 2004	7-Lamat	8	Oct 20 2004	10-Cib	4
Jun 7 2004	5-Imix	4	Aug 14 2004	8-Muluc	9	Oct 21 2004	11-Caban	5
Jun 8 2004	6-Ik	5	Aug 15 2004	9-Oc	1	Oct 22 2004	12-Etz'nab	6
Jun 9 2004	7-Akbal	6	Aug 16 2004	10-Chuen	2	Oct 23 2004	13-Cauac	7
Jun 10 2004	8-Kan	7	Aug 17 2004	11-Eb	3	Oct 24 2004	1-Ahau	8
Jun 11 2004	9-Chicchan	8	Aug 18 2004	12-Ben	4	Oct 25 2004	2-Imix	9

Date	Day-Sign	L		Date	Day-Sign	L		Date	Day-Sign	L
Oct 26 2004	3-Ik	1		Jan 2 2005	6-Oc	6		Mar 11 2005	9-Etz'nab	2
Oct 27 2004	4-Akbal	2		Jan 3 2005	7-Chuen	7		Mar 12 2005	10-Cauac	3
Oct 28 2004	5-Kan	3		Jan 4 2005	8-Eb	8		Mar 13 2005	11-Ahau	4
Oct 29 2004	6-Chicchan	4		Jan 5 2005	9-Ben	9		Mar 14 2005	12-Imix	5
Oct 30 2004	7-Cimi	5		Jan 6 2005	10-Ix	1		Mar 15 2005	13-Ik	6
Oct 31 2004	8-Manik	6		Jan 7 2005	11-Men	2		Mar 16 2005	1-Akbal	7
Nov 1 2004	9-Lamat	7		Jan 8 2005	12-Cib	3		Mar 17 2005	2-Kan	8
Nov 2 2004	10-Muluc	8		Jan 9 2005	13-Caban	4		Mar 18 2005	3-Chicchan	9
Nov 3 2004	11-Oc	9		Jan 10 2005	1-Etz'nab	5		Mar 19 2005	4-Cimi	1
Nov 4 2004	12-Chuen	1		Jan 11 2005	2-Cauac	6		Mar 20 2005	5-Manik	2
Nov 5 2004	13-Eb	2		Jan 12 2005	3-Ahau	7		Mar 21 2005	6-Lamat	3
Nov 6 2004	1-Ben	3		Jan 13 2005	4-Imix	8		Mar 22 2005	7-Muluc	4
Nov 7 2004	2-Ix	4		Jan 14 2005	5-Ik	9		Mar 23 2005	8-Oc	5
Nov 8 2004	3-Men	5		Jan 15 2005	6-Akbal	1		Mar 24 2005	9-Chuen	6
Nov 9 2004	4-Cib	6		Jan 16 2005	7-Kan	2		Mar 25 2005	10-Eb	7
Nov 10 2004	5-Caban	7		Jan 17 2005	8-Chicchan	3		Mar 26 2005	11-Ben	8
Nov 11 2004	6-Etz'nab	8		Jan 18 2005	9-Cimi	4		Mar 27 2005	12-Ix	9
Nov 12 2004	7-Cauac	9		Jan 19 2005	10-Manik	5		Mar 28 2005	13-Men	1
Nov 13 2004	8-Ahau	1		Jan 20 2005	11-Lamat	6		Mar 29 2005	1-Cib	2
Nov 14 2004	9-Imix	2		Jan 21 2005	12-Muluc	7		Mar 30 2005	2-Caban	3
Nov 15 2004	10-Ik	3		Jan 22 2005	13-Oc	8		Mar 31 2005	3-Etz'nab	4
Nov 16 2004	11-Akbal	4		Jan 23 2005	1-Chuen	9		Apr 1 2005	4-Cauac	5
Nov 17 2004	12-Kan	5		Jan 24 2005	2-Eb	1		Apr 2 2005	5-Ahau	6
Nov 18 2004	13-Chicchan	6		Jan 25 2005	3-Ben	2		Apr 3 2005	6-Imix	7
Nov 19 2004	1-Cimi	7		Jan 26 2005	4-Ix	3		Apr 4 2005	7-Ik	8
Nov 20 2004	2-Manik	8		Jan 27 2005	5-Men	4		Apr 5 2005	8-Akbal	9
Nov 21 2004	3-Lamat	9		Jan 28 2005	6-Cib	5		Apr 6 2005	9-Kan	1
Nov 22 2004	4-Muluc	1		Jan 29 2005	7-Caban	6		Apr 7 2005	10-Chicchan	2
Nov 23 2004	5-Oc	2		Jan 30 2005	8-Etz'nab	7		Apr 8 2005	11-Cimi	3
Nov 24 2004	6-Chuen	3		Jan 31 2005	9-Cauac	8		Apr 9 2005	12-Manik	4
Nov 25 2004	7-Eb	4		Feb 1 2005	10-Ahau	9		Apr 10 2005	13-Lamat	5
Nov 26 2004	8-Ben	5		Feb 2 2005	11-Imix	1		Apr 11 2005	1-Muluc	6
Nov 27 2004	9-Ix	6		Feb 3 2005	12-Ik	2		Apr 12 2005	2-Oc	7
Nov 28 2004	10-Men	7		Feb 4 2005	13-Akbal	3		Apr 13 2005	3-Chuen	8
Nov 29 2004	11-Cib	8		Feb 5 2005	1-Kan	4		Apr 14 2005	4-Eb	9
Nov 30 2004	12-Caban	9		Feb 6 2005	2-Chicchan	5		Apr 15 2005	5-Ben	1
Dec 1 2004	13-Etz'nab	1		Feb 7 2005	3-Cimi	6		Apr 16 2005	6-Ix	2
Dec 2 2004	1-Cauac	2		Feb 8 2005	4-Manik	7		Apr 17 2005	7-Men	3
Dec 3 2004	2-Ahau	3		Feb 9 2005	5-Lamat	8		Apr 18 2005	8-Cib	4
Dec 4 2004	3-Imix	4		Feb 10 2005	6-Muluc	9		Apr 19 2005	9-Caban	5
Dec 5 2004	4-Ik	5		Feb 11 2005	7-Oc	1		Apr 20 2005	10-Etz'nab	6
Dec 6 2004	5-Akbal	6		Feb 12 2005	8-Chuen	2		Apr 21 2005	11-Cauac	7
Dec 7 2004	6-Kan	7		Feb 13 2005	9-Eb	3		Apr 22 2005	12-Ahau	8
Dec 8 2004	7-Chicchan	8		Feb 14 2005	10-Ben	4		Apr 23 2005	13-Imix	9
Dec 9 2004	8-Cimi	9		Feb 15 2005	11-Ix	5		Apr 24 2005	1-Ik	1
Dec 10 2004	9-Manik	1		Feb 16 2005	12-Men	6		Apr 25 2005	2-Akbal	2
Dec 11 2004	10-Lamat	2		Feb 17 2005	13-Cib	7		Apr 26 2005	3-Kan	3
Dec 12 2004	11-Muluc	3		Feb 18 2005	1-Caban	8		Apr 27 2005	4-Chicchan	4
Dec 13 2004	12-Oc	4		Feb 19 2005	2-Etz'nab	9		Apr 28 2005	5-Cimi	5
Dec 14 2004	13-Chuen	5		Feb 20 2005	3-Cauac	1		Apr 29 2005	6-Manik	6
Dec 15 2004	1-Eb	6		Feb 21 2005	4-Ahau	2		Apr 30 2005	7-Lamat	7
Dec 16 2004	2-Ben	7		Feb 22 2005	5-Imix	3		May 1 2005	8-Muluc	8
Dec 17 2004	3-Ix	8		Feb 23 2005	6-Ik	4		May 2 2005	9-Oc	9
Dec 18 2004	4-Men	9		Feb 24 2005	7-Akbal	5		May 3 2005	10-Chuen	1
Dec 19 2004	5-Cib	1		Feb 25 2005	8-Kan	6		May 4 2005	11-Eb	2
Dec 20 2004	6-Caban	2		Feb 26 2005	9-Chicchan	7		May 5 2005	12-Ben	3
Dec 21 2004	7-Etz'nab	3		Feb 27 2005	10-Cimi	8		May 6 2005	13-Ix	4
Dec 22 2004	8-Cauac	4		Feb 28 2005	11-Manik	9		May 7 2005	1-Men	5
Dec 23 2004	9-Ahau	5		Mar 1 2005	12-Lamat	1		May 8 2005	2-Cib	6
Dec 24 2004	10-Imix	6		Mar 2 2005	13-Muluc	2		May 9 2005	3-Caban	7
Dec 25 2004	11-Ik	7		Mar 3 2005	1-Oc	3		May 10 2005	4-Etz'nab	8
Dec 26 2004	12-Akbal	8		Mar 4 2005	2-Chuen	4		May 11 2005	5-Cauac	9
Dec 27 2004	13-Kan	9		Mar 5 2005	3-Eb	5		May 12 2005	6-Ahau	1
Dec 28 2004	1-Chicchan	1		Mar 6 2005	4-Ben	6		May 13 2005	7-Imix	2
Dec 29 2004	2-Cimi	2		Mar 7 2005	5-Ix	7		May 14 2005	8-Ik	3
Dec 30 2004	3-Manik	3		Mar 8 2005	6-Men	8		May 15 2005	9-Akbal	4
Dec 31 2004	4-Lamat	4		Mar 9 2005	7-Cib	9		May 16 2005	10-Kan	5
Jan 1 2005	5-Muluc	5		Mar 10 2005	8-Caban	1		May 17 2005	11-Chicchan	6

Date	Day-Sign	L	Date	Day-Sign	L	Date	Day-Sign	L
May 18 2005	12-Cimi	7	Jul 25 2005	2-Ix	3	Oct 1 2005	5-Ik	8
May 19 2005	13-Manik	8	Jul 26 2005	3-Men	4	Oct 2 2005	6-Akbal	9
May 20 2005	1-Lamat	9	Jul 27 2005	4-Cib	5	Oct 3 2005	7-Kan	1
May 21 2005	2-Muluc	1	Jul 28 2005	5-Caban	6	Oct 4 2005	8-Chicchan	2
May 22 2005	3-Oc	2	Jul 29 2005	6-Etz'nab	7	Oct 5 2005	9-Cimi	3
May 23 2005	4-Chuen	3	Jul 30 2005	7-Cauac	8	Oct 6 2005	10-Manik	4
May 24 2005	5-Eb	4	Jul 31 2005	8-Ahau	9	Oct 7 2005	11-Lamat	5
May 25 2005	6-Ben	5	Aug 1 2005	9-Imix	1	Oct 8 2005	12-Muluc	6
May 26 2005	7-Ix	6	Aug 2 2005	10-Ik	2	Oct 9 2005	13-Oc	7
May 27 2005	8-Men	7	Aug 3 2005	11-Akbal	3	Oct 10 2005	1-Chuen	8
May 28 2005	9-Cib	8	Aug 4 2005	12-Kan	4	Oct 11 2005	2-Eb	9
May 29 2005	10-Caban	9	Aug 5 2005	13-Chicchan	5	Oct 12 2005	3-Ben	1
May 30 2005	11-Etz'nab	1	Aug 6 2005	1-Cimi	6	Oct 13 2005	4-Ix	2
May 31 2005	12-Cauac	2	Aug 7 2005	2-Manik	7	Oct 14 2005	5-Men	3
Jun 1 2005	13-Ahau	3	Aug 8 2005	3-Lamat	8	Oct 15 2005	6-Cib	4
Jun 2 2005	1-Imix	4	Aug 9 2005	4-Muluc	9	Oct 16 2005	7-Caban	5
Jun 3 2005	2-Ik	5	Aug 10 2005	5-Oc	1	Oct 17 2005	8-Etz'nab	6
Jun 4 2005	3-Akbal	6	Aug 11 2005	6-Chuen	2	Oct 18 2005	9-Cauac	7
Jun 5 2005	4-Kan	7	Aug 12 2005	7-Eb	3	Oct 19 2005	10-Ahau	8
Jun 6 2005	5-Chicchan	8	Aug 13 2005	8-Ben	4	Oct 20 2005	11-Imix	9
Jun 7 2005	6-Cimi	9	Aug 14 2005	9-Ix	5	Oct 21 2005	12-Ik	1
Jun 8 2005	7-Manik	1	Aug 15 2005	10-Men	6	Oct 22 2005	13-Akbal	2
Jun 9 2005	8-Lamat	2	Aug 16 2005	11-Cib	7	Oct 23 2005	1-Kan	3
Jun 10 2005	9-Muluc	3	Aug 17 2005	12-Caban	8	Oct 24 2005	2-Chicchan	4
Jun 11 2005	10-Oc	4	Aug 18 2005	13-Etz'nab	9	Oct 25 2005	3-Cimi	5
Jun 12 2005	11-Chuen	5	Aug 19 2005	1-Cauac	1	Oct 26 2005	4-Manik	6
Jun 13 2005	12-Eb	6	Aug 20 2005	2-Ahau	2	Oct 27 2005	5-Lamat	7
Jun 14 2005	13-Ben	7	Aug 21 2005	3-Imix	3	Oct 28 2005	6-Muluc	8
Jun 15 2005	1-Ix	8	Aug 22 2005	4-Ik	4	Oct 29 2005	7-Oc	9
Jun 16 2005	2-Men	9	Aug 23 2005	5-Akbal	5	Oct 30 2005	8-Chuen	1
Jun 17 2005	3-Cib	1	Aug 24 2005	6-Kan	6	Oct 31 2005	9-Eb	2
Jun 18 2005	4-Caban	2	Aug 25 2005	7-Chicchan	7	Nov 1 2005	10-Ben	3
Jun 19 2005	5-Etz'nab	3	Aug 26 2005	8-Cimi	8	Nov 2 2005	11-Ix	4
Jun 20 2005	6-Cauac	4	Aug 27 2005	9-Manik	9	Nov 3 2005	12-Men	5
Jun 21 2005	7-Ahau	5	Aug 28 2005	10-Lamat	1	Nov 4 2005	13-Cib	6
Jun 22 2005	8-Imix	6	Aug 29 2005	11-Muluc	2	Nov 5 2005	1-Caban	7
Jun 23 2005	9-Ik	7	Aug 30 2005	12-Oc	3	Nov 6 2005	2-Etz'nab	8
Jun 24 2005	10-Akbal	8	Aug 31 2005	13-Chuen	4	Nov 7 2005	3-Cauac	9
Jun 25 2005	11-Kan	9	Sep 1 2005	1-Eb	5	Nov 8 2005	4-Ahau	1
Jun 26 2005	12-Chicchan	1	Sep 2 2005	2-Ben	6	Nov 9 2005	5-Imix	2
Jun 27 2005	13-Cimi	2	Sep 3 2005	3-Ix	7	Nov 10 2005	6-Ik	3
Jun 28 2005	1-Manik	3	Sep 4 2005	4-Men	8	Nov 11 2005	7-Akbal	4
Jun 29 2005	2-Lamat	4	Sep 5 2005	5-Cib	9	Nov 12 2005	8-Kan	5
Jun 30 2005	3-Muluc	5	Sep 6 2005	6-Caban	1	Nov 13 2005	9-Chicchan	6
Jul 1 2005	4-Oc	6	Sep 7 2005	7-Etz'nab	2	Nov 14 2005	10-Cimi	7
Jul 2 2005	5-Chuen	7	Sep 8 2005	8-Cauac	3	Nov 15 2005	11-Manik	8
Jul 3 2005	6-Eb	8	Sep 9 2005	9-Ahau	4	Nov 16 2005	12-Lamat	9
Jul 4 2005	7-Ben	9	Sep 10 2005	10-Imix	5	Nov 17 2005	13-Muluc	1
Jul 5 2005	8-Ix	1	Sep 11 2005	11-Ik	6	Nov 18 2005	1-Oc	2
Jul 6 2005	9-Men	2	Sep 12 2005	12-Akbal	7	Nov 19 2005	2-Chuen	3
Jul 7 2005	10-Cib	3	Sep 13 2005	13-Kan	8	Nov 20 2005	3-Eb	4
Jul 8 2005	11-Caban	4	Sep 14 2005	1-Chicchan	9	Nov 21 2005	4-Ben	5
Jul 9 2005	12-Etz'nab	5	Sep 15 2005	2-Cimi	1	Nov 22 2005	5-Ix	6
Jul 10 2005	13-Cauac	6	Sep 16 2005	3-Manik	2	Nov 23 2005	6-Men	7
Jul 11 2005	1-Ahau	7	Sep 17 2005	4-Lamat	3	Nov 24 2005	7-Cib	8
Jul 12 2005	2-Imix	8	Sep 18 2005	5-Muluc	4	Nov 25 2005	8-Caban	9
Jul 13 2005	3-Ik	9	Sep 19 2005	6-Oc	5	Nov 26 2005	9-Etz'nab	1
Jul 14 2005	4-Akbal	1	Sep 20 2005	7-Chuen	6	Nov 27 2005	10-Cauac	2
Jul 15 2005	5-Kan	2	Sep 21 2005	8-Eb	7	Nov 28 2005	11-Ahau	3
Jul 16 2005	6-Chicchan	3	Sep 22 2005	9-Ben	8	Nov 29 2005	12-Imix	4
Jul 17 2005	7-Cimi	4	Sep 23 2005	10-Ix	9	Nov 30 2005	13-Ik	5
Jul 18 2005	8-Manik	5	Sep 24 2005	11-Men	1	Dec 1 2005	1-Akbal	6
Jul 19 2005	9-Lamat	6	Sep 25 2005	12-Cib	2	Dec 2 2005	2-Kan	7
Jul 20 2005	10-Muluc	7	Sep 26 2005	13-Caban	3	Dec 3 2005	3-Chicchan	8
Jul 21 2005	11-Oc	8	Sep 27 2005	1-Etz'nab	4	Dec 4 2005	4-Cimi	9
Jul 22 2005	12-Chuen	9	Sep 28 2005	2-Cauac	5	Dec 5 2005	5-Manik	1
Jul 23 2005	13-Eb	1	Sep 29 2005	3-Ahau	6	Dec 6 2005	6-Lamat	2
Jul 24 2005	1-Ben	2	Sep 30 2005	4-Imix	7	Dec 7 2005	7-Muluc	3

Date	Day-Sign	L
Dec 8 2005	8-Oc	4
Dec 9 2005	9-Chuen	5
Dec 10 2005	10-Eb	6
Dec 11 2005	11-Ben	7
Dec 12 2005	12-Ix	8
Dec 13 2005	13-Men	9
Dec 14 2005	**1-Cib**	1
Dec 15 2005	2-Caban	2
Dec 16 2005	3-Etz'nab	3
Dec 17 2005	4-Cauac	4
Dec 18 2005	5-Ahau	5
Dec 19 2005	*6-Imix*	6
Dec 20 2005	7-Ik	7
Dec 21 2005	8-Akbal	8
Dec 22 2005	9-Kan	9
Dec 23 2005	10-Chicchan	1
Dec 24 2005	11-Cimi	2
Dec 25 2005	12-Manik	3
Dec 26 2005	13-Lamat	4
Dec 27 2005	**1-Muluc**	5
Dec 28 2005	2-Oc	6
Dec 29 2005	3-Chuen	7
Dec 30 2005	4-Eb	8
Dec 31 2005	5-Ben	9
Jan 1 2006	6-Ix	1
Jan 2 2006	7-Men	2
Jan 3 2006	8-Cib	3
Jan 4 2006	9-Caban	4
Jan 5 2006	10-Etz'nab	5
Jan 6 2006	11-Cauac	6
Jan 7 2006	12-Ahau	7
Jan 8 2006	*13-Imix*	8
Jan 9 2006	**1-Ik**	9
Jan 10 2006	2-Akbal	1
Jan 11 2006	3-Kan	2
Jan 12 2006	4-Chicchan	3
Jan 13 2006	5-Cimi	4
Jan 14 2006	6-Manik	5
Jan 15 2006	7-Lamat	6
Jan 16 2006	8-Muluc	7
Jan 17 2006	9-Oc	8
Jan 18 2006	10-Chuen	9
Jan 19 2006	11-Eb	1
Jan 20 2006	12-Ben	2
Jan 21 2006	13-Ix	3
Jan 22 2006	**1-Men**	4
Jan 23 2006	2-Cib	5
Jan 24 2006	3-Caban	6
Jan 25 2006	4-Etz'nab	7
Jan 26 2006	5-Cauac	8
Jan 27 2006	6-Ahau	9
Jan 28 2006	*7-Imix*	1
Jan 29 2006	8-Ik	2
Jan 30 2006	9-Akbal	3
Jan 31 2006	10-Kan	4
Feb 1 2006	11-Chicchan	5
Feb 2 2006	12-Cimi	6
Feb 3 2006	13-Manik	7
Feb 4 2006	**1-Lamat**	8
Feb 5 2006	2-Muluc	9
Feb 6 2006	3-Oc	1
Feb 7 2006	4-Chuen	2
Feb 8 2006	5-Eb	3
Feb 9 2006	6-Ben	4
Feb 10 2006	7-Ix	5
Feb 11 2006	8-Men	6
Feb 12 2006	9-Cib	7
Feb 13 2006	10-Caban	8

Date	Day-Sign	L
Feb 14 2006	11-Etz'nab	9
Feb 15 2006	12-Cauac	1
Feb 16 2006	13-Ahau	2
Feb 17 2006	**1-Imix**	3
Feb 18 2006	2-Ik	4
Feb 19 2006	3-Akbal	5
Feb 20 2006	4-Kan	6
Feb 21 2006	5-Chicchan	7
Feb 22 2006	6-Cimi	8
Feb 23 2006	7-Manik	9
Feb 24 2006	8-Lamat	1
Feb 25 2006	9-Muluc	2
Feb 26 2006	10-Oc	3
Feb 27 2006	11-Chuen	4
Feb 28 2006	12-Eb	5
Mar 1 2006	13-Ben	6
Mar 2 2006	**1-Ix**	7
Mar 3 2006	2-Men	8
Mar 4 2006	3-Cib	9
Mar 5 2006	4-Caban	1
Mar 6 2006	5-Etz'nab	2
Mar 7 2006	6-Cauac	3
Mar 8 2006	7-Ahau	4
Mar 9 2006	*8-Imix*	5
Mar 10 2006	9-Ik	6
Mar 11 2006	10-Akbal	7
Mar 12 2006	11-Kan	8
Mar 13 2006	12-Chicchan	9
Mar 14 2006	13-Cimi	1
Mar 15 2006	**1-Manik**	2
Mar 16 2006	2-Lamat	3
Mar 17 2006	3-Muluc	4
Mar 18 2006	4-Oc	5
Mar 19 2006	5-Chuen	6
Mar 20 2006	6-Eb	7
Mar 21 2006	7-Ben	8
Mar 22 2006	8-Ix	9
Mar 23 2006	9-Men	1
Mar 24 2006	10-Cib	2
Mar 25 2006	11-Caban	3
Mar 26 2006	12-Etz'nab	4
Mar 27 2006	13-Cauac	5
Mar 28 2006	**1-Ahau**	6
Mar 29 2006	*2-Imix*	7
Mar 30 2006	3-Ik	8
Mar 31 2006	4-Akbal	9
Apr 1 2006	5-Kan	1
Apr 2 2006	6-Chicchan	2
Apr 3 2006	7-Cimi	3
Apr 4 2006	8-Manik	4
Apr 5 2006	9-Lamat	5
Apr 6 2006	10-Muluc	6
Apr 7 2006	11-Oc	7
Apr 8 2006	12-Chuen	8
Apr 9 2006	13-Eb	9
Apr 10 2006	**1-Ben**	1
Apr 11 2006	2-Ix	2
Apr 12 2006	3-Men	3
Apr 13 2006	4-Cib	4
Apr 14 2006	5-Caban	5
Apr 15 2006	6-Etz'nab	6
Apr 16 2006	7-Cauac	7
Apr 17 2006	8-Ahau	8
Apr 18 2006	*9-Imix*	9
Apr 19 2006	10-Ik	1
Apr 20 2006	11-Akbal	2
Apr 21 2006	12-Kan	3
Apr 22 2006	13-Chicchan	4

Date	Day-Sign	L
Apr 23 2006	**1-Cimi**	5
Apr 24 2006	2-Manik	6
Apr 25 2006	3-Lamat	7
Apr 26 2006	4-Muluc	8
Apr 27 2006	5-Oc	9
Apr 28 2006	6-Chuen	1
Apr 29 2006	7-Eb	2
Apr 30 2006	8-Ben	3
May 1 2006	9-Ix	4
May 2 2006	10-Men	5
May 3 2006	11-Cib	6
May 4 2006	12-Caban	7
May 5 2006	13-Etz'nab	8
May 6 2006	**1-Cauac**	9
May 7 2006	2-Ahau	1
May 8 2006	*3-Imix*	2
May 9 2006	4-Ik	3
May 10 2006	5-Akbal	4
May 11 2006	6-Kan	5
May 12 2006	7-Chicchan	6
May 13 2006	8-Cimi	7
May 14 2006	9-Manik	8
May 15 2006	10-Lamat	9
May 16 2006	11-Muluc	1
May 17 2006	12-Oc	2
May 18 2006	13-Chuen	3
May 19 2006	**1-Eb**	4
May 20 2006	2-Ben	5
May 21 2006	3-Ix	6
May 22 2006	4-Men	7
May 23 2006	5-Cib	8
May 24 2006	6-Caban	9
May 25 2006	7-Etz'nab	1
May 26 2006	8-Cauac	2
May 27 2006	9-Ahau	3
May 28 2006	*10-Imix*	4
May 29 2006	11-Ik	5
May 30 2006	12-Akbal	6
May 31 2006	13-Kan	7
Jun 1 2006	**1-Chicchan**	8
Jun 2 2006	2-Cimi	9
Jun 3 2006	3-Manik	1
Jun 4 2006	4-Lamat	2
Jun 5 2006	5-Muluc	3
Jun 6 2006	6-Oc	4
Jun 7 2006	7-Chuen	5
Jun 8 2006	8-Eb	6
Jun 9 2006	9-Ben	7
Jun 10 2006	10-Ix	8
Jun 11 2006	11-Men	9
Jun 12 2006	12-Cib	1
Jun 13 2006	13-Caban	2
Jun 14 2006	**1-Etz'nab**	3
Jun 15 2006	2-Cauac	4
Jun 16 2006	3-Ahau	5
Jun 17 2006	*4-Imix*	6
Jun 18 2006	5-Ik	7
Jun 19 2006	6-Akbal	8
Jun 20 2006	7-Kan	9
Jun 21 2006	8-Chicchan	1
Jun 22 2006	9-Cimi	2
Jun 23 2006	10-Manik	3
Jun 24 2006	11-Lamat	4
Jun 25 2006	12-Muluc	5
Jun 26 2006	13-Oc	6
Jun 27 2006	**1-Chuen**	7
Jun 28 2006	2-Eb	8
Jun 29 2006	3-Ben	9

Date	Day-Sign	L
Jun 30 2006	4-Ix	1
Jul 1 2006	5-Men	2
Jul 2 2006	6-Cib	3
Jul 3 2006	7-Caban	4
Jul 4 2006	8-Etz'nab	5
Jul 5 2006	9-Cauac	6
Jul 6 2006	10-Ahau	7
Jul 7 2006	11-*Imix*	8
Jul 8 2006	12-Ik	9
Jul 9 2006	13-Akbal	1
Jul 10 2006	**1-Kan**	2
Jul 11 2006	2-Chicchan	3
Jul 12 2006	3-Cimi	4
Jul 13 2006	4-Manik	5
Jul 14 2006	5-Lamat	6
Jul 15 2006	6-Muluc	7
Jul 16 2006	7-Oc	8
Jul 17 2006	8-Chuen	9
Jul 18 2006	9-Eb	1
Jul 19 2006	10-Ben	2
Jul 20 2006	11-Ix	3
Jul 21 2006	12-Men	4
Jul 22 2006	13-Cib	5
Jul 23 2006	**1-Caban**	6
Jul 24 2006	2-Etz'nab	7
Jul 25 2006	3-Cauac	8
Jul 26 2006	4-Ahau	9
Jul 27 2006	5-*Imix*	1
Jul 28 2006	6-Ik	2
Jul 29 2006	7-Akbal	3
Jul 30 2006	8-Kan	4
Jul 31 2006	9-Chicchan	5
Aug 1 2006	10-Cimi	6
Aug 2 2006	11-Manik	7
Aug 3 2006	12-Lamat	8
Aug 4 2006	13-Muluc	9
Aug 5 2006	**1-Oc**	1
Aug 6 2006	2-Chuen	2
Aug 7 2006	3-Eb	3
Aug 8 2006	4-Ben	4
Aug 9 2006	5-Ix	5
Aug 10 2006	6-Men	6
Aug 11 2006	7-Cib	7
Aug 12 2006	8-Caban	8
Aug 13 2006	9-Etz'nab	9
Aug 14 2006	10-Cauac	1
Aug 15 2006	11-Ahau	2
Aug 16 2006	12-*Imix*	3
Aug 17 2006	13-Ik	4
Aug 18 2006	**1-Akbal**	5
Aug 19 2006	2-Kan	6
Aug 20 2006	3-Chicchan	7
Aug 21 2006	4-Cimi	8
Aug 22 2006	5-Manik	9
Aug 23 2006	6-Lamat	1
Aug 24 2006	7-Muluc	2
Aug 25 2006	8-Oc	3
Aug 26 2006	9-Chuen	4
Aug 27 2006	10-Eb	5
Aug 28 2006	11-Ben	6
Aug 29 2006	12-Ix	7
Aug 30 2006	13-Men	8
Aug 31 2006	**1-Cib**	9
Sep 1 2006	2-Caban	1
Sep 2 2006	3-Etz'nab	2
Sep 3 2006	4-Cauac	3
Sep 4 2006	5-Ahau	4
Sep 5 2006	6-*Imix*	5

Date	Day-Sign	L
Sep 6 2006	7-Ik	6
Sep 7 2006	8-Akbal	7
Sep 8 2006	9-Kan	8
Sep 9 2006	10-Chicchan	9
Sep 10 2006	11-Cimi	1
Sep 11 2006	12-Manik	2
Sep 12 2006	13-Lamat	3
Sep 13 2006	**1-Muluc**	4
Sep 14 2006	2-Oc	5
Sep 15 2006	3-Chuen	6
Sep 16 2006	4-Eb	7
Sep 17 2006	5-Ben	8
Sep 18 2006	6-Ix	9
Sep 19 2006	7-Men	1
Sep 20 2006	8-Cib	2
Sep 21 2006	9-Caban	3
Sep 22 2006	10-Etz'nab	4
Sep 23 2006	11-Cauac	5
Sep 24 2006	12-Ahau	6
Sep 25 2006	13-*Imix*	7
Sep 26 2006	**1-Ik**	8
Sep 27 2006	2-Akbal	9
Sep 28 2006	3-Kan	1
Sep 29 2006	4-Chicchan	2
Sep 30 2006	5-Cimi	3
Oct 1 2006	6-Manik	4
Oct 2 2006	7-Lamat	5
Oct 3 2006	8-Muluc	6
Oct 4 2006	9-Oc	7
Oct 5 2006	10-Chuen	8
Oct 6 2006	11-Eb	9
Oct 7 2006	12-Ben	1
Oct 8 2006	13-Ix	2
Oct 9 2006	**1-Men**	3
Oct 10 2006	2-Cib	4
Oct 11 2006	3-Caban	5
Oct 12 2006	4-Etz'nab	6
Oct 13 2006	5-Cauac	7
Oct 14 2006	6-Ahau	8
Oct 15 2006	7-*Imix*	9
Oct 16 2006	8-Ik	1
Oct 17 2006	9-Akbal	2
Oct 18 2006	10-Kan	3
Oct 19 2006	11-Chicchan	4
Oct 20 2006	12-Cimi	5
Oct 21 2006	13-Manik	6
Oct 22 2006	**1-Lamat**	7
Oct 23 2006	2-Muluc	8
Oct 24 2006	3-Oc	9
Oct 25 2006	4-Chuen	1
Oct 26 2006	5-Eb	2
Oct 27 2006	6-Ben	3
Oct 28 2006	7-Ix	4
Oct 29 2006	8-Men	5
Oct 30 2006	9-Cib	6
Oct 31 2006	10-Caban	7
Nov 1 2006	11-Etz'nab	8
Nov 2 2006	12-Cauac	9
Nov 3 2006	13-Ahau	1
Nov 4 2006	**1-Imix**	2
Nov 5 2006	2-Ik	3
Nov 6 2006	3-Akbal	4
Nov 7 2006	4-Kan	5
Nov 8 2006	5-Chicchan	6
Nov 9 2006	6-Cimi	7
Nov 10 2006	7-Manik	8
Nov 11 2006	8-Lamat	9
Nov 12 2006	9-Muluc	1

Date	Day-Sign	L
Nov 13 2006	10-Oc	2
Nov 14 2006	11-Chuen	3
Nov 15 2006	12-Eb	4
Nov 16 2006	13-Ben	5
Nov 17 2006	**1-Ix**	6
Nov 18 2006	2-Men	7
Nov 19 2006	3-Cib	8
Nov 20 2006	4-Caban	9
Nov 21 2006	5-Etz'nab	1
Nov 22 2006	6-Cauac	2
Nov 23 2006	7-Ahau	3
Nov 24 2006	8-*Imix*	4
Nov 25 2006	9-Ik	5
Nov 26 2006	10-Akbal	6
Nov 27 2006	11-Kan	7
Nov 28 2006	12-Chicchan	8
Nov 29 2006	13-Cimi	9
Nov 30 2006	**1-Manik**	1
Dec 1 2006	2-Lamat	2
Dec 2 2006	3-Muluc	3
Dec 3 2006	4-Oc	4
Dec 4 2006	5-Chuen	5
Dec 5 2006	6-Eb	6
Dec 6 2006	7-Ben	7
Dec 7 2006	8-Ix	8
Dec 8 2006	9-Men	9
Dec 9 2006	10-Cib	1
Dec 10 2006	11-Caban	2
Dec 11 2006	12-Etz'nab	3
Dec 12 2006	13-Cauac	4
Dec 13 2006	**1-Ahau**	5
Dec 14 2006	2-*Imix*	6
Dec 15 2006	3-Ik	7
Dec 16 2006	4-Akbal	8
Dec 17 2006	5-Kan	9
Dec 18 2006	6-Chicchan	1
Dec 19 2006	7-Cimi	2
Dec 20 2006	8-Manik	3
Dec 21 2006	9-Lamat	4
Dec 22 2006	10-Muluc	5
Dec 23 2006	11-Oc	6
Dec 24 2006	12-Chuen	7
Dec 25 2006	13-Eb	8
Dec 26 2006	**1-Ben**	9
Dec 27 2006	2-Ix	1
Dec 28 2006	3-Men	2
Dec 29 2006	4-Cib	3
Dec 30 2006	5-Caban	4
Dec 31 2006	6-Etz'nab	5
Jan 1 2007	7-Cauac	6
Jan 2 2007	8-Ahau	7
Jan 3 2007	9-*Imix*	8
Jan 4 2007	10-Ik	9
Jan 5 2007	11-Akbal	1
Jan 6 2007	12-Kan	2
Jan 7 2007	13-Chicchan	3
Jan 8 2007	**1-Cimi**	4
Jan 9 2007	2-Manik	5
Jan 10 2007	3-Lamat	6
Jan 11 2007	4-Muluc	7
Jan 12 2007	5-Oc	8
Jan 13 2007	6-Chuen	9
Jan 14 2007	7-Eb	1
Jan 15 2007	8-Ben	2
Jan 16 2007	9-Ix	3
Jan 17 2007	10-Men	4
Jan 18 2007	11-Cib	5
Jan 19 2007	12-Caban	6

Date	Day-Sign	L	Date	Day-Sign	L	Date	Day-Sign	L
Jan 20 2007	13-Etz'nab	7	Mar 29 2007	3-Cimi	3	Jun 5 2007	6-Ix	8
Jan 21 2007	**1-Cauac**	8	Mar 30 2007	4-Manik	4	Jun 6 2007	7-Men	9
Jan 22 2007	2-Ahau	9	Mar 31 2007	5-Lamat	5	Jun 7 2007	8-Cib	1
Jan 23 2007	3-*Imix*	1	Apr 1 2007	6-Muluc	6	Jun 8 2007	9-Caban	2
Jan 24 2007	4-Ik	2	Apr 2 2007	7-Oc	7	Jun 9 2007	10-Etz'nab	3
Jan 25 2007	5-Akbal	3	Apr 3 2007	8-Chuen	8	Jun 10 2007	11-Cauac	4
Jan 26 2007	6-Kan	4	Apr 4 2007	9-Eb	9	Jun 11 2007	12-Ahau	5
Jan 27 2007	7-Chicchan	5	Apr 5 2007	10-Ben	1	Jun 12 2007	13-*Imix*	6
Jan 28 2007	8-Cimi	6	Apr 6 2007	11-Ix	2	Jun 13 2007	**1-Ik**	7
Jan 29 2007	9-Manik	7	Apr 7 2007	12-Men	3	Jun 14 2007	2-Akbal	8
Jan 30 2007	10-Lamat	8	Apr 8 2007	13-Cib	4	Jun 15 2007	3-Kan	9
Jan 31 2007	11-Muluc	9	Apr 9 2007	**1-Caban**	5	Jun 16 2007	4-Chicchan	1
Feb 1 2007	12-Oc	1	Apr 10 2007	2-Etz'nab	6	Jun 17 2007	5-Cimi	2
Feb 2 2007	13-Chuen	2	Apr 11 2007	3-Cauac	7	Jun 18 2007	6-Manik	3
Feb 3 2007	**1-Eb**	3	Apr 12 2007	4-Ahau	8	Jun 19 2007	7-Lamat	4
Feb 4 2007	2-Ben	4	Apr 13 2007	5-*Imix*	9	Jun 20 2007	8-Muluc	5
Feb 5 2007	3-Ix	5	Apr 14 2007	6-Ik	1	Jun 21 2007	9-Oc	6
Feb 6 2007	4-Men	6	Apr 15 2007	7-Akbal	2	Jun 22 2007	10-Chuen	7
Feb 7 2007	5-Cib	7	Apr 16 2007	8-Kan	3	Jun 23 2007	11-Eb	8
Feb 8 2007	6-Caban	8	Apr 17 2007	9-Chicchan	4	Jun 24 2007	12-Ben	9
Feb 9 2007	7-Etz'nab	9	Apr 18 2007	10-Cimi	5	Jun 25 2007	13-Ix	1
Feb 10 2007	8-Cauac	1	Apr 19 2007	11-Manik	6	Jun 26 2007	**1-Men**	2
Feb 11 2007	9-Ahau	2	Apr 20 2007	12-Lamat	7	Jun 27 2007	2-Cib	3
Feb 12 2007	10-*Imix*	3	Apr 21 2007	13-Muluc	8	Jun 28 2007	3-Caban	4
Feb 13 2007	11-Ik	4	Apr 22 2007	**1-Oc**	9	Jun 29 2007	4-Etz'nab	5
Feb 14 2007	12-Akbal	5	Apr 23 2007	2-Chuen	1	Jun 30 2007	5-Cauac	6
Feb 15 2007	13-Kan	6	Apr 24 2007	3-Eb	2	Jul 1 2007	6-Ahau	7
Feb 16 2007	**1-Chicchan**	7	Apr 25 2007	4-Ben	3	Jul 2 2007	7-*Imix*	8
Feb 17 2007	2-Cimi	8	Apr 26 2007	5-Ix	4	Jul 3 2007	8-Ik	9
Feb 18 2007	3-Manik	9	Apr 27 2007	6-Men	5	Jul 4 2007	9-Akbal	1
Feb 19 2007	4-Lamat	1	Apr 28 2007	7-Cib	6	Jul 5 2007	10-Kan	2
Feb 20 2007	5-Muluc	2	Apr 29 2007	8-Caban	7	Jul 6 2007	11-Chicchan	3
Feb 21 2007	6-Oc	3	Apr 30 2007	9-Etz'nab	8	Jul 7 2007	12-Cimi	4
Feb 22 2007	7-Chuen	4	May 1 2007	10-Cauac	9	Jul 8 2007	13-Manik	5
Feb 23 2007	8-Eb	5	May 2 2007	11-Ahau	1	Jul 9 2007	**1-Lamat**	6
Feb 24 2007	9-Ben	6	May 3 2007	12-*Imix*	2	Jul 10 2007	2-Muluc	7
Feb 25 2007	10-Ix	7	May 4 2007	13-Ik	3	Jul 11 2007	3-Oc	8
Feb 26 2007	11-Men	8	May 5 2007	**1-Akbal**	4	Jul 12 2007	4-Chuen	9
Feb 27 2007	12-Cib	9	May 6 2007	2-Kan	5	Jul 13 2007	5-Eb	1
Feb 28 2007	13-Caban	1	May 7 2007	3-Chicchan	6	Jul 14 2007	6-Ben	2
Mar 1 2007	**1-Etz'nab**	2	May 8 2007	4-Cimi	7	Jul 15 2007	7-Ix	3
Mar 2 2007	2-Cauac	3	May 9 2007	5-Manik	8	Jul 16 2007	8-Men	4
Mar 3 2007	3-Ahau	4	May 10 2007	6-Lamat	9	Jul 17 2007	9-Cib	5
Mar 4 2007	4-*Imix*	5	May 11 2007	7-Muluc	1	Jul 18 2007	10-Caban	6
Mar 5 2007	5-Ik	6	May 12 2007	8-Oc	2	Jul 19 2007	11-Etz'nab	7
Mar 6 2007	6-Akbal	7	May 13 2007	9-Chuen	3	Jul 20 2007	12-Cauac	8
Mar 7 2007	7-Kan	8	May 14 2007	10-Eb	4	Jul 21 2007	13-Ahau	9
Mar 8 2007	8-Chicchan	9	May 15 2007	11-Ben	5	Jul 22 2007	**1-Imix**	1
Mar 9 2007	9-Cimi	1	May 16 2007	12-Ix	6	Jul 23 2007	2-Ik	2
Mar 10 2007	10-Manik	2	May 17 2007	13-Men	7	Jul 24 2007	3-Akbal	3
Mar 11 2007	11-Lamat	3	May 18 2007	**1-Cib**	8	Jul 25 2007	4-Kan	4
Mar 12 2007	12-Muluc	4	May 19 2007	2-Caban	9	Jul 26 2007	5-Chicchan	5
Mar 13 2007	13-Oc	5	May 20 2007	3-Etz'nab	1	Jul 27 2007	6-Cimi	6
Mar 14 2007	**1-Chuen**	6	May 21 2007	4-Cauac	2	Jul 28 2007	7-Manik	7
Mar 15 2007	2-Eb	7	May 22 2007	5-Ahau	3	Jul 29 2007	8-Lamat	8
Mar 16 2007	3-Ben	8	May 23 2007	6-*Imix*	4	Jul 30 2007	9-Muluc	9
Mar 17 2007	4-Ix	9	May 24 2007	7-Ik	5	Jul 31 2007	10-Oc	1
Mar 18 2007	5-Men	1	May 25 2007	8-Akbal	6	Aug 1 2007	11-Chuen	2
Mar 19 2007	6-Cib	2	May 26 2007	9-Kan	7	Aug 2 2007	12-Eb	3
Mar 20 2007	7-Caban	3	May 27 2007	10-Chicchan	8	Aug 3 2007	13-Ben	4
Mar 21 2007	8-Etz'nab	4	May 28 2007	11-Cimi	9	Aug 4 2007	**1-Ix**	5
Mar 22 2007	9-Cauac	5	May 29 2007	12-Manik	1	Aug 5 2007	2-Men	6
Mar 23 2007	10-Ahau	6	May 30 2007	13-Lamat	2	Aug 6 2007	3-Cib	7
Mar 24 2007	11-*Imix*	7	May 31 2007	**1-Muluc**	3	Aug 7 2007	4-Caban	8
Mar 25 2007	12-Ik	8	Jun 1 2007	2-Oc	4	Aug 8 2007	5-Etz'nab	9
Mar 26 2007	13-Akbal	9	Jun 2 2007	3-Chuen	5	Aug 9 2007	6-Cauac	1
Mar 27 2007	**1-Kan**	1	Jun 3 2007	4-Eb	6	Aug 10 2007	7-Ahau	2
Mar 28 2007	2-Chicchan	2	Jun 4 2007	5-Ben	7	Aug 11 2007	8-*Imix*	3

Date	Day-Sign	L
Aug 12 2007	9-Ik	4
Aug 13 2007	10-Akbal	5
Aug 14 2007	11-Kan	6
Aug 15 2007	12-Chicchan	7
Aug 16 2007	13-Cimi	8
Aug 17 2007	**1-Manik**	9
Aug 18 2007	2-Lamat	1
Aug 19 2007	3-Muluc	2
Aug 20 2007	4-Oc	3
Aug 21 2007	5-Chuen	4
Aug 22 2007	6-Eb	5
Aug 23 2007	7-Ben	6
Aug 24 2007	8-Ix	7
Aug 25 2007	9-Men	8
Aug 26 2007	10-Cib	9
Aug 27 2007	11-Caban	1
Aug 28 2007	12-Etz'nab	2
Aug 29 2007	13-Cauac	3
Aug 30 2007	**1-Ahau**	4
Aug 31 2007	2-*Imix*	5
Sep 1 2007	3-Ik	6
Sep 2 2007	4-Akbal	7
Sep 3 2007	5-Kan	8
Sep 4 2007	6-Chicchan	9
Sep 5 2007	7-Cimi	1
Sep 6 2007	8-Manik	2
Sep 7 2007	9-Lamat	3
Sep 8 2007	10-Muluc	4
Sep 9 2007	11-Oc	5
Sep 10 2007	12-Chuen	6
Sep 11 2007	13-Eb	7
Sep 12 2007	**1-Ben**	8
Sep 13 2007	2-Ix	9
Sep 14 2007	3-Men	1
Sep 15 2007	4-Cib	2
Sep 16 2007	5-Caban	3
Sep 17 2007	6-Etz'nab	4
Sep 18 2007	7-Cauac	5
Sep 19 2007	8-Ahau	6
Sep 20 2007	9-*Imix*	7
Sep 21 2007	10-Ik	8
Sep 22 2007	11-Akbal	9
Sep 23 2007	12-Kan	1
Sep 24 2007	13-Chicchan	2
Sep 25 2007	**1-Cimi**	3
Sep 26 2007	2-Manik	4
Sep 27 2007	3-Lamat	5
Sep 28 2007	4-Muluc	6
Sep 29 2007	5-Oc	7
Sep 30 2007	6-Chuen	8
Oct 1 2007	7-Eb	9
Oct 2 2007	8-Ben	1
Oct 3 2007	9-Ix	2
Oct 4 2007	10-Men	3
Oct 5 2007	11-Cib	4
Oct 6 2007	12-Caban	5
Oct 7 2007	13-Etz'nab	6
Oct 8 2007	**1-Cauac**	7
Oct 9 2007	2-Ahau	8
Oct 10 2007	3-*Imix*	9
Oct 11 2007	4-Ik	1
Oct 12 2007	5-Akbal	2
Oct 13 2007	6-Kan	3
Oct 14 2007	7-Chicchan	4
Oct 15 2007	8-Cimi	5
Oct 16 2007	9-Manik	6
Oct 17 2007	10-Lamat	7
Oct 18 2007	11-Muluc	8

Date	Day-Sign	L
Oct 19 2007	12-Oc	9
Oct 20 2007	13-Chuen	1
Oct 21 2007	**1-Eb**	2
Oct 22 2007	2-Ben	3
Oct 23 2007	3-Ix	4
Oct 24 2007	4-Men	5
Oct 25 2007	5-Cib	6
Oct 26 2007	6-Caban	7
Oct 27 2007	7-Etz'nab	8
Oct 28 2007	8-Cauac	9
Oct 29 2007	9-Ahau	1
Oct 30 2007	10-*Imix*	2
Oct 31 2007	11-Ik	3
Nov 1 2007	12-Akbal	4
Nov 2 2007	13-Kan	5
Nov 3 2007	**1-Chicchan**	6
Nov 4 2007	2-Cimi	7
Nov 5 2007	3-Manik	8
Nov 6 2007	4-Lamat	9
Nov 7 2007	5-Muluc	1
Nov 8 2007	6-Oc	2
Nov 9 2007	7-Chuen	3
Nov 10 2007	8-Eb	4
Nov 11 2007	9-Ben	5
Nov 12 2007	10-Ix	6
Nov 13 2007	11-Men	7
Nov 14 2007	12-Cib	8
Nov 15 2007	13-Caban	9
Nov 16 2007	**1-Etz'nab**	1
Nov 17 2007	2-Cauac	2
Nov 18 2007	3-Ahau	3
Nov 19 2007	4-*Imix*	4
Nov 20 2007	5-Ik	5
Nov 21 2007	6-Akbal	6
Nov 22 2007	7-Kan	7
Nov 23 2007	8-Chicchan	8
Nov 24 2007	9-Cimi	9
Nov 25 2007	10-Manik	1
Nov 26 2007	11-Lamat	2
Nov 27 2007	12-Muluc	3
Nov 28 2007	13-Oc	4
Nov 29 2007	**1-Chuen**	5
Nov 30 2007	2-Eb	6
Dec 1 2007	3-Ben	7
Dec 2 2007	4-Ix	8
Dec 3 2007	5-Men	9
Dec 4 2007	6-Cib	1
Dec 5 2007	7-Caban	2
Dec 6 2007	8-Etz'nab	3
Dec 7 2007	9-Cauac	4
Dec 8 2007	10-Ahau	5
Dec 9 2007	11-*Imix*	6
Dec 10 2007	12-Ik	7
Dec 11 2007	13-Akbal	8
Dec 12 2007	**1-Kan**	9
Dec 13 2007	2-Chicchan	1
Dec 14 2007	3-Cimi	2
Dec 15 2007	4-Manik	3
Dec 16 2007	5-Lamat	4
Dec 17 2007	6-Muluc	5
Dec 18 2007	7-Oc	6
Dec 19 2007	8-Chuen	7
Dec 20 2007	9-Eb	8
Dec 21 2007	10-Ben	9
Dec 22 2007	11-Ix	1
Dec 23 2007	12-Men	2
Dec 24 2007	13-Cib	3
Dec 25 2007	**1-Caban**	4

Date	Day-Sign	L
Dec 26 2007	2-Etz'nab	5
Dec 27 2007	3-Cauac	6
Dec 28 2007	4-Ahau	7
Dec 29 2007	5-*Imix*	8
Dec 30 2007	6-Ik	9
Dec 31 2007	7-Akbal	1
Jan 1 2008	8-Kan	2
Jan 2 2008	9-Chicchan	3
Jan 3 2008	10-Cimi	4
Jan 4 2008	11-Manik	5
Jan 5 2008	12-Lamat	6
Jan 6 2008	13-Muluc	7
Jan 7 2008	**1-Oc**	8
Jan 8 2008	2-Chuen	9
Jan 9 2008	3-Eb	1
Jan 10 2008	4-Ben	2
Jan 11 2008	5-Ix	3
Jan 12 2008	6-Men	4
Jan 13 2008	7-Cib	5
Jan 14 2008	8-Caban	6
Jan 15 2008	9-Etz'nab	7
Jan 16 2008	10-Cauac	8
Jan 17 2008	11-Ahau	9
Jan 18 2008	12-*Imix*	1
Jan 19 2008	13-Ik	2
Jan 20 2008	**1-Akbal**	3
Jan 21 2008	2-Kan	4
Jan 22 2008	3-Chicchan	5
Jan 23 2008	4-Cimi	6
Jan 24 2008	5-Manik	7
Jan 25 2008	6-Lamat	8
Jan 26 2008	7-Muluc	9
Jan 27 2008	8-Oc	1
Jan 28 2008	9-Chuen	2
Jan 29 2008	10-Eb	3
Jan 30 2008	11-Ben	4
Jan 31 2008	12-Ix	5
Feb 1 2008	13-Men	6
Feb 2 2008	**1-Cib**	7
Feb 3 2008	2-Caban	8
Feb 4 2008	3-Etz'nab	9
Feb 5 2008	4-Cauac	1
Feb 6 2008	5-Ahau	2
Feb 7 2008	6-*Imix*	3
Feb 8 2008	7-Ik	4
Feb 9 2008	8-Akbal	5
Feb 10 2008	9-Kan	6
Feb 11 2008	10-Chicchan	7
Feb 12 2008	11-Cimi	8
Feb 13 2008	12-Manik	9
Feb 14 2008	13-Lamat	1
Feb 15 2008	**1-Muluc**	2
Feb 16 2008	2-Oc	3
Feb 17 2008	3-Chuen	4
Feb 18 2008	4-Eb	5
Feb 19 2008	5-Ben	6
Feb 20 2008	6-Ix	7
Feb 21 2008	7-Men	8
Feb 22 2008	8-Cib	9
Feb 23 2008	9-Caban	1
Feb 24 2008	10-Etz'nab	2
Feb 25 2008	11-Cauac	3
Feb 26 2008	12-Ahau	4
Feb 27 2008	13-*Imix*	5
Feb 28 2008	**1-Ik**	6
Feb 29 2008	2-Akbal	7
Mar 1 2008	3-Kan	8
Mar 2 2008	4-Chicchan	9

Date	Day-Sign	L
Mar 3 2008	5-Cimi	1
Mar 4 2008	6-Manik	2
Mar 5 2008	7-Lamat	3
Mar 6 2008	8-Muluc	4
Mar 7 2008	9-Oc	5
Mar 8 2008	10-Chuen	6
Mar 9 2008	11-Eb	7
Mar 10 2008	12-Ben	8
Mar 11 2008	13-Ix	9
Mar 12 2008	**1-Men**	1
Mar 13 2008	2-Cib	2
Mar 14 2008	3-Caban	3
Mar 15 2008	4-Etz'nab	4
Mar 16 2008	5-Cauac	5
Mar 17 2008	6-Ahau	6
Mar 18 2008	*7-Imix*	7
Mar 19 2008	8-Ik	8
Mar 20 2008	9-Akbal	9
Mar 21 2008	10-Kan	1
Mar 22 2008	11-Chicchan	2
Mar 23 2008	12-Cimi	3
Mar 24 2008	13-Manik	4
Mar 25 2008	**1-Lamat**	5
Mar 26 2008	2-Muluc	6
Mar 27 2008	3-Oc	7
Mar 28 2008	4-Chuen	8
Mar 29 2008	5-Eb	9
Mar 30 2008	6-Ben	1
Mar 31 2008	7-Ix	2
Apr 1 2008	8-Men	3
Apr 2 2008	9-Cib	4
Apr 3 2008	10-Caban	5
Apr 4 2008	11-Etz'nab	6
Apr 5 2008	12-Cauac	7
Apr 6 2008	13-Ahau	8
Apr 7 2008	**1-Imix**	9
Apr 8 2008	2-Ik	1
Apr 9 2008	3-Akbal	2
Apr 10 2008	4-Kan	3
Apr 11 2008	5-Chicchan	4
Apr 12 2008	6-Cimi	5
Apr 13 2008	7-Manik	6
Apr 14 2008	8-Lamat	7
Apr 15 2008	9-Muluc	8
Apr 16 2008	10-Oc	9
Apr 17 2008	11-Chuen	1
Apr 18 2008	12-Eb	2
Apr 19 2008	13-Ben	3
Apr 20 2008	**1-Ix**	4
Apr 21 2008	2-Men	5
Apr 22 2008	3-Cib	6
Apr 23 2008	4-Caban	7
Apr 24 2008	5-Etz'nab	8
Apr 25 2008	6-Cauac	9
Apr 26 2008	7-Ahau	1
Apr 27 2008	*8-Imix*	2
Apr 28 2008	9-Ik	3
Apr 29 2008	10-Akbal	4
Apr 30 2008	11-Kan	5
May 1 2008	12-Chicchan	6
May 2 2008	13-Cimi	7
May 3 2008	**1-Manik**	8
May 4 2008	2-Lamat	9
May 5 2008	3-Muluc	1
May 6 2008	4-Oc	2
May 7 2008	5-Chuen	3
May 8 2008	6-Eb	4
May 9 2008	7-Ben	5

Date	Day-Sign	L
May 10 2008	8-Ix	6
May 11 2008	9-Men	7
May 12 2008	10-Cib	8
May 13 2008	11-Caban	9
May 14 2008	12-Etz'nab	1
May 15 2008	13-Cauac	2
May 16 2008	**1-Ahau**	3
May 17 2008	*2-Imix*	4
May 18 2008	3-Ik	5
May 19 2008	4-Akbal	6
May 20 2008	5-Kan	7
May 21 2008	6-Chicchan	8
May 22 2008	7-Cimi	9
May 23 2008	8-Manik	1
May 24 2008	9-Lamat	2
May 25 2008	10-Muluc	3
May 26 2008	11-Oc	4
May 27 2008	12-Chuen	5
May 28 2008	13-Eb	6
May 29 2008	**1-Ben**	7
May 30 2008	2-Ix	8
May 31 2008	3-Men	9
Jun 1 2008	4-Cib	1
Jun 2 2008	5-Caban	2
Jun 3 2008	6-Etz'nab	3
Jun 4 2008	7-Cauac	4
Jun 5 2008	8-Ahau	5
Jun 6 2008	*9-Imix*	6
Jun 7 2008	10-Ik	7
Jun 8 2008	11-Akbal	8
Jun 9 2008	12-Kan	9
Jun 10 2008	13-Chicchan	1
Jun 11 2008	**1-Cimi**	2
Jun 12 2008	2-Manik	3
Jun 13 2008	3-Lamat	4
Jun 14 2008	4-Muluc	5
Jun 15 2008	5-Oc	6
Jun 16 2008	6-Chuen	7
Jun 17 2008	7-Eb	8
Jun 18 2008	8-Ben	9
Jun 19 2008	9-Ix	1
Jun 20 2008	10-Men	2
Jun 21 2008	11-Cib	3
Jun 22 2008	12-Caban	4
Jun 23 2008	13-Etz'nab	5
Jun 24 2008	**1-Cauac**	6
Jun 25 2008	2-Ahau	7
Jun 26 2008	*3-Imix*	8
Jun 27 2008	4-Ik	9
Jun 28 2008	5-Akbal	1
Jun 29 2008	6-Kan	2
Jun 30 2008	7-Chicchan	3
Jul 1 2008	8-Cimi	4
Jul 2 2008	9-Manik	5
Jul 3 2008	10-Lamat	6
Jul 4 2008	11-Muluc	7
Jul 5 2008	12-Oc	8
Jul 6 2008	13-Chuen	9
Jul 7 2008	**1-Eb**	1
Jul 8 2008	2-Ben	2
Jul 9 2008	3-Ix	3
Jul 10 2008	4-Men	4
Jul 11 2008	5-Cib	5
Jul 12 2008	6-Caban	6
Jul 13 2008	7-Etz'nab	7
Jul 14 2008	8-Cauac	8
Jul 15 2008	9-Ahau	9
Jul 16 2008	*10-Imix*	1

Date	Day-Sign	L
Jul 17 2008	11-Ik	2
Jul 18 2008	12-Akbal	3
Jul 19 2008	13-Kan	4
Jul 20 2008	**1-Chicchan**	5
Jul 21 2008	2-Cimi	6
Jul 22 2008	3-Manik	7
Jul 23 2008	4-Lamat	8
Jul 24 2008	5-Muluc	9
Jul 25 2008	6-Oc	1
Jul 26 2008	7-Chuen	2
Jul 27 2008	8-Eb	3
Jul 28 2008	9-Ben	4
Jul 29 2008	10-Ix	5
Jul 30 2008	11-Men	6
Jul 31 2008	12-Cib	7
Aug 1 2008	13-Caban	8
Aug 2 2008	**1-Etz'nab**	9
Aug 3 2008	2-Cauac	1
Aug 4 2008	3-Ahau	2
Aug 5 2008	*4-Imix*	3
Aug 6 2008	5-Ik	4
Aug 7 2008	6-Akbal	5
Aug 8 2008	7-Kan	6
Aug 9 2008	8-Chicchan	7
Aug 10 2008	9-Cimi	8
Aug 11 2008	10-Manik	9
Aug 12 2008	11-Lamat	1
Aug 13 2008	12-Muluc	2
Aug 14 2008	13-Oc	3
Aug 15 2008	**1-Chuen**	4
Aug 16 2008	2-Eb	5
Aug 17 2008	3-Ben	6
Aug 18 2008	4-Ix	7
Aug 19 2008	5-Men	8
Aug 20 2008	6-Cib	9
Aug 21 2008	7-Caban	1
Aug 22 2008	8-Etz'nab	2
Aug 23 2008	9-Cauac	3
Aug 24 2008	10-Ahau	4
Aug 25 2008	*11-Imix*	5
Aug 26 2008	12-Ik	6
Aug 27 2008	13-Akbal	7
Aug 28 2008	**1-Kan**	8
Aug 29 2008	2-Chicchan	9
Aug 30 2008	3-Cimi	1
Aug 31 2008	4-Manik	2
Sep 1 2008	5-Lamat	3
Sep 2 2008	6-Muluc	4
Sep 3 2008	7-Oc	5
Sep 4 2008	8-Chuen	6
Sep 5 2008	9-Eb	7
Sep 6 2008	10-Ben	8
Sep 7 2008	11-Ix	9
Sep 8 2008	12-Men	1
Sep 9 2008	13-Cib	2
Sep 10 2008	**1-Caban**	3
Sep 11 2008	2-Etz'nab	4
Sep 12 2008	3-Cauac	5
Sep 13 2008	4-Ahau	6
Sep 14 2008	*5-Imix*	7
Sep 15 2008	6-Ik	8
Sep 16 2008	7-Akbal	9
Sep 17 2008	8-Kan	1
Sep 18 2008	9-Chicchan	2
Sep 19 2008	10-Cimi	3
Sep 20 2008	11-Manik	4
Sep 21 2008	12-Lamat	5
Sep 22 2008	13-Muluc	6

Date	Day-Sign	L
Sep 23 2008	**1-Oc**	7
Sep 24 2008	2-Chuen	8
Sep 25 2008	3-Eb	9
Sep 26 2008	4-Ben	1
Sep 27 2008	5-Ix	2
Sep 28 2008	6-Men	3
Sep 29 2008	7-Cib	4
Sep 30 2008	8-Caban	5
Oct 1 2008	9-Etz'nab	6
Oct 2 2008	10-Cauac	7
Oct 3 2008	11-Ahau	8
Oct 4 2008	*12-Imix*	9
Oct 5 2008	13-Ik	1
Oct 6 2008	**1-Akbal**	2
Oct 7 2008	2-Kan	3
Oct 8 2008	3-Chicchan	4
Oct 9 2008	4-Cimi	5
Oct 10 2008	5-Manik	6
Oct 11 2008	6-Lamat	7
Oct 12 2008	7-Muluc	8
Oct 13 2008	8-Oc	9
Oct 14 2008	9-Chuen	1
Oct 15 2008	10-Eb	2
Oct 16 2008	11-Ben	3
Oct 17 2008	12-Ix	4
Oct 18 2008	13-Men	5
Oct 19 2008	**1-Cib**	6
Oct 20 2008	2-Caban	7
Oct 21 2008	3-Etz'nab	8
Oct 22 2008	4-Cauac	9
Oct 23 2008	5-Ahau	1
Oct 24 2008	*6-Imix*	2
Oct 25 2008	7-Ik	3
Oct 26 2008	8-Akbal	4
Oct 27 2008	9-Kan	5
Oct 28 2008	10-Chicchan	6
Oct 29 2008	11-Cimi	7
Oct 30 2008	12-Manik	8
Oct 31 2008	13-Lamat	9
Nov 1 2008	**1-Muluc**	1
Nov 2 2008	2-Oc	2
Nov 3 2008	3-Chuen	3
Nov 4 2008	4-Eb	4
Nov 5 2008	5-Ben	5
Nov 6 2008	6-Ix	6
Nov 7 2008	7-Men	7
Nov 8 2008	8-Cib	8
Nov 9 2008	9-Caban	9
Nov 10 2008	10-Etz'nab	1
Nov 11 2008	11-Cauac	2
Nov 12 2008	12-Ahau	3
Nov 13 2008	*13-Imix*	4
Nov 14 2008	**1-Ik**	5
Nov 15 2008	2-Akbal	6
Nov 16 2008	3-Kan	7
Nov 17 2008	4-Chicchan	8
Nov 18 2008	5-Cimi	9
Nov 19 2008	6-Manik	1
Nov 20 2008	7-Lamat	2
Nov 21 2008	8-Muluc	3
Nov 22 2008	9-Oc	4
Nov 23 2008	10-Chuen	5
Nov 24 2008	11-Eb	6
Nov 25 2008	12-Ben	7
Nov 26 2008	13-Ix	8
Nov 27 2008	**1-Men**	9
Nov 28 2008	2-Cib	1
Nov 29 2008	3-Caban	2

Date	Day-Sign	L
Nov 30 2008	4-Etz'nab	3
Dec 1 2008	5-Cauac	4
Dec 2 2008	6-Ahau	5
Dec 3 2008	*7-Imix*	6
Dec 4 2008	8-Ik	7
Dec 5 2008	9-Akbal	8
Dec 6 2008	10-Kan	9
Dec 7 2008	11-Chicchan	1
Dec 8 2008	12-Cimi	2
Dec 9 2008	13-Manik	3
Dec 10 2008	**1-Lamat**	4
Dec 11 2008	2-Muluc	5
Dec 12 2008	3-Oc	6
Dec 13 2008	4-Chuen	7
Dec 14 2008	5-Eb	8
Dec 15 2008	6-Ben	9
Dec 16 2008	7-Ix	1
Dec 17 2008	8-Men	2
Dec 18 2008	9-Cib	3
Dec 19 2008	10-Caban	4
Dec 20 2008	11-Etz'nab	5
Dec 21 2008	12-Cauac	6
Dec 22 2008	13-Ahau	7
Dec 23 2008	**1-Imix**	8
Dec 24 2008	2-Ik	9
Dec 25 2008	3-Akbal	1
Dec 26 2008	4-Kan	2
Dec 27 2008	5-Chicchan	3
Dec 28 2008	6-Cimi	4
Dec 29 2008	7-Manik	5
Dec 30 2008	8-Lamat	6
Dec 31 2008	9-Muluc	7
Jan 1 2009	10-Oc	8
Jan 2 2009	11-Chuen	9
Jan 3 2009	12-Eb	1
Jan 4 2009	13-Ben	2
Jan 5 2009	**1-Ix**	3
Jan 6 2009	2-Men	4
Jan 7 2009	3-Cib	5
Jan 8 2009	4-Caban	6
Jan 9 2009	5-Etz'nab	7
Jan 10 2009	6-Cauac	8
Jan 11 2009	7-Ahau	9
Jan 12 2009	*8-Imix*	1
Jan 13 2009	9-Ik	2
Jan 14 2009	10-Akbal	3
Jan 15 2009	11-Kan	4
Jan 16 2009	12-Chicchan	5
Jan 17 2009	13-Cimi	6
Jan 18 2009	**1-Manik**	7
Jan 19 2009	2-Lamat	8
Jan 20 2009	3-Muluc	9
Jan 21 2009	4-Oc	1
Jan 22 2009	5-Chuen	2
Jan 23 2009	6-Eb	3
Jan 24 2009	7-Ben	4
Jan 25 2009	8-Ix	5
Jan 26 2009	9-Men	6
Jan 27 2009	10-Cib	7
Jan 28 2009	11-Caban	8
Jan 29 2009	12-Etz'nab	9
Jan 30 2009	13-Cauac	1
Jan 31 2009	**1-Ahau**	2
Feb 1 2009	*2-Imix*	3
Feb 2 2009	3-Ik	4
Feb 3 2009	4-Akbal	5
Feb 4 2009	5-Kan	6
Feb 5 2009	6-Chicchan	7

Date	Day-Sign	L
Feb 6 2009	7-Cimi	8
Feb 7 2009	8-Manik	9
Feb 8 2009	9-Lamat	1
Feb 9 2009	10-Muluc	2
Feb 10 2009	11-Oc	3
Feb 11 2009	12-Chuen	4
Feb 12 2009	13-Eb	5
Feb 13 2009	**1-Ben**	6
Feb 14 2009	2-Ix	7
Feb 15 2009	3-Men	8
Feb 16 2009	4-Cib	9
Feb 17 2009	5-Caban	1
Feb 18 2009	6-Etz'nab	2
Feb 19 2009	7-Cauac	3
Feb 20 2009	8-Ahau	4
Feb 21 2009	*9-Imix*	5
Feb 22 2009	10-Ik	6
Feb 23 2009	11-Akbal	7
Feb 24 2009	12-Kan	8
Feb 25 2009	13-Chicchan	9
Feb 26 2009	**1-Cimi**	1
Feb 27 2009	2-Manik	2
Feb 28 2009	3-Lamat	3
Mar 1 2009	4-Muluc	4
Mar 2 2009	5-Oc	5
Mar 3 2009	6-Chuen	6
Mar 4 2009	7-Eb	7
Mar 5 2009	8-Ben	8
Mar 6 2009	9-Ix	9
Mar 7 2009	10-Men	1
Mar 8 2009	11-Cib	2
Mar 9 2009	12-Caban	3
Mar 10 2009	13-Etz'nab	4
Mar 11 2009	**1-Cauac**	5
Mar 12 2009	2-Ahau	6
Mar 13 2009	*3-Imix*	7
Mar 14 2009	4-Ik	8
Mar 15 2009	5-Akbal	9
Mar 16 2009	6-Kan	1
Mar 17 2009	7-Chicchan	2
Mar 18 2009	8-Cimi	3
Mar 19 2009	9-Manik	4
Mar 20 2009	10-Lamat	5
Mar 21 2009	11-Muluc	6
Mar 22 2009	12-Oc	7
Mar 23 2009	13-Chuen	8
Mar 24 2009	**1-Eb**	9
Mar 25 2009	2-Ben	1
Mar 26 2009	3-Ix	2
Mar 27 2009	4-Men	3
Mar 28 2009	5-Cib	4
Mar 29 2009	6-Caban	5
Mar 30 2009	7-Etz'nab	6
Mar 31 2009	8-Cauac	7
Apr 1 2009	9-Ahau	8
Apr 2 2009	*10-Imix*	9
Apr 3 2009	11-Ik	1
Apr 4 2009	12-Akbal	2
Apr 5 2009	13-Kan	3
Apr 6 2009	**1-Chicchan**	4
Apr 7 2009	2-Cimi	5
Apr 8 2009	3-Manik	6
Apr 9 2009	4-Lamat	7
Apr 10 2009	5-Muluc	8
Apr 11 2009	6-Oc	9
Apr 12 2009	7-Chuen	1
Apr 13 2009	8-Eb	2
Apr 14 2009	9-Ben	3

Date	Day-Sign	L
Apr 15 2009	10-Ix	4
Apr 16 2009	11-Men	5
Apr 17 2009	12-Cib	6
Apr 18 2009	13-Caban	7
Apr 19 2009	1-Etz'nab	8
Apr 20 2009	2-Cauac	9
Apr 21 2009	3-Ahau	1
Apr 22 2009	4-Imix	2
Apr 23 2009	5-Ik	3
Apr 24 2009	6-Akbal	4
Apr 25 2009	7-Kan	5
Apr 26 2009	8-Chicchan	6
Apr 27 2009	9-Cimi	7
Apr 28 2009	10-Manik	8
Apr 29 2009	11-Lamat	9
Apr 30 2009	12-Muluc	1
May 1 2009	13-Oc	2
May 2 2009	1-Chuen	3
May 3 2009	2-Eb	4
May 4 2009	3-Ben	5
May 5 2009	4-Ix	6
May 6 2009	5-Men	7
May 7 2009	6-Cib	8
May 8 2009	7-Caban	9
May 9 2009	8-Etz'nab	1
May 10 2009	9-Cauac	2
May 11 2009	10-Ahau	3
May 12 2009	11-Imix	4
May 13 2009	12-Ik	5
May 14 2009	13-Akbal	6
May 15 2009	1-Kan	7
May 16 2009	2-Chicchan	8
May 17 2009	3-Cimi	9
May 18 2009	4-Manik	1
May 19 2009	5-Lamat	2
May 20 2009	6-Muluc	3
May 21 2009	7-Oc	4
May 22 2009	8-Chuen	5
May 23 2009	9-Eb	6
May 24 2009	10-Ben	7
May 25 2009	11-Ix	8
May 26 2009	12-Men	9
May 27 2009	13-Cib	1
May 28 2009	1-Caban	2
May 29 2009	2-Etz'nab	3
May 30 2009	3-Cauac	4
May 31 2009	4-Ahau	5
Jun 1 2009	5-Imix	6
Jun 2 2009	6-Ik	7
Jun 3 2009	7-Akbal	8
Jun 4 2009	8-Kan	9
Jun 5 2009	9-Chicchan	1
Jun 6 2009	10-Cimi	2
Jun 7 2009	11-Manik	3
Jun 8 2009	12-Lamat	4
Jun 9 2009	13-Muluc	5
Jun 10 2009	1-Oc	6
Jun 11 2009	2-Chuen	7
Jun 12 2009	3-Eb	8
Jun 13 2009	4-Ben	9
Jun 14 2009	5-Ix	1
Jun 15 2009	6-Men	2
Jun 16 2009	7-Cib	3
Jun 17 2009	8-Caban	4
Jun 18 2009	9-Etz'nab	5
Jun 19 2009	10-Cauac	6
Jun 20 2009	11-Ahau	7
Jun 21 2009	12-Imix	8

Date	Day-Sign	L
Jun 22 2009	13-Ik	9
Jun 23 2009	1-Akbal	1
Jun 24 2009	2-Kan	2
Jun 25 2009	3-Chicchan	3
Jun 26 2009	4-Cimi	4
Jun 27 2009	5-Manik	5
Jun 28 2009	6-Lamat	6
Jun 29 2009	7-Muluc	7
Jun 30 2009	8-Oc	8
Jul 1 2009	9-Chuen	9
Jul 2 2009	10-Eb	1
Jul 3 2009	11-Ben	2
Jul 4 2009	12-Ix	3
Jul 5 2009	13-Men	4
Jul 6 2009	1-Cib	5
Jul 7 2009	2-Caban	6
Jul 8 2009	3-Etz'nab	7
Jul 9 2009	4-Cauac	8
Jul 10 2009	5-Ahau	9
Jul 11 2009	6-Imix	1
Jul 12 2009	7-Ik	2
Jul 13 2009	8-Akbal	3
Jul 14 2009	9-Kan	4
Jul 15 2009	10-Chicchan	5
Jul 16 2009	11-Cimi	6
Jul 17 2009	12-Manik	7
Jul 18 2009	13-Lamat	8
Jul 19 2009	1-Muluc	9
Jul 20 2009	2-Oc	1
Jul 21 2009	3-Chuen	2
Jul 22 2009	4-Eb	3
Jul 23 2009	5-Ben	4
Jul 24 2009	6-Ix	5
Jul 25 2009	7-Men	6
Jul 26 2009	8-Cib	7
Jul 27 2009	9-Caban	8
Jul 28 2009	10-Etz'nab	9
Jul 29 2009	11-Cauac	1
Jul 30 2009	12-Ahau	2
Jul 31 2009	13-Imix	3
Aug 1 2009	1-Ik	4
Aug 2 2009	2-Akbal	5
Aug 3 2009	3-Kan	6
Aug 4 2009	4-Chicchan	7
Aug 5 2009	5-Cimi	8
Aug 6 2009	6-Manik	9
Aug 7 2009	7-Lamat	1
Aug 8 2009	8-Muluc	2
Aug 9 2009	9-Oc	3
Aug 10 2009	10-Chuen	4
Aug 11 2009	11-Eb	5
Aug 12 2009	12-Ben	6
Aug 13 2009	13-Ix	7
Aug 14 2009	1-Men	8
Aug 15 2009	2-Cib	9
Aug 16 2009	3-Caban	1
Aug 17 2009	4-Etz'nab	2
Aug 18 2009	5-Cauac	3
Aug 19 2009	6-Ahau	4
Aug 20 2009	7-Imix	5
Aug 21 2009	8-Ik	6
Aug 22 2009	9-Akbal	7
Aug 23 2009	10-Kan	8
Aug 24 2009	11-Chicchan	9
Aug 25 2009	12-Cimi	1
Aug 26 2009	13-Manik	2
Aug 27 2009	1-Lamat	3
Aug 28 2009	2-Muluc	4

Date	Day-Sign	L
Aug 29 2009	3-Oc	5
Aug 30 2009	4-Chuen	6
Aug 31 2009	5-Eb	7
Sep 1 2009	6-Ben	8
Sep 2 2009	7-Ix	9
Sep 3 2009	8-Men	1
Sep 4 2009	9-Cib	2
Sep 5 2009	10-Caban	3
Sep 6 2009	11-Etz'nab	4
Sep 7 2009	12-Cauac	5
Sep 8 2009	13-Ahau	6
Sep 9 2009	1-Imix	7
Sep 10 2009	2-Ik	8
Sep 11 2009	3-Akbal	9
Sep 12 2009	4-Kan	1
Sep 13 2009	5-Chicchan	2
Sep 14 2009	6-Cimi	3
Sep 15 2009	7-Manik	4
Sep 16 2009	8-Lamat	5
Sep 17 2009	9-Muluc	6
Sep 18 2009	10-Oc	7
Sep 19 2009	11-Chuen	8
Sep 20 2009	12-Eb	9
Sep 21 2009	13-Ben	1
Sep 22 2009	1-Ix	2
Sep 23 2009	2-Men	3
Sep 24 2009	3-Cib	4
Sep 25 2009	4-Caban	5
Sep 26 2009	5-Etz'nab	6
Sep 27 2009	6-Cauac	7
Sep 28 2009	7-Ahau	8
Sep 29 2009	8-Imix	9
Sep 30 2009	9-Ik	1
Oct 1 2009	10-Akbal	2
Oct 2 2009	11-Kan	3
Oct 3 2009	12-Chicchan	4
Oct 4 2009	13-Cimi	5
Oct 5 2009	1-Manik	6
Oct 6 2009	2-Lamat	7
Oct 7 2009	3-Muluc	8
Oct 8 2009	4-Oc	9
Oct 9 2009	5-Chuen	1
Oct 10 2009	6-Eb	2
Oct 11 2009	7-Ben	3
Oct 12 2009	8-Ix	4
Oct 13 2009	9-Men	5
Oct 14 2009	10-Cib	6
Oct 15 2009	11-Caban	7
Oct 16 2009	12-Etz'nab	8
Oct 17 2009	13-Cauac	9
Oct 18 2009	1-Ahau	1
Oct 19 2009	2-Imix	2
Oct 20 2009	3-Ik	3
Oct 21 2009	4-Akbal	4
Oct 22 2009	5-Kan	5
Oct 23 2009	6-Chicchan	6
Oct 24 2009	7-Cimi	7
Oct 25 2009	8-Manik	8
Oct 26 2009	9-Lamat	9
Oct 27 2009	10-Muluc	1
Oct 28 2009	11-Oc	2
Oct 29 2009	12-Chuen	3
Oct 30 2009	13-Eb	4
Oct 31 2009	1-Ben	5
Nov 1 2009	2-Ix	6
Nov 2 2009	3-Men	7
Nov 3 2009	4-Cib	8
Nov 4 2009	5-Caban	9

Date	Day-Sign	L
Nov 5 2009	6-Etz'nab	1
Nov 6 2009	7-Cauac	2
Nov 7 2009	8-Ahau	3
Nov 8 2009	9-Imix	4
Nov 9 2009	10-Ik	5
Nov 10 2009	11-Akbal	6
Nov 11 2009	12-Kan	7
Nov 12 2009	13-Chicchan	8
Nov 13 2009	1-Cimi	9
Nov 14 2009	2-Manik	1
Nov 15 2009	3-Lamat	2
Nov 16 2009	4-Muluc	3
Nov 17 2009	5-Oc	4
Nov 18 2009	6-Chuen	5
Nov 19 2009	7-Eb	6
Nov 20 2009	8-Ben	7
Nov 21 2009	9-Ix	8
Nov 22 2009	10-Men	9
Nov 23 2009	11-Cib	1
Nov 24 2009	12-Caban	2
Nov 25 2009	13-Etz'nab	3
Nov 26 2009	1-Cauac	4
Nov 27 2009	2-Ahau	5
Nov 28 2009	3-Imix	6
Nov 29 2009	4-Ik	7
Nov 30 2009	5-Akbal	8
Dec 1 2009	6-Kan	9
Dec 2 2009	7-Chicchan	1
Dec 3 2009	8-Cimi	2
Dec 4 2009	9-Manik	3
Dec 5 2009	10-Lamat	4
Dec 6 2009	11-Muluc	5
Dec 7 2009	12-Oc	6
Dec 8 2009	13-Chuen	7
Dec 9 2009	1-Eb	8
Dec 10 2009	2-Ben	9
Dec 11 2009	3-Ix	1
Dec 12 2009	4-Men	2
Dec 13 2009	5-Cib	3
Dec 14 2009	6-Caban	4
Dec 15 2009	7-Etz'nab	5
Dec 16 2009	8-Cauac	6
Dec 17 2009	9-Ahau	7
Dec 18 2009	10-Imix	8
Dec 19 2009	11-Ik	9
Dec 20 2009	12-Akbal	1
Dec 21 2009	13-Kan	2
Dec 22 2009	1-Chicchan	3
Dec 23 2009	2-Cimi	4
Dec 24 2009	3-Manik	5
Dec 25 2009	4-Lamat	6
Dec 26 2009	5-Muluc	7
Dec 27 2009	6-Oc	8
Dec 28 2009	7-Chuen	9
Dec 29 2009	8-Eb	1
Dec 30 2009	9-Ben	2
Dec 31 2009	10-Ix	3
Jan 1 2010	11-Men	4
Jan 2 2010	12-Cib	5
Jan 3 2010	13-Caban	6
Jan 4 2010	1-Etz'nab	7
Jan 5 2010	2-Cauac	8
Jan 6 2010	3-Ahau	9
Jan 7 2010	4-Imix	1
Jan 8 2010	5-Ik	2
Jan 9 2010	6-Akbal	3
Jan 10 2010	7-Kan	4
Jan 11 2010	8-Chicchan	5

Date	Day-Sign	L
Jan 12 2010	9-Cimi	6
Jan 13 2010	10-Manik	7
Jan 14 2010	11-Lamat	8
Jan 15 2010	12-Muluc	9
Jan 16 2010	13-Oc	1
Jan 17 2010	1-Chuen	2
Jan 18 2010	2-Eb	3
Jan 19 2010	3-Ben	4
Jan 20 2010	4-Ix	5
Jan 21 2010	5-Men	6
Jan 22 2010	6-Cib	7
Jan 23 2010	7-Caban	8
Jan 24 2010	8-Etz'nab	9
Jan 25 2010	9-Cauac	1
Jan 26 2010	10-Ahau	2
Jan 27 2010	11-Imix	3
Jan 28 2010	12-Ik	4
Jan 29 2010	13-Akbal	5
Jan 30 2010	1-Kan	6
Jan 31 2010	2-Chicchan	7
Feb 1 2010	3-Cimi	8
Feb 2 2010	4-Manik	9
Feb 3 2010	5-Lamat	1
Feb 4 2010	6-Muluc	2
Feb 5 2010	7-Oc	3
Feb 6 2010	8-Chuen	4
Feb 7 2010	9-Eb	5
Feb 8 2010	10-Ben	6
Feb 9 2010	11-Ix	7
Feb 10 2010	12-Men	8
Feb 11 2010	13-Cib	9
Feb 12 2010	1-Caban	1
Feb 13 2010	2-Etz'nab	2
Feb 14 2010	3-Cauac	3
Feb 15 2010	4-Ahau	4
Feb 16 2010	5-Imix	5
Feb 17 2010	6-Ik	6
Feb 18 2010	7-Akbal	7
Feb 19 2010	8-Kan	8
Feb 20 2010	9-Chicchan	9
Feb 21 2010	10-Cimi	1
Feb 22 2010	11-Manik	2
Feb 23 2010	12-Lamat	3
Feb 24 2010	13-Muluc	4
Feb 25 2010	1-Oc	5
Feb 26 2010	2-Chuen	6
Feb 27 2010	3-Eb	7
Feb 28 2010	4-Ben	8
Mar 1 2010	5-Ix	9
Mar 2 2010	6-Men	1
Mar 3 2010	7-Cib	2
Mar 4 2010	8-Caban	3
Mar 5 2010	9-Etz'nab	4
Mar 6 2010	10-Cauac	5
Mar 7 2010	11-Ahau	6
Mar 8 2010	12-Imix	7
Mar 9 2010	13-Ik	8
Mar 10 2010	1-Akbal	9
Mar 11 2010	2-Kan	1
Mar 12 2010	3-Chicchan	2
Mar 13 2010	4-Cimi	3
Mar 14 2010	5-Manik	4
Mar 15 2010	6-Lamat	5
Mar 16 2010	7-Muluc	6
Mar 17 2010	8-Oc	7
Mar 18 2010	9-Chuen	8
Mar 19 2010	10-Eb	9
Mar 20 2010	11-Ben	1

Date	Day-Sign	L
Mar 21 2010	12-Ix	2
Mar 22 2010	13-Men	3
Mar 23 2010	1-Cib	4
Mar 24 2010	2-Caban	5
Mar 25 2010	3-Etz'nab	6
Mar 26 2010	4-Cauac	7
Mar 27 2010	5-Ahau	8
Mar 28 2010	6-Imix	9
Mar 29 2010	7-Ik	1
Mar 30 2010	8-Akbal	2
Mar 31 2010	9-Kan	3
Apr 1 2010	10-Chicchan	4
Apr 2 2010	11-Cimi	5
Apr 3 2010	12-Manik	6
Apr 4 2010	13-Lamat	7
Apr 5 2010	1-Muluc	8
Apr 6 2010	2-Oc	9
Apr 7 2010	3-Chuen	1
Apr 8 2010	4-Eb	2
Apr 9 2010	5-Ben	3
Apr 10 2010	6-Ix	4
Apr 11 2010	7-Men	5
Apr 12 2010	8-Cib	6
Apr 13 2010	9-Caban	7
Apr 14 2010	10-Etz'nab	8
Apr 15 2010	11-Cauac	9
Apr 16 2010	12-Ahau	1
Apr 17 2010	13-Imix	2
Apr 18 2010	1-Ik	3
Apr 19 2010	2-Akbal	4
Apr 20 2010	3-Kan	5
Apr 21 2010	4-Chicchan	6
Apr 22 2010	5-Cimi	7
Apr 23 2010	6-Manik	8
Apr 24 2010	7-Lamat	9
Apr 25 2010	8-Muluc	1
Apr 26 2010	9-Oc	2
Apr 27 2010	10-Chuen	3
Apr 28 2010	11-Eb	4
Apr 29 2010	12-Ben	5
Apr 30 2010	13-Ix	6
May 1 2010	1-Men	7
May 2 2010	2-Cib	8
May 3 2010	3-Caban	9
May 4 2010	4-Etz'nab	1
May 5 2010	5-Cauac	2
May 6 2010	6-Ahau	3
May 7 2010	7-Imix	4
May 8 2010	8-Ik	5
May 9 2010	9-Akbal	6
May 10 2010	10-Kan	7
May 11 2010	11-Chicchan	8
May 12 2010	12-Cimi	9
May 13 2010	13-Manik	1
May 14 2010	1-Lamat	2
May 15 2010	2-Muluc	3
May 16 2010	3-Oc	4
May 17 2010	4-Chuen	5
May 18 2010	5-Eb	6
May 19 2010	6-Ben	7
May 20 2010	7-Ix	8
May 21 2010	8-Men	9
May 22 2010	9-Cib	1
May 23 2010	10-Caban	2
May 24 2010	11-Etz'nab	3
May 25 2010	12-Cauac	4
May 26 2010	13-Ahau	5
May 27 2010	1-Imix	6

Date	Day-Sign	L	Date	Day-Sign	L	Date	Day-Sign	L
May 28 2010	2-Ik	7	Aug 4 2010	5-Oc	3	Oct 11 2010	8-Etz'nab	8
May 29 2010	3-Akbal	8	Aug 5 2010	6-Chuen	4	Oct 12 2010	9-Cauac	9
May 30 2010	4-Kan	9	Aug 6 2010	7-Eb	5	Oct 13 2010	10-Ahau	1
May 31 2010	5-Chicchan	1	Aug 7 2010	8-Ben	6	Oct 14 2010	*11-Imix*	2
Jun 1 2010	6-Cimi	2	Aug 8 2010	9-Ix	7	Oct 15 2010	12-Ik	3
Jun 2 2010	7-Manik	3	Aug 9 2010	10-Men	8	Oct 16 2010	13-Akbal	4
Jun 3 2010	8-Lamat	4	Aug 10 2010	11-Cib	9	Oct 17 2010	**1-Kan**	5
Jun 4 2010	9-Muluc	5	Aug 11 2010	12-Caban	1	Oct 18 2010	2-Chicchan	6
Jun 5 2010	10-Oc	6	Aug 12 2010	13-Etz'nab	2	Oct 19 2010	3-Cimi	7
Jun 6 2010	11-Chuen	7	Aug 13 2010	**1-Cauac**	3	Oct 20 2010	4-Manik	8
Jun 7 2010	12-Eb	8	Aug 14 2010	2-Ahau	4	Oct 21 2010	5-Lamat	9
Jun 8 2010	13-Ben	9	Aug 15 2010	*3-Imix*	5	Oct 22 2010	6-Muluc	1
Jun 9 2010	**1-Ix**	1	Aug 16 2010	4-Ik	6	Oct 23 2010	7-Oc	2
Jun 10 2010	2-Men	2	Aug 17 2010	5-Akbal	7	Oct 24 2010	8-Chuen	3
Jun 11 2010	3-Cib	3	Aug 18 2010	6-Kan	8	Oct 25 2010	9-Eb	4
Jun 12 2010	4-Caban	4	Aug 19 2010	7-Chicchan	9	Oct 26 2010	10-Ben	5
Jun 13 2010	5-Etz'nab	5	Aug 20 2010	8-Cimi	1	Oct 27 2010	11-Ix	6
Jun 14 2010	6-Cauac	6	Aug 21 2010	9-Manik	2	Oct 28 2010	12-Men	7
Jun 15 2010	7-Ahau	7	Aug 22 2010	10-Lamat	3	Oct 29 2010	13-Cib	8
Jun 16 2010	*8-Imix*	8	Aug 23 2010	11-Muluc	4	Oct 30 2010	**1-Caban**	9
Jun 17 2010	9-Ik	9	Aug 24 2010	12-Oc	5	Oct 31 2010	2-Etz'nab	1
Jun 18 2010	10-Akbal	1	Aug 25 2010	13-Chuen	6	Nov 1 2010	3-Cauac	2
Jun 19 2010	11-Kan	2	Aug 26 2010	**1-Eb**	7	Nov 2 2010	4-Ahau	3
Jun 20 2010	12-Chicchan	3	Aug 27 2010	2-Ben	8	Nov 3 2010	*5-Imix*	4
Jun 21 2010	13-Cimi	4	Aug 28 2010	3-Ix	9	Nov 4 2010	6-Ik	5
Jun 22 2010	**1-Manik**	5	Aug 29 2010	4-Men	1	Nov 5 2010	7-Akbal	6
Jun 23 2010	2-Lamat	6	Aug 30 2010	5-Cib	2	Nov 6 2010	8-Kan	7
Jun 24 2010	3-Muluc	7	Aug 31 2010	6-Caban	3	Nov 7 2010	9-Chicchan	8
Jun 25 2010	4-Oc	8	Sep 1 2010	7-Etz'nab	4	Nov 8 2010	10-Cimi	9
Jun 26 2010	5-Chuen	9	Sep 2 2010	8-Cauac	5	Nov 9 2010	11-Manik	1
Jun 27 2010	6-Eb	1	Sep 3 2010	9-Ahau	6	Nov 10 2010	12-Lamat	2
Jun 28 2010	7-Ben	2	Sep 4 2010	*10-Imix*	7	Nov 11 2010	13-Muluc	3
Jun 29 2010	8-Ix	3	Sep 5 2010	11-Ik	8	Nov 12 2010	**1-Oc**	4
Jun 30 2010	9-Men	4	Sep 6 2010	12-Akbal	9	Nov 13 2010	2-Chuen	5
Jul 1 2010	10-Cib	5	Sep 7 2010	13-Kan	1	Nov 14 2010	3-Eb	6
Jul 2 2010	11-Caban	6	Sep 8 2010	**1-Chicchan**	2	Nov 15 2010	4-Ben	7
Jul 3 2010	12-Etz'nab	7	Sep 9 2010	2-Cimi	3	Nov 16 2010	5-Ix	8
Jul 4 2010	13-Cauac	8	Sep 10 2010	3-Manik	4	Nov 17 2010	6-Men	9
Jul 5 2010	**1-Ahau**	9	Sep 11 2010	4-Lamat	5	Nov 18 2010	7-Cib	1
Jul 6 2010	*2-Imix*	1	Sep 12 2010	5-Muluc	6	Nov 19 2010	8-Caban	2
Jul 7 2010	3-Ik	2	Sep 13 2010	6-Oc	7	Nov 20 2010	9-Etz'nab	3
Jul 8 2010	4-Akbal	3	Sep 14 2010	7-Chuen	8	Nov 21 2010	10-Cauac	4
Jul 9 2010	5-Kan	4	Sep 15 2010	8-Eb	9	Nov 22 2010	11-Ahau	5
Jul 10 2010	6-Chicchan	5	Sep 16 2010	9-Ben	1	Nov 23 2010	*12-Imix*	6
Jul 11 2010	7-Cimi	6	Sep 17 2010	10-Ix	2	Nov 24 2010	13-Ik	7
Jul 12 2010	8-Manik	7	Sep 18 2010	11-Men	3	Nov 25 2010	**1-Akbal**	8
Jul 13 2010	9-Lamat	8	Sep 19 2010	12-Cib	4	Nov 26 2010	2-Kan	9
Jul 14 2010	10-Muluc	9	Sep 20 2010	13-Caban	5	Nov 27 2010	3-Chicchan	1
Jul 15 2010	11-Oc	1	Sep 21 2010	**1-Etz'nab**	6	Nov 28 2010	4-Cimi	2
Jul 16 2010	12-Chuen	2	Sep 22 2010	2-Cauac	7	Nov 29 2010	5-Manik	3
Jul 17 2010	13-Eb	3	Sep 23 2010	3-Ahau	8	Nov 30 2010	6-Lamat	4
Jul 18 2010	**1-Ben**	4	Sep 24 2010	*4-Imix*	9	Dec 1 2010	7-Muluc	5
Jul 19 2010	2-Ix	5	Sep 25 2010	5-Ik	1	Dec 2 2010	8-Oc	6
Jul 20 2010	3-Men	6	Sep 26 2010	6-Akbal	2	Dec 3 2010	9-Chuen	7
Jul 21 2010	4-Cib	7	Sep 27 2010	7-Kan	3	Dec 4 2010	10-Eb	8
Jul 22 2010	5-Caban	8	Sep 28 2010	8-Chicchan	4	Dec 5 2010	11-Ben	9
Jul 23 2010	6-Etz'nab	9	Sep 29 2010	9-Cimi	5	Dec 6 2010	12-Ix	1
Jul 24 2010	7-Cauac	1	Sep 30 2010	10-Manik	6	Dec 7 2010	13-Men	2
Jul 25 2010	8-Ahau	2	Oct 1 2010	11-Lamat	7	Dec 8 2010	**1-Cib**	3
Jul 26 2010	*9-Imix*	3	Oct 2 2010	12-Muluc	8	Dec 9 2010	2-Caban	4
Jul 27 2010	10-Ik	4	Oct 3 2010	13-Oc	9	Dec 10 2010	3-Etz'nab	5
Jul 28 2010	11-Akbal	5	Oct 4 2010	**1-Chuen**	1	Dec 11 2010	4-Cauac	6
Jul 29 2010	12-Kan	6	Oct 5 2010	2-Eb	2	Dec 12 2010	5-Ahau	7
Jul 30 2010	13-Chicchan	7	Oct 6 2010	3-Ben	3	Dec 13 2010	*6-Imix*	8
Jul 31 2010	**1-Cimi**	8	Oct 7 2010	4-Ix	4	Dec 14 2010	7-Ik	9
Aug 1 2010	2-Manik	9	Oct 8 2010	5-Men	5	Dec 15 2010	8-Akbal	1
Aug 2 2010	3-Lamat	1	Oct 9 2010	6-Cib	6	Dec 16 2010	9-Kan	2
Aug 3 2010	4-Muluc	2	Oct 10 2010	7-Caban	7	Dec 17 2010	10-Chicchan	3

Date	Day-Sign	L	Date	Day-Sign	L	Date	Day-Sign	L
Dec 18 2010	11-Cimi	4	Feb 24 2011	1-Ix	9	May 3 2011	4-Ik	5
Dec 19 2010	12-Manik	5	Feb 25 2011	2-Men	1	May 4 2011	5-Akbal	6
Dec 20 2010	13-Lamat	6	Feb 26 2011	3-Cib	2	May 5 2011	6-Kan	7
Dec 21 2010	1-Muluc	7	Feb 27 2011	4-Caban	3	May 6 2011	7-Chicchan	8
Dec 22 2010	2-Oc	8	Feb 28 2011	5-Etz'nab	4	May 7 2011	8-Cimi	9
Dec 23 2010	3-Chuen	9	Mar 1 2011	6-Cauac	5	May 8 2011	9-Manik	1
Dec 24 2010	4-Eb	1	Mar 2 2011	7-Ahau	6	May 9 2011	10-Lamat	2
Dec 25 2010	5-Ben	2	Mar 3 2011	8-Imix	7	May 10 2011	11-Muluc	3
Dec 26 2010	6-Ix	3	Mar 4 2011	9-Ik	8	May 11 2011	12-Oc	4
Dec 27 2010	7-Men	4	Mar 5 2011	10-Akbal	9	May 12 2011	13-Chuen	5
Dec 28 2010	8-Cib	5	Mar 6 2011	11-Kan	1	May 13 2011	1-Eb	6
Dec 29 2010	9-Caban	6	Mar 7 2011	12-Chicchan	2	May 14 2011	2-Ben	7
Dec 30 2010	10-Etz'nab	7	Mar 8 2011	13-Cimi	3	May 15 2011	3-Ix	8
Dec 31 2010	11-Cauac	8	Mar 9 2011	1-Manik	4	May 16 2011	4-Men	9
Jan 1 2011	12-Ahau	9	Mar 10 2011	2-Lamat	5	May 17 2011	5-Cib	1
Jan 2 2011	13-Imix	1	Mar 11 2011	3-Muluc	6	May 18 2011	6-Caban	2
Jan 3 2011	1-Ik	2	Mar 12 2011	4-Oc	7	May 19 2011	7-Etz'nab	3
Jan 4 2011	2-Akbal	3	Mar 13 2011	5-Chuen	8	May 20 2011	8-Cauac	4
Jan 5 2011	3-Kan	4	Mar 14 2011	6-Eb	9	May 21 2011	9-Ahau	5
Jan 6 2011	4-Chicchan	5	Mar 15 2011	7-Ben	1	May 22 2011	10-Imix	6
Jan 7 2011	5-Cimi	6	Mar 16 2011	8-Ix	2	May 23 2011	11-Ik	7
Jan 8 2011	6-Manik	7	Mar 17 2011	9-Men	3	May 24 2011	12-Akbal	8
Jan 9 2011	7-Lamat	8	Mar 18 2011	10-Cib	4	May 25 2011	13-Kan	9
Jan 10 2011	8-Muluc	9	Mar 19 2011	11-Caban	5	May 26 2011	1-Chicchan	1
Jan 11 2011	9-Oc	1	Mar 20 2011	12-Etz'nab	6	May 27 2011	2-Cimi	2
Jan 12 2011	10-Chuen	2	Mar 21 2011	13-Cauac	7	May 28 2011	3-Manik	3
Jan 13 2011	11-Eb	3	Mar 22 2011	1-Ahau	8	May 29 2011	4-Lamat	4
Jan 14 2011	12-Ben	4	Mar 23 2011	2-Imix	9	May 30 2011	5-Muluc	5
Jan 15 2011	13-Ix	5	Mar 24 2011	3-Ik	1	May 31 2011	6-Oc	6
Jan 16 2011	1-Men	6	Mar 25 2011	4-Akbal	2	Jun 1 2011	7-Chuen	7
Jan 17 2011	2-Cib	7	Mar 26 2011	5-Kan	3	Jun 2 2011	8-Eb	8
Jan 18 2011	3-Caban	8	Mar 27 2011	6-Chicchan	4	Jun 3 2011	9-Ben	9
Jan 19 2011	4-Etz'nab	9	Mar 28 2011	7-Cimi	5	Jun 4 2011	10-Ix	1
Jan 20 2011	5-Cauac	1	Mar 29 2011	8-Manik	6	Jun 5 2011	11-Men	2
Jan 21 2011	6-Ahau	2	Mar 30 2011	9-Lamat	7	Jun 6 2011	12-Cib	3
Jan 22 2011	7-Imix	3	Mar 31 2011	10-Muluc	8	Jun 7 2011	13-Caban	4
Jan 23 2011	8-Ik	4	Apr 1 2011	11-Oc	9	Jun 8 2011	1-Etz'nab	5
Jan 24 2011	9-Akbal	5	Apr 2 2011	12-Chuen	1	Jun 9 2011	2-Cauac	6
Jan 25 2011	10-Kan	6	Apr 3 2011	13-Eb	2	Jun 10 2011	3-Ahau	7
Jan 26 2011	11-Chicchan	7	Apr 4 2011	1-Ben	3	Jun 11 2011	4-Imix	8
Jan 27 2011	12-Cimi	8	Apr 5 2011	2-Ix	4	Jun 12 2011	5-Ik	9
Jan 28 2011	13-Manik	9	Apr 6 2011	3-Men	5	Jun 13 2011	6-Akbal	1
Jan 29 2011	1-Lamat	1	Apr 7 2011	4-Cib	6	Jun 14 2011	7-Kan	2
Jan 30 2011	2-Muluc	2	Apr 8 2011	5-Caban	7	Jun 15 2011	8-Chicchan	3
Jan 31 2011	3-Oc	3	Apr 9 2011	6-Etz'nab	8	Jun 16 2011	9-Cimi	4
Feb 1 2011	4-Chuen	4	Apr 10 2011	7-Cauac	9	Jun 17 2011	10-Manik	5
Feb 2 2011	5-Eb	5	Apr 11 2011	8-Ahau	1	Jun 18 2011	11-Lamat	6
Feb 3 2011	6-Ben	6	Apr 12 2011	9-Imix	2	Jun 19 2011	12-Muluc	7
Feb 4 2011	7-Ix	7	Apr 13 2011	10-Ik	3	Jun 20 2011	13-Oc	8
Feb 5 2011	8-Men	8	Apr 14 2011	11-Akbal	4	Jun 21 2011	1-Chuen	9
Feb 6 2011	9-Cib	9	Apr 15 2011	12-Kan	5	Jun 22 2011	2-Eb	1
Feb 7 2011	10-Caban	1	Apr 16 2011	13-Chicchan	6	Jun 23 2011	3-Ben	2
Feb 8 2011	11-Etz'nab	2	Apr 17 2011	1-Cimi	7	Jun 24 2011	4-Ix	3
Feb 9 2011	12-Cauac	3	Apr 18 2011	2-Manik	8	Jun 25 2011	5-Men	4
Feb 10 2011	13-Ahau	4	Apr 19 2011	3-Lamat	9	Jun 26 2011	6-Cib	5
Feb 11 2011	1-Imix	5	Apr 20 2011	4-Muluc	1	Jun 27 2011	7-Caban	6
Feb 12 2011	2-Ik	6	Apr 21 2011	5-Oc	2	Jun 28 2011	8-Etz'nab	7
Feb 13 2011	3-Akbal	7	Apr 22 2011	6-Chuen	3	Jun 29 2011	9-Cauac	8
Feb 14 2011	4-Kan	8	Apr 23 2011	7-Eb	4	Jun 30 2011	10-Ahau	9
Feb 15 2011	5-Chicchan	9	Apr 24 2011	8-Ben	5	Jul 1 2011	11-Imix	1
Feb 16 2011	6-Cimi	1	Apr 25 2011	9-Ix	6	Jul 2 2011	12-Ik	2
Feb 17 2011	7-Manik	2	Apr 26 2011	10-Men	7	Jul 3 2011	13-Akbal	3
Feb 18 2011	8-Lamat	3	Apr 27 2011	11-Cib	8	Jul 4 2011	1-Kan	4
Feb 19 2011	9-Muluc	4	Apr 28 2011	12-Caban	9	Jul 5 2011	2-Chicchan	5
Feb 20 2011	10-Oc	5	Apr 29 2011	13-Etz'nab	1	Jul 6 2011	3-Cimi	6
Feb 21 2011	11-Chuen	6	Apr 30 2011	1-Cauac	2	Jul 7 2011	4-Manik	7
Feb 22 2011	12-Eb	7	May 1 2011	2-Ahau	3	Jul 8 2011	5-Lamat	8
Feb 23 2011	13-Ben	8	May 2 2011	3-Imix	4	Jul 9 2011	6-Muluc	9

Date	Day-Sign	L	Date	Day-Sign	L	Date	Day-Sign	L
Jul 10 2011	7-Oc	1	Sep 16 2011	10-Etz'nab	6	Nov 23 2011	13-Cimi	2
Jul 11 2011	8-Chuen	2	Sep 17 2011	11-Cauac	7	Nov 24 2011	**1-Manik**	3
Jul 12 2011	9-Eb	3	Sep 18 2011	12-Ahau	8	Nov 25 2011	2-Lamat	4
Jul 13 2011	10-Ben	4	Sep 19 2011	13-*Imix*	9	Nov 26 2011	3-Muluc	5
Jul 14 2011	11-Ix	5	Sep 20 2011	**1-Ik**	1	Nov 27 2011	4-Oc	6
Jul 15 2011	12-Men	6	Sep 21 2011	2-Akbal	2	Nov 28 2011	5-Chuen	7
Jul 16 2011	13-Cib	7	Sep 22 2011	3-Kan	3	Nov 29 2011	6-Eb	8
Jul 17 2011	**1-Caban**	8	Sep 23 2011	4-Chicchan	4	Nov 30 2011	7-Ben	9
Jul 18 2011	2-Etz'nab	9	Sep 24 2011	5-Cimi	5	Dec 1 2011	8-Ix	1
Jul 19 2011	3-Cauac	1	Sep 25 2011	6-Manik	6	Dec 2 2011	9-Men	2
Jul 20 2011	4-Ahau	2	Sep 26 2011	7-Lamat	7	Dec 3 2011	10-Cib	3
Jul 21 2011	5-*Imix*	3	Sep 27 2011	8-Muluc	8	Dec 4 2011	11-Caban	4
Jul 22 2011	6-Ik	4	Sep 28 2011	9-Oc	9	Dec 5 2011	12-Etz'nab	5
Jul 23 2011	7-Akbal	5	Sep 29 2011	10-Chuen	1	Dec 6 2011	13-Cauac	6
Jul 24 2011	8-Kan	6	Sep 30 2011	11-Eb	2	Dec 7 2011	**1-Ahau**	7
Jul 25 2011	9-Chicchan	7	Oct 1 2011	12-Ben	3	Dec 8 2011	2-*Imix*	8
Jul 26 2011	10-Cimi	8	Oct 2 2011	13-Ix	4	Dec 9 2011	3-Ik	9
Jul 27 2011	11-Manik	9	Oct 3 2011	**1-Men**	5	Dec 10 2011	4-Akbal	1
Jul 28 2011	12-Lamat	1	Oct 4 2011	2-Cib	6	Dec 11 2011	5-Kan	2
Jul 29 2011	13-Muluc	2	Oct 5 2011	3-Caban	7	Dec 12 2011	6-Chicchan	3
Jul 30 2011	**1-Oc**	3	Oct 6 2011	4-Etz'nab	8	Dec 13 2011	7-Cimi	4
Jul 31 2011	2-Chuen	4	Oct 7 2011	5-Cauac	9	Dec 14 2011	8-Manik	5
Aug 1 2011	3-Eb	5	Oct 8 2011	6-Ahau	1	Dec 15 2011	9-Lamat	6
Aug 2 2011	4-Ben	6	Oct 9 2011	7-*Imix*	2	Dec 16 2011	10-Muluc	7
Aug 3 2011	5-Ix	7	Oct 10 2011	8-Ik	3	Dec 17 2011	11-Oc	8
Aug 4 2011	6-Men	8	Oct 11 2011	9-Akbal	4	Dec 18 2011	12-Chuen	9
Aug 5 2011	7-Cib	9	Oct 12 2011	10-Kan	5	Dec 19 2011	13-Eb	1
Aug 6 2011	8-Caban	1	Oct 13 2011	11-Chicchan	6	Dec 20 2011	**1-Ben**	2
Aug 7 2011	9-Etz'nab	2	Oct 14 2011	12-Cimi	7	Dec 21 2011	2-Ix	3
Aug 8 2011	10-Cauac	3	Oct 15 2011	13-Manik	8	Dec 22 2011	3-Men	4
Aug 9 2011	11-Ahau	4	Oct 16 2011	**1-Lamat**	9	Dec 23 2011	4-Cib	5
Aug 10 2011	12-*Imix*	5	Oct 17 2011	2-Muluc	1	Dec 24 2011	5-Caban	6
Aug 11 2011	13-Ik	6	Oct 18 2011	3-Oc	2	Dec 25 2011	6-Etz'nab	7
Aug 12 2011	**1-Akbal**	7	Oct 19 2011	4-Chuen	3	Dec 26 2011	7-Cauac	8
Aug 13 2011	2-Kan	8	Oct 20 2011	5-Eb	4	Dec 27 2011	8-Ahau	9
Aug 14 2011	3-Chicchan	9	Oct 21 2011	6-Ben	5	Dec 28 2011	9-*Imix*	1
Aug 15 2011	4-Cimi	1	Oct 22 2011	7-Ix	6	Dec 29 2011	10-Ik	2
Aug 16 2011	5-Manik	2	Oct 23 2011	8-Men	7	Dec 30 2011	11-Akbal	3
Aug 17 2011	6-Lamat	3	Oct 24 2011	9-Cib	8	Dec 31 2011	12-Kan	4
Aug 18 2011	7-Muluc	4	Oct 25 2011	10-Caban	9	Jan 1 2012	13-Chicchan	5
Aug 19 2011	8-Oc	5	Oct 26 2011	11-Etz'nab	1	Jan 2 2012	**1-Cimi**	6
Aug 20 2011	9-Chuen	6	Oct 27 2011	12-Cauac	2	Jan 3 2012	2-Manik	7
Aug 21 2011	10-Eb	7	Oct 28 2011	13-Ahau	3	Jan 4 2012	3-Lamat	8
Aug 22 2011	11-Ben	8	Oct 29 2011	**1-Imix**	4	Jan 5 2012	4-Muluc	9
Aug 23 2011	12-Ix	9	Oct 30 2011	2-Ik	5	Jan 6 2012	5-Oc	1
Aug 24 2011	13-Men	1	Oct 31 2011	3-Akbal	6	Jan 7 2012	6-Chuen	2
Aug 25 2011	**1-Cib**	2	Nov 1 2011	4-Kan	7	Jan 8 2012	7-Eb	3
Aug 26 2011	2-Caban	3	Nov 2 2011	5-Chicchan	8	Jan 9 2012	8-Ben	4
Aug 27 2011	3-Etz'nab	4	Nov 3 2011	6-Cimi	9	Jan 10 2012	9-Ix	5
Aug 28 2011	4-Cauac	5	Nov 4 2011	7-Manik	1	Jan 11 2012	10-Men	6
Aug 29 2011	5-Ahau	6	Nov 5 2011	8-Lamat	2	Jan 12 2012	11-Cib	7
Aug 30 2011	6-*Imix*	7	Nov 6 2011	9-Muluc	3	Jan 13 2012	12-Caban	8
Aug 31 2011	7-Ik	8	Nov 7 2011	10-Oc	4	Jan 14 2012	13-Etz'nab	9
Sep 1 2011	8-Akbal	9	Nov 8 2011	11-Chuen	5	Jan 15 2012	**1-Cauac**	1
Sep 2 2011	9-Kan	1	Nov 9 2011	12-Eb	6	Jan 16 2012	2-Ahau	2
Sep 3 2011	10-Chicchan	2	Nov 10 2011	13-Ben	7	Jan 17 2012	3-*Imix*	3
Sep 4 2011	11-Cimi	3	Nov 11 2011	**1-Ix**	8	Jan 18 2012	4-Ik	4
Sep 5 2011	12-Manik	4	Nov 12 2011	2-Men	9	Jan 19 2012	5-Akbal	5
Sep 6 2011	13-Lamat	5	Nov 13 2011	3-Cib	1	Jan 20 2012	6-Kan	6
Sep 7 2011	**1-Muluc**	6	Nov 14 2011	4-Caban	2	Jan 21 2012	7-Chicchan	7
Sep 8 2011	2-Oc	7	Nov 15 2011	5-Etz'nab	3	Jan 22 2012	8-Cimi	8
Sep 9 2011	3-Chuen	8	Nov 16 2011	6-Cauac	4	Jan 23 2012	9-Manik	9
Sep 10 2011	4-Eb	9	Nov 17 2011	7-Ahau	5	Jan 24 2012	10-Lamat	1
Sep 11 2011	5-Ben	1	Nov 18 2011	8-*Imix*	6	Jan 25 2012	11-Muluc	2
Sep 12 2011	6-Ix	2	Nov 19 2011	9-Ik	7	Jan 26 2012	12-Oc	3
Sep 13 2011	7-Men	3	Nov 20 2011	10-Akbal	8	Jan 27 2012	13-Chuen	4
Sep 14 2011	8-Cib	4	Nov 21 2011	11-Kan	9	Jan 28 2012	**1-Eb**	5
Sep 15 2011	9-Caban	5	Nov 22 2011	12-Chicchan	1	Jan 29 2012	2-Ben	6

Date	Day-Sign	L		Date	Day-Sign	L		Date	Day-Sign	L
Jan 30 2012	3-Ix	7		Apr 7 2012	6-Ik	3		Jun 14 2012	9-Oc	8
Jan 31 2012	4-Men	8		Apr 8 2012	7-Akbal	4		Jun 15 2012	10-Chuen	9
Feb 1 2012	5-Cib	9		Apr 9 2012	8-Kan	5		Jun 16 2012	11-Eb	1
Feb 2 2012	6-Caban	1		Apr 10 2012	9-Chicchan	6		Jun 17 2012	12-Ben	2
Feb 3 2012	7-Etz'nab	2		Apr 11 2012	10-Cimi	7		Jun 18 2012	13-Ix	3
Feb 4 2012	8-Cauac	3		Apr 12 2012	11-Manik	8		Jun 19 2012	1-Men	4
Feb 5 2012	9-Ahau	4		Apr 13 2012	12-Lamat	9		Jun 20 2012	2-Cib	5
Feb 6 2012	10-Imix	5		Apr 14 2012	13-Muluc	1		Jun 21 2012	3-Caban	6
Feb 7 2012	11-Ik	6		Apr 15 2012	1-Oc	2		Jun 22 2012	4-Etz'nab	7
Feb 8 2012	12-Akbal	7		Apr 16 2012	2-Chuen	3		Jun 23 2012	5-Cauac	8
Feb 9 2012	13-Kan	8		Apr 17 2012	3-Eb	4		Jun 24 2012	6-Ahau	9
Feb 10 2012	1-Chicchan	9		Apr 18 2012	4-Ben	5		Jun 25 2012	7-Imix	1
Feb 11 2012	2-Cimi	1		Apr 19 2012	5-Ix	6		Jun 26 2012	8-Ik	2
Feb 12 2012	3-Manik	2		Apr 20 2012	6-Men	7		Jun 27 2012	9-Akbal	3
Feb 13 2012	4-Lamat	3		Apr 21 2012	7-Cib	8		Jun 28 2012	10-Kan	4
Feb 14 2012	5-Muluc	4		Apr 22 2012	8-Caban	9		Jun 29 2012	11-Chicchan	5
Feb 15 2012	6-Oc	5		Apr 23 2012	9-Etz'nab	1		Jun 30 2012	12-Cimi	6
Feb 16 2012	7-Chuen	6		Apr 24 2012	10-Cauac	2		Jul 1 2012	13-Manik	7
Feb 17 2012	8-Eb	7		Apr 25 2012	11-Ahau	3		Jul 2 2012	1-Lamat	8
Feb 18 2012	9-Ben	8		Apr 26 2012	12-Imix	4		Jul 3 2012	2-Muluc	9
Feb 19 2012	10-Ix	9		Apr 27 2012	13-Ik	5		Jul 4 2012	3-Oc	1
Feb 20 2012	11-Men	1		Apr 28 2012	1-Akbal	6		Jul 5 2012	4-Chuen	2
Feb 21 2012	12-Cib	2		Apr 29 2012	2-Kan	7		Jul 6 2012	5-Eb	3
Feb 22 2012	13-Caban	3		Apr 30 2012	3-Chicchan	8		Jul 7 2012	6-Ben	4
Feb 23 2012	1-Etz'nab	4		May 1 2012	4-Cimi	9		Jul 8 2012	7-Ix	5
Feb 24 2012	2-Cauac	5		May 2 2012	5-Manik	1		Jul 9 2012	8-Men	6
Feb 25 2012	3-Ahau	6		May 3 2012	6-Lamat	2		Jul 10 2012	9-Cib	7
Feb 26 2012	4-Imix	7		May 4 2012	7-Muluc	3		Jul 11 2012	10-Caban	8
Feb 27 2012	5-Ik	8		May 5 2012	8-Oc	4		Jul 12 2012	11-Etz'nab	9
Feb 28 2012	6-Akbal	9		May 6 2012	9-Chuen	5		Jul 13 2012	12-Cauac	1
Feb 29 2012	7-Kan	1		May 7 2012	10-Eb	6		Jul 14 2012	13-Ahau	2
Mar 1 2012	8-Chicchan	2		May 8 2012	11-Ben	7		Jul 15 2012	1-Imix	3
Mar 2 2012	9-Cimi	3		May 9 2012	12-Ix	8		Jul 16 2012	2-Ik	4
Mar 3 2012	10-Manik	4		May 10 2012	13-Men	9		Jul 17 2012	3-Akbal	5
Mar 4 2012	11-Lamat	5		May 11 2012	1-Cib	1		Jul 18 2012	4-Kan	6
Mar 5 2012	12-Muluc	6		May 12 2012	2-Caban	2		Jul 19 2012	5-Chicchan	7
Mar 6 2012	13-Oc	7		May 13 2012	3-Etz'nab	3		Jul 20 2012	6-Cimi	8
Mar 7 2012	1-Chuen	8		May 14 2012	4-Cauac	4		Jul 21 2012	7-Manik	9
Mar 8 2012	2-Eb	9		May 15 2012	5-Ahau	5		Jul 22 2012	8-Lamat	1
Mar 9 2012	3-Ben	1		May 16 2012	6-Imix	6		Jul 23 2012	9-Muluc	2
Mar 10 2012	4-Ix	2		May 17 2012	7-Ik	7		Jul 24 2012	10-Oc	3
Mar 11 2012	5-Men	3		May 18 2012	8-Akbal	8		Jul 25 2012	11-Chuen	4
Mar 12 2012	6-Cib	4		May 19 2012	9-Kan	9		Jul 26 2012	12-Eb	5
Mar 13 2012	7-Caban	5		May 20 2012	10-Chicchan	1		Jul 27 2012	13-Ben	6
Mar 14 2012	8-Etz'nab	6		May 21 2012	11-Cimi	2		Jul 28 2012	1-Ix	7
Mar 15 2012	9-Cauac	7		May 22 2012	12-Manik	3		Jul 29 2012	2-Men	8
Mar 16 2012	10-Ahau	8		May 23 2012	13-Lamat	4		Jul 30 2012	3-Cib	9
Mar 17 2012	11-Imix	9		May 24 2012	1-Muluc	5		Jul 31 2012	4-Caban	1
Mar 18 2012	12-Ik	1		May 25 2012	2-Oc	6		Aug 1 2012	5-Etz'nab	2
Mar 19 2012	13-Akbal	2		May 26 2012	3-Chuen	7		Aug 2 2012	6-Cauac	3
Mar 20 2012	1-Kan	3		May 27 2012	4-Eb	8		Aug 3 2012	7-Ahau	4
Mar 21 2012	2-Chicchan	4		May 28 2012	5-Ben	9		Aug 4 2012	8-Imix	5
Mar 22 2012	3-Cimi	5		May 29 2012	6-Ix	1		Aug 5 2012	9-Ik	6
Mar 23 2012	4-Manik	6		May 30 2012	7-Men	2		Aug 6 2012	10-Akbal	7
Mar 24 2012	5-Lamat	7		May 31 2012	8-Cib	3		Aug 7 2012	11-Kan	8
Mar 25 2012	6-Muluc	8		Jun 1 2012	9-Caban	4		Aug 8 2012	12-Chicchan	9
Mar 26 2012	7-Oc	9		Jun 2 2012	10-Etz'nab	5		Aug 9 2012	13-Cimi	1
Mar 27 2012	8-Chuen	1		Jun 3 2012	11-Cauac	6		Aug 10 2012	1-Manik	2
Mar 28 2012	9-Eb	2		Jun 4 2012	12-Ahau	7		Aug 11 2012	2-Lamat	3
Mar 29 2012	10-Ben	3		Jun 5 2012	13-Imix	8		Aug 12 2012	3-Muluc	4
Mar 30 2012	11-Ix	4		Jun 6 2012	1-Ik	9		Aug 13 2012	4-Oc	5
Mar 31 2012	12-Men	5		Jun 7 2012	2-Akbal	1		Aug 14 2012	5-Chuen	6
Apr 1 2012	13-Cib	6		Jun 8 2012	3-Kan	2		Aug 15 2012	6-Eb	7
Apr 2 2012	1-Caban	7		Jun 9 2012	4-Chicchan	3		Aug 16 2012	7-Ben	8
Apr 3 2012	2-Etz'nab	8		Jun 10 2012	5-Cimi	4		Aug 17 2012	8-Ix	9
Apr 4 2012	3-Cauac	9		Jun 11 2012	6-Manik	5		Aug 18 2012	9-Men	1
Apr 5 2012	4-Ahau	1		Jun 12 2012	7-Lamat	6		Aug 19 2012	10-Cib	2
Apr 6 2012	5-Imix	2		Jun 13 2012	8-Muluc	7		Aug 20 2012	11-Caban	3

Date	Day-Sign	L	Date	Day-Sign	L	Date	Day-Sign	L
Aug 21 2012	12-Etz'nab	4	Oct 28 2012	2-Cimi	9	Jan 4 2013	5-Ix	5
Aug 22 2012	13-Cauac	5	Oct 29 2012	3-Manik	1	Jan 5 2013	6-Men	6
Aug 23 2012	1-Ahau	6	Oct 30 2012	4-Lamat	2	Jan 6 2013	7-Cib	7
Aug 24 2012	2-Imix	7	Oct 31 2012	5-Muluc	3	Jan 7 2013	8-Caban	8
Aug 25 2012	3-Ik	8	Nov 1 2012	6-Oc	4	Jan 8 2013	9-Etz'nab	9
Aug 26 2012	4-Akbal	9	Nov 2 2012	7-Chuen	5	Jan 9 2013	10-Cauac	1
Aug 27 2012	5-Kan	1	Nov 3 2012	8-Eb	6	Jan 10 2013	11-Ahau	2
Aug 28 2012	6-Chicchan	2	Nov 4 2012	9-Ben	7	Jan 11 2013	12-Imix	3
Aug 29 2012	7-Cimi	3	Nov 5 2012	10-Ix	8	Jan 12 2013	13-Ik	4
Aug 30 2012	8-Manik	4	Nov 6 2012	11-Men	9	Jan 13 2013	1-Akbal	5
Aug 31 2012	9-Lamat	5	Nov 7 2012	12-Cib	1	Jan 14 2013	2-Kan	6
Sep 1 2012	10-Muluc	6	Nov 8 2012	13-Caban	2	Jan 15 2013	3-Chicchan	7
Sep 2 2012	11-Oc	7	Nov 9 2012	1-Etz'nab	3	Jan 16 2013	4-Cimi	8
Sep 3 2012	12-Chuen	8	Nov 10 2012	2-Cauac	4	Jan 17 2013	5-Manik	9
Sep 4 2012	13-Eb	9	Nov 11 2012	3-Ahau	5	Jan 18 2013	6-Lamat	1
Sep 5 2012	1-Ben	1	Nov 12 2012	4-Imix	6	Jan 19 2013	7-Muluc	2
Sep 6 2012	2-Ix	2	Nov 13 2012	5-Ik	7	Jan 20 2013	8-Oc	3
Sep 7 2012	3-Men	3	Nov 14 2012	6-Akbal	8	Jan 21 2013	9-Chuen	4
Sep 8 2012	4-Cib	4	Nov 15 2012	7-Kan	9	Jan 22 2013	10-Eb	5
Sep 9 2012	5-Caban	5	Nov 16 2012	8-Chicchan	1	Jan 23 2013	11-Ben	6
Sep 10 2012	6-Etz'nab	6	Nov 17 2012	9-Cimi	2	Jan 24 2013	12-Ix	7
Sep 11 2012	7-Cauac	7	Nov 18 2012	10-Manik	3	Jan 25 2013	13-Men	8
Sep 12 2012	8-Ahau	8	Nov 19 2012	11-Lamat	4	Jan 26 2013	1-Cib	9
Sep 13 2012	9-Imix	9	Nov 20 2012	12-Muluc	5	Jan 27 2013	2-Caban	1
Sep 14 2012	10-Ik	1	Nov 21 2012	13-Oc	6	Jan 28 2013	3-Etz'nab	2
Sep 15 2012	11-Akbal	2	Nov 22 2012	1-Chuen	7	Jan 29 2013	4-Cauac	3
Sep 16 2012	12-Kan	3	Nov 23 2012	2-Eb	8	Jan 30 2013	5-Ahau	4
Sep 17 2012	13-Chicchan	4	Nov 24 2012	3-Ben	9	Jan 31 2013	6-Imix	5
Sep 18 2012	1-Cimi	5	Nov 25 2012	4-Ix	1	Feb 1 2013	7-Ik	6
Sep 19 2012	2-Manik	6	Nov 26 2012	5-Men	2	Feb 2 2013	8-Akbal	7
Sep 20 2012	3-Lamat	7	Nov 27 2012	6-Cib	3	Feb 3 2013	9-Kan	8
Sep 21 2012	4-Muluc	8	Nov 28 2012	7-Caban	4	Feb 4 2013	10-Chicchan	9
Sep 22 2012	5-Oc	9	Nov 29 2012	8-Etz'nab	5	Feb 5 2013	11-Cimi	1
Sep 23 2012	6-Chuen	1	Nov 30 2012	9-Cauac	6	Feb 6 2013	12-Manik	2
Sep 24 2012	7-Eb	2	Dec 1 2012	10-Ahau	7	Feb 7 2013	13-Lamat	3
Sep 25 2012	8-Ben	3	Dec 2 2012	11-Imix	8	Feb 8 2013	1-Muluc	4
Sep 26 2012	9-Ix	4	Dec 3 2012	12-Ik	9	Feb 9 2013	2-Oc	5
Sep 27 2012	10-Men	5	Dec 4 2012	13-Akbal	1	Feb 10 2013	3-Chuen	6
Sep 28 2012	11-Cib	6	Dec 5 2012	1-Kan	2	Feb 11 2013	4-Eb	7
Sep 29 2012	12-Caban	7	Dec 6 2012	2-Chicchan	3	Feb 12 2013	5-Ben	8
Sep 30 2012	13-Etz'nab	8	Dec 7 2012	3-Cimi	4	Feb 13 2013	6-Ix	9
Oct 1 2012	1-Cauac	9	Dec 8 2012	4-Manik	5	Feb 14 2013	7-Men	1
Oct 2 2012	2-Ahau	1	Dec 9 2012	5-Lamat	6	Feb 15 2013	8-Cib	2
Oct 3 2012	3-Imix	2	Dec 10 2012	6-Muluc	7	Feb 16 2013	9-Caban	3
Oct 4 2012	4-Ik	3	Dec 11 2012	7-Oc	8	Feb 17 2013	10-Etz'nab	4
Oct 5 2012	5-Akbal	4	Dec 12 2012	8-Chuen	9	Feb 18 2013	11-Cauac	5
Oct 6 2012	6-Kan	5	Dec 13 2012	9-Eb	1	Feb 19 2013	12-Ahau	6
Oct 7 2012	7-Chicchan	6	Dec 14 2012	10-Ben	2	Feb 20 2013	13-Imix	7
Oct 8 2012	8-Cimi	7	Dec 15 2012	11-Ix	3	Feb 21 2013	1-Ik	8
Oct 9 2012	9-Manik	8	Dec 16 2012	12-Men	4	Feb 22 2013	2-Akbal	9
Oct 10 2012	10-Lamat	9	Dec 17 2012	13-Cib	5	Feb 23 2013	3-Kan	1
Oct 11 2012	11-Muluc	1	Dec 18 2012	1-Caban	6	Feb 24 2013	4-Chicchan	2
Oct 12 2012	12-Oc	2	Dec 19 2012	2-Etz'nab	7	Feb 25 2013	5-Cimi	3
Oct 13 2012	13-Chuen	3	Dec 20 2012	3-Cauac	8	Feb 26 2013	6-Manik	4
Oct 14 2012	1-Eb	4	Dec 21 2012	4-Ahau	9	Feb 27 2013	7-Lamat	5
Oct 15 2012	2-Ben	5	Dec 22 2012	5-Imix	1	Feb 28 2013	8-Muluc	6
Oct 16 2012	3-Ix	6	Dec 23 2012	6-Ik	2	Mar 1 2013	9-Oc	7
Oct 17 2012	4-Men	7	Dec 24 2012	7-Akbal	3	Mar 2 2013	10-Chuen	8
Oct 18 2012	5-Cib	8	Dec 25 2012	8-Kan	4	Mar 3 2013	11-Eb	9
Oct 19 2012	6-Caban	9	Dec 26 2012	9-Chicchan	5	Mar 4 2013	12-Ben	1
Oct 20 2012	7-Etz'nab	1	Dec 27 2012	10-Cimi	6	Mar 5 2013	13-Ix	2
Oct 21 2012	8-Cauac	2	Dec 28 2012	11-Manik	7	Mar 6 2013	1-Men	3
Oct 22 2012	9-Ahau	3	Dec 29 2012	12-Lamat	8	Mar 7 2013	2-Cib	4
Oct 23 2012	10-Imix	4	Dec 30 2012	13-Muluc	9	Mar 8 2013	3-Caban	5
Oct 24 2012	11-Ik	5	Dec 31 2012	1-Oc	1	Mar 9 2013	4-Etz'nab	6
Oct 25 2012	12-Akbal	6	Jan 1 2013	2-Chuen	2	Mar 10 2013	5-Cauac	7
Oct 26 2012	13-Kan	7	Jan 2 2013	3-Eb	3	Mar 11 2013	6-Ahau	8
Oct 27 2012	1-Chicchan	8	Jan 3 2013	4-Ben	4	Mar 12 2013	7-Imix	9

Date	Day-Sign	L
Mar 13 2013	8-Ik	1
Mar 14 2013	9-Akbal	2
Mar 15 2013	10-Kan	3
Mar 16 2013	11-Chicchan	4
Mar 17 2013	12-Cimi	5
Mar 18 2013	13-Manik	6
Mar 19 2013	**1-Lamat**	7
Mar 20 2013	2-Muluc	8
Mar 21 2013	3-Oc	9
Mar 22 2013	4-Chuen	1
Mar 23 2013	5-Eb	2
Mar 24 2013	6-Ben	3
Mar 25 2013	7-Ix	4
Mar 26 2013	8-Men	5
Mar 27 2013	9-Cib	6
Mar 28 2013	10-Caban	7
Mar 29 2013	11-Etz'nab	8
Mar 30 2013	12-Cauac	9
Mar 31 2013	13-Ahau	1
Apr 1 2013	**1-Imix**	2
Apr 2 2013	2-Ik	3
Apr 3 2013	3-Akbal	4
Apr 4 2013	4-Kan	5
Apr 5 2013	5-Chicchan	6
Apr 6 2013	6-Cimi	7
Apr 7 2013	7-Manik	8
Apr 8 2013	8-Lamat	9
Apr 9 2013	9-Muluc	1
Apr 10 2013	10-Oc	2
Apr 11 2013	11-Chuen	3
Apr 12 2013	12-Eb	4
Apr 13 2013	13-Ben	5
Apr 14 2013	**1-Ix**	6
Apr 15 2013	2-Men	7
Apr 16 2013	3-Cib	8
Apr 17 2013	4-Caban	9
Apr 18 2013	5-Etz'nab	1
Apr 19 2013	6-Cauac	2
Apr 20 2013	7-Ahau	3
Apr 21 2013	8-Imix	4
Apr 22 2013	9-Ik	5
Apr 23 2013	10-Akbal	6
Apr 24 2013	11-Kan	7
Apr 25 2013	12-Chicchan	8
Apr 26 2013	13-Cimi	9
Apr 27 2013	**1-Manik**	1
Apr 28 2013	2-Lamat	2
Apr 29 2013	3-Muluc	3
Apr 30 2013	4-Oc	4
May 1 2013	5-Chuen	5
May 2 2013	6-Eb	6
May 3 2013	7-Ben	7
May 4 2013	8-Ix	8
May 5 2013	9-Men	9
May 6 2013	10-Cib	1
May 7 2013	11-Caban	2
May 8 2013	12-Etz'nab	3
May 9 2013	13-Cauac	4
May 10 2013	**1-Ahau**	5
May 11 2013	2-Imix	6
May 12 2013	3-Ik	7
May 13 2013	4-Akbal	8
May 14 2013	5-Kan	9
May 15 2013	6-Chicchan	1
May 16 2013	7-Cimi	2
May 17 2013	8-Manik	3
May 18 2013	9-Lamat	4
May 19 2013	10-Muluc	5

Date	Day-Sign	L
May 20 2013	11-Oc	6
May 21 2013	12-Chuen	7
May 22 2013	13-Eb	8
May 23 2013	**1-Ben**	9
May 24 2013	2-Ix	1
May 25 2013	3-Men	2
May 26 2013	4-Cib	3
May 27 2013	5-Caban	4
May 28 2013	6-Etz'nab	5
May 29 2013	7-Cauac	6
May 30 2013	8-Ahau	7
May 31 2013	*9-Imix*	8
Jun 1 2013	10-Ik	9
Jun 2 2013	11-Akbal	1
Jun 3 2013	12-Kan	2
Jun 4 2013	13-Chicchan	3
Jun 5 2013	**1-Cimi**	4
Jun 6 2013	2-Manik	5
Jun 7 2013	3-Lamat	6
Jun 8 2013	4-Muluc	7
Jun 9 2013	5-Oc	8
Jun 10 2013	6-Chuen	9
Jun 11 2013	7-Eb	1
Jun 12 2013	8-Ben	2
Jun 13 2013	9-Ix	3
Jun 14 2013	10-Men	4
Jun 15 2013	11-Cib	5
Jun 16 2013	12-Caban	6
Jun 17 2013	13-Etz'nab	7
Jun 18 2013	**1-Cauac**	8
Jun 19 2013	2-Ahau	9
Jun 20 2013	*3-Imix*	1
Jun 21 2013	4-Ik	2
Jun 22 2013	5-Akbal	3
Jun 23 2013	6-Kan	4
Jun 24 2013	7-Chicchan	5
Jun 25 2013	8-Cimi	6
Jun 26 2013	9-Manik	7
Jun 27 2013	10-Lamat	8
Jun 28 2013	11-Muluc	9
Jun 29 2013	12-Oc	1
Jun 30 2013	13-Chuen	2
Jul 1 2013	**1-Eb**	3
Jul 2 2013	2-Ben	4
Jul 3 2013	3-Ix	5
Jul 4 2013	4-Men	6
Jul 5 2013	5-Cib	7
Jul 6 2013	6-Caban	8
Jul 7 2013	7-Etz'nab	9
Jul 8 2013	8-Cauac	1
Jul 9 2013	9-Ahau	2
Jul 10 2013	*10-Imix*	3
Jul 11 2013	11-Ik	4
Jul 12 2013	12-Akbal	5
Jul 13 2013	13-Kan	6
Jul 14 2013	**1-Chicchan**	7
Jul 15 2013	2-Cimi	8
Jul 16 2013	3-Manik	9
Jul 17 2013	4-Lamat	1
Jul 18 2013	5-Muluc	2
Jul 19 2013	6-Oc	3
Jul 20 2013	7-Chuen	4
Jul 21 2013	8-Eb	5
Jul 22 2013	9-Ben	6
Jul 23 2013	10-Ix	7
Jul 24 2013	11-Men	8
Jul 25 2013	12-Cib	9
Jul 26 2013	13-Caban	1

Date	Day-Sign	L
Jul 27 2013	**1-Etz'nab**	2
Jul 28 2013	2-Cauac	3
Jul 29 2013	3-Ahau	4
Jul 30 2013	*4-Imix*	5
Jul 31 2013	5-Ik	6
Aug 1 2013	6-Akbal	7
Aug 2 2013	7-Kan	8
Aug 3 2013	8-Chicchan	9
Aug 4 2013	9-Cimi	1
Aug 5 2013	10-Manik	2
Aug 6 2013	11-Lamat	3
Aug 7 2013	12-Muluc	4
Aug 8 2013	13-Oc	5
Aug 9 2013	**1-Chuen**	6
Aug 10 2013	2-Eb	7
Aug 11 2013	3-Ben	8
Aug 12 2013	4-Ix	9
Aug 13 2013	5-Men	1
Aug 14 2013	6-Cib	2
Aug 15 2013	7-Caban	3
Aug 16 2013	8-Etz'nab	4
Aug 17 2013	9-Cauac	5
Aug 18 2013	10-Ahau	6
Aug 19 2013	*11-Imix*	7
Aug 20 2013	12-Ik	8
Aug 21 2013	13-Akbal	9
Aug 22 2013	**1-Kan**	1
Aug 23 2013	2-Chicchan	2
Aug 24 2013	3-Cimi	3
Aug 25 2013	4-Manik	4
Aug 26 2013	5-Lamat	5
Aug 27 2013	6-Muluc	6
Aug 28 2013	7-Oc	7
Aug 29 2013	8-Chuen	8
Aug 30 2013	9-Eb	9
Aug 31 2013	10-Ben	1
Sep 1 2013	11-Ix	2
Sep 2 2013	12-Men	3
Sep 3 2013	13-Cib	4
Sep 4 2013	**1-Caban**	5
Sep 5 2013	2-Etz'nab	6
Sep 6 2013	3-Cauac	7
Sep 7 2013	4-Ahau	8
Sep 8 2013	*5-Imix*	9
Sep 9 2013	6-Ik	1
Sep 10 2013	7-Akbal	2
Sep 11 2013	8-Kan	3
Sep 12 2013	9-Chicchan	4
Sep 13 2013	10-Cimi	5
Sep 14 2013	11-Manik	6
Sep 15 2013	12-Lamat	7
Sep 16 2013	13-Muluc	8
Sep 17 2013	**1-Oc**	9
Sep 18 2013	2-Chuen	1
Sep 19 2013	3-Eb	2
Sep 20 2013	4-Ben	3
Sep 21 2013	5-Ix	4
Sep 22 2013	6-Men	5
Sep 23 2013	7-Cib	6
Sep 24 2013	8-Caban	7
Sep 25 2013	9-Etz'nab	8
Sep 26 2013	10-Cauac	9
Sep 27 2013	11-Ahau	1
Sep 28 2013	*12-Imix*	2
Sep 29 2013	13-Ik	3
Sep 30 2013	**1-Akbal**	4
Oct 1 2013	2-Kan	5
Oct 2 2013	3-Chicchan	6

Date	Day-Sign	L
Oct 3 2013	4-Cimi	7
Oct 4 2013	5-Manik	8
Oct 5 2013	6-Lamat	9
Oct 6 2013	7-Muluc	1
Oct 7 2013	8-Oc	2
Oct 8 2013	9-Chuen	3
Oct 9 2013	10-Eb	4
Oct 10 2013	11-Ben	5
Oct 11 2013	12-Ix	6
Oct 12 2013	13-Men	7
Oct 13 2013	**1-Cib**	8
Oct 14 2013	2-Caban	9
Oct 15 2013	3-Etz'nab	1
Oct 16 2013	4-Cauac	2
Oct 17 2013	5-Ahau	3
Oct 18 2013	*6-Imix*	4
Oct 19 2013	7-Ik	5
Oct 20 2013	8-Akbal	6
Oct 21 2013	9-Kan	7
Oct 22 2013	10-Chicchan	8
Oct 23 2013	11-Cimi	9
Oct 24 2013	12-Manik	1
Oct 25 2013	13-Lamat	2
Oct 26 2013	**1-Muluc**	3
Oct 27 2013	2-Oc	4
Oct 28 2013	3-Chuen	5
Oct 29 2013	4-Eb	6
Oct 30 2013	5-Ben	7
Oct 31 2013	6-Ix	8
Nov 1 2013	7-Men	9
Nov 2 2013	8-Cib	1
Nov 3 2013	9-Caban	2
Nov 4 2013	10-Etz'nab	3
Nov 5 2013	11-Cauac	4
Nov 6 2013	12-Ahau	5
Nov 7 2013	*13-Imix*	6
Nov 8 2013	**1-Ik**	7
Nov 9 2013	2-Akbal	8
Nov 10 2013	3-Kan	9
Nov 11 2013	4-Chicchan	1
Nov 12 2013	5-Cimi	2
Nov 13 2013	6-Manik	3
Nov 14 2013	7-Lamat	4
Nov 15 2013	8-Muluc	5
Nov 16 2013	9-Oc	6
Nov 17 2013	10-Chuen	7
Nov 18 2013	11-Eb	8
Nov 19 2013	12-Ben	9
Nov 20 2013	13-Ix	1
Nov 21 2013	**1-Men**	2
Nov 22 2013	2-Cib	3
Nov 23 2013	3-Caban	4
Nov 24 2013	4-Etz'nab	5
Nov 25 2013	5-Cauac	6
Nov 26 2013	6-Ahau	7
Nov 27 2013	*7-Imix*	8
Nov 28 2013	8-Ik	9
Nov 29 2013	9-Akbal	1
Nov 30 2013	10-Kan	2
Dec 1 2013	11-Chicchan	3
Dec 2 2013	12-Cimi	4
Dec 3 2013	13-Manik	5
Dec 4 2013	**1-Lamat**	6
Dec 5 2013	2-Muluc	7
Dec 6 2013	3-Oc	8
Dec 7 2013	4-Chuen	9
Dec 8 2013	5-Eb	1
Dec 9 2013	6-Ben	2

Date	Day-Sign	L
Dec 10 2013	7-Ix	3
Dec 11 2013	8-Men	4
Dec 12 2013	9-Cib	5
Dec 13 2013	10-Caban	6
Dec 14 2013	11-Etz'nab	7
Dec 15 2013	12-Cauac	8
Dec 16 2013	13-Ahau	9
Dec 17 2013	**1-Imix**	1
Dec 18 2013	2-Ik	2
Dec 19 2013	3-Akbal	3
Dec 20 2013	4-Kan	4
Dec 21 2013	5-Chicchan	5
Dec 22 2013	6-Cimi	6
Dec 23 2013	7-Manik	7
Dec 24 2013	8-Lamat	8
Dec 25 2013	9-Muluc	9
Dec 26 2013	10-Oc	1
Dec 27 2013	11-Chuen	2
Dec 28 2013	12-Eb	3
Dec 29 2013	13-Ben	4
Dec 30 2013	**1-Ix**	5
Dec 31 2013	2-Men	6
Jan 1 2014	3-Cib	7
Jan 2 2014	4-Caban	8
Jan 3 2014	5-Etz'nab	9
Jan 4 2014	6-Cauac	1
Jan 5 2014	7-Ahau	2
Jan 6 2014	*8-Imix*	3
Jan 7 2014	9-Ik	4
Jan 8 2014	10-Akbal	5
Jan 9 2014	11-Kan	6
Jan 10 2014	12-Chicchan	7
Jan 11 2014	13-Cimi	8
Jan 12 2014	**1-Manik**	9
Jan 13 2014	2-Lamat	1
Jan 14 2014	3-Muluc	2
Jan 15 2014	4-Oc	3
Jan 16 2014	5-Chuen	4
Jan 17 2014	6-Eb	5
Jan 18 2014	7-Ben	6
Jan 19 2014	8-Ix	7
Jan 20 2014	9-Men	8
Jan 21 2014	10-Cib	9
Jan 22 2014	11-Caban	1
Jan 23 2014	12-Etz'nab	2
Jan 24 2014	13-Cauac	3
Jan 25 2014	**1-Ahau**	4
Jan 26 2014	*2-Imix*	5
Jan 27 2014	3-Ik	6
Jan 28 2014	4-Akbal	7
Jan 29 2014	5-Kan	8
Jan 30 2014	6-Chicchan	9
Jan 31 2014	7-Cimi	1
Feb 1 2014	8-Manik	2
Feb 2 2014	9-Lamat	3
Feb 3 2014	10-Muluc	4
Feb 4 2014	11-Oc	5
Feb 5 2014	12-Chuen	6
Feb 6 2014	13-Eb	7
Feb 7 2014	**1-Ben**	8
Feb 8 2014	2-Ix	9
Feb 9 2014	3-Men	1
Feb 10 2014	4-Cib	2
Feb 11 2014	5-Caban	3
Feb 12 2014	6-Etz'nab	4
Feb 13 2014	7-Cauac	5
Feb 14 2014	8-Ahau	6
Feb 15 2014	*9-Imix*	7

Date	Day-Sign	L
Feb 16 2014	10-Ik	8
Feb 17 2014	11-Akbal	9
Feb 18 2014	12-Kan	1
Feb 19 2014	13-Chicchan	2
Feb 20 2014	**1-Cimi**	3
Feb 21 2014	2-Manik	4
Feb 22 2014	3-Lamat	5
Feb 23 2014	4-Muluc	6
Feb 24 2014	5-Oc	7
Feb 25 2014	6-Chuen	8
Feb 26 2014	7-Eb	9
Feb 27 2014	8-Ben	1
Feb 28 2014	9-Ix	2
Mar 1 2014	10-Men	3
Mar 2 2014	11-Cib	4
Mar 3 2014	12-Caban	5
Mar 4 2014	13-Etz'nab	6
Mar 5 2014	**1-Cauac**	7
Mar 6 2014	2-Ahau	8
Mar 7 2014	*3-Imix*	9
Mar 8 2014	4-Ik	1
Mar 9 2014	5-Akbal	2
Mar 10 2014	6-Kan	3
Mar 11 2014	7-Chicchan	4
Mar 12 2014	8-Cimi	5
Mar 13 2014	9-Manik	6
Mar 14 2014	10-Lamat	7
Mar 15 2014	11-Muluc	8
Mar 16 2014	12-Oc	9
Mar 17 2014	13-Chuen	1
Mar 18 2014	**1-Eb**	2
Mar 19 2014	2-Ben	3
Mar 20 2014	3-Ix	4
Mar 21 2014	4-Men	5
Mar 22 2014	5-Cib	6
Mar 23 2014	6-Caban	7
Mar 24 2014	7-Etz'nab	8
Mar 25 2014	8-Cauac	9
Mar 26 2014	9-Ahau	1
Mar 27 2014	*10-Imix*	2
Mar 28 2014	11-Ik	3
Mar 29 2014	12-Akbal	4
Mar 30 2014	13-Kan	5
Mar 31 2014	**1-Chicchan**	6
Apr 1 2014	2-Cimi	7
Apr 2 2014	3-Manik	8
Apr 3 2014	4-Lamat	9
Apr 4 2014	5-Muluc	1
Apr 5 2014	6-Oc	2
Apr 6 2014	7-Chuen	3
Apr 7 2014	8-Eb	4
Apr 8 2014	9-Ben	5
Apr 9 2014	10-Ix	6
Apr 10 2014	11-Men	7
Apr 11 2014	12-Cib	8
Apr 12 2014	13-Caban	9
Apr 13 2014	**1-Etz'nab**	1
Apr 14 2014	2-Cauac	2
Apr 15 2014	3-Ahau	3
Apr 16 2014	*4-Imix*	4
Apr 17 2014	5-Ik	5
Apr 18 2014	6-Akbal	6
Apr 19 2014	7-Kan	7
Apr 20 2014	8-Chicchan	8
Apr 21 2014	9-Cimi	9
Apr 22 2014	10-Manik	1
Apr 23 2014	11-Lamat	2
Apr 24 2014	12-Muluc	3

Date	Day-Sign	L
Apr 25 2014	13-Oc	4
Apr 26 2014	**1-Chuen**	5
Apr 27 2014	2-Eb	6
Apr 28 2014	3-Ben	7
Apr 29 2014	4-Ix	8
Apr 30 2014	5-Men	9
May 1 2014	6-Cib	1
May 2 2014	7-Caban	2
May 3 2014	8-Etz'nab	3
May 4 2014	9-Cauac	4
May 5 2014	10-Ahau	5
May 6 2014	*11-Imix*	6
May 7 2014	12-Ik	7
May 8 2014	13-Akbal	8
May 9 2014	**1-Kan**	9
May 10 2014	2-Chicchan	1
May 11 2014	3-Cimi	2
May 12 2014	4-Manik	3
May 13 2014	5-Lamat	4
May 14 2014	6-Muluc	5
May 15 2014	7-Oc	6
May 16 2014	8-Chuen	7
May 17 2014	9-Eb	8
May 18 2014	10-Ben	9
May 19 2014	11-Ix	1
May 20 2014	12-Men	2
May 21 2014	13-Cib	3
May 22 2014	**1-Caban**	4
May 23 2014	2-Etz'nab	5
May 24 2014	3-Cauac	6
May 25 2014	4-Ahau	7
May 26 2014	*5-Imix*	8
May 27 2014	6-Ik	9
May 28 2014	7-Akbal	1
May 29 2014	8-Kan	2
May 30 2014	9-Chicchan	3
May 31 2014	10-Cimi	4
Jun 1 2014	11-Manik	5
Jun 2 2014	12-Lamat	6
Jun 3 2014	13-Muluc	7
Jun 4 2014	**1-Oc**	8
Jun 5 2014	2-Chuen	9
Jun 6 2014	3-Eb	1
Jun 7 2014	4-Ben	2
Jun 8 2014	5-Ix	3
Jun 9 2014	6-Men	4
Jun 10 2014	7-Cib	5
Jun 11 2014	8-Caban	6
Jun 12 2014	9-Etz'nab	7
Jun 13 2014	10-Cauac	8
Jun 14 2014	11-Ahau	9
Jun 15 2014	*12-Imix*	1
Jun 16 2014	13-Ik	2
Jun 17 2014	**1-Akbal**	3
Jun 18 2014	2-Kan	4
Jun 19 2014	3-Chicchan	5
Jun 20 2014	4-Cimi	6
Jun 21 2014	5-Manik	7
Jun 22 2014	6-Lamat	8
Jun 23 2014	7-Muluc	9
Jun 24 2014	8-Oc	1
Jun 25 2014	9-Chuen	2
Jun 26 2014	10-Eb	3
Jun 27 2014	11-Ben	4
Jun 28 2014	12-Ix	5
Jun 29 2014	13-Men	6
Jun 30 2014	**1-Cib**	7
Jul 1 2014	2-Caban	8

Date	Day-Sign	L
Jul 2 2014	3-Etz'nab	9
Jul 3 2014	4-Cauac	1
Jul 4 2014	5-Ahau	2
Jul 5 2014	*6-Imix*	3
Jul 6 2014	7-Ik	4
Jul 7 2014	8-Akbal	5
Jul 8 2014	9-Kan	6
Jul 9 2014	10-Chicchan	7
Jul 10 2014	11-Cimi	8
Jul 11 2014	12-Manik	9
Jul 12 2014	13-Lamat	1
Jul 13 2014	**1-Muluc**	2
Jul 14 2014	2-Oc	3
Jul 15 2014	3-Chuen	4
Jul 16 2014	4-Eb	5
Jul 17 2014	5-Ben	6
Jul 18 2014	6-Ix	7
Jul 19 2014	7-Men	8
Jul 20 2014	8-Cib	9
Jul 21 2014	9-Caban	1
Jul 22 2014	10-Etz'nab	2
Jul 23 2014	11-Cauac	3
Jul 24 2014	12-Ahau	4
Jul 25 2014	*13-Imix*	5
Jul 26 2014	**1-Ik**	6
Jul 27 2014	2-Akbal	7
Jul 28 2014	3-Kan	8
Jul 29 2014	4-Chicchan	9
Jul 30 2014	5-Cimi	1
Jul 31 2014	6-Manik	2
Aug 1 2014	7-Lamat	3
Aug 2 2014	8-Muluc	4
Aug 3 2014	9-Oc	5
Aug 4 2014	10-Chuen	6
Aug 5 2014	11-Eb	7
Aug 6 2014	12-Ben	8
Aug 7 2014	13-Ix	9
Aug 8 2014	**1-Men**	1
Aug 9 2014	2-Cib	2
Aug 10 2014	3-Caban	3
Aug 11 2014	4-Etz'nab	4
Aug 12 2014	5-Cauac	5
Aug 13 2014	6-Ahau	6
Aug 14 2014	*7-Imix*	7
Aug 15 2014	8-Ik	8
Aug 16 2014	9-Akbal	9
Aug 17 2014	10-Kan	1
Aug 18 2014	11-Chicchan	2
Aug 19 2014	12-Cimi	3
Aug 20 2014	13-Manik	4
Aug 21 2014	**1-Lamat**	5
Aug 22 2014	2-Muluc	6
Aug 23 2014	3-Oc	7
Aug 24 2014	4-Chuen	8
Aug 25 2014	5-Eb	9
Aug 26 2014	6-Ben	1
Aug 27 2014	7-Ix	2
Aug 28 2014	8-Men	3
Aug 29 2014	9-Cib	4
Aug 30 2014	10-Caban	5
Aug 31 2014	11-Etz'nab	6
Sep 1 2014	12-Cauac	7
Sep 2 2014	13-Ahau	8
Sep 3 2014	**1-Imix**	9
Sep 4 2014	2-Ik	1
Sep 5 2014	3-Akbal	2
Sep 6 2014	4-Kan	3
Sep 7 2014	5-Chicchan	4

Date	Day-Sign	L
Sep 8 2014	6-Cimi	5
Sep 9 2014	7-Manik	6
Sep 10 2014	8-Lamat	7
Sep 11 2014	9-Muluc	8
Sep 12 2014	10-Oc	9
Sep 13 2014	11-Chuen	1
Sep 14 2014	12-Eb	2
Sep 15 2014	13-Ben	3
Sep 16 2014	**1-Ix**	4
Sep 17 2014	2-Men	5
Sep 18 2014	3-Cib	6
Sep 19 2014	4-Caban	7
Sep 20 2014	5-Etz'nab	8
Sep 21 2014	6-Cauac	9
Sep 22 2014	7-Ahau	1
Sep 23 2014	*8-Imix*	2
Sep 24 2014	9-Ik	3
Sep 25 2014	10-Akbal	4
Sep 26 2014	11-Kan	5
Sep 27 2014	12-Chicchan	6
Sep 28 2014	13-Cimi	7
Sep 29 2014	**1-Manik**	8
Sep 30 2014	2-Lamat	9
Oct 1 2014	3-Muluc	1
Oct 2 2014	4-Oc	2
Oct 3 2014	5-Chuen	3
Oct 4 2014	6-Eb	4
Oct 5 2014	7-Ben	5
Oct 6 2014	8-Ix	6
Oct 7 2014	9-Men	7
Oct 8 2014	10-Cib	8
Oct 9 2014	11-Caban	9
Oct 10 2014	12-Etz'nab	1
Oct 11 2014	13-Cauac	2
Oct 12 2014	**1-Ahau**	3
Oct 13 2014	*2-Imix*	4
Oct 14 2014	3-Ik	5
Oct 15 2014	4-Akbal	6
Oct 16 2014	5-Kan	7
Oct 17 2014	6-Chicchan	8
Oct 18 2014	7-Cimi	9
Oct 19 2014	8-Manik	1
Oct 20 2014	9-Lamat	2
Oct 21 2014	10-Muluc	3
Oct 22 2014	11-Oc	4
Oct 23 2014	12-Chuen	5
Oct 24 2014	13-Eb	6
Oct 25 2014	**1-Ben**	7
Oct 26 2014	2-Ix	8
Oct 27 2014	3-Men	9
Oct 28 2014	4-Cib	1
Oct 29 2014	5-Caban	2
Oct 30 2014	6-Etz'nab	3
Oct 31 2014	7-Cimi	4
Nov 1 2014	8-Ahau	5
Nov 2 2014	*9-Imix*	6
Nov 3 2014	10-Ik	7
Nov 4 2014	11-Akbal	8
Nov 5 2014	12-Kan	9
Nov 6 2014	13-Chicchan	1
Nov 7 2014	**1-Cimi**	2
Nov 8 2014	2-Manik	3
Nov 9 2014	3-Lamat	4
Nov 10 2014	4-Muluc	5
Nov 11 2014	5-Oc	6
Nov 12 2014	6-Chuen	7
Nov 13 2014	7-Eb	8
Nov 14 2014	8-Ben	9

Date	Day-Sign	L	Date	Day-Sign	L	Date	Day-Sign	L
Nov 15 2014	9-Ix	1	Jan 22 2015	12-Ik	6	Mar 31 2015	2-Oc	2
Nov 16 2014	10-Men	2	Jan 23 2015	13-Akbal	7	Apr 1 2015	3-Chuen	3
Nov 17 2014	11-Cib	3	Jan 24 2015	1-Kan	8	Apr 2 2015	4-Eb	4
Nov 18 2014	12-Caban	4	Jan 25 2015	2-Chicchan	9	Apr 3 2015	5-Ben	5
Nov 19 2014	13-Etz'nab	5	Jan 26 2015	3-Cimi	1	Apr 4 2015	6-Ix	6
Nov 20 2014	1-Cauac	6	Jan 27 2015	4-Manik	2	Apr 5 2015	7-Men	7
Nov 21 2014	2-Ahau	7	Jan 28 2015	5-Lamat	3	Apr 6 2015	8-Cib	8
Nov 22 2014	3-Imix	8	Jan 29 2015	6-Muluc	4	Apr 7 2015	9-Caban	9
Nov 23 2014	4-Ik	9	Jan 30 2015	7-Oc	5	Apr 8 2015	10-Etz'nab	1
Nov 24 2014	5-Akbal	1	Jan 31 2015	8-Chuen	6	Apr 9 2015	11-Cauac	2
Nov 25 2014	6-Kan	2	Feb 1 2015	9-Eb	7	Apr 10 2015	12-Ahau	3
Nov 26 2014	7-Chicchan	3	Feb 2 2015	10-Ben	8	Apr 11 2015	13-Imix	4
Nov 27 2014	8-Cimi	4	Feb 3 2015	11-Ix	9	Apr 12 2015	1-Ik	5
Nov 28 2014	9-Manik	5	Feb 4 2015	12-Men	1	Apr 13 2015	2-Akbal	6
Nov 29 2014	10-Lamat	6	Feb 5 2015	13-Cib	2	Apr 14 2015	3-Kan	7
Nov 30 2014	11-Muluc	7	Feb 6 2015	1-Caban	3	Apr 15 2015	4-Chicchan	8
Dec 1 2014	12-Oc	8	Feb 7 2015	2-Etz'nab	4	Apr 16 2015	5-Cimi	9
Dec 2 2014	13-Chuen	9	Feb 8 2015	3-Cauac	5	Apr 17 2015	6-Manik	1
Dec 3 2014	1-Eb	1	Feb 9 2015	4-Ahau	6	Apr 18 2015	7-Lamat	2
Dec 4 2014	2-Ben	2	Feb 10 2015	5-Imix	7	Apr 19 2015	8-Muluc	3
Dec 5 2014	3-Ix	3	Feb 11 2015	6-Ik	8	Apr 20 2015	9-Oc	4
Dec 6 2014	4-Men	4	Feb 12 2015	7-Akbal	9	Apr 21 2015	10-Chuen	5
Dec 7 2014	5-Cib	5	Feb 13 2015	8-Kan	1	Apr 22 2015	11-Eb	6
Dec 8 2014	6-Caban	6	Feb 14 2015	9-Chicchan	2	Apr 23 2015	12-Ben	7
Dec 9 2014	7-Etz'nab	7	Feb 15 2015	10-Cimi	3	Apr 24 2015	13-Ix	8
Dec 10 2014	8-Cauac	8	Feb 16 2015	11-Manik	4	Apr 25 2015	1-Men	9
Dec 11 2014	9-Ahau	9	Feb 17 2015	12-Lamat	5	Apr 26 2015	2-Cib	1
Dec 12 2014	10-Imix	1	Feb 18 2015	13-Muluc	6	Apr 27 2015	3-Caban	2
Dec 13 2014	11-Ik	2	Feb 19 2015	1-Oc	7	Apr 28 2015	4-Etz'nab	3
Dec 14 2014	12-Akbal	3	Feb 20 2015	2-Chuen	8	Apr 29 2015	5-Cauac	4
Dec 15 2014	13-Kan	4	Feb 21 2015	3-Eb	9	Apr 30 2015	6-Ahau	5
Dec 16 2014	1-Chicchan	5	Feb 22 2015	4-Ben	1	May 1 2015	7-Imix	6
Dec 17 2014	2-Cimi	6	Feb 23 2015	5-Ix	2	May 2 2015	8-Ik	7
Dec 18 2014	3-Manik	7	Feb 24 2015	6-Men	3	May 3 2015	9-Akbal	8
Dec 19 2014	4-Lamat	8	Feb 25 2015	7-Cib	4	May 4 2015	10-Kan	9
Dec 20 2014	5-Muluc	9	Feb 26 2015	8-Caban	5	May 5 2015	11-Chicchan	1
Dec 21 2014	6-Oc	1	Feb 27 2015	9-Etz'nab	6	May 6 2015	12-Cimi	2
Dec 22 2014	7-Chuen	2	Feb 28 2015	10-Cauac	7	May 7 2015	13-Manik	3
Dec 23 2014	8-Eb	3	Mar 1 2015	11-Ahau	8	May 8 2015	1-Lamat	4
Dec 24 2014	9-Ben	4	Mar 2 2015	12-Imix	9	May 9 2015	2-Muluc	5
Dec 25 2014	10-Ix	5	Mar 3 2015	13-Ik	1	May 10 2015	3-Oc	6
Dec 26 2014	11-Men	6	Mar 4 2015	1-Akbal	2	May 11 2015	4-Chuen	7
Dec 27 2014	12-Cib	7	Mar 5 2015	2-Kan	3	May 12 2015	5-Eb	8
Dec 28 2014	13-Caban	8	Mar 6 2015	3-Chicchan	4	May 13 2015	6-Ben	9
Dec 29 2014	1-Etz'nab	9	Mar 7 2015	4-Cimi	5	May 14 2015	7-Ix	1
Dec 30 2014	2-Cauac	1	Mar 8 2015	5-Manik	6	May 15 2015	8-Men	2
Dec 31 2014	3-Ahau	2	Mar 9 2015	6-Lamat	7	May 16 2015	9-Cib	3
Jan 1 2015	4-Imix	3	Mar 10 2015	7-Muluc	8	May 17 2015	10-Caban	4
Jan 2 2015	5-Ik	4	Mar 11 2015	8-Oc	9	May 18 2015	11-Etz'nab	5
Jan 3 2015	6-Akbal	5	Mar 12 2015	9-Chuen	1	May 19 2015	12-Cauac	6
Jan 4 2015	7-Kan	6	Mar 13 2015	10-Eb	2	May 20 2015	13-Ahau	7
Jan 5 2015	8-Chicchan	7	Mar 14 2015	11-Ben	3	May 21 2015	1-Imix	8
Jan 6 2015	9-Cimi	8	Mar 15 2015	12-Ix	4	May 22 2015	2-Ik	9
Jan 7 2015	10-Manik	9	Mar 16 2015	13-Men	5	May 23 2015	3-Akbal	1
Jan 8 2015	11-Lamat	1	Mar 17 2015	1-Cib	6	May 24 2015	4-Kan	2
Jan 9 2015	12-Muluc	2	Mar 18 2015	2-Caban	7	May 25 2015	5-Chicchan	3
Jan 10 2015	13-Oc	3	Mar 19 2015	3-Etz'nab	8	May 26 2015	6-Cimi	4
Jan 11 2015	1-Chuen	4	Mar 20 2015	4-Cauac	9	May 27 2015	7-Manik	5
Jan 12 2015	2-Eb	5	Mar 21 2015	5-Ahau	1	May 28 2015	8-Lamat	6
Jan 13 2015	3-Ben	6	Mar 22 2015	6-Imix	2	May 29 2015	9-Muluc	7
Jan 14 2015	4-Ix	7	Mar 23 2015	7-Ik	3	May 30 2015	10-Oc	8
Jan 15 2015	5-Men	8	Mar 24 2015	8-Akbal	4	May 31 2015	11-Chuen	9
Jan 16 2015	6-Cib	9	Mar 25 2015	9-Kan	5	Jun 1 2015	12-Eb	1
Jan 17 2015	7-Caban	1	Mar 26 2015	10-Chicchan	6	Jun 2 2015	13-Ben	2
Jan 18 2015	8-Etz'nab	2	Mar 27 2015	11-Cimi	7	Jun 3 2015	1-Ix	3
Jan 19 2015	9-Cauac	3	Mar 28 2015	12-Manik	8	Jun 4 2015	2-Men	4
Jan 20 2015	10-Ahau	4	Mar 29 2015	13-Lamat	9	Jun 5 2015	3-Cib	5
Jan 21 2015	11-Imix	5	Mar 30 2015	1-Muluc	1	Jun 6 2015	4-Caban	6

Date	Day-Sign	L
Jun 7 2015	5-Etz'nab	7
Jun 8 2015	6-Cauac	8
Jun 9 2015	7-Ahau	9
Jun 10 2015	*8-Imix*	1
Jun 11 2015	9-Ik	2
Jun 12 2015	10-Akbal	3
Jun 13 2015	11-Kan	4
Jun 14 2015	12-Chicchan	5
Jun 15 2015	13-Cimi	6
Jun 16 2015	**1-Manik**	7
Jun 17 2015	2-Lamat	8
Jun 18 2015	3-Muluc	9
Jun 19 2015	4-Oc	1
Jun 20 2015	5-Chuen	2
Jun 21 2015	6-Eb	3
Jun 22 2015	7-Ben	4
Jun 23 2015	8-Ix	5
Jun 24 2015	9-Men	6
Jun 25 2015	10-Cib	7
Jun 26 2015	11-Caban	8
Jun 27 2015	12-Etz'nab	9
Jun 28 2015	13-Cauac	1
Jun 29 2015	**1-Ahau**	2
Jun 30 2015	*2-Imix*	3
Jul 1 2015	3-Ik	4
Jul 2 2015	4-Akbal	5
Jul 3 2015	5-Kan	6
Jul 4 2015	6-Chicchan	7
Jul 5 2015	7-Cimi	8
Jul 6 2015	8-Manik	9
Jul 7 2015	9-Lamat	1
Jul 8 2015	10-Muluc	2
Jul 9 2015	11-Oc	3
Jul 10 2015	12-Chuen	4
Jul 11 2015	13-Eb	5
Jul 12 2015	**1-Ben**	6
Jul 13 2015	2-Ix	7
Jul 14 2015	3-Men	8
Jul 15 2015	4-Cib	9
Jul 16 2015	5-Caban	1
Jul 17 2015	6-Etz'nab	2
Jul 18 2015	7-Cauac	3
Jul 19 2015	8-Ahau	4
Jul 20 2015	*9-Imix*	5
Jul 21 2015	10-Ik	6
Jul 22 2015	11-Akbal	7
Jul 23 2015	12-Kan	8
Jul 24 2015	13-Chicchan	9
Jul 25 2015	**1-Cimi**	1
Jul 26 2015	2-Manik	2
Jul 27 2015	3-Lamat	3
Jul 28 2015	4-Muluc	4
Jul 29 2015	5-Oc	5
Jul 30 2015	6-Chuen	6
Jul 31 2015	7-Eb	7
Aug 1 2015	8-Ben	8
Aug 2 2015	9-Ix	9
Aug 3 2015	10-Men	1
Aug 4 2015	11-Cib	2
Aug 5 2015	12-Caban	3
Aug 6 2015	13-Etz'nab	4
Aug 7 2015	**1-Cauac**	5
Aug 8 2015	2-Ahau	6
Aug 9 2015	*3-Imix*	7
Aug 10 2015	4-Ik	8
Aug 11 2015	5-Akbal	9
Aug 12 2015	6-Kan	1
Aug 13 2015	7-Chicchan	2

Date	Day-Sign	L
Aug 14 2015	8-Cimi	3
Aug 15 2015	9-Manik	4
Aug 16 2015	10-Lamat	5
Aug 17 2015	11-Muluc	6
Aug 18 2015	12-Oc	7
Aug 19 2015	13-Chuen	8
Aug 20 2015	**1-Eb**	9
Aug 21 2015	2-Ben	1
Aug 22 2015	3-Ix	2
Aug 23 2015	4-Men	3
Aug 24 2015	5-Cib	4
Aug 25 2015	6-Caban	5
Aug 26 2015	7-Etz'nab	6
Aug 27 2015	8-Cauac	7
Aug 28 2015	9-Ahau	8
Aug 29 2015	*10-Imix*	9
Aug 30 2015	11-Ik	1
Aug 31 2015	12-Akbal	2
Sep 1 2015	13-Kan	3
Sep 2 2015	**1-Chicchan**	4
Sep 3 2015	2-Cimi	5
Sep 4 2015	3-Manik	6
Sep 5 2015	4-Lamat	7
Sep 6 2015	5-Muluc	8
Sep 7 2015	6-Oc	9
Sep 8 2015	7-Chuen	1
Sep 9 2015	8-Eb	2
Sep 10 2015	9-Ben	3
Sep 11 2015	10-Ix	4
Sep 12 2015	11-Men	5
Sep 13 2015	12-Cib	6
Sep 14 2015	13-Caban	7
Sep 15 2015	**1-Etz'nab**	8
Sep 16 2015	2-Cauac	9
Sep 17 2015	3-Ahau	1
Sep 18 2015	*4-Imix*	2
Sep 19 2015	5-Ik	3
Sep 20 2015	6-Akbal	4
Sep 21 2015	7-Kan	5
Sep 22 2015	8-Chicchan	6
Sep 23 2015	9-Cimi	7
Sep 24 2015	10-Manik	8
Sep 25 2015	11-Lamat	9
Sep 26 2015	12-Muluc	1
Sep 27 2015	13-Oc	2
Sep 28 2015	**1-Chuen**	3
Sep 29 2015	2-Eb	4
Sep 30 2015	3-Ben	5
Oct 1 2015	4-Ix	6
Oct 2 2015	5-Men	7
Oct 3 2015	6-Cib	8
Oct 4 2015	7-Caban	9
Oct 5 2015	8-Etz'nab	1
Oct 6 2015	9-Cauac	2
Oct 7 2015	10-Ahau	3
Oct 8 2015	*11-Imix*	4
Oct 9 2015	12-Ik	5
Oct 10 2015	13-Akbal	6
Oct 11 2015	**1-Kan**	7
Oct 12 2015	2-Chicchan	8
Oct 13 2015	3-Cimi	9
Oct 14 2015	4-Manik	1
Oct 15 2015	5-Lamat	2
Oct 16 2015	6-Muluc	3
Oct 17 2015	7-Oc	4
Oct 18 2015	8-Chuen	5
Oct 19 2015	9-Eb	6
Oct 20 2015	10-Ben	7

Date	Day-Sign	L
Oct 21 2015	11-Ix	8
Oct 22 2015	12-Men	9
Oct 23 2015	13-Cib	1
Oct 24 2015	**1-Caban**	2
Oct 25 2015	2-Etz'nab	3
Oct 26 2015	3-Cauac	4
Oct 27 2015	4-Ahau	5
Oct 28 2015	*5-Imix*	6
Oct 29 2015	6-Ik	7
Oct 30 2015	7-Akbal	8
Oct 31 2015	8-Kan	9
Nov 1 2015	9-Chicchan	1
Nov 2 2015	10-Cimi	2
Nov 3 2015	11-Manik	3
Nov 4 2015	12-Lamat	4
Nov 5 2015	13-Muluc	5
Nov 6 2015	**1-Oc**	6
Nov 7 2015	2-Chuen	7
Nov 8 2015	3-Eb	8
Nov 9 2015	4-Ben	9
Nov 10 2015	5-Ix	1
Nov 11 2015	6-Men	2
Nov 12 2015	7-Cib	3
Nov 13 2015	8-Caban	4
Nov 14 2015	9-Etz'nab	5
Nov 15 2015	10-Cauac	6
Nov 16 2015	11-Ahau	7
Nov 17 2015	*12-Imix*	8
Nov 18 2015	13-Ik	9
Nov 19 2015	**1-Akbal**	1
Nov 20 2015	2-Kan	2
Nov 21 2015	3-Chicchan	3
Nov 22 2015	4-Cimi	4
Nov 23 2015	5-Manik	5
Nov 24 2015	6-Lamat	6
Nov 25 2015	7-Muluc	7
Nov 26 2015	8-Oc	8
Nov 27 2015	9-Chuen	9
Nov 28 2015	10-Eb	1
Nov 29 2015	11-Ben	2
Nov 30 2015	12-Ix	3
Dec 1 2015	13-Men	4
Dec 2 2015	**1-Cib**	5
Dec 3 2015	2-Caban	6
Dec 4 2015	3-Etz'nab	7
Dec 5 2015	4-Cauac	8
Dec 6 2015	5-Ahau	9
Dec 7 2015	*6-Imix*	1
Dec 8 2015	7-Ik	2
Dec 9 2015	8-Akbal	3
Dec 10 2015	9-Kan	4
Dec 11 2015	10-Chicchan	5
Dec 12 2015	11-Cimi	6
Dec 13 2015	12-Manik	7
Dec 14 2015	13-Lamat	8
Dec 15 2015	**1-Muluc**	9
Dec 16 2015	2-Oc	1
Dec 17 2015	3-Chuen	2
Dec 18 2015	4-Eb	3
Dec 19 2015	5-Ben	4
Dec 20 2015	6-Ix	5
Dec 21 2015	7-Men	6
Dec 22 2015	8-Cib	7
Dec 23 2015	9-Caban	8
Dec 24 2015	10-Etz'nab	9
Dec 25 2015	11-Cauac	1
Dec 26 2015	12-Ahau	2
Dec 27 2015	*13-Imix*	3

Date	Day-Sign	L	Date	Day-Sign	L	Date	Day-Sign	L
Dec 28 2015	1-Ik	4	Mar 5 2016	4-Oc	9	May 12 2016	7-Etz'nab	5
Dec 29 2015	2-Akbal	5	Mar 6 2016	5-Chuen	1	May 13 2016	8-Cauac	6
Dec 30 2015	3-Kan	6	Mar 7 2016	6-Eb	2	May 14 2016	9-Ahau	7
Dec 31 2015	4-Chicchan	7	Mar 8 2016	7-Ben	3	May 15 2016	10-Imix	8
Jan 1 2016	5-Cimi	8	Mar 9 2016	8-Ix	4	May 16 2016	11-Ik	9
Jan 2 2016	6-Manik	9	Mar 10 2016	9-Men	5	May 17 2016	12-Akbal	1
Jan 3 2016	7-Lamat	1	Mar 11 2016	10-Cib	6	May 18 2016	13-Kan	2
Jan 4 2016	8-Muluc	2	Mar 12 2016	11-Caban	7	May 19 2016	1-Chicchan	3
Jan 5 2016	9-Oc	3	Mar 13 2016	12-Etz'nab	8	May 20 2016	2-Cimi	4
Jan 6 2016	10-Chuen	4	Mar 14 2016	13-Cauac	9	May 21 2016	3-Manik	5
Jan 7 2016	11-Eb	5	Mar 15 2016	1-Ahau	1	May 22 2016	4-Lamat	6
Jan 8 2016	12-Ben	6	Mar 16 2016	2-Imix	2	May 23 2016	5-Muluc	7
Jan 9 2016	13-Ix	7	Mar 17 2016	3-Ik	3	May 24 2016	6-Oc	8
Jan 10 2016	1-Men	8	Mar 18 2016	4-Akbal	4	May 25 2016	7-Chuen	9
Jan 11 2016	2-Cib	9	Mar 19 2016	5-Kan	5	May 26 2016	8-Eb	1
Jan 12 2016	3-Caban	1	Mar 20 2016	6-Chicchan	6	May 27 2016	9-Ben	2
Jan 13 2016	4-Etz'nab	2	Mar 21 2016	7-Cimi	7	May 28 2016	10-Ix	3
Jan 14 2016	5-Cauac	3	Mar 22 2016	8-Manik	8	May 29 2016	11-Men	4
Jan 15 2016	6-Ahau	4	Mar 23 2016	9-Lamat	9	May 30 2016	12-Cib	5
Jan 16 2016	7-Imix	5	Mar 24 2016	10-Muluc	1	May 31 2016	13-Caban	6
Jan 17 2016	8-Ik	6	Mar 25 2016	11-Oc	2	Jun 1 2016	1-Etz'nab	7
Jan 18 2016	9-Akbal	7	Mar 26 2016	12-Chuen	3	Jun 2 2016	2-Cauac	8
Jan 19 2016	10-Kan	8	Mar 27 2016	13-Eb	4	Jun 3 2016	3-Ahau	9
Jan 20 2016	11-Chicchan	9	Mar 28 2016	1-Ben	5	Jun 4 2016	4-Imix	1
Jan 21 2016	12-Cimi	1	Mar 29 2016	2-Ix	6	Jun 5 2016	5-Ik	2
Jan 22 2016	13-Manik	2	Mar 30 2016	3-Men	7	Jun 6 2016	6-Akbal	3
Jan 23 2016	1-Lamat	3	Mar 31 2016	4-Cib	8	Jun 7 2016	7-Kan	4
Jan 24 2016	2-Muluc	4	Apr 1 2016	5-Caban	9	Jun 8 2016	8-Chicchan	5
Jan 25 2016	3-Oc	5	Apr 2 2016	6-Etz'nab	1	Jun 9 2016	9-Cimi	6
Jan 26 2016	4-Chuen	6	Apr 3 2016	7-Cauac	2	Jun 10 2016	10-Manik	7
Jan 27 2016	5-Eb	7	Apr 4 2016	8-Ahau	3	Jun 11 2016	11-Lamat	8
Jan 28 2016	6-Ben	8	Apr 5 2016	9-Imix	4	Jun 12 2016	12-Muluc	9
Jan 29 2016	7-Ix	9	Apr 6 2016	10-Ik	5	Jun 13 2016	13-Oc	1
Jan 30 2016	8-Men	1	Apr 7 2016	11-Akbal	6	Jun 14 2016	1-Chuen	2
Jan 31 2016	9-Cib	2	Apr 8 2016	12-Kan	7	Jun 15 2016	2-Eb	3
Feb 1 2016	10-Caban	3	Apr 9 2016	13-Chicchan	8	Jun 16 2016	3-Ben	4
Feb 2 2016	11-Etz'nab	4	Apr 10 2016	1-Cimi	9	Jun 17 2016	4-Ix	5
Feb 3 2016	12-Cauac	5	Apr 11 2016	2-Manik	1	Jun 18 2016	5-Men	6
Feb 4 2016	13-Ahau	6	Apr 12 2016	3-Lamat	2	Jun 19 2016	6-Cib	7
Feb 5 2016	1-Imix	7	Apr 13 2016	4-Muluc	3	Jun 20 2016	7-Caban	8
Feb 6 2016	2-Ik	8	Apr 14 2016	5-Oc	4	Jun 21 2016	8-Etz'nab	9
Feb 7 2016	3-Akbal	9	Apr 15 2016	6-Chuen	5	Jun 22 2016	9-Cauac	1
Feb 8 2016	4-Kan	1	Apr 16 2016	7-Eb	6	Jun 23 2016	10-Ahau	2
Feb 9 2016	5-Chicchan	2	Apr 17 2016	8-Ben	7	Jun 24 2016	11-Imix	3
Feb 10 2016	6-Cimi	3	Apr 18 2016	9-Ix	8	Jun 25 2016	12-Ik	4
Feb 11 2016	7-Manik	4	Apr 19 2016	10-Men	9	Jun 26 2016	13-Akbal	5
Feb 12 2016	8-Lamat	5	Apr 20 2016	11-Cib	1	Jun 27 2016	1-Kan	6
Feb 13 2016	9-Muluc	6	Apr 21 2016	12-Caban	2	Jun 28 2016	2-Chicchan	7
Feb 14 2016	10-Oc	7	Apr 22 2016	13-Etz'nab	3	Jun 29 2016	3-Cimi	8
Feb 15 2016	11-Chuen	8	Apr 23 2016	1-Cauac	4	Jun 30 2016	4-Manik	9
Feb 16 2016	12-Eb	9	Apr 24 2016	2-Ahau	5	Jul 1 2016	5-Lamat	1
Feb 17 2016	13-Ben	1	Apr 25 2016	3-Imix	6	Jul 2 2016	6-Muluc	2
Feb 18 2016	1-Ix	2	Apr 26 2016	4-Ik	7	Jul 3 2016	7-Oc	3
Feb 19 2016	2-Men	3	Apr 27 2016	5-Akbal	8	Jul 4 2016	8-Chuen	4
Feb 20 2016	3-Cib	4	Apr 28 2016	6-Kan	9	Jul 5 2016	9-Eb	5
Feb 21 2016	4-Caban	5	Apr 29 2016	7-Chicchan	1	Jul 6 2016	10-Ben	6
Feb 22 2016	5-Etz'nab	6	Apr 30 2016	8-Cimi	2	Jul 7 2016	11-Ix	7
Feb 23 2016	6-Cauac	7	May 1 2016	9-Manik	3	Jul 8 2016	12-Men	8
Feb 24 2016	7-Ahau	8	May 2 2016	10-Lamat	4	Jul 9 2016	13-Cib	9
Feb 25 2016	8-Imix	9	May 3 2016	11-Muluc	5	Jul 10 2016	1-Caban	1
Feb 26 2016	9-Ik	1	May 4 2016	12-Oc	6	Jul 11 2016	2-Etz'nab	2
Feb 27 2016	10-Akbal	2	May 5 2016	13-Chuen	7	Jul 12 2016	3-Cauac	3
Feb 28 2016	11-Kan	3	May 6 2016	1-Eb	8	Jul 13 2016	4-Ahau	4
Feb 29 2016	12-Chicchan	4	May 7 2016	2-Ben	9	Jul 14 2016	5-Imix	5
Mar 1 2016	13-Cimi	5	May 8 2016	3-Ix	1	Jul 15 2016	6-Ik	6
Mar 2 2016	1-Manik	6	May 9 2016	4-Men	2	Jul 16 2016	7-Akbal	7
Mar 3 2016	2-Lamat	7	May 10 2016	5-Cib	3	Jul 17 2016	8-Kan	8
Mar 4 2016	3-Muluc	8	May 11 2016	6-Caban	4	Jul 18 2016	9-Chicchan	9

Date	Day-Sign	L
Jul 19 2016	10-Cimi	1
Jul 20 2016	11-Manik	2
Jul 21 2016	12-Lamat	3
Jul 22 2016	13-Muluc	4
Jul 23 2016	**1-Oc**	5
Jul 24 2016	2-Chuen	6
Jul 25 2016	3-Eb	7
Jul 26 2016	4-Ben	8
Jul 27 2016	5-Ix	9
Jul 28 2016	6-Men	1
Jul 29 2016	7-Cib	2
Jul 30 2016	8-Caban	3
Jul 31 2016	9-Etz'nab	4
Aug 1 2016	10-Cauac	5
Aug 2 2016	11-Ahau	6
Aug 3 2016	*12-Imix*	7
Aug 4 2016	13-Ik	8
Aug 5 2016	**1-Akbal**	9
Aug 6 2016	2-Kan	1
Aug 7 2016	3-Chicchan	2
Aug 8 2016	4-Cimi	3
Aug 9 2016	5-Manik	4
Aug 10 2016	6-Lamat	5
Aug 11 2016	7-Muluc	6
Aug 12 2016	8-Oc	7
Aug 13 2016	9-Chuen	8
Aug 14 2016	10-Eb	9
Aug 15 2016	11-Ben	1
Aug 16 2016	12-Ix	2
Aug 17 2016	13-Men	3
Aug 18 2016	**1-Cib**	4
Aug 19 2016	2-Caban	5
Aug 20 2016	3-Etz'nab	6
Aug 21 2016	4-Cauac	7
Aug 22 2016	5-Ahau	8
Aug 23 2016	*6-Imix*	9
Aug 24 2016	7-Ik	1
Aug 25 2016	8-Akbal	2
Aug 26 2016	9-Kan	3
Aug 27 2016	10-Chicchan	4
Aug 28 2016	11-Cimi	5
Aug 29 2016	12-Manik	6
Aug 30 2016	13-Lamat	7
Aug 31 2016	**1-Muluc**	8
Sep 1 2016	2-Oc	9
Sep 2 2016	3-Chuen	1
Sep 3 2016	4-Eb	2
Sep 4 2016	5-Ben	3
Sep 5 2016	6-Ix	4
Sep 6 2016	7-Men	5
Sep 7 2016	8-Cib	6
Sep 8 2016	9-Caban	7
Sep 9 2016	10-Etz'nab	8
Sep 10 2016	11-Cauac	9
Sep 11 2016	12-Ahau	1
Sep 12 2016	*13-Imix*	2
Sep 13 2016	**1-Ik**	3
Sep 14 2016	2-Akbal	4
Sep 15 2016	3-Kan	5
Sep 16 2016	4-Chicchan	6
Sep 17 2016	5-Cimi	7
Sep 18 2016	6-Manik	8
Sep 19 2016	7-Lamat	9
Sep 20 2016	8-Muluc	1
Sep 21 2016	9-Oc	2
Sep 22 2016	10-Chuen	3
Sep 23 2016	11-Eb	4
Sep 24 2016	12-Ben	5

Date	Day-Sign	L
Sep 25 2016	13-Ix	6
Sep 26 2016	**1-Men**	7
Sep 27 2016	2-Cib	8
Sep 28 2016	3-Caban	9
Sep 29 2016	4-Etz'nab	1
Sep 30 2016	5-Cauac	2
Oct 1 2016	6-Ahau	3
Oct 2 2016	*7-Imix*	4
Oct 3 2016	8-Ik	5
Oct 4 2016	9-Akbal	6
Oct 5 2016	10-Kan	7
Oct 6 2016	11-Chicchan	8
Oct 7 2016	12-Cimi	9
Oct 8 2016	13-Manik	1
Oct 9 2016	**1-Lamat**	2
Oct 10 2016	2-Muluc	3
Oct 11 2016	3-Oc	4
Oct 12 2016	4-Chuen	5
Oct 13 2016	5-Eb	6
Oct 14 2016	6-Ben	7
Oct 15 2016	7-Ix	8
Oct 16 2016	8-Men	9
Oct 17 2016	9-Cib	1
Oct 18 2016	10-Caban	2
Oct 19 2016	11-Etz'nab	3
Oct 20 2016	12-Cauac	4
Oct 21 2016	13-Ahau	5
Oct 22 2016	**1-Imix**	6
Oct 23 2016	2-Ik	7
Oct 24 2016	3-Akbal	8
Oct 25 2016	4-Kan	9
Oct 26 2016	5-Chicchan	1
Oct 27 2016	6-Cimi	2
Oct 28 2016	7-Manik	3
Oct 29 2016	8-Lamat	4
Oct 30 2016	9-Muluc	5
Oct 31 2016	10-Oc	6
Nov 1 2016	11-Chuen	7
Nov 2 2016	12-Eb	8
Nov 3 2016	13-Ben	9
Nov 4 2016	**1-Ix**	1
Nov 5 2016	2-Men	2
Nov 6 2016	3-Cib	3
Nov 7 2016	4-Caban	4
Nov 8 2016	5-Etz'nab	5
Nov 9 2016	6-Cauac	6
Nov 10 2016	7-Ahau	7
Nov 11 2016	*8-Imix*	8
Nov 12 2016	9-Ik	9
Nov 13 2016	10-Akbal	1
Nov 14 2016	11-Kan	2
Nov 15 2016	12-Chicchan	3
Nov 16 2016	13-Cimi	4
Nov 17 2016	**1-Manik**	5
Nov 18 2016	2-Lamat	6
Nov 19 2016	3-Muluc	7
Nov 20 2016	4-Oc	8
Nov 21 2016	5-Chuen	9
Nov 22 2016	6-Eb	1
Nov 23 2016	7-Ben	2
Nov 24 2016	8-Ix	3
Nov 25 2016	9-Men	4
Nov 26 2016	10-Cib	5
Nov 27 2016	11-Caban	6
Nov 28 2016	12-Etz'nab	7
Nov 29 2016	13-Cauac	8
Nov 30 2016	**1-Ahau**	9
Dec 1 2016	*2-Imix*	1

Date	Day-Sign	L
Dec 2 2016	3-Ik	2
Dec 3 2016	4-Akbal	3
Dec 4 2016	5-Kan	4
Dec 5 2016	6-Chicchan	5
Dec 6 2016	7-Cimi	6
Dec 7 2016	8-Manik	7
Dec 8 2016	9-Lamat	8
Dec 9 2016	10-Muluc	9
Dec 10 2016	11-Oc	1
Dec 11 2016	12-Chuen	2
Dec 12 2016	13-Eb	3
Dec 13 2016	**1-Ben**	4
Dec 14 2016	2-Ix	5
Dec 15 2016	3-Men	6
Dec 16 2016	4-Cib	7
Dec 17 2016	5-Caban	8
Dec 18 2016	6-Etz'nab	9
Dec 19 2016	7-Cauac	1
Dec 20 2016	8-Ahau	2
Dec 21 2016	*9-Imix*	3
Dec 22 2016	10-Ik	4
Dec 23 2016	11-Akbal	5
Dec 24 2016	12-Kan	6
Dec 25 2016	13-Chicchan	7
Dec 26 2016	**1-Cimi**	8
Dec 27 2016	2-Manik	9
Dec 28 2016	3-Lamat	1
Dec 29 2016	4-Muluc	2
Dec 30 2016	5-Oc	3
Dec 31 2016	6-Chuen	4
Jan 1 2017	7-Eb	5
Jan 2 2017	8-Ben	6
Jan 3 2017	9-Ix	7
Jan 4 2017	10-Men	8
Jan 5 2017	11-Cib	9
Jan 6 2017	12-Caban	1
Jan 7 2017	13-Etz'nab	2
Jan 8 2017	**1-Cauac**	3
Jan 9 2017	2-Ahau	4
Jan 10 2017	*3-Imix*	5
Jan 11 2017	4-Ik	6
Jan 12 2017	5-Akbal	7
Jan 13 2017	6-Kan	8
Jan 14 2017	7-Chicchan	9
Jan 15 2017	8-Cimi	1
Jan 16 2017	9-Manik	2
Jan 17 2017	10-Lamat	3
Jan 18 2017	11-Muluc	4
Jan 19 2017	12-Oc	5
Jan 20 2017	13-Chuen	6
Jan 21 2017	**1-Eb**	7
Jan 22 2017	2-Ben	8
Jan 23 2017	3-Ix	9
Jan 24 2017	4-Men	1
Jan 25 2017	5-Cib	2
Jan 26 2017	6-Caban	3
Jan 27 2017	7-Etz'nab	4
Jan 28 2017	8-Cauac	5
Jan 29 2017	9-Ahau	6
Jan 30 2017	*10-Imix*	7
Jan 31 2017	11-Ik	8
Feb 1 2017	12-Akbal	9
Feb 2 2017	13-Kan	1
Feb 3 2017	**1-Chicchan**	2
Feb 4 2017	2-Cimi	3
Feb 5 2017	3-Manik	4
Feb 6 2017	4-Lamat	5
Feb 7 2017	5-Muluc	6

Date	Day-Sign	L	Date	Day-Sign	L	Date	Day-Sign	L
Feb 8 2017	6-Oc	7	Apr 17 2017	9-Etz'nab	3	Jun 24 2017	12-Cimi	8
Feb 9 2017	7-Chuen	8	Apr 18 2017	10-Cauac	4	Jun 25 2017	13-Manik	9
Feb 10 2017	8-Eb	9	Apr 19 2017	11-Ahau	5	Jun 26 2017	1-Lamat	1
Feb 11 2017	9-Ben	1	Apr 20 2017	12-Imix	6	Jun 27 2017	2-Muluc	2
Feb 12 2017	10-Ix	2	Apr 21 2017	13-Ik	7	Jun 28 2017	3-Oc	3
Feb 13 2017	11-Men	3	Apr 22 2017	1-Akbal	8	Jun 29 2017	4-Chuen	4
Feb 14 2017	12-Cib	4	Apr 23 2017	2-Kan	9	Jun 30 2017	5-Eb	5
Feb 15 2017	13-Caban	5	Apr 24 2017	3-Chicchan	1	Jul 1 2017	6-Ben	6
Feb 16 2017	1-Etz'nab	6	Apr 25 2017	4-Cimi	2	Jul 2 2017	7-Ix	7
Feb 17 2017	2-Cauac	7	Apr 26 2017	5-Manik	3	Jul 3 2017	8-Men	8
Feb 18 2017	3-Ahau	8	Apr 27 2017	6-Lamat	4	Jul 4 2017	9-Cib	9
Feb 19 2017	4-Imix	9	Apr 28 2017	7-Muluc	5	Jul 5 2017	10-Caban	1
Feb 20 2017	5-Ik	1	Apr 29 2017	8-Oc	6	Jul 6 2017	11-Etz'nab	2
Feb 21 2017	6-Akbal	2	Apr 30 2017	9-Chuen	7	Jul 7 2017	12-Cauac	3
Feb 22 2017	7-Kan	3	May 1 2017	10-Eb	8	Jul 8 2017	13-Ahau	4
Feb 23 2017	8-Chicchan	4	May 2 2017	11-Ben	9	Jul 9 2017	1-Imix	5
Feb 24 2017	9-Cimi	5	May 3 2017	12-Ix	1	Jul 10 2017	2-Ik	6
Feb 25 2017	10-Manik	6	May 4 2017	13-Men	2	Jul 11 2017	3-Akbal	7
Feb 26 2017	11-Lamat	7	May 5 2017	1-Cib	3	Jul 12 2017	4-Kan	8
Feb 27 2017	12-Muluc	8	May 6 2017	2-Caban	4	Jul 13 2017	5-Chicchan	9
Feb 28 2017	13-Oc	9	May 7 2017	3-Etz'nab	5	Jul 14 2017	6-Cimi	1
Mar 1 2017	1-Chuen	1	May 8 2017	4-Cauac	6	Jul 15 2017	7-Manik	2
Mar 2 2017	2-Eb	2	May 9 2017	5-Ahau	7	Jul 16 2017	8-Lamat	3
Mar 3 2017	3-Ben	3	May 10 2017	6-Imix	8	Jul 17 2017	9-Muluc	4
Mar 4 2017	4-Ix	4	May 11 2017	7-Ik	9	Jul 18 2017	10-Oc	5
Mar 5 2017	5-Men	5	May 12 2017	8-Akbal	1	Jul 19 2017	11-Chuen	6
Mar 6 2017	6-Cib	6	May 13 2017	9-Kan	2	Jul 20 2017	12-Eb	7
Mar 7 2017	7-Caban	7	May 14 2017	10-Chicchan	3	Jul 21 2017	13-Ben	8
Mar 8 2017	8-Etz'nab	8	May 15 2017	11-Cimi	4	Jul 22 2017	1-Ix	9
Mar 9 2017	9-Cauac	9	May 16 2017	12-Manik	5	Jul 23 2017	2-Men	1
Mar 10 2017	10-Ahau	1	May 17 2017	13-Lamat	6	Jul 24 2017	3-Cib	2
Mar 11 2017	11-Imix	2	May 18 2017	1-Muluc	7	Jul 25 2017	4-Caban	3
Mar 12 2017	12-Ik	3	May 19 2017	2-Oc	8	Jul 26 2017	5-Etz'nab	4
Mar 13 2017	13-Akbal	4	May 20 2017	3-Chuen	9	Jul 27 2017	6-Cauac	5
Mar 14 2017	1-Kan	5	May 21 2017	4-Eb	1	Jul 28 2017	7-Ahau	6
Mar 15 2017	2-Chicchan	6	May 22 2017	5-Ben	2	Jul 29 2017	8-Imix	7
Mar 16 2017	3-Cimi	7	May 23 2017	6-Ix	3	Jul 30 2017	9-Ik	8
Mar 17 2017	4-Manik	8	May 24 2017	7-Men	4	Jul 31 2017	10-Akbal	9
Mar 18 2017	5-Lamat	9	May 25 2017	8-Cib	5	Aug 1 2017	11-Kan	1
Mar 19 2017	6-Muluc	1	May 26 2017	9-Caban	6	Aug 2 2017	12-Chicchan	2
Mar 20 2017	7-Oc	2	May 27 2017	10-Etz'nab	7	Aug 3 2017	13-Cimi	3
Mar 21 2017	8-Chuen	3	May 28 2017	11-Cauac	8	Aug 4 2017	1-Manik	4
Mar 22 2017	9-Eb	4	May 29 2017	12-Ahau	9	Aug 5 2017	2-Lamat	5
Mar 23 2017	10-Ben	5	May 30 2017	13-Imix	1	Aug 6 2017	3-Muluc	6
Mar 24 2017	11-Ix	6	May 31 2017	1-Ik	2	Aug 7 2017	4-Oc	7
Mar 25 2017	12-Men	7	Jun 1 2017	2-Akbal	3	Aug 8 2017	5-Chuen	8
Mar 26 2017	13-Cib	8	Jun 2 2017	3-Kan	4	Aug 9 2017	6-Eb	9
Mar 27 2017	1-Caban	9	Jun 3 2017	4-Chicchan	5	Aug 10 2017	7-Ben	1
Mar 28 2017	2-Etz'nab	1	Jun 4 2017	5-Cimi	6	Aug 11 2017	8-Ix	2
Mar 29 2017	3-Cauac	2	Jun 5 2017	6-Manik	7	Aug 12 2017	9-Men	3
Mar 30 2017	4-Ahau	3	Jun 6 2017	7-Lamat	8	Aug 13 2017	10-Cib	4
Mar 31 2017	5-Imix	4	Jun 7 2017	8-Muluc	9	Aug 14 2017	11-Caban	5
Apr 1 2017	6-Ik	5	Jun 8 2017	9-Oc	1	Aug 15 2017	12-Etz'nab	6
Apr 2 2017	7-Akbal	6	Jun 9 2017	10-Chuen	2	Aug 16 2017	13-Cauac	7
Apr 3 2017	8-Kan	7	Jun 10 2017	11-Eb	3	Aug 17 2017	1-Ahau	8
Apr 4 2017	9-Chicchan	8	Jun 11 2017	12-Ben	4	Aug 18 2017	2-Imix	9
Apr 5 2017	10-Cimi	9	Jun 12 2017	13-Ix	5	Aug 19 2017	3-Ik	1
Apr 6 2017	11-Manik	1	Jun 13 2017	1-Men	6	Aug 20 2017	4-Akbal	2
Apr 7 2017	12-Lamat	2	Jun 14 2017	2-Cib	7	Aug 21 2017	5-Kan	3
Apr 8 2017	13-Muluc	3	Jun 15 2017	3-Caban	8	Aug 22 2017	6-Chicchan	4
Apr 9 2017	1-Oc	4	Jun 16 2017	4-Etz'nab	9	Aug 23 2017	7-Cimi	5
Apr 10 2017	2-Chuen	5	Jun 17 2017	5-Cauac	1	Aug 24 2017	8-Manik	6
Apr 11 2017	3-Eb	6	Jun 18 2017	6-Ahau	2	Aug 25 2017	9-Lamat	7
Apr 12 2017	4-Ben	7	Jun 19 2017	7-Imix	3	Aug 26 2017	10-Muluc	8
Apr 13 2017	5-Ix	8	Jun 20 2017	8-Ik	4	Aug 27 2017	11-Oc	9
Apr 14 2017	6-Men	9	Jun 21 2017	9-Akbal	5	Aug 28 2017	12-Chuen	1
Apr 15 2017	7-Cib	1	Jun 22 2017	10-Kan	6	Aug 29 2017	13-Eb	2
Apr 16 2017	8-Caban	2	Jun 23 2017	11-Chicchan	7	Aug 30 2017	1-Ben	3

Date	Day-Sign	L
Aug 31 2017	2-Ix	4
Sep 1 2017	3-Men	5
Sep 2 2017	4-Cib	6
Sep 3 2017	5-Caban	7
Sep 4 2017	6-Etz'nab	8
Sep 5 2017	7-Cauac	9
Sep 6 2017	8-Ahau	1
Sep 7 2017	9-Imix	2
Sep 8 2017	10-Ik	3
Sep 9 2017	11-Akbal	4
Sep 10 2017	12-Kan	5
Sep 11 2017	13-Chicchan	6
Sep 12 2017	1-Cimi	7
Sep 13 2017	2-Manik	8
Sep 14 2017	3-Lamat	9
Sep 15 2017	4-Muluc	1
Sep 16 2017	5-Oc	2
Sep 17 2017	6-Chuen	3
Sep 18 2017	7-Eb	4
Sep 19 2017	8-Ben	5
Sep 20 2017	9-Ix	6
Sep 21 2017	10-Men	7
Sep 22 2017	11-Cib	8
Sep 23 2017	12-Caban	9
Sep 24 2017	13-Etz'nab	1
Sep 25 2017	1-Cauac	2
Sep 26 2017	2-Ahau	3
Sep 27 2017	3-Imix	4
Sep 28 2017	4-Ik	5
Sep 29 2017	5-Akbal	6
Sep 30 2017	6-Kan	7
Oct 1 2017	7-Chicchan	8
Oct 2 2017	8-Cimi	9
Oct 3 2017	9-Manik	1
Oct 4 2017	10-Lamat	2
Oct 5 2017	11-Muluc	3
Oct 6 2017	12-Oc	4
Oct 7 2017	13-Chuen	5
Oct 8 2017	1-Eb	6
Oct 9 2017	2-Ben	7
Oct 10 2017	3-Ix	8
Oct 11 2017	4-Men	9
Oct 12 2017	5-Cib	1
Oct 13 2017	6-Caban	2
Oct 14 2017	7-Etz'nab	3
Oct 15 2017	8-Cauac	4
Oct 16 2017	9-Ahau	5
Oct 17 2017	10-Imix	6
Oct 18 2017	11-Ik	7
Oct 19 2017	12-Akbal	8
Oct 20 2017	13-Kan	9
Oct 21 2017	1-Chicchan	1
Oct 22 2017	2-Cimi	2
Oct 23 2017	3-Manik	3
Oct 24 2017	4-Lamat	4
Oct 25 2017	5-Muluc	5
Oct 26 2017	6-Oc	6
Oct 27 2017	7-Chuen	7
Oct 28 2017	8-Eb	8
Oct 29 2017	9-Ben	9
Oct 30 2017	10-Ix	1
Oct 31 2017	11-Men	2
Nov 1 2017	12-Cib	3
Nov 2 2017	13-Caban	4
Nov 3 2017	1-Etz'nab	5
Nov 4 2017	2-Cauac	6
Nov 5 2017	3-Ahau	7
Nov 6 2017	4-Imix	8

Date	Day-Sign	L
Nov 7 2017	5-Ik	9
Nov 8 2017	6-Akbal	1
Nov 9 2017	7-Kan	2
Nov 10 2017	8-Chicchan	3
Nov 11 2017	9-Cimi	4
Nov 12 2017	10-Manik	5
Nov 13 2017	11-Lamat	6
Nov 14 2017	12-Muluc	7
Nov 15 2017	13-Oc	8
Nov 16 2017	1-Chuen	9
Nov 17 2017	2-Eb	1
Nov 18 2017	3-Ben	2
Nov 19 2017	4-Ix	3
Nov 20 2017	5-Men	4
Nov 21 2017	6-Cib	5
Nov 22 2017	7-Caban	6
Nov 23 2017	8-Etz'nab	7
Nov 24 2017	9-Cauac	8
Nov 25 2017	10-Ahau	9
Nov 26 2017	11-Imix	1
Nov 27 2017	12-Ik	2
Nov 28 2017	13-Akbal	3
Nov 29 2017	1-Kan	4
Nov 30 2017	2-Chicchan	5
Dec 1 2017	3-Cimi	6
Dec 2 2017	4-Manik	7
Dec 3 2017	5-Lamat	8
Dec 4 2017	6-Muluc	9
Dec 5 2017	7-Oc	1
Dec 6 2017	8-Chuen	2
Dec 7 2017	9-Eb	3
Dec 8 2017	10-Ben	4
Dec 9 2017	11-Ix	5
Dec 10 2017	12-Men	6
Dec 11 2017	13-Cib	7
Dec 12 2017	1-Caban	8
Dec 13 2017	2-Etz'nab	9
Dec 14 2017	3-Cauac	1
Dec 15 2017	4-Ahau	2
Dec 16 2017	5-Imix	3
Dec 17 2017	6-Ik	4
Dec 18 2017	7-Akbal	5
Dec 19 2017	8-Kan	6
Dec 20 2017	9-Chicchan	7
Dec 21 2017	10-Cimi	8
Dec 22 2017	11-Manik	9
Dec 23 2017	12-Lamat	1
Dec 24 2017	13-Muluc	2
Dec 25 2017	1-Oc	3
Dec 26 2017	2-Chuen	4
Dec 27 2017	3-Eb	5
Dec 28 2017	4-Ben	6
Dec 29 2017	5-Ix	7
Dec 30 2017	6-Men	8
Dec 31 2017	7-Cib	9
Jan 1 2018	8-Caban	1
Jan 2 2018	9-Etz'nab	2
Jan 3 2018	10-Cauac	3
Jan 4 2018	11-Ahau	4
Jan 5 2018	12-Imix	5
Jan 6 2018	13-Ik	6
Jan 7 2018	1-Akbal	7
Jan 8 2018	2-Kan	8
Jan 9 2018	3-Chicchan	9
Jan 10 2018	4-Cimi	1
Jan 11 2018	5-Manik	2
Jan 12 2018	6-Lamat	3
Jan 13 2018	7-Muluc	4

Date	Day-Sign	L
Jan 14 2018	8-Oc	5
Jan 15 2018	9-Chuen	6
Jan 16 2018	10-Eb	7
Jan 17 2018	11-Ben	8
Jan 18 2018	12-Ix	9
Jan 19 2018	13-Men	1
Jan 20 2018	1-Cib	2
Jan 21 2018	2-Caban	3
Jan 22 2018	3-Etz'nab	4
Jan 23 2018	4-Cauac	5
Jan 24 2018	5-Ahau	6
Jan 25 2018	6-Imix	7
Jan 26 2018	7-Ik	8
Jan 27 2018	8-Akbal	9
Jan 28 2018	9-Kan	1
Jan 29 2018	10-Chicchan	2
Jan 30 2018	11-Cimi	3
Jan 31 2018	12-Manik	4
Feb 1 2018	13-Lamat	5
Feb 2 2018	1-Muluc	6
Feb 3 2018	2-Oc	7
Feb 4 2018	3-Chuen	8
Feb 5 2018	4-Eb	9
Feb 6 2018	5-Ben	1
Feb 7 2018	6-Ix	2
Feb 8 2018	7-Men	3
Feb 9 2018	8-Cib	4
Feb 10 2018	9-Caban	5
Feb 11 2018	10-Etz'nab	6
Feb 12 2018	11-Cauac	7
Feb 13 2018	12-Ahau	8
Feb 14 2018	13-Imix	9
Feb 15 2018	1-Ik	1
Feb 16 2018	2-Akbal	2
Feb 17 2018	3-Kan	3
Feb 18 2018	4-Chicchan	4
Feb 19 2018	5-Cimi	5
Feb 20 2018	6-Manik	6
Feb 21 2018	7-Lamat	7
Feb 22 2018	8-Muluc	8
Feb 23 2018	9-Oc	9
Feb 24 2018	10-Chuen	1
Feb 25 2018	11-Eb	2
Feb 26 2018	12-Ben	3
Feb 27 2018	13-Ix	4
Feb 28 2018	1-Men	5
Mar 1 2018	2-Cib	6
Mar 2 2018	3-Caban	7
Mar 3 2018	4-Etz'nab	8
Mar 4 2018	5-Cauac	9
Mar 5 2018	6-Ahau	1
Mar 6 2018	7-Imix	2
Mar 7 2018	8-Ik	3
Mar 8 2018	9-Akbal	4
Mar 9 2018	10-Kan	5
Mar 10 2018	11-Chicchan	6
Mar 11 2018	12-Cimi	7
Mar 12 2018	13-Manik	8
Mar 13 2018	1-Lamat	9
Mar 14 2018	2-Muluc	1
Mar 15 2018	3-Oc	2
Mar 16 2018	4-Chuen	3
Mar 17 2018	5-Eb	4
Mar 18 2018	6-Ben	5
Mar 19 2018	7-Ix	6
Mar 20 2018	8-Men	7
Mar 21 2018	9-Cib	8
Mar 22 2018	10-Caban	9

Date	Day-Sign	L
Mar 23 2018	11-Etz'nab	1
Mar 24 2018	12-Cauac	2
Mar 25 2018	13-Ahau	3
Mar 26 2018	1-Imix	4
Mar 27 2018	2-Ik	5
Mar 28 2018	3-Akbal	6
Mar 29 2018	4-Kan	7
Mar 30 2018	5-Chicchan	8
Mar 31 2018	6-Cimi	9
Apr 1 2018	7-Manik	1
Apr 2 2018	8-Lamat	2
Apr 3 2018	9-Muluc	3
Apr 4 2018	10-Oc	4
Apr 5 2018	11-Chuen	5
Apr 6 2018	12-Eb	6
Apr 7 2018	13-Ben	7
Apr 8 2018	1-Ix	8
Apr 9 2018	2-Men	9
Apr 10 2018	3-Cib	1
Apr 11 2018	4-Caban	2
Apr 12 2018	5-Etz'nab	3
Apr 13 2018	6-Cauac	4
Apr 14 2018	7-Ahau	5
Apr 15 2018	8-Imix	6
Apr 16 2018	9-Ik	7
Apr 17 2018	10-Akbal	8
Apr 18 2018	11-Kan	9
Apr 19 2018	12-Chicchan	1
Apr 20 2018	13-Cimi	2
Apr 21 2018	1-Manik	3
Apr 22 2018	2-Lamat	4
Apr 23 2018	3-Muluc	5
Apr 24 2018	4-Oc	6
Apr 25 2018	5-Chuen	7
Apr 26 2018	6-Eb	8
Apr 27 2018	7-Ben	9
Apr 28 2018	8-Ix	1
Apr 29 2018	9-Men	2
Apr 30 2018	10-Cib	3
May 1 2018	11-Caban	4
May 2 2018	12-Etz'nab	5
May 3 2018	13-Cauac	6
May 4 2018	1-Ahau	7
May 5 2018	2-Imix	8
May 6 2018	3-Ik	9
May 7 2018	4-Akbal	1
May 8 2018	5-Kan	2
May 9 2018	6-Chicchan	3
May 10 2018	7-Cimi	4
May 11 2018	8-Manik	5
May 12 2018	9-Lamat	6
May 13 2018	10-Muluc	7
May 14 2018	11-Oc	8
May 15 2018	12-Chuen	9
May 16 2018	13-Eb	1
May 17 2018	1-Ben	2
May 18 2018	2-Ix	3
May 19 2018	3-Men	4
May 20 2018	4-Cib	5
May 21 2018	5-Caban	6
May 22 2018	6-Etz'nab	7
May 23 2018	7-Cauac	8
May 24 2018	8-Ahau	9
May 25 2018	9-Imix	1
May 26 2018	10-Ik	2
May 27 2018	11-Akbal	3
May 28 2018	12-Kan	4
May 29 2018	13-Chicchan	5

Date	Day-Sign	L
May 30 2018	1-Cimi	6
May 31 2018	2-Manik	7
Jun 1 2018	3-Lamat	8
Jun 2 2018	4-Muluc	9
Jun 3 2018	5-Oc	1
Jun 4 2018	6-Chuen	2
Jun 5 2018	7-Eb	3
Jun 6 2018	8-Ben	4
Jun 7 2018	9-Ix	5
Jun 8 2018	10-Men	6
Jun 9 2018	11-Cib	7
Jun 10 2018	12-Caban	8
Jun 11 2018	13-Etz'nab	9
Jun 12 2018	1-Cauac	1
Jun 13 2018	2-Ahau	2
Jun 14 2018	3-Imix	3
Jun 15 2018	4-Ik	4
Jun 16 2018	5-Akbal	5
Jun 17 2018	6-Kan	6
Jun 18 2018	7-Chicchan	7
Jun 19 2018	8-Cimi	8
Jun 20 2018	9-Manik	9
Jun 21 2018	10-Lamat	1
Jun 22 2018	11-Muluc	2
Jun 23 2018	12-Oc	3
Jun 24 2018	13-Chuen	4
Jun 25 2018	1-Eb	5
Jun 26 2018	2-Ben	6
Jun 27 2018	3-Ix	7
Jun 28 2018	4-Men	8
Jun 29 2018	5-Cib	9
Jun 30 2018	6-Caban	1
Jul 1 2018	7-Etz'nab	2
Jul 2 2018	8-Cauac	3
Jul 3 2018	9-Ahau	4
Jul 4 2018	10-Imix	5
Jul 5 2018	11-Ik	6
Jul 6 2018	12-Akbal	7
Jul 7 2018	13-Kan	8
Jul 8 2018	1-Chicchan	9
Jul 9 2018	2-Cimi	1
Jul 10 2018	3-Manik	2
Jul 11 2018	4-Lamat	3
Jul 12 2018	5-Muluc	4
Jul 13 2018	6-Oc	5
Jul 14 2018	7-Chuen	6
Jul 15 2018	8-Eb	7
Jul 16 2018	9-Ben	8
Jul 17 2018	10-Ix	9
Jul 18 2018	11-Men	1
Jul 19 2018	12-Cib	2
Jul 20 2018	13-Caban	3
Jul 21 2018	1-Etz'nab	4
Jul 22 2018	2-Cauac	5
Jul 23 2018	3-Ahau	6
Jul 24 2018	4-Imix	7
Jul 25 2018	5-Ik	8
Jul 26 2018	6-Akbal	9
Jul 27 2018	7-Kan	1
Jul 28 2018	8-Chicchan	2
Jul 29 2018	9-Cimi	3
Jul 30 2018	10-Manik	4
Jul 31 2018	11-Lamat	5
Aug 1 2018	12-Muluc	6
Aug 2 2018	13-Oc	7
Aug 3 2018	1-Chuen	8
Aug 4 2018	2-Eb	9
Aug 5 2018	3-Ben	1

Date	Day-Sign	L
Aug 6 2018	4-Ix	2
Aug 7 2018	5-Men	3
Aug 8 2018	6-Cib	4
Aug 9 2018	7-Caban	5
Aug 10 2018	8-Etz'nab	6
Aug 11 2018	9-Cauac	7
Aug 12 2018	10-Ahau	8
Aug 13 2018	11-Imix	9
Aug 14 2018	12-Ik	1
Aug 15 2018	13-Akbal	2
Aug 16 2018	1-Kan	3
Aug 17 2018	2-Chicchan	4
Aug 18 2018	3-Cimi	5
Aug 19 2018	4-Manik	6
Aug 20 2018	5-Lamat	7
Aug 21 2018	6-Muluc	8
Aug 22 2018	7-Oc	9
Aug 23 2018	8-Chuen	1
Aug 24 2018	9-Eb	2
Aug 25 2018	10-Ben	3
Aug 26 2018	11-Ix	4
Aug 27 2018	12-Men	5
Aug 28 2018	13-Cib	6
Aug 29 2018	1-Caban	7
Aug 30 2018	2-Etz'nab	8
Aug 31 2018	3-Cauac	9
Sep 1 2018	4-Ahau	1
Sep 2 2018	5-Imix	2
Sep 3 2018	6-Ik	3
Sep 4 2018	7-Akbal	4
Sep 5 2018	8-Kan	5
Sep 6 2018	9-Chicchan	6
Sep 7 2018	10-Cimi	7
Sep 8 2018	11-Manik	8
Sep 9 2018	12-Lamat	9
Sep 10 2018	13-Muluc	1
Sep 11 2018	1-Oc	2
Sep 12 2018	2-Chuen	3
Sep 13 2018	3-Eb	4
Sep 14 2018	4-Ben	5
Sep 15 2018	5-Ix	6
Sep 16 2018	6-Men	7
Sep 17 2018	7-Cib	8
Sep 18 2018	8-Caban	9
Sep 19 2018	9-Etz'nab	1
Sep 20 2018	10-Cauac	2
Sep 21 2018	11-Ahau	3
Sep 22 2018	12-Imix	4
Sep 23 2018	13-Ik	5
Sep 24 2018	1-Akbal	6
Sep 25 2018	2-Kan	7
Sep 26 2018	3-Chicchan	8
Sep 27 2018	4-Cimi	9
Sep 28 2018	5-Manik	1
Sep 29 2018	6-Lamat	2
Sep 30 2018	7-Muluc	3
Oct 1 2018	8-Oc	4
Oct 2 2018	9-Chuen	5
Oct 3 2018	10-Eb	6
Oct 4 2018	11-Ben	7
Oct 5 2018	12-Ix	8
Oct 6 2018	13-Men	9
Oct 7 2018	1-Cib	1
Oct 8 2018	2-Caban	2
Oct 9 2018	3-Etz'nab	3
Oct 10 2018	4-Cauac	4
Oct 11 2018	5-Ahau	5
Oct 12 2018	6-Imix	6

Date	Day-Sign	L
Oct 13 2018	7-Ik	7
Oct 14 2018	8-Akbal	8
Oct 15 2018	9-Kan	9
Oct 16 2018	10-Chicchan	1
Oct 17 2018	11-Cimi	2
Oct 18 2018	12-Manik	3
Oct 19 2018	13-Lamat	4
Oct 20 2018	**1-Muluc**	5
Oct 21 2018	2-Oc	6
Oct 22 2018	3-Chuen	7
Oct 23 2018	4-Eb	8
Oct 24 2018	5-Ben	9
Oct 25 2018	6-Ix	1
Oct 26 2018	7-Men	2
Oct 27 2018	8-Cib	3
Oct 28 2018	9-Caban	4
Oct 29 2018	10-Etz'nab	5
Oct 30 2018	11-Cauac	6
Oct 31 2018	12-Ahau	7
Nov 1 2018	*13-Imix*	8
Nov 2 2018	**1-Ik**	9
Nov 3 2018	2-Akbal	1
Nov 4 2018	3-Kan	2
Nov 5 2018	4-Chicchan	3
Nov 6 2018	5-Cimi	4
Nov 7 2018	6-Manik	5
Nov 8 2018	7-Lamat	6
Nov 9 2018	8-Muluc	7
Nov 10 2018	9-Oc	8
Nov 11 2018	10-Chuen	9
Nov 12 2018	11-Eb	1
Nov 13 2018	12-Ben	2
Nov 14 2018	13-Ix	3
Nov 15 2018	**1-Men**	4
Nov 16 2018	2-Cib	5
Nov 17 2018	3-Caban	6
Nov 18 2018	4-Etz'nab	7
Nov 19 2018	5-Cauac	8
Nov 20 2018	6-Ahau	9
Nov 21 2018	*7-Imix*	1
Nov 22 2018	8-Ik	2
Nov 23 2018	9-Akbal	3
Nov 24 2018	10-Kan	4
Nov 25 2018	11-Chicchan	5
Nov 26 2018	12-Cimi	6
Nov 27 2018	13-Manik	7
Nov 28 2018	**1-Lamat**	8
Nov 29 2018	2-Muluc	9
Nov 30 2018	3-Oc	1
Dec 1 2018	4-Chuen	2
Dec 2 2018	5-Eb	3
Dec 3 2018	6-Ben	4
Dec 4 2018	7-Ix	5
Dec 5 2018	8-Men	6
Dec 6 2018	9-Cib	7
Dec 7 2018	10-Caban	8
Dec 8 2018	11-Etz'nab	9
Dec 9 2018	12-Cauac	1
Dec 10 2018	13-Ahau	2
Dec 11 2018	**1-Imix**	3
Dec 12 2018	2-Ik	4
Dec 13 2018	3-Akbal	5
Dec 14 2018	4-Kan	6
Dec 15 2018	5-Chicchan	7
Dec 16 2018	6-Cimi	8
Dec 17 2018	7-Manik	9
Dec 18 2018	8-Lamat	1
Dec 19 2018	9-Muluc	2

Date	Day-Sign	L
Dec 20 2018	10-Oc	3
Dec 21 2018	11-Chuen	4
Dec 22 2018	12-Eb	5
Dec 23 2018	13-Ben	6
Dec 24 2018	**1-Ix**	7
Dec 25 2018	2-Men	8
Dec 26 2018	3-Cib	9
Dec 27 2018	4-Caban	1
Dec 28 2018	5-Etz'nab	2
Dec 29 2018	6-Cauac	3
Dec 30 2018	7-Ahau	4
Dec 31 2018	*8-Imix*	5
Jan 1 2019	9-Ik	6
Jan 2 2019	10-Akbal	7
Jan 3 2019	11-Kan	8
Jan 4 2019	12-Chicchan	9
Jan 5 2019	13-Cimi	1
Jan 6 2019	**1-Manik**	2
Jan 7 2019	2-Lamat	3
Jan 8 2019	3-Muluc	4
Jan 9 2019	4-Oc	5
Jan 10 2019	5-Chuen	6
Jan 11 2019	6-Eb	7
Jan 12 2019	7-Ben	8
Jan 13 2019	8-Ix	9
Jan 14 2019	9-Men	1
Jan 15 2019	10-Cib	2
Jan 16 2019	11-Caban	3
Jan 17 2019	12-Etz'nab	4
Jan 18 2019	13-Cauac	5
Jan 19 2019	**1-Ahau**	6
Jan 20 2019	*2-Imix*	7
Jan 21 2019	3-Ik	8
Jan 22 2019	4-Akbal	9
Jan 23 2019	5-Kan	1
Jan 24 2019	6-Chicchan	2
Jan 25 2019	7-Cimi	3
Jan 26 2019	8-Manik	4
Jan 27 2019	9-Lamat	5
Jan 28 2019	10-Muluc	6
Jan 29 2019	11-Oc	7
Jan 30 2019	12-Chuen	8
Jan 31 2019	13-Eb	9
Feb 1 2019	**1-Ben**	1
Feb 2 2019	2-Ix	2
Feb 3 2019	3-Men	3
Feb 4 2019	4-Cib	4
Feb 5 2019	5-Caban	5
Feb 6 2019	6-Etz'nab	6
Feb 7 2019	7-Cauac	7
Feb 8 2019	8-Ahau	8
Feb 9 2019	*9-Imix*	9
Feb 10 2019	10-Ik	1
Feb 11 2019	11-Akbal	2
Feb 12 2019	12-Kan	3
Feb 13 2019	13-Chicchan	4
Feb 14 2019	**1-Cimi**	5
Feb 15 2019	2-Manik	6
Feb 16 2019	3-Lamat	7
Feb 17 2019	4-Muluc	8
Feb 18 2019	5-Oc	9
Feb 19 2019	6-Chuen	1
Feb 20 2019	7-Eb	2
Feb 21 2019	8-Ben	3
Feb 22 2019	9-Ix	4
Feb 23 2019	10-Men	5
Feb 24 2019	11-Cib	6
Feb 25 2019	12-Caban	7

Date	Day-Sign	L
Feb 26 2019	13-Etz'nab	8
Feb 27 2019	**1-Cauac**	9
Feb 28 2019	2-Ahau	1
Mar 1 2019	*3-Imix*	2
Mar 2 2019	4-Ik	3
Mar 3 2019	5-Akbal	4
Mar 4 2019	6-Kan	5
Mar 5 2019	7-Chicchan	6
Mar 6 2019	8-Cimi	7
Mar 7 2019	9-Manik	8
Mar 8 2019	10-Lamat	9
Mar 9 2019	11-Muluc	1
Mar 10 2019	12-Oc	2
Mar 11 2019	13-Chuen	3
Mar 12 2019	**1-Eb**	4
Mar 13 2019	2-Ben	5
Mar 14 2019	3-Ix	6
Mar 15 2019	4-Men	7
Mar 16 2019	5-Cib	8
Mar 17 2019	6-Caban	9
Mar 18 2019	7-Etz'nab	1
Mar 19 2019	8-Cauac	2
Mar 20 2019	9-Ahau	3
Mar 21 2019	*10-Imix*	4
Mar 22 2019	11-Ik	5
Mar 23 2019	12-Akbal	6
Mar 24 2019	13-Kan	7
Mar 25 2019	**1-Chicchan**	8
Mar 26 2019	2-Cimi	9
Mar 27 2019	3-Manik	1
Mar 28 2019	4-Lamat	2
Mar 29 2019	5-Muluc	3
Mar 30 2019	6-Oc	4
Mar 31 2019	7-Chuen	5
Apr 1 2019	8-Eb	6
Apr 2 2019	9-Ben	7
Apr 3 2019	10-Ix	8
Apr 4 2019	11-Men	9
Apr 5 2019	12-Cib	1
Apr 6 2019	13-Caban	2
Apr 7 2019	**1-Etz'nab**	3
Apr 8 2019	2-Cauac	4
Apr 9 2019	3-Ahau	5
Apr 10 2019	*4-Imix*	6
Apr 11 2019	5-Ik	7
Apr 12 2019	6-Akbal	8
Apr 13 2019	7-Kan	9
Apr 14 2019	8-Chicchan	1
Apr 15 2019	9-Cimi	2
Apr 16 2019	10-Manik	3
Apr 17 2019	11-Lamat	4
Apr 18 2019	12-Muluc	5
Apr 19 2019	13-Oc	6
Apr 20 2019	**1-Chuen**	7
Apr 21 2019	2-Eb	8
Apr 22 2019	3-Ben	9
Apr 23 2019	4-Ix	1
Apr 24 2019	5-Men	2
Apr 25 2019	6-Cib	3
Apr 26 2019	7-Caban	4
Apr 27 2019	8-Etz'nab	5
Apr 28 2019	9-Cauac	6
Apr 29 2019	10-Ahau	7
Apr 30 2019	*11-Imix*	8
May 1 2019	12-Ik	9
May 2 2019	13-Akbal	1
May 3 2019	**1-Kan**	2
May 4 2019	2-Chicchan	3

Date	Day-Sign	L	Date	Day-Sign	L	Date	Day-Sign	L
May 5 2019	3-Cimi	4	Jul 12 2019	6-Ix	9	Sep 18 2019	9-Ik	5
May 6 2019	4-Manik	5	Jul 13 2019	7-Men	1	Sep 19 2019	10-Akbal	6
May 7 2019	5-Lamat	6	Jul 14 2019	8-Cib	2	Sep 20 2019	11-Kan	7
May 8 2019	6-Muluc	7	Jul 15 2019	9-Caban	3	Sep 21 2019	12-Chicchan	8
May 9 2019	7-Oc	8	Jul 16 2019	10-Etz'nab	4	Sep 22 2019	13-Cimi	9
May 10 2019	8-Chuen	9	Jul 17 2019	11-Cauac	5	Sep 23 2019	**1-Manik**	1
May 11 2019	9-Eb	1	Jul 18 2019	12-Ahau	6	Sep 24 2019	2-Lamat	2
May 12 2019	10-Ben	2	Jul 19 2019	*13-Imix*	7	Sep 25 2019	3-Muluc	3
May 13 2019	11-Ix	3	Jul 20 2019	**1-Ik**	8	Sep 26 2019	4-Oc	4
May 14 2019	12-Men	4	Jul 21 2019	2-Akbal	9	Sep 27 2019	5-Chuen	5
May 15 2019	13-Cib	5	Jul 22 2019	3-Kan	1	Sep 28 2019	6-Eb	6
May 16 2019	**1-Caban**	6	Jul 23 2019	4-Chicchan	2	Sep 29 2019	7-Ben	7
May 17 2019	2-Etz'nab	7	Jul 24 2019	5-Cimi	3	Sep 30 2019	8-Ix	8
May 18 2019	3-Cauac	8	Jul 25 2019	6-Manik	4	Oct 1 2019	9-Men	9
May 19 2019	4-Ahau	9	Jul 26 2019	7-Lamat	5	Oct 2 2019	10-Cib	1
May 20 2019	*5-Imix*	1	Jul 27 2019	8-Muluc	6	Oct 3 2019	11-Caban	2
May 21 2019	6-Ik	2	Jul 28 2019	9-Oc	7	Oct 4 2019	12-Etz'nab	3
May 22 2019	7-Akbal	3	Jul 29 2019	10-Chuen	8	Oct 5 2019	13-Cauac	4
May 23 2019	8-Kan	4	Jul 30 2019	11-Eb	9	Oct 6 2019	**1-Ahau**	5
May 24 2019	9-Chicchan	5	Jul 31 2019	12-Ben	1	Oct 7 2019	*2-Imix*	6
May 25 2019	10-Cimi	6	Aug 1 2019	13-Ix	2	Oct 8 2019	3-Ik	7
May 26 2019	11-Manik	7	Aug 2 2019	**1-Men**	3	Oct 9 2019	4-Akbal	8
May 27 2019	12-Lamat	8	Aug 3 2019	2-Cib	4	Oct 10 2019	5-Kan	9
May 28 2019	13-Muluc	9	Aug 4 2019	3-Caban	5	Oct 11 2019	6-Chicchan	1
May 29 2019	**1-Oc**	1	Aug 5 2019	4-Etz'nab	6	Oct 12 2019	7-Cimi	2
May 30 2019	2-Chuen	2	Aug 6 2019	5-Cauac	7	Oct 13 2019	8-Manik	3
May 31 2019	3-Eb	3	Aug 7 2019	6-Ahau	8	Oct 14 2019	9-Lamat	4
Jun 1 2019	4-Ben	4	Aug 8 2019	*7-Imix*	9	Oct 15 2019	10-Muluc	5
Jun 2 2019	5-Ix	5	Aug 9 2019	8-Ik	1	Oct 16 2019	11-Oc	6
Jun 3 2019	6-Men	6	Aug 10 2019	9-Akbal	2	Oct 17 2019	12-Chuen	7
Jun 4 2019	7-Cib	7	Aug 11 2019	10-Kan	3	Oct 18 2019	13-Eb	8
Jun 5 2019	8-Caban	8	Aug 12 2019	11-Chicchan	4	Oct 19 2019	**1-Ben**	9
Jun 6 2019	9-Etz'nab	9	Aug 13 2019	12-Cimi	5	Oct 20 2019	2-Ix	1
Jun 7 2019	10-Cauac	1	Aug 14 2019	13-Manik	6	Oct 21 2019	3-Men	2
Jun 8 2019	11-Ahau	2	Aug 15 2019	**1-Lamat**	7	Oct 22 2019	4-Cib	3
Jun 9 2019	*12-Imix*	3	Aug 16 2019	2-Muluc	8	Oct 23 2019	5-Caban	4
Jun 10 2019	13-Ik	4	Aug 17 2019	3-Oc	9	Oct 24 2019	6-Etz'nab	5
Jun 11 2019	**1-Akbal**	5	Aug 18 2019	4-Chuen	1	Oct 25 2019	7-Cauac	6
Jun 12 2019	2-Kan	6	Aug 19 2019	5-Eb	2	Oct 26 2019	8-Ahau	7
Jun 13 2019	3-Chicchan	7	Aug 20 2019	6-Ben	3	Oct 27 2019	*9-Imix*	8
Jun 14 2019	4-Cimi	8	Aug 21 2019	7-Ix	4	Oct 28 2019	10-Ik	9
Jun 15 2019	5-Manik	9	Aug 22 2019	8-Men	5	Oct 29 2019	11-Akbal	1
Jun 16 2019	6-Lamat	1	Aug 23 2019	9-Cib	6	Oct 30 2019	12-Kan	2
Jun 17 2019	7-Muluc	2	Aug 24 2019	10-Caban	7	Oct 31 2019	13-Chicchan	3
Jun 18 2019	8-Oc	3	Aug 25 2019	11-Etz'nab	8	Nov 1 2019	**1-Cimi**	4
Jun 19 2019	9-Chuen	4	Aug 26 2019	12-Cauac	9	Nov 2 2019	2-Manik	5
Jun 20 2019	10-Eb	5	Aug 27 2019	13-Ahau	1	Nov 3 2019	3-Lamat	6
Jun 21 2019	11-Ben	6	Aug 28 2019	**1-Imix**	2	Nov 4 2019	4-Muluc	7
Jun 22 2019	12-Ix	7	Aug 29 2019	2-Ik	3	Nov 5 2019	5-Oc	8
Jun 23 2019	13-Men	8	Aug 30 2019	3-Akbal	4	Nov 6 2019	6-Chuen	9
Jun 24 2019	**1-Cib**	9	Aug 31 2019	4-Kan	5	Nov 7 2019	7-Eb	1
Jun 25 2019	2-Caban	1	Sep 1 2019	5-Chicchan	6	Nov 8 2019	8-Ben	2
Jun 26 2019	3-Etz'nab	2	Sep 2 2019	6-Cimi	7	Nov 9 2019	9-Ix	3
Jun 27 2019	4-Cauac	3	Sep 3 2019	7-Manik	8	Nov 10 2019	10-Men	4
Jun 28 2019	5-Ahau	4	Sep 4 2019	8-Lamat	9	Nov 11 2019	11-Cib	5
Jun 29 2019	*6-Imix*	5	Sep 5 2019	9-Muluc	1	Nov 12 2019	12-Caban	6
Jun 30 2019	7-Ik	6	Sep 6 2019	10-Oc	2	Nov 13 2019	13-Etz'nab	7
Jul 1 2019	8-Akbal	7	Sep 7 2019	11-Chuen	3	Nov 14 2019	**1-Cauac**	8
Jul 2 2019	9-Kan	8	Sep 8 2019	12-Eb	4	Nov 15 2019	2-Ahau	9
Jul 3 2019	10-Chicchan	9	Sep 9 2019	13-Ben	5	Nov 16 2019	*3-Imix*	1
Jul 4 2019	11-Cimi	1	Sep 10 2019	**1-Ix**	6	Nov 17 2019	4-Ik	2
Jul 5 2019	12-Manik	2	Sep 11 2019	2-Men	7	Nov 18 2019	5-Akbal	3
Jul 6 2019	13-Lamat	3	Sep 12 2019	3-Cib	8	Nov 19 2019	6-Kan	4
Jul 7 2019	**1-Muluc**	4	Sep 13 2019	4-Caban	9	Nov 20 2019	7-Chicchan	5
Jul 8 2019	2-Oc	5	Sep 14 2019	5-Etz'nab	1	Nov 21 2019	8-Cimi	6
Jul 9 2019	3-Chuen	6	Sep 15 2019	6-Cauac	2	Nov 22 2019	9-Manik	7
Jul 10 2019	4-Eb	7	Sep 16 2019	7-Ahau	3	Nov 23 2019	10-Lamat	8
Jul 11 2019	5-Ben	8	Sep 17 2019	*8-Imix*	4	Nov 24 2019	11-Muluc	9

Date	Day-Sign	L	Date	Day-Sign	L	Date	Day-Sign	L
Nov 25 2019	12-Oc	1	Feb 1 2020	2-Etz'nab	6	Apr 9 2020	5-Cimi	2
Nov 26 2019	13-Chuen	2	Feb 2 2020	3-Cauac	7	Apr 10 2020	6-Manik	3
Nov 27 2019	**1-Eb**	3	Feb 3 2020	4-Ahau	8	Apr 11 2020	7-Lamat	4
Nov 28 2019	2-Ben	4	Feb 4 2020	*5-Imix*	9	Apr 12 2020	8-Muluc	5
Nov 29 2019	3-Ix	5	Feb 5 2020	6-Ik	1	Apr 13 2020	9-Oc	6
Nov 30 2019	4-Men	6	Feb 6 2020	7-Akbal	2	Apr 14 2020	10-Chuen	7
Dec 1 2019	5-Cib	7	Feb 7 2020	8-Kan	3	Apr 15 2020	11-Eb	8
Dec 2 2019	6-Caban	8	Feb 8 2020	9-Chicchan	4	Apr 16 2020	12-Ben	9
Dec 3 2019	7-Etz'nab	9	Feb 9 2020	10-Cimi	5	Apr 17 2020	13-Ix	1
Dec 4 2019	8-Cauac	1	Feb 10 2020	11-Manik	6	Apr 18 2020	**1-Men**	2
Dec 5 2019	9-Ahau	2	Feb 11 2020	12-Lamat	7	Apr 19 2020	2-Cib	3
Dec 6 2019	*10-Imix*	3	Feb 12 2020	13-Muluc	8	Apr 20 2020	3-Caban	4
Dec 7 2019	11-Ik	4	Feb 13 2020	**1-Oc**	9	Apr 21 2020	4-Etz'nab	5
Dec 8 2019	12-Akbal	5	Feb 14 2020	2-Chuen	1	Apr 22 2020	5-Cauac	6
Dec 9 2019	13-Kan	6	Feb 15 2020	3-Eb	2	Apr 23 2020	6-Ahau	7
Dec 10 2019	**1-Chicchan**	7	Feb 16 2020	4-Ben	3	Apr 24 2020	*7-Imix*	8
Dec 11 2019	2-Cimi	8	Feb 17 2020	5-Ix	4	Apr 25 2020	8-Ik	9
Dec 12 2019	3-Manik	9	Feb 18 2020	6-Men	5	Apr 26 2020	9-Akbal	1
Dec 13 2019	4-Lamat	1	Feb 19 2020	7-Cib	6	Apr 27 2020	10-Kan	2
Dec 14 2019	5-Muluc	2	Feb 20 2020	8-Caban	7	Apr 28 2020	11-Chicchan	3
Dec 15 2019	6-Oc	3	Feb 21 2020	9-Etz'nab	8	Apr 29 2020	12-Cimi	4
Dec 16 2019	7-Chuen	4	Feb 22 2020	10-Cauac	9	Apr 30 2020	13-Manik	5
Dec 17 2019	8-Eb	5	Feb 23 2020	11-Ahau	1	May 1 2020	**1-Lamat**	6
Dec 18 2019	9-Ben	6	Feb 24 2020	*12-Imix*	2	May 2 2020	2-Muluc	7
Dec 19 2019	10-Ix	7	Feb 25 2020	13-Ik	3	May 3 2020	3-Oc	8
Dec 20 2019	11-Men	8	Feb 26 2020	**1-Akbal**	4	May 4 2020	4-Chuen	9
Dec 21 2019	12-Cib	9	Feb 27 2020	2-Kan	5	May 5 2020	5-Eb	1
Dec 22 2019	13-Caban	1	Feb 28 2020	3-Chicchan	6	May 6 2020	6-Ben	2
Dec 23 2019	**1-Etz'nab**	2	Feb 29 2020	4-Cimi	7	May 7 2020	7-Ix	3
Dec 24 2019	2-Cauac	3	Mar 1 2020	5-Manik	8	May 8 2020	8-Men	4
Dec 25 2019	3-Ahau	4	Mar 2 2020	6-Lamat	9	May 9 2020	9-Cib	5
Dec 26 2019	*4-Imix*	5	Mar 3 2020	7-Muluc	1	May 10 2020	10-Caban	6
Dec 27 2019	5-Ik	6	Mar 4 2020	8-Oc	2	May 11 2020	11-Etz'nab	7
Dec 28 2019	6-Akbal	7	Mar 5 2020	9-Chuen	3	May 12 2020	12-Cauac	8
Dec 29 2019	7-Kan	8	Mar 6 2020	10-Eb	4	May 13 2020	13-Ahau	9
Dec 30 2019	8-Chicchan	9	Mar 7 2020	11-Ben	5	May 14 2020	**1-Imix**	1
Dec 31 2019	9-Cimi	1	Mar 8 2020	12-Ix	6	May 15 2020	2-Ik	2
Jan 1 2020	10-Manik	2	Mar 9 2020	13-Men	7	May 16 2020	3-Akbal	3
Jan 2 2020	11-Lamat	3	Mar 10 2020	**1-Cib**	8	May 17 2020	4-Kan	4
Jan 3 2020	12-Muluc	4	Mar 11 2020	2-Caban	9	May 18 2020	5-Chicchan	5
Jan 4 2020	13-Oc	5	Mar 12 2020	3-Etz'nab	1	May 19 2020	6-Cimi	6
Jan 5 2020	**1-Chuen**	6	Mar 13 2020	4-Cauac	2	May 20 2020	7-Manik	7
Jan 6 2020	2-Eb	7	Mar 14 2020	5-Ahau	3	May 21 2020	8-Lamat	8
Jan 7 2020	3-Ben	8	Mar 15 2020	*6-Imix*	4	May 22 2020	9-Muluc	9
Jan 8 2020	4-Ix	9	Mar 16 2020	7-Ik	5	May 23 2020	10-Oc	1
Jan 9 2020	5-Men	1	Mar 17 2020	8-Akbal	6	May 24 2020	11-Chuen	2
Jan 10 2020	6-Cib	2	Mar 18 2020	9-Kan	7	May 25 2020	12-Eb	3
Jan 11 2020	7-Caban	3	Mar 19 2020	10-Chicchan	8	May 26 2020	13-Ben	4
Jan 12 2020	8-Etz'nab	4	Mar 20 2020	11-Cimi	9	May 27 2020	**1-Ix**	5
Jan 13 2020	9-Cauac	5	Mar 21 2020	12-Manik	1	May 28 2020	2-Men	6
Jan 14 2020	10-Ahau	6	Mar 22 2020	13-Lamat	2	May 29 2020	3-Cib	7
Jan 15 2020	*11-Imix*	7	Mar 23 2020	**1-Muluc**	3	May 30 2020	4-Caban	8
Jan 16 2020	12-Ik	8	Mar 24 2020	2-Oc	4	May 31 2020	5-Etz'nab	9
Jan 17 2020	13-Akbal	9	Mar 25 2020	3-Chuen	5	Jun 1 2020	6-Cauac	1
Jan 18 2020	**1-Kan**	1	Mar 26 2020	4-Eb	6	Jun 2 2020	7-Ahau	2
Jan 19 2020	2-Chicchan	2	Mar 27 2020	5-Ben	7	Jun 3 2020	*8-Imix*	3
Jan 20 2020	3-Cimi	3	Mar 28 2020	6-Ix	8	Jun 4 2020	9-Ik	4
Jan 21 2020	4-Manik	4	Mar 29 2020	7-Men	9	Jun 5 2020	10-Akbal	5
Jan 22 2020	5-Lamat	5	Mar 30 2020	8-Cib	1	Jun 6 2020	11-Kan	6
Jan 23 2020	6-Muluc	6	Mar 31 2020	9-Caban	2	Jun 7 2020	12-Chicchan	7
Jan 24 2020	7-Oc	7	Apr 1 2020	10-Etz'nab	3	Jun 8 2020	13-Cimi	8
Jan 25 2020	8-Chuen	8	Apr 2 2020	11-Cauac	4	Jun 9 2020	**1-Manik**	9
Jan 26 2020	9-Eb	9	Apr 3 2020	12-Ahau	5	Jun 10 2020	2-Lamat	1
Jan 27 2020	10-Ben	1	Apr 4 2020	*13-Imix*	6	Jun 11 2020	3-Muluc	2
Jan 28 2020	11-Ix	2	Apr 5 2020	**1-Ik**	7	Jun 12 2020	4-Oc	3
Jan 29 2020	12-Men	3	Apr 6 2020	2-Akbal	8	Jun 13 2020	5-Chuen	4
Jan 30 2020	13-Cib	4	Apr 7 2020	3-Kan	9	Jun 14 2020	6-Eb	5
Jan 31 2020	**1-Caban**	5	Apr 8 2020	4-Chicchan	1	Jun 15 2020	7-Ben	6

Date	Day-Sign	L	Date	Day-Sign	L	Date	Day-Sign	L
Jun 16 2020	8-Ix	7	Aug 23 2020	11-Ik	3	Oct 30 2020	**1-Oc**	8
Jun 17 2020	9-Men	8	Aug 24 2020	12-Akbal	4	Oct 31 2020	2-Chuen	9
Jun 18 2020	10-Cib	9	Aug 25 2020	13-Kan	5	Nov 1 2020	3-Eb	1
Jun 19 2020	11-Caban	1	Aug 26 2020	**1-Chicchan**	6	Nov 2 2020	4-Ben	2
Jun 20 2020	12-Etz'nab	2	Aug 27 2020	2-Cimi	7	Nov 3 2020	5-Ix	3
Jun 21 2020	13-Cauac	3	Aug 28 2020	3-Manik	8	Nov 4 2020	6-Men	4
Jun 22 2020	**1-Ahau**	4	Aug 29 2020	4-Lamat	9	Nov 5 2020	7-Cib	5
Jun 23 2020	2-*Imix*	5	Aug 30 2020	5-Muluc	1	Nov 6 2020	8-Caban	6
Jun 24 2020	3-Ik	6	Aug 31 2020	6-Oc	2	Nov 7 2020	9-Etz'nab	7
Jun 25 2020	4-Akbal	7	Sep 1 2020	7-Chuen	3	Nov 8 2020	10-Cauac	8
Jun 26 2020	5-Kan	8	Sep 2 2020	8-Eb	4	Nov 9 2020	11-Ahau	9
Jun 27 2020	6-Chicchan	9	Sep 3 2020	9-Ben	5	Nov 10 2020	12-*Imix*	1
Jun 28 2020	7-Cimi	1	Sep 4 2020	10-Ix	6	Nov 11 2020	13-Ik	2
Jun 29 2020	8-Manik	2	Sep 5 2020	11-Men	7	Nov 12 2020	**1-Akbal**	3
Jun 30 2020	9-Lamat	3	Sep 6 2020	12-Cib	8	Nov 13 2020	2-Kan	4
Jul 1 2020	10-Muluc	4	Sep 7 2020	13-Caban	9	Nov 14 2020	3-Chicchan	5
Jul 2 2020	11-Oc	5	Sep 8 2020	**1-Etz'nab**	1	Nov 15 2020	4-Cimi	6
Jul 3 2020	12-Chuen	6	Sep 9 2020	2-Cauac	2	Nov 16 2020	5-Manik	7
Jul 4 2020	13-Eb	7	Sep 10 2020	3-Ahau	3	Nov 17 2020	6-Lamat	8
Jul 5 2020	**1-Ben**	8	Sep 11 2020	4-*Imix*	4	Nov 18 2020	7-Muluc	9
Jul 6 2020	2-Ix	9	Sep 12 2020	5-Ik	5	Nov 19 2020	8-Oc	1
Jul 7 2020	3-Men	1	Sep 13 2020	6-Akbal	6	Nov 20 2020	9-Chuen	2
Jul 8 2020	4-Cib	2	Sep 14 2020	7-Kan	7	Nov 21 2020	10-Eb	3
Jul 9 2020	5-Caban	3	Sep 15 2020	8-Chicchan	8	Nov 22 2020	11-Ben	4
Jul 10 2020	6-Etz'nab	4	Sep 16 2020	9-Cimi	9	Nov 23 2020	12-Ix	5
Jul 11 2020	7-Cauac	5	Sep 17 2020	10-Manik	1	Nov 24 2020	13-Men	6
Jul 12 2020	8-Ahau	6	Sep 18 2020	11-Lamat	2	Nov 25 2020	**1-Cib**	7
Jul 13 2020	9-*Imix*	7	Sep 19 2020	12-Muluc	3	Nov 26 2020	2-Caban	8
Jul 14 2020	10-Ik	8	Sep 20 2020	13-Oc	4	Nov 27 2020	3-Etz'nab	9
Jul 15 2020	11-Akbal	9	Sep 21 2020	**1-Chuen**	5	Nov 28 2020	4-Cauac	1
Jul 16 2020	12-Kan	1	Sep 22 2020	2-Eb	6	Nov 29 2020	5-Ahau	2
Jul 17 2020	13-Chicchan	2	Sep 23 2020	3-Ben	7	Nov 30 2020	6-*Imix*	3
Jul 18 2020	**1-Cimi**	3	Sep 24 2020	4-Ix	8	Dec 1 2020	7-Ik	4
Jul 19 2020	2-Manik	4	Sep 25 2020	5-Men	9	Dec 2 2020	8-Akbal	5
Jul 20 2020	3-Lamat	5	Sep 26 2020	6-Cib	1	Dec 3 2020	9-Kan	6
Jul 21 2020	4-Muluc	6	Sep 27 2020	7-Caban	2	Dec 4 2020	10-Chicchan	7
Jul 22 2020	5-Oc	7	Sep 28 2020	8-Etz'nab	3	Dec 5 2020	11-Cimi	8
Jul 23 2020	6-Chuen	8	Sep 29 2020	9-Cauac	4	Dec 6 2020	12-Manik	9
Jul 24 2020	7-Eb	9	Sep 30 2020	10-Ahau	5	Dec 7 2020	13-Lamat	1
Jul 25 2020	8-Ben	1	Oct 1 2020	11-*Imix*	6	Dec 8 2020	**1-Muluc**	2
Jul 26 2020	9-Ix	2	Oct 2 2020	12-Ik	7	Dec 9 2020	2-Oc	3
Jul 27 2020	10-Men	3	Oct 3 2020	13-Akbal	8	Dec 10 2020	3-Chuen	4
Jul 28 2020	11-Cib	4	Oct 4 2020	**1-Kan**	9	Dec 11 2020	4-Eb	5
Jul 29 2020	12-Caban	5	Oct 5 2020	2-Chicchan	1	Dec 12 2020	5-Ben	6
Jul 30 2020	13-Etz'nab	6	Oct 6 2020	3-Cimi	2	Dec 13 2020	6-Ix	7
Jul 31 2020	**1-Cauac**	7	Oct 7 2020	4-Manik	3	Dec 14 2020	7-Men	8
Aug 1 2020	2-Ahau	8	Oct 8 2020	5-Lamat	4	Dec 15 2020	8-Cib	9
Aug 2 2020	3-*Imix*	9	Oct 9 2020	6-Muluc	5	Dec 16 2020	9-Caban	1
Aug 3 2020	4-Ik	1	Oct 10 2020	7-Oc	6	Dec 17 2020	10-Etz'nab	2
Aug 4 2020	5-Akbal	2	Oct 11 2020	8-Chuen	7	Dec 18 2020	11-Cauac	3
Aug 5 2020	6-Kan	3	Oct 12 2020	9-Eb	8	Dec 19 2020	12-Ahau	4
Aug 6 2020	7-Chicchan	4	Oct 13 2020	10-Ben	9	Dec 20 2020	13-*Imix*	5
Aug 7 2020	8-Cimi	5	Oct 14 2020	11-Ix	1	Dec 21 2020	**1-Ik**	6
Aug 8 2020	9-Manik	6	Oct 15 2020	12-Men	2	Dec 22 2020	2-Akbal	7
Aug 9 2020	10-Lamat	7	Oct 16 2020	13-Cib	3	Dec 23 2020	3-Kan	8
Aug 10 2020	11-Muluc	8	Oct 17 2020	**1-Caban**	4	Dec 24 2020	4-Chicchan	9
Aug 11 2020	12-Oc	9	Oct 18 2020	2-Etz'nab	5	Dec 25 2020	5-Cimi	1
Aug 12 2020	13-Chuen	1	Oct 19 2020	3-Cauac	6	Dec 26 2020	6-Manik	2
Aug 13 2020	**1-Eb**	2	Oct 20 2020	4-Ahau	7	Dec 27 2020	7-Lamat	3
Aug 14 2020	2-Ben	3	Oct 21 2020	5-*Imix*	8	Dec 28 2020	8-Muluc	4
Aug 15 2020	3-Ix	4	Oct 22 2020	6-Ik	9	Dec 29 2020	9-Oc	5
Aug 16 2020	4-Men	5	Oct 23 2020	7-Akbal	1	Dec 30 2020	10-Chuen	6
Aug 17 2020	5-Cib	6	Oct 24 2020	8-Kan	2	Dec 31 2020	11-Eb	7
Aug 18 2020	6-Caban	7	Oct 25 2020	9-Chicchan	3			
Aug 19 2020	7-Etz'nab	8	Oct 26 2020	10-Cimi	4			
Aug 20 2020	8-Cauac	9	Oct 27 2020	11-Manik	5			
Aug 21 2020	9-Ahau	1	Oct 28 2020	12-Lamat	6			
Aug 22 2020	10-*Imix*	2	Oct 29 2020	13-Muluc	7			

TABLE TWO

MAYAN NEW YEAR DATES

Date	Year	Year Bearer
Apr 26 1919	12-South	Eb
Apr 25 1920	13-East	Caban
Apr 25 1921	1-North	Ik
Apr 25 1922	2-West	Manik
Apr 25 1923	3-South	Eb
Apr 24 1924	4-East	Caban
Apr 24 1925	5-North	Ik
Apr 24 1926	6-West	Manik
Apr 24 1927	7-South	Eb
Apr 23 1928	8-East	Caban
Apr 23 1929	9-North	Ik
Apr 23 1930	10-West	Manik
Apr 23 1931	11-South	Eb
Apr 22 1932	12-East	Caban
Apr 22 1933	13-North	Ik
Apr 22 1934	1-West	Manik
Apr 22 1935	2-South	Eb
Apr 21 1936	3-East	Caban
Apr 21 1937	4-North	Ik
Apr 21 1938	5-West	Manik
Apr 21 1939	6-South	Eb
Apr 20 1940	7-East	Caban
Apr 20 1941	8-North	Ik
Apr 20 1942	9-West	Manik
Apr 20 1943	10-South	Eb
Apr 19 1944	11-East	Caban
Apr 19 1945	12-North	Ik
Apr 19 1946	13-West	Manik
Apr 19 1947	1-South	Eb
Apr 18 1948	2-East	Caban
Apr 18 1949	3-North	Ik
Apr 18 1950	4-West	Manik
Apr 18 1951	5-South	Eb
Apr 17 1952	6-East	Caban
Apr 17 1953	7-North	Ik
Apr 17 1954	8-West	Manik
Apr 17 1955	9-South	Eb
Apr 16 1956	10-East	Caban
Apr 16 1957	11-North	Ik
Apr 16 1958	12-West	Manik
Apr 16 1959	13-South	Eb
Apr 15 1960	1-East	Caban
Apr 15 1961	2-North	Ik
Apr 15 1962	3-West	Manik
Apr 15 1963	4-South	Eb
Apr 14 1964	5-East	Caban
Apr 14 1965	6-North	Ik
Apr 14 1966	7-West	Manik
Apr 14 1967	8-South	Eb
Apr 13 1968	9-East	Caban
Apr 13 1969	10-North	Ik

Date	Year	Year Bearer
Apr 13 1970	11-West	Manik
Apr 13 1971	12-South	Eb
Apr 12 1972	13-East	Caban
Apr 12 1973	1-North	Ik
Apr 12 1974	2-West	Manik
Apr 12 1975	3-South	Eb
Apr 11 1976	4-East	Caban
Apr 11 1977	5-North	Ik
Apr 11 1978	6-West	Manik
Apr 11 1979	7-South	Eb
Apr 10 1980	8-East	Caban
Apr 10 1981	9-North	Ik
Apr 10 1982	10-West	Manik
Apr 10 1983	11-South	Eb
Apr 9 1984	12-East	Caban
Apr 9 1985	13-North	Ik
Apr 9 1986	1-West	Manik
Apr 9 1987	2-South	Eb
Apr 8 1988	3-East	Caban
Apr 8 1989	4-North	Ik
Apr 8 1990	5-West	Manik
Apr 8 1991	6-South	Eb
Apr 7 1992	7-East	Caban
Apr 7 1993	8-North	Ik
Apr 7 1994	9-West	Manik
Apr 7 1995	10-South	Eb
Apr 6 1996	11-East	Caban
Apr 6 1997	12-North	Ik
Apr 6 1998	13-West	Manik
Apr 6 1999	1-South	Eb
Apr 5 2000	2-East	Caban
Apr 5 2001	3-North	Ik
Apr 5 2002	4-West	Manik
Apr 5 2003	5-South	Eb
Apr 4 2004	6-East	Caban
Apr 4 2005	7-North	Ik
Apr 4 2006	8-West	Manik
Apr 4 2007	9-South	Eb
Apr 3 2008	10-East	Caban
Apr 3 2009	11-North	Ik
Apr 3 2010	12-West	Manik
Apr 3 2011	13-South	Eb
Apr 2 2012	1-East	Caban
Apr 2 2013	2-North	Ik
Apr 2 2014	3-West	Manik
Apr 2 2015	4-South	Eb
Apr 1 2016	5-East	Caban
Apr 1 2017	6-North	Ik
Apr 1 2018	7-West	Manik
Apr 1 2019	8-South	Eb
Mar 31 2020	9-East	Caban

TABLE THREE
PHASES OF VENUS

Date	Phase	Phenomena
Thu Jan 1 1920	Morning Star	
Tue May 11 1920	Superior	
Sat Jul 3 1920		Superior Conjunction
Mon Aug 9 1920	Evening Star	
Wed Feb 9 1921		Max. Eastern Elongation
Fri Apr 1 1921		Stationary Retrograde
Tue Apr 19 1921	Inferior	
Fri Apr 22 1921		Inferior Conjunction
Wed Apr 27 1921	Morning Star	
Fri May 13 1921		Stationary Direct
Fri Jul 1 1921		Max. Western Elongation
Mon Dec 19 1921	Superior	
Thu Feb 9 1922		Superior Conjunction
Sun Mar 19 1922	Evening Star	
Fri Sep 15 1922		Max. Eastern Elongation
Sat Nov 4 1922		Stationary Retrograde
Wed Nov 22 1922	Inferior	
Sat Nov 25 1922		Inferior Conjunction
Thu Nov 30 1922	Morning Star	
Fri Dec 15 1922		Stationary Direct
Sun Feb 4 1923		Max. Western Elongation
Tue Jul 24 1923	Superior	
Mon Sep 10 1923		Superior Conjunction
Mon Oct 22 1923	Evening Star	
Mon Apr 21 1924		Max. Eastern Elongation
Tue Jun 10 1924		Stationary Retrograde
Sat Jun 28 1924	Inferior	
Tue Jul 1 1924		Inferior Conjunction
Sun Jul 6 1924	Morning Star	
Wed Jul 23 1924		Stationary Direct
Wed Sep 10 1924		Max. Western Elongation
Fri Feb 27 1925	Superior	
Fri Apr 24 1925		Superior Conjunction
Thu May 28 1925	Evening Star	
Sat Nov 28 1925		Max. Eastern Elongation
Sun Jan 17 1926		Stationary Retrograde
Thu Feb 4 1926	Inferior	
Sun Feb 7 1926		Inferior Conjunction
Fri Feb 12 1926	Morning Star	
Sun Feb 28 1926		Stationary Direct
Sun Apr 18 1926		Max. Western Elongation
Wed Oct 6 1926	Superior	
Sun Nov 21 1926		Superior Conjunction
Tue Jan 4 1927	Evening Star	
Sun Jul 3 1927		Max. Eastern Elongation
Sat Aug 20 1927		Stationary Retrograde
Wed Sep 7 1927	Inferior	
Sat Sep 10 1927		Inferior Conjunction
Thu Sep 15 1927	Morning Star	
Sun Oct 2 1927		Stationary Direct

Date	Phase	Phenomena
Mon Nov 21 1927		Max. Western Elongation
Tue May 8 1928	Superior	
Sun Jul 1 1928		Superior Conjunction
Mon Aug 6 1928	Evening Star	
Thu Feb 7 1929		Max. Eastern Elongation
Sat Mar 30 1929		Stationary Retrograde
Wed Apr 17 1929	Inferior	
Sat Apr 20 1929		Inferior Conjunction
Thu Apr 25 1929	Morning Star	
Sat May 11 1929		Stationary Direct
Sat Jun 29 1929		Max. Western Elongation
Tue Dec 17 1929	Superior	
Thu Feb 6 1930		Superior Conjunction
Mon Mar 17 1930	Evening Star	
Fri Sep 12 1930		Max. Eastern Elongation
Sun Nov 2 1930		Stationary Retrograde
Wed Nov 19 1930	Inferior	
Sat Nov 22 1930		Inferior Conjunction
Thu Nov 27 1930	Morning Star	
Sat Dec 13 1930		Stationary Direct
Mon Feb 2 1931		Max. Western Elongation
Tue Jul 21 1931	Superior	
Tue Sep 8 1931		Superior Conjunction
Mon Oct 19 1931	Evening Star	
Tue Apr 19 1932		Max. Eastern Elongation
Tue Jun 7 1932		Stationary Retrograde
Sun Jun 26 1932	Inferior	
Wed Jun 29 1932		Inferior Conjunction
Mon Jul 4 1932	Morning Star	
Wed Jul 20 1932		Stationary Direct
Thu Sep 8 1932		Max. Western Elongation
Sat Feb 25 1933	Superior	
Fri Apr 21 1933		Superior Conjunction
Fri May 26 1933	Evening Star	
Sat Nov 25 1933		Max. Eastern Elongation
Mon Jan 15 1934		Stationary Retrograde
Fri Feb 2 1934	Inferior	
Mon Feb 5 1934		Inferior Conjunction
Sat Feb 10 1934	Morning Star	
Sun Feb 25 1934		Stationary Direct
Mon Apr 16 1934		Max. Western Elongation
Thu Oct 4 1934	Superior	
Sun Nov 18 1934		Superior Conjunction
Wed Jan 2 1935	Evening Star	
Sun Jun 30 1935		Max. Eastern Elongation
Sun Aug 18 1935		Stationary Retrograde
Thu Sep 5 1935	Inferior	
Sun Sep 8 1935		Inferior Conjunction
Fri Sep 13 1935	Morning Star	
Sun Sep 29 1935		Stationary Direct
Mon Nov 18 1935		Max. Western Elongation
Wed May 6 1936	Superior	
Mon Jun 29 1936		Superior Conjunction
Tue Aug 4 1936	Evening Star	
Fri Feb 5 1937		Max. Eastern Elongation

Date	Phase	Phenomena
Sat Mar 27 1937		Stationary Retrograde
Thu Apr 15 1937	Inferior	
Sun Apr 18 1937		Inferior Conjunction
Fri Apr 23 1937	Morning Star	
Sun May 9 1937		Stationary Direct
Sun Jun 27 1937		Max. Western Elongation
Wed Dec 15 1937	Superior	
Fri Feb 4 1938		Superior Conjunction
Tue Mar 15 1938	Evening Star	
Sat Sep 10 1938		Max. Eastern Elongation
Sun Oct 30 1938		Stationary Retrograde
Thu Nov 17 1938	Inferior	
Sun Nov 20 1938		Inferior Conjunction
Fri Nov 25 1938	Morning Star	
Sat Dec 10 1938		Stationary Direct
Mon Jan 30 1939		Max. Western Elongation
Wed Jul 19 1939	Superior	
Tue Sep 5 1939		Superior Conjunction
Tue Oct 17 1939	Evening Star	
Wed Apr 17 1940		Max. Eastern Elongation
Wed Jun 5 1940		Stationary Retrograde
Sun Jun 23 1940	Inferior	
Wed Jun 26 1940		Inferior Conjunction
Mon Jul 1 1940	Morning Star	
Thu Jul 18 1940		Stationary Direct
Fri Sep 6 1940		Max. Western Elongation
Sat Feb 22 1941	Superior	
Sat Apr 19 1941		Superior Conjunction
Fri May 23 1941	Evening Star	
Sun Nov 23 1941		Max. Eastern Elongation
Tue Jan 13 1942		Stationary Retrograde
Fri Jan 30 1942	Inferior	
Mon Feb 2 1942		Inferior Conjunction
Sat Feb 7 1942	Morning Star	
Mon Feb 23 1942		Stationary Direct
Tue Apr 14 1942		Max. Western Elongation
Thu Oct 1 1942	Superior	
Mon Nov 16 1942		Superior Conjunction
Wed Dec 30 1942	Evening Star	
Mon Jun 28 1943		Max. Eastern Elongation
Sun Aug 15 1943		Stationary Retrograde
Thu Sep 2 1943	Inferior	
Sun Sep 5 1943		Inferior Conjunction
Fri Sep 10 1943	Morning Star	
Mon Sep 27 1943		Stationary Direct
Tue Nov 16 1943		Max. Western Elongation
Wed May 3 1944	Superior	
Tue Jun 27 1944		Superior Conjunction
Tue Aug 1 1944	Evening Star	
Fri Feb 2 1945		Max. Eastern Elongation
Sun Mar 25 1945		Stationary Retrograde
Thu Apr 12 1945	Inferior	
Sun Apr 15 1945		Inferior Conjunction
Fri Apr 20 1945	Morning Star	
Sun May 6 1945		Stationary Direct

Date	Phase	Phenomena
Sun Jun 24 1945		Max. Western Elongation
Wed Dec 12 1945	Superior	
Fri Feb 1 1946		Superior Conjunction
Tue Mar 12 1946	Evening Star	
Sun Sep 8 1946		Max. Eastern Elongation
Mon Oct 28 1946		Stationary Retrograde
Thu Nov 14 1946	Inferior	
Sun Nov 17 1946		Inferior Conjunction
Fri Nov 22 1946	Morning Star	
Sun Dec 8 1946		Stationary Direct
Tue Jan 28 1947		Max. Western Elongation
Wed Jul 16 1947	Superior	
Wed Sep 3 1947		Superior Conjunction
Tue Oct 14 1947	Evening Star	
Wed Apr 14 1948		Max. Eastern Elongation
Thu Jun 3 1948		Stationary Retrograde
Mon Jun 21 1948	Inferior	
Thu Jun 24 1948		Inferior Conjunction
Tue Jun 29 1948	Morning Star	
Fri Jul 16 1948		Stationary Direct
Fri Sep 3 1948		Max. Western Elongation
Sun Feb 20 1949	Superior	
Sat Apr 16 1949		Superior Conjunction
Sat May 21 1949	Evening Star	
Sun Nov 20 1949		Max. Eastern Elongation
Tue Jan 10 1950		Stationary Retrograde
Sat Jan 28 1950	Inferior	
Tue Jan 31 1950		Inferior Conjunction
Sun Feb 5 1950	Morning Star	
Mon Feb 20 1950		Stationary Direct
Tue Apr 11 1950		Max. Western Elongation
Fri Sep 29 1950	Superior	
Mon Nov 13 1950		Superior Conjunction
Thu Dec 28 1950	Evening Star	
Mon Jun 25 1951		Max. Eastern Elongation
Mon Aug 13 1951		Stationary Retrograde
Fri Aug 31 1951	Inferior	
Mon Sep 3 1951		Inferior Conjunction
Sat Sep 8 1951	Morning Star	
Tue Sep 25 1951		Stationary Direct
Wed Nov 14 1951		Max. Western Elongation
Thu May 1 1952	Superior	
Tue Jun 24 1952		Superior Conjunction
Wed Jul 30 1952	Evening Star	
Sat Jan 31 1953		Max. Eastern Elongation
Mon Mar 23 1953		Stationary Retrograde
Fri Apr 10 1953	Inferior	
Mon Apr 13 1953		Inferior Conjunction
Sat Apr 18 1953	Morning Star	
Mon May 4 1953		Stationary Direct
Mon Jun 22 1953		Max. Western Elongation
Thu Dec 10 1953	Superior	
Fri Jan 29 1954		Superior Conjunction
Wed Mar 10 1954	Evening Star	
Sun Sep 5 1954		Max. Eastern Elongation

Date	Phase	Phenomena
Mon Oct 25 1954		Stationary Retrograde
Fri Nov 12 1954	Inferior	
Mon Nov 15 1954		Inferior Conjunction
Sat Nov 20 1954	Morning Star	
Sun Dec 5 1954		Stationary Direct
Tue Jan 25 1955		Max. Western Elongation
Thu Jul 14 1955	Superior	
Thu Sep 1 1955		Superior Conjunction
Wed Oct 12 1955	Evening Star	
Thu Apr 12 1956		Max. Eastern Elongation
Thu May 31 1956		Stationary Retrograde
Tue Jun 19 1956	Inferior	
Fri Jun 22 1956		Inferior Conjunction
Wed Jun 27 1956	Morning Star	
Fri Jul 13 1956		Stationary Direct
Sat Sep 1 1956		Max. Western Elongation
Mon Feb 18 1957	Superior	
Sun Apr 14 1957		Superior Conjunction
Sun May 19 1957	Evening Star	
Mon Nov 18 1957		Max. Eastern Elongation
Wed Jan 8 1958		Stationary Retrograde
Sat Jan 25 1958	Inferior	
Tue Jan 28 1958		Inferior Conjunction
Sun Feb 2 1958	Morning Star	
Tue Feb 18 1958		Stationary Direct
Wed Apr 9 1958		Max. Western Elongation
Fri Sep 26 1958	Superior	
Tue Nov 11 1958		Superior Conjunction
Thu Dec 25 1958	Evening Star	
Tue Jun 23 1959		Max. Eastern Elongation
Mon Aug 10 1959		Stationary Retrograde
Sat Aug 29 1959	Inferior	
Tue Sep 1 1959		Inferior Conjunction
Sun Sep 6 1959	Morning Star	
Tue Sep 22 1959		Stationary Direct
Wed Nov 11 1959		Max. Western Elongation
Fri Apr 29 1960	Superior	
Wed Jun 22 1960		Superior Conjunction
Thu Jul 28 1960	Evening Star	
Sun Jan 29 1961		Max. Eastern Elongation
Mon Mar 20 1961		Stationary Retrograde
Fri Apr 7 1961	Inferior	
Mon Apr 10 1961		Inferior Conjunction
Sat Apr 15 1961	Morning Star	
Tue May 2 1961		Stationary Direct
Mon Jun 19 1961		Max. Western Elongation
Thu Dec 7 1961	Superior	
Sat Jan 27 1962		Superior Conjunction
Wed Mar 7 1962	Evening Star	
Mon Sep 3 1962		Max. Eastern Elongation
Tue Oct 23 1962		Stationary Retrograde
Fri Nov 9 1962	Inferior	
Mon Nov 12 1962		Inferior Conjunction
Sat Nov 17 1962	Morning Star	
Mon Dec 3 1962		Stationary Direct

Date	Phase	Phenomena
Wed Jan 23 1963		Max. Western Elongation
Thu Jul 11 1963	Superior	
Fri Aug 30 1963		Superior Conjunction
Wed Oct 9 1963	Evening Star	
Thu Apr 9 1964		Max. Eastern Elongation
Fri May 29 1964		Stationary Retrograde
Tue Jun 16 1964	Inferior	
Fri Jun 19 1964		Inferior Conjunction
Wed Jun 24 1964	Morning Star	
Sat Jul 11 1964		Stationary Direct
Sun Aug 30 1964		Max. Western Elongation
Mon Feb 15 1965	Superior	
Mon Apr 12 1965		Superior Conjunction
Sun May 16 1965	Evening Star	
Mon Nov 15 1965		Max. Eastern Elongation
Wed Jan 5 1966		Stationary Retrograde
Sun Jan 23 1966	Inferior	
Wed Jan 26 1966		Inferior Conjunction
Mon Jan 31 1966	Morning Star	
Tue Feb 15 1966		Stationary Direct
Wed Apr 6 1966		Max. Western Elongation
Sat Sep 24 1966	Superior	
Tue Nov 8 1966		Superior Conjunction
Fri Dec 23 1966	Evening Star	
Wed Jun 21 1967		Max. Eastern Elongation
Tue Aug 8 1967		Stationary Retrograde
Sat Aug 26 1967	Inferior	
Tue Aug 29 1967		Inferior Conjunction
Sun Sep 3 1967	Morning Star	
Wed Sep 20 1967		Stationary Direct
Thu Nov 9 1967		Max. Western Elongation
Fri Apr 26 1968	Superior	
Thu Jun 20 1968		Superior Conjunction
Thu Jul 25 1968	Evening Star	
Sun Jan 26 1969		Max. Eastern Elongation
Tue Mar 18 1969		Stationary Retrograde
Sat Apr 5 1969	Inferior	
Tue Apr 8 1969		Inferior Conjunction
Sun Apr 13 1969	Morning Star	
Tue Apr 29 1969		Stationary Direct
Tue Jun 17 1969		Max. Western Elongation
Fri Dec 5 1969	Superior	
Sat Jan 24 1970		Superior Conjunction
Thu Mar 5 1970	Evening Star	
Mon Aug 31 1970		Max. Eastern Elongation
Tue Oct 20 1970		Stationary Retrograde
Sat Nov 7 1970	Inferior	
Tue Nov 10 1970		Inferior Conjunction
Sun Nov 15 1970	Morning Star	
Tue Dec 1 1970		Stationary Direct
Thu Jan 21 1971		Max. Western Elongation
Fri Jul 9 1971	Superior	
Fri Aug 27 1971		Superior Conjunction
Thu Oct 7 1971	Evening Star	
Fri Apr 7 1972		Max. Eastern Elongation

Date	Phase	Phenomena
Sat May 27 1972		Stationary Retrograde
Wed Jun 14 1972	Inferior	
Sat Jun 17 1972		Inferior Conjunction
Thu Jun 22 1972	Morning Star	
Sun Jul 9 1972		Stationary Direct
Sun Aug 27 1972		Max. Western Elongation
Tue Feb 13 1973	Superior	
Mon Apr 9 1973		Superior Conjunction
Mon May 14 1973	Evening Star	
Tue Nov 13 1973		Max. Eastern Elongation
Thu Jan 3 1974		Stationary Retrograde
Sun Jan 20 1974	Inferior	
Wed Jan 23 1974		Inferior Conjunction
Mon Jan 28 1974	Morning Star	
Wed Feb 13 1974		Stationary Direct
Thu Apr 4 1974		Max. Western Elongation
Sat Sep 21 1974	Superior	
Wed Nov 6 1974		Superior Conjunction
Fri Dec 20 1974	Evening Star	
Wed Jun 18 1975		Max. Eastern Elongation
Wed Aug 6 1975		Stationary Retrograde
Sun Aug 24 1975	Inferior	
Wed Aug 27 1975		Inferior Conjunction
Mon Sep 1 1975	Morning Star	
Thu Sep 18 1975		Stationary Direct
Fri Nov 7 1975		Max. Western Elongation
Sat Apr 24 1976	Superior	
Fri Jun 18 1976		Superior Conjunction
Fri Jul 23 1976	Evening Star	
Mon Jan 24 1977		Max. Eastern Elongation
Wed Mar 16 1977		Stationary Retrograde
Sun Apr 3 1977	Inferior	
Wed Apr 6 1977		Inferior Conjunction
Mon Apr 11 1977	Morning Star	
Wed Apr 27 1977		Stationary Direct
Wed Jun 15 1977		Max. Western Elongation
Sat Dec 3 1977	Superior	
Sun Jan 22 1978		Superior Conjunction
Fri Mar 3 1978	Evening Star	
Tue Aug 29 1978		Max. Eastern Elongation
Wed Oct 18 1978		Stationary Retrograde
Sat Nov 4 1978	Inferior	
Tue Nov 7 1978		Inferior Conjunction
Sun Nov 12 1978	Morning Star	
Tue Nov 28 1978		Stationary Direct
Thu Jan 18 1979		Max. Western Elongation
Fri Jul 6 1979	Superior	
Sat Aug 25 1979		Superior Conjunction
Thu Oct 4 1979	Evening Star	
Sat Apr 5 1980		Max. Eastern Elongation
Sat May 24 1980		Stationary Retrograde
Thu Jun 12 1980	Inferior	
Sun Jun 15 1980		Inferior Conjunction
Fri Jun 20 1980	Morning Star	
Sun Jul 6 1980		Stationary Direct

Date	Phase	Phenomena
Mon Aug 25 1980		Max. Western Elongation
Wed Feb 11 1981	Superior	
Tue Apr 7 1981		Superior Conjunction
Tue May 12 1981	Evening Star	
Wed Nov 11 1981		Max. Eastern Elongation
Thu Dec 31 1981		Stationary Retrograde
Mon Jan 18 1982	Inferior	
Thu Jan 21 1982		Inferior Conjunction
Tue Jan 26 1982	Morning Star	
Wed Feb 10 1982		Stationary Direct
Fri Apr 2 1982		Max. Western Elongation
Sun Sep 19 1982	Superior	
Thu Nov 4 1982		Superior Conjunction
Sat Dec 18 1982	Evening Star	
Thu Jun 16 1983		Max. Eastern Elongation
Wed Aug 3 1983		Stationary Retrograde
Mon Aug 22 1983	Inferior	
Thu Aug 25 1983		Inferior Conjunction
Tue Aug 30 1983	Morning Star	
Thu Sep 15 1983		Stationary Direct
Fri Nov 4 1983		Max. Western Elongation
Sun Apr 22 1984	Superior	
Fri Jun 15 1984		Superior Conjunction
Sat Jul 21 1984	Evening Star	
Tue Jan 22 1985		Max. Eastern Elongation
Wed Mar 13 1985		Stationary Retrograde
Sun Mar 31 1985	Inferior	
Wed Apr 3 1985		Inferior Conjunction
Mon Apr 8 1985	Morning Star	
Thu Apr 25 1985		Stationary Direct
Wed Jun 12 1985		Max. Western Elongation
Sat Nov 30 1985	Superior	
Sun Jan 19 1986		Superior Conjunction
Fri Feb 28 1986	Evening Star	
Tue Aug 26 1986		Max. Eastern Elongation
Wed Oct 15 1986		Stationary Retrograde
Sun Nov 2 1986	Inferior	
Wed Nov 5 1986		Inferior Conjunction
Mon Nov 10 1986	Morning Star	
Wed Nov 26 1986		Stationary Direct
Fri Jan 16 1987		Max. Western Elongation
Sat Jul 4 1987	Superior	
Sun Aug 23 1987		Superior Conjunction
Fri Oct 2 1987	Evening Star	
Sat Apr 2 1988		Max. Eastern Elongation
Sun May 22 1988		Stationary Retrograde
Thu Jun 9 1988	Inferior	
Sun Jun 12 1988		Inferior Conjunction
Fri Jun 17 1988	Morning Star	
Mon Jul 4 1988		Stationary Direct
Tue Aug 23 1988		Max. Western Elongation
Wed Feb 8 1989	Superior	
Tue Apr 4 1989		Superior Conjunction
Tue May 9 1989	Evening Star	
Wed Nov 8 1989		Max. Eastern Elongation

Date	Phase	Phenomena
Fri Dec 29 1989		Stationary Retrograde
Mon Jan 15 1990	Inferior	
Thu Jan 18 1990		Inferior Conjunction
Tue Jan 23 1990	Morning Star	
Thu Feb 8 1990		Stationary Direct
Fri Mar 30 1990		Max. Western Elongation
Sun Sep 16 1990	Superior	
Thu Nov 1 1990		Superior Conjunction
Sat Dec 15 1990	Evening Star	
Fri Jun 14 1991		Max. Eastern Elongation
Thu Aug 1 1991		Stationary Retrograde
Mon Aug 19 1991	Inferior	
Thu Aug 22 1991		Inferior Conjunction
Tue Aug 27 1991	Morning Star	
Fri Sep 13 1991		Stationary Direct
Sat Nov 2 1991		Max. Western Elongation
Sun Apr 19 1992	Superior	
Sat Jun 13 1992		Superior Conjunction
Sat Jul 18 1992	Evening Star	
Tue Jan 19 1993		Max. Eastern Elongation
Thu Mar 11 1993		Stationary Retrograde
Mon Mar 29 1993	Inferior	
Thu Apr 1 1993		Inferior Conjunction
Tue Apr 6 1993	Morning Star	
Thu Apr 22 1993		Stationary Direct
Thu Jun 10 1993		Max. Western Elongation
Sun Nov 28 1993	Superior	
Mon Jan 17 1994		Superior Conjunction
Sat Feb 26 1994	Evening Star	
Wed Aug 24 1994		Max. Eastern Elongation
Thu Oct 13 1994		Stationary Retrograde
Sun Oct 30 1994	Inferior	
Wed Nov 2 1994		Inferior Conjunction
Mon Nov 7 1994	Morning Star	
Wed Nov 23 1994		Stationary Direct
Fri Jan 13 1995		Max. Western Elongation
Sat Jul 1 1995	Superior	
Sun Aug 20 1995		Superior Conjunction
Fri Sep 29 1995	Evening Star	
Sun Mar 31 1996		Max. Eastern Elongation
Mon May 20 1996		Stationary Retrograde
Fri Jun 7 1996	Inferior	
Mon Jun 10 1996		Inferior Conjunction
Sat Jun 15 1996	Morning Star	
Tue Jul 2 1996		Stationary Direct
Tue Aug 20 1996		Max. Western Elongation
Thu Feb 6 1997	Superior	
Wed Apr 2 1997		Superior Conjunction
Wed May 7 1997	Evening Star	
Thu Nov 6 1997		Max. Eastern Elongation
Fri Dec 26 1997		Stationary Retrograde
Tue Jan 13 1998	Inferior	
Fri Jan 16 1998		Inferior Conjunction
Wed Jan 21 1998	Morning Star	
Thu Feb 5 1998		Stationary Direct

Date	Phase	Phenomena
Sat Mar 28 1998		Max. Western Elongation
Mon Sep 14 1998	Superior	
Fri Oct 30 1998		Superior Conjunction
Sun Dec 13 1998	Evening Star	
Fri Jun 11 1999		Max. Eastern Elongation
Fri Jul 30 1999		Stationary Retrograde
Tue Aug 17 1999	Inferior	
Fri Aug 20 1999		Inferior Conjunction
Wed Aug 25 1999	Morning Star	
Sat Sep 11 1999		Stationary Direct
Sat Oct 30 1999		Max. Western Elongation
Mon Apr 17 2000	Superior	
Sun Jun 11 2000		Superior Conjunction
Sun Jul 16 2000	Evening Star	
Wed Jan 17 2001		Max. Eastern Elongation
Fri Mar 9 2001		Stationary Retrograde
Tue Mar 27 2001	Inferior	
Fri Mar 30 2001		Inferior Conjunction
Wed Apr 4 2001	Morning Star	
Fri Apr 20 2001		Stationary Direct
Thu Jun 7 2001		Max. Western Elongation
Mon Nov 26 2001	Superior	
Mon Jan 14 2002		Superior Conjunction
Sun Feb 24 2002	Evening Star	
Thu Aug 22 2002		Max. Eastern Elongation
Thu Oct 10 2002		Stationary Retrograde
Mon Oct 28 2002	Inferior	
Thu Oct 31 2002		Inferior Conjunction
Tue Nov 5 2002	Morning Star	
Thu Nov 21 2002		Stationary Direct
Sat Jan 11 2003		Max. Western Elongation
Sun Jun 29 2003	Superior	
Mon Aug 18 2003		Superior Conjunction
Sat Sep 27 2003	Evening Star	
Mon Mar 29 2004		Max. Eastern Elongation
Mon May 17 2004		Stationary Retrograde
Sat Jun 5 2004	Inferior	
Tue Jun 8 2004		Inferior Conjunction
Sun Jun 13 2004	Morning Star	
Tue Jun 29 2004		Stationary Direct
Wed Aug 18 2004		Max. Western Elongation
Fri Feb 4 2005	Superior	
Thu Mar 31 2005		Superior Conjunction
Thu May 5 2005	Evening Star	
Thu Nov 3 2005		Max. Eastern Elongation
Sat Dec 24 2005		Stationary Retrograde
Wed Jan 11 2006	Inferior	
Sat Jan 14 2006		Inferior Conjunction
Thu Jan 19 2006	Morning Star	
Fri Feb 3 2006		Stationary Direct
Sat Mar 25 2006		Max. Western Elongation
Tue Sep 12 2006	Superior	
Fri Oct 27 2006		Superior Conjunction
Mon Dec 11 2006	Evening Star	
Sat Jun 9 2007		Max. Eastern Elongation

Date	Phase	Phenomena
Fri Jul 27 2007		Stationary Retrograde
Wed Aug 15 2007	Inferior	
Sat Aug 18 2007		Inferior Conjunction
Thu Aug 23 2007	Morning Star	
Sat Sep 8 2007		Stationary Direct
Sun Oct 28 2007		Max. Western Elongation
Tue Apr 15 2008	Superior	
Mon Jun 9 2008		Superior Conjunction
Mon Jul 14 2008	Evening Star	
Thu Jan 15 2009		Max. Eastern Elongation
Fri Mar 6 2009		Stationary Retrograde
Tue Mar 24 2009	Inferior	
Fri Mar 27 2009		Inferior Conjunction
Wed Apr 1 2009	Morning Star	
Fri Apr 17 2009		Stationary Direct
Fri Jun 5 2009		Max. Western Elongation
Mon Nov 23 2009	Superior	
Mon Jan 11 2010		Superior Conjunction
Sun Feb 21 2010	Evening Star	
Thu Aug 19 2010		Max. Eastern Elongation
Fri Oct 8 2010		Stationary Retrograde
Tue Oct 26 2010	Inferior	
Fri Oct 29 2010		Inferior Conjunction
Wed Nov 3 2010	Morning Star	
Thu Nov 18 2010		Stationary Direct
Sat Jan 8 2011		Max. Western Elongation
Mon Jun 27 2011	Superior	
Tue Aug 16 2011		Superior Conjunction
Sun Sep 25 2011	Evening Star	
Mon Mar 26 2012		Max. Eastern Elongation
Tue May 15 2012		Stationary Retrograde
Sun Jun 3 2012	Inferior	
Wed Jun 6 2012		Inferior Conjunction
Mon Jun 11 2012	Morning Star	
Wed Jun 27 2012		Stationary Direct
Wed Aug 15 2012		Max. Western Elongation
Sat Feb 2 2013	Superior	
Thu Mar 28 2013		Superior Conjunction
Fri May 3 2013	Evening Star	
Fri Nov 1 2013		Max. Eastern Elongation
Sat Dec 21 2013		Stationary Retrograde
Wed Jan 8 2014	Inferior	
Sat Jan 11 2014		Inferior Conjunction
Thu Jan 16 2014	Morning Star	
Fri Jan 31 2014		Stationary Direct
Sun Mar 23 2014		Max. Western Elongation
Tue Sep 9 2014	Superior	
Sat Oct 25 2014		Superior Conjunction
Mon Dec 8 2014	Evening Star	
Sun Jun 7 2015		Max. Eastern Elongation
Sat Jul 25 2015		Stationary Retrograde
Wed Aug 12 2015	Inferior	
Sat Aug 15 2015		Inferior Conjunction
Thu Aug 20 2015	Morning Star	
Sun Sep 6 2015		Stationary Direct

Date	Phase	Phenomena
Mon Oct 26 2015		Max. Western Elongation
Tue Apr 12 2016	Superior	
Mon Jun 6 2016		Superior Conjunction
Mon Jul 11 2016	Evening Star	
Thu Jan 12 2017		Max. Eastern Elongation
Sat Mar 4 2017		Stationary Retrograde
Wed Mar 22 2017	Inferior	
Sat Mar 25 2017		Inferior Conjunction
Thu Mar 30 2017	Morning Star	
Sat Apr 15 2017		Stationary Direct
Sat Jun 3 2017		Max. Western Elongation
Tue Nov 21 2017	Superior	
Tue Jan 9 2018		Superior Conjunction
Mon Feb 19 2018	Evening Star	
Fri Aug 17 2018		Max. Eastern Elongation
Fri Oct 5 2018		Stationary Retrograde
Tue Oct 23 2018	Inferior	
Fri Oct 26 2018		Inferior Conjunction
Wed Oct 31 2018	Morning Star	
Fri Nov 16 2018		Stationary Direct
Sun Jan 6 2019		Max. Western Elongation
Mon Jun 24 2019	Superior	
Wed Aug 14 2019		Superior Conjunction
Sun Sep 22 2019	Evening Star	
Tue Mar 24 2020		Max. Eastern Elongation
Wed May 13 2020		Stationary Retrograde
Sun May 31 2020	Inferior	
Wed Jun 3 2020		Inferior Conjunction
Mon Jun 8 2020	Morning Star	
Thu Jun 25 2020		Stationary Direct
Thu Aug 13 2020		Max. Western Elongation

TABLE
CALCULATION NOTES

THE TZOLKIN DAY-SIGN AND TRECENA

The tzolkin data displayed in table 1 was calculated using the Goodman-Martinez-Thompson (GMT) benchmark of Julian day number 584,283. This correlation is generally accepted by most scholars, and is reaffirmed by the exhaustive work of Munro S. Edmonson in *The Book of the Year.* According to this correlation, the start of the current Mayan era occurred on August 11, 3114 BC. Based on data obtained by cross-referencing tzolkin dates with Long Count dates found on Mayan inscriptions, it has been determined that day zero of the Long Count occurred on the tzolkin date 4-Ahau.

In order to determine the day-sign and day number for a particular date, the Julian day number for that date is first calculated using a standard algorithm. The benchmark number of 584,283 is then adjusted by 159 days to compensate for the difference between 4-Ahau and the first day of the tzolkin (1-Imix), and the result is subtracted from the Julian day number. The day number and day-sign are calculated by dividing this difference by 13 and 20 respectively, and examining the remainders.

A single, invariable form of the day count was universally observed across Mesoamerica. As Edmonson points out, "Any particular day always had and still has the same position in the day count everywhere." (Edmonson, p. 5) Therefore, assuming the GMT correlation is correct, calculation of the tzolkin is straightforward.

THE LORD OF THE NIGHT CALCULATION

References to the Lords of the Night are found in a series of Classic Mayan monumental inscriptions known as the lunar glyph series. Within the series, Glyph G in particular referred to the Lord of the Night, and the glyphs provided a means of cross-referencing the Lords of the Night to Long Count dates.

In terms of the Long Count, we know that on August 11, 3114 BC, the ninth Lord of the Night (G-9) ruled the day, and we can make calculations accordingly from this base date.

THE YEAR CALCULATION

As described in chapter 4, the Maya had a concept of a 365-day civil year, which complemented and interacted with the tzolkin 260-day calendar. This solar calendar was also known as the "haab" (or "vague") year. As explained below, a variety of these 365-day calendars were in use throughout Mesoamerica; they differed in specific details that have been categorized and described by Edmonson in *The Book of the Year.*

In all systems, the haab consisted of eighteen months of twenty days each, followed by a period of five intercalated days named "Uayeb." The names of the Mayan months are listed below:

Pop	Mol	Muan
Uo	Ch'en	Pax
Zip	Yax	Kayeb
Zotz'	Zac	Cumku
Tzec	Ceh	Uayeb (five days)
Xul	Mac	
Yaxkin	Kankin	

Possible astrological meanings of the months (insofar as such meanings make sense in a civil calendar) have not been well preserved and have yet to be reconstructed. What is clear, however, is that the five-day Uayeb period was "generally viewed as a kind of calendrical hiatus between years—a time of special danger or even horror, and its days were said to be useless, lost, or even nameless." (Edmonson, p. 10)

Days of the month were identified by their number and month name, similar to modern months. The day numbers most commonly started with 0 and ended at 19, but some systems started with 1 and ended with 20. So, using the more common notation, the first day of the first month would be "0-Pop," the second day "1-Pop," etc., all the way through "19-Pop." The first day of the second month was "0-Uo," and so on.

While the 260-day count was invariable and universal in Meso-america, a multitude of 365-day calendars were in use (especially in the Postclassic period), varying by region and culture. Edmonson describes over sixty such calendars in *The Book of the Year*. To explain how we decided which one might be appropriate for use in our current study of Mayan astrology, we must first look at why so many different civil calendars existed.

An obvious issue with any 365-day calendar relates to the fact that the solar year is actually 365.2422 days long, not 365. In many calendrical systems, in order to keep the calendar from drifting out of sync with the seasons, some kind of leap year adjustment is typically made. Without this adjustment, the summer solstice (for example) would occur later and later in the 365-day calendar at the rate of one day every four years. According to Edmonson, however, a simple leap-year adjustment was not used in Mesoamerica. Instead, the calendar makers understood that 1508 vague years equate to 1507 "real" (tropical) years. In order to synchronize the two calendars, they effectively removed the extra year by subtracting one twenty-day month every eighty-three years. Edmonson calls this an "anti-leap-year" correction.

Edmonson explains that this change was not applied to ongoing calendar systems. Instead, the adjustments were made as new calendars were established. Existing calendars were allowed to run their course without changing the date of New Year, thereby drifting out of sync with the seasons. New calendars were often created when deemed necessary to meet the cultural and religious needs of a particular Mesoamerican people. The introduction of these new calendars provided the opportunity to resynchronize the civil calendar with the seasons and, in some cases, the tzolkin.

For calculating the year information displayed in table 2, we have decided to settle on the Tikal calendar, as described by Edmonson. It was the primary calendar of the Eastern Maya from the first century on, and is the one found in the *Dresden Codex*. Day zero of the Long Count in this system was the date "8-Cumku." (Thus, including the tzolkin date mentioned previously, the complete date notation for Long Count day zero was "4-Ahau 8-Cumku.") One will note that the New Years' dates in table 2 occur earlier in the modern calendar with each passing year. This shift is because no leap year-type adjustments have been made.

For the Tikal calendar displayed in the table, the day-signs of the yearbearers are Ik, Manik, Eb, and Caban. Note that the table lists the day numbers before the directions of the corresponding day-signs, and that they run sequentially from 1 to 13. Thus, one can read the tzolkin New Year date of April 2, 2012, for example, as 1-Caban, with Caban being a sign of the east.

The software that generated table 2 uses the parameters as defined by Edmonson to calculate the haab calendar dates. There are four factors to consider:

1. The start date of a New Year's day in the Julian or Gregorian calendar. When considered with the corresponding Long Count date, this date also determines the type of yearbearer system employed. For the Tikal calendar, Edmonson lists an example base date of July 14, 1549 (Julian).
2. The name of the first month of the year, i.e., the first month following Uayeb, the five-day month. For the Tikal calendar, this is month Pop.
3. Whether the month starts with the number 0 (and ends with 19) or starts with 1 (and ends with 20). The Tikal calendar starts with 0.
4. Whether the year is named for its first day (day 0) or the last day before Uayeb (day 359). Some calendars name the year for the day-sign on which it begins, while others name for its last day. This is yet another variation on yearbearer assignment. The Tikal calendar names the year for the first day, which is the day-sign of 0-Pop.

Table 2 illustrates that throughout the twentieth century, New Year's day in the Tikal calendar always fell in the month of April, and that all of the preceding five-day Uayeb periods did, as well. Thus, in the context of the Mayan calendar, April can be seen as a month of transition, analogous to December in our modern (Julian) calendar. Because of the negative implications of the Uayeb as a kind of "no man's land" between years, the authors can speculate that April was a month of difficulty, bringing to mind the line "April is the cruellest month," from T. S. Eliot's "The Waste Land."

VENUS PHASE CALCULATION

The data in table 3 was generated by a custom program written by one of the authors (Orr). The dates of the canonical periods (listed in the Mayan Phase column) are approximate, and are based on a speculative mapping of the Mayan division of the Venus synodic period. Using the date of the inferior conjunction just prior to the birth date as a starting point, the Venus phase is determined by calculating the proportional position of the birth date within the 584-day Venus synodic cycle. All dates shown in the table are calculated based on Greenwich time. Phenomena dates are accurate to within one day of the actual astronomical events.

BIBLIOGRAPHY

Argüelles, José A. *The Mayan Factor*. Santa Fe: Bear & Company, 1987.

Aveni, Anthony F. *Skywatchers of Ancient Mexico*. Austin: University of Texas Press, 1980.

Bierhorst, John. *The Mythology of Mexico and Central America*. New York: William Morrow and Company, 1990.

Bricker, Harvey and Victoria Bricker. "Zodiacal References in the Maya Codices." In *The Sky in Mayan Literature*. Edited by Anthony Aveni. New York: Oxford University Press, 1992.

Brotherston, Gordon. *Image of the New World: The American Continent Portrayed in Native Texts*. London: Thames and Hudson, 1979.

Brotherston, Gordon. *Book of the Fourth World*. Cambridge University Press, 1992.

Burland, C. A. *The Gods of Mexico*. New York: G. P. Putnam's Sons, 1967.

Carlson, John B. *Venus-Regulated Warfare and Ritual Sacrifice in Mesoamerica: Teotihuacan and the Cacaxtla "Star Wars" Connection*. College Park, Md.: The Center for Archaeoastronomy, 1991.

Carrasco, David. *Quetzalcoatl and the Irony of Empire*. Chicago: University of Chicago Press, 1982.

Caso, Alfonso. *Los Calendarios Prehispanicos*. Mexico City: Universidad Nacional Autonoma de Mexico, 1967.

Casteneda, Carlos. *Tales of Power*. New York: Simon and Schuster, 1974.

Craine, Eugene R., and Reginal C. Reindorp, eds. and trans. *Codex Perez and the Book of Chilam Balam of Mani*. Norman, Okla.: University of Oklahoma Press, 1979.

Codice Chimalpopoca. Mexico City: Universidad Nacional Autonoma de Mexico, 1975.

Coe, Michael D. *Breaking the Maya Code*. London: Thames and Hudson, 1992.

———. *The Maya*. London: Thames and Hudson, 1993.

Cook de Leonard, Carmen. "A new astronomical interpretation of the four ballcourt panels at Tajin, Mexico." In *Archaeostronomy in Pre-Columbian America*. Edited by A. Aveni. Austin, Tx.: University of Texas Press, 1975.

Edmonson, Munro S. *The Book of the Year: Middle American Calendar Systems*. Salt Lake City: University of Utah Press, 1988.

Hay, Clarence L., Ralph Linton, Samuel K. Lothrop, Harry L Shapiro, eds. *The Maya and Their Neighbors: Essays on Middle American Anthropology and Archaeology*. New York: Dover Publications, 1977.

Jenkins, John Major. *Tzolkin: Visonary Perspectives and Calendar Studies*. Garberville, Calif.: Borderland Sciences, 1994.

———. *Maya Cosmogenesis 2012*. Rochester, Vt.: Bear & Company, 1998.

Kelly, David H. "Astronomical Identities of Mesoamerican Gods." *Archaeoastronomy*, no. 2 (1980): S1–S54.

Krupp, Dr. E. C. *In Search of Ancient Astronomies*. New York: McGraw Hill, 1978.

———. *Echoes of the Ancient Skies*. New York: Harper and Row, 1983.

de Landa, Friar Diego. *Yucatan Before and After the Conquest*. Translated by William Gates. New York: Dover Publications, 1978.

Leon-Portilla, Miguel. *Time and Reality in the Thought of the Maya*. Translated by C. L. Boiles and F. Horcasitas. Boston: Beacon Press, 1973.

Makemsom, Maud W. *The Book of the Jaguar Priest: A Translation of the Book of Chilam Balam of Tizimin, with Commentary*. New York: Henry Schuman, 1951.

Malmstrom, Vincent H. *Cycles of the Sun, Mysteries of the Moon.* Austin: University of Texas Press, 1997.

Markman, Roberta H., and Peter T. Markman. *The Flayed God: The Mesoamerican Mythological Tradition.* San Francisco: Harper, 1992.

Men, Hunbatz. *Secrets of Mayan Science/Religion.* Santa Fe: Bear & Company, 1990.

Morley, Sylvanus Griswold. *The Ancient Maya.* Stanford: Stanford University Press, 1956.

————. *An Introduction to the Study of Maya Heiroglyphs.* New York: Dover Publications, 1975.

Roys, R. L. *The Book of Chilam Balam of Chumayel.* Norman, Okla.: University of Oklahoma Press, 1967.

de Sahagun, Fray Bernardino. *Florentine Codex: General History of the Things of New Spain, Books 4 and 5.* Translated by C. E. Dibble and A. J. O. Anderson. Ogden: University of Utah Press, 1957.

Schele, Linda, and David Freidel. *A Forest of Kings: The Untold Story of the Ancient Maya.* New York: William Morrow and Company, 1990.

Schele, Linda. *Maya Cosmos: Three Thousand Years on the Shaman's Path.* With Joy Parker. New York: William Morrow and Company, 1993.

Scofield, Bruce. *Day-Signs: Native American Astrology from Ancient Mexico.* Amherst, Mass.: One Reed Publications, 1991.

————. *Signs of Time: An Introduction to Mesoamerican Astrology.* Amherst, Mass.: One Reed Publications, 1994.

Seler, Eduard. *The Tonalamatl of the Aubin Collection.* Berlin and London: Hazell, Watson & Viney, 1901.

————. *Codex Fejervary-Mayer: An Old Mexican Picture Manuscript in the Liverpool Free Public Museum.* Translated by A. H. Keane. Edinburgh: T. and A. Constable, 1901–1902.

————. *Codex Vaticanus B.* Edinburgh: T. and A. Constable, 1902–1903.

Severin, Gregory M. *The Paris Codex: Decoding an Astronomical Ephemeris.* Philadelphia: The American Philosophical Society, 1981.

Stevens, John L. *Incidents of Travel in Yucatan*. 2 vols. New York: Harper, 1843. Reprinted by Dover Publications, New York, 1961.

Tedlock, Barbara. *Time and the Highland Maya*. Albuquerque: University of New Mexico Press, 1982.

Tedlock, Dennis. *Popol Vuh*. New York: Simon and Schuster, 1985.

Thompson, J. Eric S. *The Rise and Fall of Maya Civilization*. Norman, Okla.: University of Oklahoma Press, 1966.

———. *Maya Hieroglyphic Writing: An Introduction*. Norman, Okla.: University of Oklahoma Press, 1960.

———. *Maya History and Religion*. Norman, Okla.: University of Oklahoma Press, 1970.

———. *Commentary on the Dresden Codex*. Philadelphia: The American Philosophical Society, 1972.

Volguine, Alexandre. *Astrology of the Mayas and Aztecs*. Kent, England: Pythagorean Publications, 1969.

Williamson, Ray A., ed. *Archaeoastronomy in the Americas*. Los Altos, Calif.: Ballena Press and College Park, Md.: Center for Archaeoastronomy, 1981.

Willson, Robert W. "Astronomical Notes on the Maya Codices." In *Papers of the Peabody Museum of American Archaeology and Ethnology*. Cambridge, Mass.: Peabody Museum, Harvard University, 1924.

MAYAN ASTROLOGY ON THE WEB

Authors Bruce Scofield and Barry C. Orr have maintained a Web site, OneReed.com, since 1999. This popular online resource contains information about a wide range of astrological topics.

"OneReed" is derived from the Aztec name for Quetzalcoatl, god of knowledge, culture, and civilization, also known as a feathered or "plumed" serpent. Quetzalcoatl had several names, including "Ce Acatl," which translates literally as One Reed. Legend had it that Quetzalcoatl arrived in Mexico in the year the Aztecs called One Reed, and was expected to return when that number and sign combination recurred, thus his name "One Reed." (Unfortunately for the Aztecs, Cortes arrived on the shores of Mexico in the year named One Reed and used the ancient prophecy to his advantage.)

The OneReed Web site includes the following features:

- An online computer report that produces a personality profile based on the elements of Mayan astrology
- A catalog of books offered by Bruce Scofield's publishing company, One Reed Publications
- An eclectic collection of articles about Mayan and Western astrology
- An experimental online divination program based on the Tzolkin (260-day sacred calendar of the Maya)
- An online journal containing current observations by the authors.

OneReed.com operates under the premise that Mayan astrology was and is a viable system that may prove to be useful not only in the quest for self-knowledge but also in understanding natural cycles and their effects on the biosphere. Its authors are dedicated to the restoration and further development of this ingenious astrological system.

BOOKS OF RELATED INTEREST

THE MAYAN CALENDAR AND
THE TRANSFORMATION OF CONSCIOUSNESS
by Carl Johan Calleman, Ph.D.

MAYA COSMOGENESIS 2012
The True Meaning of the Maya Calendar End-Date
by John Major Jenkins

GALACTIC ALIGNMENT
*The Transformation of Consciousness According to
Mayan, Egyptian, and Vedic Traditions*
by John Major Jenkins

SECRETS OF MAYAN SCIENCE/RELIGION
by Hunbatz Men

TIME AND THE TECHNOSPHERE
The Law of Time in Human Affairs
by José Argüelles

ASPECTS IN ASTROLOGY
A Guide to Understanding Planetary Relationships in the Horoscope
by Sue Tompkins

HOW TO PRACTICE VEDIC ASTROLOGY
*A Beginner's Guide to Casting Your Horoscope
and Predicting Your Future*
by Andrew Bloomfield

THE ARABIC PARTS IN ASTROLOGY
A Lost Key to Prediction
by Robert Zoller

Inner Traditions • Bear & Company
P.O. Box 388
Rochester, VT 05767
1-800-246-8648
www.InnerTraditions.com

Or contact your local bookseller